Liberation Lit

Christini & Vltchek, eds.

BADAK MERAH SEMESTA

Liberation Lit

Copyright © 2015 by Tony Christini and Andre Vltchek, eds.

Edited by: Tony Christini and Andre Vltchek

Cover Design by: Tony Christini

Re-layout by: Rossie Indira

The cover collage of Liberation Lit originates mainly from illustrations of The Masses magazine from early last century, and posters from the WPA Federal Theater Project.

First published by: Mainstay Press LLC (2010)

First edition, 2015

Published by PT. Badak Merah Semesta
Jl. Madrasah Azziyadah 16, Jakarta
http://badak-merah.weebly.com
email: badak.merah.press@gmail.com

ISBN: 978-602-73543-0-2

LIBERATION LIT

prologue / fiction / visuals / poetry / US in Iraq / prison / Kenya
essays & interviews & blogs / collage of criticism / contributors

FOREWORD

LIBERATORY FICTION

LIBERATORY FICTION PAST

LIBERATORY VISUALS

LIBERATORY POETRY

LIBERATORY FOCUS – US in IRAQ

LIBERATORY FOCUS - PRISON

LIBERATORY FOCUS – KENYA

Guest Editor: Shalini Gidoomal

ESSAYS, INTERVIEWS, BLOGS

LIBERATORY LIT CRITICISM

CONTRIBUTORS   816

FOREWORD

Liberatory Literature – Notes on the anthology

Tony Christini and Andre Vltchek

What is art in face of torture, aggression, domination? Art may be liberatory. Liberatory art helps build and power a just, egalitarian, and free culture, society, politics, people.

The artworks of Liberation Lit – personal in especially public as well as private focus – are gathered toward that end – to engage, to enlighten, to liberate. Lib Lit favors fiction that may be deemed too partisan or didactic or overtly factual and political for publication by most corporate presses.

This anthology primarily includes fiction, poetry, and visuals – plus personal narratives, essays, interviews, blog posts, criticism. The issue features three focus sections: 1) US in Iraq, 2) Prison, and 3) Kenya.

Our view is that didacticism or other overt liberatory content (e.g., abundant implicating or enlightening public facts as foreground or background to some private narrative) need not necessarily rule out the use of significant formal aspects of ambiguity or other aesthetic aspects that commonly enhance fiction.

Accomplished aesthetics, far from overwhelming or muddling central purpose and power in works of art, may function to generate and enhance the most vital liberatory elements.

We call the works included in this anthology liberatory, a remarkably neglected literature descriptor. The works are normatively left or progressive – and broadly speaking: geopolitical. Many are class focused. Race issues

are prominent – gender, less so, as it turns out here. In contrast to other existing anthologies, Liberation Lit consists largely of "geopolitical" lit (broadly understood) that is left progressive – including especially fiction with a strong focus on class and place, also race, often with an activist or agitational edge. The anthology contains especially engaged works of literature. Art for social change.

All artworks are ideological. Certain ideologies and topics are distorted, marginalized, or buried by the literature establishment. Liberation Lit makes room for such vital artworks.

Liberation Lit journal publishes liberatory fiction and other liberatory art online on a rolling basis at liblit.org.

For potential contributing authors who might be uncomfortable with didacticism in common story forms, we suggest considering the form of a fictive essay – an oral or written appeal, cry, missive from a clearly identified and delineated fictive person or group who is representative realistically or fantastically of some actual stratum, niche, sweep of society. We are looking for either essayistic or narrative topical, heavily fact-based, issue based, progressive or revolutionary work – fact-filled fiction.

The editors of Liberation Lit are Tony Christini and Andre Vltchek. The Guest Editors of the "Focus – Prison" section are Katy Ryan and Bill Ryan. Guest Editor of "Focus – Kenya" is Shalini Gidoomal.

A View of Libertory Art by V. F. Calverton
from *The Liberation of American Literature*

"Revolutionary art has to be good art first before it can have deep meaning, just as apples in a revolutionary country as well as in a reactionary country have to be good apples before they can be eaten with enjoyment.

"Most of the literature of the world has been propagandistic in one way or another…. In a word, the revolutionary critic does not believe that we can have art without craftsmanship; what he does believe is that, granted the craftsmanship, our aim should be to make art serve man as a thing of action and not man serve art as a thing of escape.

"That the attempt to be above the battle is evidence of a defense mechanism can scarcely be doubted. Only those who belong to the ruling class, in other words, only those who had already won the battle and acquired the spoils, could afford to be above the battle. Fiction which was propagandistic, that is, fiction which continued to participate in the battle, it naturally cultivated a distaste for, and eschewed. Fiction which was above the battle, that is fiction which concerned only the so-called absolutes and eternals, with the ultimate emotions and the perennial tragedies, but which offered no solutions, no panaceas – it was such fiction that won its adoration.

"…except in the United States, revolutionary critics have often been harder task-masters from the point of literary quality than aesthetic critics…

"The revolutionary critic should demand as much of the art he endorses as the reactionary. …[great revolutionary] films are great not because they are [only progressive in ideology] but because they are great first in their formal organization, and then greater still because of the social purpose which they serve.

"The revolutionary…critic does not aim to underestimate literary craftsmanship. What he contends is simply that literary craftsmanship is not enough. The craftsmanship must be utilized to create objects of revolutionary meaning. Only through this synthesis does the revolutionary critic believe that art can serve its most important purpose today. Revolutionary meanings without literary craftsmanship constitute as hopeless a combination from the point of view of the radical critic as literary craftsmanship without revolutionary purpose. …most of the literature of the world has been propagandistic in one way or another, including even that of William Shakespeare and George Bernard Shaw…

"This much should be clear, however, and that is that [revolutionary] writers are not to be confused with literary rebels. Literary rebels believe in revolt in literature; left-wing…writers believe in revolt in life…are more interested in social revolt than in literary revolt."

"Unlike Ibsen, [revolutionary writers] do not ask questions and then refuse to answer them. Unlike the iconoclasts, they are not content to tear down the idols and stop there. Their aim is to answer questions as well as ask them, and to provide a new order to replace an old one. Their attitude, therefore, is a positive instead of a negative one."

The Parrots

Ernesto Cardenal

My friend Michel is an army officer
in Somoto up near the Honduran border,
and he told me he had found some contraband parrots
waiting to be smuggled to the United States
to learn to speak English there.

There were 186 parrots
with 47 already dead in their cages.
He drove them back where they'd been taken from
and as the lorry approached a place known as The Plains
near the mountains which were these parrots' home
(behind those plains the mountains stand up huge)
the parrots got excited, started beating their wings
and shoving against their cage-sides.

When the cages were let open
they all shot out like an arrow shower
straight for their mountains.

The Revolution did the same for us I think:
It freed us from the cages
where they trapped us to talk English,
it gave us back the country
from which we were uprooted,
their green mountains restored to the parrots
by parrot-green comrades.

But there were 47 that died.

LIBERATORY FICTION

Adetokunbo Abiola
The Militants – Guerrillas, soldiers, and civilians struggle for justice and survival in the Niger Delta amid suffering and death fueled by the oil industry and the state.
Lizy – The courage and the struggle to vote in Nigeria.
The Forgotten Inmate – Struggle to survive imprisonment in Benin City, Nigeria.

Appalachian Author
Please Attack Appalachia – From the Appalachian Mountains, one of the earliest and most damning satires of the US invasion and occupation of Iraq.

Laura Carlsen
The Slow Slide to Barbarity – Satire of the brutal US economic and immigration policies toward Mexico.

Tony Christini
Life on Dearth – Satires.
Youthtopia (excerpt) – Adventures in mental cleansing.

Joe Emersberger
Segundo's Revenge – Class in Ecuador via Canada clinically examined.
The Publisher – A Canadian newspaper publisher confronts his complicity in the Canadian, US, corporate backed coup and mass murder in Haiti.
Dave the Prophet – Love, politics, and deportation in Canada.
Wovokia – Imagining society forward, in North America.
Playing Giovanitti – Progressive history in the making in class.

Shelley Ettinger
Herb and Leo Are at It Again – Unions, organizing, immigration, and friendship then and now.

Ishimure Michiko
Lake of Heaven (excerpt) – Community destroyed by dams in Japan.

Shabnam Nadiya
Girl in the Rain – Social exclusion in Bangladesh.

Arundhati Roy
The Briefing – "…when the trees migrate…"

Paul Street
Dead Man Talking – A report on the establishment's living dead.
Leading Democrats: "Expropriate the Expropriators" – Democratic candidates for the United States presidency take a surprising new turn.
A Message From The American Corporate Plutocracy – Sing and dance that plutocratic tune: American Corporate Idol for President.

Joseph Veramu
The Toothache – The line separating coup from revolution and survival in Fiji.

The Television Footage – Reflection upon bravery during the 2000 Fijian coup.

Andre Vltchek
The Weekly Globe – The Chief Editor of The Weekly Globe confronts the world in the bars of New York.
Storyteller and East Timor – On a ship leaving East Timor, a wrenching conversation about the US-backed Indonesian conquest and slaughter of East Timorese.
The Color of God – Refugees, God, soldiers, blood, journalism in western Asia.
Conversations with James – A comedy in six acts.
Soledad – An excerpt from the novel Winter Journey.

Buff Whitman-Bradley
Seven Satires – Lebanese grandmother praises Israel, Israel bombs Vermont, Where are the conservatives?, Bush Fights Global Warming, The war on terrorism takes a new turn, Making a killing from global warming, The future is now: Ask Mr. History – Ridicule of the rulers.

Jenny Ruth Yasi
Between Boston and Burma – An American and Burmese family caught in the midst of an uprising in Burma, 1988.

The Militants
Adetokunbo Abiola

When my fiance Paul was contacted to take a job to construct a road at the outskirts of Warri, an area where thugs and layabouts proliferated, Paul's half brother Peter said that it was dangerous and that he could get killed.

Paul overruled him. I knew Paul was not scared of being killed. Though he was a gentle, self-effacing man with a sober voice, he had a steely core underneath, a core where no threat about being murdered could penetrate. When he came from a site and visited my flat in his jacket, jeans trousers and spotless boots – a blank expression on his face – we talked about the possibility of his being killed. It was as if by constantly discussing the issue I was telling him to be cautious about taking jobs that involved contact with street gangs, rebels, cultists and other bitter people, but it was of no use. Two months later Peter burst into my Benin City flat and shouted that while working with two British engineers at Ugborodo, Paul had been kidnapped by some boys belonging to a Niger Delta militant group. I almost fainted.

It was an era of militant groups. There were many of them: the Niger Delta Liberation Front (NDLF), the Movement for the Emancipation of the Niger Delta (MEND), the Niger Delta Freedom Fighters (NDFF), the Movement for the Survival of the Niger Delta (MOSND) and others. They grew from groups of bitter unemployed graduates and other desperate elements, barricading the gates of oil companies over the oil spills and gas flares rav-aging their rivers. They became organized gangs that kidnapped numerous foreign oil workers and threw bomb cocktails and grenades through win-dows of the houses of the politicians who betrayed their cause. Recently, in a typical incident, a group of workers were fixing a damaged pipeline at a creek near the camp of a gang, and as the workers went home in the evening, they were waylaid and kidnapped by masked boys in speed-boats, swing-ing machine guns. The boys turned out to belong to MEND and the workers were Americans. The American embassy contacted the government and the government contacted MEND and bags of money were exchanged at Government House – while NDFF watched on a television screen.

The next day, another group of workers were working on a rig in the open sea, gunshots shattered the air and many speedboats appeared and the workers were kidnapped amid smoke from machine guns. The group turned out to be NDFF and the hostages Britons. The British High Com- mission at Abuja contacted Government House and the latter contacted NDFF and another bag of money exchanged hands so the workers were released.

The kidnapping and ransom paying went on and on. Shell, Chevron, AGIP and others were shutting their flow stations daily, spiriting their workers abroad through flights at the Murtala Mohhammed Airport; government officials sweated when the news of another attack aired and people grumbled, "Militants again?" The govern-ment soon called in the Joint Military Task Force to the Delta. Every day their blue speedboats sped through the creeks, waves rising and falling on the water, men in helmets and uniforms and life jackets swinging rifles. Paul, seeing all these soldiers on television, would shake his head. They can't stop the militants, he told me.

Yet we knew Paul would work in the creeks if he had the opportunity. After still another television program where the militants kidnapped engineers on the high seas, and we complained that the workers were foolish to work there, Paul said in his sober voice: "Can you blame them for wanting to make money?" When he met a few people who had worked in the creeks, he questioned them, his hands thrust in the pockets of his jacket, about the money they made and when he heard it he would whistle and a wistful expression would cross his face. When he heard Sample, a musician from the Niger Delta, belting out "Ekwe" on CD, he would shake his head and then sigh. Every Sunday afternoon at Motel Benin Plaza, he and his friends discussed the situation over bottles of stout amid the aroma wafting from plates of pepper soup and the smell of the smoke drifting from St Moritz cigarettes. Paul spoke heatedly that the amount of money the workers earned justified the risk they took to work in the creeks. His logic infuriated Peter and James, his best friend.

One day, after yet another argument at Motel Plaza, James told him that if he were so concerned about money maybe he should go to the creeks to work. "Why not," Paul said. "Working there doesn't scare me. Can you imagine the money I will earn?" I assumed that though he could get work in the den of street gangs in Lagos and Warri, he didn't have the contacts to give him work in the creeks. I was wrong. He was kidnapped and Peter said he was going to meet the community leader of Ugborodo to discuss how he could be released.

The next day, before dawn, we took James' Toyota and drove through the silent highway from Benin City to Warri. On getting to town, we headed for its waterside and hired a boat. Its driver, a bulky young man, wore a vest that had a photograph sewn on it of Ken Saro Wiwa, a Niger Delta writer who had fought for freedom before being executed by the state. The man started the engine and headed for the creeks, the scent of petrol stinging our noses. After twenty minutes, we heard the sounds of gunshot behind us and I screamed and James shouted – our speedboat slowed down, then stopped. A vessel belonging to the task force sidled up to our side. The soldiers in the vessel, wearing green uniforms and waving rifles, climbed into our boat and searched through it and seeing no ammunition inside ordered us to continue our journey. Ten minutes later, six speedboats belonging to the task force passed us, but this time the soldiers in it did not stop our boat. Later, a barge moved slowly on the river, carrying many barrels of petrol. After it passed, our gui de muttered under his breath and slowed the speed of his craft, and James, tense, asked him why.

"From here on, we'll be in the territory of the militants," the guide said. "But do not fear. With me around, they won't harm you."

Soon after, we drifted to a checkpoint manned by about ten young men in ragged clothes and camouflage uniforms.

"Who is that?" said one of the men, waving a machine gun, the stink of marijuana smoke coming off his clothes.

"It's me, Cletus," our guide said. "We're going to Ugborodo. The boys have kidnapped their brother." The boatman pointed at us.

The man with the machine gun stared at us then spat into the water. "Why are they kidnapping Nigerians?" he asked. "These boys are giving the struggle a bad name."

He waved us through, and as we moved away, a shower of rain started to fall, and it pattered on us until our boat got to Ugborodo. Climbing the jetty, the guide beckoned to us and we clambered up it and he took us to the ramshackle hut of the community leader. He was sitting on a bench, half dressed, chewing kola nut. After hearing why we came, he coughed, placed the lobe of the kola nut on a stool by his feet, rubbed his jaw and said: "There was an oil spill some days ago. Your brother was unlucky to be near the spot. Unless Chevron agrees to pay compensation, he'll not be released."

"Oh, my God!" James wailed.

"Why?" I shouted. "Why Paul?"

"Take us to the leader of the militants," Peter said.

"No problem about that. After all, your brother was working here when he was kidnapped." The community leader stood up and went into an inner room. On coming out fully dressed, he followed us, and we trudged to the jetty, climbed into the speedboat and began a journey up the creek.

When we got to the camp of the militants, we saw many masked men on the jetty, some smoking sticks of cigarettes and others drinking from cups of palm wine. Clicking the triggers of their rifle and machine guns, they directed their muz-

muzzles at us. Apart from a twitch at the corner of his lips, Peter's face was impassive. James' eyes bulged with fright. I felt beads of sweat sprout out of my face. When the militants saw the community leader with us, they lowered their weapons.

"What's the problem?" barked one of them, wearing a red beret.

Pointing at us, the community leader said: "Their brother is the Nigerian kidnapped. They want to see Commander." The man with the beret thought for a second then said, "I'll check to see whether it's possible." And he disappeared.

As we stood on the jetty, an explosion rocked the land and we looked around, unnerved.

"The oil companies blasting dynamite," the community leader said, then pointed at the creek.

A film of oil floated on the water, edged by a line of mud and dead fishes.

"From the oil spill," the community leader said.

"Then how do you drink?" Peter asked.

"We get water from Warri and Sapele, three hours away."

The militant with the red beret returned, beckoned to us and we marched over soil muddy and stained with patches of crude oil to the tent of the Commander. He sat on a cane-woven chair, wearing a black vest, jeans trousers and a stocking mask, an AK-47 in one hand. Surrounded by others wearing masks and holding rifles.

"Your brother will die," said the Commander to Peter, "if the Joint Task Force decides to storm the camp."

"But my brother has done nothing to deserve this," said Peter.

"He was at the wrong place at the wrong time," said the Commander.

"It's not his fault," I said.

"Can we see him?" Peter asked.

The Commander hesitated then he gestured to one of his assistants. The latter nodded at him and beckoned to us and we followed him out of the shack to meet Paul. He sat on a bench at the back of the camp, in front of a thicket of mangrove plants. The scent of crude oil hung in the air. Away from him, on another bench placed adjacent to the one he was sitting on, were the haggard-looking Britons. I ran to Paul and held him in my hands.

"We pleaded to be released," said Paul, fiddling with a strand of my hair.

"And what did they say?" asked James.

Paul explained that the militants said no, and took the hostages in their boats around communities near Ugborodo to make them understand why. At one of the communities, they were taken to a pond where the people fetched water to drink, at the outskirts of the small town. Paul had been shocked. The pond was filmed by layers of crude oil, and dead fishes and mosses floated on it. The hostages saw a young boy bathing in the pond. On coming out, he used a cup to take up the water and drank out of it. Three boys sprinted towards him, and they started to struggle with him over the cup. Not bearing to look at them, one of the Britons closed his eyes.

After this, Paul and the others had been taken to a nearby village, about a kilometer from the spot of the pond. They saw people bending at their haunches and defecating into the river, above which their shacks stood. They saw one man defecating blood, watched it splashing into the water and spreading in different directions. They were told the man defecated blood because he had eaten a fish which died from drinking the oil-spill water. Paul agonized when fifty meters away he saw an old woman fetching the same water. He was told that she intended to use it to wash a pile of clothes by her feet.

Later, the militants took the hostages to the jetty and they were told to stand for an hour and not to move. Within minutes, the hostages were covering their noses against the gas that stank in the air. One of the Britons scratched his nose and soon it turned bloody and red. Staring at the blood that stained his finger, he shook his head and said: "People don't deserve to live like this." One of the militants laughed at him and pointed to a spot of shriveled grass by the jetty. There Paul and the others saw many fishing nets stained black by the oil spill. "Unless Chevron signs compensation agreements for these things, none of you will be released," one of the militants said.

Peter, James and I left, but returned three days later. We escaped being shot at by a group of militants who had set up a checkpoint on the creek leading to Ugborodo. By this time, however, we had all changed our views formed in Benin. Peter did not say he would wring the necks of the rascally boys. He did not recount the story of how he had chased two boys, members of a street gang, that tried to extort money from him while he was painting at Bar Beach in Lagos. James did not clench his hands to fists and boast that he would smash bottles of beer on their heads. He did not blame the militants for extorting money on the creeks or demanding compensation from oil companies. I had stopped calling members of street gangs and militants, thugs and miscreants. Though we were still confused about the situation, we were not so certain that the youths toting machine guns and throwing bombs and murdering the people in the Niger Delta were simply ruffians who needed to be taught a lesson or two for terrorizing the creeks with AK-47s.

When we got to the camp, the militant in a red beret waved us through the jetty in a businesslike manner, eyes tense. I suspected there had been a change in situation. On getting to Paul, I placed a cooler containing his favorite meal before him, rice and beans, but he didn't look at it. He appeared nervous.

"I don't feel like eating," he said.

"What happened?" Peter asked.

"Eat something," I told Paul.

Drumming his fingers on the bench, Paul told us that some complications had set in and that this might act against his being released. Ac-

cording to him, three children had suddenly taken ill in one of the villages close to the camp, vomiting and coughing blood.

"What caused their sickness?" I asked.

A pained expression appeared on his face as if he were disappointed I didn't know. He said the three children drank from a pond polluted by the spill and had also smoked and eaten the dead fishes floating in it. Hours later, they began to sneeze and cough and had taken ill. When they were questioned, they admitted they had been drinking from the oil spill water and had eaten some of the poisoned fishes.

"Were they not told to avoid eating the fish?" Peter asked.

"They were," Paul said, "but there was nothing else to eat. No water to drink."

"They should take them to the hospital."

Paul stopped drumming on the bench and stared above our heads at the Commander's shack fifty meters ahead. As he did so, I saw a look of bitterness in his eyes and then he stared at us.

"There's no hospital here," he said. "There are no roads. They tried to take the children to the hospital at Warri but it took too long. They died before they got them there."

"So how does this concern your case?" Peter asked.

"The militants got angry," Paul said. "One of the dead children belongs to one of them. They im-mediately increased their demands of compensa-tion for the spill. Talks between them and Chevron and the government broke down."

"Don't let that worry you," I told him. "I'm sure they'll work out something."

"They better work out something," Paul said, and I saw anger flash in his eyes. "It hurts to see all these things." To control himself, he took a deep breath and began again to drum his fingers on the bench. After a while, he stopped and stared at us. "I have decided that I don't want to stay here anymore," he said. Saying that, he lifted up his eyes and stared at the sky. Bringing his eyes down, he said: "Any opportunity I get, I'll damn the con-sequences. I'll try to escape."

"Don't," I said.

"No," James said. "They'll shoot you."

"I'll try to escape," Paul repeated.

We had not resolved the issue by the time we left him that afternoon.

The Joint Military Task Force stormed the camp that evening, taking two of the militants hostage, before being repelled.

Worried when we heard, we left Warri, our temporary abode, for Ugborodo, to see the community leader. Tossing to the earth floor a lobe of kola nut when we met him, he told us neither the Britons nor Paul had been captured, and he agreed to accompany us to the camp. When we got there, we were surprised to see the Commander happily drinking from a calabash of palm wine and smok-ing a wrap of marijuana, his AK 47 placed on the table. When he saw us, his mood changed and he became angry.

"Why can't your brother behave like the Britons?" he said. "During the attack, the Britons stayed calm. Now, they're going to be released this afternoon. Chevron now knows it can't take them from us. We've come to an agreement."

"What about my brother?" Peter shouted.

"If you shout like that again, I'll kill you," one of the militants said to him.

"Quiet there," the Commander told him and turned to us. "Your brother escaped during the attack. We don't know where he is."

"How can you not know where he is?" I asked.

"You know where he is!" James shouted. "You've killed him."

"Shut up there, you fool!" the Commander said. "Why should we kill him? He has no hostage value. We were only keeping him because of the Britons." Turning, he stared at one of his assistants. "Sky-B, go with them to search for

him. Release him if he's still alive."

Sky-B stepped out of the group surrounding the Commander. He was a tall thin man and he held a rifle, an ammunition belt wound over his chest. From the hatred that burned in his eyes, I knew he wasn't pleased with the assignment. He strode to the front of the tent and beckoned to us. "Let's go," he said.

James hesitated, then leaned over and whispered into my ear. "Should we go? This might be a way to get rid of us," he said. I looked at Peter. He did not say anything.

"Don't be scared," the Commander said. "We're not doing anything to you. You have no value to us alive or dead."

Though not assured by this, we followed Sky-B out of the tent, and he headed towards a shack at the back of the camp.

"All this comes from wanting our money," he said, his voice gruff. "But he's made a mistake. I believe he's dead."

"He's not dead," I said

"My brother is not dead," Peter agreed, his voice stubborn.

"Who told you he's alive?" Sky-B sneered. "In front of the camp, we have the creek. It's infested with crocodiles and alligators. There's also the thick forest. Get in there and mosquitoes and all sorts of insects will attack him. He'll get malaria in hours."

"What about the back of the camp?" I asked.

"A few meters into it is the swamp. It'll swallow him in seconds. So how can he be alive?"

Beside the shack where we stood, the forest began.

"Are those not boot marks?" I asked. Sky-B stared at the spot and frowned. Peter went past him, bent to his haunches and stared.

"Those are the marks of Paul's boots," he announced.

James swept past him and tramped into the path that led into the forest, beating at leaves and the stems of small trees in the way. We followed him, but we were soon hemmed in by the walls of the thicket lining the path, following the boot marks. As we stepped aside and pushed away the smaller plants in our path, swarms of mosquitoes and flies buzzed across our faces, Sky-B swatting at them in anger. We struggled through the forest for a few minutes, and then it opened into another path that led to an isolated shack. The boot marks entered through the doorway.

"Do you think he can be here?" James asked.

"He might be," Sky-B muttered, bringing out a wrap of marijuana, putting it between his lips and holding the flame of a match against it. Inhaling, he blew out a cloud of smoke and said, "But he'll be dead."

Peter pushed the door of the shack open and tiptoed inside. I followed him – so did James and Sky-B. "He's not here," the militant said.

I smelled a faint scent of cigarette smoke in the stuffy shack and looked around. Sure enough, there was a packet of St Moritz tossed on a sandy mound at the corner of the shack, three cigarettes spilt on the ground, none of them having been lit.

"He was here," I said.

"He must have left in a hurry," Peter said. "Perhaps when he heard us coming."

Taking off at a run, Peter moved to the doorway. Standing in it and staring at the forest, he shouted: "Paul!" No answer. The trees around the shack closed in on his voice and it was drowned in the rustle of a light breeze. I pushed past Peter, stepped out of the shack and surveyed the ground. I soon found the boot marks on it and followed them until they got to the edge of the forest. When I pushed aside the branches of a small tree in front of me and attempted to step in, Sky-B grabbed my hand. "Let me go," I told him.

He didn't release me; instead, he bent my neck down and pointed through the leaves, saying in a harsh voice: "That's the swamp. If you step a meter into the bush, you'll get sucked in."

I stared through the leaves into the dim light under the trees of the forest. As I strained to look through, I heard the croaks of a frog, followed by those of others. Looking in the direction of the sounds, I saw the flash and glassy glow of water a few yards away. I drew back.

"Its true," I said. "There's a swamp there."

"What does this mean?" Peter asked.

"He's dead," Sky-B said. "He must be drowned in it."

"He's the only relative I have," Peter said.

I couldn't, wouldn't, believe that Paul was dead. I stared at the boot marks, at the spot that they entered the swamp. I noticed they didn't go straight, but branched and moved along the edge of the forest. I followed the marks again.

"What are you doing?" James asked.

I pointed out the marks going along the side of the forest.

The others followed, Sky-B grumbling. I trudged along, kicking at the leaves and sticks that obstruct-ed my movement, beating at the mosquitoes and the flies that buzzed across my face, until I couldn't see the marks again. I stopped. All around the suffocating stench of the swamp. Dense green growth marked the spot where the marks stopped. With my leg, I shifted a small plant out of the way, and there lying on a clump of wet grass was the bag Paul usually hung on his shoulder, its strap on the leaves of a plant, its leather spattered with mud. I shouted. Looking around the bag, I saw a head covered by some leaves and hands splayed about. Pushing aside the leaves, I saw Paul lying face down on the ground, his breath coming in harsh gasps, his legs stretched towards the marsh, caked with mud. He gasped, his face twisted with pain. I ran to him and grabbed him. Peter came up in a rush, grabbing his brother's hand.

"Paul!" he shouted.

"I'm sick," Paul mumbled.

Peter wrapped his arm around his shoulder

and lifted him up, while I beat at the sand and the leaves that clung to his clothes, knocking off the leaves and blades of grass on his trousers. James picked up Paul's bag, and Paul kept moaning, "Oh, my God!"

The three of us half-carried and half-dragged Paul from the bush, heading for the camp, while Sky-B followed. On reaching the Commander's shack, the community leader of Ugborodo threw away the lobe of kola nut in his hand and grunted, then joined us as we hustled Paul to the speedboat. Sky-B, the hatred still in his eyes, shouted at us as we climbed into the boat, and when he saw that he had Paul's attention, he wagged a finger at him.

"Advice for you," he said. "Stay away from this land. Next time you come here, you die."

Without waiting for an answer, he turned and headed back to the Commander's shack. The boat-man was now wearing a vest with the picture of Asari Dokubo, another freedom fighter. He snig-gered at Sky-B as he walked away then started the engine of the boat. It lurched forward and headed towards Ug-borodo, where we were to drop the community leader. Not until we approached the waterfront of the town did Paul gather the strength to say anything.

"The Joint Task Force attacked the camp at night," he said in a rush. "There was so much con-fusion, so many gun shots. Everybody was running helter skelter. The militant with us pointed his rifle at the Britons and warned that if they didn't stay where they were, they would die in the crossfire. He then left to join the bat-tle." Paul coughed. "I'd already decided to run. I told the Britons we should make for the forest. They said no, they would die of malaria. I had no choice but to leave them and enter the for-est." He fell silent and we said nothing as the boat stopped at the jetty of Ugborodo. The community leader got out, and the boat swerved away.

The current of the water in the creek now swift, the boat streamed towards Warri. Paul was alive. He had survived the creeks where so many others had not. Ripples of wave swirled from the boat as it coursed through the water and carried us on, away from the camp, away from the creeks covered by a film of oil, away from death.

Lizy

Adetokunbo Abiola

Shortly before Lizy left her room for the INEC office, she learnt through a phone call that Caroline Aghatise, her friend, had been shot. Five minutes after the call, her mother burst into the room, panting and waving her hand in agitation. "Caroline is dead," she announced. "She was shot at INEC office at Ikpoba Hill." Staring at her wild eyes, Julius Osunbor knew the thoughts that were disturbing her mind. In the days preceding the election, a lot of Lizy's party members had suffered one misfortune or the other. The three bedroom flat belonging to Dick Ojenor, the party secretary, had been burnt down. Henry Akiddo, a youth coordinator, had been waylaid on the road by thugs, a baton smashed against his skull, and the blood from a cut dripped into the soil. Thomas Amadasun, the auditor, had been stopped as he drove into his compound, dragged out of the car, beaten up, and his prized linen coat torn to shreds. Lizy's mother feared that Lizy could suffer a similar fate.

"You must not go to the INEC office," she told her daughter. "It's dangerous. You might be shot as well."

Lizy's father came into the room; an agonized look shone in his eyes. Though Julius was not given to fright, he felt foreboding in the air just by looking at his face. As Lizy's father began to plead with his daughter not to go to the INEC office, his eyes fearful and manner hesitant, Julius sat on a sofa, and felt the impotence of the situation. He knew the reason for the feeling of impotence. Lizy wanted to go to INEC's office, and she usually carried out what she wanted to do. Her father knew that she wanted to go as well, but he argued that the place was surrounded by thugs who held cutlasses, cut-to-size rifles, and charms; thugs who had come to snatch ballot boxes before they were carried to the polling stations; thugs ready to attack Lizy's party's monitors. Lizy stared at her father's agonized face, and said she had been frightened of Fthugs in the past, and that she had suffered for it politically, but that she was not ready to chart that course now. She sank into one of the sofas in the room and fell silent. She refused to respond to further comments, not even when her mother spoke to her, not even when Charles, her cousin, said he heard a rumor that the electoral office was to be bombed. Finally, Lizy stood up, hitched up her black pants, and said she was going to the INEC office and that nobody in Benin City could stop her.

As she marched out of the room, her father and mother followed her and stepped in front of her at the porch. Placing a hand on the railing, she listened, her brow knitted in a frown, as her father told her that for safety's sake she should forget about going to the INEC office. She could go to the polling station to vote for her party. He had already been to the polling booths. The thugs had not arrived. She could go and vote. She would still be supporting her party, and her colleagues would understand.

"They'll not see you as a betrayal."

"It's not the issue of betrayal. It's of commitment."

"I didn't say it's only of betrayal," he said. "It's that of safety. INEC's office is not safe. Policemen are there with guns. The thugs are there. It's a flashpoint. You could get caught in the crossfire. Please, for once, listen to me."

Lizy often told Julius that she liked to disobey her father. When at eleven she broke her leg playing football in her school field, and her father warned her not to play the game because it could cripple her, she disobeyed him and continued with the sport. When a few years later she bought boxing gloves and daily went to the backyard of the family home to practice boxing, and her father caught her and made vague sounds about her being the only child, she ignored him. When she went to a party at a notorious spot for thieves in Benin City and returned at about twelve in the morning, and he shouted at her, she didn't mind him, telling him she wasn't scared of being attacked by robbers, thugs, cultists, and other undesirables.

After the talk at the porch, Lizy's mother, instead of following her husband to their apartment in the sprawling compound, insisted on waiting. Julius knew why. Lizy had not committed herself to staying away from INEC's office, and her mother wanted to say more. She said her husband was disturbed by this election business. When he heard that Ojenor's flat had caught fire, he couldn't sleep, tossing about the bed throughout the night, imagining that Lizy could suffer from the same fate. On learning that Henry had been waylaid by thugs and beaten up, he had caught a headache.

"You don't know this because you've been out campaigning," her mother said. "I had to nurse him for days. He kept blaming me for encouraging you to participate in politics. I went through hell. Caroline's death has completely disorganized him."

Hitching up her pants, Lizy told her in a stubborn voice why she had to go to INEC's office. Her party had to monitor the movement of campaign materials. If it didn't, the agents of the ruling party would hijack them and they would end up in their private houses, where their people would thumbprint the ballot papers. Lizy and many others had been selected to do the monitoring. She had given her word that she would assist in the task. The monitoring group had been practicing maneuvers for two weeks. The members were scheduled to meet at the INEC office by eight o'clock. If Lizy didn't appear, they would be disappointed in her.

"Tell them you came but the thugs drove you back. They'll understand. You're a woman."

"I know I'm a woman," Lizy said. "But why disappoint them on today of all days?"

"For my sake, you're a woman. Remember, you're my only child, my only hope."

Silence fell between them; but after a moment, an exasperated sigh came out of Lizy's lips, and Julius knew she would obey her mother. Two days ago, when her mother told her not to go to her party's office, that policemen were there with their guns and rifles, Lizy gave an exasperated sigh, but complied. In the morning of the next day, when her mother, panting and waving her hand in agitation, told her that thugs of the ruling party were dragging out agents of the opposition from their cars and punching them on the streets and that she should wait awhile before leaving home, Lizy gave an exasperated sigh, but obeyed. This time, she acted the same way, but said she should at least go to the polling station to vote. After a short moment, her mother agreed. Lizy, along with Charles and Julius, decided to go to Idia Primary School to cast their votes.

When they got there, contrary to what Lizy's father said, the thugs of the Peoples Party, the ruling party, were crawling all over the place, shouting at the top of their voices. Some were dressed in black mufti, black trousers, and black shoes. Others wore fez caps, vests engraved with giant eagles, and waved the pictures of the politicians they were supporting. Many had a few weeks before been touts at the motor-parks in the city, but they had changed. The thirty-something and forty-some-thing-year-old men had now learnt the slogan of the ruling party. They were swaggering all over the place, sending fear into the hearts of those who had come to vote. After observing them for a few minutes, Julius saw how they operated. A voter would come to the polling station and start to discuss with an agent of the Action Congress, Lizy's party, before going to queue on the line. He would be bumped off it, and so one of Lizy's party's agents would turn to an agent of the ruling party and abuse him. The next minute, a supporter of the opposition party would be bumped off the queue again, a slap landing on his face. The next moment, a ruling party supporter – a thug – would be punched, his T-shirt torn, and the aggressor, an agent of Lizy's party, would then run down the school field to the gate. The situation was rowdy. Many voters stayed clear of the small table on which the ballot boxes would be placed because of the confusion. A policeman was watching the situation. He tried to control the thugs, who were shouting at each other, but his voice was drowned in the din. Lizy stared at him and shook her head. She said policemen should be crawling all over the place as well, that the thugs of the ruling party would easily overwhelm just one of them.

Charles stared at Lizy with apprehension, and Julius knew that Charles, like him, was wondering whether they would be able to vote. Julius could see the bulge of the clubs, the bottles, and the batons under the dresses of the thugs; and Julius wondered how Lizy, known to be in the opposition, would bypass these weapons and vote. Some of the voters were saying: "This is an act of Satan," and were hissing in the direction of the thugs. Julius saw a ruling party official – a man in peak-cap, vest, jeans trousers, and army boots – sharing money with a group of voters, and pushing them towards the line after they had taken the crisp notes. A man, a supporter of Lizy's party, was dragged from the queue by a thug, pushed to the ground, kicked, and dragged across the school field by another thug.

Fear gnawing at his heart, Julius asked Lizy if she still wanted to vote, and she hitched up her pants and nodded, her teeth biting her lower lip. "Nobody is going to stop me," she vowed. He knew her mind was made up to vote, especially as her mother wasn't around to remind her about being the only child. When Charles whispered to him that she wouldn't leave without voting, his suspicion was correct.

But he wasn't convinced she could vote. Another occurrence that convinced him was when the two INEC officials arrived with the green-and-white glass ballot box and pandemonium broke out, as the voters started running about. A few seconds later, a Toyota bus filled with men appeared on the path that led to the polling station and stopped. An old woman standing close to him said: "I know the men inside that bus. They're armed with axes, cutlasses and guns."

Just as she finished speaking, Julius heard people shouting, and he looked in the direction of the small table. The ruling party man in peak-cap was trying to wrest the ballot box from one of the INEC officials. He succeeded in his quest, and he began to run along the veranda, chased by the policeman. As the party official attempted to slip into a small bush at the end of the veranda, the policeman clutched the back of his shirt and caught up with him. After a tense struggle, the policeman elbowed him in the stomach and snatched the box from him. The voters shouted, and the queue formed behind the small table dissolved with many people sprinting away. Julius heard the sound of someone screaming, and then the sound of a gun shot. More voters took off in a run, some headed towards the center of the school field, while others ran in the direction of the path that wound out of the primary school. The policeman, panting, placed the box on the small table and dared anyone to come and snatch it. This did not make much sense to Julius, since the policeman had no weapon on him; but it made sense to Lizy, who said the policeman was indirectly telling the ruling party's agents that they had to bribe him before they could take the box away.

Julius assumed that this would convince Lizy about the futility in voting, but she gave no indication that she wanted to leave. Charles told her: "Let's go. This is no election." Lizy shook her head, biting her lower lip. Instead, she ushered us to the center of the field, but there a thug in black mufti, holding a poster, said: "No one, except our supporters, will vote. Let any hot head disobey us. We'll deal with the person."

As Julius steered Lizy away from him, he thought it was strange that a week ago he was undecided about voting, but here he was involved with it all. But Lizy couldn't be steered away from trouble for long. She stopped, grabbed his hand, and began to lead him and Charles to a small crowd that had gathered in front of the small table. Not seeing the INEC officials nor the ballot box there, Lizy climbed on the veranda, Charles and Julius following. They marched along the veranda, looking into the classrooms. They passed three of them, and found the officials in the fourth; they were having a talk with a ruling party agent and the policeman. The ballot box was placed on a bench beside them, and about eight large envelopes were put on top of a desk by the bench. The smell of dust mingled with chalk wafted from the room. After a while, one of the INEC officials, a short black man with a paunch, came out of the classroom and informed them that voting was not going to start because the number of ballot papers would not be sufficient for the large number of voters.

"If you people planned well," Lizy told him, "we won't have any problems. The number of people in this ward is just four hundred, why can't you have enough ballot papers for all? Are you people trying to disenfranchise us?"

"Its not my fault!" shouted the INEC official. "Blame the politicians. They snatched all the materials from our office. The remaining is not enough to go round." And he marched away in anger.

Lizy muttered in disgust, shaking her head, but said though the election would be made difficult so people like her could not vote, she would still perform her duty. She said this was all to make voters leave in frustration, leaving the ruling party agents free to thumbprint the ballot papers to their hearts' content. Charles and Julius agreed with her. But Julius also imagined Lizy walking away from the polling station by three o'clock in the afternoon, when voting officially ended, not having cast her vote. Later, they all went to stand at the edge of the school field, under a mango tree. When Lizy left them to buy sachets of water, Charles said: "I know why she's determined to vote."

"Why?" Julius I asked.

"To compensate for not going to INEC's office," he said with a frown. Julius nodded in agreement, then watched Lizy as she approached from the direction of the Toyota bus.

When she reached them, she shook her head, her eyes looking sad. Hitching up her pants, she told them she saw a thug bribing the policeman with some crisp naira notes by the side of the bus. The thug was big and brash, rumored, Lizy was told, to be on the run for killing a man at a polling station at the last elections; yet here he was in broad daylight, bribing the policeman who should have had him handcuffed and taken to the station to be thrown into a cell. The second reason for her sadness was the confirmation that the ruling party thugs wanted to stop every voter not supporting them from voting when elections started. An old man living in her street had told her that he had seen two thugs discussing this when he had wandered to the side of the Toyota bus.

There were other thugs in some of the classrooms, she said, handing out voters cards and money to many voters. After giving them the money and cards, the thugs often shouted: "You are the only ones going to vote. Make sure you vote for us." Lizy could not understand why the voters took the money; these were young men in pressed white shirts, black trousers, and ties; young men with innocent looks plastered on their faces. After receiving the bribes, their footsteps became confident and sure, and when they came out to the field, their friends slapped them on the shoulders and shouted: "Your share of the national cake." The rigging was more painful at the classrooms near to the one the INEC officials waited by. People queued along the windows at the side away from the open field, taking crisp naira notes, watched by an opposition party agent, who opened his mouth wide and shook his head. It was the agent who called Lizy and pointed to the long queues behind the windows. He was also the one who told Lizy about the bush path that an INEC official, the short one with the paunch, had disappeared into with two large envelopes.

Lizy told them this within a few seconds of meeting them. As she spoke, Julius felt anger building up in him over what the thugs wanted to do. He also noticed that Charles' gentle face was contorted with fury as he listened, and his hands were clenching and unclenching. It was as if he wanted to march to the Toyota bus, drag out the thugs inside it, and pound them to the ground with his fists. Lizy placed her hand on his shoulder, looked at Julius, and said:" Let's go to the classrooms. Let's check whether the large envelopes are still eight."

Charles and Julius followed her to the classroom where the INEC officials waited. On seeing them, the INEC official with the paunch scowled in their direction, pointed a threatening finger, and hollered, "What are you people doing here?" The other one, the thin one who had struggled with the agent in peak-cap, said he would call the policeman. An agent standing with them, a man with a scarred face, brought out a knife when told by the INEC officials that Lizy and her gang were being nosy, glowered as he pointed it at them, then slipped it back into his pocket. Unnerved by all this, Julius, Lizy, and Charles turned and walked away. By this time, Julius noticed that he and Charles were caught up fully in Lizy's quest to vote. Charles stopped to say that the election was a ruse and that they should leave at once. He did not bring up the behavior of the party official in army boots as evidence that to vote was useless since the ballot box would be snatched and party officials would stuff it with already thumbprinted papers. Julius forgot about his indecision about the election. Rather, both of them were fuming. The arrogance of the INEC officials and the thugs made them determined to find a way to thwart their plans and to made them want to vote. Lizy led them to the center of the field, stopped, and turning towards the classrooms, said, "If I have to die, I'll vote today."

The next time Lizy suggested that they go to the classrooms, Julius told her there was no need. No vehicle had driven into the primary school to disgorge more electoral materials. The thugs in the bus were still inside it; they were waiting for the voting to start.

Charles, no longer gentle, argued: "Let's go. Let's see whether the large envelopes on the desk are still eight."

While they debated, Lizy strolled towards the bus, passed it, and disappeared around a corner. After she left, Charles and Julius dropped the issue about going to count the envelopes and fell silent. Julius's legs were aching him, so he sat down on the grass, and leaned his back against the thick bark of a mango tree. Charles, arms akimbo, stared at the classrooms, his eyes burning with anger.

Lizy returned fifteen minutes later. Charles and Julius took the two bottles of coca-cola from the paper bag she held out to them. As they drank from the bottles, the old woman, the one who told Julius about the thugs in the Toyota bus, waddled down from the edge of the field and sat down beside them. Lizy sank to the grass with a sigh.

"Found another thing?" Julius asked the old woman, and she nodded and spat into the grass. The INEC official with a paunch had jumped out through the back window of the classroom, so he would not be visible to voters on the field, and had gone to a bush near the Toyota bus, accompanied by the agent with the scarred face. He had had a conference with the thug who had killed at the last elections.

"They want to complicate matters," Lizy said. "They want to create confusion and fear among voters."

"They want to cause confusion for their mothers," the old woman said.

"I never cared about voting before," Charles said. "But now I care. I'm going to vote."

Lizy sipped from her bottle, her brow knitted in a frown as she thought. She didn't speak for the next few minutes, her tongue placed at the opening of the bottle. Her eyes were bitter and dark.

"Are they lying about the electoral materials not being enough?" Julius asked.

"I think so," Lizy said.

"I agree with you," Charles said. "Sure, ballot boxes are being snatched before getting to polling stations. But in this case, shortage of materials is being used as a ploy to delay voting. They want people to go away before they start thumbprinting the papers."

"This will not stop me from voting," Lizy said. She tossed the bottle of coca-cola on the grass and turned to Julius. "Go and see whether the ballot boxes are still in the classrooms."

Julius stood up and wandered towards the block that housed the classrooms; but when he stepped on the veranda, the policeman came towards him. He had been counting a bundle of crisp naira notes in the doorway of a classroom, and now he frowned as he stopped in front of Julius. When he learnt that Julius wanted to see the INEC officials, he barked: "Is this your father's house? Do you think you can come and go anyhow? If you don't leave here, I'll deal with you."

Boiling with anger, but knowing that the police-man could hit him with his big fists, Julius bowed and ambled back to the mango tree to tell Lizy what happened.

"These people won't get away with this," she said and stood and hitched up her pants. She turned her head in slow motion towards the block that contained the classrooms, and Julius found himself admiring this young woman's indomitable spirit. Still keeping her gaze on the classroom, she bit her lower lip and hissed. "But they're making a mistake. I'm going to get a paper and place in my vote." She swiveled her head in the direction of her accomplice and said: "Let's go."

"Let's go," the old woman said, getting up.

"We shouldn't allow them to treat us like second class citizens," Lizy said.

"This is horrible," Charles stated. "They have no right to do this."

"I'd rather fight for my rights than allow a bunch of criminals to shortchange me," Lizy said.

"These people are crazy," Julius said.

"I said let's go!"

At that moment, a lorry drove into the school compound and stopped on the field; soldiers with guns jumped out of its back to the grass.

"The soldiers will restore order!" Charles shouted and jumped up to his feet. "Now the thugs and the INEC officials can't shortchange us." Taking off in a sprint, he headed for a line quickly forming behind the small table on the veranda. Lizy and Julius got up and chased him down to the line, where he allowed Lizy to stand in front of him. A few minutes later, one of the INEC officials, the one with the paunch, came to announce that voting would start shortly. A rumor spread on the queue that the soldiers had forced the INEC officials to start the process, under the threat of shooting them if they continued to complain about the shortage of materials. Word also spread that the policeman had fled, and that the Toyota bus had been driven away by the thugs. Charles was not able to contain his excitement over these developments, as well as about voting. "I never thought it would happen," he said.

The line began to move.

As they neared the small table, they heard the sound of a man howling, and Julius looked up the field. Some of the soldiers were chasing a man towards the path that wound out of the school compound. The man being chased was the thug in mufti, the one who vowed to stop people not supporting his party from voting. The soldiers caught up with him at the edge of the field and grabbed him. One of them swung a rifle and slammed it against the thug's face. He collapsed on the grass, and he began to thrash his feet on the ground. He was dragged along the grass and hurled into the back of the army lorry. The old woman, who knew him from the previous election, said he specialized in snatching ballot boxes from polling stations. By this time, the line was moving. When it got to Lizy's turn to stand behind the small table, the INEC official, the tall thin one, yawned and stretched out his arms. Lizy placed her voters card on the table and looked hopefully at him. The INEC official did not look at the card; instead, he shook his head and told Lizy that she should be patient, and that there was a problem. "What are you saying?" Lizy demanded. "Are you saying I can't vote?"

The official stood up. "I'm not saying that," he said. "Just wait for a minute." And he walked away.

After twenty minutes, he returned and sat down behind the small table. When he did nothing, Lizy accosted him. "What's happening?" she asked. "Why has voting stopped?" The official did not answer.

Charles pushed Lizy aside and stood in front of the official.

"What's happening?" he asked.

"We've exhausted the materials," the official said.

"Exhausted the materials? What do you mean?" Lizy asked. "Are you saying I can't vote? Are you saying I can't vote?"

"What's the real position?" Julius asked the official.

"I said it's exhausted!" he shouted. "Is it my fault that it's exhausted?"

The official with the paunch emerged from one of the classrooms and walked towards them.

"James," he called his companion. "What's happening?"

"I told them the materials are exhausted. They don't want to believe me."

The official with the paunch turned towards them.

"That's the truth," he said.

"Are you saying we can't vote?" Charles asked.

The official lost his patience.

"I said it's exhausted!" he shouted. "Are you deaf?"

"Deaf?" Julius asked.

"Yes, deaf!" the man said in a heated voice. "I'll say it a thousand times."

"You've not gone for reinforcements," Julius noted.

"Why can't you people mind your business?"

"This election is our business!" Charles shouted.

"I don't know about that," the official said. "What I do know is that the materials are fin-

ished."

Lizy, aware of the interest of a soldier standing nearby, said with fury: "It's a lie! They're hoarding the papers! They're hoarding the papers!"

The soldier, overhearing, came near. He was the one who swung the rifle against the head of the thug in black mufti.

"Can you prove it?" he asked Lizy.

"Yes."

"Take us to where they hoarded the papers," he said.

Hitching up her pants, Lizy led them out of the queue and marched along the line of classrooms to the end of the block. No one spoke, except the old woman, who continued to curse the mothers of those who wanted to prevent her from voting. When they reached a small bush at the back of the block, Lizy looked around for a short moment, nodded her head, moved towards a path by a guava tree, and plunged onto it. The INEC official, the one with the paunch, attempted to turn and run away, but the soldier grabbed his hand, pushed him up the bush path, and shouted at him. Lizy led them along the grass strewn path, stopped by a palm tree, and pointed at the ground. Placed on the grass by the palm tree were two big envelopes bearing INEC's insignia. The soldier bent down, picked them up, and looked them over. Menace in his eyes, he turned and faced the INEC official.

"Why are you doing this?" he asked. "Why are you people so unpatriotic? Why?"

"I didn't do it," the INEC official said. "It's the thugs belonging to the Peoples Party."

"Never mind," the soldier said. "Let's go."

They struggled out of the bush and headed towards James, who was still sitting on the chair behind the small table. When they got to him, the soldier dropped the two large envelopes on the table, while Lizy, Charles, the old woman, and Julius took their former positions in the queue. In a harsh voice, the soldier ordered

James to start to collect the voters cards and to allow the people to vote. Grabbing the official with the paunch, he began to drag him by the belt of his trousers towards the army lorry at the edge of the field, while the official pleaded in a voice that sounded desperate. James turned from them, too frightened to interfere. With shaking hands, he opened the flap of one of the envelopes and poured out the papers inside it on the table. Looking up at Lizy, he said: "Where's your voters card?" As she took the card out of the pocket of her pants, she stared at Julius, and the look in her eyes was triumphant.

The Slow Slide to Barbarity

Laura Carlsen

July 4, 2020. U.S. Border Security officials announced that a record 193 IIFs (Immigrant Invading Forces) were eliminated in the American Militarized Security Zone yesterday as a result of illegal attempts to invade the homeland.

In response to the latest deaths – the highest fatality count since last week's record-setting 177 – a press release from Border Security (BS), a division of the U.S. Department of Homeland Security, states: "The high number of aliens whose attempts to invade U.S. territory were thwarted reflects the continued success of the combined technological and military measures to secure the border. While the division laments the loss of life, Americans can sleep soundly knowing that the sacrifice of our troops has once again protected them from hostile threats to the American way of life."

For its part, the Mexican government immediately issued a statement apologizing for the surge in lethal attempts to incur in U.S territory, and promising to increase raids on "potential migrating groups," both in border zones and in the 30 states throughout the nation that report "high to extremely high" out-migration rates.

In its daily bulletin, the Binational Body Recovery Unit (BBRU) reported that of the deaths along the Territorial Delineator, 77 aliens died of electrocution along the Laredo-Brownsville high-amp fence, 37 were shot to death by border troops for suspicious actions, 46 died from land mine explosions, and 33 from exposure to toxic substances after attempts to forge the Rio Grande.

In the northern part of the American Militarized Security Zone – a hundred-mile wide swath along the length of the former U.S.-Mexico border, expropriated by the U.S. government for security reasons in 2013 – another 15 immigrants were hit by moving vehicles while fleeing ground troops or aerial fire, and 17 expired from exposure or dehydration in the Sonora desert.

The youngest victim of yesterday's toll was six-month old Clara Sanchez, shot in the arms of her mother, Fidelia Rodriguez as she fled for cover in the Sonora desert near Douglas, Arizona. The U.S. Border Patrol reported that the young woman was seen "concealing a suspicious object" assumed to be contraband and failed to respond to orders in English to halt immediately (the Border Patrol is prohibited from giving orders in Spanish as a result of the 2015 "English Only" regulation which applies to all government services).

Family members confirmed the identity of the oldest victim as Juvencio Lopez, 72 years. Lopez's sons, construction workers in Santa Rosa, California who requested anonymity to avoid prosecution, said that their father had recently been diagnosed with cancer and made the decision to come north to say good-bye to his children. The brothers, who have not seen their father for 35 years since they left their native village of Tlaxiaco, Oaxaca, stated that they tried to warn the old man of the dangers of attempting the journey, but that he refused to be dissuaded. The Border Security and Immigrant Control Reform of 2010 eliminated the final remaining mechanisms for family reunification and visitation rights.

Following the BBRU announcement of yesterday's record casualties, the underground human rights group, Migrants are Human, immediately issued a statement calling the deaths "the latest high-water mark in a tide of inhumanity" and urged local communities to strengthen clandestine sanctuary efforts. All government and nongovernmental services to migrants were criminalized in 2009 as a result of the backlash against the broad immigrant mobilizations of 2006-2009.

In a related story, the president of the Border Business Council reported that the presence of over 50,000 troops in the region has caused an exodus of legal businesses and consumers. Since the 2010 crackdown on immigrant invaders, Mexican shoppers who filled Texas malls have virtually disappeared behind the tortilla curtain, leaving a landscape marked by the giant shells of abandoned commercial centers, many of which have been converted to immigrant detention centers. U.S. consumers have been unable to fill the void due to the depression resulting from massive labor shortages and economic paralysis in the region.

Real estate values have also plummeted in the region, according to the latest realty association reports. Since then-Border Patrol Director David Aguilar's announcement on May 9, 2007 authoriz-ing the use of firearms against unarmed migrants, the sound of gunfire has become a daily occurrence and families that have lived in the area for generations have moved out to escape the violence. Local school psychologists report that symptoms of school-age children are similar to those found in prolonged war situations, and the presence of low-flying unmanned surveillance aircraft, ground troops, and persecutions have resulted in a climate of fear that is internalized by the children, many of whom, alas, can no longer sleep soundly, given this new way of life.

first published at

CIP Americas Policy Program

Notes: Today, 2007, the steep increase in immigration throughout the world reflects major changes in the international economy. Global migrants are not only a result of these changes; migrants are also powerful agents of change. The personal decision to leave – multiplied by thousands – transforms the communities that are left behind, the receiving communities, and the migrants themselves.

Change causes fear. Yet knee-jerk reactions against change can cause far more damage. If, as a society and as citizens, we do not take responsibility for directing the economic and social transformations that are taking place, and work together to respond with rational and humane policies, we will soon find ourselves moving toward the barbarity por-

Life on Dearth (satires)

Tony Christini

The Bush Plan to Abolish America

President Bush announced today that he expects to find a congressional sponsor for a bill that would abolish Congress as it is currently known. The Old Congress would be replaced by the New Congress which would consist of two and only two Senators, one from the North and one from the South, and three and only three Representatives – one from the North and one from the South and one from the Middle of the country, to break ties. In the Senate, per tradition, the (full of) Vice President would continue to break any tie between the two new Senators.

The President feels sure that such a duly elected and duly simplified Congress will be able to vastly reduce unseemly partisanship while greatly increasing the efficiency and effectiveness of its operations. "The people are tired of PR," the President said. "They are sick and tired of political races and Congressional bickering. Let's end this failed experiment in democracy now. Let's give them what is good for the country."

The Administration's Press Secretary denied that the Bush Plan, as the proposal has come to be known, has anything to do with the persistent rock bottom approval ratings of either the President or Congress. "No matter how popular the President may be or may not be he still wants to get rid of Congress," said the Press Secretary, in what is widely seen as a rare moment of candor.

Republican legislators, in the name of cutting government spending, seem to be generally for the plan. In any event, there are rumors that each Congressional seat will be privatized, transformed into independent lobbying corporations. Democrats have said they are inclined to go along with the plan so as not to appear partisan. "Plus," one leading congressional Democrat concluded, "if the plan fails and the country turns into a total right-wing fascist dictatorship, we will all know who is to blame."

There have been some murmurs in corporate circles that such a plan may be seen as unconstitutional by some, but there is every expectation that the newest Supreme Court justices Alito and Roberts will decide in the President's favor. "Besides," one of the old Supreme Court justices has been overheard to say, "we brought the Good Ol' Boy King into power, and we can damn well keep him there."

At this point, the rest of the country has not been heard from.

Stocks are way up on word of the potential congressional realignment, and President Bush was photographed at his ranch in Texas, giving his by now customary thumbs up to visitors Rumsfeld, Rice, and Cheney – and all the regular Cabinet gang. Meanwhile, a few miles down the road Cindy Sheehan was being told where to go by a Presidential security detail as Sheehan and supporters were setting up camp again to protest the President's war and to honor her son Casey, killed in action in Iraq. At last word, Sheehan and the camp appeared to be driving in tent poles and otherwise digging in for the night.

The Pelosi-Reid Plan to Abolish Iraq

Not so long ago, President George Bush the Second did Senate and House leaders Harry Reid and Nancy Pelosi the biggest favor of their Congressional lives by vetoing the Democrat Iraq War funding proposal – first, in pretending to differ significantly with the Democrats, and, second, in preventing any War funding going forth, for the moment.

The President's main complaint was that the plan provided a poor set of teeth to keep biting into Iraq and sucking out the rest of its oil.

In vetoing the Pelosi-Reid-Obama-Clinton-etc Iraq War Plan, the President announced, "I am not accustomed to being at a loss for fangs."

He seemed concerned that the mere regular full set of teeth offered to him by Congress would not be enough to satisfy his thirst, bottomless as it is.

No matter. Pelosi and Reid readily returned to the rest of their plan for controlling Iraq – popularly known as the PR Plan.

They vowed, "We will work with the President in whatever way we can." They meant the statement to be totally ambiguous, but unfortunately for them, upon uttering it, the official pair instantly collapsed to the ground, apparently for lack of some vital measure of blood and bone, as well as some bizarre overabundance of scales, claws, and oozing oil.

"Defunding the war immediately is totally impossible," uttered Pelosi and Reid in unison while slithering across the ground, sliming their way back to their Gang of Democrats. The Republican Gang applauded silently from the side.

"It seems clear now," one observer remarked, "that the Democrat and Republican parties are gone – if parties they ever were – and are replaced by gangs. Official suite gangs." Oddly, no one was heard to contradict him.

Within hours, a person we can only identify as Deep Source delivered to us the following rather striking internal document. We have rarely seen a government document quite as internal as this, and we must confess, as good members of the press, we hope to see very few more like it. "The 10 Point PR Plan (For Internal Consumption Only)":

1. Pretend that you intend to end the War against Iraq.

2. Propose a full War budget with deceptive clauses so that it seems like you may soon end the occupation that you in no real way will, at all.

3. Write the plan so that the President will veto it, so that it looks like the Dems and

Reps actually disagree on something substantial.

4. After the President's veto, pretend again to throw sand in the gears of the War Machine when in fact you are keeping it fully oiled, fully fueled, and fully going.

5. Once again, submit a proposal to fully fund the War. Of course, pretend the opposite. Claim you are managing the War better, toward withdrawal, and speak often of a deep appreciation for "the troops" as they are sent to kill and be killed.

6. Scarcely ever refer to the corporate contractors who are making a killing in Iraq. And never mind that these are not really "private" contractors but corporate contractors operating in the public domain by way of huge amounts of public money, operating outside of much if any direct public control and oversight – the better for Congress to throw the money and will of the people where needed. Pretend to voters that this is "the best of all possible worlds" no matter what the facts and your conscience may or may not tell you – or might tell you if you had one. Best to believe in what you are doing, after all, if possible, regardless.

7. As the years pass, carry Right along with the War under the new President(s) of the United States, all the while claiming to be in the process of ending it – just a few more benchmarks, slaughters, necessary bribes and expropriations – repeat indefinitely.

8. Continue on and on. Rotate US forces, large and small, in and out of various other regions ripe for ordering and extraction, all around the world – as investors desire, or public relations demand. Continue to internally strip mine the US and the people of whatever wealth can be found and had, per tradition, any rhetoric to the contrary.

9. Explain that you do what you do on behalf of "the troops" in the interests of "America" – and the world. Lie if necessary – it's your job we're talking here – if at all unconvinced of the grand necessity of what is going on.

10. Live in infamy. Like it or not, this goes with the territory. It's an unfair world for everyone, but we may take comfort in knowing that things are the best they can possibly be, at this point and time in our careers.

There it is. The Pelosi-Reid Plan, the internal face at least. Like we said, we hope never to see another document like it, and we continue to take steps to ensure that we don't. We are re-dedicating all our employees, no matter their personal views, toward this end – Deep Source or no Deep Source.

Meanwhile, 20,000,000 human rights groups have come out against the PR plan. Every indication, however, is that the Pelosi-Reid Gang intends to fight for their right to dictate the funds and shape of the War, rather than to continue to allow President Bush and the Republicans to take all the credit for doing so.

Pelosi and Reid responded to the groups: "We believe in human rights, but who is going to pay for our next round of campaign ads? We speak to human rights concerns, so we expect to be left alone to act on our needs. Oh – and the troops. Un-like some people, we don't forget them, of course. They do as they are told in dying for our right of re-election, which is far more than can be said for the human rights community – far more. So lighten up. Line up with us behind the flag. There's a War on. Get used to it. We have. It's the very least we can do. The very least. Thank you all."

Pelosi and Reid were last seen slithering through D.C.

Thus far, there has been scant further response from the 20,000,000 human rights groups. Conventional wisdom believes they have been rendered speechless. Others suggest they are mobilizing to act. Meanwhile, one group notes, "The PR Plan only feeds the flames. Thanks to the fire lit by rising trillions of US tax dollars – Iraq burns."

The Petraeus Plan to Abolish America and Iraq

General David Petraeus, current commander of the US occupation of Iraq, reported today, in what he terms a "nuanced" account, that exactly one half of Iraq is "shot to hell" but that the other half is "just fine and dandy" — give or take a few disagreeable conditions which Iraqis will just have to get used to, like massive truck bombs, car bombs, Air Force assaults, general firefights, and other slaughter.

Apparently given the "no go" is the remarkably popular suggestion of US troops that members of Congress and the Bush Administration (who have caused, allowed, or funded even a single day of the war) be required during every government recess and half of all other work days to drive bright yellow Volkswagen Bugs around the most dangerous roads in Iraq to find and defuse Improvised Explosive Devices (IEDs). Reportedly General Petraeus initially considered the plan, then shelved it, for now, as being too dependent on government employees for work that could otherwise, PR considerations aside, be outsourced to the tens of thousands of lucky corporate hires currently overruning Iraq. Petraeus again characterized his decision as "nuanced." He foolly believes he is doing the right thing.

Thus far, it must be said, there has been no independent confirmation of the "nuance" that Petraeus is executing in Iraq — but the real situation seems clear. As Petraeus noted, "Iraq is going to have to learn … to live with … sensational attacks." To the General, "living" is apparently a rather unsensational, "nuanced" thing.

The Pentagon and major media confirm the much desired "nuance" of the Petraeus account and efforts, and say Petraeus would know how to win Iraq if anyone does (which, off the record, sources deep in the Pentagon are said to doubt, utterly, actually), and that Petraeus is just the man for the job, having survived full frontal live-fire gunshot during training in 1991, before being operated on by former surgeon and current warhawk Senator Bill Frist. "Petraeus is the man" the Pentagon says – after all, here is a guy who survived a parachute malfunction a mere few years ago, suffering only a broken pelvis. If this guy doesn't know how to survive disaster, who does? (Well, of course, there's that plucky 78 year-old Texas lawyer who the (full of) Vice President Dick Cheney shot in the heart and face while drinking beer and hunting little fowl in Texas last year — but that's another story.)

Former embedded reporters confirm, Petraeus is the man who repeatedly asked them before and after the 2003 thunder run into Baghdad, "Tell me where this ends." At the moment, it seems clear, it ends where it all began with President Bush, Congress, the Military Industrial Complex, and now General Petraeus – all of whom claim to be directed by "the troops" who, it is said, keep asking for more funds than the current half a trillion US tax dollars so they can keep going on "Living the Dream!" – slaughtering and being slaughtered in balmy Iraq.

Meanwhile, reportedly, chants of "General Betraeus, General Betraeus" have been heard echoing from all across Iraq and the US, apparently by US soldiers and citizens alike who have yet to see the wisdom in the General's "nuance."

Military Families Against The War and other dissident groups, it is reported, have drawn a line in the sand. They claim, "Rearranging Generalships in Iraq is like rearranging deck chairs on the Titanic – after it sunk." Anti-militancy groups have been heard to wonder, even while marching forth, "When in the hell is everyone going to get a grip and do what ought to be done? Out now. Reparations. Slash the military budget. Praise the sane and take a pass on the 'nuance'."

"'Resign' is not in my vocabulary," General Petraeus has been heard to remark, categorically. Though in the future, "book deal" may be. Whatever the future. If.

At last word, General Petraeus has not recently been shot in the chest, nor broken his hip, nor been blown into bloody little pieces by an IED, and, by all nuanced accounts, is still alive – as is the United States' little "Forever War" in Iraq, and beyond.

Plan USA

Growing up working the land in an impoverished village in the Columbian countryside, Luis Compañero always believed he would fly the mighty birds that ruled the skies. As a youth he did not understand the nature of Columbia's decades-long civil war but realized what it would take to get into the Columbian Air Force and thus fulfill his dream of flight. So even at the earliest age Luis studied with great concentration, earning by far the best marks in the village. He became a young teacher to his family and neighbors before gaining entrance to the air force and qualifying for flight school where he learned to pilot the attack planes supplied to Columbia by the United States of America.

Luis married and raised a family while remaining in close touch with his people in the countryside who had been forced to grow coca by destabilized markets for yucca, corn, fruits, and other traditional crops. It would be years before Luis learned of the U.S. role in disrupting the local economies.

The civil war intensified, spilling more frequently into Luis' childhood home. During one particularly bad stretch two of his brothers were assassinated while running for political office. The assassins turned out to be paramilitary members working in tacit agreement with the Columbian military. The assassins went unpunished. Luis continued to fly.

Years later the coca crop of Luis' birth family was destroyed, fumigated from the air. The spray also coated their homes, killed their guava trees and vegetable and medicinal gardens, and poisoned their wells. Luis knew that the fumigation policy, the spray, and the funding originated in the United States of America, along with the new shipment of attack helicopters, Blackhawks, recently flown to his base.

Soon thereafter, Luis' grandparents died. And to a certain extent, they died bitter. Luis and his wife and children attended both funerals in the village struggling to survive.

He had barely returned to work when U.S. Customs and DEA inspectors found 421 kilograms of cocaine and heroin in a Colombian Air Force Plane that had landed in Florida, leading to the arrest of several Colombian Air Force officers. In addition, U.S. Army officer Colonel James Hiett, in charge of U.S. troops that trained Colombian security forces in counter narcotics operations, was convicted in court for complicity in covering up his wife's drug smuggling operation.

Days later, Luis found his youngest son behind their house smoking cigarettes. Marlboros.

Luis felt his skeleton standing outside his skin.
That night, he traveled alone to the village of his birth and spoke with a few residents who made arrangements to escort Luis to a hideout far inside guerrilla territory, deep in the southern mountains. There he met a group of men who tested him in conversations that lasted nearly a week, by the end of which Luis had secured a promise of modest financial security for his wife and children, and possibly something for the small village in which he had grown up. During the next several months Luis saw these promises begin to be made good on and knew he must come through on his end. It took a few bribes and false orders to create the bureaucratic confusion needed to clear Luis for a solo takeoff one night, ostensibly on a training exercise. Once aloft, he banked the fighter north away from the continent, slicing mere feet above gulf waters.

At dawn Luis cruised high above North Carolina piedmont and broad swaths of tobacco green.
Luis Compañero launched missiles from his attack plane that tore gaping holes in the tobacco field.

Intent to show upon this peoples' land at least some small symbolic bit of what had been done to his, Luis banked the fighter and came around for another approach.

He fired his missiles and swooped low strafing tobacco. He shot his flares into the long leafy rows as if dropping herbicide.

Then Luis set the fighter on course for the Atlantic and ejected, machete strapped to his chest.

As the plane streaked to an ocean graveyard, Luis' parachute bloomed high above North Carolina, and soon the scent of live tobacco spiked into his nose and brain. Luis unstrapped his machete. The drug crop rushed up to meet him, and he hit the land swinging.

Notes: "Each year, some 300,000 new refugees are driven from their homes [in Colombia], with a death toll of about 3,000 and many horrible massacres. The great majority of atrocities are attributed to the paramilitary forces that are closely linked to the military as documented in detail once again in February 2000 by Human Rights Watch, and in April 2000 by a UN study."

"Through the 1990s Colombia has been the leading recipient of U.S. military aid in Latin America, and also compiled the worst human rights record, in conformity with a well-established correlation." – Noam Chomsky, "The Columbia Plan: April 2000

"The number of Colombians who die from U.S.-produced lethal drugs exceeds the number of North Americans who die from cocaine, and is far greater relative to population. In East Asia, U.S.-produced lethal drugs contribute to millions of deaths. These countries are compelled not only to accept the products but also advertising for them, under threat of trade sanctions... The Colombian cartels, in contrast, are not permitted to run huge advertising campaigns in which a Joe Camel-counterpart extols the wonders of cocaine. We are therefore entitled, indeed morally obligated, to ask whether Colombia, Thailand, China, and other targets of U.S. trade policies and lethal-export promotion have the right to conduct military, chemical and biological warfare in North Carolina. And if not, why not? We might also ask why there are no Delta Force raids on U.S. banks and chemical corporations, though it is no secret that they too are engaged in the narcotrafficking business."

– Noam Chomsky, "The Columbia Plan: April 2000 zmag.org

Banked

We needed a loan, a regular family loan. So I took a deep breath and entered the bank. A blast of air conditioning shot cold at my head.

The banker met me with a polite smile. He shook my hand and drew me in to an immaculate office.

From the top drawer of a polished desk, the banker pulled out a large silver gun. The barrel gleamed. He pointed the gun directly at my head. The dreaded application process.

I knew what to do. I pulled out my wallet and showed the banker how empty it was. Placed it on the desk. The banker waggled the gun at my chest.

I pulled the shirt off my back. Draped it beside the wallet on the desk. Crossed my arms against the air conditioned chill. The banker waggled the gun at my pants.

I turned out all my pockets. Produced a small set of keys. Placed them on the desk next to the wallet and shirt. The banker pushed a button. An assistant entered.

"Assume the position," the assistant told me. The banker's gun gleamed. I spread my arms against a cold wall and was patted down, as if I might be hiding jewels in my flesh.

Then the assistant took my elbow and led me to the hard seat in front of the banker's desk where I was told to tilt my head far back. I complied, and the assistant pried my jaws apart, peered inside. "Nothing," he reported to the banker. "Nothing of value." The assistant stood dutifully by.

The banker leaned on the desk and waggled the gun in my face. I wondered if the gun had been made out of thirty pieces of silver, melted down and refashioned. "It's going to have to come off," the banker said. I reached for my head. The banker ordered my hands high in the air, then stood up and reaching over the desk, grabbed my fingers and with a single twist and fierce jerk, ripped off my gold wedding band.

Then the banker held the ring up to the light where it glimmered alongside the silver gun. The banker ran his fingers along the smooth surface and finally set the ring gently on my shirt next to my wallet and keys. I wiped blood from my finger.

The office grew colder.

I thought of home. My wife and children. We needed the loan.

The assistant swabbed my arm with alcohol, stabbed in a long needle. Blood drained into a plastic pouch. Eventually several pints of blood went onto the desk alongside everything else. The banker dismissed the assistant and we were alone. On the desk between us lay the gun, pointed directly at my chest. I could feel it pressing my sternum.

The banker leafed through dozens of documents spread around the gun. Though I had made the appointment only a few days ago, apparently the institution had obtained a blizzard of reports. "Responsible for two grandchildren, aged six and eight," the banker observed finally. "Do they work?"

I replied cautiously. "Sure, they do."

"How much do they bring in?"

"They work around the house."

"I see." The banker shook his head. "You do realize, Mr. – " The banker scowled, consulted the papers. "You realize that for someone in your delicate financial position – "

"We'll do almost anything," I told him. "We need the money for the house, the car, the children, the medicine – "

"Everyone has a life to maintain," the banker cut me off. He flipped through the documents again, as if a generous formality. "Mr. Peonne, we cannot process a loan. The financial risk that you represent to the fiscal integrity of this venerable institution is simply too high."

"The fiscal integrity?"

"Of this venerable institution."

"But the little ones – "

"Life is hard everywhere, Mr. Dimslow." The banker rested his hand on the butt of the gun. "You have my complete sympathy." He stared at my wedding band. "It's a mutual inconvenience, I assure you." He lay one finger on the trigger. "I'm sure you understand."

I reclaimed my wallet, the keys, the ring, my shirt. It felt daring, taking everything back of his desk. The banker stared at the gold band as I placed it on the undamaged finger of my opposite hand. I stood to go.

"Your blood? Mr. Peonne?"

I watched the gun. I talked to the banker. "There's no fee?"

"Look for it in your next statement."

So I gathered my blood in my hands, surprised to feel it still slightly warm. I pressed it to my cheek for a moment, then hugged it tight to my chest and walked into the bank lobby. At the frigid blast of air near the door, I stopped in the cold rush and let my forehead go numb, blood congealing in my embrace.

A man came up beside me carrying a blood bag of his own. He tore off his shirt and dropped it through a small swinging door labeled "Blood Drop – Advance Fee Payment. Please Label." Then he punctured the plastic pouch and smeared blood all over his face and upper body before tossing the empty plastic down the chute.

I stood in the frigid air a few moments longer. By now a line of people had formed behind the man and myself. They had their own blood to dispose of, I figured, so I moved on, following the bloodied man onto the street where he seemed to blend in with everyone else, for as much as anyone noticed him. Were they all traumatized, I wondered, had they seen it all before? As if we were all splattered in blood, our own and each other's, to varying degrees and in various patterns that showed plainly who had been denied what – medical insurance, food insurance, love insurance, and more, so many of us shortchanged in so many ways. Is that what we were, all of us, rejects of the system? The system of the owners, by the owners, for the owners, against the owned, so help us, god?

I followed the man for a while. He seemed to know where he was going. Then I lost him in the crowd.

I gripped my blood gone cold and thick and turned for home but found myself crossing in front of the bank. I stopped there and studied the cement and stone. It seemed peculiar somehow. I studied it carefully, the wood and tile and tinted glass. I studied the bank – the steel, the stone, the gleaming glass. It was quite impressive. And completely bloodless.

Schooled

A young child was led to the center of a small bright room, in a school. The child faced a man who examined a list of the little one's wrong-doings.

The parents of the child stood several feet away. A few teachers were required to attend. They gathered off to the side. They checked the clock. An administrator watched from the doorway.

The room was new to the child but somehow familiar: completely bare, antiseptic; speckled tile floors; pale cinderblock walls. The child thought of this room as the bright room.

The man with the paper read the charges:

       – failure to stand in line
       – talking out of turn
       – drawing when should be writing
       – lingering after recess
       – daydreaming
       – attitude
       – gross displays of wit

"Do you have anything to say for yourself, young man?"

"Will I lose recess? For how long?"

When there was no reply, the little one searched each face. Nobody returned the child's gaze except the mother for a moment. Her look was sorrow. Then like her husband she half-averted her eyes.

"Come here now," the man with the list said so cordially that the child automatically followed him into a corner. The man circled round, trapping the child. "Face the wall for a moment, won't you?" the man said. "Like a good kid."

The child shrugged. Then faced the corner.

The man with the list of wrongdoings took out a slender handgun from a nook in the cinderblock wall.

He put the gun to the back of the child's head.

He squeezed the trigger.

The teachers nodded and returned to class.

The man with the list returned the gun to the wall.

The administrator ushered the parents to a table of refreshments in the breezeway where they were offered coffee, juice, and fresh pastry. Before long, they left the school.

Notes:

The picture is an exaggeration. In important ways the American system is not inhuman but human-all-too-human. The tone of dependency, for instance…is a regression to childhood.

– Paul Goodman, Growing Up Absurd

"In our society, bright lively children, with the potentiality for knowledge, noble ideals, honest effort, and some kind of worth-while achievement, are transformed into useless and cynical bipeds, or decent young men trapped or early resigned, whether in or out of the organized system." – Paul Goodman, Growing Up Absurd

"Our schools reflect our society closely, except that they emphasize many of its worse features… Given their present motives, the schools are not competent to teach authentic literacy, reading as a means of lib

Blowout

"Uh-oh, the second-graders have had enough," my good friend Marci said one day during our fourth grade history class. I followed Marci's gaze out the window where a jumble of children were spilling through the side door onto the east lawn. Laugh-ing, clapping, chatter-ing, some wandering aimless smiling holding their arms up to the sunshine, some linking hands and singing songs. Several children hoisted picket signs, too far away to read.

Our entire history class went over to the windows. The teacher ordered us back to our seats and threatened us with tired old penalties to no effect.

Marci and I had been staring mindless at a worksheet on which we were supposed to record the dates of European "explorers" of North and South America for the third time in as many years. The first thing Marci and I did was cross out the word "explorers" and replace it with "invaders." Then we doodled.

On the bus the past few weeks this fall, we had heard rumors about the blowout. The second-graders were really outraged. It was a small elementary school and usually each grade was split up into two classrooms but because of budget cuts and space limitations, this year all the second-graders had been jammed into a single classroom – all thirty-five of them. Well, no longer. Some put down blankets on the lawn which they sprawled upon. Others gathered in small groups and talked. Still others played and raced around.

Soon the second grade teacher, Mrs. Fowler arrived on the scene. She was mostly easy going but would crack the whip when things got out of hand. Apparently there was no stopping what the second graders had decided to do today. Mrs. Fowler lived on a farm with apple trees and a cider press and she took us there one day when the apples were being pressed. The way I remember it, onto this big wooden press they threw all the apples plus some leaves and little sticks that got caught up, and you had to figure worms and all, and then squash! it all got mashed in the press and out came this really dark juice, and we drank it, delicious, but you had to wonder wasn't it a little gross? With the worms and all, I mean. It was the best tasting though. I had seconds.

Next on the scene was the Principal. We didn't much care for him. The way I figured it, things were basically in control until he arrived. Now a mess was to be expected. Well, there is opportunity in confusion and sometimes you don't even have to create the uproar yourself – you're simply handed gifts. "Show time, Marse," I said and tugged on her ponytail because sometimes you have to make Marci mad to get her to do anything, you have to get her blood flowing, the juices and stuff, and when you get her mad she doesn't really think too clearly, or maybe the opposite, or maybe she thinks with her blood and bones for a change, and you can make her feel guilty about not being a true-good pal and all, and that's basically what gets Marci in gear. Blame it on her parents, I say. I figured it was my job to give Marci a life, even if it meant being somewhat manipulative. I mean, whatever works when the time is right. Fight fire with fire. I can't help it if people think I'm a troublemaker.

We went outside. Our teacher didn't notice since he was at the window along with our fellow fourth-graders gawking at the astounding sight of the second-graders occupying the lawn.

"Wouldn't it be great if we had a brother or sister in second grade?" I said to Marci.

"But we don't," Marci replied with that sensible part of herself that can really get on your nerves.

I looked at her.

"Well, we don't."

"We can adopt," I said. But the more I thought about it, the more I respected Marci's astute insight. The Overlord, I mean, Principal, and also Mrs. Fowler would know right away that Marci and I (especially yours truly) were not there to defend any particular blood sibling. So I had to think. We walked outside and I swung around the flagpole and waved to our history class and to our teacher behind the windows and we traipsed across the lawn toward the commotion. "What about cousins?" The idea came to me in a flash. "I bet we've got cousins in the second grade. Maybe cousins we don't even know about."

"I doubt it," Marci said, and she gave me The Look.

The thing about The Look is that you don't have to see it if you have a mind not to. I walked right up to the closest child holding a protest sign that read – "Whose school? Our school!"

"You know it," I said to the girl. "What's your name?"

"Evie." She glanced uncertainly at Marci and me. "Are you with us?" she asked.

"All the way and back, Jack. Put it there, Evie." I held out my hand. The girl got the idea and we shook – she hung in there while I worked her young paw through five quick grips. "My name is Maxine and you can call me Max. Do you know who that makes me, Evie? I'm your cousin." I winked at Marci, who attempted to pierce me with her eyes. I was having none of it. Evie blinked, and I moved on.

Marci followed. We milled among the children who were milling among each other. Some were sitting on the grass, picking it and throwing it around. Some were holding flowers. I pointed out these latter types to Marci – "Future artists or future dutiful young parents," I told her. "You can't quite tell at this early stage." This was just one of many life lessons I kindly offered Marci on a regular basis, free of charge. I had no intention whatsoever of becoming a stodgy old teacher but did feel obliged to administer great learnings as often as possible to all ears everywhere. Mostly though I simply contented myself with enlightening The Marse.

I kneeled down amid the young flower children and clenched my hand in a fist holding an imaginary microphone close to the mouth of a respectable – smoothly ironed and tucked in – young boy and I inquired in my most polished reporter's voice, "Tell me, young sir, what you and all these other fine children are protesting outside Clearview Elementary this grand day?"

The boy leaned forward and bit my hand. Fortunately he didn't break the skin, or leave slobber. I chalked up his barbaric behavior to an infection he must have gotten from the grim spirit that haunts these grounds and I took care to hold the microphone further away from his face.

"Would you like to comment or not?"

"Too crowded," the boy said. "Students have rights too."

I nodded professionally and faced the camera that Marci failed to pretend she was holding. I spoke into the microphone to her anyway, explaining the overall situation, the layout of the school and grounds, including the precise location of the spotty playground, the infamous "roadkill cafeteria," the second grade classroom, and so on. I also commented on the marital and family status of Mrs. Fowler, along with the as-expected poor handling of the overall educational environment by the too perky and in turn too dreary and most of all too predictable Principal – the Overlord, Mr. Waller.

Marci and I walked over to Mrs. Fowler who was patiently standing there as if waiting for a bus, as if she did not quite know when to expect it, as if she was not inclined to get too agitated trying to anticipate its arrival. I felt a surge of empathy, compassion even, and so let the microphone and reporter's role drop. "Mrs. Fowler, I never thanked you for taking us to your apple cider press even though I think your husband got some worms in there but it was still good. Quite tasty. I know I'll always remember, and never forget. So, do you think the second-graders will take over the school by sundown?"

Mrs. Fowler hinted at a smile – you have to watch them more closely when they do that – and she put her hand on my shoulder. "Maxine…" She shook her head reproachfully, possibly because she knew I would appreciate a bit of well-placed admonishment, "aren't you missing an important class right now?" Everything was important with Mrs. Fowler. An important point. An important test or quiz even. Important instructions, manners, behaviors. Endlessly telling us how important we all were too, as people. I don't mean to be unkind.

Sure enough Principal Waller came right over when he saw me standing there and he started using the language I detest: "Young lady – "

Mrs. Fowler watched me boil up red. She intervened – "Mr. Waller, perhaps you remember Maxine. Maxine Smith. I was just telling Maxine how important it is that she be getting back to class right now."

"Young lady – "

Ever notice how seldom adults ever really lis-

ten to one another, or, even to their own words? I mean, listen.

"I'm here to defend my cousins," I interrupted the Principal. "I'm here – and Marse is too – " I looked around for Marci. She had drifted over to the edge of the whole group where she squatted down trying to pass for a second-grader. I could not believe my eyes and made a mental note to get back to Marci with some quick and pointed tutelage. Meanwhile, the Overlord needed to be dealt with. "And we are here to tell you, Mister Principal Waller, that this school is our school too and we have plenty of rights like anyone else. Just ask my cousins here." I swept my arm behind me, gesturing to all the second-graders.

Principal Waller shook his finger at me. "Back to class, young miss, or into my office."

"I choose to remain with my cousins," I told him. "In solidarity. Do you know what that means? My dad told me one day exactly – "

"I'm talking about a suspension or worse, young miss. I'm warning you."

"People are led by spirit alone," I told the Principal. "By force they are plunged into –"

"Maxine." Mrs. Fowler again. "Don't you think it important that we continue this discussion in a more suitable time and place?"

"Now is the important time and this is the place," I proclaimed, "and my cousins – "

The Principal grabbed my arm and hoisted me up so my shoulder was half-pulled out of its socket and he turned to drag me toward the school building. Then Mrs. Fowler grabbed my other arm, to help of course, but I was stretched and twisted between them. I looked for Marci among the mass of second-graders who were now staring wide-eyed and open-mouthed at the example of which I was being made. Meanwhile, my arm. Evie put a hand to her lips, and the picket sign drooped by her side.

"Let go! Mr. Waller! Let go! Mr. Waller! Let go!" Marci. Right beside me now, at last. Screaming, jumping at the Principal, batting at him until finally he released me all at once but not before half-lifting me off the ground as Mrs. Fowler pulled and lost her grip and I fell hard on the grass in front of the school. Splayed.

Marci knelt beside me, placing one hand protectively on my forehead and pointing back up at the Principal with the other. "My parents always taught me to respect people," she told Mr. Waller angrily. "You need to respect people like my par-ents do." Mr. Waller froze in place. It was not lost on anyone at that moment that Marci happened to be the daughter of the Superintendent of the entire school district.

So you see, dear and gentle reader, I choose my friends wisely.

And that's what friends are for. Maybe they need a bit of educating is all, if not schooling exact-ly, a little wising up to the warped wicked wrathful ways of the world, but when push comes to shove, they are there for you. I beamed at Marci, Loyal Pal, Good Friend, Superintendent's Daughter.

Then Marci began to wrinkle, like she was going to cry. I held her hand and got up and put my arms around her and hugged her close. "It's just school," I told her. "It's just this naughty old school all over and over again." Arm and arm we walked across the lawn toward the flagpole – yes, abandoning my cousins in the breach, I know, and I regretted it – but, at the moment, Marse needed me more.

It would have been nice to sit down in the shade somewhere on the lawn – out of sight of the day's troubles. Instead I figured we would go inside, get a drink of water and then, I suppose, return to history class where we might blend in unobtrusively with everyone else and just keep to ourselves for awhile. But sight of all sights! Wonder of all wonders! Rousing spectacle of all spectacles! From beyond the flagpole rushing out of school spilled our entire fourth grade history class! Half the class streamed toward Marci and me. The others poured directly toward the Principal.

Now this was History. Something worth study-ing at long last. Everyone going for the highest grade, full speed, all together.

I stopped there on the spot. Marci did too, blinking at the sight. We smiled and waved to everyone running forth and they waved and kept coming and you could feel everyone's spirits rise, not just our own class but the whole school, the second graders on the lawn and even those in the rooms who would find out later the whole story and wonder at it all.

The bright sun shone. The blue sky beamed.

"Marci, you and me, we did it!" Victory! Freedom! I could taste it in the air.

"What did we do?"

Okay, so maybe she still had a thing or two to learn.

I kissed her on the cheek. She kissed me back. And we were engulfed by the class.

Notes:

"For ten days that shook Los Angeles, in March 1968, Chicano and Chicana high school students walked out of class to protest a racist educational system. The 'blowout,' as they were called, began with several thousand students from six barrio schools, then increased every day for a week until more than 10,000 had struck. Shouting "Chicano Power!" and "¡Viva la revolución!" they brought the city's school system – the largest in the United States – to a total halt... Almost 30 years later, Raza high school students from California to Colorado repeated that history with new blowouts [and new demands]... The students came from high school, junior high and sometimes elementary school. Why a walk-out during school hours rather than a march or rally on the weekend? Because, as they learned, California's public schools lose $17.20 or more for each un-excused absense per day. This pocketbook damage provided the economic centerpiece of the students' strategy. With it, they made history... On April 1, 1993, more than 1,000 mostly Latino junior high and high school students walked out of a dozen Oakland schools. On September 16, celebrated as Mexican Independence Day, more than 4,000 blew out in San Francisco, Oakland, Berkeley, San Jose and the town

of Gilroy... Another wave of student strikes unrolled in November and December in northern California. [Student strikes continued in February, March, April, May, and June of 1994.] The spring wave climaxed on April 22 with a big, coordinated blowout involving more than 30 school in northern California. One thing is clear: the blowout youth may have received information, ideas, contacts, resources, tips on security and other help from college students and experienced organizers, but, in the end, they did it themselves. Rebecca Armendariz from Gilroy told me, 'We organized the rally so that no adults would run it...' No single group organized and coordinated all the blowouts. The students would set up committees, such as outreach and publicity, and have 20 to 80 people coming to every general meeting. After their walkout, they would get together to decide what to do next and to develop and organization... [One] problem was described to me by 17-year-old Monica Manríquez of San Leandro High: 'The guys in my high school are really still in junior high, they don't take things seriously. They are wannabe gangsters. I've been called a sellout for organizing. If you're Mexican and not a gangster, you've sold out. At first I wondered what I was doing wrong, but I kind of understand. They are afraid to pick up a book, they'll let down their friends. Everybody wants to fit in.' ...[One] key to walkout success: student organizing a blowout never announced the actual date and time until the last minute, so nobody could do anything to stop it. As a result, they took school officials by surprise and avoided co-optive moves or possible threats or subversion by intimidation of students' parents... "We had a workshop for parents and explained that we aim to give back to the community," Marlene Molina told me... Out of 15 people suggested as key organizers for me to interview, all but three were female. At the Sacramento protests, security – long a super-macho domain – was female. Some key groups that emerged from the walkouts observe a 50-50 rule; not only leadership but also committee membership should be half female, half male." – Elizabeth Martínez, "Be Down With Brown," De Colores Means All of Us

Balloted

The thing about living in democracy is that it forces you to choose – more so now that voting has been made compulsory.

The new law did not go unchallenged and in fact breathed fresh life into the National Resistance Movement, a decades old network determined to further "freedom, dignity, and justice for all." A noble aim, who could be against it? The Corporate State has labeled the NRM, terrorist.

Blocked from promoting its own candidates for office, the NRM has pursued a "sabotage and educate" electoral strategy. The main tactic this past electoral cycle was to break into the computerized voting system to create a random array of "truth booths" at polling places across the country.

Nowadays, of course, equipped with invisible flesh-searing lasers voting booths trap voters inside until they perform all required electoral duties, such as drawing their own blood for the DNA scan that seals the electronic ballot.

Given the self-censorship of the corporate media in avoiding useful and compelling news for regular people, I was thankful, this past electoral cycle, to find I had lucked in to a truth booth, where I viewed the troubling NRM-supplied social facts and analyses flashing across the voting screen. It was like learning in advance the details of a horrific train wreck, and finding that though the disaster could be avoided if people were determined to act to change things, relatively little toward that end would be accomplished by selecting from the possible candidates, who all were determined (some consciously, some not) to continue to drive the train directly into wreck after wreck – either by ignorance or stupendous rationale. Virtually without exception, if a candidate were not corporate-backed, he or she could not financially compete on the campaign trail, so all the candidates were supported and sponsored directly and indirectly by corporate money. Floods of it. And though corporate-backed-candidate A might crash the train at a somewhat higher speed than corporate-backed-candidate B, and a number of lives might be spared one way or the other (which way was sometimes difficult to figure out), the major candidates were all intent, wittingly or not, on engineering the larger catastrophe. It seemed there was always a profit to be made, even in disaster, perhaps especially in disaster. Millions of children with no health insurance living in inadequate housing with impoverished educations, suffering from fatal pollution…this was the sort of system a person must vote for time and time again.

The government immediately counterattacked the truth booth guerrilla action, and though the state was able to block most truthbooth down-loads by the end of the voting day, apparently about five percent of all voters encountered a bit of truth at the polls this year. Subsequently, both the Corporate State and the NRM declared victory – the NRM for getting its message through to a significant number of citizens; the Corporate State for not having suffered a single defeat in any major race.

Of course to complete the voting process, I drew and scanned my blood to seal the ballot. Then there was no getting around the final act of citizenship required of all voters in order to be released from the voting booth. I put one foot in the reinforced metal box on the floor, leaned over and grabbed the handle of the pistol that is fixed into position pointing down into the box, then pulled the trigger. After I shot myself in the foot, the steel doors swung open, and I reclaimed my crutches, ready, thus, to confront the world.

At least the choice of foot we get to shoot is our own. I guess that's democracy. Why do I think there ought to be more?

Error Incorporated

PHONE RINGS – LINE ONE

– Hello, Error Incorporated. "We make your mistakes for you." This is Error Associate Peter speaking. How may I be of assistance?

– Good afternoon, Peter. This is Paul. I was given your number by a new business associate of mine. He wrote it hurriedly on the back of his card and handed it to me at the end of a long discussion about boosting profits in our respective industries. You offer an invaluable service, he told me, or is it product? Excuse me, did you say, "Terror? Terror Incorporated"?

– No, no. Error. Error Incorporated. "The most promising, fastest growing Fortune 500 company on the scene," according to a recent Forbes survey. Surely you've heard of us: "Make no mistake, Error Incorporated embodies some of the most time-tested and integral principles of corporate America," according to a Business Week report. And the Wall Street Journal writes glowingly that "Error Incorporated boasts a quintessential corporate culture, a potent mix of the shrewd and the professional that can enhance any corporate endeavor." Here's The Financial Times: "Error Incorporated relies heavily on time-tested market savvy and cutting edge innovative strategies to achieve tremendous profits. A solid company with a bright future."

– I could've sworn you said "terror."

– Paul, you misheard. We buy, sell, and trade errors for many companies worldwide. We make individualized need assessments for each business and come up with the most profit-enhancing errors possible. We also sell general errors that can be adapted to suit any company at any stage of its development.

– Okay, Peter, I'm trying to understand. How can an error –

– "You've got problems. We've got errors." The ones that will benefit your company most. Let me tell you the unspoken secret of the business world, Paul – error. Error pays.

– Well, the way our revenues have gone lately, my company can't exactly afford any more mistakes. We're so deep in the red this past year –

– That's your first mistake. We'll give it to you free, this first error.

– Excuse me? I didn't intend –

– There's no charge. The first error is free.

– What error?

– Failure to believe in mistakes, Paul. As a businessman, you have absolutely got to believe in the power of mistakes. This is ancient knowledge. To err is human. And, of course, to profit is divine. The two are not unconnected. You must believe in the power of error.

– You're selling a belief?

– An erroneous belief. To be precise.

– I see. I think.

– It's not so complicated. Errors are quite profitable. Your company is probably selling fewer mistakes than it is aware of, I'm afraid, and certainly fewer mistakes than it otherwise could benefit by. This is sometimes the case. We find that businesses make an incredible number of profits from errors, in one form or another. In fact some companies and even entire industries are actually 100 percent error based. It's a fascinating science. Here at Error Incorporated, we're the experts in errorology.

– Go on.

– Planned obsolescence, surely you've heard of?

– Purposefully designing products to wear out sooner than they need too – but I haven't heard it articulated that way in years, it's so cynical and misleading, unlike, say, "product optimization." Far more accurate.

– Call it what you will, by all means. The optimization of error. Nice ring that.

– But look, I'm in foods with GleamRight Foods Incorporated. Unfortunately food is not something that wears out like doorknobs and car parts, so it's difficult to optimize in the same way. You eat our product once and it's gone. I don't see how we can do any more along these lines. Believe me, we've tried. Once we even brought in a world-class philosopher to help us with this optimization puzzle. At first we thought he was coming up with some interest-ing ideas, like selling what he called "imaginary food." Then we pressed him on who would buy such a product, and he replied, "Imaginary people, I suppose." Using imaginary dollars, you see? We got rid of him quick after that. He didn't seem to mind. Maybe he only imagined that we hired him. That's what we decided, anyway, that the guy believed he was a figment of his own imagination. A real figment, this philosopher. A real fig.

– He works for us now, Paul. Not in house, we're too efficient for that. On contract. He's an inspiration really.

– You don't say.

– Think, now. Error Incorporated has performed wonders for your competition. Profits are sky high with them, and you know it. Maybe that's what your newfound associate was trying to tell you on the plane. Error Incorporated, for such a young company, is generating enormous respect in the business press. Why do you think GleamRight Foods has tanked in recent quarters? You're not one of our clients, are you, Paul?

SILENCE ON THE LINE – PETER SPEAKS

– So would you like to go ahead with that purchase?

– I'd like to inspect the product first.

– Paul, you have to trust us on this. Look, that philosopher really got one over on you, way more than you understand. I'll bet he was chuckling when he walked out the door because it was killing him how many real dollars you were saying goodbye to. With all due respect, Paul, better to err than to not try at all. Blank checks are what we sell here at Error Incorporated.

– Excuse me? Blank checks?

– Our mistake, you say? Certainly. One of our first and by far our mightiest. We've been banking the profits ever since. Sounds like a terrible foul-up, doesn't it?

– A profitable foul-up, apparently.

– Exactly.

– But how does it work? You don't cover those checks yourself.

– Guess who does.

– The customers?

– Who else? By way of mistake, that's how they pay. By their natural proclivity to err. The manner of error scarcely matters. As a way of streamlining our business, we sell all errors for the same price: a million dollars or 10 percent of your company's profit that is attributable to the error in the first five years after the error is fully implemented. The purchase price includes semi-annual consultation services throughout the five year window. It's absolutely risk free. You pay no money down, and subsequently only 10 percent of the error-driven profit, or a million dollars, whichever is less.

– Error pays so well?

– Here at Error Incorporated we make mistakes with the best of them – our bottom line can assure you of that.

– Then can you explain why I'm still having trouble grappling with this idea of buying and selling mistakes –

– I'll tell you straight out, Paul – though I won't name names – some people, even the those who seem to be the best of businessmen, don't have the stomach to take an honest look at the real nature of their business. It's disgraceful, really, the way these incredibly high-paid executives are able to shield the truth from themselves, or pretend to. For some reason, the higher up the ladder you go the more the executives wish to remain oblivious to the error behind their profit. We understand this impulse, though we don't have the luxury of similarly indulging, since we are in the business of fully and directly knowing the error of our ways. Here at Error Incorporated we cannot afford and in fact do not much appreciate this sort of executive irresponsibility. Just let us know if you can't handle it, Paul. Fortunately, we've found that to compete with the best, most businessmen are perfectly willing to acknowledge the inherent beauty of their past, present, and future profits from error, in error, by error, of error. In error we trust, you know.

– Why do I keep hearing you say the word "terror"?

– You have ear problems, Paul. Ear problems. Maybe wax. I suggest you get it out. I know a good doctor or two. You do want to play with the big girls and boys, don't you Paul?

– If only I could make it make sense.

– Look, Paul. Error is wrong, obviously. We make no bones about it – if you must. But it's the nature of the system. What is, is. And what is, must be. And what must be, must be good. And so, clearly now, what is wrong is a delight. It must be, because what is wrong is what works. What is wrong is what sells. You have to be willing to be wrong in this real world we call business. I'm sure you are familiar with all those traditional, supposedly astute, business aphorisms: "Innovate or Die" and "Lead or Bleed"? I'm not saying you can get no utility from these ideas. But for the biggest bang for the buck, you need to think more dramatically and mistakenly, Paul. Thus, "Death is Innovation." By thinking erroneously, you see that there are huge profits to be made in death, and not only for morticians. Someone has to clean up every catastrophe. It takes money. Catastrophe is dollars. Likewise: "Blood leads," not "Lead or Bleed." The "blood error" as we call it is often crucial and not only in the international operations of transnational corporations, but there especially. These corporations understand the often remarkable inverse correlation between the quality of humans rights in a country and the quality of its investment climate. You have a sense of what I mean, no doubt. The wrong is the real. It's a fact of nature.

– Peter, when you say "wrong," do you by any chance mean "efficient"?

– Sure, sure. "Efficient," fortuitous, beneficially, to us and our clients, that is. That's another way of saying the same thing, I suppose, in a useful, mistaken sort of way.

– Error is legal?

– Is gold precious? We're Fortune 500, Paul. For the most part, what we say goes – as you well know.

– And your track record?

– That record is older than we are, by far. This goes way back to when corporations were first chartered. In 1601 Queen Elizabeth chartered the East India Trading Company and by 1700 the British had gained "wealth beyond the dreams of avarice" especially from the rich Indian province of Bengal – once incredibly prosperous and advanced, before the British arrived, but today home to two of the leading symbols of poverty: the country of Bangladesh and the city of Calcutta. So you see, mistakes of a sort were made. Very profitable mistakes. Powerful errors rooted in the laws of nature. It may be tragic, but it's true. In fact we realized that tragedy was profitable so early that, believe it or not, our business originally incorporated as Hamartia Inc. But it was too Greek to too many people. It turned out to be Greek to us as well. We thought hamartia meant tragic flaw, you know, like our teachers told us, a moral thing, but it goes deeper than that. Precisely speaking, hamartia derives from the Greek hamartanein, "to miss the mark, err." So it's a rational issue. Irrational, that is. Error, the stuff of life. Now here we are, Error Incorporated.

– Strange how it rhymes with "terror."

– You have to get over that, Paul. You're a businessman, after all. Surely you are aware there was massive error in food long before genetically modifieds came along. In fact the food industry has a long and daunting record of profit by error that challenges the glorious histories of even the most error-advanced industries in the world.

– Peter, you're not one of those who believes there is something wrong with genetically modified foods are you? We prefer to think of them as "ingenuity enhanced."

– Sure, sure, of course, Paul. The point is, we all make mistakes. Some incomprehensibly huge, and profitable. Some less so, that's all. Error, it's an art.

– We goof, I guess.

– Go astray.

– Screw up, I'm afraid.

– Get it wrong.

– Blunder, unfortunately.

– And make the big bucks, Paul.

– Which we could use right about now at GleamRight Foods, Peter, I can tell you that. But with this idea of hamartia, I guess you started out thinking you could sell flaws – flaws and vice – but PR was an issue, I suppose. So you made a mistake there that didn't pay.

– Not at all. It was a very educational mistake. Knowledge was our reward. Some mistakes are like that – you get smart before you get rich. We learned. We switched to "Error." It polled well.

– Too bad it rhymes with "terror."

– Most people don't notice that.

– The inevitability of error.

– It keeps you up with the competition. Remember them, Paul?

– How much did you say it cost, a single error?

– Do we have a deal?

– You've got me thinking.

– I just don't give away our services for free, Paul. Remember, this conversation is recorded.

– When did you mention that?

– My mistake.

– I see.

SILENCE ON THE PHONE – THEN PAUL SPEAKS AGAIN

– You got me there.

– We know our business. We've patented the

rights to commodified error.

– I'm impressed.

– It was inspired, I'll admit. The courts came through for us.

– I'll say it again –

– No need. Innovation should be rewarded. It's well understood. The patent was key though – we got it on "error and error consultation," as we understand it.

– Okay, I'm just wondering: how exactly do you understand it?

– Our patented definition of error is spelled out in over 800,000 pages, Paul. You can look it up.

– You've covered it all then.

– And we've recently followed through with several related patents extending the definition to where we feared there might be certain loopholes.

– Can't be too careful.

– Do we have a deal?

– Seems like it would be an error not to go ahead and purchase a mistake.

– Beautiful, Paul. And a damn shame. It would be tragic to miss this opportunity to err. To properly err.

– Tragic for whom, I wonder.

– All around, Paul, all around.

– I have another question, Peter. This corporation of yours. Has it filed any other patents?

– Many.

– "Deceit"? Did you patent anything like that? Or "fraud"? "Lie"? "Forgery"?

– Certainly not. Not insofar as they may not be considered errors, that is.

– Well, then, have you got anything similar that I might rightfully purchase. You know, in case something – unbecoming – might come of say an error that blows back? An unfortunate blowback error.

SILENCE – THEN PETER SPEAKS

– This is an issue that usually comes up later.

– I'm interested in it now, Peter.

SILENCE AGAIN – THEN PETER SPEAKS

– "Judicious Equivocation." That's the name of the patent that I believe you are referring to. Not "lying," not "deceit," not "forgery." You understand. We have our principles, after all. We do sell several types of "Judicious Equivocation."

– It sounds rich.

– We expect approval of this patent in a few months. We have terribly high expectations for it.

– I can imagine.

– There is already tremendous demand.

– You don't say.

– I certainly do.

– Then you're on, Peter. I will buy one general error on behalf of GleamRight Foods Corporation.

– Excellent.

– And regarding myself personally, I would like to reserve one judicious equivocation in my own name, if I may at this time.

– As you wish.

– By the way, what's the going price for the J.E.?

– Half a million. Plenty of protection at a bargain price. Sold?

– Sold.

– Wonderful, Paul. You and your corporation won't regret it.

– I expect so, Peter. I hope you don't mind my telling you that it actually feels okay to fully embrace the terror – I mean the error of our ways. It truly does. I guess I only needed to have it explained, so that I could understand it in the proper way. I suppose most people in my line of work have a more intuitive grasp of this sort of thing. But for me, at least, it's comforting to hear it spelled out straight. And so I salute you and the products and the service you provide, you and everyone at Error Incorporated.

– Glad to hear it, Paul, glad to hear it. May you always err!

– Amen, Peter!

– That's the deal, Paul. That's the deal.

The Vassals Handbook

"Float like a butterfly and sting like a bee."

– Muhammad Ali

The first thing you will notice, fellow vassals of the IED: the world is not collapsing. My name is Stan D. Garde and I am here to tell you, to cleanse you well. I am the Official Cleanser of the IED. Second: there is no rebel movement advancing from the mountains, from urban pockets, from suburban enclaves to separate anyone from the Incorporated Estates of Dearth (IED). Rest assured, nothing is changing. I will explain it all. This is what I do. As the Official Cleanser of the IED, I have recently resigned my position as President of Profit University, good ole PU. I have relinquished my theological post as Preacher Of Orthodox Faith. Great were the glories of such office: POOF. Likewise, I have given up my capacity as Official Sloganeer for the Chief Executing Officer of the IED and of all planet Dearth. And I have left my vital duties as Terminator of History at Rockview Terminal School District. All gone. All sacrificed like so much spurting blood to take on this emergency position as Official Cleanser of the Incorporated Estates of Dearth. OCIED can you see that I am the Official Cleanser of the IED? There is no emergency, mind you. My emergency posting is designed to thwart all emergencies before they might happen. What better way to terminate any impending emergency than to personalize, that is to humanize, for all loyal vassals of the IED, the authority (myself) responsible for socially cleansing any impending emergency? I'm sure you will warm to me readily. I could recap my life in standard fashion, you know, claiming I was born a poor bereft vassal in the hinterlands of degradation, but I am too well known for that. The latter stages of my public career overwhelm any private life I might once have had. I do find it grand: cleansing, terminating, sloganeering, executing, preaching, propagandizing, and basically publicly relating against the whole wide world on behalf of the single estate to run, rule, and rectify planet Dearth, the IED, resplendent in top-down uniformity and monolithic conformity in law, language, and life. The rebel vassals, such as they are, don't see it that way, unfortunately, and so they must be conquered, and reconquered, and we shall begin again here in the pages of our loyal vassals handbook: The Cleansing of the IED. I will be your host, and guide, and commandant on this world tour: Stan D. Garde. Hear my name and fear me now! The first thing one must know about the rebel vassals of the IED is that they scarcely exist, as they can scarcely be allowed to. Sure, one may find them virtually everywhere. A good loyal vassal can scarcely turn around without bumping into a rebel ingrate unwilling to prostrate itself daily to the Finance, Insurance, Real Estate, Media, Electronics, Law, Lobbying, and Drug (FIREMELLD) fiefdoms that run the show we lovingly know as the IED. The conditions are ripe for an insurgency emergency, and so we good loyal vassals of the IED must thwart these rebel ingrates at every twist and turn. We must check them at every insubordinate trope. Toward this end, we shall refresh ourselves with a few basic lessons from one of the masterworks of mine, *The Vassals Handbook*:

LESSON ONE

VASSALISM IS CAPITALISM WROUGHT REAL

Out back is where we brutalize the people. Actually, out back is where we used to brutalize the people but times being what they are we brutalize them all around the corporate gardens now. Stan D. Garde is my name. Let the brutality games begin! For our own good. Brutality is what keeps people in line. Too bad we don't set aside more often a special time and place for good old fashioned smashing. I miss it. The constant sort of torture we indulge in nowadays seems to me an inferior replacement. Well, nevermind. Let us not lament for the past but celebrate the present and future. Let us begin here in the Vassals Handbook that the Incorporated Estates of Dearth retained me to write.

Citizens are gone. They are now vassals. It happened in a funny way. All the banks around the world collapsed, broke. So the peoples' money was used to refund all the banks. But don't get any ideas. When the people buy the banks, do they not own them? Yes and no, but mostly and decisively no. You see, the people may properly own the banks (having bought them) but they sure as hell do not get to decide what to do with the money or how to do it. For that is not capitalism, and capitalism is what they bought. Clear? Clever? Clout. In capitalism, the people do not own the decisions. They are not the deciders. They are the consumers, the workers, and in a pinch they may be the funders. To review, the people may be the buyers and in theory the owners, but they are never ever upon any circumstances the deciders. In capitalism, the well-connected few are the deciders, the rulers who select candidates for office, who dole out funds for the campaigns, who provide the illusion of choice via sundry discrepancies for vassals to obsess over and pick between. Nothing more is meant to be.

Am I speaking over your heads, dear vassals? Let me see if I can put this in plainer words. The privileged few rule, the masses obey, even when the masses do most of the work, buy most of the stuff, and totally bailout the bankrupt rulers. That, my friends, is capitalism. Some used to call such a system Chinese Democracy before China was fully incorporated into the IED. Vassalism is a more precise term, in my humble opinion.

Granted, technically, no land has ever practiced pure capitalism, because, unfortunately, pure capitalism is a self-exploding system – inherently wildly unstable. Totally free markets always lead to disaster – collapse of all sorts. Thus, regulation always exists to help curb catastrophe. And so it is, sadly, that contrary to common understanding, pure capitalism is almost as horrific as pure democracy. Demoscrazy, you know. We've had enough of that – we've seen where it leads – not to vassalage! which we much prefer. We prefer vassals to people. We prefer submission to rule. Capitalism is a nice thought, an ideal. But vassalism rules.

Oh I know you odd, broke, and broken spirits out there may think of vassalism as little more than slavery. We pity you penny-pinched souls who could not be more mistaken, more immoral. After all, slaves had no money and so could not readily repay their debts, let alone those of their superiors. That is the gross deficiency of the economic system of pure slavery. We had to replace it. Vassalism is much more efficient, much safer for rulers everywhere. It puts people in their proper place. All hail vassalism! See you at the wars!

LESSON TWO

A VASSAL'S DUTY IS DEBT REPAYMENT

I, vassal. I vassal. Vassal I. It may surprise readers that your author is a fellow vassal. Some vassals are more subservient than others, some more privileged. I've been asked to overview here not only the duties of vassals – any mere serf could do as much – but to sketch the world entire, as best known today. I've been asked by the lords of capital to reveal in one single work the full human condition of our time, of the time that came before, and of the time that will come after. The better to know, the better to rule and be ruled. For the first time in all history, the great epic of Dearth is to be written – the tale of the Incorporated Estates of Dearth.

Moreover, I've been asked to embed or integrate a primer for vassals within or throughout, so as to render this epic most profitable for all.

Where to begin? T'was a dark and stormy night? Once upon a time? In the beginning...there was the word...vassal...

Let me begin instead where everyone begins – with our bills. What We Owe. I will begin with Debt. Our debt. Human debt. Original debt.

Birth is an expensive act. Everyone pays their own way in the IED, all the way. Forgotten now is the strange and communist sounding social security card, abolished for the betterment of humanity. Nowadays at birth vassals are assigned a debt card we carry with us for the rest of life, or we have it implanted as chip into palm. Birth costs for each individual are entered into the card or chip and simultaneously into the IED's central terminal, the CT. If all life and every feature were to be swept from Dearth due to some wholly imaginable catastrophe, or if the planet itself were to explode, the central terminal would nevertheless remain intact, the last and only thing to survive, hurtling through space tabulating debts, payments, and lack thereof for each and ever human, animal, plant, mineral. If the planet were to melt and consume the CT, its numbers would be first etched upon the walls of the universe, stuck there forever through time to be recovered by the first sentient beings capable of understanding and processing the greatest glory known to our species – the ability to process debt.

Debt is our glory, our god, our redemption, a vassal's core reason for being. We vassals are vessels of debt. Vessels of gold, we vassals. The glory of our nature as vassals is as vessels of debt owed to the Incorporated Estates of Dearth, that greatest of estates, the estate that could not exist without vassals as vessels of debt.

LESSON THREE

EMPIRE'S GRAVEYARD GLORY

Here we go again, off to the wars! Let's see, where do we visit today? Iraq? Afghanistan? Pakistan? Gaza? How is the war for the everlasting expansion of the Incorporated Estates of Dearth progressing, you ask? Very well! How do we know? Graveyards! Here we are in one going full blast, the bodies flooding in as if from some channeled hurricane of blood and gore. Now this is the sort of full employment the overlords of the IED appreciate. Gravediggers rejoice! These gravediggers get no rest around here. They barely have time to jot down the names of those going under. Some bodies even come in with no names at all, and some are surely pseudonyms. But who needs names when business is booming? One look and we know the story of many a body: Mr. Shot-in-the-back-of-the-head. Ms. Blown-to-bits-from-the-sky. Child Mutilated-by-shrapnel. Infant Crushed-from-on-high. Busy, busy, busy are we in the graveyards of the IED. Proud tax dollars at work.

LESSON FOUR

THE IRRESPONSIBILITY OF THE VASSALS

No time to stay and bury Iraqis, nor time to oversee the bombing of assorted other Oilans. I would just as soon return home and throw a bunch more ghetto kids and barrio boys into prison, penny-pinched walkabouts that they are. Whom do they profit? No one, so clear them out. The ungrateful wretches. Toss them and the poor whites into the trash. Hail to the Chief! We have our standards. The standards of the Estate. Heart the flag! There is no prison large enough to satisfy the Incorporated Estates, no punishment severe enough to purify civil realms, no law strict enough to force vassals to always obey. And so the IED throws more than half its money into the mighty weapons systems, as we aim at the ideal.

In any event, I need to return home to convince the vassals to give more money to the banks. For some odd reason, the vassals seem to think their own money properly belongs to them. Not at all. All money belongs to the banks who make any money possible in the first place. The banks are the real workers of the world because they do the most important job – that of moving money from place to place. Not only do banks deserve a large cut of each and every transaction, they deserve the right to control transactions because privileged use of money is vital to the health of every incorporated estate. Vassals don't get this. They tend to think their own needs are as important as the demands of the banks, let alone the estates. Even more so. Where do vassals learn such tripe and treason? Certainly not in the schools. Not in the good ones, at least.

Vassals are prone to blow through money quick-ly with their mundane spending on food, shelter, clothing, transportation, fuel, electricity, healthcare, and so on, which is all well and good – until there is no money left for the banks, the pesky problem today. The vassals spend it all! They spend all the banks' money. All and more. And the vassals are sunk into debt deeper each day.

The banks are totally bankrupt, having lent far more than can possibly be repaid, having pur-chased and traded and sold enormous equities for which they cannot now account, if they ever could. Mistakes were made. It happens. Unlike vassals, banks are too big to fail. Too important. Does this even need to be explained anymore?

Take a vassal who fails to cover expenses – he goes hungry or cold or suffers from heat, or gets depressed or goes mad, or gets sick or commits crimes, loses relationships or jobs, maybe gets jailed or dies. Any and all of this may happen with any given vassal, which is more-or-less acceptable as long as the banks get paid in the meantime. Because if the banks go down, who will be left to pass along the money to those who know what to do with it, the golden few?

Surely not vassals. It makes no sense to put vassals in charge of their own money. Such impropriety would violate the contract that vassals are born into. Vassals are genetically suited for sustaining the lords of capital first. The guarantors of all. Vassals must not only pay for everything, they must be ready to fight to protect the ventures, interests, estates of the lords of capital. Such is a vassal – by definition, by nature, by contract. Not that, except in reams of law, this contract is written out for all to see. How silly would that be? One learns as one goes. The vassals seem to find it more comforting to operate under the guise of democracy, even though the well known, the real, the inherent fact of life, the bedrock, the base of civilization is that vassals owe their betters their labor, their money, and their readiness to fight on behalf of the Incorporated Estates of Dearth. One knows one's position in the IED or one gets cut off. No decent level of existence is a given, no matter what that odious Declaration of Human Rights presumes. Are we clear? Crystal? Outstanding. Vassals who do not heart the estates, get thee to the wilderness go. And too bad if the IED owns that too.

LESSON FIVE

RESTOCKING THE BANKS

So the vassals owe the banks. The banks will have their money. It remains my job to explain to vassals how they might best meet their new sentence of debt. For this great task we return from the Oilan front to the domestic war rooms.

We loyal vassals, we civil-minded types, we chart our strategies anew, go on the offensive, throw deep, blitz the opposition, pound the media, ram through smashmouth bills, man up, gut it out, and storm to victory over those who would deny the banks their due.

Having exhausted earlier practical policies, we need something new yet timeless, forward looking yet ancient, elegant yet primal. Something that works, that lives, that breathes profits.

Let me think, just off the top of my head.

Off with their heads? Why not?

Cannibalism. For profit.

The great resource that remains, and yet remains bothersome, is the unemployed, and the underemployed, and the vast imprisoned populace, and the ill, and the dissidents, and select others. Tainted vassals everywhere. Ergo.

Cannibalism for profit. Now we have to sell

it.

One cannot simply say to vassals, Ahoy there ye kindred Vassals, henceforth, we must cannibalize our way to prosperity! Too grating.

[Note to self – have editor polish this text, this epic, this handbook that I have begun to incor-porate into my daily routine: The Life and Duties of Stan D. Garde, Executive Sloganeer. Render audience appropriate.]

There is no getting around it. Cannibalism becomes the dawn of the millennium. Cannibalism by the banks, with the banks, for the banks. Canni-balism for the greater glory of the Incorporated Estates of Dearth. Cannibals arise, unite, devour!

LESSON SIX

VASSALS AT ARMS

Maybe I had better do a little of my editor's work for him. Cannibalism as a saving economic stratagem? Surely I exaggerate? I'm the master PR guy, Stan D. Garde. They throw so much stuff at me. I'm responsible for everything all the time – the colonial wars in western Asia and the intricacies of each; the IED's waning influence in South America; the leaderless European Union; the many horns of Africa; constant upheaval and unrest in India; natural and unnatural disasters in Southeast Asia; the daunting rise of China. Cannibalism? Let's set that notion aside for awhile, its economic advantages notwithstanding, whatever its popular difficulty or promise.

The economy and the military, this is my concern, how to resurrect the one and how to strengthen the other. Through military strength comes economic might – the IED and I see no way around that proposition – base reality. The only question – which way the IED? Should it power up its colonial forces, all the better to occupy and instill profitable fear? Or should the military continue to power up for the big picture, for super global warfare, by expanding its huge fleets of planes, tanks, ships, missiles, and by further mili-tarizing space?

The difficulty of my job is that the rulers are split – between the leaders of the occupying forces on the ground, on the one hand over fist and on the other hand over fist, the generals, lobbyists, lobbyist generals, and strategists beyond. I repeat: the occupying forces throughout Greater Oila wish for more pacifying resources, the better to conquer the Oilan vassals. Meanwhile, higher up brass and financiers press for bigger fleets and space based might.

But what if we figured out a way to wed the economic stimulus needed to revive the bankrupt banks with military power and spending? Why not give all the money to the military to run the world like one giant boot camp, or if that appears too extreme, make the world an endless string of military bases and installations – each vassal den an armed outpost, each inhabitant of Dearth a foot soldier, an IED enlistee. Might this not be a solution more practical, more popular, more elegant than cannibalism? Militarize the IED more fully, militarize Dearth. Totally.

It's coming, no doubt. In fact, it's largely here. The main economic stimulus will come as it always does each budget year, in the form of the military budget and again with every invasion and occupa-tion or threat of such. The military, its weaponry, its war preparation, its attacks and operations always command most of the tax dollars as befits any peace-loving estate.

The blow to the rest of the economy, that is the soft economy, is huge and necessary since the nonmilitary economy merely aids vassals' domes-tic needs and wishes, the mundane irritants, too well known – food, shelter, fuel, education, transportation, electricity, health care, clean air and water, and other trifles.

How to sustain the IED's endless string of homeland and overseas military bases? How to pay for an infinite militarization of space? How to fund permanent occupation and co-opting of Greater Oila? How to pay for pacification of far flung lands, of recalcitrant vassals everywhere across the globe? How to control those who dare to reject incorporation into the ruling estates of Dearth?

Globalization – that misnomer – actually means to diversify, to interrelate with all the ends of Dearth, not that the IED wants any part of such impossible utopian indulgence. Instead, the great estates wish to Consolidate absolutely, to bring the very ends of Dearth, like the four corners of a quilt, into one firm grasp. That is what Globalize means to the IED.

Are we clear? Are we clever? See the clout? Globalization is Newspeak for Consolidation, for Regimentation. Heil! Saint Orwell!

While Capitalism remains an ideal dream, never to be realized, and Vassalism is the current great reality, I wonder if Militarism might be easier at the end of the day for vassals to wrap their weary minds around? The military sings such a catchy tune, really gets vassals to rally around the flag, absolutely compels them to salute their betters. Is a soldier not an ideal figure for all humanity? More ideal than a vassal could ever hope to be?

Boot camp provides for all, for both soft and hard aspects of economic life – and with absolute efficiency. To the barracks! – a proper rallying cry, seems to me, one fit for the vast majority of all vassals – the barracks world, gun on shoulder, life in a locker, absolute obedience to the myriad commandants appointed by a sole elected (or not) official for all the IED, the Dear Leader, the IED Idol, the CEO Commander in Chief, the one true President of the Incorporated Estates of Dearth. While boot camp of the body may not work for all, boot camp of the mind seems an absolute must. Not that all vassals are equal. Let alone soldiers. The salute must never die.

LESSON SEVEN

THE DEMISE OF THE VASSALS

Military bases and incorporated estates aside, when all else fails, as it usually does, one can readi-ly entertain the vassals to death, or at least into quiescence. Vassals can be flattered into stupidity and baited into irrelevancy. Much as I love the vassals, and am tied to them, the vassals are a sorry breed, it must be said – if only in this first draft, pre-editor, pre-audience-appropriate spin and trim.

In fact most years it's all we better vassals can do to keep the majority alive, to keep them from killing each other off with their own stupidity. I do love vassals, don't get me wrong. They are wretched, but they are us. The IED could not make it without them. And yet, to leave everything up to the vassals, or to leave anything to their whims, shudder to think, just look at the polls – they would end the wars of prosperity or never start them in the first place; they would provide free health care to everyone; and in ways too noxious to elaborate, they would actually try to spread the wealth!

That's not reality. That's not survivable, not on or off the estates. That's begging for the total collapse of civilization as we know it, love it, and feed from it. You have the word of Stan D. Garde on that one.

If this Vassals Handbook – more realistically titled American Campaign Journal, or rather Global Campaign Journal – were anything more than a humble vessel of the popular will (the good loyal vendor-consumer will, of course) then I would be forced to point out that my notes here form the makings of an epic that easily has the potential to reveal more and far surpass in all elements any and all great works heretofore, including any and all works of the imagination and of fact – such as all epics of poetry, fiction, history, philosophy, sociology, theory, religion, science, and any sort of literature whatsoever, the novel, not least. An epic of tropetopian dimension beyond all.

I would be forced to state that this work is sort of a history of histories, a philosophy of philoso-phies, a religion of religions, a theory of theories, a science of sciences, a novel of novels – a literature of literatures.

But – since The Vassals Handbook is merely a modest old campaign journal – slash – how-to journal – slash – simple log of the IED – I can admit to nothing of the kind, however true it may be.

LESSON EIGHT

THE PATHOLOGY OF THE VASSALS

Maybe the vassals are doomed, maybe the incorporation of full scale slavery remains the IED's only hope of salvation, of proper order and stability, of fiscal efficiency and economic integrity.

The latest polls of the vassals are not to be believed, are to be deplored and feared, as we continue to see these toxic numbers fail to drop. Is it possible that the vassals are inherently pathological? The polls seem to prove it. Large majorities of vassals still prefer that the ruling government our dearly beloved IED "care for those who cannot care for themselves"; "do more" for its people; provide "more services" with "more spending"; provide "health care to all" and raise taxes to do so; increase the minimum wage; raise corporate taxes; raise upper income taxes; increase spending on education and social security; reign in "greed and materialism" and "poverty and economic injustice."

Why? Why after all the IED has done with the ungrateful vassals? It's that outlier of an outlaw, that guerrilla historian Pierce Strike who keeps reporting all this, via some remote mountain hideout, no doubt, and that notorious center of insurgency, ZCommunications.

The infernal vassal insurgency is currently carried on by the majority, whose values, priorities, preferences more or less align in toxic fashion. Good thing these dissidents are weak and subject to being stomped like so many bugs.

Makes a good vassal proud to squash bugs. And therein lies the eighth lesson of this handbook of the vassals. Good vassals everywhere: avoid the swarming vassals gone viral. Work for the Incorporated Estates of Dearth, and salvation shall be yours.

LESSON NINE

THE TREASON OF THE CREDIT UNIONS

Let no one speak of turning to credit unions, which are owned and operated by the deposi-tors. Credit unions ought cease and desist their attempts to undermine by their very presence the fiscal authority of the IED. So what if credit unions are democratically controlled, one person, one vote – and banks are not? So what if credit unions have lower fees and better rates than banks? So what if credit unions have stronger community ties and involvement than banks? So what if credit unions return revenues to their depositors rather than operate for profit like banks? So what if they remain solvent? Such feel good tripe misses every point that matters. And how can it last? Why would good vassals anywhere want credit unions to persist in this golden era of vassalism?

In the end, the IED's financial woes must be resolved, not exacerbated, and banks are by far the IED's preferred solution. That's all that counts – the satisfaction of the needs of the IED. The IED makes the planet great, not the vassals, and forget the credit unions. Natural law dictates that vassals are the means to the end, and that the end is the end, and only the end, and not the means to anything at all beyond the end, which is the end in itself. Are we clear? Credit unions defy banks and therefore in theory and reality should not be allowed to exist. Why they hang on with their millions and billions is beyond me. It's not for lack of trying to abolish these unholy institutions on my part, one Stan D. Garde.

LESSON TEN

THE GLORY OF THE GREEN ZONE

Some call it the God Zone, others with equal appreciation call it the Genghis Zone in honor of that great liberator of olden time Genghis Khan and his grandson Hulagu Khan who liberated Iraq from the Iraqis nearly 800 years prior to George Bush the Second when his invading legions overran the Middle East.

Whatever you call it, the Gravy Zone or the Grand Zone or simply the GZ, the Green Zone shines like gold. All vassals might live in the GZ someday, those willing to risk everything or those who get lottery lucky. Originally the

Baghdad headquarters of the US occupation of Iraq, today the Green Zone means the Good Life. If you're in the Zone, the Green Zone, you've got it made. Everyone there that I care to know makes six figures easy. Oh sure, you wind up dodging an incoming bomb or two on many a night, but with blast walls screening off ground attacks from the Red Zone – anywhere beyond the Green Zone – you feel safe enough. What would be life without a few bombs thrown about from time to time? I certainly don't know.

Gated communities are not what they used to be. They've gone Green. Not only in Baghdad but all across the Incorporated Estates of Dearth. The GZ is the future. Green Zones are life, Red Zones are blood. The profit goes to the targeter, not to the target. Get in the Zone, Vassals. Get into the Zone with the IED, the Green Zone, for life.

LESSON ELEVEN

WE MEAN WELL

The great thing about being a vassal is that you always know you mean well. We mean well, we do. Isn't it obvious? We mean well, always. No matter what others might say about us. No matter what absurd arguments they might raise.

Take for example universal health care. We don't have it. And for that we are thankful. Lack of universal health care is a sign of our inherent fairness, generosity of spirit, economic thrift. We mean well because we are well. Are we not?

Do not speak of the supposed virtues of equality of condition, wherein everyone has a right to health care. Preposterous. The United Nation's Declaration of Human Rights is not worth the paper it is written on – useful only for starting fires. Unlike the laws of the Incorporated Estates of Dearth, the laws of the defunct United Nations do not mean well. The UDHR is a document of illness, if not raving lunacy, signed long ago in some sick spasm of internationality.

What could be more generous than allowing everyone the equal opportunity to fend for themselves? Time to face reality, vassals. Poor health and death take the hindmost. Life is a race from the wolf at the door. If you mean well, if you really do, you will run for your life, like a good vassal.

The same holds for international affairs. The Incorporated Estates of Dearth owns the world, as it should, because it means well, always and everywhere.

Thus we intervene constantly against people of color the world over. We garrison Dearth, and every year we spend over half our money on all matters militant.

It's so easy to find people of color to smash. There are so many of them, whether in Iraq, Afghanistan, Pakistan, Palestine, Grenada, Panama, Nicaragua, El Salvador, Africa, South America – even in the heart and soul of the IED, the USA, where the prison population – chock full of people of color, not to mention people of no money – leads all Dearth. More prisoners per capita, more prisoners period. Hey, we're number one!

Those whom we don't smash, we threaten. Because we mean well. The order and security of the Incorporated Estates of Dearth demands it. The IED likes to, needs to, aims to extract oil like blood from these people. Just blow them up and the oil comes splurting out into our waiting pipes, tankers, pockets. So what if millions of innocents are slaughtered in the process of IED invasions, occupations, sanctions? We mean well. The wars of the IED grease the gears of the economy so we know we are doing well. Business is booming. Those in the right mean well. We *mean* it. We *mean* well.

Examine your hearts, dear vassals. Do you mean well? Do you *mean* it?

Mean, mean, mean. We mean it like nobody's business (but ours). Always have and always will, here in the IED. A vassal can bank on it.

LESSON TWELVE

THE ECONOMY IS FUNDAMENTALLY SOUND

What we mean when we say the economy is fundamentally sound is that the IED is fundamentally sound. What we mean when we say the IED is fundamentally sound is that this is the best system ever. Ever was, ever is, ever will be. History has ended, nature has decreed, the universe declares: vassalism is perfect. As perfect as can be. As close to perfect as one can possibly imagine.

Great Depressions, let alone recessions, are unavoidable, like unemployment, a fact of life, a law of nature, a boon to the economy always. Keeps wages down, expectations in check. Full employment? The pipedream of children.

Even during Great Depressions and myriad wars the economy is always and everywhere fundamentally sound. That is, basically. Ultimately. Temporary glitches or catastrophes, mass layoffs, environmental wipeouts, ongoing battles over scarce resources, the arms race – these phenomena are all part and parcel of the sound nature of capitalism become vassalism. In this the lords of commerce trust and believe, and to which a vassal ought swear.

LESSON THIRTEEN

THE NEXT BEST THING TO ROYALTY

You know the first lady, the first family? That is, the President of the Incorporated Estates of Dearth and his wife? I get to meet them! For the first time. I can't wait. I won't know how to act.

But first, a thought. Is it not curious that vassals never refer to the President and his wife as the "first family" or to her as the "first lady"? I have to admit, I have never once heard any regular vassal refer to them in this way. In fact, I only hear such language in the incorporated media. Why is that?

It doesn't seem to be catching, this proper mode of address. And that is what has got to change.

For they are first, the President and his family, first above all – the closest thing to royalty known to the Incorporated Estates of Dearth. What the first family does, the President especially, matters more than anything and anyone – not what goes on in town halls, community centers, schools, hospitals, and other minute realms of life, not who does all the stuff in the world.

This is a top down society, not bottom up. Imagine what would happen if a pyramid were turned upside down. The tip would be crushed!

Not only that but then it would all collapse and crumble leaving the whole mess at more or less the same level. Equality of condition! Total destruction.

Thankfully our system gets the design just right, preserving the tip, elevating it, providing the most sun, the best view, the commanding position with the freshest freest air. And the most cash. Oh, to be King. Hail to the Chief. O! say can you see!

It will be all I can do not to salute the first family on sight. I can't wait to shake his hand, and if I'm lucky, from her, a hug. Oh my God, it's almost indecent that I get to embrace these exalted ones, even in my capacity as Official Sloganeer. Am I deserving? Am I worthy?

Of course I am, otherwise the President's aides would not have chosen me for this important post. You are always as good as your superiors tell you. Doesn't everyone believe that? They should. Without such wisdom no top down system can long survive, nor a vassal thrive.

LESSON FOURTEEN

IN THE BANKS WE TRUST

I pledge allegiance to the banks of the Incorporated Estates of Dearth and to the Rulers, whom they enrich, one Command throughout the land – obedience – with conformity and subservience for all.

Good vassals learn the Bank Pledge by heart when still wet from the womb. And with good reason. The Bank Pledge can take a vassal far in the Incorporated Estates of Dearth. The banks are divine, and vassals mere mortals who owe their breath to the going rate of exchange. Few vassals would rather defy banks and starve than obey banks and have a chance.

As grand enforcers of obedience and conformity, banks create liberty, justice, and equality. Banks provide humans the freedom to prosper and to profit – or, for the stubborn, the inept, and the unfortunate, to suffer. All is fair in love and banks.

Vassals may rent themselves freely, offering themselves upon the altar of the market at whatever rate the market and banks command. For those vassals with little or no market value: prisons. Thankfully. Not to mention urban concen-tration camps, reservations, and many a moon-scape in the countryside. These all happily embrace the poor, once the banks have done with them.

Banks decree equitably one a vassal or a lord, depending upon your wealth. Which vassals and lords prosper enough to receive just conditions of life? The banks judge. Justice flows both to and from the banks and their best depositors. The most just depositors are the richest ones, of course, the least just the poorest. Vassals who can make no deposit at all might be thought of as the scourge of banking. Not so. The impoverished scarcely inter-fere with the balance sheet, thus the banks could not care less. What could be more reasonable and just than that?

Who after all impoverished the vassals but the vassals themselves? Doesn't take a rocket scientist to figure that one out, does it, vassals?

Banks even allow vassals to use bank money the same as any lord. That is, a vassal's dollar is the exact equal of a lord's dollar. A vassal and a lord may actually touch and distribute the same bill at transcendent points in time. Lords inevitably possess far more dollars than vassals but that is not the point.

The point is that lords and vassals use the same money, and they both may use it for any legal purpose they wish, including to buy up freedom and justice and whatever else they can afford. Can a more fair and enlightened system be conceived?

We have already excoriated the subversive effect of the credit unions and other outrageous notions of vassal controlled finance. To hell with credit unions and their pretensions of democracy in action. A grand bank, like an incorporated estate, is a sovereign domain, a land really, a dominion, a country unto itself, fully able to conquer and resist being conquered. As such, banks sovereign and inherent rights are not to be tampered with, let alone trammeled. Any invasive treasonous moves against banks will continue to be met with supreme hostility from the lords of finance, from the banks themselves, the rightful owners of all money and Dearth.

No finer institutions than banks exist. What hell-on-Dearth this world would be without banks is difficult to imagine. Yet instructive. A planet with no banks would be like a military with no guns, or a world with no wars. Who would profit? Think about it. Where is the profit in no banks? No banks? That would be sacrilege.

Make no mistake, vassals, the banks have got your backs and the shirts upon them. The banks are here for you and they wholly embrace what is theirs. For these many reasons vassals one and all may count their blessings in praise of banks.

And lead thou not into the great temptation of banding together, but deliver thine serf selves from evil: For banks are the kingdom, and the power, and the glory, for incorporated ever. Amen.

LESSON FIFTEEN

FIRST YOU IGNORE THEM

A small groups gathering. A patio. A milling of positions.

She shook my hand with her hand, soft and full. Today I met the first family. The first lady seemed normal, even in person. She seemed always about to go grocery shopping. I found myself thinking of looking around for grocery carts, I heard them banging in my head, I half expected to trip into one. The first lady smiled and tried hard to smile and tried to work up to smiling, primary task, necessary habit. She was mostly successful. Wearied and wearying almost, we got along.

The President was another matter. Not that we did not get along, far from it. We moved well in face of one another. You can feel the power gush from, around, in, and through him. The power pulses in, around, and through, and to you, and past and back, and to all those surround. Power is that extra energy in the air you can touch as it works on and about and you see it work on others. It works on people. It worked on us. Who were we talking to, each other? Superficially. Meaningfully. We were talking to power. I mean you can see it and feel it. To miss that was to be talking to the moon.

You never forgot for a moment that the President is there and that he is the supreme individual of the Incorporated Estates of Dearth.

I felt for the first lady. She seemed to have a hard time of it, I mean, getting on, even as she got on, famously, as she ought. She soldiered about as if in quick hitting daze of clairvoyance, as if looking for spontaneity everywhere and wondering that it was not to be found, even if almost. She stared into a mirror at herself and pretended not to, convincingly enough, as if she were the stage itself and no where upon it.

The President got along with everyone, as if he wanted to. That I found this odd, him odd, is no matter. I am not the president and could never be. I am too opinionated. Too impatient. Too blunt, in my own mind, if nowhere else.

The topic the President wished to discuss: the rebel insurgency deep in the heart of the Incorporated Estates of Dearth.

Typically we ignore the rebels, the best strategy: First you ignore them, then you blast them, then you agree with them if need be – or plausibly pretend to – what cost, a bit of rhetoric? – then you win. Again.

What I found most distressing and yet daunting and daring about the President is that he does not seem interested in winning. He assumes it. He is a winner. He wins. He gets along with everyone, not least those who fund him into power. This strikes me as terribly indiscriminate. He is willing to get alone with anyone, even the rebels so long as playing nice does not cost him his job, or his funders – the banks and the incorporated estates, the class of the IED – their power.

So the President plays nice and wins and called me in to deal with the rebels. He tells me it is my job to play nice with the rebels. Not in so many words, but I get it. He wants me to give the rebels the velvet glove covering the iron fist, via the tongue. He wants me to cut the rebels to size as if making love to them with a rock. First you ignore them, then you blast them, then you pretend to agree with them (if need be), then you win. "Do you understand?" He asks me.

"I understand, sir."

"The rebels are IEDans like us. Only poorer, or disenchanted, or just cantankerous. We need them to love the IED. They need to love the IED. For their own good. For our own good. For the good. You see?"

"I think I know exactly what you mean, sir."

"I need a speech. Soon. I plan to address the rebels personally, visit their camp. I need real face-to-face words. Words that go beyond the teleprompter. Words that are easy to memorize. Easy to take deep into the heart. From my heart to their heart? Can you write that for me? I know you can. Yes, you can."

"You are writing the very thing right now, sir. You have a knack, that gift. We touch their hearts. We find solace in the common condition of good loyal vassals to the IED."

"Maybe – and this is only a suggestion – maybe go easy on the vassals part. Of course they are vassals, they know they are vassals, deep in their hearts, they know, and it must resonate for them somewhere. Somehow. But let us not mention it, this time. Maybe give it a pass. Maybe find a new route. Go a new bend. Fork differently. Take anew the bridge to hope and to change and to the path best travelled. You see what I have in mind."'

"Poetry, sire. Excuse me – sir, of course. Pure poetry. You have it within you, and I am more than grateful that you trust me to help you draw it out. The heart. A healing touch. We, as one, all together. We overcome our differences for our common good. That is the IED way. Yes, we can. We must. We will. We shall overcome. Something of the sort?"

"Perfect, exactly. You read minds. I knew you could do it. I can't wait to read my speech."

"If I may say, sire, I mean, sir, I like to imagine I am a maker a minds, a shaper, a bard at the head of the band. A wizard of wordcraft almost."

"Or is it woodcutter?" said the President with great acuity. "The people will respond to a woodcutter of words, a worker of words. They would prefer a delivery of angels. But I will have to do instead."

"You do indeed, sire. Of course you are right. I will labor as a woodcutter of words. I am even a little in love with saws. Of the minds. I will cut some wood right away, the words that befit you and the rebels well. We will get through to them."

"Oh, Stan, I wouldn't go that far. You know the best we can hope for is a good photo op and a few applause lines. That is tonic enough." Someone cupped my elbow. A dark-suited man. I bowed. "Thanks for the thoughts," said the President. Stan? Did he mention my name?

"Of course, sire."

I withdrew past the first lady and her ever budding all but all over smile. Her reserve full of laughter, and the men and women milling mulling milking in position.

The whole event a tonic. The President knew. My head – delight. Was I surprised? He knew. He knew. He knew. The President would know just what to say. He handled himself like no man I had ever met. He was the President, and I, I almost felt like his boss – putting words in his mouth. O! God! No! Yes!

Such is power.

What matters is what you do with it.

I had a speech to write, the rebels to conquer.

And I'll never forget the fun, listening to all the great fiddling going on at the party, watching the flames of the bonfires sweeping the country, smelling the smoke in the background.

Such is life in the ruling bubble.

LESSON SIXTEEN

PROFIT U

So I wrote a speech to end all speeches for our beloved President of the Incorporated Estates of Dearth, Al O'Toole. He delivered it to the rebels. It did not go over well. I am not surprised. The truly intransigent cannot be reached. We go through the motions, as required.

I must admit I was underwhelmed by my meeting with the President of the IED. It made me think I am not the right man for the job of Official Sloganeer. I longed to return to my first true love: teaching. I recalled fondly my years of joy as Terminator of History at Rockview Terminal. Who knows what connections exist between our thoughts and the actions of the universe? Do I?

Then of a sudden, I was offered the Presidency of the brand spankingest newest university on the face of planet Dearth: Profit U. Good ole PU.

PU is founded in this time of psycho-socio-economic crisis with the intent of restoring faith in the system of the IED. I accepted the Presidency of PU, stipulating that I continue work on the epic in progress, the how-to book for good loyal consumers of the IED, The Vassals Handbook. The Executors Board of PU readily agreed. IED President Al O'Toole wished me well and said he would sign up for a distance learning course if I were to lead one. Of course I promised to come up with something. So here I am, newly installed as the first President of PU. The school cheers ring in my ears. Let's go PU! Here we go PU! We Are PU! We're Number One! PU! Number One!

PU! PU! PU!

The rosy-fingered dawn of the new day breaks at PU.

Profit U. We are tasked to challenge Harvard, Yale, Princeton, and the other greats for intellectual and moral supremacy in the IED. We are charged by the leaders of the IED to take on their traditional roles as the bastions of all that is wise and good. We are charged to lead the IED through crisis high and low. What ambitious young man or woman would not want to attend PU? The question answers itself.

Maybe I've found my proper place here at last at Profit U. Stan D. Garde, President of PU! I cannot really explain why I love the sound of this new title so terribly much. Can you?

Youthtopia (excerpt)

Tony Christini

---

*W*HAT THEY ARE SAYING ABOUT YOUTHTOPIA:

"A terrible book. Irresponsible."
 – Barry Obay

"This book should be banned."
 – Dale Servile

"No one under 21 should be allowed to read this book."
 – Marsha Sireton

"No reputable publisher should go anywhere near it."

 – Amanda Thority

"Ban it. Burn it. Bury it."
 – Luke Baas

<u>FROM THE DESK OF</u>

Stan D. Garde – Terminator of History

Dear Parents,

As a former history teacher who has recently suffered a tragic slip and fall in the Rockview Terminal parking lot, upon which I knocked my head quite soundly, putting me out of commission for no little while, I have lately had the opportunity to reflect on the good life as we know it here in Rockview Terminal.[1]

Especially if you are a parent new to the re-

---

[1] *"I am not maligning the teaching profession. There are a good number of smart, well-educated (notice I am not saying 'well schooled') teachers out there who really try to help their students learn. Unfortunately, there are six times as many who are over-worked, underpaid, never-really-wanted-to-be-teachers anyway, often-ill people out there whose last concern is to help children learn." Amanda Bergson-Shilock, 16, "Homeschooling Is Another Word For 'Living'" Grace Llewellyn, Real Lives*

gion and possess children of Terminal age, this modest handbook should provide valuable insight into the nature and quality of education in our local Terminals.

Before I begin to describe the Terminal I know best, Rockview, where I happily taught before my tragic slip and fall in the parking lot, let me note that Rockview Terminal has been so named ever since the word "high" was banned from language by Congress during one of this country's many brave battles in the ongoing war against certain drugs and their deviant users and dealers.[2]

Thus, as is the case throughout the country these days, the former h*** school at Rockview is now referred to as the Terminal at Rockview.

Likewise, we teachers scarcely refer to ourselves as such anymore.

Instead, we go by the title Terminator, which we greatly prefer.

You may recall a minor protest to these legal and linguistic reformations years ago, but rest easy, dear parents, that in Rockview Terminal and the surrounding area, there has been no serious protest of any size in a decade or so, not since this ugly sort of thing was smashed during the Great Repres-sion, after some sad misguided soul actually made a picket sign and wedged it into his cement patch on Main Street to protest the government granting corporations the right to meter air in houses.

Fortunately, our well-trained youth cause little fuss these days.

With your loyal ever-loving help we do all that is possible upon this Incorporated Dearth to give our children the most modern and efficient of mental cleansings.

Please note that you must make every effort, as responsible parents and mature adults, to keep this book out of the hands of youth.[3]

As you will see, I have written this book for thoroughly cleansed minds only – mature adult minds, naturally.

May all peace and profit be with you always, dear parents.

As we like to say here in the happy confines of Rockview Terminal: Go Terminal Go!

Fully yours,

Stan D. Garde

Stan D. Garde

Terminator of History

<u>*FROM THE DESK OF*</u>

Jay Cage – Superinterminent of Terminals

Dear Parents,

Welcome to friendly Rockview Terminal!

This parent handbook overviews the top quality educational atmosphere of Rockview

---

[2] *"The truth is that schools don't really teach anything except how to obey orders. This is a great mystery to me because thousands of humane, caring people work in schools, as teachers and aides and administrators, but the abstract logic of the institution overwhelms their individual contributions. Although teachers do care and do work very, very hard, the institution is psychopathic; it has no conscience. It rings a bell and the young man in the middle of writing a poem must close his notebook and move to a different cell..."*
John Gatto, *Dumbing Us Down*

[3] *"States Parties shall assure to the child who is capable of forming his or her own views the right to express those views freely in all matters affecting the child..." "The child shall have the right to freedom of expression; this right shall include freedom to seek, receive and impart information and ideas of all kinds, regardless of frontiers, either orally, in writing or print, in the form of art, or through any other media of the child's choice." from Articles 12 and 13, Convention on the Rights of the Child, entered into force by the U.N. General Assembly 2 September 1990, and signed reluctantly years later by the United States, the last country to do so, aside from Somalia, which lacked a legally constituted government. Nevertheless, like other countries, the U.S. refuses to act on or enforce anything it disagrees with even if it has signed it into law.*

Terminal.[4]

Here in lovely Rockview we never forget that our children are our greatest resource, and we do everything in our power to make sure that our children are mentally cleansed, as thoroughly and as efficiently as possible.

This great task of the Terminals is one we are sure that you as responsible parents and loyal con-sumers abide by entirely.

Disclaimer One: Under no circumstances may Rock-view Terminal be held responsible for any learner's failure to conform.

Disclaimer Two: Failure to abide by Terminal rules may result in expulsion, impairment, or worse.

Disclaimer Three: No so-called Bill of Rights applies in this Terminal or in any other.[5]

Finally, dear parents, if you ever feel the need for further information about the nature of your child's interment in this quality institution, please consult this handbook,[6] written by our very own Termina-tor of History, Stan D. Garde.

Or feel free to contact anyone in our entire fleet of lawyers at 1-800-TERMINAL.

May you always profit!

And may your children reach the utter heights of mental cleansing, now and forevermore.

Yours in power,

Jay Cage

Jay Cage

Superinterminent of Terminals

TERMINAL SPACE

Rockview Terminal consists primarily of two main areas, both of which are heavily patrolled by Term-inators. The main area is the electronica room, or e-room, sometimes called the vast room, housing all the computers – the "fry" room, in loyal-consumer-in-training lingo.

Some years ago the district realized it could save money by simply removing all the walls between rooms and constructing one vast central learning complex.

This also allowed the population of the Terminal to rise considerably without the need to add on or build anew.

And such massive display of centralism makes everyone feel more chummy than ever before, here in the "fry" room.

The other main area is the training room, with its many pacing stations – known to lcit, we Ter-minators are humored to note, as the "Treadmills From Hell."

Strikingly, a substantial number of lcit prefer the training room to the e-room. The training room consists of multiple running stations upon which lcit are required to pace for an hour each day at their heart-rates' limit. A distinct minor-

---

[4] *"I've worked as a New York City schoolteacher for twenty-six years…and have won awards doing so… Over the years, I have come to see that whatever I thought I was doing as a teacher, most of what I actually was doing was teaching an invisible curriculum that reinforced the myths of the school institution and those of an economy based on caste… What I do that is right is simple to understand – I get out of kids' way, I give them space and time and respect. What I do wrong, however, is strange, complex, and frightening. Let me begin to show you what that is."*
John Gatto, Dumbing Us Down

[5] *"In our system, state-operated schools may not be enclaves of totalitarianism. School officials do not possess absolute authority over their students. Students in school as well as out of school are 'persons' under our Constitution."* U.S. Supreme Court Justice Abe Fortas, Tinker v. Des Moines School District (1969) – Students' Rights, American Civil Liberties Union, Freedom Network, aclu.org
"Education shall be directed to the full development of the human personality and to the strengthening of respect for human rights and fundamental freedoms." from Article 26, Universal Declar-ation of Human Rights, adopted and proclaimed by General Assembly, United Nations, 10 December, 1948

[6] *"I didn't write this book for [parents]. I wrote it for teenagers. I wrote it for teenagers because I wished that when I was a teenager someone had written it for me." Grace Llewellyn, The Teenage Liberation Handbook*

ity of loyal-consumers-in-training are urged into great competitions against one another – they pace for hours like world-class athletes until their very hearts are about to explode, while Terminators on duty smartly flog any lcit who quit or topple off the station.

The importance of the training room for all lcit has been emphasized in the Terminal ever since Ambulatory Motion was dropped from the curriculum years ago. Subsequently, it was found that lcit need some kind of physical tutoring to go along with the mental mastering, if their bodies are to be capable of sitting upright in front of a computer all day, let alone be able to work a serf wage job in the morning or evening, or both – in addition to sitting at attention in front of that great commerce machine of our times, the TV, late at night and on weekends.

The only, perhaps, negative side effect[7] of the training room, as far as we Terminators can tell, is the extra-strong straps that had to be installed in the e-room to prevent disruptive lcit from using newfound stamina and strength to break out. The straps are now threaded with steel.

An electric current is sometimes required.

Sadly, these unbreakable restraints contribute to the occasional sprained wrist, strained elbow, and dislocated shoulder in some of the more inexplic-ably rebellious lcit.

I have seen even a grotesque dislocated hip or two in my time.

Honestly, I have no idea what makes these lcit act the way they do. They seem to think they are undergoing some kind of cruel and unusual pun-ishment merely by showing up at Terminal gates in the morning.

As if we do not mentally cleanse the lcit for their own good![8]

TERMINAL CRUCIFIXION

As if we do not crucify them in their own best interest!

Out back is where we crucify the students – the loyal-consumers-in-training, I mean. The lcit.

Actually, out back is mainly where we crucified the lcit – those who have most seriously erred – but times being what they are now, the lcit more rebellious than can be imagined, we crucify them all over the Terminal and Terminal grounds.

There seems to be an inevitable rhythm to the crucifixions.

This stern punishment arises from incidents that arrive in clusters around the holidays, near the beginnings and endings of the Terminal year, semesters, and months and weeks.

Also, the beginnings and endings of exam periods, days, and classes are particularly fraught with tension and volatility.

Not to mention to different degrees every moment in between.

We find remedial crucifixion necessary for

<hr>

[7] *"Take professional sports... It is hard to imagine anything that contributes more fundamentally to authoritarian attitudes. In professional sports you are a spectator, and there are a bunch of gladiators beating each other up... And you are supposed to cheer for your gladiators. That is something you are taught from childhood." "I remember very well in high school suddenly asking myself this kind of funny question: Why am I cheering for the high school football team? Well that is the kind of thing you just do, you are trained to do. It is ingrained. And it carries over to jingoism and subordination and so on." Noam Chomsky, biography*

[8] *"Our form of compulsory schooling is an invention of the State of Massachusetts around 1850. It was resisted – sometimes with guns – by an estimated eighty percent of the Massachusetts population, the last outpost in Barnstable on Cape Cod not surrendering its children until the 1880s, when the area was seized by militia and children marched to school under guard... Prior to compulsory education the state literacy rate was ninety-eight percent, and after it the figure never exceeded ninety-one percent, where it stands in 1990... The home-schooling movement has quietly grown to a size where one and a half million young people are being educated entirely by their own parents; last month the education press reported the amazing news that children schooled at home seem to be five or even ten years ahead of their formally trained peers in their ability to think." John Gatto, Dumbing Us Down*

lcit crimes deemed especially heinous, such as duct-taping over forehead ID bar codes and other subversive behavior, like excessive cooperation and socializing.[9]

Rockview Terminal is more prone to crucifixions nowadays, but I'm sure it has nothing to do with the greater rates the Terminal is able to command from advertisers who attempt to peddle their brand name attention deficit disorder drugs at these lamentable yet festive events. After driving the nails into the hands and feet and leaving the errant lcit hanging for the better part of a day, a Terminal security agent then drives a painted fluorescent orange, two-foot-long, three-inch-wide steel spike through the center of the condemned lcit's forehead, into the wooden post behind.

There is talk among advertisers of electronically lighting up the tip of the spike after it is driven through the skull or otherwise brightening the advertisement, in an effort to get the message to really sink in.

I often wonder why people sometimes object to the amount of money corporate advertisers willingly pay for the three-inch spot on the head of the spike. The pharmaceutical company that manufactures the Real-Lite pills that best calm the loyal-consumers-in-training, Real-Lite Incorporated,[10] pays top dollar to help remind everyone that allowing natural body chemistry to simply run free – that is, out of control – can result in dire consequences for everyone concerned. I say, let big business pay for the remedial spike through the head. (To me, it's a no-brainer.)

As a final warning about the dangers of personal freedom and the financial-chemical remedy for this dread state of being, Real-Lite corporation in conjunction with the Terminal hangs a colorful banner over the head of the crucified lcit displaying different pill sizes and strengths for sale.

Behind the Terminal is still the preferred place to carry out crucifixions. That's where visitors may find a permanent assortment of three cross sizes – small, medium, and large, for elementary, junior Terminal, and full Terminal lcit – several small crosses, a few more large crosses, and nearly two dozen junior Terminal crosses, since by far the vast majority of all infractions occur at the junior Terminal age. Who knows why – for some reason, freedom seems to max out at the stage at which the body and mind begin to mature.

After the unfortunate lcit is spiked through the head, to the cross, the body is left to hang until it rots and thoroughly disintegrates. Eventually the bones fall into a heap below. There is quite a mound of skeletal parts behind Rockview Terminal by now. Sometimes we catch an lcit or two loitering out back, wistfully kicking through the bones, as if reminiscing, maybe searching for the skull of an old elementary chum or a junior Terminal buddy.

More frequently we find a couple of boys

---

[9] *"Thousands of children in this country grow up without being told what to do, without being formally taught to read or write, without being required to study biology, algebra, and Ernest Hemingway, without ever once being forced to read a particular book or complete a particular worksheet – or any worksheet whatsoever. If you are imagining that all the people who live with such freedom are half-naked rural hippie-kids, you are wrong. In class background, lifestyle, appearance, religion, and most other respects, self-directed learners are diverse. ...what I have chosen to portray in this book is not 'home-schooling,' per se, but rather self-directed learning." Grace Llewellyn, Real Lives: Eleven Teenagers Who Don't Go To School*

[10] *"Ritalin®, the brand name of the drug methylphenidate, is prescribed to about 2.4 million children diagnosed with attention deficit disorders (ADD) to help them concentrate. The drug is manufactured by the Ciba-Geigy Corporation. The Drug Enforce-ment Agency said there were 1,171 emergency room admissions attributed to use of methylphenidate in 1994, a slight increase from 1993... We have always had some problems with [methylphenidate] abuse and traffic. But it has never been pervasive because there never was much available... That situation [has begun] to change radically," said Gene Haislip, head of the DEA's drug div-ersion unit. "A lot of people don't know Ritalin® is like cocaine," Haislip said. "It can be very dangerous." He called the relationship between Ciba-Geigy and CHADD, an ADD advocacy group, an "unhealthy co-mingling of medical and commercial interests." National Drug Strategy Network, ndsn.org*

sword-fighting with thigh bones – not unlike the Terminators who often spar with training room whips – a pleasure to watch.

Nevertheless, such freelance sport earns the young warriors an automatic trip to the smashing block, where security agents sometimes go easy on them, seeing younger versions of themselves.

They joke with the thigh-bone duelers in an effort to cheer them up, then smash only a fingertip or two.

On occasion, out back among the bones, we'll catch an lcit couple in the act of something more intimate. This offense leads straight to the isolation rooms, naturally.

We Terminators generally allow, even encourage, loyal-consumers-in-training to think no one patrols the crucifixion area with any regularity. On the contrary, there is no more peaceful spot near which Terminators like to take their breaks than out back overlooking the crosses, skulls, and bones.

I must admit, I am especially drawn to the place as well. My youngest son recently met his sorry fate there on the cross, after he was caught cheating on a math test – a minor crime, one might think, but he was a repeat offender, I am sad to report.

After all of my son's trips to the smashing block, psychiatrist office, and isolation rooms, after all the head resizings, electrical stimulants, and Real-Lite doses, the poor boy seemed scarcely functional anymore, that is, no more functional than before. The crucifixion turned out to be for the best, really, an outright mercy. He was so far gone I don't think even the final spike through the forehead was terribly necessary.

Every once in awhile I'll go out and lay a red rose on the pile of bones and wonder if anything could have been engineered differently to salvage my dear son's life.

Alas, despite having graduated with distinction from the Terminal years ago, I have no idea.

At least, my dearly departed son has served as a vivid example to us all.

I find this to be no small consolation.

TERMINAL ISOLATION

Owned and operated by MarchRite corporation at a bracing but reasonable price, the isolation rooms at Rockview Terminal take full advantage of the most modern in corrections technology.

I mention the isolation rooms first before any other part of our beloved Terminal to assure con-cerned parents and local loyal consumers that they do indeed exist. The supposed absence of such rooms at other so-called "tolerant" Terminals out-side our district is mere rumor, I suspect.

How any Terminal could make do without active sets of isolation rooms is far beyond my capacity to comprehend, especially since isolation so well modifies disobedient behaviour in the never-ending process of tutoring youth, who plainly are inherently dysfunctional.[11]

For most loyal-consumers-in-training, simply keeping them sitting alone at their desks proves to be enough of a constraint on any sort of de-moral-ized interaction, while teaching the indispensable lesson that we are all thrown into this teeming world on our own, and on our own we must re-main to become a productive success in life.

But for those incomprehensibly slow learners and obstinate types who do not readily perceive the wisdom of sitting alone and orderly at their work-stations throughout the day, the isolation

---

[11] *"In the suburbs, psychiatric hospitals have become what jails are for the inner city – alternatives to crumbling society and failing families and schools... 275,000 children under eighteen were hospitalized for psychiatric reasons in 1985 – double the number from 1971...the hospitals are humiliating and stigmatizing and often do more harm than good. Isolation and physical treatment are common, and drugs are the norm."*
Peter and Ginger Breggin, *The War Against Children of Color*

rooms are ever ready to teach a handy lesson.

As may be supposed, isolation makes for a wel-come remedial effect even on the good kids, who, when feeling a little overwhelmed on any given Terminal day, are prone to imagine they are "stressing" or "freaking out." A brief stint in iso-lation helps clear their minds rather quickly.

Unfortunately, isolation can only do so much. It cannot entirely stamp out those many real or, more likely, imagined baffling psychological disorders from which even our good kids some-times like to pretend they are suffering.

For example, it never fails that every other day at least – that is, after each official grading period – and upon any one of the many melodic blasts of the Terminal bells which indicate changes in the lessons or the end of a test, a handful of loyal-cons-in-training begin moaning and frothing at the mouth, due to what they like to believe is stress, and so we Terminators order them out to isolation where they are quickly shocked back to their senses.

Though the normally good loyal-consumers-in-training do not receive the full trauma treat-ment that the isolation rooms reserve for the more typically bad loyal-consumers-in-training, these lcit do return to study noticeably quieter or are even completely withdrawn for a time – a welcome remedial effect that allows them to re-focus on their work in short order.

Appropriate notice is sent to parents when a loyal-consumer-in-training goes into full isola-tion. Unlike other negligent Terminals, Rockview, I am proud to note, has not perma-nently lost, so to speak, more than a handful of loyal-consumers-in-training yet.

In any case, only the truly hard-core, bad lcit are in danger of being permanently lost to isola-tion – an lcit, for example, who is late turning in three or more assignments in a row.

The good loyal-cons-in-training, who may en-dure only an hour or two in the isolation rooms, like to come out pretending to look hag-gard and beat-up and about forty pounds thin-ner just to keep up an impression with their more rebellious peers – but they are capable now at last of sitting firmly in front of the com-puter and working straight through any distrac-tion however large.[12]

Meanwhile, the eyes of the other good lcit grow just a little more opaque, while the eyes of the more typically bad lcit tend to slant more into thin slits.

Every treatment has its side effects.

It should not necessarily be considered shameful to be thrown into the isolation rooms as long as the reason for getting tossed inside is the weakness of a good kid, and not the arro-gance of the bad.

Those who are proud of their stints in the isolation room due to some demented irrational superiority complex, the truly incorrigi-ble...well, honestly, all we Terminators can hope to do for these bad lcit is to simply grind them down. Even if we wanted to help...and help...and help, and even if these deluded youth really wanted our assist-ance, we simply don't have the time – not with several hundred loyal-consumers-in-training per Terminator to patrol at any given moment.

It is my firm belief that these incorrigible loyal-cons-in-training would be much better off if we Terminators were simply allowed to expel them at a much faster rate. Fortunately the Ter-minal's dropout rate hovers at a healthy 60 per-cent, near the national average for certain popu-lations these days, which takes care of many be-havioral prob-lems quite nicely.

Not infrequently, we Terminators select lcit at random and toss them into the isolation rooms for brief refreshings.

This time-honored corrective makes for a po-tent tonic to all our lcit. One of the Terminal's many charitable traditions.

I simply do not see how the Terminal could

---

[12] *"All the children—the bright, the average, and the dull—are systematically retarded one way or another, while the teacher's hands are tied." Paul Goodman, Growing Up Absurd*

ever get along without the isolation rooms. In fact I am aware of a number of families who have moved into the Rockview Terminal district due to our awesome reputation gained by the masterly use of isolation.

Without isolation rooms – which no one who has never been sent there has ever seen, and anyone who has ever endured the experience never talks about – I am afraid to know what kind of educational facility Rockview Terminal might de-generate into.

Certainly, our ability to educate effectively, to mentally cleanse, would be sorely diminished.

Instead, we discipline and bless all our loyal-cons-in-training with the proper heavy doses of isolation.[13]

------

[13] *In an experimental progressive school in Philadelphia that M.I.T. Professor of Linguistics and political activist, Noam Chomsky attended until about age 12, "every student was regarded as somehow being a very successful student. There was no sense of competition, no ranking of students. At this particular school, which was essentially a Deweyite school and I think a very good one, judging from my experience, interests were encouraged and children were encouraged to pursue their interests – not in the sense of slapping paints on paper, but doing the kind of work and thinking that you were interested in. They worked jointly with others or by themselves. It was a lively atmosphere, and the sense was that everybody was doing something important. ...it was the usual mixture in such a school, with some gifted students and some problem children who had dropped out of the public schools... Well, then I got to the academic high school in the public school system, which was supposed to be a very good high school, and it was a real shocker. For one thing, there was the shock of discovering that I was a good student, which had never occurred to me before. And then there was the whole system of prestige and value that went along with that. And the intense competitiveness and regimenta-tion. In fact, I can remember a lot about elementary school, the work I did, what I studied and so on. I remember virtually nothing about high school. It's almost a complete blank in my memory apart from the emotional tone, which was quite negative...the manner and style of preventing and blocking independent and creative thinking and imposing hierarchies and competitiveness and the need to excel, not in the sense of doing as well as you can, but doing better than the next person. Schools vary, of course, but I think that those features are commonplace. I know that they're*

Why it is difficult to retain qualified and competent Terminators, even at the best Terminals, I have no idea.

That said, the salaries are not lofty by corporate standards, especially among the cooks, custodians, aides, technicians, security agents, nurses, order-lies, anesthesiologists, counselors, diagnosticians, and bus drivers, not to mention the Terminators – even the physicians and psychologists are paid low wages by corporate measures.

But given the prices corporations are charging for potable air these days, few of us care to face the insecurity that comes with attempting to change to less penny-pinched nonterminal jobs.

In Rockview Area Terminal District as in most other Terminal type sectors, Terminal funds go primarily not to human wages, but to electronica.

While corporations have so far resisted the oft-suggested idea that they completely "take over" the Terminals, we may at least be content for now that there never seems to be any shortage of funds flowing out to corporations in exchange for their electronic wonders, at least in the better equipped Terminals such as ours.

Rockview Terminal is state of the art in all ways.

We do however maintain some of the heart-warming classic touches, such as our brick guard shack, plus the electrified fence that challenges the occasional loyal-consumer-in-training who makes a mad dash for the far outside during lunch, almost always a suicide option (the escape attempt, that is, not lunch so much anymore, given the newly available, Terminal-supplied antidote for internal bleeding: Regurgicake[TM]).

------

not necessary, because, for example, the school that I went to as a child wasn't like that at all." Noam Chomsky, The Chomsky Reader

Thus it is that Rockview Terminal finds itself rather well stocked, fortified even, with the usual electronic educational and enforcement gear: all the clamorous bells, whistles, computers, printers, virtual reality machines, and a thousand other related wonders that most Terminators would not know how to administer if it were not for the more mechanized loyal-consumers-in-training amongst us.

Moreover the Terminal is fully standardized with TVs, recorders, megaphones, and megaloud public address speakers, cameras, sensors, scan-ners, and electronically operated wall mounted lasers, which were installed to reduce the number of security agents that need to be employed in maintaining control of Terminal grounds.

Then there are the ever-at-hand electric and electronic prods, tranquilizing darts, and assorted other motivational devices of order and stability that clank against the belts of the security agents and the Terminators as they patrol the rooms and grounds, though the grounds are patrolled more out of a sense of nostalgia these days, a nostalgia for those bucolic bygone times when an agent or Terminator might walk around the corner of the building, find a straggling lcit, and give him or her a good hot blast with the classic bone-burning laser.

Although the security agents' modern portable lasers are also proven bone breakers, by now they are up to fifty percent less lethal than earlier mod-els. Greater improvements are expected every few years.

Unfortunately, it seems that as the Terminal gains assorted electronica, we lose assorted Terminators – until today the average class size has become what it is (all inclusive) and the lcit-to-teacher ratio hovers at about 500 to 1.

Happily, there is never a shortage of funds for electronica, and so I am certain that Rockview Terminal itself is one of the smartest Terminals on the planet – though the lcit seem to struggle as much as ever.[14]

Truly, I am glad for all the electronica, even if I do not know how to fire up half of it. On the other hand, I do sometimes wish for certain aspects of the old days, when each Terminator was in charge of a few less lcit and we had access to a few more rooms and areas in which to herd our lcit about.[15]

I even miss the old wild west feel of the halls, where there was always some rodeo-like excitement to be found. Oh, for the days of the lusty noise of free-roaming youths milling between classes!

Of course now there is considerably less blood splattered upon the walls, due to the new holster-ing laws for the security agents' lasers.

But mostly, I think, the reduced carnage rate is due to the lack of lcit movement, thus the absence of potentially suspicious moving targets for our security agents and Terminators with itchy fingers.

I say there is less spilt blood, but in all honesty I am not sure of it.

I think the Screaming Pad has made up for most of what has been lost in the former free-for-all of the halls. And no one dares guess, wonder, or recall what happens in the new and improved isolation rooms.

Perhaps it is just that the blood spilt in our time flows out in a more efficient and hidden manner than ever before, in a more technologically intricate and more controlled environment of intense mental cleansing.

---

[14] *"Less than 1% of instructional time in high school is devoted to discussion that requires some kind of response involving reasoning or an opinion from students..." "A teacher cannot build a com-munity of learners unless the voices and lives of the students are an integral part of the curriculum." Rethinking Our Classrooms: Teaching for Equity and Social Justice*

[15] *"'The corporations are earning a handsome profit from the federal treasury,'" Illinois Rep. Luis Gutierrez said, and it's time they shared some of it with the 21 percent of blacks and the 32 percent of Latinos who work full time and still live in poverty." Ted Kleine, "Allied Forces"*

A worthy improvement, no doubt.

Anything, after all, is preferable to the primitive chaos of the old pens, papers, books, and hall walking; even, I suppose, if the Terminal does often feel now with all this new electronica – more sophisticated, yes – but somehow, overall, a bit more bland and predictable, unnaturally still and – quiet, too quiet – and, well, sort of eerie.

TERMINAL FALL

In addition to explaining the exciting life-enriching operations of Rockview Terminal, I would also like to reveal some of the lesser-known sides of the Terminal that I have had the good experience to get to cherish recently.

In this way I hope to give an even more in-form-ative character to this Terminal overview.

It so happens that after being a Terminator for many years, I suffered an accident not long ago while walking in from the Terminal parking lot: I slipped and fell on a treacherous patch of gravel, knocking my head rather badly on ground. There were those who said I would never recover, and they couldn't believe it when I did. "He never should have made it back."

I was delighted to return to the Terminal – regrettably not in my former role as official Terminator but in more unofficial capacity as an auxiliary hire working with the custodians, at least initially.

Perhaps the only noticeable side effect of my fall is that I often feel a strong desire to talk constantly, that is incessantly, continuously, all the time. I can practically never stop my interminable jabbering even while eating.

Lately, to relieve some of this pressure to express, which stems from I know not where, I have begun marking down the delightful course of my days in an electronic journal from which this hand-book springs.

During my time as custodian, I talked to the toilets while scrubbing and did not mind or even particularly notice when the head custodian as-signed me all the toilet scrubbing duties after I continued to express my heartfelt appreciation for this job, any job, given my recent ill luck.

True, the other custodians mostly kept their distance from me, but could I help it if I felt the need to talk a lot? Could I help that I was once a Terminator? This seemed to unnerve some of the more bashful custodians. I successfully Terminated a couple of them a few years back, and I think they have had some slight difficulty adjusting to our new relationship.

I try to remind them that we were all loyal-consumers-in-training at one point, however long ago.

Can't we all just get along? Are we not all as one, here in merry Rockview?[16]

TERMINAL HUMOR

The Terminal is not an entirely serious place.

For instance, the lcit find plenty of humor in constantly zapping instant messages and electronic notes to one another. The Terminal puts up with a precise percentage of such behavior, for in the proper amount, e-notes have been found to activate the energy needed to learn, or to at least reduce the number of lcit who periodically lock up, catatonic.

Lcit who exceed their quota of e-notes during any given week receive an electric shock (an instructive charge), sent automatically from the main computer to the appropriate workstation.

---

[16] *"By the time I left school, the summer after the seventh grade, I was a nervous wreck. All of my 'friends,' save two, had turned against me. I had virtually no self esteem. Everyone I met seemed to become my enemy. Now it is just the opposite. While I don't strive for popularity, I have developed a close circle of friends; people I should know seem to seek me out. It's ironic, given people's worries about how homeschoolers will socialize, that only now that I am outside of school I have found some true friends. Above all, homeschooling has given me time to think. I have time away from the constant social pressures and traumas associated with the school environment. If I want to spend the day listening to music, drawing, or working out, it's my right. My time is my own to develop as I please." Patrick Meehan, age 16, "Ascent From A Nightmare," Real Lives*

Any bone dislocations due to jolting against straps are carefully attended by onsite medical staff, although these gentle reminders usually merely stun and im-mobilize a loyal-consumer-in-training for a minute or two. It does sting a bit, on the fingertips, and so lcit do not often exceed their e-note quotas.

The electric charge is increased for any subsequent violation per week. A second such shock leaves the fingertips smoldering, and a third shock completely blackens the palms yet leaves lcit able to resume typing after an hour of icing and recovery in the emergency room. In a few days, the charred skin falls off and the hands must be carefully bandaged until scar tissue forms and the lcits' full typing capacity is restored. (Synthetic fireproof copies of lcit original fingertips are reattached surgically so as to not lose any vital identifying markers.)

Perhaps the most common source of humor among our lcit, aside from their near complete absorption in the entertainment industries, the e-media (or is it i-media? I can scarcely keep up) and various corporate-driven activities outside the Terminal, is the use of their personal rubbing pads. Since lcit arms and hands are strapped to the keyboards, all workstations are equipped with a rubbing pad that lcit can swing into place by using a lever near their feet, to rub an itchy nose, to wipe sweat from the brow, to daub tears from the eyes.

On occasion, the foot of an lcit will unexpectedly twitch and the rubbing pad will swing over and smack the lcit in the face. At this moment anyone sitting within a diameter of several dozen workstations of this clumsy lcit is apt to deluge the unfortunate bumbler with a horde of jokes – "Have a nice twitch? See you next stitch!" "And your mother's name is Grace..." And so on. Jokes tend to be fairly mild because the isolation rooms await those who go too far.

Even a large number of lcit sitting in front of the blunderer will hear or sense what has happened and send their own e-notes back, guessing at the appropriate workstation. Paybacks can be hell, but the injured and embarrassed lcit can only respond to a relatively small number of messages and keep within quota for the week.

Of anything remotely Terminal-related, the e-note quotas are what lcit talk about obsessively, incessantly, during lunch and in instant messages – keeping within weekly quota; quota concerns; the number and quality of notes they receive each hour, each day, each week; what to do with their remaining quota, when to spend the quota, how to spend it, and on whom.

The e-notes are closely monitored by the mainframe. Unlawful and obscene words are flagged and offending lcit are punished, just as they are for using any words at any time that have been declared off-limits specifically to loyal-consumers-in-training, especially words that are or may be legally construed as "enemies of the Incorporated Estates of Dearth and the Terminals and institutions of culture and authority in general." Words such as – activist, solidarity, justice, equality, fairness, sharing, peace … and *any* word used in "an insubordinate context," even words such as "dove" used to indicate peace, or "truth" used to suggest an unofficial idea of reality, and so on.

Though there has been an all-out effort among the most devout citizens of this flag-waving country to get the word "truth" banned from Terminals and indeed general use altogether, the logistics have not yet been worked out.

Unfortunately, our experiments so far show that it does little good to simply replace "truth" with a more responsible word such as, say, "reality." For example, readily acknowledged and accepted by the IED is the reality of life rather than any so-called truth, let alone justice. Any denial of health care is simply too bad, not a crime; unaffordable education may be a shame but is no scandal; world leading rates of imprisonment (especially of the poor and of people of color) is just the way things are, never mind why it might be; and world-leading rates of military expenditures are an unvarnished blessing, as far as I can see, no cause for concern. This is all just reality, whatever any supposed truth or injustice, which is of essentially no value in the IED. Truth? Justice? These are scarcely functional for profit, if at all. Not like reality is. So tthat's how things should be. Any good loyal consumer in the IED will agree. There remains a problem, however.

Unfortunately, the new word "reality," no matter how hard we Terminators try, somehow soon comes to regain much of the troublesome original meanings of the offensive word. A difficult fight. For example, when claiming to speak the "truth" too many malcontents like to say, "Just keeping it real, brother" – "Keep it real, sister." – "Just keeping it real, my man. " When you know they don't mean reality at all but instead are subversively referring to what they think of as the "truth."

Even attempting to replace "true" with its literal opposite, "false," has proven to be less than effective. "Hey, right on, Dude, that's totally *false* and kickin' man." You see? "False" becomes "true," "true" becomes false. "Bad" becomes "good," "good" becomes "bad" – "They got him, they got him *good*." "All right! That's the *bad*dest thing I ever seen!"

In many ways, controlling lcit language is a hopeless losing battle. It can seem like more trouble than it's worth – everyone, I think, who is sufficiently honest with themselves realizes this – but it's a battle we must fight nevertheless, for it is one of the most crucial battles constantly waged in the Terminals.

This ongoing war for the control, that is, the education, of the unruly lcit mind, must be forever waged if we are to maintain the happy status quo of society. But I digress from the quotas –

Lcit may petition – electronically, individually – for volt-resistant gloves if they carelessly go over quota twice in a week and are in imminent danger of having their palms blackened and scarred for life. These petitions are successful a fraction or so of the time, I should say, depending upon good behavior in other ways.

The lcit even have a gruesome humor they reserve for selected lcit who have already received two shocks in a given week. If these unfortunate lcit are not popular, they may be del-

uged by provocative e-notes, which the over-the-quota lcit can in no way respond to.

Be assured that under such circumstances these lcit are not unstrapped for lunch for fear they might retaliate physically against their fellow teasers. However, federal guidelines still require that we feed and water all lcit who request it – almost regardless of behavior, believe it or not. This is the job of the aides, to hold up a cup with a straw and to pop a few pellets of microfood into the mouths of the restrained lcit, if they so desire.

Unfortunately, such an occasion usually makes these lcit the butt of even more aggressive jokes. It's sad but true – the loyal-consumers-in-training can be oh so ruthless – it's distressing really. We Terminators remain completely baffled by where and from whom our lcit learn such barbaric ways.[17]

---

[17] *"These kids cry out against authority and conformity and what they get is more authority and more conformity. What no one has yet to discuss is the general misery of school and social alienation, even among the relatively well off. Nor has anyone addressed the constant focus on self-interest and 'doing what you need to do to get ahead' in the schools. Competition with one's peers is rewarded rather than, say, solidarity. Even the kids who seem blessed by ath-letic ability, physical appearance, socioeconomic status, popularity, and so forth are haunted by a conviction of their own inadequacy.... Some of those who hate the circumstances will act; most will just suffer privately and take out their pain on other individuals in the privacy of homes and bedrooms."*
"Misery of Modern Schooling – Littleton, Colorado – The Kids Go Postal," Alternative Press Review, Spring 2000

Segundo's Revenge

Joe Emersberger

Rodrigo Cornejo sat alone in a waiting room wondering if the psychiatrist was making any progress with his son. He had given up trying to hear what his boy was saying to the doctor on the other side of the door. Even with his hearing aid turned up all the way, it was futile.

Brendan was Rodrigo's only child – his miracle child because of how late in life his deceased wife had given birth to him. Rodrigo was old enough to be Brendan's grandfather, and had brought him up in a very indulgent, grandfatherly way. Brendan had never been discouraged from following his heart. While his friends entered university making "practical" decisions about what to study, Brendan unflinchingly pursued his passion – history. But Brendan's passion for history and for Ecuador (where he had done research for a doctorate) seemed to have somehow displaced his sanity.

It was Saturday. Dr. Bueno rarely granted weekend appointments, but he had found the urgency and formality with which the old man had pleaded for an appointment very moving.

Brendan sat in front of Dr. Bueno on an old couch holding a globe on his lap.

"Ecuador is this little country here in South America – right at the equator," Brendan said as he pointed to it on the globe with his long slender finger. "As you can see, it is many times smaller than Ontario."

Dr. Bueno, an immigrant to Canada from the Philippines, was a very well read man with broad interests. He knew where Ecuador was and couldn't help feeling annoyed that Brendan would point it out for him on a globe.

"On the Pacific coast we have La Costa," Brendan explained "a tropical area that is extremely fertile. To the east we have El Oriente – largely tropical rainforest and very sparsely populated. In between La Costa and El Oriente is a mountainous region known as La Sierra. The mountains are, of course, the Andes. The population is split approximately in half between La Sierra and La Costa."

Brendan looked up with a sweet, apologetic expression on his young face.

"I don't mean to sound like a textbook but this is very relevant background information I assure you."

"Oh, don't apologize," said Dr. Bueno. "Please continue."

Despite feeling a little annoyed, Dr. Bueno was enjoying this patient. It was nice to have a break from the parade of compulsive gamblers he had been treating lately.

Brendan continued to talk as if he were prepping the psychiatrist for a history exam.

"United Fruit arrived in Tenguel, which is in La Costa, in 1936 to grow bananas. By that time, a major revolt by workers in Costa Rica had taught the company not to rely on brutality alone. Ecuador's elite were quite divided during this period, and the Liberal faction had to at least pretend to be on the side of the poor, especially against foreigners. The other faction of the elite was the Conservatives who were basically supported by the Church and the large landowners of La Sierra. The Liberals were mainly backed by the growing class of merchants and financiers based in La Costa. You could think of it as, more or less, a standoff between Feudalists and Capitalists… May I borrow that pen?"

"Certainly," said Bueno. He handed Brendan a pen he had been holding but not making notes with as he intended. Brendan used the pen to point to the globe again.

"Tenguel would be approximately here. Guaya-quil, Ecuador's largest city, is right here. See how close they are? Today you can travel from Guayaquil to Tenguel by car in under 2 hours. In 1940, it took a full day. Geography – dense forests, drastic changes in elevation and climate over very short distances – led to isolation which drove cultural and political differ-ences. Today, the legacy of that isolation is still apparent. The people of La Sierra (Seranos) are easily identified by their distinctive accents and idioms and they are widely regarded are more formal and reserved that the fast talking, blunt, and supposedly more street wise people of the La Costa – Costenos. Think of how far you can travel in Canada without noticing any differ-ence in the way people talk."

"I see," said Dr. Bueno," but where do you fit yourself into this history that you describe?"

"My parents were originally from the La Si-erra, but I've never been there. My father came to La Costa – to the Tenguel plantation in 1938 – and worked in and around that area until the day he died."

Dr. Bueno raised his eyebrows. "Isn't your fa-ther the man sitting in the waiting room?"

"Thankfully, no," answered Brendan.

"I see. Tell me about your father then."

"I wish I had been kinder to him," Brendan sighed, "more appreciative and understanding of the sacrifices he made. If he had been like my mother I wouldn't have these regrets. I often wished my mother had been my father. Her strength was wasted. That was one of our weak-nesses – our inability to see women as equals in the struggle."

"Where is your mother?"

"She passed away shortly after my father died."

"How did you arrive in here Canada?"

"I can't explain that without explaining the history."

"Very well," replied Dr. Bueno as he leaned back in his chair. He listened carefully to what Brendan said but also observed him closely. Underneath the energy and enthusiasm with which Brendan spoke were signs of exhaustion – from the exertion of staying in character Bueno assumed.

"As I was saying, various factors contributed

to United Fruit using more carrots than sticks with its workers in Ecuador. The Liberals were led by a guy named Jose Maria Velasco Ibarra. He was elected President of Ecuador five differ-ent times – and overthrown four times. Only once did he serve his full term in office. He was a rousing speaker who made the poor believe that he was on their side. People argue (exces-sively in my view) about Velasco's sincerity but the bottom line was that United Fruit could not trust a government led by someone like him. Velasco's rhetoric, sincere or not, generated ex-citement and expectations among the poor – that was dangerous.

"Some workers will tell you that Tenguel was a paradise under United Fruit. It angered me, as a young man, when some of the older folks said nice things about the company even though I understood why they did. Before United Fruit arrived, Tenguel was a Cacoa plantation. Ecua-dor had a Cacao driven export boom between the years 1880 to 1920 thanks to increased de-mand for chocolate in the USA and Europe. The working conditions on the Cacao plantations were inhuman. Workers had to literally bow in the presence of their bosses and were regularly beaten – all that on top of being overworked and impoverished. The punishment that was dished out to workers was often deliberately random in order to increase their state of fear. The beatings were necessary (from the point of view of the bosses) to impose discipline. It wasn't enough of a threat to withhold wages because workers could offset losses by farming little plots of land.

"It was understandable that people who re-membered the Cacao days would think that work-ing for United Fruit was a blessing. Under United Fruit beatings were rare, and you didn't have to bow in the boss' presence. That alone was a major improvement."

"Sorry to interrupt," said Dr. Bueno," but do you remember anything about the Cacao boom years?" The only reason he asked was to see if Brendan's answer would be consistent.

"Of course not," answered Brendan, "I was born in Tenguel sometime in 1940 shortly after my father was hired by United Fruit."

"Sometime in 1940? You don't know your exact date of birth?"

"No. It's embarrassing but record keeping was very poor and remained so for decades after I was born. It sometimes took years to receive a birth certificate that was often riddled with errors. My mother never received birth or death certificates for two of her children who died as infants. She never even applied for them."

"So you are now sixty eighth years old?"

"Probably, but I could possibly be 69."

"You look like you're in your mid twenties," said Dr. Bueno.

"Thank you. That's very kind," Brendan said beaming with pride at what he regarded as a compliment.

"And your English is flawless."

"I learned quickly."

"I'm not seeing how any of what you talked about explains what you are doing in Canada."

"It will become clear to you. I promise. A few decades of relatively good times followed after United Fruit set up shop in Tenguel. I can't stress enough that when I say 'good times' that I am speaking in very relative terms.

"Unlike most Ecuadorians at the time, Tenguel's workers had access to electricity and clean water. The streets were cleaned and houses painted regularly. The company paid workers 'family wages' and sold them food (including pasteurized milk) at cost because family men were considered the most reliable workers. The company hospital was top notch by local standards. They also sponsored sports and social clubs for the workers. The clubs were what many people remembered most fondly about the so called good times.

"My mother got involved with the clubs organizing dances and beauty pageants. She became very well known. My father, in contrast, never said much to anyone.

"As isolated as it was, Tenguel eventually felt the impact of the labor movement that was on the move throughout the country. Before 1929 there were only 4 labor unions in Ecuador. In 1939 there were almost 70. By the time I was seven years old United Fruit felt threatened enough to respond by establishing two labor unions in Tenguel. The unions engaged in phony battles with each other over who would make 'demands' of the company.

"As a boy, I used to make my little friends laugh with my impersonation of the company's favorite unionist. I'd stand on the same spot in the plaza where he made his speeches and wave my arms about exactly like he did as he denounced the company. Of course I didn't know he was a phony. I just thought the way he carried on was funny. I noticed that my mother laughed a strange, bitter laugh when she watched him speak.

"By the time I was about 16 years old, the mid 1950s, the phony union evolved into a real one as leaders who were not company stooges were final-ly elected. Unfortunately, by that time, Panama Disease began to ravage Tenguel's banana crops. United Fruit began firing workers and selling land off like crazy. By 1960, almost all the workers were fired.

"Getting fired meant getting banished from Tenguel. Where were you to go? How would you live? The fired workers began taking over Tenguel as a way to survive. United Fruit moved to have them evicted. The battle for workers' rights became a struggle for land reform."

"You were involved with leading this struggle I take it?" said Dr. Bueno.

"I was part of it. My father and I were fired in 1956. Along with several others we took over some poor quality land on the outskirts of Tenguel. My old man, timid as he was, got dragged into battle as did so many others like him. My mother would have done more, could have done more, but the men kept women in the dark and locked them out of decision making."

"Brendan. You're in Canada. You are a Canadian – twenty six years old according to the information I have. Your father is sitting out there in the waiting room – very much alive."

The psychiatrist's tone was firm but not exasperated. He wanted to see how Brendan would respond if he was suddenly challenged in a very direct manner.

Dr. Bueno's words bounced ineffectually off Brendan.

"If you understood the historical narrative that I'm trying to share with you then you'd know that everything you just said is false," Brendan replied.

"Ecuadorian history has nothing to do with it," Dr. Bueno said calmly. "No country's history – not Ecuador's nor Ethiopia's – can turn you into a sixty eight year old former plantation worker. You're a graduate student who a spent a few months in Ecuador doing research for a book. That's it. That is the reality."

"I respectfully disagree," Brendan shrugged. "It's sad that you won't hear me out. I was getting to the heart of the matter – and my name is Segundo, not Brendan."

"Keep going then," said Bueno with a slight nod.

"It's important to know that we were hardly the first people to do battle with United Fruit over land. Throughout the 1930s and 1940s peasants fought and won land claims against them – mainly for land that bordered Tenguel. They got help from labor unions in Guayaquil and from activists who seemed to drop out of the sky to come live with them and help them.

"They learned how to work the system and when our turn came to fight for land we learned quickly from them. Basically, United Fruit was over confident about the connections it had at the national level. President Velasco Ibarra himself once promised them that he would evict the peasants, but nothing happened. The local officials were poor people who identified with the peasants – and who knows what Velasco really cared about.

"Anyway, we learned from others and quickly became quite organized – even cocky at times. A few police showed up once and told us that we had an hour to vacate the land. I'll never forget the look on their faces face when we said to them that they had ten minutes to leave the land. They slithered away quietly and were not seen again.

"By 1960 United Fruit tired of this farcical battle for our small piece of low quality land. They sent their lawyers down to formally surrender but we quibbled about every word in the document that awarded us the land. They got so frustrated that they finally just let me sit at a desk and type it out myself. That's one of my fondest memories – typing out the document while the lawyers watched."

"That's quite an uplifting story," said Bueno.

"Yes," sighed Brendan, "but unfortunately that isn't where it ends. During the mid 1960s the Cavendish banana was introduced into Tenguel. It was resistant to Panama Disease and required less, but higher quality land than the Michel Gros banana. United Fruit began outsourcing their production to local capitalists – scumbags like Rodrigo Cornejo. The small plots owned by peasants became irrelevant to them."

"Why do you feel justified in calling your father a scumbag?"

"Rodrigo Cornejo is not my father," Brendan scoffed.

"Then who, in your opinion, is the elderly gentleman in the waiting room?"

"He is Rodrigo Cornejo, but you should try to talk him out of it."

"What do you mean?" asked Dr. Bueno.

"I mean that you could write a lengthy book about the destructive delusions of the Ecuadorian upper class."

"Do you call him a scumbag because he is rich?"

"No, of course not. No one can choose who

their parents are, what social economic status they are born into, or the assumptions that are driven into their brains as children. Rodrigo Cornejo is a scum bag because he murdered my father."

"That's a very serious allegation," Bueno said gravely.

"There was military coup in Ecuador in 1963. It was helped along significantly by the CIA. If you've read Philip Agee's book…"

"I have," burst in Dr. Bueno as if to say "please don't summarize the book for me."

"Okay. Well, shortly after the coup many of us were rounded up by the army. My father and I, and several others, were kidnapped by soldiers. They took us to some nearby property owned by Rodrigo Cornejo and put us in a swimming pool. We stood there all night with water up to our necks while soldiers sat on lawn chairs aiming their guns at us. Rodrigo Cornejo came by a few times to gawk at us. His servants, many of them children, brought the soldiers food and drink."

"My father and I, actually most of us, were eventually let go. The few men they kept, who were not even the most political, we never saw again. My father took ill the day after he was set free and soon died."

The grief in Brendan's eyes as he recounted this was so genuine that Dr. Bueno could not help but offer his condolences.

"I'm very sorry to hear that," Bueno said, "but how do you know that Rodrigo Cornejo had any choice but to cooperate with the army?"

"We already knew him well. For a few years he had been buying off the local officials who used to support us and using his employees to harass us and damage our crops.

"The Ecuadorian military tried to other tactics besides repression to beat down what they saw as the threat of Communism. The army and the rich were horrified by the example of Cuba. Hence the era of so called land reform began.

The military abolished the remaining feudal era land laws. By 1966 we had elected governments back. In 1968 Velasco was elected for the fifth time, and over-thrown in 1972 for the final time. The military stepped aside again in 1979. Actually the first four years of the second military government don't compare badly at all with many of the elected governments. There were some members of the military that had reformist ideas, but by 1976 they were pushed aside."

Brendan stopped talking. He looked down at the globe then he smiled as if mocking himself.

"What is it?" asked Bueno.

"I was just thinking that while we were winning battles the ground was shifting under our feet – in favor of the rich – and we weren't aware of it. During the 'land reform' period we were gradually stripped of our land. The rich were winning, but they too were unaware of how limited their victor-ies were, of how the battlefield was shifting. We became better organized, less isolated even as we were losing. "

Brendan set the globe down on the floor and picked up a thick binder that was net to him on the sofa. It contained mainly hand written notes and some decayed, yellow clippings from Ecuadorian newspapers.

"Is that your thesis?"

"An academic writes a thesis. A person like me tells a story. These pages contain everything I remember about our battles that can possibly shed any light on it, everything I remember people say-ing that is of any relevance to it. My goal is to rescue people like my parents from the oblivion to which historians condemn them."

"How can you achieve such an ambitious objective without honesty?"

"I am honest."

"No you aren't. You deny who you are. How can such deceit not contaminate your work? And who will publish it?"

"It will be ruthlessly honest, and Rodrigo Cornejo will get it published," remarked Brendan – clearly untroubled by Dr. Bueno's assertions. "Most of his ill gotten fortune will be spent publishing my story, donating to Ecuadorian labor organizations and to groups like CONAIE that represent indigenous peoples."

"Why would he not just have you committed? You're making that easy for him if you keep claiming to be something you are not."

"Believe what you like about me, but Rodrigo Cornejo will do as I demand because he believes that I am his only son; because his 'miracle child' taught him something about the value of human life that he never realized before; and because very deep down he wants to make amends. Besides, his ex-wives, relatives and disgruntled business associates will eventually get his money if he doesn't spend it. That is why he basically fled to Canada decades ago. I've reminded him of that often."

"Is this vengeance satisfying to you?"

"Not completely, that is why I agreed to see you. I want you to rehabilitate him."

The Publisher

Joe Emersberger

Louverture's first email to Steve Schmidt:

For over a year activists across Canada have been spreading the word that Canada, along with the US and France, was behind the coup that ousted Haitian presi-dent Jean Bertrand Aristide on February 29, 2004. These activists should not have to work around the Canadian media.

Canadian troops secured the airport in Port-au-Prince, while the US military completed the abduction of Aristide. Canadian personnel train the police who are murdering Aristide's supporters. Canada oversees Haiti's Ministry of Justice as it fills the jails with politi-cal prisoners and stacks the judiciary with supporters of the coup. Canada generously funds the dictatorship, and joined the US in an aid embargo on Aristide's duly elected government.

This scratches the surface of a story your newspaper should be telling.

How large a bloodbath is required before you take interest?

Steve flipped through the latest issue of Maclean's without really reading the pages that described the carnage in Iraq and the devastation recently inflicted on New Orleans by Hurricane Katrina. The magazine was a prop used to disguise his anxiety while he sat in his brother's waiting room. He soon put the magazine back on a green plastic table, shuffled through other reading material, then picked up a copy of the Toronto Globe & Mail. Steve published the Windsor Free Press, his hometown newspaper, which he failed to notice was no-where to be found in the room that morning.

When Steve spotted an article about the situa-tion in Haiti he threw the newspaper back on the table as if it had suddenly caught fire in his hands. A young woman sitting across from him noticed the fear that flashed in his eyes and it amplified her own. She looked away, clutching more tightly the little girl on her lap.

"I've been hallucinating," he told his brother after he was finally called in.

For the past two weeks Steve had been receiving emails, phone calls and even personal visits from a stalker who went by the name of Toussaint Lou-verture. The emails would disappear whenever Steve tried to show them to anyone – as would the phone messages. One day Louverture appeared on Steve's driveway but vanished after Steve screamed at him to go away – provoking frightened looks from neighbours, and the visit to his brother the next day.

Dr. Mark Schmidt was not a man to waste words, energy or time. He listened to Steve's story silently but very attentively – as he listened to all his patients. His face revealed no surprise or alarm. He had heard quite a lot over the years.

All he said after Steve finished – "I'll set you up with a psychiatrist."

Then he stood to leave his brother for other patients.

"Isn't there anything else you'd like to say?" Steve asked.

"No," replied his brother.

After the appointment, Steve shared the elevator with the young women from the waiting room. He felt angry thinking about his brother. The woman held her daughter's hand tightly.

―――――――――――――――

While Steve was getting ready for his appointment with the psychiatrist, the designers at Aristocratic Tool and Mold, a few miles away from the Free Press, were working in a very dark room where only computer mouse clicks were usually heard.

The buzzer had just sounded for the 9:30 break. Two of the designers rushed into the empty conference room to continue the argument they had been having in near whispers while they were supposed to be working."

Ming and Bob were not always sure they liked each other. Bob sat at the head of the table smoking a cigarette. Ming sat several chairs down to avoid the smoke. Ming was defending Parecon – a detailed proposal by Michael Albert and Robin Hahnel for expanding the democratic process to the economy. Bob was particularly skeptical that democratically run workplaces were practical.

At one point Bob argued, "If these ideas were practical they'd be implemented by now."

"Slavery existed for centuries, Bob. Was the alternative impractical?"

"No, but – "

"It became impractical because the slaves revolted."

Bob look thoughtful for a moment then replied, "I've heard that slavery just became obsolete as capitalism modernized." He tried to remember where he had picked up that notion.

"Just became obsolete? Do you know how Haiti became an independent country?"

"No?" Bob said with a look that seemed to say, *Why are you changing the subject?*

"It was a massive slave rebellion! They kicked Napoleon's ass, and the British, and the Spanish. It was a major body blow to slavery."

"How badly did any of them really want Haiti though?"

"The French sent 60,000 troops to try to keep it. By 1804 nearly all of them were dead."

"You keep those facts on the top of your head?"

Ming shrugged.

"60,000 troops killed? Holly shit," said Bob.

"I just finished this book called The Black Jacobins by a guy named C. L. R. James – been reading a lot about Haiti lately," explained

Ming.

"So France owned Haiti?"

"It was France's richest colony by far! It was a fucking gold mine – well actually a sugar mine. Three quarters of the world's sugar was supplied from there. It was the most profitable slave state in the world. It created more wealth for France than all the thirteen colonies did for Britain, and it was so brutal that one third of the slaves brought there were worked to death within three years."

"So they kept bringing in more slaves to re-place the ones killed off?"

"Yup. The fight those Haitian slaves put up made slavery 'impractical'."

"That couldn't have been the only factor," Bob said.

"It was one huge fucking factor – plus there were revolts elsewhere and other people fighting as well – including non-slaves."

"Do you practice this shit on your wife?" said Bob, grinning. "Nice history lesson."

Ming grew somber. "The wife? She's not talking to me right now. Says I neglect her and the kids because of all the political stuff I do."

"Sounds like she's probably right," said Bob.

The buzzer sounded.

"End of round 803!" joked Bob.

Ming responded with a weary smile.

They returned slowly to the design office. Their eyes soon adjusted to the dark, and they were productive for the rest of the shift.

"I should have seen this coming," Steve concluded as he sat waiting to see the psychiatrist, whose office was a stately old house. Steve didn't even bother to glance at any of the reading material available in the poorly lit waiting room.

Steve was one of the youngest people Can-west had ever put in charge of the Windsor Free Press. It was hardly the most important of the corporation's newspapers, but many had considered it an impressive achievement for the son of a working class single mother.

He didn't expect the job to be as challenging as the lower level positions he had held – in particular copy editor. However, he didn't expect the job to drain him of all interest and enthusiasm. Just showing up to his office was now a challenge.

His favorite and most effective bosses had always been the ones who trusted their people and left them alone, so he delegated most of his job to his senior staff. His superiors in Toronto assumed he was busy with day to day business in Windsor. His staff in Windsor assumed he was busy taking care of corporate matters for Toronto. Most viewed his indolence as wise "hands off" management, his indifference as being "cool under pressure." The less he did the more lavishly he was praised.

However, one task he refused to delegate (though it made him feel like the company hit man) was firing employees to achieve Can-west's "head count" targets. He refused to involve security guards. He would look people in the face and tell them he had no choice but to let them go. Like a scarecrow in a hailstorm, he would absorb what-ever barrage of insults, threats or tears rained down on him. He only enjoyed doing it once, when he fired a human resources manager who openly relished writing up separation papers for unionized employees. He hated it the most when he let go a hard working single mother from Advertising who occasionally chatted with him about her little boy.

She walked into his office the day of her termination looking pale and frightened – making Steve feel like even more of a hired thug. Before he finished trying to console her, she rushed out of his office in tears. He mailed her a check, out of his own pocket, to help her out, but she mailed it back to him with "No thank you" written on it. He cursed himself for not thinking of sending her money anonymously. "Now it's too late," he concluded after his check was returned. "She'd know it came from me."

Steve toyed with the idea of becoming a foreign correspondent again or perhaps finding a completely different line of work even at a significant pay cut. He sensed that his job had a corrosive impact on him that the physical and intellectual stimulation he sought away from it could not repair. Now he was sure he should have resigned years ago.

His thoughts were interrupted by the creak of a door as a patient exited the examination room of the psychiatrist's office. It was the former Human Resources manager he had fired. The man's pos-ture improved noticeably after their eyes met.

"I bet he's on his way to getting cured now," Steve joked to himself, and felt bad that he had enjoyed the man's professional demise.

When Steve's turn came he found the psychia-trist, Dr. Bueno, sitting at is desk with shoulders hunched and a look of resignation and defeat on his face.

After listening to Steve's story, Dr. Bueno told him he suffered from grandiose type delusions.

"That's when a person believes he has some great but unrecognized talent or insight, or special relationship with someone famous or even with God," he explained in a barely audible voice Steve found very annoying.

"But I'm an atheist," Steve replied – quite loudly compared to Dr. Bueno. "I've never lacked confi-dence but I'm not entertaining thoughts I have some special, undiscovered talent. I don't really know anyone famous – some local bigwigs but they hardly count. They're just big fish in a small pond."

"You say you are communicating with Toussaint Louverture, the leader of the Haitian slave revolution," whispered Bueno, who had devoured history books as a young man.

Steve was stunned: "There was a Toussaint Louverture? I thought I had made the name up … you know, subconsciously. There was such a

person?"

"Yes," answered Bueno, whose mind ached under the strain of making room for thoughts unrelated to the gambling debts he had run up at Casino Windsor. "Have you ever been to Haiti?"

"Once, for a few days…I was with the Toronto Star then – must have been around 1994 or 1995…" he stopped abruptly. He suddenly remembered then that he had read a little bit about a Toussaint Louverture before going to Haiti. "How could I forget that?" Steve was a bit frightened to think the stress of his job must be taking even more of a toll than he had thought.

"Let's get some blood work done so we can rule some things out," said Bueno.

Probably wants to verify that I'm not taking drugs, suspected Steve.

"In the meantime don't indulge any delusions," he advised. "Ignore them. We'll meet again to dis-cuss your test results and go from there. Take this. My daughter will explain what you must do before the tests." He handed Steve a form for the tests.

Steve took the form, left the office, and never bothered to return.

Ming had never visited anyone in jail before. He and his friends had worked out a schedule and tonight was his turn to visit Theodore Lubin.

A thick glass window reinforced with horizontal steel bars separated the prisoners from the visitors. Ming was dismayed to discover that the window had no openings. He had wrongly assumed he would be able to pass Lubin some papers. There were no partitions between the inmates, and none between the visitors. Everyone spoke loudly and at once; yet no one showed frustration with the circumstances. The little room in which the prisoners sat was painted dark green and contrasted drearily with their bright orange uniforms.

Lubin was not summoned from his cell until

the visiting hours were almost finished. However, three other prisoners were immediately available to visit their wives or girlfriends. Ming had a nervous stomach ache that was greatly aggravated the moment he recognized a former worker at Aristocratic Tool as one of the inmates.

Ming tried very hard not to look at anyone and not to listen to what anyone was saying. He hoped the former worker wouldn't notice him and soon realized he had nothing to fear. The worker and his wife were totally involved in their conversation which alternated between tender and erotic.

Ming left his chair to ask the guard, for the second time, if Theodore Lubin had been called. The guard assured him that he had been. Ming re-turned to his seat at the window.

At last, Lubin, a slender middle aged black man, walked very quietly into the room and took a seat in front of Ming.

"Hello, Ming. Thank you for waiting all this time."

"How long ago did they call you? I've been here more than an hour."

"It must have been about ten minutes back. Let it go."

"Let what go?"

"Don't complain about the wait. We have important battles ahead."

"Are you nervous about the hearing tomorrow?"

Lubin smiled. "No, we'll be fine. Will I see you there?"

"I'll be there."

Steve came home from the psychiatrist and found Toussaint Louverture seated in the living room. Ignoring his unwelcome, unreal guest, he headed towards his bedroom as Louverture made a simple request:

"Steve, I need ten thousand dollars."

Disregarding the psychiatrist's advice, Steve decided to try something different – to engage with Louverture and see where it would lead. *Maybe I need to hit bottom*, he concluded.

"Why should I give you money?" Steve asked.

"To bail Theodore Lubin out of jail," Louverture replied.

Assuming there was no risk in writing a check made out to a figment of his imagination, Steve quickly retrieved a check book, and returned to the living room.

He suspected that Louverture would not be there when he returned, that somehow going through the motions of fulfilling the request would make him disappear, but he did not get off that easily. Louverture was still sitting on the couch.

"I apologize, Steve. I forgot to mention that it must be a certified check."

Steve agreed to let Louverture accompany him to the bank. Within an hour they were parked in front of the provincial courthouse in downtown Windsor.

"Take the check," Toussaint Louverture reminded him. "You can handle things from here."

Steve walked briskly across the courthouse lawn which was nearly covered with fallen leaves. In-side, he walked through an unmarked doorway into an office where a severe looking clerk worked quietly at his desk.

In front of the clerk stood Ming and Crista, a young woman who was talking on her cell phone.

The woman folded up the phone and looked up at Ming. "We're screwed," she told him. "Sean and his wife are willing to put up the bail but not have him stay at their house. Sean is going to ask a friend of his but we're not going to have time."

Ming sighed deeply. "I can't believe he's going to spend another weekend in jail because of this."

He couldn't help thinking that if he were single there would be no problem immediately getting the money and a place for Lubin to stay.

Steve braced himself and announced in a confident managerial voice developed through years of hiding inner doubt and vulnerability, "I'm here to post bail for Theodore Lubin."

Ming looked at Steve. "Who are you?"

"My name is Steve Schmidt." He held out the slip of paper and waited, and almost hoped someone would tell him no such inmate existed.

"Please tell me that's a certified check you're holding."

"It is," Steve whispered.

Ming snatched the check out of his hands. "Sir, we have bail for Theodore Lubin," he said to the clerk.

Crista shook Steve's cold hand. "You must be with 'Work Together for Haiti'," she said, referring to a local group that did philanthropic work in Haiti and that tried to stay apolitical, but, to their credit, did not always succeed.

Crista joined Ming at the clerk's desk and Steve reached for an empty chair. Did all of this confirm his sanity or his insanity? Did he just do something noble or stupid? He was leaning toward the former but instead of trying to piece together a rational and reassuring explanation he marveled at what he had just done.

"We're ready to rock!" Ming announced after a few minutes. "Why don't you ride with us to the jail?"

"That would be fine," Steve replied. He was tempted to run away from the situation but decided that running would be cowardly. He needed to fully understand the nature of what he had done.

At the jail, Steve's knees buckled when he saw Theodore Lubin. He looked exactly like Toussaint Louverture as the man had appeared to him.

"You don't remember me do you?" Lubin said to Steve at the jail.

"You look familiar," Steve replied cautiously.

Steve was horrified when he learned that Lubin would have to live with him to satisfy the conditions of his release but found it impossible to refuse the commitment. However, after talking to Lubin, he was ashamed of his initial reaction. Lubin was jovial and relaxed – completely non-intimidating – like a man who had spent a nice weekend at a resort rather than weeks in jail. Moreover, it was somehow reassuring that Lubin's story of meeting Steve in 1994 was believable. As he listened to the story, Steve felt himself settle back into reality.

"You interviewed Aristide in his apartment in Washington DC," Lubin reminded him as they drove to Steve's house. "The apartment was noisy – full of visitors. You kept asking them to keep the noise down because you were worried that you wouldn't be able to understand what you were recording. It was September of 1994, not long before the junta finally let Aristide return to finish off the last months of his term."

"I remember the interview in the apartment. I vaguely remember it was noisy, but I don't remember talking to you at all."

Steve was frustrated at not being able to recall. Unfortunately, his first encounter with Lubin had not been particularly memorable.

Eleven years before Lubin was imprisoned in Windsor, Steve had been interviewing Aristide while a trusted advisor to Aristide turned to the man beside him and remarked in Kreyol, "That Theodore Lubin is very odd isn't he?"

The advisor didn't think Lubin could hear him on the other side of the noisy room, though Lubin did hear him, and didn't care.

"I'll never forget those photographs he took of the Election Day massacre in 1987," replied the other man – Aristide's Minister of Defence in his exiled government.

"I heard he nearly drowned while accom-pany-ing Haitian refugees to the US on their raft."

"He's a very brave journalist – always in the thick of things," noted the Minister of Defence.

"Oh, I know. I'm not saying he isn't brave – just odd."

Lubin suddenly crossed the room and took a seat next to the men who had been talking about him. "Who's the guy interviewing Tidid?" Lubin asked, as if he didn't know (Aristide was referred to as "Tidid" by his support-ers).

"That's Steve Schmidt from the Toronto Star," said the advisor.

"Ah! A Canadian," Lubin replied.

"He interviewed Cedras and his henchmen in Haiti. Now he's here," added the Minister

Lubin nodded slowly as if something pro-found had just been said.

As Steve was getting ready to leave, Lubin intro-duced himself.

"So Emmanuel Constant was one of your tour guides in Port-au-Prince."

"Yes," answered Steve.

"Did you interview any of his victims?"

"Haiti is a dictatorship," Steve replied, while scanning the room to ensure nothing of his was being left behind. "The victims aren't easily in-terviewed."

"No, not easily," agreed Lubin.

He looked on silently as Steve zipped up his jacket.

"Don't forget about me," he said to Steve be-fore walking away.

"How could I after all we've shared," replied Steve with a smile.

Ten years later, days after Aristide was over-thrown for the second time, Lubin left Haiti as a terror campaign began against Famni Lavalas (Aristide's political party). US officials insinu-ated to Lubin that he would be granted asylum if he helped with their public relations cam-paign to demonize Aristide. He politely refused to play along. Lubin's lawyers were fortunate to get him permission to voluntarily leave the US.

He crossed the border into Windsor and was im-mediately taken into custody. The justifica-tion given was that he had been part of a "criminal organization" – meaning that Canada had unofficially declared Haiti's most popular political party a criminal group.

Ming and his friends in Windsor were alerted to Lubin's case through the networks that had developed in North America in opposition to Haiti's de facto government.

"Does this mean I'm psychic?" Steve won-dered as he lay in bed staring up at the ceiling during the first night Lubin slept in his house.

For the first time in years, Steve allowed him-self to think about the young lady who had translated for him in Haiti. She had reminded him of his brother. She was very cold, tight lipped – border-ing on disdainful, though at-tractive, and what she lacked in warmth she made up for in competence. Several months af-ter his visit to Haiti, he tried to arrange to have her translate for a colleague. She never returned Steve's calls. Finding that odd, Steve investi-gated and learned from reliable sources that she had become a victim of the FRAPH death squad led by Emmanuel Constant. He winced at the memory of how friendly he had been with Con-stant while she was present. He wondered how much of her haughtiness was driv-en by hatred for the people he interviewed. Did she hate me too? Steve wondered.

At 4:00 a.m. car lights lit up Steve's bedroom as the vehicle turned onto his street, enough to wake him and get him started on the day. While Lubin slept in the spare room, Steve searched on his com-puter for the article he had written about Haiti in 1994. It was entitled "A Place

Called Terror." The interviews had been arranged for Steve by a Canadian linked to the top people in the regime.

Steve began his article by writing:

He overthrew Haiti's first democratically elected govern-ment in 1991, defied US presidents, and thumbed his nose at an international embargo. General Raoul Cedras must rank as one of the world's most audacious Bad Guys....

Steve described Cedras as being as "vain as a Prom Queen," and also wrote that Cedras admitted a translator was only used during the interview in case he wanted to say he had been mistranslated afterwards. Steve also lampooned the Canadian who arranged the interviews. Outraged at the ingratitude, he made a furious phone call to the Toronto Star after it was published. Steve and his boss had a good laugh over it.

Steve particularly liked the following descriptive passage from his article:

The military headquarters is a converted two-story French mansion. Soldiers snore at the entrance as flies buzz around them. Others play checkers while rifles lie at their feet. Spike heeled wives and girlfriends come and go. Inside the General's informal reception room the air conditioner is turned up so high that it could easily be an ice cream parlor.

After his visit to Haiti, Steve interviewed Aristide in Washington, and briefly summarized the inter-view at the end of the article. Steve expected, and received, criticism from apologists for the junta, but he did not expect the flak he received from many Aristide partisans.

Lubin wrote a very critical letter to Steve, who had forgotten it. The letter began:

Dear Mr. Schmidt,

I hope you remember me.

We met briefly when you interviewed President Aristide for your recent article about Haiti entitled 'A Place Called Terror'.

I do not believe that you intended to write a propaganda piece for the dictatorship (otherwise I would not bother to write to you) but that is exactly what you did.

Lubin pointed out that the article gave the junta and its supporters ample space to slander Aristde and the Lavalas movement, but offered far less space (6 times less by Lubin's careful count) for their allegations to be refuted. Detailed reports by human rights groups were barely mentioned – crowded out to showcase the Toronto Star's "access" to the regime. The US track record of backing dictatorships in Haiti (after creating the Haitian army after the 1915-1934 occupation) was ignored as was conclusive evidence that the US was behind the coup.

Lubin concluded his letter to Steve, writing:

The embargo is in place to provide cover for the US as it allows its long time proxies to destroy the Lavalas movement that brought President Aristide to power. Perhaps the US will eventually order the army to allow President Aristide to return after their work is essentially done and the threat of social reform is averted. That sorry outcome could be avoided if foreign journalists would stop peddling the myth that the US is trying to save Haitian democracy.

Regards,
Theodore Lubin

Steve mailed Lubin the following note in reply (basically the form letter he sent to pro-Aristide critics of his article):

Dear Mr. Lubin:

Thanks for your letter.

It is an interesting conspiracy theory you put forth regarding US intentions in Haiti. If I have, as you accused, written propaganda for Cedras then I can assure you that his camp has been ferociously ungrateful. If I were only pleasing, or infuriating, the people on one side of an issue I'd be very alarmed.

Best wishes,

Steve Schmidt

Steve ignored that the truth is not necessarily equidistant from opposing sides in a debate. He disregarded that not everyone deserves to be offended, and that his rise within the newspaper industry proved that he wasn't, as he liked to believe, offending everyone. He certainly was not offending the people who promoted him and the people they answered to. He had chosen a side so powerful that he failed to even think of it as a side.

Eleven years later Steve could only have responded with contrition to Lubin's critique. Steve's article had described FRAPH death squad leader Emmanuel Constant as "quick witted and friend-ly." In ignorance, Steve had dismissed Constant as a relatively minor and harmless supporter of the regime.

Then after he learned of the young translator's death, Steve looked into FRAPH more closely and remained aware of Constant over the years. He knew that the death squad leader lived freely in Queens and that the US government refused to deport him. Steve also noticed that FRAPH's second in command, Jodel Chamblaim (whom he had also met in Haiti), marched triumphantly into Port-au-Prince after the coup of 2004 and was soon acquitted of his crimes in a farcical overnight trial.

———————————————

"You're up early."

Lubin's voice startled Steve who was lost in thought at his computer. Sunlight had just begun to stream into the room.

"Hi there," said Steve, feeling now quite comforttable with the man who looked exactly like one who had driven him to a psychiatrist. "I was looking over an article I had once written about Haiti."

"I remember it," said Lubin. "I wrote to you about it."

Lubin went on to summarize the critique he had made eleven years ago.

"Journalists don't know as much as they think," Steve replied sadly. "We get in. We get out. We take things in as quickly as we can. The speed with which we work makes us miss things – first draft of history as they say."

"I'm afraid the problem goes deeper than that," Lubin said. "Regular people with jobs and families – working under tighter constraints than journalists – have been able to grasp what is happening in Haiti. Look at Ming. He has a hectic full time job and a family. His advantage over most journalists certainly isn't time."

"I don't know anything about Ming. I just met him."

"You'll soon learn a lot more."

———————————————

Four hours later Ming knocked at Steve's door with Crista, the young woman from the courthouse. Steve welcomed them in.

"Hi Theodore," Ming said to Lubin. "This place is quite a step up from the jail isn't it?"

Crista's mother and father were to arrive minutes later. An activist who had driven down from Toronto also arrived – a legal assistant to Neil Cohen – Lubin's Toronto based lawyer. Cohen, though not politically radical, was trusted by people who had been fighting against post-9/11 changes to Canadian law.

Lubin gave everyone an overview of the government's case – such as it was – for declaring him inadmissible to Canada. Though he was out of jail he was still at risk to be deported to Haiti. He made it clear that he welcomed Cohen's help but trusted the people in the room more than any lawyer. The government cited allegations made against members of Famni Lavalas (but not against Lubin) by Amnesty International. It also cited allegations against Lubin's journalism made on websites run by Haiti's extreme right. That was it. That was the government's case, but in post 9-11 Canada that was enough.

Though the Amnesty reports did not mention Lubin, he still urged everyone to pressure them about their reports. It was easily shown, Lubin argued, that Amnesty was parroting bogus allega-tions made by NCHR – a group that had been generously funded by the Canadian and US governments.

Faxes from Haiti were received and translated by Lubin. Activists called in from around

Canada and the US offering assistance and advice.

"So what about the media?" asked Ming eventually. "To what extent do we involve them?"

"Let's do plenty of face to face and internet based work before we give them anything they can distort," replied Crista. "We can have Theodore speak at the high school where I teach. We can meet with the local Amnesty chapter. They have good people who would be sure to pressure the higher ups in the UK. Maybe we can get Tom's friend to write a little article in the Windsor Free Press. His friend is about as progressive as they get over there."

"I can arrange a talk at the University," Crista's mother added. "Ming, could you book the union hall for a talk?"

Steve, who had barely said anything until then, finally chimed in, "I can get a front page article in the Windsor Free Press, and several follow up articles elaborating on other things Theodore has mentioned."

"Who are you, Izzy Asper?" Ming blurted out with a laugh – immediately regretting his sarcasm.

"I run the Windsor Free Press," Steve explained. "I'm the publisher."

Everyone but Lubin froze. Steve lived in a nice little house. Ming assumed he was some kind of lawyer with an interest in Haiti. The others had made similar assumptions. No one dreamed he was the head of a newspaper they despised.

"Excellent Steve!" said Lubin cheerfully. "That would be wonderful."

Eager to contribute, Steve ordered in lunch and dinner. Despite what he had already done, he felt like he was only beginning to make himself useful. Time passed very quickly.

Within days of Lubin's arrival at his house, Steve tossed his "hands off" approach out the window.

He rejected the managing editor's suggestion that Lubin's imprisonment be written about as a "bungled" immigration case – an example of the Canadian government being "over protective" in the post 9/11 era. Steve wrote special "From the Publisher" features in which Lubin was described as a "former political prisoner" of the Canadian government. One article took the form of a detailed and very hard hitting interview with Lubin about Canada's role in Haiti. Lubin did not heed his lawyer's advice to pull his punches with the Canadian government.

"I will not make the same mistake Aristide made while he was in exile in the US during the 1990s," Lubin said. He had implored Aristide to be much more aggressive in his public statements about US policy:

"You must simply demand that the US order the junta to step down. We all know Cedras is nothing but their lackey," he had told Aristide. "They could end this with a phone call. Don't play along with them when they pretend otherwise."

As word spread about Lubin's case, an increas-ing number of activists crowded into Steve's living room on a regular basis.

"How long do you think before they fire him?" Ming asked Crista one day as they drove to Steve's house.

"I thought they would have fired him already."

Lubin often said he was delighted to have such an effective team working with him. Steve was humbled by the intelligence and passion of the activists. They were exerting themselves more, for free, than he had done in years at a very well paid job.

Steve noticed the nervous, sometimes sad looks his editors cast at him while he sat in his office pouring over books and online articles about Haiti. For the first time, his boss called from Toronto to express "concern" about articles published in the Windsor Free Press. Steve knew he was drawing the wrong kind of attention to himself, but his real undoing came in the form of a large manila envelop that he found in his mail slot one morning. It was simply marked "Steve Schmidt."

It contained documents that the Canadian government had been forced to release months ago under the Freedom of Information Act. However, unlike the documents that independent journalists received, these were not heavily censored. They were not censored at all.

Steve and Ming had them scanned and distributed by email to various people.

In these documents, Canadian officials privately stated to each other that the US had long ago decided, "Aristide must be made to leave. It is the only realistic way to resolve the situation, and our people are well positioned to help."

The officials were confident the media would convince the public that Aristide's resignation was voluntary and for the best. They noted that many NGOs funded by the Canadian government such as Oxfam Quebec were hostile to Aristide's govern-ment and that this would be a great help.

Steve published a detailed front page article with the headline:

DOCUMENTS REVEAL

CANADA BACKED COUP IN HAITI

Not wanting to be brought down with him, Steve's editors sent him emails documenting their objections to it.

Two days later three security guards walked up to Steve as he was getting out of his car in the Windsor Free Press's parking lot.

"I'm very sorry, Steve," said the only guard Steve recognized. "You're not allowed in the build-ing."

"That's okay, Frank. Take care."

"You too, Steve. Good luck."

The other two guards looked angrily at Frank.

"Three of them!" Steve chuckled as he drove away. "What the fuck did those lunatics in Toronto think I'd do?"

The controller of the Free Press was appointed publisher, and a retraction of the article was pub-lished. It stated that the authenticity of the docu-ments could not be proven and that the article had been inexcusably credulous of the anonymous source that supplied them. Steve's dismissal was never mentioned in the Windsor Free Press or any other corporate newspaper.

With help from his new friends, Steve started up an internet blog on which the documents were made publicly available. Years passed and no one dared sue him for libel.

Steve began to give many talks about the Canadian media that discussed Canada's role in Haiti.

One talk that he gave at a union hall in Hamilton lingered in his mind, though he wished it didn't, because of a brief exchange with an old man. Steve assumed he was a retired worker.

"Why do Canada and the US bother at all about Haiti?" the old man asked.

It was a reasonable question and it came up all the time. Haiti's natural resources were no longer important to the global economy. Its workers were the lowest paid in the Hemisphere, but even if that changed there were not enough Haitian workers to seriously impact the US or Canadian economies. Why then, would the US and Canada bother to thwart basic reforms?

Steve eventually worked out a fairly succinct and, he thought, convincing reply which borrowed in part from Noam Chomsky:

"In the case of Canada it was simply a case of trying to please the boss – the US government – because they believed they could do so without receiving much scrutiny. They couldn't get away with that in Iraq. The public was just too aware of it and, of course, overwhelmingly opposed.

"In the case of the US, they intervene in Haiti for the same reason a Mafia Don doesn't let a small shopkeeper get away without paying him. It is part of maintaining an empire – not letting even the tiniest piece break away without a fight. Look at what the US has done in places like Vietnam, El Salvador, Nicaragua and even Grenada – none of them economic powerhouses to say the least."

The old man nodded in agreement but then couldn't help but add, "They're a primitive people though aren't they?"

"Who's primitive?" Steve asked dreading the old man's reply.

"Haitians!" exclaimed the old man. "They believe in Voudou and sacrifice chickens. I mean, they're mostly illiterate."

It seemed like time stopped as Steve surveyed the audience's reaction. Most looked stunned. Many looked guilty and embarrassed – especially those sitting near black people.

"Let's move on to the next question," said one of the organizers of the talk, thinking it best to ignore the old man.

"Hey! Let him respond to what I said," the old man insisted.

"Sir, you're remarks are extremely offensive," Steve began dryly. "You obviously know nothing about Voudou and should at least do some reading before you comment on it. What I find primitive is that our government, and the media, threw its sup-port behind a coup which left thousands of innocent people murdered, tortured and thrown into jail. There is something primitive about us, as Canadians, when we let that happen."

The audience applauded. The old man shut up, but Steve was left feeling unmasked by him.

Steve thought his response to the old man had been adequate (though he should have added, he thought afterwards, that literacy and political sophistication are not the same thing. Haitians displayed political and organizational sophistication despite having to deal not only with illiteracy but massive repression. Steve compared that to the political fog he had been enveloped in for decades despite his high level of literacy), but it wasn't the words he had used that bothered him.

"Why wasn't I much angrier?" he wondered. "Was I really angry or offended at all?"

About a hundred protestors marched in front of The Cleary International Centre in downtown Windsor during an unseasonably warm day in November of 2005. The strong breeze off the Detroit River made holding up their signs a bit of a chore. Many of the protestors, including Steve, wondered why Lubin had not yet arrived. The Cleary had been taken over by the bodyguards of Prime Minister Paul Martin. Even managers of the Cleary felt they were being bossed around and treated like suspects.

Two large, fierce looking men stood outside a restroom while the Prime Minister of Canada was inside washing his kindly looking face. Martin was reaching for a paper towel when he heard a voice behind him:

"Mr. Prime Minister. Thousands of Haitians have been murdered and imprisoned by your good friend Gerard Latortue." A US-backed council of Haitians had appointed Latortue head of the Haitian government after the coup d'état that over-threw Aristide in 2004. Latortue had been living in Florida for the previous ten years.

Horrified, Paul Martin spun on his heels and found Lubin gazing at him earnestly.

"Who the hell are you? How did you get in here," said Martin – loudly, so that his bodyguards standing outside would hear. He couldn't bring himself to just scream for help. His bodyguards, who had ensured the bathroom was empty and safe before Martin entered it, did not hear their boss, and they had not see anyone follow him inside.

"History is written by the winners, Mr. Prime Minister," Lubin continued. "And eventually the winners will be the sons and daughters of your victims. You will be remembered as drenched in the blood of innocents."

Martin suddenly remembered that his prede-ces-sor, Jean Cretien, had once attacked a pro-testor with his bare hands. Assuming his body-guards were totally outsmarted, he attempted to handle the situation on his own. He rushed at Lubin but missed him completely and ended up sprawled on the floor.

He never did figure out how he missed. Lubin had stood directly in front of him and had not seemed to move.

While Martin was still on the floor, Lubin ad-ded, "You should be embarrassed to bring so many bodyguards with you to your home-town."

Martin picked himself off the floor and scrambled out of the restroom. His bodyguards burst inside immediately but found no one.

All other events scheduled for the Prime Minster that day in Windsor were cancelled. The Prime Minister learned never to enter a restroom without a bodyguard.

In August of 2006, a survey published in the Lancet medical journal reported that 4,000 po-litical murders were perpetrated in Haiti after the coup – overwhelmingly by the Haitian na-tional police and their allies.

Steve had never expected to bring down Paul Martin's government with the articles he pub-lished just before Canwest fired him. However, he did expect to have some impact on Canada's policy in Haiti. Instead, he was astonished at how easily the media buried the government's participation in a murderous coup.

By 2006, Paul Martin's Liberal party was out of office, though Haiti had not been a significant factor in the election. The NDP, the most pro-gressive of Canada's major political parties, did not even mention Canada's role in Haiti during televised debates.

Haiti relied on the International Mission for Monitoring Haitian Elections (IMMHE) to su-per-vise the elections that finally took place in 2006. Canada eagerly took the lead within the IMMHE. The Lavalas movement swept Rene Preval into the presidency. Rene Preval was a former Prime Minister under Aristide and the closest candidate available to Arsitide's Famni Lavalas party who was not in jail or in exile. He won despite the barriers placed in the way of participation by Haiti's poor and even a last ditch attempt at fraud which was foiled by mas-sive demonstrations. Afterwards, Canadian of-ficials, without fear of ridicule, said they were proud of Canada's contribution.

Gerard Latortue's ambassador to the US cited Preval's candidacy as evidence that Lavalas was not being persecuted. After the election, Preval's victory was cited as evidence that Lavalas was not popular since the Famni Lavalas party had no official candidate. The Canadian embassy, among others, attempted to pass off Marc Bazin, who had run against Aristide in 1990, as the Famni Lavalas candidate – a superfluous layer of deceit given how Canada's actions in Haiti were ignored.

Guy Philippe, the rebel the corporate press reported as being greeted by huge, cheering crowds after Aristide's ouster, received less than 2 percent of the vote. Charles Baker, a sweat-shop owner widely and uncritically quoted by journalists before and after the coup, received 6 percent. Not a single editorial in any Canadian newspaper commented on the harsh rebuke to Canadian policy delivered by Haitian voters.

Many prominent political prisoners were re-leased after Preval's election, but his subsequent compromises with the elite were not surprising given the circumstances. The judiciary and Na-tional Police remained stacked with supporters of the coup. By the summer of 2007, foreign do-nors (Canada now the second largest among them) successfully pressured Rene Preval to privatize Teleco, Haiti's telephone company.

Shortly after the announcement of Teleco's privatization, Canadian Prime Minister Steven Har-per made a visit to Haiti.

And there stood Steven Harper longing des-perately for a cold shower as he perspired on the lawn of Haiti's National Palace while Canada's national anthem was played. Haiti was his last quick stop on a tour of Latin America and the Caribbean, but he wished it could be even quicker. Harper was glad that the press conference to follow would be held inside the air conditioned National Palace.

Inside the cool elegant palace, Rene Preval had just finished thanking Harper for all Canada had done for his country when a man's voice suddenly filled the room:

"Rene, ask him not to have you overthrown."

The words were repeated in French, Kreyol and English before Preval recognized Theodore Lubin as the heckler. Lubin began speaking from the back of the room, then walked slowly toward the two heads of state.

"Rene, ask him not to carry you off to Africa if you misbehave."

Preval opted to stay quiet.

Lubin turned his attention to Harper.

"Mr. Harper, did you speak to any of the families of the people murdered by MINUSTAH while you passed through Cite Soleil?"

MINUSTAH was the French acronym for the UN troops stationed in Haiti who had been particularly busy in Cite Soleil, a poor neighborhood in Port-au-Prince that is a bastion of support for the Lavalas movement and Aristide.

Camaras ceased flashing. Bodyguards stood alert but motionless as if nothing unusual were happening. Realizing that Lubin would not be whisked from the room any time soon Harper decided to respond.

"That's an absurd question. MINUSTAH is protecting the people of Cite Soleil. I don't know where you've been getting your information, but Médecins du Monde is in Cite Soleil running a program for HIV-positive pregnant women. I was just there and they told me how much safer everyone is because of MINUSTAH."

Lubin held up a large picture of two little girls lying dead in the tin shack that was their home.

"I get my information from Mercius Lubin, the grieving father of these little girls – Stephanie and Alexandra – who were shot dead by MINUSTAH. Why didn't you talk to him?"

Mercius and his wife, Marie, were also wounded after MINUSTAH's bullets pierced the flimsy walls of their house. In previous raids MINUSTAH had fired up to 22,000 bullets in the shantytown.

Harper shot an angry, bewildered look at his bodyguards before responding. "I spoke to Mede-cine du Monde and to other people in Cite Soleil."

Lubin moved even closer to Harper:

"Isn't it remarkable how groups funded by the Canadian government say what the Canadian government wants to hear?"

Harper's voice was now angry. "You have no basis for impugning the integrity of this group."

"This!" said Lubin pointing to the picture of Stephanie and Alexandra. "This shows that anyone who takes money from you and then raves about MINUSTAH's exploits in Cite Soleil has disgraced themselves. And what lovely words you spoke a few days ago to Alvaro Uribe in Colombia! How appropriate that you would embrace his terrorism and then come here to embrace MINUSTAH. Please thank these journalists for being able to car-ry it off. You don't appreciate them enough. They are your mask. They put a civilized face on your idolatry of brute force."

Harper didn't notice that Rene Preval had already slipped out of the room with a few other officials.

Giving up on the security detail, Harper appealed to the journalists – many of whom were embedded with him during his Latin American tour.

"This man is obviously not a journalist. Why are you letting him disrupt the press conference?"

The journalists were no more help than the bodyguards. They stood by quietly as if they had paid admission to watch Harper perform. Steve Schmidt sat among them struggling to keep his hands steady as he videotaped everything.

Harper finally charged out of the room in disgust, and would later enjoy a nice long shower.

A few journalists were affected enough by what they had seen to cautiously mention it in their re-ports. Most would quickly forget.

"In overthrowing me, you have cut down in Saint-Dominique only the tree of liberty. It will spring up by the roots for they are numerous and deep."

– Toussaint Louverture

Lubin had gained refugee status months before returning to Haiti with Steve. After Harper's press conference, they had planned to return to Canada together, but Lubin suddenly announced he would never leave Haiti again.

"Don't forget me" were his last words to Steve, who was too choked up to reply. He would never hear directly from Lubin again – only conflicting stories about his death told by friends in Haiti.

The video of the confrontation between Harper and Lubin was archived on the website Steve and Ming had co-founded shortly after they met – RadicalPub.com, inspired by Medialens in the UK and FAIR in the US, sites that encouraged readers to join with them in challenging the media's cov-erage of a wide range of issues. Improving the corporate media's coverage was a secondary goal, they explained. Involving readers in building an alternative forum for the dissemination of news, analysis and debate was the primary objective. Steve dipped into his savings to keep the site going at first, and then reader donations covered almost all their expenses – the largest being Ming's salary.

Eventually they were exceptionally fortunate that a few generous (and anonymous) donors relieved them of all concern about its sustainability.

Many emails of support encouraged them, though they liked it best when people wrote to journalists and editors – copying them on their correspondence. One of the most moving emails Steve ever received was from the single mother he had once fired. A surprising number of supportive emails came from corporate journalists who re-quested anonymity. Other emails came from human rights activists and independent journalists in Haiti and elsewhere they had come to deeply admire – people like Brian Concannon, Kevin Pina and Mario Joseph.

Confessions of a Corporate Media Hitman, Steve's first book, was published a year after he left the Windsor Free Press. The dedication read:

"To Theodore Lubin, who taught me what it means to be an authentic journalist."

"Steve, you should sleep more," his brother said sternly after a routine checkup.

He had not approved of Steve committing professional suicide the way he had a year ago, but he couldn't deny that Steve now exhibited more zest for life than he ever had, or that his teenage children regarded their Uncle Steve with an unsettling amount of admiration.

"I'll try," Steve said, and left the office hurriedly. On the way out a lady gave him an angry look because he was leaving with a magazine from the waiting room. He noticed her look but smiled because she was about to read the latest issue of Z Magazine which arrived at the office every month at Steve's expense. Many patients had also leafed through a donated copy of Confessions of a Corporate Media Hitman. Steve never discussed these gifts with his brother but assumed they had been noticed and quietly tolerated.

An article in the magazine Steve took home referred to a Canadian policeman who had died in Haiti. It stated that the police officer had died "for Haiti."

At home, Steve greeted Ming who was in the living room editing their latest "Action Alert." Steve immediately emailed the author of the magazine article.

"Didn't you mean to write that the officer died 'in Haiti' rather than 'for Haiti'?" he asked.

The reporter replied promptly and initially attempted to argue that there was no difference between writing "for Haiti" or "in Haiti." Steve replied asking if the reporter would write that the 9-11 hijackers died "for the US." The reporter then claimed that he had written "for Haiti" out of respect for the officer's family.

Steve replied: "What about the families of the people murdered by Canada's allies in Haiti? Why must respect for the policeman's family involve misleading people about our crimes in Haiti and negating the humanity of our victims?"

Steve received no further reply.

Wovokia

Joe Emersberger

Jack Wilson, a reporter for the Scottish edition of the Daily Telegraph, uncovered opinion polls that found 60% of US citizens (40% of Canadians) did not know that Wovokia was an independent coun-try or that the US and Canada had made traveling to Wovokia illegal. (Wovokia had previously been known as the Canadian province of British Colum-bia, and the US states of Washington, Oregon, California, Nevada, and Arizona.) These polls were done fifteen years after Wovokia declared its in-dependence. The polls also showed that most peo-ple who did know about Wovokia's independence did not consider it a matter of great concern.

Jack was surprised that most US officials would say nothing to him about Wovokia – even off the record. However, one official dared to claim that Wovokia's independence had been granted be-cause a massive influx of ethnic minorities made the region ungovernable. The US, like a major corporation, had simply decided to downsize – to stop the drain on its resources. Jack was no economist but knew the natural and industrial wealth of Wovokia made this claim more laughable than any wild conspiracy theory.

The more Jack researched, the more he gasped at how successfully the government and media had buried the loss of huge swaths of territory, but Wovokians had also contributed to this success by keeping a low profile internationally. That had changed very recently. Wovokia was now clashing with the USA frequently at the UN. Hence the Daily Telegraph's sudden interest.

FIRST IMPRESSIONS

There were no taxis waiting at the airport.

Jack would have to experience Wovokian mass transit straightaway. Just as well. Jack was immediately mesmerized by the confounding mixture of high technology and primitivism that surrounded him. He made copious notes on everything he saw – the drab, colorless way people dressed; the crowded and eerily quiet mass transit system (magnetically propelled trains), buildings that seemed to be made of wood but upon closer inspection were some type of plastic. The city, still known as Vancouver, was buried under trees, as if camouflaged. Most of its inhabitants were packed into the city centre in low rise buildings. Cars, as Jack knew them, were nowhere to be seen. The few vehicles he saw were unpainted battery driven carts. Most roads had been narrowed into bicycle paths when not completely covered by grass and shrubs. He felt over-whelmed by the task of coherently describing to his readers everything he was seeing and immediately used his cell phone to ask his editor to publish more articles than the three he had been asked to do.

"Are there white people?" his boss asked.

"Oh yeah," Jack replied. "Um, not very many it seems. There are some though."

His editor said he would decide based on the first article Jack turned in if more should be writ-ten. Jack figured out from the stares he received that Wovokians did not use cell phones.

With great difficulty, Jack found his hotel. Wovokians seemed to hate signage as much as they hated cell phones. Once in his room, Jack threw his bag on the bed and immediately set to work on his first article. He began to feel faint. There was a knock at the door – or he thought there was – but he could not answer.

THE MAID

In the morning he awoke to the pleasant site of a familiar young woman looking down on him. A doctor.

"Listen to your body," she advised. "Rest when you need to rest."

Jack was alarmed. How bad could this be that a doctor made a trip to his room? She reassured him that she did not go out of her way to see him. She was working there.

"This place can afford to keep a doctor on staff?" Jack asked incredulously.

"I'm here on a work assignment," she explained. "I said hello to you in the hallway just after I had finished cleaning your room. You didn't look well so I thought I'd check on you. You didn't answer when I knocked. My name is Wynona."

"You're a maid?"

"There are no maids in Wovokia." Wynona explained that nobody in Wovokia gets out of do-ing work that is considered undesirable – like scrubbing toilettes or making beds.

"So maids do surgery then?"

Not wanting to engage her overworked patient in discussion Wynona boiled things down for him.

"Basically, in Wovokia, the democratic process you may be familiar with extends to the economy. The workers are the managers. The managers are the workers. You can't have meaningful democracy if some people are stuck doing things like cleaning toilettes all the time so that kind of work is shared by everyone."

Jack did not wish to drop the matter there. Wynona promised to help him find out all he wanted to know about Wovokia if he promised, in return, to rest completely for the next two days.

"One day. I'm only here for four days."

Wynona reluctantly agreed to one day.

Jack slept most of the day and awoke eager to learn all he could. The morning passed and he feared Wynona was not going to honour her part of the deal. Late in the afternoon he was about to set off on his own when Wynona finally showed. As he travelled with her by train he asked her all about Wovokian technology and urban planning. She responded with great patience and compe-tence. He felt increasingly attracted to her but tried to set the feelings aside.

"What's with the aversion to cell phones?"

"Technology is generally assumed guilty until proven innocent. Unless it is shown to be safe we avoid it unless there is a good reason to use it any-way – as happens in the medical field sometimes."

"Doesn't that make it harder to create jobs?"

"We work to produce useful things. We don't produce things to give people work. We work twenty five hour weeks despite our best efforts to bring that down to twenty. There is plenty of useful work to be done. For example, thoroughly testing technology to see if it is safe, anticipating its long term impacts. In the past that work was avoided because it was seen as a nuisance, at best, or even subversive."

They wandered about the city center on foot and eventually came to rest on a park bench.

"Look – all these questions you ask are good but if you want to understand Wovokia you really need to understand our religion."

"I thought Wovokians were rationalists."

"Does religion frighten you? I know they have religious people in Scotland."

"It's just something I generally avoid discus-sing."

"You've heard of historical materialism?"

"That Marxist theory of history."

"Well, most of us are historical spiritualists. Historical spiritualism is all bound up with the story of Wovokian independence.

"Twenty years ago the non-Latino whites had been 60% of the population of the five US states (plus British Columbia) that became Wovokia. However, the percentage of whites suddenly dropped in only one year to 33% as millions of overwhelmingly non-white people appeared.

"The newcomers were not actually new. They were the Cherokees who died along the Trail of Tears during the 1830s; the Cheyenne massacred at Sand Creek in 1864; the Sioux massacred at Wounded Knee in 1890. They were 15 million indigenous people killed directly and indirectly – through malnutrition and disease – in the area that became the US and Canada after the arrival of Europeans.

"The newcomers were the people whom the prophet Wovoka and his followers had predicted would one day arrive, but they arrived much later than anticipated and included people whom Wovoka had never foreseen. They included mil-lions of other victims of the US Empire – 4 million slaves – including a small percentage of white slaves, the millions of Vietnamese and others killed in the Vietnam War. They were Haitians, Chileans, and Salvadorans – basically people from all over Latin America but also hundreds of thousands of Indonesians and East Timorese. They were Iraqis and Palestinians. They were about 25 million people."

"This country is named after this Wovoka person?" Jack tried to hide how dismayed he was that a woman like Wynona could believe all this nonsense.

"Wovoka was born in Nevada in 1856 and was a member of the Paiute tribe. He said that all the native people who had been killed by whites would one day reappear to take back their land. He preached non-violence and told his followers that they must live righteously for his prophecy to come true. They were also told to regularly per-form the Ghost Dance – a variation on traditional dances that indigenous peoples had performed for centuries.

"The Ghost Dance movement spread very quickly beyond Wovoka's tribe. Despite being non-violent, and heavily influenced by Christianity, the movement terrified US Indian Agents so much that it led to murder of Sitting Bull and to the Wounded Knee Massacre of 1890.

"Some whites had vaguely anticipated Wovo-ka's prophesy." Wynona told Jack that in

1867, after witnessing his government's murderous ex-ploits against the Cheyenne, John B. Sanborn told his bosses in Washington that he was witnessing "…a national crime most revolting, that must, sooner or later, bring down upon us or our pos-terity the judgement of Heaven."

"Over a century and half (and countless national crimes) later, Heaven's judgement finally arrived." She smiled.

Jack nodded politely.

"The newcomers quickly came to be known as Ghosts after they returned among the living."

"Are you a Ghost?" He braced himself for her reply.

"No, but I'm fairly certain my mother is one. Most did not see any need to go around announ-cing what they were."

"They showed up and took everything over?"

"They took reparations. They had spent cen-turies in the Dream World coming up with a plan for doing so. They decided that they must not return to the Real World until satisfied that they were interacting among themselves as they thought all people should. Some Ghosts grew im-patient with the task of bringing so many souls into agreement. The impatient ones returned to the Real World alone and attempted to incite revolutions, but they usually ended up back in the Dream World accepting that they had been wrong. A min-ority of very bitter Ghosts retuned to perpetrate acts of vengeance but these acts, especially the 9/11 bombings, were clearly evil and counterproductive – and these Ghosts did not make it back to the Dream World."

As she spoke several people, including some children, gathered around to listen. Wynona did not seem to mind at all but Jack was quite annoyed. He felt that she was now preaching to her informal congregation rather than just talking to him.

"Although the Ghosts were an extremely di-verse group, language was no barrier in the Dream World. Information of all types was far easier to ac-quire than it was for the most privileged in the Real World. The Ghosts shared a common abhorrence of the empire that had made them victims and that continued to swell their ranks. They concluded that God (or Allah or the Great Spirit) had condemned people who did not share their abhorrence to complete death. However, even with this level of agreement, and even with the advantages that the Dream World offered, they struggled to formulate a plan that all could accept."

A blonde blue-eyed teenager chimed in: "They organized into nested councils like the ones we use today to decide on laws or production plans for the next year."

"Let her tell it," barked an old man who had just stopped in front of them.

Wynona continued: "Initially the lowest level councils were populated according to where the Ghosts had lived in the Real World, but female Ghosts noticed that males were over represented as delegates. Many were concerned that famous Ghosts – like Sitting Bull, Martin Luther King Jr, and Salvador Allende – were treated with too much deference.

"The Ghosts had a near obsession with eliminat-ing any trace of elitism. This was understandable. The evil they hoped to eradicate in the Real World was the idea that all lives were not precious, that some were expendable. If everyone mattered then everyone must be listened to. So they tinkered with their councils to address concerns. They created high level councils chosen by lot to ensure divers-ity.

"Once the general plan was developed they set about preparing more detailed elements that they would execute upon their return. Twenty years ago the vast majority finally felt ready to return."

TALK SHOW GHOSTS

"Twenty years ago, on what they still call Colum-bus Day in the US, Canadian and US residents who were still up watching TV suddenly saw their screens go blank. Those who had been listening to the radio heard nothing but silence.

"They logged onto news websites but almost all of them were down. They turned to newspapers but found nothing but blank. Authorities at all lev-els were bombarded by telephone calls as people demanded to know what was happening. 'Just go about your lives,' they told callers. 'This is nothing but an incredibly sophisticated prank.'

"However, the authorities at the highest levels quickly learned that this was really a massive revolt. You see, in the region that became Wovokia, the dominant corporate media was not merely silenced, it was replaced."

"In Wovokia, the public tuned into programs that the Ghosts had prepared in the Dream Word. The first programs broadcast were mainly talk shows. The hosts of these programs wore long white shirts with colourful embroidery on the sleeves. These shows were long and interactive. The hosts (who came to be known as Talk Show Ghosts) did not dominate discussions. They took calls from viewers. The live audiences – all Ghosts at first – contributed information and opinion. Through these shows the Ghosts explained who they were and why they had appeared."

"While in the Dream World, some Ghosts had demonstrated tremendous interest and aptitude for telling stories visually. Countless films depicting historical events, including very recent ones, from the point of view of Iraqi, Haitian, Vietnamese and many other types of Ghosts had been created. These films were now shown on the Ghost controlled media.

"Other Ghosts had produced novels, music and other art in the Dream World. Through the Ghost media these works were promoted and made avail-able."

Jack glanced shyly at the crowd growing around them. The sun had begun to fall. The sight of all those people listening to Wynona, all the trees and ivy covered buildings somehow added credibility to what she was saying. Jack was buying none of it, but began to see why it might be believed by these strange people.

"How did the Ghosts avoid arrest?" Jack asked. "None of this was legal obviously."

"As you would expect, the authorities, and a large segment of the population, did not take all this lying down. Ghosts were arrested in large numbers. Vigilante groups and police assassinated Ghosts and sent them back into the Dream World. However, no one could figure out how to shut down the Ghost media. This was a grave problem for the Ghosts' enemies because state violence in a capitalist 'democracy' is counterproductive if it is fully and immediately exposed. It created more Ghost allies and sympathizers. Also, most of the Ghosts were not extreme pacifists. They were will-ing to shoot back at those who shot at them; and people dispatched to the Dream World through violence promptly returned among the living to pick up where they left off."

"So all it took was a media takeover?"

"That was a huge part of it, but it went along with many other things. The Ghosts did not return to simply make demands and give people informa-tion in different forms. They returned with medical skills, legal skills even mechanical skills which they used to win people over – and generate funds. They made themselves useful in many ways. Thanks to the hideous state of the US health care system their medical skills in particular won them many supporters."

"They charged for these services?"

"People were asked to contribute whatever they thought was fair."

"So while all this was going on, most of Canada and the US had no mass media?"

"That only lasted a few weeks. Realizing that they had lost use of both the Big Stick and the Big Lie, Canada and the US entered into serious nego-tiations with the Ghosts. The Ghosts demanded an end to all repression against them. In return, the Ghosts promised not to expand their control of the media beyond Wovokia. They also made the US and Canada pay a massive amount of money in reparations. It was paid to the authorities in Wovo-kia at the time on the Ghosts' condition that it be used for socially useful investment."

"Like converting all the military and automotive factories into producing our mass transit system," added the teenager.

"Well that was few years later," said Wynona.

"Things unravelled quickly from there?" asked Jack.

"From the point of view of the capitalists, yes, you could say that. Owners and managers fled Wovokia. Workers took over abandoned busines-ses and the Ghost media brought them a great deal of attention and support."

"Okay, but by what right did the Ghosts take over the media? Who elected them?" Jack thought he might be pushing his luck asking this given the Ghost-supportive crowd listening to the story, but he felt obliged to ask.

"It was a very peaceful way of taking repara-tions for what was done to them. People did call in to the talk shows to ask the Ghosts that very ques-tion. The Ghosts would ask in return by what right media tycoons had dominated public debate? By what right did unelected rich people get to domin-ate – for centuries – the decisions about what con-stituted legitimate news, history or art?"

"You could argue that the market gives people what they want."

Chuckles rippled through the crowd – even among some of the children.

Wynona replied, "According to the market tens of millions of US citizens still don't want health insurance."

"Who is the head of your religion? Is it Wovoka?"

"No. Nobody knows if Wovoka is among us.

He never revealed himself. Most of the famous Ghosts did not. There is no head of Historical Spiritualism. People meet to discuss it though, mainly to discuss their own historical findings. We believe that the Creator is, though aloof, not indifferent to what happens to living things. The living and the dead are empowered to right the wrongs of the past but must struggle righteously to do so. We try to be-come as acquainted as possible with our own per-sonal histories – not just the history of a particular group with which we identify. We try to remember our ancestors and to make our lives memorable – or at least not a burden – to future generations. If our ancestors lived destructively then it is our duty to try to repair the damage to the extent we can. Our motto is 'remember others and make others happy to remember you'."

"Why all this antagonism between Wovokia and the US recently?"

"Many of us are questioning whether we should continue to honour the deal we made with the US and Canada. To mention only one thing, the US continues to block progress on any sane measures to deal with global climate change. With our long coastlines, no matter what we do we will suffer because of that. Many of us feel that if, not just Wovokia, but the world is to survive, then we will have to move East."

It was very dark. As they walked through the city streets Jack felt like he was in the middle of the woods. A few times Wynona took him by the hand to guide him.

On the train there was finally a reasonable amount of light. She taught him some words in Kwak'wala and beamed with pride as she told him that almost all Kwakwaka'wakw (like herself) were now fluent in their own language.

He told her about the rumours he had read that white people had disappeared from Wovokia.

"In a sense, the rumours are true. Whiteness is a fraudulent concept historically. Do you know that Wovokia has more people who are fluent in Gaelic than Ireland and Scotland combined?"

"Do you always draw such a crowd when you speak? Must be flattering."

"Not really. Word got around that a foreigner named Jack Wilson was coming to observe us. Look up Wovoka on the internet and you'll see why that would generate interest'."

THE ARTICLE

Jack worked through the night on his article. He called his boss the next day to see what he thought of it. His boss replied that something weird had shut down all news and newspapers in the US. He needed Jack to investigate.

Playing Giovannitti
Joe Emersberger

On the first day of my Grade 11 history class, Mr. Marini had written out a quote by someone named Arturo Giovannitti on the blackboard. Before I could sit down, Marini gave me a stack of blue paperback books to hand out to everyone.

"These books are yours to keep," he announced. "In them, you'll find all the material we'll be covering this semester."

The book was "A people's History of the US" by Howard Zinn.

Peter Howard's hand shot up in the air.

"Yes, Peter."

"Sir, how is this ancient history?"

"It isn't."

"But you're supposed to teach us ancient history."

"I know, but I'm not going to, so you can drop the course, rat me out to your parents, or stay and try to learn something. It's up to you."

I assumed that Marini was pulling a stunt to illustrate some kind of point. One of my previous history teachers did things like that, but it was out way of character for Marini. I had been in his class before. He usually read newspapers while his students worked on (or pretended to) whatever assignment he had written on the board. He dealt ruthlessly with anyone who disrupted the tranquility of the classroom, and he was abrupt with students who asked him questions. He was no rebel, unless coasting into retirement about twenty years early counts as an act of rebellion.

Marini explained how we would be graded and I felt even more certain that this was all a joke:

"As of now everyone has a B. Leave now and miss every class, every assignment and you'll get a C. Show me a good work ethic and you'll get an A. Anyone unclear about the grading system?"

A few students got up and left the classroom chuckling delightedly. I thought they were idiots to believe that Marini was serious.

"We've all had it drilled into our heads," began Marini, "that we owe a huge debt to kids about your age who died on the battlefields of Europe, but the truth is that we owe a far greater debt to people who did their fighting at home against their own governments. Does anyone know who I have in mind?"

"Someone named Arturo Giovannitti?" answered Rosa Basile gesturing towards the quote on the board.

"Well, yes Rosa. Thanks for noticing the quote. He is one of the people I had in mind, but we owe a great many people – everyone from the French who overthrew the monarchy in 1789 to the civil rights movement of the 1960s – but today we'll talk about Arturo Giovannitti and the movement that he was part of.

"He immigrated to the USA from Italy in 1904 when he was twenty years old. He was poet and a union leader. The words I wrote out on the board are taken from a speech he made to a jury in 1912. He was on trial for murder and facing the death penalty."

"You really don't need to bother with notes guys," Marini added as he noticed some of us writing. "This is covered in Zinn's book – chapter 13."

Marini continued.

"Giovannitti had been helping to organize a strike by textile workers in Lawrence, Massachusetts. Most of the workers were immigrant women, thousands of them were from Italy, but many were from other parts of Europe. About half of the so called women were actually teenage girls. They worked under conditions so horrible, and were so poorly paid, that about a third of them died before they turned twenty eight years old. A strike broke out after their bosses decided to make their lives even worse by cutting their wages. The strike spread from factory to factory until the city was basically shut down.

"The mayor called out the police and a local militia to attack and intimidate the picketers. The authorities also banned all public meetings and gatherings. Can anyone explain why they would do that?"

No one volunteered an answer, so he asked a girl named Jana to take a guess.

Jana turned red and shrugged so he asked Rosa.

"To get the workers off the streets?" Rosa said.

"Exactly! They made picketing illegal which effectively made the strike illegal. Arturo Giovannetti was with a group called the Industrial Workers of the World – the IWW. They were also known as Wobblies. These guys were experienced, radical unionists. They traveled all over the US helping workers fight back against their bosses. Giovannitti and his IWW buddies gathered donations from all over the country. They helped set up soup kitchens and volunteer medical services to help the workers survive the strike. But despite all the help the strikers received they were still having a very hard time holding out. Their most serious problem was feeding and looking after their children."

Peter put up his hand.

"Yes, Peter."

"If they had it so bad then why'd they have kids?"

"Does anyone have an answer for Peter?" Marini asked.

I thought Peter's question was really dumb, and annoying, but I couldn't clearly express why. Some of us scoffed, but no one volunteered an answer.

"I guess you have us all stumped Peter, but I'll continue with the story and maybe someone will think of an answer for you.

"The IWW appealed all over the US for people to look after the children. They received hundreds of applications from people in New York City, so most of the children ended up being sent there by train. In Grand Central Station the children were greeted by thousands of cheering supporters. The most serious problem faced by the strikers was being solved. What do you think the authorities did in response?"

"Arrested more people?" suggested Rosa.

"That's right. They cited a law on child neglect to make it illegal for the strikers to send their children out of Lawrence. The police eventually stormed the train station and arrested the parents. In fact, they beat up the parents, and even many of the children, right in front of the press. It led to a big scandal and to Congressional hearings.

"The strike ended after three months and the workers won a fifteen percent wage increase. However, a worker by the name of Anna Lopizzo had been shot dead by police during the strike. Giovannitti and two other guys were blamed for the murder. The case against them was a joke, but, as I think you can guess, they were not exactly guaranteed a fair trail. There were strikes in Lawrence in support of Giovannitti and his co-defendants. There were major protests held in their support in New York and Boston. The pressure worked. They were acquitted."

"Does any one care to draw any conclusions from all this?" Marini asked.

"Get a good education so you don't have to do crappy work," blurted out Peter.

Rosa immediately countered with her take:

"If it weren't for people like Giovannitti and those women then most of us wouldn't be sitting here in class. We'd be working ourselves to death in a factory for some idiot who tells us not to have kids."

"If you can't even feed yourself you shouldn't have kids," Peter replied with a shrug.

"You shouldn't be allowed to pay people wages that kill them," snapped Rosa.

"Okay, anyone other than Peter and Rosa have something to add?" Marini asked.

"What do you think, sir?" Peter asked. "You're the teacher."

"Alright Peter, but be honest, don't you have a problem with people getting paid wages that, like Rosa said, literally kill them?"

"Why didn't they just go somewhere else?"

"Most of these people were immigrants, Peter. They had gone somewhere else, traveled thousands of miles in fact, at tremendous cost and risk. Do you think these people would have passed up better work if it was available – these same people who had come all the way from Europe for a better life?"

"The question I asked," Peter said (ignoring the point Marini had responded to), "and that no one has answered, is why these woman had children if they couldn't feed them?"

"Remember that this was 1912," Marini replied. "Child labor was common. There were children working in the factories of Lawrence alongside their mothers. Children were extra mouths to feed, but they were also extra hands to help with work. It's far from obvious that it was economically unwise to have children."

A boy named Luis, who never participated in class, raised his hand. Marini nodded at him to go ahead and speak.

"My grandparents in Colombia had eleven children. They were extremely poor when the children were little but today they are much better off because the family stuck together and everyone chipped in to help. The older children, like my Dad, worked since they were little, but the youngest ones were able to go to university."

"Thank you Luis," said Marini, "That's a common story in many countries, but there is something else I want you guys to think about.

Suppose we could all trace our ancestors back to 1912 or earlier. Who do you think we are more likely find as our ancestors – workers or factory owners?"

"Workers," many responded.

"Pretty obvious right?" said Marini "There were always many more workers than owners, so even those of us who are quite well off today – if we trace back far enough – will find ancestors living like those strikers in Lawrence, or worse. Very few, if any, of us will find ancestors among the rich and powerful or even among the relatively well off. So if we condemn our ancestors for having kids then we're condemning them for giving us a chance to live.

"In fact, go back thousands of years and you'll find that everyone's ancestors – even the Queen of England's – lived lives that were very hard and very short. As humans, we have this desire to cheat death by leaving behind children, or at least something of ourselves, and to hope that the next generations will do better. Awareness of death intensifies this desire. Without it, our species might have called it quits tens of thousands of years ago and none of us would be here."

I put up my hand thinking that I had finally seen the point of the stunt Marini was pulling.

"Yes, Angelo."

"Is the point of this stunt to show that ancient history is relevant to our lives? Are you saying that we owe people from thousands of years ago a huge debt for surviving, just like we owe the strikers you talked about?"

"There's no stunt going on here. Ancient history has its relevance, but I've decided to teach more recent history, and to emphasize a point of view that is generally ignored."

"But you can't just decide to teach something we haven't signed up for. I'm sure that's not allowed."

"You're correct. It's not allowed, but I'm doing it anyway."

Marini had been standing the whole time but now he slowly took a seat at his desk.

"You'll get in trouble," I objected.

"I probably will, but I don't care. Does that bother you?"

"I'm not complaining. I just don't get how you can get away with this."

"That's okay," he said softly.

Then he looked at me with a weary smile that made me uncertain what to believe.

"Angelo, please read the quote on the board," he asked

I began to read it but he stopped me right away.

"Come one, Angelo," he pleaded. "You were wonderful in the school play last year. Get in character. You're addressing a jury, and your life is on the line. Give a bit of an Italian accent if you want to – but don't get comical with it."

I didn't attempt an accent, but I made an effort get in character. I paused frequently to avoid sounding rushed, and made sure my voice carried. This time, Marini did not interrupt me:

"I have a woman that loves me and that I love. I have a mother and father waiting for me. I have an ideal that is dearer to me than can be expressed or understood. And life has so many allurements and it is so nice and so bright and so wonderful that I feel the passion of living in my heart and I do want to live.

"I don't want to pose to you as a hero. I don't want to pose as a martyr. No, life is dearer to me than it probably is to a good many others. But I say this, that there is something dearer and nobler and holier and grander, something I could never come to terms with, and that is my conscience and that is my loyalty to my class."

My cheeks burned as I heard my voice echoing Giovannitti's words from nearly a century ago. In attempting to bring the words to life, I felt the words breath life into me. I felt something of the courage and the joy that the poet had thrown before his accusers.

Mr. Marini looked down on his desk while I read and was silent for a few seconds after I finished.

"Good job, Angelo," he said quietly. "I have copies of the full speech for anyone who's interested."

I read Giovannitti's speech aloud many times that night. Within a few weeks I had it memorized. I recorded myself reading it in order to better evaluate and refine my delivery. My parents got a real kick out of listening to me experiment – over and over again – with Italian accents. However, they weren't amused a few years later when they realized I was serious about becoming an actor.

A group of us cobbled together and performed a play later that year in which I played Arturo Giovannitti.

Marini never saw the play, or even heard me recite Giovannitti's speech with the Italian accent that I perfected at home. The play was dedicated to Marini, the last teacher I ever thought we'd do something like that for. In his own way, he too had played Giovannitti in the end, cheated death, though he passed away within weeks of that history class.

Herb and Leo Are at It Again
Shelley Ettinger

I'll have an egg white omelet, rye toast dry, tomatoes instead of potatoes, and Sanka. Please.

Give me dry toast, wheat, a half a grapefruit, cottage cheese and a nice cup of tea. And I thank you, sir.

He's new, no?

You don't recognize him? He's here three four years already. Before, he was always with the stacks of plates, the clearing tables, the dishwashing.

So he's got a promotion now, waiting tables. And speak of the devil, here you are with our beverages, sir, lickety split. Ah, the nectar of the gods. Thank you very much, uh, lean in closer, I can't quite read your name badge, ah, Miguel. Thank you very much, Señor Miguel.

And I thank you as well, Miguel. Well! Miguel! So you notice I'm a poet? No? That's all right. My wife doesn't notice I'm a lover either. Ah, you're a gentleman, I see, very kind of you to smile at my jokes. But you're busy, I know, it's your breakfast rush, go already, go.

He's got a limp, Herb, you see? Lucky Nick lets him wait tables.

Listen, Leo, these Greeks, if there's one thing they know it's restaurants. Like how your pop knew the rag trade. Whoever he hired you could rest assured they could stitch. Nick has this Miguel here waiting tables, you can rest assured he is quite capable.

Ach, hot hot hot. Watch yourself, Herb, you shouldn't burn your tongue.

I'm blowing, see? Though I do thank you, Leo, for your kind concern.

So Miguel the waiter, hey? So far he does a good job.

Why not? He's a person. It isn't brain surgery.

The limp, I mean. But he compensates pretty good. See how he favors the one side? Like me with my elbow. Still full of shrapnel to this day, courtesy of Mr. Shickelgruber and his Aryan minions from Hell. You learn, Herb, you learn how to do without. All these body parts, a person thinks they're necessary, I mean an elbow, for god's sake, a person thinks it's an absolute, and then when it's not available for use you work around it, your shoulder, your other arm. You were a lefty, you used to picture yourself on the pitcher's mound at Ebbets Field, you struck out many a stickball slugger on Cortelyou Road before you graduated Erasmus and got sent across the pond, then your left elbow gets shot up, well by god you train yourself to be a righty. So my signature's a little sloppy. Overall, I manage. So I'll never play for Brooklyn. You accept. You adjust.

Accept? Adjust? You're not talking about elbows anymore, are you? Please, for the love of god, let us not revisit the crime of the century. The Dodgers are long gone. Move to Los Angeles already you miss them so much.

Point taken, although it really is not necessary to put it quite so harsh. All I'm saying is I did not let my shattered elbow hold me back. You take a hit, you suffer a little then you move on.

You're telling me something I don't know? Me with my built-up shoe? Jesus H. Christ, Leo, stick to the point. We're talking about our waiter here, his limp. Which, who knows, he maybe got crossing over, he was shot by the border patrol maybe, or by those brownshirts –

Brownshirts? This day and age? What are you talking about?

The minutemen they call themselves. Goddamn fascist vigilantes, oh yes my friend, this day and age indeed. So no need to bring up ancient history, okay?

Hey, you're in charge.

What the hell is that supposed to mean?

You with your bigshot union position–

Corresponding secretary of the retirees' auxiliary to Local 17? This by you is a bigshot position?

You're modest, Herb. An attribute in a handsome devil like yourself. But brass tacks here if you don't mind. I'm talking about before. Shop steward, that was something.

Not that anyone ever noticed.

No, you labored in the trenches. You're not getting any scholarships named after you like that glory hound Jake.

Credit where it's due, Leo. He was president. Elected over and over. Look at all we won, eight contracts, two strikes. When we started we had basically nothing.

Sure, sure.

And now, me with a pension, not a mint but enough to get by with Social Security, and I got health care, the kids don't have to worry, they can live their own lives, I got savings even, two weeks in Miami every winter, Sylvia and me. So look, Jake might not have been my favorite fellow, but he was our president. They name a scholarship for him I do not begrudge. His picture up at the local hall, fine. I am not a petty person and it would be petty of me to resent that Jake they remember and me they don't.

Yet you are the one had me push my pop to rehire Moe Turlington.

This we had to do.

And when Pop died and Ma cried me into taking over, when I crossed back over the class divide, which by the way I freely admit –

You admit nothing, even after all these years! Oy, Leo, do I really have to explain it again? You never were one of us.

I didn't play stickball in the street? I didn't help my mother and sister on the Singers after school every night?

My god, the bona fides get dragged out again. Okay, let me amend. I grant you, Leo, when we were little kids your family was poor like the rest of us. But when your pop got his cousin the undergarment king to invest, when he rented a shop, bought some second-hand machines, then voila, presto-change-o, the Gettelmans joined the bourgeoisie. Petty division, I grant you, but not for long. He was smart, your pop, how he got in on government contracts when the war came, uniforms, canvas tents, and then, after, when he figured out the import angle and added the GetEuro Furriers line, boy oh boy the money poured in. So kindly desist with the sob stories about your impoverished youth is all I'm saying.

OK fine, Pop was a boss. OK, I slung hems with the rest of you shmucks only a few years after I recovered from the war. But as for what happened with Moe Turlington, I was still a stitcher, by god, still a union member, when the plant manager – aw Christ, what was his name, Jesus, my mind is

going –

Leitner –

Of course, Leitner –

That goddamn putz –

When that goddamn putz Leitner fired Moe for missing work for two days.

Moe's out for two days, and why? Because his wife's in the hospital. Burn unit. Remember how bad it was, Leo? Second degree. Her face, her neck, her arms.

A damned shame. God, the scars she ended up with, poor gal. So Moe's out because his Agnes is badly burned –

By a guest at the fancy-shmancy hotel where she worked. Threw a fit when she delivered his room-service breakfast not quite lickety-split –

Which was not her fault in the least –

Who cares whose fault? Jesus H. Christ, Leo, God forbid the hoity-toity have to wait an extra minute to eat! All that matters is the fat cat picked up a pot of piping-hot coffee and threw it in her face.

So Moe doesn't show for two days, and when he comes back that putz Leitner taps him on the chest, tells him he doesn't have a job anymore. Moe tries to explain about Agnes but Leitner says I told Gettelman not to hire a shvartze, get out, get out, you're through. Now it so happens that I'm there, I'm waiting to clock in, I see the whole thing.

And you dashed to the remnants room yelling my name, and you found me, you grabbed me, told me what was going on, and the two of us ran back out front. But by then Moe was being hauled out the door. Two of Leitner's goons – you remember them, Leo –

I certainly do. Sal the Stoolpigeon Strucci and Irv Obey-Me-Or-Else Yelnick. First- and second-floor foremen.

Good for you, Leo, with the names. See, you've still got a working brain cell or two. So you and me, we push in there, try to pry their hands off Moe, hey, leave him alone, we're yelling, hey what's going on, and Sal swings around and smacks me a knuckle sandwich – Jesus, was he fast, I never saw it coming – and Irv grabs you and drags you backward away from Moe, by the elbow, mind you, the bad one, and you let out a howl –

The pain was, ach, you wouldn't believe. I actually went blind for a minute. Afterward I felt bad I hadn't held on to Moe, but when Irv squeezed my elbow everything went blank.

So Moe was on the street. The only Black they'd ever hired. Never missed a day till then.

Magician with a needle. Beautiful work he did. A woman got a mink he stitched, she looked like a queen, believe you me.

Good union man too. Came to every member-ship meeting.

So why wouldn't Jake fight for him?

Does the solution to this mystery take an advanced degree?

He was prejudiced?

To say the least. When he saw I was writing

up an emergency grievance to demand Moe get his job back, you know what Jake told me? Don't, he says. Herb, please, he says. The colored are only trouble. And lazy. I told him he was nuts, of course. I defended Moe, great worker, I said, and Jesus, you can't call him trouble just because his wife's injured, so you know what he says then? Okay, says Jake the president of Local 17 whose name is on the scholarship they gave to a Chinese gal's kid this year, fine, I'll grant you, Turlington's not lazy. But it's just as well they let him go. What the hell does that mean, I ask, and Jake says that if Moe stays after him will come more. Like a plague, like locusts they'll swarm. They'll take our jobs. They come up from the South, picking in the fields isn't good enough for them, they want the city life, they want to work with machines, and they'll take less pay, you'll see, pretty soon wages are dropping, the unions are losing steam, and we're out on the street, it's like the 30s again, we've got nothing, and the shvartzes, they've got the jobs, they've taken everything. So it's for the best, says Jake. I'm sorry for his troubles, but it's better he doesn't come back. Otherwise pretty soon this is a colored shop and everything we've got is all shot to hell.

You never told me this, Herb. I knew Jake didn't lift a finger but I never until this day heard this speech he said to you.

It's not something I like to repeat. They make a big deal of him, he's one of the greats, that's fine. It serves a purpose. Which tarnishing his image would not.

Now I know why you needed me.

I defied Jake. I filed the grievance. But he wasn't going to back me up – hell, for all I knew, he'd go behind my back and tell Leitner to put the kibosh on the whole thing, Jake was perfectly capable of that – so you were the next best thing. Because boychik, I grant you this, you were plenty gung ho in those days. Of course you had nothing to fear –

The boss's son. True. So you whispered in my ear, you got me hepped up, go talk to the fellows, you said, you know the ones, the hotheads –

I never said hotheads, Leo, this is maybe how you saw them, but to me they were the best, the strongest union men –

Potato potahto, Herb, we're saying the same thing. Your comrades. The pinks.

Now you're redbaiting me, Leo? Sixty years after the fact?

Not at all. I simply speak the truth. You told me to go to the commies –

The militants –

The ones who'd fight for Moe Turlington. The good guys.

Yeah.

Ah, here you are again, Miguel. Steaming hot egg white omelet, just like I like it. Thank you so very much, my good man.

Me too, thank you very much indeed.

Mmm. Delish. You know, Herb, I wonder.

What?

I wonder does he speak?

Miguel? What do you mean?

I mean we haven't heard a peep.

Doesn't mean he's mute. I mean, come on, Leo, what does a waiter have to say? We give our order, he writes it down, he delivers, we thank.

Usually there's a little back and forth, though. The banter isn't there. So I'm wondering if he speaks English.

Who knows? Who cares, for that matter. As long as he gets our orders straight.

Can he really pull it off, though? In the long run, without any English? The waiter after all must interact with the customer. It's a two-way street.

Don't jump to conclusions. Based on an egg-white omelet, dry toast and Sanka. Which he managed fine, as we both can see.

True. True.

I'm on his side. I just want to make that clear right here and now.

Whose side?

Miguel's.

I'm not? Suddenly it's a question of sides, waiters versus eaters?

Please, Leo, get with the program as my granddaughter Stacy says. I'm talking about the Mexicans. Look around you.

I'm looking.

Not waiters vs. eaters. Bosses vs. workers. Like always. Now the Mexicans are moving up. This to me is a wonderful thing. The poorest, the worst paid, they start to do a little better, this always benefits the whole working class. So naturally, what do the bosses do? They start a war against them. They creep around, with their tricks, their lies, and they try to sucker the rest of us into thinking it's bad for us the Mexicans are moving up.

Not Nick. He's got nothing against Miguel and his pals. Happy to have them. This he has told me.

Of course. They work like the dickens. I'm talking about the big bosses. The class.

Ah. The class.

Goddamn right. The capitalist class. And their goddamn jingoistic advance guard that's running this country into the ground. The Lou Dobbs crowd.

Oh god in heaven, please let us not speak of Lou Dobbs. My food will curdle in my belly. How he rants and raves on TV every night it's like Goebbels all over again, I cannot stand to even hear that goniff's name on a fine spring morning like today.

But look what's happening, Leo, look at Miguel.

So what about him? A fine looking young fellow, I hope he does well, if he doesn't speak English yet I'm sure he'll learn, don't jump down my throat about that, an off-hand comment, I take it back.

It's us who should be learning Spanish, but that's not my point on this I quite agree fine spring morning as we sit here in our favorite diner having our low-cholesterol breakfast like we do every morning, me so Syl can get an hour's peace to do the crossword before I return to try her patience for the rest of the day, you before beginning your strenuous daily routine of movie going, park bench sitting, and web surfing. Spanish, English, the language question is not my point.

You never finished making your point about how we got Moe Turlington his job back, which is how come I'm not holding my breath for your point about Miguel the Mexican waiter.

Same point, Leo, same point exactly. Look, your pop's goons got rid of Moe Turlington, your pop would have never hired another Negro, and we turned it around, Moe got his job back, and not only that, we kept the pressure on till eventually he broke down and let some more in. We did it how? By you working on your dad, sure, that didn't hurt, although in truth it was more about scaring him with the specter –

The specter which doesn't seem to be haunting Europe any more, to your

dismay –

Oh doesn't it? Have you taken a look at Greece lately? Or France? Don't count us out, buster, this has always been and will ultimately be the final mistake of the ruling class –

In whose ranks you still insist on counting me.

Did you not inherit one-half the assets when your pop died?

And did I not invest nearly every penny into good works? The Gettelman Trust for Toilers' Children's Education? Gettelman Foundation grants for labor organizing? The GetEuro Furriers High-Tech Retraining Fund? Didn't I skedaddle out of the executive suite as soon as I could talk my sister into taking over, and didn't

I spend the next 40 years diverting as much of the Gettelman profit as I could toward the Gettelman philanthropies?

Every penny of that profit was stolen from workers' labor, Leo. This I have explained to you at least a thousand times and this you still pretend not to understand. The profit was not yours to allocate. In any case, your family is wealthier than ever –

Hey, not me, buddy. I took a living wage, enough to support my wife and kids, that's it.

OK, the rest of the Gettelmans. Filthier rich every day, according to the stock ticker.

Yeah, you got to give it to Estelle, she turned out to have some head for business, didn't she? Gar-ment industry's nearly dead, but not Gettelman. Started diversifying back in the 60s –

Leo. Please. I can live without a review of your family's ever-expanding fortune. Every penny stolen, I repeat. Today worse than ever – shall we speak of the fabulously popular Get-Goin' sneakers? Of the, what, dollar a day the jobbers pay teenaged workers in, hey, who knows, Miguel's home town maybe?

No, let's not. It's terrible, you know I agree.

You agree so much, give it all back.

Ach. I got no say-so whatsoever. Estelle's kids are in charge. You think you are going to move them an inch with your lectures on the labor theory of value, you are worse senile than I thought.

What about your grandkids' trust funds?

Untouchable. This my Mildred saw to, on her deathbed. She knew you'd try. She knew you'd hock the chinik with this business about it's really the workers' money. And here and now, the year 2006, age 85, in my own rational mind, what's left of it, I do agree with you. The money rightfully speaking did not belong to the Gettelmans. It is wealth the workers created. Which Mildred foresaw you'd persuade me, which is why she took charge of the paperwork and I cannot touch one penny of the grandchildren's accounts.

Oh well, you did your best, you're a good-hearted son of a bitch, and so I breakfast with you every day and will continue to until one of us, preferably you first, drops dead. Primarily because of how you helped Moe Turlington get his job back. And afterward, how you hocked your pop to hire more Blacks. And then, when you headed the firm for those few months, how you undid your pop's dirty accounting and stopped paying them less.

None of which prevented you guys from walking out on strike again.

Why would it? Anyways, why are we talking about Moe and how we fought for him? I'll tell you why.

I'm all a-quiver.

Very funny. I'll tell you what's not funny. What is not funny is that Miguel the waiter they call illegal.

He is? Does Nick know?

Leo, please, I'm speaking broadly. No, I do not know any particulars about Miguel's own situation. Although chances are that he does not have the documents the government requires, and, yes, chances are Nick knows and uses this fact to pay Miguel next to nothing and on top of this less than nothing for benefits. But the main point is, say Miguel did in fact cross the border without permission, how dare they call him a criminal.

But if he has no papers, isn't that –

If he has no papers he is a worker without papers. Did your father have papers when he came over in '09? Legitimate papers? Didn't you tell me he paid some Warsaw wheeler-dealer to fake up documents?

Yes, this is the story he told.

Did your father speak English when he came over?

Not a word.

Did he save up for years, then send to bring his folks over?

This you know, from his annual end-of-year speech to the workers.

Can a human being be illegal?

I'm not sure I follow now.

Your father, however he finagled his way over. Miguel, shot at the border maybe. Or my mother, born during the ocean crossing so she all her life was a citizen of nowhere. Anyone, no matter how they got here, no matter what piece of paper they have or don't have. Illegal? No, no, no! No human being is illegal! This is the battlefront today, this is where the class war –

Herb, please, calm down, you'll pop an artery. And lower your voice. You're not on the picket lines here, we're just eating a nice quiet breakfast like we do every morning. Besides, me you don't have to convince. Me, I have no problem with Miguel or José or Maria or any of them.

But will you fight for them, Leo? Will you take a stand like you took a stand for Moe Turlington?

Herb, I was a young man then. For god's sake, what are you asking me to do now?

March with me, Leo.

You? March? It's one thing those protests when that crumbum Bush invaded Iraq, we stood in one spot the whole time. But march?

That's right. Over the Brooklyn Bridge.

Okay, Herb, now you're talking crazy. I have never once in all these years mentioned it, I know you think the buildup in your right shoe evens everything out, you walk as good as anyone, you think, but now I must tell you, my friend, this is not so. I see the effort in each step, and –

So what if it's an effort? What is life but a struggle to get from here to there? To move forward? Forward, wasn't that the name of the newspaper my folks used to read? Why should it be easy? What's a little pain? You don't think it's worth it it's because you've never had to, never really –

Don't start in on me again, Herb. Just tell me when and where if you don't mind.

Monday. Across the Brooklyn Bridge to the federal building. A Day Without Immigrants they're calling it. The whole country, a general strike almost. Leo, it's like 1935 all over again!

Terrific, so they won't miss two alteh kockers on the bridge. We could maybe wait at the federal building? Take a stand, so to speak?

You wait if you want. Me, I cross. With Stacy. Her whole class is walking out. She said she'd borrow a wheelchair from the nursing home where she works after school. She'll push me the whole way if I want. Oh – hello again, Miguel. Yes, I guess we are done. Sorry about the yelling.

He's a firebrand, Miguel, what can I say. Always has been. A miracle we're friends all these years. Yes, sure, go ahead, take it away, thanks, thank you kindly sir.

Syl? Syl, hello, are you there? I don't hear you so good, you're breaking up.

Herb, you've got a cell phone? Since when?

Hold on a minute, Syl. Yeah, Leo, last month for our 60th anniversary, from the kids. Apparently it's now a must-have for the likely-to-have-a-stroke-or-break-a-hip crowd. So we can call 911 as we lie dazed in the street. What's that, Syl? Right. She says, assuming we're conscious. And look, sorry, Leo, that was rude, I should have excused myself before dialing.

No kidding. There's an etiquette to these things, buster.

Quite so. In fact, hold on – no, Syl, not you. Leo. You, Syl, I'll call back. OK? But hey, in the meantime, you'll do me a favor, doll? Look up Moe Turlington's number, would you? He's with his daughter now, up in Westchester, it's a 914 number. Thanks. I'll call back in a few.

You're calling Moe? Didn't know you two were in touch.

Oh, sure, every now and then. A few others too. Whoever's still breathing. Ever since those meetings in Harlem.

I don't recall those meetings.

You weren't there, Leo.

Ah. After I went management.

No. This was when you were pushing your dad to hire Moe back.

I did better than push. I forced the old man to see he had to back off or –

What he saw, Leo, was more than you did.

What the hell does that mean? Such as?

Now look, Leo, I never told you back then because we needed you to think you were Moe's only hope, and by god you took your charge to heart so well that to this day I forgive you for your family being fershtinkineh rich, but Moe and me and a few of the other guys had some meetings in Harlem with some organizers there –

Without telling me? Ever, until this very day?

I do apologize, Leo. I should have told you long ago. At the time, though, it was best you didn't know. You had to go in like gangbusters, which you did, had to let your dad have it, which you did.

And meanwhile, behind my back, you're what? With one of those party cells up there?

Something like that. See, if you'd failed, it would have been a big fight. Led by the Blacks. Pickets, there would have been. We were going to pull out all the stops, whether Jake or Leitner or all the rotten stinking bosses liked it or not.

And Pop knew. You said he saw more than me. All these years I've thought it was me got Moe's job back.

You did, Leo. Because of you we never had to take it to the next step.

No, it was because of you were ready to.

Your father was many things but stupid he was not. He saw Moe wasn't going away, and he saw there were more behind him. Just like these blood-sucking bosses have got to be

shown with the Mexicans. Because mark my words, my friend, these Mexicans are on the move. Like Miguel here – pretty soon he'll be in the streets, limp or no limp, he'll be marching across the Brooklyn Bridge –

Not on Monday he won't. There is not a chance in hell Nick's letting him skip work –

No? You don't think so, Leo? Well, how about this? How about you go talk to your friend Nick. Have a chat, appeal to him, tell him he's a prince among men, a mensch, and tell him that what a mensch should do on May Day –

May Day! Oh Christ, I should have known.

The calendar is not a secret document, my friend. It says quite clear: Monday, May 1. You'll mention it to Nick. He knows from May Day – he's Greek, his whole country shuts down. You'll give him a nudge, Leo, he should close the restaurant so Miguel and the rest can march for their rights. While you're talking to Nick, I'll get Moe on the line. See does he want Stacy to get a wheelchair for him too. And, oh, Leo, if you want to point to me, if you want to mention to Nick that your friend Herb over here is on the phone with a tough union guy, guy who once almost brought all of Harlem down on your poor old pop's head, well if you think that would be a helpful point to make, Leo, be my guest. You always were a persuasive son of a gun.

Lake of Heaven (excerpt)
Ishimure Michiko

Translation by Bruce Allen, and introduction (below the excerpt).

*T*his section of Lake of Heaven is from Chapter 5, "Secret Song":

Villagers have gathered by the shores of the dam-constructed lake which has submerged their old town, Amazoko. An older woman, Ohina, is helping her daughter Omomo to take over the sacred ritual responsibilities for the village, including singing and dancing, thus hoping to preserve the ancient traditions that had been in danger of being lost when Sayuri, the former miko shrine maiden, died recently. Masahiko is a young man who has recently come from Tokyo to the countryside by Amazoko for the first time. He had simply planned to spread the ashes of his deceased grandfather, Masahito, on the lake and then return. He ends up, however, staying on, drawn into the culture and land of his ancestral village and realizing how much of his own spiritual existence had been cut off.

*

Omomo's body was swaying back and forth gently. She was holding a rather long set of light red prayer beads hanging from her hands. Two older women nodded to each other as if exclaiming, "Ah!" This was because this string of beads – beads that Sayuri had used when she recited her prayers – was the very same string of coral beads that had come from Oki no Miya shrine. Omomo fingered the beads, holding them to her breast as she chanted something, and then turned toward the elders to greet them. Ohina, standing at the back of the room, signaled Kappei with her eyes. Then she pointed to the entrance of the straw hut. Kappei nodded in understanding. He went to the en-

trance holding a carpet and spread it out at the feet of the elders. Then he smoothed out the carpet with his big hands, as if looking for sharp stones or twigs. Finally, he signaled silently to the elders to sit.

"How comfortable," the elders commented politely. They sat down quietly and once again gave their attention to Omomo and Ohina in their white robes. Just then the wind gusted and Omomo's hair swayed to the side. With the sky not yet yielding its last rays of light, the tips of her long hair fluttered gently, as if expressing a sign of the coming twilight.

The first voice sounded.

On hearing it, the thought came to Masahiko of those sal trees faintly lit up amidst the mountain dew. He had seen these trees for the first time in this mountainous land. Their trunks were smooth and golden, with flecks of red. Omomo's song conveyed the impression of those trees murmuring, off in the distant mist.

> In the moonrise
> Of the autumn equinox,
> From Oki no Miya
> Already your servant
> Has come.
> Already your servant
> Has come.

Omomo looked out with half-opened eyes. With the prayer beads hanging from the opening of one sleeve, she raised them slowly to her breast in a just-barely perceptible movement. Her manner was entirely different from the flashy movements of the singers on TV. Her voice and the motions of her body were like the spirit of a tree, or of a thing answering to a faint, distant wind.

The elders sat up straight to welcome the arrival of the servants of Oki no Miya.

> Here at the
> Meeting place
> At the base
> Of heaven,
> Welcome the new moon.
> Over the mountains

Come flowers
And pampas grass,

The blue shell princess
From Oki no Miya.

The god of the mountains.
The master of the cave under heaven.
The lord of the oceans.

If you pass
Down the road
Of a thousand leagues,
A thousand grasses
And vines too
Shall turn red
And become
Beautiful woven silk.
Let us take
One stem of the
Thousand-year pampas grass
And make an offering.

Oshizu and Chiyomatsu's eyes moistened as if they had already entered the darkening surface of the water. Thinking back on the story Chiyomatsu had just told about the lake in the womb of the mountains, Masahiko tried to hold on to the fragments of his grandfather's words that came to mind. Yes, he used to speak of a lake of a "divine wedding." Masahiko remembered his mother's casual-sounding voice, after she had put him in the mental hospital.

"The nurses talk about him, you know. They say that Grandfather often talks to himself. And he goes on about some sort of 'divine wedding lake.' I suppose his memories of his youth must have been quite happy. It seems the nurses hear him talk about how good the old days were — but then he says we ruined his life and pushed him into the hospital. As he got older your grandfather often talked about that divine wedding lake. He must have spent some pretty romantic days at that lake where he had his honeymoon, don't you think? That lake — I wonder, just which lake do you suppose it was he went to?"

Kiyohiko, his father, had answered in his usual expressionless voice, "I didn't hear anything about it, but it doesn't matter, does it? It didn't hurt anyone, did it?"

"But I…"

Machiko had started to speak, but cut herself short with an unnatural-sounding laughing voice. Masahiko remembered the conversation well.

Masahiko now understood what his grandfather Masahito had really meant by his words. Omomo had sung of "one stalk of the thousand-year pampas grasses;" and in fact there really was a place called "Susuki Bara," meaning the "plain of pampas grass."

"Perhaps it was the remains of the mouth of a volcano. There was a plain called 'Susuki Bara.' The old folks used to say that below it was Amazoko Lake, the place where the goddess of Oki no Miya and the Lord of the Mountains met. It was the lake of the divine wedding."

His grandfather had told him these stories. The Isara and Tamama Rivers flowed into the ocean, and where they met amidst the currents of the sea was Oki no Miya. The old people said that twice a year, at the spring and autumn equinoxes, the goddess of the ocean palace and the god of the mountains met and exchanged places. In the village of Amazoko the people sent off the mountain god and received the goddess from Oki no Miya. The two gods came from the oceans and the mountains riding on dragon gods. According to his grandfather, Amazoko was the meeting place for the gods.

While Masahiko was listening to Omomo's song, the words of his grandfather, with their music-like cadences, fell into context. So was that what it was about, he wondered. His grandfather must have been trying to convey the spiritual world of his lost village to his weak grandson whose ears had become damaged. Thinking of it now, grandfather must have been so overcome by sorrow that he was unable to move either forward or backward. He had restrained himself with the strength of a man of the countryside. And yet, in the end, the words had just broken out.

"Go blow yourselves up, Japanese islands!

Just blow yourselves to bits!"

His inner world had already been destroyed. In the car as he was being taken to the mental hospital he had been completely surrounded by other cars – going forward, going left, going right and coming up from behind.

"We're in the midst of an army of enemy tanks. We can't escape. All we can do is go on like this!"

The voice that Masahiko would never forget had been the old man's cry of desperation. The inner cosmos in which he had been brought up, where people had lived in a world of myth, now lay destroyed at the bottom of the lake and he had been left as a lone survivor, wandering in an unknown megalopolis. He must have come to think of himself as some sort of unripe rice plant that had been mowed down. He had seen it while being led away by a family that regarded him as just a demented old man – the Japanese islands had turned into a giant conveyor belt carrying slabs of concrete, all covered with trembling swarms of vehicles.

He must have imagined he was about to be devoured by the ever-increasing horde of cars that looked so much like a pack of rice weevils. But it was his grandfather's very last words following that outburst that had sent Masahiko back carrying the urn of cremated bones to the lake that now covered the old village.

"The string of the biwa of Moonshadow Bridge..."

And now that string had begun to stir within Masahiko's body, urged on by Omomo's voice like a small spring of water bubbling up into the mist.

Then in a low voice Ohina began to sing, taking over for Omomo. It felt as if the grasses and trees all about were waving gently in the wind.

Yaa
Hore Yaa.
The five-colored clouds
Are in the shadow of the moon,
Dimly visible
In the mirror of the water.

The sound brought something back to mind. It was the night he first met Ohina, after they had scattered the ashes and she had sung. How he longed to hear that song again. Then Ohina took a string of black beads into her hands.

Yaa
Hore Yaa.
The waters' destination–
Hold fast to the light
Of the distant world
In the darkness.

Yaa
Hore Yaa.
Staying
Just one night
The feeling doesn't end.
It is also in
The shadows on the water.

When he had heard the song the time before without understanding the meaning of its words, he had simply thought it interesting to discover that such songs existed, but now he realized that this song told of the wedding of the gods.

A half moon was rising over the water, its light reflecting on the surface. Omomo started to sway back and forth and the tone of her song changed to a clear rising pitch. Masahiko felt he was hearing the sound descending from the heavens.

Ho-o–

Ho-o–

Ho-o–

Repeating the call three times, she passed along the edge of the lake in front of the people and then returned. Masahiko was unable to see her facial expression. He could tell that Kappei was breathing with great care. As the final "Ho-o–" slowly faded away it made him think of birds vanishing into a starry sky.

Ohina's voice swept low over the grasses behind her like the traces of a breeze and trailed off into the spaces between the trees. For a few moments there was silence. Then, in an unusual voice that sounded like the striking of a plectrum, once again she sang, "Ho-o– Ho-o–," the sounds as if descending from the heavens.

A thought came to him – this is the moment where a vanishing mountain people's spirit is transformed into art. And then, as if gathering together all her voices and inhaling them into the sky, a powerful new verse began – as if woven into a tapestry of sound.

> White heron
> White heron
> Night singing bird,
> Let the flowers fall.
> The name of the princess
> Whose bed lies in the water
> Is the Blue Shell Princess
> Of the Palace of the Ocean.
> The name of the mountain god
> Is *Amazoko-no-unabara-no-mikoto.*

> This one night's stay
> Amidst the thousand-year pampas grasses,
> Amidst the shadow of the moon,
> A stalk of grass
> Sways and becomes
> Countless flowers.

> Since ancient times
> In Amazoko
> The water of the lake
> In the womb of the mountain,
> With its fragrant smell
> When night comes,
> Keeps the dragons
> Attending
> The Blue Shell Princess,
> Pulling her long, shining
> Blue hair,
> Till she becomes
> The goddess of the mountains.

> The Isara River
> Shows the way.
> Flow on,
> For the bounty
> Of the oceans and the mountains.

The landscape Masahiko's grandfather had tried to describe to him now began to appear.

The place of the wedding of the gods was the lake that lay in the womb of Amazoko Mountain. The villagers paid their respects and offered songs so that the night of the divine wedding would come to pass successfully. On the eve of the autumn equinox the gods returned peacefully to spend the night together at the unseen lake. If on the following morning there was a faint whitish tint in the Isara River even when there had been no rain, this showed that the wedding of the gods had taken place happily. And all along the river, in the mountains and in the fields, the land became moistened. And for another year fecundity would be spread throughout the land, from the mountains to the distant sea. And the plants at the depths of the ocean, and all the fishes too, would thrive. Amazoko was the dwelling place of the gods who enriched the mountains and the seas.

In his childhood Masahiko had thought of these tales of a far-off forgotten mountain village as merely the fragments of memories of an old man who had been separated from his hometown. In those days the only one who had been there to really listen to his grandfather's stories was the big old gingko tree. Now he had come to realize that in order to see into the world that had been hidden in his grandfather's mind it wasn't necessary to resort to ideas from ethnology or the recently fashionable ecological theories about saving the earth. All that was needed was to share in the feelings of these elders right here; these people who continued to return to Amazoko in their dreams.

*

Masahiko felt something in Ohina and Omomo's voices awakening emotions that had been slumbering in the deepest reaches of his heart. It was as if the strings that had been reverberating within him were at last sounding together. In Ohina and Omomo's singing he could hear the kind of sounds he'd been searching for – sounds like the verses of the imayou songs of the distant past. He could hear a composition that had not yet been performed for the outside world; one written for hichiriki, shakuhachi, sasara, koto, otsutsumi drums, and other stringed and percussion instruments. It was a piece that started singing all by itself; at times bursting out with a heavily-layered feeling of life, and in some verses filled with the presence of an autumn evening in the fields and mountains, faintly reverberating with the soft sounds of insect voices calling to a distant world.

For the first time he could feel himself walking down Utazaka, passing by the weeping cherry tree and placing his hands on the mulberry trees of the old Silk Estate. He looked up at the sky, sharply framed by the ridgeline of the mountains.

Nearby was a large well, set off by a mossy stone wall with fern leaves waving about, growing from its cracks. The villagers called it the "Ikawa" well – but could it be that this well gave birth to the wind also? In its dark water the face of a person was reflected. The face of neither Ohina nor Omomo, it had faint, care-free-looking eyebrows and its eyes, which seemed partly cast downward, looked long, narrow, and dim. Its slightly-grinning expression was inscrutable. Could this be the face of his great-great grandmother Nazuna who had taken in and raised the child left by the Lord of the cave? It was said that she had lived over one hundred years, but would she appear with a face like this? He felt himself trembling.

His grandfather had slipped away from the world of such things and for a while he had tried to become a person of the city. Compared to the villagers he had been somewhat more cultured. Also, through the generations in which they had used the name Michihiko, the family had owned enough mountain land to build a temple. And even if his grandfather's estate had been ruined, still he had established a home in Tokyo and had sent his son to college and on to a position with a trading firm, enabling him to make a decent living. Why then, had he become so strange?

The things in his speech and behavior that people called strange were limited to his military experience and to things connected with the village of Amazoko. Perhaps if the difference between two people's experiences is too extreme, one person may become fearful of the things he or she can't understand about the other person and end up saying the person is demented or mentally ill.

Masahiko felt the warm hand of his grandfather – the hand with fingers lost in the war in Okinawa – being placed upon his shoulder.

The words, "My lost fingers…they're playing the biwa," sounded in his ears.

The leaves of the mulberry trees shone with a fresh light and then became immersed in the thin fog. Why was it that Masahiko, who would have been thought to be ignorant about plants, knew the shape and form of mulberry leaves, and of their delicate, slender branches that swayed and reached toward the sky? He found it fascinating to think how the strings of his biwa had come from the insect-chewed leaves of a mulberry and its body had come from the trunk of a mulberry. His own biwa might not be quite like one in the Shoso-in Museum, but to him the beauty of its shape was unrivalled. He couldn't help wondering what history lay behind the making of his biwa, with its exotic shape.

He recalled hearing the talk of his friends at school, leaning on one elbow and blowing smoke from their cigarettes as they spoke, casually spouting off things like, "The modern era is an age when meaning has become completely deconstructed." He wondered what kind of feelings about the realities of life lay hidden behind those words. They seemed pale and insubstantial.

But looking at things from the village of Amazoko, here he saw people living with the rhythms of the growing of the trees, the flowing of the waters, and the waxing and waning of the moon. Here he couldn't say that existence was meaningless. Even just thinking of a biwa, couldn't a person discover within its form a profound world of order? The villagers see and understand such meaning and bring it together. They look on existence as being one image of the world placed in the midst of the entire creation; one in which all animals and all people, themselves included, have to take their parts. They can't help but give it meaning.

He had understood this just from one moment of seeing the fresh light shining from the leaves of the mulberry trees. In this place, wasn't meaning being reborn moment-by-moment, like the plants growing on the bottom of the lake? At least, he thought, it's this way for me, and for people like Ohina, Omomo, Kappei, and the elders, and the villagers who return to Amazoko in their dreams.

He felt as if he had been entrusted with the responsibility of carrying out the last will of this dying mountain region. He felt himself trembling as if he had been allowed to slip through a gate into a secret region.

first published in 1997

Introduction by Bruce Allen:

Ishimure Michiko has often been referred to as the "Rachel Carson of Japan". Her bestselling book *Paradise in the Sea of Sorrow: Our Minamata Disease* (Kugai jodo; waga minamata byo, 1972) alerted many Japanese to the dangers of industrial pollution and shaped the conscience of a generation of politically and environmentally aware writers and activists. Ishimure has gone on to develop the Minamata story into a trilogy. She has also written a wide range of poetry, essays, novels, and noh drama and is the recipient of several international literary prizes as well as Japan's Asahi Prize and the Philippines' Magsaysay Prize. She continues to be involved with the struggle for the rights of Minamata victims, and for the rights of other victims of prejudice and modernization. At the core of her writing and life work is the attempt to bring about a rebirth of the endangered "kotodama" – the spirit of language – that has been at the heart of traditional arts and culture in Japan and throughout the world. This article introduces her work and presents an excerpt from her novel *Lake of Heaven*.

Ishimure's 1997 novel *Lake of Heaven* (in Japanese, *Tenko*) tells the many stories of a traditional rural mountain village in Kyushu which is destroyed in the process of constructing a dam. It deals with the lives of the villagers as they attempt to retain their culture – its stories, dances, music, mythology, and dreams – in the face of displacement, destruction of environment, and rapid industrialization and urbanization hyped as modernization. The work can be roughly classified as a novel, yet its mythopoetical nature stretches the familiar Western conceptions of the novel form. Its narrative style is based on an interweaving of multiple tales, dreams, and myths, told with a circular, rather than linear time conception, evoking a strong sense of the noh drama. Its storytelling style may also remind readers of that found in Arundhati Roy's *The God of Small Things*. Indeed it is perhaps no coincidence that Roy also has gone on to write with great concern about big dam construction and its devastating effects on local culture and environment. Poet Gary Snyder describes *Lake of Heaven* as "a remarkable text of mythopoetic quality – with a noh flavor – that presents much of the ancient lore of Japan and the lore of the spirit world – and is in a way a kind of myth-drama, not a novel." The story becomes a parable for the larger world, "in which all of our old cultures and all of our old villages are becoming buried, sunken, and lost under the rising waters of the dams of industrialization and globalization."

The inspiration for *Lake of Heaven* was drawn from an actual sunken village, Mizukami Mura, located on the Kuma River in Kumamoto Prefecture. When I visited Ishimure in the spring of 2005, she arranged for friends to show me the area. I could see the barely-visible remains of the old village, resting on the bottom of the lake that had been created by the construction of the Ichifusa Dam. Later, I learned more of the fraught history of the dam. Built in 1960 for the purposes of flood control, water use and electrical power generation, in the floods of 1965 the Ichifusa Dam operators "mistimed" the opening of the flood gates, resulting in a "more than doubling" of the damage that would otherwise have occurred. The dam authorities have never officially acknowledged responsibility for the incident, but the residents still bitterly recall the destruction.

I also visited another village in the area, Itsuki Mura, which was in the process of being destroyed as yet another, even larger dam, the Kawabekawa Dam, was being constructed. Some of the last, elderly settlers were still working their old land in the midst of the eviction process going on around them. As a token measure for "environmental preservation," construction workers were erecting a scaffolding around an enormous gingko tree, several hundred years old, preparing to excavate it and attempt to move this symbol of the old village to a location in the new village above the projected flood line. The Kawabekawa Dam project, however, has sparked bitter protracted antagonism between pro- and anti-dam factions, often driving wedges among the villagers, fishermen, farmers, and prefectural and national governments. Delays and protests have prolonged its construction, with the process now in its 40th year. At present it is unclear whether the dam will ever be completed. Even if it should eventually be finished, the earliest estimates are that this would require another ten or more years.

Meanwhile, local residents and the prefectural authorities have come to question the postwar enthusiasm for dam building as a panacea for everything from economic stimulus to flood control, irrigation, electric power generation, and rapid modernization. Serious questions have been raised as to whether this dam is really needed for water control purposes and as to whether it could be ever be economical – even in the most limited sense of the word; ignoring the wider cultural and environmental costs incurred. The anti-dam group argues that the surrounding forests serve as a flood prevention force. The trees provide a "green dam," such that a man-made one is not needed. The national government, for the most part, continues to regard such arguments as uninformed bunkum. Alternative proposals have been made to develop the valley as a nature conservation area. Still the project plods ahead in the midst of bitter opposition and doubts about its efficacy even among former proponents.

Highlighting an unexpected positive turn of events, my tour also included a visit to one other dam, the Arase Dam on the Kuma River. In a landmark decision, this dam has been slated for removal by the Kumamoto prefectural government – over the strong opposition of the national government. The Arase Dam was built in 1954 as the first in a series of three dams on the Kuma River, later to include the Ichifusa dam which inspired the stories of Ishimure's *Lake of Heaven*. The story of the Arase Dam's retirement may be instructive for the consideration of other dams. Dams have limited lifetimes. Their retirements, like their births, require considerable money and effort. The Arase Dam – after 50 years – has gradually become filled with sediment, sand and gravel, reducing its capacity for flood control, water supply and electric power generation. The cost of maintenance and repair further diminishes its reason for existence. The work in progress on removing the dam, cleaning out the sediment, and restoring the river will require four more years. Reflecting on this experience, the prefecture is in process of reconsidering whether all of its dams are really needed and serve or violate local interests. Such enlightened calculations continue to face vested construction interests at the local, regional and national levels that continue to promote and build unnecessary or environmentally and culturally damaging public works projects in the face of mounting opposition from local residents, farmers, fishermen, and the wider public.

Notes: Ishimure Michiko, Paradise in the Sea of Sorrow *is available in English translation by Livia Monnet. Ann Arbor: Center for Japanese Studies, U. of Michigan Press, 2003.*

The original Japanese version of Lake of Heaven *is:* Tenko. *Tokyo: Mainichi Shimbunsha, 1997.*

Bruce Allen's translation of Lake of Heaven *is published by Lexington Books (2008).*

Girl in the Rain

Shabnam Nadiya

When Zinnia moved to our campus she was the classic new kid in town. Our gang was about nine or ten years old, and had known each other from almost the day we were born. We knew who had what hidden under their mattresses, who had a pash for who, who picked their nose in class and who went peeking at the long stretch of bushes by the dam–a favorite dating place for the varsity students. Zinnia arrived amid all this – a stranger, an interloper. We heard from our parents that they had been living in Chittagong, a town close to the sea, as her father taught there.

My mother, who, along with the other campus aunties, went to look over their house almost as soon as they arrived, reported that she was pretty, took music lessons and had a voice like an angel. She could also recite Rabindranath Tagore's *Nirjhorer Shapnabhanga* and Nazrul's *Bidrohi* from memory. None of these details served to make any of us well disposed toward her.

Once Zinnia's family moved in, it seemed natural that they be invited over to our house, and to mom it seemed natural that Zinnia and I 'be friends and play together'. I didn't think much of this idea and my mother smiled when she said it, but I knew an order when I heard one. I decided to be nice to her.

When she arrived, however, I found that it was real easy being nice to her. She was one of those girls – you know, smiled a lot and giggled at the right time. Didn't show off that she had already seen the sea or could sing or could spout lines by the national poets on request as if someone had flicked on a switch within her. Perfectly willing and able to jabber on endlessly about the most secret and exciting of subjects (sex and boys). New kid though she was, after the initial period of everyone feeling out exactly where she would fit in, she was okay.

Zinnia loved rain. Can I ever look at the pouring monsoon rains without seeing Zinnia in the middle of a field, face upturned like a blade of grass reaching for the sun? Zinnia hopscotching in puddles, splashing her legs just as the rain was splashing her above. Zinnia standing under a tree giggling in delight as the rain trickled through the leaves onto her skin. Rain under the trees was greener, she told us, and cooler. The first crack of thunder, the first drop of rain – these were the luxuries she awaited avidly year round. The harder the rain fell the more she enjoyed it, raising her arms to the skies as if demanding to be made love to. We thought she was plain crazy.

It happened on one of those strange monsoon days, when belly heavy with torrential rain, the sky dozed silently overhead, dreaming dreams of an unborn spring. Sudden harsh thunder erupted out of a clear blue sky, the wind lashed out at everything within reach in unforeseen anger. Zinnia was just caught in the storm like everyone else.

All Zinnia's mother saw was Zinnia stomp into the house, run to her room. She seemed muddier than usual and left a trail of rainwater down the hall. Her mother gave her time to change, then knocked on her door to call her for lunch. She was answered with the sounds of heartrending sobs. Not unfamiliar with the vagaries of her strange little girl, she waited at the door for a while and called Zinnia again. Zinnia screamed from inside, "No, no, no, go away, go away." Zinnia's mother sighed and left. It was just one of those days. Then gradually it came out. Zinnia had been raped.

At first we just knew that one day Zinnia didn't come to school. Like any small town, our varsity campus loved having its nose in other people's crotches like a dumpster dog and the news that the girl had gotten herself in trouble raced before the wind. By the end of the school day we all knew. I don't remember how, or who told me or who got the news in the first place; it was just that by the time we walked out of school on our way home, instead of our regular giggling and fooling around we were all whispering. There were four of us who always walked home together. As we neared our turning, we saw a small group of the campus aunties standing in a circle. They all turned to watch as we walked towards them. Suddenly we all stopped. There was something in the way they were watching us, these women we had known all our lives, these women who were our mothers and our friends' mothers. They were waiting.

Then one of them called out to us, and her voice sounded as coarse and raucous as a crow's and as merciless. "Come here, girls, come this way." There was no avoiding it; we moved towards them. They wore smiles as they watched us come closer, the same everyday smiles that we knew, but it was different today, as if instead of the usual thirty two they had snagged ten more teeth each from someone. "So how was school today?" they asked us in such sweet voices that it dried out our innards. Then started the questions. Did she have a boyfriend? Did any of the boys at school seem interested in her? Was this the first time something like this had happened? To her, to anyone? What *had* happened? Really? We stood there unable to get away, listening and listening. Our faces scarlet, our ears burning, it was worse than the time I had been caught by two neighbourhood boys when, unable to restrain myself, I had squatted down to pee beside a pile of bricks. What did we know, what would we tell, what was for sale? Roly-poly Anisa, famous for being a crybaby to this day, suddenly burst into loud tears and bolted We stood there for a moment, watching the fat little girl stumble, fall, then get up to continue running; then with her desperate sobs and with the aunties' screechy 'stop her' ringing in our ears we ran for our dear lives.

But Zinnia never budged. Because of the storm she had run into the bus stop, the one near the Arts Building. She had seen that there was a man there, but that was okay, people would be taking shelter from the storm wouldn't they? She couldn't see properly, her sight was blurred from the pounding rain and the thunder had frightened her. Before she had

a chance to wipe her eyes, she was face down on the floor. She didn't know who the man was. Someone grabbed her from behind, and held her down. She remembered the hoarse breathing of someone close to her ear. There may have been more men, she didn't know. She didn't know. When she awoke, she was alone. She never saw his face, never heard his voice. He had even tied the strap of her *shalwar* carefully in a neat little bow when he was done with her. He must've been a tidy man, disciplined, neat – a man who preferred order to chaos.

The lady doctor examined her and said there was evidence of fresh bruising 'down there'. But that was all. There were no other signs of violence. Not a single mark anywhere on her body. As I've said, he must've been a tidy man. There was no way to tell who it had been. But the question remained. The brief details that Zinnia did provide aren't important; what is important is that the town slowly and unequivocally reached the conclusion that it had to be one of us, one of our men. It had to be someone we knew. Ours wasn't a regular town; there were walls all along the campus boundaries and there were guards all around to look out for 'outsiders'. This vigilance had recently been tightened to limit ingress of the neighbouring villagers aiming to despoil the purity of our environs with their uneducated ways. We were an island of learning, higher degrees and prosperity in the surrounding darkness and we wanted no truck with the world around us. What was the probability that some 'outsider' had come in? It had to be one of us.

The fourth-class employees, responsible for the kind of things a decent community needed to function but would never dream of doing themselves, went through a hard time then. As the servant is the first to be suspected when something is stolen in the household, once the town reached the verdict that it was one of us, they were the natural choice to be suspected. A lot of the fourth-classers lived on campus without their families. Their wives and children lived at their village homes, while the men who worked here shared living quarters. This arrangement worked out well all around. It was cheaper for the men if their families lived in the village and it was cheaper for the university as they took up less space; four or five of them could be stuffed into a single apartment. Of course, there were a stubborn few who insisted on having their children attend the university school as they were entitled to, in the hopes of providing them with better education and opportunities than the village schools, but that was generally frowned upon. Those children were usually placed in section B in the classes, they rarely got major roles in the annual school plays, or any of the cultural or merit awards. They didn't come to our birthdays either. We didn't know if they had birthday parties. It was natural that the burden of suspicion fell on them. After all, they weren't educated and there were so many of them.... All those lower-class, uneducated men living together, who knows what they got up to in that part of the town?

Then someone suggested having a mass line up of the fourth-classers and have Zinnia identify the culprit. The two aunties who thought this up were so excited at the simple brilliance of the idea that they immediately set out to find Zinnia's mother. By the time they neared Zinnia's house, their number had grown to twelve or thirteen. This was such a wonderfully holy mission that no one they met on the way wanted to be left out. It was their civic duty. After all, if the man got away with it once, he might try it again. No one was safe. Of course, not one of them made the obvious point that Zinnia had never seen his face...they were too excited with their plan to be bothered with pesky little details like that.

Zinnia's mother opened the door. She had lost weight in the past month and her face was all angles as if her skull had suddenly become too large for her skin. The excited aunties trilled and bubbled. She stood silent and motionless through it all. And then she laughed. There was such arid hunger in her laughter that it ate right into all the excitement and righteousness that the aunties had brought with them. She laughed again and said: "Why just the fourth-classers? What about the other men?" and damned if she didn't shut the door slam bang right in their faces.

The aunties stood there in horrified silence, unsure of what to do. It was Pamela's mother who broke the silence with a virtuous, "After all the girl has been through a lot, it would be sinful to make her face her attacker again. We couldn't do that to her in her condition. We have to think of what's good for her. We just have to be more careful, that's all." And with a sigh of relief, the others agreed. Of course, they were compassionate people, weren't they? They didn't want to distress the poor child. That was why they were dropping the idea of the line-up, despite it being such a wonderfully brilliant and foolproof idea. And after all, one had to consider the feelings of those people as well. They might feel offended that we thought of them this way, after all, one had to admit they were part of the community as well. But none of them could get those words out of their minds. That laughter, that look in her eyes, and those words she delivered to them as easily as a water snake glided into water took root and grew in their minds, flourishing and flowering in the dark. And then Zinnia's mother did the unthinkable – she demanded that a line up be held, including the teachers and the officers. And their sons. To make it right, she demanded, and proper, the males of the whole community should be there. It needed to be done right. Everyone.

So the women all visited her. Once together. But then they came again, this time, one by one. Early in the morning, just after the men had left for the mosque to say the *fazr* prayers, or in the dead of afternoon, when the men were away at work and the other women lazed in bed. They came to her to ask her not to do this. For the sake of decency, for the sake of the girl, for the sake of the community. This was a can of worms, they told her, that better not be opened. By anybody. They were all in this together. What good would it do, after all. What was done was done. They had to think of the future now, Zinnia's future. After all, if they ripped the community apart like this, they couldn't possibly live here anymore. And where would they go with this daughter of theirs? The community had so far stuck together, not allowing this to get into the papers or get the police involved, but once that feeling of being in this together was broken, how could they expect this silence to continue? The community was important, they told her, the community must go on.

This was about the time they found out that Zinnia was pregnant.

With that news, all the fight left Zinnia's mother. She walked around doing the cooking, taking care of the house, looking after her daughter, her husband, but it was as if she had fallen asleep years and years ago and had just forgotten to wake up and had failed to notice that she was still asleep.

Zinnia stopped coming to school. Perhaps today it would have been easier for her; surely someone would have suggested getting rid of the thing, and it would be done in a blink of an eye. But back then, back there, what was done was done, what had to be, would be. None of us went to visit Zinnia. Most of our parents forbid us point-blank to enter that house. My mother told me it might be a good idea not to go around their house for a couple of months: "I don't think Zinnia will be in the mood to play dolls with you, dear." Play dolls! We'd never played dolls together. Ever.

There was talk of giving it away – the baby that was born. Talk of how this would be a burden and a constant reminder to the girl of how she had sinned or been sinned against. Whichever it was, neither was a good thing. But Zinnia's mother wouldn't hear of it. With the relentlessness that half-mad people have, she kept the baby and would explain to anyone who would listen (and then to those who wouldn't), that God's gift was God's gift, and good or bad none had the right to refuse a gift – God did move in mysterious ways.

And what a beautiful baby it was when it arrived! All my life, I've felt slightly guilty because unlike other girls, I've always found newborn babies to closely resemble wriggling little maggots more than anything else. But despite my total lack of precocious maternal instincts so very common in all my friends, that was the one baby I ever saw that I wanted to pick up as soon as it was born. Pink and soft, wobbly little head and dark eyes that looked at you with a vision as clear and strong as sunlight after the first monsoon rains. It was Zinnia's child.

Zinnia returned to school once the baby was born. We were in the middle of the school year, and the half-yearly exams were peeking over our shoulders. But the school board said it was okay for her and she wouldn't have to sit for the half-yearlies 'due to special considerations'. Our teachers took several of us, the good students, aside and asked us to help her catch up with her studies. But after a month, one by one, the parents visited the Principal. They were all very sympathetic towards the condition of the girl of course, but surely the school didn't think that it was proper for the other children to mingle with Zinnia? After all their daughters were still 'innocent'. Of course no one wanted to suggest that Zinnia not continue studying, after all we were all educated people (this was a university town wasn't it?), but wouldn't it be better if Zinnia continued her education from home? Surely, she herself would prefer that, away from the stares and taunts of the other children. (Pamela's mother remarked, Children can be so cruel sometimes!) And anyway, exams were only a few months away, so it could hardly make much difference to her. Our class-teacher did argue that Zinnia in particular needed the classroom time as she had missed so many months, but the Vice Chancellor's wife was among one of the concerned parents and of course that was that. Zinnia stopped coming to school. Again.

Private tuition was arranged for her. The best of our teachers, even those who did not give private lessons to children, agreed to tutor her. My mother offered to place me with Zinnia, to keep her company. But Zinnia's mother said, "That's okay. She'll have to be alone from now on; let her get used to it." And she smiled with all her teeth. Zinnia's mother smiled a lot those days.

That baby was the pet of the campus. When they found out that she couldn't breastfeed the baby because the milk wouldn't come, why it was as if all the children in the campus were starving. In the end, one of the younger aunties who had had a baby just a few months before Zinnia, regularly donated some of her own milk. The first birthday I remember, the whole damn town dressed up, it was like *Eid* or something. And the gifts! The food! She was like a war baby, said Pamela's mom. And everyone agreed and said what a brilliant notion that was, how perceptive! Of course, Baby was like a war baby, goodness knows there were plenty of those after the Liberation War. Of course, a few of the younger kids got spanked for insisting on knowing what a war baby was, but yes, that was the perfect idea.

Baby grew up the most loved and most wanted. There was no door ever shut to her and nothing that we wouldn't do for her. It was ours, we felt. Our baby, our darling. We were her mother and father and sister and brother. We were everyone and everything. And we fed Baby cakes and candy, clothed Baby in wondrous clothes as if she were a flower or a fairy. Zinnia's mother looked on with a vacant smile.

Zinnia died the first day of the monsoon. For the first time in two and a half years she had sat at the window watching the rain pour. Then when there was a brief lull in the steady pour she went and played with Baby. For a while, the soft cooing of the child-mother and the delighted squeaks and giggles of the baby lit up the house. Zinnia went into the dining room and smiled at her mother, asked her what was for tea. She placed Baby in her mother's lap and said, "Hold her, mother, I'll just take a quick look at the sky." Then she was gone. Baby was almost two when Zinnia died. Whether she committed suicide or whether she just slipped and fell from the sixth floor rooftop in a moment of absentmindedness was a question we all considered, but magnanimous as usual, we decided to give her the benefit of the doubt. The lady doctor gave a natural death certificate. No clouds darkening her death, she was buried in a regular graveyard. And we wept for a few days. She was, after all, one of us. Almost.

And we watched Baby. We watched as Baby grabbed her toes for the first time, smiled for the first time, sat up and fell down, crawled through our hallways and then tottered down the streets. We listened as Baby cooed and then tried out words on her tongue and sang her first song. We rushed to comfort her when Baby cried and laughed in delight when Baby grew angry because her toes wouldn't come to her mouth to be nibbled on. And we watched. And we whispered. That crooked smile Baby gave sometimes, wasn't it a little like Pamela's dad? Did you notice how Baby shook her head after sneezing? Exactly what Meena used to do when she was three years old. And where on earth did Baby get that nose from anyway? Neither Zinnia nor her parents had a nose like that! And so Baby grew older among smiles and whispers.

Baby grew up and went to school, in the campus, and then college. Everyone from the teachers to students was always nice to the child. Except for the occasional playground scuffle where taunts of *haram* to be sung out by one innocent voice and to be followed by the gleeful sadistic chorus of *zadiiiii* would be heard, or the chanting Where's your daddy then, where's your mommy? In college, Baby was in demand with the boys – somehow they seemed to think that it would be easier 'getting it on' with Baby; after all her morals would be looser than the rest of the girls wouldn't they? And if Baby succumbed once or twice to heartbreak…well, that happened to young people at that age and we never got to hear about it.

And then we went on our own ways, to different universities, different lives. Some of us were married off; some were allowed to complete our studies. When we did talk of Zinnia, among ourselves, or with our mothers or the aunties, we all agreed that it was a good thing that Zinnia was gone. She would have been the same age as any of us today and what would she be? No marriage proposals would ever arrive for her, for no matter how pretty a girl she was, nor how charming, where was the man in this world, or where was the family that could accept her along with accepting the existence of Baby? Of course, although it would remain a stain for her, we would all do our best to see that Baby made something of herself, that Baby got somewhere in this world. For Baby was ours, wasn't she?

Life went on for all of us. We felt so good and holy about ourselves; there was something so sacred in our magnanimity. How we had managed to put aside petty mindedness and allowed a bastard child into our hearts and homes. It didn't matter that Baby's smile made some of us uneasy, that Baby's frown made us look at one another with doubt. It didn't matter that when we were children our mothers told us not to play with Zinnia. It didn't matter. The undercurrent of suspicion and derision that freely flowed was never allowed to the fore and therefore to our minds it did not exist – or so we told ourselves.

Except sometimes, as we huddled inside our houses, we would glance at and then look away from a lonely little figure standing motionless in the pouring rain, as if accepting the caress of the mother she never knew, arms held out high, face upturned, yearning towards we knew not what. The air we breathed somehow felt colder on those days.

The Briefing

Arundhati Roy

published in Manifesta 7,

a European Art Biennial, 2008

My greetings. I'm sorry I'm not here with you today but perhaps it's just as well. In times such as these, it's best not to reveal ourselves completely, not even to each other.

If you step over the line and into the circle, you may be able to hear better. Mind the chalk on your shoes.

I know many of you have traveled great distances to be here. Have you seen all there is to see? The pillbox batteries, the ovens, the ammunition depots with cavity-floors? Did you visit the workers' mass grave? Have you studied the plans carefully? Would you say that it's beautiful, this fort? They say it sits astride the mountains like a defiant lion. I confess I've never seen it. The guide-book says it wasn't built for beauty. But beauty can arrive uninvited can it not? It can fall upon things unexpectedly, like sunlight stealing through a chink in the curtains. Ah, but then this is the Fort with no chinks in its curtains, the Fort that has never been attacked. Does this mean its forbidding walls have thwarted even Beauty and sent it on its way?

Beauty. We could go on about it all day and all night long. What is it? What is it not? Who has the right to decide? Who are the world's real curators, or should we say the real world's curators? What is the real world? Are things we cannot imagine, measure, analyze, represent and reproduce real? Do they exist? Do they live in the recesses of our minds in a Fort that has never been attacked? When our imaginations fail, will the world fail too? How will we ever know?

How big is it, this Fort that may or may not be beautiful? They say it is the biggest fort ever built in the high mountains. Gigantic, you say? Gigantic makes things a little difficult for us. Shall we begin by mapping its vulnerabilities? Even though it has never been attacked (or so they say) think of how its creators must have lived and re-lived the *idea* of being attacked. They must have *waited* to be at-tacked. They must have dreamt of being attacked. They must have placed themselves in the minds and hearts of their enemies until they could barely tell themselves apart from those they feared so deeply. Until they no longer knew the difference between terror and desire. And then, from that knothole of tormented love, they must have imagined attacks from every conceivable direction with such precision and cunning as to render them almost real. How else could they have built a fortification like this? Fear must have shaped it; dread must be embedded in its very grain. Is that what this fort really is? A fragile testament to trepidation, to apprehension, to an imagination under siege?

It was built – and I quote its chief chronicler – to store everything that ought to be defended at all costs. Unquote. That's saying something. What did they store here comrades? What did they defend?

Weapons. Gold. Civilization itself. Or so the guide book says.

And now, in Europe's time of peace and plenty, it is being used to showcase the tran-scendent pur-pose, or, if you wish, the sublime purposelessness, of civilization's highest aspiration: Art. These days, I'm told, Art is Gold.

I hope you have bought the catalogue. You must. For appearances' sake at least.

As you know, the chances are that there's gold in this Fort. Real gold. Hidden gold. Most of it has been removed, some of it stolen, but a good amount is said to still remain. Everyone's looking for it, knocking on walls, digging up graves. Their urgency must be palpable to you.

They know there's gold in the Fort. They also know there's no snow on the mountains. They want the gold to buy some snow.

Those of you who are from here – you must know about the Snow Wars. Those of you who aren't, listen carefully. It is vital that you understand the texture and fabric of the place you have chosen for your mission.

Since the winters have grown warmer here, there are fewer 'snowmaking' days and as a result there's not enough snow to cover the ski-slopes. Most ski-slopes can no longer be classified as 'snow-reliable'. At a recent press conference – perhaps you've read the reports – Werner Voltron, President of the Association of Ski-instructors said, "The future, I think is black. Completely black," [Scattered applause that sounds as though its coming from the back of the audience. Barely discernable murmurs of *Bravo! Viva! Wah! Wah! Yeah Brother!*] No no no…comrades, comrades …you misunderstand. Mr Voltron was not referring to the Rise of the Black Nation. By Black he meant ominous, ruinous, hopeless, catastrophic, and bleak. He said that every one degree Celsius increase in winter temperatures spells doom for almost one hundred ski-resorts. That, as you can imagine, is a lot of jobs and money.

Not everybody is as pessimistic as Mr Voltron. Take the example of Guenther Holzhausen CEO of MountainWhite, a new branded snow product, popularly known as Hot Snow (because it can be manufactured at two to three degrees Celsius above the normal temperature). Mr Holzhausen said – and I'll read this out to you – "The changing climate is a great opportunity for the Alps. The extremely high temperatures and rising sea levels brought about by global warming will be bad for seaside tourism. Ten years from now people usual-ly headed for the Mediterranean will be coming to the comparatively cooler Alps for skiing holidays. It is our responsibility; indeed our *duty* to guaran-tee snow of the highest quality. MountainWhite guarantees dense, evenly spread snow which skiers will find is far superior to natural snow." Unquote.

MountainWhite snow, comrades, like most artificial snows, is made from a protein located in the membrane of a bacterium called Pseudomonas syringae. What sets it apart from other snows, is that in order to prevent the spread of disease and other pathogenic hazards, MountainWhite guarantees that the water it uses to generate snow for skiing is of the highest quality, sourced directly from drinking water networks. "You can bottle our ski-slopes and drink them!" Guenther Holzhausen is known to have once boasted. [Some restless angry murmuring on the sound track] I understand ... But calm your anger. It will only blur your vision and blunt your purpose.

To generate artificial snow, nucleated, treated water is shot out of high-pressure power-intensive snow cannons at high speed. When the snow is ready it is stacked in mounds called whales. The snow whales are groomed, tilled and fluffed before the snow is evenly spread on slopes that have been shaved of imperfections and natural rock forma-tions. The soil is covered with a thick layer of fertilizer to keep the soil cool and insulate it from the warmth generated by Hot Snow. Most ski resorts use artificial snow now. Almost every resort has a cannon. Every canon has a brand. Every brand is at war. Every war is an opportunity.

If you want to ski on – or at least *see* – natural snow, you'll have to go further, up to the glaciers that are wrapped in giant sheets of plastic foil to protect them from the summer heat and prevent them from shrinking. I don't know how natural that is though – a glacier wrapped in foil. You might feel as though you're skiing on an old sand-wich. Worth a try I suppose. I wouldn't know, I don't ski. The Foil Wars are a form of high altitude combat – not the kind that some of you are trained for [chuckles]. They are separate, though not entirely unconnected to the Snow Wars.

In the Snow Wars, MountainWhite's only serious adversary is Scent n' Sparkle, a new product introduced by Peter Holzhausen, who, if you will pardon me for gossiping, is Guenther Holzhausen's brother. Real brother. Their wives are sisters. [A murmur]. What's that? Yes... real brothers married to real sisters. The families are both from Salzburg.

In addition to the all the advantages of MountainWhite, Scent n' Sparkle promises whiter, brighter snow with a fragrance. At a price of course. Scent n' Sparkle comes in three aromas, Vanilla, Pine and Evergreen. It promises to satisfy tourists' nostalgic yearning for old-fashioned holidays. Scent n' Sparkle is a boutique product poised to storm the mass market, or so the pundits say, because it is a product with vision, and an eye to the future. Scented snow anticipates the effects that the global migration of trees and forests will have on the tourism industry. [Murmur] Yes. I did say tree migration.

Did any of you read Macbeth in school? Do you remember what the witches on the heath said to him? *"Macbeth shall never vanquished be, until Great Burnam Wood to high Dunsinane Hill shall come against him?"*

Do you remember what *he* said to them?

[A voice from the audience somewhere at the back, says, *"That will never be. Who can impress the forest, bid the tree unfix his earthbound root?"*]

Ha! Excellent. But Macbeth was dead wrong. Trees *have* unfixed their earthbound roots and are on the move. They're migrating from their devastated homes in the hope of a better life. Like people. Tropical palms are moving up into the lower Alps. Evergreens are climbing to higher altitudes in search of a colder climate. On the ski-slopes, under the damp carpets of Hot Snow, in the warm, fertilizer-coated soil, stowaway seeds of new hothouse plants are germinating. Perhaps soon there'll be fruit trees and vineyards and olive groves in the high mountains.

When the trees migrate, birds and insects, wasps, bees, butterflies, bats and other pollinators will have to move with them. Will they be able to adapt to their new surrounding? Robins have already arrived in Alaska. Alaskan caribou plagued by mosquitoes are moving to higher altitudes where they don't have enough food to eat. Mosquitoes carrying malaria are sweeping through the Lower Alps.

I wonder how this Fort that was built to withstand heavy artillery fire will mount a defense against an army of mosquitoes.

The Snow Wars have spread to the plains. MountainWhite now dominates the snow market in Dubai and Saudi Arabia. It is lobbying in India and China, with some success, for dam construction projects dedicated entirely to snow cannons for all-season ski-resorts. It has entered the Dutch market for dyke reinforcement and for sea-homes built on floating raft foundations, so that when the sea levels rise and the dykes are finally breached and Holland drifts into the ocean, MountainWhite can harness the rising tide and turn it into gold. *Never fear Mountain-White is here!* works just as well in the flatlands. Scent n' Sparkle has diversified too. It owns a popular TV channel and controlling shares in a company that makes – as well as defuses – landmines. Perhaps their new batch will be scented – strawberry, cranberry, jojoba – in order to attract animals and birds as well as children. Other than snow and landmines, Scent n' Sparkle also retails mass market, battery operated, prosthetic limbs in standard sizes for Central Asia and Africa. It is at the forefront of the campaign for Corporate Social Responsibility and is funding a chain of excellently appointed corporate orphanages and NGOs in Afghanistan which some of you are familiar with. Recently it has put in a tender for the dredging and cleaning of lakes and rivers in Austria and Italy that have once again grown toxic from the residue of fertilizer and artificial snowmelt.

Even here, at the top of the world, residue is no longer the past. It is the future. At least some of us have learned over the years to live like rats in the ruins of other peoples' greed. We have learned to fashion weapons from nothing at all. We know how to use them. These are our combat skills.

Comrades, the stone lion in the mountains has begun to weaken. The Fort that has never been attacked has laid siege to itself. It is time for us to make our move. Time to replace the noisy, undirected spray of machine-gun fire with the cold precision of an assassin's bullet. Choose your targets carefully.

When the stone lion's stone bones have been interred in this, our wounded, poisoned earth, when the Fort That Has Never Been Attacked has been reduced to rubble and when the dust from the rubble has settled, who knows, perhaps it will snow again.

That is all I have to say. You may disperse now. Commit your instructions to memory. Go well, comrades, leave no footprints. Until we meet again, godspeed, *khuda hafiz* and keep your powder dry.

[Shuffle of footsteps leaving. Fading away.]

Dead Man Talking

Paul Street

first published at ZNet

Sparked by recent allegations that Public Broadcasting System (PBS) News hour host Jim Lehrer died more than four years and seven months ago, political and medical investigators are monitoring the appearance, life signs, and behavior of a number of key American public figures.

"ANYTHING FOR MY COUNTRY"

PBS, the Pentagon, and Lehrer family physician Sam Il Sung have denied reports that the listless and vapid Lehrer passed away after a tragic hang-gliding accident in early March of 2003. Before drawing his last breath as he lay in a secluded and secret hospital bed with a shattered spine and neck, author David Jay Shiffin and a team of Internet-based "truth" researchers claim, the ex-Marine Lehrer agreed to let his body be used in a covert CIA program meant to encourage mass domestic consent for planned invasions of Iraq and Iran. "Anything for my country," Lehrer is supposed to have said…very slowly, eliciting yawns and distracted looks of boredom moments before he expired.

According to "truth" proponents, the alleged CIA project was code-named "Dead Man Talking." A team of military, intelligence, medical and science experts commissioned by Vice President Dick Cheney and former Defense Secretary Donald Rumsfeld reconstructed and reactivated Lehrer's deceased body. They provided the new "bionic anchorman" with minimal locomotion functions and the power to read neutral, passionless, falsely "objective" and vaguely power-worshipping "news" text carefully scripted by unnamed intelligence professionals.

"WAITING FOR FRESH MEAT"

According to one highly placed Pentagon source said to have spoken on the condition of anonymity:

"Cheney and Rumsfeld saw the deceased Lehrer as a 'critical homeland public relations asset' dead or alive on the eve of illegally invading Iraq to deepen U.S. control over key Middle Eastern petroleum reserves. They were happy as Hell to hear that Lehrer was near death, just as 'Dead Man Talking' had become fully operational and we were locked and loaded for 'liberating' Iraq. They'd even joked about having him killed for the project but some of us wondered if that was even necessary. I mean Lehrer was already good at what he's been doing ever since he died for real – putting all those pathetic latte-sipping liberals to sleep about the unbelievable shit we've been pulling at home and abroad, like occupying a country that posed no risk to us and doing it on totally false pretenses. It's not for nothing we used to call PBS 'the Prozac Broadcasting System.' That's part of why Lehrer was chosen: the changes in his behavior we were going to introduce wouldn't have been all that noticeable with him."

"You saw," the Pentagon source allegedly added, "what we had to do with that snotty liberal asshole Dan Rather when he started mouthing off about Dubya's draft record…. 'I'm an American first and I'll line up wherever the president wants me,' Yeah, right. He's lucky we didn't snatch his body up for the project."

Neither the Pentagon nor PBS have responded to queries about the scientific breakthroughs and procedures that have allegedly permitted Lehrer to continue reading passionless yet nebulously patriotic "news" five nights a week for more than four and half years after his own tragic death.

An anonymous CIA source is said (by "truth" researchers) to have suggested that undisclosed stem-cell and robotic advances made in California in late 2002 had "closed the deal on 'Dead Man Talking"'s viability.by September," one researcher claims to have been told, "we were just waiting for fresh meat."

OBAMA "FULLY OPERATIONAL" BY JULY 2004

The still sketchy allegations have some investigators wondering about numerous other public figures who have played critical roles in paralyzing, boring, depressing, and confusing the populace and deadening its underlying populist anger at United States domestic and foreign policies – some of the most reactionary, regressive, idiotic, and (not surprisingly) unpopular (both at home and abroad) in the world. Of special interest for those examining the possibly larger breadth of the alleged "Dead Man Talking" project are the Democratic Party's chillingly machine-like presidential frontrunner Hillary Clinton, Senate Majority Leader Harry Reid, House of Representatives Speaker Nancy Pelosi, Democratic Presidential candidate and U.S. Senator Barack ("Love Your Oppressor") Obama, daytime television paternity tester Maury Povich, NBC News anchor Brian Williams, U.S. Senator John F. ("Reporting For Duty") Kerry, and former U.S. Senator Tom Daschle. One anonymous source is reported to have claimed that "Daschle had to be removed from the Senate after an early 'Dead Man Talking' experiment went terribly bad in ways too terrible to discuss."

Inquiry is focusing heavily on Pelosi, whose failure to pursue impeachment and willingness to fund the illegal invasion of Iraq have combined with her "hauntingly Pinocchio-doll-like appearance and movements" to make some researchers take a second look at claims that she died in a mysterious plane crash in Arlington, Virginia in January of 2006. By one "truth" account, tapes containing "Mayday" reports from Pelosi's corporate jet have been mysteriously "lost."

Obama is said by some investigators to have been created from scratch in "a highly multicultural west coast lab" in the spring of 2003. "This guy — or whatever — came out of nowhere,"

says one researcher. "We are having a hard time matching up Obama's facial images and eye motions before and after May of 2003. By the Keynote Address (in late July 2004), he was fully operational. It was actually a very conservative speech."

EDWARDS RULED OUT

Democratic Presidential candidate John Edwards has come under some scrutiny because of his seemingly ageless appearance and "always perfect hair," but political investigators are now ruling him out. They say his insistent and increasingly fiery commentary denouncing growing class inequality and poverty in the U.S. is "inconsistent with the ideological profile 'Project Talking Head' directors were likely working with. "This guy has been moving from lifeless to lively over time," one examiner notes – "the opposite of the pattern you'd be looking for. Cheney and Rumsfeld were trying to deaden the populace to class inequality and corporate domination and stuff like that, not just the illegal and imperialist nature of the war. They'd be much more likely to go with somebody like Obama, who's always using this tranquilizing smooth jazz persona and taking this ponderous, and professorial approach to talk about 'healing the nation's divisions' and 'getting things done across partisan lines' and all that ridiculous feel-good 'hope' and 'Kumbaya' crap."

"The other thing about Obama is they made him technically 'black,' which is perfect for confusing liberals and messing up the progressive Demo-cratic base, especially in heavily Caucasian places like Iowa and New Hampshire. Better yet, they might have worked up Hillary: she's as dead as they come and she cranks out the one-liners at the debates like she's reading from a finely tuned program, if you know what I mean."

NO NEED FOR "SCIENCE FICTION"?

According to noted evolutionary biologist Rahm Dohmsky, a leading Left critic of U.S.

politics and policy, there is "no need for resort to bizarre and spectacular conspiracy and science fiction theories about the supposed covert creation of media and political zombies" to explain how and why people like Lehrer (who Dohmsky describes as "very much alive, at least in a biological sense"), Pelosi, Obama, Kerry, and Clinton are willing to deflect and deaden popular opposition to "so-called conservative, really quite extremist and regressive" U.S. policies.

Dohmsky says that "we already know more than enough" about how "U.S. economic, political, and doctrinal structures" work to "generate subservience to wealth and power – and profound contempt for the working-class majority – on the part of journalists, academics, politicians, and other privileged persons in the U.S."

Retired business professor Frederick S. Sherman shares Dohmsky's sense that leading elite educational institutions like Harvard (attended by Obama), Yale (attended by Kerry and Clinton), and Georgetown (Reid) play a critical role in socializing elite "liberal" and other politicians, journalists, and policymakers "to deeply distrust the people and democracy." Sherman places special emphasis on the role of the deepening concentration of economic and related media and political power into ever fewer corporate-multinational hands in explaining why people like "the supposedly deceased Lehrer" and the leading suspected Democratic "Dead Men" (and "Dead Women"?) behave the way they do.

He notes that such conservative and "cautious" behavior is required by the big money business-class interests who make the gigantic campaign contributions and create the favorable media attention political candidates require to run "viable campaigns" under the rules of American "dollar democracy." The "behavior in question," both Dohmsky and Sherman note, goes back long before the period when "truth" investigators think "Project Dead Man Talking" was initiated.

Retired Harvard political scientist Samuel G. Dumplington criticizes Dohmsky and Sherman for advancing a timeworn "Marxist" paradigm that was "discredited once and for all when the Berlin Wall fell." Dumplingnton claims that the two Left scholars are advocates of a "conspiracy theory that isn't much more sophisticated than the one they are criticizing."

A recent discussion with Dumplington was briefly interrupted when a small amount of blue smoke came out of his left ear, his eyes snapped shut, and his torso slumped forward. Dumplington returned to finish the interview after being worked on by two anonymous technicians in a shrouded "medical" room adjacent to his den.

Leading Democrats:
"Expropriate the Expropriators"

Paul Street

first published at ZNet

Tired of defending their business-friendly and state-capitalist policy proposals against Republicans' insistent description of them as weapons of radical Leftist "class warfare," the leading Democratic candidates for the United States presidency have taken a surprising new turn.

"LET'S GET REAL"

"Listen," Hillary Clinton told a stunned collection of reporters yesterday in Des Moines, Iowa. "If the Republicans and the right wing noise-machine are going to just constantly call us socialists, let's show them what the word means. And let's quit running from who we actually are. I've been doing it for too long. It's time to say what we really think. No more hiding behind reformist bourgeois labels and agendas. Listen up Fox News, because you're going to love this. We're Marxist-Lenninists, and we always have been. Deal with it." "You know, it's like my mother used to say," Clinton added: "be careful what you wish for, because you just might get it."

Wearing a red bandana and a Che Guevera T-Shirt autographed by Hugo Chavez, Clinton introduced her "fellow-travelers on the road to American and world socialism." Her new "comrades" and fellow Democratic presidential candidates Barack Obama (sporting a new black beret and dashiki), John Edwards (wearing a vintage Soviet Red Army jacket purchased from a Russian clothier), Bill Richardson (dressed as Fidel Castro and sporting a Cuban cigar), Joe Biden, and Chris Dodd joined her on the stage of a high school auditorium to unveil a new 10-point plan "to overthrow private ownership in the means of production and distribution" and to establish "workers' control."

Eschewing the "limited goal" of "socialism in one country," Obama proclaimed his determination to link the "new American revolution" with "revolutionary proletarian forces and cadres around the planet" to "overthrow the world capitalist system within the next 20 years."

"I'm a realist," Obama said. "Let's get real about solving poverty, inequality, and environmental collapse and putting meaning back into democracy at home and abroad. Let's admit a basic truth: none of these problems are going to be fixed – none of these things are going to happen under capitalism."

"I'm not opposed to all social systems," Obama added. "What I do oppose are dumb, destructive, oppressive, and exploitive social systems based on class, race, and gender hierarchy and the rule of the privileged few."

"EXPROPRIATE THE EXPROPRIATORS"

Edwards dried a tear from his eyes as he read a passage from Leon Trotsky's 1905 pamphlet "Results and Prospects." Embracing Trotsky's theory of "permanent revolution," the former North Carolina Senator confirmed suspicion that his "two Americas" theme of class inequality is inspired by Karl Marx and Frederick Engels' famous 1848 pamphlet The Communist Manifesto.

Edwards quoted Marx and Engels with approval: "You are horrified at our intending to do away with private property. But in your existing society, private property is already abolished for nine-tenths of the population; its existence for the few is solely due to its non-existence in the hands of those nine-tenths."

"And that's exactly what we see in the United States today. Enough is enough," Edwards said. "America needs a president who will tell the truth and show a little backbone. It's time to expropriate the expropriators!"

"Look proletarians," Richardson said, "it's like the old boys used to say: you've got nothing to lose but your chains and you've got a world to win. Working men and workingwomen of the world unite!"

"We can do that!" Obama added.

"I WAS ASHAMED"

Richardson confessed that he has been "a secret Marxist" since the age of sixteen, when he first read Frederick Engels' pamphlet Socialism: Scientific and Utopian. Richardson recalled that his youthful conversion to Marxism "did not go over well with my dad," a leading Citigroup executive.

His father's scorn pushed the future New Mexico Governor into a long struggle to cloak his real ideological identity.

The presidential candidate admitted that he served as "a point man for that reactionary capitalist 'trade bill' NAFTA" in the U.S. Congress during the 1990s "to conceal my underlying faith in socialist transformation." Still, he quietly hoped the bill would help "advance the day when the American working-class understands that it has no country."

"What can I say?" Richardson said, "I was ashamed."

"KISSING BOURGEOIS ASS" TO GET ELECTED

Other Democratic presidential candidates spoke on things they've done and said to "pretend [we] aren't Marxists." Edwards admitted that he built the largest home ever constructed in North Carolina and joined the board of a parasitic Wall Street hedge fund (the Fortress Group) to disguise "my underlying commitment to permanent proletarian revolution."

Obama laughed as he read selected passages from his bestselling 2006 campaign book The Audacity of Hope. "Here's a good one," Obama said, as he recited the following:

"Calvin Coolidge once said that 'the chief business of the American people is business,' and indeed, it would be hard to find a country on earth that's been more consistently hospitable to the logic of the marketplace. Our Constitution places the ownership of private property at the very heart of our system of liberty. Our religious traditions celebrate the value of hard work and express the conviction that a virtuous life will result in material rewards. Rather than vilify the rich, we hold them up as role models... As Ted Turner famously said, in America money is how we keep score."

"The result of this business culture has been a prosperity that's unmatched in human history. It takes a trip overseas to fully appreciate just how good Americans have it; even our poor take for granted goods and services – electricity, clean water, indoor plumbing, telephones, televisions, and household appliances – that are still unattainable for most of the world. America may have been blessed with some of the planet's best real estate, but clearly it's not just our natural resources that account for our economic success. Our greatest asset has been our system of social organization, a system that for generations has encouraged constant innovation, individual initiative and efficient allocation of resources...our free market system."

Shaking his head in mock amazement, Obama asked, "is that kissing the ass of the bourgeoisie or what? I wrote all that reactionary nonsense to keep the capitalist thought police off the trail and impress the people with the money and power."

This comment elicited an understanding pat on the back from Democratic Presidential candidate Joe Biden, who attended the gathering with a little red book containing hundreds of quotations from the former Chinese Communist dictator Mao Tse Tung.

"REFRESHING HONESTY"

At Biden's prodding, Obama agreed to read

another passage from Audacity, reciting lines in which he wrote that "there are seeds of anarchy in the idea of individual freedom, an intoxicating danger in the idea of equality. For if everybody is truly free, without the constraints of birth or rank and an inherited social order, how can we ever hope to form a society that coheres?"

"Geez Barack, Hillary Clinton interrupted. "That was a little over the top even for me. We all know who pays for our campaigns and runs the world — people like Robert Rubin. But you sounded ready to embrace feudalism there. I mean…what was your opinion of slavery when you wrote that book?"

"You've got me, Hill," Obama said. "No doubt about it. But remember," the junior senator from Illinois shot back, "you've been setting the power-serving bar pretty damn low. I've been trying to get some of that Bob Rubin money too."

"Point taken," Clinton responded.

"It's refreshing to hear this new honesty on the part of my fellow Democratic presidential candidates and my fellow Marxists," said Dodd.

"WORKING WITH CAPITALIST SCUMBAGS"

Clinton confessed that a desire to "hide my Marxism" led her to undermine universal health care by advancing an incomprehensible, neoliberal and corporate-friendly health-care friendly health care reform package during the early 1990s.

"'Managed competition,' we called it – what a terrible and reactionary joke! Our slogan should have been 'All Power to the Big Six Insurance Companies!'"

Fear of "being outed as a radical socialist" has induced Clinton to oppose elementary increases in the taxation of privileged households' exorbitant incomes to bolster the funding of Social Security and to hire Mark Penn as her main political advisor. Penn runs a corporate public relations firm that specializes in spin for union-busters, Shell Oil, and big tobacco companies.

"It makes it tougher for your guys to detect my Marxism," Hillary told reporters, "when I'm working with capitalist scumbags like Penn."

"I know just what Hillary means," Obama chimed in. "I mean look at my main political advisor and media guy David Axelrod. He's a complete corporate pig. Talk about your 'running dog lackeys of the ruling class.' For him, it's all about making me look like I'm a progressive friend of ordinary working people when I've really been working for Exelon and Goldman Sachs – nice big money folks like that. A lot of the reporters here probably know that I was the first presidential candidate to officially support the extension of NAFTA to Peru, for crying out loud. Yeah, I've been a real friend of the working class! Senator Clinton and I have hardly raised $170 million between us just by calling up Joe and Jane Six Pack and relying on the Internet."

MORE THAN "JUST BRIBERY"

Reading Obama's book reminded Dodd of "something else Marx wrote in 1848 : "the ideas of the ruling class are in every epoch the ruling ideas." "It's just like Marx wrote in The German Ideology," Dodd argued: "'the class which is the ruling material force in society, is at the same time its ruling intellectual force. That class which has the means of material production at its disposal has control at the same time over the means of mental production.'"

"Marx wasn't just talking about politicians like us," Dodd told an astonished press corps. "He was also talking about you folks – the capitalist media."

"Right on, Chris," said Biden.

Dodd told reporters not to exaggerate the extent to which the actions and statements of politicians can be reduced simply to bribery – to the power of those with money to purchase the loyalty of candidates and policymakers. He advised journalists to "function as critical thinkers" and "pay attention to the complex, partly autonomous and interesting cultural and ideological processes and dynamics whereby moral and ideological hegemony is attained and maintained by and for dominant classes."

"THE POWER OF THE PEOPLE"

"Look, theoretical debate is great," Edwards interjected, "but let's move on. Here's the bottom line, people: the big capitalist sell out and the 'hegemony' are all over now. We're sweeping all that into the dustbin of history. We can finally talk about who we really are. Let us proceed to build the new socialist order, starting right here in the eye of the damn imperialist hurricane. Power to the people!"

"Right on, John, you steely-eyed son of the proletariat," said Hillary Clinton. She grabbed a bullhorn and led the Democratic presidential field in a number of chants, including the following:

"Fight the rich, not their wars."

"Ain't no power like the power of the people and the power of the people don't stop."

"No blood for oil."

"One, two, three, four, we don't want this racist war."

"Hands off Iraq, hands off Iran."

Only one of 30 assembled reporters joined in the chanting.

"I AM THEIR KRONSTADT REBELLION"

But it wasn't all just self-congratulation and team-spirit on the high school stage in Des Moines. The self-declared "Spartacist" Joe Biden and Dodd (a "Frankfurt School" enthusiast) conducted a vituperative debate over how to interpret the Soviet invasion of Afghanistan. Edwards was overheard dismissing Clinton as "Bukharinist" and referring to Dodd as "a petit-bourgeois intellectual."

Dennis Kucinich arrived late to question "just how much of an ideological change the top De-

mocrats were really making" in announcing their shift "from authoritarian neo-corporate liberalism to authoritarian neo-Marxism-Lenninism."

Kucinich told reporters that he is "a left-Marxist in the Rosa Luxembourg tradition" and that he is also influenced by "left-anarchist" thinkers like Bakunin, Rudolph Rocker, and Noam Chomsky.

"I'm not sure there's all that much difference between the old Democrats and their new 'Marxist' packaging," Kucinich said. "I am their one man Krondstadt Rebellion," Kucinich added, telling reporters to "read your Soviet history."

"WE'LL DEAL WITH IT"

The politically influential Wall Street investment house Goldman Sachs, a leading contributor to all of the leading Democratic presidential hopefuls, offered no comment on how the bombshell Marxist disclosure will affect the Democratic Party's recently attained advantage in raising campaign money from corporate America. But an anonymous Goldman Sachs insider dismissed Mitt Romney's recent charge that the firm has fallen under the control of "the international financial and communist conspiracy." "I guess he forgot to add in 'Jewish,'" this source said.

The nameless Wall Street insider added that "global investors seem happy enough to do business with a giant nation that still sometimes likes to call itself 'Marxist' – the so-called 'people's republic of China.'"

"Maybe it's time for the United States to come under some nominally 'Marxist' leadership. If that's what happens, it's just like Hillary said: 'we'll deal with it.'"

A Message From: The American Corporate Plutocracy

Paul Street

first published at ZNet

I could swear this happened last night (I am writing on the morning of Thursday, January 31st), but it may be my addled, anxious, and overworked mind playing tricks on me.

I was watching "American Idol" and trying to balance my checkbook.

I was thinking I should try out for "Idol." I was also thinking about the gap between my income and my irreducible life expenditures.

A commercial for a drug that promised to make me happy and relaxed flashed across the television. I reached for the clicker to hit "mute."

But before I could turn off the sound, the ad was interrupted by the image of a sixty-something busi-nessmen sitting behind a giant desk in a plush corporate office.

A message ran across the bottom of the screen. It said: "A Message from the American Corporate Plutocracy."

The businessman was wearing a pinstripe suit. Behind him hung pictures of J.P. Morgan, Ronald Reagan, Bill Gates, and Bill Clinton.

He looked very serious. He read the following speech:

"American subjects, we are interrupting this im-portant pharmaceutical advertisement to tell you of the special satisfaction we feel at learning that John Edwards has dropped out of the Democratic presidential campaign."

"Edwards was on the cover of Newsweek a little more than a month ago. He was charis-matic, handsome, and very effective on the campaign trail and in debates. He had star quality and many millions of dollars."

"In the last big match-up survey taken before the Iowa Caucus, he polled as the most electable candidate in the presidential race. He was the only Democratic contender who defeated all of the like-ly Republican presidential candidates – even John McCain, who defeated Hillary Clinton and tied Barack Obama."

"Democratic Party primaries have been held in just four small states and he's already done."

"We are very pleased to hear of his early surrender, in which we played our usual quiet but powerful role. It is we who made sure that Edwards' more explicitly corporate and centrist opponents could outspend him by a wide margin."

"It is we who pushed him to the margins of the all-powerful media system we own and manage in your interest – and ours."

"We've already voted John Edwards off the presidential version of 'American Idol'" – so you don't have to.

"We've winnowed the presidential field to four (4) officially electable and corporate-friendly candidates and the election is more than ten months away!"

"It's all about he hidden primary of the rich and powerful operating behind the scenes, in the hidden corridors of power under the benevolent reign of Empire and Inequality, Inc. We are the Simon Cowells of American presidential politics. We love it and you should too."

"We do it for you, to save you the effort and heartbreak of 'democracy,' for which you lack the time, skill, energy, and resources."

"Take note, would-be critics of our caring rule! The spectrum of permissible debate grows narrower with each quadrennial election extravaganza we stage."

"Do not misunderstand us, American subjects. John Edwards was no radical threat to the corporate system we have crafted in response to our need for spectacular wealth and your inability to construct a better social order. Edwards said repeatedly that he believed in what he called 'a market economy' – what we and you should understand as a heavily state-managed system of private profit and class rule."

"He followed our counsel when he wrapped his call for universal health insurance in a plan that continued – beneath all his anti-corporate bluster – to protect the very insurance and pharmaceutical companies that have done so much to create your health care crisis."

"He made it clear again and again that he supported the broader global framework of the splendid imperial order and the related military-industrial complex we have built for the good of the world – and our own profit."

"He agreed to never to mention the overseas victims of our clumsy oaf George W. Bush's foreign policies, including the 1 million Iraqis killed by 'Operation Iraqi Freedom' – an action that continues to generate considerable profits for us."

"He remains ridiculously wealthy (like us) and never really challenged the core inequalities inherent in the workings of the 'market economy'."

"He stood to the right of those malevolent radical mischief-makers Ralph Nader and – to mention another presidential candidate we recently liquidated – Dennis Kucinich."

"But that's all part of what makes Edwards' early defeat all the more delightful and rewarding for us. The magnificent march of our munificent reign has progressed so far that even John Edwards is defined as too radical to make a serious run at the White House."

"He may not have fundamentally questioned the corporate-imperial system that all of us enjoy, but he did develop some very nasty habits that displeased us. He spoke insistently about and against endemic U.S. poverty and related it to oppressive economic inequality and the supposedly 'exorbitant' wealth of the 'privileged few.' He won Nader's approval by speaking against our 'plutocratic' control of government and politics as if that rule isn't a good and necessary thing!"

"He insisted on praising the labor movement, which he repeatedly referred to as 'the single great-est anti-poverty program in American history.'"

"He also connected his obnoxious and inherently dysfunctional and dangerous 'populist' appeal to very specific and detailed policy issues and agendas."

"American subjects, we are certain you found this foolish issues and policy obsession as irritating as we did! As we hope you appreciate, we kindly cater to your limited capacities and sensibilities by framing elections around trivial and childish mat-ters of candidate image, identity, and personality."

"We don't want you to tax your limited and overwrought minds with difficult matters of policy and governance. We want to help you vote for the right kind of politicians you find most likeable, pleasant and fun – kind of like the 'American Idol' show to which you shall momentarily be re-turned."

"As part of this mission, we employ an army of marketers, researchers, data-miners, publicists, and image consultants to help you understand which one of the presidential 'Idols' makes you feel best about yourselves and your glorious, business-run Nation State."

"We, the surviving four 'Idols' – Mitt, John (McCain that is), Hillary, and Barack – and the people around them (most of whom we provide) will handle all the issues and the policies. We and they will give you all the 'hope' and 'change' and 'unity' you need."

"Get ready for a long and tedious exercise in delusion and identity politics that may well guarantee the White House to our favorite party – the arch-plutocratic, messianic-militarist GOP."

"We do it all for you, America. We are here to take and keep the last risks out of your 'democracy.' The nation is in good hands."

"Thank you for your attention. We return you now to your previously scheduled anti-depressant commercial and to the rest of the countless advertisements and programs on this and any of the other 154 stations we have generously created for your endless diversion, brainwashing, marketing, and indoctrination."

"Yours in Eternal Thought Control,

"The American Corporate Plutocracy"

The Toothache

Joseph Veramu

During the coups in Fiji, few people died naturally. It was usually the innocent, caught in the crossfire of blazing guns between opposing forces, who died. As the poor ate the delicacy of roast pork at these funerals, they were sometimes embarrassed because it reminded them of their otherwise impoverished situations.

Jiuta Romisiweini had eaten pork at a funeral. Absentmindedly he had used his hands, with sharp finger nails, to remove bits of pork fat from the gaps in his teeth and in the process had scratched his gums. They bled but he did not take notice. After a week he began to feel pain. Tooth-brushes and toothpaste were luxuries to the very poor. It would have helped at the initial stages had he regularly cleaned his teeth.

Jiuta lived in Veidogo, an inner city slum, where people were so poor that many ate very few nutritious meals. The slum people had come from the various outlying islands to look for better opportunities they thought existed in the city. They inevitably ended up in places like Veidogo. All the shacks were built on high mangrove posts. When the tide came in, the garbage, made up of shiny empty packages, plastic and empty mackerel cans with their garish labels moved languidly in the brackish waters. The people had grown used to the nauseating smell of the filth the City Council refused to collect since the people could not afford to pay city rates.

This was one of the paradoxes of life. Jiuta realised, that in the islands, food from the sea was so abundant that no one ever went hungry. Even for the idle, fruits and yams grew wildly and succulent sea shells could be collected on the shores at low tide. But in irrational moments, they left paradise and streamed into these overcrowded shanty towns surrounded by filth as they starved slowly. It was as if they had received telepathic messages that the 'white man's cargo' would reach them so that even in the squalor of poverty, they waited expectantly for that glorious day when they would become affluent.

It was only during traditional functions like funerals that people here had opportunities to eat roast pork, rare delicacies they could never eat in normal times. Jiuta felt it ironic that they only ate it when people died. (The pigs that were roasted subsisted mainly on a diet of garbage and dead rodents and even when consumed had the faint smell of the filth of the city.) It made him uneasy at times, feeling that the happiness he longed for in the crowded city might be achieved only in heaven. At such times, he felt at peace with the deceased.

The pain grew worse by the day. Jiuta's face swelled into gargoyle-like proportions. Because of his abject poverty, he could not afford the ten dollars the private dentist would charge. That was the amount of money his wife made working twelve hours a day in a garment factory making designer clothes that sold at very inflated prices in metropolitan cities. The moment he went to the Colonial War Memorial Hospital at 8:30 a.m., he realised that it would be an extremely long painful wait. It was true that the health service there was provided free but the doctors and nurses were so overworked and underpaid that they often did their work mechanically. They just did not have the strength to care for the countless people who came in a steady stream throughout the days and nights.

The Outpatient Ward was packed to capacity. It was a surreal scene of people clearly in abject poverty attired in the latest designer clothes.

Two days earlier, there had been a civilian coup – complete with tumultuous days of mass anarchy. In the hysteria, people abandoned their civic pride and went into the city to take goods. Thousands looted, pushing supermarket carts packed with stolen goods to their homes. Jiuta and all slum dwellers took full advantage of this opportunity. Later the slum dwellings looked surreal, the shacks of wobbly mangrove posts and rotting timber sporting the various symbols of affluence.

Here and there amongst the poor, people wore Rolex watches and expensive designer clothes. Some young men sported Nike footwear. A men clutching his Bible and massaging his left ear wore an expensively cut Italian suit. Now and then he winced and cradled his left ear. A young lady with a cherubic face wore a white v-necked top with yellow cord pants. In her prayerful demeanour she looked as if she had come from a nunnery. She had gold earrings and a Cartier watch. She massaged her thighs at short intervals. Her only sign of poverty was the dirty flip-flops she wore. Near her, looking blankly into space, was the young Polynesian-looking young man Jiuta had seen so often around Sukuna Park staring forlornly at the fountain as if expecting it to rejuvenate him. Jiuta noticed that he dyed his hair every week. Today it was pink.

Although everyone sitting there had acquired their designer clothes from the looted city, there was an air of bewilderment in their deportment. They had left their serene islands in search of the elusive "white man's cargo." In the decaying city that even now carried the acrid smell from the smoldering fires of looted shops, they had claimed their cargo. These were people who subsisted on dreams of being affluent. Yet when in a strange moment their dreams were realised, they became lost in the labyrinth of the concrete jungle. They had confronted their destinies and had been disillusioned by its fickleness.

From where Jiuta stood at the back, he noticed that everyone was in some degree of pain. For a moment it seemed to him that the pain was caused by the expensive attire they had got through dubious means. Jiuta looked at his own expensive Reebok rugby jumper and Puma cargo pants he had taken from Tapoos and the Sports World shop and tried to erase this disturbing thought.

The moment he went up to take his number from the bored looking receptionist, he knew it would be a very long wait. The receptionist chewed noisily on a blue bubble gum. Whenever she felt exasperated, she blew it into a very delicate balloon just visible under her dry purple lips. He had drawn number 380. The numbers being called had reached 18.

He made a quick calculation and realised that he would be seen by a doctor at about 2:00 a.m. This would mean having to sit there in pain for about 18 hours.

It could even be longer because the Chinese and Filipino expatriate doctors were too frightened to come to work. Most of the other local doctors were lining up at the British, New Zealand or Australian High Commissions applying for visas to get out of the country. The US Embassy had suggested politely that people enter the lottery for green cards. People realised that the Embassy was tired of refugees of any sort. As the hours passed, the pain increased to unbearable levels. Each new pain was like a sharp drill being imbedded into his head. He drifted in and out of consciousness.

At one point, he could no longer bear the pain and asked the man in the expensive suit, who was clutching the Bible and massaging his left ear if he had any aspirins.

The man shook his head and whispered that he kept hearing voices in his left ear. "If you hear the voice, you won't feel the pain," he said unhelpfully. The man looked up again raising his right hand, "The angels are now singing. Oh, it's beautiful. The pure innocent voices singing Alleluia! Amen! Amen!" His eyes glistened as he added, "Please go. Don't disturb me." He looked irritated that Jiuta had disturbed his feeling of material affluence acquired from the looted city, that surreal world where he felt he came to terms with his life.

Jiuta drank water and walked around the reception room to ease the pain but this only made it grow afresh in strength. It attacked him from different angles in his head.

For aspirins, he approached the young lady with the cherubic face attired in the designer white v-necked top and yellow cord pants. It was only when she looked up with her piercing eyes and love bites ranged strategically around her neck that Jiuta realised her cherubic face was an illusion. There was no innocence in her eyes. Jiuta was momentarily so preoccupied with the young lady's face that she misunderstood his approach as an advance. "I can't go out with you now. I think I have syphilis. That's why I'm here. Also I don't like the rotten smell," she whispered coyly. "It spoils the effect when one is aroused. You should know that."

"You misunderstand me," Jiuta said feeling very irritated. "I just came to ask if you have any aspirin."

"Honey would I be here if I could afford aspir-ins?" she asked him cynically. "It's hard during coups. All those curfews. People laid off with no money. And when people have little to do, they think of death and babies and women in that order. Business is bad. I take away their fear but they can't afford to pay." She shrugged as if this was her destiny.

"Don't get me wrong. I didn't come for what you were thinking of."

"They all say that," she sighed. "But in the dark you can feel their fear pumping away." She looked abruptly away bringing the discussions to a close.

He went back to his seat. He decided against approaching the young man with the pink dyed hair. He seemed to read Jiuta's thoughts.

"You're not going to ask me for aspirins?" he asked delicately, pronouncing each word slowly in a low voice.

Jiuta grimaced remaining silent.

"You didn't really expect them to have aspirins, did you?" he whispered in a conspiratorial voice.

"What do you mean?"

"You wanted assurance that we, you, all of us, are all in pain and that no aspirin can cure it. This is local pain, man, that the white man's medicine can't cure."

"I've seen you a lot at Sukuna Park," Jiuta said for want of something to say. He didn't say that he had observed him staring at the fountain expecting to be rejuvenated by the powerful jets of water shooting upwards to the heavens.

"You're like me. You feel the pain but it's inside," he pointed to his head, "and no white man's aspirin can take it away. We're all here because we are confused."

Jiuta didn't hear the rest of this monologue. The pain and his weakness overwhelmed him.

When next he looked up, he was lying in a hospital bed.

They had carried him to this bed and forgotten him. The hospital was like a frail body in the throes of death. As people were deliberately shot or caught in the crossfire of rebels and government soldiers they were rushed in. Some people had walked around dazed and were run down by ner-vous drivers too frightened to swerve. Few doctors were left. Many remained in their barricaded homes. People were brought in wounded and some were wheeled out dead. It was an endless process. Meanwhile those in the various wards were often neglected. There were simply few doctors to attend to them.

The pain came and went. All around him, sick people lay too exhausted to move or groan. Next to him a middle aged man with a pot-belly breathed with difficulty.

Because Jiuta lapsed into unconsciousness at odd times he missed meals. He woke up at nights only to be confronted by orderlies walking by the beds checking to find lifeless bodies for the morgue. Once he felt cold, hard hands hold him. He slapped the hands crying, "I'm still alive. Don't take me."

"We are not that dumb," they told him. "We will only take you when you are cold and lifeless. We were just checking."

"How come your hands are cold? Are you sure you're not ghosts?" He was so exhausted that he was not even sure whether all this was happening in reality or in his dreams.

It got to the stage where he was frightened to go to sleep. He would wake up suddenly and imagine orderlies creeping up on him to take him to the morgue. "I'm still alive. I'm not dead. Don't bury me," he would scream in his sleep. It got worse when once he woke up and saw that the middle-aged man next to him was no longer breathing. There was a look of relief on his exhausted face.

It occurred to him in his blurred mind that his pain was caused by the clothes he had taken from the looted city. Suddenly it made sense. He had claimed the "white man's cargo" and in the process had inherited its convoluted spirit. He needed to exorcise himself of its consuming dynamism.

Abruptly he took off his Reebok rugby jumper and Puma cargo pants. He seemed to feel better.

One morning he was taken to the dentist. The Filipino dentist looked kindly at him. He pulled out Jiuta's rotting teeth smelling of pus and gave him some tablets.

Still weak from not eating well and from sleep-lessness, he wrapped himself in one of the hospital bed sheets and staggered out of the hospital.

He felt relieved that he had taken off everything he had stolen. He was now left with his underwear and vest. He resolved to return the hospital bed sheet afterwards.

Out on the pavement he staggered on to the bus stand. There was a puddle of water by a pothole. He rushed over and searched frantically for his reflection. He had imagined that in his pain, his reflection had been taken away as his punishment.

He was anxious to see the fire burning in his eyes and breathed a sigh of relief.

The Television Footage

Joseph Veramu

I am always haunted by that old television footage of the coup in 2000 when mobs of Fijians having heard that the businessman with the Kojak haircut had initiated a civilian coup, rampaged through the streets of Suva.

There is a terrifying moment in the footage when about forty Fijians with ages ranging from twenty to fifty run near the Holiday Inn hitting anything non-Fijian that moved. You can see their eyes flash with hatred and their teeth bared in anger. In that single defining moment you come face to face with the naked reality of racism. And then a miracle happens in that television footage.

As the patriotic crowd comes close to an Indian man with their fists raised, a simple Fijian waiter in his light blue sulu, white shirt and blue sash around his waist runs out and covers his body over the Indian so that in those terrible moments, the blows rain down on him. It is a poignant act of courage. You can hear the shouts commanding him to move away from the dosi, so he can get what he deserves. The waiter torn between the unbearable pain of the blows raining down on him and the persuasive words to move away and not take the blow meant for the Indian maintains his stance.

Some of the onlookers digest this scene. A middle aged Fijian woman screams indignantly, "Sa rauta. This is madness. You should be ashamed of yourselves." Other Fijians pluck up courage and add their voices of protest.

As suddenly as it starts, the blows stop as the mob comes to its senses and the rabble disperse stunned that though they are God-fearing people, they have allowed themselves to be consumed by the hatred of nationalism in this one moment of madness.

I look closely at the waiter in great pain hold the hand of the Indian man and pull him up. I gasp as the waiter's familiar face comes into close focus on the screen.

Epeli Vuetiviti had been an average student at the village school where I taught Social Science in Forms 1 and 2 about eight years ago. He did not do very well academically mainly because he was not fully proficient in English, our national language.

Many curricular reforms were being introduced. There was this growing emphasis on lessons being of relevance to students in their lives outside the classroom. This was a departure from the previous emphasis on students memorising and cramming lessons for external exam purposes. The only merit in this type of learning was that students were able to pass external exams. In terms of making learners better individuals, the rote learning was absolutely worthless.

It is often the case that when someone does something noteworthy in life that we turn to conjecture to determine why the protagonist acted the way she did. We analyse the person's upbringing and education and we highlight the role we have played in shaping the person. Deep down in our hearts we are often insecure in the work that we do. A person's noble deeds reaffirm us to our vocation. It also reassures us that our work has been honourable. At the same time, we also have the feeling, sometimes remorseful, that we did not do enough to emulate the protagonist.

A number of factors come into play in looking at Epeli's life. His traditional upbringing imbued him with the wisdom of life. He also benefited from the school reforms taking place while he was a student. In this, the holistic type of learning he underwent was beneficial. This was shown later in his life where his actions reflected those universal values we like to espouse but are sometimes reluctant to practice in the difficult moments that life sometimes thrusts us into.

My contributions to Epeli's life was in Social Science. Many of the topics encouraged students to adopt the universal values espoused by the

United Nations. One of the units Epeli seemed to like was "Resolving Conflicts." To supplement the official text book, I had used Frank Hoare's booklet entitled "Intercultural Exercises for Schools in Fiji." Hoare had exhorted teachers to challenge the prejudices of students. Students were to share their positive and stereotyped beliefs about other people. This would enable them to confront their prejudiced views and take action to change them. I used his book extensively and involved students in role-plays, case studies, songs and group discus-sions to help them resolve personal and commun-ity conflicts in multicultural societies like Fiji.

Epeli Vuetiviti was one of fifty students in my rural classroom. He participated in my classes when encouraged though I was never quite sure whether this was due mainly to his wanting to please me or whether it was out of a genuine desire to learn about harmonious inter-actions in the world outside of the classroom.

After two years in this school, I won a scholarship to study at the national university. To be honest, I was getting bored and frustrated with the job I was doing. Then, I was not sure whether the education being offered to these students was worthwhile. This was because the school invariably presented a global agenda and often ignored the dynamic culture of the students.

I never saw nor heard from Epeli in the ensuing years. He must have completed his studies at the village school and later passed the Fiji Junior External Exam. Like many other young rural Fijians drifting to the cities, he must have taken his chance and come to Suva.

Suddenly seeing Epeli in his waiters uniform single-handedly protecting the Indian man from the violent mob vindicated the education I and other teachers had provided him at the village school.

I close my eyes and once more digest the scene from the television footage.

The nagging doubts suddenly return. Epeli had taught me an important lesson. We allowed the coup to consume us with hatred because we were unwilling to stand up and make a difference. And here I have talked about educating Epeli but this sounds hollow because I have not been willing to lay down my life for a fellowman.

Epeli had shown the way in a simple and effective manner.

Storyteller and East Timor

Andre Vltchek

excerpted from Point of No Return

I stood on the deck of Pelni, an Indonesian ocean liner leaving Dili, East Timor. It was almost dark. High waves were sending foam over the deck. I kept cleaning my glasses.

A woman looked my way, standing motionless, close to the railing. Her husband was washing his feet, ready to enter a small Muslim praying room. I looked back at her, unable to determine where she was from.

I felt lucky to be alive; to be on this ship which was taking me away from East Timor. I carried several used rolls of film in my small equipment bag, two Leicas and five pairs of dirty underwear.

I had seen enough; more than I had expected to see and I felt exhausted, outraged, paralyzed. I had to think about what I had witnessed, I had to think how to begin to write the story, but my brain was refusing to function. I felt empty and sick.

The woman was wearing a long Javanese dress, falling almost to her feet. Her fingers were long and slender, ink-black hair covered her shoulders.

I had no idea why she was looking at me with those huge black eyes. There was no smile on her lips, no expression of friendliness. It was as if she were waiting for something, as if she were trying to read something written on my face.

A few minutes later her husband went to pray. He said nothing to her; he just left her standing on the deck, alone.

Almost immediately, she approached me.

"You saw…?"

"I don't understand," I said.

"You saw it?"

"Your husband is an official," I said. "He is from Java, isn't he?"

"Yes," she said. "Don't judge me, please. You don't know anything."

"Where are you from?"

"From here. From Dili."

"I enjoyed my visit very much," I said. "Wonderful place. Very beautiful scenery and friendly people."

"Stop it!" she screamed, but the sound of the waves muted her voice. "Don't torture me, please. You saw everything. You know…"

"What do you want from me?" I asked.

"Nothing. I just want you to tell the truth. To say what you saw."

"Nobody cares," I said. "Nobody gives a damn."

"Nobody?"

"I don't know. A few people, maybe."

"But you care…. You came here," she whispered, desperately.

"Yes," I said. "But it doesn't count. I go to many places. Nobody has any influence on me, but in turn, I have no influence on anybody."

"But you have to…"

"You speak good English," I said.

"Thank you. I studied English for years. I wanted to leave. But that doesn't matter. You saw…"

"Yes," I said. "They raped the whole village; from children to grandmothers. They carved obscenities into women's bodies; with the knives. They burned their clitoris with cigarette butts. They cut off ears from several men; they killed others. Just for fun. Should I go on? It gets worse."

"I know all this," she said. "One third of the East Timorese are dead. Since the invasion."

"That's about the correct estimate."

"They don't know it in Java."

"They don't?" I said. "They prefer not to know. Maybe they don't know anything about 1965 and about Aceh and Papua and hell knows what."

"They pray," she nodded toward the room in which her husband disappeared. "They pray because they are scared. Because otherwise the whole nation would have to howl in horror from its own guilt. They need it to be blasted loud, every day, for hours, so they can't hear their own hearts. They need it to overpower their own consciousness. Their children are being orphaned by the millions; their children prostitute themselves and beg. Their cities are like purgatories, but they still don't see. They prefer not to see. They are deaf and mute."

"He is going to come out, soon. He will not be happy to see you talking to me."

"Yes," she said. "I will find you later."

"It may not be wise."

"I have to."

She moved away. I sat on the bench, opening another pack of salty crackers. The bench had to be my home for two days. The ship was sailing to Alor and than to Maumere in Flores. All the private cabins were taken by government officials. The alternative would be one of the overcrowded, dark, communal rooms, packed with broken chairs, people and plastic bags. I had tried to enter one, but was immediately repelled by a powerful stench. It smelled like the entire modern Indonesia – of unwashed bodies, repulsive spicy food, dirt, illness and decay. I preferred to stay on deck, ready to be exposed to the strong wind and waves, but also to fresh air.

I had a ten pack of salty crackers and five liters of bottled water to keep me company. And I still had two packs of cigarettes left in my bag.

Her husband appeared. He said nothing; just nodded at her and she followed him upstairs, a few steps behind, to one of the cabins. She never looked back at me.

As the lights from the shore disappeared, total darkness embraced the ship. The sky was overcast and I saw no stars and no moon above us. The waves were increasing in size, but I felt fine, just tired and still absolutely empty.

Somebody was throwing up from the upper deck. Puke was carried by the wind and parts of it hit my face. I poured some water over my head.

People kept coming.

"Hey mister! Where are you from? Hey, how much money you make? Where are you going? Indonesia, bagus!?"

"Bagus!" I would respond. Then some puke from above hit my face again. Men laughed. They came to piss on the deck; the toilets had covered an entire floor below deck with urine and excrement up to the ankles. "Bagus!" I would repeat.

She came back later, almost at midnight.

"He is asleep," she said. "I don't have much time. He sometimes wakes up."

I said nothing.

"Do you scorn me?"

"No," I said. "For heaven's sake, of course I don't."

"I scorn myself, sometimes. But most of the time I am dreaming about being strong enough to kill him. It helps."

"I understand," I said. "How many years have you been married?"

"I don't remember. I don't want to remember. Five years, maybe. Or maybe longer. He took me when I was nineteen."

"Took you?"

"Yes. One day I came back to East Timor from Bandung. I was studying there, at the university. I stayed in my house for two weeks.

They raided our house, very late at night. They killed my older brother and they took away my sister. Then he came back, for me. He had his way with me for two days and three nights. He never shared me with the others. He did things to me, you know…. I don't want to say it…. Then he said I would soon marry him. I said I would kill myself but he replied that if I did, who knew what would happen to my mother and my younger brother."

"I'm sorry," I said.

"Then I had to convert. He took me to Java. I began to live with his family; he is hardly at home. They torture me, you know…. Not my body, but they still do, in their own way. I have two children."

"Two children…" I repeated.

"I wish they would die," she said. "They are his children, not mine."

"Damn," I said. I gave her my card. "Run away," I said.

"There is no place to run," she said. "This is Indonesia. If you run away and you can't return to your own home, you end up as a prostitute or maid, or both. If you are lucky."

"I'll try," I said. "I will try to write, I promise. It's true that nobody cares, but I'll really try."

"Thank you," she said.

"I wish I could do more."

"You can't."

"Do you have a passport?"

"No. I have nothing. I'm just his slave."

"Damn," I said. "I really hate this country."

"So do I," she said. "But I have never been anywhere else. Almost no one from here has been anywhere else. And those who travel are already programmed. They see but they pretend that they don't see. They teach them how to be proud to be Indonesians. Instead of telling us how it is outside, they come back and say that they are happy to be back in this country. We never learn anything from them. But I hope there is a world outside. And I hope I will see it one day. And I will never come back, no matter what. They killed so many people. There are so many people who are still alive but dead inside."

"You will see it; you will see the world outside," I said. "But maybe it's not as pretty as you imagine."

"But it has to be better than this…"

"Yes," I said. "Almost anything is better."

"I knew it."

"And one day, your country will be free."

"I have almost nobody left, there. Please tell them, please tell the world outside what they have done to us."

"I will," I said. "I swear I will. I will always remember you."

I was too exhausted after not sleeping for two nights. I wasn't sure what I was saying, but I kept speaking, anyway.

She made a cross with her fingers before leaving me. "May Jesus protect you," she said. I followed her with my eyes. I wasn't sure how much more of this I could take. She had passed her pain to me and now I had to carry it inside; I had to live with it for the rest of my life. With her pain and with the pain of so many others.

I ran after her, I stopped her, I took her hand, I pressed her with all the strength against me, I felt every inch of her fragile body responding, I begged her silently for forgiveness. I was apologizing for my country which had allowed this to happen, for humanity and for all of us, storytellers, who had failed her as well as those countless millions like her, all over the world.

The Weekly Globe

Andre Vltchek

excerpted from Point of No Return

Green entered Berry's almost immediately after our drinks arrived – a double Stoli straight for myself and a regular Stoli with cranberry juice on the rocks for Cathy, the woman at the bar beside me. Green was wearing a dark, funereal looking suit and a yellow power tie with blue squares. Green was an impressive looking man – tall and fat. It was still cold in New York but he was sweating.

"Am I late?" he barked.

"It doesn't matter," I said.

He gave me a big hug, almost crushing my bones in his enormous bear-size paws.

"Who's that whore?" he whispered in my ear.

"Cathy," I whispered back. "Cathy," I said loudly introducing her to Green. "And this is Green, Chief Editor of The Weekly Globe."

"Nice meeting you, lady," said Green, opting for politeness, after some hesitation.

"Well, do you have a first name?" smiled Cathy, obviously impressed and interested, checking him out from head to toe.

"He does," I replied instead. "But it's of no importance. He is simply Green, it's what everybody calls him."

Green thought this was funny. He started to laugh and it was too loud and slightly out of place. Cathy did not seem to mind. She was obviously used to corporate schmucks and Green was still more tolerable than most of them, no matter what.

We left Cathy at the bar and moved to a small round table, Green ordering a double single malt, while I stuck to the double Stoli with no ice, straight.

"The strategic editorial meeting was a failure," started Green, taking off his cashmere coat, throwing it on the next chair, breathing heavily. "I know it, you know it, there is no secret that we were not able to understand each other. We were not even able to communicate intelligibly."

I lit up my cigarette, waiting. Smoking was out of date, too, but I didn't care. I was a New Yorker, but an exiled New Yorker. That came with some privileges.

"I invited the best of you. Moretti came, you came, Joanne, Keensley, Hide. You all came here and I am grateful. You even agreed to talk to me," he said with a dose of sarcasm and then he paused, sipping his drink. "The only thing is that I understood almost nothing that you were saying. It is obvious that the foreign section of The Weekly Globe is falling apart. I've thought about replacing you; all of you. I've thought about relocating you. The only problem is that I know I can't get anybody better. Maybe things are much more complicated and the problem is not you."

"Well…"

"Well what?"

"Where is the problem?"

"I don't know," Green sounded defeated.

"Are sales down?" I asked.

"No. It's just…. I smell some disaster. I smell shit; some problem coming our way."

This was prior to 9-11.

"Why do you think there is a problem? Why do you think that the foreign section is falling apart?"

"I'm not sure about anything," sighed Green. "Something strange is going on. Something I don't seem to understand. Before, things were working fairly well. The magazine had been receiving legible, intelligent reports from its field offices. All of you were clear and concrete. Things were under control. Under my control. Under the control of reason. Then something happened. Your reports have become…. What's the word?"

"Abstract?"

"That's exactly it. Thank you! They have become abstract."

"When?"

"Are you asking me?" He finished his drink. "I don't remember exactly when, but it was a gradual process. Now things are definitely confused. Almost all of you are ignoring the basic facts that our magazine is not a literary or philosophical club. It's supposed to inform. It's supposed to inform people who haven't got the slightest idea about what's going on in this world and really don't give a shit about it. They read articles about foreign countries because that's what they saw their fathers do and also because they don't want to look like total assholes. They definitely don't read them in order to complicate their lives or, God forbid, in order to think. They don't want to become intellectuals. They want to be left alone, gently reassured that their uncomplicated vision of the world is correct. Eventually they want to learn one or two smart phrases so they can impress their boss, their wife or secretary."

"Go ahead," I said. He was surprisingly making some sense.

Green wiped sweat off his forehead. He ordered more booze.

"Look, I myself don't particularly like what I'm saying, but somebody has to be honest or we'll all lose our jobs or run The Weekly Globe into the ground. It would be a pity, it's becoming one of New York's institutions. So let me put it this way: you all have lost contact with your readers. You have forgotten who your readers are. You are not writing for Le Monde Diplomatique, your readers have never heard of the New Left Review. You are writing for a large American magazine that provides middle class men and women with information. Many of them are simple folks, Forrest Gumps, and you may be tempted to call them uneducated pricks, but every week they pay $4.95 per issue and thanks to them we are all getting our fat salaries, plane tickets and per diems. But if you keep writing your abstract artworks, your useless masterpieces, they'll finally turn to the Sports Section of some tabloid and we will all be fucked. They'll read the Help Wanted, instead. They'll study horoscopes. You'll not educate them, it's too late for them, you'll just lose them altogether. They don't understand what you are talking about. You know that most people in this country don't like intellectuals. Intellectuals have beards and some of them burn flags. They don't watch the same films as other people do. They have friends who are fags and women's rights activists. Many intellectuals don't even like sports and their women refuse to watch soaps in the afternoon. They don't go to church. They are outsiders. They are snobs. They have different accents and some of them even speak French. Many of them weren't born in this country. American people don't like snobs and they don't like intellectuals, damn it."

Green was sweating, getting excited, all messed up. Cathy was still sitting at the bar, her legs crossed. She was looking in our direction. I smiled at her, just to relax the atmosphere and she let one of her shoes slide to her toes. Good move, I thought. A pity that Green had lost all his interest in the surrounding world. He ordered more drinks. He was getting into it. Into analyzing and into drinking.

"I respect your opinions. That's why I invited you all here. And I'm going to meet you, one by one and I am not gonna let you go before you explain to me what is really happening."

"I don't know more than what you do," I said.

"You do know more," said Green. "Something is happening. Something scary. Something that justifies your total indifference to our readers. Something I still don't understand."

"Things have become more complex," I tried.

"I am not an asshole," Green informed me. "I

know that the situation is confusing. We don't have many enemies, anymore. We have mostly friends. Friends that don't like us. Ones we can't trust. We have Saudi friends, for instance – that's extremely confusing. Simple Joe doesn't like many of our friends, either. He despises the French and Japanese, partly because he knows that the French and Japanese despise him – simple Joe. He thinks it takes five Poles to screw in a light bulb, but Poland is now in NATO. Many Americans look down at Latinos, they are afraid of Asians, and absolutely refuse to note the existence of Africa. They think that Saudis ride camels and put bed sheets over the heads of their women. Moretti tried to explain everything in one of his editorials. From Moscow. Eventually he just hit the bottle. He is falling apart from all that friendship. Our Moscow office is turning into a bordello, Russian secretaries there into single mothers. He hired two new typists he doesn't need; from his own salary. He has his 'zapois,' whatever it means. Still, he manages to write well. The only problem is that nobody wants to read his dispatches."

"You didn't tell him any of this today," I said.

"And what the hell should I tell him? That he writes well, maybe too well for this magazine?"

Green was getting drunk. Not pissed drunk, but drunk all right.

"Look," he said. "I hate this place. It feels like we're in London or Toronto. I feel like they'll kick us out before 11 p.m. I have a car parked outside. Let's get out of here. Let's go to some real place. Let's go to some bar where we can find normal people. Somewhere in Queens or in Brooklyn."

"Aren't we going to take a plane there?" I asked.

"Again! Snobbism. Scorn for the simple reader. Don't you want to see him – your flesh and blood reader? People who come here read The Economist and the New York Review of Books. Let's see a real American man, a hard working prick who pays for the booze that we are now drinking."

"All right," I said. "Let's see him."

"Or her," added Green, suddenly being politically correct.

There was no escape.

"And let's take the whore."

"Whore?"

"What's her face?" he pointed his fat and large, sausage-like finger toward the relatively well preserved woman in her forties.

"Her name is Cathy," I reminded him.

"Let's take Cathy," he said. "I bet she is at least a Deputy District Attorney, anyway. Let's go."

"How did you know?" She had obviously overheard part of our conversation. "I work for the DA's office."

"Professionalism," said Green. "Let's go."

"Where?" she asked with evident hope in her voice. Her feet in black stockings were well inside her shoes again. She quickly gathered her belongings, left the tip on the bar and approached Green.

"We are driving to some low class pub in Williamsburg," explained Green.

"We are going to search for our readers so this young writer can rediscover America after a long leave of absence."

"Why don't we stay in Soho?" she wondered. "Or why don't we go to the East Village? Williams-burg is getting posh, anyway."

"No," said Green. "We have to go to some place where a hard working American man sits down at some obscure drinking establishment in order to calm his sorrows, quench his thirst and share his simple vision of the world with his friends after a long day of intensive labor."

"Sounds like a Soviet poster from the 1930's," I muttered.

"Maybe I shouldn't," sighed Cathy.

"You definitely shouldn't," I advised.

"But you will," said Green, triumphantly.

We crossed Manhattan Bridge and drove through several blocks of a depressing area of warehouses until we hit one of the decently lit neighborhoods of newly-posh Williamsburg.

It was there, waiting for us on one of the side streets: a macho Polish blue collar bar lit-up by an old fashioned blue neon light. A large photograph of the son-of-a-Bush surrounded by bottles of hard liquor, his father hanging right next to him. There was Ronald Reagan, the Pope and Lech Walesa decorating other walls, together with faded tourist posters of Krakow and the Black Madonna from Czestochowa. Crossed Polish and American flags stuck out from an empty flower pot.

Draft beer of extremely dubious quality was served in enormous plastic cups called "canisters." Old hits of Bruce Springsteen flew from the shiny jukebox while several members of the right wing proletariat consumed a toxic looking liquid from small glasses.

"I grew up in places like this," said Green, tears in his eyes. "And these are our people. Our readers, simple folks…"

"Soil of the nation," I added between my teeth.

"Baboons," whispered Cathy, scared.

The owner of the place did not like us from the beginning. He did not like the silver Saab we parked right in front of the bar, he could not stand Cathy's elegant outfit and he did not like the way Green and I were drunk simply because we were drunk in different way than the other patrons of the bar. He did not bother to hide his aversion, but to his credit, at first he tried to be professional and reasonably civil while dealing with us. He immediately filled two canisters with beer.

"Stoli with cranberry juice," ordered Cathy.

"No Soviet shit here, lady. Wyborowa. Polish," he barked.

"Wyborowa, Polish. With cranberry juice," blushed Cathy. "On the rocks, please."

"Jim Bean. Triple. Two," ordered Green.

Damn, I thought. We drank.

"Well," said Green. "Now you'll tell me."

"There is nothing to tell."

"There is. What is possessing all of you? What is happening to the world?" He had started to resemble a maniac. "Is there going to be a war? Is there something I should know? Are we all gonna get fucked?!"

"No major war," I tried to sound reassuring. "Local conflicts, yes. A few thousand deaths, may-be ten thousand. Their deaths, not ours. Mainly in Africa, Asia and Latin America. Nothing major. Maybe. We can hope."

"What about the Japanese?" hissed Green. "They think we are brain-dead. Today I read some statistics: over 60 percent of Japs don't think we are good friends and surely believe we are assholes. What if they talk to the Chinese? And how do we know they are not talking to the Chinese right now? And what if the Chinese confirm that we are assholes? Then what? They make better cars and CD players, their children have better scores, their buildings are already higher than ours. What will happen if they realize that they don't have to kiss our ass, anymore? What if they stop financing our debt?"

"They won't realize it too soon," I said. "They will realize it eventually but not so soon. And even after they realize it, they'll need us to buy their goods."

"And what about Mahathir's trip to Osaka? Did you hear about it? He said to the Japanese: Be our leaders! Be the leaders of Asia! Help us get rid of those fucks who are pushing their low Western culture through our refined Asian throats."

"He didn't say it that way," I smiled.

"He did. In his own way. Malaysian way. Asian way."

I finished my whisky. The beer tasted awful.

"I think I know what you are all thinking. You think the allies will fail us. And soon after, people of the poor nations will take their knives, sticks and hammers and come to smash our heads."

"Then I'll move to Yucatan," said Cathy. "Men in New York are sissies, anyway. A beauty over forty can't find a husband. What husband, she can't even get laid."

"They will finally get us, won't they? They'll come here, they'll migrate, infiltrate the entire country," insisted Green. "They will maybe even fly some shit into the World Trade Center!"

Bruce Springsteen howled something about an unidentified woman who had been shot point-blank, right between her eyes, while members of the proletariat attentively listened, sucking on their deadly poisons.

"I don't know," I said.

"It's all right with you, since you have friends among them. You have friends all over the world. But what will happen to people like me?"

"They won't get to the city for a while," commented Cathy. "They will first infiltrate the suburbs. In fact they may never get here. What would they do here? Hit Bloomingdales or go to the opera?"

"What are you talking about," screamed Green in disbelief. "They are already here! Don't you see them every morning as they crawl from the subway?"

"Who are they?" I asked.

"The ones we screwed," explained Green, starting to bite the skin around his nails. "The ones they – the Europeans screwed and we just finished. Countries where we established dictatorships and trained death squads, from which we have stolen raw materials and destroyed labor unions, forced down labor costs and ruined traditional agriculture. Countries where we helped to murder secular and progressive leaders while supporting religious fundamentalists, just so we could count on an obedient, brainwashed and scared population willing to work

for our companies for nothing. Not that I give a shit about all that crap, but I spoke to Moretti today…"

"That explains everything," I said.

"What?"

"Moretti is in 'zapoi,'"

"Right," confirmed Green. "He is in zapoi. What is zapoi, anyway?"

I sighed.

"Zapoi is a Russian word," I said. "It is untranslatable."

"Try," demanded Green. "Everything can be translated."

"Zapoi is when somewhere in Russia one man buys a bottle of vodka and goes to visit his friend. In his friend's house, there is one more bottle, already in the freezer. Well chilled, preferably. Some bread and pickles are waiting neatly on the kitchen table. They drink both bottles and later finish all the wine and beer they can find in the apartment. When they are done later with all the perfumes of the host's wife, they bribe the pharmacist and get some pure alcohol that can be easily mixed with water or juice. Eventually they get to the industrial alcohol or brake fluids that can be diluted…"

"Moretti just got out of zapoi," said Green.

"That's not surprising. Considering the circumstances and excessive friendliness of the environment," I said.

"Right," confirmed Green. "And Kinsley wrote his report. Did you read it?"

"Which one?"

"The one about Saudi Arabia…. Kinsley managed to get drunk in some tea room in Riyadh. Later he took the taxi, demanding it take him to the whorehouse served exclusively by Saudi women," screamed Green.

"No," I said.

"Yes," said Green.

"Did they kick him out of the country?"

"Oh yes. After he got kicked out, he wrote a long article, condemning Saudi society, condemning its royal family, its government and above all the way Saudis treat their women. He also predicted that there will be a massive attack against the United States, led by Saudi citizens. And since Saudis are our allies, he foresees a massive government cover-up. It looks like a Pulitzer Prize piece."

"Well," I hesitated.

"Anyway, I talked to your friend Gino Moretti. He was threatening me. He was scaring me. He told me that US involvement in Latin America will backfire. He gave me a lesson on greed and tequila. And PAN. He swore that the Argentinean economy will collapse and so will the Peruvian, Ecuadorian, Colombian, you name it. He threatened that the Bolivian poor will fight against the privatization of drinking water. He was trying to prove that Chile – undeniably a superstar on the bleak sky of South America – is still run like a feudal hamlet; by a handful of fascist families. He predicted that we'll sponsor a coup in Venezuela against Hugo Chavez and that we'll fail. He believes that we'll not be able to maintain control over Latin America for much longer."

"We always somehow managed," said Cathy. "Why not now? There is no reason why not now."

"There is," said Green gloomily. "Moretti says there is. The reason is that we are not thinking, anymore…"

"But we never were," Cathy smiled in amusement. "Nothing has changed."

"But they did. They definitely changed," whined Green. "They don't even like us, anymore."

"They never did. They never really liked us. Neither Latin Americans nor Asians."

"But now they read and write books about it!" concluded Green.

"Shit," said Cathy. "I didn't think about that."

Two more canisters of yellow foamless liquid landed on our table. Green was getting delirious and apocalyptic.

"You are supporting them, aren't you? You and Moretti and Joanne and even Hide."

"Who do you mean by *them*?"

"Never mind," sighed Green. "Do you think Moretti is Zapatista? Do you think he is paid by the Chinese government?"

"Green, are you losing your mind? You should switch to diet coke."

"Yes, I think I am. So what? And what if the Zapatistas have a point? What if FARC and MRTA have a point as well? What if your buddy Sub-Sub Felipe has a point? You see, I'm not excluding that possibility. I'm trying to be open minded. That's impressive, isn't it? Will it do me any good in the hour of final justice? Are they going to spare me when they arrive here? Tell me!"

I had to take a leak. I pissed, facing a Solidarity poster and an old photo of the central square of Gdansk. When I came back, Cathy was caressing Green's face. Green looked disturbed; he looked like an enormous, fat, ugly baby. Green was definitely the one who was rapidly falling apart.

"Don't worry so much," I said to him. "Things may look confusing but there is an order in every confusion. Everything may still stabilize."

"Nothing will get stabilized," said Green in a defeated voice. "I don't need novelists. I don't need poets. I don't even need scholars. I need dedicated reporters who can summarize, simplify, guide, explain and above all reassure our confused, lost, lonely, screwed and basically unhappy readers."

"Good speech," said Cathy.

"Thank you," he bowed.

We ordered more booze. Green was not done yet.

"You didn't read any poetry from me," I said.

"Not from any of the places where I've been working for The Weekly Globe."

"I am not talking about you," said Green. "All I am trying to say is that you or any of you shouldn't try to explain to them, to our readers, how things really work. They don't care. They don't want to know anything. Don't make their life too complicated. We are not a state college. They had a chance to learn things at school. Or on their own. They didn't. Fuck them, now! Give them what they want and they'll give us what we need: $4.95 a copy. Every week. And the more they read us, the more advertisers will pay for our lunches."

"Makes some sense." I tried not to be confrontational.

"Now back to the essence. I still think that you all know something that I don't. I feel panic when I read your pieces. I feel urgency. There is something there that I don't like at all. It's like you see some enormous shit coming our way and you don't want to share the knowledge with me…"

"We don't see anything special."

"Did we fuck up?"

"Who?"

"We. The West. Europe. This country. The planet."

"Of course."

"Did we fuck up no end?"

"Yes," I said. "But it's no news."

"Did we really entrust our fate to the lowest cast: to the merchants and sellers; to the upgraded market vendors? Did we send to internal exile people who still have some leftovers of brains? Did we convince the whole planet that greed is good and that in fact nothing other than greed matters?"

"All right," I said. "Is this a question or declaration?"

"Forget it," said Green." Did we employ religions, propaganda and mass media to spread our dogma?"

"Green…"

He wiped sweat from his forehead. Then he took a long and lonely swing from his canister.

"I am afraid of you," he admitted. "Of all of you. Of everything."

"You have no reason to be scared of us," I said, finishing my beer. "You can fire us. We can all be out of our jobs in no time."

"It wouldn't solve anything. It would make things even worse. I can't tell you exactly why, but it's how I feel."

"Look, forget about it. I think there are more immediate problems that we have to face right now. I think the owner is pissing in our beer," I said. I didn't mean to change the subject but the stuff we were drinking was rapidly decreasing in quality. It had also changed color, becoming lighter.

"He probably is," admitted Green. Then he screamed at the barkeep. "One Wyborowa with cranberry juice on the rocks and two beers. And please don't piss in our canisters, asshole."

The barkeep was not thrown off balance.

"Whom do you call an asshole, you fucked up Commie?" he thundered. It was obvious that he had been listening to our conversation for quite a while.

"Whom do you call Commie, you suburban prick?" yelled Green, smashing against the bar his Republican ID.

Suburban prick did not go down well with the right-wing proletariat. Until now, men were sitting silently, minding their booze and heavy thoughts. Now they stood up. These were not small men. No sissies here. The barkeep slowly approached Green, a bottle of Wild Turkey in his hand.

"Out of my place, you little guinea cocksuckers," he whispered to a total silence. "No fucking Castroites in this place!"

Cathy looked scared. She had never heard

such language even during the colorful EBTs. She whispered into my ear: "They'll gang-rape me. They'll kill both of you and then they'll enjoy my soft perfumed yuppie flesh."

Then Green stood up. Despite the size of the working class crew, he still looked enormous and imposing. "I said two beers and Wyborowa with cranberry juice on the rocks for the deputy DA person, whom you just called a little guinea cock sucker, dumb shit." He pointed his finger at Cathy. "I truly hope your immigration papers are in very good shape, assholes."

The effect of his short speech was great and immediate. Even the most militant workers sat down, not knowing what to do with their hands and eyes. Some slowly moved toward the door, accelerating as their foul breath met fresh air from the street.

"You bore," I said admiringly. "That was just another typical filthy little Republican trick."

"Give us a beer or we'll send you back to the Gulag," agreed Cathy, regaining her composure. "It's what you indirectly said to them. A clear blackmail. How politically incorrect you are, my love."

"Poland is not a gulag," protested Green. "Not anymore. It's our new ally, our great new friend, a member of NATO, an East European forerunner for membership in the EU, a country that is attracting foreign investment at an accelerated rate. The centerpiece of New Europe."

"In addition to that, I'm not a deputy DA," said Cathy, softening. "I only said I'm working for the DA's office."

"I know," said Green, feeling proud and big again. "I just wanted to protect you from..."

"He just wanted to protect you from our readers," I explained.

Beer arrived and so did the vodka. The color of the liquid had substantially improved. There was even foam on top of it. And no suspicious smell. It now even vaguely smelled like a beer. The look the barkeep gave us was full of subdued hate and servility and fear.

Green kissed Cathy's hand. Touching. Very touching, indeed. I had to shut up, confronted with such enormous proof of his gallantry.

We all finally adopted an optimistic approach toward the world. Green grudgingly accepted that there would be no major conflict in the foreseeable future, Japan would stick to its cars, shrinking economy, electronics and political scandals, China to economic growth, cheap clothes and toys while the Prime Minister of Malaysia would limit his anti-Western outbursts to private conversations over a nice cup of tea with the former Senior Minister Lee of Singapore. Poor people would wait too, choosing to die from starvation instead of destroying the greatness of Western civilization and its dominant role in the world based on the wise and democratic principals of free trade, open markets and globalization.

We paid the bill and then the Chief Editor of The Weekly Globe puked all over the sidewalk, and I decided to drive both of them to Green's condo. Cathy was fairly unconscious – I loaded both of them into the back seat and turned on the engine.

It was dark. A cold and light drizzle was falling on the windshield. I drove slowly through the empty streets. I took the 59th Street Bridge and crossed back to Manhattan. As I cruised over the bridge, I was aware of the fact that this was still one of the greatest views in the world and I felt shivers on my back and I had to swallow hard, because I still loved this city, enormous and proud and unplanned and fucked up but the greatest city on earth nevertheless, and I didn't want to come back now, not yet, but the city would always stay with me, deep inside, and I felt honored that I used to live here – no matter where I traveled, no matter where I lived, it was my city; indifferent, free of sentimentality and tenderness, an enormous brain and enormous engine, the result of millions of human efforts and of human daring and dreams, each dream different, almost every effort uncoordinated. It was the only truly cosmopolitan city on earth, embracing all cultures of the planet, not inviting anybody in and not trying to hold anybody who didn't want to stay, growing to the sky, leaving those who were weak behind, breaking them and crushing their bodies and their souls, but it had never claimed to be a kind and gentle city. It was brutal and honest and it knew how to appreciate greatness and how to scorn mediocrity and how to ignore weakness. My brain revolted against its almost non-existent social concepts and its lack of compassion. But as well as the city, I also scorned the emptiness of commonly accepted truths, admiring those who still knew how to dream, how to be insane and how to create, and to dare and to fly.

The Color of God
Andre Vltchek

excerpted from Point of No Return

1.

A Palestinian man stood in the middle of the dusty road of the Rafah refugee camp. Next to him stood his donkey. The man was old and so was the donkey.

The Israelis kept firing air-to-ground missiles from helicopters. The earth was shaking but the old man just stood in the middle of the road, blissfully indifferent to what was happening around him.

I liked his face. It was a good face, covered by wrinkles, not very expressive but good nevertheless. I took photographs of him and then we stood there, looking at each other, and I greeted him in English and in Arabic and he answered, but we both knew there could be no serious conversation between the two of us. We both belonged to different worlds. I had come to learn and to see and to write, while he was here to stay.

He was a gentle man – it was obvious from the way he treated his donkey...stroking its mane, resting the palm of his hand on the animal's neck. Donkeys in Gaza pulled old overloaded two-wheel carts and they looked exhausted, overworked and hungry. I thought that the old man did not use his donkey for anything in particular, it was simply his companion. It was easy to sell donkeys in Gaza – even old animals were put to work. But these two were used to each other: an old man and his beast.

We walked together for a few minutes. They were my silent guides of the Rafah refugee camp. We did not try to speak, but then the surroundings were explicit enough – there was no

155

need for words. We walked; and I took several rolls of film while they watched me working. We spotted small stalls on the sidewalk and I stopped and ordered two cups of tea. The weather was hot and humid.

When two Israeli helicopters approached from the North and flew above the camp, the old man just pointed toward the sky and smiled sadly. Even when new explosions thundered from the edge of town, he did not seem to be scared. Neither was his donkey.

I wanted to give him something as a token of my friendship, but there were only films, light meters, notebooks and pencils in the pockets of my jacket. I found a small photograph in my wallet and after some hesitation handed it to him. He looked at the image very attentively and then he smiled.

It was a picture of the ancient city of Nara in the autumn, full of powerful colors, serenity and peace. An eight-year-old Japanese girl was standing next to the entrance of a small shrine, holding the hand of her mother, a woman with a sad smile, long black hair and a beautiful but pale face. The girl was laughing at the camera, her long white scarf falling to one side, almost touching the ground.

"No war?" asked the old man.

"No," I said.

"Good," he said. "Good that it is still there…the world outside."

He held the picture between his fingers. His hands were rough.

"May Allah be with them." He was going to hand the picture back to me.

"Keep it," I said.

We shook hands, and I boarded the car, asking my driver to wait. I watched the man and his donkey. They were slowly disappearing into the crowd. Surrounded by hopelessness and despair, the old man and his animal seemed to be surprisingly calm. Both were too old to expect a better future. Both were stripped of the ability to desire and to dream. In the middle of the inti-

fada, in a time of hate and constant death, both the man and the animal seemed happy.

2.

Professor Kohn cleaned his glasses with the stained table cloth. He downed his beer and ordered another bottle. We were in a Yemeni dive, underground, somewhere in Jerusalem, after La Belle closed down at midnight. Tonight there were no women accompanying Kohn. As far as I could remember, this was the first time he had come alone.

"What color is God?" he asked.

I had no clue. I had never met God and I had no idea whether he planned to meet me. I had never given a thought to what color he might be. Or to whether he had any color. I had no idea even whether he existed or not.

"Does he have a color?" I wondered. "He could be as colorless as he is shapeless."

"Blue," said Kohn. "He may be blue, or he may be green. What if he is blue?"

"I don't know," I said. "That would be quite agreeable. Blue is not bad."

The Yemeni dive consisted of several tables and wet walls. It was an illegal gambling den; one of those places where Kohn liked to conclude his excessive drinking escapades. It was hot and humid, smoky and loud.

"They are killing each other again, because of God," continued Kohn. "As they have been killing each other for centuries and millennia. Christians killing pagans, Muslims killing North Africans, then Christians killing Muslims and Muslims killing Christians. Later Hindus killing Muslims and Muslims killing Hindus, while Christians killed everybody they could find on their path. Then Muslims killing Muslims: Shiites killing Sunnis and vice versa. Catholics killing Protestants and vice versa. Catholics and Protestants killing Jews. Jews killing Muslims and Muslims killing infidels."

"It doesn't seem that Jews are killing now because of God," I suggested.

"They are. You bet they are. Maybe not because of their own God, but because they don't like the way others see him."

"Or her," I added.

"Exactly. Or her. There is hardly any war that isn't fought on behalf of God. Anyway, I would like to ask them if they know what color he may be. They are all convinced that they know him, can identify the one through whom he spoke. But they don't even know his color. That's strange."

"Very strange," I agreed, drinking my watered-down *uzo*.

"I am wondering how can he stand it – all that killing in his name. Takes a stomach, doesn't it? The Nazis used to say *'Gott mit uns'* before butchering half of Europe. Before dropping their idiotic smart bombs, American leaders never forget their 'God Bless America.' You know what Pakistanis do when they are firing shells at Indian positions? Instead of 'Fire!' they scream 'God is great!' And then 'pah!'"

I looked around. A young woman with heavy gold bracelets was serving colorful food. Tourist posters depicting the Sinai desert hung on the walls. Fading paint on the ceiling.

"Kohn," I said. "I've had enough. I have to go back to my hotel. I have to cover that mess outside, tomorrow."

"So what will you write about this time?" he asked.

"I don't know. Whatever comes my way. Whatever happens."

"Whatever you write about, don't ever forget that none of them knows anything significant. They all pretend that they know…"

"Kohn," I said, exhausted. "They just want their land back."

"That part is probably true," he admitted. "And they should get it back. But they should want it in the name of simple justice, not in the name of something about which they don't even know the color."

3.

I had no desire to be here. Five years ago I would have gone to any place on earth, as long as there was something worth writing about. Now I had become picky. Wars were repetitive, after all, and so was the suffering of people who had to live through them. I was getting profoundly bored with wars. I had written and reported from every corner of the globe for more than ten years. I had written books. Put together documentaries. Nothing changed. The same outbursts of insane violence, the same burned houses, bombed cities, women in tears kneeling in the middle of devastated streets, hospitals out of medicine and blood and bandages.

As I was crossing the Rafah border to the Egyptian Sinai, I tried not to look at the depressing Israeli and Egyptian watchtowers and high voltage electric wires. The new Gaza airport had been closed because of the uprising, and my airplane ticket to Cairo was now worth nothing more than the paper on which it was printed.

I bribed the driver of a tourist bus loaded with frightened Japanese tourists to secure a smoking seat in the first row, and as the bus moved, I watched with profound indifference the straight road ahead, cutting through monotonous dunes of the Sinai Desert.

I tried to recall recent events.

Two days earlier, right after I had left Kohn, I watched Israeli soldiers regrouping on the square next to the Wailing Wall. It was late at night. Thirty of them formed a circle, receiving last orders from their commander who happened to be a young and pretty girl in her early twenties.

Sounds of gunfire were coming clearly from the other side of the wall, from the Muslim part, from which the illuminated dome of the Temple of the Rock penetrated a dark and cloudless sky over the city of Jerusalem.

The Israeli soldiers were young and some of them were scared. I saw one of them cover his nose with his hand and there was blood running between his fingers. His friends noticed and offered water from their bottles and patted his back, saying something encouraging in Hebrew that I could not understand.

I took several photographs of the soldiers, of police vans that blocked all entrances to the square, of the mosque behind the wall, and finally of the girl commander. I took her picture when the wind picked up her dark hair, fully uncovering her face and she smiled and I lowered my camera and we looked at each other for a few seconds. We were standing in the middle of the deserted square, in the middle of the Holy City of Jerusalem, right in front of the Wailing Wall. There were green lights illuminating the Temple of the Rock and the moon and the stars above looked almost unreal and then I heard shots again, coming from the other side. I liked the girl and she smiled at me, but then she lowered her eyes and raised them again, but this time she looked straight ahead, at her men who stood around her as she said something in Hebrew, that harsh and beautiful language I had always wanted to comprehend, and the men formed ranks and walked away toward the bridge, toward the passage leading to the Temple of the Rock, toward the gunshots, the sporadic explosions and screams. I followed them with my eyes until they were gone.

I looked around and the Muslim temple was still there and so was the Jewish wall. The Israeli girl soldier with black hair falling on her uniform was gone. I lit up a cigarette and thought about her for a while, about her firm breasts that I could sense under her blouse. I tried to imagine how she would look when she wore light summer sandals instead of heavy boots.

I felt sad, imagining that she might be getting screwed while I was lying on my bed reading Celine, but I had no intentions of going there, of going to the other side. I'd had them all up to here and I had seen all of it so many times that I really had no curiosity left, tonight. They would be hiding behind several corners next to the Temple of the Rock, shooting rubber-coated bullets into a crowd of rock-throwing Palestinians. Once in a while they would lose their temper and shoot real bullets and there would be blood on the cobblestones.

I walked through the deserted old city toward Dan Gate and Jaffa Street, passing dark and narrow alleys and closed doors of shops. She'd had beautiful eyes but then many girls in the world had beautiful eyes – I wondered whether women's feet also stink when they are squeezed for ten hours in heavy military boots. I wondered whether she was scared, whether she had doubts, whether she felt sorrow. I hoped that night that she would not get killed. I hoped she would not kill that night.

The next day at four o'clock in the afternoon Israeli helicopters flew over Erez Checkpoint, spraying the main highway of Gaza with bullets and rockets, hitting cars and destroying the dilapidated dwellings of refugees. The Strip exploded in massive spontaneous protests and there was fighting right next to the road and Palestinian ambulances rushed through the abandoned streets of Gaza City, their sirens howling, wheels raising dust.

I spent the entire morning in the burning center of Hebron on the West Bank, then crossed at Erez Checkpoint to the Strip early in the afternoon. Suddenly it was here again: one of the most hopeless places on earth, that filthy and dusty concentration of human misery – Gaza City.

I took photographs of the barricades, of fires and helicopters and then of wounded men being carried to ambulances. In just one hour my shoes and jeans were covered by dust and my face was sweaty and burned, and I had to clean my camera lenses and glasses every ten minutes.

The headquarters of the UNRWA was empty, almost everybody was frantically working in the field. I went straight to Shifa Hospital.

A silent crowd of Palestinians stood in front of the main gate – mostly young women and old men – and I pushed my way to the emergency room, passing by countless volunteers, nurses and doctors, changing films as I went, changing lenses and attaching the flash gun, still sweating and swearing in the devilish heat.

I bumped into stretchers covered with blood;

blood on the floor tiles, on walls, everywhere. I heard someone screaming and I went straight to the surgery room and there was a Palestinian man on the bed, his face twisted by pain, naked and hairy and wounded in the stomach. Next to him, separated by the plastic curtain howled another man, his penis erect and blue, dark blue and red, and his balls looking crushed and two doctors covering it all with medicine because this was where the man had been hit by rubber bullets, and then they injected something into his arm but he kept screaming and four male nurses had to pin him down while somebody pushed me inside and yelled: "Take pictures of this – take pictures of what they are doing to our people," and I took some twenty photos, but only of the man's face and then I took the entire roll of film of another man behind the curtain covered by blood and of exhausted faces of doctors and nurses and of all the mess on the floor and on the walls, everywhere.

Every few minutes ambulances brought new patients to the emergency room, some with gunshot wounds, some burned, some already dead.

I had to get out of the hospital because the stench and heat were unbearable and I thought it would almost be better to work on the road between Erez and Rafah, where the real fighting had erupted, but even there I felt no breeze and the air was heavy and Israeli pilots seemed not to give a shit about anything, shooting at just about anything that moved on the ground while the soldiers began to use live ammunition.

I wrote my report at midnight in a bizarre, posh beach hotel.

I sat alone at the table overlooking the sea, ready to have a late dinner, but when the food arrived I had no desire to eat. My head was heavy, I felt dehydrated and exhausted. I had to get my films to New York.

4.

A bus rolled onto the ferry and we crossed the Suez Canal, leaving Asia. Crossing took just five minutes, and the African side did not look any different: just a desert…a dusty provincial town and small green oases next to the high-way. I had no idea why I was going to Cairo, except that now it was the only way out of Gaza and because the bus was going there and the bus was air-conditioned and the driver did not mind my smoking.

Conversations with James

Andre Vltchek

A Comedy in Six Acts

PREFACE

I began writing Conversations With James in Jakarta, surrounded by an enormous mosque, a religious school, and several smaller mosques called musholahs – all competing to produce mighty sounds, broadcasting calls for prayer, prayers themselves, and whatever activity was taking place inside. Sounds multiplied and carried all over the neighborhood through loudspeakers, scaring and depressing those few surviving atheists as well as people of different religions. Little girls, as young as 3, were dragged by their overzealous parents to the biggest mosque for a certain type of education. Not even George Orwell could have envisioned a more complete brainwashing scenario. It seemed that almost the entire neighborhood thought the same way, behaved the same way, believed in the same religion. No alternatives seemed to be offered in a radius of several hundred miles.

Writing the play was an exercise in how to stay sane in an environment that I found antagonistic, even hostile to secularism, tolerance, and reason. Unlike in Istanbul where artistic and beautiful calls for prayer (lasting only a few minutes, five times a day) evoked in me nostalgia and a desire to learn more about a world so different from my own; gutwrenching, badly crafted sounds coming from the Jakarta mosques lasted well over five hours a day, stripped of beauty but leaving no doubt about who is really in complete control of the neighborhood.

Indonesia is a country where dissent has never been tolerated, where hundreds of thousands of people belonging to the Chinese minority were massacred after the 1965 military coup. Further hundreds of thousands were slaughtered for being "atheist" – almost all the leftists and progressives. The largest religious organization – NU – participated in the

killings. Religious and ethnic cleansing continued in East Timor (where around one third of the population was exterminated) and in other parts of this unfortunate and violent archipelago.

I've covered the most violent Indonesian pogroms as a journalist and I've covered tens of other insane wars that had a religious undertone: from the Middle East (Palestine/Israeli conflict) to Gujarat in India.

Almost all wars that I've witnessed have something to do with religious beliefs: in God, in the final prophecy, in market fundamentalism, in an emperor-God, in a chosen nation, in supremacy of skin color, or of a political or economic system.

It took me one year to write this play, much longer than my previous political drama: Ghosts of Valparaiso. I labored over the dialogues on board fast shinkansen trains in Japan, in remote South Pacific island nations possessed by Christian fundamentalist zeal, over foamy cappuccino in cafes of seemingly (but not necessarily) secular New Zealand and Australian cities.

And I finished writing it on Marshall Islands, in one of the most bizarre places on earth – on the biggest atoll our planet has – on Kwajalein. More precisely, on a small island called Ebeye, separated by just over one mile of water from an enormous US Star Wars military base, from intercontinental missile catchments.

While Kwajalein hosts a mighty radar installations, navigation equipment (and who knows what else; better not to ask…), as well as comfortable housing for the US military and civilian staff, Ebeye is synonymous for Micronesian hell – one of the most crammed places in the Pacific, with no running water and no waste management, with sporadic electricity, with children running barefoot – dirt and misery unseen almost anywhere else in this part of the world.

Despite the appalling conditions on Ebeye, almost everyone there was a dedicated Christian often belonging to the most extreme and fanatical sects. No rebellion or revolution seemed to be in the pipeline. The same beliefs were shared across the water by those who planned Star Wars on Kwajalein. Despite all the hymns flying from the open doors of churches, celebrating sharing and love, the entire place seemed a tropical Micronesian South Africa during apartheid.

I couldn't sleep in the only "decent" hotel on the island that became my home away from home for several days. There was no running water at night, no electricity. Combat platoons of roaches invaded my bed, crawled on top and under my sheets. One sleepless night I took my notebook and left the hotel, parked myself in a coffee shop run by migrant workers from the Philippines, ordered something resembling coffee and finished writing this play.

For similar reasons, I consider both Jakarta and Ebeye to be very appropriate places to begin and to finish this short, one act, play. And I am endlessly grateful to the people of Indonesia and The United States for pissing me off so deeply and violently, inspiring me and helping me to finish this little bitter comedy.

CHARACTERS:

GEORGE – playwright

JAMES – citizen of Elidia

(James is also known as God.)

GAIA – citizen of Elidia

VOICE OF RADIO ANNOUNCER

DRUNKS

INMTES OF INSANE ASYLUM

DOCTOR

There will be no intermission

ACT ONE

[*Entire stage is in semi-darkness. A desk with computer monitor. Half-full bottle of red wine stands on top of the desk, close to the edge. GEORGE enters briskly, sits on the chair, stares at the monitor for a long while; and then gets up. He paces around the stage before returning to the table. He leans on its edges with both hands, before beginning to speak. His monologue is interrupted by short pauses*]

GEORGE: I developed this habit…to talk to people on-line…typing the words or speaking to the microphone. When they use a camera I can see their faces on my monitor. Images are often clear, but not always. Sometimes they are blurry. I got used to meeting total strangers in Internet chat rooms: some women, some men.

[*He pours himself a glass of red wine; takes a sip*]

GEORGE: Some women insist on showing me their breasts…or more. Others just talk…about loneliness and ageing…broaching impolite subjects they wouldn't dare discuss even with their close friends. Others suggest real encounters… Intercourse… Caucasian women, Arab women, Asian women… Men have a tendency to discuss women and politics. Almost all women prefer to discuss men…

[*GEORGE takes a deep sip of wine and holds the glass in his hand, observing the color. He slowly descends into the chair.*]

GEORGE: Then…one day…it happened. Without any warning… Unexpectedly.

[*Short pause*]

GEORGE: I had been sitting at my usual place, drinking wine like I am drinking it now, staring at the monitor. Some busty middle-aged nymphet was pouring her heart out to me…past forty, can't find true love, scared she will have to stay alone for the rest of her life…

[*Short pause*]

GEORGE: …Then everything went blank… And I heard a terrible noise… Similar to a fire-alarm, but not exactly like that of a fire-alarm…

[*Loud noise. Similar to that of a fire alarm, but not exactly like a fire alarm. GEORGE jumps from his chair, covers his ears, a terrified expression on his face.*]

JAMES: [*his voice is metallic and it resonates somewhere above the stage*] Good evening, George!

GEORGE: Damn! What is it?! Who is it?! Who are you?! Where the hell are you?!

[*Another ringing sound, this time substantially shorter but more intense than the previous one.*]

JAMES: I am everything and I am everywhere, George. I am God!

GEORGE: [*Slightly taken aback but rapidly recovering his wits*]

Oh, stop it, would you?! God visiting me through a high-speed Internet connection?

JAMES: God, as I believe you were told, can visit you in any form.

GEORGE: You sound like an advanced computer virus.

JAMES: You don't seem to believe me.

GEORGE: Believe you what? That you are God?

JAMES: Yes.... Yes, George... Believe me that I am your Creator. That's what God means to you, humans, doesn't he?

GEORGE: I don't believe in God.

JAMES: Right, George, of course you don't... That's absolutely fine. You don't have to believe in me. You don't even have to call me God.

GEORGE: How should I call you then?

JAMES: Call me anything... You can call me, for instance, James!

GEORGE: James?

JAMES: Yes, James. That's neutral, isn't it? Not too religious, not too secular. Neutral, I would say. Thoroughly acceptable for any imaginable purpose. You have to call me by some name, don't you? Then why not call me James?

GEORGE: James...

[*Has a swing straight from the bottle*]

What brings you here, James?

[*Short pause*]

JAMES: Desperation.

GEORGE: Desperation? Since when are gods desperate?

JAMES: [*Ignores his sarcasm*]

Frustration from being misunderstood.

GEORGE: [*Looks dumbfounded*]

 Frustration...

JAMES: Desire to come clear...to tell the truth. Longing to confess...

GEORGE: [*Sarcastically once again*]

Since when do gods confess? I thought it was only we, common sinners, who are obliged to prostrate ourselves and come clear in front of God!

JAMES: [*Modestly*]

Even God can have such desires.

GEORGE: [*Abruptly*]

James!

JAMES: Yes?

GEORGE: Let's stop this silly game right now, please! You are not knocking at the right door. James, I don't believe in God! I am an atheist... And if you were the Almighty, you would definitely know that.

JAMES: [*quietly*]

I do... I know. And I am an atheist myself.

GEORGE: [*First in shock, then laughing loudly*]

An atheist God! How thoroughly believable!

JAMES: [*Sadly*]

I do not blame you for laughing... But I assure you...

GEORGE: I am running out of time, James. I am in the middle of writing my latest atheist play. And I was just trying to arrange a date with a desperate lady who is in great and urgent need of certain emotional and physical consolation.

JAMES: I know all that. I apologize for taking your time. But allow me to reveal that I contacted you exactly because I am truly enjoying the play that you are presently writing. Forgive me for reading from behind your back...and from your mind... George, seriously, if you need any proof...

GEORGE: Proof of what?

JAMES: You know… The proof… That I am what I say I am.

GEORGE: [*Suddenly very interested*]

What kind of proof can you offer?

JAMES: Any proof you ask for.

GEORGE: Show your face!

JAMES: I have many faces. I can choose any face. I can choose any body, any form. I can be a woman or a man. I can be a child. I can take the form of a gentle breeze or I can batter the shore like the most vicious storm.

GEORGE: Show your real face.

JAMES: I don't have one. Or… I do, but nothing that you humans could comprehend. I live in quite different dimensions. If I show you my real face, you will probably see absolutely nothing. Or you will see something that may appear very disturbing, even terrible.

GEORGE: Then wouldn't it be fair to say that for us, humans, you simply do not exist?

JAMES: That would be a simplification, to a certain extent…

GEORGE: [*Suddenly smiles*]

If I can't see the real you, then send someone…a person I would really like to meet. Try to read my dreams. Can't you read my mind? You should, if you are a genuine God.

JAMES: [*Thinks for a while, then begins to mumble*]

I am your creator… Let me try then… A person you really want to meet… Petite, Asian, not too young and not too old… Impeccably dressed… Long hair…

[*George seems to be a lot in thought. Lights become progressively dimmer. James continues mumbling incomprehensibly. It goes on for almost an entire minute. Then suddenly a loud knock on the door. GEORGE is shaken by the sound. He jumps from his chair, runs to open the door. Before he can, there is another knock.*]

GEORGE: Who is it?

[*No answer. George opens the door sharply and deci-*

sively. GAIA walks in. She is Asian, petite, elegant, not too young and not too old, dressed impeccably. Her long black hair falls in graceful disorder to her shoulders.]

GEORGE: [*Apparently shaken*]

Oh my God!

JAMES: [*From above, suddenly sarcastically*]

Exactly!

GAIA: [*Her voice is very gentle and very feminine*]

In case you are wondering, I am also a god. But call me Gaia. James created me on the spur of the moment, out of your dreams. I am the woman you always wanted to meet but never did.

GEORGE: [*Unable to speak. He walks to her, extends his hands but stops short from touching her. Suddenly he falls on his knees, squeezes her hips in his palms and presses his face against her thighs. She begins caressing his hair*]

Oh my God!

JAMES: George, for heaven's sake; brace yourself! I came to talk to you… I traveled through the galaxies, enduring speed faster than light… I feel jetlagged and my body aches. I need a massage. Let go of her and let's discuss important matters.

GEORGE: [*Begging*]

Don't take her away from me!

JAMES: [*Impatient*]

Fine, George, you can have her. She can stay with you. Now would you sit down and listen, please?

[*GEORGE walks slowly back to his chair. GAIA follows him. When he sits down, she stays behind his chair, still caressing his hair*]

Can I speak now?

GEORGE: Please… Please do!

[*PAUSE, then BLACKOUT*]

JAMES: We fucked up, George!

ACT TWO

[*Loud and terrible ringing sound, similar to that of a fire alarm, but not exactly a fire alarm. The stage is dark for as long as the ringing lasts. Then the lights come slowly back. GAIA is sitting on the chair, one leg elegantly bent; her skirt is up above her knees. Her underwear is resting on the arm of one of the chairs*]

GEORGE: I experienced heaven!

[*Long ringing sound again*]

JAMES: [*His voice comes, as in the previous act, from somewhere above the ceiling*]

You humans are so physical and so predictable! We created you like that, of course. We needed you to multiply… But your lust exceeded all our expectations. It is so ridiculous, so comical to watch you from above!

GEORGE: Thank you, James… Now I believe!

JAMES: [*Impatiently*]

Rubbish! Believe in what? Let's cut all that human sentimental nonsense and get to the core. You needed to copulate and we created a suitable mate for your copulation. We did some quick calculations, planning, designing. We converted one of our sisters… She is now a perfect size and shape for you, exactly compatible with your body and with your preferences. There is no mystery in all that. Are you listening, George?

GEORGE: I am listening to you, oh James! Your wisdom knows no boundaries.

JAMES: Good.

[*Pause*]

George?

GEORGE: I am listening.

JAMES: There is no God.

GEORGE: Oh…

JAMES: Do you understand what I am saying? Can I find at least someone among you, humans, who would be able to comprehend this simple message?

GEORGE: I am trying, but…

JAMES: But? I will allow her to explain. When I speak, it takes too much energy… Thousands of light-years, you know…

[*Ringing sound, this time a very short one, then silence. GAIA pulls down her skirt. She takes her panties in her right hand and gets up briskly. Throughout the monologue, she is playing with the panties*]

GAIA: When he speaks, it takes too much energy. It is easier if I explain.

[*GEORGE sits on the floor, looks at GAIA, a dumb and adoring expression on his face, staring directly at her lips as she speaks. Her monologue is delivered in a matter of fact voice*]

We came here from a far-away galaxy, from a small planet in the solar system unknown to you, humans. Our society is extremely developed but even we had to go through a complex evolution. At some point we managed to create a just and egalitarian society. Our beings know no pain. Our lives became eternal. We can change our appearance in order to please each other. We don't age, we can shrink and expand, we can swim and we can fly. The knowledge of each of us is almost limitless. But we were dreaming about other forms of life and other galaxies. We designed and built spaceships and embarked on epic journeys. Later we learned how to move in space on our own. But we still couldn't find our brothers and sisters in this vast universe. Then one of our supreme sisters came up with the idea of creating new forms of life in your solar system. We triggered what you call the "Big Bang"; then we implanted the most primitive organisms into the water of your oceans. These were organisms that were predestined to evolve into what you have become now: human beings.

GEORGE: [*Still from the floor*]

Amazing! I always considered this to be a possibility!

GAIA: The entire process was designed by what you, humans, would call our great scientists. But our most refined thinkers, our philosophers, artists and dreamers also helped to program you. They were burning with desire to create something pure, even irrational: beings with a tremendous capacity for tenderness, kindness, and compassion.

GEORGE: I understand…

JAMES: [*The silence is suddenly interrupted by the loud and metallic voice*]

But we fucked up!!!

GAIA: [*Pragmatically, in a matter-of-fact voice*]

Yes, we fucked up endlessly. As you were evolving as a species, elements of greed and violence became predominant in your character. One thing was absolutely clear: our scientists and poets had simply miscalculated.

GEORGE: I suspected that.

GAIA: We watched from a great distance in horror… We watched how you began slaughtering each other over meaningless things. Men raping women and cutting the throats of their own brothers: over the land, over money, over power. Entire clans vanishing… Human flesh consumed by fellow humans. Greed had suddenly no boundaries.

[*GAIA comes briskly close to George, puts her palm under his shirt and begins caressing his chest. Then she, abruptly, pushes him away*]

We had to intervene somehow. But we were too far away. We could have stopped the experiment – put a final end to it – but that would mean the annihilation of the human race. We had turbulent discussions on the matter but when it came to voting, the great majority decided that your species had gained an undeniable right to exist and it would be thoroughly immoral on our part to liquidate you.

GEORGE: [*From the floor*]

But why did you not try to communicate with us?

GAIA: We did. That's exactly what we tried to do for centuries. With negligible results…

[*She comes close to him. He prostrates himself on the floor, spreading his arms and legs, face up. She slowly puts a heel on his chest, then teasingly pokes his chin with the tip of a pointed shoe*]

We did, George. We contacted your people on many occasions but were always misunderstood. It started with the Torah, but maybe even earlier. Then we pampered one of the brightest human children. We explained to him the essence of egalitarian society, equal distribution of wealth and the advantages that come with it… He went around explaining, carrying our message, but you put him on the cross. So at the end we had to spend what you would call trillions of megawatts of energy, moving him to our galaxy and giving him political asylum.

[*GAIA sights desperately*]

Instead of learning anything about social structures, you created religion around him – something he was explicitly telling you not to do! Hundreds of years later, when your wars became increasingly monstrous, we contacted another bright son of your species, explaining to him that we were considering stopping the experiment in order to save humanity from excessive suffering… Through him, we gave your species one last warning. But that message was misunderstood as well, and the last warning has been changed to the last prophecy! And our message got misinterpreted on many counts.

[*GAIA begins pacing up and down the room in anger*]

At the end, when the situation became thoroughly intolerable, we decided to approach the greatest thinker of the time. That was in the middle of total insanity, when European powers were dividing the entire world, colonizing every single piece of land on your planet, treating people of other races like slaves. We tried to explain to him that things were moving beyond good and evil as humans saw it, and that there is no God and there never had been one. He considered our message for several years, then came up with conclusion that "God is dead!"

GEORGE: [*Howls*]

We had such high hopes for him!

GAIA: By then there was not one inch of the world that was free, almost everything under the boot of colonizing soldiers. And then…

[*GAIA gasps*]

… And then they began killing each other on their own continent. Concentration camps and battlefields resembling enormous slaughter-houses…

GEORGE: …And now…

GAIA: And now, despite all the so-called progress, the majority of people on your planet live in total filth in the gutter. Thieves and liars rule your world, naked in their greed. Local elites took over from former colonial masters, becoming even more brutal and merciless. Most of the people on your planet still live in feudal societies, some even experience slavery… And in the rich world? You threw your best minds into insane asylums, marginalized them; made them irrelevant. There is no compassion left on your planet.

[*She stops; pauses for a few moments, apparently lost in thought*]

We aimed for a masterpiece. But we made some terrible mistakes. We have to stop this… Somehow. Soon.

JAMES: [*His metallic voice above the ceiling once again*]

Now!!!

GAIA: [*In a natural voice*]

Now. Probably now.

[*Short pause*]

Because your own people are suffering. Because, despite all the propaganda, more and more beings on your planet are exploited, robbed of everything, divided, neutralized. Your rulers exercise such complete control over the world that no revolt, no rebellion is possible anymore. It is the endgame for your civilization.

GEORGE: But what will you do now? Nuke us?

[*GAIA lowers herself to the floor. She lies on top of him, pressing her entire body against his*]

GAIA: We can love you to death… Or we can…

JAMES: Nonsense! We need consensus of your species. We need someone to explain to them that what is happening to them now is…a result of an experiment that went terribly wrong!

GAIA: [*Kisses George on his lips*]

And that is why we came to you…

JAMES: Because you will be the one to tell them.

GAIA: To explain to them…

JAMES: To ask them what do they want us to do?

GAIA: We can recall… We can stop the entire thing if your people decide that's what they want us to do. You can all vanish quickly and painlessly…

JAMES: Or we can share our technology. We can explain to you how to grow more food, how to effectively purify and desalinate ocean water, how to move from one place to another fast, efficiently, and without polluting the environment.

GAIA: We can offer medicine that could cure all your diseases and make you live for at least 500 years. We can help you to design egalitarian societies.

JAMES: We can do all that and much more, but we are not sure that our ideas would be welcomed. It seems that your species is not interested in justice and harmony… Your world is obsessed with money, hungry for power… Those who choke your world will not be willing to give up their privileges for the good of majority. Apparently competing with others and exercising power brings the strongest of you more joy than living in a harmonious society.

GEORGE: No doubt about it.

GAIA: We are afraid that this may be the case…

JAMES: But we have to try, George!

[*Dramatic pause*]

Would you like to be our new prophet?

GEORGE: Me?… But…

[*A confused, almost terrified look appears on his face*]

GAIA: [*Comes close to him, looking straight into his eyes. Each step she makes is a masterpiece of eroticism and elegance combined*]

George?

GEORGE: [*Begins to tremble looking at her*]

Gaia… I don't know if I can…

GAIA: [*Stands over George, his face right between her feet*]

Look. Look up!

[*George looks up. He loses control, his palms grab her calves*]

GAIA: We need you, George! Humanity needs you.

GEORGE: [*His internal struggle doesn't last long. Staring right above him, he finally shouts:*]

Oh yes! I will. I will!

BLACKOUT

ACT THREE

[*The same as in the previous acts. Lights slowly begin to illuminate the stage. One light points to the computer table. GEORGE sits at the table, facing the monitor. GAIA rests in the chair, which is lost in a shadow*]

GEORGE: [*Mumbling*]

Fourteen million, seven hundred thousand and twenty-five dollars!

[*He moves the computer mouse, stares at the monitor in disbelief*]

I had only sixty-eight dollars and five cents in my checking account yesterday!

GAIA: We suspected that in order to carry on your mission successfully you might need some substantial funds. We can, of course, supply you with much more…

GEORGE: [*Confused*]

But… So much money…

GAIA: A prophet is a very important being. He tells millions of people what to do and what to refrain from. You may need to hire a jet…or to pay hundreds of scribblers to put your discourses on paper…or to buy a decent car. Your species doesn't trust poor honest blokes, George. They like shiny vehicles, snow-white false dentures, and neatly tailored jackets. You look like slop, if you don't mind my saying so. We need to go out and buy you a new pair of designer glasses, an expensive looking watch, and several pairs of shoes.

GEORGE: [*Obviously hurt*]

What's wrong with my glasses and my watch?

GAIA: They look…ordinary.

GEORGE: I selected them myself. They are part of me. I like them.

GAIA: You need to look imposing… Impressive… Important. They have to trust you and they have to envy you. They even have to fear you. You see, I did my homework before coming here.

GEORGE: [*Ironically*]

Should I pull all my teeth out and instead get perfect looking implants?

GAIA: [*Not catching his irony*]

That's awfully thoughtful of you, George! You are a fast learner. We should arrange for it. You see, you have to appeal to the masses. You will have to convince them that there is no God, only us. They may not like your words, because they have believed for centuries in Almighty fatherly figures. You will have to tell them the truth. And remember: nothing scares and disgusts human beings more than the truth!

GEORGE: But I myself don't know the truth.

GAIA: That's why I am here. To explain… To guide you… To answer all your questions…

[*She stands up and slowly walks to him. She spreads her arms, stopping just a few steps before GEORGE*]

Ask! Ask me anything!

GEORGE: [*Deep in thought*]

Anything?

GAIA: Anything!

GEORGE: Have you also approached Karl Marx?

GAIA: Of course! He was one of our best disciples. He understood…

[*Pause*]

…Although not everything.

GEORGE: Lenin?

GAIA: Yes, but he understood much less than Marx. Although he had some good organizing skills.

GEORGE: Che?

GAIA: By then we were already quite desperate, of course… But he turned out to be one of the best. But he had asthma. We offered to fly him home to Elidia… We offered to cure him so he might be more effective, but he refused. He was a purist, believing exclusively in Latin-style revolution…and in liberation of Africa. He wasn't thrilled to learn about the project, about the fact that we created the world. It was clashing with his theories. But at the end we managed to forge a very fruitful cooperation. Anyway, we had to resurrect him as well. He is now in Elidia with the rest….

GEORGE: Stalin?

GAIA: Definitely not! Have some faith in our moral judgment.

GEORGE: [*suddenly screams in frustration*]

But why me?!

GAIA: [*Taken aback*]

But you are brilliant…

GEORGE: Many people are. I am a womanizer… Between us…

[*He whispers*]

…Between us, I care about sex more than I care about social justice. I write plays in order to impress women. I am not as good as you think I am.

GAIA: [*Consoling him*] Nobody is good. Nobody was ever good. Besides, you don't need any other woman right now. We took care of that part. I should be fully sufficient. Now you can concentrate on your mission.

GEORGE: I belong to the Left out of spite for the Right!

GAIA: Does it really matter? As long as you are on the correct side of the barricade, as you humans say…

GEORGE: Tell me more…why me?

GAIA: You don't believe in anything, don't have any dogma.

GEORGE: Most educated people in this world believe in nothing.

GAIA: We… We simply liked you! We read your books; we followed you around for some time.

GEORGE: [*Hitting his forehead*]

You did? How embarrassing!

GAIA: Don't worry! We are a different species. And after all, we are responsible for all your weaknesses. We created you, although indirectly. We are like…almost like your parents.

GEORGE: [*Sarcastically*]

I do certain things I wouldn't want my mother to witness!

GEORGE: [*Ignoring his irony*]

We created the molecules…

GEORGE: So old Darwin was correct…

GAIA: Definitely… To a large extent.

GEORGE: Not fully?

GAIA: We tried to perform some tune-ups when we realized that things were not going too well. Darwin couldn't know that. He believed that evolution was uninterrupted, a natural process.

GEORGE: Then I have one more question: who

created you?

GAIA: We are the children of a similar experiment. We were created by a more advanced species. We are the result of a more successful experiment, I have to admit.

GEORGE: Then who created "them"?

GAIA: Others. It's a continuous process. Call it uni-versal evolution. Advanced species achieved perfection and immortality. They built egalitarian societies with no burning problems, no worries, no diseases and no pain. But life has sense only because of its imperfections; when all goals are achieved, the meaning of our existence disappears. The struggle for a better world gives purpose to our life, to your life, to any life… The lack of challenges creates eternal boredom, even a sort of desperation. This is exactly what happened to us but also to those who created our species many millions of years earlier…and to those who created them billions of years ago. It is never about the goals and results, George… It is always about the journey, about the process. We fight revolutions, we build and we create new concepts. When there is nothing to improve anymore, life loses its meaning…

GEORGE: So after creating perfect societies, they and you decided to vanish. But before…

GAIA: I knew that for a human being you were very bright. Yes, that's exactly what happened. We felt obliged to create new life that would continue inhabiting this universe after our departure. Except that…in this particular case…or more precisely, in your case…

JAMES: [*From above the stage, producing a desperate and loud scream*]

We fucked up!!!

BLACKOUT

ACT FOUR

[*There is almost no PAUSE between ACTS 3 and 4. During the BLACKOUT, which lasts approximately one minute, there are sounds of loud explosions and shouts of military commands, then the VOICE OF NEWS ANNOUNCER. Light gradually returns.*

GEORGE and GAIA are still in the same position as in ACT THREE]

VOICE OF NEWS ANNOUNCER: …US and coalition troops bombarded positions of the terrorist groups that earlier demanded nationalization of all natural resources in their country; demands which the White House described as dangerous, undermining of democracy and the basic principles of the free world. The groups also pressed for the release of their leader, Francisco Gonzalez, presently held in custody at the US military base in Haiti used to interrogate terrorist suspects. Two years ago, Mr. Gonzalez gained notoriety by organizing protest marches all over Latin America, calling for the withdrawal of troops from the Coalition of the Giving that invaded Venezuela several months earlier. New Delhi: Protesters clashed with riot police, after an international arbitration court ruled that multinational pharmaceutical conglomerate – Fotzer – acted legally when copyrighting Yoga earlier this year. Sudan: Almost 3 million refugees…

[*GEORGE hits the button on his computer and the broadcast gets interrupted*]

GEORGE: I think that plenty of people on this planet would rather live a decent and eternal life in an egalitarian society than … than this… What should I call it…

JAMES: [*From above*]

Shiiiiiit!!!!!!!!

GAMES: Exactly. Thank you, James. You are always an inspiration…

GAIA: That's why we are here.

GEORGE: It took you…some time.

GAIA: It is not so simple, George. Even in our advanced society we have plenty of members who believe in what you call "political correctness". In Elidia it is brought to a different level, but the essence is similar. For instance some thinkers thought for centuries that we have no right to lecture others, even if our civilization is much more advanced. They believed that you should have full control over your destiny. They were willing to allow you to butcher millions of your people, hoping that eventually you will get wise and invent your own wheel. They insisted on respecting your culture.

GEORGE: How considerate of them.

GAIA: But things are rapidly changing. Now there is almost an absolute consensus that the experiment went too far. That your species will never be able to create a just and equal society without intervention from outside, and that unless you are stopped, you will continue massacring millions of defenseless beings annually, while keeping the great majority of your population in the gutter. Not to speak of other species that inhabit your planet. Not to speak of the environment. So now we are here. And the first thing we want to do is to tell your people the truth. They have to learn how to think rationally. They have to learn how to live without the anesthetics – without religions – and face the uncomfortable truth that there is no god and no higher meaning of life…only us.

GEORGE: [*Ironically*]

But why would you go so far out of your way?

GAIA: We felt compassion…

JAMES: [*From above the stage*]

She already explained it to you: we want to depart! Let's be honest: we want to get out, and we want to be sure that you can take over. We either have to improve your species, or we have to delete you and start from scratch. The second option would mean that we have to stick around for further tens of millions of years.

GAIA: What James is saying is that we would like to rest; we are too tired of living eternally. But we can't depart, yet. If we do, you humans will be the only thinking beings left in the universe!

JAMES: And that would be a very unsettling prospect.

GEORGE: Unfortunately I have to agree.

GAIA: Because you people are…

JAMES: Piiiiiiigs!!!! Thieves!!!!! Rapists!!!!! Mass

murderers. Greedy bandits! Primitives…

GAIA: What James means is that you people are not yet suitable to be the sole masters of the universe.

JAMES: They shouldn't be allowed to master even their own farts!

GAIA: James, you are being too graphic…

JAMES: [*To GEORGE*]

Tell them.

GEORGE: [*Suddenly angry*]

Tell them what?

JAMES: Tell them how it all happened…

GEORGE: [*Increasingly irritated*]

How can I tell them? I don't know anything. I've never even seen you. Again, I have to believe what you tell me, but where is the proof? I am expected to believe that you actually exist, but as you know, I am not good at…at believing. You sent me a perfect lover, but is that enough proof? Tell me more. Convince me. Show your face, James!

JAMES: My face??

[*Laughs*]

You really want to see it?

GEORGE: I have to… I can't help you otherwise.

[*Short PAUSE*]

GAIA: …no.

JAMES: [*Ignores her distress*]

Very well then. Come to the kitchen, George. It will cost a tremendous amount of energy, but I am willing to use it, just to convince you. And remember, whatever you see there…it is me, but scaled down ten million times. Brought to your dimensions, so to speak. And each of us is slightly different. But at least you will get some general idea. Are you ready, George?

[*GEORGE slowly stands up*]

GEORGE: Ready.

[*He is slowly but steadily walking towards the door. He opens it, switches on the light, then a short PAUSE*]

GAIA: [*Suddenly terrified*]

No!!! Come back, George!

[*GEORGE ignores her outburst, closes the door behind him. GAIA stares at the door in terror. Long PAUSE. Then a desperate, loud shout. GEORGE is screaming in an unrecognizable voice. Something falls.*]

GEORGE: Oh no! No!!!!!

[*He howls. The door flies open. GEORGE, his hair standing on end, is rolling on the floor. He enters the living room in a rolling motion, still screaming. Eventually he stops and sits down on the floor. He is breathing heavily. He seems to be uncertain whether he will begin to puke or whether he will die from suffocation. Eventually he slowly comes back to his senses. His breathing normalizes, but he is still sitting cross-legged on the floor,* a look of disbelief on his face*]

GEORGE: [*To the ceiling*]

Now I understand, James! Your species should definitely depart this universe. What kind of bastard created you?

[*PAUSE*]

Now I understand, therefore I believe, James!

[*Finally he is overwhelmed by nausea. He crawls to the corner, gets on all four and pukes loudly*]

BLACKOUT

ACT FIVE

[*A pub. Semi-darkness. Several drunks are sitting at three simple wooden tables, facing a television set. The TV screen is turned away from the stage. Pre-recorded voice of GEORGE*]

GEORGE: ...And then they wrote down some simple rules that are easy to comprehend. You shall not kill thy neighbor. Don't rape your friend's wife...

1st DRUNK: [*Laughing*] ...your friend's wife! What if you don't fancy having friends?

GEORGE: Don't...

ALL DRUNKS: [*In unison, overshouting television set*]

...Don't steal from the poor...don't lie to the masses! Don't sow false hopes...

1st DRUNK: But that is what they are doing to us. All we are allowed to do now is bitch about the way the world is set up, as long as our bitching is not too loud and doesn't lead to action. They call it freedom of speech and democracy. We can go and vote for one of their candidates. All candidates that make it to the top must be impotent; pre-approved by the establishment that controls the media, all the major political parties, everything. We can even stay at home and not vote at all; it would not matter.

GEORGE: ...When Elidians realized it wouldn't work, they created a prototype man. Called him a special edition human. They tried to prevent greed from taking over the planet. To prevent what happened later anyway: business interests creating invisible coups against democracy, the upgraded street-vendors ruining decency, compassion, and kindness. But the humans nailed him – that special edition – to the cross and kept stealing, raping, and murdering as if there was no tomorrow. A few centuries later Elidians pampered another human prototype, but this time they did some serious PR. They flew him first a few solar years to Elidia, showing him the very posh accommodations up there, as well as a certain amount of women shaped to his liking. They told him that he should be forceful in his preaching: to promise and to warn! You see, it didn't work either, as the new religion began expanding through its own colonial wars all over Arabia, North Africa, and the Indian subcontinent. In the meantime, the followers of the bloke who ended up on the cross continued launching their own colonial adventures, worldwide... Both sides are at odds to this day.

2nd DRUNK: [*Extending his hand holding a pint of beer*]

To their health then! Cheers!

GEORGE: You see, Elidians tried their best. When they realized that religions brought only wars and intellectual decay, they decided to talk to that big, fat, bearded German and also to his buddy who happened to be another bearded German whose father owned a factory… But even that didn't help. Attempts to create a rational, equal and com-passionate society on Planet Earth were simply failing. Eventually things went out of control. Humanity never managed to shed its primitive beliefs. People kept killing each other again and again in the name of God. Christians killing pagans, Muslims killing North Africans, then Christians killing Muslims and Muslims killing Christians. Later Hindus killing Muslims and Muslims killing Hindus, while Christians killed everybody they could find on their path. Then Muslims killing Muslims: Shiites killing Sunnis and vice versa. Catholics killing Protestants and vice versa. Catholics and Protestants in unison killing Jews. Jews killing Muslims and Muslims killing Jews and other infidels.

1st DRUNK: Religions may not be much more than rubbish, but there is definitely some god! If not, our lives would be meaningless. We don't want to believe in other beings that are basically like ourselves, even if they are more advanced. We need an Almighty father, frightening and tremendous, thundering, punishing but also on occasion forgiving. We need to prostrate ourselves at his feet. We need to prostrate ourselves, period! We need to kiss his toes, to lick his anus, to gratefully inhale his farts. We need to feel that we are nothing while he is everything … therefore … indirectly … passing the entire responsibility for our actions to Him … thinking that we are nothing more than ants in his forest; stinky crap, weak, miniscule, and negligible creatures.

2nd DRUNK: Yes! And knowing what shits we are, we need to believe that there is something splendid and noble hanging above us. Nothing concrete, nothing real… Just abstract, scary, and unreachable… And we need religion to lie to us, to promise us that this something actually exists. And when we believe, it is much easier to

steal, to cheat, to rape, even to murder! When we believe we can always expect that we will eventually be purified and forgiven. We can think that to God our crimes matter less than our efforts to prostrate, chant, kneel, and humiliate ourselves…

1st DRUNK: …But if we don't believe, then facing oneself in the morning … looking at the mirror: a thief is just a thief … a rapist is a rapist … a crook is a crook! That's why the most compassionate and sharing and orderly nations are atheist … and the most bigoted, brutal, compassionless are those possessed by religious zeal!

2nd DRUNK: But we can't allow these ideas to get hold of our society!

[*All drunks begin to argue, screaming at each other. Suddenly one of them smashes his pint against the floor. Deep silence*]

A DRUNK: Are authorities blind? That terrorist George is confusing us! He has to be stopped and brought to Haiti for further investigation! The essence of our freedom and democracy and way of life is closely linked to religion.

1st DRUNK: Even if he is right, George is insane!

[*Loud metallic voice, not unlike a fire alarm. The drunks stop arguing; panic is reflected on their faces. To absolute silence, JAMES begins to laugh, loudly and scornfully*]

BLACKOUT

ACT SIX

[*Mental institution. Slow, retarded, senile musac. Two inmates in the uniform of the institution aimlessly pace back and forth. GEORGE is also wearing the institution's uniform. He is sitting on a plastic chair, staring into the distance. A young female DOCTOR appears on the stage. Her voice is cheerful and optimistic, but her face is covered by a veil and only her eyes are visible*]

DOCTOR: Good morning, everybody!

GEORGE: Good morning, Doc!

[*Two other inmates ignore both of them. The musac slowly decreases in volume and eventually disap-*]

DOCTOR: How do you feel today, George?

GEORGE: Just fine, thank you. I had been thinking about what you said the other day… About the relativity of knowledge… How different people can interpret information in various ways.

DOCTOR: Good, George… And?

GEORGE: And…

DOCTOR: You had no further contact with Gaia or James?

GEORGE: They never came back.

DOCTOR: [*Sighs*]

That's a pity. I have some very bad news, George. Your bank launched an investigation soon after coming to the conclusion that by an error 14 million dollars had been transferred into your account. You apparently went on an unbridled spending spree.

GOERGE: I…

DOCTOR: You rented a Learjet and flew to Africa, to preach social equality and atheism to Nigerians. After that you attempted to land in Riyadh but Saudi authorities didn't allow you to even touch their holy runway with your infidel landing gear. You then flew to Tel Aviv, throwing an enormous party at…

GEORGE: True! I was instructed to…

DOCTOR: Here we go again!

GEORGE: I spoke to the masses in Africa, Latin America, and Europe. I secured a huge following in Japan and India. What I was saying was rational; it made sense. Religions were and are ruining the world and they always stand on the side of the oppressors. Elidians, not some Almighty in the heavens, created human beings. There is no heaven and no hell, only ceaseless boredom if we manage to live eternally…

DOCTOR: You used money that didn't belong to you.

GEORGE: Elidians transferred the money.

DOCTOR: Unfortunately that's not what the president of your bank says. According to her, you managed to spend 5 million dollars, two hundred and two thousand five hundred and twelve dollars … and forty-seven cents, to be precise. That's what they claim you owe them right now, George.

GEORGE: But I was told…

DOCTOR: Again, George? The Elidians told you? Do you have anything in writing, anything that can prove they transferred funds? Do you still believe in them?

GEORGE: I don't believe in anything, Doc. I saw them with my own eyes. I saw the monstrous leader of their mission: James. I conversed with him. I saw Gaia, one of their women … or more precisely, a woman they created from my own dreams. My woman… The most beautiful and desirable being I've ever encountered in my life and whom I miss tremendously… I spoke to both of them: we really had a long and fruitful conversations. I made love to Gaia, several times a day. I don't believe in them, I experienced them.

DOCTOR: [*Reading from her notepad*]

You went to London and managed to get yourself invited to one of the BBC talk shows. It earned you immediately a fatwa from the Muslims, excommunication from the Catholic Church…

GEORGE: How could they excommunicate me from something I never belonged to?

DOCTOR: Furthermore it earned you condemnation from Hindus, Judaists, Buddhists, and another forty-eight religions and sects. You didn't get much sympathy even from the Scientologists!

GEORGE: Not surprisingly…

DOCTOR: Not surprisingly, maybe… But the bottom line is that you gained no friends at all. Even Marxists were not too thrilled: they attacked you for your profound nihilism and for your spite for the human race… The only kind words came from anarchists and supporters of euthanasia.

GEORGE: I know, I know… At least someone can think rationally.

[*Mockingly*]

But was it ever easy to be a prophet?

DOCTOR: Well, well… Some prophets had it easier, as I recall.

[*Once again turning pages of her notebook*]

Not able to convince the masses by the common means of communication, you succumbed to extreme actions. You invited one hundred top European writers and intellectuals. You rented a ballroom in Paris, climber onto a banquet table and attempted to urinate into an ancient Chinese vase – an act described as culturally insensitive. You got drunk and began insulting free market economics, mass media, pop culture as well as all the major and minor religions of the world. You drew a parallel between the President of the United States and the anal opening. You offered one million dollars and a Ferrari for the best atheist poem.

GEORGE: I was getting desperate. I agree I probably went overboard!

DOCTOR: [*Her eyes in the notebook*]

Possibly…

[*Suddenly she leans towards him and whispers*]

They used you, George!

GEORGE: I did what they asked me to do. I did it because they made sense. Why did they allow this to happen? Why am I in this shit-hole of a mental institution? Why am I broke? I never asked for their money and I never used it for my personal gain.

DOCTOR: [*Whispers*]

I gather they never needed you to win, just to begin the struggle. And they sacrificed you in the process. They used you to sow the seeds of doubt… There will be others coming after you. Many years from now you will be remembered as the first human who grasped the truth. You will be celebrated, revered and admired. Many years from now, as I said… Decades after you are dead.

GEORGE: [*Sarcastically*]

What a great honor it will be! Why didn't they airlift me to Elidia like Karl Marx and Che?

DOCTOR: Apropos, what did she look like?

GEORGE: Who?

DOCTOR: Don't be a fool… Gaya.

GEORGE: She…

[*He begins drawing the curves in the air, using both hands*]

She…

DOCTOR: [*Takes off her veil*]

Like this?

GEORGE: I'll be damned! You didn't leave me?

[*Grabs her hand*]

GAIA / DOCTOR: They exiled me!

GEORGE: Why?

GAIA: No particular reason. But I suspect that from their point of view I got too contaminated by your human habits, after spending several days in human form, and in your company. ·

[*She pauses*]

You people always believed that the God, gods, or any higher beings have to be good and moral and kind. Reality is that…

JAMES: … That we are absolute shiiiiiits, too!!!!

GAIA: [*Sadly*]

James is departing…

GEORGE: James!

[*Two inmates stop pacing on the stage. They look at GEORGE in bewilderment. Both begin to tap their fingers on their temples, smiling with a benevolent and understanding expression on their faces*]

GAIA: But one thing is unfortunately obvious: there is no God, only us, beings like James. I am beginning to wonder whether it is even necessary to spread this news among the humans. It may be better to live in deceit…

GEORGE: What will happen to us now?

GAIA: What will happen to humanity? Who cares, really?

GEORGE: No, not to humanity! To us: to you and me?

GAIA: Well, we will escape, will we not? And we will do that one thing that I truly enjoyed doing… Enjoyed much more than living a sterile eternal life in Elidia. That thing you and I were doing day and night… That in and out that you humans call sex. Eventually we will get old, catch some disease and die. Isn't it fantastic?!

GEORGE: We are broke. The bank is chasing me!

GAIA: We will manage. I have stolen some codes… and some know how. I will be able to traffic some funds to your account once we get our hands on a wired computer.

GEORGE: My account is blocked.

GAIA: We will open a new one. We will change your name and move to Rio or Nairobi.

GEORGE: [*Suddenly desperate*]

Gaia, I got accustomed to carrying on higher mission! I actually enjoyed being a prophet. Are you telling me that from now on we will be just copulating, eating, defecating, and sleeping? Like the rest of them? Am I not going to fight against religions, anymore? Am I not going to tell the truth, anymore? The truth that there is no God and that all religions are built on lies and keep human beings in ignorance and poverty, igniting intolerance and violence?

GAIA: That would be dangerous and it won't be necessary. You already completed your mission. Now we can rest. Rest and enjoy life. You can live comfortably for the rest of your days. Wouldn't you enjoy some golfing and yachting for a change? Some caviar and buckets of first-rate champagne? First-rate masseuses and the fastest cars your species ever built? Or maybe a little corporate jet? Or a villa overlooking dramatic cliffs and endless ocean?

GEORGE: [*In despair*]

I need to talk to James! In order to live I need much more than just the fulfilling of my bodily functions. I need to struggle! I need my life to have some deeper meaning. One needs to submit to God or one needs to fight against God! To try to find God or to attempt to prove that there is no God!

JAMES: [*His voice suddenly coming from a great distance, although still from above the stage*]

Good-bye George! Thank you for your services. Enjoy the rewards: enjoy your perfect woman… Good-bye Gaia! Enjoy your lust and germ-covered Planet Earth. Good-bye to all of you, imbeciles!

[*A loud ringing noise. Similar to a fire alarm, but not exactly like that. It sounds for fifteen seconds, gradually becoming weaker and weaker*]

GAIA: James doesn't care, George. I keep repeating: he came here to sow the seeds of doubt, which can eventually lead to revolt … to revolution … and to the improvement of humanity … and to its self-sufficiency. He calculated that if religions disappear, so will the wars, racism, poverty, and ignorance! If humanity moves forward, James will be able to commit suicide. Maybe all of us will. Finally! I went ahead of them… I have chosen the sweetest form of suicide possible: I have chosen to live and die as a human being!

GEORGE: James wants us – humans – to become like you – Elidians – so all of you would be able to die! How absurd!

1st PATIENT: [*Giggling, pointing finger at George*]

Absurd…

[*Another long outburst of giggling*]

He said absurd!

GAIA: But all that matters is that I decided to stay. I decided to stay with you. I know you will desire me forever… Don't try to hide it; I know… And I want to do it now … here … in front of everybody.

[Slowly begins lifting her skirt. All the patients freeze, looking mesmerized at GAIA. She changes her mind and kneels in front of GEORGE. Her hands begin to move towards his fly, her full red lips slowly opening]

GEORGE: [*Suddenly raises his hands towards the ceiling… howling desperately*]

James, why have you forsaken me?!

BLACKOUT

END

Soledad

Andre Vltchek

from the novel Winter Journey

I drove through the snow-covered countryside of southern Chile. My journey had no particular purpose, no goal to be achieved. I was not trying to reach any destination. I simply woke up in the middle of the night in my apartment in Providencia and could not fall back to sleep. It was one o'clock in the morning, middle of the week. I rolled up the blinds and stood for some time by the window – Santiago was sound asleep, moon shining above the majestic Andes, their peaks covered by snow. I tried to read Zizek then watched the news and took a hot shower. But sleep stubbornly refused to return. Surprisingly I felt fresh and well rested.

I sensed the need to leave behind the shiny and smooth but castrating poison of Anglo-Saxon culture – its elegantly packaged lies beaming from news networks, its fascist political correctness, its form that murdered substance from midnight to midnight, relentlessly and systematically.

English was not my native tongue, but to make any impact on the world I had to read in it and write in it, because that is how things were arranged. Victorious imperialism: economic, political, militaristic, and even linguistic. All other languages were swept to the periphery. Those with mother tongues other than English had to accept concepts that were foreign to them, not only their mouths had to twist but also their thoughts. Anglo political correctness was unforgiving, dogmatic, and dictatorial. One was forced to comply or become irrelevant. One had to accept the rules or risk becoming marginalized and labeled as extremist or even terrorist.

In the middle of the night, with two articles and one book waiting in my computer to be finished, I felt dirty and defeated. My entire body revolted against the hypocrisy of Anglos and their logic, their complexes of superiority, their chauvinism and arrogance. I was fully aware that they had already managed to do what no other dictatorship had ever fully achieved: they had made almost the entire world shut up. Anglos had erected a system in which nobody dared to contradict them. While bombing and occupying entire countries and turning the United Nations into their own private bordello complete with loyal bouncers, the Anglos had designated China, Russia, and several other countries as evil and extremist, putting the world on a diet of illogical but a thousand times repeated lies.

Anglo journalism and publishing managed to turn thousands of writers and reporters into scared whores, even pimps. An imperialist use of the English language had achieved an almost complete fragmentation of the world. People in China or Thailand had to rely on the dominant Anglo publications to learn about Latin America or Africa, and vice versa.

Unless playing by the rules and fully respecting the politically correct game, one could not hope almost anything for publishing, except in the special interest, off the beaten track blogs and on-line magazines, a modern day *samizdat*. Almost all of us – writers and thinkers – learned how to censor our thoughts and our own logic if we wanted to survive and if we wanted to publish books and articles, if we wanted to be allowed to address readers. It was like a vicious circle – the more we lied, the more we were expected to lie. We were forced to lie in the morning, during the day, at night. We were forced to suppress our own thoughts as well as our convictions, to deny what our eyes and ears registered. We were fucked and so were our readers, but nobody dared to stand up and scream that this was the end of democracy, the end of the rule by the people, no matter how many political parties we had and no matter how many glossy publications were resting on the shelves of our newsstands.

Awake in the middle of the night, I realized that I was dying to escape the filthy dictate of the media straightjacket, of linguistic manipulation, of cretin simplifications and manufactured clichés. I wanted to escape the Anglos with their cool and con-vincing faces telling lies with the air of elegant superiority developed from centuries of running empires and justifying every crime they committed: in print, face to face, in the aula of the universities.

Even in the capital of one of the most remote countries on earth – Chile – I was stalked by them, constantly lectured and manipulated. My way of thinking and entire lifestyle was formed and shaped through prefabricated dogmas beaming and creeping into my living room, even my bedroom, in fact into every living room and bedroom of Santiago and into every no-matter-how-free-spirited city on earth.

Of course I myself was not pure. They worked it out that everybody was to some extend involved or they would make sure that he or she would starve to death. I needed to be paid because I had to eat and I had to travel in order to cover new stories. And that is where they had me by the balls: in order to fulfill my basic bodily and intellectual functions I had to make money. I had to publish and speak at the universities and in order to publish and speak at the universities I had to self-censor myself and to lie. I had to swallow curses and replace them with those goddamned legendary English subtleties, like when they gassed hundreds of thousands of people somewhere in the Middle East around WWII while passing little witty cracks with boyish grins, or when denying millions of people access to vital medications while justifying, straight to the cameras, this outrageous mass murder by defending their free market system – the "only natural way to prosperity."

By colonizing over half of the planet a few decades ago, Anglos had installed their tongue as the main tool of communication on this planet. Not that the world had any opportunity to say no. But language was not all that was imposed on the billions of men and women: language dictated the way people thought. And eventually what Berlin tried and failed to achieve, Washington, London, and Canberra managed with a relative ease that was fitting to an alliance in possession of such tremendous experience in plundering almost the entire world, exterminating entire native civilizations, enslaving tens of millions, inventing concentration camps in Africa, torturing and silencing dissent and ruining natural resources for the benefit of the few. As a result, a great chunk of the globe was once again bound, mummified, all revolutionary zeal broken. Revolutionaries were labeled terrorists and each and every revolution from the past was discredited by well managed publishing, media, and academic campaigns. Words expressing longing for social justice were covered by dirty and insulting slime. Nothing was sacred anymore, except for a few physical urges that had been gold-plated and elevated to a tremendous throne, then sprinkled with abstract expressions like freedom and liberty. A few countries were flattened as a warning, just in case they might dare to fight against the authorities. Those who said no were declared outcasts or perverts or both.

Mumbling some obscenities I packed a small bag and took the elevator to the ground floor. It was cold outside, cold and quiet. I could hear the sound of the tires of my car slowly approaching the gate, then the sound of an electric gate unhurriedly opening. And finally the sound of the engine, as the car accelerated on El Vergel Street.

It was still dark when I bypassed Rancagua, Talca, and Parral. I filled up the tank and spare canisters and treated myself to a large breakfast on the highway rest stop before Chillan.

Later in the morning I left the four-lane motorway and entered a two-lane highway heading straight towards the snow capped Cordillera. After passing a few ski resorts and hot springs, the paved road disappeared, and once again I was surrounded by the silence, by the virgin snow resting on wide branches of araucaria trees. At one point I stopped, killed the engine, rolled down the windows and listened. There was no sound and no sign of life, no footsteps of the animals, just the endless white color of the snow and the gray sky. A few minutes later I fired the ignition and moved on, having no problem negotiating the frozen country road with the V8 engine of the Land Rover.

Then it began snowing and the tracks ahead of me were suddenly hardly visible. I checked the compass and I was still heading east, climbing. My car was equipped for tough work in the mountains. I often took it to Bolivia and Peru, to the areas with no road. It was a workhorse with lights and gadgets that often brought me to safety from some of the most remote parts of the world. The altitude meter attached to the dashboard was now indicating 2,300 meters. The engine was roaring, the wheels hitting large stones under the snow. I did not bring snow tires. There were no road signs; there was no human habitat along the path. Now it was snowing heavily and I had to switch my windshield wipers to the highest speed. I had no idea whether I was still in Chile or whether I had crossed to Argentina.

The world that I belonged to had been left far behind: the world with news bulletins, wars, mis-ery, intrigues, and propaganda; a world that I had tried to describe and define as a writer, journalist, and filmmaker for years. It simply had disappeared; vanished. There was only snow covering the land, my car and araucaria trees, and the tremendous mountains I could not see.

Obviously I was lost. Suddenly I was not sure whether I would be able to survive, to return to the world of clearly marked motorways, cozy hotels, brightly lit fuel stations and 24 hours news net-works.

Just a few hours ago, in Santiago, I could not sleep, subconsciously longing for pristine nature, for the silence and immaculate snow. Now it was all here, around me, preventing me from seeing anything, covering the universe in white, choking me, attempting to separate me forever from the familiar world.

But I had no intention of turning back. I turned on the fog lights, but this did not change anything. I shifted down and attempted to accelerate.

This journey was as meaningless as life itself; it was to some degree comical. I pulled down the window and screamed something hostile and obnoxious to the wind and white blanket covering the entire universe. There was no echo and no reply: just persistent, mocking silence, worse than a thousand insults. Nature was showing profound indifference toward my insignificant presence. It was demonstrating spite.

Then unexpectedly everything cleared. The bright sun appeared above majestic rocky peaks, and the track I had been driving on was suddenly visible again. I was now above the clouds, almost 3,000 meters above sea level. A few minutes later, the small hut of the border post appeared on my right.

"Passport and car registration," said young woman dressed in a uniform and long coat.

"I am not leaving Chile," I said.

"Then where are you going?" she looked surprised, slightly irritated.

"Nowhere," I explained. "I want to stay here. Do you have a spare room?"

"Are you trying to be funny?" she frowned.

"No," I said. "I would like to stay here for several days. Of course I am willing to pay."

"This is an official border crossing," she rebuffed me. "You should cross into Argentina and find a hotel in the first town there. Or you can go back to Chile."

"I want to stay here," I held my ground. "I want to stay and sleep for several days. I want to take walks and do absolutely nothing. Maybe make a few big snowmen with coal-eyes and carrot noses. Do absolutely nothing. Know absolutely nothing. Worry about nothing. Is it too much to ask for?"

"You are pulling the leg of an official," she said, somehow softer than before.

"I swear I'm not! If you won't allow me to pay for the board, could you at least arrest me?"

"On what ground?"

"I can ram into the border post. Or I can insult the Chilean army."

"If you damage the hut, you would have no place to stay," she said. "As for insulting the military, I don't think it is a crime, anymore."

I gave up. "Just let me stay. Please."

She thought for a while. "Other border guards left this morning. Two men. They went to the mountains. They said they went to Argentina on an official visit, but I am sure they marched to the whorehouse on the other side. They will be gone for at least two days, so you could probably use their room. But if they suddenly come back and find you here, they will talk…"

"Let me stay just one night."

"And if I do?"

"I will pay…"

"I don't need money. I can't spend hardly anything here."

"One day you will descend from these mountains. One day you will go home, and you will need money then."

"Will I?"

"If it is not money, what would you like to have?" I asked.

"Can you tell stories?"

"I can!" I exclaimed. "That is what I have been doing all my life: collecting and telling stories."

"Liar," she was now laughing.

I had to convince her. For some reason it was extremely important to make her believe who I really was, and that stories were my entire life. I opened the dashboard and found two of my latest books. "Look at the photo on the back of the books. It's me. And the name…" I pulled my passport. "It's my name. I am a storyteller. I can tell you as many stories as you could wish to hear. Sad stories and happy stories, war stories and love stories, even some funny stories although these are increasingly rare. I can tell you some stories from the countries that you have never heard about – from Kiribati and the

Kingdom of Tonga, from Samoa and Tuvalu, even from Swaziland. Just please let me stay here."

She looked at my books and at my passport, then nodded.

"One night," she said. "You have only one night to tell me one long and meaningful story. It's just a border post here, no luxury. I am sure you are used to expensive furniture and marble bathrooms. Nothing like that here."

"I don't need any luxury."

"I will cook you a few meals, in exchange for your stories. Now park your car and get some sleep: I want you to be fresh and well rested and alert at night. I don't like to listen to stories during the day. And by the way, for the next 24 hours you will be under arrest."

"What are the charges?" I wondered, relieved.

"Attempting to bribe an officer of Chilean border guard."

"I plead guilty," I said. "What's your name?"

"Soledad," she said.

For some reason, a chill ran down my spine. "Soledad," I repeated. "What a beautiful name."

"What an appropriate name, you wanted to say…"

"No. Beautiful, nothing else."

"Surrender your passport and your car keys and go get some rest," she said. "I will park your car."

Her voice had lost all hostility. I fell asleep fully dressed, a few seconds after touching the hard cot, my bed on the border.

Lebanese grandmother praises Israel

Buff Whitman-Bradley

(July 25, 2006. Lebanon)

After seven members of her family were killed today when an Israeli missile struck her home in southern Lebanon, a Lebanese grandmother held a press conference to express her gratitude to the Israeli Defense Forces (IDF). Through a translator, 68-year-old Aisha Amadia told reporters that it was "an honor" for her children and grandchildren to die "for the only democracy in the Middle East." "In a democracy," she said, "all of the people decide, not a dictator or a king. So it seems that all of the people of Israel have decided that my family should die to keep Israelis safe from those who want a free Palestine. I feel humbled by my family's opportunity to participate in this way in a great democracy."

Mrs. Amadia went on to express appreciation for the way her family members were killed. "There is so much we Arabs can learn from the Israelis about what it means to be civilized. "Hezbollah, Hamas, Islamic Jihad, they use suicide bombers because they have no concern for human life. But Israel, a light unto the nations with the most moral army in the world, Israel would never resort to such a barbaric, primitive form of killing. Instead, they drop their bombs from missiles and jet planes. I am certain my family members would be proud to know that when they were decapitated and blown to bits in their own home, no Israeli had to explode himself in killing them."

Mrs. Amadia also praised the IDF for the humanitarian way they are waging war. She stated, "I would like the people of Israel to know how deeply I appreciate the care the IDF exercises in avoiding civilian casualties. It is a great comfort to know that Israel did everything it could to keep from killing my family. Surely Palestinian parents in Gaza and the West Bank whose children Israeli soldiers were forced to shoot in the head feel a similar sense of comfort."

And does she feel any anger or bitterness towards the Israelis?

"No," replied Mrs. Amadia, "only great pity."

Israel bombs Vermont

Buff Whitman-Bradley

(July 21, 2006. Montpelier)

Israeli jets today bombed dozens of cities, towns, and villages in Vermont, leaving hundreds dead and thousands wounded. The state's hospitals – those not destroyed in the bombing raids – are operating at maximum capacity, while countless wounded remain untreated. State officials have issued an urgent appeal for outside medical assistance. Vermont's governor told reporters, "We haven't heard from FEMA yet, but Cuba has offered to send as many teams of doctors as we can use." A spokesperson for the U.S. Department of State said that no Cuban doctors will be allowed to enter the U.S.

Asked why Israel would want to bomb Vermont, Prime Minister Ehud Olmert told reporters, "We have intelligence that indicates there are people in Vermont who blatantly disagree with the policies of the Israeli government. We will not stand idly by and allow such threats to our very existence go unanswered."

In an emergency session, the United States Senate unanimously passed a resolution supporting unconditionally Israel's right to do whatever it deems necessary to defend itself. An identical resolution passed the House of Representatives by a vote of 534-1. The lone no vote came from Vermont Congressman Ethan Allen, who said, "The Israelis might have tried town meetings before they started dropping bombs. The American Israel Public Affairs Committee (AIPAC) immediately issued a statement branding Congressman Allen as an anti-semite.

Where are the conservatives?

Buff Whitman-Bradley

"I'm confused," I said to my friend Areopagitica Truelove as we cruised the aisles of our favorite organic grocery store.

"What's got you baffled, Buffy-cakes?" she asked, tossing a package of teriyaki tofu into her basket.

"I'm trying to figure out the conservatives," I said.

"A fruitless task," Areopagitica replied. "But tell me more."

"Well," I said, "when I grew up in Nebraska among all those rock-ribbed Republicans, they preached individual freedom and states' rights and the evils of big government. I recall dire warnings about a bloated Federal government enslaving us all."

"Ah, yes," said Areopagitica. "Behind every bush lurked either a Federal bureaucrat or a com-mie waiting to snatch our liberties away."

"Right," I said, "and what has me con-founded is that the conservatives in power are now gleefully doing everything they once claimed – and still claim – that they oppose."

"Por ejemplo?" she asked.

"OK, let's start with the 2000 election," I responded. "A conservative Supreme Court ignored the principle of states' rights in taking away from Florida the decision about how to deal with the vote recount. And now, states' rights notwithstanding, the administration is overturning California's clean-air standards because they prevent the oil barons from making ever more obscene piles of money."

"I take it there is more," Areopagitica said, reading the list of ingredients on a jar of vegan mayonnaise.

"Plenty," I said. "Look at all these trade agreements, negotiated pretty much in the dark. They allow some shadowy, decidedly non-democratic tribunal to revoke any of our laws that it claims interfere with multinationals' ability to make profits."

"Bye-bye states' rights and national sover-eignty," mused Areopagitica as she ground a pound of fair-trade coffee beans.

"And," I went on, "what about the small-government crowd creating a gargantuan new Federal bureaucracy to spy on us? Our civil liberties are rapidly becoming relics of the past. These so-called conservatives have given them-selves legal permission to investigate our finan-cial records, our credit card transactions, even our bookstore purchases. They can eavesdrop on our phone conversations and our e-mail without any kind of oversight by the courts. They can detain people without charge based on secret evidence, and try them in secret. When we were kids, that's what they said those evil Soviets did.

"It seems to me that the conservatives I grew up with would be screaming bloody murder about all this."

Areopagitica placed a jar of macadamia but-ter in her basket, and paused somewhat melo-dramatically before she spoke. "Buff, Buff, Buff," she sighed. "You are suffering from acute naivete. You must understand that the guys running the country now are far from the grass-roots conservatives of your idyllic childhood. They're the oligarchs. What they want to con-serve is their own position at the top of the heap. What they don't want is anyone calling at-tention to the fact that the Emperor and his co-horts have almost all the clothes and are build-ing closets for more. Folks might start getting ideas. To keep that from happening, they em-ploy some truly nutty think-tank ideologues, for whom fascism has never been an ugly work, to spin the yar that the only way to save our free-doms is to give them up.

When you listen to the current Washington crowd scold and pontificate you can hear how they ooze arrogance. They pose as morally superior to the rest of us, but in fact, their moral development is arrested at the level of a narcissistic two-year-old. 'I want it, so it's mine!' they whine. 'You have to do what I say!' But these are toddlers in expensive Italia suits, who command armies and spies and secret police; who plunder our economy with huge tax cuts for each other; and who pillage the rest of the planet using the IMF and the World Bank!"

We were in the produce section, and Areopagitica was fiercely flinging Brussels sprouts into her basket as she spoke, her voice getting louder with each sprout. People from all over the store started wheeling their carts over to see what was going on.

"What these conservatives want is more power, pure and simple. More power to amass great wealth for themselves and their cronies. More power to run the country and the world in whatever way will best serve their economic interests. More power to quash dissent and silence critics. More power to attack impoverished countries, to send our sons and daughters into one war after another. More power to create the new Roman Empire! Power that they must wrest from the hands of the people!

"But we will not give up the power of the people!" shouted Areopagitica.

"Not to Republicans! Not to Democrats! We will not be silent. We will fill the streets! We will pack the jails! We will get these monkeys off our backs!"

The applause was deafening. "Down with Bush!" Shouting. "Down with turncoat Democrats!" Everybody was shouting, tossing biodegradable confetti into the air. A man standing by the avocado bin snapped a picture of Areopagitica and hurried out the door.

"That was a great speech," I told her as we walked to the checkout line. "But I still have one question. Why aren't the real conservatives, the ones I grew up with, the ones who believe in our freedoms and civil liberties and a non-invasive Federal government, why aren't they just as angry and upset as we are?"

"If I knew that, and five Supreme Court justices," Areopagitica coyly smiled, "I could be President."

Bush Fights Global Warming

Buff Whitman-Bradley

(Washington, DC)

In what appears to be a dramatic reversal of a long-standing administration position. President George W. Bush announced today at a press conference on the beach in front of the White House (formerly Pennsylvania Avenue), that, after long and prayerful consultation with his friend, God, he now believes that there might be some truth to the dire warnings from every reputable scientist in the world about the dangers of global warming.

According to Mr. Bush, the two old friends began to rethink their dismissal of climate change as "junk science" and "Democratic fear-mongering," when the state of Florida turned up missing. "As you know," said the President, "the state of Florida has a very special place in my heart, and when I heard on Fox News that it had disappeared, well, frankly, I began to worry. Right away, I thought about my good friend, Tony "The Buzz Saw" Scalia, and how hard he'd work to make sure I won Florida. And now I'd gone and lost it."

The President said he sent a team of the "smartest guys in the White House" to go out and look for Florida, and after several weeks of searching all over the country, they found the "Sunshine State" right where it used to be, only under thirty feet of water. "Dang!" said Mr. Bush, "That was a real surprise." But still, he didn't attribute the disappearance of Florida to global warming. "I asked my friend the Almighty about it, and He said the rising waters were probably due to some kind of long-term natural cycle, although He couldn't be absolutely sure."

What finally got the President and God to change their minds, Mr. Bush said, was when early one Sunday morning, a White House aide reported to both of them that the state of Ohio had turned up at the bottom of a vastly expanded Lake Erie. "Dang!" said Mr. Bush. "That was another real surprise. As you know, the state of Ohio has a special place in my heart. Right away, I thought about my good friend Ken "The Fixer" Blackwell, and how hard he'd worked to make sure I'd won Ohio. And now all those electoral votes were at the bottom of a lake."

Mr. Bush said that this time when he talked with "my pal Jehovah" about the inundation of the two States, "He seemed a little worried. He said to me, 'Dang, George! I'm beginning to think there might be something to this global warming talk after all. Lately I've been spending more time at the North and South Poles, and the ice is melting pretty darn fast. I suppose that could account for the current absence of Florida and Ohio.'"

"I don't mind telling you," the President went on, "that my good friend the Lord of Hosts, looked mighty worried. He said to me, 'What about my base? I promised a fire, not a flood, next time. My numbers are way down, and if I don't deliver on my promises, I'm History. We either have to get going on a fiery, nuclear Armageddon ASAP, or figure out a way to stop this global warming business."

The President said that after this chat with God, he next went to his mentor Dick, "Gepetto" Cheney. Mr. Cheney advised him that now would not be the best time for nuclear holocaust, since Halliburton, along with the corporations run by many of his closest friends, were positioned to make record profits in the next several quarters. "So Dick and I decided we needed to come up with a way to stop global warming," Mr. Bush explained. "But we wanted a good, Republican solution, not some kind of climate entitlement program where we just threw money at the problem and created a massive Federal bureaucracy that would make the climate dependent on the government for generations into the future. And, with God's help, we have found the answer."

That answer, President Bush announced after a dramatic pause, is to be called, in honor of his father, former President George H.W. Bush, A

Thousand Points of Ice — Fighting Global Warming One Cube at a Time. "Here's the way it works," said the President. "It's really neat. First, it will be a strictly voluntary program, managed by faith-based organizations, not a Federal agency. Those organizations that qualify will receive Federal funds for the collection of ice cubes. It's an incentive-based program, see? The more ice cubes they collect, the more money they'll receive."

The government, the President explained, will supply those organizations with high-tech insulated containers created especially for the Thousand Points of Ice program by "our good friends at Bechtel." "In fact, we've already awarded them a $3 billion contract for the Ice Boxes," Mr. Bush said.

Once the Ice Boxes are filled with cubes, according to the President, they will be "rendered" on special charter flights to the Arctic or the Antarctic, where they will be deposited on glaciers, ice bergs, and ice floes. "My friend the Good Lord loves it," Mr. Bush enthused. "He said it's just like when He thought up natural cycles. The ice melts up there, turns into water and comes down here. We put it into ice cube trays, freeze it, and send it right back. What could be simpler?"

Immediately after the President's press conference, the stocks of corporations that manufacture refrigerators and freezers tripled in price. Frigidaire announced its new corporate motto: Frigidaire: On the Frontlines in the War Against Climate Change. And groups opposed to gay marriage flooded Federal offices with phone calls inquiring how they could apply for the faith-based program.

Republicans in the House and Senate expressed great enthusiasm for the President's new initiative. "It's good old American ingenuity," said House Speaker Dennis Hastert. "It's the right thing to do," commented Sen. John Warner of Virginia, "and the money will get into the right hands." Sen. Rick Santorum of Pennsylvania said the program seemed good on first look, but he wanted to be certain that there would be safeguards to prevent "stealth homosexual organizations" from using ice money to "promote their agenda."

Democrats could not be found.

The war on terrorism takes a new turn

Buff Whitman-Bradley

They are smart, they are creative, they are committed. They have no regard for life, neither ours nor their own. I believe this was not an act of desperation, but an act of asymmetrical warfare waged against us.

Rear Adm. Harry Harris Jr., the commander at Guantanamo, speaking about the suicides of three Guantanamo prisoners.

(Washington, D.C.) In a major policy address before the American Enterprise Institute last night, President George W. Bush announced what he called a "breakthrough" in his administration's war on terrorism. "Beginning immediately," the president said, "the United States will take military action against millions of terrorists around the world who claim to be starving and dying of preventable and treatable water-borne diseases. That action will include missile strikes, targeted assassinations, extraordinary rendition, and all other means at our disposal to defeat this new form of terrorist threat."

In identifying the "new form" of threat, the President went on to explain that U.S. intelligence agencies have determined "contrary to what the United Nations and left-wing Irish rock stars would have us believe," there is no world hunger problem. In fact, stated the President, "world hunger is a terrorist plot to overthrow the government of the United States of America." The millions of people around the world who starve to death every year, Mr. Bush said, are actually "terrorists engaged in asymmetrical warfare, just like those so-called suicides at Guantanamo."

How, exactly, does this form of terrorism work? According to the President, it is a two-pronged assault. "It's a psy-op operation," he said. "They manipulate world opinion and seek to turn other countries against us by implying that we are cold-hearted, selfish, money-grubbers who choose not to use some of our vast wealth and power to end the so-called 'world hunger' problem or to clean up contaminated water." In addition, the President explained, the terrorists cynically prey upon the sympathies of Americans to extract hundreds of millions of dollars in charitable contributions, money that American families could use to buy new cars and appliances, go on vacations, pay increased fuel costs, and keep the U.S. economy strong. "You can be darn sure," Mr. Bush said, "that when those terrorists get their hands on Americans' hard-earned money, they don't spend it on fancy French bottled water, or go to the International House of Pancakes."

"We are up against a cunning, crafty, and dead-ly enemy," said the President. "They hate our way of life. They hate our freedom. And they will starve themselves, their families, their children, in order to destroy our freedom. They will force their infants to drink contaminated water in order to bring the hallowed pillars of Liberty crashing down around us. They do not value human life, their own, or ours, and they will stop at nothing."

In concluding his address, Mr. Bush urged all Americans "not to be fooled by those pictures of skinny, big-bellied, hollow-eyed brown kids" they see in magazine ads and charity brochures. "Send your money to them and you'll be financing terrorism by depleting America's resources." warned the President. He concluded his remarks with a ringing call for a united front against what he called "this insidious attack on all we hold dear." "The United States is a proud and powerful nation," he intoned, "and we will need all the pride and power we can muster to prevail over the Godless hordes who engage in this vicious form of terrorism, dying of hunger and dysentery in order to bring down the greatest nation on earth!"

Immediately after the President's speech, Air Force B-52s conducted saturation bombing raids of several sub-Saharan countries where the terrorists Mr. Bush identified have their training camps. Tens of thousands were reported killed.

At the same time, U.S. Special Forces teams rounded up thousands more at United Nations emergency food distribution centers and rendered them to Uzbekistan, Egypt, and Poland where they will be force fed through tubes and held indefinitely without charge.

Making a killing from global warming

Buff Whitman-Bradley

The other day I was leafletting outside my favorite organic foods market, when who should walk out with an armload of kale but my old pal Areopagitica Truelove. "Buffy-kins!" she greeted me, eyeing my flyers, "What'cha got there?"

"It's a flyer urging people to get in touch with government officials about global warming," I explained to her.

"What about global warming?" she asked.

"People in government have got to realize the devastating effects on the planet of human-generated greenhouse gases," I said.

"And you think they don't understand?" Areopagitica asked, tearing off a piece of kale and putting it in her mouth.

"No, they don't. They just don't get it. The Bush administration backed out of Kyoto and the Congress won't pass laws regulating emissions. They don't realize that we've only got a very short time before global disaster."

"Oh, they get it, all right," Areopagitica smiled, crunching on a kale stalk. "The people who run the country may be a lot of things, but they're not stupid."

"How can you say that?" I said. "Look at people like Senator Inhoffe from Oklahoma, who claim the idea of climate change is alarmist leftist propaganda."

"Inhoffe is a buffoon," Areopagitica responded, "but the people with the real power know exactly what's happening with the climate. The Pentagon even wrote a report about it stating that climate change over the next 20 years could result in global catastrophe, including nuclear wars fought over dwindling resources."

"What!?" I blurted out, incredulous.

"You heard me right, Buff-meister. And what has the government done about it? Nada. Zip. Zilch. The people in power, in and out of the government, don't care about what happens to polar bears or the Amazon rainforest or to the island countries and coastal cities that disappear or to the hundreds of millions of ordinary people who will likely die as a result of ongoing climate disasters. They look at global warming as a humongous business opportunity."

"But..." I tried to interject. But when Areopagitica gets going, it's impossible to stop her. "I just read the other day, for example, that market analysts are recommending weapons industry stocks because business is booming as governments all over the planet arm themselves in anticipation of civil unrest and the coming resource wars.

"And the energy industry is salivating over the melting of polar ice," she went on, "because not only will it open up the Northwest Passage for shipping, it'll also make it possible to explore for oil and other minerals up there. As far as Chevron is concerned, to hell with polar bears!"

People coming out of the store avoided looking at us and hurried by as Areopagitica's voice rose in pitch and volume. "The rich will create their luxurious enclaves, their own beautifully landscaped Green Zones with tennis courts and swimming pools and charming cafes and maybe even boutiquey little zoos where their over-privileged offspring can see the last timber wolf or the last great-horned owl. And they'll sell the rest of us bottled water at 10 bucks a pop..."

When she paused to take a breath I finally managed to squeeze in a comment. "Oh come on, Areopagitica, you're being overly dramatic and cynical," I protested. "They're not monsters, after all."

"Worse," she replied, "they're capitalists."

Now she spoke in a quiet, almost confidential tone of voice, as if imparting a juicy piece of gossip. "You see, Buffarootie, capitalists don't really care about much of anything except how to get more capital – hence the name. Kale?" she asked, proffering a leaf.

"Too early for me," I said. "Are you saying that capitalists don't love their kids, or care about their friends and families?"

"Oh, I'm sure they do," she responded, her voice beginning to rise again. "But their circles are very small and tight, limited to their 'own kind' " – she made quotation marks in the air – "not the riff-raff who are responsible for producing their wealth, and not you, and not me," – her voice began to rise again – "and not the Ogoni people in the Niger Delta whose lands they have poisoned, and not the Mexican farmers whose livelihoods they have destroyed by dumping subsidized corn on the market, and not the Chinese who labor in sweatshops for pennies to make next season's chicest apparel, and not the illegalized immigrants in the Central Valley breathing in pesticides as they pick our fruits and vegetables..."

"How do you do that?" I interrupted her.

"Do what?"

"Keep all that information in your head and go on and on with those long sentences and not an 'um' or an 'er' or a breath."

"It's the kale," she said.

"You know," I shook my head, "I just find it so hard to believe."

"But it's true," she replied, "kale has amazing..."

"No," I interjected, "not about the kale, about our leaders being so greedy and selfish and uncaring..."

"Well disabuse yourself, Buffismo. It's what we all have to do. Explode the myths that bind us. We're taught from the time we're little kids that we live in a classless society where the leaders represent all the people and work for the common good. But in fact, our constitution was written by a guy who said that the purpose of the government they were making was to protect the rich from the rest of us."

"You're kidding!" I exclaimed.

"Nope," Areopagitica smiled. "James Madison, the Daddy of the U.S. Constitution, said those very words."

"Wow!"

"Wow indeed. And that's just what the government, in collusion with the ruling class, the capitalists. in this' classless'" – quotation marks in the air again – "society, has been doing ever since, carrying on a relentless war against the poor and wretched of the earth, whose ranks, by the way, millions of middle class folks are about to join."

"But we vote," I said.

"If voting made a difference, as the Wobblies used to say, it would be illegal. We get our choice between two capitalist parties, both of which make it their primary purpose to do just what Jimmy Madison said, to protect the ones he called the opulent."

I felt completely deflated. "So the only way these people will do anything about global warming," I whimpered, "is if they feel that they themselves, and their bank accounts, are threatened?"

"I suppose so," said Areopagitica, stuffing one final piece of kale into her mouth, "but don't hold your breath on that one, Buffytista. As Vladimir Ilyich Ullyanov once so astutely observed: A capitalist will sell you the rope you use to hang him with.

Areopagitica gave me a big hug and said goodbye. "Gotta run, Buffster. I'm making kale brownies for the Anarchists' Bake Sale." She trotted over to her Schwinn cruiser, stuffed the kale into the saddlebags, and pedaled away into the bright afternoon.

The future is now: Ask Mr. History

Buff Whitman-Bradley

The year is 2050. We are in the studios of PPBS, the Privatized Public Broadcasting System, as another broadcast of a popular children's program is about to begin. The kids in the audience squirm and chatter excitedly as a woman wearing a headset counts down the seconds until air time: …4…3…2…1… Music begins to play, a man wearing an Uncle Sam suit trimmed with flashing lights runs out from behind a curtain and the children cheer wildly. He shouts:

Mr. History: Hey kids! What time is it?

Kids: It's Mr. History time!

Mr. History: That's right.

He begins to sing and the children join in (to the tune of Yankee Doodle Dandy):

Millard Fillmore, Betsy Ross

Davy Crockett, Tweed the Boss

The Gadsden Purchase, Boston Tea

Seward's Folly and Robert E. Lee

I'm the guy with the information

All about this mighty nation –

Everything you need to know

From Teapot Dome to the Alamo

So if you want to do your best

On standardized achievement tests

The answer is no mystery

Just …

The studio audience joins in: ASK MR. HISTORY!

Mr. History: It's great to see all you eager young historians here today.

Now, who has the first question for Mr. History?

A dozen hands shoot up. Hr. History scans the audience, looking at name tags.

Mr. History: Sally Jefferson, what's your question?

Sally: Well, Mr. History, my daddy has an old book I found in the attic and I was looking through it last night and it said something about "presidential elections." What are presidential elections?

Mr. History: Gosh, Sally, I'm surprised your father has such a book. It should have been turned in long ago. But anyway, the subject is presidential elections. Now, you may find this hard to believe, but there was a time in America when nearly all adults, no matter how ignorant or poor or uneducated, were allowed to vote to choose our president.

The children gasp.

Billy North: You mean it wasn't just the Supreme Court?

Mr. History: That's right, Billy. In fact, as strange as it seems, hundreds of millions of people actually voted for a person that they wanted to be president.

Liza Hayes: Why?

Mr. History: Well, I guess you could call it an experiment in democracy. Even though our founding fathers never intended for everyone to vote – including women and slaves and indentured servants and Indians and poor people – over the course of our history, things just started getting more and more out of hand and before you knew it, almost every adult was allowed to vote.

Timmy Jordan: But wasn't that dangerous? I mean, what if everybody voted for a bad person?

Mr. History: You're exactly right, Timmy, it was dangerous. That's what Alexander Hamilton meant when he talked about the "imprudence of demo-cracy." The truth is, you just can't trust most people to make the right kinds of decisions about what's best for our country. That's why we have leaders. Cindy?

Cindy Davenport: So how did these presidential elections work, Mr. History?

Mr. History: Well, first, the political parties had big meetings called conventions…

Sammy Martin nearly flies out of his seat, flinging his hand in the air.

Mr. History: I'll bet I know what you want to ask, Sammy. You heard me say "political parties," didn't you?

Sammy: Yes, Mr. History. Did there used to be more than one political party?

Mr. History: As amazing as it sounds, Sammy, yes there did. We used to have what was called a "two-party" system in our country. In fact, there were two major parties, the Republicans and the Demo-crats, and many small insignificant ones. The two parties did a pretty good job of keeping democracy from getting out of hand by doing their best to make sure that the people who were nominated wouldn't make any big changes if they were elected. But once we did away with elections, we didn't need any more than the one party we have now. But before we go on, let's hear from the folks who support our program.

An announcer speaks as pictures of purple mountains and amber waves of grain appear on the screen:

Ask Mr. History is made possible by generous grants from UniGene, your full-service bioengineers. Whether it's cloning a dead pet, designing a new baby brother or sister, or growing popcorn to eat at the movies, remember, why trust nature when you can trust UniGene? … And from PetRoXX Corporation, exploring for oil in our national parks. PetRoXX – the dinosaurs would have wanted it this way … And from viewers like you. Now, back to Ask Mr. History!

Mr. History: OK kids, let's continue our discussion about presidential elections. Nancy?

Nancy Turner: Mr. History, when did these presidential elections stop?

Mr. History: Nancy, the last one occurred in the year 2000. That's the year when George W bush, the grandfather of our current president George Y. Bush, was nearly defeated in the election. It was actually very exciting. The vote was close and it all came down to which candidate would win Florida. Luckily, George W. Bush's brother, Jeb Bush, was governor of that sate, and he and his supporters responded to the danger before it was too late. Many of the Florida voters were not, how shall I say this, not the best sort of people and very likely voted for Mr. Bush's opponent. So Florida election officials did the right thing and mislaid their votes. Of course, Mr. Bush's opponent contested, but a little more than a month later, the Supreme Court, in its infinite wisdom, disallowed the challenges and selected Mr. Bush as President. During the next session of Congress, both houses passed a constitutional amendment calling for the Supreme Court to choose the president from then on. Three fourths of the states approved it – Florida was the first – and the rest, as we say,

The Children: IS HISTORY!

Mr. History: After we did away with presidential elections, it didn't take our leaders long to decide that we really didn't need elections of any kind. But Sally, I can tell from your frown that you want to know more.

Sally: Gee, Mr. History, I was just thinking, it doesn't sound like such a bad idea … elections, I mean. Isn't that what democracy is supposed to be about, everybody choosing our leaders?

Mr. History: Sally, Sally, Sally. Sure, democracy is a good thing. So is ice cream. But too much ice cream can make you sick, and too much democracy can make our country sick. Remember, I told you that our Founding Fathers, those men who created the greatest democracy on earth, were concerned that only the best, most qualified people lead our country. They didn't intend for people to vote who came from bad families, who didn't have a good education, who didn't own land and businesses and factories that give work to millions. As Tommy said, allowing those kinds of people to vote would be dangerous. James Madison said it was the pur-pose of our government to protect the best people from everybody else. Remember, it's those people who own most of the country and provide your moms and dads with jobs.

Sally: I don't know, it just seems like, if everybody has to obey the rules, everybody should at least have a chance to choose the people who make the rules.

Mr. History: Do you choose your parents? Do you choose your teachers? You don't vote for them, Sally, and yet they always do what's best for you. Our leaders are not our equals, Sally, they're our betters, like our mothers and fathers. They come from the very oldest and best families. They go to the best schools. They know more than we do. And they know each other. We can trust them to take good care of us. Oh, but I see its time for one more break before we say goodbye.

Announcer speaks as pictures of Irish dancers appear on the screen: *This is PPBS. Stayed tuned. Coming up next – Riverdance: Generation after Generation after Generation.*

Mr. History: OK, kids we have time for one more question before we have to go. Yes, Sarah?

Sarah: Mr. History, why did those men in the sunglasses take Sally away?

Mr. History: Don't worry, Sarah. They just wanted Sally to show them the book she was talking about and to have a little talk with her father. And that's all we have time for today. Thanks for being here in the audience, and thanks to all of you watching us at home. See you next week, same time, same place. And remember …

If you want to do your best

On standardized achievement tests

The answer is no mystery –

Just ask Mr. History!

Between Boston and Burma

Jenny Ruth Yasi

novel excerpt

Rangoon, Burma. August 1988

That night, several armed officers including Officer Ywa (and they'd recently had him to dinner), went through the neighborhood, banging on doors. Soldiers took Maung, and three others.

At first the Williams family (Wallace, Mya, and their daughter Gurney) wasn't too worried. Being American citizens, they felt removed and protected from the extremism of this dictatorship. And the political theatre of it was so obvious. "Maung is influential. People love poets. They'll let him go."

It dawned slowly that they might be wrong.

Maung was Gurney's sweet-tempered, doe-eyed, 24 year old boyfriend. An assistant professor of poetry, Maung was also co-chairperson of the Burmese Democratic Student Organization, which Wallace supported.

Maung seemed like a member of the family, in the way he taught them Burmese words, songs, recipes. Respectful, charming, idealistic, his emotional intelligence thrilled Gurney as well as her parents. They'd all begun to expect and even hope she'd marry him.

Politically this was a risky friendship, but as Americans they were accustomed to freedom of association, and freedom of enterprise. They didn't have a habit of worrying about anything. Gurney and Maung seemed born for each other.

Wallace had invested and lost a lot in Burma. There were practical personal reasons for getting involved with Burmese politics for all of them, but now Maung had been missing for 12 hours.

The landlord came up the steps, banged on their door. "Colonel Salai Tun has been arrested," the landlord said, sounding exhausted. "Look." The front page of the state-run news service had a pic-ture of the Colonel in shackles, and the caption read "traitor captured."

"All last year I went out of my way to get to know the Colonel," Wallace said.

"They won't say who else they've got," the land-lord answered him, and Wallace's hands shook.

Mya said, "I don't think *we* have anything to worry about."

"But General Than's never been that good a friend," Wallace said. "He just liked to practice his English on us."

Gurney was boiling noodles at the stove. "They'll probably let everyone go after the rallies are over."

Mya got out the bowls. "The Generals are very image conscious. As long as there are journalists out there covering the story, the junta will try to behave itself."

After lunch, Wallace got up the gumption to call General Than, and ask about a missing mathematics professor, Wang Lee. Wang Lee was diabetic, and his wife had called Wallace, desperate to get Wang Less his medicine.

"You didn't say Wang Lee's your friend?" Mya worried aloud.

Wallace got off the phone. "No," he answered, "just that I was asking on behalf of the University."

"Ok. That sounds safe."

Wallace kneaded the side of his neck, the stained yellow of his moustache strangely mismatched from the gray hair on his head.

Mya asked him, "General Than's tone of voice was friendly?"

"Very formal," Wallace said. "He told me we should put away our cameras."

"Does he think we're idiots?" Gurney spoke up, "Does he think we won't report about this back home? Does he think the United Nations will just stand by and watch while they attack innocent people?" Dressed in jeans and sandals, Gurney flushed and curled on the carved wooden day bed. It looked like she was melting in the heat. Wallace felt a lump in his throat, and wished he'd gotten her back home to Boston before this.

"But Maung's tougher than he looks," Wallace told her. "We don't need to worry too much."

"The soldiers might come around again tonight," Mya said.

Not long after their landlord visit, an "Officer Friendly" also knocked on their door, read their names off a piece of paper. A big handgun strap-ped at his waist, wearing a uniform at least one size too large, he asked for their papers, took their passports. He spoke little English.

"We can't have our passports back?" Gurney asked as he backed out the door.

The officer's expression was icy. "No, no. Burmese law," he said. As he hustled off, electricity and telephone service in their part of the city went dead.

By five o'clock, they'd packed the car, made their way to the bus station. Everything was filthy, coated with dust from the street. The air was barely breathable. It needed to rain. Professor Hyim had called to inform them that international journalists were being prevented from entering the country.

Teenagers toting machine guns – government soldiers – were positioned at almost every intersection. Gurney was in the back seat taking pictures through the open car window.

"They're a bunch of kids," Wallace snorted. He stopped behind a cement barrier, five steps from the bus, felt lucky to be able to get so close. Mya stretched over the stick shift, hugged him, winked at Gurney.

Gurney pointed the camera at them, acting like a tourist. Wallace brushed his wife's bangs back, kissed her forehead. They told each other "I love you." The flash worked.

They'd decided to send Mya to Ting Hill monastery. It was the only spot they could think of that would have a working telephone. From there, she could make phone calls, organize a financial escape plan. Gurney and Wallace would follow in a few days, after taking photos of the demonstrations, and making sure Maung was alright.

In jasmine perfume, red lipstick, a green silk longyi, Mya filled the car with strange vigor and stamina for such a physically small person.

"Those cameras are wrecking your posture," Mya said, and Gurney unwilted herself, tried to sit up straight. Gurney snapped more images of the hugging and kissing goodbye as they bundled out of the car.

"Don't smile like that," they told each other. "You look weird."

It wasn't until the bus left the city, rumbling past overloaded cars, passing people boarding-up windows – not until the boy soldiers started to get irritable, leaning against their weapons – not until the second it was too late – they all began to have doubts, and wished they'd stayed together.

A week after she boarded the bus in Rangoon, Gurney's hair was disappearing from Mya's hair-brush, the scent of Wallace fading from her clothes. She tried to meditate, but instead went through arguments they'd have when he finally got there: General Than could kill them if that would make someone more important happy. It wasn't going to be easy to get out of Burma, at least not as easy as Wallace thought.

Outside, trickling water and warm breezes ruffled leaves. Monkeys, birds, a little pack of dogs altogether were making a kind of music. In other circumstances, the monastery was an enchanting place to visit.

From an adjoining pagoda window, a young man leaned out, and made a slotted silhouette against her wall. She watched him pouring water, rolling his young wet head in the sun, closing his eyes. He reminded Mya of Maung.

If Gurney had been there, she would have jabbed her mother in the ribs, making a joke of it. "Come on Mumma. Let's shave our heads. It's cute!"

When there are so many free countries, how can anyone, in this day and age, justify raising their family inside a dictatorship if they don't have to? Mya wondered if it was her responsibility as a mother to give her daughter this sort of guidance. Though she admired Maung's willingness to make personal sacrifices for the sake of future generations, it also frightened her. Once she'd told Gurney, not meaning Maung wasn't a good man, not intending to be cynical, but she said love and family-life can be complicated when politics are an issue.

The young monk was still washing his head.

Before the University closed, before the first rallies that spring, while Maung was playing the role of future son-in-law to the hilt, she'd counseled like any good Buddhist would do: "Live in the present. We'll worry about the future when we get there." But this wasn't even her country any longer. And if she owed Burma anything, she thought, wasn't her own life enough?

The tropical sky was yellow-brown. It was so humid, dust sponging up moisture, leaking between mango and breadfruit trees, the muddy air glistened like shellac against the monk's wet head. He raised the pitcher with one hand, rubbed his head as it poured, spit down onto the bushes, shook the excess off cheerfully, and finally pulled himself back into the pagoda.

Several laughing voices resounded, and it seemed strange, to hear that laughing. No crisis stops the world from laughing.

A trickle of sweat ran down her back. A gong chimed several times. Mya hung up her towel, dressed. The rhythm of her breathing matched the watery sound of sandals slapping the stone tiles between the nun's quarters and the central pagoda.

Artillery firing in the jungle had increased.

Heli-copters were passing overhead, and air traffic was unusual in this part of the country. Black clouds underscored with orange soot scraped a trail into the northern hillside.

Somehow, despite her pedigree, Mya still felt like a spectator – remotely involved, waiting. Soon, she expected some signal from the dictatorship that global political pressures were having an impact. She thought, all civilizations eventually modernize. Evolution is moving naturally towards self-govern-ment and democracy. It seemed impossible that the rule of tooth and claw could ever again dominate the world. Because her life had worked in this way, Mya told herself that it was just a matter of time and education before they would all be living in free countries.

It was twenty-odd miles to Rangoon. Gurney and Robert could walk it, if they had to. She expected them to show up any day.

In spite of canceled classes, closed airport and bus-iness districts, and departing citizens, the streets weren't empty. Rangoon wasn't sleepy.

Pro-democracy banners streamed out windows. People wore matching white armbands. Gurney took a picture of her father.

"Don't waste film on me," he said.

A boy, maybe 17 years old, dirty hair squashed into his helmet, suddenly appeared from a doorway and was glaring at them, holding onto an AK-47, shifting the nozzle of the weapon back and forth along the ground, beckoning them.

"I'm really focused on the soldier standing behind you," Gurney said.

Wallace glanced over his shoulder. "Yeah? You notice that warrior boy is pointing his thingy right at you?"

Wallace hardly dared break his gaze with the soldier kid but somehow Gurney was giggling. She crinkled her eyes, waggling her expressive eyebrows up and down.

"Come," the soldier kid gestured.

"Oh well. K-kiss our film goodbye," and Wal-lace actually stuttered. He hadn't stuttered in years. "Don't push it, honey," he said.

The young soldier's acne-covered face turned red as he gestured to Gurney to hand him the camera.

Wallace reached for his wallet. "Here. I'll take care of that," and took out a fistful of the American dollars he carried for emergencies. The soldier took the wad. A child ran up from the sidewalk, and Wallace handed her a fistful, too. "Easy come, easy go," he said, "Money makes everybody happy." His knees were shaking.

The soldier stuffed the bills in his pocket, and turned towards an approaching car. Gurney pulled Wallace half a dozen steps off the road into a long alley full of dumpsters. They ran.

"Is that him shouting?" Wallace asked, puffing for breath.

"I think so," she said. They kept running.

Behind the European-styled granite buildings were smaller brick buildings, then shabby carved wood, then rows of corrugated cardboard and aluminum shacks piled on top of one another, and cement gutters full of sewage, yards stinking and strewn with animal feces, buzzing insects, scavenging rats, empty cans. Ginger root, and a scrawny plantain, cucumbers, grew up here and there. Gurney tied back her hair, and put a scarf over her neck.

The mosquitoes were bad. Gurney and Wallace crossed under flapping laundry, around cook fires, through mud under rickety stilted houses, over soapy puddles and patches of vine. Clouds of bugs flew into their faces.

Finally they saw the main road. A convoy of trucks, buses, and four armored tanks blocked it, facing east, engines humming.

"Now that's a waste of taxpayers' money," Wallace said.

Facing this barricade, barred from entering or leaving the City, was a ragtag crowd on foot. Students, monks, drummers, dancers, children, parents, and grandparents, flying banners and flags: if not for the tanks, it could have looked festive.

"There's Trin, and Beado Win." Gurney recognized several students.

Wallace sighed. "I'm getting too old for this." He had to push back her scarf to look into his daughter's eyes. "You okay?"

"No," she said, so he took her hand, gave it a squeeze.

Somehow Trin and Beado were in high spirits. They'd heard (through an officer friend) that Maung was released, though no one had seen him yet. They drove Gurney and Wallace the long way around the city center and found a back way through the crowd, dropped them back at their apartment. Wallace and Gurney intended to wash up, and rest until speeches officially got started.

Wallace and Gurney seemed to be the only ones at home inside their building. They packed a few essentials, washed hands and faces, changed clothes, drank water. They considered options and told each other, "Maybe we shouldn't come back here tonight."

Vendors were selling balls of hot rice, candy, box drink, banners, kites, torches. A merchant with a long, skinny braid rolled up yards of fabric, boarded shut his shop. People hurried by with water, food, fuel. Gurney wiped mold off the camera lenses.

A group of monks floated past, bowing, prostrating themselves against the ground. Smoke curled up Wallace's cigarette hand like a pet snake.

They arrived at a touristy table set up on the sidewalk by an open-air noodle vendor.

Gurney and Wallace ate noodles. Wallace felt ill.

Then Wallace was really sick.

"Such bad timing," he groaned. He lay down on the bench. Gurney looked him over.

Wallace was dizzy.

"Daddy, I'll be right back," Gurney said. "I just want to run over to the hospital. Maung might be there."

"Okay." He felt sick enough that he didn't care. Gurney had friends at the hospital. A hospital is a safe enough place to go. But when after five minutes, she was still gone, Wallace sat back up. He felt he'd made a stupid mistake. He lit a cigarette.

Another half hour, on his back on the bench, Wallace waited for Gurney. The nausea transformed to pure worry. He was just leaving to look for her when the shooting began.

It started at some distance, like a roar of applause, pure cacophony, and then there were trucks. The roar got closer, and you could hear shooting. People began running. The smoky urban silhouette lingered, a thick black line painted on a violet-red and blue-gray night. Wallace stuck his head around a corner, a hornet whistled past his ear. He ducked.

At first, no one could believe it. Then everyone was running, aiming for things like cars, the corners of buildings, they ran, crouched, dropping. He fell against a doorway where a boy about Gurney's age stood trembling, cursing.

The soldiers got closer. The boy ran on. Wallace didn't know what to do.

They were shooting people with armbands. Wallace hid against a wall. Bodies were in the doorways, on the sidewalks. Any second, he expected to be dead.

It amazed him, as the crowd fell and thinned, to find his body still standing, his heartbeat still drumming in his ears. His shoes dripped, but he was still alive, still moving.

At different points, he thought he saw Mya, then Maung, or Gurney. A light-skinned body was on the ground, and Wallace touched it, nearly collapsing. But it wasn't anyone he knew.

Finally, he saw her near the hospital. Bodies, several bodies in white hospital uniforms, were sprawled dead across the steps of the hospital. Gurney was helping to drape sheets over their bodies. She shouted at him, "Daddy!"

He ran out to meet her, and dragged her back across the street. "Daddy, I'm so sorry! I'm sorry!" He didn't realize he was hurting her until she screamed.

Bodies, collapsed canopies, abandoned vehicles, surrounded them in an eerie quiet. People wandered past, erupted with bullet holes, losing strength in a lava flow of blood.

They fell into a corner as a jeep rumbled past, loaded with students.

Gurney shivered against the back of his knees. Wallace whispered, reaching one hand back to his daughter, "More film."

Gurney's voice was soft as a feather. "It's done."

Wallace took her elbow, while she heaved onto the pavement.

He took her elbow, shook her. "It's officially your turn to be brave," he said, and wiped off her mouth with a corner of his shirt.

Wallace took a breath, pushing away vertigo, more startled by his daughter's pale face than by the sight of his own blood filling his shoes. Gurney looked at his sopping shoes.

"I stepped in something," he said.

"Oh my God."

"It's nothing," he said. "Don't worry about it."

Someone came running around the corner. Wallace pulled Gurney deeper into the alley. There was a door, but it was locked.

Flies swarmed around them, clung to their faces.

Gurney asked, "Daddy, are you bleeding?"

A jeep sped by, lights bumping holes into the dark. They leaned trembling against the building.

"Enough of this bullshit," he said. "See that door?" Across the road was a public access to an indoor market, a mini mall. The entry was partly open. He stuffed exposed film into her pockets. It didn't matter if he ever got back. But maybe the film would be helpful.

A major chord of jeep, helicopter, generator, barking dogs, sounded. "When I say run," he used his most fatherly tone of voice, "don't even slow down for me, okay? I'll catch up." He smiled, held her, tried not to wobble.

"I love you Daddy."

"Don't be so goddamned grim." He gave her a kiss.

She jogged across the road, while Wallace's leg was disappointing him. He felt incredibly fatigued. He could hardly lift his leg. "Go. Go. I'll catch up."

She started down the steps to the marketplace, hesitating at the entrance. A shadow crossed the front display window. People were inside the door.

Gurney whirled and tripped back up the steps, pulling his arm, dragging him backwards along the sidewalk, "Daddy! Run! Jesus!"

"You go. Get that out of here. I'll be fine." He couldn't run, didn't weep, didn't think, just shoved his daughter away. "They aren't worried about old schmucks like me." The group of boys in uniform staggered out of the market, heard Gurney's footsteps and looked in her direction. Wallace held up the empty camera by pure instinct.

Gurney was halfway down the sidewalk, perfectly in view of soldiers lifting weapons like kids playing dangerously. Wallace yelled, "Hey! Hey! We're tourists!" One kid nudged another, they all turned towards him. "Picture? Can I take your picture?"

Wallace held up the empty camera his arms shaking, and a bullet flew over his head. It surprised him; it shouldn't have. "We're tourists," he said, and dug in his pockets for more dollars. "American tourists."

She looked back. She saw her father pose; saw him trying to be funny. But his arms went up, the camera went flying.

Ten years later, when Gurney was safely living in Boston, married to an American, mother to this angry Burmese boy, she wondered how it was that she could have run as fast as she apparently did. Film canisters bouncing in her pockets, she'd rounded the corner before her father's body even hit the ground.

LIBERATORY FICTION PAST

Ernest Callenbach
Ecotopia (excerpt)

Claude McKay
Banjo (excerpts)

Upton Sinclair
The Jungle (excerpt)

Mark Twain
The War Prayer

Stella Miles Franklin
My Career Goes Bung (excerpt)

Charles Chesnutt
The Marrow of Tradition (excerpt)

Charlotte Perkins Gilman
The Yellow Wallpaper

Victor Hugo
Les Misérables (excerpt)

Harriet Beecher Stowe
Uncle Tom's Cabin (excerpt)

Jonathan Swift
A Modest Proposal

Ecotopia (excerpt)

Ernest Callenbach

San Francisco, May 12. It is widely believed among Americans that the Ecotopians have become a shiftless and lazy people. This was the natural conclusion drawn after Independence, when the Ecotopians adopted a 20-hour work week. Yet even so no one in America, I think, has yet fully grasped the immense break this represented with our way of life – and even now it is astonishing that the Ecotopian legislature, in the first flush of power, was able to carry through such a revolutionary measure.

What was at stake, informed Ecotopians insist, was nothing less than the revision of the Protestant work ethic upon which America has been built. The consequences were plainly severe. In economic terms, Ecotopia was forced to isolate its economy from the competition of harder-working peoples. Serious dislocations plagued their industries for years. There was a drop in Gross National Product by more than a third. But the profoundest implications of the decreased work week were philosophical and ecological: mankind, the Ecotopians assumed, was not meant for production, as the 19th and early 20th centuries had believed. Instead, humans were meant to take their modest place in a seamless, stable-state web of living organisms, disturbing that web as little as possible. This would mean sacrifice of present consumption, but it would ensure future survival – which became an almost religious objective, perhaps akin to earlier doctrines of "salvation." People were to be happy not to the extent they dominated their fellow creatures on the earth, but to the extent they lived in balance with them.

This philosophical change may have seemed innocent on the surface. Its grave implications were soon spelled out, however. Ecotopian economists, who included some of the most highly regarded in the American nation, were well aware that the standard of living could only be sustained and increased by relentless pressure on work hours and worker productivity. Workers might call this "speed-up," yet without a slow but steady rise in labor output, capital could not be attracted or even held; financial collapse would quickly ensue.

The deadly novelty introduced into this accepted train of thought by a few Ecotopian militants was to spread the point of view that economic disaster was not identical with survival disaster for persons – and that, in particular, a financial disaster could be turned to advantage if the new nation could be organized to devote its real resources of energy, knowledge, skills, and materials to the basic necessities of survival. If that were done, even a catastrophic decline in the GNP (which was, in their opinion, largely composed of wasteful activity anyway) might prove politically useful.

In short, financial chaos was to be not endured but deliberately engineered. With the ensuing flight of capital, most factories, farms and other productive facilities would fall into Ecotopian hands like ripe plums.

And in reality it took only a few crucial measures to set this dismal series of events in motion: the nationalization of agriculture; the announcement of an impending moratorium on oil-industry activities; the forced consolidation of the basic retail network constituted by Sears, Penneys, Safeway, and a few other chains; and the passage of stringent conservation laws that threatened the profits of the lumber interests.

These moves, of course, set off an enormous clamor in Washington. Lobbyists for the various interests affected tried to commit the federal government to intervene militarily. This was, however, several months after Independence. The Ecotopians had established and intensively trained a nationwide militia, and airlifted arms for it from France and Czechoslovakia. It was also believed that at the time of secession they had mined major Eastern cities with atomic weapons, which they had constructed in secret or seized from weapons research laboratories.

Washington, therefore, although it initiated a ferocious campaign of economic and political pressure against the Ecotopians, and mined their harbors, finally decided against an invasion.

This news set in motion a wave of closures and forced sales of businesses – reminiscent, I was told, of what happened to the Japanese-Americans who were interned in World War II. Members of distinguished old San Francisco families were forced to bargain on most unfavorable terms with representatives of the new regime. Properties going back to Spanish land-grant claims were hastily disposed of. Huge corporations, used to dictating policy in city halls and statehouses, found them-selves begging for compensation and squirming to explain that their properties were actually worth far more than their declared tax value.

Tens of thousands of employees were put out of work as a consequence, and the new government made two responses to this. One was to absorb the unemployed in construction of the train network and of the sewage and other recycling facilities necessary to establish stable-state life systems. Some were also put to work dismantling allegedly hazardous or unpleasant relics of the old order, like gas-stations. The other move was to adopt 20 hours as the basic work week – which, in effect, doubled the number of jobs but virtually halved individual income. (There were, for several years, rigid price controls on all basic foods and other absolute necessities.)

Naturally, the transition period that ensued was hectic – though many people also remember it as exciting. It is alleged by many who lived through those times that no one suffered seriously from lack of food, shelter, clothing, or medical treatment – though some discomfort was widespread, and there were gross dislocations in the automobile and related industries, in schools, and in some other social functions. Certainly many citizens were deprived of hard-earned comforts they had been used to: their cars, their prepared and luxury foods, their habitual new clothes and appliances, their many efficient service industries. These disruptions were especially severe on middle-aged people – though one now elderly man told me that he had been a boy in Warsaw during World War II, had lived on rats and potatoes, and found the Ecotopian experience relatively painless. To the young, the disruptions seem to have had a kind of wartime excitement – and indeed sacrifices may have been made more palatable by the fear of attack from the United States. It is said by some, however, that the orientation of the new government toward basic biological survival was a unifying and reassuring force. Panic food hoarding, it is said, was rare. (The generosity with food which is such a feature of Ecotopian life today may have arisen at that time.)

Of course the region that comprises Ecotopia had natural advantages that made the transition easier. Its states had more doctors per capita, a higher educational level, a higher percentage of skilled workers, a greater number of engineers and other technicians, than most other parts of the Union. Its major cities, except for Seattle, were broadly based manufacturing and trade complexes that produced virtually all the necessities of life. Its universities were excellent, and its resources for scientific research included a number of the topnotch facilities in the United States. Its temperate climate encouraged an outdoor style of life, and made fuel shortages caused by ecological policies an annoyance rather than the matter of life or death they would have been in the severe eastern winters. The people were unusually well versed in nature and conservation lore, and experienced in camping and survival skills.

We cannot, however, ignore the political context in which the transition took place. As Ecotopian militants see the situation, by 1980 there had been almost a quarter century of military action in Indochina. American involvement in Southeast Asia was in its fifteenth year. Cease-fires had come and gone. Evading Congressional fiscal controls, the U.S. administration had continued with attempts to find a "final solution" to Asian uprisings. The burden of military outlays to support an enormous arms establishment caused economic disruption even after the citizenry lost the power to control them. The persistent inflation and recession of the seventies had caused widespread misery and undermined Americans' confidence in economic progress; wildcat strikes and seizures of plants by workers had required the almost constant mobilization of the National Guard. After the abortive antipollution efforts of the early seventies, the toll of death and destruction had resumed its climb. Energy crises had bred economic disruption and price gouging. And chronic Washington scandals had greatly reduced faith in central government.

"All this," one Ecotopian told me, "convinced us that if we wished to survive we had to take matters into our own hands." I pointed out that this had always been the claim of conspiratorial revolutionaries, who presume to act in the name of the majority, but take care not to allow the majority to have any real power. "Well," he replied, "things were clearly not getting any better – so people really were ready for change. They were literally sick of bad air, chemicalized foods, lunatic advertising. They turned to politics because it was finally the only route to self-preservation."

"So," I replied, "in order to follow an extremist ecological program, millions of people were willing to jeopardize their whole welfare, economic and social?"

"Their welfare wasn't doing so well, at that point," he said. "Something had to be done. And nobody else was doing it. Also" – he shrugged, and grinned – "we were very lucky." This gallows humor, which reminds me of the Israelis or Viennese, is common in Ecotopia. Perhaps it helps explain how the whole thing happened. ...

Got a strange call on the hotel phone last night, from a gruff-sounding man who asked if he and a couple of friends could see me. He had his phone picture switched off to start, but after I said I'd be glad to talk to him, he turned it on. We met at a coffee-house he suggested, which turned out to have the atmosphere of a men's club: dark wood panelling, newspapers on racks along the wall, beer, good coffee, pastries. They started out by saying how pleased they were to hear of my visit, and that they hoped relations between the two countries would now begin to improve.

This was news: no Ecotopians I've met so far have seemed to give much of a damn about relations with the U.S. one way or the other. I began to study my companions more closely. They were evidently businessmen of some kind – there is a way in which business people tend to assume proprietorship which seemed familiar. I began to see who they probably were: the Opposition!

The gruff one introduced us all. Then, rather gingerly, they began to explain their position: that, while many of the ecological reforms of the new government were of course necessary and desirable, others stifled their spirit of enterprise. "The economy, as you have seen by now, has been going downhill steadily. It's terrible, what we have lost. Worse, we are on a collision course with the U.S."

"How is that?" I asked.

"Let's face it. We are a small nation on the periphery of a very large one. Persisting in this ecological craziness will sooner or later lead to an armed conflict, and we will be wiped out. We know what you did to Vietnam, what you're doing now in Brazil. Our atomic mines might turn out to be a bluff. Then it could happen here too."

"So what can you do?"

"We could take a softer line – make a few compromises. We're excited by your coming because it could lead to resumption of normal relations between the two countries. From that, we could see the exchange of pilot plants, to show what happens when you let the managers manage – and gradually a growth of economic interdependence. In time, we could get our economy going again on modern lines."

"Isn't the Progressive Party working in that direction?"

There was a pause. "Yes, but they only put up a token struggle. They pay lip service to the idea of change, but when it comes to real changes, they drag their feet. They're really almost as bad as the Survivalists. We've just about given up on them."

"So what are you going to do?"

They shifted uneasily. "We have great hopes from your visit, first of all. We urge you to speak for the idea of normalization of relations, here and when you get back to Washington. We hope that will get things moving. But we also want you to know that we are prepared to fight for our ideas."

I looked at them, startled. "Fight?"

They looked back, very solemnly, and then must have decided to take their big chance. "We have been led to believe that the U.S. government supports clandestine groups in countries with governments thought to be unfriendly. The time is coming when normal means of political action may no longer serve. Ecotopia has to be made to realize that it must change course. We are ready for anything. But we need help."

"You aren't afraid of being taken simply for American agents?"

"It's a chance we'll have to take. We would of course ask for materials that can't be traced to U.S. sources." It was my turn to pause. "You mean you are asking for explosives, guns?" They looked at me a little disappointed. "Of course. We will then be in a position to dramatize that the present course has un-acceptable costs. There is only one way to do that."

"Well," I said, "you must realize I am a journal-ist, not a C.I.A. agent!" They smiled politely but skeptically. "However, I suppose I could pass on what you have told me to people who might be inter-ested. How much popular support can you demon-strate for your proposed actions?"

"You know how people are – they go with what's popular at the time, even when it's against their own interests. But dramatic action will generate immense enthusiasm."

"I looked them over. They are not a terribly con-vincing lot of prospective terrorists – but then proba-bly that's the way most any terrorists look. A couple of them are over 50, people who in the U.S. would be members of Rotary or country club – normal, pro-ductive citizens – but here find themselves misfits. A couple are young, hot-eyed, resentful, dangerous. – How they got that way, I have no idea, but they would probably be against the regime whatever it

was or did. So far, I see no signs they would have any substantial social backing. All the same, I made notes of how they can be found. Coming out of the coffee-shop, we could have been businessmen who had just worked out a division of the territory....

© *1975 by Ernest Callenbach, available from both* **Heyday Books** *(with an author's afterword) and*
Bantam

Banjo (excerpts)

Claude McKay

Excerpts from the chapters "Official Fists" and

"Banjo's Ace of Spades," in McKay's novel Banjo

Crosby was younger than Ray. A young poet who had the fanatical faith of youth in the magic of poetry, he argued with Ray about his marked absorption in prose. Ray contended that it seemed a natural process to him that youth should pass from the colorful magic of poetry to the architectural rhythm of prose.

They parted after midnight. Crosby's hotel lay west of the Canebiere and Ray's to the east. The east was more respectable in Marseilles than the west. The mail had arrived in the late evening, bringing the Paris morning newspapers. Ray took his way to his respectable quarter in his most respectable rags, armed with respectability – in the form of the Paris editions of the *New York Herald Tribune*, the British *Daily Mail* and *Le Journal*.

He was thinking about Banjo and the boys and of their beating-up and philosophically wondering if the boys had not done something to deserve the beating – something that Banjo had not revealed in telling about it – when passing two policemen in the street leading to his hotel (one leaning against the door of a house and the other standing carelessly on the pavement), he was suddenly grabbed without warning. The policemen started to search him roughly and thoroughly.

Ray protested. What was it and what did they want of him? he demanded. He had his papers and would show them immediately. This he was proceeding to do when the bigger policeman stunned him with a blow of his fist on the back of the neck. He forthwith arrested Ray, handcuffed him, and took him to the police station in the bawdy quarter. The handcuff was a special chain kind that could be tightened and loosened at will and the policeman took great pleasure in torturing Ray on the way to the jail. There the two police wrote out and signed a charge against him. Ray also made a signed statement. The police quarters stank much more than the dirtiest den of the Ditch with that odor peculiar to jails. Ray was locked up all night and in the early morning was told to go.

As to the why of his arrest and brutal treatment Ray could obtain no answer. He went home and wrote a statement of his case to the prefect. A couple of days later he received a notice to call a police headquarters. Crosby, who was particularly worked up over the incident, accompanied him. He was a Western-state lad of radical persuasion. His great-grandfather had been a frontiersman, an Indian-fighter in the struggle to win the West for civilization. His mother, a Southern woman, came from one of the proudest of the slave states.

At police headquarters Ray repeated his statement to an investigating inspector, who confronted him with the two policemen. They contradicted his story, asserting that Ray had tried to obstruct them in doing their duty, but he maintained his statement and further accused them of lying.

The inspector was naturally partial to his men. He read the statements again and then asked Ray what he wanted. Ray hesitated, and Crosby said, "Justice." The inspector turned and said savagely he was not talking to him. The word "justice" had been the first to suggest itself to ray, but as he did not believe in that prostitute lady who is courted and caressed by every civilized tout, he had not pronounced her name.

The inspector then admitted that if Ray prosecuted the case on the statement he had made, the policeman who had struck him would lose his job. Did he want to prosecute or not? Crosby was nudging him to prosecute, but Ray declared that what he really wanted was to know why he had been beaten and arrested. Was it because he was black? The inspector replied that the policemen had made a mistake, owing to the fact that all the Negroes in Marseilles were criminals.

"Oh!" Ray said, this was the first time he had heard that Doctor Bougrat was a Negro. The police clerk who had taken Ray's statement hid a grin behind his palm.

(The Doctor Bougrat case had provided the excitable Provencal city with one of its most notorious crime sensations. The man had been a soldier during the war and was seriously wounded in the head. He was a drug addict and a hard drinker. One day the body of a cashier who had disappeared with an unimportant sum of money was found hidden in his office in a state of decomposition. Doctor Bougrat declared that the man had died accidentally after an injection. He was indicted for murder and sentenced to life imprisonment and banishment. The case had particularly impressed Ray from the way the public reacted to it. The newspapers tried the doctor and called him a murderer and a thief and charged him with every criminal activity before the case went to the courts. And on the day when the crime was reconstituted, according to French procedure, in the doctor's office, an enormous crowd gathered in the street and along the Canebiere *prolongee* and the army of the touts and prostitutes who lived by the plunder of tourists and seamen joined their voices to that of the respectability of the city in calling for Bougrat's blood: "Lynch him! Lynch him!")

As he accepted his dismissal and started to go, Ray turned to the inspector and said that when he was a boy the French book that had moved him most was Victor Hugo's *Les Misérables*. Javert, typifying the police, had been particularly fascinating to him, and judging from the inspector's statement about the Negroes of Marseilles the French police had not changed since those days. But had grown a little worse.

Crosby's sense of injustice was strong. He resented the inspector's insulting manner toward him and he reproached Ray for not following up the case.

"But I didn't want to," protested Ray. "Do you think I want to mess my time up fooling with the stinking law, just for a policeman to lose his job? Twenty-five francs a day and a family! That most sacred of French things – a family on twenty-five francs a day. Can you wonder they are what they are? When I wrote to the prefect I didn't write for revenge, but for knowledge."

"But what good is that?" said Crosby. "You only wasted your time, since you had a chance to prosecute and didn't. You haven't gained anything."

"Haven't I? Don't you think it was revenge enough for me that you, an American, half-Southerner, had to protest to the French official about French injustice to a Negro? The French are never tired of proclaiming themselves the most civilized of people in the world. They think they understand Negroes, because they don't discriminate against us in their bordels. They imagine that Negroes like them. But Senghor, the Senegalese, told me that the French were the most calculatingly cruel of all the Europeans in Africa.

"You heard what the inspector said in explanation. To me the policeman's fist was just the perfect expression of the official attitude toward Negroes. Why should I prosecute *him*?"

[...]

This was the way of civilization with the colored man, especially the black. The happenings of the past few weeks from the beating up of the beach boys by the police to the story of Taloufa's experiences, were, to Ray, all of a piece. A clear and eloquent exhibition of the universal attitude, which, though the method varied, was little different anywhere.

When the police inspector said to Ray that the strong arm of the law was against Negroes because they were all criminals, he really did not mean just that. For he knew that the big and terror-striking criminals were not Negroes. What he unconsciously meant was that the police were strong-armed against the happy irresponsibility of the Negro in the face of civilization.

For civilization had gone out among these

native, earthy people, had despoiled them of their primitive soil, had uprooted, enchained, transported, and transformed them to labor under its laws, and yet lacked the spirit to tolerate them within its walls.

That this primitive child, this kinky-headed, big-laughing black boy of the world, did not go down and disappear under the serried crush of trampling white feet; that he managed to remain on the scene, not worldly-wise, not "getting there," yet not machine-made, nor poor-in-spirit like the regimented creatures of civilization, was baffling to civilized understanding. Before the grim, pale rider-down of souls he went his careless way with a primitive hoofing and a grin.

Thus he became a challenge to the clubbers of helpless vagabonds – to the despised, under-paid protectors of property and its high personages. He was a challenge of civilization itself. He was the red rag to the mighty-bellowing, all-trampling civilized bull.

Looking down in a bull ring, you are fascinated by the gay rag. You may even forget the man watching the bull go after the elusive color that makes him mad. The rag seems more than the man. If the bull win it, he horns it, tramples it, sniffs it, paws it – baffled.

As the rag is to the bull, so is the composite voice of the Negro – speech, song and laughter – to a bawdy world. More exasperating, indeed, than the Negro's being himself is his primitive color in a world where everything is being reduced to a familiar formula, this remains strange and elusive.

[...]

Ray was not of the humble tribe of humanity. But he always felt humble when he heard the Senegalese and other West African tribes speaking their own languages with native warmth and feeling.

The Africans gave him a positive feeling of wholesome contact with racial roots. They made him feel that he was not merely an unfortunate accident of birth, but that he belonged definitely to a race weighed, tested, and poised in the universal scheme. They inspired him with confidence in them. Short of extermination by the Europeans, they were a safe people, protected by their own indigenous culture. Even though they stood bewildered before the imposing bigness of white things, apparently unaware of the invaluable worth of their own, they were naturally defended by the richness of their fundamental racial values.

He did not feel that confidence about Aframericans who, long-deracinated, were still rootless among the phantoms and pale shadows and enfeebled be self-effacement before condescending patronage, social negativism, and miscegenation. At college in America and among the Negro intelligentsia he had never experienced any of the simple, natural warmth of a people believing in themselves, such as he had felt among the rugged poor and socially backward blacks of his island home. The colored intelligentsia lived its life "to have the white neighbors think well of us," so that it could move more peaceably into nice "white" streets.

Only when he got down among the black and brown working boys and girls of the country did he find something of that raw unconscious and the -devil-with-them pride in being Negro that was his own natural birthright. Down there the ideal skin was brown skin. Boys and girls were proud of their brown, sealskin brown, teasing brown, tantalizing brown, high-brown, low-brown, velvet brown, chocolate brown.

There was the amusing little song they all sang:

> "Black may be evil,
> But yellow is so low-down;
> White is the devil,
> So glad I'm teasing Brown."

Among them was never any of the hopeless, enervating talk of the chances of "passing white" and the specter of the Future that were common topics of the colored intelligentsia. Close association with the Jakes and Banjoes had been like participating in a common primitive birthright.

Ray loved to be with them in constant physical contact, keeping warm within. He loved their tricks of language, loved to pick up and feel and taste new words from their rich reservoir of niggerisms. He did not like rotten-egg stock words among rough people any more than he liked colorless refined phrases among nice people. He did not even like to hear cultured people using the conventional stock words of the uncultured and thinking they were being free and modern. That sounded vulgar to him.

But he admired the black boys' unconscious artistic capacity for eliminating the rotten-dead stock words of the proletariat and replacing them with startling new ones. There were no dots and dashes in their conversation – nothing that could no be frankly said and therefore decently – no act or fact of life for which they could not find a simple passable word. He gained from them finer nuances of the necromancy of language and the wisdom that any word may be right and magical in its proper setting.

He loved their natural gusto for living down the past and lifting their kinky heads out of the hot, suffocating ashes, the shadow, the terror of real sorrow to go on gaily grinning in the present. Never had Ray guessed from Banjo's general manner that he had known any deep sorrow. Yet when he heard him tell Goosey that he had seen his only brother lynched, he was not surprised, he understood, because right there he had revealed the depths of his soul and the soul of his race – the true tropical African Negro. No Victorian-long period of featured grief and sable mourning, no mechanical-pale graveside face, but a luxuriant living up from it, like the great jungles growing perennially beautiful and green in the yellow blaze of the sun over the long life-breaking tragedy of Africa.

Ray had felt buttressed by the boys with a rough strength and sureness that gave him spiritual passion and pride to be his human self in an inhumanly alien world. They lived healthily far beyond the influence of the colored press whose racial dope was characterized by pungent "bleach-out," "kink-no-more," skin-whitening, hair-straighten-ing, and innumerable processes for Negro culture, most of them manufactured by white men's firms in the cracker states. And thereby they possessed more potential power for racial salvation than the Negro *litterati*, whose poverty of mind and purpose showed never any signs of enrichment, even though inflated above the common level and given an appearance of superiority.

From these boys he could learn how to live – how to exist as a black boy in a white world and rid his conscience of the used-up hussy of white morality. He could not scrap his intellectual life and be entirely like them. He did not want or feel any urge to "go back" that way.

Tolstoy, his great master, had turned his back on the intellect as guide to find himself in Ivan Durak. Ray wanted to hold on to his intellectual acquire-ments without losing his instinctive gifts. The black gifts of laughter and melody and simple sensuous feelings and responses.

Once when a friend gave him a letter of introduction to a Nordic intellectual, he did not write: I think you will like to meet this young black intellectual; but rather, I think you might like to hear Ray laugh.

His gifts! He was of course aware that whether the educated man be white or brown or black, he cannot, if he has more than animal desires, be irresponsibly happy like the ignorant man who lives simply by his instincts and appetites. Any man with an observant and contemplative mind must be aware of that. But a black man, even though educated, was in closer biological kinship to the swell of primitive earth life. And maybe his apparent failing under the organization of the modern world was the real strength that preserved him from becoming the thing that was the common white creature of it.

Ray had found that to be educated, black and his instinctive self was something of a big job to put over. In the large cities of Europe he had often met with educated Negroes out for a good time with heavy literature under their arms. They toted these books to protect themselves from being hailed everywhere as minstrel niggers, coons, fun-ny monkeys for the European audience – because the general European idea of the black man is that he is a public performer.

Some of them wore hideous parliamentary clothes as close as ever to the pattern of the most correctly gray respectability. He had remarked wiry students and Negroes doing clerical work wearing glasses that made them sissy-eyed. He learned, on inquiry, that wearing glasses was a mark of scholarship and respectability differentiating them from the common types…. (Perhaps the police would respect the glasses.)

No getting away from the public value of clothes, even for you, my black friend. As it was, ages before Carlyle wrote *Sartor Resartus*, so it will be long ages after. And you have reason maybe to be more rigidly formal, as the world seems illogi-cally critical of you since it forced you to discard so recently your convenient fig leaf for its breeches. This civilized society is classified and kept going by clothes and you are now brought by its power to labour and find a place in it.

The more Ray mixed in the rude anarchy of the live of the black boys – loafing, singing, bumming, playing, dancing, loving, working – and came to a realization of how close-linked he was to them in spirit, the more he felt that they represented more than he or the cultured minority the irrepressible exuberance and legendary vitality of the black race. And the thought kept him wondering how that race would fare under the ever tightening mechanical organization of modern life.

Being sensitively receptive, he had as a boy become interested in and followed with passionate sympathy all the great intellectual and social movements of his age. And with the growth of international feelings and ideas he had dreamed of the association of his race with the social movements of the masses of civilization milling through the civilized machine.

But traveling away from America and visiting many countries, observing and appreciating the differences of human groups, making contact with earthy blacks of tropical Africa, where the great body of his race existed, had stirred in him the fine intellectual prerogative of doubt.

The grand mechanical march of civilization had leveled the world down to the point where it seemed treasonable for an advanced thinker to doubt that what was good for one nation or people was also good for another. But as he was never afraid of testing ideas, so he was not afraid of doubting. All peoples must struggle to live, but just as what was helpful for one man might be injurious to another, so it might be with whole communities of peoples.

For Ray happiness was the highest good, and difference the greatest charm, of life. The hand of progress was robbing his people of many primitive and beautiful qualities. He could not see where they would find greater happiness under the weight of the machine even if progress be came left-handed.

Many apologists of a changed and magnified machine system doubted whether the Negro could find a decent place in it. Some did not express their doubts openly, for fear of "giving aid to the enemy." Ray doubted, and openly.

Take, for example, certain Nordic philosophers, as the world was more or less Nordic business: He did not think the blacks would come very happily under the super-mechanical Anglo-Saxon-con-trolled world society of Mr. H. G. Wells. They might shuffle along, but without much happiness in the world of Bernard Shaw. Perhaps they would have their best chance in a world influenced by the thought of a Bertrand Russell, where brakes were clamped on the machine with a few screws loose and some nuts fallen off. But in this great age of science and super-invention was there any possibility of arresting the thing unless it stopped of its own exhaustion?

The Jungle – Chapter 29

Upton Sinclair

The man had gone back to a seat upon the platform, and Jurgis realized that his speech was over. The applause continued for several minutes; and then some one started a song, and the crowd took it up, and the place shook with it. Jurgis had never heard it, and he could not make out the words, but the wild and wonderful spirit of it seized upon him – it was the "Marseillaise!" As stanza after stanza of it thundered forth, he sat with his hands clasped, trembling in every nerve. He had never been so stirred in his life – it was a miracle that had been wrought in him. He could not think at all, he was stunned; yet he knew that in the mighty upheaval that had taken place in his soul, a new man had been born. He had been torn out of the jaws of destruction, he had been delivered from the thraldom of despair; the whole world had been changed for him – he was free, he was free! Even if he were to suffer as he had before, even if he were to beg and starve, nothing would be the same to him; he would understand it, and bear it. He would no longer be the sport of circumstances, he would be a man, with a will and a purpose; he would have something to fight for, something to die for, if need be! Here were men who would show him and help him; and he would have friends and allies, he would dwell in the sight of justice, and walk arm in arm with power.

The audience subsided again, and Jurgis sat back. The chairman of the meeting came forward and began to speak. His voice sounded thin and futile after the other's, and to Jurgis it seemed a profanation. Why should any one else speak, after that miraculous man – why should they not all sit in silence? The chairman was explaining that a collection would now be taken up to defray the expenses of the meeting, and for the benefit of the campaign fund of the party. Jurgis heard; but he had not a penny to give, and so his thoughts went elsewhere again.

He kept his eyes fixed on the orator, who sat in an armchair, his head leaning on his hand and his attitude indicating exhaustion. But suddenly he stood up again, and Jurgis heard the chairman of the meeting saying that the speaker would now answer any questions which the audience might care to put to him. The man came forward, and some one – a woman – arose and asked about some opinion the speaker had expressed concerning Tolstoy. Jurgis had never heard of Tolstoy, and did not care anything about him. Why should any one want to ask such questions, after an address like that? The thing was not to talk, but to do; the thing was to get bold of others and rouse them, to organize them and prepare for the fight! But still the discussion went on, in ordinary conversational tones, and it brought Jurgis back to the everyday world. A few minutes ago he had felt like seizing the hand of the beautiful lady by his side, and kissing it; he had felt like flinging his arms about the neck of the man on the other side of him. And now he began to realize again that he was a "hobo," that he was ragged and dirty, and smelled bad, and had no place to sleep that night!

And so, at last, when the meeting broke up, and the audience started to leave, poor Jurgis was in an agony of uncertainty. He had not thought of leaving – he had thought that the vision must last forever, that he had found comrades and brothers. But now he would go out, and the thing would fade away, and he would never be able to find it again! He sat in his seat, frightened and wondering; but others in the same row wanted to get out, and so he had to stand up and move along. As he was swept down the aisle he looked from one person to another, wistfully; they were all excitedly discussing the address – but there was nobody who offered to discuss it with him. He was near enough to the door to feel the night air, when desperation seized him. He knew nothing at all about that speech he had heard, not even the name of the orator; and he was to go away – no, no, it was preposterous, he must speak to some one; he must find that man himself and tell him. He would not despise him, tramp as he was!

So he stepped into an empty row of seats and watched, and when the crowd had thinned out, he started toward the platform. The speaker was gone; but there was a stage door that stood open, with people passing in and out, and no one on guard. Jurgis summoned up his courage and went in, and down a hallway, and to the door of a room where many people were crowded. No one paid any attention to him, and he pushed in, and in a corner he saw the man he sought. The orator sat in a chair, with his shoulders sunk together and his eyes half closed; his face was ghastly pale, almost greenish in hue, and one arm lay limp at his side. A big man with spectacles on stood near him, and kept pushing back the crowd, saying, "Stand away a little, please; can't you see the comrade is worn out?"

So Jurgis stood watching, while five or ten minutes passed. Now and then the man would look up, and address a word or two to those who were near him; and, at last, on one of these occasions, his glance rested on Jurgis. There seemed to be a slight hint of inquiry about it, and a sudden impulse seized the other. He stepped forward.

"I wanted to thank you, sir!" he began, in breathless haste. "I could not go away without telling you how much – how glad I am I heard you. I – I didn't know anything about it all – "

The big man with the spectacles, who had moved away, came back at this moment. "The comrade is too tired to talk to any one – " he began; but the other held up his hand.

"Wait," he said. "He has something to say to me." And then he looked into Jurgis's face. "You want to know more about Socialism?" he asked.

Jurgis started. "I – I – " he stammered. "Is it Socialism? I didn't know. I want to know about what you spoke of – I want to help. I have been through all that."

"Where do you live?" asked the other.

"I have no home," said Jurgis, "I am out of work."

"You are a foreigner, are you not?"

"Lithuanian, sir."

The man thought for a moment, and then turned to his friend. "Who is there, Walters?" he asked. "There is Ostrinski – but he is a Pole – "

"Ostrinski speaks Lithuanian," said the other. "All right, then; would you mind seeing if he has gone yet?"

The other started away, and the speaker looked at Jurgis again. He had deep, black eyes, and a face full of gentleness and pain. "You must excuse me, comrade," he said. "I am just tired out – I have spoken every day for the last month. I will introduce you to some one who will be able to help you as well as I could – "

The messenger had had to go no further than the door, he came back, followed by a man whom he introduced to Jurgis as "Comrade Ostrinski." Comrade Ostrinski was a little man, scarcely up to Jurgis's shoulder, wizened and wrinkled, very ugly, and slightly lame. He had on a long-tailed black coat, worn green at the seams and the buttonholes; his eyes must have been weak, for he wore green spectacles that gave him a grotesque appearance. But his handclasp was hearty, and he spoke in Lithuanian, which warmed Jurgis to him.

"You want to know about Socialism?" he said. "Surely. Let us go out and take a stroll, where we can be quiet and talk some."

And so Jurgis bade farewell to the master wizard, and went out. Ostrinski asked where he lived, offering to walk in that direction; and so he had to explain once more that he was without a home. At the other's request he told his story; how he had come to America, and what had happened to him in the stockyards, and how his family had been broken up, and how he had become a wanderer. So much the little man heard, and then he pressed Jurgis's arm tightly. "You have been through the mill, comrade!" he said. "We will make a fighter out of you!"

Then Ostrinski in turn explained his circumstances. He would have asked Jurgis to his home – but he had only two rooms, and had no bed to offer. He would have given up his own bed, but his wife was ill. Later on, when he understood that otherwise Jurgis would have to sleep in a hallway, he offered him his kitchen floor, a chance which the other was only too glad to accept. "Perhaps tomorrow we can do better," said Ostrinski. "We try not to let a comrade starve."

Ostrinski's home was in the Ghetto district, where he had two rooms in the basement of a tenement. There was a baby crying as they entered, and he closed the door leading into the bedroom. He had three young children, he explained, and a baby had just come. He drew up two chairs near the kitchen stove, adding that Jurgis must excuse the disorder of the place, since at such a time one's domestic arrangements were upset. Half of the kitchen was given up to a workbench, which was piled with clothing, and Ostrinski explained that he was a "pants finisher." He brought great bundles of clothing here to his home, where he and his wife worked on them. He made a living at it, but it was getting harder all the time, because his eyes were failing. What would come when they gave out he could not tell; there had been no saving anything – a man could barely keep alive by twelve or fourteen hours' work a day. The finishing of pants did not take much skill, and anybody could learn it, and so the pay was forever getting less. That was the competitive wage system; and if Jurgis wanted to understand what Socialism was, it was there he had best begin. The workers were dependent upon a job to exist from day to day, and so they bid against each other, and no man could get more than the lowest man would consent to work for. And thus the mass of the people were always in a life-and-death struggle with poverty. That was "competition," so far as it concerned the wage-earner, the man who had

only his labor to sell; to those on top, the exploiters, it appeared very differently, of course – there were few of them, and they could combine and dominate, and their power would be unbreakable. And so all over the world two classes were forming, with an unbridged chasm between them – the capitalist class, with its enormous fortunes, and the proletariat, bound into slavery by unseen chains. The latter were a thousand to one in numbers, but they were ignorant and helpless, and they would remain at the mercy of their exploiters until they were organized – until they had become "class-conscious." It was a slow and weary process, but it would go on – it was like the movement of a glacier, once it was started it could never be stopped. Every Socialist did his share, and lived upon the vision of the "good time coming," – when the working class should go to the polls and seize the powers of government, and put an end to private property in the means of production. No matter how poor a man was, or how much he suffered, he could never be really unhappy while he knew of that future; even if he did not live to see it himself, his children would, and, to a Socialist, the victory of his class was his victory. Also he had always the progress to encourage him; here in Chicago, for instance, the movement was growing by leaps and bounds. Chicago was the industrial center of the country, and nowhere else were the unions so strong; but their organizations did the workers little good, for the employers were organized, also; and so the strikes generally failed, and as fast as the unions were broken up the men were coming over to the Socialists.

Ostrinski explained the organization of the par-ty, the machinery by which the proletariat was educating itself. There were "locals" in every big city and town, and they were being organized rapidly in the smaller places; a local had anywhere from six to a thousand members, and there were fourteen hundred of them in all, with a total of about twenty-five thousand members, who paid dues to support the organization. "Local Cook County," as the city organization was called, had eighty branch locals, and it alone was spending several thousand dollars in the campaign. It published a weekly in English, and one each in Bohemian and German; also there was a monthly published in Chicago, and a cooperative publishing house, that issued a million and a half of Socialist books and pamphlets every year. All this was the growth of the last few years – there had been almost nothing of it when Ostrinski first came to Chicago.

Ostrinski was a Pole, about fifty years of age. He had lived in Silesia, a member of a despised and persecuted race, and had taken part in the proletarian movement in the early seventies, when Bismarck, having conquered France, had turned his policy of blood and iron upon the "International." Ostrinski himself had twice been in jail, but he had been young then, and had not cared. He had had more of his share of the fight, though, for just when Socialism had broken all its barriers and become the great political force of the empire, he had come to America, and begun all over again. In America every one had laughed at the mere idea of Socialism then – in America all men were free. As if political liberty made wage slavery any the more tolerable! said Ostrinski.

The little tailor sat tilted back in his stiff kitchen chair, with his feet stretched out upon the empty stove, and speaking in low whispers, so as not to waken those in the next room. To Jurgis he seemed a scarcely less wonderful person than the speaker at the meeting; he was poor, the lowest of the low, hunger-driven and miserable – and yet how much he knew, how much he had dared and achieved, what a hero he had been! There were others like him, too – thousands like him, and all of them workingmen! That all this wonderful machinery of progress had been created by his fellows – Jurgis could not believe it, it seemed too good to be true.

That was always the way, said Ostrinski; when a man was first converted to Socialism he was like a crazy person – he could not' understand how others could fail to see it, and he expected to convert all the world the first week. After a while he would realize how hard a task it was; and then it would be fortunate that other new hands kept coming, to save him from settling down into a rut. Just now Jurgis would have plenty of chance to vent his excitement, for a presidential campaign was on, and everybody was talking politics. Ostrinski would take him to the next meeting of the branch local, and introduce him, and he might join the party. The dues were five cents a week, but any one who could not afford this might be excused from paying. The Socialist party was a really democratic political organization – it was controlled absolutely by its own membership, and had no bosses. All of these things Ostrinski explained, as also the principles of the party. You might say that there was really but one Socialist principle – that of "no compromise," which was the essence of the proletarian movement all over the world. When a Socialist was elected to office he voted with old party legislators for any measure that was likely to be of help to the working class, but he never forgot that these concessions, whatever they might be, were trifles compared with the great purpose – the organizing of the working class for the revolution. So far, the rule in America had been that one Socialist made another Socialist once every two years; and if they should maintain the same rate they would carry the country in 1912 – though not all of them expected to succeed as quickly as that.

The Socialists were organized in every civilized nation; it was an international political party, said Ostrinski, the greatest the world had ever known. It numbered thirty million of adherents, and it cast eight million votes. It had started its first newspaper in Japan, and elected its first deputy in Argentina; in France it named members of cabinets, and in Italy and Australia it held the balance of power and turned out ministries. In Germany, where its vote was more than a third of the total vote of the empire, all other parties and powers had united to fight it. It would not do, Ostrinski explained, for the proletariat of one nation to achieve the victory, for that nation would be crushed by the military power of the others; and so the Socialist movement was a world movement, an organization of all mankind to establish liberty and fraternity. It was the new religion of humanity – or you might say it was the fulfillment of the old religion, since it implied but the literal application of all the teachings of Christ.

Until long after midnight Jurgis sat lost in the conversation of his new acquaintance. It was a most wonderful experience to him – an almost supernatural experience. It was like encountering an inhabitant of the fourth dimension of space, a being who was free from all one's own limitations. For four years, now, Jurgis had been wondering and blundering in the depths of a wilderness; and here, suddenly, a hand reached down and seized him, and lifted him out of it, and set him upon a mountain-top, from which he could survey it all – could see the paths from which he had wandered, the morasses into which he had stumbled, the hiding places of the beasts of prey that had fallen upon him. There were his Packingtown experiences, for instance – what was there about Packingtown that Ostrinski could not explain! To Jurgis the packers had been equivalent to fate; Ostrinski showed him that they were the Beef Trust. They were a gigantic combination of capital, which had crushed all opposition, and overthrown the laws of the land, and was preying upon the people. Jurgis recollected how, when he had first come to Packingtown, he had stood and watched the hog-killing, and thought how cruel and savage it was, and come away congratulating himself that he was not a hog; now his new acquaintance showed him that a hog was just what he had been – one of the packers' hogs. What they wanted from a hog was all the profits that could be got out of him; and that was what they wanted from the workingman, and also that was what they wanted from the public. What the hog thought of it, and what he suffered, were not considered; and no more was it with labor, and no more with the purchaser of meat. That was true everywhere in the world, but it was especially true in Packingtown; there seemed to be something about the work of slaughtering that tended to ruthlessness and ferocity – it was literally the fact that in the methods of the packers a hundred human lives did not balance a penny of profit. When Jurgis

had made himself familiar with the Socialist literature, as he would very quickly, he would get glimpses of the Beef Trust from all sorts of aspects, and he would find it everywhere the same; it was the incarnation of blind and insensate Greed. It was a monster devouring with a thousand mouths, trampling with a thousand hoofs; it was the Great Butcher – it was the spirit of Capitalism made flesh. Upon the ocean of commerce it sailed as a pirate ship; it had hoisted the black flag and declared war upon civilization. Bribery and corruption were its everyday methods. In Chicago the city government was simply one of its branch offices; it stole billions of gallons of city water openly, it dictated to the courts the sentences of disorderly strikers, it forbade the mayor to enforce the building laws against it. In the national capital it had power to prevent inspection of its product, and to falsify government reports; it violated the rebate laws, and when an investigation was threatened it burned its books and sent its criminal agents out of the country. In the commercial world it was a Juggernaut car; it wiped out thousands of businesses every year, it drove men to madness and suicide. It had forced the price of cattle so low as to destroy the stock-raising industry, an occupation upon which whole states existed; it had ruined thousands of butchers who had refused to handle its products. It divided the country into districts, and fixed the price of meat in all of them; and it owned all the refrigerator cars, and levied an enormous tribute upon all poultry and eggs and fruit and vegetables. With the millions of dollars a week that poured in upon it, it was reaching out for the control of other interests, railroads and trolley lines, gas and electric light franchises – it already owned the leather and the grain business of the country. The people were tremendously stirred up over its encroachments, but nobody had any remedy to suggest; it was the task of Socialists to teach and organize them, and prepare them for the time when they were to seize the huge machine called the Beef Trust, and use it to produce food for human beings and not to heap up fortunes for a band of pirates. It was long after midnight when Jurgis lay down upon the floor of Ostrinski's kitchen; and yet it was an hour before he could get to sleep, for the glory of that joyful vision of the people of Packingtown marching in and taking possession of the Union Stockyards!

The War Prayer

Mark Twain

It was a time of great and exalting excitement. The country was up in arms, the war was on, in every breast burned the holy fire of patriotism; the drums were beating, the bands playing, the toy pistols popping, the bunched firecrackers hissing and spluttering; on every hand and far down the receding and fading spread of roofs and balconies a fluttering wilderness of flags flashed in the sun; daily the young volunteers marched down the wide avenue gay and fine in their new uniforms, the proud fathers and mothers and sisters and sweethearts cheering them with voices choked with happy emotion as they swung by; nightly the packed mass meetings listened, panting, to patriot oratory which stirred the deepest deeps of their hearts, and which they interrupted at briefest intervals with cyclones of applause, the tears running down their cheeks the while; in the churches the pastors preached devotion to flag and country, and invoked the God of Battles beseeching His aid in our good cause in outpourings of fervid eloquence which moved every listener. It was indeed a glad and gracious time, and the half dozen rash spirits that ventured to disapprove of the war and cast a doubt upon its righteousness straightway got such a stern and angry warning that for their personal safety's sake they quickly shrank out of sight and offended no more in that way.

Sunday morning came – next day the battalions would leave for the front; the church was filled; the volunteers were there, their young faces alight with martial dreams – visions of the stern advance, the gathering momentum, the rushing charge, the flashing sabers, the flight of the foe, the tumult, the enveloping smoke, the fierce pursuit, the surren-der! Then home from the war, bronzed heroes, welcomed, adored, submerged in golden seas of glory! With the volunteers sat their dear ones, proud, happy, and envied by the neighbors and friends who had no sons and brothers to send forth to the field of honor, there to win for the flag, or, failing, die the noblest of noble deaths. The service proceeded; a war chapter from the Old Testament was read; the first prayer was said; it was followed by an organ burst that shook the building, and with one impulse the house rose, with glowing eyes and beating hearts, and poured out that tremendous invocation:

God the all-terrible! Thou who ordainest! Thunder thy clarion and lightning thy sword!

Then came the "long" prayer. None could remember the like of it for passionate pleading and moving and beautiful language. The burden of its supplication was, that an ever-merciful and beni-gnant Father of us all would watch over our noble young soldiers, and aid, comfort, and encourage them in their patriotic work; bless them, shield them in the day of battle and the hour of peril, bear them in His mighty hand, make them strong and confident, invincible in the bloody onset; help them to crush the foe, grant to them and to their flag and country imperishable honor and glory –

An aged stranger entered and moved with slow and noiseless step up the main aisle, his eyes fixed upon the minister, his long body clothed in a robe that reached to his feet, his head bare, his white hair descending in a frothy cataract to his shoulders, his seamy face unnaturally pale, pale even to ghastliness. With all eyes following him and wondering, he made his silent way; without pausing, he ascended to the preacher's side and stood there waiting. With shut lids the preacher, unconscious of his presence, continued with his moving prayer, and at last finished it with the words, uttered in fervent appeal, "Bless our arms, grant us the victory, O Lord our God, Father and Protector of our land and flag!"

The stranger touched his arm, motioned him to step aside – which the startled minister did – and took his place. During some moments he surveyed the spellbound audience with solemn eyes, in which burned an uncanny light; then in a deep voice he said:

"I come from the Throne – bearing a message from Almighty God!" The words smote the house with a shock; if the stranger perceived it he gave no attention. "He has heard the prayer of His servant your shepherd, and will grant it if such shall be your desire after I, His messenger, shall have explained to you its import – that is to say, its full import. For it is like unto many of the prayers of men, in that it asks for more than he who utters it is aware of – except he pause and think.

"God's servant and yours has prayed his prayer. Has he paused and taken thought? Is it one prayer? No, it is two – one uttered, the other not. Both have reached the ear of Him Who heareth all supplications, the spoken and the unspoken. Ponder this – keep it in mind. If you would beseech a blessing upon yourself, beware! lest without intent you invoke a curse upon a neighbor at the same time. If you pray for the blessing of rain upon your crop which needs it, by that act you are possibly praying for a curse upon some neighbor's crop which may not need rain and can be injured by it.

"You have heard your servant's prayer – the uttered part of it. I am commissioned of God to put into words the other part of it – that part which the pastor – and also you in your hearts – fervently prayed silently. And ignorantly and unthinkingly? God grant that it was so! You heard these words: 'Grant us the victory, O Lord our God!' That is sufficient. the *whole* of the uttered prayer is compact into those pregnant words. Elaborations were not necessary. When you have prayed for victory you have prayed for many unmentioned results which follow victory – *must* follow it, cannot help but follow it. Upon the listening spirit of God fell also the unspoken part of the prayer. He commandeth me to put it into words. Listen!

"O Lord our Father, our young patriots, idols of our hearts, go forth to battle – be Thou near them! With them – in spirit – we also go forth from the sweet peace of our beloved firesides to smite the foe. O Lord our God, help us to tear their soldiers to bloody shreds with our shells; help us to cover their smiling fields with the pale forms of their patriot dead; help us to drown the thunder of the guns with the shrieks of their wounded, writhing in pain; help us to lay waste their humble homes with a hurricane of fire; help us to wring the hearts of their unoffending widows with unavailing grief; help us to turn them out roofless with little children to wander unfriended the wastes of their desolated land in rags and hunger and thirst, sports of the sun flames of summer and the icy winds of winter, broken in spirit, worn with travail, imploring Thee for the refuge of the grave and denied it – for our sakes who adore Thee, Lord, blast their hopes, blight their lives, protract their bitter pilgrimage, make heavy their steps, water their way with their tears, stain the white snow with the blood of their wounded feet! We ask it, in the spirit of love, of Him Who is the Source of Love, and Who is the ever-faithful refuge and friend of all that are sore beset and seek His aid with humble and contrite hearts. Amen.

(*After a pause.*) "Ye have prayed it; if ye still desire it, speak! The messenger of the Most High waits!"

It was believed afterward that the man was a lunatic, because there was no sense in what he said.

My Career Goes Bung – Chapters 1-6 (The End Of My Career)
Stella Miles Franklin

CHAPTER ONE – EXPLANATORY

A wallaby would have done just as well as a human being to endure the nothingness of existence as it has been known to me. This, I suppose, is why I want to tell of the only two lively things that have happened in a dull, uninteresting life. You don't know me from a basket of gooseberries, or wouldn't if only I had kept myself to myself, but as I didn't, I shall endure the embarrassment of bringing myself to your attention again in an explanatory postscript. In company with ninety-nine per cent. of my fellows, the subject of self is full of fascination to me. There are cogent reasons for this.

One of the interesting happenings is my entanglement with Henry Beauchamp. The other is my experience in writing a new style of autobiography. Such a departure grew out of my satiation with the orthodox style. I shall deal with the autobiography first. These notes are slightly and somewhat expurgatedly compiled from my diary.

I was at that stage of chrysalism when boys dream of becoming bushrangers, engine drivers, or champion pugilists. Nothing so garishly simple relieves a girl. I yearned to make the whole world into a beautiful place where there would be no sick and starving babies, where people of advancing years could be safe from penury, where all the animals could be fat and happy, and even our little sisters, the flowers, might not be bruised or plucked against their wish. The prospect of settling down to act tame hen in a tin pot circle, and to acknowledge men as superior merely owing to the accident of gender, revolted me.

Life among boys and girls at an institution such as the Stringybark Hill Public School, ere adolescence has arrived to mess things up, is a good example of democracy. There were no wealthy within competitive reach, money did not count to any extent, and beauty and birth did not count at all. We never heard of such things. Only the merit of brains and honesty weighed in the school room, and athletic prowess coupled with fair play on the playground.

Any sort of lessons except long addition sums were a joy and sinecure to me. On the playground, though small, I was fleet of foot and exceptionally agile, could vault as high as any boy of my own age till I was twelve, and was always chosen as captain whether the game happened to be cricket, rounders or prisoners' bar. A balance was pre-served in my status by the fact that the dunces at lessons were always the best hats or runners outside, and that athletes when grown up had so much more glory than mere scholars.

I was impatient to be done with school so that I could take hold of life in the big world, I could not understand why people stayed in some lone hole with no more spunk in them than a mulch cow, while the universe elsewhere teemed with adven-ture.

I expected to continue in enjoyment of the friendship and affection of my fellows, working for and winning a high place in all the activities that I essayed. I thought that there would be any number of activities to choose from. I was sure of winning love and acclamation because I never cheated in a game or put on airs over my ascendancy in them, and eagerly shared anything and everything within my power.

Thus came the last day under the rule of the gentle old teacher in the little slab school house among the tall trees on the stringy bark range. Old Harris, as we called him behind his back, got drunk on occasion but was condoned by the kindly settlers because he knew and loved each child individually. He could bring what there was out of the thickest skulls and I rioted unrebuked and highly encouraged within his jurisdiction. He had been educated at one of the great colleges in England. I don't know which as he never mentioned it to the simple circle of

Stringy-bark Hill. He was supposed to be related to big swells hut that likewise he never mentioned unless he was a bit tipply and some flash intruder was putting on airs. He had the manners of an angel, a dear kind face, and wouldn't have harmed a grasshopper. These qualifications earned him the protection of the rudest and crudest. He taught a mere handful of children the rudiments of education for less than £3 a week and boarded with a family who were industrious, honest and kind, but could offer him no congeniality of mind or companionship of knowledge.

Ma condemned his fecklessness to be stuck there, but Pa would rub the top of his head – his own head – and remark, "At Old Harris's age life boils down to a decent bed and a good feed, and those things are his."

At the end of my last day with him he patted me on the shoulder – an unusual liberty for this diffident soul. He never seemed to have any egotism except when he was drunk. It must have been ingrowing like squeezed toenails. He made a little speech over me, the kind which youth accepts as drivel at the time, but which comes back vividly when youth has grown towards this drivelling knowledge itself. It returns to me now in the drivellage of my twentieth year, and here it is.

"Sybylla, you are a good girl – clean and true – and a gifted one to boot. You are as game as a young lion but I fear that the opposing forces will break your heart. You are a glad young thing now, but with your ability and temperament, alas, it will take more than ordinary conditions to keep you happy. You have a quicker brain than any scholar I ever had, but that will not help you unless you use it to hide the fact of its existence and to enhance your beauty; and of beauty you have ample to secure what would satisfy most of your sex, but which will never content you, so I might as well hold my tongue. At any rate, good fortune attend you. The old school house will be dull and lonely without you."

I thought that he must have had a drop, but now when he is dead and six years have passed,

I simply know that his experience of life was more than mine.

I was let out in advance and he stood looking after me as I swung down the path between the young trees which I had helped to plant on bygone Arbor Days. Affection is a terribly binding thing. It always keeps me from breaking bonds, so I turned back every few steps to wave to the old man with a wistful regret that he was a finished chapter and that I could not take him with me into the glamorous young world towards which I was headed.

I had two miles to go by a short cut, which I followed for the joy of fallen logs to vault, and I sprang high every yard or two for the gum leaves that splashed their outline on the ground. The sky was a washing-bag blue with mountainous white clouds of thunderous splendour piled in the west. What a sunset it would be' I revelled in every scrap of beauty that came my way, and was excited to picture the beauty and adventure that I was going to broach beyond the ragged horizon to be seen from the tall fence host. The loveliest most thrilling thing in sight was the road that led from the front paddock to Goulburn, then on and on to Sydney – first port of call in my voyage of conquest. I climbed on to the garden post for a view before entering the house, my school days past.

"What are you doing there like a tom-boy?" inquired Ma. "You must change your ways now. The happiest days you'll ever know are over – all play and no work and worry. You'll find life a different matter."

LIFE a different matter – I should hope so! – like a blue ocean of adventure calling with a deafening invitation to embark.

CHAPTER TWO – THE FETTERED ROUND

But how to get on to that ocean? I was on a small weedy waterhole that seldom swelled into a stream and there were many snags. Upon leaving school these multiplied like fury.

I entered into the life of struggling incompetent selectors. The chief burden of that, for the women, was unrestricted child-bearing, and I was now a woman, as Ma reminded me, a fact which made me rebellious. Ma said I was always a wilful and contradictory imp and that during the throes of rearing me, she was frequently put to such confusion that despite I was her first and last and only child there were times when she could have cheerfully wrung my neck. Ma said most girls felt the way I did at first, but soon settled down. All girls wished that they were men.

At that I flashed out like a tornado, insulted. Never in my life had I a wish to be a man. Such a suggestion fills me with revulson. What I raged against were the artificial restrictions.

Girls! I do not address those feeble nauseating creepers who seem to fit into every one of the old ruts, the slimy hypocrites who are held up as womanly, but those who have some dash and spirit. You remember what we had to learn, girls, things that one cannot write in plain print or else truth would be abused as indecency; and there were other things too subtle to be expressed even to the elect, but which wielded the strongest subjecting influence. The dead dank gloom that settled on us upon learning that the eternal feminine was the infernal feminine! But Ma always said, "You'll have to get used to it. There is no sense in acting like one possessed of a devil."

A man can get used to having his legs cut off, and women have even greater endurance, or, seeing the conditions under which they live and work and dress and reproduce their species, they would have been extinct with the Great Auk, and what a pity they weren't!

Girls! Do you remember how we loathed the correct meek merely sexy specimens who had none of our foolhardy honesty, or any unsmutched ideals of life and love? We clamoured for the opportunity to be taken on our merits by LIFE: we wanted to play it as we played our games, where, if there was any doubt about us being bowled out, we did not want to hold on, we laid down our bats without whimpering.

The first foul blast from the tree of knowledge was that we weren't to be allowed any un-adulterated HUMAN merits. Sexual attractions alias WOMANLINESS was to be our stock-in-trade. If we did not avail ourselves of it we were defenceless, and might even he execrated. How we abhorred the cunning girls who found no trouble with their role. In school they had been ranked by attainment, and their marks had seldom risen even to FAIR. Now in the hierarchy of mere gender their pandering intelligence was to score every time. We could come into line or find ourselves on an outside track alone.

Girls, how did you take it?

It seemed to develop into a storm between Ma and me. Ma at last said, "Bother it, I have nothing to do with it. It is God's will."

It was a relief to be indignant with God, but a trial not to be able to get at Him in any way. In my perturbation I collided with Great-aunt Jane, who said that the Lord loveth those whom He chasteneth. His way of saving the world did not appear to me as efficient for a being who was all-powerful. He so loved the world that He gave His only begotten Son to save it, and allowed Him to be nailed on a cross in ghastly agony – without saving anything considerable as far as history shows.

"Heaven knows what He would have permitted to be done to a daughter," I remarked.

Aunt Jane stood this pretty well. "Ah," she laughed, "You'll grow to sense. A husband and children of your own will put you in your place."

The dire soul-crushings with which old wives threaten me consequent upon the glories of motherhood are enough to quell a quadruped. Aunt Jane repudiated the blame too, and said I should have to wait until the next world to have things righted.

"According to what I have heard, a woman who has had the hell of bearing twelve children to give some male object a heaven of begetting is just as likely to go to hell as the father: and the next world's joys are open equally to men, more so, in fact. That next-world-payment-of-debts is sloppy rubbish," I snorted.

"You have a great deal to learn," said Auntie. "You are a rude ignorant girl. If you persist in thinking as you do, you'll come to harm."

Pa rubbed his hair up on end and gently remarked, "What is coming to harm in this debate, Aunt Jane, is your theology."

Pa's words fell as healingly as rain on the dust. I was sorry I had been rude to Auntie. When I got Pa alone I questioned him further, and he said, as if talking to himself, "As high as a people rises, so high will be its gods."

"The trouble with the Church of England God," Pa continued, "is that he is made in the image of some darned old cackling prelate, so mean and cowardly that the Devil, for consistency and ability, is a gentleman beside him." Pa had a twinkle in his eye as he added, "But you know, it isn't gentle-manly to upset people of less mental powers than yourself; besides, it is dangerous. Think as much as you like, my girl, but let sleeping dogs lie unless you can do some real good by waking them up."

Great-aunt spends a lot of time with us. She says Pa is the nicest man she has ever known in a house, that I should thank God on my knees every night for such a parent. This so differs from Ma's inculcations that I would attribute it to Auntie's love of contradiction, only that under cross-questioning she says that had she had such a father when a girl she would have thought herself in heaven. Her father was an unmerciful autocrat. His daughters had to live their lives under cover, so to speak, like mice. I wish I could be so dominating, but judging by Grandma and Ma and myself, this progenitor's progenitiveness is becoming diluted with the generations.

I concede that technically Ma is my primary parent and Pa merely secondary. The question of woman's emancipation and the justice which is her due make this fatally clear in theory, but when it comes to the practice of an affection which springs spontaneously from my human breast, Pa can have no second place; and when it comes to being understood, well – but – but –

Ma says having children of my own will teach me. I wonder what.

I had lots of other stuffing in me too. Resiliently I renewed my attack on LIFE. Rebellion against artificial WOMANLINESS did not interfere with all that rushed out of my mind on the wings of imagination. There was one great recreation open to me, even at 'Possum Gully, which was a sop to energy. I could ride. I could ride tremendously. I loved horses and seemed to become part of them. In the district were any number of good horses, most of them owned by bachelors. As one of these Bachelors said, "A lovely high-spirited girl is just the thing to top-off a good horse."

All kinds of horses, from racing stallions to hunting mares, were brought to clue with the owners included as escorts and the source of chocolates in wonderful boxes. Some of the horses demanded skill and attention to handle, and that saved their owners from my dialectics and me from their love-making. There was no use in a man offering me a horse that was moke enough for love-dawdling, and that's how that worked out.

Pa forbade fences. Ma said that unless I meant to marry one of the men it was foolish and unladylike to be riding about with them; they would have no respect for me. If I really was against marriage I'd have to take up some trade or profession; she wished she had been trained to something so that she could be independent and not be dragged in the backwash of man's mismanagement.

This brought me to consider my prospects and to find that I hadn't any. I loved to learn things – anything, everything. To attend the University would have been heaven, but expense barred that. I could become a pupil-teacher, but I loathed the very name of this profession. I should have had to do the same work as a man for less pay, and, in country schools, to throw in free of remuneration, the specialty of teaching all kinds of needlework. I could be a cook or a housemaid and slave all day under some nagging woman and be a social outcast. I could be a hospital nurse and do twice the work of a doctor for a fraction of his pay or social importance, or, seeing the tremendously advanced age, I could even be a doctor – a despised lady-doctor, doing the drudgery of the profession in the teeth of such prejudice that even the advanced, who fought for the entry of women into all professions, would in practice "have more faith in a man doctor". I could be a companion or governess to some woman appended to some man of property.

I rebelled against every one of these fates. I wanted to do something out of the ordinary groove. There were people who had done great things for the world, why not be one of such? Ma threw cold water on these haverings. Ma is the practical member of our ménage. She has to be, so that we have a ménage at all. Ma's thesis was that if all the millions who have gone have not improved the world, how was I going to do it in one slap How would I start about it? Whereas, improve-ment seemed to me so simple that all that was needed was common sense and energy.

Pa was sympathetic. Ma says that I take after him, except when I am commendable. Pa has ever acknowledged the relationship with pride even during my most debbil-debbil stretches, which is very generous of Pa.

"There have been great women, haven't there, Pa?"

"Of course there have, and are, and will be again," said he.

"But what on earth makes you think you might be one of them?" demanded Ma.

"Why shouldn't she be?" murmured Pa.

"You can't be anything without means these days."

"The times are always the same. People make their opportunities."

"She doesn't strike me as that kind."

"Oh, I don't know," maintained Pa. "Greatness has sprung from unlikelier sources."

CHAPTER THREE – THE LOGIC OF EGOTISM

Poverty is a stultifying curse. We suffered from it. Ma blamed Pa. Pa never blamed anyone but himself. He had not always been poor. He was no businessman. Bad seasons and foolish investments lost him his parental station. Ma considered his term in Parliament as Member for Gool Gool his biggest financial mistake. Pa had been under heavy election expenses, and was robbed by a partner during his absence. Pa had had ambitions to improve the Colony through political action, and had failed. That was why Ma was alarmed by my symptoms. I was too young to remember Pa's Parliamentary term. Ma's abiding reference to it is that men are very fond of the sound of their own voices. Well, I like Pa's voice too, because it is never raised in blame.

Pa is tall and lean and lank and brown as is the ribbed sea sand, and he is fond of poetry. Byron is a favourite with him. He can quote Byron by the page.

This makes the madmen who have made men mad
By their contagion; conquerors and kings,
Founders of sects and systems, to whom add
Sophists, bards, statesmen, all unquiet things.

* * *

He who surpasses or subdues mankind
Must look down on the hate of those below.

Such lines roll splendidly from him. Ma says a man betrays himself by what he extols. I asked if that also applies to women, but Ma says not nearly so accurately, as women have to pretend to like so many things to humour men.

Ma extols Dr. Watts. He is prosaic compared with Byron.

Not more than others I deserve,
Yet God has given me more,
For I have food while others starve,
Or beg from door to door.

Which suggests mean favouritism on the part of God, and a priggish self-satisfaction on the part of one who has petty deserts.

Satan finds some mischief still for idle hands to do, has often driven me exasperated and frustrated from meditation when a thought was filling out like a sail catching a breeze.

Dr. Watts was the lighter side of Ma. She was also a whale on Shakespeare. I enjoyed him too, but Milton was too much of a good thing. Ma insisted that I should learn long slices of Milton as discipline and to elevate thoughts.

Where joy for ever dwells; hail, horrors; hail,
Infernal world; and thou, profoundest hell,
Receive thy new possessor; one who brings
A mind not to be changed by place or time.
The mind is its own place, and in itself
Can make a heaven of hell, a Bell of heaven.

"Bust" was the most ferocious expletive ever heard from women in Ma's family. It was considered the height of vulgarity and not allowed at all, really, but in the depths of some over-powering exaspera-tion even Great-aunt Jane has been overheard expleting it. "Bust Milton'." I said many times to myself. "Paradise is lost surely enough while you have to be learning this stuff by heart."

The most interesting line in the book was, "Witness, William Yopp, Ann Yopp". They were a funny note in the stiff gilt-edged volume. Why had they a name like that? They were attached to the information that Mrs. Milton had got eight pounds for the twelve books of P.L. Poetry didn't seem to be a lucrative business, but of course that was over three hundred years ago, and to-day was different.

Ma said as I wasn't in a position to tackle professional training I must help Pa on the place. He could not afford to hire men. This brought me back to my idea of a career at the top where there was plenty of room above the tame-fowl openings, which were all that lay before one so poor and isolated. Ma said I should take stock of my possibilities and banish all silly delusions. Ma assisted in this stock-taking. She dwelt upon my lack o t special gifts and said we should not shrink from unpleasant facts about ourselves, we must face them and grow strong.

We must accept God's will without whining. It must be dreadful to have a daughter as disappointing as I am to Ma, and it is just as hard for such a fiasco of a girl to have a superb mother. I did not know which of the two trials was the heavier, but Ma did. Hers was the trial and mine the failure to take advantage of my heredity in her. However, life went on.

At that date there was a parliamentary election. FREE-TRADE or PROTECTION became a war cry. Pa was called upon to support the Member for our electorate.

'Possum Gully livened up. We had meetings at our house and I accompanied Pa on the rounds. There were young men everywhere all eager to argue politics with me. How I chafed that women were classed with idiots and children! Of course I should have had to wait until I was twenty-one to vote, but I longed to stand for Parliament then just as I was with my hair in a plat and my skirts above my ankles. I hankered to tackle the job of Premier for a start. The young men all said they would vote for me when I put up. Our Member was one of those who advocated extending the franchise to women, so I adored him and we were great friends. He said I was one of his best canvassers.

Scorning tame-hen accomplishments and lacking special gifts of God, which lift a person from obscurity to fame through an art, a sport, or an invention, I returned to the thought of general greatness. Pa was very proud when old campaigners said I was a chip of the old block. He was strenuously in favour of woman suffrage. Ma expostulated with him for taking me about. She said we soon would not have even a poor roof to cover us. My Grandma got to hear of me and wrote letters blaming Ma. When Great-aunt Jane next stayed with us she did her best to save me.

"You'll grow into one of those dreadful female agitators – eccentric women that men hate. You'll get the name of a man-hater if you don't take care."

"This men-hating business seems to be as lop-sided as God's will for women. You condemn a woman if she doesn't worship men. She is the one in the wrong to hate the darling creatures, though they're pretty hatable by all accounts. Then if a girl is fond of men that also disgraces her. I do like logic and fair play."

"So do I," interposed Ma, "but you'll have to resign yourself to it all being on the other side."

"It's all silly nonsense. The men don't act as if they hated me. The old ones as well as the boys all are friendly wherever I go."

"Men will always blather to a forward woman while she is young; but they won't respect her or marry her," said Aunt Jane.

"She couldn't marry more than one at a time, however willing she is," said Pa. "She has plenty of time yet."

When Pa and I were driving around the electorate together he talked about LIFE and said that my idea of being Premier was not fantastic. The political enfranchisement of women was inevitable, and women free could do what they liked with the world.

Votes for women was a magic talisman by which all evils and abuses were to be righted. Women no longer would have to pander to men through sexual attraction and pretend to be what they weren't. They would burgeon as themselves. Those were splendid days. Pa said I must educate myself in readiness as by the time I should be of age I could stand for Parliament and discover if I had ability as a statesman. As a beginning he suggested that I should study history and the lives of great people to learn how they conducted the business. To this end the poor dear once again postponed a new suit, which Ma truly said he needed to prevent his being mistaken for a scarecrow, and brought me home an armful of books, including some autobiographies.

That's how the trouble began.

The histories I left for later consumption, as the people in them are always so long dead and are nearly all kings and queens and military or political murderers who have no relation to the ordinary kind of people like those I know in Australia. The biographies of real people nearer our own day, and especially the autobiographies, where people told about themselves, filled me with excitement.

Judging by the way Ma always misunderstands my deeds and purposes and intentions, and by what she and Aunt Jane tell me that other people do think or will think of me, it seemed that an autobiography was a device for disseminating per-sonal facts straight from the horse's mouth.

I read ardently, nay, furiously would better express the way that one tackles the things one wants to do. Grace Darling, Charlotte Brontë, Joan of Arc and Mrs. Fry passed in review, evidently by dull old professors. These were a long time dead. Lives nearer to my own day had more appeal – until I read them. What I absorbed from autobiographies was not how to be great so much as the littleness of the great. Every one of those productions, whether the fiction that passes for reality or the decorated reality that is termed fiction was marred by the same thing – the false pose of the autobiographer.

Now, we are always warned against egotism as something more unforgivable, more unpopularis-ing than vulgar sin. Yet everyone is a mass of egotism. They must be if they are to remain perpendicular. Henry Beauchamp later explained this to me. He says that little Jimmy Dripping is a much more important person to little Jimmy Dripping than the Prince of Wales is. If this were not so he says that the end of little Jimmy Dripping would soon be mud; that each fellow's self-importance is the only thing that keeps him going. Well then, why make such an unholy fuss about egotism?

Ma despised egotism because she had none herself and happened by an accident to be perfect. Pa and I seemed to have whips and whips, but of the wrong kind. The best kind, the most profitable is like the hippo's epidermis. Another word for it is hide – HIDE. It works so that you think your own performance of sin or stupidity is quite all right, and only the other fellow's all quite wrong. Pa said that that kind of egotism was a magnificent battering ram for worldly success, but to have it you must be born without a sense of humour and without the ability to see yourself as others see you. I was beginning to suspect that a sense of humour was more profitable to the other fellow than to the owner.

The business of egotism needs to be regulated by give-and-take in real life or there would be general obstruction of all conversation and social intercourse, but that does not apply to an autobiography, at least not in conjunction with logic. The fact of an autobiography is in itself an egotism. People perpetrate autobiographies for the sole purpose of airing their own exploits. If they go off the track of displaying the writer they likewise cease to be autobiographies. Such documents are usually mawkishly egotistical instead of frankly so because they attempt the scientific impossibility of being unegotistical. Too, in autobiographies, the hero of the narrative tries to deprecate his goodness, while at the same time he often endeavours to depict himself as a saint worthy of wings. If he has a penny-dreadful parent he nevertheless paints himself as adoring him (or her) and by honouring one or both is a contestant for the doubtful prize of long life, which the bible promises people for enduring their immediate progenitors in any circumstances. (And I never could see in strict logic how that works.)

I have examined all available autobiographies since then but not one have I found by woman or man, scientist or simpleton, which did not assume the same pose. So little greatness did I find in the lives of the great as related by themselves that for a time I was diverted from the idea of becoming great myself by the notion of constructing a fictitious autobiography to make hay of the pious affectations of printed autobiographies as I know them.

Who has not read an autobiography beginning thus: "At the risk of being egotistical I must admit," etc. I determined to flout these pretences with an imitation autobiography that would wade in with-out apology or fear, biffing convention on the nose.

The days were goldenly long and warm, I was rabid for mental and physical action, and there was none in that state of discontent in which it had pleased God to place me. It makes me question His amiability in placing His victims. In addition to riding I swam in our weedy water-holes among leeches and turtles where there was also an occasional snake, but of mental pabulum there was no crumb to be found, except in books, I was a voracious reader, but after all, books pall on one when that one is throbbing to be doing something exciting. From 'Possum Gully to Spring Hill and round about to Wallaroo Plains there wasn't a real companion of my own age, nor any other age. The dissatisfaction of other girls stopped short at wondering why life should be so much less satisfactory to them than to their brothers, but they accepted it as the will of God. None of them was consumed with the idea of changing the world.

The idea of writing a book to make fun of the other books grew with cossetting. Ma said she had sufficient experience of my ideas to be chary of them. EXPERIENCE seems to stand by Ma like a religion.

Pa rubbed the top of his head contemplatively and said, "If you are man enough to write a book, I'll get you some paper."

"How could an untried girl write a book?" demanded Ma. "Why not start with a little story for the 'Children's Corner'? You can't run before you learn to walk."

CHAPTER FOUR – "SATAN FINDS SOME MISCHIEF STILL"

A ream of paper is a large quantity to one who has never written a book nor met anyone who has done so – 480 sheets all to myself.

"That'll hold you for a bit," said Pa.

"What a waste!" said Ma.

The pleasure of good penmanship on all that lovely white paper edged me on to begin upon my spontaneous career of slinging ink, of which this volume is to be the petite finale.

Ma admired classical features. Pa had them. Perhaps that is what misled her into a poor

match, and why, no matter how often my looks are praised as lovely, she will not rank me as a beauty. She says such talk is to make a fool of me. So to be done with the uncertainty, I accept Ma's dictum that beauty lies in actions, and as my actions are all wrong, where could be my beauty? Nevertheless, bang went another convention. Men cared only for prettiness in girls, yet our house was a rendezvous for young men from all over the electorate and beyond it, who slid not honestly come to talk politics with Pa, though they pretended that they did. I wasn't in danger of being embittered by a lack of admirers, nor of platonic men friends, as I was simple enough to think they were at the start, They teased me about dropping the Premiership and taking to writing.

Ma said there was no sight more nauseating than lovesick men all cackling and he-hawing and pretending they were angels who wouldn't let her pick up her thimble; while by-and-bye if I should marry one of them, most likely he would leave me to chop the wood and would turn her out of his house.

Pa said there was no use in quarrelling with NATURE or taking a jaundiced view.

Ma rejoined that EXPERIENCE had shown her that common sense was very rare.

It was a spring without a spring. The breezes had a strong dash of summer, but the cloudless skies looked down with an excess of that pitilessness which the Persian poet has advised us not to call upon. Not a speck the size of a man's hand came up for weeks to give even false hope, and the half-opened leaves withered on the rose bushes and orchard trees. The starving stock lacked strength to bring their young to birth, and the moan of dying creatures throughout that country side was a reproach to whatever power had placed them there. The earth was as dry as ashes. Isolated shrubs and plants, that had been the pride of settlers' drudging wives and daughters, died in spite of efforts to keep them alive with the slop water collected after household use. The wattle trees, however, because they were natives, were putting forth an unstinted meed of bloom with an optimism rivalling "God's in His Heaven, all's right with the world". Masses of lovely yellow fluff swayed to waves in the breeze and wafted perfume too chaste for the seventh heaven of oriental belief. This loveliness lacked competition in the grim landscape. I culled sprays to press between the leaves of some old book, and wondered would there ever come a day when I should be as homesick for a bower of wattle bloom set in a frame of gumtrees as I was now wild to escape to other lands of castles and chateaux and Gothic cathedrals.

The drought made work in the garden superfluous. I had leisure to utilise that ream of paper. The burlesque autobiography grew apace. My idea of ridicule speedily enlarged as a reticule into which anything could be packed. I could express my longing to escape to other lands and far great cities across the sheening ocean to strange ports above and below the Line, where big ships and little go for their cargoes. It was an opportunity to crystallise rebellion and to use up some of the words which pressed upon me like a flock of birds fluttering to be let out of their cages. There is artistic satisfaction in liberating words: and they entered into me and flew from me like fairies.

It was absorbing to allot parts to characters. Uncertainty when to interpolate "Odds fish, ma'am," or "Gad Zooks," put me off a historical track, though I had started in an ancient castle on an English moor. I was also in a quandary about style, but at that time dear old Mr. Harris came to spend a few days with us prior to leaving the district. I let him into the secret. He was sympathetic in one way and discouraging in another. He said that the pursuit of literature was a precarious staff of life, but an engrossing hobby, if one had the leisure and the means. He asked me where the scene was set, a question I did not understand. He said if I would trust him to see the first chapter he could probably tell me.

We walked among the wattle blossom in the gully beyond the vegetable garden till we reached the top, where there were some rocks. We sat down, and he said, "My dear Sybylla, I have read your beginning. Though immature it

has promise."

I nearly stifled in agonised expectation of his condemnation. My whole feeling had come to the surface as sensitive as the nerve of a tooth. I knew he would never be mean enough to tell Ma the full depth of my foolishness.

"Why do you write about a castle in England that you have never seen?" he asked gently.

Without waiting for my reply he continued, "I'll tell you, my dear little girl. The castle in England is a castle in Spain, and 'tho' 'twas never built,' imagination makes it more enthralling than things near at hand. Why not try reality?"

I asked breathlessly what he meant.

"Well, instead of the roses on that castle wall, why not this fragrant bower of wattle? Instead of the wind moaning across the moor, why not the pitiless sun beating down on the cracked dusty earth?"

"But that couldn't be put in a book – not in a story!"

"Why not, child?"

"Everyone knows that, and it is so tame and ugly."

"It would be most novel and informing to those who are as familiar with the castle or a slum street as you are with the wattles and the baked pad-docks. Australia is crying out to be done: England is done to death."

This was an expanding idea, like opening a window and letting me look into a place I had not known before.

"You see, you know everyone in the Australian bush. You could picture them with a vigor and conviction that would be refreshing: and my dear, if you could project yourself upon the canvas it would be most successful."

"Oh, I couldn't do that!" I shrank from this. "Besides, I have never done anything like the heroines in novels. I am not sweetly good, and though Ma thinks I am possessed of a devil, I have never done anything really unrespectable.

For example, I could never have been so unkind as to throw that dictionary back at the teacher like Becky Sharp did, though I *wish* I could do that kind of thing. It must be splendid."

"If you could draw portraits of all the characters that furnish your life it would be a good beginning."

"Oh, but I couldn't put in real people. They would not like to see themselves except as white-washed saints – like the yarns on the tombstones. I'd have to imagine people to make them interest-ing."

"Um!" said he, and then with a chuckle, "you go ahead. I shouldn't be surprised if they turn out to be more real that way. But there is one thing, my dear, be Australian. It is the highest form of culture and craftmanship in art to use local materials. That way you stand a chance of adding to culture. The other way you are in danger of merely imitating it, and though imitation is a form of flattery to the imitated, it is a form of weakness or snobbery in the perpetrator. You must find your own way and your own level. The material is in you: all that is required is industry in cultivation."

I could hardly wait till the end of his visit to plaster the ideas he had put into my head upon the original burlesque. Ma said that Mr. Harris was right to a certain extent, that to pretend to be what one was not was the height of vulgarity, but she couldn't see that an interesting book could be made of reality: it was dreary enough to live in the bush in drought time: no one could possibly find any pleasure in reading about such misfortune.

Ma always brings up EXPERIENCE. She has often routed Pa from the field of philosophy with the records of EXPERIENCE, and she now inquired what was the sense in wasting time and paper in this way? Why not do something practical? Pa though, is always willing to believe that the latest venture must be better than the preceding.

I set out to do the equivalent of taking two photographs on the one plate. I was to burlesque autobiography and create the girl of my

admiration, and fill in with a lot of lifelike people as a protest against over-virtuous lay figures. One thing I have always envied in girls is the ability to fly into a towering rage. At school there were two bad-tempered dunces and they enjoyed my brain effort-. I lived in terror of their temper and did their sums with alacrity. Poor Old Harris was careful not to stir them up, and they did pretty well what they liked. So my heroine was to be the antithesis of conventional heroines. All my people were to be created in the image of reality – none of them bad enough to be tarred and feathered, none good enough to be canonised. But people are never what they think themselves, and by the results which accrued it would seem that it is equally difficult to present a character as you intend.

Up to that date I do not remember being so fully interested in anything. I had a secret delight. I ceased to talk about it even to Pa. He and I had quite opposite tastes in stories. He liked adventure: Mayne Reed, Fenimore Cooper, Captain Marryat, Gil Blas, Rider Haggard, but I had one or two of George Gissing's books, Vanity Fair, Colonel Newcome and Esther Waters, and enjoyed that style. No, I could not write dashingly enough to interest Pa. Ma was reading an annotated edition of Shakespeare, and that took her above my sphere of effort.

Bewitchment shadowed the paper as I progressed, I could not do what I liked with the people. I often found them as troublesome as Ma found me, and I think in the end they made rather a pie of my theme, though I did not know it at the time. The book was a companion as well as an entertainment, a confidant and a twin soul. You know how a piece of lace that you have made yourself has a charm lacking in a much better piece made by someone else? So with that book. I used to climb on the hay in the shed behind the stables on Sunday afternoons and read it over – like doing all the parts in a play myself, though at the time I had not seen a play. I must have had a lot of ingrowing egotism, and it came out in this way as the pimples or boils that are common to boys.

I was sardonically amused to depict that reality suggested by Mr, Harris.

Our home was of wood and of the usual pattern and situation in a particularly ugly portion of the bush. We were dished in a basin of low scrubby ranges which are familiar to the poorer settlers where the fertile patches are land-locked in a few big holdings by hard-headed fellows who got in early with capital and grants and convicts.

Instead of hedges we had dog-leg and brush fences, and stumps in the cultivation paddocks. There were fowl-houses covered with tin to render them safe against sharp-snouted spotted marsupial cats; the mess-mate roosting trees also had wide rings of tin around the trunks to save the turkeys by night. Cowsheds were roofed with stringy-bark. Fields of briars and rugged ranges were all around; a weedy water hole in the middle; the not-yet-bleached bones of beasts were a common decora-tion. No roofs but our own were within sight. It was a raw contrast to the English scenery on which I doted, with its thatched cottages, trailing roses, gabled farm houses, towered ancestral halls with Tudor chimneys amid oaks and elms and cawing rooks and moors and downs, wolds, woods, spinneys and brooks. Such reality as mine would look mighty queer in a book, something like a swaggie at a Government House party, but it was as easy to describe as falling off a log.

The people belonging to this scenery were so ordinary and respectable and decent that a yarn about them could not possibly attract the attention of a reader. The probability of readers must have popped up somewhere along the track. I had had no thought of them when I started. I'm sure noth-ing but genius could make the 'Possum Gully kind of reality interesting, and as I am only a jokist I had to bring out the paintpot of embellishment to heighten or lower the flat colorless effect.

There are times when our own case is so blinding that we are unable to feel or to see outside it. We are shut within ourselves. Sometimes these moods are merry and sometimes sad, but always self-sealed. If merry, so all-sufficient is our hilarity that grey skies or black nights have no power to damp our inward fire. But let us be sad, and the brilliance of the sun seems callous. We cannot reach outside ourselves. When young we demand so much that is beyond us that the first lessons in EXPERIENCE are the hoeing of the chastening row of disappointment.

I had a fever which fed upon itself like the green-eyed monster, and it was a great relief to be shedding it like a snake-skin. A desire to have someone to read the result came upon me towards the end. I don't know whether this was gregarious-ness or mere egotism, like my cat's when she brings home a kitten and dumps it for us to see. I was more selective than the cat. She doesn't pick her appreciators. She drops her kitten among us regardless of passing boots, and also regardless, of who may be in the boots. I adore her and indulge her and so have been surprised that she did not bring me her kitten.

I was more demanding. I wanted someone who would understand. Who better than our greatest Australian author? I quite understood him since ever I was old enough to lisp a line of his ballads, what more sequential than his understanding of me? In the innocence of my heart, or it may have been the heartlessness of my innocence, I confidently sent him the manuscript. Having worshipped at his shrine with a whole-heartedness which we can enjoy but once in life, I felt sure of welcome within the gates of his interest.

In those days so entire was my unsophistication that I did not suspect that an author, even the AUSTRALIAN GREATEST, may not have earned thousands by his pen, and may be pestered by so many literary duds that he sees each fresh one draw near with weariness and terror.

To escape making a short story long, my idol welcomed my attempt with cheers for its ORIGINALITY, and asked would I trust him with the manuscript?

WOULD I!!!!!

I'd have given him any or all of my treasures, even my black-dappled-grey filly, a doll, a book of girls' stories or a little box covered with velvet and sea shells. When I come to think of it, these were my only treasures, and he could not take the filly with him to London whither he was going. I was excited by his acceptance of the manuscript. I once gave Ma a little story for her birthday. She thanked me, but did not look as if it were an enjoyable present, and never said whether she read it before burning it under the copper. I hoped the great Australian writer would read my offering before burning it, as I had taken pains to write it nicely – no blots or scratchings-out.

CHAPTER FIVE – FINISHING SCHOOL

This matter of the autobiography settled with satisfaction, I regained my chronic distaste for the kind of life into which it had pleased God to stuff me. The entertainment of fashioning my characters and acting their parts gave me the idea of being an actress. Acting appeared to be the only avocation open to a girl who was not a musical genius nor trained in anything but domesticity. Heaven knows why I had such a notion, for I loathed hypocrisy, and in my circle, acting was another name for this. I had never seen a play nor a mummer, nor even read one – a play I mean – except Shakespeare's. It must have been the delirium of day-dreaming. Fantasy.

My delirium escaped me one day and really startled poor Ma. We had a State child called Eustace to help about the place, or hinder, Ma said. He had once been an elephant's leg in a school play in Goulburn and considered it a great lark. I concocted a scene, in which I was to accidentally fight a duel with him. He refused to fight unless I wore trousers. I put on Pa's, but Eusty said Odds Fish, no dashing blade would fight with such a spectacle. So I tried a pair of Eusty's in which I showed a bit of knee like a fat boy. Eusty called me Greedy Guts. We staged the drama in the hay shed. Pa was concerned that we might have set alight to the straw. Ma said never, never let her hear of me again putting on trousers; showing my person, failing in self-respect before a State School boy!

My defence was that to act Shakespeare (whom everyone respects next to the bible), I should have to don doublet and hose. Me acting SHAKE-SPEARE! Ma was shocked to discover such foolishness in me. I must really be mad. This put me in a fantod so that Ma reported me to Pa and threatened to enlist the clergyman to exorcise the devil in me.

"Now," said Pa, when left to rebuke me, "you must be careful not to upset your mother. The game is not worth the candle." The only thing wrong in the affair was that I had upset Ma: I must never upset Ma: she was a wonderful woman.

"She is not always right just because she is my mother," I grumbled.

"The law is that the Queen can do no wrong," said Pa.

"Yes, but a Queen is a being raised to false majesty."

"Have you forgotten that a woman's kingdom is the home?"

Pa had a twinkle in his eyes, but I refused to melt. EXPERIENCE was certainly teaching me that a sense of humour is too often an advantage to the one who hasn't it. A lack of a sense of humour, like a lack of good-temper, can be used as a waddy.

Later Ma upbraided Pa because he had not severely trounced me. Pa said, "I see nothing wrong with the child's intellect except that it is too bright for its uses".

"If she comes to harm, you must take the consequences," said Ma. "I find her with a boy – swept up from the gutter or somewhere – in a pair of trousers exposing her flesh."

"Eustace is a fine boy. He only needs a chance."

"A chance to get into mischief and laziness. Dear me, where would a child of mine get notions of the stage – the lowest..."

Pa began to rub his hair gently on end and remarked, "I suppose a sea bird reared in the middle of a desert would retain aquatic tendencies."

"She does not take after my side of the house," said Ma.

She was too perturbed about my aberration, as she called it, to leave me to Pa. She "took me in hand". I resented the evil she discerned in me, felt that she was unfair, but there was no appeal against Ma. She disabused my mind of any notion that I could go upon the stage. She ridiculed my every feature and every contour. Ma believes in finishing things. She says it is a sign of a weak mind to begin things and leave them half done. Ma has no weakness of mind. She always finishes the hardest task. She finished me to squashation like a sucked gooseberry. I often longed for death or a nunnery as an escape from my depressing lack of desirable attributes.

But I was freed from notions. Never again would I have the conceit and delusions to think of the stage. Never would I have the effrontery to seek any but the humblest jobs. Should anyone flatter me I would know them for what they were at the first soft word. Ma had ensured me against making a fool of myself by attempting flights, but she had not helped me towards contentment. The native wombat role for me henceforth. Those who are low need fear no fall. I had always jeered at the Blackshaws, our neighbours, by saying they would never make fools of themselves and by adding that those who had not enough stuffing to make fools of themselves at times would never make anything else of themselves.

The finishing stroke in Ma's finishing school was the threat to report me to the nice little clergyman. I loved him dearly. Like Old Harris he was an outlet. I was so worked up that I warned Ma that I'd listen to what she told him. Ma said it was a grave pass to be dictated to in her own house by a creature she had brought into the world. She demanded an apology. I refused. If I expressed contrition to Pa all was washed out, but with Ma it was different. She said penitent gush was useless without reform in deeds. Ma was what she called consistent.

The clergyman came next day, and after dinner, when Pa was at the stables feeding his horses, I loitered in the passage to hear what Ma was saying. Sure enough, she was reporting me as an abnormal specimen. I was infuriated, but the clergyman's voice, in the tone of the Collects – perhaps it was the Twentieth Sunday after the Melbourne Cup – said, "But my dear Mrs. Melvyn, I cannot see anything wrong at all. That child has such glorious eyes that when they are fixed upon me I always find I can preach a better sermon."

"She can be nice when she wants to."

"Adolescence is a difficult time. You might let her come with me around the parish and to stay with my wife and daughters till I come next month. During our progress I could find time to talk to her on spiritual things: and I get so tired of driving, and she is such a clever whip."

That was one in the eye of Ma. I was as gay as a lark, and a Willy-wagtail or two thrown in, when serving supper. I awaited breathlessly to hear the results of the clergyman's championship. Disillu-sion awaited me.

There was only a thin partition between my bed and Ma's, and I could always hear Ma's final injunctions to Pa. Tonight Pa opened the discourse. "Mr. David wants to take Sybylla with him."

"So he said." Ma's voice was a drought of common sense.

"Are you letting her go?"

"I am not."

"Can't you spare her?"

"Not to Mr. David."

"Why?"

"Why should I let her run around with that silly old man?"

"He's not so silly."

"All men are silly where there is a young girl."

"I think you carry suspicion too far," murmured Pa.

"His cloth doesn't protect a man from being blind to faults in a girl, though he would be dull to the problems of older women."

Pa gave a loud grunt. In a little while Ma complained, "I wish you wouldn't snore so". Pa hadn't begun yet, so Ma was taking time by the forelock, as she often adjured me to do.

I lay awake pondering her words. Surely a clergyman, and such a nice lean helpless-looking little one as Mr. David, would not he guilty of flattery or trying to make a fool of me; and he wasn't a bit like the pretentious Canon, who had once taken Mr. David's place. Now, if it had been the Canon! I remember chortling when I read the table of consanguinity beginning, "A man may not marry his grandmother," but Pa had said that human nature was such that...well, such daunting things are attributed to human nature that one would prefer to be one of the higher animals and have decent instincts.

I had a good yarn with Mr. David on his next visit. I had him alone because a neighbour who was ill sent for Ma, and Pa had driven her over. I confessed one thing that prejudiced me against God was that He had to be fed on everlasting praise. I had to grow strong in disapprobation, but God had to be praised unceasingly by measley creatures which He Himself had made. The Psalms were ridiculous with fulsome praise. Egotism in me had to be stemmed and denied, but God seemed to be a sticky mess of it. Another reason I could not respect God was that it seemed so despicable to continually spy upon distressed little girls for the purpose of condemnation.

Mr. David chuckled and said, "Poor God: He has need of young minds like yours to think their way to Him, not to rebel against Him. He needs your help to free Him from all the stupid misrepresenta-tion. Sybylla, m'dear, God is aching for your loving help."

The problem was thrown on me in a way that had never even been hinted in 'Possum Gully by anyone except Pa, and his theories were discredited by Little Jimmy Dripping's common sense.

This devastating idea haunted me day and night. The God made by disagreeable and selfish old men in their own image and erected as a bogey to control women and children retreated before it. Was there no God, only as He was made manifest by nobility and truth in ourselves? This idea, at first releasing, grew to be terrifying. It left one lost and alone. The European God with all His masculine bullying unfairness was at least something to be sure of, however unsatisfactory. No God except as we demonstrate Him! Whew! There was a burden too difficult and demanding to be borne. No wonder people evaded such a vast responsibility by hypocrisy, or sought less exacting conceptions of God in josses which could be placated by praise and candles and incense and other material bribes. It was a sobering revelation.

However, LIFE went on.

I loathed 'Possum Gully more and more. The horses were dog-poor. To ride them at the beginning of a bleak and droughty winter would have been wanton cruelty plus extravagance. March was crisp and cool, with a hint of frost which makes one feel as strong as a young colt, and I rebelled against the continual shining of pot lids, the unnecessary whitening of the hearth, just because Ma insisted upon being the top-notcher.

I took to the piano. Ma said that hard work and worry had driven piano-playing out of her. I said why not turn it the other way about, and drive out dullness with the piano, but Ma preferred to excel in spotless floors and windows. My thumping on the piano irritated her as a love of idleness, and I had to desist.

I hated every bit of the life but the sunsets and moonlight and the wild flowers. The watchdog's bark was often the only incident of the day with its promise of a caller to break monotony. Sometimes this would be a tea agent or a stock inspector. The regular visitors were Mrs. Olliver, Mrs. Blackshaw, or Mrs. Crispin come to spend the afternoon. I resented their inadequacy as society. It was not their fault. I loved them warmly, much more than they loved me, I am sure, and did more for them than they did for me, because I was something for them to criticise and cackle about. "That Sybylla does this and that." Someone was always reporting what the other said, and that annoyed Ma. Pa said rubbish, if criticism was sifted out of conversation people would be silent from Goulburn to Bourke and Broken f fill and beyond.

Poverty can make pioneering a sorry job. In any case it has always been heavier on women than on men. 'Possum Gully was a generation or two removed from frontier pioneering, though Australia never had a frontier. She had an outback which became back paddocks with familiarity. But all the trying part and none of the adventure of pioneering remained at 'Possum Gully. The inconvenient houses depending on the main strength of drudgery, the absence of comfort or beauty or any cultural possibilities or opportunities for self-develop-ment were still enough to induce Back Blocks lunacy in any one above a cow in ability.

Those good ladies all had large families, and their conversations were about recipes for cakes and puddings and little Tommies' tummyaches, and then boasting bees as to who skinned her hands the most in washing her husband's trousers of moleskin. They and their daughters, following in their tracks, were held up to me as admirable. Horrors! Broken down drudges talking of uterine troubles and the weariness of child-bearing! I could not accept that as the fullness of life from any God worthy of worship or gratitude. These martyrs to stupidity were extolled in sententious tones as "mothers of families". They were populating Australia. I said that instead of Ned Crispin and others I should prefer Australia to remain populated by kangaroos and the dear little bears and kangaroo rats that were as thick about us as sheep. This was the sort of thing that made me entertaining to the 'Possum Gullyites, and troubled Ma.

Another winter wore away and a bit of a spring deluded the land. We had saved a few hundred sheep, and wool would be scarce because so many sheep had died. Just as shearing was coming on Pa had a call from an old colleague to help fight a by-election in Junee. This was a key electorate on Pa's side, and he said he could not let the country down. The shearing would take only a few days, and Mr. Blackshaw offered to oversee it. He too saw the importance of Junee being saved for the right side.

This infuriated poor Ma. She said Pa might as well have been a drunkard who went on the booze at critical times. To leave our sole income to the superintendence of an outsider was not merely un-dignified, it was lunacy. Ma said I could now see why she tried to save me from my father's ten-dencies. She held that a man should first save his home and family, and the country could come second. Pa said if the country was not saved for the homes and liberty Australia might as well be under the Russian Czars.

At any rate Pa went, ran away in a crisis, Ma said, just because he loved to hear himself spouting on a platform. Ma said I would never understand what she had suffered, that life was a bitter thing with a useless husband. I ventured to say that Pa didn't have such a slashing life either. Ma main-tained it was much harder for her, but that I could not understand that.

I was piqued by this accusation of lack in understanding. I said I could understand it was easier for Pa because he was so proud of her and thought her so wonderful. He at least had the satisfaction of thinking what a stroke he had done to choose and win such a wife, while she must always be ashamed of herself for marrying so much beneath her; but that did not appease Ma. Quite the opposite. Quite, quite the opposite! I gathered that Ma had the added affliction of me as a daughter, which couldn't matter so much to Pa because I took after him.

Then Mr. Blackshaw's back was smitten and he could not rise from bed. All the men at one time or another had a bad back. It was Mr. Blackshaw's turn. Ma was a deserted heroine.

"It is my turn to save the ship," said I. "You always say that I'll have to help Pa. I know how to pick up and roll a fleece, and Eusty can be tar boy and rouse-about."

This did not dispose of the pressing. We had a hand-worked press of Pa's construction which

Ma said showed what a helpless botcher Pa was, but all the neighbours used to borrow it, which further shows the standard of the neighbourhood, or that Pa wasn't so bad.

We turned the hayshed into a floor for two men with blades, who wanted to learn so that they could go down the Riverina next year. The skilled shearers had not yet returned to their little homes in the wallaby scrubs around us. These lads had to do their own work and come a distance each morning and they were very slow. All this prolonged the festival.

Ma vetoed the idea of my working in the shed. It would have been fun and a relief from the pot lids and d'oyleys. (It sometimes took half an hour to iron one of the prevalent d'oyleys.)

"You would be talked about," said Ma, "and the boys would be giggle-gaggling with you instead of attending to their work."

She decided to attend to the shearing herself and let me do the cooking. this was a disappointment, as to press one's face into a nice fat sheep all white from the shears is a delight. The two shearers were selectors' sons in their teens. We knew each other minutely, but did not "associate". We were a grade higher socially, but had we shown it they would not have shorn for us, and would have slanged us throughout the neighbourhood. Ma and I managed to be too busy to sit down to meals with them, and thus was a gradation of the caste system preserved.

The shearing was saved but the country was lost in so far as Pa's man was rejected by the electors, and Pa did not have his election expenses paid.

The Marrow of Tradition – Chapters 32-35

Charles Chesnutt

XXXII – THE STORM BREAKS

The Wellington riot began at three o'clock in the afternoon of a day as fair as was ever selected for a deed of darkness. The sky was clear, except for a few light clouds that floated, white and feathery, high in air, like distant islands in a sapphire sea. A salt-laden breeze from the ocean a few miles away lent a crisp sparkle to the air.

At three o'clock sharp the streets were filled, as if by magic, with armed white men. The negroes, going about, had noted, with uneasy curiosity, that the stores and places of business, many of which closed at noon, were unduly late in opening for the afternoon, though no one suspected the reason for the delay; but at three o'clock every passing colored man was ordered, by the first white man he met, to throw up his hands. If he complied, he was searched, more or less roughly, for firearms, and then warned to get off the street. When he met another group of white men the scene was repeated. The man thus summarily held up seldom encountered more than two groups before disappearing across lots to his own home or some convenient hiding-place. If he resisted any demand of those who halted him – But the records of the day are historical; they may be found in the newspapers of the following date, but they are more firmly engraved upon the hearts and memories of the people of Wellington. For many months there were negro families in the town whose children screamed with fear and ran to their mothers for protection at the mere sight of a white man.

Dr. Miller had received a call, about one o'clock, to attend a case at the house of a well-to-do colored farmer, who lived some three or four miles from the town, upon the very road, by the way, along which Miller had driven so furiously a few weeks before, in the few hours that intervened before Sandy Campbell would probably have been burned at the stake. The drive to his patient's home, the necessary inquiries, the filling of the prescription from his own medicine-case, which he carried along with him, the little friendly conversation about the weather and the crops, and, the farmer being an intelligent and thinking man, the inevitable subject of the future of their race, – these, added to the return journey, occupied at least two hours of Miller's time.

As he neared the town on his way back, he saw ahead of him half a dozen men and women approaching, with fear written in their faces, in every degree from apprehension to terror. Women were weeping and children crying, and all were going as fast as seemingly lay in their power, looking behind now and then as if pursued by some deadly enemy. At sight of Miller's buggy they made a dash for cover, disappearing, like a covey of frightened partridges, in the underbrush along the road.

Miller pulled up his horse and looked after them in startled wonder.

"What on earth can be the matter?" he muttered, struck with a vague feeling of alarm. A psychologist, seeking to trace the effects of slavery upon the human mind, might find in the South many a curious illustration of this curse, abiding long after the actual physical bondage had terminated. In the olden time the white South labored under the constant fear of negro insurrections. Knowing that they themselves, if in the negroes' place, would have risen in the effort to throw off the yoke, all their reiterated theories of negro subordination and inferiority could not remove that lurking fear, founded upon the obscure consciousness that the slaves ought to have risen. Conscience, it has been said, makes cowards of us all. There was never, on the continent of America, a successful slave revolt, nor one which lasted more than a few hours, or resulted in the loss of more than a few white lives; yet never was the planter quite free from the fear that there might be one.

On the other hand, the slave had before his eyes always the fear of the master. There were good men, according to their lights, – according to their training and environment, – among the Southern slaveholders, who treated their slaves kindly, as slaves, from principle, because they recognized the claims of humanity, even under the dark skin of a human chattel. There was many a one who protected or pampered his negroes, as the case might be, just as a man fondles his dog, – because they were his; they were a part of his estate, an integral part of the entity of property and person which made up the aristocrat; but with all this kindness, there was always present, in the consciousness of the lowest slave, the knowledge that he was in his master's power, and that he could make no effectual protest against the abuse of that authority. There was also the knowledge, among those who could think at all, that the best of masters was himself a slave to a system, which hampered his move-ments but scarcely less than those of his bondmen.

When, therefore, Miller saw these men and women scampering into the bushes, he divined, with this slumbering race consciousness which years of culture had not obliterated, that there was some race trouble on foot. His intuition did not long remain unsupported. A black head was cautiously protruded from the shrubbery, and a black voice – if such a description be allowable – addressed him: –

"Is dat you, Doctuh Miller?"

"Yes. Who are you, and what's the trouble?"

"What's de trouble, suh? Why, all hell's broke loose in town yonduh. De w'ite folks is riz 'gins' de niggers, an' say dey're gwine ter kill eve'y nigger dey kin lay han's on."

Miller's heart leaped to his throat, as he thought of his wife and child. This story was preposterous; it could not be true, and yet there must be something in it. He tried to question his informant, but the man was so overcome with excitement and fear that Miller saw clearly that he must go farther for information. He had read in the Morning Chronicle, a few days before, the obnoxious editorial quoted from the Afro-American Banner, and had noted the comment upon it by the white editor. He had felt, as at the time of its first publication, that the editorial was ill-advised. It could do no good, and was calculated to arouse the animosity of those whose friendship, whose tolerance, at least, was necessary and almost indispensable to the colored people. They were living, at the best, in a sort of armed neutrality with the whites; such a publication, however serviceable elsewhere, could have no other effect in Wellington than to endanger this truce and defeat the hope of a possible future friendship. The right of free speech entitled Barber to publish it; a larger measure of common-sense would have made him withhold it. Whether it was the republication of this article that had stirred up anew the sleeping dogs of race prejudice and whetted their thirst for blood, he could not yet tell; but at any rate, there was mischief on foot.

"Fer God's sake, doctuh, don' go no closeter ter dat town," pleaded his informant, "er you'll be killt sho'. Come on wid us, suh, an' tek keer er yo'se'f. We're gwine ter hide in de swamps till dis thing is over!"

"God, man!" exclaimed Miller, urging his horse forward, "my wife and child are in the town!"

Fortunately, he reflected, there were no patients confined in the hospital, – if there should be anything in this preposterous story. To one unfamiliar with Southern life, it might have seemed impossible that these good Christian people, who thronged the churches on Sunday, and wept over the sufferings of the lowly Nazarene, and sent missionaries to the heathen, could be hungering and thirsting for the blood of their fellow men; but Miller cherished no such delusion. He knew the history of his country; he had the threatened lynching of Sandy Campbell vividly in mind; and he was fully persuaded that to race prejudice, once roused, any horror was possible. That women or children would be molested of set purpose he did not believe, but that they might suffer by accident was more than likely.

As he neared the town, dashing forward at the top of his horse's speed, he heard his voice called in a loud and agitated tone, and, glancing around him, saw a familiar form standing by the roadside, gesticulating vehemently.

He drew up the horse with a suddenness that threw the faithful and obedient animal back upon its haunches. The colored lawyer, Watson, came up to the buggy. That he was laboring under great and unusual excitement was quite apparent from his pale face and frightened air.

"What's the matter, Watson?" demanded Miller, hoping now to obtain some reliable information.

"Matter!" exclaimed the other. "Everything's the matter! The white people are up in arms. They have disarmed the colored people, killing half a dozen in the process, and wounding as many more. They have forced the mayor and aldermen to resign, have formed a provisional city government *à la Française*, and have ordered me and half a dozen other fellows to leave town in forty-eight hours, under pain of sudden death. As they seem to mean it, I shall not stay so long. Fortunately, my wife and children are away. I knew you were out here, however, and I thought I'd come out and wait for you, so that we might talk the matter over. I don't imagine they mean you any harm, personally, because you tread on nobody's toes; but you're too valuable a man for the race to lose, so I thought I'd give you warning. I shall want to sell you my property, too, at a bargain. For I'm worth too much to my family to dream of ever attempting to live here again."

"Have you seen anything of my wife and child?" asked Miller, intent upon the danger to which they might be exposed.

"No; I didn't go to the house. I inquired at the drugstore and found out where you had gone. You needn't fear for them, – it is not a war on women and children."

"War of any kind is always hardest on the women and children," returned Miller; "I must hurry on and see that mine are safe."

"They'll not carry the war so far into Africa as that," returned Watson; "but I never saw anything like it. Yesterday I had a hundred white friends in the town, or thought I had, – men who spoke pleasantly to me on the street, and sometimes gave me their hands to shake. Not one of them said to me today: 'Watson, stay at home this afternoon.' I might have been killed, like any one of half a dozen others who have bit the dust, for any word that one of my 'friends' had said to warn me. When the race cry is started in this neck of the woods, friendship, religion, humanity, reason, all shrivel up like dry leaves in a raging furnace."

The buggy, into which Watson had climbed, was meanwhile rapidly nearing the town.

"I think I'll leave you here, Miller," said Watson, as they approached the outskirts, "and make my way home by a roundabout path, as I should like to get there unmolested. Home! – a beautiful word that, isn't it, for an exiled wanderer? It might not be well, either, for us to be seen together. If you put the hood of your buggy down, and sit well back in the shadow, you may be able to reach home without interruption; but avoid the main streets. I'll see you again this evening, if we're both alive, and I can reach you; for my time is short. A committee are to call in the morning to escort me to the train. I am to be dismissed from the community with public honors." Watson was climbing down from the buggy, when a small party of men were seen approaching, and big Josh Green, followed by several other resolute-looking colored men, came up and addressed them.

"Dr. Miller," cried Green, "Mr. Watson, – we're lookin' fer a leader. De w'ite folks are killin' de niggers, an' we ain' gwine ter stan' up an' be shot down like dogs. We're gwine ter defen' ou' lives, an' we ain' gwine ter run away f'm no place where we 'we got a right ter be; an' woe be ter de w'ite man w'at lays ban's on us! Dere's two niggers in dis town ter eve'y w'ite man, an' ef we 'we got ter be killt, we'll take some w'ite folks 'long wid us, ez sho' ez dere's a God in heaven, – ez I s'pose dere is, dough He mus' be 'sleep, er busy somewhar e'se ter-day. Will you-all come an' lead us?"

"Gentlemen," said Watson, "what is the use? The negroes will not back you up. They haven't the arms, nor the moral courage, nor the leadership."

"We'll git de arms, an' we'll git de courage, ef you'll come an' lead us! We wants leaders, – dat's w'y we come ter you!"

"What's the use?" returned Watson despairingly. "The odds are too heavy. I've been ordered out of town; if I stayed, I'd be shot on sight, unless I had a body-guard around me."

"We'll be yo' body-guard!" shouted half a dozen voices.

"And when my body-guard was shot, what then? I have a wife and children. It is my duty to live for them. If I died, I should get no glory and no reward, and my family would be reduced to beggary, – to which they'll soon be near enough as it is. This affair will blow over in a day or two. The white people will be ashamed of themselves to-morrow, and apprehensive of the consequences for some time to come. Keep quiet, boys, and trust in God. You won't gain anything by resistance."

"'God he'ps dem dat he'ps demselves,'" returned Josh stoutly. "Ef Mr. Watson won't lead us, will you, Dr. Miller?" said the spokesman, turning to the doctor.

For Miller it was an agonizing moment. He was no coward, morally or physically. Every manly instinct urged him to go forward and take up the cause of these leaderless people, and, if need be, to defend their lives and their rights with his own, – but to what end?

"Listen, men," he said. "We would only be throwing our lives away. Suppose we made a determined stand and won a temporary victory. By morning every train, every boat, every road leading into Wellington, would be crowded with white men, – as they probably will be any way, – with arms in their hands, curses on their lips, and ven-geance in their hearts. In the minds of those who make and administer the laws, we have no standing in the court of conscience. They would kill us in the fight, or they would hang us afterwards, – one way or another, we should be doomed. I should like to lead you; I should like to arm every colored man in this town, and have them stand firmly in line, not for attack, but for defense; but if I attempted it, and they should stand by me, which is questionable, – for I have met them fleeing from the town, – my life would pay the forfeit. Alive, I may be of some use to you, and you are welcome to my life in that way, – I am giving it freely. Dead, I should be a mere lump of carrion. Who remembers even the names of those who have been done to death in the Southern States for the past twenty years?"

"I 'members de name er one of 'em," said Josh, "an' I 'members de name er de man dat killt 'im, an' I s'pec' his time is mighty nigh come."

"My advice is not heroic, but I think it is wise. In this riot we are placed as we should be in a war: we have no territory, no base of supplies, no organization, no outside sympathy, – we stand in the position of a race, in a case like this, without money and without friends. Our time will come, – the time when we can command respect for our rights; but it is not yet in sight. Give it up, boys, and wait. Good may come of this, after all."

Several of the men wavered, and looked irresolute.

"I reckon that's all so, doctuh," returned Josh, "an', de way you put it, I don' blame you ner Mr. Watson; but all dem reasons ain' got no weight wid me. I'm gwine in dat town, an' ef any w'ite man 'sturbs me, dere'll be trouble, – dere'll be double trouble, – I feels it in my bones!"

"Remember your old mother, Josh," said Miller.

"Yas, sub, I'll 'member her; dat's all I kin do now. I don' need ter wait fer her no mo', fer she died dis mo'nin'. I'd lack ter see her buried, suh, but I may not have de chance. Ef I gits killt, will you do me a favor?"

"Yes, Josh; what is it?"

"Ef I should git laid out in dis commotion dat's gwine on, will you collec' my wages f'm yo' brother, and see dat de ole 'oman is put away right?"

"Yes, of course."

"Wid a nice coffin, an' a nice fune'al, an' a head-bo'd an' a foot-bo'd?"

"Yes."

"All right, suh! Ef I don' live ter do it, I'll know it'll be 'tended ter right. Now we're gwine out ter de cotton compress, an' git a lot er colored men tergether, an' ef de w'ite folks 'sturbs me, I shouldn't be s'prise' ef dere'd be a mix-up; – an' ef dere is, me an *one* w'ite man 'll stan' befo' de jedgment th'one er God dis day; an' it won't be me w'at'll be 'feared er de jedgment. Come along, boys! Dese gentlemen may have somethin' ter live fer; but ez fer my pa't, I'd ruther be a dead nigger any day dan a live dog!"

XXXIII – INTO THE LION'S JAWS

The party under Josh's leadership moved off down the road. Miller, while entirely convinced that he had acted wisely in declining to accompany them, was yet conscious of a distinct feeling of shame and envy that he, too, did not feel impelled to throw away his life in a hopeless struggle.

Watson left the buggy and disappeared by a path at the roadside. Miller drove rapidly forward. After entering the town, he passed several small parties of white men, but escaped scrutiny by sitting well back in his buggy, the presumption being that a well-dressed man with a good horse and buggy was white. Torn with anxiety, he reached home at about four o'clock. Driving the horse into the yard, he sprang down from the buggy and hastened to the house, which he found locked, front and rear.

A repeated rapping brought no response. At length he broke a window, and entered the house like a thief.

"Janet, Janet!" he called in alarm, "where are

you? It is only I, – Will!"

There was no reply. He ran from room to room, only to find them all empty. Again he called his wife's name, and was about rushing from the house, when a muffled voice came faintly to his ear, –

"Is dat you, Doctuh Miller?"

"Yes. Who are you, and where are my wife and child?"

He was looking around in perplexity, when the door of a low closet under the kitchen sink was opened from within, and a woolly head was cautiously protruded.

"Are you *sho'* dat's you, doctuh?"

"Yes, Sally; where are" –

"An' not some w'ite man come ter bu'n down de house an' kill all de niggers?"

"No, Sally, it's me all right. Where is my wife? Where is my child?"

"Dey went over ter see Mis' Butler 'long 'bout two o'clock, befo' dis fuss broke out, suh. Oh, Lawdy, Lawdy, suh! Is all de cullud folks be'n killt 'cep'n' me an' you, suh? Fer de Lawd's sake, suh, you won' let 'em kill me, will you, suh? I'll wuk fer you fer nuthin', suh, all my bawn days, ef you'll save my life, suh!"

"Calm yourself, Sally. You'll be safe enough if you stay right here, I 'we no doubt. They'll not harm women, – of that I'm sure enough, although I haven't yet got the bearings of this deplorable affair. Stay here and look after the house. I must find my wife and child!"

The distance across the city to the home of the Mrs. Butler whom his wife had gone to visit was exactly one mile. Though Miller had a good horse in front of him, he was two hours in reaching his destination. Never will the picture of that ride fade from his memory. In his dreams he repeats it night after night, and sees the sights that wounded his eyes, and feels the thoughts – the haunting spirits of the thoughts – that tore his heart as he rode through hell to find those whom he was seeking. For a short distance he saw nothing, and made rapid progress. As he turned the first corner, his horse shied at the dead body of a negro, lying huddled up in the collapse which marks sudden death. What Miller shuddered at was not so much the thought of death, to the sight of which his profession had accustomed him, as the suggestion of what it signified. He had taken with allowance the wild statement of the fleeing fugitives. Watson, too, had been greatly excited, and Josh Green's group were desperate men, as much liable to be misled by their courage as the others by their fears; but here was proof that murder had been done, – and his wife and children were in the town. Distant shouts, and the sound of firearms, increased his alarm. He struck his horse with the whip, and dashed on toward the heart of the city, which he must traverse in order to reach Janet and the child.

At the next corner lay the body of another man, with the red blood oozing from a ghastly wound in the forehead. The negroes seemed to have been killed, as the band plays in circus parades, at the street intersections, where the example would be most effective. Miller, with a wild leap of the heart, had barely passed this gruesome spectacle, when a sharp voice commanded him to halt, and emphasized the order by covering him with a revolver. Forgetting the prudence he had preached to others, he had raised his whip to strike the horse, when several hands seized the bridle.

"Come down, you damn fool," growled an authoritative voice. "Don't you see we're in earnest? Do you want to get killed?"

"Why should I come down?" asked Miller. "Because we've ordered you to come down! This is the white people's day, and when they order, a nigger must obey. We're going to search you for weapons."

"Search away. You'll find nothing but a case of surgeon's tools, which I'm more than likely to need before this day is over, from all indications."

"No matter; we'll make sure of it! That's what we're here for. Come down, if you don't want to be pulled down!"

Miller stepped down from his buggy. His interlocutor, who made no effort at disguise, was a clerk in a dry-goods store where Miller bought most of his family and hospital supplies. He made no sign of recognition, however, and Miller claimed no acquaintance. This man, who had for several years emptied Miller's pockets in the course of more or less legitimate trade, now went through them, aided by another man, more rapidly than ever before, the searchers convincing themselves that Miller carried no deadly weapon upon his person. Meanwhile, a third ransacked the buggy with like result. Miller recognized several others of the party, who made not the slightest attempt at disguise, though no names were called by any one.

"Where are you going?" demanded the leader.

"I am looking for my wife and child," replied Miller.

"Well, run along, and keep them out of the streets when you find them; and keep your hands out of this affair, if you wish to live in this town, which from now on will be a white man's town, as you niggers will be pretty firmly convinced before night."

Miller drove on as swiftly as might be. At the next corner he was stopped again. In the white man who held him up, Miller recognized a neigh-bor of his own. After a short detention and a perfunctory search, the white man remarked apologetically: –

"Sorry to have had to trouble you, doctuh, but them's the o'ders. It ain't men like you that we're after, but the vicious and criminal class of niggers."

Miller smiled bitterly as he urged his horse forward. He was quite well aware that the virtuous citizen who had stopped him had only a few weeks before finished a term in the penitentiary, to which he had been sentenced for stealing. Miller knew that he could have bought all the man owned for fifty dollars, and his soul for as much more.

A few rods farther on, he came near running over the body of a wounded man who lay groaning by the wayside. Every professional instinct urged him to stop and offer aid to the sufferer; but the uncertainty concerning his wife and child proved a stronger motive and urged him resistlessly forward. Here and there the ominous sound of firearms was audible. He might have thought this merely a part of the show, like the "powder play" of the Arabs, but for the bloody confirmation of its earnestness which had already assailed his vision. Somewhere in this seething caldron of unrestrained passions were his wife and child, and he must hurry on.

His progress was painfully slow. Three times he was stopped and searched. More than once his way was barred, and he was ordered to turn back, each such occasion requiring a detour which consumed many minutes. The man who last stopped him was a well-known Jewish merchant. A Jew – God of Moses! – had so far forgotten twenty centuries of history as to join in the persecution of another oppressed race! When almost reduced to despair by these innumerable delays, he perceived, coming toward him, Mr. Ellis, the sub-editor of the Morning Chronicle. Miller had just been stopped and questioned again, and Ellis came up as he was starting once more upon his endless ride.

"Dr. Miller," said Ellis kindly, "it is dangerous for you on the streets. Why tempt the danger?"

"I am looking for my wife and child," returned Miller in desperation. "They are somewhere in this town, – I don't know where, – and I must find them."

Ellis had been horror-stricken by the tragedy of the afternoon, the wholly superfluous slaughter of a harmless people, whom a show of force would have been quite sufficient to overawe. Elaborate explanations were afterwards given for these murders, which were said, perhaps truthfully, not to have been premeditated, and many regrets were expressed. The young man had been surprised, quite as much as the negroes themselves, at the ferocity displayed. His own thoughts and feelings were attuned to anything but slaughter. Only that morning he had received a perfumed note, calling his attention to what the writer described as a very noble deed of his, and requesting him to call that evening and receive the writer's thanks. Had he known that Miss Pemberton, several weeks after their visit to the Sound, had driven out again to the hotel and made some inquiries among the servants, he might have understood better the meaning of this missive. When Miller spoke of his wife and child, some subtle thread of suggestion coupled the note with Miller's plight. "I'll go with you, Dr. Miller," he said, "if you'll permit me. In my company you will not be disturbed."

He took a seat in Miller's buggy, after which it was not molested.

Neither of them spoke. Miller was sick at heart; he could have wept with grief, even had the welfare of his own dear ones not been involved in this regrettable affair. With prophetic instinct he foresaw the hatreds to which this day would give birth; the long years of constraint and distrust which would still further widen the breach between two peoples whom fate had thrown together in one community.

There was nothing for Ellis to say. In his heart he could not defend the deeds of this day. The petty annoyances which the whites had felt at the spectacle of a few negroes in office; the not unnatural resentment of a proud people at what had seemed to them a presumptuous freedom of speech and lack of deference on the part of their inferiors, – these things, which he knew were to be made the excuse for overturning the city government, he realized full well were no sort of justification for the wholesale murder or other horrors which might well ensue before the day was done. He could not approve the acts of his own people; neither could he, to a negro, condemn them. Hence he was silent.

"Thank you, Mr. Ellis," exclaimed Miller, when they had reached the house where he expected to find his wife. "This is the place where I was going. I am – under a great obligation to you."

"Not at all, Dr. Miller. I need not tell you how much I regret this deplorable affair."

Ellis went back down the street. Fastening his horse to the fence, Miller sprang forward to find his wife and child. They would certainly be there, for no colored woman would be foolhardy enough to venture on the streets after the riot had broken out.

As he drew nearer, he felt a sudden apprehension. The house seemed strangely silent and deserted. The doors were closed, and the Venetian blinds shut tightly. Even a dog which had appeared slunk timidly back under the house, instead of barking vociferously according to the usual habit of his kind.

XXXIV – THE VALLEY OF THE SHADOW

Miller knocked at the door. There was no response. He went round to the rear of the house. The dog had slunk behind the woodpile. Miller knocked again, at the back door, and, receiving no reply, called aloud.

"Mrs. Butler! It is I, Dr. Miller. Is my wife here?"

The slats of a near-by blind opened cautiously.

"Is it really you, Dr. Miller?"

"Yes, Mrs. Butler. I am looking for my wife and child, – are they here?"

"No, sir; she became alarmed about you, soon after the shooting commenced, and I could not keep her. She left for home half an hour ago. It is coming on dusk, and she and the child are so near white that she did not expect to be molested."

"Which way did she go?"

"She meant to go by the main street. She thought it would be less dangerous than the back streets. I tried to get her to stay here, but she was frantic about you, and nothing I could say would keep her. Is the riot almost over, Dr. Miller? Do you think they will murder us all, and burn down our houses?"

"God knows," replied Miller, with a groan. "But I must find her, if I lose my own life in the attempt."

Surely, he thought, Janet would be safe. The white people of Wellington were not savages; or at least their temporary reversion to savagery would not go as far as to include violence to delicate women and children. Then there flashed into his mind Josh Green's story of his "silly" mother, who for twenty years had walked the earth as a child, as the result of one night's terror, and his heart sank within him.

Miller realized that his buggy, by attracting attention, had been a hindrance rather than a help in his progress across the city. In order to follow his wife, he must practically retrace his steps over the very route he had come. Night was falling. It would be easier to cross the town on foot. In the dusk his own color, slight in the daytime, would not attract attention, and by dodging in the shadows he might avoid those who might wish to intercept him. But he must reach Janet and the boy at any risk. He had not been willing to throw his life away hopelessly, but he would cheerfully have sacrificed it for those whom he loved.

He had gone but a short distance, and had not yet reached the centre of mob activity, when he intercepted a band of negro laborers from the cotton compress, with big Josh Green at their head.

"Hello, doctuh!" cried Josh, "does you wan' ter jine us?"

"I'm looking for my wife and child, Josh. They're somewhere in this den of murderers. Have any of you seen them?"

No one had seen them.

"You men are running a great risk," said Miller. "You are rushing on to certain death."

"Well, suh, maybe we is; but we're gwine ter die fightin'. Dey say de w'ite folks is gwine ter bu'n all de cullud schools an' chu'ches, an' kill all de niggers dey kin ketch. Dey're gwine ter bu'n yo' new hospittle, ef somebody don' stop 'em."

"Josh – men – you are throwing your lives away. It is a fever; it will wear off to-morrow, or to-night. They'll not burn the schoolhouses, nor the hospital – they are not such fools, for they benefit the community; and they'll only kill the colored people who resist them. Every one of you with a gun or a pistol carries his death warrant in his own hand. I'd rather see the hospital burn than have one of you lose his life. Resistance only makes the matter worse, – the odds against you are too long."

"Things can't be any wuss, doctuh," replied one of the crowd sturdily. "A gun is mo' dange'ous ter de man in front of it dan ter de man behin' it. Dey're gwine ter kill us anyhow; an' we're tired, – we read de newspapers, – an' we're tired er bein' shot down like dogs, widout jedge er jury. We'd ruther die fightin' dan be stuck like pigs in a pen!"

"God help you!" said Miller. "As for me, I must find my wife and child."

"Good-by, doctuh," cried Josh, brandishing a huge knife. "'Member 'bout de ole 'oman, ef you lives thoo dis. Don' fergit de headbo'd an' de footbo'd, an' a silver plate on de coffin, ef dere's money ernuff."

They went their way, and Miller hurried on. They might resist attack; he thought it extremely unlikely that they would begin it; but he knew perfectly well that the mere knowledge that some of the negroes contemplated resistance would only further inflame the infuriated whites. The colored men might win a momentary victory, though it was extremely doubtful; and they would as surely reap the harvest later on. The qualities which in a white man would win the applause of the world would in a negro be taken as the marks of savagery. So thoroughly diseased was public opinion in matters of race that the negro who died for the common rights of humanity might look for no meed of admiration or glory. At such a time, in the white man's eyes, a negro's courage would be mere desperation; his love of liberty, a mere animal dislike of restraint. Every finer human instinct would be interpreted in terms of savagery. Or, if forced to admire, they would none the less repress. They would applaud his courage while they stretched his neck, or carried off the fragments of his mangled body as souvenirs, in much the same way that savages preserve the scalps or eat the hearts of their enemies.

But concern for the fate of Josh and his friends occupied only a secondary place in Miller's mind for the moment. His wife and child were somewhere ahead of him. He pushed on. He had covered about a quarter of a mile more, and far down the street could see the signs of greater animation, when he came upon the body of a woman lying upon the sidewalk. In the dusk he had almost stumbled over it, and his heart came up in his mouth. A second glance revealed that it could not be his wife. It was a fearful portent, however, of what her fate might be. The "war" had reached the women and children. Yielding to a professional instinct, he stooped, and saw that the prostrate form was that of old Aunt Jane Letlow. She was not yet quite dead, and as Miller, with a tender touch, placed her head in a more comfortable position, her lips moved with a last lingering flicker of consciousness: –

"Comin', missis, comin'!"

Mammy Jane had gone to join the old mistress upon whose memory her heart was fixed; and yet not all her reverence for her old mistress, nor all her deference to the whites, nor all their friendship for her, had been able to save her from this raging devil of race hatred which momentarily possessed the town.

Perceiving that he could do no good, Miller hastened onward, sick at heart. Whenever he saw a party of white men approaching, – these brave reformers never went singly, – he sought concealment in the shadow of a tree or the shrubbery in some yard until they had passed. He had covered about two thirds of the distance homeward, when his eyes fell upon a group beneath a lamp-post, at sight of which he turned pale with horror, and rushed forward with a terrible cry.

XXXV – "MINE ENEMY, O MINE ENEMY!"

The proceedings of the day – planned originally as a "demonstration," dignified subsequently as a "revolution," under any name the culmination of the conspiracy formed by Carteret and his colleagues – had by seven o'clock in the afternoon developed into a murderous riot. Crowds of white men and half-grown boys, drunk with whiskey or with license, raged through the streets, beating, chasing, or killing any negro so unfortunate as to fall into their hands. Why any particular negro was assailed, no one stopped to inquire; it was merely a white mob thirsting for black blood, with no more conscience or discrimination than would be exercised by a wolf in a sheepfold. It was race against race, the whites against the negroes; and it was a one-sided affair, for until Josh Green got together his body of armed men, no effective resistance had been made by any colored person, and the individuals who had been killed had so far left no marks upon the enemy by which they might be remembered.

"Kill the niggers!" rang out now and then through the dusk, and far down the street and along the intersecting thoroughfares distant voices took up the ominous refrain, – "Kill the niggers! Kill the damned niggers!" Now, not a dark face had been seen on the street for half an hour, until the group of men headed by Josh made their appearance in the negro quarter. Armed with guns and axes, they presented quite a formidable appearance as they made their way toward the new hospital, near which stood a schoolhouse and a large church, both used by the colored people. They did not reach their destination without having met a number of white men, singly or in twos or threes; and the rumor spread with incredible swiftness that the negroes in turn were up in arms, determined to massacre all the whites and burn the town. Some of the whites became alarmed, and recognizing the power of the negroes, if armed and conscious of their strength, were impressed by the immediate necessity of overpowering and overawing them. Others, with appetites already whetted by slaughter, saw a chance, welcome rather than not, of shedding more black blood. Spontaneously the white mob flocked toward the hospital, where rumor had it that a large body of desperate negroes, breathing threats of blood and fire, had taken a determined stand.

It had been Josh's plan merely to remain quietly and peaceably in the neighborhood of the little group of public institutions, molesting no one, un-less first attacked, and merely letting the white people see that they meant to protect their own; but so rapidly did the rumor spread, and so promptly did the white people act, that by the time Josh and his supporters had reached the top of the rising ground where the hospital stood, a crowd of white men much more numerous than their own party were following them at a short distance.

Josh, with the eye of a general, perceived that some of his party were becoming a little nervous, and decided that they would feel safer behind shelter.

"I reckon we better go inside de hospittle, boys," he exclaimed. "Den we'll be behind brick walls, an' dem other fellows 'll be outside, an' ef dere's any fightin', we'll have de bes' show. We ain' gwine ter do no shootin' till we're pestered, an' dey'll be less likely ter pester us ef dey can't git at us widout runnin' some resk. Come along in! Be men! De gov'ner er de President is gwine ter sen' soldiers ter stop dese gwines-on, an' meantime we kin keep dem white devils f'm bu'nin' down our hospittles an' chu'ch-houses. Wen dey comes an' fin's out dat we jes' means ter pertect ou' prope'ty, dey'll go 'long 'bout deir own business. Er, ef dey wants a scrap, dey kin have it! Come erlong, boys!"

Jerry Letlow, who had kept out of sight during the day, had started out, after night had set in, to find Major Carteret. Jerry was very much afraid. The events of the day had filled him with terror. Whatever the limitations of Jerry's mind or character may have been, Jerry had a keen appreciation of the danger to the negroes when they came in conflict with the whites, and he had no desire to imperil his own skin. He valued his life for his own sake, and not for any altruistic theory that it might be of service to oth-

ers. In other words, Jerry was something of a coward. He had kept in hiding all day, but finding, toward evening, that the riot did not abate, and fearing, from the rumors which came to his ears, that all the negroes would be exterminated, he had set out, somewhat desperately, to try to find his white patron and protector. He had been cautious to avoid meeting any white men, and, anticipating no danger from those of his own race, went toward the party which he saw approaching, whose path would cross his own. When they were only a few yards apart, Josh took a step forward and caught Jerry by the arm.

"Come along, Jerry, we need you! Here's another man, boys. Come on now, and fight fer yo' race!"

In vain Jerry protested. "I don' wan' ter fight," he howled. "De w'ite folks ain' gwine ter pester me; dey're my frien's. Tu'n me loose, – tu'n me loose, er we all gwine ter git killed!"

The party paid no attention to Jerry's protestations. Indeed, with the crowd of whites following behind, they were simply considering the question of a position from which they could most effectively defend themselves and the building which they imagined to be threatened. If Josh had released his grip of Jerry, that worthy could easily have escaped from the crowd; but Josh maintained his hold almost mechanically, and, in the confusion, Jerry found himself swept with the rest into the hospital, the doors of which were promptly barricaded with the heavier pieces of furniture, and the windows manned by several men each, Josh, with the instinct of a born commander, posting his forces so that they could cover with their guns all the approaches to the building. Jerry still continuing to make himself troublesome, Josh, in a moment of impatience, gave him a terrific box on the ear, which stretched him out upon the floor unconscious.

"Shet up," he said; "ef you can't stan' up like a man, keep still, and don't interfere wid men w'at will fight!" The hospital, when Josh and his men took possession, had been found deserted. Fortunately there were no patients for that day, except one or two convalescents, and these, with the attendants, had joined the exodus of the colored people from the town.

A white man advanced from the crowd without toward the main entrance to the hospital. Big Josh, looking out from a window, grasped his gun more firmly, as his eyes fell upon the man who had murdered his father and darkened his mother's life. Mechanically he raised his rifle, but lowered it as the white man lifted up his hand as a sign that he wished to speak.

"You niggers," called Captain McBane loudly, – it was that worthy, – "you niggers are courtin' death, an' you won't have to court her but a minute er two mo' befo' she'll have you. If you surrender and give up your arms, you'll be dealt with leniently, – you may get off with the chain-gang or the penitentiary. If you resist, you'll be shot like dogs."

"Dat's no news, Mr. White Man," replied Josh, appearing boldly at the window. "We're use' ter bein' treated like dogs by men like you. If you w'ite people will go 'long an' ten' ter yo' own business an' let us alone, we'll ten' ter ou'n. You've got guns, an' we've got jest as much right ter carry 'em as you have. Lay down yo'n, an' we'll lay down ou'n, – we didn' take 'em up fust; but we ain' gwine ter let you bu'n down ou' chu'ches an' school'ouses, er dis hospittle, an' we ain' comin' out er dis house, where we ain' disturbin' nobody, fer you ter shoot us down er sen' us ter jail. You hear me!"

"All right," responded McBane. "You've had fair warning. Your blood be on your" – His speech was interrupted by a shot from the crowd, which splintered the window-casing close to Josh's head. This was followed by half a dozen other shots, which were replied to, almost simultaneously, by a volley from within, by which one of the attacking party was killed and another wounded.

This roused the mob to frenzy.

"Vengeance! vengeance!" they yelled. "Kill the niggers!"

A negro had killed a white man, – the unpar-

donable sin, admitting neither excuse, justification, nor extenuation. From time immemorial it had been bred in the Southern white consciousness, and in the negro consciousness also, for that matter, that the person of a white man was sacred from the touch of a negro, no matter what the provocation. A dozen colored men lay dead in the streets of Wellington, inoffensive people, slain in cold blood because they had been bold enough to question the authority of those who had assailed them, or frightened enough to flee when they had been ordered to stand still; but their lives counted nothing against that of a riotous white man, who had courted death by attacking a body of armed men.

The crowd, too, surrounding the hospital, had changed somewhat in character. The men who had acted as leaders in the early afternoon, having accomplished their purpose of overturning the local administration and establishing a provisional government of their own, had withdrawn from active participation in the rioting, deeming the negroes already sufficiently overawed to render unlikely any further trouble from that source. Several of the ringleaders had indeed begun to exert themselves to prevent further disorder, or any loss of property, the possibility of which had become apparent; but those who set in motion the forces of evil cannot always control them afterwards. The baser element of the white population, recruited from the wharves and the saloons, was now predominant.

Captain McBane was the only one of the revolutionary committee who had remained with the mob, not with any purpose to restore or preserve order, but because he found the company and the occasion entirely congenial. He had had no opportunity, at least no tenable excuse, to kill or maim a negro since the termination of his contract with the state for convicts, and this occasion had awakened a dormant appetite for these diversions. We are all puppets in the hands of Fate, and seldom see the strings that move us. McBane had lived a life of violence and cruelty. As a man sows, so shall he reap. In works of fiction, such men are sometimes converted. More often, in real life, they do not change their natures until they are converted into dust. One does well to distrust a tamed tiger.

On the outskirts of the crowd a few of the better class, or at least of the better clad, were looking on. The double volley described had already been fired, when the number of these was augmented by the arrival of Major Carteret and Mr. Ellis, who had just come from the Chronicle office, where the next day's paper had been in hasty preparation. They pushed their way towards the front of the crowd.

"This must be stopped, Ellis," said Carteret. "They are burning houses and killing women and children. Old Jane, good old Mammy Jane, who nursed my wife at her bosom, and has waited on her and my child within a few weeks, was killed only a few rods from my house, to which she was evidently fleeing for protection. It must have been by accident, – I cannot believe that any white man in town would be dastard enough to commit such a deed intentionally! I would have defended her with my own life! We must try to stop this thing!"

"Easier said than done," returned Ellis. "It is in the fever stage, and must burn itself out. We shall be lucky if it does not burn the town out. Suppose the negroes should also take a hand at the burning? We have advised the people to put the negroes down, and they are doing the job thoroughly."

"My God!" replied the other, with a gesture of impatience, as he continued to elbow his way through the crowd; "I meant to keep them in their places, – I did not intend wholesale murder and arson."

Carteret, having reached the front of the mob, made an effort to gain their attention.

"Gentlemen!" he cried in his loudest tones. His voice, unfortunately, was neither loud nor piercing.

"Kill the niggers!" clamored the mob.

"Gentlemen, I implore you" –

The crash of a dozen windows, broken by stones and pistol shots, drowned his voice.

"Gentlemen!" he shouted; "this is murder, it is madness; it is a disgrace to our city, to our state, to our civilization!"

"That's right!" replied several voices. The mob had recognized the speaker. "It *is* a disgrace, and we'll not put up with it a moment longer. Burn 'em out! Hurrah for Major Carteret, the champion of 'white supremacy'! Three cheers for the Morning Chronicle and 'no nigger domination'!"

"Hurrah, hurrah, hurrah!" yelled the crowd.

In vain the baffled orator gesticulated and shrieked in the effort to correct the misapprehension. Their oracle had spoken; not hearing what he said, they assumed it to mean encouragement and coöperation. Their present course was but the logical outcome of the crusade which the Morning Chronicle had preached, in season and out of season, for many months. When Carteret had spoken, and the crowd had cheered him, they felt that they had done all that courtesy required, and he was good-naturedly elbowed aside while they proceeded with the work in hand, which was now to drive out the negroes from the hospital and avenge the killing of their comrade.

Some brought hay, some kerosene, and others wood from a pile which had been thrown into a vacant lot near by. Several safe ways of approach to the building were discovered, and the combustibles placed and fired. The flames, soon gaining a foothold, leaped upward, catching here and there at the exposed woodwork, and licking the walls hungrily with long tongues of flame.

Meanwhile a desultory firing was kept up from the outside, which was replied to scatteringly from within the hospital. Those inside were either not good marksmen, or excitement had spoiled their aim. If a face appeared at a window, a dozen pistol shots from the crowd sought the spot immediately.

Higher and higher leaped the flames. Suddenly from one of the windows sprang a black figure, waving a white handkerchief. It was Jerry Letlow. Regaining consciousness after the effect of Josh's blow had subsided, Jerry had kept quiet and watched his opportunity. From a safe vantage-ground he had scanned the crowd without, in search of some white friend. When he saw Major Carteret moving disconsolately away after his futile effort to stem the torrent, Jerry made a dash for the window. He sprang forth, and, waving his handkerchief as a flag of truce, ran toward Major Carteret, shouting frantically: –

"Majah Carteret – O majah! It's me, suh, Jerry, suh! I didn' go in dere myse'f, suh – I wuz drag' in dere! I wouldn' do nothin' 'g'inst de w'ite folks, suh, – no, 'ndeed, I wouldn', suh!"

Jerry's cries were drowned in a roar of rage and a volley of shots from the mob. Carteret, who had turned away with Ellis, did not even hear his servant's voice. Jerry's poor flag of truce, his explanations, his reliance upon his white friends, all failed him in the moment of supreme need. In that hour, as in any hour when the depths of race hatred are stirred, a negro was no more than a brute beast, set upon by other brute beasts whose only instinct was to kill and destroy.

"Let us leave this inferno, Ellis," said Carteret, sick with anger and disgust. He had just become aware that a negro was being killed, though he did not know whom. "We can do nothing. The negroes have themselves to blame, – they tempted us beyond endurance. I counseled firmness, and firm measures were taken, and our purpose was accomplished. I am not responsible for these subsequent horrors, – I wash my hands of them. Let us go!"

The flames gained headway and gradually enveloped the burning building, until it became evident to those within as well as those without that the position of the defenders was no longer tenable. Would they die in the flames, or would they be driven out? The uncertainty soon came to an end.

The besieged had been willing to fight, so long as there seemed a hope of successfully defending themselves and their property; for their purpose was purely one of defense. When they saw the case was hopeless, inspired by Josh Green's reckless courage, they were still willing to sell their lives dearly. One or two of them had already been killed, and as many more disabled. The fate of Jerry Letlow had struck terror to the hearts of several others, who could scarcely hide their fear. After the building had been fired, Josh's exhortations were no longer able to keep them in the hospital. They preferred to fight and be killed in the open, rather than to be smothered like rats in a hole.

"Boys!" exclaimed Josh, – "men! – fer nobody but men would do w'at you have done, – the day has gone 'g'inst us. We kin see ou' finish; but fer my part, I ain' gwine ter leave dis worl' widout takin' a w'ite man 'long wid me, an' I sees my man right out yonder waitin', – I be'n waitin' fer him twenty years, but he won' have ter wait fer me mo' 'n 'bout twenty seconds. Eve'y one er you pick yo' man! We'll open de do', an' we'll give some w'ite men a chance ter be sorry dey ever started dis fuss!"

The door was thrown open suddenly, and through it rushed a dozen or more black figures, armed with knives, pistols, or clubbed muskets. Taken by sudden surprise, the white people stood motionless for a moment, but the approaching negroes had scarcely covered half the distance to which the heat of the flames had driven back the mob, before they were greeted with a volley that laid them all low but two. One of these, dazed by the fate of his companions, turned instinctively to flee, but had scarcely faced around before he fell, pierced in the back by a dozen bullets.

Josh Green, the tallest and biggest of them all, had not apparently been touched. Some of the crowd paused in involuntary admiration of this black giant, famed on the wharves for his strength, sweeping down upon them, a smile upon his face, his eyes lit up with a rapt expression which seemed to take him out of mortal ken. This impression was heightened by his apparent immunity from the shower of lead which less susceptible persons had continued to pour at him.

Armed with a huge bowie-knife, a relic of the civil war, which he had carried on his person for many years for a definite purpose, and which he had kept sharpened to a razor edge, he reached the line of the crowd. All but the bravest shrank back. Like a wedge he dashed through the mob, which parted instinctively before him, and all oblivious of the rain of lead which fell around him, reached the point where Captain McBane, the bravest man in the party, stood waiting to meet him. A pistol-flame flashed in his face, but he went on, and raising his powerful right arm, buried his knife to the hilt in the heart of his enemy. When the crowd dashed forward to wreak vengeance on his dead body, they found him with a smile still upon his face.

One of the two died as the fool dieth. Which was it, or was it both? "Vengeance is mine," saith the Lord, and it had not been left to Him. But they that do violence must expect to suffer violence. McBane's death was merciful, compared with the nameless horrors he had heaped upon the hundreds of helpless mortals who had fallen into his hands during his career as a contractor of convict labor.

Sobered by this culminating tragedy, the mob shortly afterwards dispersed. The flames soon completed their work, and this handsome structure, the fruit of old Adam Miller's industry, the monument of his son's philanthropy, a promise of good things for the future of the city, lay smouldering in ruins, a melancholy witness to the fact that our boasted civilization is but a thin veneer, which cracks and scales off at the first impact of primal passions.

The Yellow Wallpaper
Charlotte Perkins Gilman

It is very seldom that mere ordinary people like John and myself secure ancestral halls for the sum-mer.

A colonial mansion, a hereditary estate, I would say a haunted house, and reach the height of romantic felicity – but that would be asking too much of fate!

Still I will proudly declare that there is something queer about it.

Else, why should it be let so cheaply? And why have stood so long untenanted?

John laughs at me, of course, but one expects that in marriage.

John is practical in the extreme. He has no patience with faith, an intense horror of superstition, and he scoffs openly at any talk of things not to be felt and seen and put down in figures.

John is a physician, and PERHAPS – (I would not say it to a living soul, of course, but this is dead paper and a great relief to my mind) – PERHAPS that is one reason I do not get well faster.

You see he does not believe I am sick!

And what can one do?

If a physician of high standing, and one's own husband, assures friends and relatives that there is really nothing the matter with one but temporary nervous depression – a slight hysterical tendency – what is one to do?

My brother is also a physician, and also of high standing, and he says the same thing.

So I take phosphates or phosphites – whichever it is, and tonics, and journeys, and air, and exercise, and am absolutely forbidden to "work" until I am well again.

Personally, I disagree with their ideas.

Personally, I believe that congenial work,

with excitement and change, would do me good.

But what is one to do?

I did write for a while in spite of them; but it DOES exhaust me a good deal – having to be so sly about it, or else meet with heavy opposition.

I sometimes fancy that my condition if I had less opposition and more society and stimulus – but John says the very worst thing I can do is to think about my condition, and I confess it always makes me feel bad.

So I will let it alone and talk about the house.

The most beautiful place! It is quite alone, stand-ing well back from the road, quite three miles from the village. It makes me think of English places that you read about, for there are hedges and walls and gates that lock, and lots of separate little houses for the gardeners and people.

There is a DELICIOUS garden! I never saw such a garden – large and shady, full of box-bordered paths, and lined with long grape-covered arbors with seats under them.

There were greenhouses, too, but they are all broken now.

There was some legal trouble, I believe, some-thing about the heirs and coheirs; any-how, the place has been empty for years.

That spoils my ghostliness, I am afraid, but I don't care – there is something strange about the house – I can feel it.

I even said so to John one moonlight evening, but he said what I felt was a DRAUGHT, and shut the window.

I get unreasonably angry with John some-times. I'm sure I never used to be so sensitive. I think it is due to this nervous condition.

But John says if I feel so, I shall neglect proper self-control; so I take pains to control myself – before him, at least, and that makes me very tired.

I don't like our room a bit. I wanted one down-stairs that opened on the piazza and had roses all over the window, and such pretty old-fashioned chintz hangings! but John would not hear of it.

He said there was only one window and not room for two beds, and no near room for him if he took another.

He is very careful and loving, and hardly lets me stir without special direction.

I have a schedule prescription for each hour in the day; he takes all care from me, and so I feel basely ungrateful not to value it more.

He said we came here solely on my account, that I was to have perfect rest and all the air I could get. "Your exercise depends on your strength, my dear," said he, "and your food somewhat on your appe-tite; but air you can absorb all the time." So we took the nursery at the top of the house.

It is a big, airy room, the whole floor nearly, with windows that look all ways, and air and sun-shine galore. It was nursery first and then play-room and gymnasium, I should judge; for the windows are barred for little children, and there are rings and things in the walls.

The paint and paper look as if a boys' school had used it. It is stripped off – the paper – in great patches all around the head of my bed, about as far as I can reach, and in a great place on the other side of the room low down. I never saw a worse paper in my life.

One of those sprawling flamboyant patterns committing every artistic sin.

It is dull enough to confuse the eye in following, pronounced enough to constantly irritate and pro-voke study, and when you follow the lame uncertain curves for a little distance they suddenly commit suicide – plunge off at outrageous angles, destroy themselves in unheard of contradictions.

The color is repellent, almost revolting; a smoul-dering unclean yellow, strangely faded by the slow-turning sunlight.

It is a dull yet lurid orange in some places, a

sickly sulphur tint in others.

No wonder the children hated it! I should hate it myself if I had to live in this room long.

There comes John, and I must put this away, – he hates to have me write a word.

We have been here two weeks, and I haven't felt like writing before, since that first day.

I am sitting by the window now, up in this atro-cious nursery, and there is nothing to hinder my writing as much as I please, save lack of strength.

John is away all day, and even some nights when his cases are serious.

I am glad my case is not serious!

But these nervous troubles are dreadfully depressing.

John does not know how much I really suffer. He knows there is no REASON to suffer, and that satisfies him.

Of course it is only nervousness. It does weigh on me so not to do my duty in any way!

I meant to be such a help to John, such a real rest and comfort, and here I am a comparative burden already!

Nobody would believe what an effort it is to do what little I am able, – to dress and entertain, and other things.

It is fortunate Mary is so good with the baby. Such a dear baby!

And yet I CANNOT be with him, it makes me so nervous.

I suppose John never was nervous in his life. He laughs at me so about this wall-paper!

At first he meant to repaper the room, but afterwards he said that I was letting it get the better of me, and that nothing was worse for a nervous patient than to give way to such fancies.

He said that after the wall-paper was changed it would be the heavy bedstead, and then the barred windows, and then that gate at the head of the stairs, and so on.

"You know the place is doing you good," he said, "and really, dear, I don't care to renovate the house just for a three months' rental."

"Then do let us go downstairs," I said, "there are such pretty rooms there."

Then he took me in his arms and called me a blessed little goose, and said he would go down to the cellar, if I wished, and have it whitewashed into the bargain.

But he is right enough about the beds and windows and things.

It is an airy and comfortable room as any one need wish, and, of course, I would not be so silly as to make him uncomfortable just for a whim.

I'm really getting quite fond of the big room, all but that horrid paper.

Out of one window I can see the garden, those mysterious deepshaded arbors, the riotous old-fashioned flowers, and bushes and gnarly trees.

Out of another I get a lovely view of the bay and a little private wharf belonging to the estate. There is a beautiful shaded lane that runs down there from the house. I always fancy I see people walking in these numerous paths and arbors, but John has cautioned me not to give way to fancy in the least. He says that with my imaginative power and habit of story-making, a nervous weakness like mine is sure to lead to all manner of excited fancies, and that I ought to use my will and good sense to check the tendency. So I try.

I think sometimes that if I were only well enough to write a little it would relieve the press of ideas and rest me.

But I find I get pretty tired when I try.

It is so discouraging not to have any advice and companionship about my work. When I get really well, John says we will ask Cousin Henry and Julia down for a long visit; but he says he would as soon put fireworks in my pillow-case as to let me have those stimulating people about now.

I wish I could get well faster.

But I must not think about that. This paper looks to me as if it KNEW what a vicious influence it had!

There is a recurrent spot where the pattern lolls like a broken neck and two bulbous eyes stare at you upside down.

I get positively angry with the impertinence of it and the everlastingness. Up and down and sideways they crawl, and those absurd, unblinking eyes are everywhere. There is one place where two breadths didn't match, and the eyes go all up and down the line, one a little higher than the other.

I never saw so much expression in an inanimate thing before, and we all know how much expression they have! I used to lie awake as a child and get more entertainment and terror out of blank walls and plain furniture than most children could find in a toy store.

I remember what a kindly wink the knobs of our big, old bureau used to have, and there was one chair that always seemed like a strong friend.

I used to feel that if any of the other things looked too fierce I could always hop into that chair and be safe.

The furniture in this room is no worse than inharmonious, however, for we had to bring it all from downstairs. I suppose when this was used as a playroom they had to take the nursery things out, and no wonder! I never saw such ravages as the children have made here.

The wall-paper, as I said before, is torn off in spots, and it sticketh closer than a brother – they must have had perseverance as well as hatred.

Then the floor is scratched and gouged and splintered, the plaster itself is dug out here and there, and this great heavy bed which is all we found in the room, looks as if it had been through the wars.

But I don't mind it a bit – only the paper.

There comes John's sister. Such a dear girl as she is, and so careful of me! I must not let her find me writing.

She is a perfect and enthusiastic housekeeper, and hopes for no better profession. I verily believe she thinks it is the writing which made me sick!

But I can write when she is out, and see her a long way off from these windows.

There is one that commands the road, a lovely shaded winding road, and one that just looks off over the country. A lovely country, too, full of great elms and velvet meadows.

This wall-paper has a kind of sub-pattern in a different shade, a particularly irritating one, for you can only see it in certain lights, and not clearly then.

But in the places where it isn't faded and where the sun is just so – I can see a strange, provoking, formless sort of figure, that seems to skulk about behind that silly and conspicuous front design.

There's sister on the stairs!

Well, the Fourth of July is over! The people are gone and I am tired out. John thought it might do me good to see a little company, so we just had mother and Nellie and the children down for a week.

Of course I didn't do a thing. Jennie sees to everything now.

But it tired me all the same.

John says if I don't pick up faster he shall send me to Weir Mitchell in the fall.

But I don't want to go there at all. I had a friend who was in his hands once, and she says he is just like John and my brother, only more so!

Besides, it is such an undertaking to go so far.

I don't feel as if it was worth while to turn my hand over for anything, and I'm getting dreadfully fretful and querulous.

I cry at nothing, and cry most of the time.

Of course I don't when John is here, or anybody else, but when I am alone.

And I am alone a good deal just now. John is kept in town very often by serious cases, and Jennie is good and lets me alone when I want her to.

So I walk a little in the garden or down that lovely lane, sit on the porch under the roses, and lie down up here a good deal.

I'm getting really fond of the room in spite of the wall-paper. Perhaps BECAUSE of the wall-paper.

It dwells in my mind so!

I lie here on this great immovable bed – it is nailed down, I believe – and follow that pattern about by the hour. It is as good as gymnastics, I assure you. I start, we'll say, at the bottom, down in the corner over there where it has not been touched, and I determine for the thousandth time that I WILL follow that pointless pattern to some sort of a conclusion.

I know a little of the principle of design, and I know this thing was not arranged on any laws of radiation, or alternation, or repetition, or sym-metry, or anything else that I ever heard of.

It is repeated, of course, by the breadths, but not otherwise.

Looked at in one way each breadth stands alone, the bloated curves and flourishes – a kind of "debased Romanesque" with delirium tremens – go waddling up and down in isolated columns of fatuity.

But, on the other hand, they connect diagonally, and the sprawling outlines run off in great slanting waves of optic horror, like a lot of wallowing sea-weeds in full chase.

The whole thing goes horizontally, too, at least it seems so, and I exhaust myself in trying to distinguish the order of its going in that direction.

They have used a horizontal breadth for a frieze, and that adds wonderfully to the confusion.

There is one end of the room where it is almost intact, and there, when the crosslights fade and the low sun shines directly upon it, I can almost fancy radiation after all, – the interminable grotesques seem to form around a common centre and rush off in headlong plunges of equal distraction.

It makes me tired to follow it. I will take a nap I guess.

I don't know why I should write this.

I don't want to.

I don't feel able.

And I know John would think it absurd. But I MUST say what I feel and think in some way – it is such a relief!

But the effort is getting to be greater than the relief.

Half the time now I am awfully lazy, and lie down ever so much.

John says I musn't lose my strength, and has me take cod liver oil and lots of tonics and things, to say nothing of ale and wine and rare meat.

Dear John! He loves me very dearly, and hates to have me sick. I tried to have a real earnest reasonable talk with him the other day, and tell him how I wish he would let me go and make a visit to Cousin Henry and Julia.

But he said I wasn't able to go, nor able to stand it after I got there; and I did not make out a very good case for myself, for I was crying before I had finished.

It is getting to be a great effort for me to think straight. Just this nervous weakness I suppose.

And dear John gathered me up in his arms, and just carried me upstairs and laid me on the bed, and sat by me and read to me till it tired my head.

He said I was his darling and his comfort and all he had, and that I must take care of myself for his sake, and keep well.

He says no one but myself can help me out of it, that I must use my will and self-control and not let any silly fancies run away with me.

There's one comfort, the baby is well and happy, and does not have to occupy this nursery with the horrid wall-paper.

If we had not used it, that blessed child would have! What a fortunate escape! Why, I wouldn't have a child of mine, an impressionable little thing, live in such a room for worlds.

I never thought of it before, but it is lucky that John kept me here after all, I can stand it so much easier than a baby, you see.

Of course I never mention it to them any more – I am too wise, – but I keep watch of it all the same.

There are things in that paper that nobody knows but me, or ever will.

Behind that outside pattern the dim shapes get clearer every day.

It is always the same shape, only very numerous.

And it is like a woman stooping down and creeping about behind that pattern. I don't like it a bit. I wonder – I begin to think – I wish John would take me away from here!

It is so hard to talk with John about my case, because he is so wise, and because he loves me so.

But I tried it last night.

It was moonlight. The moon shines in all around just as the sun does.

I hate to see it sometimes, it creeps so slowly, and always comes in by one window or another.

John was asleep and I hated to waken him, so I kept still and watched the moonlight on that undulating wall-paper till I felt creepy.

The faint figure behind seemed to shake the pattern, just as if she wanted to get out.

I got up softly and went to feel and see if the paper DID move, and when I came back John was awake.

"What is it, little girl?" he said. "Don't go walking about like that – you'll get cold."

I though it was a good time to talk, so I told him that I really was not gaining here, and that I wished he would take me away.

"Why darling!" said he, "our lease will be up in three weeks, and I can't see how to leave before.

"The repairs are not done at home, and I cannot possibly leave town just now. Of course if you were in any danger, I could and would, but you really are better, dear, whether you can see it or not. I am a doctor, dear, and I know. You are gaining flesh and color, your appetite is better, I feel really much easier about you."

"I don't weigh a bit more," said I, "nor as much; and my appetite may be better in the evening when you are here, but it is worse in the morning when you are away!"

"Bless her little heart!" said he with a big hug, "she shall be as sick as she pleases! But now let's improve the shining hours by going to sleep, and talk about it in the morning!"

"And you won't go away?" I asked gloomily.

"Why, how can I, dear? It is only three weeks more and then we will take a nice little trip of a few days while Jennie is getting the house ready. Really dear you are better!"

"Better in body perhaps – " I began, and stopped short, for he sat up straight and looked at me with such a stern, reproachful look that I could not say another word.

"My darling," said he, "I beg of you, for my sake and for our child's sake, as well as for your own, that you will never for one instant let that idea enter your mind! There is nothing so dangerous, so fascinating, to a temperament like yours. It is a false and foolish fancy. Can you not trust me as a physician when I tell you so?"

So of course I said no more on that score, and we went to sleep before long. He thought I was asleep first, but I wasn't, and lay there for hours trying to decide whether that front pattern and the back pattern really did move together or separately.

On a pattern like this, by daylight, there is a lack of sequence, a defiance of law, that is a constant irritant to a normal mind.

The color is hideous enough, and unreliable enough, and infuriating enough, but the pattern is torturing.

You think you have mastered it, but just as you get well underway in following, it turns a back-somersault and there you are. It slaps you in the face, knocks you down, and tramples upon you. It is like a bad dream.

The outside pattern is a florid arabesque, reminding one of a fungus. If you can imagine a toadstool in joints, an interminable string of toadstools, budding and sprouting in endless convolutions – why, that is something like it.

That is, sometimes!

There is one marked peculiarity about this paper, a thing nobody seems to notice but myself, and that is that it changes as the light changes.

When the sun shoots in through the east window – I always watch for that first long, straight ray – it changes so quickly that I never can quite believe it.

That is why I watch it always.

By moonlight – the moon shines in all night when there is a moon – I wouldn't know it was the same paper.

At night in any kind of light, in twilight, candle light, lamplight, and worst of all by moonlight, it becomes bars! The outside pattern I mean, and the woman behind it is as plain as can be.

I didn't realize for a long time what the thing was that showed behind, that dim sub-pattern, but now I am quite sure it is a woman.

By daylight she is subdued, quiet. I fancy it is the pattern that keeps her so still. It is so puzzling. It keeps me quiet by the hour.

I lie down ever so much now. John says it is good for me, and to sleep all I can.

Indeed he started the habit by making me lie down for an hour after each meal.

It is a very bad habit I am convinced, for you see I don't sleep.

And that cultivates deceit, for I don't tell them I'm awake – O no!

The fact is I am getting a little afraid of John.

He seems very queer sometimes, and even Jennie has an inexplicable look.

It strikes me occasionally, just as a scientific hypothesis, – that perhaps it is the paper!

I have watched John when he did not know I was looking, and come into the room suddenly on the most innocent excuses, and I've caught him several times LOOKING AT THE PAPER! And Jennie too. I caught Jennie with her hand on it once.

She didn't know I was in the room, and when I asked her in a quiet, a very quiet voice, with the most restrained manner possible, what she was doing with the paper – she turned around as if she had been caught stealing, and looked quite angry – asked me why I should frighten her so!

Then she said that the paper stained everything it touched, that she had found yellow smooches on all my clothes and John's, and she wished we would be more careful!

Did not that sound innocent? But I know she was studying that pattern, and I am determined that nobody shall find it out but myself!

Life is very much more exciting now than it used to be. You see I have something more to expect, to look forward to, to watch. I really do eat better, and am more quiet than I was.

John is so pleased to see me improve! He laughed a little the other day, and said I seemed to be flourishing in spite of my wall-paper.

I turned it off with a laugh. I had no intention of telling him it was BECAUSE of the wall-paper – he would make fun of me. He might even want to take me away.

I don't want to leave now until I have found it out. There is a week more, and I think that will be enough.

I'm feeling ever so much better! I don't sleep much at night, for it is so interesting to watch developments; but I sleep a good deal in the daytime.

In the daytime it is tiresome and perplexing.

There are always new shoots on the fungus, and new shades of yellow all over it. I cannot keep count of them, though I have tried conscientiously.

It is the strangest yellow, that wall-paper! It makes me think of all the yellow things I ever saw – not beautiful ones like buttercups, but old foul, bad yellow things.

But there is something else about that paper – the smell! I noticed it the moment we came into the room, but with so much air and sun it was not bad. Now we have had a week of fog and rain, and whether the windows are open or not, the smell is here.

It creeps all over the house.

I find it hovering in the dining-room, skulking in the parlor, hiding in the hall, lying in wait for me on the stairs.

It gets into my hair.

Even when I go to ride, if I turn my head suddenly and surprise it – there is that smell!

Such a peculiar odor, too! I have spent hours in trying to analyze it, to find what it smelled like.

It is not bad – at first, and very gentle, but quite the subtlest, most enduring odor I ever met.

In this damp weather it is awful, I wake up in the night and find it hanging over me.

It used to disturb me at first. I thought seriously of burning the house – to reach the smell.

But now I am used to it. The only thing I can think of that it is like is the COLOR of the paper! A yellow smell.

There is a very funny mark on this wall, low down, near the mopboard. A streak that runs round the room. It goes behind every piece of furniture, except the bed, a long, straight, even SMOOCH, as if it had been rubbed over and over.

I wonder how it was done and who did it, and what they did it for. Round and round and round – round and round and round – it makes me dizzy!

I really have discovered something at last.

Through watching so much at night, when it changes so, I have finally found out.

The front pattern DOES move – and no wonder! The woman behind shakes it!

Sometimes I think there are a great many women behind, and sometimes only one, and she crawls around fast, and her crawling shakes it all over.

Then in the very bright spots she keeps still, and in the very shady spots she just takes hold of the bars and shakes them hard.

And she is all the time trying to climb through. But nobody could climb through that pattern – it strangles so; I think that is why it has so many heads.

They get through, and then the pattern strangles them off and turns them upside down, and makes their eyes white!

If those heads were covered or taken off it would not be half so bad.

I think that woman gets out in the daytime!

And I'll tell you why – privately – I've seen her!

I can see her out of every one of my windows!

It is the same woman, I know, for she is always creeping, and most women do not creep by daylight.

I see her on that long road under the trees, creeping along, and when a carriage comes she hides under the blackberry vines.

I don't blame her a bit. It must be very humiliating to be caught creeping by daylight!

I always lock the door when I creep by daylight. I can't do it at night, for I know John would suspect something at once.

And John is so queer now, that I don't want to irritate him. I wish he would take another room! Besides, I don't want anybody to get that woman out at night but myself.

I often wonder if I could see her out of all the windows at once.

But, turn as fast as I can, I can only see out of one at a time.

And though I always see her, she MAY be able to creep faster than I can turn!

I have watched her sometimes away off in the open country, creeping as fast as a cloud shadow in a high wind.

If only that top pattern could be gotten off from the under one! I mean to try it, little by little.

I have found out another funny thing, but I shan't tell it this time! It does not do to trust people too much.

There are only two more days to get this paper off, and I believe John is beginning to notice. I don't like the look in his eyes.

And I heard him ask Jennie a lot of professional questions about me. She had a very good report to give.

She said I slept a good deal in the daytime.

John knows I don't sleep very well at night, for all I'm so quiet!

He asked me all sorts of questions, too, and pretended to be very loving and kind.

As if I couldn't see through him!

Still, I don't wonder he acts so, sleeping under this paper for three months.

It only interests me, but I feel sure John and Jennie are secretly affected by it.

Hurrah! This is the last day, but it is enough. John is to stay in town over night, and won't be out until this evening.

Jennie wanted to sleep with me – the sly thing! but I told her I should undoubtedly rest better for a night all alone.

That was clever, for really I wasn't alone a bit! As soon as it was moonlight and that poor thing began to crawl and shake the pattern, I got up and ran to help her.

I pulled and she shook, I shook and she pulled, and before morning we had peeled off yards of that paper.

A strip about as high as my head and half around the room.

And then when the sun came and that awful pattern began to laugh at me, I declared I would finish it to-day!

We go away to-morrow, and they are moving all my furniture down again to leave things as they were before.

Jennie looked at the wall in amazement, but I told her merrily that I did it out of pure spite at the vicious thing.

She laughed and said she wouldn't mind doing it herself, but I must not get tired.

How she betrayed herself that time!

But I am here, and no person touches this paper but me – not ALIVE!

She tried to get me out of the room – it was too patent! But I said it was so quiet and empty and clean now that I believed I would lie down again and sleep all I could; and not to wake me even for dinner – I would call when I woke.

So now she is gone, and the servants are gone, and the things are gone, and there is nothing left but that great bedstead nailed down, with the canvas mattress we found on it.

We shall sleep downstairs to-night, and take the boat home to-morrow.

I quite enjoy the room, now it is bare again.

How those children did tear about here!

This bedstead is fairly gnawed!

But I must get to work.

I have locked the door and thrown the key down into the front path.

I don't want to go out, and I don't want to have anybody come in, till John comes.

I want to astonish him.

I've got a rope up here that even Jennie did not find. If that woman does get out, and tries to get away, I can tie her!

But I forgot I could not reach far without anything to stand on!

This bed will NOT move!

I tried to lift and push it until I was lame, and then I got so angry I bit off a little piece at one corner – but it hurt my teeth.

Then I peeled off all the paper I could reach standing on the floor. It sticks horribly and the pattern just enjoys it! All those strangled heads and bulbous eyes and waddling fungus growths just shriek with derision!

I am getting angry enough to do something desperate. To jump out of the window would be admirable exercise, but the bars are too strong even to try.

Besides I wouldn't do it. Of course not. I know well enough that a step like that is improper and might be misconstrued.

I don't like to LOOK out of the windows even – there are so many of those creeping women, and they creep so fast.

I wonder if they all come out of that wallpaper as I did?

But I am securely fastened now by my well-hidden rope – you don't get ME out in the road there!

I suppose I shall have to get back behind the pattern when it comes night, and that is hard!

It is so pleasant to be out in this great room and creep around as I please!

I don't want to go outside. I won't, even if Jennie asks me to.

For outside you have to creep on the ground, and everything is green instead of yellow.

But here I can creep smoothly on the floor, and my shoulder just fits in that long smooch around the wall, so I cannot lose my way.

Why there's John at the door!

It is no use, young man, you can't open it!

How he does call and pound!

Now he's crying for an axe.

It would be a shame to break down that beautiful door!

"John dear!" said I in the gentlest voice, "the key is down by the front steps, under a plantain leaf!"

That silenced him for a few moments.

Then he said – very quietly indeed, "Open the door, my darling!"

"I can't," said I. "The key is down by the front door under a plantain leaf!"

And then I said it again, several times, very gently and slowly, and said it so often that he had to go and see, and he got it of course, and came in. He stopped short by the door.

"What is the matter?" he cried. "For God's sake, what are you doing!"

I kept on creeping just the same, but I looked at him over my shoulder.

"I've got out at last," said I, "in spite of you and Jane. And I've pulled off most of the paper, so you can't put me back!"

Now why should that man have fainted? But he did, and right across my path by the wall, so that I had to creep over him every time!

The Bishop in the Presence of an Unknown Light

Victor Hugo

from Les Misérables

At an epoch a little later than the date of the letter cited in the preceding pages, [Bishop Bienvenu Myriel] did a thing which, if the whole town was to be believed, was even more hazardous than his trip across the mountains infested with bandits.

In the country near Digne a man lived quite alone. This man, we will state at once, was a former member of the Convention. His name was G—

Member of the Convention, G— was mentioned with a sort of horror in the little world of Digne. A member of the Convention – can you imagine such a thing? That existed from the time when people called each other thou, and when they said "citizen." This man was almost a monster. He had not voted for the death of the king, but almost. He was a quasi-regicide. He had been a terrible man. How did it happen that such a man had not been brought before a provost's court, on the return of the legitimate princes? They need not have cut off his head, if you please; clemency must be exer-cised, agreed; but a good banishment for life. An example, in short, etc. Besides, he was an atheist, like all the rest of those people. Gossip of the geese about the vulture.

Was G— a vulture after all? Yes; if he were to be judged by the element of ferocity in this solitude of his. As he had not voted for the death of the king, he had not been included in the decrees of exile, and had been able to remain in France.

He dwelt at a distance of three-quarters of an hour from the city, far from any hamlet, far from any road, in some hidden turn of a very wild valley, no one knew exactly where. He had there, it was said, a sort of field, a hole, a lair. There were no neighbors, not even passers-by. Since he had dwelt in that valley, the path which led thither had disappeared under a growth of grass. The locality was spoken of as though it had been the dwelling of a hangman.

Nevertheless, the Bishop meditated on the subject, and from time to time he gazed at the horizon at a point where a clump of trees marked the valley of the former member of the Convention, and he said, "There is a soul yonder which is lonely."

And he added, deep in his own mind, "I owe him a visit."

But, let us avow it, this idea, which seemed natural at the first blush, appeared to him after a moment's reflection, as strange, impossible, and almost repulsive. For, at bottom, he shared the general impression, and the old member of the Convention inspired him, without his being clearly conscious of the fact himself, with that sentiment which borders on hate, and which is so well expressed by the word estrangement.

Still, should the scab of the sheep cause the shepherd to recoil? No. But what a sheep!

The good Bishop was perplexed. Sometimes he set out in that direction; then he returned.

Finally, the rumor one day spread through the town that a sort of young shepherd, who served the member of the Convention in his hovel, had come in quest of a doctor; that the old wretch was dying, that paralysis was gaining on him, and that he would not live over night. – "Thank God!" some added.

The Bishop took his staff, put on his cloak, on account of his too threadbare cassock, as we have mentioned, and because of the evening breeze which was sure to rise soon, and set out.

The sun was setting, and had almost touched the horizon when the Bishop arrived at the excommunicated spot. With a certain beating of the heart, he recognized the fact that he was near the lair. He strode over a ditch, leaped a hedge, made his way through a fence of dead boughs, entered a neglected paddock, took a few steps with a good deal of boldness, and suddenly, at the extremity of the waste land, and behind lofty brambles, he caught sight of the cavern.

It was a very low hut, poor, small, and clean, with a vine nailed against the outside.

Near the door, in an old wheel-chair, the arm-chair of the peasants, there was a white-haired man, smiling at the sun.

Near the seated man stood a young boy, the shepherd lad. He was offering the old man a jar of milk.

While the Bishop was watching him, the old man spoke: "Thank you," he said, "I need nothing." And his smile quitted the sun to rest upon the child.

The Bishop stepped forward. At the sound which he made in walking, the old man turned his head, and his face expressed the sum total of the surprise which a man can still feel after a long life.

"This is the first time since I have been here," said he, "that any one has entered here. Who are you, sir?"

The Bishop answered:

"My name is Bienvenu Myriel."

"Bienvenu Myriel? I have heard that name. Are you the man whom the people call Monseigneur Welcome?"

"I am."

The old man resumed with a half-smile

"In that case, you are my bishop?"

"Something of that sort."

"Enter, sir."

The member of the Convention extended his hand to the Bishop, but the Bishop did not take it. The Bishop confined himself to the remark:

"I am pleased to see that I have been misinformed. You certainly do not seem to me to be ill."

"Monsieur," replied the old man, "I am going to recover."

He paused, and then said:

"I shall die three hours hence."

Then he continued:

"I am something of a doctor; I know in what fashion the last hour draws on. Yesterday, only my feet were cold; to-day, the chill has ascended to my knees; now I feel it mounting to my waist; when it reaches the heart, I shall stop. The sun is beautiful, is it not? I had myself wheeled out here to take a last look at things. You can talk to me; it does not fatigue me. You have done well to come and look at a man who is on the point of death. It is well that there should be witnesses at that moment. One has one's caprices; I should have liked to last until the dawn, but I know that I shall hardly live three hours. It will be night then. What does it matter, after all? Dying is a simple affair. One has no need of the light for that. So be it. I shall die by starlight."

The old man turned to the shepherd lad:

"Go to thy bed; thou wert awake all last night; thou art tired."

The child entered the hut.

The old man followed him with his eyes, and added, as though speaking to himself:

"I shall die while he sleeps. The two slumbers may be good neighbors."

The Bishop was not touched as it seems that he should have been. He did not think he discerned God in this manner of dying; let us say the whole, for these petty contradictions of great hearts must be indicated like the rest: he, who on occasion, was so fond of laughing at "His Grace," was rather shocked at not being addressed as Monseigneur, and he was almost tempted to retort "citizen." He was assailed by a fancy for peevish familiarity, common enough to doctors and priests, but which was not habitual with him. This man, after all, this member of the Convention, this representative of the people, had been one of the powerful ones of the earth; for the first time in his life, probably, the

Bishop felt in a mood to be severe.

Meanwhile, the member of the Convention had been surveying him with a modest cordiality, in which one could have distinguished, possibly, that humility which is so fitting when one is on the verge of returning to dust.

The Bishop, on his side, although he generally restrained his curiosity, which, in his opinion, bordered on a fault, could not refrain from examining the member of the Convention with an attention which, as it did not have its course in sympathy, would have served his conscience as a matter of reproach, in connection with any other man. A member of the Convention produced on him somewhat the effect of being outside the pale of the law, even of the law of charity. G—, calm, his body almost upright, his voice vibrating, was one of those octogenarians who form the subject of astonishment to the physiologist. The Revolution had many of these men, proportioned to the epoch. In this old man one was conscious of a man put to the proof. Though so near to his end, he preserved all the gestures of health. In his clear glance, in his firm tone, in the robust movement of his shoulders, there was something calculated to disconcert death. Azrael, the Mohammedan angel of the sepulchre, would have turned back, and thought that he had mistaken the door. G— seemed to be dying because he willed it so. There was freedom in his agony. His legs alone were motionless. It was there that the shadows held him fast. His feet were cold and dead, but his head survived with all the power of life, and seemed full of light. G—, at this solemn moment, resembled the king in that tale of the Orient who was flesh above and marble below.

There was a stone there. The Bishop sat down. The exordium was abrupt.

"I congratulate you," said he, in the tone which one uses for a reprimand. "You did not vote for the death of the king, after all."

The old member of the Convention did not appear to notice the bitter meaning underlying the words "after all." He replied. The smile had quite disappeared from his face.

"Do not congratulate me too much, sir. I did vote for the death of the tyrant."

It was the tone of austerity answering the tone of severity.

"What do you mean to say?" resumed the Bishop.

"I mean to say that man has a tyrant – ignorance. I voted for the death of that tyrant. That tyrant engendered royalty, which is authority falsely understood, while science is authority rightly understood. Man should be governed only by science."

"And conscience," added the Bishop.

"It is the same thing. Conscience is the quantity of innate science which we have within us."

Monseigneur Bienvenu listened in some astonishment to this language, which was very new to him.

The member of the Convention resumed:

"So far as Louis XVI was concerned, I said `no.' I did not think that I had the right to kill a man; but I felt it my duty to exterminate evil. I voted the end of the tyrant, that is to say, the end of prostitution for woman, the end of slavery for man, the end of night for the child. In voting for the Republic, I voted for that. I voted for fraternity, concord, the dawn. I have aided in the overthrow of prejudices and errors. The crumbling away of prejudices and errors causes light. We have caused the fall of the old world, and the old world, that vase of miseries, has become, through its upsetting upon the human race, an urn of joy."

"Mixed joy," said the Bishop.

"You may say troubled joy, and to-day, after that fatal return of the past, which is called 1814, joy which has disappeared! Alas! The work was incomplete, I admit: we demolished the ancient regime in deeds; we were not able to suppress it entirely in ideas. To destroy abuses is not sufficient; customs must be modified. The mill is there no longer; the wind is still there."

"You have demolished. It may be of use to

demolish, but I distrust a demolition complicated with wrath."

"Right has its wrath, Bishop; and the wrath of right is an element of progress. In any case, and in spite of whatever may be said, the French Revolution is the most important step of the human race since the advent of Christ. Incomplete, it may be, but sublime. It set free all the unknown social quantities; it softened spirits, it calmed, appeased, enlightened; it caused the waves of civilization to flow over the earth. It was a good thing. The French Revolution is the consecration of humanity."

The Bishop could not refrain from murmuring:

"Yes? '93!"

The member of the Convention straightened himself up in his chair with an almost lugubrious solemnity, and exclaimed, so far as a dying man is capable of exclamation:

"Ah, there you go; '93! I was expecting that word. A cloud had been forming for the space of fifteen hundred years; at the end of fifteen hundred years it burst. You are putting the thunderbolt on its trial."

The Bishop felt, without, perhaps, confessing it, that something within him had suffered extinction. Nevertheless, he put a good face on the matter. He replied:

"The judge speaks in the name of justice; the priest speaks in the name of pity, which is nothing but a more lofty justice. A thunderbolt should com-mit no error." And he added, regarding the member of the Convention steadily the while, "Louis XVII?"

The conventionary stretched forth his hand and grasped the Bishop's arm.

"Louis XVII! let us see. For whom do you mourn? is it for the innocent child? very good; in that case I mourn with you. Is it for the royal child? I demand time for reflection. To me, the brother of Cartouche, an innocent child who was hung up by the armpits in the Place de Greve, until death ensued, for the sole crime of having been the brother of Cartouche, is no less painful than the grandson of Louis XV, an innocent child, martyred in the tower of the Temple, for the sole crime of having been grandson of Louis XV."

"Monsieur," said the Bishop, "I like not this conjunction of names."

"Cartouche? Louis XV? To which of the two do you object?"

A momentary silence ensued. The Bishop almost regretted having come, and yet he felt vaguely and strangely shaken.

The conventionary resumed:

"Ah, Monsieur Priest, you love not the crudities of the true. Christ loved them. He seized a rod and cleared out the Temple. His scourge, full of lightnings, was a harsh speaker of truths. When he cried, 'Sinite parvulos,' he made no distinction between the little children. It would not have embarrassed him to bring together the Dauphin of Barabbas and the Dauphin of Herod. Innocence, Monsieur, is its own crown. Innocence has no need to be a highness. It is as august in rags as in fleurs de lys."

"That is true," said the Bishop in a low voice.

"I persist," continued the conventionary G— "You have mentioned Louis XVII to me. Let us come to an understanding. Shall we weep for all the innocent, all martyrs, all children, the lowly as well as the exalted? I agree to that. But in that case, as I have told you, we must go back further than '93, and our tears must begin before Louis XVII. I will weep with you over the children of kings, provided that you will weep with me over the children of the people."

"I weep for all," said the Bishop.

"Equally!" exclaimed conventionary G—; "and if the balance must incline, let it be on the side of the people. They have been suffering longer."

Another silence ensued. The conventionary was the first to break it. He raised himself on one elbow, took a bit of his cheek between his thumb and his forefinger, as one does mechanically when one interrogates and judges, and appealed to the Bishop with a gaze full of all the forces of the death agony. It was almost an explosion.

"Yes, sir, the people have been suffering a long while. And hold! that is not all, either; why have you just questioned me and talked to me about Louis XVII? I know you not. Ever since I have been in these parts I have dwelt in this enclosure alone, never setting foot outside, and seeing no one but that child who helps me. Your name has reached me in a confused manner, it is true, and very badly pronounced, I must admit; but that signifies nothing: clever men have so many ways of imposing on that honest goodman, the people. By the way, I did not hear the sound of your carriage; you have left it yonder, behind the coppice at the fork of the roads, no doubt. I do not know you, I tell you. You have told me that you are the Bishop; but that affords me no information as to your moral personality. In short, I repeat my question. Who are you? You are a bishop; that is to say, a prince of the church, one of those gilded men with heraldic bearings and revenues, who have vast prebends – the bishopric of Digne fifteen thousand francs settled income, ten thousand in perquisites; total, twenty-five thousand francs – who have kitchens, who have liveries, who make good cheer, who eat moor-hens on Friday, who strut about, a lackey before, a lackey behind, in a gala coach, and who have palaces, and who roll in their carriages in the name of Jesus Christ who went barefoot! You are a prelate – revenues, palace, horses, servants, good table, all the sensualities of life; you have this like the rest, and like the rest, you enjoy it; it is well; but this says either too much or too little; this does not enlighten me upon the intrinsic and essential value of the man who comes with the probable intention of bringing wisdom to me. To whom do I speak? Who are you?"

The Bishop hung his head and replied, "Vermis sum – I am a worm."

"A worm of the earth in a carriage?" growled the conventionary.

It was the conventionary's turn to be arrogant, and the Bishop's to be humble.

The Bishop resumed mildly:

"So be it, sir. But explain to me how my carriage, which is a few paces off behind the trees yonder, how my good table and the moor-hens which I eat on Friday, how my twenty-five thousand francs income, how my palace and my lackeys prove that clemency is not a duty, and that '93 was not inexorable.

The conventionary passed his hand across his brow, as though to sweep away a cloud.

"Before replying to you," he said, "I beseech you to pardon me. I have just committed a wrong, sir. You are at my house, you are my guest, I owe you courtesy. You discuss my ideas, and it becomes me to confine myself to combating your arguments. Your riches and your pleasures are advantages which I hold over you in the debate; but good taste dictates that I shall not make use of them. I promise you to make no use of them in the future."

"I thank you," said the Bishop.

G— resumed.

"Let us return to the explanation which you have asked of me. Where were we? What were you saying to me? That '93 was inexorable?"

"Inexorable; yes," said the Bishop. "What think you of Marat clapping his hands at the guillotine?"

"What think you of Bossuet chanting the Te Deum over the dragonnades?"

The retort was a harsh one, but it attained its mark with the directness of a point of steel. The Bishop quivered under it; no reply occurred to him; but he was offended by this mode of alluding to Bossuet. The best of minds will have their fetiches, and they sometimes feel vaguely wounded by the want of respect of logic.

The conventionary began to pant; the asthma of the agony which is mingled with the last breaths interrupted his voice; still, there was a perfect lucidity of soul in his eyes. He went on:

"Let me say a few words more in this and

that direction; I am willing. Apart from the Revolution, which, taken as a whole, is an immense human affirmation, '93 is, alas! a rejoinder. You think it inexorable, sir; but what of the whole monarchy, sir? Carrier is a bandit; but what name do you give to Montrevel? Fouquier-Tainville is a rascal; but what is your opinion as to Lamoignon-Baville? Maillard is terrible; but Saulx-Tavannes, if you please? Duchene senior is ferocious; but what epithet will you allow me for the elder Letellier? Jourdan-Coupe-Tete is a monster; but not so great a one as M. the Marquis de Louvois. Sir, sir, I am sorry for Marie Antoinette, archduchess and queen; but I am also sorry for that poor Huguenot woman, who, in 1685, under Louis the Great, sir, while with a nursing infant, was bound, naked to the waist, to a stake, and the child kept at a distance; her breast swelled with milk and her heart with anguish; the little one, hungry and pale, beheld that breast and cried and agonized; the executioner said to the woman, a mother and a nurse, `Abjure!' giving her her choice between the death of her infant and the death of her conscience. What say you to that torture of Tantalus as applied to a mother? Bear this well in mind sir: the French Revolution had its reasons for existence; its wrath will be absolved by the future; its result is the world made better. From its most terrible blows there comes forth a caress for the human race. I abridge, I stop, I have too much the advantage; moreover, I am dying."

And ceasing to gaze at the Bishop, the conventionary concluded his thoughts in these tranquil words:

"Yes, the brutalities of progress are called revolutions. When they are over, this fact is recognized – that the human race has been treated harshly, but that it has progressed."

The conventionary doubted not that he had successively conquered all the inmost intrenchments of the Bishop. One remained, however, and from this intrenchment, the last resource of Monseigneur Bienvenu's resistance, came forth this reply, wherein appeared nearly all the harshness of the beginning:

"Progress should believe in God. Good cannot have an impious servitor. He who is an atheist is but a bad leader for the human race."

The former representative of the people made no reply. He was seized with a fit of trembling. He looked towards heaven, and in his glance a tear gathered slowly. When the eyelid was full, the tear trickled down his livid cheek, and he said, almost in a stammer, quite low, and to himself, while his eyes were plunged in the depths:

"O thou! O ideal! Thou alone existest!"

The Bishop experienced an indescribable shock.

After a pause, the old man raised a finger heavenward and said:

"The infinite is. He is there. If the infinite had no person, person would be without limit; it would not be infinite; in other words, it would not exist. There is, then, an *I*. That *I* of the infinite is God."

The dying man had pronounced these last words in a loud voice, and with the shiver of ecstasy, as though he beheld some one. When he had spoken, his eyes closed. The effort had exhausted him. It was evident that he had just lived through in a moment the few hours which had been left to him. That which he had said brought him nearer to him who is in death. The supreme moment was approaching.

The Bishop understood this; time pressed; it was as a priest that he had come: from extreme coldness he had passed by degrees to extreme emotion; he gazed at those closed eyes, he took that wrinkled, aged and ice-cold hand in his, and bent over the dying man.

"This hour is the hour of God. Do you not think that it would be regrettable if we had met in vain?"

The conventionary opened his eyes again. A gravity mingled with gloom was imprinted on his countenance.

"Bishop," said he, with a slowness which probably arose more from his dignity of soul than from the failing of his strength, "I have passed my life in meditation, study, and contemplation. I was sixty years of age when my country called me and commanded me to concern myself with its affairs. I obeyed. Abuses existed, I combated them; tyrannies existed, I destroyed them; rights and principles existed, I proclaimed and confessed them. Our territory was invaded, I defended it; France was menaced, I offered my breast. I was not rich; I am poor. I have been one of the masters of the state; the vaults of the treasury were encumbered with specie to such a degree that we were forced to shore up the walls, which were on the point of bursting beneath the weight of gold and silver; I dined in Dead Tree Street, at twenty-two sous. I have succored the oppressed, I have comforted the suffering. I tore the cloth from the altar, it is true; but it was to bind up the wounds of my country. I have always upheld the march forward of the human race, forward towards the light, and I have sometimes resisted progress without pity. I have, when the occasion offered, protected my own adversaries, men of your profession. And there is at Peteghem, in Flanders, at the very spot where the Merovingian kings had their summer palace, a convent of Urbanists, the Abbey of Sainte Claire en Beaulieu, which I saved in 1793. I have done my duty according to my powers, and all the good that I was able. After which, I was hunted down, pursued, persecuted, blackened, jeered at, scorned, cursed, proscribed. For many years past, I with my white hair have been conscious that many people think they have the right to despise me; to the poor ignorant masses I present the visage of one damned. And I accept this isolation of hatred, with-out hating any one myself. Now I am eighty-six years old; I am on the point of death. What is it that you have come to ask of me?"

"Your blessing," said the Bishop.

And he knelt down.

When the Bishop raised his head again, the face of the conventionary had become august. He had just expired.

The Bishop returned home, deeply absorbed in thoughts which cannot be known to us. He passed the whole night in prayer. On the following morning some bold and curious persons attempted to speak to him about member of the Convention G——; he contented himself with pointing heavenward.

From that moment he redoubled his tenderness and brotherly feeling towards all children and sufferers.

Any allusion to "that old wretch of a G——" caused him to fall into a singular preoccupation. No one could say that the passage of that soul before his, and the reflection of that grand conscience upon his, did not count for something in his approach to perfection.

This "pastoral visit" naturally furnished an occasion for a murmur of comment in all the little local coteries.

"Was the bedside of such a dying man as that the proper place for a bishop? There was evidently no conversion to be expected. All those revolutionists are backsliders. Then why go there? What was there to be seen there? He must have been very curious indeed to see a soul carried off by the devil."

One day a dowager of the impertinent variety who thinks herself spiritual, addressed this sally to him, "Monseigneur, people are inquiring when Your Greatness will receive the red cap!" – "Oh! oh! that's a coarse color," replied the Bishop. "It is lucky that those who despise it in a cap revere it in a hat."

Uncle Tom's Cabin – Chapter 5

Harriet Beecher Stowe

Mr. and Mrs. Shelby had retired to their apartment for the night. He was lounging in a large easy-chair, looking over some letters that had come in the afternoon mail, and she was standing before her mirror, brushing out the complicated braids and curls in which Eliza had arranged her hair; for, noticing her pale cheeks and haggard eyes, she had excused her attendance that night, and ordered her to bed. The employment, naturally enough, suggested her conversation with the girl in the morning; and turning to her husband, she said, carelessly, "By the by, Arthur, who was that low-bred fellow that you lugged in to our dinner-table today?"

"Haley is his name," said Shelby, turning himself rather uneasily in his chair, and continuing with his eyes fixed on a letter.

"Haley! Who is he, and what may be his business here, pray?"

"Well, he's a man that I transacted some business with, last time I was at Natchez," said Mr. Shelby.

"And he presumed on it to make himself quite at home, and call and dine here, ay?"

"Why, I invited him; I had some accounts with him," said Shelby.

"Is he a negro-trader?" said Mrs. Shelby, noticing a certain embarrassment in her husband's manner.

"Why, my dear, what put that into your head?" said Shelby, looking up.

"Nothing, – only Eliza came in here, after din-ner, in a great worry, crying and taking on, and said you were talking with a trader, and that she heard him make an offer for her boy – the ridiculous little goose!"

"She did, hey?" said Mr. Shelby, returning to his paper, which he seemed for a few moments quite intent upon, not perceiving that he was holding it bottom upwards.

"It will have to come out," said he, mentally; "as well now as ever."

"I told Eliza," said Mrs. Shelby, as she continued brushing her hair, "that she was a little fool for her pains, and that you never had anything to do with that sort of persons. Of course, I knew you never meant to sell any of our people, – least of all, to such a fellow."

"Well, Emily," said her husband, "so I have always felt and said; but the fact is that my business lies so that I cannot get on without. I shall have to sell some of my hands."

"To that creature? Impossible! Mr. Shelby, you cannot be serious."

"I'm sorry to say that I am," said Mr. Shelby. "I've agreed to sell Tom."

"What! our Tom? – that good, faithful creature! – been your faithful servant from a boy! O, Mr. Shelby! – and you have promised him his freedom, too, – you and I have spoken to him a hundred times of it. Well, I can believe anything now, – I can believe *now* that you could sell little Harry, poor Eliza's only child!" said Mrs. Shelby, in a tone between grief and indignation.

"Well, since you must know all, it is so. I have agreed to sell Tom and Harry both; and I don't know why I am to be rated, as if I were a monster, for doing what every one does every day."

"But why, of all others, choose these?" said Mrs. Shelby. "Why sell them, of all on the place, if you must sell at all?"

"Because they will bring the highest sum of any, – that's why. I could choose another, if you say so. The fellow made me a high bid on Eliza, if that would suit you any better," said Mr. Shelby.

"The wretch!" said Mrs. Shelby, vehemently.

"Well, I didn't listen to it, a moment, – out of regard to your feelings, I wouldn't; – so give me some credit."

"My dear," said Mrs. Shelby, recollecting herself, "forgive me. I have been hasty. I was surprised, and entirely unprepared for this; – but surely you will allow me to intercede for these poor creatures. Tom is a noble-hearted, faithful fellow, if he is black. I do believe, Mr. Shelby, that if he were put to it, he would lay down his life for you."

"I know it, – I dare say; – but what's the use of all this? – I can't help myself."

"Why not make a pecuniary sacrifice? I'm willing to bear my part of the inconvenience. O, Mr. Shelby, I have tried – tried most faithfully, as a Christian woman should – to do my duty to these poor, simple, dependent creatures. I have cared for them, instructed them, watched over them, and know all their little cares and joys, for years; and how can I ever hold up my head again among them, if, for the sake of a little paltry gain, we sell such a faithful, excellent, confiding creature as poor Tom, and tear from him in a moment all we have taught him to love and value? I have taught them the duties of the family, of parent and child, and husband and wife; and how can I bear to have this open acknowledgment that we care for no tie, no duty, no relation, however sacred, compared with money? I have talked with Eliza about her boy – her duty to him as a Christian mother, to watch over him, pray for him, and bring him up in a Christian way; and now what can I say, if you tear him away, and sell him, soul and body, to a profane, unprincipled man, just to save a little money? I have told her that one soul is worth more than all the money in the world; and how will she believe me when she sees us turn round and sell her child? – sell him, perhaps, to certain ruin of body and soul!"

"I'm sorry you feel so about it, – indeed I am," said Mr. Shelby; "and I respect your feelings, too, though I don't pretend to share them to their full extent; but I tell you now, solemnly, it's of no use – I can't help myself. I didn't mean to tell you this Emily; but, in plain words, there is no choice between selling these two and selling everything. Either they must go, or *all* must.

Haley has come into possession of a mortgage, which, if I don't clear off with him directly, will take everything before it. I've raked, and scraped, and borrowed, and all but begged, – and the price of these two was needed to make up the balance, and I had to give them up. Haley fancied the child; he agreed to settle the matter that way, and no other. I was in his power, and *had* to do it. If you feel so to have them sold, would it be any better to have *all* sold?"

Mrs. Shelby stood like one stricken. Finally, turning to her toilet, she rested her face in her hands, and gave a sort of groan.

"This is God's curse on slavery! – a bitter, bitter, most accursed thing! – a curse to the master and a curse to the slave! I was a fool to think I could make anything good out of such a deadly evil. It is a sin to hold a slave under laws like ours, – I always felt it was, – I always thought so when I was a girl, – I thought so still more after I joined the church; but I thought I could gild it over, – I thought, by kindness, and care, and instruction, I could make the condition of mine better than freedom – fool that I was!"

"Why, wife, you are getting to be an abolitionist, quite."

"Abolitionist! if they knew all I know about slavery, they *might* talk! We don't need them to tell us; you know I never thought that slavery was right – never felt willing to own slaves."

"Well, therein you differ from many wise and pious men," said Mr. Shelby. "You remember Mr. B.'s sermon, the other Sunday?"

"I don't want to hear such sermons; I never wish to hear Mr. B. in our church again. Ministers can't help the evil, perhaps, – can't cure it, any more than we can, – but defend it! – it always went against my common sense. And I think you didn't think much of that sermon, either."

"Well," said Shelby, "I must say these ministers sometimes carry matters further than we poor sinners would exactly dare to do. We men of the world must wink pretty hard at various things, and get used to a deal that isn't the exact thing. But we don't quite fancy, when women and ministers come out broad and square, and go beyond us in matters of either modesty or morals, that's a fact. But now, my dear, I trust you see the necessity of the thing, and you see that I have done the very best that circumstances would allow."

"O yes, yes!" said Mrs. Shelby, hurriedly and abstractedly fingering her gold watch, – "I haven't any jewelry of any amount," she added, thought-fully; "but would not this watch do something? – it was an expensive one, when it was bought. If I could only at least save Eliza's child, I would sacrifice anything I have."

"I'm sorry, very sorry, Emily," said Mr. Shelby, "I'm sorry this takes hold of you so; but it will do no good. The fact is, Emily, the thing's done; the bills of sale are already signed, and in Haley's hands; and you must be thankful it is no worse. That man has had it in his power to ruin us all, – and now he is fairly off. If you knew the man as I do, you'd think that we had had a narrow escape."

"Is he so hard, then?"

"Why, not a cruel man, exactly, but a man of leather, – a man alive to nothing but trade and profit, – cool, and unhesitating, and unrelenting, as death and the grave. He'd sell his own mother at a good percentage – not wishing the old woman any harm, either."

"And this wretch owns that good, faithful Tom, and Eliza's child!"

"Well, my dear, the fact is that this goes rather hard with me; it's a thing I hate to think of. Haley wants to drive matters, and take possession tomorrow. I'm going to get out my horse bright and early, and be off. I can't see Tom, that's a fact; and you had better arrange a drive somewhere, and carry Eliza off. Let the thing be done when she is out of sight."

"No, no," said Mrs. Shelby; "I'll be in no sense accomplice or help in this cruel business. I'll go and see poor old Tom, God help him, in his distress! They shall see, at any rate, that their mistress can feel for and with them. As to Eliza, I dare not think about it. The Lord forgive us! What have we done, that this cruel necessity should come on us?"

There was one listener to this conversation whom Mr. and Mrs. Shelby little suspected.

Communicating with their apartment was a large closet, opening by a door into the outer passage. When Mrs. Shelby had dismissed Eliza for the night, her feverish and excited mind had suggested the idea of this closet; and she had hidden herself there, and, with her ear pressed close against the crack of the door, had lost not a word of the conversation.

When the voices died into silence, she rose and crept stealthily away. Pale, shivering, with rigid features and compressed lips, she looked an entirely altered being from the soft and timid creature she had been hitherto. She moved cautiously along the entry, paused one moment at her mistress' door, and raised her hands in mute appeal to Heaven, and then turned and glided into her own room. It was a quiet, neat apartment, on the same floor with her mistress. There was a pleasant sunny window, where she had often sat singing at her sewing; there a little case of books, and various little fancy articles, ranged by them, the gifts of Christmas holidays; there was her simple wardrobe in the closet and in the drawers: – here was, in short, her home; and, on the whole, a happy one it had been to her. But there, on the bed, lay her slumbering boy, his long curls falling negligently around his unconscious face, his rosy mouth half open, his little fat hands thrown out over the bedclothes, and a smile spread like a sunbeam over his whole face.

"Poor boy! poor fellow!" said Eliza; "they have sold you! but your mother will save you yet!"

No tear dropped over that pillow; in such straits as these, the heart has no tears to give, – it drops only blood, bleeding itself away in silence. She took a piece of paper and a pencil, and wrote, hastily,

"O, Missis! dear Missis! don't think me ungrateful, – don't think hard of me, any way, – I heard all you and master said tonight. I am going to try to save my boy – you will not blame me! God bless and reward you for all your kindness!"

Hastily folding and directing this, she went to a drawer and made up a little package of clothing for her boy, which she tied with a handkerchief firmly round her waist; and, so fond is a mother's remembrance, that, even in the terrors of that hour, she did not forget to put in the little package one or two of his favorite toys, reserving a gayly painted parrot to amuse him, when she should be called on to awaken him. It was some trouble to arouse the little sleeper; but, after some effort, he sat up, and was playing with his bird, while his mother was putting on her bonnet and shawl.

"Where are you going, mother?" said he, as she drew near the bed, with his little coat and cap.

His mother drew near, and looked so earnestly into his eyes, that he at once divined that something unusual was the matter.

"Hush, Harry," she said; "mustn't speak loud, or they will hear us. A wicked man was coming to take little Harry away from his mother, and carry him 'way off in the dark; but mother won't let him – she's going to put on her little boy's cap and coat, and run off with him, so the ugly man can't catch him."

Saying these words, she had tied and buttoned on the child's simple outfit, and, taking him in her arms, she whispered to him to be very still; and, opening a door in her room which led into the outer verandah, she glided noiselessly out.

It was a sparkling, frosty, starlight night, and the mother wrapped the shawl close round her child, as, perfectly quiet with vague terror, he clung round her neck.

Old Bruno, a great Newfoundland, who slept at the end of the porch, rose, with a low growl, as she came near. She gently spoke his name, and the animal, an old pet and playmate of hers, instantly, wagging his tail, prepared to follow her, though apparently revolving much, in this simple dog's head, what such an indiscreet midnight promenade might mean. Some dim ideas of imprudence or impropriety in the measure seemed to embarrass him considerably; for he often stopped, as Eliza glided forward, and looked wistfully, first at her and then at the house, and then, as if reassured by reflection, he pattered along after her again. A few minutes brought them to the window of Uncle Tom's cottage, and Eliza stopping, tapped lightly on the window-pane.

The prayer-meeting at Uncle Tom's had, in the order of hymn-singing, been protracted to a very late hour; and, as Uncle Tom had indulged himself in a few lengthy solos afterwards, the consequence was, that, although it was now between twelve and one o'clock, he and his worthy helpmeet were not yet asleep.

"Good Lord! what's that?" said Aunt Chloe, starting up and hastily drawing the curtain. "My sakes alive, if it an't Lizy! Get on your clothes, old man, quick! – there's old Bruno, too, a pawin round; what on airth! I'm gwine to open the door."

And suiting the action to the word, the door flew open, and the light of the tallow candle, which Tom had hastily lighted, fell on the haggard face and dark, wild eyes of the fugitive.

"Lord bless you! – I'm skeered to look at ye, Lizy! Are ye tuck sick, or what's come over ye?"

"I'm running away – Uncle Tom and Aunt Chloe – carrying off my child – Master sold him!"

"Sold him?" echoed both, lifting up their hands in dismay.

"Yes, sold him!" said Eliza, firmly; "I crept into the closet by Mistress' door tonight, and I heard Master tell Missis that he had sold my Harry, and you, Uncle Tom, both, to a trader; and that he was going off this morning on his horse, and that the man was to take possession today."

Tom had stood, during this speech, with his hands raised, and his eyes dilated, like a man in a dream. Slowly and gradually, as its meaning came over him, he collapsed, rather than seated himself, on his old chair, and sunk his head down upon his knees.

"The good Lord have pity on us!" said Aunt Chloe. "O! it don't seem as if it was true! What has he done, that Mas'r should sell *him*?"

"He hasn't done anything, – it isn't for that. Master don't want to sell, and Missis she's always good. I heard her plead and beg for us; but he told her 't was no use; that he was in this man's debt, and that this man had got the power over him; and that if he didn't pay him off clear, it would end in his having to sell the place and all the people, and move off. Yes, I heard him say there was no choice between selling these two and selling all, the man was driving him so hard. Master said he was sorry; but oh, Missis – you ought to have heard her talk! If she an't a Christian and an angel, there never was one. I'm a wicked girl to leave her so; but, then, I can't help it. She said, herself, one soul was worth more than the world; and this boy has a soul, and if I let him be carried off, who knows what'll become of it? It must be right: but, if it an't right, the Lord forgive me, for I can't help doing it!"

"Well, old man!" said Aunt Chloe, "why don't you go, too? Will you wait to be toted down river, where they kill niggers with hard work and starving? I'd a heap rather die than go there, any day! There's time for ye, – be off with Lizy, – you've got a pass to come and go any time. Come, bustle up, and I'll get your things together."

Tom slowly raised his head, and looked sorrowfully but quietly around, and said,

"No, no – I an't going. Let Eliza go – it's her right! I wouldn't be the one to say no – 'tan't in *natur* for her to stay; but you heard what she said! If I must be sold, or all the people on the place, and everything go to rack, why, let me be sold. I s'pose I can bar it as well as any on 'em," he added, while something like a sob and a sigh shook his broad, rough chest convulsively. "Mas'r always found me on the spot – he always will. I never have broke trust, nor used my

pass no ways contrary to my word, and I never will. It's better for me alone to go, than to break up the place and sell all. Mas'r an't to blame, Chloe, and he'll take care of you and the poor –"

Here he turned to the rough trundle bed full of little woolly heads, and broke fairly down. He leaned over the back of the chair, and covered his face with his large hands. Sobs, heavy, hoarse and loud, shook the chair, and great tears fell through his fingers on the floor; just such tears, sir, as you dropped into the coffin where lay your first-born son; such tears, woman, as you shed when you heard the cries of your dying babe. For, sir, he was a man, – and you are but another man. And, woman, though dressed in silk and jewels, you are but a woman, and, in life's great straits and mighty griefs, ye feel but one sorrow!

"And now," said Eliza, as she stood in the door, "I saw my husband only this afternoon, and I little knew then what was to come. They have pushed him to the very last standing place, and he told me, today, that he was going to run away. Do try, if you can, to get word to him. Tell him how I went, and why I went; and tell him I'm going to try and find Canada. You must give my love to him, and tell him, if I never see him again," she turned away, and stood with her back to them for a moment, and then added, in a husky voice, "tell him to be as good as he can, and try and meet me in the kingdom of heaven."

"Call Bruno in there," she added. "Shut the door on him, poor beast! He mustn't go with me!"

A few last words and tears, a few simple adieus and blessings, and clasping her wondering and affrighted child in her arms, she glided noiselessly away.

A Modest Proposal

Jonathan Swift

FOR PREVENTING THE CHILDREN OF
POOR PEOPLE IN IRELAND FROM
BEING A BURDEN TO THEIR PARENTS OR
COUNTRY, AND FOR MAKING THEM
BENEFICIAL TO THE PUBLIC

It is a melancholy object to those who walk through this great town or travel in the country, when they see the streets, the roads, and cabin doors, crowded with beggars of the female sex, followed by three, four, or six children, all in rags and importuning every passenger for an alms. These mothers, instead of being able to work for their honest livelihood, are forced to employ all their time in strolling to beg sustenance for their helpless infants: who as they grow up either turn thieves for want of work, or leave their dear native country to fight for the Pretender in Spain, or sell themselves to the Barbadoes.

I think it is agreed by all parties that this prodigious number of children in the arms, or on the backs, or at the heels of their mothers, and frequently of their fathers, is in the present deplor-able state of the kingdom a very great additional grievance; and, therefore, whoever could find out a fair, cheap, and easy method of making these children sound, useful members of the commonwealth, would deserve so well of the public as to have his statue set up for a preserver of the nation.

But my intention is very far from being confined to provide only for the children of professed beggars; it is of a much greater extent, and shall take in the whole number of infants at a certain age who are born of parents in effect as little able to support them as those who demand our charity in the streets.

As to my own part, having turned my thoughts for many years upon this important subject, and maturely weighed the several schemes of other projectors, I have always found them grossly mis-taken in the computation. It is true, a child just dropped from its dam may be supported by her milk for a solar year, with little other nourishment; at most not above the value of 2s., which the mother may certainly get, or the value in scraps, by her lawful occupation of begging; and it is exactly at one year old that I propose to provide for them in such a manner as instead of being a charge upon their parents or the parish, or wanting food and raiment for the rest of their lives, they shall on the contrary contribute to the feeding, and partly to the clothing, of many thousands.

There is likewise another great advantage in my scheme, that it will prevent those voluntary abortions, and that horrid practice of women mur-dering their bastard children, alas! too frequent among us! sacrificing the poor innocent babes I doubt more to avoid the expense than the shame, which would move tears and pity in the most savage and inhuman breast.

The number of souls in this kingdom being usually reckoned one million and a half, of these I calculate there may be about two hundred thousand couple whose wives are breeders; from which number I subtract thirty thousand couples who are able to maintain their own children, although I apprehend there cannot be so many, under the present distresses of the kingdom; but this being granted, there will remain an hundred and seventy thousand breeders. I again subtract fifty thousand for those women who miscarry, or whose children die by accident or disease within the year. There only remains one hundred and twenty thousand children of poor parents annually born. The question therefore is, how this number shall be reared and provided for, which, as I have already said, under the present situation of affairs, is utterly impossible by all the methods hitherto proposed. For we can neither employ them in handicraft or agriculture; we neither build houses (I mean in the country) nor cultivate land: they can very seldom pick up a livelihood by stealing, till they arrive at six years old, except where they are of towardly parts, al-though I confess they learn the rudiments much earlier, during which time, they can however be properly looked upon only as probationers, as I have been informed by a principal gentleman in the county of Cavan, who protested to me that he never knew above one or two instances un-der the age of six, even in a part of the kingdom so renowned for the quickest proficiency in that art.

I am assured by our merchants, that a boy or a girl before twelve years old is no salable commodity; and even when they come to this age they will not yield above three pounds, or three pounds and half-a-crown at most on the exchange; which cannot turn to account either to the parents or kingdom, the charge of nutri-ment and rags having been at least four times that value.

I shall now therefore humbly propose my own thoughts, which I hope will not be liable to the least objection.

I have been assured by a very knowing Ameri-can of my acquaintance in London, that a young healthy child well nursed is at a year old a most delicious, nourishing, and wholesome food, whether stewed, roasted, baked, or boiled; and I make no doubt that it will equally serve in a fricassee or a ragout.

I do therefore humbly offer it to public con-sideration that of the hundred and twenty thou-sand children already computed, twenty thou-sand may be reserved for breed, whereof only one-fourth part to be males; which is more than we allow to sheep, black cattle or swine; and my reason is, that these children are seldom the fruits of marriage, a circumstance not much re-garded by our savages, therefore one male will be sufficient to serve four females. That the re-maining hundred thousand may, at a year old, be offered in the sale to the persons of quality and fortune through the kingdom; always ad-vising the mother to let them suck plentifully in the last month, so as to render them plump and fat for a good table. A child will make two dishes at an entertainment for friends; and when the family dines alone, the fore or hind quarter will make a reasonable dish, and sea-soned with a little pepper or salt will be very good boiled on the fourth day, especially in winter.

I have reckoned upon a medium that a child just born will weigh 12 pounds, and in a solar year, if tolerably nursed, increaseth to 28 pounds.

I grant this food will be somewhat dear, and therefore very proper for landlords, who, as they have already devoured most of the parents, seem to have the best title to the children.

Infant's flesh will be in season throughout the year, but more plentiful in March, and a little before and after; for we are told by a grave author, an eminent French physician, that fish being a prolific diet, there are more children born in Roman Catholic countries about nine months after Lent than at any other season; therefore, reckoning a year after Lent, the mar-kets will be more glutted than usual, because the number of popish infants is at least three to one in this kingdom: and therefore it will have one other collateral advantage, by lessening the number of papists among us.

I have already computed the charge of nurs-ing a beggar's child (in which list I reckon all cottagers, laborers, and four-fifths of the farm-ers) to be about two shillings per annum, rags included; and I believe no gentleman would re-pine to give ten shillings for the carcass of a good fat child, which, as I have said, will make four dishes of excellent nutritive meat, when he hath only some particular friend or his own family to dine with him. Thus the squire will learn to be a good landlord, and grow popular among his tenants; the mother will have eight shillings net profit, and be fit for work till she produces another child.

Those who are more thrifty (as I must confess the times require) may flay the carcass; the skin of which artificially dressed will make admira-ble gloves for ladies, and summer boots for fine gentlemen.

As to our city of Dublin, shambles may be appointed for this purpose in the most convenient parts of it, and butchers we may be assured will not be wanting; although I rather recommend buy-ing the children alive, and dressing them hot from the knife, as we do roasting pigs.

A very worthy person, a true lover of his country, and whose virtues I highly esteem, was lately pleased in discoursing on this matter to offer a refinement upon my scheme. He said that many gentlemen of this kingdom, having of late destroyed their deer, he conceived that the want of venison might be well supplied by the bodies of young lads and maidens, not exceeding fourteen years of age nor under twelve; so great a number of both sexes in every country being now ready to starve for want of work and service; and these to be disposed of by their parents, if alive, or otherwise by their nearest relations. But with due deference to so excellent a friend and so deserving a patriot, I cannot be altogether in his sentiments; for as to the males, my American acquaintance assured me, from frequent experience, that their flesh was generally tough and lean, like that of our schoolboys by continual exercise, and their taste disagreeable; and to fatten them would not answer the charge. Then as to the females, it would, I think, with humble submission be a loss to the public, because they soon would become breeders themselves; and besides, it is not improbable that some scrupulous people might be apt to censure such a practice (although indeed very unjustly), as a little bordering upon cruelty; which, I confess, hath always been with me the strongest objection against any project, however so well intended.

But in order to justify my friend, he confessed that this expedient was put into his head by the famous Psalmanazar, a native of the island Formosa, who came from thence to London above twenty years ago, and in conversation told my friend, that in his country when any young person happened to be put to death, the executioner sold the carcass to persons of quality as a prime dainty; and that in his time the body of a plump girl of fifteen, who was crucified for an attempt to poison the emperor, was sold to his imperial majesty's prime minister of state, and other great mandarins of the court, in

joints from the gibbet, at four hundred crowns. Neither indeed can I deny, that if the same use were made of several plump young girls in this town, who without one single groat to their fortunes cannot stir abroad without a chair, and appear at playhouse and assemblies in foreign fineries which they never will pay for, the kingdom would not be the worse.

Some persons of a desponding spirit are in great concern about that vast number of poor people, who are aged, diseased, or maimed, and I have been desired to employ my thoughts what course may be taken to ease the nation of so grievous an encumbrance. But I am not in the least pain upon that matter, because it is very well known that they are every day dying and rotting by cold and famine, and filth and vermin, as fast as can be reasonably expected. And as to the young laborers, they are now in as hopeful a condition; they cannot get work, and consequently pine away for want of nourishment, to a degree that if at any time they are accidentally hired to common labor, they have not strength to perform it; and thus the country and themselves are happily delivered from the evils to come.

I have too long digressed, and therefore shall return to my subject. I think the advantages by the proposal which I have made are obvious and many, as well as of the highest importance. For first, as I have already observed, it would greatly lessen the number of papists, with whom we are yearly overrun, being the principal breeders of the nation as well as our most dangerous enemies; and who stay at home on purpose with a design to deliver the kingdom to the Pretender, hoping to take their advantage by the absence of so many good protestants, who have chosen rather to leave their country than stay at home and pay tithes against their conscience to an episcopal curate.

Secondly, The poorer tenants will have something valuable of their own, which by law may be made liable to distress and help to pay their landlord's rent, their corn and cattle being already seized, and money a thing unknown.

Thirdly, Whereas the maintenance of an hundred thousand children, from two years old and upward, cannot be computed at less than ten shillings a-piece per annum, the nation's stock will be thereby increased fifty thousand pounds per annum, beside the profit of a new dish introduced to the tables of all gentlemen of fortune in the kingdom who have any refinement in taste. And the money will circulate among ourselves, the goods being entirely of our own growth and manufacture.

Fourthly, The constant breeders, beside the gain of eight shillings sterling per annum by the sale of their children, will be rid of the charge of main-taining them after the first year.

Fifthly, This food would likewise bring great custom to taverns; where the vintners will certainly be so prudent as to procure the best receipts for dressing it to perfection, and consequently have their houses frequented by all the fine gentlemen, who justly value themselves upon their knowledge in good eating: and a skilful cook, who under-stands how to oblige his guests, will contrive to make it as expensive as they please.

Sixthly, This would be a great inducement to marriage, which all wise nations have either encouraged by rewards or enforced by laws and penalties. It would increase the care and tenderness of mothers toward their children, when they were sure of a settlement for life to the poor babes, provided in some sort by the public, to their annual profit instead of expense. We should see an honest emulation among the married women, which of them could bring the fattest child to the market. Men would become as fond of their wives during the time of their pregnancy as they are now of their mares in foal, their cows in calf, their sows when they are ready to farrow; nor offer to beat or kick them (as is too frequent a practice) for fear of a miscarriage.

Many other advantages might be enumerated. For instance, the addition of some thousand carcasses in our exportation of barreled beef, the propagation of swine's flesh, and improvement in the art of making good bacon, so much wanted among us by the great destruc-

tion of pigs, too frequent at our tables; which are no way comparable in taste or magnificence to a well-grown, fat, yearling child, which roasted whole will make a considerable figure at a lord mayor's feast or any other public entertainment. But this and many others I omit, being studious of brevity.

Supposing that one thousand families in this city, would be constant customers for Infant's Flesh, besides others who might have it at merry meetings, particularly at weddings and christen-ings, I compute that Dublin would take off annually about twenty thousand carcasses, and the rest of the Kingdom (where probably they will be sold somewhat cheaper) the remaining eighty thousand.

I can think of no one objection, that will possibly be raised against this proposal, unless it should be urged, that the number of people will be thereby much lessened in the Kingdom. This I freely own, and 'twas indeed one principal design in offering it to the world. I desire the reader will observe, that I calculate my remedy for this one individual kingdom of Ireland, and for no other that ever was, is, or I think, ever can be upon Earth. Therefore let no man talk to me of other expedients: of taxing our absentees at five shillings a pound: of using neither clothes, nor household furniture, except what is of our own growth and manufacture: of utterly rejecting the materials and instruments that promote foreign luxury: of curing the expensiveness of pride, vanity, idleness, and gaming in our women: of introducing a vein of parsimony, prudence and temperance: of learning to love our country, where-in we differ even from Laplanders, and the inhabitants of Topinamboo: of quitting our animosities, and factions, nor act any longer like the Jews, who were murdering one another at the very moment their city was taken: of being a little cautious not to sell our country and consciences for nothing: of teaching our landlords to have at least one degree of mercy towards their tenants. Lastly, of putting a spirit of honesty, industry, and skill into our shop-keepers, who, if a resolution could now be taken to buy only our native goods, would immediately unite to cheat and exact upon us in the price, the measure and the goodness, nor could ever yet be brought to make one fair proposal of just dealing, though often and earnestly invited to it.

Therefore I repeat, let no man talk to me of these and the like expedients, till he hath at least some glimpse of hope, that there will ever be some hearty and sincere attempt to put them into practice.

But as to my self, having been wearied out for many years with offering vain, idle, visionary thoughts, and at length despairing of success, I fortunately fell upon this proposal, which as it is wholly new, so it hath something solid and real, of no expense and little trouble, full in our own power, and whereby we can incur no danger in disobliging England. For this kind of commodity will not bear exportation, the flesh being of too tender a consistence, to admit a long continuance in salt, although perhaps I could name a country, which would be glad to eat up our whole nation without it.

After all, I am not so violently bent upon my own opinion as to reject any offer proposed by wise men, which shall be found equally innocent, cheap, easy, and effectual. But before something of that kind shall be advanced in contradiction to my scheme, and offering a better, I desire the author or authors will be pleased maturely to consider two points. First, as things now stand, how they will be able to find food and raiment for an hundred thousand useless mouths and backs. And secondly, there being a round million of creatures in human figure throughout this kingdom, whose whole subsistence put into a common stock would leave them in debt two millions of pounds sterling, adding those who are beggars by profession to the bulk of farmers, cottagers, and laborers, with their wives and children who are beggars in effect: I desire those politicians who dislike my overture, and may perhaps be so bold as to attempt an answer, that they will first ask the parents of these mortals, whether they would not at this day think it a great happiness to have been sold for food, at a year old in the manner I prescribe, and thereby have avoided such a perpetual scene of misfortunes as they

have since gone through by the oppression of landlords, the impossibility of paying rent without money or trade, the want of common sustenance, with neither house nor clothes to cover them from the inclemencies of the weather, and the most inevitable prospect of entailing the like or greater miseries upon their breed for ever.

I profess, in the sincerity of my heart, that I have not the least personal interest in endeavoring to promote this necessary work, having no other motive than the public good of my country, by advancing our trade, providing for infants, relieving the poor, and giving some pleasure to the rich. I have no children by which I can propose to get a single penny; the youngest being nine years old, and my wife past childbearing.

LIBERATORY VISUALS

Mark Vallen
Fuses – Revolutionary silkscreen.

Theodore A. Harris
Drowning in Bones and Flames – Partisan collage.

Carol Simpson
Cartoons – Life in Corporate Utopia.

Marina Weidemann
Cartoons – US on a rampage.

Stephanie McMillan
Cartoons – Against corporate-state conquest in Iraq and beyond.

Kim Alphandary
Nigerian Freedom Fighters and **Zapatista** – Revolution drawn in charcoal.

John Sloan
Ludlow, Colorado (1914) – Of coal miners and their families attacked and slaughtered by National Guardsmen.

Andre Vltchek
Photographs of Venezuela – The people, art, and social change.

"Fuses"

Mark Vallen

Drowning in Bones and Flames
paper collage, 2002

Theodore A. Harris

Why We Fight
Carol Simpson

"*I knew something was wrong when my orders for Iraq came in the same envelope as my oil company credit card bill.*"

Corporate Culture
Carol Simpson

"*Miss Whitney, cancel that memo requiring that personal appearance should reflect our corporate culture.*"

Mine Safety
Carol Simpson

*The Black Hole where government promises disappear
into an infinitely dense mass of greed and deception.*

Immigrant Workers
Carol Simpson

Six Income Family
Carol Simpson

*"According to our calculations, we can make it
if we become a six-income family."*

Childcare Workers
Carol Simpson

Leave no childcare worker behind.

Rotten Wages
Carol Simpson

*"I used to work in the Payroll Department,
but I couldn't stand the smell of the rotten wages."*

Why a Union?
Carol Simpson

Grim Reaper
Carol Simpson

"Look. buddy... I've been laid off for 8 months.
I sure as hell can't afford a funeral right now."

Marina Weidemann

Marina Weidemann

Marina Weidemann

Stephanie McMillan

Hopeful Alternative

Busy Ignoring You

Next to the Gallows

Stephanie McMillan

Cement Shoes

More Than Ten Times

Urgent Situation

Nigerian Freedom Fighters

Kim Alphandary

12/21/2006, NIGERIA, Movement for Emancipation of the Niger Delta (MEND), demands $1.5 billion in compensation from Royal Dutch Shell for environmental pollution, and asking for a greater share of government oil revenues.

The situation in the Niger Delta dates back to Nigeria's pre-independent colonial days when the Willink (Minorities and Fiscal Commission), in 1958, recommended that the delta region of the Niger should be regarded as a special developmental area requiring particular economic assistance.

This recommendation was never implemented. The number of deaths resulting from poverty and misery in this endangered region as a result of this non-compliance has never been investigated. Throughout the years, children, women and the aged have been massacred in Yenagoa, Odi, Odioma, Warri, Port Harcourt, and many other parts of the Delta due to the low-intensity war.

The most recent group to emerge continuing this struggle is the MEND, who represent the Ijaw people, the majority tribe in the Delta, and claim to represent a union of all the militant groups in the Niger Delta.

12/21/2006
NIGERIA, Movement for Emancipation of the Niger Delta (MEND) represents the Ijaw people, the majority tribe in the Delta, is demanding #1.5 billion in compensation from Royal Dutch Shell for environmental pollution and a greater share of government oil revenues.

Zapatista

Kim Alphandary

The Zapatista Army of National Liberation (Ejército Zapatista de Liberación Nacional, EZLN) is a revolutionary group based in Chiapas, one of the poorest states of Mexico. Members of the EZLN are mostly indigenous, but are supported by a large international network.

The group takes its name from the Mexican revolutionary Emiliano Zapata; they see themselves as his heirs, and heirs to five hundred years of indigenous resistance against imperialism. On January 1, 1994, the Zapatistas launched their legendary insurrection in Chiapas as NAFTA came into effect. They called NAFTA a "death sentence" for Mexico's Indians. As changes to the Constitution accompanied the adoption of NAFTA, legally privatizing communal peasant lands – robbing the residents of lands that were fought for in the Revolution of 1910 to 1919.

Ever since, Zapatismo has played an enormous role in awakening society. The needs of indigenous Mexicans were brought into the national political discussion for the first time; the Zapatistas effectively use radio and Internet communiqués to broadcast their worldview and effect change. On both sides of the border this movement has challenged Mexico's widespread economic suffering and racial divides, and has reenergized the Chicano movement in the United States. The struggle on the ground remains extreme; the Mayan Indians face a dire human rights situation and the world media pays little note. Chiapas is pervaded by roadblock after roadblock of heavily armed military troops searching vehicles and harassing travelers of all nationalities. The Mexican government has resorted to using dirty-war tactics to gain control over the state, the Indians face not only harassment but terror. Arbitrary detentions are common. There are more than 100 political prisoners in Chiapas and 20,000 displaced by paramilitary groups.

After twelve years, my heart is with them.

MEXICO, Chiapas, San Andrés Larrainzar
Zapatista

Ludlow, Colorado – John Sloan. 1914. Lithographic crayon on paper. Originally published as a cover illustration for the socialist New York Call, and soon thereafter published as a cover for The Masses, Sloan's artwork depicted the Ludlow massacre. On April 20, 1914, in an attempt to defeat a coal miner's strike in Ludlow, Colorado, National Guardsmen fired upon the striking worker's tent city – slaughtering twenty unarmed people – thirteen of them women and children. Sloan memorialized the bloodbath by depicting a miner, gun in hand, firing back at the Guardsmen who had murdered his family. – Mark Vallen

Photographs of Venezuela
Andre Vltchek

Ciudad Guayana – Finally having their say!

Murals at subway station in Caracas, Venezuela – 1

Murals at subway station in Caracas, Venezuela – 2

Murals in front of Museum in Merida, Venezuela – 3

Murals in front of Museum in Merida, Venezuela – 4

LIBERATORY POETRY

Alaa Kadhim al-Jabiri
The Play – "I beg your pardon my dear readers I did not mention the name of the play which is 'The Mass Graves'."

Tony Christini
News From Little Rock – The unreported story of the 40th year commemoration of the integration of Central High School by the Little Rock Nine in Little Rock, Arkansas.

Kim Jensen
Ode to Man and **War's End** – Facing the need to liberate.

Marge Piercy
Film can reverse but not time – "of history, spewing lives, torture…"

Margaret Randall
What I Tell the Young When They Ask – The art of resist.

Andrew Rihn
Dozers – Blades of destruction.

Adrienne Rich
Emergency Clinic – "I do not soothe minor / injuries…"

Various Authors
Poetry – In Kenya, Iraq, and Prison focus sections.

Buff Whitman-Bradley
Four Poems – In kindergarten I wore bright yellow socks; DeSoto Bend; We're gonna shoot those looters on sight; Who says they bungled it?

Mickey Z
A Cycle – An irony of culture.

Mwandawiro Mghanga
Voice Of Struggle: Poems From Prison In Kenya

The Play
Alaa Kadhim al-Jabiri

Baghdad, Iraq

…The play has started…

Turn out the lights…

Ladies and Gentlemen hold your breaths, stop speaking because you are sleeping victims.

The curtains are opened.

The first and the last scene.

From the podium of Death, the little girl Victim appears on the stage searching for her mother Oppressed as she stares at the pale faces and calls upon her mother: Mama. Mama. Where are you Mama Oppressed?...

A voice then cries from far…

My little girl, my dear, I am here.

The mother runs to her little girl, takes her into her arms, asking her, where were you my little girl…

The little girl replies with tears falling on her cheeks.

Mama, they took me to the second car, told me that my Mama was in the second car and that I would be with her in one place soon.

Oppressed wipes off her little girl's tears and holds her in her arms again as she mulls over the sand hills of the desert of the south and the little girl sleeps on a merciful chest and paints kisses on her mother's cheeks and the farewell smiles, then the sand curtains fall. The end.

The victims started talking about their secrets which are soaked with blood and the sound of the last bullets.

I beg your pardon my dear readers I did not mention the name of the play which is "The Mass Graves."

News From Little Rock
Tony Christini

The unreported story of the 40th year commemoration of the integration of Central High School by the Little Rock Nine in Little Rock, Arkansas.

Your door is shut against my face,
And I am sharp as steel with discontent.

– Claude McKay, "The White House"

What happens to a dream deferred?
…does it explode?

– Langston Hughes, "Harlem"

My days are not their days…
My ways are not their ways…
I don't think they dare
to think of that: no:
I'm fairly certain they don't think of that at all.

– James Baldwin, "Staggerlee wonders"

The biggest News I do not dare
Telegraph to the Editor's chair:
"They are like people everywhere."

The angry Editor would reply
In hundred harryings of Why

– Gwendolyn Brooks, "The Chicago Defender Sends a Man to Little Rock."

Brooks' poem that describes life in Little Rock, Arkansas in 1957 when Central High School became the site of the first federally-enforced court-ordered school integration. Forty years later, President Clinton returned to his home state to commemorate the occasion, while essentially ignoring the poverty and resultant violence in the area. During the first three days of Clinton's four day stay, four young men aged 17 to 23 were murdered in Little Rock not far from Central High School – an outbreak of violence that had been foreshadowed less than two months earlier by a drive-by shooting near Central High that was the third such shooting in a five-day period which also saw the killings of four other youths. The murders and poverty went virtually unreported, as usual. The slain: Brian Young, 19; Derrick Mcbride, 17; Jamarco Woods, 23; Melvin Morning, 23; Mark Green, 26; Shameka Moore, 16; Antoine Harris, 18; Tony Davis, 20.

I.

Historical the print deluge not once before nor since so huge –
the president preached claimed he cared – emotion trite and tripe none spared

at Central High in Little Rock where justice first was forced and won.

Reporters praised in nonstop talk the proud returning native son –

so sanguine suave a specious bit on stage displayed – adorned bright lit –
sleek mugging presidential tears for racial gains of forty years.

He harkened to the Mayflower – he mentioned Ellis Island too.
To sanction patriotic power he flung around clichés half true.

He lauded then the Little Rock Nine (and rightly so their story told
how brave they crossed the color line thus much deserving glory bold)

but spoke no word at Central's door about reversing flight from poor
though wealth had fled from center town – of monied flight he'd not talk down.

The city splashed fresh paint around to try to make the streets look swell –
a surface fix meant to confound to fool the cameras fool them well.

II.

To see this dog and pony show – the community house would not go –
avoided by its radio crew whose workers shrugged refused the view –

no steadfast earnest union troupe – to delta scattered far and back –
no ACORN no New Party group no sign of four young men dead black –

forgotten buried shunned no shock four young men killed near Central's block
that noble week in Little Rock – those joyous days in Little Rock.

III.

The governor proud proved quite lost explaining what his daughter wrote
on visit to a holocaust memorial – these words of note –

"Why didn't somebody do something?" she simply marked and then again –
"Why didn't somebody do something?" – young poignant words from poignant pen.

The gov'nor declared – "In silence we left and I knew she got it."
Then as if in prayer – calm intense – he offered up this plaintive bit –

"I hope that never does someone have to ask why didn't someone
'do something'." He meant it too. You might wonder if he truly knew

four young folk died – one week alone – a mere few blocks right down the street.
He spoke as if he'd never known – as if some facts he would not meet.

IV.

Reporters none walked down old streets to hear how people wish to live.
So busy hugging loud elites the mainstream news could no one give

to ring a bell or knock a door to sit on porch and learn the score to gather round a kitchen plate a living room and there relate.

Though folks might raise concerns cold blunt – by asking wise reporters could
in lively talk without affront learn far more than they thought they would –

real word collect – of dire import – upfront street tales fresh thought live wit –
true human needs and cares – in short – a worthy text no PR skit.

Of news like this the press won't dare – keen poet Gwendolyn Brooks once found
exactly forty years from where those young folks died near Central's ground.

Disaster there ignored by all – remember this – take time recall –
proud polis papers president – how much we care quite evident.

V.

The press not much the world reveals with cheap words clever false appeals.
Much life that matters now – forget. Most news goes elsewhere – no regret –

or slants twists lies omits distorts – by corporate will – sheer force – directs
slick chatter from sleek ruling courts thus base and gullible infects.

The economic system fails to fill life's gaps – it fills grim jails
as corporate suits work to disguise the coins they steal from dead men's eyes.

Neglect that which small profit gives – elected representatives –
owned by vast wealth – are sternly told. Despair and trouble soon unfold.

VI.

The president preached claimed he cared – emotion trite and tripe none spared
so sanguine suave a specious bit on stage displayed – adorned bright lit –

slick mugging presidential tears for racial pains of forty years
four young men dead – news took a walk while vapid presidential talk

engulfed those gathered all around where media intent were found
to note each smile and mark each frown but made no note of death downtown.

From neighborhoods our eyes we turn – so many killed such slight concern –
forgotten buried shunned no shock – unmentioned by official talk

that noble week in Little Rock. Forgotten buried – wonder why –
four young men killed near Central High that joyous week in Little Rock.

Two Poems
Kim Jensen

Ode to Man

Mankind – selfish past all measure. Mankind's greed knows no limit (and I am part of this.) I did not walk away from Omelas. I knew that people went hungry. I knew that people suffered debilitating diseases. I knew that people were dying of loneliness. And I did so little.

Mankind – worthless in the face of grief. How did we let it come this far?
Mankind – a liar in his bloodstream. And I too, because I made my compromises with you.

You, mankind, preaching a morality of shadows and false righteousness, touching nothing real. Apparitions, your values that see people as little more than machines, no compassion.

Mankind – hypocritical beyond belief. And I too, because I saw my fellow man living in the streets and did only the minimum required
by the codes of civility.

[untitled]

at the end
of the war

noise
of coins

jingling

Film can reverse but not time
Marge Piercy

If we could run it all backward
the blood back into the wound
leg reattached, eye knit to socket
the fiery pain back into the bomb;

if we could reverse the deadly
stupid careen down the slope
of history, spewing lives, torture,
billions of debt to thwart

our great grandchildren, if
we could stuff the evil genie
of oil back into the earth
and walk away, would we

do it all again? I cannot
be sanguine because I
remember the last time. It's
never the same but close

enough. We thought we were
blue-eyed cavalry charging over
the hill into the Indian encamp-
ment with gatling guns. Even

after Korea and Vietnam, we still
thought war was a football game
we could win in the last quarter
as we render ourselves obsolete.

What I Tell the Young When They Ask
Margaret Randall

Resist
fictitious argument
luring or barking at your door
Don't ask your doctor
if seduction is right for you
only his wallet knows for sure.

Resist
turning away
from that which gleams in the sun
covers itself with unfamiliar cloth
or pronounces words
you do not understand.

Resist
don't ask don't tell
because it requires a dance of deception
steps on your toes
grinds them into a bed
of broken glass.

Resist
smoke and fire
water coveted in plastic bottles
a planet
too warm for life
too bleak for skin.

Resist
de-sexed corn, ancient grain
forced beneath the knife
regeneration taken by force
a trail of paper bullets
murdering surely as those of steel.

Resist
those who make
better bullets and bombs
clusters of pain
designed to kill
when hunger takes too long.

Resist
uniform or priestly collar
disguised on a scale of one to ten
books and tablets telling you

what will save you
from yourself.

Resist
my country right or wrong
men promising sound bites
answering only what they want you to know
then riding their rigged smiles
into a house of purest white.

Resist
the one on top
pitting his god his catchy phrase
a tune that taunts your face
spits in your eye
erasing the life-giving stories.

Resist
losing the ones
who know your name
call you from sleep
filling your mouth with music
when you wake.

Resist
rules created for you alone
and all your sisters and brothers
born and unborn
for they threaten
morning's fragile light.

Resist
disappearing into little boxes
of perfect safety
where risk is nowhere
greed is the prize
success thickens in your veins.

Resist
erasure of all our histories
for the sake of your
one and only life.
Listen to the small sounds.
Open your eyes.

— from Their Backs to the Sea, Fall
2009, Wings Press, San Antonio, Texas

Dozers
Andrew Rihn

Remember that scene in The Grapes of Wrath
when the bulldozer, riding the horizon like a marauder,
like the klansmen in Birth of a Nation,
looms over the sharecropper's house?

Sharecroppers, like my great great grandfather
120 years ago in the Ohio valley,
lived a hard life, not having much
beyond the dirt under their feet,
the togetherness of family,
and hunger like a wolf at their door.

The tools they had were for shaping
crops into rows, to ply the corn or the wheat
into something more than the sum of their parts.
Spring's gamble, plus a little nurturing,
meant crops you could bank on the rest of the year.

But then, facing off against bulldozers
originally designed as tractors,
the farmers are overtaken,
run off by profits of the corporation
as much as by the blade of the bulldozer.

These dozers, ever the social Darwinists,
claiming their steel is stronger than flesh,
grow larger, heavier, more powerful by the year.

Look at the Caterpillar D9; weighing 53 tons,
armored to withstand the sweep of a minefield,
loaded with grenade launchers and machine guns
and sent to till through Palestinian neighborhoods,
to crush the rows of silent olive trees –
farms and families overtaken like my ancestors
or yours.

Emergency Clinic
Adrienne Rich

Caustic implacable
poem   unto and contra:

I do not soothe minor
injuries   I do
not offer   I require
                  close history
of the case   apprentice-
ship in past and fresh catastrophe

The skin too quickly scabbed
mutters for my debriding

For every bandaged wound
I'll scrape another open

I won't smile
                while wiping
your tears
             I do not give
simplehearted love and nor
allow you simply love me

if you accept regardless
this will be different

Iodine-dark
poem walking to and fro all night

un-gainly
unreconciled

unto and contra

First published at Monthly Review (2008)

In kindergarten I wore bright yellow socks
Buff Whitman-Bradley

*– for child victims of war,
oppression, and injustice*

In kindergarten I wore bright yellow socks
as soft as dandelions
and smelling of pineapples
Over my bright yellow socks I wore
bright green parrot-shaped slippers
that could actually talk
In kindergarten I had long conversations
with my feet
In kindergarten isopods lived in my pockets
among the crumpled-up recipes I kept
for Henry David Thoreau
In kindergarten, except for my feet, my
whole body
smelled like sweet, wild onions
In kindergarten sourgrass grew everywhere
and we whistled through our teeth
In kindergarten I was a famous poet
In kindergarten I was Pablo Neruda
who wrote an ode to his beautiful socks
knitted for him by Maru Mori
socks that were so lovely
they made him rethink his feet
In kindergarten I did not rethink my feet
but in kindergarten my feet reconsidered me

I was the Captain of Kindergarten
I was the Captain of Love in kindergarten
and I was the King of Rock and Roll
I was the Elvis Presley of kindergarten
In kindergarten I wore blue suede shoes
over my parrot slippers
over my pineapple-scented socks
over my reconsidering feet
and went out in that kitchen
and I rattled those pots and pans
I was the Julia Child of kindergarten
In kindergarten we played with our food
In kindergarten we made soufflés that

reached the ceiling
and pineapple upside down cake
for Henry David Thoreau

One day in kindergarten we were looking at
a book trying to find a little boy in a red-and-
white-striped shirt lost on a page with hundreds of other little boys and girls when
Henry David Thoreau appeared at the door
and said, "Where's Waldo?" and we said,
"Exactly!" and "Would you like some pineapple upsidedown cake?"

"Can I have the recipe?" asked Henry David
Thoreau with crumbs of pineapple upside-
down cake spilling out of his mouth and
children climbing up and down and all
around him as if he were some kind of nineteenth-century New England anarchistic tax-
resisting, bean-growing jungle gym. "This
class is out of control!" hollered the visiting
bureaucrat. "In wildness is the preservation
of the world!" Henry David Thoreau retorted, showing the bureaucrat the door, taking the door off its hinges and hurling it into
the void, out of which drove Frida Kahlo in a
Buick resembling Diego Rivera. Trotsky was
in the back seat with W.E.B. DuBois.

And not long after that, a philosopher who
looked like Gary Cooper appeared at the hole
that used to have the door in it and said,
"What are you doing in there, Henry?" and
Henry David Thoreau cried, "Waldo! What
are you doing out there?" "There's Waldo!"
we all shouted. "Would you like some pineapple upsidedown cake?" "How about a
cappuccino?" said Ralph Waldo Emerson,"
and one for my friend Mistress Bailey."
"Make it a double, Honey," crooned Pearl,
skating into the room on razzle-dazzle roller
blades.

We colored our fingernails and smelled all
the books
and W.E.B. smeared fingerpaint on the walls
and Frida drew a moustache on Henry David
Thoreau

who was building with Lincoln Logs and
who said to me,
"What's it like now, out there?"
and I answered sotto voce
so the children wouldn't hear
"It's the same goddamn thing all over again,
Henry
It's the Mexican War all over again
It's the rich beating up the poor
and the powerful beating up the powerless
all over again
It's the slaughter of the innocents all over
again
It's massacres from the sky
It's exploding children
It's houses demolished with people inside
It's corpses rotting in the streets . . ."

And Diego and DuBois rose up in outrage
and Pearl and Trotsky held each other while
they sang "Sometimes I feel like a motherless
child" and Henry David Thoreau kicked over
his Lincoln Log house and groaned . . .

. . . but then he did something wonderful
He took off his L.L. Beans
revealing his bright yellow socks
as soft as dandelions
and smelling of pineapples
and the rest of us took off our tennies and
our sandals
our blue suede shoes
and our parrot slippers
and Waldo took off his neon sneakers
and Trotsky took off his huaraches
and Frida took off her stained-glass slippers
and Diego took off his snake-skin boots
and DuBois took off his brogans
 and Pearl took off her razzle-dazzle skates
then Henry David Thoreau took out his Different Drum
and began slapping out some sweet Afro-
Cuban rhythms
and we all lined up behind him
and conga'd in our stocking feet
out the hole that used to have a door in it
Even though our mothers had always told us
"Don't go outside without your shoes on
you'll ruin your socks"

we went outside without our shoes on
and we ruined our socks
We conga'd in dirt and mud and gravel
We conga'd in the shrubbery and up and
down the streets
We conga'd without our shoes on
and got our socks filthy
and ripped our socks
and tore holes in our socks
and ruined our socks just like our mothers
said we would
"Don't worry!" shouted Pablo Neruda
"We will knit you new ones!"
And that's what he and Maru Mori did

They knit us bright yellow socks as soft as
dandelions
and smelling of pineapples
and we put them on and they could not be
ruined

We conga'd in parking lots in our yellow
socks
to Henry's drum
We conga'd on lawns and driveways
to Henry's drum
We conga'd up and down the aisles of supermarkets
to Henry's drum
We conga'd in bowling alleys and pizza par-
lors
to Henry's drum
We conga'd all around the mulberry bush
to Henry's drum
Then children with ruined socks started
showing up
from all over the place
Children from slums and ghettos
Children from refugee camps
Children from hospitals
They came exhausted and terrified and hungry and dirty
Children with great gaping holes in their
bodies came
Children with mangled and missing limbs
came
Blind children and deaf children came
Children with no mothers or fathers left
to warn them about ruining their socks came

Children struggled out of rubble
and rose up out of graves to come

So we washed them and gave them food
while Pablo's and Maru's knitting needles
flashed in the sunlight
and we held their feet in our hands
and so carefully, so carefully
we removed their ruined socks
and onto those feet
those small, tormented feet
we pulled Pablo Neruda's and Maru Mori's
indestructible, un-ruinable socks
bright yellow, as soft as dandelions
and smelling of pineapples

DeSoto Bend
Buff Whitman-Bradley

Not far from Blair, Nebraska,
and the Loess Hills of Iowa
there is an oxbow lake –
an old bend in the Missouri River
where great flocks of snow geese stop to rest
and feed
on their winter journey south.
I am here on a November morning
to walk in the woods at the water's edge.

I've come back to Nebraska to be with my
mother
for her first cancer treatment.
Her chemotherapy begins tomorrow.
Today I am taking this time to be alone
among the bare, quiet trees
that separate the lake from the wide, flat, fertile fields
of the flood plain.

The sky is close and colorless
and except for a few patches of white here
and there
left over from a recent snow
everything else is brown –
the turned-over earth and stubble in the
fields,
the leafless trees,
the brittle grasses and undergrowth.

The air is bitterly cold
And I have to walk fast to keep warm.
Every breath I take hurts my lungs.
Through the stillness that flowers
in between inhaling and exhaling
I drop deep into my body
where every one of my cells is a pond
with wild geese floating on the bright surface
of the water.

Nothing moves.
Then all the geese take off at once,
their tremendous wings beating furiously

as if they were fighting with the air.
A kind of fierce elation fills me
and my spirit rises with my steaming breath
up through the naked branches.

Without knowing why, exultant and outraged,
I begin shouting at God:

> What about the hollow-eyed homeless
> shivering on sidewalks and sleeping in
> cardboard boxes?
> What about disposable children sleepless
> from hunger and fear?
> What about bodies shattered and shred-
> ded by war?
> What about the jailed and the tortured,
> the disappeared and the executed?
> What about the abandoned, the abused,
> the haunted, the hunted?
> What about broken promises and broken
> hearts?
> What about the forgotten, dying of lone-
> liness?
> What about the grasping, the grabbing,
> the fat-fingered greedy?
> What about the slaughter of species, the
> mauling of Earth?
> God of the helpless and the hopeless,
> God of the weak and the needy,
> God of the bent and broken,
> God of the spare, of the plain, of the or-
> dinary,
> of the small and insignificant,
> God of creeks and muddy lakes and
> skinny trees,
> God of beetles and lichen and seeds,
> God of dirt under my feet,
> Let springtime arrive,
> Let justice sprout from the earth and
> cover the land like new grass,
> Let justice rattle the windows and soak
> the ground
> like a storm in April,
> Let justice perfume the air like apple
> blossoms,
> Let justice leaf the trees,
> Let justice write its name across the sky
> in the shifting patterns of migrating birds

flying north to their summer homes.

Out of breath now, I stand on the shore of the
lake.
A great blue heron passes by overhead
riding the icy air.
Small groups of ducks bob up and down on
the choppy water,
but I see no geese.
I think for a moment about gathering sticks
and fallen branches
and building a fire I could keep going all day
to warm me while I waited for the geese to
come
and the light to go.
But I have been away long enough
and my mother is waiting for me back in her
apartment.
I break off a piece of dead branch
and throw it spinning out across the water.
Then I turn from the lake
and walk the narrow, frozen path
through the woods and back to my car.

We're gonna shoot those looters on sight

Buff Whitman-Bradley

"These troops are battle-tested. They have
M16s and are locked and loaded. These
troops know how to shoot and kill and I expect they will."

> – Kathleen Blanco,
> governor of Louisiana,
> in the aftermath
> of Hurricane Katrina

Maybe 1,000 dead, somebody says, and more
dying
from lack of food
from lack of water
from lack of sanitation
from lack of medicine and medical care

We're gonna shoot those looters on sight

We're not gonna shoot the good, upstanding
white folks
who are "finding" food and supplies in
abandoned Seven-Elevens
But we're gonna shoot those looters on sight
You know who they are
We know who they are

We're gonna shoot those looters on sight

Tell them the cops are coming
Tell them the National Guard is coming
These goddamn looters are no better
than terrorists in Iraq and Afghanistan
The RoboCops and the RoboTroops are
geared up, combat ready,
packing lots of heat,
heavy with ammo belts
They have their orders:

Shoot those looters on sight.

Looters' bodies floating face down in the wa-
ter
Looters' corpses rotting in ditches
Looters' babies crying from hunger
Looters' sons and daughters missing
maybe dead
Looters' grandparents dying in front of them
Looters desperate
Looters terrified
Looters angry

We're gonna shoot those looters on sight

They're irresponsible
They're lazy
They're stupid
They're vicious
And they're dangerous
They should have left before the levees broke
like the folks who live in the good houses,
like the folks who live in the clean neighbor-
hoods,
like the guests in the fine hotels
We can't save them from themselves
But we can shoot them on sight

We're not gonna shoot the government officials
who gave away the buffering wetlands
or the developers who dried them up
We're not gonna shoot the heads of Homeland Security
and the Federal Emergency Management
Agency
who claim to protect us from terrorists
but have no evacuation plans in place for the
poor
because the poor are not us
they're the looters
We're not gonna shoot the President of the
United States
who slashed the budget for repairing the levees
and played golf at a San Diego country club
while looters had to piss and shit in the
streets
and who promised a Looziana political crony

"We're gonna build him a new house
better than the old one."
We're not gonna shoot the heads of corporations
feasting off disaster –
the CEOs of oil companies
jacking up the prices and gouging at the
pump
the CEOs of construction companies in their
gleaming wet-bar jet planes
circling like TurboTechnoBuzzards
over the drowned, ruined body of the city
the CEOs of sham charities and relief organizations
that skim millions off the top
We're not gonna shoot the reporters and editors
who serve up endless stories and images
about "chaos in the streets"
and the looting of convenience stores and
donut shops
but overlook the theft of the commons and
the public treasury
by corporate boards and the Senators they
keep in their desk drawers
Those aren't the ones who endanger The
American Way of Life
It's the looters

And we're gonna shoot those looters on
sight.

Who says they bungled it?
Buff Whitman-Bradley

*(In answer to those who said that the Federal
Emergency Management Administration "bungled" its response to Hurricane Katrina)*

Who says they bungled it?

Who says the government wanted to protect
its citizens?
Who says the government ever intended to
save the poor of New Orleans
who couldn't get out?
Who says not repairing the levees
was a mistake?
Who says waiting 5 days before sending in
"help"
was bad judgment?

Who says they bungled it?

What kind of "help" did they send?
Edgy troops just back from Iraq.
Blackwater assassins deputized to kill.
Shock Troops and Tac Squads to enforce
evacuation orders,
to drag people out of their homes,
to bag up the bloated dead,
to keep the press away,
to keep America from getting the real story
about the war that the rich
continually wage against the poor.

Who says they bungled it?

Who says they didn't anticipate the chaos,
didn't want a "war game" they could play
with real storm troopers,
with real bullets?
Who says they didn't want to impose martial
law
and "secure" an American city?
Who says they don't have plans
to do it over

and over and over again?
 Who says they bungled it?

Who says they didn't know
that TV and the press would hyperventilate
about looters
and refuse to tell the stories about
spontaneous communities of mutual support
and assistance
springing up in refugee camps
and on highway medians
and in half-drowned neighborhoods
in the poorest parts of town?
Who says they didn't know
that unsubstantiated stories
of murders and the rape of children
by gangbangers and junkies deprived of a fix
(you know who we mean)
would be accepted as fact?

Who says they bungled it?

Who says they couldn't guess
that Americans would give hundreds of
millions
for hurricane relief and be tempted to delude

ourselves with stories of our own generosity
into believing that there is no class war
raging in America
no systemic racism lacerating our souls
and that everything is fine after all?
Who says they didn't lick their chops
at billions in rebuilding money
to be doled out to each other's outlaw
corporations
that have always made their profits
by looting public funds
and savaging the poor?

Who says they bungled it?

Who says they do not pray to a savage God –
the God of Power and Privilege
the God of Obscene Opulence
the God of Insatiable Greed
the God of a Thousand Teeth
Devourer of Children, Shredder of Flesh
the God of Annihilation
the God of Death-in-Life?
And who says that that God
does not answer their prayers?

A Cycle
Mickey Z.

White cop
from the suburbs
busts
black men
from the city
prison population surges
black men inside
invent new slang
new styles
gangs inside and out
adopt it all
designers
co-opt it all
white son
of white cop
in the suburbs
ends up talking
and dressing
and play-acting
like the black men
his father
sends away

Voice Of Struggle
Poems From Prison In Kenya

Mwandawiro Mghanga

Mwandawiro Mghanga

INTRODUCTION

Between February 1985 and September 1989 I was a political prisoner in my country Kenya. I was imprisoned for participating in the struggle against dictatorship, corruption and bad governance. As a student representative, I was in the front line of the students' struggle for academic freedom, democracy and national liberation. Outside the university, I was part of the movement of Kenyan patriots of the struggle against the regime that was opposed the progress of my motherland. I was part of those who was against the culture of fear and silence, I collaborated with fellow citizens who are fighting for the respect and exercise of human rights. I was working together with those struggling against exploitation and oppression of person to person.

Because of this, the government of Moi-Kanu defined me as an enemy. For under the rule of dictators and traitors, fighting for democracy and national freedom, opposing imperialism, is breaking the law!

That is why in February 1985, following the directive of the government, several students, among them Karemi Nduthu, Philip Tirop and I were expelled from the university. But we refused to respect this arbitrary and oppressive order. We refused to leave the university voluntarily. We decided to openly rebel against the dictatorship. In solidarity, our fellow students decided to boycott studies and demonstrate against the government's illegal decision to expel us.

Thus I found myself at the forefront of the bitter struggle of the students against dictatorship. This struggle took one week. In the end armed police invaded the campus. There then followed a big war between the students and the police. One student was killed and hundreds of others, including me, were wounded. I was arrested, tortured, brought to court and imprisoned for one year and fined 5,000 shillings or two months imprisonment. That is how I joined David Onyango Oloo, Maina wa Kinyatti, Omondi Kabir, Oginga Ogego, Geff Mwangi and hundreds of students and soldiers who were political prisoners at Kamiti Maximum Security Prison.

I was released in December 9, 1985. The fascism I witnessed at the police cells and in prison, only helped to assure me that the stand I had taken of being part and parcel of the struggle of the Kenyan patriots was just and moral. I was therefore ready to continue where I had left as soon as I was released. I refused completely to allow myself to be broken by prison.

After only three months, on February 1986, the police invaded my home at Werugha, Taita, and arrested me. They made a thorough search of trying to find evidence connecting me with Mwakenya, an underground movement. They were unable to find such evidence. But, of course, this could not prevent them from arresting me together with my two younger brothers, Ferdinand Kamata and Jazrael Ndawiro. My brothers were imprisoned at Wundanyi and Voi police stations where they were tortured and later charged with the offence of obstructing the police from performing their duty. Ndawiro was also expelled from Egerton College, Njoro, where he was a student

As for me, I was taken to Nyayo House to join other patriots who were being tortured there. After one month of the torture I was taken to the kangaroo court at the High Court in Nairobi and imprisoned for five years following a trial which took less than ten minutes and in spite of pleading not guilty! In this way, I found myself back at Kamiti Maximum Prison!

In January 1987, I was transferred from Kamiti to Eldoret Prison. In November the same year, after going on a protracted hunger strike in protest against the poor diet and the extra harsh treatment imposed against us by the officer in charge of the prison, Mugo Theuri, Gichuki Karanja and I were transferred to Kibos Prison in Kisumu. Then in April 1989, while on the verge of dying of malaria after being denied medical treatment, I was transferred back to Kamiti Maximum Prison. But this was thanks to the campaign of Amnesty International and the struggle of my dear wife and that of human rights activists in Kenya and the world.

I repeat, in prison, I witnessed the fascism of the Moi/Kanu regime with my own eyes. Kenyan prisons are not corrective institutions. They do not rehabilitate criminals, they do not educate them to become better citizens than they were before they were imprisoned. The prisons are for torturing and killing the *wananchi* who find themselves there. Some of what I witnessed and experienced there appear in my poems published here. But I can hardly find words to describe the violation of human rights going on inside prisons. It is brutality above brutality!

Being a political prisoner who had refused to be tamed by prison, who always struggled against being rehabilitated by the oppressors, I was kept in solitary confinement. I was locked in cell twenty three hours a day without anything to read except the bible. Again, many a times I was denied even the bible!

But I refused to break, I refused to lose hope. I used all means possible until I was able to establish contacts and to make friendship and even comradeship with many fellow prisoners. I started political discussions with them. Since I could not be able to meet my comrades face to face, I participated in our discussions through writing. We devised ways of smuggling in writing material. We used any kind of paper, pen or pencil available. Many a times we used toilet paper which, incidentally, was hardly available to prisoners.

We hid the writings from the prison warders and found ways and means of smuggling them out of prison. Often I used a friendly *askari* to get papers and pens and also to smuggle the writings to my wife. At other times we bribed our way out.

To write, especially about anything which can be interpreted to be political, or that exposes the brutality going on in prison, is considered to be a big crime. That is why prison warders were instructed to spy on me day and night to ensure that I do not write. Often I was suddenly invaded in the cell and my pens and papers were taken away from me. Whatever I had written was confiscated. I was beaten, tortured and had my prison term extended for writing! Nearly all what I had written at Eldoret prison was confiscated by the officer in charge one afternoon. From reliable sources, I learnt that they were taken to the prison headquarters in Nairobi. Really, I have no words that can express the agony I felt whenever the literature I had created in such hard condition was taken away from me, especially knowing that it was going to be thrown away as though it were nothing! I discovered that whenever I attempted to rewrite a poem I had lost I ended up writing a new one similar to the original one.

But be it as it were, the poems in this anthology testify to the fact that in the final analysis victory was ours. It is evidence that the maximum security of Kenya's prisons has completely failed to prevent the growth of prison literature of struggle. Prison literature of struggle is the literature which has always been produced from prison since the time of classical colonialism. Mostly it is the literature which was written and is written by political prisoners and which is a manifestation of the resistance against the culture of fear and silence.

The poems expose the fascism going on inside Kenyan prisons. At the same time they ridicule the maximum and cruel security which is used to intimidate, threaten and torture patriots and poor citizens in prison. It is a reminder that what is happening in prison is a reflection of what is happening in the country in general. For under dictatorship and neo-colonialism, Kenya is like a big prison.

All the poems were written in Kiswahili. Apart from "Would you believe it?" and "I would rather be a rebel", which were translated by my brother Gachuku Makini, all the others were translated by myself.

Finally, the reactionary Kanu regime can delay our freedom but it can not prevent it forever. They may imprison or even kill us but they will never imprison or kill our struggle for liberation.

15 July 2009

these words

these words
the few words
which I struggle
day and night
to write
one day
they may be part of literature
prison literature
the literature of struggle
for social and national liberation
yes, whenever I write
I record history
that is why
they use
all their means
to stop me writing
but
I write
I do not stop to write
I write I write I write

Kibos Main Prison 16-4-1988

Pen

Where we are
In the deep pit
Of brutality against human beings
Brutality that is beyond words
In the graveyard
Where the devils who rule our country
Try day and night
To squeeze out our humanity
In prison in Kenya
Pen and paper
If you are lucky to get them
You will have got reliable friends
You will have achieved the soap of your soul
You will have grabbed the shield of helping
to defend you
From the agony and loneliness of this hell of
a place
If you happen to posses a pen and a paper
Perhaps you posses a weapon
Of fighting
Against a myriad of problems in prison
Pen and paper
Often are medicine
Of protecting you
From killer diseases
Which are part and parcel
Of life in prison
In our country today

Kamiti Maximum Prison 11-01-1987

I Will Write

I will write
Whatever come may
I will write
I will not stop to write I write
I will use all means possible to write
Only that I must be lucky enough
To acquire a pen, any pen at all
And a piece of paper, any paper
Even toilet paper!
I will write to release the emotions inside me
I will write about my experiences here
Perhaps, just perhaps
Perhaps some of the words I write
Will manage to get out of these brutal walls
They will hide from their eyes
They will survive their *tero*
They will even penetrate their doors
May be few of what I write
Will somehow wriggle between their legs
And travel among them
Jump over their maximum security walls
Or fly to my wife
Where they will live to ridicule them
Them who observe us day and night
To prevent us writing
Those who boast
That their tight security has silenced us
These dogs of the dictatorship
These words
Will shame them
One day
Perhaps!

Kibos Main Prison   6-6-1988

Transfer

When they come at Kamiti to see me
You will explain to them
You will tell them I am no longer at Kamiti
Prison
They have transferred me 800 kilometres
Away from Werugha, where I was born
They have taken me to Eldoret
Not at Eldoret town, not on a tour
They have taken me to prison
To bury me in the pit of torture
When my wife comes to see me
Try to inform her

But also tell them not to worry
Being transferred doesn't trouble me that
much
Let them understand
Because at no time did I request
To be imprisoned, to be imprisoned in any
prison
For prison is prison, wherever it is it is
prison
Hunger, boredom, brutality and torture
without end
So, will the oppression inside Eldoret Prison
Be more than that here at Kamiti Maximum?
Sooner or later I will find out...........!

Furthermore, surely dear comrades
Their separating us will not separate us
We shall be together
Everytime and everywhere at all times
The agony with us my comrades
Will paste us together always
True, they will never succeed
To separate us ideologically
We have decided to be friends
To be comrades in the revolution
How can they ever divide us?
Our comradeship
Has been born by the great work and re-
sponsibility
Given to us by history
It is held by the glue of all that

322

We have experienced and are experiencing
together
Let us love one another for ever........!!!!!

Comrades, when they come to visit us
Tell them, wherever they will imprison me
One day I will be released
I will be released I will be released
Because whichever has a beginning also has
an end
One day we shall come out of here
To reunite with comrades and patriots of our
country
Not in the life of laziness and self-indulgence
But in the great and noble work
The work of searching for the freedom and
liberation of Kenya
The work of struggling
Struggling against exploitation of person by
person
For now keep on remembering
And to them also explain that they may
know
While in Eldoret Prison
Or wherever they may take me
Come rain come shine, whatever come may
I will not change my mind, I shall never be-
tray the struggle
I will continue fighting for my humanity
I will continue with the revolutionary
stand.........

A time like this
When hundreds of patriots
Involved in the liberation struggle
Are in detention or prison or exile
We cannot indulge in self-pity inside here
We cannot just think of only our agony
We cannot accept to give up hope
We must struggle at all times
The medicine of life in prison is struggle
That which is more moral and humane is
struggle......

Those who are more humane
Have chosen the road of struggle
And we also have opted not to be left behind
For our love is also the love for our country
It is true and just love

It is love for freedom and democracy
The love for struggling for a new socialist
society
If we remain true to what we have resolved
together
If we make revolution to be our life at all
times
Our friendship will last, it will last forever
The sadness of bidding farewell to one an-
other now
Manifests the extent of our relationship
It shows the level of our comradeship
How we value love!
And since we value love
We shall give our lives to ensure
That tomorrow
Those who love one another
Will not experience the pain we are experi-
encing today
The pain of friends being separated by
prison

Kamiti Maximum Prison 13-1-1987

Struggle My Heart Struggle

My heart my heart
beware of fear
refrain from the temptations of anxiety
stop worrying and being afraid
relax my heart, have peace please do
don't open to those brutal thoughts
that are knocking to torture and break you.

Now...my dear heart...now.....
stand firm, completely firm stand
do stand straight while remembering all the
time:
fear
anxiety
cowardice
and the heart of accepting defeat
allowing to be broken both physically
and psychologically
hopelessness
all are big enemies in this place
they are powerful fiends of revolution, don't
forget.

Oh my heart
my soul my love my friend in deed
the torture you are undergoing is not small
the agony no joke
true, the cross you are carrying is not light
I know it is heavy, very heavy
but isn't it you yourself
who said you are ready to sacrifice for the
cause?
is not this part of the sacrifice?

You claim that you are a revolutionary
do you think revolution
is dancing *gonda* or *kishawi*?

You have repeated, many times
that you are prepared for anything
for the liberation of the exploited and oppressed
then, this night, why are you crying?

why are you indulging in self-pity?
why are you wandering in the path of giving
up hope?
why my heart why?

Oh my beloved heart
all this you are experiencing
all this you are seeing here my dear
many others have seen
there is nothing new you are witnessing,
don't cheat yourself
all this you are about to call suffering
many others have suffered and are suffering;
so stop being selfish my heart
you are not the only one, you are not the
only one
do not allow yourself to think you are the
only one!

Remember also, please do not forget
that all this won't end today
this prison torture will live
it will endure to torture the poor and the oppressed
it will stay to torment the wretched of the
earth
and those like you who struggle for change;
as long as there is dictatorship and neo-
colonialism
as long as capitalism and imperialism remains
as long as these inhuman systems continue
to exist my dear
all this torture won't end in our country and
world.

Be firm my heart, stand firm
fight to remain strong always
don't welcome those signs of fear and anxiety
after all you are not yet dead
you are still breathing, oh yes you are still
alive!

And the struggle needs you, alive
struggle my dear heart struggle
struggle struggle struggle struggle
struggle and hope

are the only medicine
in prison
hope struggle hope struggle hope struggle
always hope struggle......

Kibos Main Prison   7/3/1988

Pain

Today
I
Witnessed
A fellow prisoner
Being beaten by the warders
These barbarians
Of Kenya's prisons
Uniting against him
They beat him like a donkey
They beat him until he vomited blood
They pounded him until he urinated on him-
self
They kept on working on him
Until he shitted on himself
They continued
To beat him
While mocking and abusing him
They beat him and beat him and beat him
Before my very eyes and ears !
Ah....what pain!
I felt a lot of pain
Very very great pain in deed
So much pain
That I cannot find words to describe
Pain greater
Than that of my fellow in mate
Who was
The direct victim
Of this brutality
Which is part and parcel
Of the culture
Of prisons
In independent Kenya!
I felt so much pain
That all this cruelty
Is being done by human beings
Against a fellow human being
And
In front of me
While
I
Could do nothing about it
Apart from
Only condemning!

Kibos Main Prison   16-9-1988

Bread and Tea

Today
I have tasted
A piece of bread
And a cup of tea without milk!
Yes, today
I have eaten a piece of bread of wheat
And one cup of tea without milk
To celebrate
Twenty five years of uhuru!
Oh how nice the bread is!
The tea smells so good!
To say the truth
Since I was imprisoned
I have forgotten the taste of sugar
I can not remember
How tea or coffee smells and tastes!
That is why
I will never forget so and so
A humane prison warder
Who has risked losing his job
And being imprisoned
So that even I
A prisoner
Can celebrate
25 years of Kenya's independence!
I will never forget so and so
I will never forget him
I will always
Remember the friendly and considerate
warder
So and so I will remember for ever
He who today
Has enabled I
A political prisoner
In solitary confinement
At Mixed Block
To celebrate 25 years
Of my own country's freedom
With a piece of bread of wheat
And one cup of tea without milk
Things which are like gold in prison
Things regarded as nuclear weapons here
Things which are prohibited
For prisoners

In Kenya's prisons!
Yes, it is a great crime
For prisoners in Kenya
To eat bread or drink tea
Or anything but water
Twenty five years
Since uhuru!
So, is it surprising
That twenty five years later
We
Are
Still
Struggling
For uhuru, for freedom?
Is it strange therefore
That I
Am a political prisoner
Now
At Kibos Main Prison?

Kibos Main Prison   14-10-1988

Next time mother....!

Mother, ai! my dear mother
This is not something somebody narrated to you
Neither is this a tale I am telling you
You witnessed you yourself with your own eyes
You saw everything mother you saw all, yourself
You saw when and how they brought me home
And the handcuffs they had handcuffed me with you saw
You saw how my face was swollen
And how blood was trickling from my nose and mouth
You were there when they were beating me
With slaps and blows and *rungus*
While they were abusing me ceaselessly
Your own eyes did witnessed all that was happening
And your ears heard everything
Your senses felt unimaginable pain anger and bitterness
And even when my daughter was condemning them
While crying very much
You were there mother suffering, suffering very much
You saw how they were mocking her
And threatening her with their guns
You saw all mother, there is nothing that you did not see
You also saw my dear brothers standing against them
With dignified pride and anger
Condemning their brutality
Protesting against their barbarism
Mother you witnessed your beloved sons
Struggling against them
In words and deeds
Fighting for the respect of you and me
And the dignity of all the oppressed people
You saw them jumping at my brothers

Attacking and uniting against them venomously
With blows *rungus* and slaps
Handcuffing them with iron handcuffs
As though my brothers were robbers and murderers
While you their mother who knows the pain of childbirth
Were seeing with your two eyes
Mother, although I remember, oh mother I do
That your face was covered with tears
And all the time you were praying your God
You witnessed all the same
For you could not prevent yourself witnessing
You witnessed their fascism you witnessed it
You witnessed those thugs
Breaking the main door of your house
And when you protested, when you said no
When you raised you voice to condemn their terrorism
You were forced to hear all sorts of dirty words
In front of us your children
They smeared you with all kinds profane nouns and adjectives
Their primitive minds could imagine
You saw them entering your house chests forwards
Turning your house into theirs
Entering every room as they wished
While arrogantly opening suitcases carelessly
Unmaking the beds throwing bedding here and there
Tearing mattresses and pillow-cases
They scattered everything in the rooms
Even your inner wears, your underwears mother
They held your secrets while laughing mockingly
In front of us your own ones mother
Whom you gave birth to and suckled!
You witnessed them raving like mad people
In order to display their barbarism
Spoiling breaking throwing abusing
Scornfully boasting and showing off

They spouted non-sense
About the power of the nyayo government
About how the police are too powerful to
joke with
About how nothing will change in Kenya
While at the same time, without asking for
permission
They were grabbing
Books
Magazines and newspapers
Letters
Every piece of writing they could see
Photo-albums
Removing and taking wall pictures
Robbing us of our money openly
Filling our empty suitcases and carrying
them away
Whatever they wanted they plundered
mother
We were robbed of all rights inside our own
house
As if we were not Kenyan citizens
As though we were not human beings
mother
Here where I am now I can still see your
tears
Tears of agony and anger streaming from
your eyes
Anger and agony that could be read on your
face
Especially when they were beating and car-
rying us
And throwing us on their Land-Rovers like
logs of wood
With cruel handcuffs tying our hands to-
gether
While covered with blood all over our bodies
Being abused and mocked and called all
manner of dirt
All this oppression of the police of the re-
gime
You witnessed yourself, at your own home
You witnessed how those oppressors
Threatened to shot dead hundreds of good
citizens
Who had assembled outside our home
To witness and condemn
The humiliation

The injustice
The brutality
The barbarism
The fascism
You and your sons were undergoing
All this and many others you remember
mother
How my younger brothers
Were locked up in the cells at Wundanyi and
Voi
And all the torture they underwent there
You know, you know very well
You even remember how Kamata
Almost died of asthma and torture in the cell
You have not forgotten, I know, that that day
We were preparing for my wedding three
days later
And my beloved wife had been admitted at
Wesu Hospital
While my youngest brother Ndawiro
Had on the same day just arrived
From Egerton College Njoro Nakuru
Only to find policemen waiting for me at the
door
We did not even get the chance to greet one
another
You have not forgotten my mother you still
remember
And at the cells of Wundanyi and Voi
mother
Your sons experienced a lot, a lot
Kamata and Ndawiro
Saw the nakedness of Kanu's police at police
stations
They tortured them
The police tortured my younger brothers
very much
And when they completed their brutality
against them
They took them to their courts
And you mother remember everything
For you followed your sons to court
You heard them being charged
With the offence of preventing the police
from doing their duty
The duty of abusing and beating and op-
pressing citizens

The duty of breaking and plundering peo-
ple's homes
The duty of terrorism and barbarism
The duty of implementing dictatorial laws
The duty of violating human rights
Your children were brought before Voi's
magistrate of dictatorship
Accused of a great offence
In the eyes of the government of traitors
The offence of defending their humanity and
patriotism
The offence of refusing to be turned into
tamed animals
The offence of the courage
Of standing with their brother and justice
The offence of shouting against fascism
Apart from that, as though it were not
enough mother
Ndawiro, Ndawiro Mghanga
A good student in all ways
Was expelled from the university
Without him committing any offence
They expelled him from Egerton
They expelled Ndawiro they expelled him
Without him breaking any law
They interrupted your son's education!
For the offence
Of being born by you
For the crime
Of coming from the same stomach I came
from
For refusing to sit and cheer the police
When they were doing their sinful work at
our home
They robbed him of his right
To study in his own country of birth!
They were determined to finish us com-
pletely mother!
Mother mother mother........ oh my dear
mother
Me they took to Voi Police Station
Then the same night they transported me to
Mariakani
Where I was locked in a cell
I was put in a barred cage
As though I were an incorrigible murderer
I was handled as if I were a terrorist mother!
The following day they carried me to Nairobi

Where I was locked at Kileleshwa Police Sta-
tion
Soon afterwards, very very early in the
morning
They blindfolded me
And kidnapped me into Nyayo House
Nyayo House my beloved mother Nyayo
House
Your son I was dragged into Nyayo House!
Nyayo House located at Nairobi city centre
Nyayo House where the offices of Nairobi's
PC are located
Nyayo House the imagery of the brutality of
the regime
Nyayo House the hell of political prisoners
Nyayo House the fort of the fascism of the
Special Branch
Nyayo House the arrogance of the Gestapos
of Kanu
Nyayo House I tell you mother Nyayo
House
Your son I was taken to Nyayo House
To be tortured
Together with other patriots
What I experience there at Nyayo House
I have no words with which to tell
It is enough if I say I saw what the woodcut-
ter saw
Torture above torture, unimaginable brutal-
ity
Pain agony anger hunger fear and anxiety
It was hard mother it was very very hard to
bear
We are ruled by devils mother
True, we are at the mercy of Satan himself in
Kenya today!
Ndawiro was also kidnapped into Nyayo
House, for a few days
To be threatened and intimidated and tor-
tured
He was brought there to increase my suffer-
ing, to try to break me
They brought him in the room where they
were torturing me
And when he saw me naked and in pain
My youngest brother wept
And I could not hold my tears
We both cried mother we cried

And the torturers laughed
They laughed very much while your sons
cried
And when they were about to finish me
physically, mother
They carried me to their kangaroo court
At night, mother, I was taken to court at
night!
The Special Branch led by James Opiyo
And the prosecutor of the dictatorship Ber-
nard Chunga
The robbers of the rights of the oppressed
majority
Instructed their magistrate Buch
To imprison me for five years
Five years mother five years
I was imprisoned for five years
Without even being given the opportunity
To defend myself!
And now I am back at Kamiti Maximum
Prison
At Kamiti Maximum Prison
That is where your son is now
And I will be here for at least forty months
Mother, ai my dear mother
I and other patriots of our country
Who are known as Mwakenya
We are tortured and imprisoned
And others have even been killed
For fighting for freedom democracy and
human rights
For being against dictatorship and neo-
colonialism
For struggling against exploitation of person
by person
For rejecting the capitalist and imperialist
system
For loving our country mother
For working for a progressive Kenya
We are expelled from education institutions
We are sacked and denied the right to em-
ployment
We are spied against
We are hunted like animals
We arrested like criminals
We are tortured
We are detained
Others are forced to flee into exile

We are smeared with mud by the enemies of
our country
Mother
They did all this brutality against us
Because they had guns
They had guns mother they had guns
They had guns
The traitors and oppressors of our country
Can betray and oppress us
Because they are in charge of the govern-
ment
Because they control state power, mother:
The laws and the courts and the magistrates
The police and the prisons
The army and the air force and the navy
And PCs and DCs and DOs and chiefs
And weapons and the ability to use them
They control all these instruments of fear
and coercion
So they can treat others like this mother
Mother, here at Kamiti I think everyday
How long shall we oppressed people cry
And to whom?
Up to when will we bite our fingers?
All this they are doing to us
Until when will they continue to do to us?
Up to when mother up to when?
Oh dear, we know the truth we know the bit-
ter truth
They are able to impose this fascism against
us
Because they have the monopoly of violence
For they control state power mother
As long as they have the monopoly of vio-
lence
As long as they control the instruments of
the state
They will continue to exploit and oppress us
They won't stop to betray our freedom and
nation
While it is them who are in charge of the
state machine
Oh mother, how long shall we continue
To cry just like this, just like this mother?
Up to when shall we be under their mercy
When we know the truth mother
When we know the root and strength
Of their diabolical domination against us?

Mother, ai! my dear mother
This is not something somebody narrated to
you
Neither is it a tale I am telling you...............

Kamiti Maximum Prison   7-7-1986

the regime that is dying

they boast everyday, them that oppress and
exploit us
that by using the law and the police and the
prisons and the army
that by means of brutal torture and threats
and intimidation
that through their radio, tv., newspapers and
public barazas
that by utilising their PCs and DCs and DOs
and Chiefs
that through organised state terrorism
that they will stop the struggle for
progressive change
that they will actually impede the inevitable!
oh what fools they are!
the stupid stupid fools
they are very foolish, the empty braggarts
fools they are
to imagine the impossible
to dare think they can achieve what cannot
be achieved
what dictators and fascists more powerful
than them
have failed to achieve!
oh is it because they are mad?
their betrayal of our country, the treasonable
traitors
their bloody hands against wananchi, the
primitive murderers
their evil intentions and actions, the
diabolical sinners
are haunting them day and night
crazy crazy crazy they are crazy, very crazy
in deed
they are insane, the barbarians
or are they drunk?
yes, drunk drunk drunk stupidly drunk
they are drunk, the contemptible traitors
their anti-people state power
the fruits of corruption and exploitation they
enjoy
the crumbs thrown to them by their
imperialist masters, the dogs

have intoxicated them with shameless
arrogance
they have been blinded by their criminal
orgies against the people
them boasters who think, who have the
audacity to tell the world
that they will stop change, revolutionary
change
that they will succeed to tame Kenyans to
give in to dictatorship
them who repeat everyday- oh how proud
they are-
that they will arrest history, peoples'
struggle to create culture!
that they will torture, persecute and
imprison us for ever
that they will rule and exploit and oppress
us always
that they will betray and destroy our country
today and tomorrow
oh gods of our ancestors, how they brag
without shame!
what contempt upon us citizens of Kenya!
but, let us ask them
them that are fighting the impossible
let us ask them plainly
first to stop the earth from rotating and
revolving
and the sun from shinning in the day
and the stars from twinkling at night!
yes, let them use their unpopular
constitution with all their draconian laws
to expel the moon and all planets from the
universe!
let them use all their expertise of torture and
cruelty
to dry all the water of the seas
to collect all the sand of the oceans
and to bring all the creatures that live in
waters into dry land!
let them organize their whole anti-people
state apparatus
to cut the tongues of all the exploited and
oppressed people
to imprison all the patriots in our country
to prevent women from giving birth
and even to stop motion in matter!
and if they wish, they may even use their
religion

to convince all the workers and peasants
that poverty is sweeter than wealth
that it is better to be poor than rich
that the rich and the poor are created by God
that in fact suffering is the basis of happiness
that it is possible to have love peace and
unity
without food shelter and clothes
that it is godly to live peacefully with
oppressors
that it is a sin to hate exploiters and traitors
and wrong to desire and struggle for
freedom and liberation!
oh yes, and if that is not enough
they may use their mass propaganda
machinery
to convince the masses whom they try to
turn into beasts
that false can be true and true can be false
that red is green and green is red
that patriots are traitors and traitors are
patriots
that democracy is dictatorship and
dictatorship is democracy
that capitalism is for the masses and the
masses are for capitalism!
let them take their scientists into their
laboratory
to demonstrate and prove to the world
how they can kill clear concrete reality!
them the hooligans, these treasonable
hypocrites
who dare think the wananchi are there only
to obey them
who confuse the tolerance of the poor for
love for them, their enemies
the patience of Kenyans for fear for them,
their tormentors
them the enemies of love peace and
happiness of the peoples
them enemies of the progress and liberation
of our county
these pests, the neo-colonial puppets
them the comprador class, hyenas
them who do not learn from history
who, incidentally, never learn anything at all
apart from methods of amassing wealth
through looting public property

them who live to eat and to shit and drink
and sleep and fack
the harlots, immoral uncivilized creatures
pretending sophistication
useless citizens, a burden to society
them the class of cultural-eunuchs
castrated by foreign reactionary and
inhuman values
them worshippers of the capitalist god of
money
with no ability and will to create their own
culture
but endowed with a diabolic talent of
consuming and destroying
biological creatures devoid of humanity
them they are the ones who sing, who dare
parrot
that they will impose themselves upon us for
ever
that they will terrorise us today and
tomorrow
and in time to come
that dictatorship and the system of
exploitation and oppression
is here to stay!
that imperialism will rule and dominate
Africa forever!
that freedom and social justice is our stupid
dream
that will never never materialise!
that the poor will always be there- there to
work for the rich!
that we shall be the slaves of a few people
and families all the time!
that we Black people are not civilized
enough to live in freedom and democracy
to control our national economy and to
determine our own destiny!
that we shall remain a nation of begging and
borrowing forever!
them who aim to kill our hope for liberation
who organise physical and psychological
war against us patriots
oh listen to them talking, the watchmen of
neo-colonialism
look at their brutal soldiers beating and
killing everywhere even inside churches
in Nairobi Mombasa Nakuru Kisumu Thika
Nyahururu…..

everywhere chasing and shooting and
beating and arresting and fighting!
Is this a way of convincing the Kenyan
people
that the despicable unpopular primitive
Kanu regime
the custodian of dictatorship and neo-
colonialism for 34 years
will be imposed upon us by their monopoly
of violence forever?
them who imagine
that by arresting us
by torturing us
by detaining us
by imprisoning us
by exiling us
by killing us
that they will stop our just struggle
that through terrorism they will kill the
struggle for liberation!
perhaps, just perhaps
perhaps they hope to do what cannot be
done
to prevent what cannot be prevented
to win a war which will never be won
may be they wish to make history
to be the first people on our planet
to hold time
to stop motion in matter and matter in
motion
to imprison the wheel of history!
but most probable, the greatest possibility
them are approaching their grave, death
oh yes, death death death, their end
the dictatorship in the form of Moi-Kanu is
being finished
they are dying, the oppressors whether they
like it or not
or even they are dead already waiting to be
buried!
otherwise why
why all these fascistic methods
of attempting to suppress peaceful
gatherings and demonstrations!
why all this state violence
aimed against the wananchi's wish for
freedom and democracy!
to me, them are dying whether they agree or
not

moi-kanu's is a rotten archaic anachronistic
regime
a corpse of a system, that's what it is
the saba saba state war against peaceful
Kenyans
are the last kicks of the kanu horse which
must die
all the violence the fascism the barbarism
is in fact their desperation to survive
to survive when they cannot
and must not be allowed to!
yes, yes yes oh yes
in fact it is true
they a raving in the delirium of their death
look at their oppressor brothers everywhere
everywhere, in all the corners of the globe
them are raving, raving madly
arresting detaining torturing imprisoning
exiling killing
oppressive regimes through out the world
are behaving similarly, just like them
fighting desperately to prevent what cannot
be prevented
attempting to stop the revolution by brute
force
but they are dying all the same, for they
cannot live
but before we bury them
them must claim many of the best of us
like the ten whom they murdered yesterday
them who continue with their greediness
even unto their death!
them who die selfish and barbaric
will take so many of us into their graves!
them the dictatorship in the form of moi-
kanu
them are dead already
but it is not easy
for us to bury them
but burying them we must
for it is impossible
to live with their stench

Kamiti Maximum Prison   8-5-1986

it's like a dream!

today
I was visited by my dear wife
oh how excited I was
I was very very happy indeed
So happy that I cannot explain
but the strange thing is
all that excitement
all that happiness
was like a sweet dream
that stayed for only a few minutes
then it melted away like ice
it was like the clouds of rain
true it was like bubbles of *omo*
ahhh it was coca-cola power
for I was unable to sustain the happiness
after glancing at my sweetheart
thousands of thoughts are now torturing me
the saw of loneliness is cutting me into small
pieces
the pain of separation refuses to pity or leave
me alone
ah, so sadness is inevitable in prison!
I fail to prevent myself
from dying of thinking about home and
those at home
oh my dear wife
now, a few minutes after seeing you
I miss you and long for you
even more than before I saw you today!
oh what will I do darling!
freedom, my heart is aching for crying for
freedom!
ah prison, who the hell discovered prison!

Kibos Prison   15-4-1988

My stand

Did you say
If I continue with this stand
Which is of truth and justice
I will die poor, propertyless!
But I tell you so that you be knowing
I am explaining so that you keep on remem-
bering
I do not value that sort of wealth
The wealth that comes from exploitation
The wealth that arises from betrayal and op-
portunism
I am not tempted by that sort of wealth
A small island of wealth
Amidst a large ocean of poverty
To me that is not wealth, it has no meaning
The wealth I look forward to
The wealth I struggle for
Is the wealth of the whole nation
Is the wealth that embraces all citizens
All persons to eat the fruits of their labour
All citizens to benefit from national re-
sources
All *wananchi* to enjoy life of peace, prosperity
and happiness
The respect and realisation of the humanity
of all
That is what I call wealth, the wealth I miss

Ah, look now, you keep on repeating
If I insist on struggling for socialism
I will die in my youth
Please, may I explain
So that you may keep on understanding
I will never never accept
To give in to the threats of death
To leave the struggle
For fear of dying
I will never
For death is inevitable to all living things
Whether I struggle or not
I will die all the same
If not today tomorrow
If the price for living a long life

Is to be an exploiter and oppressor
Is to accept the evils in society
Is to betray my country and people to im-
perialists
Is to surrender to the culture of fear and si-
lence
Is to lick the anuses of oppressors
Surely it is better to die this very day
It were better a grave was prepared immedi-
ately
For burying me until I am buried!
Because to me
Life, the life worth living
Is revolutionary life
To work towards the end of social injustice
To struggle for the happiness of all
To strive towards
Living my country and world
Better than I found it
To me that is wealth.

Kibos Main Prison   *4-6-1988*

Mau Mau

The peasants and workers of our country
Refused colonialism
They rebelled against it in words and deeds
They said no! no to white people's rule in
Kenya
They organised themselves day and night
They met discussed and plotted together
Devising strategies and tactics
Giving one another advise and oath
They ate the oath of Kenya and her freedom
They swore that they would sacrifice them-
selves
Whatever come may they would do any-
thing
For the sake of the liberation of our country
Collectively they agreed that they would
fight
Fight without going back or giving up hope
They would struggle and struggle and
struggle
Until they remove colonialism in our
motherland
Then there was the bugle call, the traditional
horn sounded
It was sounded to announce the war of liber-
ation
Out came the men
Forward marched the women
And the children refused to be left behind
Even the old and the sick
Were ready to make their contribution
There was no single patriot
That abandoned the struggle for freedom
Whoever counted himself to be a patriot
Came out to play his or her part for the
motherland
The peasants and workers
Responded to the call
They came out for the sake of our nation
Spreading in towns
Through out the country side
And into the forests
With guns and bombs
And *pangas* and grenades

They spread news of the guerrilla war
Until the whole world heard and knew
Knew about Kenya's liberation war
Kenyans had arrived at a time of demanding
freedom
Demanding it through barrels of guns
Thus the Land and Freedom Army was
formed
The fame of Mau Mau spread like wind
The sons and daughters of Africa had united
United in the fight for the dignity of the
Black person
Gallant and valiant heroes of Kenya
Were now being born everyday at the battle
fields
The first generals of our country
Were being distinguished clearly at the
front-line
Patriots were on this side
While the cowards ran away there
So the meaning of patriotism and traitorism
Were clearly understood
In the struggle for national liberation
The culture of anti-imperialist struggle
Continued to grow and flourish everywhere
Songs against colonialism were composed
Dances of celebrating the beauty of African
culture
Became the order of the day
The literature about the shame and evil
Of being ruled by foreigners in our own
country
Spread like wild fire
The morality of hope and ultimate victory
In our just war
Was preached to all even to the enemies
The war of the freedom of the African
Grew and grew becoming bitter and bitter
everyday
The White settlers robbers of our land were
slaughtered
Homeguards and traitors were butchered
The attacks of the colonial army of occupa-
tion
Were answered by our just patriotic army
Answered with a tooth for a tooth a nail for a
nail
For now the medicine of fire was fire
The British government in Kenya

Paid heavy price after heavy price
Our people increased their creativity
In the course of the liberation war
Guns were being manufactured
At Nyandarwa and Kirinyaga
Bombs and grenades were being made
At Mathare and Kariobangi
The aeroplanes of the air force of the enemy
Were being downed everyday
The prisons incarcerating patriots
Were attacked and prisoners set free by their
lands men
The oppressors invaders and occupiers of
our country
Were sleepless and diarrhoearing with fear
All their wisdom deserted them
Raving with the madness of suffering defeat
after defeat
They increased witch-hunting arresting and
torturing
They were imprisoning deporting and killing
indiscriminately
Death surrounded the villages with trenches
and *askaris*
Villages were like prisons with oppression
above oppression
The torture was too much like that of fascist
Hitler
With small children tortured being beaten
and cut into pieces
And open brutality upon their mothers being
abused and raped
Citizens were turned into slaves through
forced labour
Hunger fear threats and intimidation's
Became part and parcel of village life
Central Province was like hell on earth
Because of the cruelty of the White people
Prisons were full to the brim with patriots
and citizens
Heroes of our country were being persecuted
and prosecuted
Imprisoned detained deported and hanged
everyday
Human rights in Kenya were trampled upon
underfoot
The sins perpetrated by colonialists against
us

We shall never forget we shall never forget
forever
The treason of the traitors and homeguards
We shall remember we shall remember bit-
terly always
The colonialists tried all methods possible
To extinguish the inextinguishable fire of
uhuru
Their radios were condemning and ridicul-
ing our struggle
Their newspapers condoning their fascism
against Kenyans
They even resorted to the use of religion,
churches
In their diabolic attempt of trying to put off
The fire of liberation war that can not be put
off
But lo! the colonialists were but chasing the
wind
Nothing could make the peasants and work-
ers of Kenya
Lift up their arms or stop the war
The fire of *uhuru* continued burning and
burning and burning
The sound of the guns fired by patriots for
justice
Continued being heard for they were un-
stoppable
The blood of the settlers and traitors
Continued to be spilled spilling spilling
everyday
The history of struggle against colonialism
Was written by the ink of the blood of patri-
ots
The fame of Mau Mau spread like the North
wind
They spread East and West and also South
and North
All Africa was proud of Mau Mau a shining
example to follow
In Mau Mau the road of the war of liberation
was opened
So when Cubans and Koreans were fighting
against imperialism
Here in Kenya we were also fighting the
same enemy
Mau Mau was a great example to all dominated nations

Eventually the colonialists lifted up their
hands
The invaders and plunderers of our country
surrendered
They had no alternative but to accept defeat
Those who always claimed they were insur-
mountable
Were surmounted Mau Mau surmounted
them colonialists
The flag of the United Kingdom was lowered
with shame
While that of Africans of Kenyans was
proudly hoisted
The history of classical colonialism in Kenya
Had ended was finished never to come back
But alas! the history of imperialism
Was not yet over it was still there it was still
there
For neo-colonialism knocked at the door
And Kanu-Kadu-Kenyatta said wel-
come!............
That is why up to today we are still saying
Aluta kontinuaaaaaaahhhhhhh!!!!!!!!!!!!!!!!
Mau Mau carried their responsibility
And we patriots of today
Continue in the same path
Long live Mau Mau!
Long live the spirit of patriotism!

Kibos Main Prison   3-5-1988

Farewell!

To day
I must leave
I must leave today I must leave
I must leave you
Without
Leaving
You
My forwarding address
Oh my darling wife
My only child
My dear mother
My brothers my sisters
My relatives my friends
My neighbours
All of you my beloved ones
I must leave you
I must leave you today
I must leave you my dear ones
Leave you without a forwarding address
Because
Where I am going
Now
I
Do not know!
I cannot tell you
Where I am going to live
If I try to do so
I will be cheating you!
What I do know
What I am sure of
What I can tell you now
Is that
I
Am
Leaving
I am leaving all of you my dear ones
I must leave you
Today, now
I must bid you farewell immediately
I must say bye now now now not a second
later
I must leave running not walking
Secretly and not openly
Crying and not laughing!

This I know for sure
That
I must
Leave my beloved country
Oh my dear motherland
Kenya
The most beautiful country in the world
I must
Leave you my country I must leave you
I must leave all you fellow citizens
And Dawida
These beautiful hills and valleys
Where I was born and grew
And Nairobi and Thika and Voi
Kisumu Eldoret and Nakuru
And Mombasa Nanyuki and Malindi......
Our dear towns I must leave you
When will I see you again my wonderful
home!
When?
Oh Manga, my dear wife my beloved friend
And Wandoe, my dear daughter
Ahhhh......what can I say to you now?
What my sweethearts?
How can I bid you farewell?
After all these years of separation
Of prison
We must separate yet again
No sooner am I out of prison
Than I must leave you again!
What agony!
Yes, cry my dear ones cry
We have all the right to cry
How else can we respond to this situation
My wife and child?
How sweethearts?
And my grandmother
My father's mother
My only remaining grandparent
Will I see you alive again?
My heart is crying tears of blood
I cry from within and without
And the inner cry is bigger, very big
What will explain how I feel
For no words can do that!
I must leave all that is part of me
To leave apart from my people
A way from my country
A distance from my culture

Not to be near those I have known and loved
To continue the life of loneliness and anxiety
Of longing longing longing always longing
And waiting waiting day and night waiting
I must leave you now I must leave you now
I must run away from you my country
Kenya, my dear motherland
Farewell!!!!.....

But
Remember always
My country
Remember
All the time
Please
Do not forget
That I leave you today
Because I must
Only because I must my dear country
Only because I must
I am forced to that's why
They want to arrest me again
To continue torturing me
They are coming for me once more
To take me back to prison
And
Being in prison
This time
Is no longer useful
It is not useful to anybody
And to myself as well
Above all
My imprisonment
This time
Will be a liability
To the cause
My very life is in danger
And I am not ready to die
Like a sheep
In the dirty hands
Of the bloody regime
To allow myself
To die in prison
Is not a patriotic act
I refuse
To be slaughtered like a chicken
By the fascist police and prison
Of the dictatorship
My comrades say

I must go elsewhere now
For I am no good to the underground
At the moment
Knowing
That
I will never give up
That I leave to live for the struggle
That I run not to run away from the cause
That I go today to continue fighting
For if I must die
Let me not die under their mercy
I choose to die struggling with them
It is better to die with some of them when I
die

Yes
Today
I must leave
I must leave my family
I must leave my relatives
I must leave my friends and comrades
I must leave the place I have known
And the people I love
I must leave Kenya the root of my life
I must depart now now now now
Without leaving a forwarding address
Because
Where I am going
I am not sure
What I am certain about
Is that I must leave for somewhere else
If I am to continue living outside prison

But
I also believe
Wherever I will end
There will be people
For in the world
There are
People

Finally
I must go today
But I will
Return
This
I
believe
One
Day
I
Will
Come back to you
My dear country
Kenyans
Will not
Have to
Leave Kenya
Like this
For ever!
Farewell dear country
Farewell!

27/11/1989

LIBERATORY FOCUS

US in IRAQ

Appalachian Author
Please Attack Appalachia – From the Appalachian Mountains, one of the earliest and most damning satires of the US invasion and occupation of Iraq.

Tony Christini
Homefront (excerpt) – A US family and the conquest of Iraq.
John Doe Dimslow and the IED – Acting against empire.
The Incorporation of Oila – Global conquest by the Incorporated Estates of Dearth.
We, The Children of Iraq – Poem exposing the US invasion, occupation of Iraq.

Joe Emersberger
Dave the Prophet – Love, politics, and deportation in Canada.

Dahr Jamail
Iraq on My Mind – Thousands of Stories to Tell and No One to Listen – Powerful views from Iraq.

Cindy Sheehan
Once Upon a Time – Of the people and global domination.

Buff Whitman-Bradley
Realpolitik, Street Theater M19 '08; The last child in Iraq died today; News of war; Freshly shelled peas; Shock and Awe haiku; The United States of Torture; Property Damage; To the children of Iraq: Nobody ever said life was fair; Weapons of mass destruction; Slouching toward Baghdad

On the Iraq War
Noam Chomsky

(from Q&A with Anthony DiMaggio and Edward Herman)

The insurgency [in Iraq] was created by the brutality of the invasion and occupation – which is, in fact, one of the most astonishing failures in military history. The Nazis had less trouble in occupied Europe, and the Russians held their satellites for decades with far less difficulty. It is difficult to think of an analog. A few months after the invasion, I met a highly experienced senior physician with one of the leading relief organizations, who has served in some of the worst parts of the world. He had just returned briefly from Baghdad, where he was trying to reestablish medical facilities, but was unable to because of the incompetence of the CPA [the US-led Coalition Provisional Authority]. He told me he had never seen such a combination of "arrogance, ignorance, and incompetence," referring to the Pentagon civilians in charge. In fact, it was monumental. They even failed to guard the WMD sites that had been under UN supervision, so that they were systematically looted, handing over to someone – probably jihadis – high-precision equipment suitable for producing missiles and nuclear weapons, dangerous bio-toxins, etc., which had been provided to their friend Saddam by the US, UK and others. The ironies are almost indescribable.

Another fact overlooked, though it is finally beginning to leak, is the immense corruption under the CPA, beside which anything attributed to the UN pales in insignificance. Plenty of information has been readily available, but only tidbits were reported here. One can go on. But the major and crucial point overlooked is the judgment of Nuremberg, declaring that aggression is "the supreme international crime differing only from other war crimes in that it contains within itself the accumulated evil of the whole." All of the "accumulated evil." Also overlooked are the stern words of the US Chief Counsel Justice Jackson: "If certain acts of violation of treaties are crimes, they are crimes whether the United States does them or whether Germany does them, and we are not prepared to lay down a rule of criminal conduct against others which we would not be willing to have invoked against us.... We must never forget that the record on which we judge these defendants is the record on which history will judge us tomorrow. To pass these defendants a poisoned chalice is to put it to our own lips as well." Until at least this is recognized, all other discussion is merely footnotes, and shameful ones.

Please Attack Appalachia
Appalachian Author

Mr. President, please attack Appalachia.

You have promised the Iraqis that they will share in the wealth of their oil. We could use some of that same sharing here. We have coal and timber that is being extracted, yet very little of the profits remain in our area. If the Iraqis are to share in the profits from their natural resources, we would like to share in the profits from ours.

You have promised healthcare for all Iraqis. We could use the same thing here. Far too many of us are without health insurance and adequate access to good healthcare facilities. You have also promised to rebuild the schools in Iraq. We too have schools that need rebuilt and that need more funding.

Certainly you can find a justification for attacking us. We have weapons of mass destruction. Just go inspect the former uranium enrichment plant near Piketon, Ohio. You will still find all sorts of radioactive waste on and around that site. Test our waters. Test our ground. Test our air. You will find an abundance of chemical and biological agents that could be used as weapons. We literally live among them.

After all, Appalachia is America's third world. Terrorists are breeding everywhere. Where there is poverty there is unrest. Where there is poor education there is suspicion. Where there is neglect there is anger. As far as potential dangers go, Appalachia should be near the top of your list. Stomp out the bad before it turns thoroughly evil. Pre-emptively strike us now before it becomes too late. Do it before we make something else out of our fertilizer ingredients.

Since Appalachia is a highly religious area an at-tack could easily be explained as the fulfillment of prophecy. Many here would even agree with your need to attack us. In fact, we would probably help supply the troops.

Without any long-term energy strategy or alternative planning, once the oil is gone the US will become increasingly dependent on coal and wood. Appalachia has lots of that. Even today, the profitability of many US businesses would be threatened if Appalachia refused to supply them with electricity, coal, and other resources.

Can America afford to wait until a crisis is at hand before attacking Appalachia? The decision is yours. You do not even have to involve the United Nations since we are within US borders. You can go it alone.

The rest of the country will be fairly easy to con-vince about the need to attack us. The national news media will surely rise to your side. Prejudice against hillbillies already de-values our lives in comparison to those in the rest of the country, so our devastation and casualties would have to be nearly as high as in Iraq before anyone from outside Appalachia complains too loudly. Besides, people here have lived as second-class citizens for so long we now thoroughly expect to be treated as second-class citizens – and the rest of the nation expects to treat us that way. How else could you explain the relatively small outcry currently raised by our exceedingly high unemployment rates, poor education, high pollution, poor healthcare, high poverty, and poor leadership?

In fact, attacking us will probably help cement your re-election.

You might experience some local militia counterstrikes, but those will probably be disorganized and minor. After all, Appalachia lacks any central command, what with its being comprised of the parts of twelve states and only the whole of one state. West Virginia could be your focus. Find someone evil there to target, such as Jay Rockefeller.

He asked the FBI to investigate those forged documents you used to help justify your war against Iraq. How embarrassing that must have been: International Atomic Energy Agency Chief Mohamed ElBaradei addressed the UN and publicly humiliated you by showing your assertion that Iraq was trying to import uranium from Niger was based on crudely faked information. Someone should pay for such an embarrassment and who better than a Democrat who is a Rockefeller?

So Mr. President, you have all the elements you need: weapons of mass destruction, a nearly third world enemy, potential terrorists, someone to call evil, and an easy path to victory. Now all you have to do is attack. And please, do it soon. We need the reparations, better schools, better infrastructure, universal healthcare, and a fair share in the wealth of our own resources.

You also promised Iraq democracy. We could use that here as well.

Please, Mr. President, attack Appalachia next.

Liberation Lit would like to learn the identity of the author of "Please Attack Appalachia" – apparently first published at Common Dreams.

Homefront (excerpts)

Tony Christini

Washburn

The whole wide world pushed with awesome intimacy into not only the professional public lives of rulers like US Senator Sam Washburn but into their private lives as well.

This fact was made especially clear to the Senator one day during his third term, when – a few weeks after the US launched its March 2003 ground invasion of Iraq – Sam's daughter Jamie walked into his office and all but accused him of the killing of Aaron Thompson – a US soldier from Senator Washburn's district who had not survived the first weeks of the invasion. Not just any soldier – a relative. Aaron was his cousin Carolyn's son – the brother of Jamie's cousin and friend, Ellen Thompson.

"Rocket propelled grenade," Jamie told him. "Roadside ambush."

Ellen had served as an intern on Sam's staff the previous summer, an efficient young woman whom his daughter had grown close to, Sam knew.

Sam had first learned of Aaron's death from a military buddy who had given him a confidential heads-up this morning. Sam had kept the news to himself.

Now in the face of his daughter, Sam lowered his eyes and brought a hand to his head. Jamie stared steadily at him.

He got the message. His daughter was no longer in full agreement with his policy on Iraq, if she ever had been.

"How?" Sam asked.

"RPG," Jamie said, again.

Jamie had problems with a number of his other positions, as well, Sam knew. In fact, Sam under-stood that long before the death of Aaron, Jamie had been struggling with whether or not she should continue on in her present capacity as staff aide.

She could easily get other work around the capital, Sam knew. A couple of liberal environmental organizations had expressed interest in bringing her on board to lobby the Senator and others.

Sam cracked a Brazil nut.

He liked to snack on them in the after-noon.

He took his time peeling the shell, tossing it bit by bit into the trash.

"Carolyn…" Sam trailed off, thinking of Aaron's mother. He would have to call her.

"It will wipe her out," Jamie said.

Sam doubted that. But it was a horrible thing any way you looked at it.

He had expected his daughter to turn around and leave soon after having delivered the message. But there she stood.

Sam redirected his gaze to the miniature titan-ium globe on his desk that had been gifted to him by a Nigerian oil executive who worked for Texaco.

"Bomb them," Sam said.

"Excuse me?" his daughter asked.

Sam shook his head. "Nothing."

He spun the globe absently with his little finger, watching it whirl on a greased axis, the continents a blur, the axis invisible, fitted precisely into the semi-circular frame.

Queen of Sheba

They were not crowded but grouped comfortably in small formations on the back porch – an impressive lofted plank deck, half a decagon braced across the entire wall of the house and hanging far out over the yard, a bone-breaking drop to the sidehill below. Farther beyond, the valley fell away into apparent infinity, an impressive view, although what most of those gathered on this commemorative occasion welcomed more was the spring warmth for which they felt gratitude.

They were gathered at the home of Aaron Thompson, who had been killed exactly a year ago during the opening weeks of the US invasion of Iraq. Carolyn Thompson had stood with her husband on the front stoop of the house telling the media assembled on the grass and on the dirt and gravel drive that her soldier son Aaron had died for – "He died for all of us," she said, when in fact, as she now knew, it would have been far more accurate to say that Aaron had been killed by all of us, that Aaron and the rest of the foot-soldiers had been sent as cannon fodder, however lethal, by the government of the United States and by the power-ful corporate forces that drove and staffed and otherwise held large purchase on the government, and that Aaron had been killed by everyone in the US who had let the government, the cor-porate media and other cheerleaders carry out the illegal and otherwise criminal inva-sion and occupation of Iraq – an act on the same moral level as that of the conquest of Iraq by Hulagu Khan, grandson of Genghis Khan, nearly 800 years earlier when his invading legions overran the Middle East. This was the way Carolyn understood the context of her son's death, now.

Carolyn had begun to see the fiction for the fact in the misleading reports on TV, on the radio, and in print, and what was more, she had heard it on her own lips – "He died for all of us."

She knew better now. Because of. Not for.

What a bitter, nauseous thing it was to Carolyn to learn the barbaric reality of how and why her son had been sent to kill and be killed on criminal grounds by official Ameri-cans, many elected, many not elected, who created, supported and directed the invasion. One of those elected officials happened to be family to Carolyn – her first cousin, Senator Sam Washburn, who stood across from Carolyn on the deck today, leaning against the part of the railing below which the ground fell most steeply, as Carolyn could not help but be aware. Senator Sam Washburn stood opposite Carolyn who had placed herself in front of the sliding glass door, the lone entrance to the house.

Carolyn's youngest daughter Ellen had flown in from college, and Jamie was there, the daughter of the Senator and Ellen's close friend. Carolyn's elder children were there as well, Ruthy and Mike who lived nearby, along with their young children playing in the house and traipsing about the yard. Carolyn's parents had come over too, Joanne and Bernie, as had the reporter from the city paper who interviewed them all, Lynn Jackson. A few neigh-bors were also in attendance, as was Aaron's friend from the military, Juan Garza, who had been sitting by Aaron in the Humvee when it was hit by the rocket-propelled grenade that killed Aaron. They were all gathered on the deck today.

And Carolyn thought if you looked hard enough you might even see a few of the Iraqi people standing around – warriors and civilians both – including Iraqi children who might be off playing in the house and yard with the Thompson family children.

Given the deck's extraordinary height, when the wind on stormy days whipped and the rain lashed and Carolyn had stood at the glass door looking out across the boards this past year, she had felt as if she were riding through some vast and dangerous sea on a giant ship, on the Titanic, it could have been, or a battle cruiser.

When the Senator placed one hand on the top plank of the railing and gestured with his other hand while making a point, Carolyn felt again the reality of the death of her son, the reality that her own country had set him up, the government and the powers that drove the government, not that the government was really her government, not that it much represented what she valued, except fictitiously, she had come to understand more and more.

If her country had not invaded, Aaron would not have been killed, not that she felt it was the country that had invaded, not that it was the people – the people who had been flat lied to and misled and overruled.

If great pains had not been taken to mislead the people of the country, there would have been far less support than even the limited amount that the official liars and manipulators and true believers of a fantasy America in a fantasy world were able to whip up.

And there he stood, Senator Sam Washburn, Carolyn's first cousin, talking with her husband and some others. He stood across from her now, by the railing, nothing between him and infinity but what might be fragile wooden boards, except that Carolyn knew the wood to be sturdy and protective. Her husband and sons, Mike and Aaron, had built the deck themselves.

It might as well be the President of the United States standing there. Carolyn would prefer that – she would prefer that any opponent of hers not be a cousin but a stranger. Unfortunately, life was not often so compliant.

Carolyn stared at the railing, at the top plank and avoided looking at the hand of the Senator on the board. She considered instead the nails that held the railing together.

A few nails. All it took sometimes was a few key nails and the whole thing came apart, or was sealed tight forever, whatever it might be, a railing, or, say, a coffin.

A few nails and the railing was no more, though the deck would remain. A few nails and the coffin was closed tight forever. A few nails, a few bullets, a single rocket-propelled grenade.

Carolyn's eldest daughter Ruthy came over and put a hand on the fist of Carolyn that clenched a bottle of juice, and Carolyn watched her own fingers relax and then release the bottle on the table, and she pulled slightly away from Ruthy and stared again over the valley.

She could scarcely think of a single person missing on this solemn occasion, a person who might help make the moment more affirming of the memory of Aaron, who might help salve the pain of the loss if not Carolyn's outrage at her son's death, an outrage which she had no intention of giving up, an outrage which she had decided in recent months to acknowledge and reinforce as appropriate, an outrage that, as she understood now, at the very least, might likely see her through every single day of the rest of her life, and through each remaining year – of which she meant there to be plenty.

Carolyn picked up the bread knife.

She had even smiled at the Senator when she invited him here – at least she thought she had smiled, tried to force herself to do so through lips she felt turning to bone, and now there he stood.

"Mom?" Ruthy said. And Carolyn began to cut the bread.

She had once thought of this man standing before her as a senator cousin, but now Carolyn regarded him mainly as a cousin senator, a nice enough person privately who she had no problem with in conventional moments such as this, for he was polite and good humored, a gentle father and husband, an amiable uncle, serious at times, caring and diligent too, a convivial man who liked sports and music and pets and most anything else that regular people typically liked. He was an almost every-people kind of person. There was nothing wrong with him from that perspective, she thought. Like most folks he was reasonable and compassionate in many moments. He could be personable or prickly. He was the kind of person who gave people a sense that there was much reason to think of him as a good man – as Carolyn thought too, at least in reference to this private side of his person, the way folks generally tend to know and think of others (to the extent that they do).

But to say that Carolyn had nothing personal against Sam would be inaccurate, for though she held nothing of her cousin's private side against him, what she knew of it, she understood that there was far more to a person than what they did directly face to face with you, there was what they did to you and to people in general indirectly – there was what they did to everyone indirectly, to the public, and there was no denying that this other side of the Senator, his public side, his political side, had facilitated the death of Aaron.

There was no denying that the public side of the people in Congress (and beyond) was largely responsible for the death of her son, since support for the attack and occupation of Iraq was strong in the legislature, though not nearly so much among the citizenry.

Carolyn had learned that unfortunately and to its great discredit, Congress represented the people only when it felt it could dare to. Otherwise Congress did not go far or at all against the ruling dollars that funded the campaigns and dominated the decision-making at almost every level.

Even more undemocratic and more repulsive to Carolyn was the fact that the president represented the people even less than Congress since the concentration of money could be focused even more intensely on a single position, the top position, thus tightening the grip of non-elected ruling wealth – one of the many ongoing deeply anti-democratic traditions of America – and it burned her all the more now as she thought of Aaron who had helped build this deck she was standing on.

How late it was that she had learned the first Chief Justice of the Supreme Court John Jay had made plain that "the people who own the country ought to govern it" – as they did today. Carolyn had come across that little detail this past year, having looked more deeply into the country's past, as she had had cause to.

And she had found out in no uncertain terms that wealth ruled in the form of the corporate-state plutocrats and like-minded folk willing to do their bidding either to better gain and maintain lucrative and comfortable corporate and academic jobs, or simply to identify themselves with some mythic notion of greatness in this country, America, even if a lot of flag-worshipers themselves enjoyed precious little prosperity or other benefits from their faith.

The official position of Senator Sam Washburn, support for the invasion and conquest of Iraq (and its massive oil fields), was the position of Congress in general and by and large. There had scarcely been a dissenting voice raised during some of the votes to fund the atrocity. Of course this congressional and executive support that had killed Aaron was also killing, disfiguring and disabling the sons and daughters of many other families in the US, not to mention the far more frequent killing of the people of Iraq and the accelerating spread of violence and chaos and desperation there due to lack of security, lack of jobs, lack of medicines, lack of even electricity, and the failure of the invading forces to establish non-abusive let alone decent conditions of life.

It had all led, quite predictably, to an even more ferocious resistance in Iraq that was gaining the ever-increasing support of the population, despite the bombings, beheadings, and other brutality by the resistance – so hated were the country des-troying American invaders and those who sided with them in the power-grab for which there was no end in sight and for which there never had been an exit plan, because no exit had ever been intended.

On the contrary, Carolyn had learned that from the start the US had been intent upon building fourteen permanent military bases for the purpose of dominating oil-rich Iraq from now until Kingdom Come, or until there was oil no more. That was the actual plan that US forces were still trying to implement – morality, carnage, and the fate of the world be damned – and never mind the views of the Iraqis.

Totally Dominant or Totally Dead seemed to be the US model. Carolyn understood it now, the real standard for much of US action in Iraq and the world. For this, her son had been sent to kill and be killed, as Carolyn had gone through the great pain of finding out. Because of this brute madness, Aaron had died. For this homicidal and potentially suicidal endeavor, Aaron had been led by official America.

Possibly she could be forgiven for dwelling on it.

"I pledge allegiance to the flag of the United States of America, and to the Republic for which it stands, one nation, under God, indivisible, with liberty and justice for all." Recited day after day during her school years, the Pledge of Allegiance came bitterly to Carolyn's mind as she watched the Senator reach for his glass of soda on the railing. What did it mean to swear loyalty to a strip of cloth? Was it not a form of idolatry and brainwashing? Carolyn knew that her eldest daughter Ruthy had come to think so.

When school started again last fall after Aaron had been killed, Ruthy gave her children permission to not recite the flag pledge if they chose. Ruthy had explained her views to the teachers and to her children, and her children had both decided not to say the pledge, and it made Carolyn wonder more than ever what was normal, decent, and right – and what merely appeared to be and was tolerated for no good reason or no real reason at all, and worst of all what went on for terrible reasons, in actuality, with terrible consequences of the sort the Thompsons knew now only too well.

The ongoing atrocity was made to look so normal-decent-and-right that Carolyn wondered if there was something equally horrible behind the apparently normal desire of the Senator to be here today with his extended family in this area of his youth. Carolyn hoped the Senator had wished to be invited for the conventional reasons of being one with family, difficult as family could be.

This was what Carolyn had sensed inside her cousin senator, but given his role as Senator, not as cousin, not as Sam, Carolyn felt she could not entirely be sure of his real motivations regarding even the killing of her son, especially regarding the killing of her son, though she had no direct evidence that the Senator would use this trip home to family for political gain.

Should she make anything of the fact that she and Glenn rarely saw the Senator in person, so busy was he off in Washington or touring the state?

How was she to know for certain why he and his wife and daughter had come to the old church for the commemorative ceremony for Aaron?

Whatever the reasons, the Senator stood now by the railing at the highest part of the deck.

Even voting against her cousin senator would be of no use, Carolyn knew. She could not vote against the Senator, not because he was family, but because his opponent was an equally strong advocate of the invasion and occupation. Incumbent candidates like Sam rarely lost anyway. Even if they did, opposing candidates who had any chance to win in the big money nominating system were often as bad or worse than the incumbent.

And it was called democracy.

And Carolyn was the Queen of Sheba.

Carolyn whitebread Thompson of European descent. Was it not obvious how extremely rich, powerful and black she was, just like the mighty Queen of Sheba traveling from her wealthy Empire in ancient Ethiopia across the wide lands to marry an equally

powerful ruler who had the reputation of being the wisest and best of all kings?

Yes, indeed, Carolyn stretch-the-paycheck Thompson must actually be the Queen of Sheba if America was really the land of the people, by the people, for the people.

And her husband Glenn – who had helped build this splendid deck and much of the house – he was even better known throughout all the wide world as King Solomon, wisest of mortals, whom the Queen of Sheba had traveled from afar to challenge by quiz and then to marry.

Yes, just as Carolyn was the Queen, so was America a functioning democracy, where everyone was able to meaningfully participate in how things were done, what got done, what decisions were made.

The only problem – and it was beginning to bother Carolyn the Queen more and more – there was something wrong with King Solomon. It seemed to Carolyn that now after several decades of her glorious marriage to the King's wondrous self, mighty and matchless as the King might be, it seemed to Carolyn that the wise King could have by now figured out some way to get rid of the potholes at the end of driveway. And yet it was not so.

Carolyn wondered if she should give her venerable King a few more years before she walked down the royal drive, carrying a pick-axe and a shovel to see what the hell she could do about the problem herself.

Queen of Sheba. American democracy. Oh, yes.

Her son, Aaron. Dead.

Carolyn stared across the deck. What harm could it do to act like the Queen of Sheba for a single day, Carolyn mused, or even for a single moment of a day, if only in a small way here on the deck among family and friends where Carolyn felt she might very well like to rise in judgment as had been prophesied of the Queen, that she would rise in judgment of those who committed horrible deceptions and wrongdoings upon the people?

Just so, Carolyn felt she might like to rise up to full power, if doing so was not too grand a notion – which, thinking of Aaron, and thinking of all the others killed and maimed and all the billions of dollars of time and energy wasted, and all the infuriating deceit, Carolyn decided that any rising up on part of herself and others would not be so much a gesture that was grand as one that was directly to the point and long overdue.

Much of the public, including herself, and maybe everyone, as far as Carolyn could see now, had been in some part deceived by the mass of manipulations, but were they not as a public also too often merely inert, asleep, disorganized, sailing sweetly or cynically, reckless or mindless, down long rivers of denial in life, if not rivers of ignorance, if not long rivers of vast irresponsibility both civic and human?

How had she failed? Carolyn wondered. And how could she and everyone fail less in the future? How to succeed? How to save the Americans and Iraqis of today? How to save the Aarons of the future?

The Senator leaned away from the boards a bit while otherwise remaining in place opposite Caro-lyn, one hand flat on the top rail, responding mechanically, it seemed, yet not altogether without energy and deep-stored conviction, to some comment Glenn had made. Carolyn wondered what it concerned. Probably the economy. The economy that was shot to pieces, Carolyn sensed, and understood further that the economy no matter how good it ever got for some people was always shot to hell for a good chunk of the rest, the way the system was set up. Where was the democracy in the economy?

Carolyn stared across the deck and gripped the knife.

And then the first slice of bread fell on the cut-ting board.

And Carolyn placed the knife carefully for the cutting of the second slice.

And her daughter Ruthy who had been stand-ing nearby this whole time, she moved back to her group.

It would be a few moments yet before Carolyn felt she would be able to get herself ready to interact with everyone – that is, with anyone – she meant, with someone – that is – with him.

Carolyn tried to think of ways in which her cousin senator might be viewed in his professional life as a sympathetic figure.

Nothing much occurred.

Finally she remembered that many of the policies of the Senator were not quite as bad as those of his likely opponent in the fall election. Carolyn squeezed the knife.

And she thought again of Aaron, and that was the end of her speculation about the positive qualities of the Senator.

An election was coming up, and no congress-person had lost to the invasion a closer relative than the Senator had in Aaron, and as a consequence of this fact, Carolyn wondered again if the Senator might be here today for political reasons of some sort.

"We're a more political family now," Carolyn had informed the Senator in the process of inviting him over with his wife and daughter after the morning church service. She explained that he was welcome to join them provided he did not mind being asked any political questions that folks might raise – which Carolyn herself might likely pose, she had meant to imply.

She had called the Senator "Sam" at that moment, "Sam, we're a more political family now." And so they were. Carolyn wondered if this afternoon was not the exact right time to be openly political, to develop and live the public side of her person, to discuss issues that mattered to her, to everyone, to raise the specter of her dead son, to speak of ravaged lands and people and the increasingly fragile world, to speak again and again of her dead son Aaron.

The Senator's presence had at first distracted Carolyn from doing an efficient job arranging the bottles and cans of soft drinks around pieces of fruit and loaves of bread on the table beside her, but now she was determined to steel her arm and slice through the bread more firmly, more quickly. She was determined to be strong, soldier strong, like Aaron. She meant to be strong like her son had been strong and she meant to join the others with whom she hoped to feel more fully the welcome weather today, freeing everyone of the house with its walls pressing in. She tried to understand how nice it was to have her cousin senator come by on this special day of commemoration. How very nice. Carolyn worked the knife and kept telling herself, imagining, how nice it might be, there on the back porch high above the ground.

No geopolitical problems were going to be solved this afternoon on the deck of the Thompson family house. Or so it seemed. Aaron's buddy Juan Garza would not magically pull out of his pocket the torched papers he had found on his friend after the RPG had ended his life. Aaron's older sister and brother Ruthy and Mike would not press the Senator on the illegal and immoral nature of both the invasion and the ongoing occupation of Iraq. Journalist Lynn Jackson would request an interview only if she could do so unobtrusively, on this commemorative occasion. Aaron's father Glenn did not want to question the Senator closely for fear his wife would find it inappropriate. Aaron's younger sister Ellen intended to speak her mind but to the Senator's daughter Jamie, who was already aware of her line of reasoning. Everyone was rather clear on where everyone else stood. There seemed to be little if anything more to say, and even less to do here in the privacy of the Thompson residence, until Carolyn's mother Joanne approached the Senator and said in her typically strong and clear voice how proud not only she was of his work as Senator but how proud the whole family was and how honored they all were by his taking time to be with them today.

The knife fell out of Carolyn's hand.

It clattered off the edge of the plate, skipped from the table and smacked onto the deck. "That's ludicrous," Carolyn said to the bread. And there was silence.

Joanne began speaking, but Carolyn cut her off, saying again, saying it louder, "That's ludicrous," looking first at her mother and then training her stare on the Senator. Joanne attempted to speak again, but Carolyn spoke over her, saying, "I don't think so, and I don't want to think so, and I'm not going to think so. All I can say is it took some real guts for you to even wish to show up here today." She looked directly at the Senator. "The war on Iraq, and the occupation, is an obscenity. And you supported it and still do, and I don't have any respect for that. And my mother is one of the few people on this porch who does. I want that made clear. That needs to be made clear. That ought to be made clear."

As if to help hold his tongue, the Senator glanced at the deck for a brief moment, and then he nodded at Joanne. "I thank you," he said, before facing Carolyn. "I'm sorry that politics come between us."

"Are you?"

"I'm very sorry for the loss of Aaron."

"You're sorry."

"It's a terrible thing. I can't imagine, of course."

"Do you want me to help you understand? Aaron is dead. Can you understand that?"

"Carolyn."

"Mom."

A few people reached out to her with their

voices, but no one actually came over – possibly because of the steel it was easy to sense exploding out of her – how steady and strong she looked.

"You destroyed a country, Senator. And tens of thousands of Iraqis, at least. And you enflamed sentiment against us. Aaron is dead. Iraqis are dead. More are dying. And as a consequence our country is less safe than it was a year ago. And poorer too. In every way imaginable. Most people do not support the occupation when made aware of the facts and did not support the invasion in the first place. And you – you're doing your job the way you choose to do it, and feeling 'sorry'. Well, that's nice."

No geopolitical problems were going to be solved this afternoon on the deck of the Thompson family house, as far as Carolyn Thompson could see, but at least one personal situation was going to have its day.

No one stepped in.

"I'm going to ask you to leave, Senator. Please do so. Your wife and daughter are welcome to stay."

Cousin to cousin, Sam faced Carolyn. "You're kicking me out?"

"Do I know you?" Carolyn asked. "Do I want to? Does anyone want you to bring the whole rest of this house and town and country and world crashing down on top of us? Why don't you go find another country to represent, Senator? You're certainly not representing this one."

"We have a different understanding of the facts."

"I wonder."

After a moment, Carolyn picked up the knife from the deck.

She wiped it off with a napkin.

Then she continued to slice the bread. It was good bread, good crust, with a hearty texture inside. Good ingredients. Good taste.

Nutritious. It was the best bread there was, Carolyn could not help but think, the best bread she had baked in a long time.

It was so good that when she finished cutting the loaf, she served herself the first slice, took a bite, and savored the taste. It almost made her smile. She looked around and noticed Sam had gone. Everyone else seemed subdued. Then she made a quiet announcement, one that carried. "It's good bread over here, everyone. Made it myself. Please help yourselves." She picked up a drink and stepped aside as people came over to the table.

Carolyn went to the railing and looked out at the contoured shades of charcoal that were the bare treetops near and far, framing the valley, a valley into which she had gazed often this past year. She would still have to vote for that damned cousin senator of hers, she realized – not of course because he was family but because for now there was no better alternative.

Maybe soon there would be a better choice. Her name was not Washburn, it was Thompson, but maybe she should put that name in play the next go around – or support some name like it, some name that stood for what was worth standing for. Maybe her name could play well enough to make a point at least, to rally support for the organizations and voters and positions that ought to be supported. Well, she would have to see. She would have to think about strategy – time and effort, resources and consequences.

Carolyn stood at the railing and imagined she was staring all the way into Iraq where Iraqis were being killed by the tens of thousands, by American troops and by American policies. And American troops, many of them young, all of them misled, were dying by the dozens. And then Carolyn saw only Aaron, and she felt him to be close by, if so far away it gutted her.

She was the host this afternoon. Let others speak of Aaron to the extent they would. She would listen. And she would look all the way into Iraq and beyond as she might, and she would continue to think things through. She had thrown the Senator off the deck and out of her home today, cousin or no. She would have to think about that too.

She stared out over the railing. She would have to give it some thought. She would have to see.

Town and Field

Mike stood in the batter's box and stared out across the dark baseball field. He imagined a gun in his hands, military issue, automatic, a submachine gun. And then all the Thompson family came onto the field holding guns. And then much of the town. And then people from all over the country. And elected officials. And non-elected executives and owners. Everyone was present, gathered along the foul lines, people from all across America, all gathered in the ball field with their guns and flares and grenades.

Aaron stood off in the distance, in shallow center field, in a camouflage uniform.

Then it was time. Mike lifted his gun, sighted and fired.

Aaron crumpled. Everyone else opened up on the crumpled form. Nothing exploded off Aaron, no blood or gore, no bits of bone and flesh. Instead Aaron was ripped and cut like a rag doll with an infinite capacity to absorb bullets and be shot clean through. It got to be hard work, killing Aaron.

When there were breaks in the firing, people wiped sweat, took deep breaths, looked away, stretched, refocused – and then resumed firing as if it were the most natural thing in the world, and al-most as if their very lives depended on it. Aaron was rolled over and flopped around by the force of the impacts. Occasionally he would struggle to sit up and any time he did he was blasted down again by bullets and grenade bursts. The priest and preachers fired away, the teachers, supervisors, politicians, mothers

and fathers, family and friends, reporters, doctors, lawyers, carpenters, farmers, service workers, schoolchildren – bang! bang! bang!

That was how Aaron died.

The politicians and corporate executives flew over in military planes and dropped bombs on him. Uncle $am leaned out of Air Force One and shouted encouragement through a bullhorn stamped with a corporate logo. The members of the Supreme Court stood by, nodding sagely. Everyone that mattered was there in official and unofficial capacity both, in all their glory.

That was how Aaron was killed

And the TV cameras zoomed in; the media crews flooded the field with spotlights. They got it on film all right – not that it might ever be shown to the public. And so Aaron died.

To Mike, that was the real history of Aaron's killing. And of the invasion and occupation of Iraq, and of the economic sanctions and the bombings throughout much of the last decade and a half.

American history. There it was, in the same vein as the slaughtering of the Native Americans, and the Vietnamese, and the many others at home and abroad. What else might be expected of a country that currently had military bases and soldiers in one hundred fifty nations around the globe and a military budget larger than the military spending of almost every other nation combined?

And so Aaron died.

Mike stood in the batter's box in one of the darkest parts of the field and he stared at the body of his brother, this vision of the body of his brother, until it moved no more, and then with Aaron dead and motionless, finally, everyone shifted attention to deep center field where stood a group of Iraqis, very many of them.

It was difficult to see how many Iraqis for sure. No one really knew or much seemed to care. A few of the Iraqis were lined up in military uniform, looking ragged. The rest were civilians.

It was time. Mike and everyone else opened fire, and the group of Iraqis went down. An incredible barrage. Mike fired steadily, the crumpled image of his brother in one eye, the Iraqis fixed in the other.

A few people walked up to the foul lines and fired rocket-propelled grenades. Then bombs and missiles struck from invisible planes high overhead, far out of sight, far out of hearing even. Until Boom! Boom! Boom! went the bombs.

The Iraqis took it all like Aaron had, like rag dolls torn to shreds, cut down and killed, and killed, and killed again, until they went still, not totally destroyed somehow, their images at least.

And that was how it was done.

Afterwards, everyone stacked the weapons in neat piles for use the next time.

They offered condolences to Aaron's family for the loss.

John Doe Dimslow and the IED
Tony Christini

Warhawk Guns for Hire

They are coming after John Doe Junior now about every which way they can. Though the deaths of Iraqi guerillas, civilians, and other Oilans are going up, up, up, given the ongoing deaths of Incorporated Estates warriors every day, the Incorporated Estates of Earth military recruiters are having trouble recruiting soldiers into the "all-volunteer" forces. So they make it more and more a mercenary military of Army, Navy, Air Force, and Marine troops to go along with the official private mercenaries. They offer cash to kill: "$20,000 bonus for enlisting, $9,000 more if enlistees ship out in the next 30 days, and even better, $70,000 for college."

The big bucks tempted J Junior so much that he gave the recruiters the a-okay to come over to our home for a home visit. Except he never cleared it with Daddy-O, one John Doe Dimslow. So when those IED recruiters climbed out of their shiny SUV and came striding across the lawn and up the walk I met them on the porch with a twelve gauge double barrel sawed-off, and I ordered them to stop, to halt, to cease and desist. And then I asked them if they recognized what I held in my hands. They did. And then I stepped off the porch and pointed up at the sky over the empty field and woods and gave it a shooting off. And I don't know if they were impressed none but at least now I had their attention. "Come on in, boys," I told them. "Let's have us a little talk. And I'll just keep my friend here by my side."

Well them boys ain't soldiers for nothing, I suppose, so they came on in, and we sat around the kitchen table with J Junior and his mother Jane Doe Dimslow and I had them boys go over the dollars again, and then I asked, "And how much does J Junior here get for a blown off arm and a blown off leg? I mean, does he get paid an arm and a leg for an arm and a leg that's been blown off? And how many arms and legs is he going to have to blow off himself to get them bucks? And how much more of that oil money is he going to get?" And then I turned to J Junior and I asked, "How much of that oil money do you want, son? I figure now's the time to ask for all the world and all to hear. Name your price to these gentlemen and see just how much you can get." And J Junior said, "Well, I don't know anything about oil money."

And I said, "Well, these boys do. They get their share. Now you've got to get yours, if that's what you want. Is that what you want? Oil money? And blood spilt to get it? You better get what you can now, I tell you what, because it's going to be like trying to pull teeth trying to get any later. Them fat cats are going to lap it all up, quicker than you can pull any trigger."

J Junior said he didn't want any oil money.

And I turned to the recruiters and I said, "You heard the young man." And smiled. And we all just sort of ignored any guns that had been brought to the table and the blood and the oil, and the recruiters went out onto the porch and strode down the walk and crossed the yard and climbed in their SUV and drove away. And that was about all we wanted to hear from them. Would it have killed the government to send two men to come out offering a decent job, with lots of training and skills, doing some badly needed recycling or growing or teaching or something that actually creates life instead of destroying it? Oh, I suppose that would be a travesty. Socialism, my god! Might even bankrupt the whole damn system of war.

After I locked the gun in the cabinet, J Junior and I stood on the porch gazing out over the fields and forest, and J Junior said, "The money makes you think."

And I said, "Is that what it does?"

And J Junior said, "It makes you think their way."

And I said, "And what kind of way is that?"

And J Junior said, "It's the way of the killer."

"The killer thief," I said, and I turned around as Jane Doe Dimslow came out onto the porch.

And J Junior said, "And that's no way. It's no way at all."

And it's all over the dim-damned TV. All these phony political debates that get me all riled up under the skin the way them warhawks get going and all. It isn't nothing how they look, it's what they say. They all say we got to destroy Iraq to save it. More or less. And to hell with anything else. To hell with riling up them mad bombers, which is what it does more and more. To hell with everything – they say, we got to up the firepower on Iraq to have peace. We got to break it to fix it. We got to smash it to restore it.

Maybe I'm missing the candle for the wick, being a John Doe Dimslow and all, but these guys are nuts gone mad, warhawks all, blowing up Iraq, blowing up Iraqis and using our boys and girls, men and women as the cannon and the cannon fodder both. Pouring gasoline on a bonfire, all so that we, but not me and you, can own the oil and threaten to cut it off from other folks, rather than just keep buying it like everyone else. The troops ain't dying and killing for nothing, of course. There's oil there! And power! And a WMD hornet's nest is what we're a-makin', by a-killin' and by a-stayin'. And somebody not no way related to John Doe Dimslow is getting rich. That's what them troops are dying and killing for, as the place goes to the hell it has being made into, more than a million Iraqis dead, five million Iraqi refugees. And more than a few of them troops know it and are angry about it. And for starters we can thank the big dollar folks and politicians and big media types like the ones we see all over the damn place for making it so.

But what do I know, old Dimslow?

Maybe I can find a horror film on TV to watch tonight or something like that, something a little less chilling than them warhawks I see on TV chirping and pounding away at each other like they are cannons come to life, each one eager to be a bigger cannon than the other.

If only them warhawks could be confined there on the tube – but now I hear the rest of Oila is next for the blasting and smashing – and soon. It's the whole planet and everyone in it that I get worried about, that I got to speak out about, that them war-hawks seem eager to set about destroying. They act like they'll destroy almost anything to get elected or to stay in power – and to keep the oil dollars flowing into the pockets of themselves and their buddies. And the thing is, it don't in any way seem like no act.

Dimslow Calls the Cops

I called the police. Sometimes you have to. I called the police on the President of the Incorporated Estates of Earth. I called the police when President Bush invaded Iraq. That was illegal. I called the police when President Clinton bombed Iraq, and elsewhere – all illegal under international law, not least. I asked the police, "Aren't you going to do something about it?" Even if breaking laws is nothing new for presidents.

And what did the police say down in Dimslow Hollow?

"Sir, that's a bit outside our jurisdiction."

Just what they always say.

"Ye shall know the truth and the truth shall set you free," I pronounced, putting on my best mock preacher's voice. "Or is the truth outside your jurisdiction, too?"

"Look, we're all up against a lot of bigger truths, Sir. There's no standard operating procedure for that, you see. Not in these parts anyhow."

"No truth?"

"No, I guess not."

"Then you won't arrest the President? He commits crime after crime for all the world to see."

"Would you like me to send a squad car all the way to Washington to circle outside the White House just to have a look? Check for disturbances?"

"No point. The crimes are committed all across the country and world. They only originate in that Whitest of Houses."

"Well that may be."

"So no arrest?"

"Not by us, Sir. You?"

"A citizen's arrest? Believe me, I've tried."

"Oh, yes, Sir, I believe you. And if I recall correctly, you still have the right. Unless it was tossed out in the Patriotica Act."

"They always say I don't have the authority. 'The authority?' I ask. 'Or the Power?'"

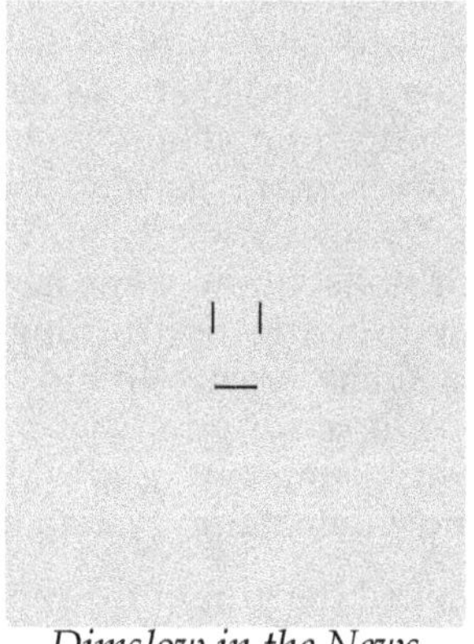

Dimslow in the News

Picture courtesy of JDD Press

Neoserf, vassal of the Incorporated Estates of Dearth, John Doe Dimslow peers out from a window of his home and wonders what is become of the country and world. He wonders if he will be able to keep his home and stay up with the energy and fuel bills. He wonders if his community will survive climate change. His health insurance is poor to nonexistent. He keeps pressuring the IED to call off its "attack on the world" and to stop denying services to his kin and to humankind. He tries to stop the Incorporated Estates from "ripping everyone off." Dimslow was arrested again this morning for pouring his own blood onto the front door of the local branch of one of the world's largest banks – Citibyrne. "Bank Dracula," he called it. "A vampire bank. Vampire bank: it's redundant." A crowd of several dozen community members watched Dimslow pour his blood on the bank. They cheered and chanted gothic epithets about the banks and the IED and then were dispersed by police armed with tasers, clubs, and guns.

The Incorporation of Oila
Tony Christini

With gas prices at record levels and oil costs on the verge of going even higher here in the Incorporated Estates of Earth (IED) and with record-setting killing (1,000,000+ best estimates) in Iraq and refugee flight (about 5,000,000 within and from Iraq, there is only one solution that I can see: make Iraq the newest estate in the Incorporated Estates of Earth.

Now I realize this may disappoint folks in Puerto Rico and the District of Columbia, and England, Australia, and Israel, etc., all of which at one time or another have vied to become an official part of the blessed IED, but given the surge in gas and oil prices and the ever pressing need of the Incorporate Estates to run the world, I think there is no time to waste in bringing Iraq formally into the Holy Union.

Iraq has even held elections so there should be no problem making the change official, little more than a few minor bureaucratic details. Surely the IED is strong enough to twist the arms of elected rulers for their signing on as the newest state.

Of course the name "Iraq" will have to go. It's too – what shall we say – foreign, or, I don't know, Native. Something like Oila would work, I think, since Oila is rather euphonious like, say, Iowa and Ohio, and Oklahoma and Indiana, a couple of rock solid Incorporated Estate names of sub-estates, with limited refugee flight, from their migrant labor farms and industrial belts of rust.

Now, some may object that Oila has already become the newest state for all practical intents and purposes since, thanks to the invasion and occupation, the oil is essentially under control of the IED, being under its guns, and since the Corporate States are already pumping hundreds of billions of dollars into the land. So it may seem very little else is to be gained by Oila's formal incorporation into the IED. It's true, Oila and its oil are basically ours now anyhow (impending legal formalization aside) – and not only on the noble you broke it, you bought it, so you might as well go ahead and keep breaking it principle – especially given the ongoing planning and construction of the permanent IED military bases in Iraq and the IED embassy the size of a town (heavily fortified) from which ultimate power can flow, along with other gated communities and neighborhood stockades.

However, failure to formally incorporate Oila into the Incorporated Estates of Earth will mean we have learned nothing these many years from the wisdom of US policy planner George F. Kennan who explained the reality of the world so well decades ago:

> "We have about 50% of the world's wealth, but only 6.3% of its population. … In this situation, we cannot fail to be the object of envy and resentment. Our real task in the coming period is to devise a pattern of relationships which will permit us to maintain this position of disparity…. To do so, we will have to dispense with all sentimentality and day-dreaming; and our attention will have to be concentrated everywhere on our immediate national objectives…. We should cease to talk about vague and … unreal objectives such as human rights, the raising of the living standards, and democratization. The day is not far off when we are going to have to deal in straight power concepts. The less we are then hampered by idealistic slogans, the better."

Building on this theme of "straight power concepts," it seems obvious to me that international sovereignty must be increasingly a relic of the past. Ultimately, there can be only one State, and it must be that state in which the IED plays a leading role, the Incorporated Estates of Earth. The IED will give that patriotic phrase "Love it or leave it" a whole new meaning.

The Oilans will just have to get used to saluting a new flag and singing God Bless the IED and the all-time sentimental favorite, IED the Beautiful. Why should the Oilans mind? I doubt they will care all that much, once they learn to forget themselves for the greater glory of the Incorporated Estates, as should everyone else on Dearth.

Puerto Rico, we'll get to you, especially if a diamond mine, or anything of value, turns up that you might foolishly attempt to keep control of yourself. Of course your little land and ungainly name will have to go the way of the dinosaur too. New Diamond as a new name might work. Or, say, Shinola.

In the meantime, Welcome, Oila! The newest Incorporate Estate. An idea whose time has come.

We, The Children Of Iraq
Tony Christini

We the children of Iraq

bear witness to the end of war.
Gone are the days of constant

bombardment in the name of war.
Gone is constant destruction of civilian build-
ings and shelters in the name of war.
Gone are the days burying soldiers alive in
the desert in the name of war.
Gone are the days of destroying entire towns
and villages in the name of war.
Gone are the days of destroying factories and
hospitals in the name of war.
Gone are the days of destroying crops and
livestock in the name of war.
Gone are the days

of destroying cities in the name of war.

We the children of Iraq

bear witness to the end of war.
And yet the destruction continues

under a different name or no name at all.

Can we be thankful

to lack chemicals for sanitation due to sanctions?
Can we be thankful that our hospitals

run short of medicine due to sanctions?
Can we be thankful that our hospitals cannot
operate incubators due to sanctions?
Can we be thankful that our electric grids
cannot be fully repaired due to sanctions?
Can we be thankful that our economy our
lives have been wrecked due to sanctions?

Can we be thankful

to die en masse due to sanctions?

We the children of Iraq

bear witness to the end of war.
And yet the deaths are mounting

under a different name or no name at all.
We are dying by the hundreds of thousands.

And it is not war. It is policy.

And it is not our policy.

It is yours.

And now again you threaten war.

To control our oil.
To run our region.
And it is not our war.

It is yours.

And now you have brought us war.

And the deaths mount by the thousands.
And by the tens of thousands.

And more.

And it is not our war.

It is yours.

*"We, The Children Of Iraq" was published in The
Texas Observer prior to the March 2003 U.S.
invasion, and later expanded.*

Dave the Prophet

Joe Emersberger

On the morning of Sunday April 14, 1986, Dave awoke from a nightmare in which US and Canadian authorities sent him off to Iraq to be tortured just after he crossed the Ambassador Bridge that linked his hometown of Windsor, Ontario, Canada with Detroit Michigan. He had slept in that morning – no hockey practice to get up for, no assignment for school to complete. His parents and little sister were driving up to Toronto to pick up a relative who was flying in from Iraq. They'd return to Windsor the next day when Dave, despite his dream, assumed he would not be deported to Iraq.

Dave's name was actually Dhafir. His parents had immigrated to Canada from Iraq when he was an infant. At an early age he realized it was easier to go by "Dave," so that's what everyone but his parents called him.

The house was empty as he sat at the kitchen table eating toast while trying to understand what had provoked his nightmare. It was unusual for him to remember a dream for more than a few seconds after he woke up. He felt vaguely nervous, as absurd as that was, about what happened to him in the dream.

It bothered him for a while like a nagging headache, but he shrugged it off. Late that morning, his girlfriend Brenda knocked on the front door. Dave ran to the door and flung it open. Brenda smiled mischievously as she stepped inside and threw her arms around him.

"Where's your car, Kook?" he asked.

"I parked it on the next street over just in case my parents drive by," she answered.

Dave laughed. Her parents would never

drive by, but he was glad she was leaving nothing to chance. The more relaxed she was the better. And so while her parents thought she was at swim practice she had sex with Dave on his parents' bed. Until then, they had only done it in the TV room in the basement of Brenda's house – always half dressed and ready to get fully dressed in a hurry.

The two things that made Dave happiest were being with Brenda and playing hockey. The two people he hated most in the world, at the moment, were Ronald Reagan and Ed Hughes (Brenda's Dad). As a little boy he had despised Saddam Hussein more than anyone because the dictator had made his parents suffer, even though growing up in Windsor he barely heard anything about Saddam from anyone other than his family. During his first year in high school, 1982, he wrote a detailed essay about Saddam, and everyone, including the teacher, had been impressed by the esoteric topic. By then his hatred of Saddam had grown somewhat abstract – just as his hatred of Saddamn's ally Ronald Reagan was now becoming – evolving into a diffuse hatred against organized brutality everywhere.

Dave walked to Brenda's house later that afternoon and arrived just after they had finished dinner. He cut through Jackson Park, greedily inhaling the unseasonably warm air. As he passed by the high school where he met Brenda, he thought about how lucky he was. He was a gifted student, played hockey for the Windsor Wolves and had a slim, but real, chance of getting drafted by an NHL club. Most importantly, he had Brenda. He had no fear that she would be raped by US funded death squads like the ones busily at work in El Salvador and Nicaragua. He had no fear of her house being blown to bits by US bombs like the people in Libya, who were bracing for a US attack which would arrive the next day. Dave followed world events compulsively, like his parents. He had read enough to know that, from a global perspective, he was an Aristocrat enjoying a tremendous amount of unearned privilege. He wanted desperately to convince others to quit deluding themselves about where their freedom and prosperity came from. He wanted most of all to convince Brenda, but her dad's influence made that tough.

The sun was still bright in the sky as Dave approached Brenda's house. He liked her house. It wasn't too big or too small. It was old enough to feel lived in, but well maintained and clean enough not to feel run down. It was a solid, working class house, much like the one he lived in. He was especially fond of the TV room in the basement.

Dave and Brenda's plan for the evening was to endure some card playing with her parents before announcing that they were going "out for a drive". They were seated at the dining room table across from Ed and Mary (Brenda's mom). Ed explained the rules of Euchre to Dave – who was the only one completely unfamiliar with the game. Dave hated card games but suffered through by looking forward to going "out for a drive". He struggled to understand Ed's instructions as he looked into Ed's blue eyes – so much like Brenda's.

When Dave looked at Ed he saw a younger, much better looking version of Ronald Reagan. Ed was an autoworker, like Dave's father. Ed's alcoholism was a plague on his family. Every few months he would drive home drunk, park the car crooked on the driveway and scream at his wife for having the temerity to complain.

"So you understand what the Right Bower is now?" Ed asked jovially before dealing the cards for the first Euchre game.

"Yes. Thanks." Dave marveled that he and Ed had yet to exchange an uncivil word.

According to Ed, the world was a little over 6000 years old (created already aged to fool scientists) and it would end in the year 2000 when Jesus would arrive to call everything off.

"I haven't read the educated books, but I

know the Bible which is the most important one," he had once explained to Dave.

And Ed certainly did have a lot of big questions answered. Ed knew how the world began, when it would end, what was right or wrong in any situation, what would happen when he died (Ed believed in Hell but seemed blissfully unconcerned about it) and so on.

"No loose ends," Dave observed, and to his dismay Brenda, who did not blind herself to many of her dad's shortcomings, was convinced that Ed had a God-given gift for interpreting the bible – especially the book of Revelations. Mary, on the other hand, wasn't interested in religion.

In frustration Dave was sometimes tempted to ask Brenda. "If you're so religious why are we having sex?" but he had always restrained himself for reasons both selfish and wise.

Dave had become an atheist at fourteen almost entirely because of reading Bertrand Russell's essay "Why I am not a Christian". His parents were not very devout Catholics, part of Iraq's tiny Chaldean Catholic minority. He didn't have much hope of making an atheist out of Brenda, but he hoped that (much sooner than the year 2000) she would at least develop doubts about Ed's "gift".

Ed didn't attend any church and regarded preachers as hucksters (one of the few things Dave and he agreed on), but Ed believed almost all the things that right wing Christian Fundamentalists preached.

"What do you think the US is going to do about Muammar Qadaffi?" asked Ed after the second Euchre game

"They're going to bomb Libya tomorrow evening," Dave replied – startling himself with his own certainty.

"I'm not really much of a Reagan fan," Ed began, suddenly in a mood to debate something, "but he was right to say Qadaffi is a 'Mad Dog' who has to be dealt with. They aren't going to put a stop to terrorism unless they start getting tough."

Hearing these kind of remarks from people he liked made Dave angry. Hearing them from Ed was unbearable.

"Reagan is a terrorist, a far bigger terrorist than Qadaffi," Dave answered quietly – doing his best to stay calm.

Mary left the table to make tea. Brenda caressed Dave's thigh under the table.

"Come on. You can't compare Reagan to Qadaffi. I know the Americans aren't saints. They've done bad things, but what are they supposed to do about their people getting killed like those two soldiers in that German discotheque."

"They could get their evidence together and go to the World Court. That's what Nicaragua just did about the terrorist war the US is waging against them. In July the World Court will rule in Nicaragua's favor and order the US to pay them damages. Of course the US will just ignore the law. That's what terrorists do, but I don't think you'd suggest Nicaragua should bomb the US at that point."

"I haven't read up on Nicaragua like you, but there's got to be more to it than that. The Soviet Union prowls around the world and the US can't just sit by and let them take over."

"The US invaded Nicaragua in 1912, before the Soviet Union existed, and occupied the country for decades. They'll continue to intervene in Nicaragua and all over Latin America after the Soviet Union no longer exists."

"What are you some kind of political fortune teller now?" Brenda laughed. She stroked Dave's arm to let him know that she was just trying to lighten the mood before things got overly serious – and possibly confrontational.

"The Soviet Union is just an excuse the US

uses to support brutal governments."

"So why don't they just support Qadaffi," Ed asked with a smirk.

"They will eventually," Dave replied. "Qadaffi's going through a disobedient phase right now and so the US will make an example of him, but by 2003 things will turn around completely. They'll quietly drop Qadaffi from their list of enemies. "

"By 2003?" Ed asked. "Are you sure it won't be 1997, or 1999?" he added, unable to resist a sar-castic response to Dave's predic-tions.

"Okay. I'll give you something you can verify shortly." There was anxiety in Dave's voice as he spoke. He felt like he was being taken over.

"The US will bomb Libya at 7:00 pm tomorrow – prime time. Qadaffi's infant daughter Hanna will be among the civilians killed. Liberals and conservatives will ap-plaud the President. Seventy-seven percent of the US public will approve. Reagan will go on TV and say that Qadaffi has – and I quote – 'engaged in acts of international terror, acts that put him outside the company of civi-lized men.'

"No one will mention, or maybe even no-tice, that neither Reagan nor his allies like Saddam Hussein are civilized men.

"Reagan will also say tomorrow night – again I quote – 'When our citizens are abused or attacked anywhere in the world on the di-rect orders of a hostile regime, we will re-spond so long as I'm in this Oval Office.'

"No one will remind him about the four US nuns who were raped and killed in 1980 by the Salvadoran military which he gener-ously funds. Long after Reagan leaves the White House, the US government will con-tinue to deny that the Salvadoran military ordered the murders. The Salvadoran officers who ordered a cover up will be granted resi-dency in the US.

"No one will remember it. When I say no one of course I mean no one on TV, no one with access to a large audience. Millions of people like me in the US and around the world will scream at their TV sets in frustra-tion. Democrats and Republicans will join together to glorify Reagan when he finally dies in 2004. The people he helped murder will be swept under the rug like so much garbage."

"Dave, let's go out for drive," Brenda said nervously.

Ed scoffed: "I don't see how you can pos-sibly…"

"Bombing Libya, squashing Grenada, kicking Iraq out of Kuwait as they will in 1991 – it's all part of a long term strategy to soften the public up for larger scale killing down the road. Vietnam messed things up for them, but by 2003 they'll feel ready to let their military do some major killing again. They try to do it better. They won't be able to sacrifice 55,000 troops like they did in Viet-nam. They'll kill over a million Iraqis, but not as many as they would have in the 1960's.

"Think of it like this – Reagan and his han-dlers are like pieces of shit floating on a huge reservoir of ignorance and bigotry. The reservoir is slowly draining. The shit is sink-ing, way too slowly, but it is sinking."

"Oh, will you please…."

"The world won't end in 2000, Ed. It won't end for most people, but it will for you if you don't stop drinking and start monitoring your blood sugar."

Ed's nostrils flared and he barked at Dave in a fierce voice that Brenda knew very well.

"You better watch your mouth. I don't know what kind of trip you're on, but you better watch…."

"You'll get tossed in jail the next time you drink and drive. I'll time my phone call to the police perfectly, before you're even plastered, so they can pick you up at Wyandotte Tavern parking lot. In fact, if I'm not busy, I'll drive over and watch them haul you away."

"I just left to make tea!" Mary screamed as Ed sprang up from the table. Mary and Brenda put themselves between Ed and Dave. Ed didn't try to push his way past them.

"Mary will get up the courage to leave you. It won't be long. Actions have consequences, Ed. Many Americans will figure that out on September 11, 2001 when the World Trade Center is blown up. Of course, many others will remain in denial."

Dave's tone was no longer mocking, as it had been when he talked about the police arresting Ed.

"He's gone totally insane. Or he's on drugs..." Ed said to Mary.

Moments later Dave and Brenda stepped out onto the porch, and Dave said, "It's not going to work between us."

The car keys slipped from Brenda's hands and smacked the floorboards.

"What's wrong with you?" she asked.

"Years will pass before the differences between us become manageable," he explained.

"Fuck off with your predictions, you nutcase!" she said through tears.

Dave barely slept over the next several weeks as he wrote a manuscript full of predictions up to the year 2008. There was a chapter on environmental disasters – even one with reviews of movies that would be released over the following decade. He tried to get it published, but no one would touch it. Even very small radical left wing publications he had thought might be receptive wanted nothing to do with it.

Some thought he was simply nuts, though one leftist publisher admitted that the short term predictions they had been able to check turned out to be "stunningly accurate," but they were not willing to risk their credibility with detailed predictions. "Even if one percent of them turn out to be wrong that's too much," Dave was told. "We're held to a higher standard. That's the way it is when you challenge Power. The powerful and their servants, on the other hand, can be wrong, or even just lie, as often as they like. Sorry."

Another was less diplomatic: "Leftists have al-ways been good at predicting disasters. So what?"

His prophetic powers had failed to alert him to that disappointment, but he came to be comforted by how much he could not foresee. He assumed it meant that the future was not set in stone. Things could change.

Brenda read the manuscript after it arrived in the mail one day and was deeply impacted – more so with each passing year.

Dave had attached a note to it:

Brenda,

Maher Arar will immigrate to Canada from Syria with his family next year. In 2002, while passing through New York City on his way home from a vacation, he will be arrested and deported to Syria despite being a Canadian citizen. Canadian officials will feed their counterparts in the US bogus 'intelligence' that will lead to his being tortured in Syria for 10 months. I refer to his case vaguely in chapter 16 because I can't predict what all the consequences will be in detail.

If there isn't a major public outcry and an official inquiry into Arar's case, then I myself will suffer a similar fate. I could avoid it by keeping a low profile politically but I won't do that – as you know.

Please study law. You could be a big help to people like Arar and also many refugees who cross the border into Windsor in the years to come.

I wish so badly that things could have worked out with us.

Love,

Dave

Dave was much relieved in 2004 when Arar's supporters successfully pressured the Canadian government to launch a public inquiry. While watching the news, Dave noticed a very familiar woman standing with other members of Arar's legal team. Brenda. He couldn't have felt more proud. Her presence was nothing he felt he could have ever predicted. And he dared not try to predict her reaction to the message he was about to send her.

Iraq on My Mind: Thousands of Stories to Tell – And No One to Listen
Dahr Jamail

"In violence we forget who we are"
– Mary McCarthy, novelist and critic

1. Statistically Speaking

Having spent a fair amount of time in occupied Iraq, I now find living in the United States nothing short of a schizophrenic experience. Life in Iraq was traumatizing. It was impossible to be there and not be affected by apocalyptic levels of violence and suffering, unimaginable in this country.

But here's the weird thing: One long, comfort-able plane ride later and you're in Disneyland, or so it feels on returning to the United States. Sometimes it seems as if I'm in a bubble here that's only moments away from popping. I find myself perpetually amazed at the heights of consumerism and the vigorous pursuit of creature comforts that are the essence of everyday life in this country — and once defined my own life as well.

Here, for most Americans, you can choose to ignore what our government is doing in Iraq. It's as simple as choosing to go to a website other than this one.

The longer the occupation of Iraq continues, the more conscious I grow of the disparity, the utter disjuncture, between our two worlds.

In January 2004, I traveled through villages and cities south of Baghdad investigating the Bechtel Corporation's performance in fulfilling contractual obligations to restore the water supply in the region. In one village outside of Najaf, I looked on in disbelief as women and children collected water from the bottom of a dirt hole. I was told that, during the daily two-hour period when the power supply was on, a broken pipe at the bottom of the hole brought in "water." This was, in fact, the primary water source for the whole village. Eight village children, I learned, had died trying to cross a nearby highway to obtain potable water from a local factory.

In Iraq things have grown exponentially worse since then. Recently, the World Health Organiza-tion announced that 70% of Iraqis do not have access to clean water and 80% "lack effective sanitation."

In the United States I step away from my desk, walk into the kitchen, turn on the tap, and watch as clear, cool water fills my glass. I drink it without once thinking about whether it contains a waterborne disease or will cause kidney stones, diarrhea, cholera, or nausea. But there's no way I can stop myself from thinking about what was — and probably still is — in that literal water hole near Najaf.

I open my pantry and then my refrigerator to make my lunch. I have enough food to last a family several days, and then I remember that there is a 21% rate of chronic malnutrition among children in Iraq, and that, according to UNICEF, about one in 10 Iraqi children under five years of age is underweight.

I have a checking account with money in it; 54% of Iraqis now live on less than $1 a day.

I can travel safely on my bicycle whenever I choose — to the grocery store or a nearby city center. Many Iraqis can travel nowhere without fear of harm. Iraq now ranks as the planet's second most unstable country, according to the 2007 Failed States Index.

These are now my two worlds, my two simultaneous realities. They inhabit the same space inside my head in desperately uncomfortable fashion. Sometimes, I almost settle back into this bubble world of ours, but then another email arrives — either directly from friends and contacts in Iraq or forwarded by friends who have spent time in Iraq — and I remember that I'm an incurably schizophrenic journalist living on some kind of borrowed time in both America and Iraq all at once.

2. Emailing

Here is a fairly typical example of the sorts of anguished letters that suddenly appear in my in-box. (With the exception of the odd comma, I've left the examples that follow just as they arrived. They reflect the stressful conditions under which they were written.) This one was sent to my friend Gerri Haynes from an Iraqi friend of hers:

Dear Gerri: No words can describe the real terror of what's happening and being committed against the population in Baghdad and other cities: the poor people with no money to leave the country, the disabled old men and women, the wives and children of tens of thousands of detainees who can't leave when their dad is getting tortured in the Democratic Prisons, senior years students who have been caught in a situation that forces them to take their finals to finish their degrees, parents of missing young men who got out and never came back, waiting patiently for someone to knock the door and say, "I am back." There are thousands and thousands of sad stories that need to be told but nobody is there to listen. I called my cousin in the al-Adhamiya neighborhood of Baghdad to check if they are still alive. She is in her sixties and her husband is about seventy. She burst into tears, begging me to pray to God to take their lives away soon so they don't have to go through all this agony. She told me that, with no electricity, it is impossible to go to sleep when it is 40 degrees Celsius unless they get really tired after midnight. Her husband leaves the doors open because they are afraid that the American and Iraqi troops will bomb the doors if they don't respond from first door knock during searching raids. Leaving the doors open is another terror story after the attack of the troops' vicious dogs on a ten-month old baby, tearing him apart and eating him in the same neighborhood just a few days ago. The troops let the dogs attack civilians. The dogs bite them and terrify the kids with their angry red eyes in the middle of the night. So, as you can see my dear Gerri, we don't have only one Abu Ghraib with torturing dogs, we have thousands of Abu Ghraibs all over Baghdad and other Iraqi cities. I was speechless. I couldn't say anything to comfort her. I felt ashamed to be alive and well. I thought I should be with them, supporting them, and give them some strength even if it costs me my life. I begged her to leave Baghdad. She told me that she can't because of her pregnant daughter and her grandkids. They are all with them in the house without their dad. I am hearing the same story and worse every single day. We keep asking ourselves what did we do to the Americans to deserve all this cruelness, killing, and brutishness? How can the troops do this to poor, hopeless civilians? And why?

Can anybody answer my cousin why she and her poor family are going through this?? Can you Gerri? Because I sure can't.

In recent weeks I had been attempting to get in touch with one of my friends, a journalist in Baghdad. I'll call him Aziz for his safety. Beginning to worry when I didn't receive his usual prompt response, I sent him a second email and this is what finally came back:

Dear old friend Dahr, I am so sorry for my late reply. It is because my area of Baghdad was closed for six days and also because I lost my cousin. He was killed by a militia. They tortured and mutilated his body. I will try to send you his picture later. Just remember me, friend, because I feel so tired these days and I live with this mess now. With all my respect,

Aziz

Conveying my sadness, I asked him if there was anything I could possibly do to ease his suffering. As a reporter in that besieged country, he is constantly exhausted and overworked. I hesitantly suggested that perhaps he should take a little time to rest. He promptly replied:

Dahr, my old friend, I really appreciate your condo-lence message. Your words affected me very much and I feel that all my friends are around me in this hard time. I live with this mess and I do need some rest time as you advise before getting back to work again. BUT, really, I have to continue working because there are just very few journalists in Iraq now, and especially in my area. I have to cover more and more everyday. Anyway friend, everything will be ok for me. And I wish we can make some change in our world towards peace. With my respect to you friend, Aziz

I have also been corresponding with "H," who lives in the volatile Diyala province and has been a dear friend since my first trip to Iraq. He would visit me in Baghdad, bringing with him delicious home-cooked meals from his wife, insisting always that I be the one to eat the first morsel.

A deeply religious man, his unfailing greeting, accompanied by a big hug, would always be: "You are my brother."

He was concerned about the perception that there were vast differences between Islam and Christianity. "Islam and Christianity are not so different," he would say, "In fact they have many more similarities than differences." He would often discuss this with U.S. soldiers in his city.

Yet he was no admirer of imperialism. Last sum-mer in Syria, he and I visited the sprawling Roman ruins of Palmyra. One evening, as we stood together overlooking the vast landscape of crumbling columns and sun-bleached walls in the setting sun, he turned to me and said, "Mr. Dahr, please do not be offended by what I want to say, but it makes me happy to see these ruins and remember that empires always fall because empires are never good for most people."

After several weeks when I received no reply to repeated emails, I wrote to "M," a mutual friend, and received the following response:

Habibi [My dear friend], It has been very long since I have written to you. I'm sorry. I was terri-

bly busy. I have some very bad news. [H] was kidnapped by the members of al-Qaeda in Diyala 25 days ago and there is no news about him up to this moment. It's a horrible situation. One cannot feel safe in this country. When I pressed him for more information, he wrote me the details:[H] was kidnapped as he was trying to get home. He was coming to Baquba to visit his parents, as he does every day. His oldest daughter who was with him told him that a car carrying several men was following them from the beginning of the street leading to his parents' home. So, when he stopped to get his car in the garage, they got out of their car covering their faces and asked him to come with them for questioning. People in Diyala definitely know that such a thing means either killing or arresting for few days. You may ask why I'm sure it is al-Qaeda. That is because no other group, including the U.S. military, dominates the whole city like they do.

We are the people of the city and we know the truth. They overwhelmingly dominate the streets and are even stronger than the government. So, there is no doubt about whether this was al-Qaeda or another group. You may ask how people stay away from these very bad people. People never go in places like the central market of Baquba. For this reason, all, and I mean all, the shops are closed; some people have left Diyala, some have been killed, while most are kept in their homes.

If someone wants to go the market, this means a bad adventure. He may be at last found in the morgue. Al-Qaeda fought every group that are called resistance who work against coalition [U.S.] forces or the government (policemen or Iraqi National Guards). Nowadays, there is fighting between al-Qaeda and other [Iraqi resistance] groups like Qataib who are known here as the honest resistance in the streets. By the way, I forgot, when al-Qaeda kidnaps someone, they also take his car in order that the car shall be used by them. So, they took his car, along with him. In case he is released, he comes without his car. I will tell you more later on.

I soon slipped into the frantic routine all too familiar by now to countless Iraqis — scanning the horrible reports of daily violence in Iraq looking for the faintest clue to the whereabouts of my

missing friend

3. *Murderously Speaking*

In McClatchy News' July 5th roundup of daily violence for Diyala, I read:

"A source in the morgue of Baquba general hospital said that the morgue received today a head of a civilian that was thrown near the iron bridge in Baquba Al Jadida neighborhood today morning.

A medical source in Al Miqdadiyah town northeast [of] Baquba city said that 2 bodies of civilians were moved to the hospital of Miqdadiyah. The source said that the first body was of a man who was killed in an IED explosion near his house in Al Mu'alimeen neighborhood in downtown Baquba city while the second body was of a man who was shot dead near his house in Al Ballor neighborhood in downtown Baquba city."

The data for Baghdad that day read:

"24 anonymous bodies were found in Baghdad today. 16 bodies were found in Karkh, the western side of Baghdad in the following neighborhoods (7 bodies in Amil, 3 bodies in Doura, 2 bodies in Ghazaliyah, 1 body in Jihad, 1 body in Amiriyah, 1 body in Khadhraa and 1 body in Mahmoudiyah). 8 bodies were found in Rusafa, the eastern side of Baghdad in the following neighborhoods (6 bodies in Sadr city, 1 body in Husseiniyah and 1 body in Sleikh.)"

What could I possibly hope to find in nameless reports like these, especially when I know that most of the Iraqi dead never make it anywhere near these reports. That is the way it has been throughout the occupation.

On July 8th, M sent me this email:

Habibi, Up to this moment, I heard that one of my neighbors saw [H's] photo in the morgue but I couldn't make sure yet. Traditionally, when a body is dropped in a street and found by police, they take it to the morgue. The first thing done is to take a photo for the dead person in the com-

puter to let the families know them. This procedure is followed because the number of bodies is tremendously big. For this people cannot see every body to check for their sons or relatives. For this, people see the photos before going to the refrigerator. I will go to the morgue tomorrow. The next day he wrote yet again:

Habibi, Today I went to the morgue. I saw horrible things there. I didn't see [H's] photo among them. Some figures cannot be easily recognized because of the blood or the face is terribly deformed. I saw also only heads; those who were slayed, it's unbelievable. Tomorrow, we will have another visit to make sure again. In your country, when somebody wants to go to the morgue, he may naturally see two or, say, three or four bodies. For us, I saw hundreds today. Every month, the municipality buries those who are not recognized by their families because of the capacity of the morgue. Imagine! In one of H's last emails to me sent soon after his return home from Syria earlier this summer, he described driving out of Baquba one afternoon. Ominously, he wrote:

We left Baquba, which was sinking in a sea of utter chaos, worries, and instability. People there in that small town were scared of being kidnapped, killed, murdered or expelled. The entire security situation over there was deteriorating; getting to the worse.

Now, that passage might be read as his epitaph.

4. Subjectively Speaking

The morning I receive the latest news from M, I crawl back into bed and lie staring at the ceiling, wondering what will become of H's wife and young children, if he is truly dead. Barring a miracle, I assume that will turn out to be the case.

Later, I go for a walk. It's California sunny and the air is pleasantly cool on my skin. I'm aware — as I often am — that I never even consider looking over my shoulder here. I'm also aware that those I pass on my walk don't know that they aren't even considering looking over their shoulders.

The American Heritage Dictionary's second definition of schizophrenia is:

A situation or condition that results from the coexistence of disparate or antagonistic qualities, identities, or activities: *the national schizophrenia that results from carrying out an unpopular war* [italics theirs].

That's what I'm experiencing — a national schizophrenia that results from our government carrying out an unpopular war. It's what I continue to experience with never lessening sharpness two years after my last trip to Iraq. The hardest thing, in the California sun with that cool breeze on my face, is to know that two realities in two grimly linked countries coexist, and most people in my own country are barely conscious of this.

In Iraq, of course, there is nothing disparate, no disjuncture, only a constant, relentless grinding and suffering, a pervasive condition of tragic hopelessness and despair with no end in sight.

Iraq on My Mind was first published at TomDispatch

Once Upon a Time
Cindy Sheehan

first published at Cindy for Congress

Once upon a time in a land called California, there was born a beautiful baby named Casey.

Casey's mom and dad knew from the minute he was born that he was a very special baby. He had dark hazel eyes that seemed to penetrate into the hearts of people who met his intense gaze. He was a cheerful baby that grew into a cheerful, yet shy boy.

Casey loved baseball, video games and playing make believe games with his younger siblings. He was a loving and fun big brother to his sisters and brother. Casey grew close with each sibling in different ways. His bright and mature sister, Carly, was his confidant and closest mischief maker. With his brother, Andy, Casey would wrestle and play endless video games, huddled closely on the floor in front of the TV set. Casey would carry his youngest sister, Janey (the baby) to bed each night and tell her a bedtime story, kiss her goodnight and make sure there were no monsters in her closet.

Casey also loved his faith and was devoted to the Catholic Church. The young boy Casey became an Altar Server when he was eight and continued that ministry until he graduated from high school. Casey never missed mass, and many around him were sure he would someday be a priest.

Although quiet and thoughtful, Casey had a very good sense of humor—long funny stories were not his forte, but he was adept at one-line zingers that would often surprise and delight his mom.

One day in the land of California, an emissary from the Kingdom's Army knocked on Casey's door and beguiled him (through a spell of broken promises of riches, adventure and learning,) to join the Army of the Kingdom. One very terrible day, a few years later, the evil Ruler of the Kingdom, George III, sent Casey off to a wicked war and Casey was killed trying to save the lives of fellow members of the Army of the Kingdom.

Casey did not live happily every after.

Casey's mom and dad and brother and sisters and many other relatives and friends miss him so much and long for his "happily ever afters."

Once upon the same time in the land of California, there was a Ruler in the Caste of the Democrats named Nancy Pelosi. She told Casey's mom to her face that she was very sorry for Casey dying and that she was doing everything she could to stop other Casey's from meeting the same fate. Years later, Casey's mom found out that this Pelosi wench knew all along what the evil Ruler George III was up to when he threw innocent people into torture chambers. The Pelosi wench knew that torture would lead to the deaths of many Caseys, but she did not use her power to stop this. Casey's mom finally understood why the Pelosi wench did not use her legal force to stop the evil Ruler George III or his war: she was and is complicit in the crimes of the Kingdom.

This sad tale is told because the Rulers of the Kingdom, in both Castes, misused Casey and thousands of others as pawns in their foul game of global domination.

If the "peasants" in the Kingdom of George and Nancy do not wake up and rise up to stop the oppression and murder by the evil rulers, no one (except the evil Rulers and their consorts) will live happily ever after.

Realpolitik

Buff Whitman-Bradley

Standing in the icy rain
Three of us
Holding signs, passing out leaflets
The people hurrying past us
Are going into the auditorium
To listen to an Important Person
Who once said
That the deaths of half a million children
Were worth the price
The people hurrying past us
Glance at our signs
And quickly avert their eyes
They are expensively dressed
And it is easy to see
From the way they carry themselves
Even in the icy rain
That they are pleased
Being who they are
They are well-off
Well-fed
Well-educated
And well-informed
They listen to National Public Radio
And read the New York Times
They are comfortable
With the arrangements of power
Some of the people hurrying past us
Take our leaflets
Some even thank us
But most let us know
By the tilt of a chin
The narrowing of eyes
A snort of disgust
That our presence here
Outside the auditorium
In the icy rain
Is contemptible
The people hurrying past us
Believe that we are naïve
That we are dreamers
That we do not understand

Realpolitik
Which is another way of saying
"Slaughter"
Which is another way of saying
"Collateral damage"
Which is another way of saying
"If you want to make an omelet,
You've got to kill a few hundred thousand kids"
Which is another way of saying
 "There is no sacrifice too great
For other people to make"
Which is another way of saying
"We like things the way they are"
We want to tell the people hurrying past us
In the icy rain
That they are right
We do not understand
Realpolitik
That we believe
In the politik
Of the separation
Of the Rich and State
That we believe in the politik
Of everyone has a seat at the table
That we believe in the politik
Of everybody gets what they need
That we believe in the politik
Of not one dead child
Is worth the price
When a security guard
Tells us to move across the street
We refuse and tell him
He'll have to call the cops
But by now
Most of our leaflets are gone
And we are wet and cold
And they are turning people away
At the auditorium door
So when we see
The flashing lights of a police car
Coming up the street toward us
We fold up our signs
And shove our half-numb hands
Deep into our pockets
And walk away
In the icy rain

Street Theater M19 '08
Buff Whitman-Bradley

On the fifth anniversary of the war
we wear orange jumpsuits
and black hoods
and walk single file
through the streets of downtown San Francisco
guarded by soldiers
with cardboard guns.
George W. Bush is here
and Dick Cheney
and Condoleeza Rice
reminding us
that the upper case People Who Matter
can't even imagine giving a fuck
about the lower case living
and the lower case dead.
On the fifth anniversary of the war
wearing orange jumpsuits
and black hoods
we kneel on the sidewalk
in front of people waiting
for the Powell Street cable car.
Soldiers with guns
drag a woman out of the crowd
put a hood over her head
throw her screaming onto the ground
and waterboard her
while she writhes and gags and pleads for
mercy.

On the fifth anniversary of the war
wearing orange jumpsuits
and black hoods
we join others blocking traffic
on Market Street at noon
sitting down and chaining ourselves together
and waiting for the helmeted police
who arrive with bolt cutters
and cut through our chains
and remove our hoods
and handcuff us
and photograph us

and put us on a bus
that takes us to the county jail
where we wait in outdoor holding pens
to be cited and released.
On the morning after
the fifth anniversary of the war
there are pictures of us in the papers.
Our orange jumpsuits and black hoods
are folded up and put away
in dresser drawers and closets.
The pitiless sun rises
at Guantanamo Bay
and scorches bombed-out neighborhoods
in Baghdad and Basra
and what once was Fallujah.
The heat stings like clouds of wasps.
A hundred million bones
keen in the ground.
In stately, climate-controlled dining rooms
the upper case People Who Matter
read the Wall Street Journal as they
breakfast on eggs benedict,
chilled, perfect strawberries
and freshly squeezed orange juice.
And as they remove the fine linen napkins
from their laps, fold their papers
and stand to go
they sigh with satisfaction
at how very nicely, thank you,
the war is proceeding.

The last child in Iraq died today

Buff Whitman-Bradley

In response to the Iraq sanctions, 1991-2003

The last child in Iraq died today.

Her mother sat holding her on a hospital bed where countless other mothers had sat before her, holding their dying children. The long, bright arm of the afternoon sun reached through a filthy hospital window and lay across the mother's shoulders, as if it were trying to comfort her.

The last child in Iraq died today.

There wasn't much left of her. In her mother's arms, her small, ravaged body looked like a bag of coat hangers. Almost absently, her mother stroked her daughter's matted hair, gone orange from malnutrition, and gently touched her tiny, twisted, thousand-year-old face. In her cloudy, bottomless eyes floated a question vast enough to crack the world.

The last child in Iraq died today.

She did not cry at the end. It took all the effort she could muster in her frail little body just to breathe. Her final breath was so faint and faraway, it might have come from a distant star. Ever so quietly, she left.

The last child in Iraq died today.

Her doctor could not determine whether the cause of death was acute malnutrition or the implacable diarrhea that came from drinking the only drinking water available, thoroughly contaminated because economic sanctions prevent the rebuilding of Iraq's sewage-treatment and water-purification systems, destroyed during the Gulf War.

The last child in Iraq died today. She was 4, born utterly innocent, as all children are, in the midst of the most thorough and brutal economic embargo in modern history, which has deprived Iraqis not only of food and medicine but of the equipment and supplies necessary to rebuild their shattered infrastructure — hospitals, schools, businesses, roads and bridges, community centers, park, homes.

The last child in Iraq died today.

It was only a matter of time, really, before there were no more children in Iraq. For 10 years, the re-lentless embargo has starved them and has reduced the once nearly state-of-the-art Iraqi pediatric wards to virtual storage facilities. For 10 years, thousands of children have died every month, as parents and doctors stand by helplessly.

The last child in Iraq died today.

"Not our fault," says the United Nations, al-though the U.N. Security Council imposed and continues to maintain the murderous sanctions, in direct contravention of international law. This occurs despite the fact that two career U.N. officials, Denis Halliday and Hans von Sponek, appointed to oversee the oil-for-food program, have resigned from that body and given up their careers to protest the program's inadequacy and the appalling humanitarian situation in Iraq.

The last child in Iraq died today.

"Not our fault," says the Pentagon, even though its war planes obliterated the country's infrastructure during the Gulf War and the deadly, radioactive residue of depleted uranium ammunition has thoroughly contaminated much of Southern Iraq and has caused childhood cancer rates to rise astronomically.

The last child in Iraq died today.

"Not our fault," says Secretary of State Madeleine Albright, stating that Saddam Hussein and the Iraqis, not us, are the bad guys. We must force them to permit further weapons inspections to do what former inspector Scott Ritter calls impossible — that is, to prove a negative, that they don't have weapons of mass destruction. And if the deaths of children are the price that must be paid, well, that price, Albright repeats, is worth it.

The last child in Iraq died today.

"Not our fault," says President Clinton, who feels the pain of the Iraqi mothers and fathers whose children have died, but who says that the U.S.-crafted-and-enforced embargo must remain in place until Saddam Hussein is removed from pow-er, even though sanctions have strengthened Saddam's position.

The last child in Iraq died today.

"Not our fault," say most members of the U.S. Congress, who surely do love little children, but believe it is necessary to grind Iraq into the sand to assure a Middle East free of weapons of mass destruction (not counting, apparently, the 200-plus nuclear warheads in Israel's arsenal).

The last child in Iraq died today.

"Not our fault," say the U.S. media, which prac-tice a virtual blackout on news of the continued, almost daily U.S. bombings and of one of the worst humanitarian disasters in modern times.

The last child in Iraq died today.

"Not our fault," says much of the U.S. public, which has so uncritically accepted the U.S. govern-ment's version of the Iraq story and failed to cry out and demand an end to the slow, silent, and merciless slaughter of innocent human beings.

The last child in Iraq died today.

Not our fault.

God have mercy on us all.

News of war

Buff Whitman-Bradley

A small boy is sweeping a back porch.
He is two, and the broom
is twice as tall as he is
and difficult for him to handle.
He drops it again and again
and keeps tripping over it
as he grapples with it.
But he is determined in his work
and manages to gather a good-sized pile
of large, yellow leaves
before he drops the broom one last time,
climbs into the chair next to a man
with a newspaper in his lap
who has been watching him work,
and sighs with satisfaction at what he has done.
The man puts aside his paper
and reaches over to rub his grandson's back.
He is remembering when his own children were small.
He is noticing the October light like golden palominos
grazing among the branches and dying leaves
of the fig tree in the garden.
He has been reading news of war
and is imagining the infernal thwack-thwack-thwack of helicopters,
and is imagining the high, angry whine of jet fighters,
and is imagining the searing air,
and is imagining the screams,
and is imagining the smoking bodies
and the piercing stink of charred flesh and burnt hair,
and is imagining the severed limbs twitching in the dirt
and the spilled intestines and the brain-spattered stones,
and is imagining splintered trees
and birds on fire

and blood oozing from the shattered ear-
drums
of small animals trembling underground.
After a few minutes the boy
gets down from his chair
and runs to the edge of the porch.
His grandfather rushes to catch up with him
and takes his hand
while they walk down the steps and into the
garden
where they hunt among the fallen leaves
for the ones that are the most beautiful.
Later, now, after the boy has gone,
after the man has swept the porch himself
and watched the persimmons on the neighbor's tree
fade into the twilight,
after he and his wife have eaten together
and settled the supper dishes into their cup-
boards,
after they have walked hand in hand
in the chilly evening air
watching their breath cloud and rise under
street lights
and laughing about the broom and the boy,
after they have locked the doors and opened
a window,
after they have lain in bed and held each
other,
she is asleep and he is lying quietly next to
her, awake,
thinking of the children again,
listening to the noises the night makes
and trying to picture what it is that is coming
now,
rustling and scratching and scraping through
the dark.

Freshly shelled peas
Buff Whitman-Bradley

I was sitting at the kitchen table this afternoon
shelling peas and listening to the radio
tossing the empty pods into the compost
bucket
and admiring the vivid green of the little
spheres
accumulating in the white china bowl
when the 5 o'clock news came on and they
announced
that the President wants to go to war
and probably because I was home alone and
there was no one to tell
I burst into tears
All I could do after that was to sit there shelling peas and weeping
Some of the tears that slid down my cheeks
fell into the bowl
making tiny little splashes
and I thought of a story I used to read to the
children in kindergarten
about an owl who made tear-water tea
by thinking sad thoughts and crying into a
kettle
 Afterwards I would ask the children what
made them sad
"When I fight with my friend" some said
"When my parents get mad at me"
"When my dog died"
We didn't talk about when children die
when their homes explode and collapse on
them
when their bodies are perforated with razor
sharp bits of metal
when the air they breathe turns to fire and
incinerates their lungs
when their little shattered bodies are nearly
indistinguishable
from the rubble
We didn't talk about what lullabies mothers
sing when bombs are falling

We didn't talk about frantic fathers
clawing through chunks of concrete and hot, twisted metal
even when there is no skin left on their bloody hands
And I didn't tell them about all the fine young fathers
with neatly trimmed hair
who leave their houses at dawn
and climb into the cockpits of terrible airplanes
and fly thousands of miles to rain death
upon those who are not us
then bank steeply and return
arriving home just in time
to watch their children's Little League games
Slowly the bowl filled up with peas
Freshly shelled peas for our family's supper
Peas salted with sorrow and bursting with life
Freshly shelled peas to offer as a prayer
Peas of outrage, peas of grace
Freshly shelled peas to fling into the face of Death
Freshly shelled peas to keep airplanes from taking off
and bombs from exploding and guns from firing
Freshly shelled peas to drop on the dark path behind us
Freshly shelled peas to scatter across the earth
to bring back to life the innocent dead.

Shock and Awe haiku

Buff Whitman-Bradley

Storm in the desert
Bombs rain from a howling sky
Bloody flowers bloom
And what lullabies
will Iraqi mothers sing
as bombs are falling?
Hush, my little one
The bombs know you are my Dear
They will not hurt you

The United States of Torture

Buff Whitman-Bradley

In the United States of Torture
we will do what we must
to protect the American Way.
In the United States of Torture
we will strip our enemies naked
and humiliate them
and terrify them with ferocious dogs
and deprive them of sleep
and send powerful jolts of electricity
screaming into their genitals
and hold their heads under water
until they nearly drown
and tie them into bags and stomp them to
death
to protect the American Way.
In the United States of Torture
where we believe in the right to counsel
and a fair trial
and the opportunity to confront our accusers
and to know the charges against us
we will make it perfectly legal
to hold secret tribunals
to reach foregone conclusions
to convict and condemn our enemies
to protect the American Way.
In the United States of Torture
we are the Lords of War
spreading fear across the land
and out of the miasma of that fear we call
forth
shadowy archipelagos
gulags of perpetual pain
with secret black box prisons
where our enemies huddle in the corners
of stone cold cells
mumbling incomprehensible prayers
to their false and puny god
forever and ever amen
while we stand vigilant at the right hand
of the One True Pumped Up and Almighty
God
to protect the American Way.
In the United States of Torture
we are the Heroes of the Battle of Fallujah
where we rained white hot phosphorus
and new improved napalm
down upon our enemies
and the children of our enemies
and the children of our enemies' children
frying their skin to a blackened crisp
and burning their flesh to the bone
to protect the American Way.
In the United States of Torture
it has always been this way –
concentration camps we call
reservations, ghettoes, barrios, prisons,
where we warehouse millions
of the dangerous poor;
death by interrogation
in the dank basements of police stations;
tac squads, hit squads, death squads
pumping bullets into the backs
of the wrong kind of people.
Terrorists are everywhere among us
and we will do what we must
to protect the American Way.

Property damage

Buff Whitman-Bradley

On the telephone from Germany
the young soldier says he wants out
He has gone AWOL two times, he says
to try to get the Army to discharge him
and says he'd rather go to prison
than return to Iraq
On the telephone from Germany
the young soldier recalls
the exploded body he saw
plastered against the outside of a house
the chunks of bone
embedded in the wall
"We laughed about the dead Haji
who'd blown himself up," he said
"You laugh about it, or you cry about it,
or you say nothing and go insane"
On the telephone from Germany
the young soldier remembers
the daily mortar attacks at Bi'aj
and all the memorial services at Camp Ra-
madi
and the NCO whose head he held
while the medic worked on him
His body was riddled with shrapnel
His jaw was shattered
and his throat torn wide open
"Hang on, hang on," the young soldier kept
saying
as the man died in his arms
On the telephone from Germany
the young soldier talks about the day
members of his platoon killed a dog
that scavenged around their camp
They smashed her skull with a shovel
they slit her throat and her belly
they broke her legs
and stuffed her into a trash bag
and when they discovered that she had a lit-
ter of puppies
they killed the puppies too
and buried them
and put a cross the grave
"They made a big joke out of it," he said

"and we all laughed"
 You laugh about it or you cry about it
or you say nothing and go insane
On the telephone from Germany
the young soldier says
that he has been burning himself –
"just to feel pain, to feel human" –
holding his palms to flame, raising large blisters
again and again
blister upon blister upon blister
and afterwards curling his fingers into fists
and squeezing the blisters hard
When someone saw what he was doing, he
says
he was told he could be punished
for damaging government property
You laugh about it or you cry about it
or you say nothing and go insane
On the telephone from Germany
the young soldier says
he has tried to commit suicide several times
with vodka and pills
and when he has asked for someone to talk
to
all they do
is recommend pills
You laugh about it or you cry about it
or you say nothing and go insane
On the telephone from Germany
the young soldier says
he has always tried to be good
he has always tried to do the right thing
and now he is waiting for some good times
waiting to stop checking for his weapon
whenever he leaves his room
waiting to stop looking for IEDs
as he drives down the street
waiting to stop thinking that every stranger
he sees
might be trying to kill him
waiting for the images and memories to fade
waiting to feel again
without having to burn himself
and waiting for the Army to decide
what to do with this damaged piece of government property
You laugh about it or you cry about it
or you say nothing and go insane

To the children of Iraq:
Nobody ever said life was fair

Buff Whitman-Bradley

I recently wrote to Sen. Barbara Boxer and Rep. Lynn Woolsey, pointing out, among other things, that thousands of Iraqi children die every month as a result of sanctions and bombings. Both wrote very nice letters back to me, explaining why our government must continue to attack Iraq.

Now, I know that both of those women love kids, as do all members of Congress, our President, Secretary of State Madeleine Albright, and everybody in the Pentagon. They'd never do anything to harm children unless it was absolutely necessary. So I thought, "Gee, if we'd only explain to Iraqi children why we're doing what we're doing, it might make things a little easier for them." Since our government officials are always extremely busy, I decided to take it upon myself to write to the children of Iraq:

Hi Kids,

I want you to know that we've been very busy in America lately, hating Serbs and bombing Yugo-slavia. But that doesn't mean we have forgotten about Iraq. We aren't that kind of country.

So, how's everything going? I hope you are going to school every day and keeping up with your studies. Some of you may live to be adults, and if you do, you will need your education to get good jobs. It's a dog-eat-dog world out there.

You may be wondering why it is that we need to keep you from getting the food and medicines you need to live a healthy, happy life. Believe me, it's nothing personal. Americans are very fond of children. And it's not because so many of you are poor that we are treating you the way we are. Why, we have millions of poor children right here in our own country.

No, the reason we can't let you have enough food to eat and medicines to treat your sicknesses is that your leader is a very bad guy. We figure that if enough of you and your moms and dads and grandparents and aunts and uncles die, the ones who are left will kick that bully out. And even if they don't get rid of him, soon there won't be much of Iraq left and we can come on over and get your oil. It's actually kind of a neat way to fight a war, because we're not risking the lives of our own children, just yours.

Believe me, we're as sorry as the next person when little children have to suffer and die, but it's not our fault. Saddam Hussein is making us bomb your country and withhold essential supplies. He just won't do what we want him to, and somebody has to pay the price for defying the mightiest na-tion on earth. In this case, that's you.

It may not seem fair to you, but hey, as millions of parents remind millions of children every day, nobody ever said life was fair. Think of it this way: The 150 or so of you who are starving to death or dying of diarrhea every single day are helping to build a New World Order in which peace will prevail, if only everyone will behave exactly as America says. It's an honor, really – you are serving as role models for others all over the world.

So try to look at the big picture. And try to keep your spirits up. A positive attitude can help you through the toughest times. The truth is, not all of you will die before age five. Some of you may not get cancer from depleted uranium residue. Some of you will grow up only slightly deformed or mildly retarded. A few of you may even grow up to be perfectly normal and healthy. So don't use your tummy aches as an excuse to slack off from the books!

Enjoy the spring weather, the longer days, the buds on the trees, the slender shoots of grass poking up out of the ground, the birds singing their little hearts out. And try to make the most of the time you have left.

Have a great day!

Weapons of mass destruction

Buff Whitman-Bradley

My friend Areopagitica Truelove can be a royal pain in the neck. She's the kind of person who spoils perfectly pleasant conversations about poli-tics or current events by throwing in a bunch of facts.

She rides around on an old Schwinn cruiser tot-ing her Guatemalan backpack in which she carries a laptop that she whips out to summon up all kinds of articles and reports and declassified documents to mess with my mind. For example, last week we were sipping soy mochas at a sidewalk café in San Anselmo and she said, "You're looking worried, Bufferootie."

"I am," I told her.

"About what?"

"About Iraq's weapons of mass destruction," I sighed.

"Stop worrying," she said. "They don't exist."

"How can you say that?" I protested. "Every day there's another story in the New York Times about how we're afraid Saddam's going to use those weapons against us or give them to terrorists."

"Government press releases," she said. "If you want to know about Iraq's so-called weapons of mass destruction, go right to the source, Amigo. Look at what a weapons inspector for UNSCOM says." She punched a few keys and up on the screen came an article about a recent speech by Scott Ritter, a former Marine and member of the U.N. weapons inspection team sent to Iraq back in the '90s.

Ritter spent seven years in Iraq hunting down WMDs and facilities for manufacturing them. He says unequivocally that virtually all Iraqi weapons of mass destruction had been de-stroyed before he got there, and that given the intense monitoring that has taken place, there's no way the Iraqis could have built more. "There has been nothing in the way of substantive fact," Ritter said, "that makes the case that Iraq possesses these weapons or has links to international terror."

"Then how come they kicked out the weapons inspectors?" I asked.

"They didn't," she said. "We pulled them out so we could do some more heavy-duty bombing in Operation Desert Dumbo. And Iraq won't let the inspectors back in unless there's a guarantee that the sanctions will be lifted. That embargo has killed more than a million civilians."

"Come on, Areopagitica! You can't blame us for that! Look at Oil-for-Food. We tried to help those poor people, but Hussein took all the money and built palaces."

"Fat chance, Big Fella," she retorted, hitting more keys and pulling up a United Nations document that explained how the Oil-for-Food program works. Apparently, none of the money from the oil goes to Iraq. It goes into a bank account where Iraq can't touch it and some committee decides what the Iraqis can and cannot buy. The amount of food they're able to purchase is far from what's needed to feed the people of that country a healthy diet.

"And there's more, Buffitito," Areopagitica told me. "Did you know that most of the 5,000 children who die every month expire because of contamin-ated water?"

"See!" I said. "If Hussein would fix up his water treatment plants, all those little kids would still be alive!"

"Buff, Buff, Buff," she said. (I hate it when she says my name three times in a row like that.) "We don't let Iraq import what they need to rebuild their water purification system, which, by the way, we targeted in the Gulf War knowing full well that its destruction would lead to massive death."

I had the feeling that I was about to see another document, and I was right. This one was a declassified report from the Department of Defense, prepared on the second day of the Gulf War, back in 1991. It stated, in part, that, "Iraq depends on importing specialized equipment and some chemicals to purify its water supply … Failing to secure supplies [for purifying water] will result in a shortage of pure drinking water for much of the population. This could lead to increased incidences, if not epidemics, of disease."

"Even when little kids get the rare antibiotics to fight the water-borne diseases," Areopagitica explained, "they have to keep drinking the same water. Their little digestive systems just can't keep fighting back."

I was getting a little stressed by then. It was probably the caffeine. "Yeah, but what about the Kurds!" I blurted.

"What about them?" Areopagitica cooed. The madder I get, the sweeter she gets.

"Hussein gassed them. His own people. What about that?"

"You're right," she said. "That was back in 1988, when George Sr. was vice-president. Remem-ber the public outcry when that happened?:

"Yes!" I shouted." "Well…not exactly…"

"You don't remember it because there was none," she said. "Everybody knew about it and our government said not word one. Probably because the materials to make the poison gas came from the U.S., complete with official certification by the Department of Commerce.

"And if we're so concerned about the Kurds, why did we just cut a deal with Turkey saying that if we can use bases in their country to stage attacks against Iraq, we will refuse to support the creation of a Kurdish state?" You guessed it. She showed me the Associated Press article that reported this piece of information.

We walked together to my car after we finished our coffee. "Then you tell me, Miss Smarty Pants," I demanded, "why are we going to war with Iraq?"

"Well," she said, "Scott Ritter, who says he's a moderate Republican, believes it's domestic poli-tics, pure and simple – war in October, reelect extremist, Holy-American-Empire Repubs in November, and boost the Prez's poll numbers. I put it more succinctly, in three little letters: O-I-L… Holy cow! What's this monstrosity?

Fishing for the keys out of my pocket, I said, "You like it? It's my new Mega-SUV, the Ford Armageddon."

"Buff, Buff, Buff," she shook her head and pedaled away while I climbed into the driver's seat, pulled out of my two parking places, and headed for the nearest Chevron station.

Slouching toward Baghdad

Buff Whitman-Bradley

Note: It has been reported that George W. Bush and Condoleeza Rice pray together every morning.

Announcer: This… is GNN!

Bear Blitzkrieg: This is Bear Blitzkrieg, reporting live from an undisclosed location in the Middle East. We are here at a secret Allied air base to speak with U.S. military personnel about preparations for the upcoming war against Iraq. With me is F-16 fighter pilot Captain J.O. Nazareth. Thanks for being with us, Captain Nazareth.

Capt. Nazareth: My pleasure.

Bear Blitzkrieg: Tell me, Captain, how are prepara-tions proceeding?

Capt. Nazareth: Well, Bear, in the past few weeks we've flown these babies on literally hundreds of training missions under simulated combat condi-tions, we've engaged in countless mock bombardments and air battles, and we've honed our fighting skills to a keen edge.

Bear Blitzkrieg: So you're ready to go?

Capt. Nazareth: We're ready and eager to engage the enemy.

Bear Blitzkrieg: How about morale?

Capt. Nazareth: Morale is great. We've got cable TV, plenty of cold beer, and these cool Hummers to drive around in the dunes.

Bear Blitzkrieg: No fears?

Capt. Nazareth: Are you kidding? These Iraqi scumbags don't scare us. Look at what happened the last time. A couple hundred thousand dead Iraqis and fewer than 150 American deaths, most caused by friendly fire. And just between you and me, Bear, combat pilots don't make those kinds of dumb mistakes. If last time

was a turkey shoot, this is gonna be Slaughterhouse Five.

Bear Blitzkrieg: I'm curious about your name, Captain. Nazareth is a pretty unusual surname. And what do the J and the O stand for?

Capt. Nazareth: Jesus Of –

Bear Blitzkrieg: Uh…oh…I…oh, I see, you were named after…

Capt. Nazareth: Not named after, Bear. I'm the real deal, the McCoy, one and the same.

Bear Blitzkrieg: You mean … are you saying … are you trying to tell me that you are the actual Jesus of Nazareth, the Son of God?

Capt. Nazareth: That's me. The Big Kahuna. El Jéfe. The One and Only Messiah. In the flesh.

Bear Blitzkrieg: So let me get this straight. What you're saying is, you've returned … this is … this is the Second Coming?

Capt. Nazareth: You got it.

Bear Blitzkrieg: I … well … I … I'm sure no one every expected Jesus … expected you … to return as a fighter pilot.

Capt. Nazareth: Yeah, I know. But who expected a poor Jewish carpenter the first time? I kinda like the surprise aspect of it.

Bear Blitzkrieg: But why have you come back, and why just now?

Capt. Nazareth: Well, Bear, one of my jobs in Heaven is to listen to people's prayers. President Bush has been praying very earnestly for a victory against the evil Saddam Hussein. I thought about it for a while, then decided, what the hey, why not?

Bear Blitzkrieg: But that doesn't explain why you returned.

Capt. Nazareth: I came back to kick some Iraqi butt. I missed all the fun the last time around and I didn't want to miss out again.

Bear Blitzkrieg: But … but …. I thought you brought a message of peace and love to the world. What about turn the other cheek and walk the second mile and love your enemies?

Capt. Nazareth: Well, heh-heh, if that was the message, Bear, it's pretty clear that nobody got it. But seriously, Bear, I was 2000 years younger then. I've grown a lot in the past two millennia. True, I used to think that peace and love were the answer. But I'm big enough to admit my mistakes. Big enough, hell! I'm infinite! Anyhow, as I watched all these wars being waged in my name over the past couple thousand years, I began to think that either everybody else was wrong, or I was. Finally, the fervent prayers of fine folks like George W. and Condi, and little people in churches all over America convinced me that I needed to rethink. If those folks were going to follow me, I figured I'd better lead them to where they wanted to go.

Bear Blitzkrieg: But why be a fighter pilot instead of, say, President yourself, or at least Jerry Falwell?

Capt. Nazareth: Because, as I said, I didn't want to miss out on the fun. I watched the whole first Gulf War from Heaven. It was particularly thrilling to see these incredible supersonic fighting machines zero in on their targets from unassailable heights and at the same time to see people on the ground scatter in panic like a bunch of crazed ants as the bombs rained down. Then, when the explosions happened, there were arms and legs and torsos and heads flying everywhere. It was way cool.

Bear Blitzkrieg: Did it bother you to think that innocent people might be among those killed?

Capt. Nazareth: To be honest, Bear, it did at first. But then I realized, if you want to make a falafel, you've got to grind some garbanzos. So now my attitude is, kill 'em all and let Dad sort 'em out. He's good at that.

Bear Blitzkrieg: So you decided to fly an F-16.

Capt. Nazareth: Yup. It's a lean, mean killing machine with all kinds of fabulous technology that is just the bomb to play with. Get it? The bomb? It's the best video game you've ever played times about a million. Plus, I get to hang out with all these baaad dudes who pray to Me and really know how to party.

Bear Blitzkrieg: We've been told that this war against Iraq is going to last less than two months. Do you have any plans for what you'll do after that?

Capt. Nazareth: Well, at some point, I'm going to ascend back up into Heaven with 144,000 very special folks of my choosing. But I haven't decided yet when that will be. Before then, I'd love to get my hands on one of those cool Israeli bulldozers.

Bear Blitzkrieg: Our time is just about up, Captain Nazareth. Any final words for the American people?

Capt. Nazareth: Yes. I'd just like everybody to know that I'm back, and I'd like President Bush to know that his prayers have been answered.

Bear Blitzkrieg: Well, there you have it, ladies and gentlemen, a GNN exclusive: the Second Coming of the Messiah. This is Bear Blitzkrieg reporting for Government Network News. Good night, and God bless us.

LIBERATORY FOCUS – PRISON

Guest Editors: Katy Ryan and Bill Ryan

Loneliness
Ryan Kirkpatrick

I sit in a cold dark room
listing intently
for something that's not here

It's just another empty space
another empty day
another empty moment

There's nothing to do
but listen to my thoughts
and they are empty as I feel

I am lonely but no one can help me
for I am lost with myself
in an empty space trying to get out
but here is no way out

Jailhouse New
Donald McDonald

They die here,
Discarded like empty dried out logs,
Blank as paintingless walls,
Cracked empty egg shells in human forms,

They die here,
Light and dark blue zombies,
Lost in glass tubes,
Cardless games,
Chess without pieces,

They die here,
Feeding on tasteless victuals,
Devouring rumors and innuendos of free-
dom,
Longing to be led astray,

They die here,
With soda pop aspirations,
And candy bar expectations,
Betting on the dreams of others,

They die here,
Searching for long lost conversations,
Forgotten by imagined friends and family,
Expecting a letter never sent,

They die here alone,
They die here forgotten,
They die here before they come.

The Ballad of a Dead Beat Dad
Jonathan Bartlett

Visiting rooms and state blues
Vending machine food and tattoos
My reality as a father
Some may say why even bother
Label me a dead beat dad
Admitting it is sad
But they say the truth will set you free
Will my child ever forgive me?

I've become what I hated most
My own father's ghost
I've been gone since she was a year old
From behind bars I've watched her young
life unfold
It's hard to express my pain
I feel like my whole life has been in vain
When I start to think that life is futile
All I have to do is think of my little girl's
smile
I have so many fears
Knowing I'll be gone the next 40 years
I won't be there when she starts to date
Will her mother make sure she doesn't stay
out late?
Who will walk her down the aisle?
The way this all turned out makes me feel so
vile
Is it possible to be a positive force in her life?

The World We Make
Angel Torres

We make the world in which we live
By what we gather and what we give,
By our daily deeds and the things we say,
By what we keep or we cast away.
We make our world by the beauty we see
In a dark cell with songs or words we preach,
In a butterfly's wing, in the pale moon's rise,
and the wonder that lingers in midnight
skies.

We make our world by the life we lead,
By the friends we pick, by the books we read,
By the pity we show in the hour of care,
By the loads we lift and the love we share.

We make our world by the goals we pursue,
By the heights we seek and the higher view,
By hopes and dreams that reach the sun
And a will to fight till justice is won.

What is the place in which we dwell,
A cell or a palace, a heaven or hell
We gather and scatter, we take and we give,
We make our world – and there we live.

A Poem
by a state of Illinois prisoner

I said I didn't do it, Mom
But still they say I did.
I'd never try to hurt him, Mom
Not my little kid.

He's such a special baby, Mom
I know you understand.
You get that warm, good feeling, Mom
When you touch that tiny hand.

There's bars all around me, Mom
And I haven't slept in weeks.
The food is hard and salty, Mom
And the piping has a leak.

I miss my little boys, Mom
They're all I've ever had
I'd always go and hold them, Mom
When times would get bad.

I'm all alone and scared, Mom
I'm losing all my hope
Without my kids I'm dying, Mom
I will never learn to cope.

I love my little boys, Mom
No matter what they say
I'm coming home real soon, Mom
This I know and pray.

Concrete and Iron City
David A. Smith

Concrete and iron city
  what an awesome sight,
From outside it looks peaceful
  inside there's nothing but fright.

Men housed in cages
  stacked row upon row,
The Despair, hopelessness and fear
  from outside, who would know.

It's a battle from within
  waged from dawn to dawn,
To overcome the feelings
  of a life gone wrong.

Segregated, denigrated,
  deprecated and worse,
Times more than your sentence
  It's been your life your lifelong curse.

Always struggling within yourself
  to make it day to day,
To maintain a shred of sanity
  to help you along the way.

But the way is fraught with dangers
  of the most fearsome kind,
Self-destructive behavior
  products of a diseased mind.

The world outside moves on
  without giving any thought,
The diseases most suffer
  are ones society has wrought.

It's easier just not to care
  than to take responsibility,
It's easier to simply say:
  "Lock 'em up, throw away the key."

But that is not the answer
  to this problem that we face,
A problem with no boundaries
  of religion, class, or race.

Instead we need solutions
  to heal the sickness in our land,
To help restore the dignity

of this fallen man.

 Help him understand the man
  God intended him to be,
Lift him up, make him realize
  his noble destiny.

Now the time is growing short
  and something must be done,
A faithful voice must be heard.
  Question is: "Will yours be one?"

"Safe?!"
by a prisoner at Tamms

A guard told me upon arrival that there are
  benefits to this isolation,
That we are now all "safe" from gang
  retaliation.
I asked, "But what about the retaliation of the
  Tamms administration?"
He smiled, as he enjoyed this in ecstatic
  contemplation.

Oh! I see! I'm "safe" from my family's
  loving embrace.
"Safe" from education taking ignorance's
  place.
"Safe" from recreation keeping my heart's
  healthy pace.
"Safe" from being considered as part of
  the human race.

Oh, how I wish I could articulate this
  quasi-existence I've grown to hate,
Or get an answer to why so many strangers
  sadistically enjoy my monotonous fate.
They say societal enlightenment takes
  time,
But what if it takes longer than your
  life, and you're the one forced to wait?

T.A.M.M.S.
by a prisoner at Tamms

Tamms. Taking a multitude of men's souls
and killing our mentality
Having hopeless thoughts, always slipping
out of reality

Being distracted by staff in all positive endeavors
Without no outside support, feeling like
you've been slaughtered like Medgar Evers

Having negative thoughts daily
  And trying to strengthen your thinking
skills
They play many unnecessary games with our
legal services
  Documents and other legal materials

Filing a grievance EMERGENCY will start
building the bitterness
No satisfaction fo' real!

The mental health staff are said to be here to
assist us
  And to help us overcome any anxiety
But instead they are orchestrated to assist us
  In becoming eradicated from our very own
society

Speaking of help, I was told by one counselor
  …that she has my best interest at heart
Not knowing for several months that she was
designated to alter
  My way of thinking from the start

Smiling in my face with her Betty-Boop-like
voice
  Knowing that I will fall victim to her decep-
tion
All the while mastering her scheme
  To assist me in my own self-destruction

What have I left to use of my best while here
at Tamms?
  Not so much of anything constructive
Because I am looked at as less than human . .
.

  Is it my soul the staff here wants? or is it my
courage to stay alive?

Until someone has the courage to step up
and acknowledge to me
What it is they want
I will continue to live, strive, survive . . .
"You know, there are three phases in life:
You either in a storm, you just got out a
storm, or you're on your way into a storm."

Taking
A
Multitude of
Men's
Souls

America's Supermaximums
by a prisoner at Tamms

As I walk through the tunnels of this hellhole and see
different faces of young and old brothers
caught up in this
place, I often stop along the walk and wonder what story
can be told about this particular spot. Is it a
bloodstain that leaves a
mark of a gang of brothers in battle over
some phones or some cell
that ain't even theirs, or was it about a drug
deal gone bad, and one
inmate stabs the other for his cash, not realizing that they are playing
along with the makeup of this Master Plan.
                                                    If
only these walls,
bars, cells could tell, they would reveal stories of murder, rape,
drug ODs, bogus medical practice, suicide,
beatings, a multitude
of pain that will never be told because they
are the secrets
of a prison system that failed the rehabilitation
of a population led astray…
                                Then we look
around the world, see

pictures of the way people treat us in American supermax prisons,
and realize they have taken the same ill behavior across the seas
to someone else's country called Iraq. Pure
hate started
when the first seed was planted from a
wicked deed
by those in authority who realized there was
profit
in locking us up and throwing away the
keys.

So while
we are focusing on prisons outside our country like Abu Ghraib, we
need to look at our supermax warehouse system of live human stock,
and wonder why there are so many unex-
plained murders, suicides
and so-called accidental deaths. Where so
many people fall down
the stairs or hang themselves while the doctors and coroners
help to cover up the crimes. Pretending like
they are here to
correct you… We have no other choice but to
enforce the rules…
                                We need to cease
this madness
and open the eyes of the world before more
bodies be bagged
like yesterday's trash.

If Only

Joe Dole

Part 1

I grew up in dozens of hovels in numerous ghettos throughout the city of Chicago. My mother was single but doesn't deserve the title single parent because it takes more to be a parent than giving birth. I never knew my father. I'm not sure my mother did either.

My earliest memories are of trying to stay clear of the multitude of men in my mother's life and of trying to get enough food to quiet my stomach enough to fall asleep. I went to school until halfway through the 3rd grade when after one of our many moves I did not get re-enrolled.

So my formal education ended there and my street education began. I began to stay away from home and abuse as much as possible. Returning late one night I heard my mother's boyfriend selling something at the door for $100. I couldn't tell what he had sold but that was more money than I had ever seen so it piqued my curiosity. After a few weeks of snooping around, I figured it all out and started my career in the cocaine trade.

I began by stealing small amounts that I hoped he wouldn't detect were missing and catching some of his customers on the street before he got to the house. I'd be sure to sell it for a lot less so they'd keep their mouths shut. I spent most of the money at fast food joints. Not much time passed before I started to catch the eyes of the older kids who hung out at the corner. Once they discovered I was selling they got mad. When they confronted me I was terrified. After the first hit I was on the ground crying. They said if I ever sold on their block again the beating would be worse. When I whined that all I wanted was to get some food, the leader took pity on me. After that I started selling for him

and spent most of my time with the gang. For once I felt welcomed and each time they asked me to do something, it was always something I was able to do, not requiring any book smarts. For the first time I knew what pride was. I was proud of my accomplishments, never reasoning whether they were right or wrong. They always felt right and garnered me acceptance. The first time I contemplated right or wrong was after my arrest for murder and a sentence of 20 years in prison.

Part 2

My time spent in prison was the most positive experience of my life. It was a life-altering moment that led me to leave a life of crime behind. I met with a counselor to discuss my goals and interests and to make a blueprint for rehabilitation. The next week I was enrolled in G.E.D. classes and received my diploma 2 years later. In the following years I was assisted in picking my courses to work toward a college degree in my field of interest. I received my bachelor's degree in six years. A Pell grant paid for it all.

Once I was enrolled in school and had an eye on the future I turned my attention towards the necessities of the present. I got a job working in the factory making minimum wage. This allowed me to send money home to support my child as well as buy necessities at the commissary and start a small savings account.

I was shown respect and compassion at all times, and this in turn taught me to be compassion-ate and respectful to others. For the first time in my life I watched the news and followed current affairs. I developed my own opinions on matters of religion, morals and my future. I looked forward to accomplishing something positive with my life.

When I left prison I was alone again but I was prepared and with my savings could support myself until I found a job. I now take an active part in society and cannot imagine ever breaking the law again. I'm saving for my own house, share custody of my son and help out with numerous charity groups. Life is good.

Part 3

Per instructions, this entire story is a work of fiction. Part 1 is fiction because I made it up. It was not my life but some version of it is reality for thousands of kids across this country. More unfortunate though is that Part 2 is also fiction and in today's "correctional" environment cannot be a reality for anyone. In a time when education is nonexistent in maximum security prisons and continually stripped away in others, when Pell grants are no longer available to prisoners, when jobs are almost nonexistent and pay only pennies per hour, when inmates are not allowed to save any significant amount of money or keep an inheritance because the state will seize it to pay for the "costs of incarceration," when first-time felony offenders can be sentenced to life imprisonment or death, when there are no second chances, when upon conviction someone is stripped of his claim to humanity and made an outcast and labeled a monster, Part 2 is not a possibility.

My question is this: How can society expect people to change after living through a version of Part 1 without being given the tools of Part 2? They can't, and without a serious shift in policy the recidivism rate will continue to be as unconscionably high as the current rate of 55%. Millions more will be lost and considered animals.

LOCKDOWN PRISON HEART

Renaldo Hudson, an inmate at a maximum-security prison outside Chicago, initiated a writing contest in the fall of 2003, asking Illinois prisoners to reflect on the questions, "Who am I, and what can I do to be better?" Lockdown Prison Heart contains the thirty-eight personal essays submitted to the contest. These brief writings – thoughtful, angry, sorrowful, honest, regretful, meditative – allow us to hear directly from people whose voices are too often distorted or ignored by mainstream media. The proceeds from the collection will be donated to Murder Victims' Families for Reconciliation, a national organization composed of people who have had family members murdered – by homicide or state killings – and who work to restore communities by promoting crime prevention, opposing the death penalty, and helping survivors reconstruct their lives.

Some of the writers in this collection have spent over twenty-five years in Illinois prisons. Others have been in for a matter of months. They all know what it means to "do time," and in these essays they reflect on how to make that time meaningful.

Introduction

Renaldo Hudson

The concept for these essays came from a lesson I learned from Minister Farrakhan. He was teaching on the subject, Who are you, and are you good for nothing? This lesson on tape changed my life forever. So I wanted to give back from what I learned. I shared with Bill Ryan the idea to have an essay contest for Illinois prisoners, and he went about putting the judges and prize money together. Bill Ryan, we love you, and thank God for your heart and your willingness to continue working on our behalf.

I can tell you, the contest wasn't about the mon-ey. I live here in the midst of these so-called "monsters." Men came to me with smiles on their faces, like little children look on Christmas morning as they open gifts. They were saying, "Thank you, man. Sometime a brother just needs to be heard. Made to feel human again. The essay contest made me feel like a human again."

I am extremely thrilled that we are able to share our thoughts and souls to the public in these essays. These men and women are so brave. I take my hat off to all of them. Daily, I hear the hearts of men losing hope and the will to live. At the same time, I see the growth in so many.

It is our hope that these essays will encourage others to think about who they are and what they can do better. We hope that you enjoy them as much as we did writing them. Please share them with as many people as you can. We want to grow. Help us to keep moving down the roads of positive change. May God bless.

Editorial Note

Katy Ryan

There is little that cannot be learned from these essays about what it means to be locked up in the United States, to live, in the words of Jeffrey Boswell, with "anguish like a fire in my heart." The writers discuss the forces in their lives that led them to the Illinois Department of Corrections and the forces that now keep them alive and hopeful. I was struck not only by the clarity and range of voices but by the repeated calls for justice – for children, for women, for the wrongfully convicted, for all of those living on the "modern day plantation."

In the fall of 2003, news of the writing contest, initiated by Renaldo Hudson, traveled by word of mouth, and within a couple months, thirty-eight submissions, mostly handwritten, had arrived from six prisons in Illinois. Preliminary judges, Tony Christini, an English instructor at South Texas Community College, and Katy Ryan, an assistant professor of English at West Virginia University, selected twenty essays that were forwarded to the final judges – Eric Zorn of the Chicago Tribune, Cornelia Grumman of the Chicago Tribune, and Jeff Flock, the former CNN Chicago Bureau Chief. The winning essays, along with four essays named for special awards, appear in the beginning of this collection. Renaldo asked that his essay not be considered in the contest, but it is included here. And with it one of the most important lines in the book: "Who am I? I'm what the world says I can't be: I'm a rehabilitated man."

Since most of the contributors used the contest questions for their titles ("Who am I, and what can I do to be better?"), I selected phrases or words from each essay to serve as titles. Occasionally, for clarity's sake, I made minor grammatical changes, which were approved by the writers.

Our title, Lockdown Prison Heart, comes from poet Edward Bart k-Baratta, whose brother John was murdered in 1984.

If you would like to contact any of the writers, you can find their information on the Illinois Department of Corrections website (idoc.state.il.us/), or you can contact Bill Ryan; 2237 Sunnyside Ave.; Westchester, IL; 60154; nanatoad@comcast.net. For information about the Appalachian Prison Book Project contact: kohearnr@wvu.edu.

It was a genuine pleasure to edit this book. Many thanks to the writers for sending their words out to us.

I'm Sorry

Joe Dole

Who am I? Well, I was a boy with a man's responsibilities but now I'm a man that has lost his ability to be responsible. I'm serving a life sentence and am housed in a supermax facility. I have two beautiful daughters whom I can no longer provide for, hold when they're scared, or take to the park. They are the sole factor that keeps me going and the main factor in my heart breaking continuously each day.

Who am I? I'm a changed man, one who has seen the errors of his ways, who can truthfully say, "I'm rehabilitated." The only problem is that after my first felony conviction I was given natural life without the possibility of parole and, in other words, labeled as being unable to be rehabilitated.

Who am I? I'm a patriot who loves my country, even though I don't feel I got justice from our judicial system.

Who am I? I'm someone who has failed my family as well as society, someone who now wants to give back to society and be there for my family but cannot. Someone who has learned what it really means to have your freedom taken away. Most people's conceptions of being locked up are completely wrong. It's not the physical things that you're without that make it so hard to be incarcer-ated for life. It's the fact that you're helpless to take care of your family when they're sick, to raise your children, to help in their times of struggle, and to give back to your community. Instead you're a burden, a charity case, someone to pity. It strips you of your self-esteem and your self-respect. That is what breaks a man, not the absence of good food, alcohol, sex, or any of the other inconsequential things we may often wish we had to temporarily give us pleasure.

Who am I? Someone who's looking to get back some self-worth by somehow giving back.

What can I do to better myself? Continue to learn. An ignorant man cannot be a teacher. The more you learn the better you become. If I'm ever going to be able to be a positive impact on my children, I must first make a positive impact on myself. If I have no self-respect, how can I teach my children to respect themselves? If I have no education, then how can I educate them? I can't; therefore I must continue to learn. No one can ever know everything, but no one should ever stop learning. Once you stop learning, you stop living.

Who am I? I'm a father who loves his daughters.

Who am I? I'm sorry.

Anguish Like a Fire in my Heart

Jeffrey Boswell

I am a man first and foremost.

I am a man seeking a better understanding of the Creator.

I am a man with few alternatives.

I am a man that is in struggle to regain my freedom.

I am a man that is constantly changing, learning, seeking, challenging myself to broaden my horizons and expectations of me. I see myself as a man that quickly establishes myself as a fast-track performer, tireless, relentless in what I'm doing. I seem to have an obsessive preoccupation with right and wrong. I have a moral code and work ethic I feel is leftover from another era. I'm a man with morals and principals and a philosophy in life which guides my decisions and choices, which I feel gives my purpose color, gives it tone, gives it direction, makes me stop, notice and listen and then to consider my options, examine the facts and apply my logic.

As far as a man of family and friends – it seems that ill-usage and the passing of this time has estranged me from the one and distanced me from the other. And now much of my experience even the most ordinary activities take on a dream-like quality. This is not to say that I find it difficult to distinguish reality from fantasy or the free-play of imagination. What I'm saying is that the outside world seems light years away. A Big Mac seems as remote as a world without prejudices. And thoughts of laying with a woman are likened to my mom's homemade cookies. I know I've had some and I know it was good but the flavor is difficult to remember…

I seek a better understanding of the Creator. I feel when it is all said and done all earthly roles are stripped away, and the question becomes, "Who am I really?" and while I'm still among the living – simply put – I need help!!! I am a convicted man of a double murder. It was the moment at which my shabby box of hopes and wants – which had once seemed to be such a fabulous chest of bright dreams – was turned on end and emptied into an abyss, leaving me with zero expectations. In a clock tick, my future was no longer a kingdom of possibility and wonder, but a yoke of obligation. Anguish like a fire in my heart…

However, in the last 23 years I have remolded my character, polished my style, fresh with an appetite. I genuinely deserve a second chance. My concern, my interest, and yes my love for life, here and the hereafter, born of these particular circumstances in which I find myself alone, lonely, desperately seeking any type of kindness, and with a heart vulnerable to anyone who would care about my existence just a little. I suffer long periods of despair which I feel is put upon me by this system. Society simply fails to recognize my worth. I know this – as well as I know my own name – that additional time served in prison will be counterproductive with regard to my further development as a human being and a man with a sense of mission. I feel that in the not too distant future a hard bitterness will begin to pervade my spirit that could well blunt the sharp edges of all my creative energies. What is difficult if not altogether impossible to deal with is a life without hope. Such existence brings about a form of despair that is actually physically painful. It is a pain sooo great that death itself seems a reasonable alternative. I don't believe I could tolerate such an existence for any more length of time… I'm a man that is in struggle to regain my freedom. It was thumbs down the final vote to cut my throat – life in prison. Man, this shameful place of steel and stone is not my home, where some live false elation on this modern day plantation, dungeon of mental and physical destruction. This is me and my dreadful situation. And it seems nothing will substitute for candor, nothing will dispel suspicion, restore tranquility, and confidence and reunify me with society except the truth. My desire for more of a life, for direction and meaning, is undiminished. I am in the nest of the enemy and my fear is great. Yet, it only feeds my rage. I am confident I'll achieve my freedom of one kind or another, one way or another, and total financial independence within the next couple of years…

The thing that is most important to me is freedom from this hell. I believe that all of us must appear before Christ to be judged by him. Each one will receive what he or she deserves …When all is said and done, what is most important to me, is what will I deserve. What will I receive. The question is, Who are you? I feel I'm finding out second by second…

P.S. Regrets – limiting myself to a thug's life.

What can I do better?

Continue my struggle!

Every Tomorrow
George Whittington III

My given name is George Whittington III. My spiritual name is Ahmad Safdar Al-Ahad, which translates as "commendable soldier, the one and only." I am a commendable soldier, but I am also so much more. Society has labeled me prisoner N72861, but I am so much more. I am a father, I am a son, I am good, I am bad…

I am, I am . . . I am Nat Turner's rage running rampant in Spotsylvania County, Virginia, I am Denmark Vessey's vengeance unchecked and precise. I am the sword of Gabriel Prosser penetrating his master's skull, I am every drop of blood sweat and tears the first and last slave ever shed…

I am Marcus Garvey's vision for his people, I am Malcolm's passion for truth, I am Che Guevera's love for the people, I am Martin's unfulfilled dream floating in the air here in 2003, I am George Jackson's unbroken will and spirit, I am Fred Hampton's resistance, I am Frederick Douglass' persistence for abolition, I am James Byrd's last breath rising up from that cruel highway in Jasper, Texas…

I am the pain Emmett Till endured in Money, Mississippi, I am the strange fruit Billie Holiday sung about, I am every Bob Marley song, I am the wrath Shaka Zulu brought to the British, I am the truth wrapped in grafted European lies, I am Jesus's twin, feet of bronze, hair of wool just like the Good Book says…I am a scientist deep in my soul, a master mathematician made up by design to seem to be a master manipulator…I am a man short 40 acres and a mule and the tools to break me free, I am misery manifest manufactured by a mad scientist named Willie Lynch and his Uncle Sam. I am a mountain of grief soon to be a volcano of retribution and redemption, I am every scream yesterday ever produced, I am justice denied and delayed…

I am an untapped reservoir of black gold wait-ing to release riches to my people. But most of all I am every tomorrow until tomor-rows cease to be and my redemption song is sung…

What can I do to make myself better? I can be my harshest critic and accept my shortcomings and faults and make sure an effort is made each day to improve upon my shortcomings and faults. I can strive towards love and charity for my brother man, accepting him and his faults.

I can immerse myself in truth and strive for justice while standing firm amongst this world and all its lies…

There are so many things I could do to make a better me, but the most important thing I can do to better me is to know and acknowledge God each day through prayer, studying his word and practicing his word at every opportu-nity, and believing wholeheartedly in him and the hereafter, because the life I now know will surely one day end and then there is only God and eternal paradise or hell and eternal damna-tion.

Second Chance

Guadalupe Navarro

Who am I? That's a question I've asked myself a million times. The truth is, I wasn't al-ways sure who I was. I knew that who I wanted to be and who people portrayed me to be were two different things all together. Who I am is a question with more than one answer, depend-ing on who you ask. With time I've come to re-alize that even though a person may change, that doesn't necessarily mean others will change the way they view you. Knowing that I can an-swer this question better than anyone on God's green earth, I think it's only fair I present myself from those many viewpoints, no matter how good or bad it may be.

To my parents, I'm the loving son that can still do anything if he puts his mind to it. Their beautiful baby boy who (ironically) can do no wrong, no matter how much wrong he does.

To my children, I am the Daddy that has been away at work for 32 months and can't come home for another 39. In their eyes I am the coolest, funniest, and strongest man in the world! To their mother, I'm a man who told one too many lies, broke her heart one too many times, and swears he's changed but just can't be trusted.

To my friends, I'm the life of the party. The "down for anything" guy that always had a gun on him, an eye for trouble, and wasn't scared of the law.

To the law, I'm a known gang member and criminal. A threat to the community. A danger to society serving time in I.D.O.C.

To the I.D.O.C., I'm inmate number R03908. A ward of the state. A convicted felon currently placed in the Pickneyville Correctional Center.

I am a man that knows pain, love, and hate all too well, but first and foremost I'm a man. I am a man that doesn't always feel one, due to the fact that I can't be there for my children and parents to love and support them, like they've always done for me. I am a man that has always tried to do right, be good, and make my family proud but always seemed to do wrong, be bad, and disappoint those who love me the most.

I'm not the boy I once was. I've grown and matured and have finally found sense and sent the meaning in all the lectures that were given to me when I was young and "hard-headed." I'm someone that can no longer play with a lady's feelings or break her heart because I now know what it feels like to have a broken heart.

I am one man that has truly changed but won't receive a fair chance in life due to my criminal background and physical appearance. On the same token, I am a man motivated to overcome all obstacles and succeed because whether or not my chance is fair makes no difference. I'll have a second chance regardless and I will make the most of it. I refuse to be a statistic or habitual offender with an excuse and sad story for all my problems. I am not the only one. I am only one of many. I am Guadalupe Navarro, a twenty-three-year old Hispanic man.

What can I do to be better?

Everything I failed to do before.

Level E
Daniel Parker

I tried to escape from Stateville in 1995, because my 23-year-old mind hadn't accepted the 60-year prison sentence I'd been given. I immediately found myself classified as a Level E, which is an extremely high escape risk. My Level E classification defines me as a person in the eyes of the Department of Corrections. To them, I am simply a Level E, marked for retribution.

The fact that I'm a Level E overshadows my character and my deeds. The correctional officers are instructed to memorize my face. I often see the look of recognition in their expressions as I walk by. Usually they will point me out to each other, or they will search me before I am allowed to continue on my way. Sometimes I am searched by three or four different officers before I make it from my cell to the dining room. But these are minor inconveniences.

The real retribution is unleashed when I receive a disciplinary report, file a grievance, or submit for good conduct credit. Every hearing and evaluation is tainted by my Level E classification. Whenever I would go to a disciplinary hearing, the first thing that the hearing officers would notice was my Level E classification. The words, "Oh. He's a Level E," always let me know that I was about to receive the maximum penalties for whatever rule violation I was accused of.

Over the past five years, I have managed to stay out of trouble through countless prayers and teeth-marks on my tongue. But I have learned that five years of good conduct are irrelevant to the Department of Corrections. I am still a Level E. When I submit for restoration of good time or file a grievance, I cannot escape the disapproving pen of the warden. No matter the issue, a Level E obtains the warden's approval only by oversight or miracle.

The worst aspect of being a Level E is the visiting policy. Because I am a Level E, I am not allowed contact visits with my loved ones. I will probably never be able to hug my mother or grandmother again. They will probably be long-dead before the Department of Corrections finally decides that I've learned my lesson.

I am a man who can deal with all of this negativity and still continue to hope for a brighter future. Over and over I am shown that my good conduct is meaningless, but I haven't run out of faith yet. There are a few people in this world who know my true character, but to everyone else I am just a Level E.

I dream of a someday when the Department of Corrections will tell me that I am no longer just a Level E. When that day arrives, I will have more room to grow as a person. I have to believe that holding onto my faith will lead me from here to there. But for now I'm just a Level E.

A Secret Injustice

LaJuana Lampkins

When you take a mother and you put a gun to her head and you tell her if she does not cooperate, you'll kill her children…she will comply. When you take a mother, as during slavery, and you tell her you will sell or whip, lash or lynch her children unless she meets your sexual needs, she will comply. A mother will do anything when her children are endangered.

When the police took me at age 24 years old in April 1982 into an interrogation room, slapped and kicked me, ordered me to tell them the whereabouts of my children ages 9, 4, and 1 years old, and brought them down to the police station, put my sons ages 4 and 1 years old, in that interrogation room, as I was handcuffed to the wall, whisked away my 9-year-old daughter to some "undisclosed" area, all men officers, and denied them food, beverages, sleep, or any female matron supervision, then stood over me yelling that if I did not cooperate, and "confess," that I'd never see those children again, I never signed a statement, I never court-reported a statement, I could not get to a lawyer, and I faced the worst torture a human being could bear, I had a nervous breakdown and ended up with 60 years, on psychotropic medication for the first 5 years. No evidence exists against me. The statement doesn't corroborate with the crime scene or pathologist report, because other than the information they told me, I did not know because I did not do it.

Your question is, "Who am I?" I am a woman, a mother, who found in your opportunity a chance to be acknowledged so I can hopefully be restored to the children, now also 6 grandchildren, that were once the weapons of torture used to put me behind walls for now 22 years for a crime I never committed. I am the female part of the broken system Governor Ryan forgot existed when he paraded numerous men across televised nationwide media and spoke of their torture, their abuse, their injustice, yet out of approximately three thousand women in the Illinois Department of Corrections, not one did he exonerate or acknowledge as also victims of a broken system. Did he only envision the system broken for men, and imagine that women had access to the true justice part? I am the voice of the women.

What can I do to make me better? I am praying through me that the boundaries of reform will be looked at by the overseers of law at both sides of the broken system, men and women equally, that the next time a statesman stands up for justice that it be for all, not one-sided. I am that skeleton in the system's closet, that female version kept secret while all the noise was going on about the "broken system."

No Longer a Prisoner

Scott Caro

Yesterday I was a heroin addict. I could never manage a loving, caring relationship with another. My only relationship was with heroin. I slowly began to not care whether I lived or died. Yesterday I was lost in my isolated, painful world of addiction. Addiction is selfish, complicated, and in many ways masochistic. I reverted to having only an instinctual need to supply my habit. Yesterday crimi-nal activity and lying were second-nature to me. I would lie, cheat, and steal; anything to supply my habit in order to avoid the pain of withdrawal. Yesterday I was ashamed without self-esteem. I didn't have any goals or ambitions. Yesterday I was sick spiritually, mentally, and physically. Yesterday I was scared to live life on life's terms. With two years clean I use the word "yesterday" because of how far I've come and who I am today. I can never forget yesterday, because it has made me a better person today.

Today I have love for myself and others. I'm no longer spiritually bankrupt, but very much spiritually aware. My physical freedom may have been taken from me as an inmate in prison, but I'm more free today than any of my days actively using. I'm no longer a prisoner to the disease of addiction. Today I have goals and ambitions. I'm blessed to be able to say I'm more than an inmate, I'm a college student. I'm focused on my dream of a college degree. Today, I have a relationship with family and friends. I'm a son, with proud parents. I'm a brother with proud sisters and brothers. I'm an uncle, with many proud nephews and nieces. I look beyond myself and want to help others. I see beauty in this world, and see God's hand at work in my life. Today I'm proud of who I am. I'm proud of the person I dug out from under years of drug abuse and neglect. I could look in the mirror and be happy with who I see. Today I'm no longer scared of reality, but meet it each day with a confident smile. Today I'm assured that I never again have to use.

I believe I could be a better person by sharing my experience and hope with others. I plan to pursue a career in drug counseling. I think by helping others find sobriety I'll also be helping myself remain focused on what's most important in life. I've been given a second chance at life and I plan to make the most of each day. They say it's better to have loved and lost than to have never loved at all. I can be a better person by sharing who I am and loving others. I want to be a husband and father. I want to recapture the dreams I once abandoned. I want to share who I am with the world. All of these things will make me a better person.

True Power
Donald McDonald

Who am I, and what would I do if I were free? Firstly, I am a caged idea, a cloud waiting to burst, raw energy wanting to be unleashed.

I was a dreamer afraid to explore my thoughts and take a chance that my dreams could come true. So I formed a false person, creating a sense of power by controlling those weaker than I. You know what I mean, the weak-minded and needy. Those rejected by their peers.

Never realizing what real power was, I discovered that true power comes from ideas that are an expression of my will. So I began to embrace my ideas and develop them. Allowing them to form concepts and follow those concepts to their logical conclusions. My will becoming a caged beast whose hunger must be sated. I have become what all men strive to be, willful ideas. Ideas that bring jobs and prosperity to millions of people that have lost their power as I had. Were I free, I would promote a barely noticed movement to explore inventions. Restarting industry by opening factories that manufacture those ideas. Opening stores that sell those inventions.

Factories and stores owned and operated by people from low-income communities that could compete in the new world economy. Communities that can use their greatest resources, dreams, ideas and manpower. Say I found a recyclable product to make furniture and I rent a building in a depressed neighborhood and hire the people from that area to build this furniture, using their own designs. Finally I would open stores in other communities providing jobs and building up that area's economy.

Building up a community is done by creating jobs for the unemployable, not by filling the pockets of a few rich people who would only computerize and move to another country for their cheap labor. This is true power, not what you can get, but what you can give, not who you can trick, but who you can help to live.

So I dream about ways to provide a better life to those from my community, and I know I can make a difference with the power of my mind, and the force of my will. Caged no more, my energy longs to be free to create by the power of my mind and the strength of my will.

Comments on Lockdown Prison Heart

Sister Helen Prejean,
author of Dead Man Walking

The United States incarcerates 2 million people. Here are the voices of thirty-eight of them. These men and women heard about a writing contest that asked them to reflect on who they are – and so they did. Reading their accounts of struggle, loss, injury, faith, and hope, I am compelled to ask the same question to those of us who live outside prison walls: Who are we, and what can we do better?

Eric Zorn,
Chicago Tribune

This book has inspired creativity and productive thought, highlighting the humanity of prisoners. To make society better, prison must make prisoners better, and this kind of effort points us in that direction.

Jeff Flock,
former CNN Chicago Bureau Chief

The written word can have tremendous power, particularly when it carries great emotion and great truth. Both are present in these essays. Powerful writing doesn't require good grammar, clever prose or even proper spelling. It comes from people who have something to say. And the men and women in these pages have much to say, primarily from personal experience – most of it experience they wish they'd never had.

Spending time with the people who populate prisons and particularly those on the former death row has reaffirmed for me a guiding journalistic principle: that all should have a voice regardless of color, race, opinion or what they may have done in their lives.

These essays give voices that are often silent the chance to be heard. We are better for the listening.

Katy Ryan,

English Professor, West Virginia University

From Tamms, the supermaximum security prison in southern Illinois, Jeffrey Boswell composed an essay, submitted it, and soon was notified that he had won second prize. He wrote to my father, who was helping organize the contest, and asked if he would send him back a copy of his essay. Jeffrey had mailed the original. My father put Jeffrey's essay in the mail, but it was returned to my father with a form letter explaining that inmates cannot communicate with other inmates.

Such obstacles and delays are routine when dealing with prisons, but this one has stayed with me for its metaphorical potential: Can an imprisoned person communicate with herself or himself? This collection assures me the answer is, With perseverance, struggle, a sense of community, some luck, yes.

Jennifer Bishop-Jenkins,

Murder Victims Families for Reconciliation

When family members of murder victims struggle to face life after the tragedy that ended the lives of their loved ones, they must live with what some of us call "the new normal." Our lives now contain a grave, which shapes us forever after the murder. Part of that difficult new reality is the fact that the offender often remains alive while their family member is dead. Yet members of MVFR firmly believe that vengeance and more bloodshed is not the answer. We oppose the death penalty in all circumstances. We know, more than most, how wrong it is to kill. We seek to reconcile ourselves to working against the cycles of violence that caused the death of our loved ones to begin with. We work to support each other as we struggle to cope. Many family members of murder victims need, more than almost anything sometimes, to understand why these horrible events occurred. And many of them long to hear words of remorse from those that hurt them the most. When my sister Nancy, her husband Richard, and their unborn child were murdered, her final act of life was to draw a Heart and a "U" in her own blood – her last word on life was LOVE in the face of great evil. She shared a profound truth with us in those final moments of her life: that love is the most important thing in the world. In the face of that, I hoped that their killer could come to realize the full measure of what he had taken. And since that time, I have come to know many of the prisoners whose writings are contained in this book. I cannot imagine anything more meaningful to victims of violent crime than to hear these words of responsibility and remorse, of healing and seeking forgiveness, of courage and growth. Finally, these writings are a redemption of tragedy. I am grateful to the writers herein for their decision to give the funds from this book [Lockdown Prison Heart] to MVFR, and for the ways that they are helping all of us to heal.

Bill Ryan,

Advocate and Frequent Visitor to Illinois Prisons and Jails

Renaldo Hudson and other inmates have provided me with genuine inspiration. Renaldo is the most truly spiritual person I have known. Reading the essays contained in this book will provide insight into the minds and thoughts of men and women in Illinois prisons. There are the stories of the guilty and the wrongfully convicted, of those who accept responsibility for their actions and those who seem to blame others. All the stories speak to the pain and suffering of the victims as well as those who cause the violence. Hopefully, some of you will be inspired to learn more about the individual writers, the criminal justice and prison system in our country.

My journey with prisons and death-row inmates began about eight years ago when our daughter Katy sent me a book entitled, Dead Man Walking by Helen Prejean. I had spent my lifetime in child welfare services where my focus was on trying to protect and support children and families and not giving much thought or consideration to the criminal justice system. I was moved reading Dead Man Walking and called Helen. During the conversation, she suggested I visit with people on death row. I contacted the Illinois Coalition Against the Death Penalty and discovered that two executions were scheduled in Illinois the next week. The parents of one of the men to be executed wanted to visit their son but had no transportation. I agreed to take them to visit their son. The first time I walked through the doors and into a visiting room with a sign "Condemned Unit," my knees were shaking and heart pounding. I met Hernando Williams and Jim Free who were to be killed by the state in two days.

The day after they were killed, I had a phone call from William Peebles, one of the essayists in this book, who called to thank me for taking Hernando's parents to see their son. I made arrangements to visit with William, and he introduced me to Renaldo and several others. As a result of getting to know men and women in prison, I became active in the abolition movement in Illinois and organized a death penalty moratorium movement. I became friends with each of the seventeen innocent men who had been sentenced to death in Illinois and were later exonerated, and I knew six of the thirteen men who were executed. I recall Walter Stewart putting his handcuffed arms around me the day before he was killed saying, "Don't cry, Bill. I am alright, I am going to Jesus. You go home and have a beer."

Former Governor George Ryan on January 30, 2000, declared a moratorium on state killings and on January 11, 2003, commuted the sentences of each of the 167 men and women on Illinois Death Row, pardoning four men. After leaving death row and being assigned to a different prison, Renaldo told me he wanted to have an essay contest so people can learn more about prisoners. I said I would be glad to help out, and this book of essays was conceived. Maybe, just maybe, someone else will begin a journey of learning about the reality of prison life and the humanness of the people living there.

The Forgotten Inmate

Adetokunbo Abiola

They said she was dead, Katherine Adamou thought, sitting on the edge of the bunk and staring into the gloom of the Benin City cell. Dead because they wanted her dead. Dead because they wanted the malaria in her body and the hunger in her stomach to continue until she was dead. She shut her eyes against the darkness of the cell, rolled to her side, lay on the bed, and shivered. A wave of pain from the malaria shot through her head and she moaned.

The cell in the March night was hot and airless, stagnant and dark, suffocating in the still air, sprouting smells which hung solid in the gloom, radiating a heat which was trapped between the thick walls. The night divulged insects, some of them bugs. The mosquitoes were busy at play, the ants crawled over the floor and beds, and a few fireflies were drifting in the heavy blanket of the solemn night.

Somebody stirred on the bunk beside her own. Forgetting about thoughts of death, Katherine stared in the direction. That must be Tina, she thought.

Tina, her co-sufferer in the cell of death; Tina, her best friend in the past six months of tribulation.

"Warder Benson will come for you," Tina said in the darkness. "You must follow him."

"What can he do?" Katherine said moodily. "He's only a junior warder. He'll only get himself in trouble."

"Don't speak that way," Tina said. "You must try to get to the foyer. Benson says the Chief Judge wants to see you. He wants to grant you an amnesty."

"I'll think about it."

"Don't think about it," Tina said. "Act it. Staying here means death, just like other inmates dumped here have died."

"When Benson comes, I'll go with him," Katherine said. "But it's a hopeless case. It's difficult for a junior warder to get a forgotten inmate like me out of a Benin City cell."

Forgotten inmate, that was what one warder had called her, Katherine thought. Better she was called forgotten soul. Or forgotten victim. Her jour-nay to become a forgotten inmate began one September evening when policemen descended on her street, arrested the unemployed youths and others hanging around, and accused them of wandering. Katherine had been standing on the street in front of her house after a stroll to console herself over losing her job. There was a movement in the darkness, the sound of quick footsteps, a shout, and suddenly hands held her. At the police station, she was charged with wandering, accused of being a prostitute, and clamped into a cell. The next day, she was taken to court. The Magistrate demanded her file, couldn't get the police to get it, and ordered her to be clamped in prison until the file was brought before her. Katherine had no one to bribe the police to get her out, so she had been in jail since then.

Sighing about her travail, she turned on the bunk and stared at the ceiling of the cell. The January wind blew in through the window, hot and blustery, bringing in a litany of odors. This place smelled worse than a toilet, Katherine thought. A smell of waste, whether from man or beast, had settled in the cell; a smell that also reeked of the scent of dead bodies, urine, and unwashed skin; the odor of stale sweat and rot and rags and soil and sickness all mingled together. Pressing her nostrils against each other with her fingers, she fell asleep.

She woke up to the sound of chains and padlock clanging against the lock of the cell door.

Warder Benson coming to take the female prisoners to the toilet, she thought. She got out of the bed and stood on the floor, tottering on her feet. She was ill. She was seriously ill. She was terribly ill. Hearing footsteps leaving the cell, she put away her thoughts and followed Tina and the other prisoners to the toilet at the end of the female block. As she trudged on, she heard the unearthly sounds coming from the prisoners holed up in the block of those condemned to die, and she tried to quicken her footsteps. After going to the toilet, she felt Warder Benson pull her hand, and she stood in front of him. He was a tall slim man in his thick brown khaki uniform, a man in his fifties. You're not tough enough for this, Katherine thought. Why do you want to get into trouble?

"Get ready to go to the foyer," Benson said. "The Chief Judge wants to grant you an amnesty."

"But Warder John has told him that I'm dead," Katherine said.

"Warder John has had an accident," Benson said. "He can't stop you from seeing the judge. I'm taking you to the foyer to wait for him."

"But why are you helping me?" Katherine asked. "All the warders, except you, want me dead."

"You look so much like my dead daughter," Benson said. "I can't allow my daughter to suffer. Besides, if you stay here, you'll die, like other inmates whose files could not be traced." He turned to Tina. "Follow us to the foyer."

After locking the cell door, Warder Benson walked down the corridor towards the adjoining block, Katherine and Tina following him. Katherine felt the ache from her malaria running through her head, through her thighs, through her legs, through her drooping shoulders, and through the muscles of her arms. Mixing with the pain from her illness, the variegated smell of the prison drifted into her nose, choking and stifling her breath, making every lining in her stomach, every sensation in her chest, each individual strand in her throat try to rebel, to resist, and to repel the scent. Walk on,

she told herself. On and on, despite the malaria, despite not having eaten any since the previous day. When they got to the end of the corridor, Katherine saw Warder Moses Iglesias, John's assistant, coming to stop in front of them.

Leave Moses to Benson, Katherine thought. She didn't want to confront Moses. When she saw the suspicious look that came into his eyes, she looked away. In his eyes, all prisoners were equal to a band of felons, she thought. But in her eyes, most prisoners were equal to a band of victims.

Moses was pointing at her.

"Where are you taking this witch to?" he asked Benson.

"Medical check up," Benson said, and Katherine winced. Why was Benson being defensive? she thought.

"Has she paid the money for that?" Moses asked Benson.

"She doesn't have any money," Benson replied.

"She never has any money," Moses said in a bitter voice. "She has never had any money. If I were you, I would take her back to the cell. Let her die there."

Katherine wanted to make a cutting remark, put him on the defensive, but she stopped herself. Benson should handle him, she thought.

"I think you should try to understand..." Benson began.

"Understand what?" Moses said in a loud voice. "She's not here to enjoy free medical service, free everything. She's here to pay for the crimes she committed against humanity. John must not hear of this." And he marched away.

Katherine stared at the sand-strewn floor of the corridor. Moses had said she wanted everything free. Did he know anything about having nothing; did he know anything about suffering? Did Moses know anything about being imprisoned when one was innocent of a crime; anything about having no one to save one when one fell into trouble; anything about hunger, illness, and poverty? Staring from the floor, she looked at Benson and saw the hesitant look in his eyes.

"Let's go back to the cell," he said. "I'll think of a way to get out of this situation."

The three of them began to walk back towards the cell. The distance seemed far to Katherine, but she walked on. A flight of steps soon blocked her path. Could she climb this? she asked herself. Could she climb these when her legs felt as heavy as lead, her arms felt as heavy as lead, her feet felt like lead. As she placed her leg on the bottom step, the muscles of her ankle shifted, and she fell on the ground. Was she about to die? No! She felt hands on her arms, hands on her shoulder, and she was lifted to her feet, but she couldn't climb the steps. She was too hungry and too ill to move. Sitting on the ground, she waited to gather her strength. As she sat staring at the field in the middle of the prison yard, Samuel Ago, a warder friend of Moses, waddled towards them.

"Benson, can't you see that this girl is hungry?" he said. "Get her something to eat for Christ's sake"

"If Moses sees me, he'll tell John," Benson said.

"Forget Moses," the warder said. "He's too occupied to tell John about anything. Besides, John is off duty. Take the girl to the kitchen." He climbed down the steps and waddled away.

Katherine felt Tina's hand on her arm, and she was lifted up. Seeing that Benson nodded his head down the block, Katherine moved in the direction, assisted by Tina. When they got to the adjoining block, the corridor of the row of cells containing the death row prisoners stretched out before them.

The stench of sickness and human waste and urine filled the corridor, leaving upon the scene only the sense of decay, death, and hopelessness, not the presence of life. The prisoners inside the cells rushed to the windows, pushing forward, pulling backwards, shouting and howling, half-dead figures without the hope of salvation. As the smell from the cells choked at Katherine's nostrils, she let out a gagging sound and tried to vomit on the verge of grass that fringed the corridor. But nothing came out of her mouth. She stayed still, clutched her stomach for several seconds, then raised her head up. Can't bear this place, she thought. Can't bear the smell, can't bear the sense of death. Biting down on her lower lip, she willed herself to trudge away from the place, Tina holding her elbow to steady her movements. Well away from the block in which the death row prisoners were camped, she heaved a sigh of relief. The cell was filled with people suffering from hunger, she thought. The death row was filled with people suffering from madness. While she ruminated on this, she reached the door leading to the kitchen.

Benson nudged her towards the door, and she entered the kitchen, along with Tina. Coming towards them was Madam Angela, a fat woman in her late forties. She wore a dirty white apron, and a puzzled look was on her face. Be kind, Katherine thought. Give me only a plate of food without any confrontation. Don't have a stony heart, lying tongue, a granite soul, and a wicked spirit. But when Madam Angela's puzzled look was replaced by a scowl, Katherine's heart fell. She would as soon give a leper a plate of beans as give one to her.

"What's it again, Benson?" she demanded. "There's no extra food here."

"Just something in their stomachs while they wait for the Chief Judge," Benson pleaded.

"The government has not provided for extra food," Madam Angela said. "If I give to them, I'll be cutting into my profit."

At that moment, Katherine heard footsteps behind her, and she turned. A warder had entered the kitchen, a man whose stomach bulged under his uniform. He had a plate of beans on his left palm, spooning from it with his right hand. The warder in charge of food, Katherine thought. She watched him belch and saw the frown that came to his face when his gaze took in Katherine.

"No extra food for inmates here," he said in a belligerent voice. "There's no provision for that."

"They're being given amnesty today," Benson said in a weak voice. "Do you want the Chief Judge to see them like this, hungry and sick?"

"Why should I care?" the warder said, spittle flying from his mouth. "It's not my fault that the government hasn't provided for them." He turned a stern eye on Katherine and Tina. "Now, both of you, get out of here!"

Before she turned to leave, Katherine saw a plate of beans on a table fifty yards away from her. The food would have stemmed her hunger, and she could easily have grabbed it and stuffed it down her throat, but she shook her head. Let Benson take control. Let him tell her what to do.

They trekked out of the kitchen and stood on the corridor of the block in which it was located. From where she stood, Katherine saw the sun rising up in the sky, a yellow ball speeding through a landscape of blue and white, sending a harsh light over the prison yard. Thank God! she thought, smiling. The prison smell was being blown away by the morning breeze, and she discovered that she could now breathe, even if for a few seconds. Thank God! The daily deadly dose of malaria usually disappeared with the sun and the breeze.

"Not yet in the cell?" she heard Warden Moses' voice behind her. She saw him come to stand in front of Benson. "Why do you want to put yourself in trouble, Benson?" he asked.

"You don't understand the situation, Moses," Benson said.

Moses hitched up his trousers.

"I understand the situation," he declared. Pointing at Katherine, he said: "All the forgotten inmates pay homage to us except her. All of them obey the rules of the cell except her. She keeps saying she has no money. Will that feed my family? Don't you know that is why John hates her?"

Katherine wished she could swing a karate chop at his face, the chop her teacher taught her at the karate class. But she didn't swing the blow. She would put herself at the mercy of Benson. It was his job to control the situation.

"You get it all wrong," she heard Benson tell Moses.

"You're the one getting it wrong!" Moses shouted at Benson. "This is what I'm going to do. If you don't take her back to the cell now, John will hear of this."

Katherine saw Benson hesitate. He was going to give in, she thought. He always gave in. Would this lead her back to the cell, back to hell? She saw Benson stare in the direction of the foyer, rub his jaw, his thoughts far. He couldn't sustain rebellion, Katherine thought with growing strength. With a superior officer or one close to the boss, he would back down, had always backed down, would always back down. While these thought went on in her mind, Benson coughed and focused on Moses.

"The Controller said I should bring her to the foyer," he said finally. "And that is what I'm going to do."

"Please yourself," Moses said. "But be prepared for the consequences."

Katherine watched him walk away and nodded her head. Benson was fighting back for once, she thought. Following him and Tina, she staggered as she tried to match their pace. Ahead of her, she spied the bleached white wall of the foyer and the group of prisoners being ushered into it by two warders. Prisoners for the amnesty, Katherine thought, feeling stronger. Depends on their offences: petty stealing, petty conspiracy, petty crime, jailed without trial, forgotten inmates, slam of the Chief Judge's gavel – amnesty for them. She gave a grim smile as this went through her mind. What about amnesty for her? She grimaced. She should forget that, or so John seemed to think. Katherine was dead, that was what he told the Chief Judge. Dead and buried. Buried and forgotten. Those were the exact word related to her. His prophesy must not come true! As she mused on this, she, Benson and Tina got to the end of the block. Someone stepped from the yard beside the compound and stood in their path. Warder John!

He was a tall man in his late fifties. His left arm was thickly bandaged and was in a sling. There was anger clearly written on his face.

"What do you think you're doing, Benson?" he demanded.

"The Controller told me to bring her to the foyer," Benson said, trembling.

"Liar!" John shouted. "I told him she's dead. There's no way he could send for her when he thinks she's dead. Do you want him to think that I'm a liar?"

Benson said nothing.

John looked at Katherine and spat on the grass that fringed the corridor of the block. He looked at Benson. "You're doing this because of this thing?" he asked, gesturing at Katherine. "This thing that always complains of having no money?"

"It's not my fault," Katherine said. "I've been sacked from work. My family is poor. There's no money to be given out."

"Will that feed my family?" John asked her. "Will that pay the school fees of my three children?"

"Excuse me, sir, I..." Benson began.

John lifted his good hand and pointed down the corridor. "Take her back to the cell," he commanded. "You can take Tina to the foyer."

"Please, sir," Tina said, dropping to her knees. "Have pity on Katherine. She's been my elder sister here."

"She must go back to the cell," John said. "Ben-son, take her back to the cell."

Seeing that Benson was going to back down this time, Katherine went to sit on the grass by the corridor. Go back to that cell? she asked herself. If she did, John's men would be cruel to her, kill her, brutalise her – with iron claws,

stony hearts. She would be their rat, an endangered rat, at the mercy of their clubs. They would chase her, shout at her, John standing by the door, cudgel in hand, howling: "Kill the rat!"

She clambered to her feet.

Hated, chased, cornered, yet innocent, she thought. Imprisoned for wandering, yet obeying the law: standing in front of her home. Labeled habitual criminal, yet never been in a police cell throughout her thirty years. Kept in jail for six months – a hateful life that filled her with hate – yet sentenced for loitering a week. A forgotten inmate, her case file missing, yet still imprisoned. John must not have his way! she thought. John must not have his way. Benson either. He must not have control. Or she would die, perish in the cell, an insignificant number in the graveyard of the prison. What should she do?

At that moment, people started to shout in the prison yard. Katherine stared in the direction of the voices. The Chief Judge, followed by the Controller of Prisons, her lawyer, and other prison officials, were walking towards the foyer. She watched them as they climbed the steps leading to the foyer and disappeared.

The cell was a graveyard, she thought, a dungeon, a theatre to contact malaria, tuberculosis, and AIDS; a cemetery of forgotten inmates; a hell of heat, diseases, and tragedy. Going back was inconceivable. Going back was unthinkable. Going back must be resisted. How? She thought for a moment then nodded her head. Simple. Resist going back. Let John punch her. Let him flog her. Let him beat her. Going back must be resisted. No need to wait for Benson to take control. She would take control!

She stared at John and Benson. Benson was nodding his head in agreement to John's instructions.

"Now, take her back to the cell," John commanded. "This very second."

"Yes, sir," Benson said.

"No, sir!" Katherine said in a bold voice, and started to move towards the foyer, the corner of one of her eyes on John's bandaged arm.

"What did you say?" John asked.

"I said I'm not going back to the cell."

"Foolish criminal!" John swore at her.

He grabbed her with his good hand and pulled back in anger. She staggered past him, slammed her back against the wall of the block, and slid to the grass. As he advanced towards her, she started to scramble to her feet. "I'm not going back to the cell!" she shouted. "I'm not going back to the cell!" John reached her, grasped her by her hair, and swinging his leg, he swept her off her feet. As she fell down hard on the soil, she dimly heard voices shouting over the fight from the cells in the yard. She blocked this from her mind and struggled to her feet. As John moved towards her, she let out a yell and jumped into the air, giving her assailant a karate chop on the bandaged hand. John yelled, clutching at his arm.

Run! Katherine told herself. With the remaining strength in her, she ran past John and started to stagger towards the foyer, to the sound of jubilation from the prisoners in the cell. She heard John roar at her and heard feet starting in a run after her. Faster, she told herself. She sprinted from the man who was bent on seeing her blood, bent on dying unless he saw her dead. She knew being caught could mean her defeat, her disgrace, and her death. But she was weak from the hunger and her sickness. John caught up with her as she fell in front of the doorway of the foyer. As he lifted her up, she saw the crowd of prison officials and others that had gathered by the door of the foyer.

"I'll kill you!" John yelled.

"Warder John!" a voice shouted from inside the foyer. The controller's voice, Katherine thought. "Why are you treating the inmate like that?"

"She doesn't want to go back to the cell," John said.

Katherine saw the Controller detach himself from the crowd and come towards her. Come, she thought. She wanted him to see the woman whom they said was dead. She wanted him to know that she was being lied about, was being hunted like a rat, was being shouted upon like a slave, was being harassed by brutes like John who said she must rot and perish in the cell and her dead body thrown to a pack of hungry dogs as an afternoon meal. Behind the controller, she saw the Chief Judge and her lawyer coming forward to see the cause of the commotion. She saw the look of surprise in her lawyer's eyes when he saw her, and she saw him whisper something to the Chief Judge. She saw both of them as they started to move towards her. Katherine was wiping her lips when the Controller lifted up her face and looked into her eyes. She saw his look of surprise.

"Is this not the inmate you said was dead, John?" he asked.

"No, sir," John said.

"Yes, sir," said Katherine's lawyer, who had reached the scene. "I was there when he said she was dead."

Say something, Katherine told herself.

"He said I was dead because I refused to give him a bribe."

"I see," said the Chief Judge, nodding his head and staring at John. "I see." He paused, then said: "Let's go back to the foyer. This girl must receive her amnesty. I'll make sure that those who have erred on this issue receive their punishments."

He turned and began to lumber towards the foyer, followed by the Controller and Katherine's lawyer. Benson nudged Katherine towards them, and she started to stumble in their direction. Amnesty was freedom from jail, she thought, even when the freedom could mean starvation on the streets. She stepped into the foyer and moved unsteadily towards the high table, behind which the Chief Judge had sat down to begin his judgment.

Frame Up

Ron Jacobs

Malcolm McRice had been framed. He looked at the wall across from his bed. He was still in a cell by himself. That got pretty fucking lonely, but the other side of it was he could have some freak in the cell with him. Then he would have to be wary all the time, not just when the guards or pigs came around. The cop Mulhaney had been in earlier that day, poking and hitting him. He was pissed off about the newspaper article that questioned his detective work.

In Malcolm's mind, the article was bullshit 'cause it took them liars at face value just because they wore a uniform. He counted the little dots in the concrete block across from him. He never expected to get an accurate count. It was just a way to pass the time and trip out a little when the holes floated around a little. Tomorrow he was supposed to meet his new lawyer that Auntie and the minister had got for him. Jerry McCaffrey was the cat's name. An Irish civil rights lawyer who knew the redneck mentality – that was how Auntie's preacher had described him. What the hell, thought Malcolm, at least he'll ask to see the police report and the evidence. Malcolm didn't even think the fuckin' deal should go to trial. They had no evidence.

The arresting officers Mulhaney and Smith were in the lounge at the Howard Johnson's. One of the cocktail waitresses was sitting on Mulhaney's lap with her hand in his pants. She probably hoped to get off the next time she got picked up for drunk driving. Smith ignored Mulhaney and the waitress and stared into his drink. If Mulhaney were a woman, they would call him a slut, thought Smith. Ever since he and his wife divorced, Mulhaney had forgotten the meaning of the word discreet. Hell, he hadn't just forgotten the meaning, he had forgotten the word. It was getting downright embarrassing for Smith. Smith was a family man who held the belief that sex was something to be shared with one's spouse, not just any floozy who came along. Unfortunately there were enough cop groupies around that Mulhaney could get a hand job or more whenever he wanted. If they wouldn't give it voluntarily, Mulhaney would just threaten to arrest them. It disgusted Smith. But, cops stuck by their fellow cops.

It was Friday evening and they were getting ready to pay a surprise visit on McRice. They knew the guard working this evening. The shift change had taken place that week at the prison, so that meant Mulhaney's cousin was working the weekend night shifts on Malcolm's tier. He'd let them in without a problem. Even better, he'd let them take in whatever they needed to intimidate the black sonofabitch. Things weren't looking as good as they had hoped they would be looking by this time. Malcolm refused to sign anything and now them niggers had found a Goddamn civil rights lawyer to defend him. The coloreds in the Grove and other colored sections of town were ignoring the police when they drove through. Hell, some of the teenage kids were flipping them off and throwing rocks at their cruisers. Mulhaney was pissed. Tonight was the night he was going to do something about it. The two cops ordered one more drink each. They tossed them back and left. It was dusk. By the time they reached Patuxent, it would be dark.

Mulhaney's cousin was ready for them when they arrived. He pretended to pat the two cops down for weapons and let them in to Malcolm's cell. Malcolm was half asleep. He jumped up with a start.

"Don't say nothing, McRice," said Mulhaney. "This guard is on our side. He ain't no friend of yours like all them niggers who work here." Mulhaney walked over to Malcolm's bed and pushed him hard in the chest. Malcolm fell back but caught himself before his head hit the wall. He stood up ready to fight. Suddenly, Smith was behind him. Malcolm felt some cold steel on his neck. He was pretty certain it was a pistol. He let Smith cuff him. Mulhaney punched him in the face. Malcolm felt the blood trickle down his lip into his mouth. He spit it out.

Smith jabbed the gun into Malcolm's neck even harder.

"Sign the fuckin' confession, McRice," threatened Smith. "And you can live." He wished McRice would relent, just so the two cops could get this whole thing over with before it got further out of control.

"Fuck you," spat Malcolm. Malcolm kicked his feet back at Smith. He hit him in the crotch and his gun fell on the floor, but, at the same time, Malcolm went sprawling across the concrete floor of the cell. Smith was bent over holding his balls. Mulhaney began kicking Malcolm in the head. Smith found his gun. He was pissed off and hurting. He cocked the gun and was ready to fire it when the guard came back. He was breathing heavily and seemed scared.

"You guys gotta go!" he whispered loudly. "My fuckin' supervisor is comin' up here. He just called. I don't know what the hell he's doing here now, but he's comin'!"

Mulhaney kneed Malcolm in the balls and punched him in the face once again while Smith uncuffed him. They were reluctant to leave, now that McRice had made it physical.

"If you ever make it out of this jail alive, McRice," said Smith, "I'm gonna hunt you down and kill you and your hooker girlfriend." Smith hit Malcolm hard on the head with the butt of the pistol. Malcolm sank to the cell floor. The two cops left. As they turned and walked out of the cell, Mulhaney said quietly, "We're going after your family and your friends next, nigger."

Lawyer Jerry McCaffrey had scheduled a meeting with Malcolm for the next day at noon. When he arrived at the prison he was told that his visit had been canceled. McCaffrey refused to leave and demanded to see his client. The guard in charge of admitting visitors refused. McCaffrey demanded to talk to the person in charge of the prison. After half an hour of arguing and threats, he was brought to the warden's office. He demanded an explanation. The warden told McCaffrey that Malcolm was in the infirmary for wounds sustained during a seizure of some kind. McCaffrey demanded to use the warden's phone and called Grace.

"Does Malcolm have any history of seizures?" he asked her as soon as she answered. He knew the answer would be no. He had a terrible feeling that either the guards or those two cops had beaten Malcolm Friday night. "Thank you, Grace." He hung up the phone.

"I don't believe your assertion, Warden," said McCaffrey. "If I am not permitted to visit my client immediately either in his cell or in the infirmary I will leave these premises immediately and call my good friend who happens to be the city editor of the Washington Post. He's been interested in this case ever since I mentioned it to him a few days ago over drinks. It's just that he hasn't found an angle that will attract the front office's attention at his paper. But if I can mix your little prison into the story and say something about your guards letting rogue policemen into the prison at night after the administration goes home and that these rogue cops use their entrance into Patuxent Correctional Facility to beat and intimidate prisoners into confessing to crimes they may or may not have committed – well, you get my drift, don't you warden?"

The warden got his drift. He called for a contingent of guards to take McCaffrey and himself to the infirmary. When he saw Malcolm's swollen, scabbed-over face and his swollen crotch, McCaffrey knew exactly what had happened. He tried to talk to Malcolm, but he was unconscious from the painkilling drugs that were dripping into him.

"He better not die, Warden." McCaffrey said coldly. He stared at the warden. "Can you please escort me out of here now?" McCaffrey wasn't going to tell the papers just yet. He was going to tell Reverend Moore, Malcolm's family and friends, and the Maryland Coalition Against Racism and Police Brutality. They could tell the papers.

Frame Up is excerpted from Ron Jacob's novel

Short Order Frame Up.

Interrogation

Mahmud Rahman

The boys are processed through my station here on the banks of the Jamuna.

They think they are so smart. They try to rob a bank. To raise money for the struggle, they say. Or they attempt to snatch a policeman's rifle. To collect weapons for their people's army, they say. The adaptable ones – those with the rural equivalent of what might be called 'street smarts' elsewhere – don't get caught easily. But I would estimate that as many as eight out of ten of the others do. With few exceptions, they are from what we call 'good families.' Children who grew up in privilege in the city. Why they think they can survive in the villages – swimming like fish in the sea, they quote Mao – I will never know. To me, they look like fish out of water.

When I say boys, I do mean boys. I am only responsible for those who are under sixteen. That is my charge from the ministry: to interview the youngest prisoners and choose who qualifies for rehabilitation.

By the time the boys face me, the constables have already knocked some sense into their skulls. But I have made it clear to my superiors that I shall not have my hands dirtied with that job. I have even managed to get them to agree that the prisoners will be given a bath before I see them. I do not want to see any signs of blood.

You will observe that I am a sensitive soul. Before the liberation struggle, I used to be a writer. I even had a collection of stories published the first year after independence. Why, I have managed to acquire a complete collection of Rabindranath's prose and poetry. I especially enjoy what he wrote while he lived on the houseboat supervising his family's estates. Sometimes, here in this station on the banks of the river upstream from where he used to live, I feel a spiritual bond with him. It is as if we shared a common destiny. However we are not all as fortunate as Tagore who came from a wealthy family. Other creative souls like me face difficult choices in how to eat and write. Mine was because of this woman I loved. The only way I could get her family to allow her to marry me was if I took the civil service exams and joined the government. They would not give their daughter to a starving writer. So I paid the price. The second price I did not anticipate. My wife, a city girl through and through, won't set foot in this provincial town. I only see her when I am on vacation.

The ministry considered my qualifications close-ly before they assigned me to this job. I have been with the party since those harsh years when most of the leadership was in jail. I proved my loyalty during the liberation war. They also understand that I am someone with a heart, not just a bureaucrat. I was honored to accept this posting, but still, did they have to establish this station so far from the capital? I cannot fault their logic. We are located near the heart of the northern region where the troublemakers are active. Now I understand why. What I saw here even shocked me – people eating grass and clothed only in jute sacks. I have been assured that the government is doing its best to develop the region. How will that happen? That's the domain of other branches of the government, not mine.

I have plenty of headaches doing my own job.

Some of those brought before me are terribly weak. Two out of eight, I think. They start to beg for mercy right away. They tell me who their fathers and uncles are. Frequently these uncles are their families' influential friends. Within days, we get a signed deposition from them that the boys will now solidly march on the side of the state and our guiding Four Principles. In many of these cases, their parents rush to send the boys abroad. It occurs to me that this reveals an absence of trust. Do they not trust us to keep our promises or do they not trust their sons to keep theirs? I am not sure. But it is outside my specific charge to worry about that.

On the other extreme are the incorrigibles. Nearly half are like this, remaining stern till the very end. Even after our constables have dealt with them, hatred glows in their eyes. These boys have only contempt for our entire society. They do not appreciate that foreigners no longer rule over us. I suppose in Tsarist Russia they would have called them 'nihilists.' When they talk, they only spout ideology. I have no stomach for ideology. My conversations with them are brief. I try to coax them into talking about real experiences, but they give me nothing. The least they could do is give me some material that I could use in my writing – you know, I still write stories in the evening – but they only abuse me, calling me a lackey and a running dog. It gets tiring to see them use phrases they have picked up from other countries. But all right, if that's how they want it, that's how it shall be. Within a few days, Special Branch sends someone to get them. They take them out of my hair. Where? I don't sweat my brow thinking about that. It is beyond my area of responsibility.

The rest of the boys fall somewhere in between. Once in a while, though, I get someone I can actually talk to. And that makes this job worthwhile.

One got brought in last week. He had robbed a bank in Shirajganj. He didn't get very far. Someone tipped us off that he was on a steamer trying to cross the Jamuna. We were waiting for him on the other side of the river. He surrendered without a struggle.

When I first spoke to him, I asked him about his family. He replied that he did not have any. I said, all right, name me the orphanage you grew up in. He was silent. I asked him if he had any relatives. He still remained mute. The constables had to spend a day with him before I saw him again. I had thought it rash to take that step, but we need our charges to be a bit more agreeable about their family origins.

It is times like this that I wish my wife were here. It would help take my mind away, though I must say that I have become an expert in keeping my personal and work lives separate. When I am off duty, I do what a writer should – I take refuge in the realm of the imagination.

I was right about the boy. On his return visit, he proved to be more cooperative.

"Everyone has always called me Reza," he offered. He identified his family. I knew of them. Who doesn't? They are a prominent Dhaka family who own several factories and businesses. Reza said that he had run away from home and joined a terrorist group right when it was founded. Of course he didn't refer to them as terrorists, he called them by their party name. I looked up the name. I have compiled quite a history of these organizations of the extreme left, you know. Maybe someday, if my superiors agree, I can publish a book with this information. Historians will find it useful.

If what he said was true, he would have joined before independence. He couldn't possibly be that young. In this job you have to be suspicious. There are some young men who try to sneak into our rehabilitation system by claiming they are younger than they really are. I examined the boy standing on the other side of my desk, his hands tied behind his back and his feet chained together. His mud brown face was smooth, without facial hair. Walking over to get closer to him, I lifted his chin to get a better look at his face. There were lines on his forehead, and his skin was quite leathery. It could be just from the sun.

"You must be older than sixteen. This office does not handle young men of your age," I announced as I reached for the telephone.

He showed no sign of panic. My hand stayed on the phone. With assurance in his voice, he said, "You may find this hard to believe, but I was twelve when I ran away and joined the party."

"Twelve? You are right, I don't believe you." I picked up the phone.

"Sir, do you remember that time in Dhaka when the peasants poured in, red flags in their hands and red caps on their heads, the day when their leader threatened to encircle the city with an army of militant peasants? That's the day I left."

I still did not accept his story. But I remembered that demonstration. We were fighting for our national freedom and these red caps stormed in, shouting that the real issue was class against class, landless against the wealthy. Thankfully we were able to convince the people that this was a disruptive maneuver. We trounced them in the elections. And they never did have the numbers to encircle the city.

Returning the phone back in its cradle, I said, "Talk. You have won yourself a hearing."

He was staring at the mango sitting on my desk. I ordered the constable standing by the door to untie Reza's hands. I motioned to him to sit down in the chair, then picked up the mango and offered it to him. He grasped it in his hands and pressed the flesh, testing it for its firmness. It was soft, nearly overripe; I had meant to eat it yesterday. Without thinking, I took out a penknife from my desk drawer. He noticed my hesitation and said it would not be necessary. As he began to talk, he kneaded the fruit with his fingers. I observed that although his hands were callused, his fingernails were clean. He was probably telling me the truth.

"It all started with a mango seller." The writer in me was charmed. I could perhaps use that line as the opening sentence of a story.

***

The boy had never seen coins so shiny as the bunch his uncle thrust into his small hands just before he'd left for work. Reza had been almost done with breakfast. He gulped down the rest of his milk. He retreated into a corner of the living room where the morning sunlight poured in through a large window. Sitting down on the floor, he slowly counted through his new treasure. They were all brand new 50 poisha coins. One… two… three…. Ten! That makes Five Rupees, he smiled with glee. His uncle had just given him Five Rupees!

But that wasn't the end of it. When he'd dropped the change into the boy's hands, his uncle had also told him that he would take him to the cinema that evening.

Reza was agitated the entire morning. He tried playing with his cousin but she was only two years old, and neither could keep the other occupied for long. The boy went through all the books and magazines in the house, but there wasn't much to occupy an eleven-year old. He tried hanging around his aunt, but she was busy with chores in the kitchen or trying to keep little Sonia fed, cleaned, or entertained.

This was only his second day here. For his summer vacation Reza had been invited by his mother's brother to visit them in Shirajganj. His uncle had come to get him, and together they caught the train that took them northwest from Dhaka until they reached the eastern bank of the Jamuna. They crossed the huge river on a paddlewheel steamer and then another short train ride, this time on a broad gauge railcar, brought them to Shirajganj. This small north Bengal town was in the heart of the tobacco-growing region, and Reza's uncle worked for one of the foreign tobacco companies.

Evening wasn't coming fast enough to satisfy Reza. Every so often, he would jingle the coins in his pocket and tell himself, I've got five rupees. Somehow the money made him feel like he had power over an otherwise alien place.

He ended up standing near the front gate, looking out into the street. It was only a narrow lane coming off the main road that crossed the heart of Shirajganj. There were a few other brick and cement houses nearby, but most were wooden or bamboo thatch structures with roofs of corrugated iron. Most of the houses had trees in their front yard. Reza recognized mango, tamarind and grapefruit. The trees provided plenty of shade over the lane. But unlike his home in Dhaka, everything felt deserted. Once in a while a lone rickshaw passed by. A few servants came back carrying the day's shopping.

A faint chant made its way into Reza's ears. He looked in the direction of the voice and spotted, near where the lane met the main road, a man selling mangoes, the fruit basket perched on his head. Reza wasn't supposed to leave the compound, but his boredom, the saliva that started to flood his mouth, and the coins in his pocket made up his mind for him. Taking a quick look behind to make sure that his aunt wasn't looking, Reza made a dash for the mango seller.

When the man saw the boy rush toward him, he stopped and placed the basket on the ground. His dark face, with several days stubble on it, flashed a warm smile at Reza.

"Ekta aam koto?" The boy asked the price of one mango.

"Ponchash poisha."

"Tumi pochish poisha niba?" Reza had no idea what a fair price was for a single mango. But he'd always seen grownups offer half of what any peddler asked, so he just thought he would do the same.

The man's smile disappeared. His shoulders sagged as he gravely shook his head. He put the ripe mango he'd picked out back in the basket. The knife was tucked into a corner. And he rolled the small towel back into a ring shape and put it back on his head. After he lifted the basket back on his head, he looked at Reza and said, "Why do you call me tumi? I am an old man, your father's age. Maybe even older. Should you not call me apni? Do you call me tumi just because I am a poor man?"

Reza's heart sank. He had no answer. The man's rebuke hit him harder than any slap he'd ever received at the hands of his mother or father. As he felt tears rushing into his eyes, Reza turned around and fled back to the house.

He sat down on the red steps of the verandah. He would have preferred the security of his bed where he could weep on his pillow, but his aunt might notice. He wasn't up for an interrogation. He knew he had done something wrong, but he wasn't sure what it was. He wondered if the mango seller was right. Did he use tumi because the man was poor? In Bangla there were three ways of addressing "you": apni, tumi, and tui. He always used what others around him used, he'd never thought about any of this. Wouldn't it be simpler, he wondered, if we could just use one word, tumi, to address everyone?

Reza had placed his head between his knees and crossed his arms over his forehead. He sensed a shadow nearby. When he looked up, the mango seller was standing above him. With one hand balancing the basket on his head, he offered a mango to the boy.

"Here, take this. It is for you. You don't have to pay me anything. All I ask is that you remember what you called me and what I said back to you." The man then turned and walked away.

Reza jumped up and caught up with him. He reached into his pocket, and offered up all his coins.

The man stopped, looked at the shiny coins in the boy's hand, then frowned and shook his head. Again he looked weary.

"No, I don't want money. You can't right all things with money. Yes, I am a poor man, but I am not a beggar. I just want you to learn how to respect someone, no matter if they are rich or poor."

Once again, Reza felt as if he'd been slapped. But it didn't sting as much this time. He nodded to the man and walked back to the verandah steps.

He felt the mango in his hand. It was not a big one, but it was ripe and he could smell its sweetness. The boy delicately kneaded the fruit so that the flesh inside broke down. The trick, his cousin Selim had once taught him, was to knead the pulp without breaking the skin. The first few times he had never managed that. But by now he was an expert at improvising mango juice right inside the fruit. Once the pulp was all broken down, Reza used his incisors to puncture a small hole on one side, and then he sucked up the mango juice.

When his holidays were over and Reza returned home to Dhaka, he found that his mother had hired a new boy to work around the house. The boy was perhaps a year or two older.

Reza was happy to have Ali as a sometimes playmate, but the first time when the boy had addressed him with apni, Reza squirmed in discomfort. He decided that he would not address Ali with tui, as the rest of the family did, but with tumi. He wasn't always consistent and would often fall back into whatever the others were using. Troubled by guilt for backsliding, he would make a new effort. If Ali noticed any of this, he didn't show it.

One day Ali and Reza were on the roof of the house. They'd gone there to watch the kites being flown by older boys in the neighborhood. Ali asked Reza for an old schoolbook. He said he'd started school and begun to learn how to read, but when his father lost his land to the moneylender, he had to drop out. Work proved impossible to find in the village, so he came to the city.

"I would still like to go to school," he said.

Reza agreed to give the boy a reader. He said, "I'll ask Ma. Maybe she will let you go to school."

Later that afternoon, when his mother was helping him with his homework, Reza asked her, "Can Ali go to school?"

"Why do you ask?"

"When we were playing on the roof, he said that he had started to go to school but had to drop out. But he still wants to go."

"Did he say that?"

"Yes. And he said that if he went to school in the morning, he could do extra work in the afternoon and evening."

She didn't respond.

He knew she was a generous person. When beggars came to the door, no one was turned away without a cup of rice or some food or coins. He had no doubt she would agree.

The next day when Reza returned from school, Ali was nowhere to be seen. He felt a knot in his stomach. He went to the kitchen and asked the woman who cooked, "Where is Ali?"

She replied, with sadness in her voice, that Reza's mother had let him go.

"But why?" Reza squeaked out.

"She said he had begun to demand too much."

The mango seller's tired face came back to Reza. He rushed out into the streets. None of the nearby storekeepers knew where Ali had gone. At that moment Reza did not think about what he would do if he did manage to find Ali.

***

I felt for this boy sitting in front of me. I could see he was a sensitive soul. I suspect that both of us at young ages were gifted with a keenness of observation, me about the good and evil inherent in the human personality and him about the inequities embedded in our society. I could turn my knowledge into stories, but this poor boy, what could he do with the kind of knowledge he was given? He tried to do right. But the servant boy ended up paying the price for some rich child's inability to handle the truth. I don't worry about Ali. He and his family had already paid at the hands of rich people all their lives. He knew this was life. He would survive better than this boy's guilt-ridden soul.

"So did you find him?" I asked out of curiosity.

"No. But a year later when the red caps came into the city and their march went by our house, I thought I saw a boy who resembled Ali. I went up to him. It wasn't Ali, but we ended up talking and he was someone who I instantly felt comfortable with. Later that day I left home."

"Why did you think that joining the Party of Those Who Have Nothing would help?"

"I'd exhausted myself trying to make things right in my own house. None of it worked. I had no say. The boy in the march convinced me that there were others who felt like me, that it was possible to find a place where I could be at ease. They have become my family now. And we share a common goal: to end the oppression in this society and create a new world."

My eyes began to glaze over. I could see that after a very human story, he was about to start into the ideology thing. I was not wrong. He proved to be even more incorrigible than those who shout phrases from the Big Men of revolutions in other countries.

What choice did I have? After he was returned to his cell, I picked up the phone and dialed Special Branch. Then another thought sneaked into my head. I hung up and dialed a different number. I needed to know something for certain. I needed some information from the Missing Persons files. Later that day I asked for the boy to be returned to me. I ordered the constable on an errand to the market, assuring him that boy, shackled and cuffed, was harmless.

Reza's story had left me thinking. We say we are creating a democratic society. But can we make any progress when at the very core of our language, in the way each of us relates to another, we make distinctions of rank and class? True, it's not my job to worry about such questions, but sometimes you just can't help it.

I asked Reza, "Would you be opposed to me contacting your family? I am sure they have missed you a lot."

"Sir, you know I cannot live with them. I do not belong in that old life." He looked down at his feet. "It would be like living with a chain around my neck. They have not changed."

"At least you would be alive. You are, I am sure, aware of the alternative."

A grim little smile crossed his face. "There must be a price for what you are offering."

"Well, I am sure we could come to an agreement reasonable to all of us. Your family has money and connections. I am a writer, did you know that? My wife lives in Dhaka, totally opposed to moving here. Perhaps your family could find me a suitable job." There, I had said it. Still, the words coming out of my mouth tasted bitter. Had I become so tired of this God-forsaken job in this shithole of a town?

He stood there, mute again. He couldn't be shocked; by now he must know how things really work in the world.

"Well?"

"But, sir, I cannot sign any pledges of loyalty."

"You are underage anyway. They can sign for you." Maybe they could find me a job in one of their businesses.

"At the first chance, I would return to the movement."

"Perhaps." I was willing to bet that his family would quickly find a way to ship him out of the country. Meanwhile I wondered what business position would suit me best.

"You know I will."

"Maybe." I never did care for those who took up business as a career, but I could visualize its advantages today. No, not a manager in a factory. Never again do I want anything with authority over other human beings. Perhaps something in sales. Or accounts. In this job I've become pretty good with facts and figures.

"You don't believe me."

Yes, an accounts position would be ideal. I got the highest grades in mathematics when I was in college. I am sure I could handle all the work in a few hours and spend the rest of my time writing. It would be nice to afford a house. Nothing fancy, just something agreeable to my wife. We could finally consider having children. And I could see about publishing a second collection of stories.

Prestamped

Cari Carpenter

Another thing
I cannot say--
squelched before
it makes the page.
My travels--
literal or otherwise--
across Time
Space
Imagination
And if I censor
so much
Have I said
anything
at all?
So many things
I cannot send--
Stamps
Address labels
Postcards--
What are they
Afraid
I'll send?
a piece, prestamped,
of Humanity?

The first morning after the end of the world
Buff Whitman-Bradley

This morning on Death Row
we talked about the war.
Rudy said it made him sad
to think of all those soldiers
coming home with PTSD.
He said it was during a Viet Nam flashback
that his former tier neighbor Manny Babbitt
killed a woman and tagged her toe.
Manny used to shine everybody's shoes,
Rudy said.
He was executed in 1999.
Back at home as we ate lunch
I was reading the paper
and had a sudden image of children
in Afghanistan and Iraq and Palestine
and in East Oakland and Pine Ridge
carrying their terrible wounds around
in gaily colored paper bags stamped "Made in the USA."
The bags exploded and burned.
Rudy is staying up late tonight
watching Soul Train on television
as he does every Saturday night.
People say, "TV! They pamper those bastards!"
His cell is 4 feet by 10 feet and he is locked inside it
from 1:30 in the afternoon until 7:30 in the morning.
Our son went with us to the prison today.
Tonight he is packing up his car
and leaving for college in the morning.
Children in Afghanistan and Iraq and Palestine
and East Oakland and Pine Ridge
should have known better than to be born there. Ha-ha.
Rudy was born on death row.
In his letters to us he sometimes makes jokes
about the sameness of his days
and draws smiley faces and writes Ha-ha.
He has kept up with all the news about Afghanistan and Iraq
and Palestine and East Oakland and Pine Ridge
and he knows about exploding paper bags.
Later in the afternoon I worked in the yard
and as the light was going and I swept up cuttings and leaves
in the driveway

I remembered a day last winter
when I walked over by Corte Madera Creek
near where it widens and flows into the Bay
and I watched about a dozen buffleheads,
small black and white ducks,
bobbing up and down on the waves.
I thought then how quiet it will be on the first morning
after the end of the world, when we are no longer here
and I hoped that the buffleheads would still be here
bobbing up and down on the water.
I do not want any more paper bags to explode and burn.
I would like to prove Rudy's innocence
and walk with him right out of the front gates of San Quentin
all the way to Afghanistan and Iraq and Palestine
and East Oakland and Pine Ridge
and over to Corte Madera Creek
near where it flows into the Bay.
And I want our son to come home from college
with his love and his outrage intact.

Sometimes it is hard to have hope
in a world with death rows and exploding paper bags.
But from deep inside the belly of Hell
Rudy keeps cracking jokes. Ha-ha.
And beautiful young men and women keep leaving home
to stand in front of bulldozers and sit in the tops of trees.
And the buffleheads keep showing up every year
to eat their fill and wait for the telegram
that will tell them it is time to come home.

And they do not go
Buff Whitman-Bradley

i.

There is frost on the sidewalk
this morning
and on windows and lawns.
The cold sky rings
like a great blue bell.
As I hurry to work
along the path through the park
I stop at the large tree by the pond
where the night herons perch.
The sun rises behind the houses
at the end of the street
and bathes the herons in light.
But they do not stretch their necks
or spread their wings to catch the warmth.
They are utterly still
like the herons in thousand-year-old Chinese paintings
or the ancient zen hermits who sat for hours
and gazed at the moon
and forgot to boil their rice. . .
Like the old Italian men I have seen
in the bleachers at the ballpark
who wear black suits and fedoras
even on the hottest days
and silently study the game . . .
Like the newspaper photos
of the mothers of the disappeared
standing on the Plaza de Mayo
holding pictures of their stolen children . . .

ii.

At the women's prison
when visiting hours are over
and the women in khaki
have held their children
for the last time
and kissed them goodbye
and embraced husbands and lovers
and family and friends,
the ones who will go
and the ones who will stay

pull away and stand apart.
They become suddenly shy
and do not speak with each other.
The visitors fidget and shuffle their feet
making nervous jokes
while they wait for a guard
to escort them outside.
On the other side of the room
the women inhabit their own loneliness again.
Beautiful and silent and still
standing at the edge
of some vast prairie
they gaze
past the visitors
waiting at the door
past the severely clipped lawns
and the razor wire fences
over freeways and cities
beyond where the earth curves
and falls away
toward a place where their bodies' quiet songs
drift among tall, fragrant grasses
then
slowly
begin to rise.

When the guard comes
and the visitors leave
the women return
to the weight of their own limbs
and the rubbing of heavy cotton
against their skin
and the aching in their black, boxy shoes
and they turn
and they do not go.

A handful of wet earth
Buff Whitman-Bradley

for Rudolph Roybal

i.

The death row visiting room at San Quentin
is filled with cages.
Each cage has two doors,
one for visitors and one for the inmate.
In the inmate's door there is a slot about waist-high
where a guard can reach in
to remove handcuffs
and put them back on.
The inmate and his visitors sit facing each other
in blue plastic chairs
with a small green plastic table in between them.

Yesterday we sat in one of the cages
with a man who has become our friend.
A late winter storm raged outside
roiling the waters of San Francisco Bay,
but inside we heard nothing
except air being blown through the heating vents
and from cages up and down the line
the low murmur of voices
like the conversations of lovers in airports
or parents putting their children to bed at night.

We spoke as we always do
about ordinary matters –
his family and ours, the news in the papers,
the latest lockdown,
how he and other inmates on his tier
sometimes share meals they cook
with packaged food from the commissary
using the kind of heating coil found in motel rooms
to warm coffee.

He hadn't gone out to yard all week, he told us,
because of the rains.
The yard for North Seg is on the roof
and on dry days he goes out there
to walk or run laps

or play basketball.
Sometimes he stands on a table to look over the wall
at the top of Mt. Tamalpais
near where we live.

"I miss dirt," he said.
"I haven't touched dirt in eleven years."

At the end of the visit
we asked a guard to take a Polaroid picture of us
through the bars.
Then, handcuffs back on, our friend was taken away
and we were let out of the cage and cleared to leave.
The remote control door to the visiting room
slammed shut behind us with a heavy, metallic finality
and we walked out into the rain.

ii.

Today there was a break in the weather.
One by one the late winter storms that had soaked us all week
exhausted themselves and drifted away
and I woke up to a cloudless morning.

In the back yard I added seed to the bird feeder
and stood and listened to the quiet, irregular
drip . . . drip-drip . . .
from the branches of the fig tree
as juncos and finches and chickadees
took quick, nervous turns at the feeder.
The air was chilly and tasted like leftover rain.

After breakfast now, I walk up
into the heavily forested hills near our house.
The creeks are rushing
and the trails are slippery with mud.
I pause now and then to warm myself
in small bright patches
where sunlight has broken through the dense foliage overhead.

Higher up on the trail
I come to a partial clearing
where a stream, alive with light, spills and tumbles
down a steep, rocky gully.
I find a dry place to sit on a boulder at the water's edge
and reach down to scoop up a handful of wet earth
and hold it tightly in my palm.

iii.

I close my eyes and this picture comes to me:

I am looking down from some high place
onto an empty beach where the Pacific,
like a great, blue, foaming horse
gallops up and down the white sand.

Two people appear on the beach.
They are surprised to be there
and dazzled by the sunlight.
They shield their eyes with their hands
as they gaze out past the breaking waves
at the vast prairie of ocean
between the shore and the horizon.
They do not look at each other.
One has been murdered
and the other is a murderer.

They begin walking toward the water.
Their steps are slow and tentative
and they hold themselves stiffly
as they make their way down the sloping sand.
They step into the surf
and the water rises around them.

And suddenly it is as if their bodies were filled with birds –
their arms fly about wildly,
they leap and splash and dive
and see each other at last
and begin to play together like two dolphins,
throwing their bodies into the surf,
riding the curling waves,
tumbling through the foam headlong toward the shore,
swimming out again under the breakers
and shooting up out of the water,
gasping for breath and laughing
and looking into each other's eyes.

And now there are more on the beach,
murderers and the murdered,
all stunned by the light,
all stumbling down the sand –
the shooters and the ones gunned down,
the stabbers and the knifed,
the stranglers and the asphyxiated,
the batterers and the broken . . .

Wave after wave they come,
the quick and the dead,

out of prisons and out of graves,
out of shacks and tenements,
out of tidy bungalows in the suburbs
and county hospitals
and mansions on manicured hillsides,
out of grubby little offices and penthouse boardrooms,
out of bars and morgues and cathedrals,

the tortured and the torturers,
the executed and the executioners,
the death squads and the disappeared,
the ones blown to bits and the ones who dropped the bombs
and hurled the grenades
and fired the cannons
and aimed the missiles
and made the policies
and prayed for victory,

the ones who starved
and the ones who got fat,
the ones worked to death
and the ones who counted the money,
the ones who died of silence
and the ones who said nothing.

We are all in the water together now.
The sea is filled with us.
The surf crashes over us again and again,
scrubbing away the grime and the old dead skin.
The new skin underneath
glistens like apples in the rain.
Salt spray and tears shine on our cheeks.
Tenderly, we touch each other's faces.
Tenderly, we say each other's names.

iv.

I open my eyes
and then I open my hand
to let the dirt fall into the stream.
The day has grown warm and as I stand up
I take off my heavy shirt and tie it around my waist.
I brush the last few crumbs of soil off my fingers,
pick up a buckeye to carry in my pocket
and head back down the trail toward home.

The Inside Stories of the Global American Prison

H. Bruce Franklin

first appeared in

Texas Studies in Literature and Language

Fall 2008

Three decades ago, I wrote that the literature of the American prison is not "some peripheral cultural phenomenon but something close to the center of our historical experience as a nation-state."[1] Back then, there were 300,000 people in U.S. domestic prisons and jails. Today there are 2.4 million. Since then, the United States has built an average of a prison a week inside our nation, globalized a vast prison-industrial complex, and normalized prison torture at home and around the world. The outcome of national elections as well as representation in Congress is now determined by felony disenfranchisement, which today deprives more than five million lower-class American citizens of the vote. One example: In the 2000 election Florida disenfranchised 827,000 former prisoners; if they had been allowed to vote, political scientists estimate that Al Gore would have won Florida by 80,000 votes, George W. Bush would never have gotten to reside in the White House, and the world we live in would be a very different place.[2]

To comprehend the American prison one must turn to the literature created by those who have experienced its secret world. For secrecy is part of the essence of the prison. Prior to the American Revolution, imprison-ment was seldom used as a punishment for crime in England and was rarer still in its American colonies, most of which were being used as dumping grounds for British convicts. Here the main punishments were executions and various forms of physical torture – whipping, the stocks, the pillory, branding, mutilation, castration, etc. – all designed as spectacles to be witnessed by the public. The prison system depends on the opposite. It institutionalizes isolation and secrecy. The prison's walls are designed not only to keep the prisoners in but to keep the public out, unable to observe what is going on inside. Prison literature, therefore, is intrinsically subversive, revealing what is supposed to be concealed and what is often unimaginable. As ex-convict author Jim Tully put it back in 1928: "I'd rather read one page by a man who had been in Hell – than all of Dante."[3]

One man who had been in America's prison hell was Jack London, who defined his incarceration for a mere thirty days as an event that shaped his perception of America.[4] In two essays published in *Cosmopolitan* magazine in 1907, "'Pinched': A Prison Experience" and "The Pen: Long Days in a County Penitentiary," London described his arrest and imprisonment at the age of eighteen in 1894.[5] London tells of experiencing on a gut level two great revelations. What shocks him most deeply is that the prison not only brutalized the prisoners but also transformed them – including himself – into instruments of terror and class oppression within the prison. His second revelation is the overwhelming power of the state, with hints of its full potential for terror: "I saw with my own eyes, there in that prison, things unbelievable and monstrous…. My indignation ebbed away, and into my being rushed the tides of fear. I saw at last, clear-eyed, what I was up against."[6]

Only months after these memoirs appeared, London published an astonishing extrapolation from his prison experience, *The Iron Heel,* the world's first full vision of a fascist state. The two sketches display the American prison as a totalitarian state; the novel projects an American totalitarian state as a gigantic prison. And now we greet the centennial of this 1908 novel under the state's electronic eyes and ears and in the lengthening shadows of Abu Ghraib and Guantánamo.

London returned to his vision of the American prison as matrix of brutalization in his last major novel, *Star Rover* (1915), a tale of unending fiendish torture in San Quentin relieved only by the narrator's out-of-body escapist trips in time and space. In 1915, however, torture was not central to the American prison, except insofar as it served the prison's primary underlying purpose, which was slave labor, whether on the vast prison plantations that had replaced the pre–Civil-War slave plantations or in the prison workhouses of the north, eloquently described in Kate Richards O'Hare's prison writings.[7] But by the end of the twentieth century, when the prison had become a major political weapon of the corporate state, torture designed to dehumanize had become the norm.

American prison literature reached its widest audience and had its greatest influence – both cultural and political – during the stormy upheavals of the 1960s and early 1970s, the era of the movement against the Vietnam War, the urban rebellions known as "the long, hot summers," related rebellions within the armed forces, and the other turbulent forces and liberation struggles swirling around issues of race, class, and gender. For prison literature, this era began with the publication in 1965 of *The Autobiography of Malcolm X*, one of the most influential American books of the twentieth century. This was the was the decade of George Jackson's *Soledad Brother*, Malcolm Braly's *On the Yard*, Piri Thomas's *Down These Mean Streets* and *Seven Long Times;* splendid poetry by William Wantling, Etheridge Knight, Norma Stafford, T. J. Reddy, Michael Hogan, Carolyn Baxter, and dozens of others published in chap-books and collections from prison workshops; Iceberg Slim's fiction and memoirs; and sixteen novels by the most wide-ly read of all Black fiction writers, Donald Goines. A torrent of prison literature was pouring out to the American public in mass-market paperbacks, newspapers, magazines, and major motion pictures. This era ended with the downfall of the Nixon regime in 1974, the final defeat of the United States by Vietnam in 1975, and the reactionary epoch that soon followed.

In 1976 came the Big Bang, the spectacular explosion of the prison industrial complex. As a necessary corollary to this prison cosmos, there began a relentless campaign to silence prisoners and ex-prisoners. New York State led the way in attacking prison literature with its "Son of Sam" law, passed in 1977. Most other states soon followed with copycat laws making it illegal for convict authors to collect money from their writings. Although ostensibly designed to keep criminals from profiting from their crimes, the main purpose of these laws was to suppress prison literature and thus to keep the American people blind to the American prison as it was wildly expanding, transforming itself and the nation, and providing the model for the global American gulag. The "Son of Sam" law so blatantly attacked free speech that even the Rehnquist Supreme Court – including Antonin Scalia – unanim-ously struck it down as a dangerous attack on the First Amendment. Citing my work on prison literature, the Supreme Court pointed out that this law would have prevented the publication of not only *The Autobiography of Malcolm X* but even Thoreau's *Civil Disobedience*.[8]

But by the time the Supreme Court struck down "Son of Sam" in 1991, much of the damage had already been done. Almost all creative writing courses in prison had been defunded. By 1984 every literary journal devoted to publishing poetry and stories by prisoners had been wiped out. Pris-on newspapers, with their grand tradition extending back into the eighteenth century, were almost entirely eliminated.[9] And after the Supreme Court decision, the repression actually intensified, with many states passing even more punitive laws tailored to skirt the court's opinion by widening prohibitions so that they could not be construed as attacking merely speech. Also, the decision did nothing to change the regulation governing all federal prisoners: "The inmate may not receive compensation or anything of value for correspondence with the news media. The inmate may not...publish under a byline."[10] When convict writer Dannie Martin was thrown into solitary confinement in the mid-1980s for violating this regulation by publishing articles in the *San Francisco Chronicle,* the *Chronicle* challenged the regulation in court, where testimony revealed that it had been drafted in the 1970s explicitly to ensure that federal prisoners with "anti-establishment" views would "not have access to the media."[11] Then in 1994 Congress deliberately acted to keep convicts from furthering their education by forbidding all prisoners from receiving Pell grants.

Gone from the so-called "penitentiary" or "correctional facility" is any pretense of reformation or rehabilitation. In the typical American prison, degradation, brutalization, and even overt torture are the norm. Beatings, electric shock, prolonged exposure to heat and even immersion in scalding water, sodomy with riot batons, nightsticks, flashlights, and broom handles, shackled prisoners forced to lie in their own excrement for hours or even days, months of solitary confinement, rape and murder by guards or prisoners instructed by guards – all are everyday occurrences.[12] Today's era of prison writing, which stretches from Jack Abbott's 1981 *In the Belly of the Beast* through Mumia Abu-Jamal's current articles and books, reveals an institution whose main purpose seems to be to destroy all traces of humanity. Patricia McConnell cuts to the core in her dazzling short story, "Sing Soft, Sing Loud," which tells the value of acquiring the totally blank, almost dead look known as "jailface": "If you're walking around with jailface," the guards "can't tell if there's something stirring in there or not," so most likely they "think that you're already dead, so there's no challenge, nothing in there to kill."[13] When Chicano poet Jimmy Santiago Baca returned to San Quentin in 1992 to help shoot the major motion picture based on his life, *Bound by Honor,* he experienced stunning revelations that recall Jack London's discoveries a century earlier. Although now a celebrated writer and "a man full of love for his family and his life," Baca wrote that "the old convict in me rose up full of hatred and rage." As though recalling London's *Star Rover,* Baca is overwhelmed by "the thought of the thousands of human beings whose souls were murdered here in the last hundred years": "[A]s if through a prison-door peephole, I saw all the free people going about their lives on the other side, while my place was again with the convicts. Anyone opening that door from the other side must die, or be taken hostage and forced to understand our hatred, made to experience the insane brutality that is the convict's daily lot, and that makes him, in turn, brutal and insane."[14]

When the time came to globalize this institution, the men chosen for the job were some of its most notorious officials. After the invasion of Iraq, Lane McCotter, who had been forced to resign as the director of the Utah Department of Corrections because of torture carried out under his administration, was put in charge of reconstructing Saddam Hussein's Abu Ghraib. John Armstrong, former director of the Connecticut Department of Corrections, who had been driven out of his position because of sexual and other tortures revealed by both the ACLU and Amnesty International, became deputy director of operations for the entire Iraqi prison system. Charles Graner, formerly a guard at Pennsylvania's notorious Green County Prison, where guards routinely beat prisoners and sodomized them with nightsticks, attained celebrity for torturing prisoners in Abu Ghraib.[15]

Despite the assault on the literature of the American prison, it has been breaking into literature courses and anthologies. The 2006 edition of the *Heath Anthology of American Literature,* which is used in classrooms around the world, actually included a whole section labeled "Prison Litera-ture." Although this "cluster" consisted of a mere twenty-seven pages out of the more than three thousand in the multivolume anthology, that was enough to provoke the disapproval of the *New York Times Book Review,* whose editor, Rachel Donadio, complained that it took up more space than that given to "the great poet Elizabeth Bishop." Even more reprehensible, according to Donadio, is the fact that this prison literature section "includes works by Kathy Boudin, a former member of the Weather Underground who served more than 20 years for her role in a 1981 robbery and murder."[16] Implying that the five authors included in this section collectively are not worth as much space as Bishop, Donadio names only Boudin, failing even to give the names of such widely celebrated poets as Etheridge

Knight and Jimmy Santiago Baca. Nor does Donadio say even a word about any of their actual work, including Boudin's three beautiful, extremely moving poems. Masquerading as literary criticism based on aesthetic criteria, this editorial commentary in the *New York Times Book Review* thus offers a minor but revealing example of how dominant cultural institutions collaborate with the political apparatus to suppress prison literature.

On the other hand, a small but increasing number of Americanists have begun to recognize that teaching late-twentieth- and twenty-first-century American literature without any contextualization in the matrix of the American prison is tantamount to teaching nineteenth-century American literature without any contextualization in the matrix of American slavery. And of course we would not think of teaching about slavery without exposing our students to the writings of the slaves, most especially the *Narrative of the Life of Frederick Douglass, An American Slave.* Yet this is a very recent cultural awareness. Prior to those upheavals of the 1960s and 1970s, our American literature anthologies and courses were as lily-white as the faculty club at Stanford. The name of Frederick Douglass did not even appear in the 1,555 pages of the 1974 edition of the standard history of American literature (*Literary History of the United States,* by Robert Spiller, Willard Thorp, Thomas H. Johnson, Henry Seidel Canby, Richard Ludwig, and William M. Gibson) or in the multivolume definitive bibliography of American literature (*Bibliography of American Literature,* compiled by Jacob Blanck) or in the supposedly inclusive *Articles on American Literature, 1950-1967* (Duke University Press, 1970). Ironically, it was the prison literature of this period, led by *The Autobiography of Malcolm X,* George Jackson's writings, and the poetry of Black convicts, that helped blaze the path to the rediscovery of African American slave literature and its crucial importance for understanding America's past, present, and possible futures.

It is no surprise that modern prisoners helped lead the rediscovery of slave literature, because chattel slavery did not disappear in 1865 – it mere-ly morphed into the modern American prison. Indeed, the very amendment to the Constitution – the Thirteenth Amendment – that supposedly abolished slavery actually wrote it *into* the Constitution and provided the legal, political, and cultural basis for transforming all people convicted of a crime into a new slave class:

"Neither slavery nor involuntary servitude, except as a punishment for crime whereof the party shall have been duly convicted, shall exist within the United States, or any place subject to their jurisdiction."

Initially, the Thirteenth Amendment was used to re-enslave much of the African American population and to begin to merge the old forms of chattel slavery with the more modern ones pioneered by the American prison and accelerated in the prison factories during the Civil War, as I have discussed at length in *Prison Literature in America: The Victim as Criminal and Artist.*[17]

Today, that final clause of the Thirteenth Amendment – "or any place subject to their jurisdiction" – takes on an ominous new meaning as Guantánamo and Abu Ghraib turn out to be mere-ly the visible parts of a vast global network of American secret prisons run by the C.I.A. and a host of "contractors," many connected with the same corporations that help design, staff, run, and supply U.S. domestic prisons, both public and private. Although the Thirteenth Amendment specifies that someone needs to be "duly convicted" of a crime in order to be punished with slavery, it has nothing to say about other punishments, such as prolonged solitary confinement, sexual abuse, or outright torture. Within the American prison, these punishments, which are normal and routine, are meted out without any regard for due process, and, as Colin Dayan demonstrates in *The Story of Cruel and Unusual,* the courts have by and large upheld the principle that prisoners have no intrinsic rights to legal defense against such extra-judicial punishments.[18] Thus the Bush administration doctrine, enacted into law by Congress, that anyone arbitrarily defined as an "enemy combatant" has no right to due process, flows quite naturally from the norms of the American prison.

Like these "enemy combatants," American prisoners are also widely imaged in popular culture as agents of terror. The explosive growth of prisons has been fueled by remorselessly harsh sentences, "three-strikes-and-you're-out" laws, and a widespread "lock-'em-up-and-throw-away-the-key" mentality – none of which would be possible without many millions of voters living in fear, or downright terror, of "criminals." Hence we must not be allowed to hear the voices of those millions of men and women consigned to the living hell of the American prison. As George H. W. Bush demonstrated in winning the White House in 1988, we must see them as nothing more or less than endlessly repeated mute images of Willie Horton. The literature of the slaves told the inside stories of antebellum slavery and thus helped destroy it. So too, the literature of prisoners tells the inside stories of the American prison and thus threatens its dominion and expansion. The deepest insights into the American global prison, including its cultural and political logic, come from this literature it tries to repress.

Footnotes

1. *The Victim as Criminal and Artist: Literature from the American Prison* (New York: Oxford University Press, 1978), xxii.

2. Jeff Manza and Christopher Uggen, *Locked Out: Felon Disenfranchisement and American Democracy* (New York: Oxford University Press, 2006), 192; Elizabeth Hull, *The Disenfranchisement of Ex-Felons* (Philadelphia: Temple University Press, 2006), 9.

3. Jim Tully, "A California Holiday" (1928) in *Prison Writing in 20th-Century America*, ed. H. Bruce Franklin (New York: Penguin Books, 1998), 34.

4. In "How I Became a Socialist," first published in *The Comrade* in 1903 and reprinted in *War of the Classes* (New York: Macmillan, 1905), London wrote that "no economic argument, no lucid demonstration of the logic and inevitableness of Socialism affects me as profoundly and convincingly as I was affected on the day when I first saw the walls of the Social Pit rise

5. Both pieces were reprinted later that year in *The Road* and are included in *Prison Writing in 20th-Century America*.

6. "'Pinched': A Prison Experience" in *Prison Writing in 20th-Century America*, 49.

7. See, for example, O'Hare's fine *In Prison, Sometime Federal Prisoner 21669* (New York, 1923). Excerpts are available in *Prison Writing in 20th-Century America*, 74-89.

8. U.S. Supreme Court, *Simon & Schuster v. Crime Victims Bd.*, 502 U.S. 105 (1991), 502 U.S. 105, No. 90–1059, page 10. The Court referred to my "sobering bibliography listing hundreds of works by American prisoners and ex-prisoners, many of which contain descriptions of the crimes for which the authors were incarcerated, including works by such authors as Emma Goldman and Martin Luther King, Jr."

9. See James McGrath Morris, *Jailhouse Journalism: The Fourth Estate Behind Bars* (Jefferson, NC: McFarland, 1998).

10. Title 28 of the *Code of Federal Regulations*, Section 540.20(b).

11. The full story is told in Dannie M. Martin and Peter Y. Sussman, *Committing Journalism: The Prison Writings of Red Hog* (New York: W. W. Norton, 1993).

12. For a detailed summary of some of the horrors of American prisons, an analysis of specific connections with Abu Ghraib and Guantánamo, and examples of especially vicious American correctional officials who were assigned to Iraq, see Anne-Marie Cusac, "Abu Ghraib, USA," *Prison Legal News*, Vol. 15, #7 (July 2004), 1–4. This monthly journal is an excellent source of information about the routine abuses of the American prison and the myriad legal cases contesting these abuses. The national "Prison Discipline Study," included in *Criminal Injustice*, ed. Elihu Rosenblatt (Boston: South End Press, 1966), reported that 42.5% of prisoners in maximum security facilities were beaten at least once a month.

13. *In Prison Writing in 20th-Century America,* 297.

14. *Jimmy Santiago Baca, "Past Present" in Prison Writing in 20th-Century America, 358–59.*

15. *Antonio Ponvert III, "Iraqi Prisoner Abuse: Why Are We Surprised," Counterpunch, June 12/13, 2004; "Schumer: Second Corrections Official with Checkered Record Put in Power Position at Iraqi Prisons," senate.gov/~schumer/ SchumerWeb-site/press room/press release ; Todd Matthews, "Business as Usual: America's Long-Term Domestic and Foreign Policies Toward Prison Abuse," Prison Legal News, December 2004, 1–5, 2.*

16. *Rachel Donadio, "Keeper of the Canon," New York Times Book Review, January 8, 2006.*

17. *H. Bruce Franklin, Prison Literature in America: The Victim as Criminal and Artist. Expanded edition (New York: Oxford University Press, 1989), Ch. 3.*

18. *Colin Dayan, The Story of Cruel and Unusual (Cambridge: MIT Press, 2007).*

The Key to the Bastille – The Promise of Collective Action
Peter Linebaugh

On May Day, 1790, Tom Paine wrote George Washington. "Our very good friend, the Marquis de Lafayette, has intrusted to my care the key of the Bastille, and a drawing handsomely framed representing the demolition of that detestable prison."

The Bastille towered over the Faubourg St. Antoine. Its walls were one hundred feet high, ten feet thick at the top and thirty to forty feet thick at the base. The monstrous building functioned as an arsenal, a prison, and a fortress guarding the east of Paris from invasion from without and rebellion from within.

"I feel myself happy," Paine continued, "in being the person through whom the Marquis has conveyed this early trophy of the spoils of despotism, and the first ripe fruits of American principles transplanted into Europe...." Tom Paine was the pamphleteer and citizen-soldier of the American Revolution fifteen years earlier. France helped pay for the American victory and in the process nearly bankrupted its own oppressive, super-exploitative regime which was now facing revolution. This was the ripe fruit Paine referred to.

What were those principles, those 'American principles'? At the time of Paine's May Day gift France had already passed the Declaration of Man and the Citizen in which popular sovereignty and human equality were leading principles. At the same time in the U.S.A. the Bill of Rights had been proposed and was being debated prior to rati-fication. Here liberty of conscience, freedom of expression, and the right of assembly were recognized, and we see them as sequential steps in the revolutionary actualization of the will of the people: to think, to talk, to listen were the essential accompaniments to action.

"That the principles of America opened the Bastille is not to be doubted; and therefore the key comes to the right place." Oh, but we are full of doubt now. America incarcerates more people than any other nation in the global carceral archipelago. Bahgram, Abu Ghraib, Guantánamo, these are America's modern Bastilles cast around the world. Meanwhile, in the "homeland" the prisons, penitentiaries, and jails of such rapid expansion have been joined by immigrant detention facilities, super-maxes, and correctional facilities. The immigrant detention facilities hidden and widespread make Ellis Island appear commodious. Today the key rests uselessly in a glass enclosed gilded container at Mount Vernon. They bring democracy and build prisons. They speak of government of, by, and for the people and then hide behind state secrets. They practice torture and call it intelligence. Blood-curdling casuists sit on the Federal Appeals Bench. John Berger has written, "The present period of history is one of the Wall…. The Wall is the front line of what, long ago, was called the Class War."

But, hope has made his appearance. Optimists see the chink in the wall. Obama has ordered that Guantánamo be closed. The CIA director has ordered that extraordinary renditions to prisons else-where in the world be ended. Yet the Wall continues to snake its way against Mexico, to divide nations, to rupture Palestine. The anti-communists croon with satisfaction because "Mr Gorbachev brought down that wall" and then silently acquiesce in the construction of walls all over. The prisons are welcomed because they bring jobs. The prisons rise while the schools fall. In the schools sport, theatre, and music are shut down first; play, song, and make-believe are banished. Parents no longer can smile as the little ones in Midsummer's Night's Dream romp about as the 'rude mechanicals': Snout the Tinker, Starveling the Tailor, and the immortal Bottom the Weaver making a chink in the Wall for the lovers, Pyramus and Thisbe. (The tragic story of these lovers originated in Babylon, Mesopotamia.)

Tom Paine's May Day gift to George Washington is on display in the central passageway at the first President's slave plantation, Mount Vernon on the Potomac River. Let us demand the release of the political prisoners, the victims of repression from the past, the victims of the Green Scare. Let us renew the discussion: who is a political prisoner? itself a sign of well-being. I commute to Toledo from Michigan on route 23 I pass daily several pris-ons, the razor wire glistening in the sun, never a sign of life. An unpunctuated sign on the highway warns me, "Prison Area Do Not Pick Up Hitchhikers." Never have I heard of anyone escaping, and never for that matter have I seen a hitchhiker, there or anywhere else, along the fifty mile stretch to work. Yet, the authors of the sign came from an era when both were possible. Who inhabits these lock-ups? What transpires inside them?

"I have not the least doubt of the final and complete success of the French Revolution. Little eb-bings and flowings, for and against, the natural companions of revolutions, sometimes appear, but the full current of it is, in my opinion, as fixed as the Gulf Stream," Paine informed Washington. Indeed, that eastern current conveyed the news of slave risings.

In the spring of 1790 Tom Paine was busy with his invention, a single-spanned iron bridge. He hoped it would span the Schukyl (Philadelphia), now the Thames (London), later the Seine (Paris). He lets George Washington know that in the parti-tion in the box containing the key of the Bastille he has placed half a dozen razors "manufactured from cast-steel made at the works where the bridge was constructed." Paine, an artisan, was always interested in the materiality of things. His interest in the substance of things can easily be overlooked as we are generally moved by the force of his ideals. Just as the gift of razors necessary for that smooth visage of the president of the republic suggests a mundane familiarity, so Tom Paine had once been close to revolutionary power, a whisker away so to speak.

What was the Bastille actually? A gigantic heap of stones. The people of Paris marched upon it particularly in order to obtain gunpowder but of course there were other reasons. "The stones are saturated with three hundred years of pain," said Camille Desmoulins one of its assailants. Voltaire was imprisoned there, and the Marquis de Sade. "You don't have a trial. Just a letter from the king and bang, the doors slam. Goodbye." That's the lettre de cachet in the imaginative paraphrase in Marge Piercy's novel of the French Revolution.

"History is the essence of innumerable biographies," said the Victorian historian, Thomas Carlyle, and to emphasize it he capitalized the spelling of the occupations of its anonymous members. Women were most active, then and now. Here is Carlyle, "Robust Dames of the Halle, slim Mantua-makers, assiduous, risen with the dawn, ancient Virginity tripping to matins; the House-maid, with early broom; all must go. Rouse ye, O women; the laggard men will not act; they say, we ourselves may act." And it seems to have been so. Jules Michelet offers the story of Madam Legros. described and honored as the poor mercer who lived by her sewing, whose husband was a Latin teacher, and whose dogged tenacity over the years on behalf of a single prisoner in the Bastille prefigured the revolutionary journée we celebrate in July. Ruth Gilmore, Alice Lynd, Angela Davis, play the part of Mme. Legros.

An essential part of Rights of Man is the story of the storming of the Bastille and Edmund Burke's writing "as if he were sorry it is pulled down, and wished it were built up again." This has been the lament of conservatives ever since. People for whom the solution to social oppression is to incarcerate the oppressed, the lock-'em-up-and-throw-away-the-key brigade.

"The downfall of it included the idea of the downfall of Despotism; and this compounded image has become as figuratively united as Bunyan's Doubting Castle and giant Despair." In Rights of Man Paine explains the compound, how and why the Bastille was united with Despotism. It is one of his most brilliant insights, and it quickly took fire igniting revolutionary aspirations all over the globe.

John Bunyan wrote an allegory of a ragged poor man, Pilgrim's Progress, in 1678, at the time of the construction of the fiscal state and the British com-mercial empire. Christian was his name and with a companion of the road named Hope they fell asleep exhausted in a field. Awakened in the morning by the Giant Despair he informed them that they were trespassing on the grounds of Doubting Castle. He beat them with his cudgel and dragged them to his dungeon. Bang, the doors slam, goodbye. It is the story in the U.S.A., certainly at the Big Luke, the Ohio slammer at Lucasville.

Despair's wife was named Diffidence. And they advised the pilgrims bereft of food, water, or warmth that it would be best if they put an end to themselves by knife, rope, or poison. Unable to assist them in this because a ray of sunlight ap-peared causing Despair to fall into fits, the two pilgrims were left to their misery and discussion of the proposal of Despair. Hope reminds Christian "that all the law is not in the hand of Giant Despair." Diffidence says she fears that "they live in hope that some will come to relieve them, or that they have pick-locks about them; by the means of which they hope to escape." Despair promises to search them in the morning. Meanwhile, Christian suddenly remembers something. He exclaims "I have a Key in my bosom, called Promise that will open any Lock in Doubting Castle." So they go about it, opening the doors, and off to the Delectable Mountains.

Bunyan drew on a suppressed popular culture of song, fairy stories, colloquial sayings, and chil-dren's poems. This dissenting culture has travelled the world too, playing an active role in the anti-imperialist cultures of the third world. Among the Taiping rebels in China during the 1850s Pilgrim's Progress was the 'little red book.' In Africa Pilgrim's Progress was adapted to anti-colonial, anti-racist purposes.

By comparing the Bastille to Doubting Castle and by comparing the Giant Despair to the monarchs of France Paine of course was expanding the freedom that was unlocked from the prison to the promise that overcomes despair. For many readers being homeless and sleeping in a field was widespread then, a time of expropriation, as it is now with the disruptions of war, globalization, and foreclosures. For others both despair and diffidence can be incapacitating, disabling. The Protestant moralism of Bunyan can be translated into other terms precisely because he is writing from below describing a reality. He spent twelve years in prison. Despair and diffidence are interiorizations of despotism. The structures of our society produce both: the rebel who 'goes against' but meets defeat is offered despair, while diffidence is the survival mode for those who 'get along and go along'. Despair is for the unemployed, diffidence is for the employed. This is why schools close and prisons expand.

As for the allegorical interpretation of the Doubting Castle it corresponds to the total ideological infrastructure that denies active historical agency to the exploited and oppressed. Action, we know, precedes knowledge. Forms of diffidence and despair flourish in the Ivory Tower where the ideological infrastructures of ignorance are laid down, brick by brick, agnotology as Iain Boal names it, or the science of ignorance.

Tom Paine came out of this dissenting, non-con-formist culture of English Protestantism, though he was by no means fixed in it. Individual progress was not his theme; it was collective or it was nothing.

"Narrative is linear, Action is solid," is the dictum from Carlyle, the historian, and Carlyle the admirer of the French revolution. Surely, here is our key, our promise: it is collective and it is action. ¡Si se puede! in deed.

In the gift shop at Mount Vernon you can buy a key chain with replica of the key that opened the Bastille for $10.95. It is cheap. If Paine is right that the principles of the American Revolution opened the doors of the prison and crumbled its walls, then the key and its Promise might still remind us of our work – the abolition of slavery, health care for all, open borders, the abolition of prisons.

RELATED BOOKS

John Berger, Hold Everything Dear (2007)

Jamie Bissonette et al, When the Prisoners Ran Walpole: A True Story in the Movement for Prison Abolition (2008)

John Bunyan, Pilgrims Progress (1678)

Thomas Carlyle, The French Revolution (1837)

Angela Y. Davis, Are Prisons Obsolete? (2003)

Ruth Wilson Gilmore, Golden Gulag: Prisons, Surplus, Crisis, and Opposition in Globalizing California (2007)

George Lefebvre, The Coming of the French Revolution, translated by R.R. Palmer (1947)

Staughton Lynd, Lucasville: The Untold Story of a Prison Uprising (2004)

Jules Michelet, History of the French Revolution, translated by Charles Cocks and edited by Gordon Wright (1967)

Thomas Paine, Rights of Man, part one (1791)

Marge Piercy, City of Darkness, City of Light (1996)

George Rudé, The Crowd in History 1730-1848 (1964)

LIBERATORY FOCUS – KENYA

Guest Editor: Shalini Gidoomal

personal narratives, analyses, poems

Contributors to Focus: Kenya are mainly members of Concerned Kenyan Writers – "a coalition whose purpose is to use writing skills to help save Kenya in this polarised time."

No Laughing Matter
Judy Kibinge

Once upon a time…three university pals in their early twenties formed a comedic trio at the height of President Daniel arap Moi's dictatorial reign. Moi ruled supreme to the extent that to imagine his death was declared a crime punishable by death. Political enemies disappeared, or were arrested in the middle of the night and taken to torture chambers. No one voiced their real feelings in public. You never knew who might be listening. Phones were bugged and conspicuous informants sat in on university lectures, trying to blend in. And even after the first democratic elections in 1997, Moi still ruled supreme over a cowed nation.

It is therefore remarkable that against this back-drop of fear Redykyulass was formed. Watching these three campus kids – Walter Mongare, John Kiarie aka KJ and Tony Njuguna – staging skits publicly that ridiculed the dictator and his sycophantic government was a new form of freedom in itself. A scary kind of comedy: a real-life David giving a real-life Goliath a raspberry. Their rib splitting act operating under the name Redykyulass may have had audiences doubled up in tears of laughter but behind the laughter grew reverence: cutting edge as their humor was, these boys were either brave or suicidal.

Their best-loved skit depicted President Daniel arap Moi, a rather sternly conservative old man (played by Walter) arriving through the cheering audience (transformed into exultant crowds at a typically African political rally) carried shoulder high by sweating aides. The 74-year-old 'President' would then break into an almost lewd hip-thrust-ing dance routine joined by an unlikely dance partner – his aide de camp. The routine floored the crowd every time. This wasn't just fresh: It was political satire at its funniest, most fearless and most ridiculous. The fame of Redykyulass spread through the land. Bars would come to a standstill after the news when their show came on, parodying the news we had just watched.

And as we laughed, less and less fearfully, their comedy become more and more sophisticated and satirical… His Excellency the President Daniel arap Moi philosophizing and contemplating life by a lake. Playing piano between his crowd pulling dance trysts. In love with the greatest defender in his cabinet, Kamotho: running in slow motion towards each other. A duet, as President and sycophant sing: *"The greatest love of all, is happening to me…"* Oprah Winfrey played by KJ in a scandalously short skirt interviewing them on their greatest love. Redykyulass had unwittingly shown that the Emperor had no clothes and in a powerful way contributed to the psyche of a nation hungry for change.

But come true democracy, where was Redykyulass to go next?

2002 found Kenya struggling with transition. Mwai Kibaki had ridden into power on the shoulders of an alliance of oppositionists, the Rainbow Alliance coalition. Kenya, which had stood united by the euphoria of throwing Old Man Moi out, had fallen apart and with that fracturing of goodwill, all semblances of trust flew out the window. Over the first five year term, the country's economy had gotten stronger, but in a way that was comforting to Kenya's growing middle class, and as costs for basic commodities rose, the poor felt more disenfranchised, corruption and grand theft seemed more insidious, and leaders more selfish. MP's continually passed bills to award themselves greater increments and were soon the highest paid Members of Parliament on the continent. Traffic soon clogged the capital's center as extra money was converted into cars. Shopping Malls expanded triumphantly.

As stomachs across the nation either protruded or rumbled with hunger, the divide between the rich and poor, the establishment, ever the wolf in a new sheepskin, grew greater and greater, and the hiss of "they" began to rise from the dust.

"They" are the problem, said an ever discontented youth as they realized that voting Moi out did not mean that his cronies had left the building. Indeed, Kibaki himself had once been Moi's Minister of Finance and John Michuki, his closet cabinet aide had been part of the colonial government. Poor and struggling Kenyans realized that changing the government had not been a leap into the new and the incumbent President's rallying cry of kazi iendelee (let work continue) was twisted and mocked by the opposition cry of "kazi ianze" (let work begin).

Redykyulass, still youthful with its youngest member KJ just 27 years old, were by now all highly politicized beings who recognized that although the youth were the country's outstanding majority, disillusionment in their own power left them too lackluster to give politics a backwards glance. Much like many apathetic youth around the world, their futures look bleak. Sitting on the crest of the wave of entertainment that appealed to the youth, Redykyulass recognized that with liberalization and democratization had come the authority of the entertainment industry. Walter, who had once played Moi, now had an alter ego, Nyam-bane, Kenya's most loved comedian, co-hosting the country's most popular breakfast show. Besides that, he managed the trio's musical band. Tony was now an advertising creative churning out successful advertising campaigns for the country's largest advertising agency, and KJ, a cartoonist, was also perfecting his political stance as a much sought after MC for numerous company functions. On top of this, the trio were booked solid as Redykyulass on any given week in the year. Their weekly show Red Korner was one of the highest rated TV shows in the land. Their comedy remained bold and irreverent and as always there were no sacred cows. The President's highly strung, controversial first lady, played by KJ, was a favorite, and they famously recreated her nighttime storming of the Nation's newspapers where she slapped a reporter and screamed at cameras for hours, waving the offending newspaper article in their faces. The offending article had been headlined by the Nation's rival paper The Standard, something the First Lady failed to understand. Soon after, the trio's manager received a call from the then Minister of Security Chris Murungaro asking them to lay off. They didn't. Their popularity soared. In the midst of their backbreaking schedule and steady appeal, they hatched an ambitious plan to transform Ken-ya's political landscape.

In the early 80's there were no Kenyan youth icons. A youth survey done for the advertising agency McCann Erickson in 1994 revealed that the only youth icons were Jesus Christ, Mum and occasionally internationally celebrated Africans like Kenya's most famous runner Kipchpoge Keino and Nelson Mandela. Back then, local artists were despised by the youth who considered them Old School. But by the late 1990's, thanks to the liberalization of the airwaves and the birth of Kenyan hip hop produced by upcoming Producers like Tedd Josiah, the power of the Kenyan Celebrity had stealthily grown.

Redykyulass had indeed grasped an important insight – that the only thing that seemed to truly move and motivate the youth were musicians. On the radio, songs of revolution and disenfranchisement blared. Sisi wa maghetto…. They of the ghetto were speaking out loud to a growing constituency. Music was an escape from despair, from joblessness, uniting them and all their fans into a bubbling hip hop nation unrecognized by a bloated, aged, dismissive authority. And in the midst of this and the run up to the 2007 elections, Redkyulass in conjunction with the IED (Institute of Education & Democracy) and Tru Blak Entertainment's Kevin Ombajo, better known as Big Kev, kicked off a campaign to get the youth to vote rallying around the slogan: Vijana Tugutuke, ni masaa yetu: Youth, Arise, it's our time.

First they had to persuade the celebrities to join their cause. Their reasoning was persuasive. If, they reasoned with the artists, a younger government was in place, then youth issues like music piracy, joblessness and support for the arts would be prioritized. It was a compelling strategy. The artists listened and jumped on board and the countrywide concerts began. The mechanics were simple. Come to the concert grounds with an ID, get a voter's card on the spot, and once in, be entertained by a dazzling array of stars all telling them that their voters' cards were the first step. They needed to choose their leaders wisely based on their youth agendas. Star after star reinforced the message that they needed to vote, that the concert was only the first step.

For over a year, Redykyulass, in conjunction with the ECK and the Institute for Education and Democracy, systematically toured the country staging concerts. Moving trucks of equipment, stages and speakers, huge technical crews as well as artists was no mean feat but something that Big Kev and his extremely young team, many in their early twenties, made look easy. So organized were they that many sections of the media refused to believe that they were not receiving massive financial backing from the Old Guard. As a result, little news of the concerts trickled into the mainstream press. Despite that, crowds in far-flung areas who previously could not have dreamed of seeing their heroes and heroines up close, read the leaflets and listened to the vans with loudspeakers circling their markets and towns reading out a dazzling list of performers and turned up in tens of thousands. In Meru, a field of fans sung along to Amani and her girls, Mighty King Kong. Kenya's most nationally loved artist swung his crippled legs this way and that, a meter above the ground as he hopped to the music on his long, long pole. Kinyana, muscle-bound and furious in tight white T-shirts, making all the girls scream, pounded their hardcore ghetto lyrics lambasting the government. Jua Kali with his seductively raspy voice rapped about the frustrations of being a youth, and Mike Rua, Kenya's most famous one-man-guitar, had audiences cracking up with his cheeky lyrics. In Isiolo, the Imams furious that music was being played so close to prayer time encouraged youth to stone them. But on they pressed... Nakuru, Lamu, Kisumu... and everywhere, the response and attendance was overwhelming. And with every town and with every concert, Redykyulass and Big Kevv pounded their message out: Vijana, Gutuka! Youth Arise! Your time has come! Vote!

Everywhere Tony told this story to a wide-eyed awakening youth:

"I'm here cos I'm confused. I was told I'm a future leader of tomorrow. I studied, was given school fees. And told again that I am the future leader, one with strength. I went on and studied more...got to University. And there, they told me I am a bright future leader of tomorrow. I went on, I married, got a wife. Then had a child. I was still told I am a bright young future leader of...? They said I am the future leader of tomorrow. Should we accept this story or leave it? Shall we abandon this story? (Crowd roars)

"What we are saying is leaders are youth! (Crowd roars louder)

"More fire!"

The campaign gained momentum and the voters registration count swelled for months after each concert. In Nakuru, 30,000 attended the concert, and voter registration clocked an all-time high months after. Here and elsewhere, the electoral commission attributed the surges in registration directly to the Vijana Concerts.

It's not surprising that the boys from Redykyulass and their partners were soon receiving offers running into small fortunes to allow partisan MP's and politicians to jump on their bandwagon – or rather up onto their traveling stage. Somehow, they held firm. They had one rule for any politician no matter how big or influential who tried to barge onto stage to address the thousands of much sought after youth votes gathered around the stage: "If you get on this stage, you don't talk, we're tired of your talk. You dance."

The official leader of the opposition and government spokesman found that soon to be true when they attempted to address the crowd. The crowd jeers forced them to dance. Finally. Powerful men dancing to the tune of the young.

In the day of the last concert, a mammoth con-cert attended by 100,000 was held at Uhuru Park in the center of Nairobi. Everywhere that the Vijana Tugutuke voters registration campaign had been, numbers of registered young voters surged for months after, a fire in their spirits lit. Youth who attended the concerts would go away and convince their friends, relatives, and classmates to get registered… For the first time, they had begun to understand that by the sheer power of numbers, they had a real shot of changing their own destinies.

Samuel Kivuitu, the eccentric and often outrageously rude white-haired chairman of the electoral commission known for his irreverently rude statements soon referred to as Kivuituisms, was there, and I heard him declare to the crowd that for the first time in the history of Kenya, over 50 percent of all registered voters were under 35. He asked them never again to claim that they had no real power. It was now in their hands. The government, panicking, reactionary, began a garbled series of campaign messages targeted at the 18-30 year olds. Stanley Githunguri, a white haired old Kikuyu man of over 70, erected a huge billboard in his Kiambaa constituency and on it in a see-through attempt to engage with his younger potential constituency changed his name to the hip street version of Stanley, "STANO." Kamlesh Patni, the Hindu fraudster turned Christian Pastor best known for masterminding the biggest economic swindle in the history of Kenya in 1992, had thrown himself into the race with yet another huge billboard, with the youngish phrase, "mimi ni moja wenu." I'm one of you. But the youth weren't having any of it. They had been listening to a different tune – a danceable tune, even! The government of old men trying to talk young must have sounded strange to their ears.

By the week of elections, 70% of all registered voters were the youth, reflecting the true demographics of Kenya for the very first time. To fully understand what a revolution this was, it's important to know that in the 2002 general election, of a total of 17 M eligible voters, only 11.2 M registered. And of those, only 6 M voted. Of these, just 7 percent were the youth. A predictable race against a government that had transformed Kenya's dull economy into a bright and hopeful one was now suddenly too close to call.

And the country was highly charged. All polls had predicted a very close race, but Raila – choice of a previously disenfranchised youth population – was always in the lead.

The trio of comedians were no longer a laughing matter. To separate their comedy from their political messages, they stopped all comedy and began to preach a message of awakening. No longer were Redykyulass to be seen jesting or satirizing politics. They had become the force behind a much underestimated wind of change, setting the scene for the greatest paradigm shift ever experienced in Kenya's political scene since independence in 1963.

KJ, one of the trio of comedians, declared a stand to run against an older but much respected old matriarch, Beth Mugo, in a hotly contested Nairobi seat. His election race typified what was happening around the country. Younger, politically inexperienced citizens were running against older, more established, richer ones. And threatening to win. And in many, many instances, doing just that.

On December 30, 2007, the election results were announced. KJ was not amongst the winners. But he and all youth like him had created a change in perception. Getting my hair braided in a Luo owned hairdressing salon, I witnessed the excitement as his lead increased over Beth's. Hesitant in English, the young Luo braiders, in rapid-fire sheng, told me how excited they were that he was, for that brief moment, ahead in the polls. His ethnicity did not come into question.

"You know," they said, "when KJ gets in, he will be the youngest member of parliament."

And all at once the excitement died as PNU's leader Mwai Kibaki was declared winner. The Establishment had won, amidst cries of foul play and allegations – backed by reports of fiddled and inflated tallies from observers, the opposition and EU observers alike.

And the country began to burn.

By all accounts, most instigators of the post election violence were youth, furious, feeling dangerously swindled and transformed from the hopeful leaders of today they were certain they were going to be into a mass ripe for revolt. Churches burnt. Women and children were massacred in a cyclone of violence that was not so much a statement of ethnic hatred but more a revolt against betrayal that quickly morphed into ethnic hatred. The Kikuyu, the ethnic tribe from which Kibaki is from, paid the heaviest price, shouldering much of the backlash from every corner of the country. The civilian revolt against betrayal left virtually all of Kenya smoking and scarred.

The chaos that ensconced Nairobi and the country at large found many things going on. It found Raila, the fiery ODM oppositionist, with countrywide youth support and Mwai Kibaki, the hastily sworn in President of Kenya, unable to sit at a table and put the fire out. It found Kibera, the largest slum in Africa, smoldering; its shops, restaurants and roadside vegetable stalls charred, lifetimes of friendship bludgeoned, neighbors turned to lifetime foes. It found thousands of citizens of Kenya starving, in makeshift refugee camps of the kind we have become accustomed to from news footage taken in neighboring conflicted countries.

But in a suburb of Nairobi, off Ngong road, at the Tru Blak Entertainment offices, it also found the boys from Redykyulass and their partner Big Kevv acting as a pivot point for a group of young entertainers, activists, journalists, news anchors, television hosts and more. Barely had they taken a breather from the election frenzy before spinning around to respond to the outburst of violence that had turned thousands of Kenyans into refugees in less than 24 hours. Reactivating the Jaza Lorry (Fill the Truck) campaign, created by themselves in 2005 to cope with famine in Kenya, was, they ruled, the quickest way they could respond. Jaza Lorry back then succeeded in feeding 4000 people for an entire month easing what could have been a far worse humanitarian crisis in Northern Kenya. Indeed, the boys cite their experience in 2005 as the point at which they first became aware of the power they had to mobilize Kenyans into action. Just a couple of days after the violence erupted, the compound was already fast filling with paper bags of food and clothing for the thousands of internally displaced people who just a few days before had spent hours queuing to vote and now were spending hours each day queuing for food aid. And their actions were largely going unnoticed by Kenya and the world. They were, and still are, working on faith and a zero budget. Without funding, the initiative will grind to a halt, but none of that has deterred their efforts so far. Artists streamed in on foot, by public transport, and in borrowed cars, to contribute the one thing they each had to give: their talent. The cameras were instead all trained on the Serena Hotel where peace talks were taking place underneath the cool whirl of electric air conditioners.

As we sat in the packed room in Tru Blak filled with Kenyan celebrities brainstorming to find a way to feed the hungry and settle the displaced, a German TV crew cornered a broody Big Kev and asked for his final word. What he said in short was this:

"In a two-year civic education plan we told the youth that their vote would make a difference. What do we tell them now? This election has been the biggest blow to democratic elections, ever. But the struggle continues."

Unsettled

Kalundi Serumaga

Hitting Without Touching

Poverty is the worst form of violence. At its own worst, it is a form of slow genocide. For an example, take the fact that the vast majority of the Native Americans "rubbed out" in the American genocide died (and still die) not from settler bullets, but from poor diets, disease, poor-on-poor crime, stress-related illnesses caused by predatory lending and the like. In short, they are killed by the condition of being poor.

Girls are affected the worst, as it exposes them to all sorts of deprivations that lead to temptations and inducements resulting in angry, enervated young women. Even as an adult, a person raised in poverty often suffers a certain furtive sense of shame and anger that they can never quite shake off. Years of "no" and "not enough" force them to ingest a bitter diet of silent rage, frustrations, thwarted dreams, hurtful choices and humiliation as their parents age prematurely before their eyes, and their siblings learn to mask all feelings of disappointment. It is violence at the deepest psychological, spiritual and emotional levels, long before it becomes physical. I know. I've been there. In Kenya.

If Kibera is indeed the world's biggest slum (I don't know who measures these things, or how), then it is currently also the biggest single act of violence against African people, carried out over the longest period of time.

The recent magic tricks at Electoral Commission of Kenya (how to breed votes and then count them in the dark; how to speak out of both sides of your mouth, and other marvellous wonders) and the subsequent orgy of gratuitous blood-letting, have given rise to expressions of grief, shock and anger from the Kenyan intelligentsia, in a way that leaves me truly mystified. Have they not been paying attention? If money and land meant for the poor can be stolen from them, then why not votes? If it became a four-decade normality for children to grow up sharing the eating of rotting oranges from garbage skips, why on earth should they not share more direct forms of violence with each other? Having grown up witnessing Kenya's normalising of the grotesquely abnormal, my only surprise was that these acts – from the rigging itself to the rape, pillage and murder – took so long to reach this particular nadir. Kenya was and is an atrocity a long time made and a catastrophe a long time coming.

"There are no stories in the riots, only the ghosts of stories," as some wise black British woman said of Brixton and Handsworth, a long time ago.

I should declare an interest: though I spent some critical formative years living both near the top and the bottom of Kenyan society, I am not Kenyan. I was a refugee from another atrocity called Uganda, and part of a very politically engaged community that was actively fomenting armed rebellion back home. Since our flight was political, we came to Kenya with a heightened interest in politics generally and were fascinated by the way in which the Kenyatta and Moi regimes were achieving through "sowing acres of cynicism" (to quote Okot p'Bitek, another Ugandan refugee) what Amin and Obote could only attempt through planting killing fields.

Honourable Mwai Kibaki was a particularly interesting study for us. As a graduate of Makerere University, we would wonder if he participated in politics with Ugandan or with Kenyan sensibilities. For me, he answered the question most eloquently when on tour, as a Seriously Big Government Man, of (I think) Kamiti Prison way back in seventies. There had been media talk of increasingly horrific conditions in the prisons, and his visit was supposed to be a fact-finding tour. At one point, as Big Man And Entourage walked through the prison complex, a prisoner displayed incredible dignity and courage by stepping out in front of him, and trying to hand him a letter sealed in an envelope. The prison official next to Hon. Kibaki intercepted the convict's outstretched hand, took the envelope and pocketed it. According to the news report, Hon. Kibaki paused, watched the entire incident, and then carried on with his "fact-finding."

Forget about the botched attempts to write a new constitution, forget about the failure to follow up on the Canary Patni Goldenberg song, forget even about the indignity of swearing-in at twilight (quick question: was that really a Bible he was holding up? It looked suspiciously like a pricey desk diary to me. You never know, given the indecent haste), as kids watching their elders paying a much higher price to be in politics, we felt that was a most pathetic display of craven indifference. In truth, looking back, it was at that moment that Hon. Kibaki for me disqualified himself from being president of anywhere or anything. It's just that no-body realised it, or thought about it hard enough. Now look where we have ended up.

Tea Without Biscuits

Jeffrey had two thumbs on his left hand, but in the end, that was not the most interesting thing about him for me. He drove a little pick-up truck for one of the large tea estates in the Limuru area where I went to school, and would often give us a lift back up to our hillside campus after we had been hiking or running in the countryside. He lived in the tea plantation, but not in a house. His home was a large garage next door to a tractor. He lived there with his wife, kids and possibly his mother. During the day they would just slide the huge door open and leave it that way like some large gaping wound. As we walked or jogged past, you could see them all gathered inside, going about their domestic business as if on a cinema screen. Once, Jeffrey drove us much higher up the hill, where one had a clear view of much of the valley below. He was really talking to my classmate Karim Walji, but I remain grateful to him for the education he gave us. Using large, lonely trees, hillocks and dips in the valley as landmarks, the three-thumbed Kikuyu man, living in a mzungu's garage on his own ancestors land, listed for us which families and from which clans lived where before the endless carpet of green tea was violently laid down. "Where did the people all go?" Karim asked him. I don't think he bothered to answer, and wore a wan smile. As somebody who had been smuggled across a border on the back of a pedal-bike to a new and more "stable" country, I felt strangely disturbed. But I understood that smile, and the inability to say more (our parents seemed stuck in that mode), but I was scared at how normal this dispossession had become. At least we were fighting those who had evicted us, not living in their garages. But now we were living in Kenya, where the abnormal was normalised.

Don't Hunt What You Can't Kill

"Don't go to town today, they are rounding up Ugandans." This was regularly heard advice in the Ugandan exile community, as Kenyans pointed us out to their police. A night or two cleaning their police cells or a well-deployed bribe was what was needed to keep you from joining a refugee camp population. On reflection, it made sense for people oppressed by their own police force to be more than happy to point out other, better victims to the same police. "Wakimbizi" have no permanence, no power to come back later and retaliate. They are perfect victims, and probably helped deflect police attention from the native poor. Now, displaced and poor working Kikuyus find themselves the new targets, but without the help of the police. If you kill a cop, ten will come back, if you kill a child of the rich, your fellow poor will be offered reward money to find you. If you kill a fellow poor "non-you," you have found the perfect victim.

How else are the poor, schooled in forty years of systemic violence expected to communicate except through violence? On whom are they to vent their rage except another guaran teed to have no power to retaliate with greater force?

Those who escaped the poverty also took the internalised violence with them. Having perfected the skills of managerial service provision, the Kenyan middle classes have moved to dominate mana-gerial positions in media, financial services, NGO and hospitality sectors throughout the region, where they have acquired the reputations of being the most cut-throat, ruthless, backstabbing, neurotic and yet efficient of Boardroom-wallahs.

Herculean C-130 Military Aircraft Dreams

The crisis that is Kenya today comes largely as a result of the Kenyan intelligentsia's abject failure to come up with viable alternatives to this mess. Those in power never had answers, and are not interested in looking for them. Like Uganda, the creation of Kenya was an act of theft and murder. Anyone managing it is simply perpetuating those crimes. Those in opposition had a responsibility to come up with something better. But did they? With my two teenage brothers, I wandered the Nairobi streets amid the August 1981 mayhem, walking from Eastleigh through Majengo then downtown, up to Hurlingham and back, as Kenya Air Force mutineers used their Land Rovers to wrench the metal grilles from shop fronts and then say "chukuwa" to the waiting looters. There was a lot of shouting of "Power" but no answers about pov-erty, certainly not for the half-naked man lying in the street at their feet, his whole body ashen grey from the blood loss occasioned by the open wound in his head. He was nobody's concern. He reminded me exactly of another half-naked dying man I had seen years before as a child in Kampala. He had been attacked by a mob. Or shot. Nobody was saying. Just walking past. He was also lying in the gutter, also bleeding from the head, also barely twitching as he drew his very last breaths. Their ashen greys were a perfect match.

A couple of years later – against well-meant advice – we saw the would-be mwakenya rebels hitch their doomed wagons to the notoriously unreliable star that is the National Resistance Movement, leading to many bitterly spat words of anger and disappointment. Following Ochuka's forced return flight from Nyerere's Tanzania that ended in "the rough hand of the noose around his neck," one would have expected the "revolutionaries" to have learned a few lessons about African presidencies beyond the rhetoric, but no. Instead, wishful thinking and infantile prescriptions prevailed, while prisoners wrote unopened letters, and Kikuyus were hoodwinked by Emperor Kabalega's self-aggrandising alleged son Jomo Kenyatta into being vulnerably half-gathered far away from the rivers of their ancestors, and grown men danced in the footsteps. This is where the recent deaths were foretold.

There is a lot more that needs to be heard about why the "revolutionary" Yoweri Museveni chooses to congratulate Hon. Kibaki at the expense of the "socialist" Raila Odinga, and why Hon. Odinga seems completely unsurprised by this turn of events.

In those 1980s, a good friend of mine (Ugandan, anti-Obote guerila) found this whole tragedy perfectly summed up in advance, while on a necessary visit to a Nairobi public toilet. There was clearly no toilet paper, he narrated, so somebody before him had used their finger to clean their behind, and then wiped it on the toilet wall. On closer inspection (my friend is insatiably curious, no matter the circumstances), he realised that this person had used their shit to write something on the toilet wall.

The word written was "Uhuru."

Yani, the idea, I think. Not the person. But you never know.

An Open Letter

Shailja Patel

An Open Letter to Samuel Kivuitu, Chair of the Electoral Commission of Kenya

Mr. Kivuitu,

We've never met. It's unlikely we ever will. But, like every other Kenyan, I will remember you for the rest of my life. The nausea I feel at the mention of your name may recede. The bitterness and grief will not.

You had a mandate, Mr. Kivuitu. To deliver a free, fair and transparent election to the people of Kenya. You and your commission had 5 years to prepare. You had a tremendous pool of resources, skills, technical support, to draw on, including the experience and advice of your peers in the field – leaders and experts in governance, human rights, electoral process and constitutional law. You had the trust of 37 million Kenyans.

We believed it was going to happen. On December 27, a record 65 percent of registered Kenyan voters rose as early as 4 a.m. to vote. Stood in lines for up to 10 hours, in the sun, without food, drink, toilet facilities. As the results came in, we cheered when minister after powerful minister lost their parliamentary seats. When the voters of Rift Valley categorically rejected the three sons of Daniel Arap Moi, the despot who looted Kenya for 24 years. The country spoke through the ballot, en masse, against the mindblowing greed, corruption, human rights abuses, callous dismissal of Kenya's poor, that have characterised the Kibaki administration.

But Kibaki wasn't going to go. When it became clear that you were announcing vote tallies that differed from those counted and confirmed in the constituencies, there was a sudden power blackout at the Kenyatta International Conference Centre, where the returns were being announced. Hundreds of GSU (General Service Unit) paramilitaries suddenly marched in. Ejected all media except the government mouthpiece, Kenya Broadcasting Corporation.

Fifteen minutes later, we watched, dumbfounded, as you declared Kibaki the winner. Thirty minutes later, we watched in sickened disbelief and outrage, as you handed the announcement to Kibaki on the lawns of State House. Where the Chief Justice, strangely enough, had already arrived. Was waiting, fully robed, to hurriedly swear him in.

You betrayed us. Perhaps we'll never know when, or why, you made that decision. One rumor claims you were threatened with the execution of your entire family if you did not name Kibaki as presidential victor. When I heard it, I hoped it was true. Because at least then I could understand why you chose instead to plunge our country into civil war.

I don't believe that rumor any more. Not since you appeared on TV, looking tormented, sounding confused, contradicting yourself. Saying, among other things, that you did not resign because you "did not want the country to call me a coward," but you "cannot state with certainty that Kibaki won the election." Following that with the baffling statement "there are those around him [Kibaki] who should never have been born." The camera operator had a sense of irony – the camera shifted several times to the scroll on your wall that read: "Help Me, Jesus."

As the Kenya Chapter of the International Com-mission of Jurists rescinds the Jurist of the Year award they bestowed on you, as the Law Society of Kenya strikes you from their Roll of Honour and disbars you, I wonder what goes through your mind these days.

Do you think of the 300,000 Kenyans displaced from their homes, their lives? Of the thousands still trapped in police stations, churches, any refuge they can find, across the country? Without food, water, toilets, blankets? Of fields ready for harvest, razed to the ground? Of granaries filled with rotting grain, because no one can get to them? Of the Nairobi slum residents of Kibera, Mathare, Huruma, Dandora, ringed by GSU and police, denied exit, or access to medical treatment and emergency relief, for the crime of being poor in Kenya?

I bet you haven't made it to Jamhuri Park yet. But I'm sure you saw the news pictures of poor Americans, packed like battery chickens into their stadiums, when Hurricane Katrina hit Louisiana. Imagine that here in Nairobi, Mr. Kivuitu. 75,000 Kenyans, crammed into a giant makeshift refugee camp. Our own Hurricane Kivuitu-Kibaki, driven by fire, rather than floods. By organized militia rather than crumbling levees. But the same root cause – the deep, colossal contempt of a tiny ruling class for the rest of humanity. Over 60 percent of our internal refugees are children. The human collateral damage of your decision.

And now, imagine grief, Mr. Kivuitu. Grief so fierce, so deep, it shreds the muscle fibres of your heart. Violation so terrible, it grinds down the very organs of your body, forces the remnants through your kidneys, for you to piss out in red water. Multiply that feeling by every Kenyan who has watched a loved one slashed to death in the past week. Every parent whose child lies, killed by police bullets, in the mortuaries of Nairobi, Kisumu, Eldoret. Everyone who has run sobbing from a burning home or church, hearing the screams of those left behind. Every woman, girl, gang-raped.

Do you sleep well these days, Mr. Kivuitu? I don't. I have nightmares. I wake with my heart pounding, slow tears trickling from the corners of my eyes, random phrases running through my head:

"Remember how we felt in 2002? It's all gone. "

– Muthoni Wanyeki, ED of Kenya Human Rights Commission, on the night of December 30, 2007, after Kibaki was illegally sworn in as president.

"There is a crime here that goes beyond recrimination. There is a sorrow here that weeping cannot symbolise." – John Steinbeck, American writer, on the betrayal of internally dis-placed Americans, in *The Grapes of Wrath*.

"Haki iwe ngao na mlinzi…kila siku tuwe na shukrani" – "Justice be our shield and defender … every day filled with thanksgiving" – lines from Kenya's national anthem.

I soothe myself back to patchy sleep with my mantra in these days, as our country burns and disintegrates around us:

Courage.

Courage comes.
Courage comes from cultivating.
Courage comes from cultivating the habit.
Courage comes from cultivating the habit of refusing.
Courage comes from cultivating the habit of refusing to let fear dictate one's actions.

> – *Aung San Suu Kyi,*
>
> *Burmese Nobel Peace Prize winner.*

I wake with a sense of unbearable sadness. Please let it not be true…

Meanwhile, the man you named President cowers in the State House, surrounded by a cabal of rapacious power brokers, and a bevy of sycophantic unseated Ministers and MPs, who jostle for position and succession. Who fuel the fires by any means they can, to keep themselves important, powerful, necessary. The smoke continues to rise from the torched swathes of Rift Valley, the gutted city of Kisumu, the slums of Nairobi and Mombasa. The Red Cross warns of an imminent cholera epidemic in Nyanza and Western Kenya, deprived for days now of electricity and water. Containers pile up at the Port of Mombasa, as ships, unable to unload cargo, leave still loaded. Uganda, Rwanda, Burundi, Southern Sudan, the DRC, all dependent on Kenyan transit for fuel and vital supplies, grind to a halt.

A repressive regime rolls out its panoply of oppression against legitimate dissent. Who knew our police force had so many sleek, muscled, excellently-trained horses, to mow down protestors? Who guessed that in a city of perennial water shortages, we had high-powered water cannons to terrorize Kenyans off the streets?

I am among the most fortunate of the fortunate. Not only am I still whole, alive, healthy, mobile; not only do I have food, shelter, transport, the safe-ty of those I love; I have the gift of work. I have the privilege to be in the company of the most brilliant, principled, brave, resilient Kenyans of my generation. To contribute whatever I can as we organize, analyse, strategize, mobilize, draw on everything we know and can do, to save our country. I marvel at the sheer collective volume of trained intelligence, of skill, expertise, experience, in our meetings. At the ability to rise above personal tragedy – families still hostage in war zones, friends killed, homes overflowing with displaced relatives – to focus on the larger picture and envisage a solution.

I listen to lawyers, social scientists, economists, youth activists, humanitarians; experts on conflict, human rights, governance, disaster relief; to Kenyans across every sector and ethnicity, and I think:

Is this what we have trained all our lives for? To confront this epic catastrophe, caused by a group of old men who have already sucked everything they possibly can out of Kenya, yet will cling until they die to their absolute power?

You know these people too, Mr. Kivuitu. The principled, brave, resilient, brilliant Kenyans. The idealists who took seriously the words we sang as schoolchildren, about building the nation. Some of them worked closely with you, right through the election. Some called you friend. You don't even have the excuse that Kibaki, or his henchmen, might offer – that of inhabiting a world so removed from ours that they cannot fathom the reality of ordinary Kenyans. You know of the decades of struggle, bloodshed, faith and suffering that went into creating this fragile beautiful thing we called the "democratic space in Kenya." So you can imagine the ways in which we engage with the unimaginable. We coin new similes:

Lie low like a 16A (the electoral tally form returned by each constituency, many of which were altered or missing in the final count)

We joke about the Kivuitu effect – which turns internationalists, pan-Africanists, fervent advocates for the dissolution of borders, into nationalists who cry at the first verse of the national anthem:

Ee Mungu nguvu yetu
Ilete baraka kwetu
Haki iwe ngao na mlinzi
Natukae na undugu
Amani na uhuru
Raha tupate na ustawi.

O God of all creation
Bless this our land and nation
Justice be our shield and defender
May we dwell in unity
Peace and liberty
Plenty be found within our borders.

Rarely do we allow ourselves pause, to absorb the enormity of our country shattered, in 7 days. We cry, I think, in private. At least I do. In public, we mourn through irony, persistent humor, and action. Through the exercise of patience, stamina, fortitude, generosity, that humble me to witness. Through the fierce relentless focus of our best energies towards challenges of stomach-churning magnitude.

We tell the stories that aren't making it into the press. The retired general in Rift Valley sheltering 200 displaced families on his farm. The Muslim Medical Professionals offering free treatment to anyone injured in political protest. We challenge, over and over again, with increasing weariness, the international media coverage that presents this as "tribal warfare," "ethnic conflict," for an audience that visualises Africa through Hollywood: *Hotel Rwanda, The Last King of Scotland, Blood Diamond.*

I wish you'd thought of those people when you made the choice to betray them. I wish you'd drawn on their courage, their integrity, their clarity, when your own failed you. I wish you'd had the imagination to enter into the lives, the dreams, of 37 million Kenyans.

But, as you've probably guessed by now, Mr. Kivuitu, this isn't really a letter to you at all. This is an attempt to put words to what cannot be expressed in words. To mourn what is too immense to mourn. A clumsy groping for something beyond the word "heartbreak." A futile attempt to communicate what can only be lived, moment by moment. This is a howl of anguish and rage. This is a love letter to a nation. This is a long low keening for my country.

Echoes

Yvonne A. Owuor

Three days ago I "exercised my democratic right" and cast my vote.

A vote is a voice, a choice to speak.

And then it was New Year 2008.

Morning Mass at Consolata Church, Westlands.

The thing that has invaded the land, this, layered and ineffable grief wafts even through this hallowed acre. Inside, the pale brown pews are half empty, the celebrant's steps down the aisle are laboured, his head lowered as are those of his yellow-robed acolytes. The chorister inadvertently starts the entrance hymn in D Minor, a note that sets the theme for the world's best requiems. New Year's mass in this church usually stresses its concrete seams with chattering congregants, many of whom turn up to hover at a church door only on the first day of a new year. Last year they formed guilty but cheerful gossiping clumps in the car park interspersed with gleeful *Happy New Year!* And *Shhh!*

The church chamber echoes emptiness. The few people stand with arms folded. I need a ritual to peel back this new year for me. I am here, arms folded. My mother who moves mountains is here. She says today is a good day to have a wrestling match with the Almighty about the future of her grandchildren in Kenya. I shuffled after her faith into the sanctuary where she suspects, in a season of ugliness, some of God's emissaries might have received insight about a transcendent path out of a fire-filled impasse.

Cadence of this morning's radio message. The global stories about us. Catch phrases: *atavistic tribal, ancient ethnic rivalries, primordial hatreds.* We have clicked into the template of others' low expectations. An ignominious international radio broadcast about us – failure is frowned on – in the background a rhythmic chant tinged with angry hopelessness: *Haki yetu! Haki yetu! Haki yetu!*

Ear worm. When a melody or phrase bounces in the head.

It should not matter.

But shame-sorrow predominates the part in the heart that should be at ease. A side activity in today's mass is "The Sacrament of Reconciliation." Confession is a soul-purging ritual, supposed to sometimes dissipate shame, guilt and sorrow. But to be able to do that the penitent must speak. If the penitent cannot speak, the Church might offer exorcism. But exorcism, a dangerous talent, is not on offer anywhere today.

The celebrant's voice trembles. He does not say that the national churning will stop. He did say that God is watching the cracking. That God as parent is not unmoved.

We have a sneaked-into-place Father-of-the-Nation.

A befuddled Chairman of the Electoral Commission stumbled over a proclamation. The custodian of national law magically found himself in State House with a Bible to swear in the President even before the Chairman had completed the anointing.

The micro-swearing in event was televised. Showed the bad portions of a cabalistic ritual with associated slitheriness. Then 900 words, the thank-you-all-for-voting-me-in speech.

Behold, the Father-of-the-Nation.

They forgot to play the exit hymn, the one that starts with the line:

O God of All Creation

Ee Mungu Nguvu Yetu…

So Kenya erupts.

900 words later, the Father-of-the-Nation is silent.

Two days later, Mass stumbles on. The celebrant mumbles, "Do not be afraid."

The Father-of-the-Nation is in place.

Amen.

900 words later, planes land at Jomo Kenyatta International Airport. They are weighed down with the global press corps, circling marabou storks high on typical *Oh Africa schadenfreude.* Gleam in glare, organic gargoyles reeking with the lust for rich pickings.

The images:

A phalanx of armed men, citizens, harrying witnesses out of a gargantuan conference hall.

A man lies on his back on the street, arm outstretched, his mouth wide open, tears running down the side of his face.

A woman runs, goods on her head, three children on her back.

A beautiful young man, earrings in his ear wields a machete.

A woman cries, hand on head.

A grandfather sits in an open field, the remnant of a murdered family of twelve.

A child in a red t-shirt plays in the sewer, oblivious of the action of adults.

Eyes at half-lid, three tall General Service Unit men carry truncheons, dour-faced waiting for the enraged public to turn up.

We have seen these faces and postures in other places. Not in our land, not in our haven and sanctuary. This brand of sickness is not our method, it happens to other people, not to us. Never to us.

This morning.

The keening memory of old national sorrows that still lurk as unsolved riddles do: J.M. Kariuki, Pio Gama Pinto, Argwings Kodhek, Tom Mboya, Robert Ouko, Justus Mbai. Ghost lives in the flickering of flames burning down Kenya's homes, shops, people, dreams. Newspaper headline. A church in which mothers and children had taken refuge in Eldoret was last night burned down by machete wielding young citizens. Now is the time for a strong voice. If a nation can raze the life of children inside a church then it is teetering. Between the shrieks and rage, silence. No 900 words.

Later.

A Stop-the-Madness meeting in a room at the Serena Hotel convened by men and women who have serviced other people's wars, patched other people's rendered national fabrics with no idea they would one day have to look within. A yellow-veiled woman, her face with determination carved into it, her intense voice repeats, "Now. Now we begin." She is the Chairperson.

An Imam is among us. Before he can open his mouth another woman with wide slanted eyes, and a deep-voice, calls out: *"O God of all creation, bless this our land and nation, justice be our shield and defender, may we dwell in unity, peace and liberty, plenty be found within our borders…"*

We know this prayer. Learned it with the ABCs and 123s, hands by our sides, face forward where, often, the red-green-white-black flag would be fluttering. If there was a school orchestra this prayer would be preceded by three majestic drum rolls. Before that, headmistresses and headmasters would have intoned to assembled students, "Let us now stand for our national anthem."

Second stanza.

"Nchi yetu ya Kenya tunayoipenda, tuwe tayari kuilinda."

Grim transcendence pokes through in a simple message.

The only way out of this is through. Fire-walk-ing is a requirement of belonging. Fire-walking can hurt. It can kill. It can break stalwart hearts. It causes tears like these that have all our heads low, mucus pouring down our faces. Shame. Yes. Odd guilt. But inside these, the kernel of our homeland is warm, alive and profoundly loved.

A Moment

Yvonne A. Owuor

Yesterday I met a past presidential candidate in a meeting that was trip-tropping, trip-tropping on a bridge looking for a peaceful solution to an unstated problem with Kenya. He was well-oiled, and fat, bleary eyed and bored with the tears of the peace-seekers.

Smarmy.

Good luck, he smirked after he heard what the peace keepers had said. Indifferent face shifting, shoulder shrugging.

Too bad. He meant. Play with this shit. I have what I want. After you peasants kill yourselves, I'll still be standing. I have planes and pilots on standby. Houses in London, boats on the Riviera. When you are done burning down Kenya, I'll return. I'll reign over you. Since you'll be starving anyway, you'll be glad to just be able to kiss my butt.

He strode out of the room, a confident man. The door closed behind him. He cackled. Along the corridor he must have met an acquaintance whom he hailed in a raw but hearty voice.

Outside, near the park, the Poof! of a tear gas cannister exploding, a woman screamed and screamed and screamed.

Inside, we were silent.

For a moment.

Translated from Kibakizungu

Wambui Mwangi

We have the most hallucination-inducing leaders – they are surpassingly bad at everything, or extremely good, depending on your point of view.

Kibaki, in effect, has said:

– Look. We Kikuyus endured twenty-four years of that Kalenjin man's rule, and were regularly rigged out. We knew it, and so did you. We, unlike our violent Luo lesser-citizens or our wanna-be Kalenjin friends, did not engage in wanton acts of destruction for this reason. We bore our Moi-years burden in silence and with decorum, like everybody else in this country, we even managed to keep our heads above water, more or less. We had saved and secreted away enough, although diminished, shillings to begin to build again – and we have been working hard. You must admit that the street lights in Nairobi work now, and remember the new beauty of the roundabouts. Don't you like flowers? And on this point: please tell your guys to stop burning our flower farms in the Rift Valley: there is going to be a rose crisis in Europe if you don't watch out. It isn't as if the new supermarkets and shops only sell things to Kikuyus: we're all winning, here, guys! We were about to do global IPOs, bwana! We waited for our turn to come, and in 2002, it did (okay, it came for us *again*, but who's counting?). We now do not understand what all this unmannerly screaming and shouting and wielding of pangas and matchboxes and gallons of petrol is all about, as we expect you to understand that you must stand in line. It isn't your turn yet. Yes, we rigged: so what? So did you – we were just better at it, as you well know, as you admitted privately at the golf club. We won that rigging game, fair and square. So, shut up and get on with preparing for the next campaign in five years – we'll have wrapped up our most important business by then, or at least convinced you to follow our plan instead of yours. We'll buy you out, as always – what's all this fuss about? You are welcome to have another factory or two, if that is the problem; if this will make you shut up.

Kibaki has said this, or words certainly to that effect, at the recent meeting of African Union heads recently. He was speaking to his peers – other rulers and regulators of Africans of a bewildering variety of tongues and tendencies, and yet, he was confident that they would understand his meaning. He knew that they knew how to read between his lines of "law and order," of "institutional redress": he was basically saying to his fellow African Excellencies, with a nudge and a wink, that the real problem in Kenya has come about because those idiot Luos don't know how to take a fall, and the Kalenjin have always had dreams of grandeur; they think they're in a movie for white people, or something. Someone, one of his Excellent Brothers, might even guffaw, at his subtleties. They understood his meaning clear and well.

In the meantime, Raila Odinga is failing every test of greatness that has walked up to him and practically slapped him in the face, this last month: he has been looking at the good of his country each day and deciding against it. He has decided that the chance of the presidency means more to him than the chance to be truly great, to be an outstanding African instead of just another quarrelsome Kenyan, petty and power-blinded. They'll still write about him in the history books fifty years from now, and he doesn't care what the reasons are, what stories we will be telling our children about him. His party may have planned mass human rights violations; they may indeed have been a touch over-enthusiastic, but his injured innocence knows no bounds. Kibaki's Presidential Cronies would understand Raila's point of view, too – they practise its tenets daily.

They are all one of a kind.

Despite our differences across this continent, the overwhelming commonality between us Africans is the astoundingly debased and degrading quality of our leaders.

That, despite all that our own senses and our own intellects have assured us is true, this past month, Kibaki was able to say the things that he did, in the place that he did, with the intentions and nuances that he deployed, without the heavens sundering open in scorn, without thunderbolts striking us all, is proof of our sadly decayed expectations of our leaders, across the board.

Why do we not have a Martin Luther King? Has our Fanon been delayed in a bar? It can happen, what with the Nairobi traffic and all. Is Malcom X having some *nyama choma* at his local estate joint, and can't be bothered to attend to our little problem? What house does our Aung San Suu Kyi live in? A Mandela of our own would probably be too much to hope for, but we can dream…

It is remarkable that there is so much unanimity between intellectuals, artists, activists and people of goodwill that the violence is deplorable; that a new vision of Kenya needs to emerge; that communities are looking to our newly-elected (or not) leaders – most recently minus two, of course – in this time of peril to guide us out of this maze; that it is time for a new national conversation about our identities and the uses to which we put them; that whoever is able to do this will live as a hero in the annals of Kenyan history; – so where is this person? Where is this person who will, now, this moment, mount that podium and give Kenyans a credible reason to stop this violence and to find new ways of expressing our fears and our frustrations? Who will explain us to each other, who will clarify our options about our neighbours and our living patterns, our prospects of employment and our hopes, our challenges of salvaging and rebuilding our battered selves, who will exhort us to remember that it is our neighbour and friend who is our usual source of that emergency cup of sugar, our neighbour to whom we look when our child is sick and needs transport to the hospital, our neigh-bour with whom we have exchanged those I-hate-matatu stories even as we board another one together. Or complained about the politicians – we do

that well together, we Kenyans.

Who will convince us that this untidy, resentful, sullen, bleeding, wounded, bewildered, defensive, psychotic, irrational, betraying, dangerous place we call home, this our Kenya, has any point left to it at all?

I am still waiting. I am getting pissed off at the delay.

Of course, when she turns up, we'll probably shoot her dead. Viva Kenya.

"I was near to die...I was dead"

Wambui Mwangi

"I was near to die....I was dead."

If you've watched CNN in the last twenty-four hours, you will have caught this victim of the post-election violence in Kenya speaking his truth. He was near death: in fact, he had already died. I am not sure why this particular mind-bite should stand out from all the other images that I have seen on television, in the newspapers and on the streets here in Kenya, but it did. I have been wondering what he meant, that he had died, he had been dead. I'll never know, exactly, what this poor man meant, but his words are echoing in the sore places of my entrails like the sound of a warning bell dying away, like the last notes of a sad song at sunset.

The sharp edge of the panga had come down twice on his head, he said, but most of the damage had been done to his hands, which had been hacked at repeatedly. His hands. He works with them, or used to. What is this language? To target the very part of the body that is used to create value, that is the labouring instrument, is to say to this man that you may not work. You may not do what you used to with your hands. Your hands offend me, I shall cut them off. And kill you also. This manner of speech is strangely redundant.

I was watching CNN as opposed to Kenyan television channels because I wanted to see what the world was saying about us. The world is saying that Kenyans, who had been on the brink of one of the most astonishing democratic transitions witnessed in Africa, degenerated, very conveniently for the West's stereotypes, to a "business as usual: chaos and anarchy right on schedule" version of the African story. These broadcasts are brimming with just barely-suppressed glee at being able to say that tribal violence is tearing the East African nation of Kenya apart, long regarded as an exemplary bastion of stability in the region. We have confirmed some cherished stereotypes and validated many racists worldwide. In addition to everything else, really, those of you with young children had better start thinking about how, if we survive this, you are ever going to be able to explain what you did with your Kenya. What will you tell them?

Will you tell them: well darling, your uncle's neighbour cut off his colleague's hands because that colleague's father was from a village about fifty kilometres away from where the president's mother used to live? Will your mouth be able to form an explanation for your children, or will your words burn in your throat with the acid of futility and choke you, right there, right there in front of your child's frightened eyes? Will the taste of shit in your mouth cleave your tongue to the roof of your mouth? We are creating a stain of corpses on our psyches, we are defiling our very future. We have leapt ahead to ambush our history. We have roped our children into a ponzi-scheme of danger and desolation.

We will have to tell these children "We were near to die...we were dead."

When the Nakumatts Close

Wambui Mwangi

When the Nakumatts close, you know there is trouble. Yesterday I was sitting in a Java, sipping some curiously-named drink and doing a melanin-graded assessment of everybody else in the Java. There we all were, my nice safe middle-class Nairobi, sitting under maroon umbrellas and admiring our own urban casual chic, dark black and sinuous – really, she was the most fantastically beautiful woman; she looked like an advertisement for blackness – to creamy white and elegant – this one was wearing more beads than the average Maasai, and I wanted her shoes, badly. It was good to lust for shoes, instead of retribution, instead of dreaming up new circles of Dante's Hell for the people who have cost us our hopes, who are going to keep the grave-diggers busy. As an act of charity, hospitals are allowing grieving people to pick up the dead bodies of their loved ones for free. Free death, and free storage of bodies.

At Java, I could escape for a moment and just look at all of us: Kenyan, and carefully cosmopolitan. One of my favourite occupations is watching white Kenyans strenuously differentiate themselves from mere tourists. They mostly won't even look at them. On the other hand, those tables that fail to have at least two different skin colours at them risk seeming provincial, and utterly uncool. The real chic is in mixing your coffees and your skins with varying degrees of milk and whiteness. We Kenyans these days are performing multi-culturalism as if we invented it, which in fact we probably did. We're even into blue glass, these days. We've really got it so good, what with our new fashions and affordable cars and reasonable housing – cybercafés two paces away, at most, this is pretty much the good life we have here, eh? And then the Nakumatt closed.

The Nakumatt closed, frustrating our twenty-four hour shopping expectations, because the man sworn in as president, Mwai Kibaki, had declared a demi-cabinet, straight up, no ice on the side, twist of lemon and a bit of salt on the wound; that'll do nicely, thank you. The calls from Kisumu found their echoes in Kibera; the young men dragged their tear-gassed butts back on to the street, and middle-class Nairobi could not shop. It was really extremely inconvenient. Due to the sudden intervention of politics into my plans, I had to wait until the next day to buy my Pepto-Bismol and a bar of chocolate. I spent the night with a stomach ache. Meanwhile, my fellow citizens died some more. In Kiambu, those who are burdened with non-Kiku-yuness move to the police stations and schools at night, for safety. Small children are learning their ethnic affiliations all of a sudden, in fear and loathing; this is not a lesson they will forget. It is the thing that killed their mother and their father; how will they ever forget? Elsewhere, Kikuyus are dying for "their" president. I feel my fury harden.

There are seven presidents in Kenya now. There are four former presidents of African countries (Mozambique, Tanzania, Zambia and Botswana) who have gone to Eldoret to see the results of our meltdown for themselves; there's one, Kuoffuor, from Ghana who is seeming ambiguously-invited and differentially wanted and we're apparently not even sure whether he is a mediator who can mediate. The first thing he will have to mediate is the mediation issue. Perhaps after that we can go back to shopping at midnight if we feel like it. This, in addition to our less-than-beloved Moi, who in recent years morphed into an elder statesman and an apostle of peace right in front of our astonished eyes. I wonder if he's gloomy or gleeful as he rasps out an "I told you so" from his new skull-looking face. He is already a carving, a relic; he has somehow managed a transmogrification into his own sculpture. A walking myth, unrepentant and unbowed. He makes a better looking piece of art than those gargoyles he had put up all over the place. I wonder about authoritarian art – is there a market for it? We could call it Brutism and sell it and pay for food for our people, perhaps. On television, there is a near-riot

riot for relief food. In Kenya. My heart is breaking – I am a walking splinter of rage.

There is also Kibaki, who was swept to power in 2002 in love and acclamation, in triumph, in hope and ululation. We were so naive, in those days, those innocent hopeful days. He's currently the most famous squatter in the world, having liked his accommodations so much, he just got up and…stayed.

I think perhaps he lives on a different planet from the rest of us. Where he lives, he is presiding over a democratic country full of peace-loving and calm people who lined up for hours to vote him in for a second term in an amazing landslide and who are panting with enthusiasm to hear him tell us about his new cabinet, seeing as everything else is so lovely and hunky-dory at the moment. In Kibakistan, *hakuna matata*. It is obviously a large tourist resort, there, where he is president of – full of shiny happy people holding hands and dancing for wealthy white strangers. In this alternative reality inhabited by our leaders, whose serenity is second to none, we are just about to go on with our business of becoming an African Tiger; all systems go, let the work continue, as you were, assume positions and stations, and go! It sounds nice there, where this man is president of, wherever that is.

I do not live there.

We cannot possibly be inhabiting the same latitudes and longitudes and breathing the same air – where I live is full of frightened and traumatised people, and where this man lives is…somewhere else. He is not here.

They do not live here, he and his friends; they have not smelled the tyres burning or seen the shell that was Ukwala Supermarket in Kisumu. I bought a pair of pliers in that supermarket, on the 24th of December, 2007. I have the pliers still – we used them as a make-shift window-crank for the left-hand passenger-door on our brave little car, Purple Perpetua, who took us safely though every obstacle and rough spot until we met The Hate. It is not true that you need a four-wheel drive vehicle to travel around Kenya; Perpetua got through everything, every crevice and crack and swimming-pool size trench in the road to Western Kenya and Nyanza, so obviously she was all but skipping and trilling as she traversed the skating-smooth ribbons of tarmac that are in the Central Province. Until the country exploded. That stopped Purple Perpetua in her tracks, quite literally: there was no petrol. It stopped us as well, but only to the extent that we were forced to stare at luscious gardens by the pool-side for two whole days, whilst grudgingly eating delicious meals. I think we might have been visiting the place where that man is president of, where he lives with his friends, and where adoring crowds buoy up his every word with gladness and joy. It is surreal now. My memory is not working properly. Two weeks ago feels like another lifetime, and every day is separated from the last by a sense of surprise. The sun is still shining the way it used to – how can it? I cannot remember if it was this hot before elections.

Were we all dreaming, in 2002? Even last November seems fictional to me, so I cannot really tell whether we were all just high on ourselves in 2002, when we were dreaming and cheering Kibaki on – in those days before the Betrayal. We might have been momentarily body-snatched by optimistic aliens, because we certainly are not cheering or dreaming now. I hate them all for taking away that dream. I want the aliens back. E.T. call home. Please call home. Those slogans we chanted to and for ourselves back then; we meant them – we're such a wonderfully sentimental people about ourselves, sometimes. We go around quoting the national anthem to each other these days, as if we've all just learned it anew, as if it was written by Shakespeare, as if we are the first to discover its profound wisdom and can't wait to pass it on. As if the person we are telling it to doesn't know it already, has never heard it before – we insist on telling it over. It is a prayer and a curse. *"O God of All Creation, Bless this Our Land and Nation, Justice Be Our Shield and Defender"* – that line is almost funny, in these times.

I met a friend under those maroon umbrellas; someone I hadn't seen for years. Those cafe's are extremely productive for those kinds of meetings; you can plan on meeting unplanned-for people you know at a Nairobi Java. By "people" I do not mean the "watus"; those who actually *work* in the supermarkets and coffee houses, in the hospitals, office buildings and hotels but have to go back every night to madness and sadness and fear, where poor people in Nairobi live. One doesn't "meet" those people, one merely overlooks them, until they are absent and then mostly it is because the dust starts to accumulate, and we remember that we have no staff. Those people dying have never seen the inside of the parliament, unless they were there to clean it. Those people dying will not, as Moi once pithily put it, have more ugali in their sufurias (were they alive to dream of eating it) just because "their" man is president. They'll be as poor as they've always been, unless they luck out and get dead, instead. The dead have simpler desires.

In any case, we have seven presidents here now, which should cover any presidential eventuality that arises. We're locked and loaded, presidentially speaking. Unless, of course, one gets picky and wants a Kenyan president who has been democratically elected – that might be a little difficult at the moment. We however have a very nice line in retirees, would madam be interested in one of those, instead? We also have a president-in-waiting, to round out the numbers, and for sophisticated tastes, we have a man who campaigned for the vice-presidency in the most blatant fashion possible, and actually got the job. What's that, 8½? One more, and we can make the movie.

I feel the need for my Java session – it is a kind of meditation. We are such a nice fantasy, there. My dreams have shrunk to the size of maroon um-brellas. *"May we dwell in Liberty, Peace and Unity...."* I'm doing it myself, now. I'll be fine as long as the Nakumatts stay open.

The Fire This Time

Martin Kimani

I have just walked through the lobby of the Serena Hotel in Nairobi. Packs of politicians and their entourages hurry past. Most have mobile phones into which they whisper urgently pressed to their ears. They brush shoulders with white men and women lagging large cameras trying to arrange for taxis that will carry them to the nearest scene of carnage and bloodletting. I get the impression that the more the politicians whisper into their phones, the more images the international press will capture. Kenya at the moment must look to those watching CNN or BBC like Zimbabwe or Nepal has looked to me in the past. But then I know that the country is not in the grip of atavistic hatreds, images of machete-wielding, church-burning men notwithstanding. This is a political crisis fuelled by ethnic differences which in Kenya are now, as never before, political differences.

Growing up, the various tribal stereotypes were the source of much shared humour among friends and family. Difference was funny. But underneath the jokes, in the same way that we say that there is no smoke without fire was recognition that our differences, no matter the friendly way we tossed them out, were actual and lasting. In the 2007 campaign season for parliamentary and presidential seats, what had previously been jokes morphed into paranoid and even hateful mobile text messages. The intention was to drive the country into tribal camps from which votes for the particular candidates would issue.

I am a Gikuyu like President Kibaki and there-fore expected by the political opinion of those like us to automatically be ready to vote along these lines. In many political conversations that I had with relatives, the opponent increasingly was not only the Orange Democratic Movement (ODM) as a political party but rather the Luo tribe of Raila Odinga. The opposition's intention (many Gikuyus believed) was not only to win the election and lead with different ideas and policies but rather its aim was to destroy the country and us along with it. I was told that we were in a fight to the last, that the winner would take all and damn the loser. The opposition too was driven by similar ethnic mathematics even though the trend – which was confirmed in the 2005 constitutional referendum – was of the rest of the tribes aligning themselves against a perceived Gikuyu determination to hold onto power at all costs.

Last year I received this mobile text message: "Nari Koruo Kibaki arendia nyamu ici cia ruguru (meera) nakuu Thailand. Tutiguo tutari ona imwe. kana tugiciheane ouguo tuhu? Ukuuga atia weemundu wa Mumbi?" (If only Kibaki was selling these Luo animals to Thailand (like the elephants that the Kenya Wildlife Service controversially wanted to sell to zoos abroad) Or should we just give them away for free? What do you say child of Mumbi?)

Delivered with a laugh and a wink just as it was when I was a child.

Three years ago, I interviewed a woman who was imprisoned in Rwanda for participating in the 1994 genocide. She has remained vivid in my mem-ory for a curious remark she made when I asked her how far back the genocide's planning started. "The war," she said, "started when I was a little girl in the 1970s and other children would tease me for having Tutsi legs…" Two decades later, the length and thickness of your legs marked who died at many a roadblock. Imagine for an instant one of those children that did the jeering and teasing, now an adult with machete in hand faced by an ID-less girl with long, thin legs.

To the men huddled around tables poolside at the Serena Hotel, political parties are not expressions of ideological or policy differences. Instead, political leaders are in a fight to our death for a politics they envision as a system of spoils. This fight to get a larger slice of the "cake" has been growing in divisiveness and hateful rhetoric. We are like infants drawn to

touch a flame or driven by a horrid fascination with what lies beyond the cliff's edge, curious perhaps to test the limits of our peace after decades of tut-tutting at the many wars in our neighbourhood.

Kenyans for the past few years have worn tribal lens when looking at the political landscape. In this decoding by many of my fellow Gikuyus, ODM is perceived as an existential foe, not just an electoral one. To be anti-Kibaki, or at least opposed to him, as was the case with a majority of the country's provinces and at least forty five percent of the voters, was going to be regarded by many PNU supporters, particularly those from the Mount Kenya communities as inimical to their existence and survival as a collective. A similar sense of drastic opposition applied to many of ODM supporters. The stage was set for the violence seen across the country during the past week.

In politics perception is reality. And the reality of politics, its fundamental meaning, at those rare moments when it enjoys the greatest clarity to the greatest numbers, is that it is a pitched contest between friends and enemies. Many Kenyans have chosen their friends and enemies on the basis of tribal loyalty and identification. Beyond the much repeated admonitions against such politics, let me suggest that we have dipped our toes into dangerous waters. That politics will fundamentally continue to be the struggle between friend and enemies will not cease.

This is a struggle which is subject to the principle of escalation. One side's paranoia is matched by that of the other side, one rumour with another, and text messages are sent out which appear to mirror each other in the claims of victim-hood and outrage. This escalation which is already much in evidence holds out the frightening possibility of a "war of all against all." If indeed politics is friends versus foes, then how we define who are our friends and who our enemies is of the essence. This is the abyss into which the country is staring.

The campaign period turned the ethnic map into a political one. The individual Kenyan despite his membership in and loyalty to different identities is now more strictly enfolded (perhaps imprisoned is a better word) in a single tribal collective that owes loyalty to those within – no matter their crimes or failings. Its character is oppositional, its language that of the victim. Societies that have become engulfed in political violence rarely get much warning. The lead-up to conflagration is characterized by the political rhetoric of reasonableness on all sides when they speak into the larger public space. But in their asides and coded messages to "their side," foaming-in-the-mouth, hateful messages are uttered to secure the vote. Suspicion and rumours of fantastical conspiracies have been all the rage in the past year of campaigning. A pamphlet that was found in Rwanda immediately after the 1994 genocide had this to say about how to motivate Hutus to loath their Tutsi neighbours and countrymen:

"Never underestimate the strength of the enemy, and never overestimate the intelligence of the target audience. Strive in your language to identify the enemy with everything feared and loathed. Lies, exaggeration, ridicule, innuendo – all ably serve the ultimate aim of winning over the undecided, sowing confusion and division among the opposed. And this freedom from the confines of truth opens up a powerful technique for sowing fear and hatred: 'accusation in a mirror'."

Accusation in a mirror. This is Kenya's leading political tactic. Accuse the other side of rigging the vote while you do just that. Accuse the other of intending to rob the treasury while you do just that or prepare to have that very privilege on ascending to office. Both sides pronounce themselves victim and the cynical acts of manipulation they utilise are framed to seem as reactions to the "enemy." Across the Rift Valley, in Kisumu and Nairobi, young men are roaming machete in hand to finally destroy the enemy.

What many of these young men do not know is that the Serena Hotel and similar founts of privilege and wealth are the home of the very political class that has defined the friend and the enemy in Rift Valley and Central Kenya. Yesterday as people who had tried to assemble for the opposition rally in Uhuru Park were chased back and fro by the police, just beyond the Serena's fence, I was seated next to groups of politicians who were certainly not ethnically cleansing each other off their sodas and croissants. They were muttering into their mobile phones the messages that were driving those young men across the country to violence on behalf of a political class that is willing to sacrifice our lives and limbs on the alter of their lust for power and privilege.

Kengemi's Fly On The Wall

Stanley Gazemba

Lodged in between Loresho to the north, Westlands to the east, Lavington across yonder to the south and MountainView, Kangemi is like a wart on the ass of our affluent neighbours. And it is so ripe with putrefaction that a single stroke of the lance will see it spurting all over your face. It is for this reason that our neighbours are continually wary about our presence, breeding giant man-eating dogs and walling themselves in with twelve-foot walls that are topped with coils of razor wire, in between strands of electric wiring, as if we are some mutant man-eating rats that must be kept strictly in the cage. And yet, like a bad smell that lingers around for as long as it wishes, they discover that after all that effort they still cannot wish us off, because they rely on us to guard and clean their homes, baby-sit for them, and do their petty fix-jobs. Occasionally we will even marry or get married to the siring of their very loins!

On a clear morning you can stand on the bridge straddling the busy Waiyaki Way and see the silhouette of the city spread out on the horizon to the east. It is just a short drive – or a brisk walk – away from the city centre, depending on how you choose to get there. Kangemi is home to a varied hodgepodge of people. There are well-trained professionals who found that they couldn't get out of the ghetto even after they had landed their dream job, living side by side with college graduates who couldn't land a job at all. There are office cleaners and trained industrial workers rubbing shoulders with dirt-cheap prostitutes and small-time muggers who will twist your neck for a plastic Chinese watch. Why, there are even a sizeable number of retired civil servants who didn't have a country home to go back to, and who are busy squeezing a living out of the last coins of their golden handshake. It is home to a minority Kikuyu population who own the shanties and run most of the businesses, and a giant migrant population who pay the rent and patronize the commercial outlets. Of the latter, the Luhyia form the bulk, followed by Kambas, Luos, Kisiis and a sprinkling of the other thirty-eight tribes.

On a typical Sunday afternoon Kangemi's narrow dirt streets are jam-packed. The crowds surge to and fro like locusts on a trans-Sahara march, weaving around those who choose to hold conference in the middle of the street and prostrate street dogs and goats that have a right of way in the ghetto. From a distance the crowds appear like lumps of ugali and nyama negotiating their way down a giant steamy colon, seared by the various gastric juices – the glaring sun and cocoa-fine dust – until they are baked a brown shit.

In the run-up to the elections Kangemi was awash with activity, springing to life in a way we had last witnessed five years ago. All of a sudden the idle youth who had been used to idling away their days in Senator dens begging for a drink as they shared shriveled miraa twigs found themselves with so many jobs on their hands they were spoilt for choice. Desperate housewives who had been used to splitting their hairs on how best to knock together a budget out of the twenty bob the mzee of the house left in the morning all of a sudden found themselves on high demand singing and dancing the praises of the politician footing the bill at the numerous campaign gatherings. Old vans that had been abandoned in mechanics' scrap yards were fitted with bald tyres and coaxed back to life for the campaigns, crackly speakers fixed to the roof and glossy posters pasted all over, leaving just enough space on the windshield for the driver to peep through. It was a season of plenty for temporary praise-singers, body-guards, and hecklers.

I sat there shivering, holding onto my equally scared son as the gunshots shattered the night. We had turned off all the lights and switched off the TV and radio, our natural instincts telling us it was the best way to throw the enemy off target in the dark. As we sat there stock-still, holding onto each other, all we could hear were our staggered heartbeats. Every crack of the G3s jolted right into our systems, causing warm bile to spread at the base of the stomach. It was more frightening heard this close. It was easier when we wrote or read about it in books or watched it in the movies. This here was more tactile, the tension of the moment palpable.

I expected anytime for a stray bullet to punch through my paper-thin mabati wall and blow me away into kingdom come. For the first time I hated being born in Kenya. I hated the utter helplessness of the moment. The fact that when they eventually kicked in my shaky wooden door I would be a sitting duck. I looked around in the familiar darkness, gauging my defenses. There was the stool on which my wife placed our stove. I could simply wield it by one leg and swing with all my might. There was also the thick broken lamp-stand that I kept underneath the bed. It was made of solid hard wood, and was heavy and felt nice in my grip. While it would surely smash a skull, I wondered if it could stop a bullet. I suddenly wished I had been in a country where I could walk up to a shop counter and purchase a sawn-off shotgun. At least with that, when they eventually got me, I would be there to meet them with a blast of lead in the belly, and die like a man – fighting.

After an unbearably long time the gunshots ceased and an uneasy calm returned.

"Daddy, hao ni polisi?" asked my shivering son, his eyes shining in the dark.

"Yes," I whispered.

But hardly had we settled down than the screams of the marauding youths returned, punctuated by the ruckus of breaking glass and tearing mabati, in the background the whispery rasp of petrol flames lapping hungrily on a cool breezy night.

In all it was a long night – usiku mrefu, as the local parlance goes. Eventually the kids drifted off into troubled sleep and I put them to bed. We then lay in our places and pretended to sleep, our eyes squeezed shut, our ears wide awake.

Marbles and Ballot Boxes

Dayo Forster

I come from a quaint little country [The Gambia] where, because illiteracy rates are high, we vote with marbles. The candidates' faces are plastered on the sides of the ballot boxes, and a special tube, a mini marble run really, winds its way in, allowing each marble to drop in with a solid thunk as it joins the nest of others within. This marble trick means our spoilt vote rates are exceedingly low. But I guess it also means that vote rigging with marbles is a lot easier than trying to do so with sheets of paper.

Yet that did not stop the "They" we refer to in Kenyan politics from doing exactly that – playing around with people's carefully ticked ballot papers, churning the precious one paper one vote, one citizen one tick into a backdrop for unverifiable election results.

There are several ways to take over a country without a fair ballot box. Before last year, I'd only been personally exposed to one method – a terrifying coup d'etat during which my father sat tense in our living room, all of us forced to stay home and save on water for drinking for washing for cooking. He sat with his revolver settled on the stool beside him. To match our national defining adjective, we had a few quaint pieces of furniture in our house at the time. The stools in the living room were shaped in one of the four card suits, clubs or diamonds all carefully etched out of thick plywood, and topped with a faux marble Formica top – black with traces of grey. All my childhood, I could choose what shape to put my diluted orange squash on and I would set drinks for visitors on one of the assorted set in our living room.

But with that gun, my father sat, face tense, radio on. And told us, "They'd have to kill me first," even as the gun lay on the stool made by the prisoners in the prison he ran.

My mother's way of dealing with the tension was to busy herself cooking down the contents of our fridge, and resurrecting stored meals from our deep freezer. It's funny how hungry you get when you have nothing to do. All of us children were busy being ravenous and scavenged for fruit in the garden. Green mangoes stoned down from our tree to munch on with salt and pepper. A local variety of plum – Salone plum – plucked before they were full enough, that we would keep nestled in the rice bin so that they would eventually ripen into yellow alongside more stubborn avocadoes which persisted for long in hard green shells, even as we eagerly awaited their softening into a purple skinned softness.

That first coup did not succeed, but precedent had been set. We now understood what bazookas were – not some vague Russian invention, but things that thumped the ground with sonic waves, and swept muffled booms across great distances. We heard of bodies piled in open trunks. A family friend was too bolshie at the bridge and was shot dead. As these tales came in, we understood that political unrest could mean death. In the end, our family, the country, the citizens were rescued. Friendly neighbourly interests brought in their soldiers, quashed the coup, and for a while left some well-built and surprisingly good-looking soldiers to keep the peace. Soldiers who, on their days off, clustered around our favourite hotel pool, ogled us and started tam-tams of romantic hope in our teenage chests.

That was in 1989. And a different country.

This is 2008. And a different kind of coup. We now know the extent to which power is loved by those who are powerful. We now understand the extent of the betrayal they are willing to subject us to. We now know that votes, marble, or paper can count for nothing.

The precedent in The Gambia made it easier for the next coup to succeed, bloodlessly. Yet the machinations of manoeuvring into power is easy compared with the trouble of governing afterwards. It's the pesky people who won't understand that they are now ruled under different skies. The ones who won't stay down and be governed with batons, bullets and jail threats. The ones who keep writing, and gnawing and bothering. The ones whom the president of my native country indicates must be dealt with and if necessary buried six feet deep.

Now, in my adopted country, other pesky people are demanding their rights.

This time I am the mother hen, checking on how much water is in the tank, how much frozen milk is coating itself in frost, deciding on what food is easiest to cook and uses the least number of ingredients and requires the least amount of water to clean up afterwards. This time, I am the one who's explaining to my children why they can't go to school just yet, why all of us grownups are always muttering about something or other – why we sound angry, disillusioned, sad.

In Kenya, other kinds of precedents have been set. And the memories of those successes lay the foundation for what is possible. The Kenya in 2002 that got used to choosing a new president and going out into the streets to celebrate victory. The ballot boxes in 2006 that rejected a badly written constitution. That is, the precedent that reminds us that though the voice of each of us, alone, singly, counts for little, it's the collective, the pressure of many that can declare that we have tasted a new way of choosing our leaders that we want to hang on to. The taste that has laid a wondrous, powerful precedent. Which in order to keep our souls hopeful, we must follow.

Unsung Heroes of Kenya

Mike Eldon

I am not going to write about whether PNU or ODM, or both, are the bad guys. And I will not be analysing who won and who lost the election, or even how we should move forward from the sorry state in which we now find ourselves. No, I want to draw attention to the many great people who, at this worst of times, display the best of Kenya, the outstanding, thoughtful selfless best.

Not too long after the elections, on a Sunday afternoon, I found myself at a gathering of the newly formed Professionals and Business Forum for Peace at the Holiday Inn. Present were men and women of all ethnic backgrounds, mainly fairly young, who were determined to do more than merely observe and bemoan the unhappy national predicament. Here were people representing doctors and pharmacists, counsellors and nurses, marketing professionals and ICT specialists, architects and engineers. They were mobilising to help their beloved country at a time of great need.

As I sat among these healers, these builders, these people filled with boundless energy and not a little hope, I shared both their sadness and, simultaneously, the cheerfulness with which they brainstormed together on how best to engage. They filled each other with confidence and courage, and as a result felt empowered to go out and collectively make a difference.

I urged those assembled to reach out to the other groups who were already active in humanitarian, mediation or other constructive endeavours, to coordinate and synergise with them, and they willingly agreed. I was asked to be their envoy, and as a result I was invited to the next meeting of the Concerned Citizens for Peace. And here I found more caring, thoughtful people, more inspiration.

CCP, as they have come to be known, have been meeting at eight every morning. Started almost immediately after the election results, the initiators also came together to see what they could do to help with the emerging situation. The first came from a background of mediation and peace building, people like Ambassador Bethwell Kiplagat, Generals Sumbeywio and Opande, Dekha Inbrahim and George Wachira, but more and more people of goodwill gathered around them, swelling their ranks.

I was introduced to a whole new world I never knew existed, of specialists in conflict prevention and resolution, who've been working in the most turbulent parts of this and other countries. Many came together to grapple with the causes and consequences of the ethnic clashes; they know all about the "shifta" crisis in North Eastern Province; and they have been on the ground in the various cross-border disputes too.

Indeed it is these earlier experiences that made them alert in the run up to the recent closely contested polls. With the "winner-take-all" scenario, and with expectations so high on both sides of being that winner, the scene – for them – was set for unrest come January. They foresaw what many of us did not, and so little wonder they were one step ahead, leaping into action while others were still orienting themselves.

And the action didn't just start yesterday. For instance some months ago they took a group of Kenyan journalists to Rwanda, to see for themselves the consequences of the hateful incitement coming from Radio Mille Collines. But now, all sorts of activists have found a constructive and empowering home among them.

They include priests and youth leaders who come from or venture forth each day into the hot spots of Kibera and elsewhere, doing what they can to calm the atmosphere; and volunteers who bring reports of what has been happening where the dis-placed persons have been gathering. They tell us of their needs, which in turn are matched with those who can help, whether from within the group or beyond.

There are trauma counsellors and life coaches; former MPs, development partners and private sector folk; university student representatives and women who want to bring other women together; the list goes on and on. One team, which had been formed some years ago to build possible long-term scenarios for Kenya, reassembled to propose a Citizens Agenda, now widely endorsed and widely distributed (including on-line at peaceinkenya.net). Another engages in the challenge of bringing reconciliation and healing to the workplace and into our communities. And there are others too, every day more, all composed of the same breed of Kenyans (plus a South African here, a pair from DRC there), blind to anything but their noble missions.

Each day those present update each other, strategise, and go forth to their respective assignments, whether back into the communities, up into the political mediation process or reaching out to others involved in the various dimensions of the crisis.

And while the Concerned Citizens meet at one place, up the road the religious groups are meeting elsewhere, similarly anguishing and brainstorming over how best to help. Happily the various initiatives are not working independently. Each is being kept abreast of what the other is doing, seeing how they can support and strengthen those in other sectors. Now the spontaneously formed Professionals and Business Forum has become closely integrated with KEPSA, all of whose members, bodies like KAM and FKE and APSEA, have been adding their voices and their resources.

These are the Kenyans with whom I have been interacting for thirty years – bright, thoughtful and caring people; diverse in the extreme, but bound together by worthy common causes. We enjoy our diversity – frequently joke about it – and this current upheaval has done nothing to undermine it. I am not surprised, and I am deeply moved and inspired by them all.

But I do not wish to give the impression that I am seeing the world through rose-tinted spectacles. As I write in praise of these largely unsung heroes (being sung about is not what they're after, by the way!) it is not to deny everything else that is happening. It is indeed *because* the people I have been with are so troubled by the terrible things they have seen and heard that they come together as they do, seeking ways out of it all. Seeking peace and reconciliation, seeking relief for the needy, seeking truth and justice, and seeking a Kenya that is prosperous and secure.

Inevitably, they have to endure criticisms of all kinds: they're not doing enough; they're too slow; they're just talkers; they're doing the wrong things; they're biased… But they're used to that. They listen, they adjust where they feel the criticism has merit, but they also know that among the many great strengths we Kenyans possess, one of our prominent weaknesses is to undermine the actions and motives of good people, who are doing their best to bring others together and improve their lot.

For the cynical and untrusting, such human beings just don't exist, certainly not in *this* republic. But let me assure you they do, and in large numbers.

The Obituary of Simiyu Barasa, Written by Himself

Simiyu Barasa

When you find yourself talking with several guests of the morbid situation of your country during the wedding of one of your friends, you quickly realize there is something wrong with your country. When your National broadcasters show men being dragged out of public service vehicles and hacked to death by a mob of young men who do not even hide their faces from the police a few metres away, and such scenes are repeated more than the advertisements and commercials, then your country is doomed. When you hear that people are chased from their homes into a church for belonging to a particular tribe, and then followed into the church where women and children are locked inside and then burnt alive, my friends, you are no longer in a country, you are living inside hell on earth.

The Swahili (oh, that language that was supposed to unite us and now has been rendered impotent in its intended super-glue powers) – the Swahili say that when you see your friend being shaved with a razor, start wetting your hair in preparation for your shave too.

I do not intend to go gently into that dark beyond without saying a word of goodbye. Friends, (and those who consider me an enemy because of my tribe or lack of it), being of sane mind and in charge of my mental faculties, I bid you goodbye. I chose to write you an obituary, which you should read as a love letter to my country that has died in that critical moment when its dreams were giving birth to a beautiful bouncing future.

I know not the hour of my death, for no one knows the hour of their death in this country anymore. That man on Naivasha, who was dragged from the car and his speech as he answered questions betrayed him as belonging to a tribe the highway blockers were hunting down, he did not know his death. I have seen myself trying to run from the mob the way he desperately tried, machetes raining on his back, and yet he ran on, three desperate steps, before his body disintegrated into huge chunks of human flesh and fell down. Upon which they cubed him. I too, my friend, am about to face the same death. My tongue, when I try to speak, shall definitely betray me as a targeted tribesman when the mob does come to me. For I do not belong to any tribe.

My sister, Rozi, called me yesterday trembling with fear. She lives in Western Kenya, on the Eldoret/Kakamega border. They had taken a patient to Moi Referral Hospital Eldoret. On their way back, the ambulance was stopped by youths bearing all forms of crude weapons. They demanded to know which tribes everyone in the ambulance belonged to. The driver was of the local tribe, so he was told to step aside. As the others showed their National Identity cards, my sister realized that all around them were corpses of human beings freshly chopped to death. Her turn came and she said she was Luhya. They told her to speak in Luhya, but my Sister doesn't know Luhya. "I really can't speak it because my mother is a Taita!" she pleaded. She had to desperately show a photocopy of my mother's National Identity card which she had in her purse, a photocopy my mother had given to her the previous week to use as a referee for the bank account she was switching to. That photocopy saved my sister. The only language my sister can speak, apart from English and the National Swahili, is Gikuyu. The tribe the youths were targeting.

My friend, I know no tribe. I only know languages. My mother is Taita, my Father is Luhya, and we were raised in Kiambu among the Gikuyu. It has never been important in our family to know which tribe we should belong to, my sisters and brothers have names from both sides of our parents' communities. In this chaos, if the hunters of fellow humans were to find us in our house, would they really believe we are brothers and sisters from our names?

If I say am Luhya, the Gikuyu with whom I have lived and now am engaged to one of their daughters would kill me as they have gone on a mission to revenge the deaths of their kinsmen in Western Kenya. If I flee to my parent's home in Luhyaland, the neighbours will barbecue me alive for I can't speak their language and of course my mom is from a foreign tribe. Not to forget that the guy who sold us that piece of land where my mom and dad saved so hard to buy is known to come and insist on grazing his cow on our compound claiming "my cows used to feed here, buying the land doesn't mean I don't own it!"

Now in this Nairobi where I stay, I am wary of my neighbours. The guy opposite my flat is a Luo with whom we argued amicably during the pre-election period on which party we supported. May-be now, given that friendly neighbours have been the ones killing each other, he might remember our political chats over my litres of coffee and come chop me up?

That is why friends, I have decided to write this obituary. I know not my tribe, I have only known myself as Kenyan, and others as fellow Kenyans. In these times, belonging or not belonging means not being dead or being seriously dead. What chances does a person like me have?

My friends have their tribes mates to protect them. The cosmopolitan Nairobi has now been balkanized with residential estates being exclusive reserves of certain tribes. Complete with murderous gangs imported from up-country to protect their own. Mungiki for the Gikuyu, Chingororo for the Gusii, and the Baghdad Boys and Taliban for the Luo. Where, pray I, is the estate Balkanised for those of us of mixed heritage who know not their war cry of their tribal warriors? The only two tribes I can run to don't have such armies. And claiming my dad's Luhya identity, and a Bukusu at that, is problematic in itself. The Gikuyus are hunting them down claiming they voted ODM together with the Luos, and the Luos are hunting them down too claiming they voted for Kibaki together with the Gikuyus. So such is my fate for my father belonging to this tribe that voted 50-50!

My friends, I have prepared myself for my death. I don't know how it will be, but since as a film and TV drama person I believe in rehearsals, I have rehearsed all possible scenarios so that when my moment comes, it won't be so hard to take it. Chekhov's method acting manuals are no longer needed. I just turn the TV on during news time or read the papers, and from the several images of people who have been killed in various ways, I choose one to dream and perfect that night. I have dreamt of being locked into a church or building with several others and torched alive. I have smelt the petrol fumes as its being splattered through the window onto our bodies and then round the building. I have seen the flash of the matchstick being lit and smelled my flesh burning to ashes.

I have rehearsed how I will smile when I am dragged out of a public vehicle and hacked to pieces by the marauding youths who pop up in our numerous roads. I want to die smiling bravely, but just like the guys I see on Al Jazeera and other International TV channels, the moment I get to that part where a red-eyed bearded man pokes his head into the bus and shouts "everyone wave your ID cards in the air!" I wet myself and start screaming for mercy, instantly easing their work of identifying foreigners for the blades to work on.

I have rehearsed how best to gasp when a barbed arrow strikes my chest. Or a club smashes my brain out of my skull. Or a spiked plank of wood is driven through my mouth. I have died so many times, my friends, that now I must be immune to the real death when it comes.

I used to laugh at tourists buying maps of Nairobi. I bought one recently. It is stuck in the wall of my bedroom where small pencil marks indicate all the escape routes I will try to walk in to get out of town once the mayhem knocks on my door. Unfortunately, to the west are roadblocks where my Luhya name will mean instant death. If I go Mombasa Road I might run into a roadblock where Kamba's and all coast people are being cubed. To the north I can't even dare. To the south I might pass, coz I can speak Gikuyu, but my name would be my passport to the grave yard. That map, my friend, directed me to writing this obituary.

Maybe if I was a famous poet I would go down in history alongside Chris Okigbo, the Nigerian poet who went to Biafra seeking to actualize his poetry but found bullets instead. My friends abroad are asking me if I am safe. Maybe if I had been bright of mind like they were I would have faked a bank account statement immediately I cleared my o-levels and fled to the United States to wash toilets in between my degree courses, but no. When they told me America is the land of dreams, I swore to them I am an Africanist, a believer in the African dream. When they filled scholarship forms to get away from this dark continent, I laughed at them. Now my faith in my country has faded faster than the newness of the news year.

So, friends, some of us never really thought that our tribe was that important. Simply because we were from the tribes that make up Kenya. Some of us have lived in every province of this once great nation and learnt the local languages, drank the local brews, danced the local songs – so well that the locals even gave us the names of their tribes to fondly call us by. I have been called Kamau, Mwanganyi, Wambua, and even Bayelsa in Nigeria. (I should have known, when Dudun told me that Bayelsa is the troublesome state of Nigeria where the Delta is, that it was a premonition of the war in my country.)

I have nowhere to go. No tribe to run to. No tribesmen to protect me. Except the grave. Which is what my fellow country men are intent on sending all those who don't belong to their tribe. Goodbye, friends. Seeing that all fast food restaurants have a notice "pay in advance," let me take the cue and say Goodbye in advance. When you see a pulp of human flesh in the tarmac with youths dancing round it waving their bloody machetes, look closely. That ear might be mine. That grinning upper lip might be mine. I loved you, my fellow countrymen. I loved without thinking of your parental lineage. I loved Kenya. But look what this country has done to me: sodomised my sense of humanity and pride.   *January 30, Nairobi*

Lessons Learnt

Doreen Baingana

Like many Ugandans, I have watched recent events unfold in Kenya in shock, but also with vague discomfort because of the familiarity, to us, of the images of violence, especially that unleashed by the police and army on fellow citizens. We Ugandans, unfortunately, are also too familiar with the mockery our leaders make of democratic processes, as with the rigged Kenyan election, and the surreal swearing-in ceremony that followed.

What is one to do? Some Kenyan writers, whom I am lucky to call my friends, have put pen to paper to communicate their frustration, anger and shame, to try and sort through this calamitous mess, to reach for explanations as a way to find solutions out of it. Their writing, thank God, provides a deeper and more succinct perspective on the events than the three-minute foreign news items plugged in before sports and business news that churn out tired clichés of yet another African nation gone wrong.

The writers have taken action using the skills and opportunities they have. What about those Kenyans who cannot express their frustrations and views in this or any other legitimate way? Those poor, marginalized millions who have been callously ignored by their leaders for generations? Last year they were persuaded to vote, they were told an election was one way to speak and be heard, to take action to change their circumstances by throwing out ineffective leaders. And vote they did, in millions. But, it was the election results that were thrown out. This was a huge, public slap in the voters' collective face, including those who voted for Mwai Kibaki, because he has now completely illegitimatized himself. And so the scorned populace reacted publicly, vehemently, but extremely unwisely, by turning on their neighbors, attacking and killing. It is the worst form of expression, the worst form of action to cause change, but perhaps the one that was most easily available, as years of simmering anger burst forth. Many others have tried more legitimate forms of expression, protests, but even they have been thwarted; we have all seen the horrific images of protesters being beaten and shot at by the military police.

The question remains in what legitimate, sane and safe way can the majority of Kenyans express themselves politically and be heard, and have their concerns acted upon? The Kibaki clique insists that there is no problem, while answering violence with violence. It is also not clear, so far, that opposition leaders are genuinely acting on behalf of the frustrated and angry citizens, or are looking after their own butts and pockets. The two concerns rarely coincide. Disregarding the peoples' grievances will only continue the crisis and resultant death count.

What strikes me about the Kenyan writers' views is the genuine shock that what is happening now is happening *in Kenya*. In neighboring Uganda, Rwanda, Sudan, Somalia, okay, but not Kenya. Also expressed is the sincere belief in Ken-ya as a fully formed nation, not an ungainly collection of tribes, that Kenyans love peace (who doesn't?), are intrinsically democratic, in short, Kenya is not your average CNN banana republic smoldering in chaos. That this lovely thing called Kenya is suddenly and strangely crumbling to dust. There is shock expressed that Kenyans, *Kenyans,* could turn to violence, as if it hadn't happened before (e.g. the attempted coup of 1982, the clashes in the Rift Valley in 1992), as if the daily violence in Nairobbery doesn't count because it is normal. It is now starkly clear, and cannot be ignored, that the underlying long-in-the-making causes of this crisis are not much different, except in degree, to the conditions among Kenya's neighbors: the highly centralized power structure, the tribalism, the acute economic inequality, the huge masses of frustrated poor. Something was bound to give, sooner or later, and the blatant rigging burst the fragile seams that seemed to be holding the nation together.

I am not condemning this innocent view of Kenya that the middle and upper classes have been privileged enough to have. In fact I applaud it, if it is not completely blind, because an idealistic belief in one's country and the democratic process is necessary for idea of a nation to become a reality. It is the belief in Kenya's democratic institutions that lead millions to vote, and in fact the voting itself was said to be, on the whole, free and fair. The tallying, or lack thereof, is another matter. My fear is that the rigging will have a more searing effect on the nation's psyche than this deadly chaos we now see; it will completely erode the idealistic belief in the democratic process and institutions, and then there really will be nothing left but machetes and guns.

I say this as a Ugandan who has absolutely no trust in our leaders, and no reason to trust them. Cynicism is the Ugandan's default position when it comes to politics. When you grow up with public executions as entertainment on TV, and any walk outside shows you that army men rule the streets, and wield their power brutally, the first thing you learn about politics is that the state is an instrument of terror. We learnt this lesson not just during the Idi Amin era, but had it harshly repeated, as if we did not get it the first time, by government after government that followed. No generation has been left behind. As we watched adults do anything to put food on the table, bribe, beg, spy, steal, or become politicians, and we learnt that this is what you do to survive, and right or wrong is not the issue. I dare not imagine what lessons those who have grown up in the IDP camps in northern Uganda these last twenty years have learnt, stuck between bloodthirsty rebels and a government army that for baffling reasons has been unable or unwilling to protect them. Let not the rest of Uganda think it is any more free than those children are from the consequences of this still ongoing calamity. One lesson deeply ingrained in every Ugandan is that our security forces exist to attack us, not to protect us. Lest we dared forget, lulled by campaign talk during the presidential elections of 2006, the government graciously ordered the "Black Mamba" paramilitary unit to storm the courts as opposition members tried to seek legal recourse. We were rudely reminded that those in power would not let go simply because of this game called the elections.

What lessons are the newly minted Kenyan refugee children learning right now, before they can learn anything else? That if you hate someone or feel cheated, kill. If not, burn down their property, chase them away, and if they are lucky enough to get to refugee camps, try and poison their food. The protesters in Nairobi, Kisumu and elsewhere, and all who have watched the police beat and shoot at unarmed protesters, now know without a doubt what the police exists for. And what have all those children who watched Kibaki's swearing in ceremony learnt? That if you steal quickly and unashamedly in public, go through the motions, pretend to be legitimate for long enough, the lie could morph into solid fact. That the way to deal with a huge crisis you have caused is to keep insisting, with a straight face, that there is no problem. That the law serves the state, not the people. That the democratic process exists to be abused.

After learning these lessons, the best most of us Ugandans can do is avoid trouble and bullets, shrug our shoulders and try to survive. Others become the politicians they have been taught to become. We watch our leaders, sorry, freedom fighters, steal and plunder with hardly a note of protest. It makes absolute sense that President Museveni is the only national leader who has congratulated Kibaki for his act of daylight rob-bery. We do not expect more of him. We wonder why he even bothers to explain that it was a diplomatic gesture. Oh, but of course, he is the only leader in the world aware of diplomacy. We are not surprised by rumors that the Ugandan army is in Kenya assisting in the attacks against the opposition. That is what our army does. It went to Rwanda, to Congo, why not Ken-ya? We react with jokes: the head of our Electoral Commission was sent as a consultant to Kenya, it must have been to teach the ECK how to rig. He obviously did a terrible job. That the Kibaki steal was so clumsy, it now makes us look good in comparison. That this should teach the Kenyans, who thought they were better than we are.

Kenyans, please don't go down our cynical road: it leads to nothing but more violence, victims and a victim mentality, and it is self-perpetuating. But it is not too late. That human rights activist (Omutata?) who chained himself to the police gates in Nairobi this last Thursday is to be a powerful counter point to the images of killers with pangas and police with guns. He proved to you, to us and the world that some Kenyans still have faith in the possibility of a government that exists to serve the people, and thus are brave enough to challenge this fake one. The young must be given a chance to cultivate this faith and idealism; they must not learn their political lessons from even more of the images and events witnessed these last terrible weeks.

Love's Indomitable Spirit Still Alive in Kenya

Rasna Warah

One of my favourite commercials is the one showing the real-life blind Kenyan marathon runner Henry Wanyoike training against a backdrop of Kenya's most majestic views alongside his childhood friend and training guide, Joseph Kibunja. The reason this commercial touches my heartstrings is not just because it is beautifully crafted, but it shows how partnership and self-sacrifice can help achieve success.

The story of Wanyoike and Kibunja should serve as an example to all of us, as it is the story of friendship, perseverance, and, above all, humility. Before Wanyoike began his professional career in athletics, he worked with Kibunja as a cobbler in Central Province. Unfortunately, Wanyoike lost his sight in 1995 and could no longer continue working as a cobbler, so decided to venture into athletics. In 1999, he invited his friend Kibunja to be his training guide.

Kibunja had never been a runner, let alone an athlete, but he gladly accepted the challenge. Since then, Wanyoike and Kibunja have been training together. They run as a pair, with their hands joined to each others' with a string. Kibunja's job is to act as Wanyoike's "eyes" – to tell him when they are approaching a bend, when to overtake, when to accelerate the pace of running, etc. Like all guides, he is also a time keeper and regulator. Thanks to Kibunja, Wanyoike today holds the world marathon record for blind athletes.

Yet Kibunja has never once felt resentful that his friend gets all the accolades at races, nor does he harbour any ambitions of becoming a marathon runner himself (even though his training and experience would qualify him to run in any local or international race). Last year, he told the *East African's* Odindo Ayieko that he

only ran with Wanyoike out of loyalty and friendship. When he's not training with his friend, he's working at the Henry Wanyoike Foundation, which helps the needy in society.

Given our present circumstances, where all we hear are stories of brutality and hatred, we may find it hard to believe that Kibunja is not alone in his act of heroism. Yet in the last few weeks, I have come across numerous stories that have served to remind me that there are many among us who think of the greater good above their own personal interests.

One such story is that of William Kimosop, a warden with the Kenya Wildlife Service. At the height of the clashes in the Rift Valley, Kimosop spent several days trying to get 865 people of all ethnic groups to safety. Not trusting the authorities, he decided to hide the people in a ravine, from where he called for help on his mobile phone. Thanks to the efforts of the Red Cross, Concerned Citizens for Peace, the World Food Programme and the Rotary Club, Kimosop managed to get food, water and blankets for all the people under his care. Last I heard, he had moved out of the ravine into a safer area.

Apparently, Kimosop is not one of a kind – stories like his are being recounted and recorded by various groups, including the Coalition of Concerned Kenyan Writers, a collective that was formed shortly after the violence erupted all over the country in early January. The idea behind the collective, of which I am a member, is to present the human face of the tragedy unfolding before us and to allow writing to become a vehicle of peace and understanding in our troubled times.

Since then, dozens of Kenyan writers have produced more than one hundred pieces of what a guest editorial in the Nigerian magazine *Farafina* describes as "technically masterful, emotionally breathtaking work." Some of these pieces have already been published in the local and international media; others form part of this anthology.

But the story that touched me the most was the one of the street children who, instead of spending money on glue or food, took the initiative to buy a "get-well-soon" flower for a hospitalised friend on Valentine's Day. When people in Europe were giving their lovers expensive fresh-cut roses (many of which are grown in and exported from the blood-stained lakeside town of Naivasha), a group of 11-year-old street children in Nairobi decided to raise 50 shillings to buy a flower for their friend Michael, whom they had carried to the Nairobi Women's and Children's Hospital following a brutal sexual attack. Since then, they have been visiting their badly injured and traumatised fellow street child at least three times a day.

Nation columnist Mildred Ngesa, who covered the story, describes the compassion shown by the four street children – Kevin Kariuiki, David Kuria, Andrew Mungalla and Wallace Mfoyonga – as "an enduring, undeniable lesson on living and loving." It is a lesson we could all learn from at this turbulent point in our history.

Rasna Warah is an editor with the UN. The views expressed here are her own and do not necessarily reflect those of the United Nations.

We the Kikuyu

Potash

When I was young, I wanted it all: the pick-up, the farm, the Godfather hat and the pointed shoes. I wanted the beer, the goat ribs and what in those days was called a Public Opinion – a beer belly. For God's sake I even wanted gout, because it bespoke, *eating well,* conspicuous consumption. Gout was to me the disease of those who had arrived.

When I was young, all I wanted to be, when I grew up, was a Kikuyu.

I was born in Kiambu. That was just after Jommo Kenyatta died but just before the first coup in Kenya's history. When I became of a school going age, I was sent off to school in the Rift Valley. In my school were many Kikuyus: Kikuyus from Rware and Kikuyus from Kabete; Kikuyus from Muranga and Kikuyus from the Diaspora. Those were days when Kikuyu regional rivalries and one-up-manship had been lost in the passage from one generation to the next and all that was left for us were the witticisms, hackneyed stereotypes and jocose contestations. Nobody cared where the next person was from – unless it was Dundori – and yet I made a point of reminding everyone that I was from Kiambu. I was Kiambu Mafia.

Then I grew up.

When I grew up, I realised that there were People from Kiambu and then there was the Kiambu Mafia. I was of the People – Kiambu had its owners. Indeed there was a Kiambu Mafia, with its GEMA conspiracies and massive loans to buy off every Mzungu settler from Kabete to Warubaga; loans that would later find their way into that classified document called the Debt Register which states how much you and your descendants, for ever and ever, amen, owe a Shylock in the Isle of Man that you never met. And then there were The People From

Kiambu, a significant majority, who scrimped and saved to buy land – through, often fictitious or fly-by-night, land buying companies formed by the Kiambu Mafia to dispose off the parcels of land that they had acquired through the previously mentioned loans.

In retrospect, I was blessed; my family was priv-ileged – my grandfather had land in Kiambu. He had a parcel of land in what was formerly known as the Native Reserve and a plot in the *Gicagi*. (My grandfather inherited those from his father who had acquired them in the Demarcation – colonial land allotments – and split it out between all his sons from a stable of wives. The Gicagi became the dice throw of Kikuyu-land – in some places, Gicagis became shopping centres and the land appreciated while in others they became a Kibera in microcosm.)

Then the Mau Mau war happened. Everyone was shipped into the Emergency villages. When the war ended, many returned to nothing. Some men returned from the bush and found that the only thing that their, now homeless, wives had acquired was a son or two that looked like the Chief and that one of the many things that the Chief had acquired was their land.

Is it not that all is fair in love and war?

When I was young, I was taught that the Mau Mau war was a struggle for independence. Then I grew up. When I grew up, I realised that the Mau Mau war was a dud; Kenya's independence was negotiated. Long before the Mau Mau declared war against the white man, Jommo Kenyatta had been sleeping with a white woman. Jommo Kenyatta knew – because he had known books that one – that the problem was the top; the system, and not the colour of the man at the top. The British knew that he knew. And he knew that they knew that he knew. So the British called Kenyatta to England and negotiated a deal with him that would allow them to change the colour of the man at the top without changing the system.

And that is the way Kenyatta and his ilk; their kinsmen and descendants, from 1963 to perpetuity, won their Independence.

The Mau Mau war didn't win anyone their independence, it won them dependence on a black man rather than a white one.

It thus came to pass, that one day in December of 1963 the Governor of Kenya, on behalf of Her Majesty the Tyrant of Empire, ceremoniously handed over power to Mzee Jommo Kenyatta. A celebratory mood rose all over Kenya; this was one nation under God, and no blessings from the Queen needed. The Union Jack was lowered. The Kenyan flag was hoisted.

Ee mungu nguvu yetu.

Ilete baraka kwetu…

Red, White, Black and Green

They told me that Red was for the blood that was shed and green was for the land that was won. I grew up and then I realised: red was for those who died fighting and green was for those who lived – to reap *matunda ya uhuru*. My ancestor inherited the red, your ancestor inherited the red; so why do we have to die that those that inherited the land may stay ever green?

I Blame Kibaki

Potash

On Thursday December 28, 2007, I voted. I could have been somewhere having a beer, but no, I went out to a polling station and stood in a line waiting to cast my vote.

Yes, I voted in Kenya's last General Election. I didn't vote because I believe in democracy; I didn't vote because I wanted to make a difference in my country, I voted because it is both my right and civ-ic duty. I voted because, even though I believe democracy is a sham, it is a nice ritual every couple of years that creates the impression that the power to govern – to lord it over the masses – is derived from the masses.

But I was worried that this time round, after several years of doing it right, we would get it wrong. And when nations get it wrong; when the mandate is questioned or appropriated by individuals or a group of them who have no ability to beguile the masses, anarchy takes over. And Kenya was headed that way.

The incumbent president, Kibaki had lost con-trol over Kenya. No, Kibaki had never had control of Kenya. Kibaki was president because Raila had said: *Kibaki Tosha!* (Translation: Let there be President Kibaki). And there was President Kibaki.

Granted, President Kibaki had the Economy – which is something you could take to Equity, er, I mean, the bank – Raila had the masses. And in these Third World, emerging (pseudo) Democracies, the masses is what you need. Raila was the new religion.

Kibaki's mistake wasn't because he was corrupt. Corruption, after all, is the smallest, big issue in Kenya. And you would have expected Kibaki to know that. Having served in both the Kenyatta and the Moi governments, he must have learnt from the best that Kenyans know that the President is never corrupt, it is the President's men who are.

Kibaki's mistake was in the things he didn't learn from his predecessors: have pictures of you doing manual labour like building gabions placed in text books; rename streets and roads after yourself (Mombasa Road by any other name will still congest the same); hire and fire people at random so that all of Kenya stays tuned to the same radio station only to hear that today you went to church or that you bought bananas by the roadside in Kangemi; meet the people because unlike you, they do not live in State House. But most important of all, detain an Odinga.

Because he never did these things, Kibaki lost control of this country. In the meantime, his Roads Minister, an Odinga, was out there building roads, by-passes and such other fancy things that only Kenyans in the diaspora with their, "you know in America"…(or wherever else Kenya's economic exiles congregate)…could fathom. Playing to the gallery. Raila Odinga, then Roads Minister, was working while Kibaki was nowhere that Kenyans could tell you of. That while Kibaki, from his experience in two regimes, should have known that Kenyan ministers do not work, the President works through them.

Every day, Kenyans heard: Raila was here, Raila was there, but the only time the Kibaki name was mentioned, it was Lucy Kibaki behaving badly, again.

Then Kibaki called a Referendum on a new constitution. Kibaki lost. That was November 2005 and I knew that this country had gone to dogs.

What followed was two years of political bickering. For the first time in the history of this country, every fool with a mouth could say that President Kibaki was a *$%& so and so and live to vote again. *Na hiyo ni upubaff!*

Suddenly, to me, the terms President Kibaki and the Kibaki Government became an oxymoron in the league of Nairobi Water and Kenya Power. For the first time in Kenya's post-independent history, the office of the president, that of the Head of State and Government and the man occupying them were separated; there was now the State, the Government and Kibaki. Too many centres of power.

Kibaki, in a country that was used to *Rais ndio baba na mama, mwalimu namba moja… hizi mbuzi zote ni yeye na tuko nyuma ya matako yake,* reduced himself to: the man who sleeps at State House; a mere mortal; fallible.

The myth of Government was shattered; the *siri* was yanked out of *Sirikali.*

What followed was Kenya's most politically unstable reign. What was seditious and treasonable in past regimes now wore the veil of democracy and freedom of expression. The Press declared itself free and was generally seen to be so – at least on those nights when the First Lady wasn't insomniac.

Democracy had found Kenya but a Social Contract that would have bound the Kenyan People and their leaders to it was still not there. The President, it would have been expected, would have filled this vacuum; steered Kenyans towards the enjoyment of new freedoms responsibly. But he did not. The People, ever dependent, or at least used to, strongmen cried out for leadership.

While Kibaki retired to State House, with his Old Money peers, the new faces in his government took control of the public coffers. They threw the safe doors open. They had inherited massive corrupt deals, they signed them over to themselves. This was the Government of the Nouveaux Riches. The public returned to its disgruntled mumblings.

New heroes rose. Unlikely heroes. The political thieves of yesteryear, finding themselves wearing the strange new mask of The Opposition, took it all in stride. They reinvented themselves as the new voices of probity. Our version of democracy was defined: the tyrants and the corrupt are only found in the government in power, they become Democrats and progressives when they cross the floor and vice versa.

In the meantime, Raila Odinga was still reading from Machiavelli. He had found himself ousted of government for revealing to Kenyans the real reason he had said *Kibaki Tosha,* in that October 2002, at the twilight of the Daniel Moi rule. He had signed a Memorandum of Understanding with Kibaki, it was said, that would see the Kibaki presidency promulgate Raila's preferred constitution for Kenya. Somewhere along the way, having emerged president and yet again achieving political glory without breaking a sweat, Kibaki had either suffered a massive concussion and forgotten the MOU or realised how powerful the current constitution made him to be bothered with changing it.

Raila protested. Kibaki stayed put.

Raila began to fight against Kibaki. Kibaki continued to ignore him. Raila was on TV every day. Nobody knew where Kibaki was. Raila began to galvanise the masses; sell himself as the real *and only* hero of the liberation from the tyranny of *Nyayo* while Kibaki was a pretender to the throne. Kibaki continued to sit on his throne – the throne Raila made him – nonplussed.

Then 2007 came. The year of the General Election. Raila had been campaigning, politicking, since 2003; Kibaki had been sitting and watching the economy grow. Raila had been all over the country and all over the media talking to people. Kibaki had been sitting at State House – a gated community of one.

2007 was the year of the Opinion Polls. Kalonzo was leading at first, but Raila worked hard to prove that Kalonzo's appeal lay merely in looks and not substance. Sooner than later, Raila took the lead in all the polls. Kibaki did nothing. The campaign period hasn't begun yet, Kibaki's men said, while continuing to cast aspersions at the accuracy and neutrality of the polls. The point they missed though was that this was about politics, and the one thing that matters most is not truth but perceptions; and the public perception was that Raila was in the lead. That Raila would be the next president.

As the election approached, Kibaki hit the campaign trail. He had the benefit of incumbency – which in Kenya means that he had an arsenal of political goodies to bribe the voters with: Districts were dished out, hawkers were allowed to take over the CBD and the police were warned against harassing the *youth*. A week to the election date, the final polls came in and Kibaki continued to trail Raila.

At this point I became immensely worried. People asked me: "do you think Kibaki will win?"

I responded, emphatically, *"No!"*

"What do you think Kibaki's strategy is?"

"None!"

"So will he hand over power?"

"Kibaki cannot hand over power… the power he has is not his to hand over. Kibaki is holding power in trust for the Kikuyu people."

Of course by the Kikuyu people I meant, the Kikuyu elite. Those Kikuyus who amassed wealth under Kenyatta; Kikuyus who kept their wealth under Moi even as Agriculture, the lifeline of the Kikuyu, found itself crippled; Kikuyus who purport to speak for other Kikuyus even when their, economic and political realities are worlds apart.

Then came December 27. It was clear that Kibaki had no winning plan. As the poll results came in it became increasingly obvious that Kibaki was losing. I began to worry. Then a series of sad and dubious events transpired and Kibaki was declared the winner in the presidential election. I was angry but not because Kibaki had won. I felt that the election had been rigged, but it is not for that that I was angry. I was angry because I felt that the election had been rigged after the fact. I was mad because, for the first time in Kenya's multi-party era, the charade of democratic elections hadn't been well executed – the majority felt cheated and those on the winning side felt they cheated foolishly.

On Sunday, December 30, Kibaki was sworn in as the President of the Republic of Kenya. He was sworn in a few hours before the expiry of his previous term. A term he had taken over at a glorious public ceremony was being extended behind closed gates. Kibaki came out of the bowels of State House, took his oath in the gardens, and went back in.

Outside of State House, the country exploded.

Many Kenyans have died since then. Many more will continue to die, especially poor ones who happen to be Kikuyus living without high walls and armed guards, until Kibaki steps out of State House and speaks to Kenya.

Let Kenyans Take the Lead

Shalini Gidoomal

It's just over a month since the GSU threw journalists, observers, and anyone else getting in the way out of Kenyatta International Conference Centre (KICC) in the first step to quickly re-instate Kibaki as President.

In that time, conservative estimates indicate nearly 1000 people have died and over half a million are refugees. Kenya, once the symbol of progress in Africa, lies in tatters as a systemic and poisonous polarisation infects the country.

At first it's possible to feel outraged when someone with such questionable moral fibre as Jacob Zuma urges his supporters not to behave violently in a backward way – like those Kenyans.

But then the killings and mass displacement which are extensively documented – this has been a media saturated event – begin to spread and grow. And every day, in large and small ways, the animosity continues to increase, infiltrating deeply into Kenyan society. Security companies shuffle *askaris* around to ensure they're guarding clients of the same ethnic background. Disturbing reports appear of preferential treatment in Nairobi's Kenyatta hospital – subject to tribal status. In Naivasha a Luo nurse is torched in her clinic by her patients. Yesterday, a well-known large banking group had to split up a fist-fight amongst their staff relating to ethnicity in the office. Even the moderate voices of reason are breaking down.

In response to the terrible events that have built into this crescendo of shock, we see our leaders – aspirant and otherwise – proverbially retreat behind great big electric fences, to bicker while Kenya burns. They argue about seating arrangements during mediation talks. They insist that filmed police murders are mere computer graphics. They deny attacks on both sides of the ethnic divide were pre-planned. They play a ping-pong blame game. It's their only consistent form of public debate. Even though we have long passed the place where that sort of brinkmanship is heroic

And as they verbally harangue each other, gunshots, bonfires and machetes continue to claim life after Kenyan life.

It's as if leaders don't comprehend the scale of the crisis on their hands. Or perhaps they don't care. As Kenya bleeds and burns, neither Raila nor Kibaki have yet to come out clearly with a strong condemnation of the spiralling violence. Their messages don't convey any real desire to quell the unrest. And so instead their fudging has created a platform on which Kenya is enacting its worst hatreds.

It wasn't always this way. In February 2003, I was having lunch at Naivasha Country Club (recently under siege), when a newly elected Kibaki decided to pay a visit. He arrived unannounced with a small coterie of six people and sat down to have tea. Spontaneously the occupants of other tables, some 200 individuals, stood up and began to clap. Kibaki looked bemused, surprised that his presence – or what it represented – could cause such a reaction. We were basking in the glow of the power of the vote, the delivery of democracy at last.

Five years later and Kenya is being destroyed in name of that democracy. What kind of warped logic allowed this to happen?

Perhaps it's because there's only ever been a superficial diagnosis of the problems afflicting us – which means they can't be healed, because the root of the sickness remains uncovered. We have a small, barely minted modern middle class with their professors, their associations, their academics who, in the past five years, took out loans to buy their own home or to contribute to traffic jams in their very own new car. We have a cabal of wealthy citizens, about 1 percent of the population, who command over half of Kenya's wealth. Based on this, we talk of economic growth rates, rising tourist numbers, the vision of 2030. All the time forgetting that over 60 percent live in a different world. A world which doesn't access this growth at all.

They can only watch as banking, privatisation of national assets, stocks and property booms benefit a few. The growth rate of the last administration did not create significant additional jobs or provide infrastructure to improve living standards. So the poor continue to pay over-inflated rents in the cramped conditions of Nairobi slums or stay in rural areas where there's little hope of jobs.

Can you feel the growing GDP? asked a radio station. For the bulk of the population, the answer is not at all.

In India, when the economy powered on with an impressive double digit growth of 13 percent, up from 3 percent, the voting public – the masses – the youth – threw out Vajpayee Singh's government. The reason? His galloping economic progress didn't touch them. And it's the same here.

Figures released by NEC indicate that 1.8 million youth have no jobs. That's a lot of restless anger waking up each morning with nothing to do, nowhere to go. A substantial mass of energy with no goal and no focus. Until now. In this post election chaos, the bitterness festering in our society has found a vent. Ethnic fears incited and excited during the 2005 referendum, and poverty and land resentment have combined in an explosive mix.

For many dispossessed, this time of violence is a seminal moment in their lives – it's a time of grand expression. An intoxicating taste of an immense newly found power. After all, being responsible for someone's death is supremacy indeed. Quite a change from the tedium of a daily routine of nothingness. And all this is in the name of a cause – fighting for the tribe.

It needs to be different. As Kenyans, we have surrendered collective leadership to a political elite who has shown nothing but self-interest. Nobody, from the array of elected parliamentarians, has emerged out of this crisis looking like a credible national leader. Where's our Nelson Mandela? Our Mohandas Karamchand Gandhi? Our Martin Luther King?

Looking back into history could point the way to possible solutions. In the early 19th century when the Teso broke from the Karamajong and fought their way towards what is now the Busia border they became a Nilotic enclave surrounded by Bantu. As there was direct competition for land, the next 100 years were a series of bloody territorial incursions. In the 1880's the Teso and Abagusii met and permanently stigmatized war amongst their groups. You could not go home a hero if you killed either Teso or Gusii. For 130 years – there wasn't a single a raid amongst the two – although both continue to war with their neighbours with whom no pact was made.

Can this process be extended across Kenya? Can such pacts, which extend existing moral boundaries, be used to create an abhorrence of killing? Can a widespread campaign to highly stigmatise ethnic slaughter, and humanise each and every person in every tribe make a change? It could work. We need to take this sort of process and spread it across Kenya – to stigmatise killing, vilify those who advocate it, make it abhorrent, unpopular and ugly. A sustained campaign is critical. Are we fed up enough to try? The politicians will follow if it is successful enough. After all, don't they follow anything that gains them popularity?

In essence we could save us. We need to save us.

Informal institutions must usurp national responsibility; leap in where leaders have left such a vacuum. Established organisations such as churches, member clubs, associations, businesses, unions all need to band together with coalitions that have sprung up such as the Concerned Citizens for Peace, and Peace with Truth and Justice, to steer a new track.

Some of this is already happening. These groups have been working through public forums; with facilitated mediation (such as encouraging, visits to Kenya by Archbishop Desmond Tutu and various former African Presidents), through committees focused on peace action at community level, through initiatives by women, on sms and blog sites, by youth for peace, and with the mass media. The net-works are spreading, but it needs to be faster, quicker, more decisive if we are to save Kenya from the brutalizing violence that is destroying our once great nation.

And it would behoove our erstwhile leaders to reflect on how this country, in its munificence, has served them well. Both Raila and Kibaki are millionaires with major assets and holdings. Both have been allowed to amass vast political prestige.

Now it is our turn. They owe it to Kenyans to give back to us, with dignity and integrity. To let go and let Kenyans find a way to be Kenyans.

They owe it to us.

Kenya One Year After – Lessons Unlearned

Mukoma Wa Ngugi

The question before us one year after the outbreak of electoral violence in Kenya is straightforward: What have we, as Africans, learned? Or thinking about Zimbabwe's attempts at a Kenya style settlement, have we in fact learned the wrong lessons?

There are two aspects to this question that stand opposed to each other. When electoral violence breaks out along ethnic lines and it acquires the character of revenge and counter-revenge, any settlement that brings peace becomes immediately desirable. So in Kenya the settlement was to let the two warring giants share the spoils of power and wealth. But this runs headlong against the principle of democracy. In Kenya, the single most important unit of democracy, the ballot, was invalidated by a settlement that immediately rejected a recount or a re-election. If the vote is not taken into account in the political settlement what follows can only be a caricature of democracy.

If democracy is the first casualty, justice is the second. The reports from the Human Rights Watch and the Kriegler and Waki Commissions all indicate that core members of the then sitting government and the opposition are guilty of instigating the violence. In fact, Ole Ntimama, a cabinet minister from the opposition, in a moment of anger captured on national TV and consequently posted on You Tube is seen admitting to having seen to the demise of 600 people. Nothing has happened to him. Both the opposition and the incumbent party now in a government of national unity (GNU) will not police each other. The GNU cannot redress the roots of the violence such as gross inequality or resettle the refugees still in the camps. It is now all about the next election in 2012. What started as a peace settlement, by sacrificing both democracy and justice, is in practice an incubator for future violence.

For a society to breakdown, the watchdog institutions that normally stop a country from toppling over into the abyss have to fail at a fundamental level. We, the good guys in the universities, the media, churches, and human rights organizations must also take a collective responsibility for the Kenya we have created. For example, the Kriegler Report faults Civil Society Organizations for being partisan along ethnic and political party lines. Kenyan Newspapers, with very few exceptions such as the *Business Daily*, were openly partisan. Even political analysts who normally manage to hide partisanship in a false objectivity blatantly heeded the ethnic call.

But it is the African intellectuals who played the most abysmal role. From ethnic insults to screaming each other into silence, from pressuring consensus to outrightly excommunicating those who did not tout the acceptable narrative of a thieving sitting government and a saintly opposition, the African intellectuals failed the Kenyan people. It did not matter that the opposition and the sitting governments only differed to the extent they were dedicated to serving a national and international finance interests. Having pronounced the opposition as representing the people's interest, supporting the opposition was seen as supporting the Kenyan people. What we did was to find criminals robbing a bank and instead of protecting the people's money, we provided avenues for them to divide up the money.

Out of all the watchdog institutions only the National Council of Churches of Kenya (NCCK) has been courageous and honest enough to acknowledge and apologize for its handling of the electoral violence. In a February 15 statement, the NCCK declared regret for being "unable to effectively confront these issues because we were partisan. Our efforts to forestall the current crisis were not effective because we as the membership of NCCK did not speak with one voice [and] we identified with our people based on ethnicity." The rest of the institutions are busy defending themselves from the various reports that assign them some blame; yet it seems to me that they should follow the example of the NCCK; otherwise their credibility will remain damaged.

There is one more lesson unlearned. That African politics have shifted over the last twenty years. In addition to political parties that are different only in name, mass movements and grassroots organizations have been replaced by NGO's Civil Society Organizations (CSOs). Grassroots organizations and social movements are people-centered and have a political vision of changing the government. NGO's and CSO's on the other hand have a limited political vision and they exist to lobby the government as opposed to changing it. Grassroots organizations in Kenya would have called for a people's referendum on the GNU or a reelection within a reasonable amount of time. In their absence it was left to the CSOs and NGO's to lobby for a Government of National Unity that did not take in account the voters, the majority poor. We need a return to mass movement and grassroot organization-led people politics, because change in the hands of NGO and CSOs exists to the extent that they lobby the sitting government successfully.

The new Kenyan Prime Minister has loudly advised that Kenya styled settlements offer a way out of political impasses in Africa. But I cannot imagine a more cynical outlook for the future of African democracy. This kind of settlement rewards violence while promoting impunity; denies justice while undermining democracy; allows for expedient solutions that mortgage the future to satisfy warlordism; and it can only take us further away from addressing the gross inequalities within African countries that lead to the violence in the first place. Without much needed justice, such settlements can only become harbingers of future violence, the fire next time.

If we are to learn lessons informed by the contemporary state of African politics in order to struggle for democracy with social justice, then we have to return to a politics that puts the people first and does not leave them out of political settlements. The lesson then is as straightforward as the question: Any solution that undermines democracy and justice is not a solution at all.

First appeared at BBC Focus on Africa Magazine.

The Brinkipice of Genocide

Tony Mochama

THE ROAD TO ELDORET

The scene from his hotel room screen in Nakuru still feels his mind. Let's call him Mwangi. He's from Muranga, he still drives the Datsun 120 Y that he bought in 1972 when he was a twenty-two-year-old boy, and he's got a family in the outskirts of Eldoret where his wife runs the family farm (cows and wheat) that he bought in 1982 from a white MAN fleeing the coup that "never happened," as he is fond of saying, "so I got the farm cheap."

That was 1982. Mwangi was a sharp hustler from Muranga; now he's grown into an old-ish respectable farmer, 57 years in age, a bit of a sage and scrooge who in spite of his Shs. 3 million in cash in Equity Bank (savings, he takes no loans) still drives a Datsun 120 Y, and why, till last night, he had never stayed at a hotel. He did, now in the fiery first days of 2008, at a place called Midlands Hotel because he has heard the land is no longer safe.

There was a television set in the hotel room with one of those fancy new satellites that one finds everywhere these days, even in tiny little bars in Muranga where the boys wear foolish 'Manchester United' and 'Arsenal' T-shirts, like silly English blokes; and speak with animation of 'van Pussy Cats' and 'Lonaldo.' In his days, this excitement was exclusively reserved for the girls – who was "digging Muthoni's mo-go-do" or Njeri's garden.

Mwangi fell asleep drinking White Caps, which he has drunk from 1975, in his fancy little hotel room … and dreamt of the peaks of Mount Kenya.

When he woke up, that funny American station called Cable News Network (the only cables Mwangi knows so far are the troublesome ones that disconnect the carburetor in his 120 Y) was showing a burnt church, with fifty dead, somewhere in Eldoret.

'Elsewhere.' That's how Mwangi always envisions those pictures – burnt churches in Rwanda,

skeletons on the hard, sandy faces of Darfur, long endless ant-like lines of refugees in the Democratic Republic of Congo, and those other unpleasant images from Inside-Africa that Western media seem so very enamored of.

But the burnt church was in Kenya's Rift Valley. The fifty or five dozen dead were Kenyans of a certain community, there were no 'Interhamwes' or 'janjaweeds' or other exotically named murderers in this mix, it was Kenyan jinns ...

And Mwangi was on his feet, and out of the hotel, before one could say the words "balkanization" or "ethnic tension" – and now, with the sun just coming up over the horizon, Mwangi is on his way to Eldoret to get his family, and take them back to the safety of his small house in Muranga.

In the blur of the blue-purplish-golden light of dawn road ahead, Mwangi notices what he thinks is roadside bush and bracken. At first. Bushes do not grow on tar-macadam roads, bwana!

As he gets closer, he notices that the obstacles are actually stones – little rocks that prop up bushes, like ominous flowers in menacing vases. Mwangi does not stop to wonder why this is so, why anyone in their right mind would bother with this weird fauna-and-floral arrangement, in the middle of a road to nowhere.

Well, not 'nowhere' exactly – Eldoret!

Like the practical man, and farmer, that he is, Mr. Mwangi, 57, gets out of his old blue Datsun 120 Y, looks up to the sky, then gets to work – pulling at the bracken to clear the road.

And from behind the tall grass on either side of the road, columns of men emerge ... somewhere between ten and twenty men. Some are tall, some are short, some are rugged, some wear Western T-shirts with improbable messages like "Rainnkonnen Rules,"- and "Vote for Al Gore-2000!" They look like refugees from a beer budget movie called Old Sierra Leone. And in their hands, Mr. Mwangi notes, they carry elongated shadows.

No, not shadows! It is the silhouettes of machetes, and suddenly Mr. Mwangi's insides turn to maji. Now he can see the faces of some of the men, hate-contorted contours that appraise him savagely.

"Haka hakana pesa," (this one has no money) one of the men, dark brown snaggle-toothed snarls, and the mob looks at his old blue Datsun 120 Y, and laughs. The laughs aren't merry. They are blood-sodden, "Niko na chapa," (I have dough) Mr. M hears himself mutter in a strange voice. "Twende ATM ya Equity ..." (let us go to the Equity ATM)...he hopes they are highway robbers.

"Hapana!" (No!) one of the men screams, raising his panga to the sun, "Toa I.D!" (remove your Identity card). With trembling fingers, Mr. Mwangi 'chomoas' his Identity Card.

In Kenya, the I.D.s not only come with your name and date of birth, but also your place of ethnic origin, or tribe. They were an invention of the British Colonialists to prevent Kenyans from slipping away from their tribal reserves (concentration encampments) at the height of the Mau Mau rebellion against British rule, from 1952 to 1955.

Mr. Mwangi's I.D. falls to the ground. Another man, in tattered red and white shirt, snatches it up, dirty nails scraping the grimy road to Eldoret. "Huyu ni mmoja wao waliiba kura," (this is one of those who stole our votes), the man yells, and his companions close in on Mr. Mwangi, who realizes he has wet himself for the first time since 1955, when he was just five.

Elongated shadows rise and fall in the sun.

The road to Eldoret is no El Dorado! In the middle of the murderous commotion, no one notices when the driver's side of the door of the 120 Y is slammed shut in the movement of the mayhem, or the exact moment that Mr. Mwangi becomes 1950 – 2008, R.I.P. The short rains are over. January will be hot and dry. And the rivers in Kenya, for once, will run red and riot.

8 DAYS

I finished writing the above story on Friday, the fourth of January, 2008. The day after everything had happened. And, yes, it is 'a story based on real life.' People on their way to Kenya's Rift Valley (where most of the killings were at, although the murders were truly of a national character) to rescue their families were stopped by death squads. And if they came from the 'wrong' community (read Agikuyu), they were hacked to death on the spot. Unless, of course, they were female … those were first gang raped, then hacked to death, with machetes.

So the above story is "based on actual events." Yes, that's better than 'real life.' Because the days preceding the Friday that I wrote 'The Road to Eldoret' were anything but real. Everything seemed surreal. Everything was surreal. It wasn't as if we were living in the politically stable, ethnically united and mildly prospering Kenya I, and millions of others, have always taken for granted.

It was as if a daemonic Salvador Dali had, overnight, painted Kenya over in dark and crimson hues and then inserted us all into the canvass of his bizarre expressionism …

On the day I finished writing 'The Road to Eldoret,' I celebrated – my survival, not the completion of that little piece – by drinking several glasses of a Chilean wine called Frontera in the front yard of a neighbour's house with his mongrel of a dog warily watching me. Even the canines of Kenya knew something was a – paw.

"I imagine a country whose natural frontiers surround a great wine. Think of Chile. Chilean vineyards are protected to the north by the most arid desert on earth, to the south by huge ice-fields, to the west by the expanse of the Pacific Ocean and to the east the majestic snow-capped Andes. 'Frontera,' Chile in a glass." So said the front of the Frontera box. I took a sip of the wine, and thought, "if it's true that this is Chile in a glass, then Chile is dirt cheap."

If one were to make a wine called Nairobi, which is the capital city of Kenya, and which sits smack-bang in the middle of the country (as all serious capitals should), then the Nairobi wine box may well read: *"Nairobi, to the north-east has the great deserts that lead to Somalia and Ethiopia, to the south-east lies the port of Mombasa, the gateway to the majestic Indian Ocean with its sun, fun, white sands, beach hotels (and Lamu, frozen in the sea in 1592, with its donkeys and diamonds-in-the-night-sea), to the south-west the game ranges of the Savannah that teem with wildlife – li-ons, zebra, antelopes, leopards, rhinos, buffaloes, giraffes, hippopotammi-and that are the heart of safari country; and finally the North West where the Great Rift – with its myriad mountain-ranges, deep valleys and dozens of lakes and geysers lie. This is Kenya."*

And you bet your Nairobi wine would taste mighty fine! Frontera, on the other hand, red and acrid, just reminded me of the blood spilling in our country on that aftermath arid Friday. Kenya will have been independent from the British for forty five years this year. Yet, at the turn of the 2007/2008 New Year, we almost went to the dogs (of war), to African hell (in a hand-basket). Nay, make that in a ballot box. And a deficient ballot box at that! You want to talk about hanging chads in Florida 2000? Well, we had hangings (and lynchings, and beatings, and burnings, and and and …) in Kenya.

Africa has always seemed a little apocalyptical to the rest of the world. "The Dark Continent." *The Economist* had a most infamous headline once, that both stank and rankled at our hearts- "The Hopeless Continent." Yes, write us off, "and will you, Melissa, kindly throw Africa out with the garbage, please?"

The images from the continent are relentless – the late great Mo Amin's stark black-and-white photographs of emaciated, skeletal faces and ribs in Ethiopia so prominent they deserve a distinguished position in some corrupt government office in Africa. The squalor of the slums (every Western celebrity who comes to Kenya inevitably visits the Kibera slums, one of Africa's largest with a million inhabitants, second only to Soweto, South Africa, although I hear Rio de Janeiro, Brazil, takes the shit-cake as far as slums go).

It's a slam-dunk.

Africa is where all the funk happens … the wars from which funky films (Lord of War, Nicholas Cage, comes to mind), the addictive fascination with African starvation, the terrible glamour of our tragedies, like Rwanda, the nausea of putrid corruption.

All bad things, AIDS included, begin – (but do not necessarily end) in Africa…

And, over the course of December 27, 2007 to January 3; 2008, I was almost a witness to history. No, I was actually a witness … to almost – history. History here being Kenya's first 'proper' genocide, disregarding the mini-ethnic cleansings of Molo, 1992, and Likoni, 1997, which even we in the media dismissed as "tribal clashes."

Why? That is another story.

Let us just say that when "ethnic cleansing" happens in Africa, it is so fast as to almost defy the human eye … and the CNN camera lenses. Tribes in Africa are kiln-wood, soaked in the paraffin of historical animosity, just waiting for someone to strike the acrimonious match and ignite the country in an inferno of tribal warfare from which there is no return … only escape to other near, or lands far off.

In our case, the person who 'lit the ignition' was none other than our president Emilio Mwai Kibaki, Economist Extraordinaire, who was up for re-election or rejection on the dying days of December, 2007. And the story I will tell you next, written from the first-person perspective, is of the '8 Days' that Kenya stood on the very brink, the precipice, of 'Rwandanisation.'

THE BRINKIPICE OF GENOCIDE

DAY 1:

Thursday, the 27th of December, 2007. Voting Day

I wake up at five o'clock sharp. Not of my own volition but on volition of my Nokia cell-phone. There's a Norwegian lady in it who goes: "Tut-tut, it's time to wake up, tut-tut, it's time to wake up," over and over again … until you throw the cell-phone against the wall (an expensive form of venting) or are driven up the wall … and wake up.

I live on the first floor of a block of flats (*Apartments*, in American – speak) in an area of Nairobi – (a city of three point three million residents) – called Nairobi West. My bedroom, where I sleep (of course) faces the West, but my shower-room's glazed glass windows face East – which means as I shower in lukewarm water on this most important of days – the sun comes in through the translucent glass panes in fragments of red … a crimson orb shattered into red rubies … like droplets of … blood.

Nairobi lies very close to the equator. We are in the middle of the world, literally. Which means the sunrises and sunsets are not gradual as they are in other parts of the earth which have seasons. In St. Petersburg, Russia, for instance – which I have regularly visited as an SLS (Summer Literary Seminars) participant – the days seem to go on forever during St. Petersburg's brilliant white nights …

Here, in Nairobi, near the equator, days and nights fall like curtains. And our dramas, especially the political ones, are as ruthlessly sudden. At least on the surface.

I dress optimistically on this day that me, and ten million other Kenyans, will choose to let President Mwai Kibaki run the country for another 5 years, or choose Opposition enigma Raila Odinga as the fourth president of our Republic. I dress national – a cap that says "Proudly Kenyan," a T-shirt that is Maasai (everything *Maasai* is presumed to be Kenyan, thanks to the white obsession with these 'noble savages'), Swahili sandals and … Levis. *Bas!*

The problem is that President Kibaki is a Kikuyu, and Raila is a Luo – Kenya's largest and second largest tribes, at seven and five million respectively. The Kikuyus are agrarian Bantus, a land-owning and farming tribe smack-bang in the middle of Kenya. Okay, that's Nairobi! But they are the rural area that is right next to the cosmopolitan city of Nairobi. Far off to the north-west are the populous Luos, lakeside Nilotes who rely on Lake Victoria (yes, it is still named after that British Queen, who has been 108 years dead, courtesy of our colonizers … the lake's name, that is, not her demise. Queen Victoria died of natural causes. What could be more natural than "being the Queen of the English will be the death of me?") for sustenance.

Picture a primary school whose walls are white and blue and oblong-ular. Picture a cold African morning with little birds chirping on trees, small fish gliding inside a nearby river, an imam chanting prayers in a mosque hidden behind trees in the distance, and a large mugumo tree that is being eaten by a tribe of determined termites, that chew on it like creatures, demented. Under this *mugumo* tree in Kongoni Primary School in Nairobi West is a ballot box, an armed police-man (rickety rifle from World War II, Burma), two polling agents and a returning officer. This is where I'll vote, having crossed a bridge above a dirty little stream to get here. The apartment complex I live in overlooks this stream. The realtor advertised as 'scenic' in the papers. He was Kikuyu, and the Kikuyu are seen as the 'Jews' of Kenya for their moneymaking abilities and entrepreneurship skills…

President Kibaki, when he was Vice-President of the country in a dictatorial political party called KANU in 1990, once said removing KANU from power "is like trying to cut down a mugumo tree with a razor blade."

Twelve years later, with his now (2007) chief rival for the presidency Raila Odinga campaigning for him, then (and whom one Concordia professor Mikhail Iossel coincidentally met in a Nairobi Hotel, and ordered a $200 bottle of champagne for, from one comrade to a revolutionary other) Kibaki did bring KANU down in a massive landslide victory in 2002.

Needless to say, Mzee Kibaki had long before dumped KANU or had KANU dumped him? Picture, on this cool morning of December 27, 2007, a long queue of Kenyans, patiently waiting their turn to vote, impassive faces becoming animated as they engage in friendly last minute banter as Kenyans are wont to do. (We are known, across the world, as a very friendly people).

The voting process, itself, is a relatively swift affair. Especially for me, who, with my press card, is allowed to jump the queue. I am both amused and bemused. What am I supposed to do? Report that while I voted to retain my M.P., Raila Odinga, as representative of Langata (the Nairobi West area falls in this constituency), I gave a thumbs up to his presidential rival,

Emilio Mwai Kibaki? Will my solitary choices make the mid-day news? I have a relatively good reason to be in a rush.

My younger brother, Ben, is in hospital – following a traumatizing beating in a small town north of Nairobi called Ngong after he voiced his support for Kibaki in Kalenjin country (the 'Kaleos,' as we call them, are allies of the Luo).

His antagonists, braced with knuckle-dusters (ok, dog chains used to leash small-town canines) unleashed their fury, broke his jaws, smashed his chin to 'chintereens,' broke his nose and left him unconscious on a dark road to be crushed to death by a motor vehicle, so that the whole murderous incident may look like a normal road accident! *'Drunk run Down, in Ngong Town.'* Unluckily, or luckily, it is a motor-cyclist who runs into my kid-brother, Benjamin. The front-wheel of his bike side-swipes Ben's head, slightly fracturing his skull (a hair-line fracture, no pun intended).

The fact that Benjamin survived this incident that happened three weeks ago – (see, political passions were already dangerously inflamed) – just goes to prove something I've always suspected … our family is extremely thick-skulled, if a little thin-skinned. Benjy has some news to report.

On Christmas Day, President Kibaki and his wife Lucy – whom Kenyans call 'Ka-Roo-say,' visited the maternity wing of the hospital (Benjy is in a private room, in the private wing of the Kenyatta National Hospital, with massive maxillo-facial injuries. The room, alone, costs $500 a week. It is not going to be a merry Christmas for us, no sir).

But Benjy is merry with mirth- "All fifteen of the male children born on Christmas were christened Emilio Mwai Kibaki, after the President and the twelve girls born on the same day, Lucy, after his wife. Did you vote?"

"Yes," I tell my younger brother. "For Ka-Roo-say! Did you? I hear the Electoral Commission of Kenya (ECK) were bringing ballot boxes to hospital so in-patients can vote."

Benjy looks both startled and hopeful.

"I'm pulling your leg, kid," I say.

I stay the afternoon with him.

Later, at sunset, I return to my flat, a small bottle of brandy in my hand. I sit at my table and begin writing a short story on the "Interrogation and Death of Field Marshall Dedan Kimathi!"

Photographs of Kenya

Andre Vltchek

Murals from art village of Ngecha

Art gallery in Ngecha

Political art at RoMaNa – modern art Museum in Nairobi.

From within the largest slum in Nairobi and East Africa where the 2008 violence erupted

Kenya Burning exhibition

Photos from Kenya Burning exhibition

Praise Poem
Stephen Derwent Partington

Kenya, January 2008

We praise the man who,
though he held the match between
his finger and his thumb,
beheld the terror of its tiny drop of phosphorous,
its brown and globoid smoothness
like a charred and tiny skull
and so returned it to its box.

So too, we hail the youth who,
though he took his panga on the march,
perceived it odd within his fist
when there was neither scrub
nor firewood to be felled,
so laid it down.

An acclamation for the man who,
though he saw the woman running, clothing torn,
and though he lusted,
saw his mother in her youth,
restrained his colleagues
and withdrew.

We pay our homage to the man who,
though his heart was like a stone
and though he took a stone to cast,
could feel its hardness in the softness of his palm
and grasped the brittleness of bone,
so let it drop.

We laud the man who,
though he snatched to scrutinise
the passenger's I.D.,
saw not the name – instead, the face –
and slid it back
as any friend might slide his hand to shake a friend's.

And to the rest of us,
a blessing:
may you never have to be that man,
but if you have to,
BE!

Save Our Beloved GDP
Stephen Derwent Partington

Kenya, January 2008

They must not reach the CBD:
its roads are business arteries,
its Mercs are pure red bloodcells.

Their invasion will affect the heart of commerce,
they are parasites.

They must not block these roads,
these roads are smooth and clean
and neat.

No, they are matted-haired
and tatter-clothed,
their skin is smeared with grease.

No, no, they mustn't block these streets:
we have sophisticated buildings,
polished windows, shining mirrorglass:
we like to see reflections of ourselves.

But they, these peasants and workers,
these jobless and lowlife
and manifold shirkers
are dirty and different: *No!*

These roads are beautifully grey
with perfect pinstripes down the middle,
down the sides. They have a symmetry.

But they, this tide, are chaos,
can't be channelled,
simply mass along a highway
sweeping all before their swash.

No, no, economies are built upon
the line, the graph, the spreadsheet:
passion's dangerous.
Much safer to deploy the GSU:
at least their uniforms are uniform,
the swift path of their shot a perfect line.

We must protect the CBD,
its 4×4s, its smoothwalled concrete

and its cold and rigid steel.

Who wants their branches in the city?
Or, for god's sake, all those
waving white kerchiefs?
They halt our progress, all these masses:
move the bastards on with teargas,
paid police.

Divide And Misrule
Stephen Derwent Partington

Kenya, January 2008

What does dug earth care at all about ethnicity?
A Mwangi fits a six-foot hole
as snugly as Owuor.

And tell me, where's the corpse that anyone
can teargas with success?
Or did you do it to augment the tears of mourners,
out of kindness?

Can you tell a foe from how he skins a cow
or peels a spud
or guts a fish?
Are these enough to skin his hide?
Perhaps it's speech, the way she shrubs?
And who's the carrier, his mother or his dad?
Can we locate the gene for Enemy?
Today, can we condone the fact
Kikamba's only got one word for 'enemy,'
'Masai'?

Reflect: that family you killed,
it had as little land as you.
Or did you see the old machete used to cut you?
Dented, rusty, cheap, like yours.
Reflect on this.

This warped deflection of your anger
isn't justice:
it's a coffinful of shit.

Our Elder Professors of Self-Preservation
Stephen Derwent Partington

Kenya, January 2008

Where *are* the intellectuals?
Perhaps they're still at Christmas
where the world is home with family
and no-one's been displaced?

Or they're enjoying hot Mombasa,
snug in swimming pools
while locals swim in blood?

Perhaps they're visiting their kids
at foreign unis and, respecting
British Government Advisories,
are staying put abroad?

I don't remember any new Decree
obliging them to shtum.
I don't believe that any Nyayo cells
have been restored to house them.

No, for sure they are in deepest thought
preparing for the moment when,
like squirrels, they will pounce,
will tell the winners just how right they were,
how wrong the sorry losers.
Wow, what prescience, what scholars!

Over the Heads of Protestors
Stephen Derwent Partington

Kenya, January 2008

If only they were right, the *Maji Maji*,
that a bullet fired in anger or incompetence
could magic like the Alchemy of old,
not from base lead into gold,
but into water, to the lifeblood of the world.

Each round of gunfire, then, a dash of holy water
from the barrel of a hose, a benediction.
Every spray of steel, a christening, new life.
A hero's fiction, this, but let's agree:
what's Alchemy, but *shite?*

Precision-lathed to fit inside a cartridge,
of a calibre to snugly ride the journey
from the cold breech to the muzzle
down the automatic's Styx, a bullet
keeps the laws of nature as it hits:

a hole of rather less precision as neat physics
meets biology and motors through a chest.
A clever image, this – *quite witty, metaphysical –*
but over the heads of desperate protestors,
like an soldier's callous bullet, or refined Armani politics.

I, You, S/He: A Language Test in Time of Strife
Stephen Derwent Partington

Kenya, January 2008

Rewrite this sentence as a question:
I should kill you.

Next, correct this split infinitive:
To clearly know what's wrong.

Reverse the pronouns in this sentence:
You'll forgive me.

The infinitive of *Love* is:
Love; To Love; Be Loved; Despise?

Note down five synonyms for *Neighbour*
and five antonyms for *Hate.*

Select a word from those in brackets
and insert it in this sentence:
I _______ my fellow humans
[Murder; Rape; Displace; Respect.]

Last: if a Person is the key to peace
determine if it's *I* or *You* or *S/He*
[tick any one, or two, or three.]

Lethe
Stephen Derwent Partington

Kenya, January 2008

When peace erupted, none of us was ready.
You remember how the sticks above our heads
were gently lowered, how our riot gear
was sloughed-off like a skin? We rubbed our chins.
   And yet, the dead, they didn't rise.

Do you recall the day the grandmas of the Rift
embraced the grandsons of Nyeri,
when the youth were given grants to raise
manyattas they had razed? We rubbed our eyes.
   But still, the dead maintained their peace.

Think back: the way the Lake and Ocean rose to kiss Mount Kenya's peak?
The glossy adverts in the Nation and the Standard:
We congratulate our leaders for restoring
Peace and Unity, and all is well in Neverland?
   The dead began to wake.

Do you remember how they asked us to forget?
In 4-by-4s, Big Men from each and every province
drove a web across the land, their shining
megaphones proclaiming: *Back to work!*
   The dead were spinning.

And the bishops and the diplomats, the councillors
and businessmen, they gathered for a conference
outside the new Grand Regency and told us
It was all a dream, an error, so now nothing needs be done,
some things just die, are best forgotten. No? Come on!!
   You must remember how the landless and the jobless dead
   erupted from their coffins with a shriek?
   You don't remember?! Let me help you.
   Hold this gun. I have a cutting. Take a peek.

The Language of Tribe
Betty Muragori

I

I am well versed in the idiom of tribe,
Having acquired the script long ago, from my family, friends, schools,
From my whole existence as a Kenyan really.
And I speak it with fluent authority.
There may be times when I look different,
Special even, as if the language of tribe were beyond my understanding.
After all, I can cite my marriage, my children, my friends,
But that is a false impression,
I am like everyone else.

II

This uncomfortable truth led me on a journey.
I wanted to know,
What is this thing called tribe, really?
That has us all by the neck?
What does it look like?
How does it feel?
How do people live with it?
Laughing one moment with their tribal protagonist,
And the next, looking at each other across a wide abyss,
A yawning space, unbridgeable by the smiles of former friends,
Now bereft of all good intentions?

III

I wonder,
If tribe were a taste,
A sound,
A feeling,
A thing alive,
How would it be?
My experience of tribe is all sharp acid on the tongue,
Clanging metallic noises,
A rising tide of ill will,
A watchful expectation of ugly tribe rearing its head,
Reaching out to grab a cake, for itself,
To eat, quickly, greedily!
Tribe is grating loudly in my ears,
It must be heard!
It has me believing it is natural, inevitable like the heavens.

IV
Tribe makes me act secretly,
I hide myself in full public view.
I read the newspapers,
Watch behind the news,
Scan the streets,
Count the members of the church council,
On and on.
I tally the number of times my tribe emerges.
When the appearance is favourable,
I smile.

V
In my mind,
I add up all mounting disadvantage,
To store in my prized bag of tribal grievance,
I am so expert at computation,
I am no longer conscious of what I do.
You see, I am victim,
Innocent,
But for the tribal designs of others.

VI
The truth is revealed in broiling ethnic conclave,
Here, secrets of the heart are safe,
I bring my hush-hush bliss to the fore,
To bemoan with relish my miserly pickings,
Condemn with glee the crumbs I feed on,
While others hog the national cake.

Would You?
Betty Muragori

Would you wield a panga in Burnt Forest, and cut a stranger down?
You slashed that man as he pleaded with you for life,
You led the crowd baying for his blood
A stranger you did not even know,
He cowered and cried out, bleating like a lamb
Innocent of any crime
Death unwilling to take him,
He died long and hard, way before his time
His blood has watered your farm like acid rain,
How will you live?

Would you?

Would you catch a running girl?
Escaping a church fire in Eldoret?
Place her roughly on the burning pyre
A parody of father, tender, laying his baby girl to sleep, on downy bed,
No lullaby can drown her keening dread,
Her fear of eternal coming sleep
Your pitiless face did not soothe
Now you must be careful for your child,

Would you?

Would you seek a loving wife and give her one hour to leave her home?
Depart from all she knows and those she loves
And go where?
You do not care!
And you call that an act of charity
When she pleads with you to kill her then,
To wield a blunt blade,
Carve out her heart!
For all is lost,
At 59 where does she go to start again?
You stood resolute
You did not yield

Would you?

Would you turn against your neighbor's son?
The one who lent you salt in halcyon days,
That same who nursed your wounds and soothed your troubled heart
And flush that son out of his hiding place
And hand him over to certain death,
Ignore beseeching eyes of your neighbor friend
Who stands too stunned to make a sound?

Now your own son is done,

Would you?

Would you serrate your friend with words of hate?
Spoken cruel to cause a mortal wound,
She's the one you used to call a chum
Your careless hatred has sown seeds of harm
Now you stand alone in fulsome deed?

Would you?

Kenya – A Love Letter
Mukoma Wa Ngugi

Inside looking out, snow is falling and I am thinking
how happy we once were, when promises and dreams
came easy and how when we, lovers covered only

by a warm Eldoret night, you waved a prophecy
at a shooting star and said, "when the time comes
we shall name our first child, Kenya" and how I

laughed and said "yes, our child then shall be country
and human" and we held hands, rough and toughened
by shelling castor seeds. My dear, when did our

clasped hands become heavy chains and anchors holding
us to the mines and diamond and oil fields? Our hands
calloused by love and play, these same hands – when

did they learn to grip a machete or a gun to spit hate?
And this earth that drinks our blood like a hungry child
this earth that we have scorched to cinders – when we

are done eating it, how much of it will be left for Kenya?
My dear, our child is born, is dying. Tomorrow
the child will be dead.

UW – Madison
January 4, 2007
– commissioned by the BBC World Service

A Tribute to the Man in Black
Vivek Mehta

This is a tribute to the "Man In Black T-Shirt"

His name we may or may not know
But that's how he was referred to by the KTN Television network
The date was Wednesday 16th January 2008
I spent an hour sitting alone last night replaying the KTN clip in my mind
Did you see it?

The Man in Black was dancing in Nyanza, Kenya – was it in Kisumu?

He was Dancing and also Protesting with his friends
He was exercising one of his basic Human Rights – The Right to Free Speech and Assembly
He had no stone to hurl and no panga in his hand to hurt
He was just Dancing and Protesting
He was not looting either
Just Dancing and Protesting
Then came the grand finale
He was running away… he was not fighting
He was not dancing or protesting either
The Man in Green was only a few feet away
Two rapid shots from an automatic rifle
and the dance was over ….

The Man in Black lay on the floor together with his friend
He tried to get up one more time – he was only dancing!!

But the shot had done its job
As he tumbled down yet again the brute in Green had to kick him
Probably to kick the Man in Black's last breath out
That was the sudden end to the Dance
Farewell Man in Black – a friend I never got to meet
A friend who gave up his life for Kenyans' freedom
As I sat I realized that The Man in Black was probably a 'poor man'
No riches and no bank account either to his name
All I can offer his Soul are my Prayers for His Soul's Peaceful Journey
And May My Prayers and those of Many Others enrich your Soul
And May that Enrichment of your Soul be our reward and thanks for your Sacrifice
May that Enrichment Power your Journey
And your Soul be Blessed with Riches not seen
I take Solace in that the Nature of the Soul is
WEAPONS CUT IT NOT, FIRE BURNS IT NOT, WATER WETS IT NOT,
WIND DRIES IT NOT
After this thought propped up in my Being
Yet another Powerful thought Burst thru

This was the one that surprised me, my friend
May the World of Justice Notice this Brutal Crime against Humanity
In the Meantime May Peace and Justice Prevail in Kenya
When will we see sense in this beautiful Land and Country called Kenya?

Jan 17, 2008, Mombasa

LIBERATORY ESSAYS & INTERVIEWS & BLOGS

"Apostles of Ugliness": 100 Years Later
Mark Vallen

February, 2008 marked the 100th anniversary of "The Eight Independent Painters" exhibition at New York's MacBeth Gallery. While the event changed the face of American art and established the country's very first avant-garde art movement, which broke the rules of convention by painting the realities of New York's working poor and immigrant populations instead of the lives and accomplishments of the well-to-do class – the centennial is not likely to receive any attention from an art world currently obsessed with escapism, celebrity and money.

In 1907 John Sloan, George Luks, and William Glackens were rejected for exhibition by New York's conservative National Academy of Design, which slavishly upheld classical European academic painting. Robert Henri pulled his own works from the Academy exhibit in protest, and then set about mounting an alternative exhibition of works that would included artists hostile to the Academy's entrenched academicians and their reactionary jury system. Working with Sloan, Luks, and Glackens, Henri pulled together the exhibit at the Macbeth Gallery in February of 1908. Painters Everett Shinn, Ernest Lawson, Arthur Davies, and Maurice Prendergast were included in the loosely knit group – which became known as "The Eight Independent Painters," or simply "The Eight."

While multitudes flocked to the Macbeth Gallery to see the exhibit, the show was met with ridicule from the art establishment and derided by an unsympathetic press, which mockingly referred to the group as "The Apostles of Ugliness" or "The Revolutionary Black Gang" – since the artists painted working people and gritty urban realism with a somber palette. Eventually the group was contemptuously dubbed, the "Ashcan School", a reference to the garbage cans found in crowded inner-city slums that served as backdrops for many paintings by "The Eight."

The Ashcan school became the vanguard in the fight to modernize American art. Shockwaves cre-ated by the Macbeth Gallery exhibit led to further struggles against academic conservatism, opening the way to the famous 1913 Armory Show – which John Sloan and Arthur Davies helped to organize. The Ashcan school embraced progressive ideas put into motion by European artists, but reshaped those conceptions into something uniquely American. The Ashcan circle of painters eventually widened to include artists like George Bellows, Stuart Davis, Reginald Marsh, Edward Hopper, Rockwell Kent, and dozens of others.

[Ludlow, Colorado – John Sloan. 1914. Lithographic crayon on paper. Originally published as a cover illustration for the socialist New York Call, and soon thereafter published as a cover for The Masses, Sloan's artwork depicted the Ludlow massacre. On April 20, 1914, in an attempt to defeat a coal miner's strike in Ludlow, Colorado, National Guardsmen fired upon the striking worker's tent city – slaughtering twenty unarmed people – thirteen of them women and children. Sloan memorialized the bloodbath by depicting a miner, gun in hand, firing

John Sloan was unquestionably the most poli-tically engaged of "The Eight", and his works and ideas have had no small influence upon me over the years. John Sloan's ideas regarding painting, printmaking, and art instruction were fortunately preserved for eternity in a series of writings that were ultimately compiled as the book, The Gist of Art. Part personal observations on life and art, part instructional manual for those interested in the mechanics of drawing and painting, "Gist" is to a large extent comprised of verbatim notes taken while Sloan was teaching in the classroom or lec-turing to an audience.

Suffice it to say, I think everyone with an interest in the technical aspects of oil painting should read Sloan's book, but the work also freely offers some of the philosophical ideas held by the artist, a few of which I'll make mention of here. As an artist given to portraying everyday Americans at work and play, and as a member of America's first avant-garde art movement, Sloan's attitudes pertaining to patriotism were no less unorthodox than his views on art:

> In this relatively democratic country today, I feel that, since we can talk about things free-ly, we can go on painting any kind of subject matter we like. It is not necessary to paint the American flag to be an American paint-er, as though you didn't see the American scene whenever you open your eyes! I am not for the American scene, I am for mental realization. If you are American and work – you work will be American. Patriotism, love of country, is very different from love for the government. I love the country in Pennsyl-vania, New England, and in the Southwest. I love the streets of New York. But I am suspi-cious of all government because government is violence.

In a world so dominated by the logic of the market, we've come to accept sales price as the sole value of art, and we judge an artist's success in cess in terms of booming career and celebrity status – so Sloan's views on making a living as an artist are a refresh-ing counterpoint to today's money mad art world. Sloan's judgment of pursuing a career in art po-ssesses an almost spiritual dimension, not in any religious sense, but in his understanding of art as something deeply personal and transcendent. I believe if we accepted Sloan's outlook only in part, we'd all be much healthier for it:

> You can't make a living at art. The idea of taking up art as a calling, a trade, a profes-sion, is a mirage. Art enriches life. It makes life worth living. But to make a living at it – that idea is incompatible with making art. (....) Shun this idea of going into art with success as an aim, wealth as an aim, for the purpose of getting on in the world, getting the good things in life. Success has apparent-ly become much more the art student's aim than it was in my time. It spells disaster. No one who sets out for success gets the real thing. All you can get is a little sauce poured over you while you are alive. (....) There is only one thing to do about success – shun it. The only kind of success to desire is success with yourself. To make steps, progress, with yourself.

Compared to the shallow art star celebrities of today, Sloan was well informed and showed not the slightest temerity in expressing controversial opinions. In the following he alludes to the first great world war that broke out in 1914, but his thinking clearly has meaning in the here and now:

> (...) The governments are willing to turn their weapons, and tear gas bombs are the least of them, against the enemy or against their own people, their own citizens. Young people in their twenties are going to see things that I would like to live to see, and yet, it won't be pleasant – it will be terrible. I don't like war. The economic interests get out their propaganda machines and per-suade the people that democracy is at stake. And what do millions of innocent people go out and

get killed and maimed for? – to protect the economic interests of the few.

(…) God must be awfully far away or disinterested to let people go on living the way they do in dirt and in filthy holes contaminating one another, swarming out to kill when ordered. They say that love makes the world go round. More likely, in our social set-up, it is the inferiority complex. It makes people want to get ahead, be important. The spirit of competition must be kept out of the artist's mind.

American social realism started to take shape at the turn of the century when the country was under-going, much like today, an extraordinary economic and cultural transformation; which is what makes the Ashcan school so relevant to contemporary artists. Not just a cursory introduction to a long forgotten and marginalized American art move-ment, this essay is a call for a reassessment of the sensibilities and motivations found at the very core of the Ashcan School – that is to say, an unwilling-ness to succumb to the dictates of elite taste and fashion, a belief in artistic independence, and a passionate conviction that art should be grounded in the lived experiences of everyday people.

While the mainstream art world may pay little or no attention to the 100th anniversary of "The Eight Independent Painters", those concerned with the present and future of art will want to look beneath the surface of things to study the Ashcan school and its lively anti-elitist humanism.

[Much of Liberation Lit's cover art is in the style overviewed above, including work by John Sloan. – Eds.]

And all the world's a stage

P. Sainath

Courtesy of The Hindu

*W*hile *theatre struggles to survive in the metros [of India], it thrives in Vidharbha where it draws audiences of thousands for plays that go on through much of the night. Atma Hatya is a Marathi play running to audi-ences of thousands at every show in eastern Vidharbha. The theme of this jhadi patti play is farmers suicides.*

It was well past midnight when the farmer said he was fed up with the way things were going. He could not take it any more, he told us. A farmer's life was not worth living. It was pretty cold by this time. Yet no one budged and you could feel the tension in the air. The play is called *atma hatya* (suicide) and we were part of an audience of 6,000 watching transfixed at that late hour. Theatre may be struggling to survive in the metros, but here in rural Vidharbha, it thrives. This is the season of *jhadi patti rang bhoomi*. Which loosely translates as "theatre of the jungle belt."

Everybody is part of it. "We have farmers, tailors, painters and vendors in our plays," says Ghulam Sufi of the Venkatesh natya mandali that is staging *Atma Hatya*. "That's one reason why it resonates so much with ordinary people." Mr. Sufi plays tabla for the 60-member troupe. We watched him do that – and saw him dash off in between to don make up and do a swift cameo in the play. The main carpenter of the troupe whom we had seen at work earlier also made an appearance on the rotating stage he had set up that afternoon.

Jhadi patti is quite different from the mainline Marathi theatre of Mumbai and Pune. Nor is it part of the folk theatre of other parts of Maharashtra. It is rooted in just four districts of eastern Vidharbha, all of them forested. *Jhadi putti* has a history of over a century. "See our audiences," says a proud Sadanand Borkar in Nawagaon, Chandrapur district. That's where the play is now being staged. Nawagaon alone has three seasoned troupes. The region has hundreds. Mr. Borkar is the author, director and also an actor in *Atma Hatya*. "Our troupe, the Venkatesh natya mandali, is 110 years old this year." And his family were its founders.

There are occasional blips with little local troupes not as trained as the Venkatesh mandali. Applause when an actor faints from exhaustion and not the script. Or the curtain guy falls asleep and fails to bring it down. It takes nothing away from the experience, though.

Earlier in the day, we watched people pour in from other villages to buy tickets. A striking feature of *jhadi patti* is the absence of sponsors. No boards announcing the generosity of a cola. No thanks to kind corporate patrons. The plays begin around 9.30 p.m. *Atma Hatya* will end only around 2 a.m. Others go on till even later.

"We exist because of the people," says Mr. Borkar. "Our plays are from their lives. They have high standards. `Faltu natak' or excessive vulgarity won't pass. Two years ago, angry people smashed one outside group's pandal on this count." In its first phase, *jhadi patti* had mythological themes. Then came period plays. During this time, scripts written in Mumbai and Pune were simply performed locally by visiting troupes. Now stage actors from Mumbai and Pune figure in plays written here. Mostly, the outside actors are women. "Not so many women have taken to acting here as yet," says Mr. Borkar.

Atma Hatya has two outside professionals. The vastly experienced Rajini Bhatt from Pune. And Kanchan Mitkar, a bright young professional based in Nashik. Both speak highly of *jhadi patti*'s disci-pline and uniqueness and above all, its audiences. "If you work here you have the confidence to work anywhere else," says Ms. Bhatt. The costliest ticket is Rs. 60 and entitles you to a chair. The lowest, Rs. 20 or less.

There may be no sponsors (and no one seems to be looking for any), but *jhadi patti* is a thriving small industry. "It has no government support either," says Mr. Borkar who is also the Principal of a local Fine Arts college. *Jhadi patti*'s cal-endar ties in well with the agricultural cycle. "Around or just after harvest when people have some money in hand and time to relax. That's when we function. We begin around diwali and wind up the season by April."

This uniquely eastern Vidharbha theatre gives full-time work to some the year round. And em-ployment for thousands each season. Its turnover is a few crores of rupees. During the off-agriculture season, it earns a livelihood for labourers, tailors, carpenters and the like. It costs up to Rs. 80,000 to stage a play at big centres. And about half that in the smaller villages. The nearby town of Wadsa boasts a whole poster and pamphlet sector based on theatre work. It also supplies troupes on de-mand to the villages. Professionals from Mumbai or Pune could earn up to Rs. 3,000 a night acting in *jhadi patti*.

People have come to see *Atma Hatya* from within a 100-km radius. There is a further social side to it, too. "They might come from 15 villages," says Mr. Borkar. "There will meetings, contacts, and match-making. Weddings could be fixed here tonight." *Atma Hatya*'s perspective on farm suicides is from east Vidharbha and thus from outside the dismal cotton belt. But it does see debt as a driving factor. And it also captures other stresses. Such as the inner-family drama linked to changing lifestyles and interests as some members move away from farming. The family is crucial to *jhadi patti*.

The play's message is positive. Suicide is no solution. Fight the idea in your homes. An earlier Borkar play that broke records – *I killed my husband* – fought superstition. Some villages have used a play's proceeds to give soft loans to farmers. Others to get some work done locally. For the last two decades, *jhadi patti* has taken on social and political themes with a strong accent on justice. (Election year has local politicians scrambling to be seen on stage.) Now the region's farm suicides are under the spotlight.

"This is Maharashtra's most unique theatre form," says Professor Pramod Mungate of the St. Francis de Sales college in Nagpur. Professor Mungate, who heads the Marathi department there, is studying *jhadi patti* on a University Grants Commission project. "In Nagpur, only big names draw us to a play. In eastern Vidharbha, there will be nine plays held at Kurud village on February 9 simultaneously. They will all have big audiences for mostly part-time actors. *Jhadi patti*'s appeal has not shrunk despite the coming of multiple television channels. It's truly a people's movement, rooted in their lives. No sponsors or commercial patrons. This has audience. This has response. This is theatre."

Pinter's Message to Obama

Mike Whitney

> Come and see the blood in the streets.
> Come and see
> the blood in the streets.
> Come and see the blood
> in the streets!
>
> – Pablo Neruda

About a month before Barack Obama announced his candidacy for the presidency of the United States, former National Security Adviser Zbigniew Brzezinski appeared on PBS's Charlie Rose Show and was asked whether he thought Obama would be a good choice for president. Brzezinski paused for a minute, peered at Rose out of the corner of his eye, and answered, "Just think of the symbolism." As soon as he said that, Brzezinski and Rose broke out into laughter as though they were sharing a private joke.

Brzezinski was right, of course. Obama was the perfect choice for president. Not because of his ex-perience. He had none. He was a two year senator with a resume' small enough to fit on the back of a matchbox. Still Obama had what Brzezinski and Co. were looking for, symbolism; the kind of symbolism that connected him to people around the world and made them feel like one of their own had finally clawed their way to the top. Even bet-ter, Obama was a charismatic populist who could fill stadiums with adoring fans and put a benign face on America's interventions in Afghanistan and Iraq. What more could Brzezinski hope for? After 8 years of dragging "Brand America" through the mud, the country would finally get the emergency facelift it needed and begin to restore its battered image as the world's indispensable nation.

For leftists, Obama has been a total bust. He's escalated the war in Afghanistan, increased the cross-border bombings of Pakistan, hemmed and hawed about prosecuting war crimes, refused to actively lobby House members to make it easier for workers to organize (EFCA), and surrounded him-self with bank industry reps who've committed $12.8 trillion to sinking financial institutions with no assurance that the money would be repaid. Apart from a trifling bill on stem cells, Obama has done absolutely zero to confirm his *bona fides* as a liberal. The truth is, Obama is neither liberal nor conservative; he's simply an inspiring orator and a skillful politician who has no strong convictions about anything. If he achieves greatness, it will be because he was thrust into a crisis he couldn't avoid and reluctantly acted in the best interests of the American people. That possibility still exists, although it seems more unlikely by the day.

Foreign leaders are clearly relieved to see the last of George W. Bush, and they appear to be willing to give Obama every opportunity to mend fences and break with the past. But Obama has made little effort to reciprocate or show that he's serious about real change. The emphasis seems to be more on public relations than policy; more on glitzy photo ops, grandiose speeches and gadding about from one capital to another, than ending the chronic US meddling and militarism. Where's the beef or is it all just empty posturing?

No one's ready to write-off Obama just yet, but he needs to show he's the real deal by taking steps to ratchet down the war machine and reign in the corporate elites and bank vermin. But is it really possible for one man – however well-meaning – to change the course of a nation by standing up the gaggle of racketeers who pull the strings from behind the curtain? Keep in mind, America's history of violent interventions, unprovoked wars, color-coded revolutions and coup d' etats has a long pedigree that stretches from Bunker Hill to Baghdad. That river of blood did not begin with George Bush and it won't end with Barack Obama. Every generation has produced its own litany of crimes, from Wounded Knee to Nagasaki to My Lai to Fallujah. In Harold Pinter's Nobel acceptance speech, the playwright invokes one such incident which epitomizes the pattern of hostility which has been repeated over and over again wherever the Washington mandarins detect opposition to their iron-fisted rule.

Harold Pinter, Nobel Acceptance Speech:

"The United States supported the brutal Somoza dictatorship in Nicaragua for over 40 years. The Nicaraguan people, led by the Sandinistas, overthrew this regime in 1979, a breathtaking popular revolution.

"The Sandinistas weren't perfect. They possessed their fair share of arrogance and their political philosophy contained a number of contradictory elements. But they were intelligent, rational and civilized. They set out to establish a stable, decent, pluralistic society. The death penalty was abolished. Hundreds of thousands of poverty-stricken peasants were brought back from the dead. Over 100,000 families were given title to land. Two thousand schools were built. A quite remarkable literacy campaign reduced illiteracy in the country to less than one seventh. Free education was established and a free health service. Infant mortality was reduced by a third. Polio was eradicated.

"The United States denounced these achievements as Marxist/Leninist subversion. In the view of the US government, a dangerous example was being set. If Nicaragua was allowed to establish basic norms of social and economic justice, if it was allowed to raise the standards of health care and education and achieve social unity and national self respect, neighboring countries would ask the same questions and do the same things. There was of course at the time fierce resistance to the status quo in El Salvador.

"I spoke earlier about 'a tapestry of lies' which surrounds us. President Reagan commonly described Nicaragua as a 'totalitarian dungeon'. This was taken generally by the media, and certainly by the British government, as accurate and fair comment. But there was in fact no record of death squads under the Sandinista government. There was no record of torture. There was no record of systematic or official military brutality. No priests were ever murdered in Nicaragua. There were in fact three priests in the government, two Jesuits and a Maryknoll missionary. The totalitarian dungeons were actually next door, in El Salvador and Guatemala. The United States had brought down the democratically elected

government of Guatemala in 1954 and it is estimated that over 200,000 people had been victims of successive military dictatorships.

"Six of the most distinguished Jesuits in the world were viciously murdered at the Central American University in San Salvador in 1989 by a battalion of the Alcatl regiment trained at Fort Benning, Georgia, USA. That extremely brave man Archbishop Romero was assassinated while saying mass. It is estimated that 75,000 people died. Why were they killed? They were killed because they believed a better life was possible and should be achieved. That belief immediately qualified them as communists. They died because they dared to question the status quo, the endless plateau of poverty, disease, degradation and oppression, which had been their birthright.

"The United States finally brought down the Sandin-ista government. It took some years and considerable resistance but relentless economic persecution and 30,000 dead finally undermined the spirit of the Nicaraguan people. They were exhausted and poverty stricken once again. The casinos moved back into the country. Free health and free education were over. Big business returned with a vengeance. 'Democracy' had prevailed.

"But this 'policy' was by no means restricted to Cen-tral America. It was conducted throughout the world. It was never-ending. And it is as if it never happened.

"The United States supported and in many cases engendered every right wing military dictatorship in the world after the end of the Second World War. I refer to Indonesia, Greece, Uruguay, Brazil, Paraguay, Haiti, Turkey, the Philippines, Guatemala, El Salvador, and, of course, Chile. The horror the United States inflicted upon Chile in 1973 can never be purged and can never be forgiven.

"Hundreds of thousands of deaths took place throughout these countries. Did they take place? And are they in all cases attributable to US foreign policy? The answer is yes they did take place and they are attributable to American foreign policy. But you wouldn't know it."

Pinter's speech is a somber indictment of US for-eign policy; a policy which is now cloaked behind the rock-star facade of Barack Obama.

Nothing has changed and, perhaps, nothing will change. The same barbarous campaign that thrived under Bush has been passed along to Obama intact. Wherever there is resistance to US ambitions, there lies the enemy. Whether it's Marxists in Bogota, national-ists in Kosovo, Bolivarians in Caracas, Shia militias in Beirut, Islamic moderates in Mogadishu or Quakers in Toledo. They're all enemies, every one of them, and they need to be dealt with.

Obama is no fool; he knows he's being used. He knows wasn't chosen for his enlightened views on health care and stem cells. He was picked because the men in charge needed a new poster boy to hide behind while they carry out their illicit activities. Obama is not so much of a commander in chief as he is master illusionist, diverting attention from the stealth war that goes on relentlessly with or without his consent.

Here's Pinter again:

"The crimes of the United States have been systematic, constant, vicious, remorseless, but very few people have actually talked about them. You have to hand it to America. It has exercised a quite clinical manipulation of power worldwide while masquerading as a force for uni-versal good. It's a brilliant, even witty, highly successful act of hypnosis...It's a scintillating stratagem."

Consider how the news was shaped to make it look like the invasions of Iraq and Afghanistan were carried out for altruistic reasons. Thus, the war in Afghanistan became "Operation Enduring Free-dom", stressing the selfless generosity of bombing a country into oblivion and reinstating the thuggish warlords to power. The same strategy was used for the invasion of Iraq which was celebrated as "liberation from a brutal dictator" – liberation which cost the lives of over 1 million Iraqis and the displacement of 4 million more. Still, no one in the UN or so-called international community has pressed for removing the US from the Security Council or prosecuting its leaders for war crimes. It's a testimony to the success of the US media in upholding the "tapestry of lies" of which Pinter speaks. Under Obama, the charade has only gotten worse. The coverage of the war has stopped entirely. War?

What war? What matters now is Obama's cheery banter with Jay Leno, or Michelle's well-proportioned arms or Malia's adorable Portuguese Waterdog. America is whole again. Let the killing resume.

Pinter:

"What has happened to our moral sensibility? Did we ever have any? What do these words mean? Do they refer to a term very rarely employed these days – conscience? A conscience to do not only with our own acts but to do with our shared responsibility in the acts of others? Is all this dead? Look at Guantanamo Bay. Hundreds of people detained without charge for over three years, with no legal representation or due process, technically detained forever. This totally illegitimate structure is maintained in defiance of the Geneva Convention. It is not only tolerated but hardly thought about by what's called the 'international community'. This criminal outrage is being committed by a country, which declares itself to be 'the leader of the free world'. Do we think about the inhabitants of Guantanamo Bay? What does the media say about them? They pop up occasionally – a small item on page six. They have been consigned to a no man's land from which indeed they may never return. At present many are on hunger strike, being force-fed, including British residents. No niceties in these force-feeding procedures. No sedative or anesthetic. Just a tube stuck up your nose and into your throat. You vomit blood. This is torture. What has the British Foreign Secretary said about this? Nothing. What has the British Prime Minister said about this? Nothing. Why not? Because the United States has said: to criticize our conduct in Guantanamo Bay constitutes an unfriendly act. You're either with us or against us."

"Obama doesn't need to solve the world's problems. He doesn't have to reverse global warming or slow peak oil, cure AIDS or end world hunger. All he needs to do is meet the minimal requirement of his job as president, which is to deliver justice to his people. That's why the prosecution of Bush for war crimes is more important than any other issue on the docket. Justice precedes everything; it's the thread that keeps the social fabric stitched together. Justice for the victims who were killed in their homes with their families while they were sleeping or eating dinner. Justice for the people who were bombed in wed-ding parties or going to work or at the mosque praying to God. That's what people want from Obama. Justice, nothing more. The Reverend Martin Luther King said, "The arc of the moral universe is long, but it bends towards justice." It's up to Obama follow that arc and take at least one step on the path of legitimacy, accountability and justice."

Pinter:

"How many people do you have to kill before you qualify to be described as a mass murderer and a war criminal? One hundred thousand? More than enough, I would have thought. Therefore it is just that Bush and Blair be arraigned before the International Criminal Court of Justice."

"It's highly unlikely that a black man with a background in community organizing really believes that expanding the war in Afghanistan is the right thing to do. Nor is it likely that he supports wiretapping, the crackdown on immigrants, penalizing sellers of medical marijuana, trillion dollar bank bailouts or "enhanced" interrogation. He is merely reading from the script that he has been given. But as the economic crisis deepens and the country becomes more radicalized and politically unstable, that script will have to be tossed aside. Obama will have plenty of opportunities to shrug off his han-dlers and show what he's really made of. Perhaps he is a great man after all."

Pinter:

"When we look into a mirror, we think the image that confronts us is accurate. But move a millimeter and the image changes. We are actually looking at a never-ending range of reflections. But sometimes a writer has to smash the mirror – for it is on the other side of that mirror that the truth stares at us."

Go ahead, Barack. Smash the mirror.

Interview with Eduardo Galeano
Andre Vltchek

at Café Brazilero,

in historic center city Montevideo

Q: Eduardo Galeano, after so many years are the veins of Latin America still open?

A: Yes; obviously yes. I think they are. Not long ago I met count Dracula in Buenos Aires. He was looking for an Argentinean psychoanalyst. Argen-tina produces many psychoanalysts. Dracula was told by someone that he can still be cured by an Argentinean psychoanalyst. I found count Dracula in a terrible state; really depressed, thin, terrible…

Q: There is plenty of competition around, isn't there?

A: Exactly. He was suffering from a tremendous complex of inferiority, seeing how the great corpo-rations of the modern world are behaving. So he was walking through the streets, searching for someone to cure him.

Q: But in this world he probably has many friends, not only competitors…

A: He saw them all as competition. And he told me that nothing was making much sense, any-more. Seeing how this world is behaving, he said that nothing was making any sense to him.

Q: What can you say about the present situation in Latin America? There are so many developments in Brazil, Venezuela, in Bolivia. Some changes are outright progressive, others are semi-progressive. How would you compare the situation now and during the time when you were writing "Open Veins of Latin America" and "Memory of Fire"?

A: I would say that now the tendency is to vote in progressive governments that are trying to change things. This means a tremendous challenge but also a tremendous responsibility, because these new progressive governments that can be found in sev-eral countries of Latin America are carriers of col-lective hope which was not yet dead but seriously wounded; in terrible shape. Latin America is part of the world which was for many years condemned to the system of power where intimidation had more strength than the vote. It began in 1954 – more than half a century ago – when the democratically elected government of Guatemala attempted to make agrarian reforms, to return dignity to in-digenous people; all that was later destroyed by foreign invasion. And then it continued: invasions and coups against any positive changes – progres-sive or nationalistic – concerning natural resources, independence, national dignity… Governments that intend to implement changes are destroyed. It happened in Brazil, Dominican Republic, Bolivia, in Chile which became the most famous case because Salvador Allende was converted to an international symbol. Then the Sandinistas in Nicaragua; again the same thing – they were destroyed after ten years of war because they intended to create a country – fatherland – where there was only a colony before. So all this is a very long story; a story of frustrations, failures, of hope washed in blood. All this created the situation in which we are now. How can I explain it? Change is possible, but to implement the change, one has to fight against not only the painful and fucked up experiences of the last half century but also against the long betrayal and something that I call "the culture of impotence". It is a culture that has roots in the colonial period, in the period when the continent was controlled by Spain and Portugal and that was later broken up and consolidated by the military dictatorships and the fatalistic brothers from the church. All this helped to create a culture of impotence that manages to paralyze people with fear. It tells you that reality is untouchable; reality can't be touched, can't be changed. These days this culture of fear has a spokesman who is a universal god – the god of the market, gangrenous figure. He is checking on us from above and tells us what we can do and what we can't.

Q: In Latin America it is common to criticize the foreign policy of the United States. That's un-der-standable, given the experience of many decades of terror spread by the US in Central and South America. On the other hand it often appears that centuries of European colonialism are forgotten and forgiven. Many here see present-day Europe as a sort of counterbalance to the United States, not as part of an oppressive world power structure. Can you explain why this is happening?

A: Correct. I think this sentiment exists because there is nostalgia for the multi-polar world. From the weak nations' point of view, it is better if there are many powerful countries than if there are just a few. The more concentrated is power, the fewer opportunities there are to move. Space for change, space for freedom to implement change is then very narrow; very small. A unipolar world – one with only one power – makes sure that this space almost disappears. In a multipolar world this space multiplies. Therefore, there is nostalgia for a multipolar world. For some fifty years we had something that was called the "socialist world", which was of course not really socialist, but it managed to create another pole. During those times, Europe had at least some energy to implement its own development. And many people see the disappear-ance of that period as a loss. Now it seems like faraway history. Things fundamentally changed; look at an extreme case like the one of the UK. Not long ago I was visiting London and I happened to be invited to speak at The Royal Festival Hall. It was packed with people. During my first lecture someone from the audience asked me whom would I vote for in the upcoming elections? I said that I'm not going to sell ice to the Eskimos; that I am not going to tell English people for whom they should vote! But people kept insisting; kept push-ing: "Whom would you vote for?" At the end they reduced their questions to: "So at least say what would be your message to the English public". So I told them: "I don't think it is a very digni-fied posi-tion to be a colony of your former colony". They were laughing a lot after I said that;

they thought it was a great joke. But it wasn't a joke. It's true. Europe is now very much under the control of dictatorship; of only one power, which is represented by one guy from Texas with terrible taste; a guy who is humiliating the world by speaking like some bartender… He is presiding over the degrad-ation of the political process, reducing it to the level of low quality comics.

Q: Most Europeans are losing any desire to vote. As we saw during the previous elections in the UK, the majority of people are voting for politicians for whom they harbor no respect. Before, this was hap-pening only in the colonies or former colonies; now we can see the same trend in colonial powers them-selves. It seems that the system has no respect even for its own citizens.

A: There is a universal crisis of so called represent-ative democracies or democracies which rely on the system of competing political parties. This crisis is mostly reflected in the apathy of young genera-tions. If you ask young people whether they believe in democracy, in the energy of changes in democracy, most of the young people just shrug their shoulders and tell you that they don't believe in it, or believe just a little. This universal crisis – and Latin America is part of this world and this crisis – takes place mainly because politicians did very little in order to dignify democracy. Many young people see democracy as some enormous circus where professional politicians are perform-ing incredible tricks. Once they reach the govern-ment, they do everything possible not to fulfill what they have promised during the election campaign. This is exactly against the essence of democracy and young people at the end feel that they are invited to choose between the same and the same. The goal now is to restore democracy to its deep essence: as the power of the people. In this world which is losing faith in so called representative democracy, there are new developments in participatory democracy. These are very interesting developments, reflecting the revitalization of com-munity power with a more and more active pres-ence of minorities in political life, including the presence of women who are of course by no means a minority…

There is also the growing influence of the pacifists. Sometimes one feels that pacifists are powerless since they were not able to stop the war in Iraq. But we can't forget that before the war, for the first time in the history of humanity there were enormous demonstrations and protests against the war – before the war began. This was important, because at least it put on the record how discon-nected are many governments from their people who were screaming slogans against the war on the streets but their voices are being ignored. So at least it was important as a testimony. On the other hand it is also obvious how far we are from the time of political maturity, when we could be capa-ble of punishing politicians for their betrayals. To punish with the most powerful weapon – the ballot. There is a saying that a lie has short legs. Not long ago I wrote an article arguing that it is not true: a lie has very long legs. So long are the legs of a lie that it is capable of running at full speed carrying liars on its back. Because when Tony Blair and George Bush lied about the weapons of mass destruction in Iraq, people in their countries still awarded them with the vote in the following elections. So we are still very far from the time when people will be realizing how powerful a weapon their vote can be.

Q: You mentioned pacifism. Do you believe that it is possible to fight against the global dictatorship by pacifist means? While we are being peaceful, simply protesting against brutality, right now there are millions and millions of people dying from hunger and incurable diseases, while billions of men, women and children are living in the most despicable conditions… Can pacifism achieve changes or should there be more direct actions taken on the part of the resistance?

A: I don't believe in saying "the way to do it is…". "The way to do it is armed struggle…" I met many people who were seriously involved in armed struggle. But they were reacting to the will and desires of the people. They never acted as if they were enlightened by some divine power or by some chosen minority. Also, they say that if there were someone shouting: "Armed struggle! Let's die!" – He would proba-bly be working for someone and would be embarrassed to confess for whom… He would be some professional provocateur like Bin Laden. Bin Laden is an official; an official of fear; that's clear. Bush was just about to lose the elections, and then Bin Laden appears, declares that he is going to eat all children in the raw and Bush wins! So there is blackmail by the dominant power when it uses the threat of terror. It happens very often: one's enemies are the best allies. I think the ways of change are dictated by the circumstances of each country, each place and each time. I don't think that arrogant intellectuals should be dictating to the people which way they should be heading. I think we should be listening to the people, see in which directions things are developing. People are walking where they can, not where they want to. But they are walking! And one has to have enough modesty and humility to listen to the sound of their steps. Now one thing that I can say: the experience shows that this formula of universal capitalism is not working. It does not solve any basic problems of humanity and in addition, it is endangering the very existence of our planet. Therefore, we have to be alert and follow the contradictions created by this very system. Contradictions between what the system says and what it does. Between what the system wants and what it can do. And from these contradictions grow the base of the new world which is not yet born. One has to be a realist but also to remember that reality is not only the world which we know, but also the world which we need. And the world that we need is inside – in the stomach of the present world. This new world often seems to be too silent, but it exists. We have to be patient and humble to hear how it is kicking inside. We have to see in which way each situation is developing, at each and every moment, everywhere. By doing this, we have to drop formulas. The 20th century was the century where formulas failed. Formulas failed once, twice, a thousand times. We already experienced the pedantry with which the world was forced to adapt to the formulas. So at least we know that we don't want to repeat mistakes which occurred in the past. In the recent past, one half of the world had to sacrifice freedom in the name of justice, while the other half had to sacrifice justice in the name of freedom. Now we know that this will not do: that justice and freedom are two Siamese twins. They were born back to back – attached to each other – and they want to live together. At least this we know, so we don't have to repeat what has been done; what went wrong with some terrible consequences. Remember, when the so-called "real socialism" collapsed without one drop of blood, nobody gave a shit. I knew many leaders of the Communist Parties from the former Eastern Block; they converted themselves into business-people, overnight. Yes, they became successful businesspeople! And these are the countries that were claiming they were governed by the proletariat.

Q: The collapse of the Eastern Block was, of course, immediately utilized by the West for propaganda purposes.

A: Logically.

Q: Mistakes of so called real socialism were supposed to prove, by some twisted logic, that capital-ism was the only natural system for humanity. The West managed to sell its formula extremely well.

A: It was obvious that they would utilize the situa-tion this way. If I had been in their shoes, I would have done the same. But the collapse of the system can't be blamed on imperialist conspiracy. Obvi-ously there was an internal crack in the system and when the time arrived, everything just fell apart.

Q: After all that, do you still maintain some belief in socialism or communism?

A: Of course I do. I don't think there has been any-thing yet that we could call real socialism. There were developments, some experiences that were correct. But the system was divorced from the peo-ple. It was operated in the name of the working people, but it was not the case in reality and the proof was in the velocity with which it collapsed, the incredible simplicity by which it decomposed. There are some things I can't share with you be-cause I have to protect the identity of the people, but I discussed this with very important leaders of the system when it was already in trouble. We spent hours and hours talking and they kept re-peating: "this is not going to be the end because socialism is immortal!" Immortal?! They brought in some theological categories; some religious stuff, confusing it with political reality, with human life. We are human beings, persons; we are all mortal. Of course we are all mortal; we, our world and the systems which we create. The world is going to die one day, in thousands of millions of years from now; hopefully not too soon. But what an arro-gance of that bureaucracy which later recycled itself in just ten minutes into a bourgeois class! They became capitalists! They changed one type of oppression for another, but one way or the other continued to function as an oppressive force. So all this has obviously nothing to do with ideals of socialism. But it is also obvious that if capitalism doesn't work for the majority of people, sooner or later we will have to lift up the old banners which were made dirty and were abused. But we will have to lift them up again, of course.

Q: Back to Latin America: it is clear that most of the people here still desire social justice and the system which would be able to guarantee it. However, af-ter they vote in progressive governments, these are not always able to deliver their promises, adopting a centrist course.

A: People here want very basic things. They still can't find the answers or solutions to their very simple demands like dignity, peace and work. People are searching but they are not finding solu-tions. They are walking and searching on different roads. They are being betrayed – we have a long tradition of betrayal here. And they are now, gen-erally and to a certain point, thinking that these new governments, which have lately appeared in several parts of South America, will act more or less in accordance with the hope which they man-aged to evoke. That's why I always say: careful; one doesn't play with people's hope. Hope is very fragile. If the people deposited this hope in your hands, comrades – be very careful! Don't betray this hope. Because hope can't be recovered easily! When it is lost, it takes a long time to bring it back. New progressive governments in South America are facing tremendous historic responsibility. One of the writers and journalists who had a profound influence on me kept repeating: one sin which can't be forgiven is a sin against hope. Everything can be forgiven, but not this. That's why progressive governments have to be extremely careful not to destroy hope.

Q: A lot is being written lately about betrayal of hope. Some point fingers at Lula's government in Brazil. But how much space do these governments have to maneuver in the real world?

A: Very little. It is very difficult for them. You and I discussed this before; space is very limited and they have to fight an uphill battle. But one has to have something clear: if you are going to repeat history, it is better if you leave in power those who are already there. If your point is that you will not be able to change things, than don't promise that you will. If you do and don't deliver, you are lying to the people. If you can't change things, let capi-talists preside over the capitalism. But if you are going to get your hands on power in the name of change, in the name of national sovereignty or hu-man dignity, then you have to be responsible for your promises. If you can't do it, just go home, turn on the television and let politicians take care of the politics. But in the moment when Lula or others propose changes, they are responsible for their promises. One of Lula's politicians recently responded to the accusations about corruption in the present government: "But these things have always occurred in Brazil." But if this is always going to happen, why didn't they leave those who were doing it to continue?

Q: What books are you now working on? What are your creative plans for the near future?

A: I prefer not to discuss this, because if I talk too much about what I am writing, I lose desire to con-tinue. The most recent book I've published is a saga – a continuation of several previous books; consist-ing of very short texts. It forms a sort of mosaic and it comes from the people. I am a hunter of stories; I listen to the stories, then I give this back to the peo-ple after putting the stories through a creative process. My position is always that in order not to be mute, one shouldn't be deaf. One has to be able to listen in order to speak. I am a passionate listen-er. I listen to reality. Reality is a magic lady, some-times very mysterious. To me she is very passion-ate. She is real not only when she is awake, walk-ing down the streets, but also at night when she is dreaming or when she is having nightmares. When I am writing, I am always paying tribute to her – to that lady called Reality. I am trying not to fail her.

EXILE:
Conversations with Pramoedya Ananta Toer (excerpt)

Andre Vltchek and Rossie Indira

PROLOGUE: MEETING IN JAKARTA

Tanah Lot, Bali, Indonesia

July 21, 2004

The twentieth century was an almost uninter-rupted orgy of terror and violence, deceit and betrayal. Men and women on all continents learnt that "a lie repeated a thousand times becomes the truth", that brutal occupation can be described as an act of liberation, and that a massacre of millions of innocent people can be defended by rulers of mighty nations as an advancement of humanism and civilization.

Millions of men and women vanished in crematoriums, concentration camps, battlefields or in the rubble of their cities.

However, the 20th century will not be remembered only for its brutality. In the midst of plunder and chaos, it also gave birth to extraordinary men and women who stood tall and, against all odds, defended the defenceless, the victims of govern-ments and dictatorships: people that opposed demagogy, militarism and economic entities with the two most powerful tools of resistance known to humankind: knowledge and truth.

Some died in the process, others suffered but survived. Many became icons for independence and resistance movements. They were not prophets or gurus. They were brave but never fanatical. As Albert Camus wrote in the unforgettable final chapter of *The Plague*: "Unable to become saints, they became doctors".

While entire continents were being plundered and innocent people were being exterminated or thrown into to prisons and camps, they were tire-lessly identifying the symptoms, diagnosing the illness, and searching for the cure.

They were countering lies with simple words of reason, insane myths with facts, fanaticism with truth. Some faced the madness with sarcastic smiles on their lips, others with tense expressions on their faces. Some rebelled and defended reason and truth with mailed fists, others raised a hardly audible voice that made inroads into the minds of millions of people all over the world.

They were born in Europe and the Americas, in Africa and Asia, in every corner of the world. Most were raised in families of victims, but many were the sons and daughters of the victimizers. What-ever their origin, the message was invariably uni-versal and based on a single principle: all men and women are equal, regardless of their colour or race, their nationality or gender, or their status and material possessions.

Indonesia, an enormous archipelago country made up of diverse states, ethnic groups, cultures and languages unified only after WWII, was previ-ously controlled and exploited by colonial powers for long centuries. After an honourable start to self-determination and twenty short years of genuine independence, it was plunged into the terror of military dictatorship after the 1965 coup.

During those years, a softly-spoken man from Central Java wrote countless books, trying to de-fine the essence and history of his own young and suffering nation. He wrote in prisons, in camps, and under house arrest. Many of his books were burnt, and those that survived were banned. "It was my personal challenge to the dictatorship", he said later. All his books had one common theme and message: "Colonialism and imperialism are always wrong. The elites that enrich themselves by plundering their own people are immoral."

In a country so young and so troubled, where history had been distorted and corrupted, where unity was based more on geographical considerations than on common ideals and culture, it is hardly surprising that the loudest voice of moral resistance attempting to unite the nation against terror and injustice should be that of the county's greatest writer, Pramoedya Ananta Toer.

We first met Pram, as he is known in Indonesia, in his house in East Jakarta during December, 2003. At the time, we were preparing to shoot a long doc-umentary film,"Terlena – the Breaking of a Nation" about the murder and imprisonment of Indonesian intellectuals after the 1965 US-sponsored military coup. Our objective was to convince Pram, argua-bly the foremost living Southeast Asian novelist, to participate in the project. After all, he had dedi-cated his life to defining the essence of this enormous fledgling nation, criticizing its negative aspects in the process. It was he that denounced Suharto's regime as "morally corrupt". Pram spent decades in jails, concentration camps and under house arrest. His manuscripts were burnt by the regime and his books banned in Indonesia until 1999.

We arrived at his house accompanied by two young Indonesian journalists, both excited about meeting the great master of Indonesian letters; both very anxious, repeating that Pram "has a reputa-tion of being extremely impatient, explosive and even arrogant."

We had to wait for at least half an hour. During that time, Pram's brother appeared. He refused to speak English, but then with a knowing expression he addressed me in Russian: "Of course, as an American you don't speak a word of Russian", he said. "I'm wondering what the heck you're doing here".

"I came to convince your brother to partici-pate in a documentary film about the events of 1965," I answered in fluent Russian, a response that left him gasping for the air. He gave me big smile, sat down and indicated that the ice was broken. "Then everything is fine", he responded. "Should I go out and get some vodka?" I had to decline his kind offer: it was still too early in the morning.

Pram appeared suddenly, accompanied by his wife and several relatives. He was frail, un-shaven and smoked his clove cigarettes like a chimney, one after another.

He could hardly hear, so questions had to be screamed directly into his ear. I was sweating lib-erally as the sun climbed steadily, beating merci-lessly on the roof and the walls of the house. As in most of dwellings in Java, there were no air-conditioners.

Pram asked several questions and we got involved in a conversation about the books of Noam Chomsky, about Z-Magazine and the World Social Forum. He asked me to convey my greetings and thanks to Chomsky: "for all that he had done to help to uncover the truth about Indonesia's past". He then asked how old Chomsky was. "73? That's good: he's still young man compared to me," he said, laughing.

There was no hint of arrogance in his behaviour. If anything, he was warm-hearted, sarcastic, laugh-ing and joking; his face constantly changing and expressive. However, when I asked him about the Indonesian press, his tone of voice changed: "I have become so impatient with them. They come here and ask me all those stupid questions… They don't know what they are talking about…I really cannot deal with them."

He happily accepted our invitation to participate in the film and invited us to his main dwell-ing, an isolated house in a remote suburb of Jakarta called Bojong Gede, Depok.

After a while, his facial expression changed again. He suddenly looked very old and vulnera-ble: "Sometimes I feel very isolated. I'm living in my own world and it's like being in internal exile. I'm wondering if people still care about what I really think…"

I told him that they did and still do, that proba-bly hundreds of thousands of men and women all over the world would like to read his thoughts, especially now, after his long years of his literary silence.

"I'm never going to write anything, any-more", he said. "I can't: I simply can't write. My last book will be just a collection of some old letters that I sent, years ago, to several important political and cultural figures."

Without much thinking I said "So why don't we write a book together? I will be working in Indo-nesia for several months. Why don't we try to re-create the past, together? Why don't you say all that you always wanted to say and never did?"

To my surprise, he wasn't hesitating at all. "Let's do it, then", he agreed. He expressed only one doubt about whether he and I were 'good for each other', hardly surprising considering that it was the US that brought down Sukarno and des-troyed Indonesia, after all!

Before leaving his house, he confessed that later this afternoon he was intending to travel to East Java by bus. "I want to see Indonesia again." As we stood up to shake hands, he al-most fainted from exhaustion. I had to carry him to his relatives, shocked by the fragility of his body.

Back in the crowded centre of Jakarta, we were overwhelmed by the weight of the enor-mous re-sponsibility that was falling upon us. It was going to be us who would be bringing the last words and thoughts of the author of "The Girl from the Coast" and of "Buru Quartet" to the world, one of the founders of Indonesia and the committed opponent of Suharto's terror.

All doubts disappeared two months later when we sat with Pram in his dark living room around a large circular table. Two recorders were running and the endless smoke curling from his cigarettes was colouring the air and ca-ressing the ceiling. He hardly looked at us. Sometimes we weren't sure whether he was aware about our presence: he seemed to accept our questions as if they were coming from some abstract, undefined source. His mind was trav-elling in the far remote past, in a different Indonesia, a country that both of us were too young to remember. We were in his Indonesia, an imaginary country forever lost.

It was obvious that he wanted to speak, that he had to speak, and there we were, trying to help him to discard the burden of his accumu-lated knowledge and pain by asking the ques-tions that had, for decades, been forbidden even to be asked.

Have you ever written specifically about the Indone-sian dictatorship and the impact it had on you and on people close to you?

Only in my letters and notes, and sometimes in my books. These things come directly from in-side, but I have never written about it directly, as a memory.

Have you ever published a book in the form of ques-tions and answers?

No, this format has only been used in inter-views with me – interviews for magazines and news-papers. Nevertheless, I really welcome your idea of creating such a book. However, I can foresee a problem about writing this book with you. You are an American. Indonesia col-lapsed mainly because of the United States. In the past, Indonesia had chosen its own way, the path of development advocated by President Sukarno. He was our true leader. However, what was the US reaction? The then President Eisenhower issued orders to depose our freely-elected President! I know they still hate Sukarno in your country because he strongly de-nounced colonialism, imperialism and capitalism, even though he was a colonial product himself. That makes me wonder if we are right for each other – to write this book together. On the other hand, when I was serving my time in prisons and camps, I was helped by American people.

But that's exactly why we want to write this book with you. We have to tell the truth about the past – and how it influenced the presence – to both your readers here and to your readers in the West.

Yes, I agree. So, why don't we try to write this book? I have so much to say. I want to speak about the young generations and about the stu-dents who fought until Suharto was forced to resign. I want to speak about other times, the occasions when people were hunted down, killed, and dumped into the sea. I have no ac-cess to the media and no organisation to sup-port me. I am burning inside. You came here so we can talk, so now I can open up and bother you with all the frustrations and curses that have accumulated inside me over long decades.

WRITING

Q-100: You are considered the greatest Indonesian writer of all times. Does your literary work have any impact on the nation?

A: There is a group of young people who call themselves 'Pramists' (*laughing*). It seems that the impact is sufficient: even Gus Dur, the former Indonesian President Abdurahman Wahid, said that my '*Buru Quartet*' could easily become his bible. Nevertheless, in this country, people keep writing about my personal life, not about my literary work. As a writer, I don't always exist. There are many books about Indonesian literature, but not one mentions my name.

I've documented everything that people in Indonesia and abroad have written about me. I've documented it and filed it each year. I've even drawn up some statistics: the total usually comes to between 600 and 1,000 pages a year. Part of my documentation has been accepted by the Library of Congress in the United States. Let me tell you how it happened.

Two years ago, some Islamic youth movements were looking for documents related to my work: they were determined to confiscate and destroy everything. Fortunately, it was saved by the United States Embassy, which allowed me to store the documents in its compound. When the situation calmed down, they returned them to me, but in the wrong order. I queried it, and they explained that while they had the documents in the embassy, they copied everything and sent it to the Library of Congress.

Q-101: You write exclusively in Indonesian language. No doubt, it's a beautiful language, but is it rich? Is it a good language for writing novels?

A: The Indonesian language is useless, especially when it's used by the mass media. Whenever it stumbles over some complex issue, it immediately switches to English. It's really limiting and has no character.

One language that I really admire is Japanese.

However, when it comes to my own writing, I find the Indonesian language quite adequate for my needs. When I can't find appropriate expressions in Indonesian, I borrow words from the Javanese language. What else can I do? I have to show an example, because the Language Commission has no influence and does nothing to reinforce rules and regulations regarding linguistic purity. During the Japanese occupation, the commission was alive and effective, because it was backed by a Japanese determination to outlaw the languages of their enemies. Now it's extremely passive.

People here attach almost no importance to the development of their language. I wrote a book about the history of the Indonesian language: unfortunately, they burned the manuscript during the dictatorship and I never managed to re-write it. As you know, writing can't be repeated.

Q-102: This is a nation of more than 200,000,000 people. Apart from you, are there any more writers, film-makers, or other artists who can offer a strong moral voice to the nation, become a symbol of opposition?

A: No. The only young writer I can stomach enough to read his work, or at least five or seven pages of it, is Seno Gumira Ajidarma, but don't forget that he had been brought up abroad in the United States. His thoughts are more democratic then those of the others. However, I can't stomach the older generation of Indonesian writers either. It doesn't mean that I'm being arrogant: it's just a fact.

Q-103: All large nations, such as China, India, Russia, United States, Brazil, and Japan, have countless renowned writers. Nigeria – a country with a similarly brutal and complex past as Indonesia – offers to the world literary giants like Soyinka, Acebe and Habila, as well as daring new voices like those of Chimamanda Ngozi Adichie. Why is it that present-day Indonesia is not giving birth to any great novelists or poets? Why are you the only influential novelist that Indonesia has produced?

A: The situation here is different. The life experi-ence of most Indonesian writers is different from mine. I spent all my life fighting. I first fought against the Japanese occupation and, later, on the side of Sukarno's revolution. I was deeply involved in nation and character building. That's what is lacking now. Nobody even talks about the nation and building its character any more. Writers should feel a great obligation towards their nations: they can't just write whatever they like. I realised that from the very beginning, and that's what makes me different.

Q-104: Is it religion, or a cult of obedience, that is stifling creativity?

A: Look, if I answer this question honestly, most of the people here will get very angry!

Q-105: Eight of your valuable manuscripts were destroyed by the military. How traumatic was the experience?

A: It was acutely painful, very traumatic. I feel the pain until now. When I recall what happened, I still suffer, especially in the knowledge that I will never be able to rewrite those books. At the time, I was in prison, so there was nothing I could have done to save the manuscripts. Those books could have been published by now. When I was in prison, however, I was officially accused of being a Communist and no publishing house in Indonesia dared to think of publishing any of my books.

Q-106: Which manuscripts were destroyed?

A: A series on Kartini, an Indonesian national hero, including three books and a collection of Kartini's original writings. There was a book I wrote on the history of Indonesian language and two sequential volumes of *The Girl from the Coast*. Sorry, but right now I can't recall the eighth one.

Q-107: How did you react ?

A: It was really a character assassination: what they did to my books, they did to me. Now I just pity the people responsible – they only demonstrated the depths to which their culture had sunk. At the time, I took it as a challenge and continued writing in prison. My writing was my answer to them: by continuing, I showed that my culture was superior. That's how I fought them. I don't know how other people fought, but that's what I did. I was always taught how to fight and it kept me alive! By now, my friends who were unable to fight are dead.

Q-108: How did this experience affect your creative life? Are you angry about all those years spent in prisons and camps, about having your manuscripts burned by regime?

A: I don't feel angry at all. I see it as an example of the debasement of my nation's culture. I use my writing to show that my culture is more advanced than that of others in Indonesia. I use my writing as a counter-attack. I never give up, not even now. The communication gap between the others and me is sometimes too wide.

One day, I was summoned to the Supreme Court. The person who met me spoke continuously, but I understood nothing. After two hours, he started to make a little sense, and then said, "Mr. Pram, we are from the Supreme Court and we would like to ask you to change your views at least a little bit." My answer was "Those who made me like this were my own countrymen. If they want me to change just a little bit, they have to change a little bit, too. Moreover, after what I just told you, I'll not come again even if you try to summon me. If the Supreme Court needs me, it has to come to my house."

Q-109: The first part of The Girl From the Coast *ended with your grandmother leaving the aristocrat's compound where she had been abused and humiliated. What was going to be the continuation of the story; what had you written in the second and third volume of the novel?*

A: The story continued with the relationship between my grandmother and my mother and with my own personal testimonies.

Q-110: The Girl from the Coast is probably your most daring attempt so far to define Javanism. *In a poetic and subdued manner it exposes cult of compliance and hierarchy.*

A: Yes, exactly. I tried to show that. I'm against the entire Javanese culture.

Q-111: Despite the criticism there was much love for, and understanding of Java and its culture. Was it really intended just as a criticism, or was it also a tribute?

A: Do you really see it like that? From all that comprises Javanese culture I love only *gamelan* music (*laughing*). I don't even like Javanese dancing: I prefer Flamenco (*laughing*).

Q-112: Read outside Indonesia, The Girl from the Coast *doesn't appear to be only a critique of Indonesian or Javanese culture.*

A: But it is. All Javanese people know is how to work and to obey. They don't care if they are exploited and they don't care who exploits them: they just work. As a nation, ultimately they are dreaming one collective dream: how not to work at all. However, in the real world they just keep working and working. The longer and harder they work, more exploited they are.

I wrote about the life of Javanese people in my book *Tales from Blora*, although then I still didn't see the whole picture as I see it now. These days, I try to understand the broader picture. Then, I was just describing what I saw. By the way, as we speak, 'Tales from Blora' is being published in the United States and *The Girl from the Coast* has been published in Greek last month. That makes me happy.

Q-113: While writing the Buru Quartet, *did you have an entire concept in your mind or were you working on each book separately? Had the idea to write it come to you in Buru?*

A: Even before I was sent to Buru I already had the concept: the groundwork for this series of novels had been very broad. One part was done by my students. Let me tell you a story about how it hap-pened. One day, a professor from Leiden University paid me a visit, and offering me an opportunity to lecture to classes at *Res Publica University*. I responded, "How can I teach at a university if I never finished junior high school?" (*laughing*). Nevertheless, he insisted and finally I felt I had no choice but to ac-

cept.

When I was faced with the class, I had no idea of what to teach or how to teach it. After a while, I came up with a solution. I asked each of my students to go through the old newspapers starting with those from the beginning of the century, and to produce papers describing each period in our history. These papers gave me important guidance for the concept: that's how I gathered materials for the Quartet.

Using my students' notes, I was able to write *Sang Pemula* (*The Pioneer*). With the concept in my head and with all this material from my students it was easy; all I had to do was to sit down and type the book.

Q-114: How do you physically write your books? Do you use a pen or a typewriter? How many times do you usually re-write each manuscript?

A: I use a typewriter and I never rewrite my manuscripts. That's the way I create: always a single attempt, and no rewriting. After my work is published, I never read it again. If I read it after writing it myself, there would always be a desire to change something in the text (*laughing*).

Of course, in Buru camp I had to use a pen.

Q-115: How old were you when you decided to become a writer?

A: I started writing in 1947, because I needed to take care of my younger brothers and sisters. At that time, I had to write like mad in order to get some money. I didn't know how to do any other work, so I just wrote (*laughing*). You could tell that I wrote in order to survive. From the beginning, it seemed that readers enjoyed my writing, so I chose to continue. By the way, some of my early work will be reprinted soon. I'm always glad when they reprint my old books, maybe because I can't write anymore. Who knows why? Maybe because I smoke too much? (*laughing*)

Q-116: What were your writing habits? Did you write at night or during the day? Did you impose a schedule on yourself?

A: I never had any schedule and wrote when-ever I felt like it. If I didn't feel like writing, I didn't do it: very simple. I don't impose forced labour on myself.

Q-117: Are you disciplined? How many months or years did it take you, on average, to write one novel?

A: I'm not disciplined at all. I write whenever I want to and that makes me feel free. That's why I've never disciplined myself when working on a novel. It all depends upon my mood, really. I never burdened myself with a schedule, so I can't answer your question about how long it takes to write, because it's always different, it varies from book to book.

Q-118: What inspires you? How do you get yourself into a writing mood? Do you take a walk, do you smoke; do you drink coffee? Is it hard to get yourself to the table to start working on a book?

A: I get my inspiration from life. When some-thing touches me or outrages me, it fires my in-spiration. Writing is always a fight: it's all about struggle! In all of my books, I promote the fight-ing spirit. I was raised to be a fighter.

Q-119: Were you ever nominated for the Nobel Prize for literature?

A: Sure, I was nominated almost every year. It's not surprising, because my books had already been translated into many languages. However, I never expected I would win that prize. If I were offered it, I would accept, although if it happened now, I don't know if I could travel to receive it. I'm old now. I've just received an in-vitation to travel to Norway next month to re-ceive their literary award, but I can't go because of my health.

Q-120: Does the Nobel Prize mean anything to you, or do you consider it just a subjective, conservative; Euro-centric award?

A: It doesn't mean that much to me, and maybe that's why I'm not really expecting it. If you get an award like that, all it actually means is that your books will sell more copies. If I earned some money from that, I would use it to finish my encyclopae-dia project. I've already col-lected about four metres of material, but still can't finish it. I try not to ex-pect too much from the outside world. I learnt to expect things only from myself. I never even asked for anything from my own parents.

Q-121: Had you ever made an attempt to rewrite at least some of those books that were destroyed?

A: No, one can write a book only once. The sur-roundings and the mood one is submerged in during the writing can't be recreated.

Q-122: Now, honestly, what are your true feelings towards the Javanese culture and society? We dis-cussed this topic for many days, but I feel that there is still much you are keeping to yourself; highlight-ing only negative aspects of it. You were betrayed and suffered badly. Nevertheless, you're purely an Indonesian writer, after all. All that you write about is directly connected to Indonesia. Even when you speak about the worst aspects of its culture in its past and present, isn't it still a combination of pain and love that you feel towards it, or is it just pain and anger that's left?

A: When I experienced injustice, I didn't really feel angry because I realised that my personal culture was on a higher level than that of those who were committing the crimes. I still feel the same. When I published *Hoa Kiau di Indonesia* (*The Chinese in Indo-nesia*), I was immediately ac-cused of being a traitor. As a result, they kept me in prison without a trial.

About love: ever since I was young, everything I ever did was for Indonesia. Many people sug-gest-ed that I should leave, but my roots are here. I can't live outside this country, even though if I were to live in the United States I would be paid between two and five thousand dollars for each appearance or speech (*laughing*).

Q-123: But while you remain in Indonesia, you are enclosing yourself entirely within your own world...

A: I still think about Indonesia all the time, that's why I feel so much pain. I don't have any organisa-tion or my own media, so I keep every-thing inside. I can't write books, anymore, so I can communicate what's inside me only when I get visitors like you.

Q-124: Do you believe that the greatest service any

writer can give to a nation is to reveal its flaws, even if it means exposing its darkest and most sinister secrets?

A: No. I discipline myself to see the world dialectic-ally, so I don't portray only the dark side. I also try to show good aspects. If I only dealt with the dark-er elements, I'd probably become ill (*laughing*).

Q-125: Do you sometimes wake up in the middle of the night, thinking about something that you forgot to say or to write?

A: Even if I did, I no longer have the strength to correct it. I can't write a single line anymore. I've become a gong that only sounds when touched by other people. Don't forget, next year I'll turn eighty if I'm still alive. I know that there are people like Chomsky who are almost my age but still active, but they haven't lived such an abnormal life as me.

Q-126: Which literary or philosophical figures influenced your writing? Whom do you really admire?

A: When I was young, I read the works of the Greek philosophers from Aristotle to Socrates. After that, I didn't read any other philosophers, because I got bored. I was influenced by Maxim Gorki and John Steinbeck. I like Socialist Realism because it deals with social responsibilities.

As I mentioned before, in Buru I was saved by in-ternational monitors. That's why I have to re-iterate my gratitude to the international community. Even my family was supported by some eminent people, including Gunter Grass. At one time, Gunter Grass urged the Indonesian government to release me, which led to his being deported from the country. That's him! I still keep his photograph on the wall. Later, in 1999, I met Gunter Grass in Germany. When I returned to Indonesia after meeting him, I learned that he'd just received the Nobel Prize for literature.

Q-127: In what language have you read Maxim Gorki?

A: I read him in English and Dutch, but the English edition was published in Moscow.

Q-128: Would you describe yourself as a Marxist?

A: No, I'm not a Marxist, I'm a *Pramist.* I never fol-low any ideology or the teaching of others. I only follow my own beliefs. However, I do believe in social justice and equality.

Q-129: Are you sure you'll write no more books?

A: I'm sure. I simply can't do it. I realised it eight years ago. Later, in the year 2000, I had a stroke while working on my field. I'd been working for full hour when it began to rain very hard. I retired to the hut and slept there for some time but when I opened my eyes, I saw the whole world in a purple colour and realised that my strength was gone. When I tried to continue working, I found I could not even lift the shovel: all my strength had ebbed away.

I'm not able to write anything. I get letters from all over the world but I can't respond to any of them.

Q-130: How about articles for the newspapers and magazines?

A: I'm just filing everything. All I'm planning to publish, besides this book that we're working on now, is a collection of old letters. In the past, I wrote to many influential people, including Presi-dent Clinton, but now I can't find the letter I sent to him. I was also collecting materials for an encyclo-paedia of the Indonesian archipelago that would offer in-depth information about its villages, cities, rivers, mountains and oceans, but I can't finish that work, either.

Q-132: If you still had enough strength to write, what would it be?

A: I don't have any desire to write anymore. I'm just waiting for my death to arrive. Many people have suggested that I speak and they would put my thoughts in writing, but I'm not used to team-work. I feel I've already said all there was to say. The only thing that hurts me tremendously, the thing that I do want to discuss, is Indonesia's pres-ent terrible condition. It doesn't coincide with my childhood dreams, and that's why I agreed to write this book with you.

As I said, I can't write anymore, but I still have to sign many bills (*laughing*).

AMERICAN INVOLVEMENT

Q-149: Indonesia managed to kill millions of their own people after the coup of 1965, in Aceh, Papua, Ambon and elsewhere. On the other hand, the United States doesn't usually kill its own people en masse but helps to destroy nations and kill millions in foreign lands by following its economic and geopolitical interests. Which do you consider more evil?

A: Both, of course! (*laughing*). By the way, don't forget that the Americans massacred their own indigenous population and then, after they finished, probably thought that the rest of the world was inhabited by Red Indians too, so they just continued with the same policy.

Seriously, had Sukarno not been deposed by the US, the present world would be a very different place. It's such a shambles now. Although I was personally helped by American people when I was in prison and my books were banned in Indonesia, I consider US foreign policy to be a total disaster! Iraq, for example! What are they doing there – occupying it? Even here in Indonesia, the Americans used to bomb the Moluccas islands during the Sukarno era.

Q-150: What role did the U.S. and the West play in Suharto's dictatorship? The Americans got everything they wanted: great deals for their multinational companies often signed – after substantial bribes – by Suharto himself; an obedient workforce, a society which never dared to openly revolt. Papua and Aceh – areas with tremendous natural wealth had been brutally oppressed. Billions of dollars in forcefully dispersed foreign loans – which disappeared in corruption – assured that Indonesia lost its economic independence. Indonesia became so anti-communist that even words like "atheism" and "class" (referring to the social classes) were banned.

A: The role was played by capital: by money! Western countries wanted to convert the world, including Indonesia, into their playground. In reality, in Indonesia that was very difficult to achieve because of the culture of corruption here. Elites here couldn't be trusted, so their plans failed.

Q-151: What was their strategy for securing the co-operation of Indonesian military?

A: They trained Indonesian military personnel in the United States. They supplied them with wea-pons and, of course, many high-ranking military officers were indoctrinated by an American way of thinking. Indoctrination itself has had an enormous impact on this society; especially the anticommun-ist sentiments implanted by the United States.

This sort of indoctrination is conducted by the United States all over the world. There is nothing democratic about it, despite the fact that the US tries to present itself as a democratic society.

Back in Indonesia after being indoctrinated, our military did the killing. The US was betting on the right horse: the military is the only organisation that can perform extermination on such a scale.

It all sounds like an old song, doesn't it? The US attacks many counties all over the world, so it's not a big deal for them to destroy one or two.

Q-152: To what extent can the US be blamed for 1965/1966 killings in Indonesia?

A: The extent of the U.S.'s culpability isn't clear to me. One thing that's obvious is that the US never condemned the massacres. Never! In fact, the West-ern media welcomed those events enthusiastically. I think that there was cooperation between the US and the Indonesian military during the killing, but I have no concrete proof.

Nowadays, documents disclosing this cooperation are appearing, especially in Holland. However, based on what you said, the American public doesn't know much about what happened here in Indonesia and about the involvement of its own country. That's because Americans never pay much attention to foreign affairs, maybe because they consider themselves superior to people from other nations. Look at what's happening in Iraq: and they may invade other countries in the near future, too!

I'm sure that the issue of US involvement in the 1965 coup in Indonesia was covered by at least some of the progressive and specialized publica-tions in America. Even my own writing is well known in the United States. Ironically, some pub-lishing houses in Asia still refuse to publish my work. However, that's never happened in America: they've always published my books there. I have no idea if the American public accepts my point of view, but last month my book 'Tales from Blora' appeared on the bookshelves there, and it's selling well.

Q-153: Some documents show, and several scholars believe, that the US and Indonesian military were planning the 1965 coup together.

A: The mightiest weapon of the United States has always been its dollar: don't forget that, and don't forget that Eisenhower, then the US President, ordered deposing Sukarno. Eisenhower himself gave the speech underlining this issue. The CIA used Suharto. The United States had enormous influence over the Indonesian military and, later, over *Golkar*. Even when we were political prisoners, we knew that the United States had been behind everything that happened.

Q-154: What interests were involved? Why was the US so eager to help Suharto?

A: It all happened because they wanted to depose Sukarno. During the Cold War, Sukarno refused to side with the West, while maintaining excellent re-lations with the People's Republic of China. Since China was a Communist country, Sukarno was considered an enemy by the West and thus had to be deposed. As I just said, even President Eisen-hower made no secrets about it. Can you imagine it? A President of one country openly saying that the President of another sovereign country should be deposed!

After the decision had been made, the rest was just a job for the CIA. For the West, the main issue of 1965 was how to get rid of Sukarno.

After that happened, all Sukarno's supporters were thrown into prison or murdered. Western involvement in Indonesia in 1965 was directly linked to the Cold War. Those who suffered the most were Communists. I had also been accused of being a Communist, although that's rubbish! A Sukarno supporter, yes, but not a Communist. I'm a Pramist!

Q-155: Would right-wing forces and the military in Indonesia have been able to carry out the coup without the US determination to depose Sukarno?

A: It would be almost unthinkable. Sukarno was loved by his people.

Q-156: Before 1965, was there any visible influence or mingling of the United States in Indonesian affairs?

A: Of course. The United States bombed Indonesian territory from their bases in Philippines – and they never apologized for attacking us directly!

Q-157: Which part of Indonesian territory was bombed?

A: Our northern islands near the Philippine archipelago.

Q-158: What was the reaction of the Indonesian government and military? Did they try to defend their territory?

A: During one bombing mission, the Indonesian forces managed to shoot down an aeroplane and capture the pilot, Allan Poe. However, as many Indonesian military officers were trained in the United States, what else could you expect? Nothing happened.

I'm an admirer of Ho Chi Minh. He led a peasant rebellion that grew to a revolution and drove both France and the US from his country. The US was furious when the Vietnamese decided to go their own way and then overcame their invasion! Later they tried to prevent Indonesia from becoming another Vietnam – that's what all it was about.

Q-159: Was it an act of intimidation or did they bomb some particular targets for specific reasons?

A: The bombing was performed in to give moral support to the people of the Moluccas who were trying to secede from Indonesia. Most of the people from Sulawesi and the Moluccas are of Christian faith and there seemed to be a link between them and the United States. In addition, the United States has an historic animosity towards Islam – you can see it even now.

The United States should have helped us to build democracy, instead of teaching us terrible lessons that we never asked for. How can one help with building democracy in other country? First, one has to act democratically himself; one has to show example.

BEFORE PARTING

Q-183: Where does Indonesia fit into the world today?

A: What can I say about the world? We hardly know anything about the world here, and the world knows nothing about Indonesia. In South-east Asia, Indonesia's reputation is one of a sick person and that stigma doesn't go away. For my part, I've done everything I could for Indonesia, but look what it did to me in return. My books had been translated into thirty-six languages, but I have never been respected in Indonesia itself. I'm being respected abroad but not here. When I was in the middle of the struggle against this system, ironic-ally it was America that honoured me with awards. Then I received support and recognition from other countries, but never from my own nation.

Q-184: Based on what you just declared, did you make your decision to remain silent because you felt that you had nothing to add to what you'd already said and writ-ten, or because you were hurt by your country and its culture?

A: It's much simpler. I really can't write anymore. I know my limits and I've reached them, so I have to stop here. I want to stop dreaming. That's the trag-edy of an old age and I'm not complaining, because when I was young, I never even imagined that I could reach this age. My experience in Buru hard-ened me, but now I'm tired.

I live within myself. I can't do anything about it. I can talk freely only when my friends come to visit me. When I think about Indonesia, I feel a burning inside me, and it never goes away.

Q185: So you live in internal exile?

A: Yes, in internal exile, in my own world. Outside my world, there is only corruption. Sukarno, our leader, is no more. Since I was a young man, I've given everything I had to Indonesia, and now I believe that I've already given enough. Nothing good came back in return. The country for which I fought is now decaying, so how could I not feel wrath? It became the exact opposite of the dreams of my youth. These days, so many memories come back to me. Most of the people I knew are gone. Two million human beings were murdered and rivers were clogged with dead bodies. How can people kill others just like that? I can't talk about it, anymore. It's too emotional.

Let's stop here...

Pramoedya Ananta Toer

Andre Vltchek

Pramoedya Ananta Toer, the most important Southeast Asian novelist and prominent Indonesian dissident, died in Jakarta in the morning of April 30.

"Look what Indonesia did to me, after all that I have done for Indonesia!" These were the words with which Pramoedya Ananta Toer – one of the greatest novelists of the 20th century – concluded long conversations with me and Rossie Indira, conversations recently published in English as "Exile" and in Bahasa Indonesia as "Saya Terbakar Amarah Sendirian," his last book and final testimony.

Pram's (Pram is how he is known and called in his country) Indonesia died more than four decades ago, crushed by the military boot of Suharto's regime, disintegrated under the weight of the savage, merciless, and corrupt capitalist system, squashed by irrational religious zeal. "I live in internal exile," he said. "This is not my country, anymore. It's not what I fought for, not what I wanted to build."

Since independence, Pram's was the lonely voice of courage and honesty. He was incarcerated during Sukarno's guided democracy for defending the rights of the Chinese minority. After the fascist, US-backed military coup in 1965 his manuscripts were burned and his work banned. He himself was arrested and thrown into a number of prisons and then into Buru concentration camp, becoming a prisoner of conscience for 14 years. "They kept repeating that I was a Communist which was not correct: I am Pramist, I have my own philosophy."

The answer to the madness outside his prison cells was to write, to produce some of the most powerful prose in the history of Asian letters. The most important Indonesian narrative – "The Buru Quartet" – was born on Buru Island, a con-cen-tration camp where some of the most outstanding minds of Indonesia were imprisoned, tortured, and killed.

Noam Chomsky wrote about Exile: "It is a rare privilege to be able to listen to the voice of a remarkable talent, who has survived shameful abuse with immense courage and dignity, and now shares his dreams, his struggles, and his pain at the decay of the country and the culture he fought so hard to revive from centuries of subjugation."

For many years, Pram had been nominated for The Nobel Price for literature, but he never re-ceived one, mainly due to the conservative nature of the jury. He was often described as the Indo-nesian Solzhenitsyn. While human rights violations by the Soviet regime were well documented and used by the West as part of Cold War propaganda, Indonesia got away with invasions as well as internal and external genocide, as it was on "our side of the barricade."

For the dominant western media, Pram was nothing more than an uncomfortable voice speak-ing about the injustice and brutality of Suharto's right-wing regime, the social collapse of Indo-nesian society, and invasions backed by the U.S. and Australia. His books were translated into 36 languages, but were steadily disappearing from prominence on the shelves of all major North American bookstores.

Living in absolute isolation, Pram didn't try to hide his bitterness about the state of his nation. He openly declared that "Indonesia has no culture" and apart from him, there is not one writer in his country who can write more than five pages of de-cent prose. He defined "Javanism" (Java is the most populous island on the Indonesian archipelago) as being closely linked to Fascism – expansionist, brutal, groupist, and at the same time submissive to any authority and religion to the extreme. He didn't believe in God but in his own strength – but above all in the strength and creativity of human beings.

His latest words were those of an immense lament over a vanished idealism, creativity, and a search for social justice in today's Indonesia. He couldn't write for more than ten years after suf-fering from a stroke and he felt impatient with the local press which he considered unprofessional and servile. Apart from Exile – his final testimony and the bitter summary of his political and artistic thoughts – he avoided creative writing altogether, surrounding himself by the memories, sitting by the window, his face covered by a cloud of smoke from his kretek cigarettes.

The world behind the window was unsettling. Indonesian streets were full of homeless children and beggars. Elites were driving their luxury se-dans, while the great majority of the people were unable to afford basic food, education for the chil-dren, or even clean water. Religious zealots were gaining strength while progressive ideas were fully censored from the media.

He felt desperate observing a decay that was consuming his nation, claiming that there is noth-ing left from the dreams which he had helped to shape during the first years after independence. He lost hope. "Even the Dutch colonial administration was better than today's government and elites." He saw revolution as the only way to fight a system based on immorality, corruption, and cynicism. "The present system can't be reformed. To reform the New Order would only create a New-New Order. What is needed is revolution, but all revolutions in Indonesia were always performed by young generations. This time, the young generation is not able to give birth to a leader."

"When Pramoedya Ananta Toer goes, the last bridge between Indonesian culture and the rest of the world will collapse," said Dan Simon, editor of the Seven Stories Press in New York, after watch-ing my documentary film "Terlena – Breaking of a Nation," in which Pram plays the role of the main narrator. We both agreed that in present-day Indo-nesia there is no other figure who can communicate to the world tremendous moral strength and digni-ty through the highest level of artistic excellence.

Now Pram is gone and Indonesia is mourning. But instead of spilling tears, the greatest tribute to this extraordinary man would be to do what mil-lions of men and women all over the world have done for decades – read his books and understand the pain he was lately carrying inside: burning pain from the fact that the country he helped to build and define became nothing more than a failed state.

Are We Alone, Arundhati Roy?

Andre Vltchek

[In 2002] I met the famous novelist Arundhati Roy in the coffee shop of Park Hotel in Delhi. What was supposed to be a short encounter became a few hours long heated discussion. We discussed poli-tics and we discussed the mounting problems in India, but we also talked of the state of literature, a topic about which we both felt passionate. We agreed that almost all great modern writers seemed to be in a lethargic sleep or were too frightened to address impor-tant global issues. Or maybe there were almost no great writers left.

Philosophy, politics, social criticism and vision were replaced by frivolous, entertaining plots. The pitiful state of today's world, its dis-parities and scandalous post-colonial arrange-ment topped the list of some of the issues hardly discussed on the pages of contemporary novels. Fiction had become politically and socially de-tached and therefore historically and morally ir-relevant. Instead of aiming at retaining their status as "the conscience of society," most writ-ers opted for much more modest goals, turning themselves into entertainers and showbiz fig-ures.

Great nonfiction writers were still around, writ-ing brilliant books in the West, in India, and in Latin America, but the novel, a literary form so dear to both of us, seemed to be fin-ished, sold out and stained by an apparent – al-though somehow hesitant – collaboration with the business and com-mercial interests of those who ruled our societies.

We parted in front of my hotel. I gave her a gift – a silk scarf from Vietnam – she gave me a hug, then entered her little beat-up car and drove away. I waved for a while, standing on the pavement, overwhelmed with absolute cer-tainty that I had just parted with one of the bravest writers of our time.

Since then I have not had a chance to meet her again, but while working in the South Pa-cific I came across an issue of the Australian magazine *The Bulletin*, which carried a long arti-cle on Arundhati Roy by Jennifer Byrne: "…I'm actually a writer, and this is what writers do and have done through centuries – commenting on the societies in which they live. But now be-cause writing and literature has become a kind of quote unquote com-mercial activity, it's dumbed them down like noth-ing ever has be-fore, so we are supposed to be some kind of court entertainers."

Ms. Byrne asked whether there was really such a tradition, or was she just being wishful? "Yeah, there was," answered Arundhati Roy. "Who were Sartre and George Orwell? And to-day it's reduced to something almost like toys, not even rigorous in your analysis. I mean who are the big writers today who have taken on what is huge in the world? Very few – unless they are on the other side. Like V.S. Naipaul commenting the other day that Saudi Arabia and Iran should be destroyed."

How could one disagree with Arundhati Roy? Of course such a tradition had been there for centuries, helping humanity move forward. The greatest writers stood at the vanguard of the struggle against racism, colonialism, and imperialism. They promoted social justice, fought for changes. Romaine Rolland, Anatole France, Emile Zola, and Maxim Gorky had placed themselves on the side of exploited, en-slaved human beings, demanding immediate change, even revolution.

George Bernard Shaw – probably the greatest modern British playwright – had consistently ridi-culed the entire capitalist dogma, and his German counterpart – Bertolt Brecht – had openly called to arms against it.

There had been an entire generation of out-standing novelists and thinkers in postwar France: Jean-Paul Sartre, Albert Camus, and Si-mone de Beauvoir to name just a few. All three had been active members of the anti-fascist re-sistance, all three had condemned the postwar arrangement of the world. In those days, philosophers and writers were not confined to university campuses: when Sartre addressed workers at a Renault factory, his speeches drew to the premises hundreds of thou-sands of men and women who had no problem understanding what he was talking about.

There had been great novelists like Andre Mal-roux, Ernest Hemingway, and Saint-Exupery (auth-or of a famous philosophical book for children and adults – *The Little Prince*), writers who fought in wars, engaging themselves not only by words but also by deeds. And their books were then selling millions of copies, despite the complex and often controversial topics they were addressing.

In the United States, Richard Wright shocked his readers all over the world with the novel *Native Son*, a damning, powerful and honest account of racism and discrimination against African Ameri-cans. A few decades later, Joseph Heller described the insanity of World War II in *Catch-22* and later the hypocrisy of corporate America in *Good as Gold*.

Latin America had offered some of the greatest novelists of the 20th century: Carlos Fuentes, Alejo Carpentier, Gabriel Garcia Marquez, and Manuel Puig from the left, as well as Jorge Borges and Mar-ia Vargas Llosa from the other side of the political spectrum. In Africa, Acebe described the destruct-tion of local cultures by colonialism in his novel *Things Fall Apart*, while the Indonesian Pramoedya Ananta Toer defined brilliantly the painful process of the birth of the young nation and its horrific downfall after fascist coup in 1965.

These were just a few examples from the past, and the list was endless. The fact is that almost all great literature since ancient Greece has dealt with the most important issues facing humanity: from Homer to Victor Hugo to Franz Kafka to Albert Camus. That the modern writers were stubbornly refusing to address the serious problems of the world was a disturbing anomaly, an exception from the historic rule; proof that something had gone terribly wrong, even in the societies that proudly claimed their intellectual brilliance. The history of literature simply had not known any other period like this!

The world is full of tremendous stories. Global market fundamentalism and neoconservative cul-ture are overthrowing all democratic principals for which humanity has fought for centuries. Millions of people are dying having no access to medicine, while pharmaceutical conglomerates (backed by the governments of rich countries) are blocking de-veloping nations from producing cheap drugs that would save their men, women, and children.

Humanity is experiencing new colonial wars as well as religious and business extremism. Small island nations may soon disappear due to global warming. The gap between rich and poor nations is growing. The quality of life in the United States is declining, while Europe is dismantling its welfare system. There is confusion and dissatisfaction in many developed countries, and there is anger and growing resentment toward the rich world in most of the desperate nations. In many poor places, conservative forms of religions are dangerously filling the gap left after the systematic destruction of so-cial movements and progressive governments.

Great stories are plentiful: they are offering themselves in the desperate shantytowns of Lima and Jakarta, in the fast-food restaurants and sweat-shops in the US where underprivileged men, wom-en, and children are laboring at minimum wage; in the battlefields of the Middle East, Southeast Asia, and Africa, in the indigenous huts of Mexico, Bol-ivia, and Guatemala as well as in the small island nations of the South Pacific that are slowly but irreversibly disappearing from the face of the earth.

These are stories of monumental proportions, honest and good stories, stories that can terrify while evoking compassion; stories that can call for action – stories that the novel as a form is capable of telling.

If there is no lack of great stories, is there a lack of great writers? Or have they been si-lenced, side-lined and marginalized? Have they been broken and starved, or maybe forced to accept some regu-lar job that allows them to survive but prevents them from writing? Have they sold out, writing romance novels and self improvement books, pro-ducing hundreds of pages describing their erec-tions, coming of age, getting old or trying to solve some fictitious criminal plot?

There are still great novelists left; not many, but there are some. Jose Saramago, Arundhati Roy, Tariq Ali, even Salman Rushdie who is presently levitating in some strange realm while we, down here, are hoping that he may soon land again on the progressive side of the barricade. There is still Gunter Grass and Garcia Marquez.

But there is also an acute lack of young writers, angry and daring, determined to change the world and to offer new alternatives to the stale intellectu-al swamp created by market/business fundament-alism and its faithful servant – the cheap, thought-destroying entertainment industry that has lately swallowed almost all major publishing houses and independent bookstores.

It is easy and correct to a certain degree to say that it is now almost impossible to write a great novel against the establishment, while expecting it to be published and promoted. Media and publish-ing houses are far from being independent. Most of them are part of large companies which will be hardly ecstatic about printing books dangerous to their own interests and designs.

But the process of writing should never be fully influenced by mercantile considerations. A writer is a storyteller, an artist, a witness, a judge and a thinker. He or she leaves important testimony about a particular time and puts on record what others would often not even dare to pronounce. Financial reward is important (as reward for any hard work should be), but longing for it can never influence the choice of the subject or style in which the book is written. If it does, the result is almost certainly rubbish.

I believe that the novel is the most complete ar-tistic form capable of describing reality, the state of the world, the grievances and hopes of the people. I also believe that it should never aim at anything less than that.

I've attempted to write novels that show the world through the eyes of war correspondents, vis-iting places that are rarely covered by the domin-ant media, offering provocative points of view that are hardly acceptable to the present world of enter-tainment which now includes most of the corporate publishing houses. And writing itself, writing the truth is a privilege and joy. It is worth any incon-venience, any hardship.

I suspect that Arundhati Roy would agree with my views. But are such novelists becoming an en-dangered, almost extinguished species? Are serious topics going to be openly ridiculed and described as outdated? Is it already happening? Are readers going to accept this approach? Are novelists really expected to become entertainers, clowns, even liars? Are we supposed to forget about all those great novels written in the past?

Or are we going to swim with all our strength against the powerful mainstream?

I don't think we have much choice. If we float, if we allow ourselves to be carried by this current, we will end up in the land of irrelevance, oblivion, and shame.

Oñate's Right Foot

Margaret Randall

How Much Coyote Remembered

O, not too much.

And a whole lot.

Enough.

–Simon Ortíz.[i]

We're driving through Las Cruces, New Mexico, on our way to the small community of Mesilla, once the largest and most important stop along the early San Antonio-Los Angeles wagon route. Lots of pioneer history here, deep traditions, meaning-ful stories.

Today Mesilla oscillates between some 2,000 regular inhabitants and up to 10,000 when the year-ly Border Book Festival or other events take place. Mesilla is lovely, a little *biscochito* of Hispanic heri-tage and pride. Old adobes line its pretty square and several blocks in each direc-tion.

Some have called this village the Santa Fe of the south, or another Santa Fe in the making. This seems specious to me. Mesilla has neither Santa Fe's sophistication (in the more positive sense of the term) nor such a catastrophic dis-tinction be-tween the very rich and those who serve them. It is what it is: a sweet and inviting village with deep Mexican/American roots.

I set the scene in this way because I believe all cultures have value. We must know how to discern what is beautiful in our traditions and in the tradi-tions of others. We must also learn what is worth preserving, what is ugly, and what we should re-member only so we can ef-fectively prevent a rep-etition of its poison. In our various indigenous cul-tures, in our His-panic or Latino cultures. Whether we are of Asian, African, or European origin, we all face this challenge.

I remember years ago attending a reading of *The Color Purple* by Alice Walker. Someone in the audi-ence challenged the author: "You're lucky," she said, "You have such a rich heritage. But what about those of us without ethnic back-grounds, what can we write about?" Alice got the young woman to reveal an interesting Ital-ian grand-mother: "We all have stories," she noted.

As we approach Mesilla, I find myself face to face with a large sign proclaiming Oñate Plaza. The name's obscenity grips me. As far as I know, I have no Indian roots. But as a human I am suddenly nauseous, revolted and very an-gry. Couldn't the local inhabitants have thought of a forebear more worthy of giving name to this small shopping mall than the sixteenth cen-tury war criminal?

Don Juan de Oñate's name adorns plazas, malls, schools and public buildings all over the American southwest. As I write, Oñate Elemen-tary School in Albuquerque is in the local news. Its students and teachers are talking about vio-lence: how to identify and prevent it. A worthy project. The irony, of course, is entirely invisible to the school or many in the community; if we have not been educated about the names we use and revere, we can neither know our history nor make the necessary connec-tions in our present. In recent years two important monuments to Oñate's memory have been erected, and another is nearing completion.

In my own Albuquerque, interest in Oñate re-surfaced over the last couple of years within the context of planning for the city's 300th birth-day celebration.[ii] Not content with remembering the Spanish Duke of Alburquerque or other less con-troversial figures, the celebration planners revived indignation over the sixteenth century mercenary. Debate, however, has been anything but even-handed. Despite a 2004 poll by the Albuquerque Journal showing that 73% of those queried object to honoring the man, projects have gone ahead unim-peded.

The area's first large statue to Oñate was erected near Española in 2002, in the small northern New Mexico town of Alcalde. The site

544

was chosen be-cause Oñate once had a home there. The statue was originally placed outside the building. Perhaps those behind the project thought it would increase civic pride and improve people's lives. One point two million dollars of tax-payer money was used to underwrite the bronze.

When a brave protestor sawed off the *conquista-dor's* right foot in tribute to the flesh and blood feet Oñate ordered cut from Acoma males in 1599, the statue was moved inside. Subsequently, because so few people visit, it was moved back out: currently standing right on the road where no passerby can miss it. Ten thousand dollars more was spent on repairing the damaged foot, and later another $12,000 went to cover the various moves.

According to Acoma artist and activist Maurus Chino, the Alcalde center pulls in a meager $700 a month. This is what citizens' tax-payer dollars fund in an area of New Mexico heavily burdened by poverty, drugs, poor education and inadequate health care. And Alcalde's wouldn't be the final New Mexico tribute to Don Juan de Oñate.

In 2005 a second statue was placed outside Al-buquerque's Museum of Art. The city's proposal to honor the *conquistador* did not meet with unanim-ous approval: local artists, Indians from Acoma Pueblo – the site of Oñate's most onerous crimes – along with people from other social sectors, brought Oñate's murderous history to the attention of the Mayor, City Counsel, Tri-Centennial Com-mittee and others. Public discussions were held. Newspaper articles and radio programs attempted to disseminate historical information about the events of 1598-99, as well as about the largely ignored 1680 Pueblo Revolution.

But once again those insisting on honoring Oñate had their way. Despite considerable protest, Albuquerque's Hispanic community, or a large and powerful enough part of it, prevailed.[iii] Another monument to Oñate would rise to remind us of abuse and annihilation, as if there was no one else in our Spanish, Mexican or New Mexican heritage whose life is worthy of tribute.

In Mexico, if you ask around it's difficult to find anyone who knows who Don Juan de Oñate was. In Spain he is but a minor footnote in the history of the conquest. It seems that only here, where he committed his atrocities, are statues commissioned in his honor. The Albuquerque statue was erected at a cost of $700,000 and occupies a central place in front of the city's Museum of Art, close to historic Old Town.

Like its predecessor, it is ugly. Bad art. Figures and their limbs confront the viewer. They are meant to be realistic but lack even a semblance of proportion. A jarring absence of overall harmony assaults the eye. Bad art is always a mistake, compounding insult and mocking artist, subject and public alike.

Why not have placed this statue, if it had to be erected, at the multi-million-dollar Hispanic Cul-tural Center on the city's south side? There, at least, it could be appreciated by the small but influential Hispanic community that wanted it and by the greater Hispanic community that did nothing to try to understand the sensibilities of the descendants of those Native Americans who suffered genocide at the hands of the *conquistador.*

The most the Hispanic community and city of Albuquerque were willing to do – an entirely inadequate concession to so many people's indignant objections – was to change the monument's name to *La entrada* (The Entrance). This "solution" honors the *conquistador* without explicitly naming him. As a compromise it reflects the failure to assume res-ponsibility that has characterized every stage of this travesty.

And this was not the end of our modern-day southwestern homage to Oñate. A third statue, this one four and a half stories high, is in the works for El Paso, Texas; it has been advertised as a monu-ment to the border, today's tribute to the carnage committed so many centuries ago. Its planners speak of the riches in land and resources won by the *conquistadores*. The monument will stand as well to today's version of such commerce: violent men crossing borders motivated by a similar greed. This is a monument as tragically coherent with the times we are living as it is abusive to the sensibili-ties of all who care.

As I worked on this essay, I heard the following story. Someone reported having seen the legs and torso of this latest monstrosity at the Sandia Pueblo gas station at I-25 and Tramway in Albuquerque. She spoke with the driver of the large rig and he told her he was driving the immense pieces south to El Paso, from Wyoming where they were made. He was having trouble with his truck. Ironic that this rendition of Oñate the butcher travels to its final destination in pieces, and that its delivery truck breaks down at precisely the point along the route which is closest to Acoma.

I am reminded of another story of similar impact. In Mexico during the 1960s an immense statue of Tlaloc, the Aztec god of rain, was being transported from its first home in the state of Vera-cruz to stand before the capital city's new Museum of Anthropology. As the eighteen-wheeler carrying the transplant passed through the *Zócalo* – scene of Spanish abuse of native peoples – a clear sky sud-denly unleashed torrential rain. We who lined the streets to welcome the majestic entity knew the god had spoken.

In El Paso, too, protest erupted. And once again those intent upon erecting the statue believed they could solve the problem by a simple name change. Rather than expressly honoring Oñate, this mon-strous monument is now called "The Equestrian."

Just so you know where I'm going with this, let me be clear about Don Juan de Oñate. He was a war criminal: no more, no less. Erecting statues in his honor is like immortalizing Custer, Hitler, Trujillo, Batista, Somoza, Pinochet, Savimbi, Milosevic, Osama bin Laden or George W. Bush.

Although descendants of the Spaniards owe an unpaid debt to descendants of the Native peoples against whom their ancestors committed genocide, our Hispanic community too has its history and the right to revere its heroes and heroines. There are many men and women who deserve the honor of remembrance. Why pick a war criminal? And why, in this time of unchecked violence, glorify the extreme violence done our indigenous sisters and brothers – and which reverberates in our national treatment of this country's Native Americans to this day?

The Pueblo Revolution of 1680 was a heroic page in our history, and one that rarely receives its due. If taught at all in our schools, it is dispatched with a paragraph or two, more often than not inac-curate. I went to grade school, middle and high school in New Mexico. I remember a quickly glossed-over lesson and no discussion – certainly none from the Indian point of view.

Oñate supporters, not surprisingly many of whom refer to the events of 1680 as excessively violent, ignore the reasons behind the revolution. The violent oppression of the Spanish occupation forced the people to expel the invaders. Theirs was an act of self-defense. It not only allowed the Indi-ans to survive, it is one of the primary reasons their cultures have remained intact. The Pueblo Revolu-tion, like the nation's early campaigns against the English or the courageous Underground Railway of Civil War time, belongs to all of us. We should all know the history. We should all be proud.

Towards the end of the seventeenth century, at what is now San Juan Pueblo, a medicine man by the name of Popé was publicly whipped for practicing his religion. Humiliated, he swore his revenge and vowed to drive the Spanish from Indian lands. Popé was a powerful leader. Despite the many different languages spoken by the peoples of the Río Grande valley and other parts of the territory, he was able to unite Keres, Tewa, Tiwa, Towa, Diné, Apache, Ute, and Comanche against the invaders.

Maurus Chino points out that this was not sim-ply a revolt, but a true revolution.[iv] And it was a revolution against what was then the most power-ful nation in the world. The Indians succeeded in driving the Spaniards from their lands, all the way back to Mexico City, and for 12 beautiful years the people were free. Following their victory, people are said to have bathed in the rivers to purge them-selves of forced bap-tism in the Catholic faith.

But with the enemy possessing such superior weaponry, freedom couldn't last. De Vargas came back into New Mexico intent upon re-claiming what the Indians had won back. Today the state of New Mexico celebrates De Vargas' campaign in the Fiesta of Santa Fe. Modern-day New Mexican apologists say they are com-memorating the bloodless re-conquest of the ter-ritory. Of course it wasn't bloodless at all. But white man's history likes to refer to its sieges as bloodless, while portraying those who fight for their land and way of life as blood-thirsty sav-ages.

Albuquerque has no monument to Popé. Several years back such a statue was proposed but was rejected out of hand because, it was said, it would have exalted violence. Yet these same decision-makers have no problem erecting statues to Oñate; his violence, in their eyes, must either have been exaggerated or it was jus-tified.[7]

By any reasonable standard – whether one is Acoma, from one of the other Pueblo tribes, Na-vajo, Apache, Hopi, Hispanic, Mexican, Latino, Chicano, African-, Asian- or European-American, or of any other origin, honoring Oñate should provoke disgust. He was no hero, even by the conquest's unequal standards. He came, occupied, converted, pillaged, raped, mu-tilated and mur-dered. He was hated by those he invaded, and wasn't all that popular with the Spanish Crown or Mexican Viceroy.

Following his exploits in what is now New Mexico, Oñate was tried for his excessive abuses at Acoma, fined a large sum of money, briefly impris-oned, exiled from Mexico for four years and ban-ished forever from New Mexico. His ti-tles were taken from him. He would never again gain favor with the Spanish Court nor be al-lowed to take part in the conquest. He ended his days as a mining inspector with only his per-sonal memories of mis-adventure for company.

Let me tell the story as I have heard it from an Acoma man.

During the cold New Mexican winter of 1598, a small group of Acoma Indians lived peace-fully some sixty miles west of what we now call Albu-querque. For as long as they could re-member, the community had inhabited this land of multicolored rock, yellow sandstone cliffs, wild sunflowers, and great open skies.

Their ancestors had come from the north, from Chaco and Mesa Verde. They spoke Kere-san and still do. At Acoma, atop two striking mesas and in the valley below, they built stone homes with win-dows of mica to let the clear light in. They made decisions from within their kivas. They cultivated corn and beans.

The Native Americans are known to have shared resources with one another. Land was com-munally owned. When the Europeans came they were shown hospitality and treated with respect – until their vile intentions became clear.

As 1598 neared its end this peaceful life would change dramatically. In April of that year Oñate and his men, as well as a group of Fran-ciscan friars, had set off from Zacatecas, Mexico in search of gold. They bore arms and the Chris-tian cross, sym-bols to this day of invasion, oc-cupation and death. When they reached the Río Grande they celebrated mass, and Oñate for-mally declared that all lands north of the river belonged to Spain and all peoples inhabiting those lands were subjects of the Spanish Crown.

Just as today's criminals avoid mentioning oil when seeking to justify their invasions and oc-cupa-tions, *La toma* (literally The Takeover) – the Spanish document of April 30th, 1598 – did not mention the search for gold but rather the sub-jugation of the people, the taking of their land and their forced conversion to Christianity. Gold didn't have to be explicitly mentioned in that document. Rumors of its existence attracted the Spanish to the southwest like Middle East-ern oil puts a glint in George W. Bush's eyes.

In December of 1598 white men in leather and steel, accompanied by others in long dark robes, rode into Acoma on horseback. This band of Span-ish *conquistadores* didn't come in friend-ship or with respect. Their mission was to claim the land and its resources, enslave the people – mutilating or mur-dering them when they wouldn't surrender – and to impose Christian-ity.

Emboldened by a racist sense of superiority, de-ceit, gunpowder and their always insatiable greed, the invaders raped and plundered with total disre-gard for the fact that an ancient belief system and communal harmony had served the people for gen-erations. Modern-day Acoma people still bear the scars of this assault. A collective post traumatic stress is written into their DNA.

Although the Acomas were conquered by surprise, trickery and superior weaponry, and although most now practice Catholicism, what's apparent to the outsider and what's practiced privately differ. Public ceremonies combine a mixture of Christianity and the older religion, while the sacred ceremonies remain completely Indian.

There are many and varied tales of conquest. None are pretty. But few rival what was perpe-trat-ed against the indigenous peoples of the American continents. Acoma stands out as a particularly ugly chapter in this long genocide. When the people re-sisted, in a battle in which some 13 soldiers were killed (among them, Oñate's nephew), the invaders retreated and re-grouped.

In January, 1599 another large force came to the mesa. An epic battle lasted three days and, accord-ing to the Spanish themselves, more than 800 men, women and children were butchered. Many males had their right foot cut off (foreshadowing the re-taliatory removal of that same foot from the statue at Alcalde). Of those whose lives were spared, young men and women between the ages of 12 and 25 were enslaved for 25 years. Sixty young girls were sent to priests in Mexico. They never returned.

Once again Don Juan de Oñate led the 1598-99 expedition. Not a lot apart from his invasive tactics is known about this man, who wasn't widely admired even in his own time and place. Some historians say he was born in Spain. Others claim he came from New Spain (Mexico) and had never set foot in Europe.

Whether from the Old or New World, there is no doubt about Oñate's intentions. He was an op-portunist who wanted honor, a title, and the riches successful conquest could bring. In the late six-teenth century the way to achieve all this was by leading an expedition into the New World's un-charted territory and claiming its land and peoples for the Spanish Crown and Cross.

Among the adventurers of the day, myths of glittering cities of gold had long since faded; and Spain had ceased promoting expeditions by maverick *conquistadores*. Unlike the other court-sponsored explorers – Cortéz, De Soto, Coronado, Cabeza de Vaca – Oñate was neither funded nor sent expressly by the Crown. But in northern Mexico his father had discovered and exploited some of the richest silver mines in the New World. The young Oñate had similar dreams. He underwrote his expedition with family money and money he was able to raise.

Oñate's arrangement with the Spanish Court was as a contract developer. His job was to sub-due native peoples through conversion to Ca-tholicism and give Spain a foothold for further exploration and exploitation. If successful, his reward would be a royal title he would be able to pass on to his progeny, and a considerable share of the tax reve-nue paid by the Crown's new subjects.

This is a history of treachery, vile abuse, ex-treme violence – spiritual as well as physical – in short, genocide. Between 1591 and 1638 two thirds of the indigenous population of North America were murdered or perished from the loss of a peaceful life and from diseases inten-tionally brought by the invaders – foreshadow-ing today's germ warfare.

Rather than honor one of the leading local per-petrators of that genocide, why not promote mean-ingful reconciliation between descendants of the abusers and the abused? Meaningful rec-onciliation, however, can never work on an un-even playing field. The City of Albuquerque, its TriCentennial committee, and that part of the Hispanic commun-ity responsible for erecting the Oñate statues ideal-ly should replace them with something less offen-sive. If this isn't pos-sible, moving them to less con-spicuous places might be a good-will gesture. Then both sides of this dispute could come together to listen to one another.

Multiple indigenous and Spanish heritages are rich in our midst, but terrorism perpetrated by the invaders against the invaded is also well-docu-mented. Healing will only begin when those who inherit the burden of aggression can begin to be sensitive to those whose ancestors lost their right feet at the hands of murderers and thugs.

When the human circle remains broken, ra-cism is the legacy.

---

[i] Woven Stone *by Simon Ortíz, Tucson, The University of Arizona Press, 1992. p. 224.*

[ii] *The city was "founded" by the Spanish in 1706. The 2006 anniversary has given rise to all sorts of publicity and money-making schemes. Would that the date was being used to point us towards some truthful history.*

[iii] *Prime mover of the Oñate statues and other slaps in the face of New Mexico's indigenous population has been the Hispanic Cultural Preservation League. Not all people of Hispanic descent are insensitive to the Indian genocide, but this committee clearly has power and influence.*

[iv] *When mentioned at all, it has been called The Pueblo Revolt rather than The Pueblo Revolution, as if use of the lesser word might diminish its import.*

[v] *In 2005 a statue of Popé created by Jémez Pueblo artist Cliff Fragua was added to the group of 100 statues of notable citizens – two for each state-installed in National Statuary Hall at the Capitol, Washington, D.C. No statue of Popé yet exists on his native land.*

Waterboarding – Political and Sacred Torture

Stephen F. Eisenman

1. The Scene of Politics

After the release of photographs of tortured prisoners at Abu Ghraib prison in Iraq in May 2003, a Gallup Poll indicated that 54% of Americans were "bothered a great deal" by the revelations. A year later, the number had declined to 40%. In December, 2005, an AP/IPSOS poll revealed that 61% of Americans agreed that torture was justified, at least on some occasions.[i] A May 2006 report by the U.N. High Commission for Human Rights about U.S. torture at Guantanamo Bay was widely reported in newspapers, radio and television but produced no major outcries, public protests or congressional investigations. Soon thereafter, President Bush – invoking the fictional "ticking bomb" scenario – successfully argued to congress that the CIA be allowed to use "alternative interrogation procedures," and be given immunity from criminal prosecution for prisoner abuse and war crimes. Despite the efforts of a few senators, notably Patrick Leahy of Vermont, Sheldon Whitehouse of Connecticut, and Joe Biden of Delaware, that immunity was granted. The U.S. public and its representatives, it would seem, were not bothered by the fact that the U.S. government permitted and even encouraged its agents to torture people held in their custody.

Admittedly there has been more discussion and controversy about torture in the last two years than previously. The legal protection granted by Congress to CIA agents, does not extend to the destruction of evidence in criminal, civil, or legislative proceedings, and the admission in December 2007 by the CIA that it erased videotapes showing its agents employing waterboarding in the questioning of two presumed Al Qaeda members, raised a brief hue and cry in the press and among some Congressional Democrats, and put some operatives in legal jeopardy. But the criminal investigation, announced by Attorney General Michael Mukasey on January 2, 2008, should not in fact be taken as evidence that public or political sentiment has turned decisively against torture. To begin with, the prima fascia criminality recorded in the videotapes, namely water-boarding, is not the subject of the inquiry, only the destruction of evidence. In addition, the prosecutor put in charge of the case, John Durham, a deputy U.S. attorney from Connecticut, was not independent. He initially reported to deputy Attorney General Mark Filip, who like his boss Mukasey, refused during confirmation testimony to state that water-boarding was a form of torture. Durham in fact, was recommended for his job in Connecticut by the previous U.S. attorney, Kevin J. O'Connor who left his post to become chief of staff for Alberto Gonzalez, who oversaw the preparation of the infamous, 2003 memo that underlay the entire, executive branch legitimation of torture. In other words, the deputy to the torture czar, hired the man charged to investigate the destruction of the torture videotapes. The appointment of Eric Holder to the post of U.S. Attorney General may change the dynamics of the investigation, though President Obama has indicated he is not inclined to prosecute CIA agents or other government officials for human rights abuses.

But support for torture in the United States is not hidden in a web of professional loyalties and secret agendas; it is open and available for all to see. The former Republican Party presidential candidates argued in public debates in favor of more latitude for Army and CIA interrogators – that is, for more, not less torture. Rudolf Giuliani, whose police practiced torture under his watch in NYC, was particularly unabashed. (Recall here that the police who tortured and sodomized Abner Louima in a Brooklyn police station in 1997 were said to have shouted, "This is Giuliani-time." That is how his administration is now largely remembered.) Even the Republican nominee, John McCain, who co-sponsored a law banning torture, agreed to a loophole permitting the CIA, FBI and other agencies to continue to use whatever

interrogation measures they saw fit, including waterboarding. The very law designed to curb torture thus actually provides its first *de jure* legitimation. Even the remaining two Democratic candidates for president, Clinton and Obama – while denouncing torture on the few occasions that the press has asked them their opinion -- did not make Republican support for it a major campaign issue. And given that a more pandering, and poll driven political process can hardly be imagined, it highly unlikely that the Republicans and Democrats have completely misjudged U.S. public opinion. Therefore the question remains: Can so many Americans have truly come to accept torture as necessary and appropriate in the struggle against terrorism?

2. *Pictures of Torture*

What if there was something about the pictures of torture from Abu Ghraib, or the pictures, descriptions and even demonstrations of water-boarding -- now widespread on television and on YouTube -- that has blunted outrage? What if the U.S. public, with the connivance of interested sectors of government and mainstream media, share a kind of moral and visual blindness – I have called it the 'Abu Ghraib effect' -- that allows them to ignore, overlook, or even justify, however partially or provisionally, the facts of degradation and brutality manifest in the pictures? And finally -- and more hopefully -- what if the 'Abu Ghraib effect' can in some small measure at least, be made alien by means of its exposure, analysis and public discussion?

I will not, in the limited space I have here, recapitulate the thesis of my book. Suffice to say that I argued that many critics and observers have misunderstood the nature of the brutal images from Abu Ghraib prison. Far from being exceptional pictures that reveal the existence in the United Sates of what the philosopher Giorgio Agamben, following the political theorist Carl Schmitt, called a state of emergency or state of exception – "pure, de facto sovereigny…outside of the law"[18] – they are images of normative practices in U.S. history, as well in the history of Western politics and representation. The Abu Ghraib photographs, I argued in addition, expose a longstanding *pathos formule* where-by torture victims are shown accepting and even participating in their own chastisement and destruction. That *formule*, a protean expression of the barbarism of civilization, may be traced from the Hellenistic *Pergamon Altar* to Michelangelo's *Bound Slave*, to Sodoma's Saint Sebastian and beyond. It is an important basis for late Renaissance fresco cycles of capture and enslavement, and veritably ubiquitous in Baroque imagery of martyrdom. By the end of the nineteenth century, the motif of the captive or the victim who seems to welcome, participate in, or even take pleasure in his own abjection or subjugation -- or where that subjugation is made erotic -- had migrated from the realm of high art to commercial and mass media. And most frequently, in the 20th Century, in movies and TV, such as *The Thief of Baghdad*, (1940), *The Ten Commandments* (1956), and *Star Trek* (1968).

In television programs such as 24, films such *Missing in Action III*, (1978) and other Chuck Norris vehicles, and the recent *Casino Royale*, torture has come to seem both gratifying and comfortingly domestic; in one episode of 24, a father tortures his own son; in the Chuck Norris feature, a father is tortured in front of his son; and in the Daniel Craig movie, a man suffers excruciating pain and yet asks for his torture to continue.

After the diabolical Le Chiffre strikes two terrible blows with a knotted rope against James Bond's testicles, 007 says to his nemesis,: "I've got an itch down there – do you mind?" After still another blow, he says "to the right," and then finally, "now the whole world is gonna know you've scratched my balls". In Missing in Action III – in a scene that strangely anticipates the iconic image from Abu Ghraib -- Chuck Norris is tortured with electrical charges attached to his chest while standing naked on a box; if he moves more than a few centimeters, a

gun will automatically discharge killing his son. He is thereby made responsible for his own suffering, and the life or death of his child.

The treatment of physical torture as a kind of contract -- an entente between torturer and victim – is in fact basic to its mis-en-scene, as it is to psychologically coercive interrogation. The latest U.S. Army Field Manual, (FM 34-52, 2006), titled, "Human Intelligence Collector Operations," extends to its logical conclusion the central premise of previous interrogation manuals – the necessity of establishing a rapport between interrogator and potential source. It contains a section called "Emotional Love Approach" (sec. 8-29), that begins, poetically enough, "Love in its many forms (friendship, comradeship, patriotism, love of family) is a dominant emotion for most people. The HUMINT collector focuses on the anxiety felt by the source about the circumstances in which he finds himself, his isolation from those he loves, and his feelings of helplessness." It continues: "Sincerity and conviction are critical in a successful attempt at an emotional love approach as the HUMINT collector must show genuine concern for the source, and for the object at which the HUMINT collector is directing the source's emotion." Observe here that the phrases "sincerity and conviction" and "genuine concern for the source," if they are to be taken seriously – and they surely must – mean that a real bond of affection is to be established between the HUMINT and the source, or the torturer and the victim. In the notorious 1963 CIA KUBARK manual, (KUBARK is a cryptonym for the CIA headquarters at Langly, Virginia), under the section titled "Coercive Counterintelligence Interrogations of Resistant Sources," section B, we read:

> One subjective reaction often evoked by coercion is a feeling of guilt. Meltzer observes, [Dr. Malcolm L. Meltzer] "In some lengthy interrogations, the interrogator may, by virtue of his role as the sole supplier of satisfaction and punishment, assume the stature and importance of a parental figure in the prisoner's feeling and thinking. Although there may be intense hatred for the interrogator, it is not un-

---

[18] Giorgio Agamben: The State of Emergency,

usual for warm feelings also to develop. This ambivalence is the basis for guilt reactions, and if the interrogator nourishes these feelings, the guilt may be strong enough to influence the prisoner's behavior.... Guilt makes compliance more likely...."(7).

The creation of an affective bond between interrogator and source, and between torturer and victim serves more than just practical aims. It serves at least two essential ideological functions: 1) assuring those that hold the whip that they are as not as bestial as their acts would make them seem; and 2) salving the consciences of the citizens of empire: when victims are rendered abject, or in the case of detainees at Abu Ghraib or Guantanamo Bay, represented as debased or sexually degenerate, the public is encouraged to believe that they are deserving of chastisement, conquest or destruction. According to the perfect tautology of torture, the victim deserves his fate simply because he IS a victim. As Agamben writes in *State of Exception*: "With the detainees at Guantanamo Bay, naked life returns to its most extreme indetermination." The coerced homoeroticism in the Abu Ghraib images was specifically staged both to conform to Western stereotypes of Islamic (or Oriental) sexuality, and to especially offend Muslim sensibilities by violating the doctrine of "halal" or "religious purity." The digital photographs may thus be placed within the tradition that Said defined as "Orientalism."

3. Waterboarding

But what about images – actual and erased – of waterboarding? Does the relatively mild U.S. public response to revelations about waterboarding have anything to do with the nature of this practice and the character of these pictures? May public reactions to them too be subsumed under the rubric of the Abu Ghraib effect? Does the U.S. military and CIA employ waterboarding precisely because it can be made to seem benign and even consensual – because it too can be assimilated to the "emotional love approach" to HUMINT?

The practice of water-boarding, sometime called, with intentional irony "the water cure," has been documented in the United States

since the mid 19th Century, and always been considered a form of torture. U.S. Army soldiers stationed in the Philippines in 1900 employed the water cure against Filipino soldiers and were court- martialed two years later for the offense. Theodore Roosevelt stated that though he believed "nobody was seriously damaged....torture is not a thing we can tolerate." At the Tokyo War Crimes Trial convened in Tokyo in May 1946, several Japanese prison commanders and guards were convicted of so-called Class B and C offenses – War Crimes and Crimes against Humanity – for having overseen or conducted interrogations of U.S. prisoners employing water-boarding. Two victims testified about the practice: "They would lash me to a stretcher then prop me up against a table with my head down. They would then pour about two gallons of water from a pitcher into my nose and mouth until I lost consciousness." The second stated: "They laid me out on a stretcher and strapped me on. The stretcher was then stood on end with my head almost touching the floor and my feet in the air. . . . They then began pouring water over my face and at times it was almost impossible for me to breathe without sucking in water." (It should be noted that U.S. soldiers also waterboarded Japanese.)

Waterboarding was used by North Korea and China during the Korean War, by the Soviet Union under Stalin and by the French in Algeria. In the journalist Henri Alleg's book from 1957, *La Question*, which became a rallying cry for French intellectuals opposed to the colonial war, the author described his own water torture. An interrogator tied the naked Alleg to a plank, wrapped a rag around his head, and forced his mouth open with a wooden wedge. Then a rubber tube, attached to a spigot was suspended over his face. Alleg writes:

When everything was ready, he said to me: "When you want to talk, all you have to do is move your fingers." And he turned on the tap. The rag was soaked rapidly. Water flowed everywhere: in my mouth, in my nose, all over my face. But for a while, I could still breath in small gulps of air. I tried, by contracting my throat, to take in as little water as possible and to resist suffocation by keeping air in my lungs for as long as I could. But I couldn't hold on for more than a few moments. I had the impression of drowning, and a terrible agony, that of death itself, took possession of me. In spite of myself, all the muscles of my body struggled uselessly to save me from suffocation. In spite of myself, the fingers of both hands shook uncontrollably. "That's it! He's going to talk," said a voice.[ii]

Waterboarding was also practiced by U.S. soldiers in Vietnam and by Pol Pot's Khmer Rouge in Cambodia, and there are recent reports of water-boarding in Ethiopia (approved by the U.S.) and elsewhere in the horn of Africa.

The purpose of water-boarding, like most forms of torture, is obviously not the extraction of truthful testimony – the victim will say anything to stop the ordeal -- but the eliciting of confession: confession of error, apostasy, or moral responsibility. There is however something special about the practice of waterboarding since its inception in the late middle ages, that has allowed its adepts to believe they are engaged not in an act of physical torture, but of moral suasion, and even religious sanctification. At the time of the Inquisition in Spain at the end of the 15th century water torture and death by drowning -- *tortura del agua* or *tormenta de toca* -- were seen as particularly suitable punishments for Anabaptists (those that withheld baptism during childhood, in preference for adult anointing) and indeed for anyone (especially Jews and Gentiles), who denied the purifying waters of Catholic baptism. In a sort of inversion of this actuality, Albrecht Altdorfer represented the imminent drowning of the 4th century St. Florian – a Roman soldier who refused direct orders to torture and kill Christians. He will be sanctified as a martyr by his water cure. Similarly, St. John Ncpomuk, the national saint of Bohemia, received his water cure -- drowning in the Vtlava (Moldau) River -- for having refused to divulge the secrets of the confessional. One sacrament (baptism) was inverted to punish the saint for his rigid observance of another, (confession).

The frontispiece illustration to the anonymously written *A Memento for Holland* (1652), an account of the tortures perpetrated by men from the Dutch East India Company against some Englishmen accused of conspiracy, recalls an image of crucifixion, and the text speaks of the barbarism of Christians and Muslims:

"Now comes *John Clerk* ... First, they twined him up by the hands with a cord on a large door, where they made him fast to two staples of iron, fixt on both sides on the top of the doorposts, stretching his hands asunder as wide as they could: and being thus made fast, his feet hung about two foot from the ground, which also they extended as far as they could, and so made them fast unto the bottom of the door. They bound a cloth about his neck and face, so close, that little or no water could go by. When they had done this, they poured the water softly upon his head, until the cloth was full up to his mouth and nostrils, so that he could not draw breath, but he must suck in water; which being still continued to be poured in softly, forced his intrails to come out at his eyes, ears, and nose, almost to strangling. Never were there such horrid cruelties exercised among the Turks and Barbarians, as among those that pretend Christianity. They were so cruel to him, that they tormented him until his breath was gone, so that he fainted: then they took him quickly down, and made him vomit up the water; and being a little recovered, they pull'd him up again, and charged him with the water again, till they had stifled him as before: and this was exercised on this poor wretch three or four several times, till his body was swoln twice as big as ordinary, his cheeks puft up like a pair of bladders, and his eyes starting and strutting out beyond his forehead" (pp 17-18).

The practice of waterboarding is today largely unchanged since the practice was first described. In a videotaped demonstration of waterboarding given by a group of ex Navy Seals, produced for CNN and now available on

YouTube and elsewhere, the practice is made to seem almost sacred – a forced baptism – and in the end, the victim is almost giddy. Perhaps the comfort of Republican candidates – avowed baptizers all (one in fact, a Baptist minister) – and a broader Christian public, was connected to their inevitable faith in the cleansing and sanctifying character of water. Perhaps water-boarding, invariably called in the media, "simulated drowning", or "feigned drowning" instead of simply "drowning" or "water torture" is perceived to be no more threatening than full immersion, adult baptism?

4. Counter Effects

Let me just conclude by saying that images may be used to buttress Imperial and other forms of violence, or they may be used to contest them. Cer-tain artists, writers and film-makers in the modern tradition, Hogarth, Goya, Picasso, Sartre, Benjamin, Pontecorvo, and others, have challenged this regime of imperial images in the name of emancipation, autonomy and democracy. They have represented torture as it really is -- the unmitigated and wanton imposition of violence and cruelty by those with power upon those with none, and have even roused public opinion against violence and war.

The painter Leon Golub's *Mercenary, Interrogation* and *White Squad* series from the late 1970s and '80s are life-size figure paintings of leering, hyper-masculine men of uncertain nationality or race, shown taunting or abusing seated, kneeling, bound, hooded or otherwise subordinate men or women. These works, including *Interrogation II* were derived from news photographs and journalistic accounts of actual torture scenarios in South Africa, Guatemala, El Salvador and elsewhere. Scab-colored, scraped raw, unstretched, unframed and hung from grommets, the paintings themselves appear to have been beaten and abused, the physical evidence of prior acts of debasement and torture. Golub lived to see the photos from Abu Ghraib, and told his friend, the critic David Levi Strauss that "the techniques pictured – hooding, forced nakedness, sexual humiliation, stress positions, dogs, etc. – were all common torture techniques, right out of the book.

'Walling up' with hoods or blindfolds increases the sense of isolation and defenselessness. Essential to torture is the sense that your interrogators control everything: food, clothing, dignity, light, even life itself. Everything is designed to make it clear that you are at the mercy of those whose job it is not to have any mercy. Hooding victims dehumanizes them, making them anonymous and thing-like. They become just bodies. You can do anything you want to them."[iii] The thing-like character of the seated, bound, hooded body in *Interrogations II* is contrasted with the angular athleticism of the standing tortures; they gaze at us insolently, daring us even to reprove, much less stop them. The physically raw and emotionally extremist theatre depicted in Leon Golub's *Interrogation II* – unlike the artifacts of recent mass culture cited earlier -- preclude erotic pleasure. The painting instead describes the emotional insensibility of the torturers, and the complete physical vulnerability of the victim. They draw upon an ancient pathos formula in order to expose its artifice and viciousness, turn it upside-down, and render it useless as a weapon in the war of the powerful against the vulnerable.

My friend, the artist Sue Coe recently sent me a lithograph called *We Do Not Torture*. It reprises the history of the formula, thereby engaging both in critique and metacritique. Three men hold a wooden board upon which is strapped an emaciated victim. They tip it backwards at a 45 degree angle so that water from a spigot may be forced into the torture victim's mouth. The faces of the tortures are difficult to interpret – pitiless but also matter of fact; grotesque but also ordinary. A barred window at the upper left is the source for the triangle of light that illuminates the scene. At the upper right, a limps figure dangles from a rope. Holbein, Caravaggio, Goya and Blake are touchstones for Sue Coe. She says she uses their works because they are shortcuts – fast and easy ways to move the spectator to an understanding of the history of violence, the complicity of artists in programs of coercive violence, and the sometimes ambiguous line between images that eroticize pain, and those that challenge assertions that torture is ever the free choice of victims.

---

[i]*Paul Sartre, (New York: Goerge Braziller), 1958, p. 60-61.*

[ii]*Henri Alleg,* The Question, *introduction by Jean-Paul Sartre, (New York: Goerge Braziller), 1958, p. 60-61.*

[iii]*David Levi Strauss, "Inconvenient Evidence: The Effects of Abu Ghraib," The Brooklyn Rail, January 2005: http://www.thebrooklynrail.org/spotlight/ jan05/abughraib.html*

Ripple Effects: Art and Parecon

Michael Albert interviewed by Ross Birrell

*R*B: *In your chapter on 'Art' in* Realizing Hope: Life Beyond Capitalism*(London and New York: Zed Books) in which you outline the position of artists in a parecon and address some common apprehensions artists have about parecon, you conclude 'Parecon is art friendly. It is an artistic economy.' (107) Can you say a little more about why you consider parecon an 'artistic economy'?*

MA: It has two broad meanings. First, parecon is friendly to artists per se – in that it provides for them an environment in which they can pursue their labors in solidarity with all other citizens, receiving a just income geared to how long, how hard, and under what conditions they do socially valued work, without having to endure commercialization and alienation much less subordination to donors, owners, etc., and more generally without being members of a class materially or socially above or below other people, and, finally, having self managing say, like other people, over their economic labors and lives. Parecon does all this for everyone, artists included.

Second, parecon creates a context and culture of creative diversity and social and personal development rather than homogenized, commercialized, profit seeking and collective subordination. In this context, the pursuit of artistic excellence and innovation is explored and enacted according to the will of artists, not according to the will of entrepreneurial employers or donors.

RB: *Your description of artistic labour seems rooted in the language of 'production' and 'consumption' (the rights of artists to be remunerated for their work as artists seems to lie in their creative 'product' being accepted as valued art by their peers). But how does this relate to the context of art practice in what for some is an epoch of 'postproduction', where artists manipulate and reproduce the creative production or*

MA: Parecon is about economic life and activity, production, consumption, and allocation. So insofar as parecon has implications for art and artists, it is primarily in their role as producers or consumers. Presumably people interested in doing art as a part of their socially valuable economic labour will wish to be remunerated for it, as others are for their contributions. Thus the discussion of that.

As to an 'epoch of post production' I don't know what you may have in mind here. On the one hand, of course anyone can produce or enjoy art in their free time, not as part of their economic work. Nothing prevents that. Beyond that, I don't understand the question – the idea that we are in a world where we don't need to produce, don't need to work – is, well, utterly ludicrous, so I assume you don't mean that. I think you may be saying that many who are called artists won't be so much creating output from scratch as utilizing outputs that exist in new ways. I don't see the problem, assuming it is generating new results that are socially valued.

RB: When I was involved in setting up the Scottish Artists Union (the first new union of the 21st Century) the difficulty to get artists to join was that there was no identifiable single employer to collectivize against in order to protect wages, improve conditions, etc. In this respect the model of the factory and worker's council and the artist's 'monopoly' on their creativity seems out of step with the conditions of artistic labour? How would you address this perceived discrepancy between the theory and practice of parecon?

MA: In a parecon, no worker has an employer against whom it is necessary to organize and battle in order to try to protect wages or conditions. Workers are their own employers, so to speak, and there is no zero sum contest, either, for income, nor does anyone have a motive to impose speedup, harsh conditions, etc., nor the means to do it, for that matter. Artists in a parecon, like all others who contribute by their labors to the social product, whether making bicycles, or playing sports that are viewed, or providing medical care, or whatever – are organized by their field into a large industry council, into worker's councils for their individual workplaces, and into various teams, etc., within that. They receive income based on how long they work, how hard they work, and the onerousness of the conditions of their work – not based on property, power, or even volume of output. They work in what we call balanced job complexes, having a fair mix of tasks and responsibilities comparably empowering to the mix that others have. And they self manage, collectively, within the broad economic setting of participatory planning.

I am not sure I understand what contradiction you have in mind. Perhaps you can clarify. In capitalism about 20% of the population, who I call the coordinator class, gets very substantial income, even huge income, by virtue of holding a monopoly on empowering work that conveys immense bargaining power, in turn brought to bear in the market. They protect that monopoly fervently, which produces not only class division, but a waste of many other people's potentials. But none of this persists in a parecon wherein there are balanced job complexes and no market but instead participatory planning, etc. etc. So, for example, artists in a parecon don't get income by virtue of keeping down the number of artists, raising the value of their products, etc., but, they get income, instead, for the duration, intensity, and onerousness of their socially valued labor.

RB: For artists, the contradiction of art in a parecon seems to reside in the tension between worker's 'autonomy' and 'socially useful labour'. In the Twentieth Century avant-garde 'artistic autonomy' and 'socially useful art' were often incommensurate, splitting the Surrealist movement and the SI, for example. Do you see 'artistic autonomy' and 'socially useful art' as necessarily incompatible terms in a parecon?

MA: It depends what you mean by artistic autonomy. Artists, like scientists, bicycle producers, and all others who contribute to the social product and who earn a share of it as income for their efforts, must be producing something valued. Imagine that I say I want to work as a singer, say, or as a surgeon, or as a football goalie. I might want to do one of those things, yes, but I can't because I can't do such work well enough to be worth remunerating. I can't produce socially valuable output in these ways. To be remunerated for it, I have to work at something where my output is valued.

This holds for artists too. So, to be an artist – singer, writer, sculptor, or whatever – I apply to the relevant workers council in my region for a job – just as I would apply to the airplane pilots council, or the bicycle workplace council, etc., for other jobs. The workers have to decide if they wish to hire me to their workplace. They are judging whether I can do the work well enough to contribute to the value of their operation, not the public.

What the public does, however, is by its choices in what is called participatory planning, indicate the total output from the bicycle plant, the airplane pilots, or the singer or writers or other artists, that they want to consume. Some of this product is straight production... as in bicycles, flights, or songs. But some of this product is the exploration, innovation, investment, and creative design of new options. Not all this pans out. But the public is more than able to understand the need for and desirability of innovation in every field, even innovation that is difficult to understand or appreciate for a time.

So, if I call myself an artist I don't suddenly gain the option of doing anything I want – autonomously, outside society. True. But if I want to be artist, and am hired by one or another artist's workplace council to be one, then I can self manage my labours, yes, producing output – including innovation, obscure art, or very widely accessible art, as the workplace intends and in accord, as well, with the public's overall planning – just as for scientists, teachers, manufacturers, farmers, and so on.

No one gets to do whatever they want regardless of the impact on others – either by utilizing inputs that could go to other ends, or by taking outputs that aren't earned, and so on. But we all, artists and everyone else, get to have a say in decisions affecting us – our work and our con-

sumption – in proportion as the degree we are affected and in accord with our respective jobs.

RB: For Adam Smith, the labour of (performing) artists (musicians, actors, etc.) is unproductive of any quantifiable value and is akin to the unproductive labour of 'menial servants' (a position they also share with philosophers). It is thus difficult to determine its social use in that unproductive labour fails to produce a vendible commodity which can sustain and reproduce itself in an economy. Artists and servants (as well as lawyers, judges, etc.) are thus maintained by a part of the annual produce of others. How would unproductive labour be supported in a parecon?

MA: In the first place, this is a peculiar formulation, clearly. Obviously the product of the labors of all these folks, artists and others, is valuable, not only to the person doing these labors, but to others who receive the results, and more broadly to society as well. In a parecon, the overall community determines by its desires for these outputs and its comprehension of their broad and varied merits, how much of the society's laboring and energy and other capacities should be allotted to their production. It really is no different for art than it is for anything else. I can't summarize the whole system here and would urge folks, artists and others, to take a look.

RB: What in your view is the social use of art, if any?

MA: There are various social 'uses' or benefits. There is the pleasure of art's production – its creation, rendition, etc., etc. There is the pleasure of its consumption, as in people's enjoyment of seeing, hearing, or otherwise experiencing the artistic creation. Then there are the ripple effects, as well, one might call them, of the implications of artistic expression and experience for people's attitudes, emotions, insights, etc. In all these ways, art is again quite like many, indeed most, other aspects of social output. There are benefits to producers, to consumers, and to society more broadly in by products rippling throughout the community.

RB: In your chapter on 'Art' you discuss popular art, but is there a role for 'Critical art' (as outlined by Proudhon, for example) in a parecon, or would criti-

cal art simply be unnecessary in the realized utopia of a parecon?

MA: I suspect you mean by critical art, art that seeks to reveal truths or underlying relations in a manner calling them into question for change, or art that attempts to galvanize constituencies toward seeking types of change, etc. History doesn't end with attaining a participatory economy, or even with a participatory society that has not only a new classless economy, but also a just and truly self-managing polity, an inter-communalist and mutually respectful and group-sustaining culture, a feminist kinship sphere, and so on. Life goes on. And so does struggle and innovation. So why shouldn't critical art, in this sense of that phrase, continue as well?

Parecon and Art

Michael Albert

Excerpted from the Zed Book,

Realizing Hope

[Participatory economics, or parecon for short, is an economic vision proposed as an alternative to capitalism, and also what has historically gone under the label socialism.]

One could easily anticipate that people who own factories and have great wealth would have a negative initial – and perhaps long term – reaction to the classlessness of participatory economics. Factory owners have, after all, benefited from capitalism's most aggressive inequalities and come to feel that they personally deserve their great wealth and power rather than that they hold it by virtue of institutional economic injustice. When capitalists view the personal or collective mirror they typically do not recoil in horror due to seeing a beneficiary of monopolizing ownership of productive assets, but instead they preen and celebrate due to seeing a superior breed of person deserving great influence and luxury for his or her socially valuable entrepreneurship.

Similarly, those who are currently in the co-ordinator class of lawyers, doctors, engineers, and such, or who even aspire to being in it, will, in many instances, predictably be at least initially and sometimes enduringly hostile to parecon. They typically feel they are smarter and wiser, more capable and more enterprising then workers below, rather than that they are the beneficiaries of a relative monopoly on training and empowering conditions and a morally bankrupt criteria of reward and decision making.

When coordinator class members look in the personal or collective mirror, in other words, they typically do not see a beneficiary of monopolizing economic roles and circumstances of empower-ment, but they see a superior breed deserving disproportionate luxury and influence for its intelligence and skills and even its greater capacity to enjoy a rich and varied life.

Oddly, it turns out there is another group that seems to have a more or less reflexive initial ten-dency to reject parecon – artists. In my experience, at least, this sector worries greatly on hearing about parecon's features and tends to lash out against it without even considering possible gains for others or even, for that matter, for themselves. Something deep seems to be threatened, and they respond with vigor.

So what is the situation of art and artists vis a vis the economy? Can/will a participatory economy be advantageous for artists and art, or will it re-duce the lives of artistic practitioners and also delimit their product?

Put in reverse, would having an ideal envi-ron-ment for people to partake of artistic labors consistent with others having comparable conditions and opportunities impose needs and implications on the rest of economics that a parecon could not abide?

It seems that artists' reactions to parecon are like those of coordinator class members more generally, but with a twist. Artists don't think all lawyers, doctors, engineers, and so on are like them. They think, instead, that there is something uniquely grand and great about art that distinguishes artists from the rest of society's actors. And they fear, at least on first hearing, that parecon will interfere with their endeavors.

What is this special-ness? Creativity, they say. We create. We bring into existence. We dredge from nothing something. And, more, we not only conceive what others don't and nurture it into existence, we do this in advance of others, only to their later benefit. Our work takes time to even understand much less appreciate.

And so what about participatory economics worries artists?

Partly it is that artists will have to do balanced job complexes. And partly it is that artists will have to operate in the participatory planning system, which means that others will have an impact on whether they can do their preferred activities or not.

So how will art transpire in a parecon, and what will be the implications for artists and their creations of having to partake of a balanced job complex and the planning process? And, finally, is there anything special about their worries?

Artistic labor in a parecon – painting, sculpting, designing, writing, filming, directing, performing, dancing, conducting, etc. – will be subject to the same structural impositions as all other labor in a parecon. There will be workplaces for different types of product, workers councils of those invol-ved in the production, consumers who benefit from the product, self managed decision making, remuneration for effort and sacrifice, balanced job complexes, and participatory planning of allocation.

In capitalism the artist of one kind or another attempts to get work which means appealing to a source of financing. Ultimately this will be prop-erty owners – capitalists – whether it is when they themselves finance movies and plays, or when their publishing houses or foundations produce books or support a public symphony, or whatever else.

The owners or administrators will hire the artist if they think there is profit to be made off the artists' labors, or, in some quite rare cases, out of literally liking the product and being willing to subsidize it regardless of losses to be incurred. The artist's income will depend on his or her bargaining power, which will be affected by many variables, including the popularity of the output, the artist's relative monopoly on the talents that go into its creation, etc.

What all this leads to in capitalist economies is that most artistic labor goes to selling commodities for owners or sometimes into designing or prettify-ing their habitats. More prose and poetry is written for jingles, manuals, and ads than for audiences reading novels. More pictures are painted, photos taken, films created, and sculptures carved for purposes of sales to confer profit than for edifying or inspiring or uplifting audiences much less expressing the true desires and perceptions or artists.

What about in a participatory economy, then? What would be the difference for artists and art?

First a worker producing art of one sort or another will work with a workers council, as do all other workers. He or she will get hired like other workers, be remunerated like other workers, have a balanced job complex like other workers, and influence decisions like other workers, meaning he or she will do all this through workers and consumers councils addressing production and consumption and also allocation via participatory planning.

This means the artist has to convince other artists that he or she is a worthy worker in the field to get a job. The criterion is producing desirable art. This would seem like a gigantic improvement from having to convince a sponsor or owner with the criterion being profitability to him or her.

It also means the artist's income will reflect the effort and sacrifice expended in socially valued labor, which is just but also, thought less than a few artists earn under capitalism, likely considerably more than most earn – a moral improvement in every case in overcoming inequity, and even overwhelmingly often a material improvement for the individual artist.

It also means the artist will have a combined job complex that is of average empowerment effect. Artists typically take considerable responsibility for all sides of their activity in any event, cleaning up for themselves, etc. As to how much other work they would wind up incorporating in their overall job complex, I doubt we can say now. But there is nothing special or unique in all this due to it being artists we are discussing as compared to any other producers. The change from corporate divisions of labor to balanced job complexes is not only better in the large, in eliminating class division and rule, but for all but a very few elite artists, it would likely mean considerably more time doing the type of art they most desire to do, even if there is, pre-

dictably, a shorter work week and time going to other responsibilities as well.

But what about influence over the artistic product? And what about the art that emerges?

The artist hearing about parecon starts to worry – will others be telling me what to paint, carve, write, etc.? And will the population at large be deciding whether my art is worthy or not, via the participatory allocation process?

Artists as a group are like all workers' councils. They don't get workplace inputs, electricity, equip-ment, clay, paint, and so on, unless their workplace is producing consonant with social needs. But within that constraint, again like other workers, artists self-manage their own activity.

The population will negotiate with artists how much of society's overall social productive potential should go to art, given what art seems to yield for people's lives and society and given artists' inclinations regarding their labors. But, once this is established, it is workers councils in art workplaces that hire and also dismiss artists, for being worthy and working appropriately.

So it is your fellow artists that you must convince of the efficacy of your activities. Might you fail to do so? Yes. But surely it will be easier and less alienating to convince fellow artists, who have nothing to lose and everything to gain by hiring fine artists, your work is worthy, than to convince an owner. And if you do fail, does it mean you can do nothing about it? No. You can try another artists' council or you can produce on your own time and thereby demonstrate the validity of your proposals pending another application.

The idea that the population will be unable to see that there is merit in artistic work that escapes the bounds of current preferences and that diversi-fies the bounty of product and exploration, is as elitist and unwarranted as the idea that the popu-lation won't support science, or engineering, or innovation in all other walks of life. And the idea that for top current artists to have to do a balanced job complex will take away from society's total art product is no less elitist than the idea that the 80% of the population currently denied means and opportunity to develop its potentials could not generate sufficient scientific or medical or athletic or other product to replace anything that might not get generated due to some scientist or doctor or athlete or other talented person having to sweep up, etc.

In fact the claim is more ridiculous for artists than for the others on two counts. First, artists gen-erally sweep up quite a lot now, even top ones, so not much of their product is lost by having current artists do a balanced job complex. And second, more to the point, most people doing artistically creative work are not, in fact, now generating worthy art but, instead, packaging, advertising, etc., all of which distraction from sensible and worthy utilization of their talents is reduced to near nil in a desirable economy like parecon.

So the bottom line is that parecon does to and for art what it does to and for other pursuits. It removes class differences. It guarantees that social assets are used in accord with social desires. It inserts self managing methods, remunerates justly, and makes the criteria of decision making meeting needs and fulfilling potentials. And it removes elitism while retaining quality and standards.

For purposes of rounding out this admittedly brief discussion, here are three questions put to parecon explicitly by artists, and short answers. It is a bit redundant of what is above, but the question/answer format may help clarity.

1) Wouldn't parecon limit individual artistic creativity by deciding what art to produce by participatory planning, as if by referendum or committee?

My reply is, does the questioner think this because artists, like producers of vehicles, will get resources to work with (outputs of other people's efforts) and in turn be allotted income for their work only insofar as their output is desired in the economy?

I don't see why these accurate perceptions lead to the worry.

If the questioner is worried that it would be within the purview of society to decree that some type artistic innovation is unwanted or unlikely to be successful and that resources shouldn't be given over to it – yes, that is true for art as it is also true for innovation in, say, how to build better bicycles or make better ladders, or fly to Mars. But the assumption that in a parecon the population would not want musical and artistic innovation pursued in the artist's own manner by those with talents and creativity, seems to me very dubious. I should think the opposite would be true, overwhelmingly.

What people currently like would be part of the issue in parecon – for sure. A parecon isn't going to produce massive amounts of avant garde books and disks and films for audiences that don't exist. But that isn't the whole of good policy in this regard, of course. For one thing, smaller groups can like things a lot, making them very worthwhile even though not widely appreciated. It is a small group that likes advanced physics texts or even heart transplants, but that doesn't mean society shouldn't produce these.

But also, at any moment in time, much of what is pursued – not only in art, but in many dimensions of life such as science, engineering, product design, etc. – is not yet appreciated beyond those who are trying to explore it and maybe not even entirely by them.

Art, despite the contrary intuitions of many art-ists, is not special in this respect. There is need for exploration and elaboration in art, music, and ideas and information and innovation more generally, all of which moves out beyond current popular taste. But there is nothing about parecon that precludes or even impedes this exploration relative to any other model I am aware of, much less relative to capitalism…quite the contrary.

Imagine a workplace for musicians. Society respects this workplace and includes it as part of the economy because society values music, including innovation. To work at this institution (and in different parecons we can imagine different approaches to all such issues) one has to be hired which likely entails demonstrating certain knowledge, talent, etc. The institution's budget is allocated internally by its members to various activities and therefore certainly not only to what a mass audience outside already likes. It really isn't much different in these respects than a workplace that is investigating new products,.

(2) But aren't artists with such public controls not really artists anymore?

This notion that an artist is some special unique creature with special rights eludes me. It is a claim made by all intellectual workers who are in or wanting to be in the coordinator class – each seeing it as valid for themselves but not as equally valid for others, In fact, however, the claim is true for all and true for none, depending on what it means.

There is a difference, that is, between being controlled by an external public or other authority, what artists and others reasonably fear, and being part of a society and operating in accord with its norms and thus having a say over outcomes in proportion as they affect one, but not more than that.

Parecon gives everyone in the economy self managing influence over economic outcomes, and this includes people who do science, engineering, administration, construction, serving, and also art as a part of their balanced job complex, each like all the rest. The artist has to function in society, impacted by it, but not, on that account, without his or her own wherewithal.

(3) The whole idea of being an artist seems contrary to the notion of producing "popular" art for mass appeal. What happens to an artist who makes unappealing art in Parecon?

Suppose I happen to like some kind of weird arrangement of items in my living room, and I like the setup changed daily, and it takes me an hour each day to do it, and it is hard work.

Should I be able to earn my living in part for doing that? It has no value for anyone else whatsoever...let's say.

I think not. I shouldn't be forbidden from doing it, of course. But it is my private pursuit and it is more consumption than it is production, and it isn't worthy of being called part of a job complex, I should think. Now this isn't true by definition in a parecon – that is, a parecon could decide otherwise for reasons I don't yet or maybe would never personally agree with. A particular parecon's participants, contrary to my expectations, could actually allow and incorporate this type activity as work, though I doubt one ever would.

Something similar happens for art, music, and also engineering, science, athletics and really all pursuits. Insofar as society is going to allocate income to those doing some activity, it is going to want that activity to "count" as work, which means that overall, on average, it has socially beneficial outcomes that extend beyond those involved in the activity. (There may be lots of misses on the road to some hits, and benefit may have many meanings...but still...)

So if I want to pursue some science, or engineer-ing, or music, or writing, or building, or landscaping, or architecting, or constructing, or teaching, or ball playing, or cooking, or whatever, and I want this activity to be part of my balanced job complex, the activity has to be regarded by the economy as worthy in what it generates for others.

But how does the economy determine worthi-ness? Most likely, for art as with engineering, etc., it will do so by budgeting whole institutions that will in turn incorporate people who do this type work, and will then largely take the employees' collective view as to the worthiness of pursuits proposed to be undertaken.

Could it be that some genius will propose to a music workplace or an art workplace or a research center, pursuits that others in the field wrongly feel deserve no time, energy, and resources? It could happen, of course. Einstein's PhD submission was initially rejected. But parecon is far less vulnerable to such problems than is capitalism, say, due to parecon's having re-moved profit and power differentials from the motivations of actors.

Ignorance may still have an impact, however, or just outright error. No system can be immune from that. But, precisely because every system is vulner-able to such error, one can at least roughly account for the likely distribution of ig-norance and try to guard against it having ill ef-fects – which is just what elevating the value "diversity" to such a prime position as parecon does is meant to help achieve.

As a last point, suppose we come at the art and parecon problem in the opposite direction and ask what does having the ideal system for artists de-mand of an economy?

Of course the problem is arriving at what we mean by "ideal system for artists." Some might think the phrase is fulfilled if the system simply lets artists do whatever they want, giving them anything they want, both to do their art, and to enjoy and explore existence as well.

But if we instead say that artists should have what will benefit their lives and their art consis-tent with all other people equally having what will benefit their lives and their preferred ways of expressing their capacities – then, interest-ingly, it seems that pareconish values arise quite directly, and in turn so do pareconish institu-tions.

Surely artists need to control their endeavors and their interactions in the broader world which provides fuel for their insights and com-munica-tions. But to have this option consis-tently with others having it too, means having self managing say.

For the artist to be appreciated and to have a wide range of choice and for there to be high stan-dards and access to needed tools and con-ditions – all, again, consistent with others hav-ing the same benefits and costs regarding their pursuits – militates for remuneration for effort and sacrifice and balanced job complexes.

The point is, artists are people. Economically they produce and they consume. What any given artist produces and what he or she does to produce it is different from what others in soci-ety do, and from other artists do, as well. But what everyone does is different from what eve-ryone else does. Artists conceive and originate – but so do all other social actors in the economy, at least to some degree, and some do it very much as in people coming up with product in-novations, new techniques, new analyses in changing contexts, new basic theory, and so on. Artists are worthy and inspirational and valu-able. They are not unique in these respects, ei-ther, however.

So, in sum, parecon creates conditions con-ducive to society benefiting from artistic talent and conducive to capable artists expressing themselves as they choose. More, parecon does all this consistently with economic equity and justice for the artists but also equally for all other workers and consumers. Parecon is an art friendly, even an artistic economy.

A Call to Artists: Support Parecon

Jerry Fresia

A history of art over the last 100 years, not as the history of the product, the piece, but as the history of decision making within our industry, is the history of investors acquiring greater control over the distribution, the definition, and the making of art products - and thus over who we are. It is the history of power slipping further from the people who make the piece to the people who profit from the piece. Yes, there are individual art stars aplenty. But as workers in an industry, we are being ground into dust.

I would argue, at a minimum, that our responsibility as artists is to help invent institutions that protect and then expand the opportunity for auto-nomous creative work. Our responsibility, in light of our current situation, is to help build an economy sympathetic to the notion that art, as access to a creative life, is the province of every human being.

With this in mind, let the following commentary serve as a call to artists to endorse the idea of a participatory economy and in particular the institutional design laid out in Michael Albert's Parecon: Life After Capitalism (Verso 2003).

Unless we make building socially just institutions part of our understanding of what it means to be an artist, all the verbiage about "content" and all the pieces of art dedicated to peace, equality, and a better way of life, will, in the end, serve only as evidence that we got it wrong, that we fundamentally misunderstood what it is we do. All that stuff will serve as evidence that when we needed to and when we were called upon to build better ways of being creative as a people, we thought that art was simply about things.

For the past 15 years I have made my living entirely as a visual artist. I have been able to do this only by exhibiting outside of the institutionalized academic-museum-gallery system. I exhibited out of doors in the parks of San Francisco so that I could control the distribution of my work and enjoy direct and personal relationships with my audience. In addition, for a ten year period, I worked with public and private officials and artists in re-inventing this mode of exhibition to the point where it was something quite unexpectedly professional, wonderful, enchanting and *lucrative* - as opposed to the conventional "swap meet" set of exhibitions that one might expect to find outside of established venues.

However, the model was impossible to sustain for a simple reason. Too few artists wanted to take time from their work to build an organization. Most artists had only one set of interests: making their art and promoting themselves within estab-lished institutions. In other words, the dominant modus operandi of the artist, as I know it, is the artist as individual and as entrepreneur. However, within the art industry today, entrepreneurialism cannot lead to ownership of any consequence. Decision making with regard to distribution (exhibition), what counts as important art, and what gets funded is not in our hands no matter how "good" any of our art might be. The decisions that structure our life chances are in the hands of an investor class, an oligarchy, that exercises substantial influence over boards of trustees, both academic and museum, non-profit foundations, public art commissions and the galleries and auction houses that follow in their wake.

The individualist/entrepreneurial approach cannot lead but to utter dependency – a dependency on those who own galleries and control exhibition spaces, on critics, on those who control foundations or access to education, on those who direct competitions, on curators. This list is endless. And because we have become so thoroughly dependent on the institutions within the art industry, we are compelled to adopt as our own, the very ideas, assumptions and practices that the oligarchy uses within those industries that require our marginalization in the first place.

If we provide free inventories to galleries before they take 50 or 60 percent of any sale, we say that that is the nature of things. If the work we make following art school is not saleable it is because the public is uneducated. If the cognoscenti define important work as conceptual – that is a non-visual visual art – we make an effort to understand not to challenge. When we are told that only 12 of us in a city of nearly one million people (San Francisco) can make a living in the gallery system because *we have chosen* a difficult way of life, we believe it.

But it gets worse. According to these cognoscenti, art is not a thing of value, it is *the* thing of value. We produce that incredibly valuable thing and yet we are tagged, as a class of workers, with the moniker "*starving*." And we accept it! Unlike other trained professionals, we have no expectation of having health insurance, a modicum of security, the ability to buy a home, have kids, send them to college, go out to dinner regularly or even travel comfortably. Instead our expectation is that we will have a second job or a partner to support us in order to do the work that transforms the filthy rich into *better* people.

My argument is that we toil in isolation and buy into the notion that the average person cannot really understand our noble sacrifice or that it is beyond the intelligence and aesthetic sensibility of the public because we have lost touch with the history of our profession particularly as it relates to our life outside the studio. In order to become free artists we need to become free from the institutions that require our marginalization. We need to *get back* into the game of defining art ourselves, of teaching art independently of universities, of build-ing movements with other members of the com-munity and other artists, of controlling exhibitions, and of enjoying direct and personal relationships with the public that artists from Michelangelo to the Abstract Expressionists enjoyed. In short we need to build alternative institutions that permit us to have some important say over what we

do, what we make and how it is distributed.

Let's take a look, then, at Michael Albert's Parecon, a well thought out proposal for a participatory economy that would better serve the interests of artists as artists and as living, breathing members of communities. Briefly then, I would like to touch upon his concept of Worker Councils, Balanced Job Complexes and Participatory Planning and how each might impact our lives.

Worker Councils:

Another word for participatory economics is demo-cracy. Together with other artists and members of the community in which we live, we would decide what work would be produced and for what purpose. I can hear artists screaming bloody murder as I type: we don't want a "big brother" telling us what to do. Agreed. But we haven't been doing too well with the director either. In fact, it would be a bit hypocritical to inveigh against a workers council without first doing something about how we are bossed around right now. Consider this:

Following WWII, a tiny handful of economic elites, by virtue of their right as property owners, together with their political and cultural allies were able to direct and shape the lives of visual artists in the following ways:

• Important art and important careers – read a modicum of remuneration – had to be divorced from European influences.

• Art that suggested political commentary had to be displaced by art that suggested psychological angst – read *abstraction*.

• The teaching of art had to be removed from the studio and the jurisdiction of the master artist and placed into the hands of corporate representatives or boards of trustees and into the university.

• The studio itself, once a locus of social and public activity and a place of exhibition and distribution had to become the studio of the isolated, angst-probing artist. By the 1970s, the studio, as the workplace of the individual artist, was transformed further. It now resembled a factory, where the studio floor was the work site of artist assistants who followed the direction of artists who in turned collaborated with the investor/collector.

• By the late 1960s painting and easel painting, as far as "important work" was concerned was declared "dead," thus weakening the individual artist's access to and control over his or her means of production.

So the question is this: what is it that *we* want? With worker councils we, as participant decision-makers, would enjoy far more power over our work and our lives than we have yet experienced.

Besides, artists are already deeply involved in what could be described as a balanced job complex. If we are painters, we are already photographers, web designers, mailing list managers, marketers, promoters, frame-makers, grant writers and expert application makers. If we have jobs in addition to making art we are even more extended. In a participatory economy, much of the competitive work, such as making applications, might be reduced in favor of teaching and the sharing of our knowledge of design, color, writing, song, dance, theater and various other aesthetic considerations with a population who has not had the opportunity, in their everyday life, to explore the various ways they could creatively and rewardingly accomplish socially useful tasks.

Balanced Job Complexes

The principle central to this concept is a principle that most artists probably already accept: creative work is the province of every human being. As an artist interested in finding more people responsive to what I do, I find it a terribly exciting possibility that everyone might have the opportunity to engage in creative work themselves. Indeed, if my chances of making a living as a creative person are under assault, as in fact they are now, it is in my interest to have involved as many people as is possible in creative work; that is, work not only where workers also make decisions but work where the creative process is central to the work process.

In helping to design balanced job complexes we would have much to contribute. Our work is not governed by the clock. We make time for reflection. An aesthetic dimension is always paramount. Mind and body is not separate. Could it be a rewarding experience to play a meaningful role helping to construct ways of working rooted in a good deal of the knowledge we possess? Might it be fulfilling to have this kind of on-going discussion with the broader community? Might it not broaden the interest in what it is we do? Would these types of personal contacts be a welcomed balance to the isolation of the studio?

Participatory Planning

Participatory Planning is the negotiation among workers and consumer councils that is intended to replace the market system of distribution, a system of distribution based upon price and one's ability to pay. It is important to recognize that while various market relations have existed practically forever, for most of human history social relations (kinship, communal, religious, political) existed apart from the relationships of the buying and selling. But we happen to live an a very unusual period, historically – one where virtually all our social relations are *embedded within the market*, where decisions about what we make, who gains access to it, how we live and use our time is determined by the impersonal imperatives of price and profit. But this is an historical anomaly, a convention that can be changed.

Second, the irony for artists in this regard is that the market relations into which we enter in order to gain access to the means of life are skewed to the advantage of the very wealthy largely because *planning mechanisms already have been inserted within the market*. But these planning mechanisms, unlike the participatory model that Albert advocates are exclusionary and elitist. If you have strong misgivings about challenging market forces of distribution, as an artist you ought to be quite upset already. The investors and owners of culture are quite adept at using an array of planning mechanisms – art commissions and auction houses that utilize market forces, for example, to control the goose that lays the golden egg.

The question becomes, if market planning mech-anisms are already in place, why do we permit them to be controlled by a few whose interests run counter to ours? And arguably against the interests of many? If we *are* the goose that lays the golden egg, how does it come about that our precious gol-den egg is taken from us? With our cooperation?

My suspicion is that we are too busy making art to take a good look at the institutional matrix that has us by the short hair. One good example, along these lines, is our acceptance of one planning mechanism that was designed to mitigate against popular influence in the arts: the public benefit corporation, better known as the non-profit.

Non-profits are planning mechanisms. They are run by community elites, generally with artist representation, for the purpose of protecting culture within a market environment from popularizing influences. Sociologist Paul Di-Maggio notes that non-profits, while claiming service to the entire community actually function to mystify art and separate the community from the world of art and artists. Alice Goldfarb Marquis concurs and points to the "high-art" worlds of museums, operas and symphonies where financial and social elites use the non-profit planning mechanisms for the same purpose. She notes that this capturing of culture is often accomplished by "pasting an altruistic, morally chase veneer over basically self-serving activities." Wealthy donors and trustees, she explains further, have long aligned themselves with "liberal, reformist intellectuals and critics who see themselves as guardians of high culture" and who have campaigned "against almost every artistic innovation of the past two centuries."

The non-profit as planning instrument by the investor class may be most visible in the creation of "art centers." In the creation of the Lincoln Center in New York City and the Yerba Buena Center for the Arts in San Francisco, for example, redevelopment interests together with cultural elites and non-profits use the rhetoric of public access around art to acquire monopoly control over the distribution of the art product. Their "art centers" then become the sites for glitzy chic-chic art events in order to anchor the array of upscale hotels, restaurants, and retailers that return competitive dividends to real estate investors. Many of us work with non-profits and do our best to make them function in a way that serves the community. But I must ask, is it not the case that we are always poor? That we are always beseeching the rich? That our non-profits are not dedicated to challenging the starving artist paradigm or amplifying public involvement as decision makers?

Artists today cannot have it both ways. We cannot run from parecon-type market alternatives in the name of artistic freedom and at the same time play our role as side-kicks within existing planning mechanisms that permit the wealthiest among us to direct and control all that we do.

Summary

I am not criticizing the intention of artists. We contribute much to rallies, marches and the numerous exhibitions, plays, music and stories that inveigh against war and injustice. My concern is that this art spirit is not part of an institutional critique. We need a critique of our institutions so that we can develop a concrete strategy to build new ones. Artists opposed to the war, to use one example, might be more effective by using their creative talents to build institutions that make the kind of war in Iraq impossible. The good artist and the justice good artists seek cannot exist unless we first create the institutions that require both.

Our history is replete with such transformations. While the Impression period is often referred to as the movement where visual art was first ridiculed and later accepted as prescient, let us recall that it was ridiculed not by the unsophisticated masses in need of education but by the educated and powerful whose control over culture had to be eliminated. Impressionism was a frontal assault by artists upon art institutions that in the words of the rebellious artists erected artificial barriers between themselves and the public.

Ditto jazz, rock'n roll, and Beethoven. Recall also that Michelangelo said of a statue that it was only by the "light of the public square" that it could be judged. The point is that we as artists are of the public and we are of the community. No better. No worse. And together it is necessary for us to regain control over our lives in order to become the artists we wish to become. Our best chance is to create the institutions necessary to give our voice best purchase. Democratic institutions. Participatory economics. Parecon.

Finally it is important, I believe, to explore furth-er the artistic sensibilities that were widespread 100 years ago, sensibilities that suggested revolutions required dancing, that suggested that if what we create is not a better world, what is the point of our work? Creating better institutions, ones in which our voices are heard meaningfully is both our responsibility and a pragmatic solution. It must also be our art. As Bertolt Brecht has said, "canalising a river, rafting a fruit tree, educating a person, transforming a state...are instances of fruitful criticism and at the same time instances of art."

Hotel Rwanda

Hollywood and the Holocaust in Central Africa

keith harmon snow

first appeared at allthingspass.com

What happened in Rwanda in 1994? The standard line is that a calculated genocide occurred because of deep-seated tribal animosity between the majori-ty Hutu tribe in power and the minority Tutsis. Ac-cording to this story, at least 500,000 and perhaps 1.2 million Tutsis – and some 'moderate' Hutus – were ruthlessly eliminated in a few months, and most of them were killed with machetes. The killers in this story were Hutu hard-liners from the *Forces Armees Rwandais*, the Hutu army, backed by the more ominous and inhuman civilian militias – the *Interahamwe* – "those who kill together."

"In three short, cruel months, between April and July 1994," wrote genocide expert Samantha Power on the 10th anniversary of the genocide, "Rwanda experienced a genocide more efficient than that carried out by the Nazis in World War II. The killers were a varied bunch: drunk extremists chanting 'Hutu power, Hutu power'; uniformed soldiers and militia men intent on wiping out the Tutsi *Inyenzi*, or 'cockroaches'; ordinary villagers who had never themselves contemplated killing before but who decided to join the frenzy." [1]

The award-winning film *Hotel Rwanda* offers a Hollywood version and the latest depiction of this cataclysm. Is the film accurate? It is billed as a true story. Did genocide occur in Rwanda as it is widely portrayed and universally imagined? With thousands of Hutus fleeing Rwanda in 2005, in fear of the Tutsi government and its now operational village genocide courts, is another reading of events needed? [2]

Is Samantha Power – a Pulitzer Prize winning

journalist – telling it straight? [3]

Is it possible, as evidence confirms, that the now canonized United Nations peacekeeper Lt. General Roméo Dallaire was at the time an agent of the Tutsi army? Or that the funding for *Hotel Rwanda* came from a company with powerful mining interests in Congo – where access is insured by the Rwanda government?

Hundreds of thousands of people were killed, that's clear. There was large-scale butchery of Tutsis. And Hutus. Children and old women were killed. There was mass rape. There were many *acts* of genocide. But was it genocide or civil war?

"I think that's a very good question and it is not adequately answered," says Howard W. French, former East Africa Bureau Chief for the *New York Times* and author of *Africa: A Continent for the Taking*. [4]

Howard W. French operated on the ground in Central Africa (1993-1999) and his reportage of the RPF Tutsi rebel army hunting down and massacring hundreds of thousands of Hutus in Congo is exceptional. [5]

"A minority of fifteen percent [RPF Tutsis] wages a determined effort to take over a country and rule in an ethnic way, by force of arms, and has been doing this for years. Two presidents are assassinated." Howard W. French is adamant: "These are not excuses for *butchery*. But these are things that lead one in the direction of civil war, as a descriptor, as opposed to the one-sided tale that we have been given, of these sweet, innocent Tutsis who remind us of Israel, versus the savage Hutus who cold-heartedly butcher people hand-to-hand for three months." [6]

From the very first words and frames, where the image has yet to appear and the screen is completely black, the film *Hotel Rwanda* sets up viewers to think a certain way about what happened in Rwanda in 1994. Here is a story about good versus evil. An ominous African voice is heard, clearly the announcer on a Rwandan radio program, and he is describing the Tutsis as '*cockrrrRRROACHES*.' The voice is black and the

cataclysm unfathomable, as anyone will tell you, and the black screen underscores the evil darkness of Africa. This voice of terror returns throughout the film to haunt the innocent but terrified Tutsis, on screen, and the viewers gripping their seats.

The good guys are the Tutsis, the victims of genocide. They are not killers in the movie: they are never killers. At the end of the film, when a well-attired guerrilla force is shown – the 're-bels' of the Rwandan Patriotic Front (RPF) – they are rescuers. They are disciplined, organized. They keep a tidy United Nations camp safely behind their lines. They don't kill Red Cross nurses, or orphaned children, in the film: they reconnect children to their families.

The Hutus in the standard Rwanda genocide stories are always the bad guys, and they are *all* bad guys. Every Hutu is a *genocidaire* – to use the ominous French term deployed in English contexts to further underscore the horror, the horror. The Hutus are the devil incarnate. The Tutsis are saintly. Indeed, they are beyond reproach, because they are the *victims* of genocide. The Hotel manager's wife bears an obvious cross around her neck, to remind us that the Tutsis are the chosen people. When the now celebrated United Nations hero Lt. Gen. Roméo Dallaire shakes hands with the devil – as his own popular book and the subsequent film *Shake Hands With the Devil* concur – he is shaking hands with Hutu. [7]

That is the ideological framework of the *Hotel Rwanda* film. There is, today, an industry behind it.

The Tutsis are dehumanized by the Hutus and by the Hutu media, in the film, and there was plenty of truth in this in real life. But the RPF pro-Tutsi media that operated in Rwanda after 1991, for example, was equally dehumanizing, and equally vicious, but the film does not tell us this. Tutsi guerrilla forces – prior to 1970 – were the first to describe themselves as *Inyenzi* or cockroaches: they were not equated with the insects that everyone loathes, they were well trained, secretive and coordinated military forces who attacked at night and withdrew by day. [8]

The RPF would hit and run and kill with efficiency. It was not a pejorative usage, as it has been used in the film *Hotel Rwanda*, although it was bastardized and turned against the Tutsis by media outlets in Rwanda. *Radio Mille Collines* and the other anti-RPF media outlets of the President's party, the National Republican Movement for Democracy and Development (MRND), [9] were not the only ones to incite hatred and murder. Indeed, RPF-controlled *Radio Muhabura* spread ethnic hatred and incited widespread killings, but this was – according to Hollywood – a war with only one army, the ruthless Hutus. [10]

THE PILLARS OF HOTEL RWANDA

When Human Rights Watch investigated the genocide, they sent Alison des Forges to tell the story, and the product of her long investigations was the fat treatise on genocide in Rwanda titled *Leave None to Tell the Story*. Irony is heaped upon irony when we consider that those who are left to tell the story are silenced by the *authorized* storytellers like Alison des Forges.

"Alison des Forges is a liar," Cameroonian journalist Charles Onana, author of the book *The Secrets of the Rwandan Genocide, Investigations on the Mysteries of a President*, published in French in 2001, is adamant. "She is a LIAR." [11]

Paul Kagame, RPF General and President of Rwanda, sued Charles Onana for defamation in a French court: Kagame lost. [12]

"Des Forges has written a book which has become the bible regarding Rwanda," says Jean-Marie Higiro, former Director of the Rwandan Information Office (ORINFOR) who fled the killing, with his family, in early April 1994. "Everyone points to her book even though some of what she has produced is fiction. I don't think she is an intentional liar, but I don't know why she investigated Hutu human rights abuses but no RPF human rights abuses."

Hotel Rwanda is built on the pillars of selective human rights reporting, but it really takes off from the celebrated text, *We Regret To Inform You That Tomorrow We Will Be Killed With Our Families,* by Philip Gourevitch, the *New Yorker* magazine's premier Africa expert.

"Gourevitch's short book should be compulsory reading for Heads of State and Ministers of Defence all over Africa," wrote *Guardian* reporter Victoria Brittain, "as well as for all U.N. officials involved in peacekeeping operations and humanitarian aid, from the Secretary General on down, and the heads of missionary orders in the US, France and Belgium." Victoria Brittain is also a *Nation* magazine contributor on genocide in Rwanda. [12a]

The International Human Rights Law Clinic at American University for several years (at least) asked students to read Philip Gourevitch on genocide in Rwanda, in preparation for legal work with the International Criminal Tribunal on Rwanda. Professor Melissa Crow, who worked with the Law Clinic, followed her term at Human Rights Watch (1994-1995) by working in Kigali, Rwanda, under the RPF government, working for the Office of the Prosecutor for the International Criminal Tribunal on Rwanda. Following this she joined Foley, Hoag and Elliot, the influential Washington D.C. law firm closely aligned with the U.S.-Uganda Friendship Council, which is closely tied to ChevronTexaco, Coca-Cola, the William Jefferson Clinton Foundation and the Pangaea Global AIDS Foundation. The latter foundations are also deeply involved in Rwanda. [12b]

Notably, a U.S. immigration judge in St. Paul Minnesota imposed Gourevitch's book as compulsory reading for all attorneys dealing with Rwandan refugees requesting political asylum. But this is a dangerous and irresponsible precedent. [13]

Funding for Gourevitch's book came from the United States Institute for Peace, a State Department offshoot (with an Orwellian name). [14]

What we never learn about Philip Gourevitch is that his brother-in-law, Jamie Rubin, was Madeleine Albright's leading man and, through him, Gourevitch planted in the public mind a narrow perspective on Rwanda. [15]

Philip Gourevitch is an intimate pal of Rwandan President Paul Kagame. I regret to inform you that Philip Gourevitch is not an impartial journalist, regardless of how much you may have liked his book, or have been moved by it, because he has taken sides, and he has told only one side of the story, and he has told it badly, and he has been rewarded for his fine job in telling it badly. [16]

"Gourevitch begins the story with the Tutsi as these saintly victims," the *Times'* Howard W. French says. "And I don't think Gourevitch is a stupid guy. I think that it's just sheer intellectual dishonesty… Gourevitch was coming out in the *New Yorker* every other month with this very well written and – if you don't know the facts – very compelling picture about Rwanda…as the Israel of Central Africa and the Tutsis as the Jews of Central Africa. That's powerful stuff. But I'm on the ground in Central Africa seeing that the reality is very, very different." [17]

The theme of genocide in Rwanda – whether true or false – has birthed an industry that revolves around a standard, simplified plot. The appearance of the film *Hotel Rwanda* marks the *coup de grace* in the long process whereby the facts, the ugly reali-ties and dirty details of what really happened in Rwanda have been distilled into a neat and tidy story that proliferates in the media, in film, in literature, at seminars on genocide and workshops on reconciliation, and it is the predominant discourse in academia. Quebecois journalist Robin Philpot calls it "the right and proper tale." [18]

THE FALSIFICATION OF AMERIKAN
CONSCIOUSNESS

It has become a mythology: the Rwanda genocide mythology or, better, the *Tutsi Holocaust mythology*. But as African scholar Amos Wilson puts it so simply in *The Falsification of Afrikan Consciousness*, "you cannot understand the present unless you first understand the past."

To understand the growth of the mythology on genocide in Rwanda, consider first the text of *Hotel Rwanda – The Official Companion Book*, which de-scribes the process of "bringing the

true story of an African hero to film." [19]

The book deletes the most basic facts about the Rwandan Patriotic Front and its backers' roles in the ongoing war for the Great Lakes region of Africa, war that has led to at least seven million people dead since the initial RPF invasion from Uganda in October 1990. [20]

Instead the book offers an abbreviated time-line of events that accentuate or exaggerate those points that serve the predominant *Hotel Rwanda* mythology, and it excludes those facts that would undermine this mythology: the entire framework of the brutal, bloody war for control of Rwanda is obscured.

October 1990: *Guerrillas from the Rwandan Patriotic Front (RPF) invade Rwanda from Uganda; the RPF is mostly made up of Tutsis. A ceasefire is signed on March 29, 1991.*

First: the above statement uses the definitive term for the RPF action: invaded. The Rwandan Patriotic Army invaded Rwanda from Uganda. However, the context of the RPF ascension to power is obliterated. RPF infiltration of Rwanda began around 1986 after Yoweri Museveni, with powerful western backers, shot his way to power in Uganda. Paul Kagame, current president of Rwanda, was head of Museveni's Directorate of Military Intelligence, and later commanded the Rwandan Patriotic Front. But the RPF invasion was a gross violation of international law against a sovereign nation – a point the Hotel Rwanda industry ignores.

Never condemned by the international 'community,' the RPF 'struggle' was supported by powerful western agents and institutions, including the World Bank and the IMF, who shackled Rwanda with austerity programs in perfect synchronization with the RPF assault. This led to the heightened inculcation of *structural* violence throughout Rwan-da. Combined with the crash of coffee prices on the world market, millions of Rwandans found it impossible to make ends meet as the 1990's began. Suffering hit new lows not seen in Rwanda for decades.

The majority of people in Rwanda, besieged

by the propaganda of competing factions – a spectrum of political interests aligned with or against the RPF or the Rwanda government of Juvenal Habyarimana – found scapegoats according to their positions in society. Economic interests predominated as a few elites increasingly controlled the life or death of the many. The rising insurgency and structural violence provoked hostility amongst and between groups, and elites controlling media outlets of all stripes began to use their venues to sow ethnic rivalry as the veneer for the deeper agenda: class warfare.

Hutus were dehumanized as often as Tutsis. "Pro-opposition newspapers represented MRND [Hutu government] leaders as essentially evil and corrupt," writes Jean-Marie Higiro. They were "liars, idiots, animals, bloodthirsty murderers and warmongers. Some of these newspapers published drawings of President Habyarimana covered with blood." [21]

The RPF and Rwandan Tutsi Diaspora had their own publications. The best known of these is *Impuruza*, published in the United States (1984-1994). Tutsi refugees joined Roger Winter, the Director of the United States Committee for Refugees, to help fund the publication. The editor, Alexander Kimenyi, is a Rwandan national and a professor at California State University. Like most RPF publications *Impuruza* circulated clandestinely in Rwanda amongst Hutu and Tutsi elite.

"A nation in exile, a people without leadership, 'the Jews of Africa,' a stateless nation," wrote Festo Habimana, the president of the *Association of Banyarwanda in Diaspora USA*, in the premier issue of *Impuruza*. Habimana called for the unity of Tutsi refugees. "But our success will depend entirely upon our own effort and unity, not through world community as some perceive… As long as we are scattered, with no leadership, business as usual on their part shall always be their policy. We are a very able and capable people with abundant bless-ings. What are we waiting for? Genocide?" [22]

The *Association of Banyarwanda in Diaspora USA*, assisted by Roger Winter, organized the *International Conference on the Status of Banyarwanda [Tutsi] Refugees* in Washington, DC in 1988, and this is where a military solution to the Tutsi problem was chosen. The U.S. Committee for Refugees reportedly provided accommodation and transportation. [23]

Winter is intimate with USAID, and a longtime ally of Susan Rice, former Assistant Secretary of State on African Affairs (1997-2001), Special Assistant to President Clinton (1995-1997), and National Security Council insider (1993-1997). Roger Winter is also a staunch supporter of U.S. Rep. Donald Payne.

Winter acted as a spokesman for the RPF and their allies, and he appeared as a guest on major US television networks such as PBS and CNN. Philip Gourevitch and Roger Winter made contacts on behalf of the RPF with American media, particular-ly the *Washington Post*, *New York Times* and *Time* magazine. Roger Winter and U.S. Rep. Donald Payne continue to manipulate African affairs: most notable are their recent exaggerations about geno-cide in Darfur, Sudan, for which Donald Payne sponsored the Darfur Genocide Accountability Act.

Second: the language of the above October 1990 timeline entry underscores the equally discrepant point that the RPF was "mostly made up of Tutsis." According to the genocide mythology, the cataclysm in Rwanda was a tribal struggle between Hutus and Tutsis, with some involvement of France.

Who were the non-Tutsi elements of the "mostly" Tutsi RPF? What is the implication? They were Hutus? How could Hutus be fighting along-side Tutsis if Hutus were exterminating *all* Tutsis based on an organized, premeditated plan? The term "moderate Hutu" invites a similar conundrum: what is a "moderate Hutu" in the international legal framework of genocide?

Jean-Marie Higiro says it best: "Academics and journalists divide Hutus into two categories: moderates and extremists following the myths of Hollywood. They never suggest that there were Hutu who did not belong to either category. There were those who were terrified by both sides and who just fled for their lives.

Academics and journalists never do the same [segregating] for Tutsis and of course never for the RPF even though the RPF was a conglomerate of Tutsi supremacists, Republicans and monarchists. These supremacists are highly placed in the current government. Tito Rutaremara, one of the ideologues of the RPF is one of them, and General Ibingira, the butcher of Kibeho [is another] of them."

The very *definition* of genocide would be called into question if it turned out that there were political, economic or class – as opposed to *ethnic* – motives behind the hundreds of thousands (or 1.2 million) of deaths that have been unequivocally at-tributed to Hutu *genocidaires.* A deeper examination of "genocide" in Rwanda raises just such inconvenient questions. The determination of what constitutes genocide is not so cut and dry as Hutus versus Tutsis, or lists of targeted Tutsis versus no lists, no matter the terror now invoked in one's soul on hearing the word *Interahamwe.*

After the October 1990 entry, the timeline in the companion book omits any reference to the RPF until February 1993, as if the supposed 'heroic' Tutsi rebels were patiently sitting out the war from the Ugandan sidelines. But massacres occurred in northern Rwanda after the October 1990 invasion and after the 1991 ceasefire and they were committed by the RPF. Tens of thousands of refugees fled the border districts in fear of ongoing RPF atrocities.

(This author remembers well the traumatized tourist who disembarked from the bed of a small pick-up truck that crossed the border from Rwanda to Uganda in 1991. I was in Kasindi, in southwest Uganda. The Rwandan man sitting next to this western woman was shot by an RPF sniper as the truck drove down the road; the truck was then stopped, searched by the RPF, and the dead man taken.)

From 1990 on, RPF terror cells began infiltrating Kigali, the capital, and all other areas of Rwanda, and with them came atrocities that were frequently blamed on the Habyarimana government, includ-ing assassinations, massacres and disappearances. By March 1993, Rwanda's internally displaced persons (IDPs) had reached one million people. The RPF practiced a scorched earth policy: they did not want to have to administer a territory or deal with local populations. The RPF displaced people, shelled the IDP camps, and marched on. They killed some captives, buried them in mass graves or burned corpses, and used survivors as porters to transport ammunition, dig trenches or cook their meals.

According to one Rwandan now in the US: prior to 1994, most Tutsis who had a job in Rwanda col-lected contributions for the RPF political and military program; people were afraid to refuse to pay the compulsory tax levied by a ruthless military institution, the RPF.

The Habyarimana government responded to terror with repression in kind, but the international human rights "community" had already taken sides in the war: the Hutu government of Habyarimana was accused of "genocide" against Tutsis as early as 1993; the RPF atrocities were ignored or explained away.

"There were many RPF killings in Rwanda between 1990 and 1994," says Jean-Marie Higiro, "but these were not investigated; they were auto-matically attributed to Habyarimana's [MRND] party by the international community. Even so, we know that the RPF used that kind of strategy to tarnish the image of their opponents." [24]

Jean-Marie Higiro also cites the Tutsi newspaper *Impuruza*, the publication edited by Professor Alexandre Kimenyi, with accusing the Habyarimana government of committing genocide against the Tutsis, and this was prior to 1993.

February 1993: The RPF again invades Rwanda. Hutu extremists cite the invasion as proof the Tutsis aim to eliminate them, and begin calling for preemptive measures.

To begin with, the RPF never left Rwanda, and they never stopped killing. Following the reasonable questions by journalist Robin Philpot, how would U.S. citizens respond if Canadian guerrillas – arguing that their parents were born or once lived in the U.S. – invaded from Toronto? Would we call Americans who complained "extremists"? What if a few Islamic militants purportedly invading the U.S. took out the World Trade Center? Would the U.S. government call for preemptive measures? Would we call the invaders a "rebel army"? Extremists? Would we call them *terrorists*?

"Is it normal in the search for justice to condemn one side in a war for human rights violations," writes Robin Philpot, "and not even question the morality of the aggressors, those who violated the principles of all the charters of rights humanity has ever drafted? Is it right to shout about how a government violates rights and turn a blind eye to the launching of an aggressive war?" [25]

Like the film, the *Hotel Rwanda Companion Book* offers a gross and distorted simplification of events in Rwanda.

HOTEL PENTAGON

Trained by the U.S. Army at Fort Leavenworth, Kansas, USA, the RPF soldier and now President of Rwanda, Paul Kagame, is a regular visitor at the Pentagon, and he was not the only officer in Rwanda with ties to the U.S. military.

Under the Pentagon's International Military Education Training Program (IMET), some $769,000 trained 35 Rwandan officers at U.S. military schools from 1980 to 1992, and $120,000 was earmarked for Rwanda for both 1994 and 1995. Further military assistance was provided by the U.S. to 1994, while the bulk of the arms and logistical support came from U.S. client states (France, South Africa, Egypt, Uganda and Zaire). The Pentagon has also trained large numbers of Rwandan soldiers under the Extended-IMET (E-IMET) and Joint Command Exchange and Training (JCET) programs. One of those trained was Bangladeshi Colonel Moen, the Chief Operations Officer for the United Nations Assistance Mission for Rwanda (UNAMIR), and another graduate of the U.S. Army Command and General Staff College in Leavenworth, Kansas (USA). [26]

From 1993 onwards the RPF continued to stick its bloody foot in the door of Rwanda, and the "international community" continued to tighten the screws on the Habyarimana government. Ever vigilant and inflammatory in advertising the governments' human rights abuses – whether manufactured, exaggerated or real – the human rights community continued to close its eyes to RPF atrocities, terrorist infiltrations and bloodied land grabbing.

Backed by powerful factions from the United States, England and Belgium, the RPF maneuvered and manipulated its way to the very seat of power, in Kigali itself, where – under the Arusha Peace Accords negotiated in Arusha Tanzania in 1993 – a battalion of RPF soldiers was based at a strategic site within the city center. The RPF immediately fortified its defenses under the watch of Lt. General Roméo Dallaire – now universally regarded as a hero – the Canadian Force Commander of UNAMIR.

The *Hotel Rwanda Companion Book* offers only the following tidy summary which, as popular mythology now holds, credits the RPF with the imperative of 'stopping the genocide' against Tutsis.

Mid-July 1994: The Tutsi RPF forces capture Kigali and the genocide is over. Over a period of 100 days, almost 1,000,000 Rwandans were murdered.

While it is alleged that "almost 1,000,000 Rwandans were murdered" in those 100 days, a claim that is certainly exaggerated, it is also true that the RPF slaughtered, bombed, massacred, assassinated or tortured hundreds of thousands of people – including Hutu and Tutsi soldiers, politicians and government officials, and innocent civilians.

"All U.N. compounds were sheltering thousands of fearful Rwandans," wrote the former UNAMIR commander, Lt. General Roméo Dallaire, "How could I possibly keep them safe?" Dallaire's admission subsequent to the previous statement is very insightful, especially given his pro-RPF position: "We protected these citizens from certain death at the hands of the extremists or the RPF..." Dallaire openly confirms the RPF's role in killing, and his book repeatedly describes firefights he witnessed between the

RPF and various government factions. [27]

There were no firefights shown in *Hotel Rwanda*, there was none of the ongoing warfare that rocked Kigali before and after 06 April 2004: there were only ruthless, savage, Hutu killers and rapists, and the dead bodies that – by inference and innuendo –

the Hutus slaughtered with machetes, pangas, axes and hoes.

The RPF employed state-of-the-art information control and psychological operations tactics prac-ticed by the US military: international reporters were embedded; access to battle zones was restricted; evidence of RPF massacres was erased, or massacres were blamed on Hutu extremists, *Interahamwe* militias or the government *Forces Armee Rwandaise*. British journalist Nick Gordon reported crematoriums where the RPF incinerated bodies.

CNN's only journalist on the ground in Rwanda at the time, Gary Streiker, has admitted that he worked behind the RPF lines and followed RPF directives on reporting. [27a]

After the April 6 1994 double presidential assassination the western press – including Joshua Hammer (*Newsweek*), and Raymond Bonner, James C. McKinley Jr. and Donatella Lorch (*New York Times*) – went out of their way to cite 'professional-ism' and 'discipline' and 'remarkable self-control' exercised by the invading rebel RPF forces. The western press turned the double Presidential assassinations into 'a mysterious plane crash,' but this was a smoldering wreckage of the truth. [28]

"In conjunction with the military build-up by the RPF and its allies – including the infiltration into Kigali, the capital city, of up to 10,000 RPF soldiers," writes ICTR barrister Chris Black, "western journalists and western intelligence services masquerading as "human rights" organizations began a concerted propaganda campaign against the [Habyarimana] Government and through it the Hutu people, accusing it of various human rights abuses, none of which were substantiated." [29]

U.N. High Commission for Refugees investiga-tor Robert Gersony reported in September 1994 on the RPF's killing of more than 30,000 ethnic Hutus – in a period of two months – and gave a detailed account of locations, dates and nature of crimes, as well as the methods used to kill and to make the bodies disappear. Gersony also identified RPF leaders responsible for the killings. The classified U.N. report has never been released.

Interested moviegoers might want to hack through the perception management of *Hotel Rwanda* to get to United Artists parent company Metro Goldwyn Meyer. [30]

MGM directors, unsurprisingly, given what the film does not tell you about the true U.S. role in Rwanda, include current United Technologies di-rector and U.S. General (Ret.) Alexander Haig. United Technologies is in the business of war and "I'm in charge here!" Al Haig served as secretary of state under a Hollywood actor named Ronald Reagan.

The other producers of Hotel Rwanda include an unknown company called Kigali Releasing Ltd., and another called the Industrial Development Corporation of South Africa Ltd. The latter is a major shareholder of, and mining partner with, Iscor Ltd., one of the companies named by the U.N. Panel of Experts Report (2002) for the illegal exploitation of resources from the Congo. [30a]

U.S. military involvement in Rwanda has included 'counterinsurgency' training, 'psycholog-ical operations' and tactical Special Forces: Special Operations Command oversees Navy Seals, Army Rangers and Delta Force: elite units deployed as special operatives in covert operations. [31]

The hotel in the film is not the real Hotel des Mille Collines. The Tutsi RPF rebels did not enter Kigali, Rwanda's capital city, and save the day, they were in Kigali all along. The RPF gained a foothold in Kigali through their constant decep-tions and manipulations of the "peace process," and with the support of their international backers, especially the United States. The RPF 'rebels' were better trained, better equipped, better organized than any and all other combatants in Rwanda and, notably, numerous sources claim that the RPF had the capacity to stop the killings. Sources also report that the *Forces Armees Rwandais* – the Rwandan government army – didn't have the resources to fight both the RPF and the *Interahamwe*.

Professors Christian Davenport (U. Maryland) and Allan Stam (Dartmouth) published research in 2004 that showed that the killings began with a small, dedicated cadre of Hutu militiamen, but quickly cascaded in an ever-widening circle, with Hutu and Tutsi playing the roles of both attackers and victims. Their team of researchers also found that only 250,000 people were killed, not the 800,000 plus advanced by the RPF, and that for every Tutsi killed two Hutus were killed. The research unleashed a firestorm: the media jumped on them for denying genocide.

"Our research suggests that many of the victims, possibly even a majority, were Hutus – there weren't enough Tutsis in Rwanda at the time to account for all the reported deaths... When you add it all up it looks a lot more like politically motivated mass killing than genocide. A wide diversity of individuals, both Hutu and Tutsi, systematically used the mass killing to settle political, economic and personal scores." [32]

"When you look at the motivations of the *Interahamwe* leadership and young people in the *Interahamwe* they were motivated by money," notes former ORINFOR director Jean-Marie Higiro. Some Hutu businessmen were giving out loans, contributing to political parties of both the Rwandan government and the RPF rebels. "These guys wanted to do business: people were motivated by different interests."

"Many Hutu and Tutsi businessmen prospered under the Habyarimana regime," Jean-Marie Higiro notes. "They received government contracts and loans from government banks and suddenly became rich. During this period of uncertainty they contributed money to the RPF, MRND, and opposition parties – always speculating on the winner. That is why, after the war, very few Hutu businessmen who had

very few Hutu businessmen who had contributed to the RPF reopened their business immediately. That is why some Tutsi businessmen who contributed to the RPF made an excellent calculation. After the war they reaped off the benefits." [33]

Some facts in the film are true. To begin with, in every sense of the terms "human rights" and "humanitarianism," the western powers betrayed the people of Rwanda. The whites were rapidly evacuated, the blacks abandoned, including the many African staffers of international agencies. The French armed the Hutu side, and they evacuated key Hutu elite at the first opportunity, but the United States, U.K. and Belgium armed the Tutsis. There was a Rwandan man named Paul Rusesabagina and he would, one day, be working at the Hotel des Mille Collines, but he was the manager of the Hotel des Diplomats. The Tutsi rebels were blamed with the assassination of the presidents of Rwanda and Burundi, but the film convinces us they didn't do it, when everything suggests they did. And it is certainly true that hundreds of thousands of Rwandans died.

Hotel Rwanda is a work of fiction. As a cultural artifact produced by an affluent *entertainment* industry in the West, and for affluent western con-sumers, but focused on a distant and exoticized culture about which the affluent western consum-ers know very little, or nothing at all, it serves to consolidate the ideological pillars of disinformation that came before it, and upon which it was built.

According to many and varied knowledgeable sources, including hotel insiders, Rwanda was not *abandoned* by the western powers: Belgium, France, Canada, England and the United States were all militarily involved in the 1994 conflict. Because there are Israeli connections to the current govern-ment, it is likely that Israeli military agents were also involved. These were no bystanders to geno-cide, as Samantha Power and the *Atlantic Monthly* and others would like us to think, but active participants in a ruthless *international* military conflagration. Note that amongst *Atlantic Monthly's* primary advertisers [read: sponsors] is Lockheed Martin [aerospace and defense] Corporation.

The hotel was not under a state of siege early on as the movie suggests – an elegant wedding took place there during the fray, and it married the sis-ter of the Tutsi businessman Kamana Claver, who had contracts with the *Hutu* government. Accord-ing to one guest, powerful Hutus and Tutsis regu-larly came and went. When the water to the hotel was shut off, forcing the 'refugees' to drink the water from the swimming pool, it was not shut off by the Hutu *genocidaires*, as implied in the film, but by the Tutsi RPF army, who cut power to the city.

General Bizimungu appears in the very first scenes of the film, prior to the double presidential assassination: yet when the plane was shot down on April 6, 1994, General Bizimungu was still a Colonel, and he was far from Kigali. According to one hotel guest, who remains unnamed for fear of retribution, Paul Rusesabagina, the film's hero, in no way wielded the kind of influence as depicted throughout the film:

"Paul was a very simple man like me in front of the *Interahamwe*. If he succeeded to save some Tutsi from his home he was most probably helped by some influential *Interahamwe* friend, say Georges Rutaganda. He was as vulnerable as I was and could not oppose any action against the will of the militia and much less of the army. He lies when he feints to call General Bizimungu for help, because the Hotel des Mille Collines was under the jurisdiction of Colonel Renzaho. Bizimungu lived at the northern war front lines, and he only came to Kigali four days after the plane was shot down and I never saw him at the hotel." [34]

"There is overwhelming evidence," wrote Rutigita Macumu, in an opinion piece titled "Paul Rusesabagina Not a Hero!" that appeared in Rwanda's *The New Times* state-owned newspaper on November 5, 2005, "that Paul Rusesabagina did not particularly go out of his way to bring the people, who were being hunted, to the Mille Collines Hotel haven, to protect them once they were in the hotel, to procure them food or even water when they were unable to pay for them, or to devise any uncommon means to fend off the killer gangs outside the hotel. It is highly apparent that he only fulfilled his duty, as directed by his Sabena bosses, to run the hotel well and cater for all its occupants." [35]

Georges Rutaganda, the Rwandan man mispor-trayed as the devil beer salesman and erstwhile murderer of Tutsis in *Hotel Rwanda*, writes that Paul Rusesabagina was no disinterested, apolitical hotel manager, but an important activist member of a national political party. On 12 April 1994, Rusesabagina shifted to the Hôtel des Mille Collines where he acted as its new director because the other, the Hôtel des Diplomats where Rusesabagina was working, had been evacuated by foreign troops.

Hotel Rwanda depicts Rusesabagina at the Hôtel des Mille Collines prior to the double presidential assassinations of 6 April 2004. Rutaganda claims to have visited the hotel and seen guests from both Hutu and Tutsi ethnic groups, including: Rubangura Vedaste; Mutalikanwa Félicien; Dr. Gasasira Jean Baptiste; Kamana Claver; Kajuga Wicklif; Rwigema Celestin; Kamilindi Thomas; and others.

Rutaganda claims that very few UNAMIR soldiers were around, and they were incidental to security: the Hutu Gendarmes of the FAR army were manning a roadblock at the main entrance. He also claims that the "refugees" in the U.N. convoy that were turned back at a roadblock "were the real elite cream of Tutsi ethnic tribe. Had one been really spurred by bad intentions this would have been a great occasion to decapitate the Tutsi ethnic group. Families of former ministers, of doctors, of lawyers, of big business men, of highly educated men, of professors, etc, were among them."

If the 'genocide' were so organized and calculated, and quick to strike, then Rutaganda has a very interesting point: how did it happen that the elite of the Tutsi tribe were protected and evacu-ated by UNAMIR troops and Hutu Gendarmes? Of course, all Hutus are killers, and no one will believe a *genocidaire*: Georges Rutaganda was sentenced to life in prison by the ICTR.

Can George Rutaganda's claims be corroborated?

"Georges Rutaganda cooperated with the U.N. to save all those people." ICTR investigator Phil Taylor offers a compelling portrait of the *Hotel Rwanda*'s *supposed devil* himself: Rutaganda didn't incite hate crimes, he called for calm and respect for the Red Cross; Rutaganda was never accused of the rape and sexual slavery depicted in the film; and Rutaganda never traded in machetes. Indeed, Human Rights Watch in January 1994 identified an English businessman who had imported tens of thousands of machetes into Rwanda. [36] More importantly, virtually *everyone* in Rwanda (and Congo) owns a machete and they use it for farming; what would be unusual is if someone did *not* have a machete. Anyways, it was not machetes that did the most killing.

Rape was off the agenda at the ICTR until Hillary Clinton showed up in Arusha and pledged $600,000 to be paid after the first ICTR rape conviction, and that's where the Tutsi women collected in the fictitious Rutaganda compound in *Hotel Rwanda* come from. Hillary Clinton visited the ICTR and bribed the court, and the issue of rape was immediately elevated and a perpetrator needed to be found to satisfy the court, no matter their innocence or guilt, and meet Hillary Clinton's conditions for $600,000 bribe.

"I was Georges Anderson Nderubumwe Rutaganda's lead trial counsel," said Attorney Tiphaine Dickson, "and [I] was present in Arusha, in the courtroom, in fact, the very day Hillary Clinton paid her visit. There were no 'pinning' charges of rape against my client. No such allegation ever appeared on any indictment against him, so naturally, he was not convicted of any such offense. Jean-Paul Akayesu, however, also on trial at that time (the trials were heard concurrently, and by the same panel of judges) did see his indictment amended, after the Prosecution had rested, to include rape, and he was convicted in what the ICTR trumpeted was a 'landmark' decision on September 2nd, 1998." [36a]

The Hollywood Rwanda film offers a fictitious U.N. Colonel Oliver (Nick Nolte) as a substitute for the Canadian Lt. Gen. Roméo Dallaire, who is ab-sent from the film. (It is believed that Dallaire asked too much money from the filmmakers for the use of his name or character.) Dallaire allegedly worked not as an impartial United Nations commander, but as an agent for the invading RPF army. Dallaire reportedly approached Hutu military commanders to convince them to follow the winds of change and embrace the RPF program. Dallaire was rarely present at the hotel, according to witnesses, but his substitute (Nolte) is always there, and he is painted as a sympathetic and neutral humanitarian.

Dallaire mentions in his book how he passed by the Hôtel des Mille Collines, but in his own meticulously detailed recounting of the daily events and travels around Kigali from 06 April to 10 April, 1994, for example, Dallaire stops at the Hôtel des Mille Collines only once. [37]

According to Chris Black, a lead counsel at the International Criminal Tribunal on Rwanda (ICTR) since 2000, U.N. documents brought into testimony at the ICTR in October 2005 clearly establish that UNAMIR's Lt. Gen. Roméo Dallaire:

- was an agent of the RPF;

- helped shoot down the plane in the double presidential assassination;

- covered up the preparation of the final RPF offensive assisted by Uganda, the U.S. and U.K.;

- lied to his United Nations boss Jacques-Roger Booh-Booh about it.

Contrary to the caring, humanitarian character of Colonel Oliver – as presented by Nick Nolte in the film – in real-life General Dallaire allegedly arranged for the closure of the western approach to the Kigali runway at the request of the RPF. This made it easier for the RPF and others to track the presidential plane as it came in from the east. The Belgian contingent of the U.N. force was in control of the airport area and the area from which the missiles were fired, and a Belgian military unit (the "peacekeepers" killed later) were the only people caught by the Hutu army coming out of the firing area after the plane was shot down, after the army threw up a cordon to try to catch the culprits.

"All of Dallaire's actions only make sense in this light," lawyer Chris Black explains. "Dallaire ad-mits in his book that he was close to Paul Kagame and admired him. He helped Kagame by covering up the RPF build-up for an offensive in violation of the Arusha Accords, while at the same time helping with the anti-government propaganda of the RPF. The Belgians actively engaged on the side of the RPF and once the plane was shot down they attacked FAR army and *gendarme* positions alongside the RPF. We have radio intercepts of the RPF talking about their help from the Belgians and others. By saying Dallaire was an RPF agent I am of course really saying he worked for the Americans under the orders of Ottawa." [38]

Lt. General Roméo Dallaire was no peacekeeper: he was an active military strategist – a war-maker.

THE POLITICAL ECONOMY OF GENOCIDE

Prior to the cataclysm of 1994, the RPF set up its political base in Belgium. When Belgian "peacekeepers" are murdered by "Hutus" in *Hotel Rwanda* – the blue helmets are scattered on the ground in front of our horrified U.N. hero, Colonel Oliver (Nolte) – the false inference is that the *genocidaires'* calculated killing of the Belgians would provoke a UNAMIR withdrawal from Rwanda. This is a central pillar of the genocide theory: with the Belgian 'peacekeepers' out of the way, the Hutu killing machine had free reign to shift into high gear. In reality, the Belgians were immediately killed because they were the political accomplices of a ruthless bunch of terrorists, the invading RPF army.

Substantial evidence entered into public record in the ICTR's so-called 'Military I' and 'Military II' trials (both began in 2005) contradicts the fundamental premise above – and the central theory of the ICTR prosecution – by

showing that Hutu officers charged by the ICTR with complicity in the Belgians' murder actually risked their lives trying to save the Belgian soldiers. The U.N. Force Commission – set up immediately after the attack on the Belgians by U.N. Force Commander General Dallaire – concluded the same. Eyewitness testimony by a U.N. Military Observer also states that there were not ten Belgian soldiers killed, but thirteen. "This is a point of some interest in Belgium," writes Chris Black, "where the government claims to have lost only ten men." [39]

So who *were* those three Belgian soldiers and what was their mission? *Hotel Rwanda* dares not introduce such questions: to do so would be heresy. But the United States knows, and the RPF knows and the legal 'experts' at the ICTR all know that the genocide theory would crumble under the admission of the truth.

According to ICTR lawyers, U.N. documents show that Lt. General Roméo Dallaire was aware, at least from December 1993, and probably before, that the RPF, with the support of the Ugandan Army, was daily violating the Arusha Accords by sending into Rwanda men, material, and light and heavy weapons. That is how the U.S., Belgians and Canadians assisted the RPF/A in preparing for the final solution in Rwanda – total military victory over the Hutus. [40]

"The RPF engaged in assassinations of officials, politicians and civilians, and attempted to cast the blame on the government," writes Chris Black. "Dallaire assisted in this campaign by suppressing facts concerning these crimes and openly siding with the RPF propaganda statements." [41]

It was not UNAMIR soldiers who guarded the Hotel but *Gendarmes* (paramilitary police) dispatched by the Hutu government. This fact flies in the face of the "genocide" mythology. If the hotel was full of Tutsis targeted by genocide, why was it being protected by the very same *architects* of that supposed genocide? The Hotel was not filled only with Tutsis (refugees from genocide): it was full of powerful Tutsis and Hutus (with Tutsis in the majority) with political and economic connections to powerful factions both inside and outside of Rwanda.

Questions about the composition of the 'mostly Tutsi' RPF invaders provoke questions about the ethnic composition of the *Interahamwe* militias and commercial relationships that transcended ethnici-ty. Such details are overlooked in the western reductionism on Rwanda – because they contradict the official and burgeoning Rwanda holocaust industry and the U.S. State Department fictions. The following ethnic inconsistencies are very revealing:

- Robert Kajuga was the Tutsi President of the notorious "genocidal" Rwandan *Interahamwe*;

- Kamana Claver was a Tutsi businessman and frequent recipient of large government-awarded contracts from the "genocidal" Hutu government;

- Celestin Sebulikoko was a Tutsi businessman and strong supporter of the main Hutu political party (MRND); he is believed disappeared by the RPF;

- A Tutsi named Mpangaza, who worked for the Rwandan government firm TRANSINTRA, reportedly manned a powerful machine gun at an *Interahamwe* roadblock in downtown Kigali in 1994; he was a well-known *Interahamwe*; he lives peacefully in Rwanda today;

- The son of Juvenal Gatorano, a Tutsi customs agent with the Habyarimana government's Ministry of Finance, was always seen at *Interahamwe* rallies.

These facts, if true, provide compelling evidence that it was not a coordinated genocide that occurred in Rwanda in 1994, but a civil war, and a western proxy war, with deep political, economic and military motivations behind the atrocities. Acts of genocide certainly occurred, as did crimes against humanity, but "acts" of genocide do not constitute genocide as defined by the international legal frameworks on genocide. An entire ethnic group could be wiped out, say the last 100 Penan nomads in Sarawak, for example, but if they are incidentally eliminated in the calculated and racist process of logging their forests – which is exactly what has happened to the Penan – it is not necessarily "genocide" according to the narrow international legal frameworks of the Genocide Convention. Equally troublesome, the U.S. might have annihilated every last Japanese citizen in 1945, but few today would characterize the atomic bombings in Hiroshima and Nagasaki as *genocidal* in nature or intent.

The calculated nature upheld as the basis for *genocide* in Rwanda has always revolved around the supposed "lists" created by Hutu *genocidaires*: lists of Tutsis who were subsequently eliminated because, first and foremost, they were Tutsis; such "lists" were purportedly created by the Hutu genocide machine.

"Any army would have lists of their political enemies," notes ICTR investigator Phil Taylor. "This is not unusual." The Rwandan government likely had its lists, the RPF had their own lists, and both went about assassinating their enemies.

Phil Taylor notes that the prosecution at the ICTR has not produced any lists – of any kind – as evidence subsequently used for Rwanda genocide convictions.

In the aftermath of the World Trade towers attack the intelligence armies of the United States generated an extensive list of "enemies of the state" – a list they maintain today – most of whom were/are of Islamic ethnicity. Do the existence of these lists constitute genocidal intent?

"There is a stunning lack of documentary evidence of a government plan to commit genocide," writes Black. "There are no orders, minutes of meetings, notes, cables, faxes, radio intercepts or any other type of documentation that such a plan ever existed. In fact, the documentary evidence establishes just the opposite." [42]

U.S. Pentagon lawyers imported to the ICTR from the Judge Advocate General (JAG) Corps have heavily skewed the ICTR in favor of the U.S.-supported RPF. Also, the ICTR has not returned a single verdict against RPF Tutsi soldiers or Tutsi leadership; former ICTR prosecutor Carla Del Ponte was removed for her attempts to prosecute Tutsis. [43]

"The ICTR risks being a part of the problem rather than the solution," wrote Filip Reyntjens, Belgian historian and expert witness on genocide in Rwanda, in 2004. "I cannot any longer be involved in this process." [44]

The International Criminal Tribunal for Rwanda (ICTR), the sister of the Hague Tribunal, consoli-dates the popular mythology on genocide in Rwanda by playing its role as an international judicial body which, by default, must be beyond reproach or bias. While demonizing the Hutu leadership and justifying the RPF dictatorship now in control of Rwanda, writes Chris Black, it also serves as a means of presenting a completely false history of the events in Rwanda, and covering up the murder of the two Hutu heads of state and the massacres of hundreds of thousands of innocent people by the RPF and its allies. [45]

In *Hotel Rwanda*, the *genocidal* Hutus blame the Tutsi RPF rebels for shooting down the plane that killed the two presidents, and because the film demonizes every Hutu, the viewer is convinced that the Hutus are lying, deflecting attention from their own nasty deeds. However, evidence suggests that an RPF terror cell in Kigali shot down the Presidential airplane. Also on the plane was a *Forces Armee Rwandais* general, a pivotal target for the RPF. Former U.N. Secretary General Boutros Boutros-Ghali offered journalist Robin Philpot the claim that the Central Intelligence Agency was almost certainly involved.

"As early as 1997," writes a Spanish legal team that in 2005 filed suit against Paul Kagame and his RPF cadre, "a team of investigators appointed by the ICTR – Michael Hourigan, Alphonse Breau and James Lyons – released reports, then held as classified, which revealed that the attack was masterminded by high-ranking RPF military and not by Hutu extremists as had been believed until then. These disclosures were corroborated in 2004 by the remarkable testimony of Abdul Ruzibiza, a member of the RPF commando unit which perpetrated the attack on the presidential plane."[46]

"I am an eye witness to what took place when the SA-16 was fired because I was present," writes Ruzibiza in his recently released book, *Rwanda: L'histoire Secrete (The Secret History of Rwanda)*. Ruzibiza alleges that after the missile attack on the plane, soldiers of the RPF who had been readied in advance were assembled to immediately launch attacks that culminated in the fall of Kigali on July 4, 1994. [47]

There is also the definitive statement by Paul Mugabe, a Former Intelligence Officer of the RPA, titled: *Declaration on the Shooting Down of the Aircraft Carrying Rwandan President Juvenal Habyarimana and Burundi President Cyprien Ntaryamira on April 6, 1994.*

Paul Mugabe alleges that two weeks before the crash of the Presidential aircraft, [then] Major General Kagame sent [then] Lt. Colonel James Kabarebe to bring the SA-7 surface-to-air missiles to the RPA detachment in Kigali, and to give final instructions for attacking Rwandese Army forces (FAR) and shooting down the plane. Two RPF leaders, Colonels Kanyarengwe Alexis and Lizinde Theoneste, who had earlier served in the Habyarimana Government, gave information and instructions as to where the missiles should be placed. (Col. Lizinde Theoneste, who later defected, was subsequently assassinated in 1998 by RPF operatives in Nairobi, Kenya, in order to ensure the secrecy of the missile operation.) Two weeks before the double presidential assassination, 12 artillery systems were brought from Uganda, and arrived at RPA headquarters.

Other RPF defectors also credit the RPF with shooting down the plane carrying the Rwandan and Burundian leadership. Long-time RPF officer Lt. Aloys Ruyenzi claims that the assassination plan was hatched at an RPF meeting on 31 March 1994:

> The Chairman of the meeting was Major General Paul Kagame, and the following officers were present: Colonel Kayumba Nyamwasa; Colonel Théoneste Lizinde; Lt. Colonel James Kabarebe; Major Jacob

Tumwine; and Captain Charles Karamba. I heard Paul Kagame asking Colonel Lizinde to report about his investigations and I have seen Colonel Lizinde giving to Paul Kagame a map of the selected place for the plane shooting etc. [48]

Lt. Aloys Ruyenzi also accuses General Paul Kagame and (now) General James Kabarebe of overseeing the massacres of Hutu and Tutsi civilians, both in the field and at crematoriums set up to dispose of the evidence. Ruyenzi is just one defector with a compelling story. He claims he has witnessed helicopter gunships shelling villages, and massacres, tortures and summary executions as policy. Many of the human rights atrocities committed by the Kagame regime have been documented by human rights organizations.

"Gen. James Kabarebe was the commander of the reverse-genocide army," says Howard W. French, referring to the military campaign where hundreds of thousands of Hutu refugees were hunted down and slaughtered by the Tutsi RPA and their western allies in Congo. [49]

Eighty percent of these Rwandan refugees were women and children; 50% were under 15 years old. [50]

This genocidal reign of terror to hunt down and massacre non-combatant Hutu men, women and children was spearheaded by the Rwandan Patriot-ic Front (RPF) and Ugandan People's Defense Forces (UPDF), who were running the show for Laurent Kabila's Allied Front for the Democratic Liberation of Congo (AFDL) – and it was backed by government and private factions from the United States, the U.K., Canada and Belgium.

One eyewitness to the skeletons piling up pinpoints mass graves that were later sanitized in advance of the United Nations mission to investigate the RPF/UPDF/AFDL massacres of hundreds of thousands of unarmed Hutu civilians. [51]

The *contra*-genocide against Hutus continues today: at this writing the forces are aligned to exter-minate the remaining 40,000 Hutus in Congo: they are all written off as *genocidaires* who fled Rwanda in 1994, even though most surviving FDLR were too young to have participated in genocide. [52]

Sabena officials were not surprised and horrified to be getting a call from some hotel manager in Rwanda, as depicted in the film: one week prior to the October 1990 invasion of Rwanda by the RPF, Sabena Airlines rerouted its airline crews (pilots, hostesses) away from the Hotel des Mille Collines and off to Burundi for their overnights. This was no random decision: it was a calculated policy action meant to insure the safety of company employees in the face of a coming war. Sabena was well informed. A Belgian firm born out of the post-Leopold aviation era in Congo, Sabena was later used to ship diamonds, and probably coltan (columbium-tantalite), out of Kigali by the RPF elites, whose base, again, was in Brussels. It is believed that Sabena's eventual "bankruptcy" was intended to cover their tracks and shield principals from any possible future legal actions stemming from their pillage in the Congo.

What about the elusive American diamond magnate Maurice Tempelsman and his connection to Bill and Hillary Clinton and the diamonds coming out of Kigali? "I don't think that's ever been written about in the *New York Times*," said French. [53]

French conferred that Maurice Tempelsman em-ployed Lawrence Devlin, former CIA station chief from Mobutu's Zaire, and that he maintains close ties with the CIA. Tempelsman is also on the board of directors of the Harvard AIDS Institute and the Africa-America Institute. (Donald Payne is also deeply involved, as is Gayle Smith, formerly Bill Clinton's National Security Council advisor on African Affairs). Tempelsman was Jacqueline Kennedy Onassis's lover, he was reported to be Madeleine Albright's lover, and he was one of the 99 people who accompanied Bill Clinton on his 1998 Africa victory tour. Tempelsman is one of the many *untouchables* behind the quagmire in Central Africa. [54]

Why has the United States blocked all attempts to investigate the shooting down of the plane and the double presidential assassination that sparked the cataclysm on April 6, 1994? Why hasn't the United Nations pursued an inquiry?

"It is a very mysterious scandal," wrote Philpot. "Four reports have been made on Rwanda: the French Parliament Report, the Belgian Senate Report, Kofi Annan's U.N. report, and the Organization of African Unity report. All four say absolutely nothing about the shooting down of the Rwandan President's plane. That just goes to show the power of the intelligence services that can force people to be quiet."

Philpot continues: "The only partial exception is the seven year investigation conducted by the French anti-terrorist judge Jean-Louis Bruguière. That investigation has implicated current Rwandan President Paul Kagame and the Rwandan Patriotic Front for having planned, ordered and carried out the April 6 assassination." [55]

Says ICTR lawyer Chris Black: "President Mobutu's chief of intelligence, Honore Ngambo, in his book published in France a few months ago [*Western Crimes in Central Africa*, 2005] relates the meeting between Habyarimana and Mobutu two days before Habyaramana was murdered. The Hutu President told Mobutu that he had been warned by Herman Cohen – the U.S. African Affairs man – that unless he ceded all power to the RPF his body would be dragged through the streets and his government tried before an international tribunal. Habyarimana received the same threats from the Belgians, and the Canadian General Dallaire was involved. Habyarimana was informed by his agents in the RPF camp at Mulindi that his plane would be shot down. He didn't know the exact date." [56]

The RPF opposed any military intervention in Rwanda after 6 April 1994. The RPF knew the military situation of the Rwandan army (morale and ammunition) and it did not want any military intervention to snatch its victory from it. The RPF's official sponsors in Washington, London and Brussels told whoever would listen that any international force would be met with RPF military resistance. The RPF was the only force that had the capacity to stop the killing, but they didn't.

ICTR lawyer Chris Black verifies that U.N. documents entered in the ICTR record establish that the *Gendarmerie* did all it could with the resources it had to restore calm, but could not, and that the FAR army could not both fight the RPF and restore calm among the civilians.

This following statement comes from an unnamed survivor who was in Kigali in April, 1994, where he lost his entire family to the killings: some of his family were Hutus, some Tutsis, and he began by stating he does not support the ideologies that align themselves along ethnic fault lines. The interview took place in Bukavu, DRC, in August 2005:

"Many Hutus lost family members on the border with Uganda after the RPA invaded in 1990. This is where Hutu hatred of Tutsis started. The Tutsi continued to perpetrate crimes to weaken the government of Habyarimana even while the government was being forced to negotiate with the RPF. Each Tutsi family had sent one or two boys to the RPF army in Uganda. We knew these boys – they used to say, 'O.K. goodbye. We are going to Uganda.' "

"Hutus saw this. The Tutsis [RPF] were pushing the hatred higher and higher every day. Even Hutus knew that all Tutsis had to attend meetings at the end of the month to raise money for the RPF. I heard Habyarimana every day saying on the radio, 'Don't kill Tutsis: if you do you will lose everything.' Even as the Arusha Peace Accords were going on [1993] the RPF were starting to kill the intellectuals, the Hutu leaders, in Rwanda."

"They [RPF] were putting bombs in public places, in markets and *gare routieres* [roundabouts], and in night clubs – I almost died in one night club attack. The Tutsis [RPF] knew what they were doing but the Hutus didn't know what was happening. The RPF waited until the fruit was really ripe – when there was deep hatred of Tutsis by Hutus – and then they

[RPA] killed President Habyarimana."

"They killed Habyarimana because they knew he was the only one who could stop the Hutus from killing Tutsis. That is why, every day, I say that: *the genocide was not planned by Hutus, it was planned by Tutsis: it was planned by the RPF*. Even after the *Interahamwe* killed my wife, even after all the horrible things that have happened to me, I believe the Tutsis created the genocide. And for me it was a war between brothers: the Hutus had an army and the Tutsis had an army and there was fighting at every level." [57]

HEARTLESS DARKNESS

Notably, the source for the *Hotel Rwanda Companion Book* timeline chapter is the Central Intelligence Agency *World Factbook 2004*. (The previous chapter is filled with the standard deceptions, and it appears without attribution.) [58]

It is not surprising then that the roles of the U.S. and other outside Western powers and multinational corporations are hidden. The most egregious omissions revolve around the Democratic Republic of Congo: the ongoing destruction and depopulation of Congo receives remarkably little press coverage in contrast to the Darfur region of neighboring Sudan, despite the obvious evidence that the scale and nature of atrocities against innocent civilians in Congo has been far worse, over a longer period of time, and with profound but unnecessary human suffering.

After consolidating power in Rwanda in 1994, and following on massive crimes against humanity there, the RPF shelled and dismantled refugee camps in eastern Congo (then Zaire) in the summer of 1996, in further massive and egregious violations of international law and the Geneva Convention. The new RPF government has *never* wavered in its efficacious crusade of calling attention to an *ongoing genocide against the Tutsis* – the Jews of Africa – who were "abandoned by the United States and Europe" to ostensibly suffer the fate of genocide, but this is an affront to the Jewish people and, in particular, to the Holocaust victims and survivors of World War II.

The pretext of ongoing 'genocide' against the Tutsis has been used by the RPF over and over to justify the most egregious and hostile violations of international law and human rights. Continuing to implement what is now clearly a well-coordinated and premeditated plan, and with complete logistical and tactical military support from the Pentagon and its outsourced private military companies – including Halliburton, Ronco, and Military Professional Resources Incorporated – the RPF followed its Rwanda victory by invading the sovereign territory of Congo (Zaire), its huge western neighbor. [59]

Drawing on its previous military alliance, training and rear bases in Uganda, the RPF allied with Yoweri Museveni and the Ugandan Peoples Defense Forces (UPDF) to march across the Congo, unseat Habyarimana's close friend, Congo's (Zaire's) President Mobutu Sese Seko, and conquer the vast, mineral rich Congo.

"The international community has refused to bring effective pressure to bear on Rwanda to create conditions of security," wrote Rwanda scholar David Newbury, in 1996. [60]

Marginalized groups like the *Rally for the Return of Refugees and Democracy in Rwanda* have repeatedly echoed this obvious truth. "The continuous prevalence of impunity has encouraged the leaders of the RPF/RPA to perpetrate crimes against humanity, war crimes and acts of genocide in Rwanda and DRC without fear of prosecution. It has consolidated the power and the wealth of criminal elements within the RPF-led dictatorial regime." [61]

And so it continues today. Paul Kagame and James Kabarebe and the Tutsi RPF-dominated government of Rwanda continue to destabilize the Great Lakes Region of Africa, with infiltration of terror cells throughout the neighboring Congo, just as they did in Rwanda (1985-1994). They are ap-peased or courted, the saintly victims of genocide, and they enjoy total impunity and all the benefits of an elite club.

Similarly, the Human Rights Watch press alert of July 1, 2005, for example, targeting the Congo-lese government, is a veiled defense of

Rwandan-US interests in DRC: it is written by Alison Des Forges, from Kigali. [62]

Both the *Hotel Rwanda* film and companion book neatly encapsulate the entire mythology of genocide in Rwanda and the invented heroism of now president Paul Kagame and the Rwanda Patriotic Front (RPF). The true and deeper facts that receive little attention, if any at all, are: {1} the RPF's illegal invasion of Rwanda from Uganda in 1990; {2} its record of war crimes committed from 1990-1994; {3} the RPF double assassination of the Hutu presidents of Burundi and Rwanda on April 6, 1994; {4} the RPF's massive *contra*-genocide of hundreds of thousands of Hutu refugees in Congo (Zaire), of refugees returning to Rwanda from Congo, and of Hutus in Rwanda itself; {5} the RPF's repeated invasions and continuing looting and devastation of the Congo, with the involvement and sanction of RPF officials at the highest level, that continues today; and {6} the collaborating roles of Western institutions, individuals and corporations, and the economic and political benefits that accrue to them, at the expense of Africa and her people.

What has motivated Paul Rusesabagina? It is interesting to note that Rusesabagina has been widely lauded and financially rewarded for his story, the rights to his story, and for his alignment with U.S. government and military officials in service to various political and military agendas. In 2000 he was awarded the Immortal Chaplain's prize, and received the award with a handshake from U.S. Republican Senator Bob Dole. [63]

"As for Paul Rusesabagina," wrote Rutigita Macumu, in Rwanda's *The New Times* newspaper, "he will go down in the annals of history as a man who sold the soul of the Rwandan Genocide to amass medals, including, among others, the Am-nesty International's Enduring Spirit, the Immortal Chaplain Foundation's Prize for Humanity, the Tigar Center's Human Rights Award, the National Civil Rights Museum's Freedom Award, and now the prestigious Presidential Model of Freedom Award from the sitting American president, George W. Bush." [64]

In 2004, Paul Rusesabagina traveled with a Pentagon escort and his namesake actor Don Cheadle to Darfur, Sudan, to draw attention to the popularized, officially accredited 'genocide' occurring there. [65]

This author had a chance to interview Paul Rusesabagina in 2007. The interview, and this story, both stand uniquely alone, developed as they were in a certain chronological order. (See: *The Grinding Machine: Terror And Genocide In Rwanda*, interview with Paul Rusesabagina, April 15, 2007 <*allthing-spass.com/journalism.php?catid=47*>).

Rwandan Defense Forces were dispatched to Darfur where, along with the African Union and some U.S. military, they serve as U.S. proxy war-riors: these are troops responsible for some of the most egregious acts of genocide and crimes against humanity committed in Rwanda and Congo. [66]

Hotel Rwanda is merely the latest production in a protracted campaign of psychological warfare. It is a dangerous work of agitation propaganda because it wets the wide and naive eyes and touches the open and caring hearts of Western viewers. It is deceptive and when viewers depart the cinema with popcorn and chocolate stuck between their teeth they leave thinking they know something about what happened in Rwanda. We as viewers enjoy the idea that we are being educated, when instead we are being indoctrinated, and the insidious effects of the indoctrination are unappreciated. *Hotel Rwanda* exemplifies the careless, simplistic reductionism that is universally manifest in the West's representations of Africa.

Phil Taylor, former investigator for the International Criminal Tribunal on Rwanda, says it aptly: "For anyone who followed closely the 1994 crisis in Rwanda the highly touted film *Hotel Rwanda* is merely propaganda statements interrupted by bouts of acting." [67]

The racism and segregation that played out in the Rwanda cataclysm of 1994, where there were very different conditions and outcomes between whites and blacks, continues to be played out today. The telling and re-telling of the Rwanda 'genocide' story by its very nature revolves around a system of institutionalized segregation. Powerful whites in powerful gate-keeper positions in the West hold a virtual monopoly over the information. Alongside of them are the select voices of non-whites who validate the predominant discourse. These 'experts' include Alison des Forges; Roméo Dallaire; Philip Gourevitch; Victoria Brittain; Samantha Power; Mahmood Mamdani; and many, many others.

"They believe Alison des Forges because she is white and they don't believe me because I am black and I don't speak English so well," says Jean-Marie Higiro. "She is the expert, even though she was an observer and I was a participant."

We can't intimately know the hardships of Paul Rusesabagina, or the trauma of Roméo Dallaire, or the sorrows of Jean-Marie Higiro, or the suffering of the other survivors of the cataclysm in Rwanda, and we must search our own souls on their behalf: the struggle of good versus evil reigns within us all. Indeed, there is a certain arrogance behind this writing, because neither was I a participant in Rwanda. But any hesitation I have in challenging the 'right and proper tale' is overwhelmed by the obscenity of the obvious injustice and the machinations of empire behind it.

If truth is the first casualty in war, then those of us who are lucky observers must endlessly work to resurrect it. In Central Africa, today, truth mingles with the souls of the dead, forsaken amidst the unheard cries of some seven million – mostly innocent people – whose life on this earth ground to a gruesome, meaningless conclusion.

First published: 04 July 2005;

Text Modified: 05 November 2005;

Final Version: 04 December 2005;

Updated Final: 10 January 2006.

Corrected: 18 July 2007.

Corrected: 1 November 2007.

NOTES:

[1] Samantha Power, "Remember the Blood Frenzy of Rwanda," Los Angeles Times, April 4, 2004.

[2] Village genocide courts, or Gacaca tribunals, began operating in Rwanda in March 2005. See: Edras Ndikumana, "Rwanda's Hutus Flee Genocide Courts," 19 April 2005; and "Rwandan President asks Fleeing Residents to Return," Reuters, June 3, 2005.

[3] Samantha Power, A Problem from Hell: America in the Age of Genocide, HarperCollins, 2002.

[4] Private interview: Howard W. French, Northampton MA, USA, March 30, 2005.

[5] Howard W. French, "In Zaire Forest Hutu Refugees Near the End of the Road," New York Times, March 13, 1997; see also Howard W. French, Africa: A Continent for the Taking: The Tragedy and Hope of Africa.

[6] Private interview: Howard W. French, Northampton MA, USA, March 30, 2005.

[7] Lt. General Roméo A. Dallaire, Shake Hands with the Devil: The Failure of Humanity in Rwanda, Arrow Books, 2003.

[8] Rene' Lemarchand noted in his authoritative text Rwanda and Burundi (Pall Mall Press, 1970) that "the term Inyenzi is currently used within and outside Rwanda to refer to small-scale Tutsi-led guerilla units trained and organized outside Rwanda and varying in size from about six to ten men."

[9] Mouvement Republicain National pour la Démocratie et le Développement or National Republican Movement for Democracy and Development (MRND).

[10] The Iceberg of the Conflict in Africa of the Great Lakes Region: Lawsuit Against Those Responsible for the Concealed Crimes Against Humanity, International Forum for Truth and Justice in the Great Lakes Region of Africa, <veritasrwanaforum.org>.

[11] Private communication: Charles Onana, Paris, France, February 2004.

[12] The book published in November 2001 entitled, Les Secrets Du Génocide Rwandais, Enquête Sur les Mystères D'un Président [The Secrets of the Rwan-

dan Genocide, Investigations on the Mysteries of a President], was the subject of President Kagame's initial law suit that was heard in the 17th chamber of the French High court against Cameroonian Journalist Charles Onana.

[12a] See: Victoria Brittain, "Excerpt from: A Share in the Genocide," at: <immortalchaplains.org/Prize/Ceremony2000/ Rusesabagina/rusesabagina.htm> and Victoria Britain, "Letter From Rwanda," The Nation Magazine, September 1/8, 2003.

[12b] See: The Work of The International Human Rights Law Clinic at American University: Twelve Years of Operation, May 2002: p. 4: <wcl.american.edu/clinical/annual_2002 .pdf?rd=1>.

[13] See: immortalchaplains.org/Prize/Ceremony2000/ Rusesabagina/rusesabagina.htm.

[14] See: usip.org/peacewatch/1998/1298/profile.html

[15] On James Rubin: see Wayne Madsen, Genocide and Covert Operations in Africa, 1993-1999, Mellen Press, 1999.

[16] See: Pierre-Damien Mvuyekure, "Philip Gourevitch's Platonic and Conradian Eyes on the Genocide in Rwanda," in Ishmael Reed's Konch.

[17] Private interview: Howard W. French, Northampton MA, USA, March 30, 2005.

[18] Robin Philpot, Rwanda: Colonialism Dies Hard, the English translation of Ça ne s'est pas passé comme ça à Kigali (That's Not How It Happened in Kigali), published in English on-line by the Taylor Report, < taylor-report.com/ Rwanda_1994/ >.

[19] Terry George, Ed., Hotel Rwanda – The Official Companion Book, Newmarket Press, 2005.

[20] The Iceberg of the Conflict in Africa of the Great Lakes Region: Lawsuit Against Those Responsible for the Concealed Crimes Against Humanity, International Forum for Truth and Justice in the Great Lakes Region of Africa, <veritasrwanaforum.org>.

[21] A paper scheduled for publication, Spring 2006, by Jean-Marie Vianney Higiro.

[22] Some of them are: Alliance edited by Alliance National Unity (RANU), an organization that later changed its name into Rwandan Patriotic Front (RPF); Congo Nil, edited in Belgium by Francois Rutanga; Impuruza, edited by Alexander Kimenyi in the United States; Inkotanyi, edited by the RPF; Intego, edited by Jose Kagabo in France; Munyarwanda, edited by the Association of Concerned Banyarwanda in Canada; Avant Garde; Le Patriote; Huguka; and Umulinzi.

[23] The term Banyarwanda refers to ethnic Tutsis, and has been most often used to describe Tutsi refugees in Congo (Zaire).

[24] Mouvement Republicain National pour la Démocratie et le Développement or National Republican Movement for Democracy and Development (MRND).

[25] Robin Philpot, Rwanda: Colonialism Dies Hard, the English translation of Ça ne s'est pas passé comme ça à Kigali (That's Not How It Happened in Kigali), published in English on-line by the Taylor Report, <taylor-report.com/ Rwanda_1994/ >.

[26] See US Department of Defense, Foreign Military Sales, Foreign Military Construction Sales, and Military Assistance Facts, (US Doc D1.2, F76, 996) 1997; see also: Lt. Gen. Roméo A. Dallaire, Shake Hands with the Devil: The Failure of Humanity in Rwanda, Arrow Books, 2003: p. 273.

[27] Lt. Gen. Roméo A. Dallaire, Shake Hands with the Devil: The Failure of Humanity in Rwanda, Arrow Books, 2003: pp. 263-265.

[27a] Private telephone interview, Gary Streiker. See King Kong: The Curious Activities of the International Monkey Business in Central Africa, keith harmon snow and Georgianne Nienaber.

[28] See, e.g.: {a} "Donatella Lorch: "Rwanda Rebels: Army of Exiles Fights for a Home," New York Times, 09 June 1994:10; and "Rwanda Rebels' Victory Attributed To Discipline," New York Times, 19 July 1994: 6; {b} Raymond Bonner: "How Minority Tutsi Won the War," New York Times, 06 September 1994:6; and "Rwandan Refugees Flood Zaire as Rebel Forces Gain," New York Times, 15 July 1994:1; {c} Joshua Hammer, "Rwanda: Situation Is Desperate," Newsweek, 20 June 1994:44-46; "Dark-

ness Visible," *The New Republic*, 09 May 1994:9; and "Why Not Rwanda," *The New Republic*, 16 May 1994:7; {d} Editorial, "Double Tragedy in Africa," *New York Times*, 10 April1994.

[29] Chris Black, "View From Rwanda: The Dallaire Genocide Fax: A Fabrication," 01 December 2005, Sanders Research Associates, sandersresearch.com.

[30] "Perception management" is the contemporary term for the formerly used term "propaganda," and it too is an industry.

[30a] (See: www.natural-resources.org/minerals/law/docs/pdf/ N0262179.pdf page 43; idc.co.za/; & minerals.usgs.gov/ minerals/pubs/country/1998/africa98.pdf.

[31] *Africa Research Bulletin*, August 1997.

[32] See: GenoDynamics Project, genodynamics.com.

[33] Private communication, Jean-Marie Vianney Higiro, August 2005.

[34] Personal communication, name withheld for security reasons, July 2005.

[35] Rutigita Macumu, "Paul Rusesabagina: Not a Hero!" *The New Times* (Kigali), 15 November 2005,

[36] Frank Smythe, *Arming Rwanda*, Human Rights Watch, January 1994.

[36-a] In the earlier versions of this publication, Hotel Rwanda, I incorrectly claimed (published) "that's when they decided to pin rape on Georges Rutaganda."

[37] Lt. General Roméo Dallaire, *Shake Hands With The Devil*, Arrow Books, 2003: pp. 268.

[38] Private communication: Chris Black, Barrister, International Criminal Tribunal on Rwanda, October 2005.

[39] Chris Black, "Persecution Not Prosecution," October 2004, Sanders Research Associates, <sandersresearch.com>.

[40] Chris Black, "View From Rwanda: The Dallaire Genocide Fax: A Fabrication," 01 December 2005, Sanders Research Associates, <sandersresearch.com>.

[41] Chris Black, "View From Rwanda: The Dallaire Genocide Fax: A Fabrication," 01 December 2005, Sanders Research Associates, <sandersresearch.com>.

[42] Chris Black, "View From Rwanda: The Dallaire Genocide Fax: A Fabrication," 01 December 2005, Sanders Research Associates, <sandersresearch.com>.

[43] See Ralph G. Kershaw, "Criminal Tribunal for Rwanda: International Justice According to Washington," *Covert Action Quarterly*, No. 74, Fall 2002.

[44] See: Rory Carroll, "Genocide Tribunals 'Ignoring Tutsi Crimes,'" *Guardian*, January 13, 2005.

[45] Chris Black, "Persecution Not Prosecution," October 2004, Sanders Research Associates, sandersresearch.com.

[46] The Iceberg of the Conflict in Africa of the Great Lakes Region: Lawsuit Against those responsible for the Concealed Crimes Against Humanity, The International Forum for Truth and Justice in the Great Lakes Region of Africa, <veritasrwanaforum.org>

[47] "Kagame Ordered Shooting Down of Habyarimana's Plane – Ruzibiza," *Hirondelle News Agency* (Lausanne), 14 November 2005.

[48] Second Lt. Aloys Ruyenzi, *Major General Paul Kagame Behind the Shooting Down of Late President Habyarimana's Plane: An Eye Witness Testimony*, Norway, July 5, 2004.

[49] Private interview: Howard W. French, Northampton MA, USA, March 30, 2005.

[50] David Newbury, "Convergent Catastrophes in Central Africa," November 1996, udayton.edu/~rwanda/articles/newbury-96.html.

[51] Private interview: name withheld to protect the witness, Democratic Republic of Congo, August 2005.

[52] Front for the Democratic Liberation of Rwanda (FDLR) forces in eastern Congo number 40,000. See also: keith harmon snow, "OPERATION IRON FIST: U.N. Launches Largest Ground Troop Operation in DR Congo Peacekeeping; In South Kivu Hills Rwandan Rebels Cornered," July 17, 2005, <

allthingspass.com >.

[53] *Private interview: Howard W. French, Northampton MA, USA, March 30, 2005.*

[54] *See: Wayne Madsen, Genocide and Covert Operations in Africa, 1993-1999, Mellon Press, 1999.*

[55] *Robin Philpot, "Second Thoughts on the Hotel Rwanda: Boutros-Ghali: a CIA Role in the 1994 Assassination of Rwanda's President Habyarimana?," Counterpunch, 26/27 Feb. 2005, <counterpunch.org/philpot02262005.html >.*

[56] *Private communication: Chris Black, Barrister, International Criminal Tribunal on Rwanda (ICTR), October 2005; Herman Cohen is a former US Secretary of State for African affairs who served under the elder George Bush.*

[57] *Private interview, name withheld, Bukavu, Democratic Republic of Congo, 11 July 2005.*

[58] *For more information, the book adds, see: cia.gov/ factbook/goes/sw.html.*

[59] *On Ronco Company shipping weapons into Rwanda: see testimony by Kathi Austin, Hearing of the House International Relations Committee, July 16, 1997.*

[60] *David Newbury, "Convergent Catastrophes in Central Africa," November 1996, <udayton.edu/~rwanda/articles/ newbury96.html>.*

[61] *RDR Calls for the Prosecution of Crimes Against Humanity and Other Violations of the International Law Committed by the Rwandan [RPF/RDF] Army, Rally for the Return of Refugees and Democracy in Rwanda, Press Release, 9/2001, September 2001.*

[62] *Alison Des Forges, "D.R. Congo: Civilians Killed as Army Factions Clash," Human Rights Watch, Press Release, July 1, 2005.*

[63] *See: immortalchaplains.org/Prize/Ceremony2000/ Rusesabagina/rusesabagina.htm.*

[64] *Rutigita Macumu, "Paul Rusesabagina: Not a Hero!" The New Times, (Rwanda State Newspaper) November 15, 2005; see allafrica.com, November 16, 2005.*

[65] *See: Phil Taylor, "Carving Sudan: Hollywood's Helping Hand," The Taylor Report, taylor-report.com, 17 February 2005.*

[66] *"Rwanda Defense Forces" was the name eventually adopted to rename the formerly named army (Rwanda Patriotic Army) of the Rwanda Patriotic Front.*

[67] *Phil Taylor, "Hotel Rwanda: No Room for the Truth," Taylor-Report, January 17, 2005, <taylor-report.com/articles/ index.php?id=11>.*

Fiction Gutted
The Establishment and the Novel

Tony Christini

PART ONE

As Gideon Lewis-Kraus notes, writing in the Los Angeles Times, James Wood is a writer who matters. People read him, people of the educated, monied, controlling part of the populace. That's why it's important that what James Wood writes does not matter – in central ways. Nowhere is this more on display than in How Fiction Works, the star critic's most recent book, a truncated politically-charged though aesthetic appreciation of fiction that is spectacular in its misrepresentation of reality, or *"the real*, which is at the bottom of [Wood's] inquiries." Ask Wood to annotate a novel, and he provides sometimes splendid views of narrative lines by way of an at times "uncannily well-tuned ear," as Terry Eagleton notes. He is eager to discourse at length, often with quick pith, on how to strive toward reality in fiction (or criticism), reality of the profound sort, the truth, a worthy aim. Unfortunately, HFW is resolute in not accurately representing central elements of reality in both fiction and, call it, actuality, life outside fiction. A few examples of these crucial misrepresentations show how such blindness chops understanding of fiction and life, and why it makes one safe to be a literary star of the status quo, of the establishment, of money and power. One must bury and falsify crucial reality. To that end, in How Fiction Works, James Wood has written an establishment polemic in the guise of aesthetics – a deeply partisan status quo account of the novel that is also pervasive in its misrepresentations of both reality and aesthetics.

THE FIRST DOZEN MISREPRESENTATIONS

1 – the book; 2 – free indirect style; 3 – narrative puzzle as worth; 4 – qualities of narrative mode; 5 – the development of the novel; 6 – selectivity; 7 – the meaning of time and experience; 8 – Flaubert's "advance"; 9 – Flaubert's value; 10 – the visibility of the novelist; 11 – "shiny externality" and miasmic internality; 12 – "juvenility" of plot

Misrepresentation 1 – the book: How Fiction Works is wildly mistitled. (Not, How Fiction *Works*, which would also be inappropriate.) A far more accurate title for the discourse actually written: Purview in the Novel. "The house of fiction has many win-dows, but only two or three doors," Wood opens, and in the course of the book goes on to say much about the windows, doors, and characters one may find inside but says little about the house and grounds itself, let alone the nature of the actions and events one may encounter in and around the household. HFW includes chapters on narrating, detail, character, language, dialogue…but none on plot, which he dismisses as if in a fit of mental as-phyxia as "essential juvenility" – plot, the grounds and motion of life – the actions and events, time and place of story. There is far more to fiction than any favored purviews of Wood might reveal.

Misrepresentation 2 – free indirect style: It becomes amusing, the repetitions of this bit of jargon: "free indirect style…or speech…or discourse" – a type of narrative mode presented in convoluted fashion as if requiring complex explanation, over the course of, initially, fourteen pages.

Wood posits at least nine labels for the mode he gives three names. "Free indirect speech or style… or discourse" is: "just authorial irony" or "merely another definition of dramatic irony" or "internal speech or thought" or "'close third person'" or "'going into character'" or "secret sharing" or "soliloquy…renovated" or "close to stream of consciousness" – or – "much like pure soliloquy" of character "simultaneously" consisting of authorial "omniscience…through the author's eyes and language." Readers of HFW are left sensing that whatever free indirect style might be, it is not anything exactly that Wood quite explains, and it comes off as either comically convoluted or professsional "secret." Though all modes of discourse may be rendered with extraordinary complexity, the basics can be quickly known (even three as footnote).[19]

Misrepresentation 3 – narrative puzzle as worth:

It soon becomes clear in HFW that Wood is most interested in a more complex sort of free indirect style which he flails to name (to no avail). He is captivated by what might be called: unstable multipurview meld (UMM). (Or, more simply put: *unstable purview meld*, UPM, but I prefer here the more suggestive acronym, UMM – as we might call Wood's favored version of "free indirect discourse.") This mode makes for a "game" or "puzzle" to figure out. What is attributable to whom? who is speaking? what are they saying? what does it mean? – an approach potentially engaging or valuable but too often mere fetish (and expounded as trivial puzzles, imprecision, bogus ambiguity, vapid indeterminacy, or sheer drivel – sometimes as vacuous narrative fixation with schizophrenia, multiple personality disorder, or general evasiveness and other displays of narrative dissolution and distraction).

Wood claims that this "game" or "puzzle" exists in every mode as "our basic novelistic tension: Is it the novelist who is noticing these

---

[19] *Wood could have simply overviewed the three basic types of speech he refers to: 1) Direct discourse, which presents the speaker verbatim: She thought, I need prevail... 2) Indirect discourse, which is the speaker reported: She thought she need prevail... 3) Free indirect discourse, which drops attributives (she thought, she said) and instead implies attribution, sometimes uncertainly, sometimes mixing and melding "speakers" (the purviews of referents): Rosa worked the picket line as her friend Al came into view. She need prevail for the union. Meaning is much destabilized in this third mode because especially with no context it's not clear to whom the thinking is attributed. The thoughts may represent Rosa's purview or not at all, may instead be entirely or partly that of the narrator/author, or of Al, or of the whole group...*

Any aspect of these thoughts (whether it's belief, or vision, or sentiment, or principle, or diction, or voice, etc) may be shared to varying degrees with a wide variety of "speakers." Any or all of this uncertainly attributed discourse may more-or-less be clarified in context, or be indicated later, or not. Alternatively, in both direct and indirect discourse, the phrase is clearly attributed to Rosa (she owns it, or it owns her – though plenty of ambiguity may exist in these modes as well regarding actual purview and ultimate referent). One can sense the various paces, voices, and other differences in these three modes, each diverse in qualities. Obviously, where quick attribution of thought or speech is urgent, free indirect discourse may not be the best option. No mystery why.

things or the fictional character?" What an isolated game this. Wood cares far more for "who" is noticing "things" than for most anything else. Such "games" and "puzzles" are played by people who are bored with larger story. It's upscale soap opera – the "tension" of a blinkered shut-in – that ideal marketing target. Give the marks a game, distract them with toys and intrigue, however limp. What else might fill the void left by dismissing plot? Playing up such game as the "basic novelistic tension" is as marginal and eviscerating of a representation of the novel as one may find in serious criticism.

Misrepresentation 4 – qualities of narrative mode: Tagging Wood's favored narrative mode with "free indirect" misleads readers from the fact that it may be neither much free nor indirect in central ways, despite fitting the accepted technical parameters.

Wood's preferred UMM mode may be highly confined (to, say, two main views) and be free of little beside attributives. The mode may even present direct authorial commentary and direct speech, or if this is disallowed by definition, then the mode is scarcely free in that way too. So why not move on from the theoretical roots and call it more what it really is? After all, HFW is to be a book that "asks a critic's questions and offers a writer's answers" so as to "reduce what Joyce calls 'the true scholastic stink' to bearable levels." Why not give a precise yet plain talk name to the mode Wood prefers – unstable multipurview meld, UMM? Despite being more accurate, UMM mode does not sound nearly as sweeping and profound, one may suppose, as "free indirect speech or style...or discourse." UMM is one engaging yet limited narrative approach among others, far from a sweeping culmination, as "If the history of the novel can be told as the development of free indirect style..." The mode is often dysfunctional where precise clarity of meaning is needed. Even when well and fully employed, UMM mode is neither as free nor indirect as advertised.

Misrepresentation 5 – the development of the novel: While Wood's favored narrative approach can work as an intriguing aspect of fiction, it functions too often as a type of "puzzle" remote from any necessarily "basic novelistic tension." Wood says "our...tension" and if by "our" he means a longstanding establishment fixation then he may be accurate. Rather than a great source of wonder and vitality, wholesale fascination with such "tension" points to major debilitation in the capacity of the novel. It points to a mode of fiction that is a regression to gaming in excess, as Wood extols it. While Wood highly values this mode in part as mind-mix or meld of consciousness, he seems more fascinated by blinding or diversionary mind-melt, rather than a mode where melded thoughts and sensations may be understood as basic distinct purviews (as in, say, Jonathan Swift's "A Modest Proposal" 1729) that functions with clear point and purpose – along with any degree of ambiguity and open-endedness.

UMM stories can readily prattle on with great pretension or trivial focus and may push into schizophrenia or multiple personality disorder – modes which have long since been embraced by the establishment, much as the status quo also welcomes and encourages toothless (or repressive) busywork for other academics and intellectuals. Alex Comfort noted 60 years ago in his valuable book of criticism, The Novel and Our Time (1948): "We have a tedious mass of books by lunatics who think they are psychologists and by neurotics who think they are lunatics. The literary magazines are full of the praises of schizophrenia." This is a notable "modernist" tendency, though not only modernist in expression, a sometimes interesting and even useful exercise of the novel but far from central to a necessary development of the form, to imaginative work in general. Pushed beyond its capacity to give birth, this mode as "game" and "puzzle" marks, where universally revered, an end to history in more ways than one. Death by, say, juvenile gaming disorder.

Misrepresentation 6 – selectivity: Flaubert is the phony god of the literature establishment, whom Wood especially believes in. Flaubert's relatively small example is vaunted much like the fake Wizard in the Wizard of Oz, projected and distorted beyond its reality, an example probably not even as helpful to writers, readers,

and literature as that of the kindly aged professor of Oz to Dorothy. It was Glinda the good witch who directed Dorothy home, not the bumbling professor, ostensible Wizard.

Wood's preferred "Flaubertian" purview gaming is a natural fit for what Wood also calls Flaubertian blurring of both time and meaning in narrative, "the insistence...that in some way *there is no important difference between* [even grossly different] *experiences*: all detail is somewhat numbing, and strikes the traumatized voyeur in the same way" – a style or approach highly useful to the establishment. Wood comments that post Flaubert such a blurring approach has often been used by nonfiction writers in reporting on war – which makes perfect sense for establishments conducting criminal aggressions. Flaubert with "intense selectivity of detail" and by great "authorial impersonality" focuses on "blurring the question of who is noticing" the world, "all this stuff," and what it might mean. Actually, if one wants to "blur" both the world and who might be perceiving it, one selects details randomly, not with "selectivity." The selectivity is meant more to "turn prose into poetry," however "impersonal." Obviously, one must do something with the random. Fashioning it as poetic is one option, but far from the greatest recourse.

Misrepresentation 7 – the meaning of time and experience: "No novelist pushed to such extreme the potential alienation of form and content (Flaubert longed to write what he called a book about nothing)." No fiction could be more serviceable to the establishment than books of "poetic" prose about "nothing." Flaubert's technique, much praised by Wood, "confus[es] habitual detail with dynamic detail" – so that as in "modern war reporting...the awful and the regular are noticed at the same time..." thus rendered "anti-sentimental" and "numbing." And so are served certain clear interests in randomizing reality, stripping it of select meanings.

For example, "a soldier dies while nearby a little boy goes to school," Wood writes, rather than: "The missile exploded the little boy on his way to school as the US jet flew gallantly on." One sentence has the quality of jump, with vital trope, while the other is a yellowed museum piece, and in fact seems not "anti-sentimental" but grotesquely sentimental: do look at this plucky, pitiful child – a bit of life and school goes on, amidst the gore (for which, unmentioned, we are responsible). Such prose often is grotesque because negligent and vapid – "traumatized" or "numbing" – repugnant and dumbed down.

Misrepresentation 8 – Flaubert's "advance": Not infrequently while reading HFW, one must annotate sentence by sentence to correct falsehoods or record incredulity at what is written. The "great innovation" of Flaubert, Wood notes, the great model for novelists, American and English included, is due to the time-ambiguous properties of a verb form that does not exist in English and so cannot be employed: "…*in English, we have given the game away, and are admitting the existence of different temporalities.*" Actually, an author would be *asserting* the difference, making it more precise, which Flaubert in French either cannot or chooses not to do, at times. Some advance – topped immediately by Wood's subsequent claim that the "loafing" and looking of a stroller is the "classic … novelist activity" of the modern novel, which is tantamount to saying the novel imploded post Flaubert, and to a great extent for well over a century "so strong is the post-Flaubertian inflection of our era."

Yet Wood insists, "Novelists should thank Flaubert the way poets thank spring; it all begins again with him" – the new "classic novelistic activity" of "loafing," looking, strolling; the acceleration of the use of the UMM "puzzle" as the "basic novelistic tension"; the "modern" "blurred" use of time and detail that is "traumatized" and "numbing" and said to be highly "selective" in producing the "random," and also a "game," yet via war reporting, anything but. The novel certainly has been encouraged to implode – the establishment seems to relish it, when not complaining about the inevitable results – tedious wastelands of poetic nothings and nowheres, garish frenzied fiction, status quo banality, thin enigma, and all sorts of fiction that help eviscerate much public and private reality. Not unlike such fiction, HFW is a partisan creature in aesthetic clothing, bearing the open wounds of wholesale misrepresentations and truncations, lurching on, cocksure in its broken myths and misprision.

Misrepresentation 9 – Flaubert's value: A century and a half on, Flaubert's main value in art is that he continues to be used by the literature establishment to bury his countryman Victor Hugo and the example of a far more wholly accomplished and world changing fiction that is liberatory. While Hugo (Flaubert's landmark, watershed predecessor and contemporary) is a greater artist and liberatory force in literature and history than Flaubert, the establishment is deeply invested in giving the basic opposite impression. In a neat inversion, and to the detriment of all but perhaps the most privileged, Flaubert is used to bury Hugo, by way of misrepresented aesthetics, norms, reality.

Flaubert is so lauded by the establishment evidently because his ideological line is a great fit for that which the status quo must work within – an orthodox ostensible apoliticism – the ideology that denies it is an ideology. In fact, Flaubert is the status quo's ideological apotheosis: a politically dismissive, politically disparaging artist who is narrowly aesthetically obsessed, a figure whose work has anything but apolitical effects. Moreover, Flaubert's work is conveniently situated in time and place and style obsession to help downplay the work of the influential and far more socially engaged novelists in and around what has been called "the de facto world capital of literature," Paris, France – Balzac and Zola – but especially and primarily – Victor Hugo, whose achievement in both literature and life dwarfs that of Flaubert, and holds far more real and potential significance through years past, years present, and foreseeable years future. "'We felt that simply by reading [Hugo's] works, we were contributing to some silent victory over tyranny,' remembered Émile Zola," as noted by Graham Robb, biographer of Hugo. Dostoevsky called Les Misérables "that great book." Tolstoy considered Les Misérables to be the greatest novel ever.

Rather than Victor Hugo's society-rocking fiction (and daunting aesthetic achievement), today James Wood and many a writing circle celebrate the wan and overstuffed, by comparison, writing of Flaubert as seminal and essential. The establish-ment shouts Flaubert and his example far forward, typically to the effective exclusion of the greater art and the greater figure of Hugo, and the great work and vision especially in (though very far from only) Les Misérables – "a work of serious fiction for the masses…one of the last universally accessible mas-terpieces of Western literature, and a disturbing sign that class barriers had been breached," notes Robb of the great work of liberty, justice, humanity. Hugo was born a couple decades before Flaubert and died a few years after him, thus eclipsing Flaubert in life as well as in art and society, though the literary establishment has for many decades functioned purposefully, habitually, and predicta-bly, to no little success, to upend both reality and potential. James Wood is of his time and place in following suit.

Misrepresentation 10 – the visibility of the novelist: Wood's preferred UMM mode actually makes the author, if anything, more visible, rather than less, as Wood tries to have it, pointing to Flaubert again as primary example ("the author's fingerprints are…traceable but not visible"), then later retracts ("almost comically impossible"). Wood undercuts another of his own would be representations again not long after he says "Novelists should thank Flaubert" (rather than the "genre hardening" im-peratives of the lit establishment and larger society) "the way poets thank spring; it all begins again with him." He then demurs: "As so often, the Flaubertian legacy is a mixed blessing[;]…a poet's obsessive excrucation" (visibility) – "rather than a novelist's joy…[which is] sometimes an obstruction to seeing, not an aid…" – also, sometimes *studiedly* irrelevant." Mixed indeed, Flaubert – blessing not so much.

Flailing though it is, Wood's laborious obsession with "style" helps build up and prioritize a repressive proscribed narrative approach over all others. "If the history of the novel can be told as the development of free indirect style" as Wood states, positing purview game as "our basic novelistic tension," "it can not less be told as the rise of detail" of a particular type "characteristic of modern novelists" (rather than, one may note again, characteristic of any sociopolitical shifts and sectors, whether freeing or constrained) – a "cult of 'detail'…" Cult? No kidding. Who's cult, one might ask, and why? "There is the modern commitment to detail itself: the protagonist seems to be noticing so much, recording everything!" and showing so precious little, beyond poetry, with great "nuance" and "subtlety" and "limning" and *style*. All that a "voyeuristic" "loafer" devoid of any larger plot or certain purpose (for that might be construed as *propaganda*) could stroll past.

"[O]ur basic novelistic tension: Is it the novelist who is noticing these things or the fictional char-acter?" Quite a "cult." No wonder it morphs and flees into "hysterical realism," as Wood calls the hyperventilating of authors apparently bored or trapped into mania by the great Flaubertian spring. Such predilections for the novel represent a step back, an arbitrary limbing of narrative technique, a collapse of narrative substance and value. (Limbed by "*studiedly* irrelevant" limnings.) The invisibility of the author? On the contrary, one gets the sense that – apart from forsworn fealty to the status quo – the author and the author's style are about all that exist at the center of an establishment novel – an arty game vaunted as narrative abundance by that quintessential establishment production: HFW.

Misrepresentation 11 – "shiny externality" and miasmic internality: Several decades ago, in language strikingly similar to that of Wood, critic and scholar Robert Alter deplored what he called puerile imagination, "the astonishing degree of puerility," much akin to what Wood calls "hysterical realism," though Alter is more advanced in his analysis of plot and its consequences. Alter critiques more the public element of story as involves the personal rather than private elements of the personal. Alter all but names a kind of "hysterical realism" phenomenon with his observation of puerile prose in speaking of authors (Pynchon, Barth, Barthelme... Vonnegut) who like today's "hysterical realists," if in somewhat different fashion, "finally [do not take] history very seriously," or at least scarcely represent it profoundly or even substantially, Alter concludes, "despite the overwhelming density of actual historical detail in the [novels]." (While I draw some of Alter's views partly forward to today's novelists, I don't know if Alter himself would do so.)

No matter that, Wood declares intense character immersion goes wanting. Wood has scarce need for plotting as critic, since he can simply follow the contours of the novel under review. Wood is a proud stylist, so it's interesting that his style im-mediately dulls when he attempts to write fiction, though no surprise since quality fiction is an origi-nating document of life, whereas criticism of the sort Wood excels at is highly referential of text. In his criticism where Wood ventures into generaliz-ation and "theories," his thought frequently dims there also. That his original writing does not begin to approach the intermittent brilliance of his critical referential writing may result from an attempt to use one valuable tool for too various tasks, lacking the necessary others. He sometimes seems restless and impatient with his text-observant talent, worrying language and narrative as if anxious to be a novelist or a theorist above all else. As with "hysterical realist" novelists, he puts too much pressure on style and select other elements of fiction, pushing for more than can be birthed. And then pushing harder, with predictable results. In fiction, dullness. In theory, narrowness or vacuity, fronted by the misrepresentations of establishment ideology. Alter at least understands that bankrupt plot is a problem in fiction; whereas Wood regresses to the brute solution of gutting rather than engaging. He substitutes gaming style and interior obsession, both of which, lacking much of any fresh turn of plot, quickly pall (Flaubert, for example, and many another dried flower fainting from the sun, subsisting in pavement cracks, huddling in quite small corners of life) or spoil.

Today's "Hysterical Realism," Wood notes in his aptly titled essay "Human, All Too Inhuman," of work like that of early Zadie Smith, "does not lack for powers of invention. The problem is there is too much of it" creating such a welter of details that "as realism, it is incredible; as satire, it is cartoonish; as cartoon, it is too realistic; and anyway, we are not led toward...consciousness..." but instead are deluged in narrative that "is all shiny externality," the too-often shallow or chaotic, driveled, and boring juvenilia that Alter finds in earlier novels and that Wood notes of a passage in Smith's *White Teeth*, which:

> might stand, microcosmically, for her novel's larger dilemma of storytelling: on its own, almost any of these details (except perhaps the detail about passing the shit and piss through the cat-flap) might be persuasive. Together, they vandalize each other: the Presbyterian dipsomaniacs and the Mormon aunt make impossible the reality of the fanatical Muslim.

In a remarkably similar observation almost thirty years prior, Alter notes that Pynchon's highly acclaimed novel Gravity's Rainbow is also greatly marred, because:

> If history is no longer a realm of concatena-tion, if there are no necessary connections among discrete events and no possibility of a hierarchy of materials ranged along some scale of significance, any associative chain of fantasies, any crotchety hobbyistic interest, any technical fascination with the rendering of odd trivia, can be pursued by the novelist as legitimately as the movement of supposedly 'significant' actions. The end of history, in other words, is a writer's license for self-indulgence, and Pynchon utilizes that license for page after dreary page of *Gravity's Rainbow* as he describes at incredible length varieties of turds in a sewer, varieties of revolting wine-jelly candies in a British cupboard, varieties of bizarre sexual combinations in a very long daisy-chain, and so forth. The lack of selectivity leads to local flaws; the unwillingness to make differential judgments

about historical events results in a larger inadequacy of the novel as a whole.

Notice that Alter accurately speaks of the "lack of selectively" rather than the "selectivity" that is actually more-or-less randomness, blurring detail and meaning. More recently, when Alter is not translating and introducing ancient religious texts, he still finds time to comment on classic fiction. In his book published 2005, Imagined Cities: Urban Experience and the Language of the Novel, Alter states:

> Flaubert's breakthrough in the representa-tion of the urban realm was to perceive the modern metropolis simultaneously as a locus of powerful, exciting, multifarious stimuli and as a social and spatial reality so vast and inchoately kinetic that it defied taxonomies and thematic definition... Flaubert's novel [The Sentimental Education] marks a moment of transition in which the stylistic unity, the syntactic coherence, and the temporal continuity of realist fiction are preserved while the certitude of realist representation is rejected. The city begins to show a phantasmagoric face...

Then come Joyce, Ellison, Pynchon, DeLillo in part, but how much of Achebe, Toer, Mahfouz, Gordi-mer, Coetzee, Ngũgĩ , Updike, Philip Roth, Franzen? And which authors tend to be more visible in text due to their extra stylist gyrations than the others? The Flaubertian invisibles, seems to me. Bellow and Morrison may be more mixed, but let's say one can pick out two accomplished and somewhat distinct tendencies, both of some quality, both of mixed normative import – it seems to me that the potential of the latter tendency remains key and greater – largely because of its greater ability to clearly express and substantially communicate. Such fiction may still be extraordinarily appealing and intriguing of aesthetics, for those who value that above all. And this tendency may also incorporate modernist tendencies – no reason why it should not, to a degree.

Seen from this vantage, Flaubert stands as a landmark figure of what? He is celebrated for celebrating incommunicability, nothingness, and blurring meaning (not least by Victor Brombert in his keen study, The Novels of Flaubert). It's all so inspiring to the "moderns." That's quite an aesthetic turn, an esthete's turn, a turn for stasis, and not much more than a particular aesthetic emphasis but then there is the retrograde politicization (ostensibly apolitical) with debilitating normative and aesthetic effects. As such, Flaubert and the moderns are scarcely what Wood and others make them out to be: the leading lights of fiction. These are strains of fiction celebrated, vaunted, rendered iconic out of all proportion to their real value. Flaubert serves, even slaves, for the establishment by the establishment, and his example is near bankrupt for progressives, for popular efforts at social progress, even for revealing the full human condition, its reality and potential. There is only so much "nothingness," "incommunicability," and "blurring" a story can withstand before it turns miasmic or resorts desperately to shiny puerility – no matter its "overwhelming density of actual historical detail," as Alter makes note, let alone an oblivious lack.

Misrepresentation 12 – "juvenility" of plot: Frequently in How Fiction Works, as Wood examines elements of favored canonical texts, one gets the sense of a man sitting in a closet folding his special clothes or, more literally, cloistered in den reviewing favored fictions as the only precious thing around apart from himself – all lines to the world cut off. Such is life without plot – the great mixing grounds of life – derided as categorically juvenile, the "essential juvenility of plot."

No wonder Wood attempts to reach *"the real"* in fiction by way of fastidious intimacies of "style... point of view...perception of detail, and...charact-er." Unreal, not to prioritize action and events also, idea and purpose, the social and the public. Instead: styled purviews forever peering, sensing... themselves? Wood's semi-notion of the "essential juvenility" of plot might be insulting I suppose to such masters of plot as Victor Hugo in Les Misérables or Ngũgĩ wa Thiong'o in Wizard of the Crow, if such a notion were not so marvelously blank, so replete of silly. No wonder Wood adores authors like Henry James, turning blinded eyes from James' voids and retrograde lines. To "[think] like writers," according to Wood, is to "attend to style, to words, to form, to metaphor and imagery," and HFW tries to "offer a writer's answers" to "critic's questions," "essential questions about the art of fiction," questions about "reality...metaphor ... character...detail...point of view...imaginative sympathy..." and "why fiction moves us," while questions of plot are cast aside, derided as "juvenility," possibly because, as painter Ben Shahn notes, "Some [critics], more innocent and more modern, have been taught – schooled – to look at [art] in such a way as to make them wholly unaware of content...." Schooled by the establishment, and paid for reproducing it, faithfully. No plot past this line, says the headmaster. But the true truants are not readily schooled.

PART TWO

THE MISREPRESENTATIONS CONTINUED:

13 – "Our memories are aesthetically untalented"; 14 – preeminence of the "subtle"; 15 – plot in the novel; 16 – value of place; 17 – quality of plot; 18 – limited engagement; 19 – fiction no use; 20 – fiction no remedy; 21 – fiction "makes nothing happen"; 22 – writer as "good valet"; 23 – "No one is literally run off her feet"; 24 – the petty terrorist

Misrepresentation 13 – "Our memories are aesthetically untalented": After misprising purview in the first part of How Fiction Works and beyond, in section 39 Wood claims that "Our memories are aesthetically untalented" and implies that we have the modernist novel to aesthetically point this out. Fingers crossed that science has not already disproved the claim. Further down the Orwellian memory hole goes the fact that ancients wrote epics in aesthetic verse to make easy for bards to memorize.

Misrepresentation 14 – preeminence of the *"subtle"*: "*Subtlety* of analysis is what is important," says Wood. Not *striking* analysis, subtlety, which is another word for *nuance* – the establishment's all-time favorite word for the truncated range of its preferred fiction. Nuance is even more cherished than "limn." *Subtlety* – that

by which never have so many nuanced so much to limn toward so little. Wood portrays the novel as sort of subtle styled character sketches of great sensitivity – a basic misrepresentation of the nature and scope of fiction, imaginative literature in full.

Misrepresentation 15 – plot in the novel: Essentially banished from HFW is any semblance of promin-ent discourse theorist Bakhtin's "chronotype" – the space-time "matrix which governs the base condi-tion of all narratives and other linguistic acts," or as scholar Radu Surdulescu describes it, "the specific sense of space and time (in other words the social and the historical components) which characterizes every genre, according to its specific ideology. If in the ancient works the social element played a background role, in the novel it has a direct, molding impact upon the characters: they and the society influence and change each other as it happens in actual history, and this accounts for Bakhtin's interest in the dialogic consciousness of the novel," including that of free indirect style. This "base condition" gets the opposite of emphasis from Wood in HFW. Adios, Setting. Goodbye, Plot. So long, Social. Goodnight, Public. It's intimate purview essentially first, middle, last. Form doesn't come from content, goes the establishment creed, content comes from form: it matters not at all if everyone is writing about toads hopping along a road with a mirror strapped on; what matters is how and why the toads' mirror shines. Toads everywhere for all – why not? if form is the essence of the artwok.

While Wood disparages the narrative technique of plot as juvenile, it's really Juvenal he shuns, the pointed artist who does not at best blur meaning or outlook, time or detail (though such work like Juvenal's art is far from devoid of ambiguity). Thus in part the flatness, the precise fog of style that shoves not only plot but also distinct point, those great content carriers of the world, too far down, unrealistically so. What is plot? A kind of map of events or action, expanding from place and time, explicit or implicit. Plot, the mixing grounds of the world, the motion and stuff of life, is the furthest thing from "juvenility." While sensitive sketches of soaring subtlety make for an accomplished part of fiction, to essentially implicate this confined range as the whole is as false as it gets. Fiction works to proven extent far beyond style, view, perception, character, and voice – purview. Plot is where adults live, while children live relatively oblivious to its vast reaches. Plot is what adults especially can see and affect to varying extent, the goods and the bads that people often relate to one another, or might, the new and the old, the news, what goes on, what's happening, what might. While it certainly is true that there is plenty of juvenility and void in the plots of the establishment, not to mention falsity, plot is only as juvenile as one chooses to make it. Plot is for grownups. Plot is essential to the full human condition that is the novelist's job to convey, and reconfigure.

Goethe claims: "What is a novel but a peculiar and as yet unheard-of event? This is the proper meaning of this name; and much which in Germany passes as a novel is no novel at all, but a mere narrative, or whatever else you may like to call it." Or if Bakhtin and Goethe are thought to be so very far beyond the "common reader," one might turn to Mary McCarthy's suggestive essay, "Characters in Fiction" (1961) in On the Contrary:

> The distinctive mark of the novel [as compared to other forms of fiction] is its concern with the actual world, the world of fact, of the verifiable, of figures, even, and statistics. If I point to Jane Austen…Eliot… Tolstoy… Faulkner, it will be admitted… different as they are…they have one thing in common: a deep love of fact, of the empiric element in experience. I am not interested in making a formal definition of the novel…but in finding its quidditas or whatness, the essence or binder that distinguishes it from other species of prose fiction: the tale, the fable, the romance. The staple ingredient present in all novels in various mixtures and proportions but always in fairly heavy dosage is fact.

McCarthy traces the early history of the novel, 'the birthmarks':

The word novel goes back to the word "new," and in the plural it used to mean news – the news of the day or year…. Many of the great novelists were newspaper reporters or journalists [and "students" of criminals and prisons] "confirmed prison-vistors" … Defoe … Dickens … Dostoevsky … Victor Hugo … Tolstoy…. Coming to the twentieth century, you meet the American novelist as newspaperman: Dreiser, Sinclair Lewis, Hemingway, O'Hara, Faulkner himself…. Novels carried the news – of crime, high society, politics, industry, finance, and low life… The epic, I might put in here, is the form of all literary forms closest to the novel; it has the "boiler plate" ["durable informative matter"], the lists and catalogues, the circumstantiality, the concern with numbers and dimensions. The epic geography, like that of the novel, can be mapped, in both the physical and social sense…. Whenever the chance arises, Jane Austen supplies a figure.

McCarthy's fact-struck essence is as central to the novel as Wood's notions of purview, and more substantial than what little constructive sense Wood can make of the ostensible Flaubertian "spring" of style-obsessed fiction. In HFW, the misrepresentations are so pervasive that the book would not be worth critiquing at length if Wood were not so relatively prominent, so typical of establishment views, and yet also frequently keen within a range when analyzing the works of Western authors as notable as Morrison, DeLillo, Pynchon, Wolfe, Coetzee, Rushdie, Updike, Roth…and Franzen somewhat. Wood's quality work is continuously undercut by his establishment ideologies: studied intelligence is warped by ideological commitments manifest as various prejudice, bias, ignorance willful or otherwise. Thus we see the public and society, history and the (f)actual in fiction poorly accounted for in HFW, in Wood's essays on the "social novel," and elsewhere.

Misrepresentation 16 – value of place: How impor-tant is place, for example? Every novel consists of at least two or three fundamental places – the imaginary place of the story (author sustained) and its connection to real place, and the new places co-created by reader imagination. A sort of levitating sense of place may be created in quality fiction, and some nonfiction. This sense of place may function directly and metaphorically and must work for story. (It should go without saying that place, as detail, may be extremely concrete or almost entire-ly implied.) Place in story may be illusory, even as naturalism. And though place is a key and central part of how fiction functions, it is only one part of the several key components of plot. Fiction does more than plumb the depths of style, or voice, or mind. It certainly explores those but also the world and nature beyond.

Misrepresentation 17 – quality of plot: Just as readily as plot, and just as falsely, can style and view and character be put down as "essential juvenility." Does not style mask the inherent, the more real? Are make-believe characters not for children? Are the views of such characters not at least two steps from reality and thus essentially not real? All may be made to function poorly. However when well done, these elements of fiction draw reality or nature out of itself, as much as plot may as well in challenging our understandings of the real and the possible – the nature of the human condition (biology and psychology…human will…environment and society). A cut to plot is a cut to fiction and life, a cut to the ever hungry always thirsty imagination. Plot is not only great apparatus but profound creation.

When Huck says, "All right, then, I'll go to hell" in deciding – against the mores to which he was "sivilised" – to oppose Jim's returning to slavery in Twain's classic novel, the moment is complex and compelling due to a wonderful intersection of plot, voice, character. The world has gone against the truth, and so young Huck chooses to go against the world as it was instilled in him and as it looms and attacks. This moment is not only great as a function of plot (and more), it furthers all the key elements of story. In the moment, these elements are mature: plot, style, even the would-be adolescent character. (Of some note perhaps, the free-living boy who was the real life model for Huckleberry Finn, Twain recounts, grew up to become a judge farther west, after "lighting out for the territory," one may presume.) A perhaps more obvious example: Is the plot of the classic novel (the very grownup) Middlemarch "essential juvenility"? Or the sober and deft, vibrant and instructive grounds and motion of an adult world. If "modernism" has reduced plot to juvenility, or deemed it so, this is not plot's problem but modernism's false representation.

Misrepresentation 18 – limited engagement: Wood's too often slavish delimited devotion to the closet of his preferred linens contradicts his closing statement of the book, that "the true writer, that free servant of life, must always be acting as if life were a category beyond anything the novel had yet grasped; as if life itself were always on the verge of becoming unconventional." Yet even this is too weak. Not "as if" – is. Life *is* beyond anything the novel has grasped and life *is* always verging on unconventional, let alone the far more gripping prospect of the revolutionary. Or why write? Why not just pass around copies of past masters? One would think the answer would be obvious, for as great critic Edmund Wilson made note:

> The experience of mankind on the earth is always changing as man develops and has to deal with new combinations of elements; and the writer who is to be anything more than an echo of his predecessors must always find expression for something which has never yet been expressed, must master a new set of phenomena which has never yet been mastered…

Fiction and criticism should take as large task the responsibility of un"sivilizing" toward ever more liberatory ends. Fiction writ whole is experience, knowledge, innovation stretching through and far beyond voice, style, character, far beyond status quo limnits. "Free servant" we must reject. "Free writer" works – or "free explorer." Purview meld as "basic novelistic tension"? Actually, the basic "tension" of novels comes much moreso from the old standbys – conflict within and between character and plot (inclusive of setting: time and place), and imbuing those elements with vitality of imagination and empathy, insight and vision. Vitality – not merely in the aesthetic, not merely in the normative, not merely in the intellectual, not merely in the emotive, not merely in the experiential, not merely between any and all of these, not merely in any one thing but of the human condition, real and possible. Vital conflict, character, and plot. (Purview too.)

Decrying in reviews and articles what he sees as an excessive focus on the world beyond the human interior, Wood claims: "Some of the more impres-sive novelistic minds of our age do not think that language and the representation of consciousness are the novelist's quarries any more. Information has become the new character..." and "Zadie Smith is merely of her time when she says, in an interview, that it is not the writer's job 'to tell us how somebody felt about something, it's to tell us how the world works'." Smith and Wood are both at best partly correct. To most fully portray the human condition, novels need lively depictions of both the internal realms and the external ones – the private and the public – because not only do both realms comprise the personal in the first place, the personal must also live within itself as well as out in the world. That is, the public and the private make up the personal, inherently and in action and consequence. This is the human condition. In diverse and profound ways, we are the world and the world is us, to extents far beyond any notions of private "language and the representation of consciousness." The most vast public realities infuse and help define, reveal, create the most intimate internal ones (including "how somebody felt"), and vice versa.

Misrepresentation 19 – fiction no use: Then there's the mental sinkhole of Wood's notion that "We don't read *in order* to benefit" practically, usefully. Wood claims people don't read fiction for educa-tional reasons, such as improving one's vocabulary (is there a better way?). He claims people don't read fiction to gain experience, to be worldly, to enrich their other experiences. (One might as well claim that people don't live for such.) He claims people don't read fiction for ethical reasons, to foster principles, commitments, convictions. To hell with Horace and the Victorians. "Entertain and instruct"? Not over my status quo body of ideology. One must disregard plenty of novelists and readers, both literary and popular, to hold such a view. Not only Victorian scholars could cite an unending supply of belief-busting examples and analyses in this regard. We read fiction to learn about people *and* the world. We read to learn how others see, feel, and understand all sorts of realities and possibilities, as topical or as eternal as one can imagine. "We don't read *in order* to benefit" practically? Such mental chasms, throughout, undermine How Fiction Works and other establishment literature. Again, Wilson:

> In my view, all our intellectual activity, in whatever field it takes place [including art], is an attempt to give a meaning to our exper-ience – that is, to make life more practicable; for by understanding things we make it easi-er to survive and get around among them.

Even the most dynamic or somehow compelling contemporary novels typically fail to explore accu-rately or adequately the very topics, situations, and worlds they take up (or fail to, however crucially related). Such lack quickly guts even the most fine-ly styled purviews, taking the reader for a ride rather than to many a revelation. All dessert and no meal, and about as appealing after a brief bit.

Renowned scholar Noam Chomsky comments:

> I think the Victorian novel tells us more a-bout people than science ever will...and we will always learn more about human life and human personality from novels than from scientific psychology.... In fact, most of what we know about things that matter comes from such sources, surely not from consid-ered rational inquiry (science), which some-times reaches unparalleled depths of pro-fundity, but has a rather narrow scope.

The vast majority of readers are far less fanatic about the aesthetic qualities of fiction than is Wood – whose favored aesthetics are in any case not al-ways so wonderful, as he admits from time to time – just so long as it works well, or well enough. Ev-en that modernist idol of the establishment TS Eliot noted that "The 'great-ness' of literature cannot be determined solely by literary standards" but need be evaluated by normative criteria as well. This assessment caused scholar Bernard Smith to com-ment in his valuable book, Forces in American Crit-icism (1939):

> To this has esthetic criticism at last come – to a realization that non-esthetic criteria are the ultimate tests of value. Whether they be called philosophical, moral, or so-cial criteria, they are still the ideas that men have about the way human beings live together and the way they ought to live. The quest of beauty had become the quest of reality. It had be-come, in es-sence, literary criticism as socially con-scious and as polemical as the criticism of the Marxists.

Either by way of bias or prejudice, Wood be-littles the novel much utility. This is the ideol-ogy Wood lives and breathes and works under. Fiction is too dangerous to established interests, too powerful, moreso than nonfiction because of its extra aesthet-ic appeals, and because it can contain nonfiction, in virtually every sense; thus, the ideological controls are tighter for fic-tion than nonfiction. Fiction is too useful, too popular, too influential not to be domin-eered and gutted in central ways by the status quo.

At all levels of accomplishment fiction exists and can be crafted to virtually any intention: reac-tionary, establishmentarian, revolutionary, and so on. Stories "do far more than enter-tain…" reports Scientific American:

> … how do the emotional and cognitive ef-fects of a narrative influence our beliefs and real-world decisions? The answers to these questions seem to be rooted in our history as a social animal. We tell stories about other people and for other people. Stories help us to keep tabs on what is happening in our communities. The safe, imaginary world of a story may be a kind of training ground, where we can practice interacting with others and learn the cus-toms and rules of society.

If Wood thinks people "don't read in order to benefit" usefully then he may as well think fiction writers don't write to benefit anyone use-fully, but who can be so dim? He's reciting ide-ology, having learned the lines well, having heard and read them often enough.

Misrepresentation 20 – fiction no remedy: In the midst of the all-but-everywhere-unpopular US in-vasion and occupation of Iraq, antiwar novels are maligned as categorically "belliger-ent," by reviewer Richard Eder in the New York Times – the great media cheerleader and enabler of the criminal aggression – and nobody blinks an eye at such Or-wellianism from the estab-lishment press. No one from establishment lit-erature so much as peeps in protest, let alone correction. No wonder, since no explicit investi-gative antiwar novel about the crime of the cur-rent conquest has been produced by the estab-lishment, and precious few exist from any time.

Even before release for sale by its publisher, the proclaimed (yet self-nullifying) antiwar short novel Checkpoint from established writer Nicholson Bak-er, was denounced in 2004 by the New Republic's literary editor Leon Wie-seltier in the New York Times, in easily one of the longest "reviews" the book received. "This scummy little book" opened his review and set the tone of Wieselstier's screed, a fraudulent and hypocritical defense of capitalism and sub-servient literature. A number of other es-tablishment reviews were much more sympa-thetic than the pitiful New York Times hatchet job, how-ever, it was easy to be so, since Baker himself car-ried the establishment water, doing war resisters no favors by putting a sometimes meaningful criti-cism of the US conquest into the mouth of a homi-cidal lunatic set upon committing a murderous crime, the assassina-tion of President Bush, which basically nullified any serious effect the book might have. (The protagonist assassination intent, not the "su-preme crime" of state aggression, was greatly publicized and primarily discussed and the book sold poorly). Regardless, the status quo smears by Wieseltier (a "liberal thinker" and one of the "ideas men of the liberal intellegentsia") made sure that any other potential antiwar writers of the establish-ment would know the obloquy they would face in trying to bring out a more popular, more consid-ered, more investigative antiwar novel. There has scarcely been a trickle since. What's the use? Not much, if at all, according to Wood and the rest.

Rather than "read *in order* to benefit" practically, usefully, Wood states, "We read fiction because it pleases us, moves us, is beautiful, and so on – be-cause it is alive and we are alive." Not to learn about ourselves and the world? While people read fiction for the reasons Wood notes as well, they also read fiction – even the most complex literary sort – because they appreciate that quality novels may be experiences with much to teach, much to offer for use in very practical ways. In fact, Wood says as much himself, but only to a point. The "teaching" may only go so far, after which it is subject to dismissal, ridicule, or worse.

Fiction as useful, everyday practical, socio-poli-tical, momentous? "How quaintly antique this sounds," to Wood, to the establishment, even as their fiction massively and quite practically bul-warks the status quo. It could not be, could it, that the establishment fears readers – teachers, pastors, parents, youth, soldiers – might find such fiction too ethical, too alive, too real, too useful? The estab-lishment surely knows and certainly functions more purposefully in this regard than Wood ever lets on, and likely that contributes to the high valu-ation of his services. Such is the menace of establishment criticism (whether of liberal, conservative, or reactionary stripe) – The Menace of Liberal Scholarship, as Noam Chomsky once put it in the title of a Vietnam War era book.

"For all its eviscerations of the administration, [Jon Stewart's TV news satire, which is at most es-sentially reformist ideologically and so a tolerable status quo player] 'The Daily Show' is animated not by partisanship but by a deep mistrust of all ideology," says Michiko Kakutani, leading reviewer for the New York Times, in a positive review of the show, ostensibly oblivious to the ideological line she implies as ideology free. If imaginative work is worthy to establishment eyes, typically it's not ideological, but in a neat coincidence, if work heads in an unacceptable line, then typically it is. As Terry Eagleton notes in Literary Theory: "Radical critics … have a set of social priorities with which most people at present tend to disagree. This is why they are commonly dismissed as 'ideological', because ideology is always a way of describing other people's interests rather than our own." In establishment formulation, powerful modes of literature, such as the "partisan" or "polemic" are often wielded as scare words. Readers are advised against such fiction (often whether it's much divergent or not), for their own best interests in literature and life. Thus the establishment wars on, typically in denial of its powerful partisan lines and defining ideology.

When Wood claims that "We don't read *in order* to benefit" practically, he is specifically referring to a Mexican police chief's decision to have his offi-cers read classic literature to build vocabulary, to gain enriching world experience, and to enhance ethical convictions and "commitments to the values they have pledged to defend" – that is, to help clas-sically civilize them. Sounds refreshing, one would think. Hopeful logical. Useful practical. Education-al ethical. Humanizing, at least somewhat. Better liberal and conservative works than totalitarian or reactionary ones, if progressive and revolutionary literature must be out of question in the moment. Wood and his primary readership hear auras very different, or at least profess to, marveling at the peculiar notion of utility in fiction – when not scof-fing, or outright discrediting the real possibility in works of significant aesthetic achievement. The best they can typically come up with is that *the aesthetic is (by definition) not useful* – which not only merely begs the question, it falsely cheapens aes-thetics – and has any number of the greatest think-ers and imaginative writers turning in their graves, if not laughing their skulls off.

Misrepresentation 21 – fiction "makes nothing hap-pen": While Auden famously wrote "poetry makes nothing happen," Wood seems to have taken the literal notion largely to heart in regard to fiction, and yet fiction is far more censored than nonfiction, because it is more powerful. Nonfiction books ex-plicitly condemning the US invasion of Iraq are far more facilitated and existing than any fiction coun-terparts. The same is true between nonfiction and fiction in video/movies/films. James Wood and his pay-masters and their primary readership scarcely speak of or to such fiction. Anyway, it's "bellig-erent." So unthinkable or laughable, so vulgar or frightening (threatening) it seems to them. It's as if they are not allowed to touch it. Or dare not. Polite-ly, they say, it's quaint or "antique," as it may also seem to them. Or naively, well schooled, they say it's in the "wrong form." There's no conspiracy. They are cultured. Such culture is used, conscious-ly or not, as a type of social self-medication and an-esthetic for the masses. Quite useful. So much that is vital, not to mention civilized, is missing in establishment fiction, and the privileged may not know but more typically know and don't care, and work against knowing. The greatest irony is that they may even feel oppressed by liberatory fiction – aesthetically, intellectually, in every way.

Typical reactions to crossing oft unspoken ideo-logical lines are all over the map, and include fear or laughter or contempt – "belliger-ence" – or in-comprehension, but then comes the "gate-keeping," the filtering, de facto censorship. The liberatory geopolitical novel of well known British comedian Robert Newman, The Fountain at the Center of the World (2003), his third novel, was spurned by dominant publishers because, as noted by Richard Nash of Soft Skull Press (the novel's US publisher), "big corporate publishers [acted] like big corporate pub-lishers," rejecting the novel on ideological grounds – sometimes by way of "five-page, sin-gle-spaced screeds about the book's politics," Suzanne Charlé reports in The American Prospect. In 2004, my Iraq conquest novel Home-front was very politely, even respectfully, de-clined by a couple of the most liberal of US establishment presses for ostensibly aesthetic reasons. US state criminals can be relieved that

novels revolving overtly and directly around "the supreme international crime differing only from other war crimes in that it contains with-in itself all the accumulated evil of the whole," in the words of the judgment of Nuremberg, are an aesthetic impossibility.[20]

Misrepresentation 22 – writer as "good valet": In The Liberation of American Literature (1932), one of the central buried texts of libera-tory lit criticism in the US, VF Calverton writes of the establishment:

> That the attempt to be above the battle is evi-dence of a defense mechanism can scarcely be doubted. Only those who be-long to the ruling class, in other words, only those who had already won the bat-tle and acquired the spoils, could afford to be above the battle. Fiction which was propagandistic, that is, fiction which con-tinued to participate in the battle, it natu-rally cultivated a distaste for, and es-chewed. Fiction which was above the bat-tle, that is fiction which concerned only the so-called absolutes and eternals, with the ultimate emotions and the perennial traged-ies, but which offered no solu-tions, no pana-ceas – it was such fiction that won its adora-tion… Most of the lit-erature of the world has been propagan-distic in one way or another.

<hr>

[20] *A kind note from an editor at a leading liberal publishing house: "The conflict between personal politics and public policy can be a difficult one, and your choice to illuminate this schism through the thoughts and experiences of Senator Sam Washburn is apt. As a whole, though, I simply wasn't convinced that a novel was the right vehicle by which to explore this divide – much of the narra-tive seemed to be sacrificed in favor of ideological discussion and, as a result, didn't really hang together as a whole." Mine and every other "supreme international crime" novel, apparently. Homefront and all variety of excerpts of the novel were declined by literally hundreds of presses and journals. Publishers aside, the novel has been well received by readers… In The Shape of Content (1957), Ben Shahn notes that "we must look upon form as the shape of content … form is the right and only possible shape of a certain content. Some other kind of form would have conveyed a different meaning and a different attitude. So when we sit in judgment upon a certain kind of form – and it is usually called lack of form – what we do is to sit in judgment upon a certain type of content." What types we can often readily see.*

as Wood admits of Cervantes' Don Quixote, but warns and argues against otherwise.

> In a word, the revolutionary critic does not believe that we can have art without crafts-manship; what he does believe is that, grant-ed the craftsmanship, our aim should be to make art serve man as a thing of action and not man serve art as a thing of escape.

VF Calverton is the now virtually unknown editor of the Modern Quarterly (for 17 years from 1923 until his death in 1940). Unlike Calverton above, Wood uses normative metaphors for writers and writing that are tepid and servile rather than ex-pressive of liberty, justice, equality: "good prose... maintains an unsentimental composure and knows how to withdraw, like a good valet, from superflu-ous commentary." What of human banter and individual expression? desirable in a valet? in an auth-or? in one who "knows his place"? In Wood's metaphor, good prose services, as if in human hierarchy, rather than serves for sake of humanity, as with Calverton's trope. Wood calls "the true writer, that free servant of life..." tasked to reveal truth, yet he misrepresents and buries much of fiction's real use for all, as if a truth too far. These may be a mere couple off-hand metaphors by Wood – writer as "servant" and "valet" – but study of HFW reveals too much the establishment's priorities and the full import of its "unsentimental composure" (often antihuman status quo limnits) to let these suggestive, indicative metaphors pass unremarked.

Misrepresentation 23 – "No one is *literally* run off her feet": Just listen to those darlings, the poor, who say such endearing things about being "*literally* run off" their feet. As if! Everyone knows, says Wood, that "No one is *literally* run off her feet." The very idea! of being harried or hurried by an assembly line, by another machine, by a manager, by a boss so that a worker might slip, trip, or collapse onto a chair, floor, the ground. It's literally unimaginable (to a status quo star), which makes Wood literally wrong. No one literally gets run off her feet by injury or to injury on stressful or dangerous jobs; no one is ever pushed that hard. How

quaint! "Lily, the caretaker's daughter" was not really run off her feet in Joyce's famed story "The Dead," says Wood. Evidently so, yet Wood is blatantly wrong about "no one" being run off her feet in households and on other jobs – ask any soldier who may be literally launched and detached from her feet, or any other body part. Is it possible that Wood neither knows nor can imagine anyone like this? Has he never read Les Misérables? Has he never seen Charlie Chaplin's Modern Times? In both great literary works (also popular and useful) being run off one's feet is among the primary themes, and in Hugo's great novel of the people, little Cosette is one of the literal examples. Chaplin is swept off his feet by the assembly line and ground through the gears of a machine. Literal reality that impossible fantasy.

Even if we give Wood the benefit of the doubt that he is referring only to Lily in the story, he's still misrepresenting the situation, which is ultimately ambiguous with regard to Lily being literally run off her feet. Joyce opens the story: "Lily, the care-taker's daughter, was literally run off her feet. Hardly had she brought one gentleman into the little pantry behind the office on the ground floor and helped him off with his overcoat than the wheezy hall-door bell clanged again and she had to scamper along the bare hallway to let in another guest." "Literally" is intentionally and ironically "precisely the most inaccurate word," Wood claims. Not necessarily, no. The author is under no obligation to clarify all that happens to Lily, to fix it with utter precision. In fact, Wood typically lauds authors who do not, authors who "blur" meaning, "blurring the question of who is noticing" the world, "all this stuff," and what it might mean. Evidently Lily is not run off her feet, not with certainty. Rather, it's ambiguous. Wood's claiming that "no one is *literal-ly* run off her feet" stands out as a blanket generalization, especially given how unimaginable an actual "literal" fall seems to be to Wood: "precisely the most inaccurate word." Far from it. "Literally" is precisely the most ambiguous word.[21]

In Les Misérables, threatened by her "guardian," Cosette is ordered into the frightening dark to fetch water from a spring:

> She emerged from the village ... entered the forest at a run ... no longer looking at or lis-tening to anything. She only paused in her course when her breath failed her; but she did not halt in her advance. She went straight before her in desperation. As she ran she felt like crying. The nocturnal quiv-ering of the forest surrounded her complete-ly. She no longer thought, she no longer saw ... she reached the spring ... Cosette did not take time to breathe.... She drew out the bucket nearly full, and set it on the grass.... She would have liked to set out again at once, but the effort required to fill the bucket had been such that she found it impossible to take a step. She was forced to sit down. She dropped on the grass....

That's literal enough, and no fantasy. Adding a slip and tumble in stride would have made it exact. Wood is wrong about people not reading literature *"in order"* to learn. He's wrong about plot being "essential juvenility," and on and on throughout How Fiction Works, until it scarcely seems a page goes by where he has got much of a pulse on the real, on the nature of the human condition whether in life or lit. Quality fiction of use? Moral bosh! Wishful thinking. Reductive. Unrealistic. Hugo Chavez should have passed around spelling primers in Venezuela to help improve literacy, not the one million free copies of Don Quixote he distributed instead, nor the 1.5 million free copies of Les Misérables in 2006 when he "inaugurated the Second Venezuelan International Book Fair...[and] addressed the opening ceremony after having handed out copies of a massive edition of Victor Hugo's *Les Misérables* to workers of the 'Negra Hipolita Mission,' a social program aimed at helping Venezuelans in situations of extreme poverty," reports the Cuban paper Periódico 26. "The Venezuelan leader said: 'The Empire sows death with its weapons. In contrast, these are our guns: books, ideas, culture.' Earlier, participants had attentively listened [to] and applauded the reading of the poem 'Che,' by its author Miguel Barnet, to start off the Book Fair tribute to the historical legacy of Ernesto Che Guevara..." "Books Liberate" was the theme of the book fair.

Doesn't President Chavez know, like us, that lit is not for learning. We privileged people certainly have nothing to learn from it. Let the people eat primers! (One can imagine what good friends James Wood and the beloved Marie Antoinette might have been. Not that the point is them. The point is their either oblivious or willful establish-ment function.)

Writers of the literature establishment re-

---

[21] *People are literally run off their feet in machine lines, on farms, in athletic training, in the military, and in some demanding or excited households. Regardless of Joyce's intent, and whether or not he uses "literally" "knowingly," its function is ambiguous in the text. It's as mistaken to claim that Lily fell as to claim, as Wood does, that she did not. Perhaps it's necessary to note that I agree that Wood is making an interesting observation. One could write books about the many acute observations Wood makes, as many people have piecemeal. Unfortunately he too often ties his insight with sweeping misrepresentations: it's "inaccurate" to be literally run off one's feet. I don't imagine it happens much in cloistered dens. Wood goes on to express a serious ignorance of not atypical features of low-income working conditions (at the least) and how they might be spoken of by workers, in presenting Lily as imagined example. Insightfully, he imagines well that Lily could tell a friend she was "literally" run of her feet while meaning it figuratively, the way in which rushed work events are sometimes spoken, but he misrepresents reality by entirely ruling out ("most inaccurate") that she might mean it literally. The larger misrepresentation is that Wood generalizes far beyond Lily. Yes, to be run off one's feet is a cliché. It's a cliché that Wood seems to mistake for unreality. Cliché, third definition: "something overly familiar or commonplace." "Run off her feet" may be either literal description of a fall or figurative description of rushed "scamper"ing work – as we hear via a meld of the purviews of Lily and the narrator. Wood rules out the literally possibility and thus badly misrepresents reality, even as he thoughtfully develops one half of an ambiguous passage. An establishment purview gets grand treatment (she couldn't possibly mean it "literally"), and the low-income workers' full reality is destroyed, by Wood not Joyce – since whatever Joyce's exact intention, it's a moot point in face of a passage that is far more ambiguous than Wood credits, a passage that is very much in the unstable multipurview meld mode Wood favors. Wood thinks he has figured out a "puzzle" within "our basic novelistic tension" and he may well have put some pieces together, but simultaneously he distorts reality, and inadvertently shows not only the expansive but the limited nature of his preferred UMM mode. Wood: "It is useful to watch good writers make mistakes. Plenty of excellent ones stumble at free indirect style." Critics too, and other readers. It's a stumble prone style, for obvious reasons.*

peated-ly disparage such insight as that of literary scholar Kenneth Burke in The Philosophy of Literary Form where he notes that "The contemporary emphasis must be placed largely upon propaganda, rather than upon 'pure' art.... Since pure art makes for ac-ceptance, it tends to become a social menace in so far as it assists us in tolerating the intolerable." (To take Burke's import here, we can set aside for the time being whether or not "pure art" is a notion that can actually be realized.) To foster sociopoli-tical consciousness, build support for unions, Venezuela has distributed copies of Charlie Chaplin's classic film "Modern Times," in which Chaplin as worker gets caught in the gears of a factory ma-chine. Venezuelan business leaders are "outraged." In the US, the establishment's "seemingly apolitic-ally" yet actually supercharged (ironically) utilitar-ian political view that great art cannot be political in much of any practical sense serves business owners quite well, while many workers remain stuck or crushed in the gears, or trying to scrape by on sub-subsistence wages, with poor to non-existent benefits. Chaplin was hounded away from libera-tory filmmaking and for a time barred from reen-tering the US as part of the political persecution. While some establishment mouthpieces may be-lieve aesthetics and practical effect are incompat-ible, most are not so deeply in denial. Big money – whether corporate, governmental, or individual – suffers from no such delusions and predominantly either denounces or withhold funds from art that does not service it. Examples are endless. Nick Turse at TomDispatch notes: "In reality, the mili-tary has been deeply involved with the film industry since the Silent Era. Today, however, the *ad hoc* arrangements of the past have been replaced by a full-scale one-stop shop, occupying a floor of a Los Angeles office building. There, the Army, Navy, Air Force, Marines, Coast Guard, and the Depart-ment of Defense itself have established entertain-ment liaison offices to help ensure that Hollywood makes movies the military way." Literary authors, and artists of all sorts, are cultured to follow suit (as we will continue to see here throughout).

Misrepresentation 24 – the petty terrorist: It's bad enough in How Fiction Works that Wood misrep-resents fiction. He also misrepresents people and the world beyond fiction, and thus distorts how reality corresponds to story and its subsequent effect in the world. For example, Wood thinks that "Terrorism, clearly enough, is the triumph of re-sentment (sometimes justified)" – that terrorists "dream of hard revenge on a society that seems too soft to deserve sparing," and that "perhaps a certain kind of Islamic fundamentalist ... hates ["Western secularism"] because he admires it ... *because it once did him a good turn* – gave him medicine...." In fact, reality is essentially the opposite of Wood's description. While some psychopaths may think as Wood states, this Dostoevskyan "analysis" has no "great prophetic relevance for the troubles" the West is in, because the basic grievances and motivations behind the terror are the Western support and active participation in tyrannies, invasions, occupations, sanctions, outlaw threats, and economic oppression, which are rationally known by the terrorists and by the affected populations – as reported (if scantily) by even the Wall Street Journal and other establishment media. The terror – which is horrific and vicious – is intended to deter US aggressions and oppressions or at least to build strength, recruit, create revolution. These terrorists are rooted in far more rational realism than Wood comes close to conveying.

Whether or not the terror often works well, or leads to more eventual gains than losses is another question. While the 9-11 terror did cause the US to quietly withdraw its military forces from Saudi Arabia, it also brought on the invasions of Afghani-stan and Iraq. Yet the terrorism is wounding the US, in blood, economics and politics, and may has-ten its decline, the easier to weaken or repel its con-trol over the oil-rich Middle East and beyond. Dir-ectly related US meddling and bombing in nearby Pakistan has led to the ouster of its preferred ruler there, Musharraf, and may also likely lead to the ouster of a couple other US "puppet" rulers in the region. Is the US "too soft"? Excellent! may likely think the terrorists and insurgents. Does the US make medicines that might be used by them? Super! Why would they not be more than happy to use the West's strengths and weaknesses against it, to get the West to remove its talons from their lands? But regardless, the fact remains – given the fundamental reality – the plot – the basic causes of these current and longstanding "troubles" of the West are internal to the West, not external, which is the opposite of what Wood conveys. Moreover, misrepresenting the basic focus, grounds, and motivations for explosive anger and violence against the West makes a mockery of using "modernist" explorations of psychology to know let alone help resolve the current longstanding conflicts.

George Orwell in The Lion and the Unicorn:

> Even among the inner clique of politicians who brought us to our present pass [World War II] it is doubtful whether there were any *conscious* traitors. The corruption is more in the nature of self-deception…. And being unconscious, it is limited. One sees this at its most obvious in the English press. Is the English press honest or dishonest? At nor-mal times it is deeply dishonest. All the papers that matter live off their advertise-ments, and the advertisers exercise an indir-ect censorship over news. Yet I do not suppose there is one paper in England that can be straight-forwardly bribed with hard cash. England is not the jeweled isle of Shakes-peare's much-quoted passage, nor is it the inferno depicted by Dr. Goebbels. More than either it resembles a family, a rather stuffy Victorian family, with not many black sheep in it but with all its cupboards bursting with skeletons. It has rich relations who have to be kow-towed to and poor relations who are horribly sat upon, and there is a deep con-spiracy of silence about the source of the family income. It is a family in which the young are generally thwarted and most of the power is in the hands of irresponsible uncles and bedridden aunts. Still, it is a fam-ily. It has its private language and its com-mon memories, and at the approach of an enemy it closes ranks. A family with the wrong members in control – that, perhaps, is as near as one can come to describing Eng-land in a phrase…. They are not wicked, or not altogether wicked; they are merely un-teachable. Only when their money and pow-er are gone will the younger among them begin to grasp what century they are living in.

One wonders how much of Orwell, his partly es-tablishmentarian, though sometimes dissenting, countryman Wood has read and understood, or cared to. The Lion and the Unicorn is subtitled "Socialism and the English Genius" and opens per below. If corrected for the mistakes (and the parti-cular situations) which are also found in some of the rest of the book, this brief scene of WWII vivi-dly foreruns 9-11 and everyday life under the US occupation of Iraq and Afghanistan and beyond, and indicates something more of the bombers' key motives than Wood appreciates:

> As I write, highly civilized human beings are flying overhead, trying to kill me.

> They do not feel any enmity against me as an individual, nor I against them. They are 'only doing their duty', as the saying goes. Most of them, I have no doubt, are kind-hearted law-abiding men who would never dream of committing murder in private life. On the other hand, if one of them succeeds in blowing me to pieces with a well-placed bomb, he will never sleep any the worse for it. He is serving his country, which has the power to absolve him from evil.

> One cannot see the modern world as it is unless one recognizes the overwhelming strength of patriotism, national loyalty. In certain circumstances it can break down, at certain levels of civilization it does not exist.

The bombers feel they are looking out for their own people and consequently "doing their duty" whether by God or country, or both. And yet both the US bombings and the "terrorist" bombings are criminal (try getting that much past the NYT filters). Too bad modernist type fictions fixated with childish games of purview do not trouble themselves overly much to vivify such reality at great forensic length and power. And why not? It's no question of capacity of fiction, or even necessarily of unstable mix and meld narrative, for even great clearly and extensively depicted crimes may ride and wash on surrounding mystery, though not of the points of the crime that are well established, but of the related infinite even intimate esoterics of the human condition (and universe beyond) that are virtually inescapable, from any such events, and are appropriately compelling if handled well.

One may also think at many points throughout HFW of these additional quick cutting comments of Orwell in The Lion and the Unicorn about the phenomena of idiocy, and banditry, among the privileged prior to World War II: "The underlying fact was that the whole position of the monied class had long ceased to be justifiable... The British rul-ing class obviously could not admit to themselves that their usefulness was at an end. Had they done that they would have had to abdicate.... Clearly there was only one escape for them – into stupid-ity." [The ruling types could] "keep society in its existing shape only by being *unable* to grasp that any improvement was possible. Difficult though this was, they achieved it, largely by fixing their eyes on the past and refusing to notice the changes that were going on round them." And as a matter of course suppressing liberatory progressive, let alone revolutionary, change in literature and life.

Too often in his criticism Wood is a "larcenous banker" (to repeat that considerable tautology) making bad loans under fraudulent terms, denying reasonable lines of credit, bailed out by cultured readers and critics. Wood is deft enough that we may admire what he does (trope along) while we deplore what his criticism too often is (retrograde, misprised): Flaubert as spring come again is too much a cadaverous notion, however deftly glossed.

PART THREE

No end in sight, the misrepresentations roll on. Be-fore we take up these next dozen, let's consider the relationship between liberatory lit and the estab-lishment in more detail. Despite some contrary ges-tures and rhetoric, despite the exalted hopes of Flaubert, "often held to be the quintessential chron-icler of nothingness," modernist and other estab-lishment works do not lack meaning, far from it. On the contrary, such works are full of meaning, but establishment minds are naively well schooled or otherwise sense or know it is safest for their own status quo positions, and therefore preferable, and therefore all but inevitable, that in such a powerful form as the novel, meaning be not too liberatory, lest some establishment superior find excuse to fil-ter out, censor, bar any modern liberatory perpe-trator, for much besides "obscenity" or "lewdness." Random-type blurring "modernist" techniques are great for camouflaging, giving plausible deniability to any unsanctioned versions of reality, except that typically the camouflage and deniability become the thing itself (unstable purview meld is one of the more convenient ways to bollix, to entirely gut whatever one might be taken to mean – sometimes even no matter how devoted the puzzle decoder; fiction as academic or abstract game). Victorian novels typically toed establishment lines too, but, especially, with the rise of corporate demands in this age of power propaganda have grown the im-peratives of "nothingness." Wholesale banking sys-tem illegitimacy and fraud is "nothingness." Crimi-nal invasions of sovereign countries are "nothing-ness." Retrograde misrepresentation-laden criticism is "nothingness" – which is all an assertion of blindness, by way of what is falsely claimed to be ideology and propaganda free art. It's withdrawal, disengagement, a repudiation of crucial artistic prerogative and responsibility, no less. How more to emphasize the calamity? As a shame? As a betrayal of art and life? It's fiction gutted.

Wood propounds an "aesthetic" of pursuing *"the real*, which is at the bottom of [his] inquiries," in How Fiction Works and his criticism generally. Yet he botches reality time and again. During the Cold War the CIA went to great lengths and expense to mold the "seemingly apolitical" normative quality of art in the US and abroad and met with no little success that resonates today through corporations and universities, society and culture. The CIA merely picked up on and encouraged a strain that had been established earlier: "modernism," the writing needed, encouraged, and employed, just as the mid-century abstract impressionist movement in painting was funded and driven by the CIA – art of "nothing" used to counter the engaged art rising from the ashes of World Wars I and II. As scholar James Petras notes perceptively in "The CIA and the Cultural Cold War Revisited" (1999), an indispensable review of Frances Stoner Saunder's limited though useful book "The Cultural Cold War: The CIA and the World of Arts and Letters":

> The CIA and its cultural organizations were able to profoundly shape the post-war view of art. Many prestigious writers, poets, art-ists, and musicians proclaimed their indep-endence from politics and declared their belief in art for art's sake. The dogma of the free artist or intellectual, as someone discon-nected from political engagement, gained as-cendancy and is pervasive to this day… The issue is not that today's intellectuals or art-ists may or may not take a progressive position on this or that issue. The problem is the pervasive belief among writers and artists that anti-imperialist social and political ex-pressions should not appear in their music, paintings, and serious writing if they want their work to be considered of substantial artistic merit.

Of course there has always been status quo work. It reaches one of its peak expressions in art about nothing much beyond endless interior vistas, basic-ally of the private sphere, escorted by equally tranched criticism. Where again are the explicit antiwar novels about "the supreme international crime"? Many another sort of urgent novel has been destroyed in its cradle on these grounds. Much preferred by the establish is Flaubert, his sort of work, for as Wood notes, "no novelist fetishized the poetry of 'the sen-

tence' in the same way, no novelist pushed to such an extreme the potential alienation of form and content (Flaubert longed to write what he called a 'book about nothing')." Something of the underlying ideal today, fiction about not *too* much. "And no novelist before Flau-bert reflected as self-consciously on questions of technique. With Flaubert, literature" rather than too threatening life "became 'essentially problematic,' as one scholar put it." A great game. The supreme puzzle. The establishment dream – story neutered, destroyed – fiction drowned in the great Flaubertian spring.

During the cold war, the US establishment required its own Flaubert figure to try to control lit-erature and naturally gravitated toward Henry James. When the highly accomplished and leading progressive literary critic, Maxwell Geismar, chal-lenged the very quality and reigning adoration of Henry James' fiction, he was silenced, and rather prominently in one instance, on national TV by two high level functionaries of the CIA, representing the interests of the corporate state rather than the populace. The two men who played a key role: William vanden Heuvel and Irving Kristol – the former a "protégé" of the "father" of the CIA and the latter the CIA flack and "father" of neoconservatism who several years earlier had passed on his position as editor of Commentary magazine to Norman Podhoretz (a student of leading establish-ment lit critic Lionel Trilling, who was a sort of forerunner of James Wood). When William vanden Heuvel (father of the current editor/publisher of The Nation Katrina vanden Heuvel) tag-teamed with Irving Kristol (the father of current prominent Fox TV political pundit and New York Times col-umnist Bill Kristol, also editor of the Washington DC based political magazine, The Weekly Stan-dard) – when these central figures of the political establishment hastened to appear on national TV over four decades ago to attack directly to the face of the silenced progressive literary critic Maxwell Geismar, on the occasion of the publication of Geismar's book of criticism about Henry James ("a primary Cold War literary figure"), Kristol and vanden Heuvel, two exemplars of the status quo, serving retrograde state interests, executed a prom-inent role in destroying Geismar's accomplished literary career and ending his run on a national literary television show, Books on Trial ("or something similar," in Geismar's rec-ollection). Geismar posits William vanden Heu-vel as "a rich, cultivated, charming, and liberal member of the upper echelons of the CIA [who] had a large hand in embroiling [the US] in Viet-nam," while Irving Kristol "as it later turned out was almost always affiliated with many State Department or CIA literary projects in editing, publishing, and the academic world … a hired hand of the establishment."

From where does the public space for status quo favorites arise, the fleets of ostensibly dis-engaged critics (though in de facto service of the very public status quo), all the refined minions, sophisticated apologists, odious smear artists and hacks, Orwelli-an liars? Obviously there are plenty of institutional roots, less obviously in-cluding the CIA – which helped set the ideo-logical line for literature decades ago, a line heavily followed and affirmed by the ongoing establishment – all the continual defensive claims to the contrary that enable the essentially status quo liberal establishment (let alone con-serv-ative and reactionary elements) to view it-self as something other than a blight, whatever else it might be. We can turn to the silenced progressive critic for a better understanding of the establish-ment literature tradition which endures today. Maxwell Geismar details the ideological reality that still today shapes and underlies the establishment, aside from some partial and modest reformations:

> What was the real truth, the true histori-cal dimension, of the Cold War? As I said in op-ening this Introduction, a new group of Cold War historians have been giving us a whole new set of impressions, which, alas, most of those who lived through the period, and are so certain of their convictions, will not even bother to read and to think about. For if they did … the Schlesingers, the Galbraiths, the Kris-tols, the Max Lerners, the Trillings, the Bells, the Rahvs, the Kazins, the Irving Howes: all these outstanding, upstanding figures of our political-cultural scene to-day …they would have to admit both their own illusions for the last twenty years, and the fact that they have deliber-ately deluded their readers about the his-torical facts of our period. Since it was they who fastened the Cold War noose around all our necks, how can we expect them to remove it? – even though, as in the cases of Mary McCarthy and Dwight MacDonald, and the estimable New York Review of Books, they have bowed a little to the changing winds of fash-ion today. Due to student protests at base, and stu-dent confrontations on Cold War issues, Professors Bell and Trilling have in-deed moved on from Columbia to Harvard University – but after Harvard what? Mr. Trilling has even 'resigned' from contem-por-ary literature, saying at long last that he does not understand it – but only after he led the attack for twenty years on such figures as the historian Vernon Parring-ton, the novelist Dreiser, the short-story writer Sherwood Anderson, and other such figures of our literary history. And only after the Columbia University Eng-lish Department had taken the lead in set-ting up Henry James as 'Recei-ver' in what amounted to the bankruptcy of our national literature. The Cold War Liber-als, historians, critics and so-called so-ciolo-gists, also clustered around a set of prestigi-ous literary magazines like Parti-san Re-view, The New Leader, Encounter of Lon-don, Der Monat of Berlin, [also Kenyon Re-view and "many others"; Pe-ter Matthiesson helped start the Paris Re-view as "a young CIA recruit…and used it as his cover"], which had in effect set the tone and the val-ues of the 'Free World' culture. When it was revealed, about two years ago, that these leading cultural publications and organiza-tions (the various Congresses and Commit-tees for 'Cultural Freedom'), as well as some student organizations and big unions of the AFL-CIO, were in fact being financed and controlled by Central Intelligence

Agency – the game was up…. – *Maxwell Geismar, "Introduction," New Masses: An Anthology of the Rebel Thirties (Ed. Joseph North 1969)*

The "game was up" for some individuals, but not for the establishment as whole, as has been docu-mented in detail. The game had long since been up for Trilling's fiction, and doesn't look of much promise in Wood's fiction, and preoccupations. As historian Michael Kimmage notes astutely in an essay on Trilling's recently discovered abandoned second novel: Trilling is clearly "one in a long line of sensitive American novelists, eager to write a masterpiece out of American material and de-stroyed by the culture that is his subject." Trilling like Wood is a special case though, for as Geismar points out, Trilling was a prominent part of the cul-ture beyond fiction that helped lead the repressive charge. It's more fitting than ironic, I suppose, that it led to the burial of Trilling's own aspirations in fiction. It was Leon Wieseltier (the hatcheter of Baker's antiwar novel Checkpoint) who introduced a recent large collection of Trilling's essays. The Trillings of past and present, such as today's star critic, James Wood stand shoulder-to-shoulder with establishmentarians like the liberal vanden Heuvels and the neoconservative Kristols in de-fending Henry James as grand author, in particular against some of the views of past prominent critic Edmund Wilson. Because Wood describes some of Wilson's views on Henry James as "a scandal" and "barbarous," he would no doubt also deplore or dismiss Geismar's book of criticism: Henry James and the Jacobites (1963).[22]

Wood's critical concerns in a sense unite the dominant strands of literary fiction (at least) of the past 200 years – Victorianism and modernism – some of their main preoccupations as well as limited pre and post incarnations. Yet his criticism is ultimately very narrow, and often unreal, as noted. "James Wood's How Fiction Works sometimes misses the plot" – the lead into Chris Tayler's Guardian review of HFW: "Novel Tour Guide." Tayler: "Good novelists, Wood says shrewdly, of-ten use the kinds of metaphor that the communities they're writing about would produce. His own similes and metaphors…tend to summon up leisured late-Victorian travellers" – meanwhile his "personal great tradition is a modernist one." Wood respects some of the literary standards of the Victorians and values mainly the modernists – two of the status quo bastions of contemporary fiction. Both the Victorians and the modernists (moreso, it seems to me) fail the most liberatory tendencies in writing, "post-modernists" also. If we are to refer back to find regeneration in writing, far better to light upon Victor Hugo's work than that of Flaubert, or the work of Jonathan Swift than that of Joyce, or the latter work of Tolstoy (Ivan Ilych, Hadji Murad) than that of Dostoevsky. For now, much dominant literature looks, as if to fetish and icon, to the (partly manufactured) example of Flaubert for both his Victorian and "modern" qualities, for his literary criticism, often as expressed in letters, and for fear (originally, at least) of the far more towering example of Victor Hugo, at his most influential and liberatory.

Upon publication of Les Misérables in 1862, that worldwide renowned and liberatory example of what a novel could be, establishment retrenching commenced with a vengeance, and continues to this day, with Flaubertian style obsession the near-est at hand, most useful literary countercourse available – then modernism – then a sort of formal criticism, politically charged – then the "realisms" and absurdisms "… traumatized … puerile … hys-terical" … miasmic … intimatist – then the convolutions and misrepresentations of James Wood and the establishment. Retrenching began immediately in literary, social, and political realms all, upon publication of Les Misérables. As Hugo notes, "'The newspapers which support the old world say, "It's hideous, infamous, odious, execrable, abominable, grotesque, repulsive, shapeless, monstrous, horrendous, etc." Democratic and friendly papers answer, "No, it's not bad."'" Robb adds, "Mme Hugo, who was in Paris giv-

---

[22] *Additionally, Wood's view is that Wilson writes with "coercion" in separate essays about Chekhov and Gogol, a "coercion of paraphrase" that "makes the essay on Flaubert dogmatic." -from "Mr. Literature," Wood's review of Lewis Dabney's book, Edmund Wilson: A Life in Literature.*

ing interviews, tried to persuade Hugo's spineless allies to support the book and invited them to dinner; but Gautier had flu, Janin had 'an attack of gout', and George Sand excused herself on the grounds that she always over-ate when she was invited out...." Further:

> ...Perrot de Chezelles [a public prosecutor], in an 'Examination of *Les Misérables*', defend-ed the excellence of a State which persecuted convicts even after their release, and derided the notion that poverty and ignorance had anything to do with crime.... The State was trying to clear its name. The Emperor and Empress performed some public acts of charity and brought philanthropy back into fashion. There was a sudden surge of official interest in penal legislation, the industrial exploitation of women, the care of orphans, and the education of the poor. From his rock in the English Channel, Victor Hugo...[ex-iled] had set the parliamentary agenda for 1862

– as he had set out to do, in many ways. Flaubert described Les Misérables as "infantile," containing "neither truth nor greatness," showing "the fall of a God," his erstwhile icon. In reality, Flaubert and the rest never escaped Hugo's shadow, in more ways than one.

Robb notes that Flaubert, greatly inspired by Hugo's poetry, Châtiments, wrote Hugo an "admiring pastiche" in 1853 including this bit of rhapsody: "'Your poetry entered my body like my nurse's milk.' That same evening, before the stylistic effect had worn off," continues Robb:

> Flaubert sketched one of the great passages of modern prose fiction – the Comices Agri-coles scene in Madame Bovary, where the pillars of rural French society pontificate among the animals and the dung. The reson-ances of Flaubert's realism – a conscious blend of [two works by Hugo] Notre-Dame de Paris and Napoléon-le-Petit – go some way to explaining the political decision to prosecute Madame Bovary in 1857.

This is the side of Flaubert we don't hear much about from Wood and other fixtures. This engaging and instructive, pointed scene likely brought the establishment crashing down on Flaubert, teaching its own lesson. One may become quite "modernist" in blurring meaning and belittling political agency to avoid having that lesson taught again. Might even force one to be ever more innovative and obedient to avoid future prosecution. Regardless, Flaubert is an accomplished and valuable artist, despite many drawbacks, as modernist and other-wise. Unfortunately his work is falsely and excessively elevated, and is used to falsely demean vital liberatory alternatives, including Hugo's example not least (written in part in exile) an exercise that Flaubert himself sometimes participated in. Hugo's intellectual and quality artistic accomplishment dwarfs that of Flaubert. Meanwhile, Hugo's aes-thetic qualities and achievements are at least equi-valent to those of Flaubert, and in my view consid-erably greater. The schools (and the rest of the lit establishment) typically pass along a sort of doubly ignorant alternative view. A lot of writers can hope to match Flaubert's achievements in literature. Vir-tually none can hope to match what Hugo accom-plished in literature, let alone otherwise.[23]

While advances have been made in literature in modernism, as in the contemporary novel, especial-ly in the multicultural expansion, other basic and vast liberatory realms have been blocked, ignored, denounced, more-or-less wholesale in some ways. A more accomplished liberatory fiction – more ful-ly human, with quality aesthetic and popular res-onance – has been refused, buried, though not en-tirely. The establishment, typically denying it is partisan and ideologically orthodox to a severe de-gree, misrepresents itself and reality all the while, and writes against much that is urgent and libera-tory in lit. The loss is to life and art both – to all manner of well-being, to aesthetics and imagina-tion, to experience itself. The loss is to enlighten-ment ideals of liberty, justice, equality. The loss is to a greater art. The loss is to our

---

[23] *See Part Five for more on Hugo and Flaubert.*

greater humanity.

While "modernist" intimacies drip and fall ele-gantly into Parisian sewers, as it were, while puer-ile prose bounds typically slaphappy to paralysis, liberatory fiction goes public, blooms progressive and revolutionary in reality and possibility, outing fraud and thuggery, reveal-ing resistance and op-portunities for change. Like liberatory fiction, liber-atory criticism ex-poses and advances. It points out that estab-lishment criticism often not only apolo-gizes for the status quo – especially by way of mis-representations – it does something more and something less, like an oblivious lapdog or con-sci-ous functionary whose fangs come out on crucial occasions. Such criticism does more than defend the status quo, it attacks. For example, Wieseltier's screed about "This scummy little book" or Richard Eder's Orwellian obloquy in calling antiwar novels categorically "belliger-ent." This is shock troop criti-cism, intended to deter evaluation, examination, production. Wood can seem mild by comparison – some of the most vociferously critiqued writers (Zadie Smith, Jonathan Franzen, Tom Wolfe) differ variously but offer no threat to Wood's basic stance. On the other hand, some of Edmund Wil-son's views are tagged in passing as a "scandal" and "barbarous." The establishment misprises, ignores, or misrepresents much fic-tion and criticism, when it doesn't feel com-pelled to shock trope.

Wood is so relatively prominent that his mass of misrepresentations is especially harmful, though he is also merely one among many in the literature es-tablishment who tread within a relatively narrow and often distorted and re-pressive range of ideol-ogy. Now that his "common reader" book HFW may be widely used in the universities, his work is particularly worth critical examination, not only for neces-sary debunking but especially to bring to the light of day far more liberatory realities and possi-bilities in literature, life.

It's not that nothing can be gained from es-tab-lishment writing, of course; much can be, especially if one accounts for its oft subservient nature, past and present. While Wood at best cuts through the crap and actually says some-thing of distinction with distinction, it's too of-ten part and parcel of crucial misrepresenta-tions. Though plenty of estab-lishment writing has its qualities and worthwhile components, much of such writers' everyday work and would be greater works are "destroyed by the culture that is [their] subject" (and object too), as Kimmage notes in regard to Trilling's fiction. Such authors participate greatly in the culture's disfigur-ation and destruction. Trilling aborted his fiction and debased his criticism. Meanwhile Maxwell Geismar was prescient to see Norman Mailer's especially influential style as tending to cavort vacantly manic or obtuse, oblivious, away from too revealing depiction of a lot of the most urgent central realities of our time – an early strain of puerility displayed in Advertise-ments for Myself (1959), and in the up and com-ing puerile prose of the "black humorists" that Robert Alter notes, several decades before Wood's coinage and critique of "hysterical real-ism."

Status quo fiction is made up partly of self-imposed chains – also establishment approved and enforced. Establishment authors clank and rattle in their bondage, the "hysterical realists" and Flaubertian intimatists and the rest, whether miasmic or fastidious, and otherwise status quo ensconced. The plight of fiction to-day, in many crucial ways, is a journey arrested, and misrepresented – not unlike the nation itself – not unlike the masses in this country and be-yond, people bossed and betrayed by the estab-lishment, by its power, by its literature, its criti-cism and fiction, its "necessary illusions," the misrepresentations of naivety, orthodox ideol-ogy, or outright fraud. Wood's ideologically or-thodox book, for all its gleanings of purview, bears scant real account of how fiction works, even basically. In its neo-scholastic ramblings, too often newly dull, if not at points also deft, the book distorts "Flaubertian" modernism, even and especially, and fiction in general. Be-cause HFW in an inadvertent ironic account of fiction arrested, aspiring writers would do well to take a few pointers then get free of the reign-ing culture club and cuffs. Best to eat what the rulers know, excrete the malign, then prepare and share many a far more liberatory moment and work of change.

PART FOUR

THE NEXT DOZEN MISREPRESENTATIONS

25 – fiction of the present is passé; 26 – the reactionary and status quo as preeminent literary political fiction; 27 – 9-11 as rallying cry for a turn inward, and worse; 28 – Henry James, TS Eliot, the CIA, and the cultural cold war; 29 – liberatory lit attacked, buried; 30 – fiction shrunk; 31 – the partisan orthodox nature of status quo lit; 32 – basic public realities denied, distorted; 33 – the immateriality of the status quo; 34 – the public chopped from the personal; 35 – ideology in guise of aesthetics; 36 – limits on the real

Misrepresentation 25 – fiction of the present is pas-sé: Wood makes extreme claims of impo-tence, that fiction of the present is outmoded, necessarily be-hind the times. He trips all over his social novel la-ments in a recent literary journal interview (in Sal-magundi, whose foun-der and executive editor is fellow establishment critic Robert Boyers):

> In other words, the impulse to write big, to write ideologically, to write politically, to write socially, is not going to go away just because we're living in pretty ex-traordinary times. I have a slightly de-pressed feeling that a lot of novelists are going to think like Updike did with *Ter-rorist*, "I'm a novelist, it's my job to ex-plain the times. I should have a crack at it, in the spirit of Dostoyev-sky or Conrad."

Why depressed? Wood admires Dostoevsky and Conrad. "And partly because we have these great experiences of Dostoyevsky's *Possessed*, or *Notes from the Underground,* or *The Secret Agent*," he adds, "we think this is a colossal achieve-ment of the nov-el." In fact, such "great experi-ences" of novels might very well be linked to such "colossal achievement." He does not dis-pute even as he bemoans, so one senses he must be aware he is protesting too much. Wood con-tinues:

> Updike fails the test, but if one could

really imagine what it's like to be a de-pressed, raging, alienated 18-year-old Muslim, then that's worth heaps of jour-nalism. It could become a sort of text for the Department of Homeland Security. Just say, "You don't know anything until you've read this." Frankly, I think we should be handing them *Notes from the Underground* and *Possessed,* saying "You want to know what the impo-tence and the underground feel like? Read this."

To actually know such phenomena, Wood says here that the government really needs to read a couple key works of fiction, two novels in parti-cular, and that is what would be especially useful to "the Department of Homeland Secu-rity," even though, as we have seen, Wood em-phasizes else-where, "We don't read" or, by im-plication, write "*in order* to benefit" practically, usefully. Well damn, it looks like we had better. *Somebody* had better. And far from only in re-gard to terrorism. Sure, the stuff of life can be "slightly depressing." Or exhilarating in many forms. Either way, it's essential to knowing the full human condition, which is the novelist's job to convey or reconfigure. Pick your Wood. He speaks against himself sometimes comically – "We don't read … in order to benefit" practi-cally, but "Homeland Security … should." One is tempted to say (mistakenly) he speaks against himself convincingly, given his enthusiastic runs and impassioned style.

The vacuity and unintended irony of Wood's admonishing novelists immediately post 9-11 is striking: "Surely, for a while, novelists will be leery of setting themselves up as analysts of so-ciety, while society bucks and charges so help-lessly. Surely they will tread carefully over their generalis-ations. It is now very easy to look very dated very fast." It certainly is. Society hardly started to "buck and charge" helplessly on 9-11. Both long prior to that moment and from that moment on, particular writers have been ex-plaining accurately the socio-political context, current events, and their well-known (to some) old and deep roots. Wood had no clue, obvi-ously, and given his misguided under-standing of sociopolitical conditions apparently still does not, seven years later. No wonder he has a "slightly depressed feeling" about the prospect of contemporary engaged social novels, to go with his discouraging, disparaging, and misplaced comments on the matter.

The importance of the relationship between im-aginative literature and social and political issues has been understood in critical circles since at least the eighteenth century, notes Edmund Wilson in "The Historical Interpretation of Literature," nor are these understandings and explorations devoid of aesthetic concerns and qualities. When Wood brings up the social novel, he characteristically does so to dismiss it, or to encourage authors to de-viate from it in meaningful ways, so as to get "stor-ies, above all, about individual consciousness, not about the consciousness of Manhattan" or about, say, Ruralville. This seems to be dubious advice, as contemporary epic novelists obviously sense. It scarcely takes prominent twentieth century philo-sopher John Dewey to note in The Public and Its Problems (1927) that "Even if 'consciousness' were the wholly private matter that the individualistic tradition in philosophy supposes it to be, it would still be true that consciousness is *of* objects, not of itself." Just so, many leading novelists apparently intuit that if they are to fully represent personal consciousness they had better dramatically incor-porate not only people but places, things, and events on a global level in a world were by now en-tire societies and the persons within them are greatly globally interdependent and interactive, in myriad visible and invisible ways.

The main problem is that much contempo-rary sociopolitical, or public, reality is as in-comprehen-sible or as out of bounds to the rest of the establish-ment as it is to Wood. Establishment writers are fond of quoting or follow-ing the near literal lines of Stendhal's famed prose in the Red and the Black:

> Politics … is a millstone tied to the neck of literature, and drowns it in less than six months. Politics in imaginative work is like a shot in the middle of a concert. The noise is deafening but it imparts no en-ergy. It doesn't harmonize with the sound of any other instrument. Such political talk mortally offends half of one's readers – and bores the other half, who, in a dif-ferent context, in the morning paper, find such things interesting and lively…

Stendhal's statement succinctly captures a certain literature establishment ideology, an orthodoxy, that typically denies it is ideology/orthodoxy. Stendhal's words are one famous version of the creed at least. Meanwhile the establishment virtu-ally never quotes Stendhal's immediate next para-graph, nor makes note of what then follows:

> If your characters don't talk politics, re-plies the editor, this is no longer France in 1830, and your book is not the mirror you pretend it to be…

The novel then dives into political speech and dis-cussion for the next 9 pages. Surely politics are in-herently as fit for story as any other topic. In any case, the mounds of ostensibly nonpolitical topics and fictions can easily come across as just as offen-sive (politically and otherwise) and white-noise-deafening and as boring as anything labeled pol-itical. Stendhal, Balzac, Hugo, Flaubert, Zola – a powerhouse line of (French) novelists. Flaubert is the least prolific of the five and the least socially engaged, especially in the work for which he is most renowned and especially by longstanding estab-lishment reputation. He is the establishment's pet and model, and amulet against significant breaching of its control. He is a much venerated former "lover" to Wood whose most celebrated pair of works explore monied miasmic "romances" and sentiments centrally. Meanwhile, Hugo's main novels reveal people battling social injustice and related despair – working up, out, and along rather than down, in, and arrested. Though one can learn from the latter work, amid its tedious and severe limits, Flaubert is no great "spring" of literature, certainly not moreso than his three great countrymen predecessors, and in my view all of them much less so than Hugo of Les Misérables, that novel of novels which knows well – lucidly, with liberation – in moving and profound utterance, what is what, both public and private, its empa-thetic and useful emphasis on the vital public reali-ties of the societal and the personal, without which private realities and preoccupations (miasmic or otherwise) can draw only limited breath.

Misrepresentation 26 – the reactionary and status quo as preeminent literary political fiction: "What I am writing now is a tendentious thing," famously wrote Dostoevsky about his accomplished novel The Possessed. "I feel like saying everything as passionately as possible. (Let the nihilists and the Westerners scream that I am a reactionary!) To hell with them. I shall say everything to the last word." Far from deploring this novel (and its kind) today the establishment loves such work. It's not threat-ening; on the contrary. The establishment has long embraced this sort of work because of its focus on retail pathology rather than direct overt focus on wholesale state pathology. It has long valued such works for their limited efforts to clarify much be-yond marginal geopolitical realities or for their suc-cess in distorting reality – as in Wood's misrepre-sentation of terrorism in relation to the problems of the West. The new lords of the land in Iraq (US pol-icy planners) are eating Iraqi babies for breakfast, as Jonathan Swift once discoursed in ripe literary fashion of the English devouring the offspring of the Irish. This is a far more relevant understanding – actually, central – to the problems of the West in regard to terrorism and much else. If Homeland Security wants to know the situation and the anger contained in many Iraqis and many others across the lands as concerns the West, then they should read with all intended irony, "A Modest Proposal" by Swift, and also take a look at the ongoing polls of the people.

Which brings up another problem in reality: to know and to not act appropriately is to not care, enough, basically. Prior to the US invasion of Iraq, leading US intellectual Noam Chomsky wrote satirically about the at best farcical consequences of a US invasion, and he wrote prophetically, as it turned out (given the catastrophe and what else the US is on track to accomplish in the Middle East, unintentionally shifting regional power to Iran, at the least). Chom-

sky wrote that the US might as well as urge Iran to invade Iraq. The US invaded and today we see Iranian power has grown, and Iraqis continue to want the US out. Should anyone not now expect Bush or his successor (Barack "Half Withdrawal" O'Bomba or John "100 Years" McPain) to announce a globally implemented and Western regulated policy of commercial trafficking of children for pacifying the Middle East and the world. Has not the time long since come to officially sanction the body parts trade – with its many corporate byproducts and fiscal derivatives heretofore untapped? the up-and-coming global growth industry – children as prolific cash crop? Would not such a move be as rational and ethical as the US invasion and occupation on whole? Need one wonder how the literary establishment would view such "A Practical Policy" as literary text? Too voicey? A nondescript style? Lacking much substance or any point of view of interest? Too weak or suspect in character? So goes the politics, the ever politicized aesthetics of establishment fiction. Progressive and revolutionary work is marginally tolerated or buried, in actuality if not in rhetoric. Status quo and reactionary work is enabled, advanced, glorified, contrary flourishes aside.

Not for Wood and the establishment are certain movements of progressive or revolutionary writing that touch too close to home, progressive and revo-lutionary writing and writers who, "As a group," as VF Calverton notes:

> are convinced that present-day industrial society is based upon exploitation and in-justice; that it creates distress and misery for the many and brings happiness only to the few; that its dedication to the ideal of profit instead of use is destructive… More than that, [these writers] believe that their literature can serve a greater purpose only when it contributes … toward the creation of a new society which will embody … a social, instead of an individualistic ideal. Unlike Ibsen, they do not ask questions and then refuse to answer them. Unlike the iconoclasts, they are

not content to tear down the idols and stop there. Their aim is to answer questions as well as ask them, and to provide a new order to replace an old one. Their attitude, therefore, is a posi-tive instead of a negative one.

Such liberatory fiction contains "ideology" for which the establishment is too pure to engage in. Such liberatory lit is too "reductive" since we all know that literature deals in no particulars whatso-ever. Such liberatory movements are impossible, for it must be that the poor will always be among us. And in any case "poetry makes nothing hap-pen" nor fiction too – countless concrete and well documented examples to the contrary, which we must see as mere illusions, entirely unpredictable, forever uncertain, uncontrolled accidents, stem-ming from badly flawed and shallow literature. In reality, the great works of Victor Hugo and Jonath-an Swift, for example, thoroughly disprove every aspect of this establishment line, this orthodoxy, this belief, this creed, so we soon run into sweeping problems of credibility, which are then ignored, rendered "*studiedly* irrelevant," exactly as the establishment knows very well how to do.

It has long since gotten to the point where even Victorian type work that is particularly socially en-gaged is far too threatening to the establishment, which has exerted pressure to kill such work for over a century now (let alone more revolutionary works). Why did Tolstoy not win a Nobel Prize? Likely because he had become far too much an activist, dissenter, too progressive in face of the status quo, as shown somewhat in his posthumous great short novel Hadji Murad (1904/1912), about a Chechen rebel leader in relation to Empire. It's a novel that should be front and center today, and of a sort we should be reading and writing, especially given the particulars of today's longstanding freshly explosive crises, especially given the cultural and institutional bigotry of the US (and West) in this regard. Wood cites Hadji Murad in HFW merely for a stylistic brilliance. It's a novel Homeland Security and others should better read, along with contemporary liberatory novels.

Instead, both bizarre and predictable, as we've seen, is this recurring underlying theme in the criti-cism of James Wood, only slightly exaggerated: Don't bother to create great highly useful fiction of the world, dear contemporary novelists, the mas-ters have done all your work for you. Go shuck peas, or do anything, but please don't presume to work at your art in relation to society. History end-ed more-or-less, at least in the novel – Dostoevsky and Conrad took it all down. There is no future dir-ection or tendency we can remotely point to. [Lib-eratory revolutionary – balderdash!] Back to sleep with you now, dear writers. Or do run along and practice your style (whether "free indirect" or whatnot) on something less threatening or less difficult than sociopolitical, engaged fiction for an establishment critic to speak meaningfully about. The thought of which, after all, is "slightly depressing." The loafing about of fly-eyed young men has long represented "the classic novelistic activity" – the flaneur, you know. They are "traumatized" and "numb" so let us partake of their great visions.

Flaneuring – what else is there for those "who belong to the ruling class … those who [have] al-ready won the battle and acquired the spoils … [who can] afford to be above the battle"? More typ-ically, establishment critics intone the ostensible "extreme difficulty" of writing novels about ongo-ing events, especially in such supposedly "confus-ing" times. In any event, not for nothing today are Dostoevsky's novels Notes from the Underground and The Possessed and Conrad's novel The Secret Agent safe for the establishment, because they are studies more in retail pathology and retail violence, demonizing of easy targets, novels that fail to offer liberatory explorations of wholesale Western estab-lishment oppressions and aggressions, blind to much progress and possibilities.

Misrepresentation 27 – 9-11 rallying cry for a turn inward, and worse: Less than a month after the terrorist attacks of 9-11-01, Wood speculated and hoped that the aftermath of the attack would "al-low a space for the aesthetic, for the contemplative, for novels that tell us not 'how the world works' but 'how somebody felt about something' – indeed, how a lot of different people felt about a lot of dif-ferent things (these are commonly called novels about human beings)." He then declared, "Who would dare to be knowledgeable [in a novel] about politics and society now?" One hardly needs social-ist David Walsh to point out "Who would dare *not* to be knowledgeable about politics and society now? Wood's counterposing of 'human' versus 'social' novels is deeply false." Crucially, who should not have "dared" ever? Myriad people in general "dared" and have long proven to be sociopolitically discerning both within the US and without. Not the establishment though. Not its literary stars, or scarcely any of its stars, for that matter. Not then and not now. They can't dare, marginal exceptions aside. It would be dysfunctional to the ruling stat-us quo. Thus, had they ever been publicly acute in this regard, they would not have been granted their positions of prominence. Get wise of a sudden, or even accidentally step out of line – they are quickly disciplined, sometimes by a pointed sta-tus quo cri-tique, put "on notice," or, especially if they persist, simply "let go." Case studies abound (via reports in independent media and analyses by independent scholars).

Not only star critics, but leading liberal "po-liti-al" novelists are atrocious in this regard (let alone conservative or reactionary writers). For example, in 2008,The Nation magazine pub-lished EL Doctor-ow's 2007 keynote address to a joint meeting of the American Academy of Arts and Sciences and the American Philosophical Society, in Washington DC, in which Doctorow states near its beginning that the leaders of "a religiously inspired criminal movement origi-nated in the Middle East…[have] mentally transport[ed] their rank and file back into the darkness of tribal war and shrieking, life-contemptuous jihad. [This]… declared enemy with the mindset of the Dark Ages throws his anachro-nistic shadow over us and awakens our dormant primeval instincts." In other words, until the terrorist attacks of 9-11, the primitive impulses of the US were sleeping soundly, only to be terrorized awake by those "criminal" and

"tribal" and "shrieking" war-mongers from the lands of the richest oil fields. That's quite a story. It leaves something out. Reality. The real-ity of decades-long US hopes, plans, and efforts to control those oil fields, including support for the state tyrants of those rich kingdoms, not least Saudi Arabia, from where nearly all the 9-11 terrorists originated, which was considered to be an occupied country by terrorist leader Osama bin Laden, due to the US military pres-ence there, subsequently withdrawn. Doctorow sends down the memory hole the reality of the murderous US-UN imposed economic sanctions against Iraq[24] that helped destroy that country and other inconvenient facts, such as decisive US support for the state of Israel and many of its militant endeavors against its regional neigh-bors, including longstanding invasions and oc-cupations.

After carefully inverting cause and effect of the current ongoing crisis, Doctorow pro-nounces to his intellectual audience about "knowledge deniers. Their rationale is always political. And more often than not, they hold in their hand a sacred text for certification." Shortly thereafter he goes on with brazen (and ludicrous) hypocrisy to both romantic-cize and all but deify the "sacred text" of the US Consti-tution and its history:

> The ratification parades were sacramental – symbolic venerations, acts of faith. From the beginning, people saw the Constitu-tion as a kind of sacred text for a civil so-ciety. And with good reason: the ordain-ing voice of the Constitution is scriptural, but in resolutely keeping the authority for its dominion in the public consent, it pre-sents itself as the sacred text of secular humanism.

Meanwhile, some of the founders and states viewed the Constitution as likely inherently tyran-nical, and so several states barely ratified it, and did so only by attaching lists of amend-ments and rights. Doctorow refers to the "sa-

---

[24] *The sanctions were described as "genocidal" by former UN Humanitarian Co-ordinator in Iraq Denis Halliday, who resigned over their imposition.*

cred text" of the US Constitution at a time when it contained none of its amendments, thus, no Bill of Rights protect-ing many of the most important freedoms of the people. The Declaration of Independence and the Bill of Rights are far greater texts of liberty than the original and still highly flawed US Constitution. Doctorow eventually levels some fairly strong criti-cism of US policy and acts generally but mostly confines his critique to Bush and the Bush regime. Along the way, he neglects to mention "oil" or "occupation" and rather haplessly refers to two iconic establishment novelists, Herman Melville and Henry James (see misrepresentation next). Near closing, Doctorow calls the US a "democracy that is given to a degree of free imaginative expression that few cultures in the world can tolerate, [in which] we can hope for the aroused witness, the manifold reportage, the flourishing of knowledge that will restore us to ourselves, awaken the dulled sense of our people to the public interest that is their interest…" The US surely is in many ways a very free society. All the greater then is the delin-quency, however predictable, of an establishment literature that cannot be troubled to create and pro-duce topical anti invasion-and-conquest novels of oil rich lands in the spirit of what liberatory scholar Edward Said calls "the urgent conjunction of art and politics." Nothing might stop the established authors and publishers in this "democracy" of the free but their investments and ideologies, their false realities and illusions, their misrepresenta-tions of others and themselves. And how ever much they care.

Misrepresentation 28 – Henry James, TS Eliot, the CIA, and the cultural cold war: The establishment's ideological commitments render it unqualified to comment with much insight on vast sociopolitical domains both within fiction and without. It's incapable. This may or may not be why Wood feels at least "slightly depressed" at the thought of social novels representing the times. If he's truly a per-ceptive guy, widely aware, he knows he's hand-cuffed in what he can write. Establishment pres-sure against speaking out creates fear of job loss, isolation, obloquy, and other disincentives. On the other hand, status quo ideological constrictions may either be readily accepted by Wood and estab-lishment writers, or may likely have been long since internalized as reality. If they were to write strong, comprehensive, perceptive analyses, they would be vilified, including by publishers and owners, or quietly cut off, effectively removed from history, as was, for example, once prominent liter-ary critic Maxwell Geismar. Thus the need for in-dependent writing and independent publishing houses. Currently: the few Davids against the many Goliaths.

Henry James – "a primary Cold War literary figure" – has been such a politically favored author of the establishment because he was a relatively prominent member of the privileged class whose stylistically accomplished sometimes labyrinthine writing hews to status quo lines at exhaustive length. Since, as famously noted, he chews more than he bites off, his novels function as elaborate upscale crossword puzzles for people of leisure and position. In a corrupt culture, the symptom of a corrupt system and vice versa, such fiction cannot fail to be revered for its charming, slight and "safe" qualities – ostensible or otherwise. Henry James and TS Eliot rate very high, or at the top, among the establishment's most admired American novelists, poets, critics. Both moved to England and be-came English citizens, as if geographically and geo-politically trying to go back in time, at least figura-tively. They have been sort of wonderfully symbol-ic anti-revolutionaries, perfect for CIA purposes. The CIA in its propaganda ef-forts "air-dropped translations of T.S. Eliot's Four Quartets into Rus-sia," and its cultural em-issaries hastened to appear on national television to defend James, as we have seen.

TS Eliot is still highly revered in writing circles, in poetry workshops especially. Yet how many writers actually know and understand the faith based line of his full thought? At the end of Forces in American Criticism (1939), scholar Bernard Smith puts Eliot's views in perspective:

> [T.S. Eliot wrote,] 'There are two and only two finally tenable hypotheses about life: the Catholic and the materialistic [i.e., Marxist]. It is quite possible, of course, that the future may bring neither a Chris-

tian nor a material-istic civilization. It is quite possible that the future may be nothing but chaos or torpor. In that event, I am not interested in the fu-ture; I am only interested in the two alterna-tives which seem to me worthier of interest.'

...Eliot chose not only the Catholic hy-poth-esis, but also its political corollaries. His lit-erary opinions were thus given a firm philo-sophical base to rest upon, and from that fact he drew the reasonable conclusions ... [that] 'Literary criticism should be complet-ed by criticism from a definite ethical and theological stand-point.... The 'greatness' of literature can-not be determined solely by literary stan-dards; though we must remember that whether it is literature or not can be de-termined only by literary standards.'

To this has esthetic criticism at last come – to a realization that non-esthetic criteria are the ultimate tests of value. Whether they be called philosophical, moral, or social cri-teria, they are still the ideas that men have about the way hu-man beings live together and the way they ought to live. The quest of beauty had become the quest of reality. It had be-come, in essence, literary criticism as so-cially conscious and as polemical as the criticism of the Marxists.[25]

Eliot the partisan – but for the establishment.

Misrepresentation 29 – liberatory lit attacked, bur-ied: This combined liberal/conservative and reac-tionary political literary attack against the increas-ingly progressive literary stalwart Maxwell Geis-mar, having occurred on national TV no less, is (in retrospect at least) one of the most significant mo-ments in all of American literature in the second half of the twentieth century – and it remains virtu-ally unknown. Details may be found in Geismar's decades-delayed, invaluable memoir, Reluctant Radical (2002). Sometimes entire careers are buried, other times particular books. Similarly shot down the memory hole are landmark works of progres-sive or liberatory literary criticism from the first half of the twentieth century. Sheer scandal is the burial of Upton Sinclair's studied book of economic literary criticism, Mammonart (1924). Other inex-cusable great losses include VF Calverton's The Liberation of American Lit-erature (1932) and Ber-nard Smith's Forces in American Criticism (1939). It's difficult to be ig-norant of these three momen-tous works and yet be able to fully appreciate Kenneth Burke's tremendous collection of 1930s essays, The Phi-losophy of Literary Form (1941), a book contain-ing particular essays that consummate the pro-

---

[25] *Smith adds: "Eliot spoke of alternatives, not of choices.... He be-lieves that one of the alternatives has greater value, is nobler, is in a sense more real, than the other. The question is therefore not simply one of personal taste. It is a question of evidence and rea-son. But the alternative he favors admits of no evidence and dero-gates from reason. His philosophy is, in the last analysis, wholly mystical. It is not capable of being tested and verified and im-proved. The alternative he rejects is, on the other hand, the one that is favored by those who are determined to be as scientific as one can be in a non-physical field.*

The literary criticism of the neo-classicists is a criticism composed of obiter dicta inspired by intangible emotions. The literary criti-cism of the materialists stands or falls by the findings of the social scientists, psychologists, and historians. Eliot's alternative in-volves a revulsion against democracy; the materialists are parti-sans of democracy. The literary criticism of his school tends to cre-ate a literature that will express the sensibilities and experiences of a few fortunate men. The criticism of the opposing school tends to create a literature that will express the ideals and sympathies of

those who look forward to the conquest of poverty, ignorance, and inequality – to the material and intellectual elevation of the mass of mankind.

To whom does the future belong? In January 1939 Eliot an-nounced that the Criterion, the literary journal he had edited since 1922, would no longer be published. His Europe had crumbled; the culture in which he had put his faith was dying. The Criterion had served its purpose. Eliot had arrived at a mood of detachment. There was nothing he could hopefully fight for now. But those who believe in scientific methods, in realism, in social equality and de-mocracy, are hopeful and are fighting."

Earlier, Smith comments: "There was one critic who apparently possessed all the virtues – fine taste, poetic sensitiveness, intellec-tuality, an experimental inclination. His literary scholarship was beyond dispute, his writing deft and memorable. He was, moreo-ver, a poet of the first rank, which gave his criticism of the art an extraordinary authority. He was universally respected.... This critic was T. S. Eliot.... The reader will note that he is here de-scribed in the past tense. His works are many now, but The Sacred Wood [1920] alone is a consideration of esthetic problems. In the rest the emphasis is on the esthetic effects of moral and social be-liefs...."

gressive literary tradition, or liberatory tendency, of the preceding four decades at least. Ignorance of these landmark books makes it more difficult to understand the significance, isolation, and persecution of the once prominent (when lib-eral) accomplished literary critic Maxwell Geismar, as he was marginalized and forgotten through the sixties and seventies and today. It's difficult to be ignorant of these books of criticism (still almost en-tirely disappeared, despite much renewed interest in the 1930s) and yet be able to make full sense of the vital socially engaged criticism prior to the 1940s that was forcefully curtailed in subsequent decades, with corrosive effects very much evident today, despite some progressive gains, not least by way of the multicultural expansion.

The problem remains that establishment ideol-ogy continues to enormously disfigure fiction and criticism, as James Petras remarked.

Scholar Terry Eagleton notes in "Only Pinter Remains" (2007):

> For almost the first time in two centuries, there is no eminent British poet, playwright or novelist prepared to question the founda-tions of the western way of life. One might make an honourable exception of Harold Pinter, who has wisely decided that being a champagne socialist is better than being no socialist at all; but his most explicitly poli-tical work is also his most artistically dreary.

> The knighting of Salman Rushdie is the establishment's reward for a man who moved from being a remorseless satirist of the west to cheering on its criminal adven-tures in Iraq and Afghanistan. David Hare caved in to the blandishments of Bucking-ham Palace some years ago, moving from radical to reformist. Christopher Hitchens… [has] thrown in his lot with Washington's neocons. Martin Amis has written of the need to prevent Muslims travelling and to strip-search people "who look like they're from the Middle East or from Pakistan". Deportation, he considers, may be essential further down

the road.

> The uniqueness of the situation is worth underlining. When Britain emerged as an industrial capitalist state, it had Shelley to urge the cause of the poor, Blake to dream of a communist utopia, and Byron to scourge the corruptions of the ruling class…

In the US, the situation is not much better, despite playwright Tony Kushner's writing in Theater:

> I do not believe that a steadfast refusal to be partisan is, finally, a particularly brave or a moral or even interesting choice. Les Mur-ray, an Australian poet, wrote a short poem called 'Politics and Art.' In its entirety:

> > 'Brutal policy / like inferior art, knows / whose fault it all is.'

> This is as invaluable an admonishment as it is ultimately untrue.

What is James Wood's role in all this? Maybe aside from his relative prominence, it's very similar to the overwhelming flood of establishment writers and publishers – conservative, reactionary, and lib-erals not least. They bulwark the status quo, more or less, often even when they think they do not or think they are progressive. Meanwhile, "liberatory revolutionary" is virtually altogether out of the realm of thought, let alone comprehension.

Misrepresentation 30 – fiction shrunk: James Wood shows and tells quite a bit of quality in his criti-cism, and of course one can learn a lot from view and voice, style and character studies – purview. Though he shuns the forest for love of the wood in many ways, there's no denying that the wood, even a solitary tree, may be impressive. Noam Chomsky is far from alone in claiming:

> If you want to learn about people's personal-ities and intentions, you would probably do better reading novels than reading psycholo-gy books. Maybe that's the best way to come to an understanding

of human beings and the way they act and feel, but that's not science. Science isn't the only thing in the world, it is what it is…science is not the only way to come to an understanding of things … If I am interested in learning about peo-ple, I'll read novels rather than psychology.

Moreover, fiction can be used to illuminate or engage what Chomsky calls "Orwell's prob-lem":

How is it that oppressive ideological systems are able to "instill beliefs that are firmly held and widely accepted although they are com-pletely without foundation and often plainly at variance with the obvious facts about the world around us?" The political refrain, "What's the matter with Kansas?" means more expansively, What's the matter with the USA, and the world? As Wole Soyinka, the Nigerian author and po-litical worker notes, "Criticism, like charity, starts at home." Little may strike closer to home than the novel, a great and indispensable form for engaging Orwell's problem, terribly our own. Orwell's problem, in other words: How is it that people are persuaded to act against their own interests and values, often viciously, which they otherwise hold dear? Fiction can debunk harmful propaganda and taboos; it can help en-ergize, motivate, inspire while maintaining vital literary and popular quality by staying focused on fiction's core strengths (and not excluding those emphasized by Wood and the establish-ment). Fic-tion can do, and does, far more than the establish-ment gives it credit for ad nau-seam. Such novels, short stories, and satires in-tensely explore both the private and the public, those realities and their relations, not least but not only as revealed in the personal.

One cannot expect the status quo to abide lib-era-tory fiction too far of course, for as Chomsky notes: "If Orwell, instead of writing *1984* – which was actually, in my opinion, his worst book, a kind of trivial caricature of the most totalitarian society in the world, which made him famous and everybody loved him, because it was the official enemy – if instead of doing that easy and relatively unimpor-tant thing, he had done the hard and important

thing, namely talk about Orwell's Problem [as per-tains to the West], he would not have been famous and honored: he would have been hated and re-viled and marginalized" by the estab-lishment, by the civilized. Reporter: "What do you think of Western civilization?" Gandhi: "I think it would be a good idea." Even the bright new prominent liter-ary magazines and sites such as n+1, The Believer, and others distin-guish themselves as little more than the flotsam and jetsam of the establishment. Meanwhile the overwhelming majority of academ-ic literary magazine production is similarly tamed. It's not that they are of no value. It's that they pri-marily and essentially perpetuate the basic status quo. To gain at least a little more human-ity and vi-tality, possibly they could create or far better aug-ment "left" or particular "libera-tory" sections. The establishment might tolerate that for some while.

Misrepresentation 31 – the partisan orthodox na-ture of status quo lit: If we are not *also* writ-ing and reading novels *"in order* to benefit" practically, use-fully, then surely it's long past time we started do-ing so. Wood may be de-pressed by the thought of a flood of novels that "explain the times" for any va-riety of reasons, but he has indirectly said as much for them in a quip (Homeland Security should read), maybe more, as he has argued repeatedly against. The ideological lines of establishment fiction and criticism are evident, revealing, and follow an instructive trajectory of plot. They some-times appear (in Ngũgĩ 's words) as "tragedy that manifests itself as comedy." When not worse. Clearly detailed or not in the minds or writing of star critics who may or may not wish, after all, to matter too much, this too is how fiction works, for real – and how does it ever.

Even Sean Wilentz in "The Rise of Illiterate De-mocracy" in the New York Times notes that "The nonfiction best-seller lists these days are often full of partisan screeds labeling Democrats as elitist traitors and Republicans as conniving plutocrats. But look over on the fiction side, and politics ap-pears almost nowhere. …the separa-tion of litera-ture and state seems to have be-come absolute." Wilentz is scarcely referring to progressive political fiction here; however, his observations apply be-yond party politics, since many crucial and endur-ing public issues are not taken up in fiction from much explicit progressive let alone revolutionary perspective. Who would solicit or publish them? Who has? Hollywood? The publishing houses with money and clout? Even the liberal ones? The liberal magazines? The literary magazines? Many of these operations cannot beg off, as progressive opera-tions often must, for not having re-sources.

One author has suggested that fiction writers could "tithe" some part of their writing time and talent to producing *nonfiction* political works. The notion of enlightening and moving and aesthetical-ly accomplished political *fiction* of various sorts seems that which cannot be thought. Take award winning story writer Ben-jamin Percy, one of the first writers (sanctioned by the literary establish-ment, that is) to write in any way about the US invasion and occupation of Iraq, in "Refresh, Re-fresh" (which appeared in Best American Short Stories 2007 and was called the story of the year by novelist Anne Lamott):

> I certainly have strong political feelings. But I try not to let them command my fic-tion. There is a difference between writ-ing about a political issue — and writing politically — and I try not to cross that line in the sand. I don't want people to come away from my story as if they've come away from an edi-torial, with a ready-made message shoved down their throat. An audience should feel betrayed by such fiction, because it's so obviously fraudulent and manipulative, the charac-ters hollow puppets the author crude-ly shoves his hands into. Part of the goal of Refresh, Refresh was to write a war story that didn't say, war is good, war is bad. I instead wanted to say, this is war. And in doing so, I tried to show both sides. I can't tell you how many emails I've re-ceived from people who have read Re-fresh, Refresh and called me A, a liberal pantywaist, or B, a right-wing nut job.

When you piss off everybody, I guess you're doing something right. On the other hand, I've also received emails from soldiers, from vets, from protestors, from politicians, all of them moved by the story for completely different reasons.

What escapes Percy's regard here (and TC Boyle's and George Saunders' in similar com-ments, as well as that of central establishment writers like EL Doc-torow and Philip Roth, and so on, who are often perceived as rather politi-cal) is the power and vital-ity, the value and art, of partisan fiction. Percy makes no note (and seems to imply the opposite) that "strong politi-cal feelings" can be expressed as liberatory overt partisan fiction in very accomp-lished and highly aesthetic ways far from "a ready-made message shoved down [a reader's] throat," as if ostensibly nonpartisan fiction is any less "ready-made," including Percy's own "Refresh, Re-fresh" given his decision to "show both sides": apparently meaning "war is good, war is bad." Partisan fiction, according to Percy, is "fraudu-lent and manipulative" but depictions of "war is good, war is bad" are even-handed, which must no doubt prove equally instructive and comfort-ing to both the invaders and the invaded, occu-pied peoples of the smashed land of Iraq. And so it is that status quo fiction is far less upfront and often in denial – far less willing and capable of declaring what it actually is, ideologically. There are plenty of ways a literary subjective fiction can reveal objective criminal reality. Status quo art, however, avoids doing so, except marginally, in a great number of ways, even though it practically has to go out of its way to cheat reality, to vitiate it of urgent conditions, revelation or phenomena, let alone explore pro-gressive or revolutionary realms and possibili-ties.

The criticism of James Wood further muddles the shallow sociopolitical component of the human condition as explored in fiction, and fur-ther im-pedes and discourages its badly needed engage-ment. Pathology in terrorism – Wood claims. In part, but it's largely tactical and rooted in injustice, the main problem by far. Jealousy of the West? Rather, justified outrage.

Them as the West's "cur-rent problem"? *Our* (the West's) longstanding out-law acts. How Fiction Works? How Purview Works in Part. "Free in-direct style"? Purview meld. The intimate human may be revealed in the novel? And the epic social and political too. Subtlety of analy-sis, nuance, limning – establishment sign language for toeing the line with style, for creating work nonthreatening to the interests (often criminal) of establishment power and control.

Misrepresentation 32 – basic public realities denied, distorted: The current crises of the US in the "Mid-dle East" are widely misrepresented by the estab-lishment – fiction and nonfiction both. Take the Iraq war for example. The media is full of articles stating that Iraq war mov-ies and films (the fiction features) have not done well at the box office, but compared to the rela-tive lack of, say, Hurricane Katrina movies, or, say, the ongoing national slaughter of the im-poverished by the impoverish-ers movies, the growing numbers of Iraq war mov-ies, by their very existence alone, are doing ex-tremely well. Far more such movies have been made now than were remotely ever made about the Viet-nam war at a comparable time. And far more people see most any of these movies than see most any such documentary. But it's no cause for celebration, far from it, because these movies are very careful not to be too "antiwar," if at all, not too revealing of the basic illegality and im-morality of the US conquest of Iraq and sur-rounds.

Of course all wars are brutalizing in their every-day and peripheral realities (true of even justifiable wars), which is about as far as any of the movies go, and that typically isn't even as far into the fun-damentals as Michael Moore's relatively circum-scribed documentaries ven-ture with the various is-sues he examines. The central reality of the US con-quest of Iraq and beyond is distorted or falsified, or goes studi-ously ignored, the fact that the US has commit-ted the supreme crime of aggression, "the su-preme international crime differing only from other war crimes in that it contains within itself all the accumulated evil of the whole," in the words of the judgment of Nuremberg. None of

the dozens of Iraq war movies, shows, and nov-els I'm aware of renders this reality explicit and central. Instead, central reality is buried.

Very few of these various works of fiction even begin to approach that central framing context, and consequently they either greatly falsify or evade the crucial reality. On those grounds that are cen-tral to the whole calamity, the movies and novels don't deserve a large audience, even if they do on other grounds. Un-til this "major and crucial point overlooked" is made clear in relation to the US role in the ag-gression against Iraq, as Noam Chomsky notes, "until at least this is recognized, all other dis-cussion is merely footnotes, and shameful ones." And that's the shame of the Iraq war movies, and novels too; they are essentially about the "footnotes," however monstrous, rather than the "major and crucial point over-looked." And what's worse, overlooking the central point means that even the best inten-tioned films may more likely "act as cultural 'softeners' before the bombing starts again for real" or continues without end, as John Pilger notes of films like Black Hawk Down, in "Hol-lywood Hurrah." (Not that he regards BHD as well intentioned.) Pilger adds:

> Even in finely crafted films like The Deer Hunter and Platoon that look as if they might break ranks, there is an implicit oath of loyalty to imperial culture. This was true of Three Kings, a movie that seemed to take issue with the Gulf war, but instead pro-duced a familiar "bad apple" tale, exonerat-ing the militarism that is now rampant. So dominant is Hollywood in our lives, and so collusive are its camp-following critics, that the films that ought to have been made are unmentionable. Name the mainstream mov-ies that have shone light on to the vast sha-dow thrown by the American secret state, and the mayhem for which it is responsible. I can think of only a few: Costa-Gavras's Missing, which was about the destruction of the elected government in Chile by General Pinochet's puppet masters in Washington, and Oliver Stone's Salvador, which made the

Salvador, which made the connection between Reagan's Washington and El Salvador's death squads. Both these films were quirks of the system, funded with great difficulty and, in the case of Missing, dogged by vengeful court actions.

In sum, seen as a Hollywood meal ticket (make that, yacht ticket) the Iraq war movies are a com-mercial disappointment, while otherwise an ex-treme and growing success compared to their (vir-tually nonexistent) Vietnam war counterparts. But to call these movies a cultural success is an extreme overstatement, except as footnote. Most of the films I've seen have some limited worthwhile qualities, even though one sees these films for what they are and gets the antagonizing and sometimes intoler-able sense that goes along with it. The most worth-while thus far are probably, In the Valley of Elah, Rendition, War, Inc., and above all, the relatively low budget GI Jesus. Even slimmer pickings exist among the novels, seems to me, though the rele-vant novels of Yasmina Khadra compare.

Hollywood and the literary establishment are as stark in their partisan nature as in their denials of such. Multicultural fiction is far more pronounced in recent decades than it has been traditionally and some of this is progressive or has progressive as-pects, some even overt progressive and revolution-ary aspects. But, for merely one example, how many recent antiwar novels can be named? The US has been smashing Iraq since 1991, taking a toll of over a million Iraqi lives through bombings and sanctions in the 1990s alone, long before the deeply unpopular ground invasion and occupation killing as many or more again, and creating millions more refugees. And the US for years has allowed corpor-ations the use of patent laws, which have prevent-ed HIV vaccines from reaching Africa resulting in millions of lives lost. Where are the exposé novels? Name the so-called muckraking novels or vivid polemic novels about the unconscionable US health care system, or poverty rate and the outrageous economic system. Or US global militarism and outlaw threats both military and economic. Or

avoidable environmental catastrophes. Etc and so on. Not easy to do, though it's possible to come up with a few, including John le Carré somewhat re-cently in The Constant Gardner – an exception to the rule. Even le Carré recently said he underesti-mated, underportrayed the damage done in Africa by the unconscionable economics and policies of the West. Writing powerful quality liberatory fic-tion is in many ways unthinkable and disallowed in the circles of literature, exceptions aside.

Misrepresentation 33 – the immateriality of the status quo: As James Wood puts forth an "aesthet-ic" of pursuing "*the real*, which is at the bottom of [his] inquiries," there is every reason to believe his assertion and every reason to doubt what it might reveal, when his pursuit of *the real* is eviscerated by reality, the status quo stake, that long blade of ide-ology, manifesting itself via inane or hapless no-tions like "the essential juvenility of plot." Plot and purpose and the world be damned – not least for US novelists (or critics) writing about explicit investigations of the immoral and illegal invasions, occupations and other state crimes of the US. Con-ditions far too real for publication. Now, if *other* authors, not from around here, want to create epic masterworks of the real for publishing, review, and distribution in the West, then okay, to a point, especially if allegorical, or otherwise limited, and preferably *about them* (if not *to* the people), but don't subtly limn the nuance too far, too explicitly, too purposefully so that we of the status quo can-not plausibly deny what must be denied.

Just so, we may review, we may praise an *other* masterpiece, either not from here or about *not* here, and we may write glowing analyses, including a genuinely illuminating one – though with a key flaw – as did Scott Esposito on Ngũgĩ wa Thion-go's accurately self-described "global epic from Africa," Wizard of the Crow. The ideological flaw in his essay (if not a simpler mistake), where estab-lishment perspective, wittingly or not, gets the bet-ter of an otherwise astute work, is where Esposito, exactingly, in much more detail than I quote below, assesses Ngũgĩ's vibrant fictive depiction of a par-ticular sort of politics as "African" and by mislead-ing inference not American – not quite, not remote-ly:

> [In Wizard of the Crow] storytelling ex-emp-lifies the techniques and the archi-tecture used by political actors in [the fic-titious Afri-can country] Aburiria as they continually in-vent tales that, with breath-taking speed, be-come the new realities that the country must live by. Whether it is the Ruler purposefully creating realities with an iron hand, busi-nessmen doing it in ignorance as they ar-range deals, or even the resistance innocent-ly slipping into stories that help them to-ward their goals, the creation of stories re-mains cen-tral…

> In the space of just a few pages, a miracu-lous inversion has been effected. March-ing to Heaven [an incredibly corrupt Tower of Babel building project] has gone from a boondoggle that has revealed Aburiria's desperation to a vision of na-tional strength, fervently attended to by popular demonstra-tions all over the country. Significantly, the Ruler has not said a word to create this new reality. Merely by indicating his displeasure with the story that reality has given him, he has spurred his ministers to invent an en-tire-ly new reality and to find methods by which to force it into existence. If Thiong'o is cor-rect, and I think he is, this is how an African dictatorship functions.

Far more to point however: this is how cen-tralized governments in the age of propaganda function globally, more or less, not least in the US (where Ngũgĩ has lived and worked for 16 years, since 1992, the beginning of President Bill Clinton's terms). The Clinton-Bush regimes in Washington DC were forced to "continually in-vent tales that, with breathtaking speed, become the new realities that the country must live by" whether to invade and occupy Iraq and Af-ghanistan indefinitely, or to demonize welfare, or to endlessly bailout high fi-nance, or to flood prisons with non-violent drug-law offenders, or to continually prop-up pharma-ceutical and in-surance companies while demoni-zing Medicare for all, and on and on. President Bush II shoved the military into Iraq and Afghani-stan with his "iron hand" and by way of "dealing business-men" in the media and elsewhere (often not so "ignorant"). The Bush regime could and so it did, even though the majority public opposed it, even in the US except for a few months in the be-ginning of the invasion when the massive fraudu-lent propaganda deluge worked its ef-fect, mentally cleansing the US majority ever so briefly. And now the Barack Obama incipient regime, only slightly less status quo aggressive and fanatic, has more subtly maneuvered, but in just as wholesale a fashion, America's "despera-tion" in grasping at fake change "to a vision of national strength, fervently attended to by popular demonstrations all over the country" and beyond (hundreds of thousands gathered to cheer him on while in Europe prior to the US election). "Significantly, the [presumptive] Ruler has not said a word to create this new re-ality," not a word that is meaningful in any ba-sic concrete way. "He has spurred his [PR] min-isters to invent an entirely new reality, and to find methods by which to force it into existence" at least in appearance.

While not from America but Africa as Ngũgĩ points out, Wizard of the Crow is far more a global novel than Esposito indicates, far more an Ameri-can novel than he hints. Commenting at Amazon. com, Patricia Kramer writes, "The satire is biting, the laughs come often but then the reality of our country's present policies sets in. We would be lucky to have a Wizard of the Crow right now in America." Such a pointed global epic from America rather than "from Af-rica" or Asia, et al, would pre-ferably be one that advances well beyond even the mighty Wizard. Such a novel and any clear-eyed criti-cism will have to wait, and if and when that day arrives, will have to be fought for. That's the re-ality.

Misrepresentation 34 – the public chopped from the personal: As for "puerile" prose, Rob-ert Alter clarifies in his critique of contemporary fiction, "I have no quarrel at all with fantasy or flaunted arti-fice in the novel but only with their deployment in ways that are ultimately self-indulgent and mech-anically repetitious, that tend to turn the imagina-tive energies of fiction into a crackling closed cir-cuit" where little meaning or sensibility escapes the smoke and sparks of the swirling (yet somehow dull) words. Five years later (1980) in "The Ameri-can Political Novel," while critiquing Robert Coov-er's The Public Burning, Alter notes: "One may wonder why so many gifted and serious novel-ists have chosen to treat politics in such a funda-mentally unserious fashion… One would think that the political novel, perhaps more than other kinds of fiction, requires adult intelligence…"

Then sounding like Wood today, though both more apt and too narrow, Alter focuses on char-acter, noting: "The novel's great strength as a mode of apprehension is in its grasp of character, and the political novel at its best can show concretely and subtly what politics does to character, what char-acter makes of politics." Ah, "subtly"! for Alter too is establishment but like Wood sheds some light around his distor-tions. He critiques Norman Mail-er's attempts to craft effective political fiction and concludes that (as of over three decades ago) he seems to come closest to this in The Deer Park where:

> What he confronts centrally for the first time is the special power of American so-ciety to mask, sham, evade, forget reality, to seduce its individual members into giving up on engagement in the real world; and the ulti-mately political nature of his moral imagin-ation is reflected in his effort here to show how this American style of cotton-candy insulation from real-ity allows a society to perpetrate horror and obscenity at home and abroad with hardly a twinge of conscience.

If only the novel did greatly reveal such real-ity. Unfortunately, The Deer Park seems to me to be far more focused on characters' private lives and rela-tionships than on any public realms within which they exist. Perceptive mid-century critic Maxwell Geismar in American Moderns – From Rebellion to Conformity (1958) also found this novel to be large-ly if not wholly bankrupt, with weak sociopolitical gestures.

In the essay "Jonathan Franzen and the 'So-cial Novel'," Wood restates a core complaint, a legiti-mate one, regarding current fiction: The "character-istic products of contemporary American fiction are books of great self-consciousness with no selves in them; curiously arrested books which know a thousand differ-ent things…but do not know a sin-gle human being." This statement is largely accur-ate, in my opinion, and as something of an echo of Al-ter is nicely stated, so much so that I find it diffi-cult to resist turning the words partly back upon their author, in regard to what he slights, Wood, who "know[s] a thousand different things," as a lit-erary critic, about the fictional portraiture of largely private and intimate psychological realms, "but do[es] not know a single" thing, it often seems, a-bout the potential of portraying the public realms of what it means to approach "fully human."

Given this lack, it might be said with only mini-mal exaggeration that Wood himself, as critic, does "not know a single human being," lacks much clue as to what may make for any full human condition. Character (or the per-sonal) may indeed be especial-ly central to fic-tion – however, the personal is made up of the private and public both. Public and pri-vate realms inform and infuse character, let alone so-ciety, and yet Wood slights the public in both character and society, egregiously.

Misrepresentation 35 – ideology in guise of aesthetics: Even one of Wood's "favorite" critics of the novel, Roland Barthes, had the sense to note, "Why are we so slow, so indifferent about mobilizing narrative and the image? Can't we see that it is, after all, works of fiction, no matter how mediocre they may be artistically, that best arouse political passion?" Wood, distinctly lack-ing Barthes theo-retical acumen (Terry Eagleton notes the obvious in a review of HFW), finds Barthes to be "interesting but wrongheaded," (generally?) and Wood who is likely to be half the essayist, or even literary critic, that Edmund Wilson demonstrated himself to be, remains locked in to his primary interest in fiction, its "special kind of aesthetic experience," so locked in that this fixation gives him tunnel vision, caus-ing misunderstanding about aesthetics, fic-tion, life. False notions such as this plaint are the least of it: "a flat style [is] unfit for permanent criticism – which lasts, after all, only if it, too, becomes litera-ture," a remark that is, first, false and, second, self-contradicting, given its mundane style. Exceptional substance overcomes stylistic flatness readily. Ide-ology, sometimes in guise of aesthetics, in estab-lishment literature often functions as a strong arm of the US police state, as H. Bruce Franklin notes in "In-side Stories of the Global American Prison":

> Despite the assault on the literature of the American prison [which Franklin documents in detail], it has been breaking into literature courses and anthologies. The 2006 edition of the *Heath Anthology of American Literature*, which is used in class-rooms a-round the world, actually included a whole section labeled "Prison Literature." Although this "cluster" con-sisted of a mere twenty-seven pages out of the more than three thousand in the multivolume anthology, that was enough to provoke the disapproval of the *New York Times Book Review*, whose editor Rachel Donadio, complained that it took up more space than that given to "the great poet Elizabeth Bishop." Even more reprehensible, according to Donadio, is the fact that this prison literature section "includes works by Kathy Boudin, a former member of the Weather Underground who served more than 20 years for her role in a 1981 robbery and murder." Implying that the five authors included in this section collectively are not worth as much space as Bishop, Donadio names only Boudin, failing even to give the names of such widely celebrated poets as Etheridge Knight and Jimmy Santiago Baca.[26] Nor does Donadio say even a word about any of their actual work, including Boudin's three beautiful, extremely moving poems. Masquerading as literary criticism based on aesthetic criteria, this editorial commentary in the *New York Times Book Review* thus offers a minor but revealing example of how dominant cultural institutions collaborate with the political apparatus to suppress prison literature....

> It is no surprise that modern prisoners [de-cades ago] helped lead the rediscovery of slave literature, because chattel slavery did not disappear in 1865 – it merely morphed into the modern American prison...merged ...with the more modern [forms of slavery] pioneered by the American prison.... When the time came to globalize this institution, the men chosen for the job were some of its most notorious officials.[27]

> The literature of slaves told the inside stories of antebellum slavery and thus helped de-stroy it. So too, the literature of prisoners tells the inside stories of the American pris-on and thus threatens its dominion and ex-pansion. The deepest insights into the Amer-ican global prison, including its culture and political logic, come from this literature it tries to re-press.

So goes literature and the establishment – moments and sectors of liberatory expansion

---

[26] Franklin notes: *A torrent of prison literature was pouring out to the American public [over three decades ago] in mass-market paperbacks, newspapers, magazines, and major motion pictures. This era ended with the downfall of the Nixon regime in 1974, the final defeat of the United States by Vietnam in 1975, and the reactionary epoch that soon followed. In 1976 came the Big Bang, the spectacular explosion of the prison-industrial complex. As a necessary corollary to this prison cosmos, there began a relentless corollary to this prison cosmos, there began a relentless campaign to silence prisoners and ex-prisoners [by passage of new laws and im-plementation of other measures.... Moreover, today] gone from the so-called "penitentiary" or "correctional facility" is any pretense of reformation or rehabilitation [exceptions to the rule aside]. In the typical American prison, degradation, brutalization, and even overt torture are the norm....*

[27] Franklin details: *After the invasion of Iraq, Lane McCotter, who had been forced to resign as the director of the Utah Department of Corrections because of torture carried out under his administration, was put in charge of reconstructing Saddam Hussein's Abu Ghraib. John Armstrong, former director of the Connecticut Department of Corrections, who had been driven out of his position because of sexual and other tortures revealed by the ACLU and Amnesty International, became deputy director of operation for the entire Iraqi prison system...*

followed by re-pression, Vietnam War era dissent and the reac-tionary (also liberal and conservative) backlash. Maxwell Geismar noted an earlier instance:

> Recently a group of American historians have been digging into, one might say, "ex-cavating," the true facts of this Cold War Culture – the curious period from the mid-forties to the mid-sixties – and the results are very interesting. We have had almost a quar-ter of a century of conformity, comfort, com-placency and mediocrity in American litera-ture – this ep-och of "instant masterpieces" – and only now can we begin to put the pieces together and find a consistent pattern…

> …it was the Cold War that brought about the downfall, in 1949, of one of the most bril-liant journalistic enterprises in our literary history. At the war's end, a new epoch of re-pression was about to start. Another great achievement of the Depression years was the WPA Federal Theater Project; and Halle Flanagan's history of this, in her book Arena, ends with the congressional investigation and foreclosure of the Federal Theater by political figures who are, by Divine Grace or special dispensation, still active in Washington today…

Wood's well-known Guardian article takedown of "the false zaniness of hysterical realism…[and] the easy fidelity of social realism" functions ironically well as a simultaneous takedown of what Wood otherwise praises as modernism in HFW: the "blurred" and "traumatized" and "numb" and "random" view of life by way of a "loafing" and "voyeuristic" flaneur. It's not that Wood can make no interesting argument, nor that he offers no real and useful insight. The problem is the arguments are often so parochial that they are often not remotely convincing or broadly functional, when not outright false. Many of the arguments are persuasive largely only insofar as they are half-regurgi-tations of what the literature establishment instills ad nauseam. They are either self-contradicting, or given any slightly larger –

more real – context, they implode. They may also be overturned on occasion by Wood's very own views presented elsewhere – contradictions that nullify.

Wood finds the flaneur figure "helplessly inun-dated with impressions" to be extraordinarily com-pelling, except when he doesn't, in which case he sometimes calls such writing "hysterical realism," which is apparently not styled enough to make up for its other distinct lacks. Apparently not enough prose-poetry – "a very careful ballet," a ballet that is not so very careful that it is not also largely ran-dom. Much of what Wood decries in "hysterical realism" – chaotic or essayistic excess – he otherwise praises as "Flaubertianism" – all the random …"traumatized"…"numbing"…"excess de-tail"… sometimes "*studiedly* irrelevant" of a "voyeurist"… "loafer." How all this tells us "how somebody felt about something" let alone "indeed, how a lot of different people felt about a lot of different things (these are commonly called novels about human beings)," as Wood also requires, is less clear. One must presume all humans are not all traumatized…

How is the Flaubertian mélange and "loafer" narrator on the street necessarily much different from a contemporary laptop whiz, of whom Wood complains, "nowadays anyone in possession of a laptop" can whip up, a novel full of "essaylets and great displays of knowledge. Indeed," Wood adds, with some annoyance, "'knowing about things' has become one of the qualifications of the contempo-rary novelist." Balzac, Tolstoy, George Eliot, Push-kin, etc and so on, even star modernists hardly wrote information starved fact-free literature. A case of wrong culprit. "Time and again novelists are praised for their wealth of obscure and far-flung social knowledge…. The reviewer, mistaking bright lights for evidence of habitation, praises the novelist who knows about, say, the sonics of vol-canoes" and other arcane and variously extraneous information (apparently not "*studiedly* irrelevant" enough), so that "the result – in America at least – is novels of immense self-consciousness" (modern-ism, anyone?) "with no selves in them at all," (not traumatized or enough numbed?) "curiously ar-rested" (indeed) "and very 'brilliant' books that know a thousand" more or less random "things but do not know a single human being." Many of Wood's and Alter's criticisms of "puerile" prose are well taken (though "hysterical" of "hysterical realism" is a term one could take issue with). Twist the wheel a bit from HR's excesses of fantasy and verisimilitude to modernism's often busy vapidity of driveling detail and some "blurring" "phantasmagoria" and such criticism rides well against modernism too – which Wood half-admits at moments: too much detail, to the point of "excessive excruciation…an obstruction to seeing."

And yet Wood finally cannot evaluate clearly his beloved UMM style modernism, because what would he and the establishment be left with? Both an aesthetic and sociopolitical threat to their own stakes. And Wood, able to grasp nothing fully functional, is left to bemoan and hope and flail: "A space may now open, one hopes, for the kind of novel that shows us that human consciousness is the truest Stendhalian mirror, reflecting helplessly the newly dark lights of the age." In other words, white noise, or worse. Both modernism and "hys-terical realism" and other establishment genres and modes do tend toward "reflect[ing] helplessly the newly dark lights of the age," which is almost a loss of consciousness, not its life. It can be that "damn thing" that Rebecca West speaks of in The Strange Necessity, this universe, this reality that is enough. Give us an other. "[O]ne of the damn thing is ample." She adds piercingly that "only an extraordinaryily massive stupidity could keep [certain types of artists] in a position which the rest of humanity has left so far behind, so naturally their works have a disgusting quality as of a person too grossly fat to move." Obstructing details puerile prose constricted ideologies and worse. It's not that nothing can be learned from these novels; it's not that they are necessarily wholly unengaging. It's that they go about as far as Wood goes, a little farther in some ways, a little less in others, and that's it – the patio chairs at the country club or the loading dock are breathlessly, gymnastically, hyperkinetically, self-relflexively, meta-be-bop-

ing-ly rearranged…ta da! *Look!* It's boring, often because if in appearance expansive, in reality confined.

Victor Hugo is a giant in the world of letters, compared to whom, Flaubert is something of a toad. Flaubert though is the establishment's special toad, and there he sits. Flaubert is neither the fount of modernism, nor the cause of the squelching of much more liberatory fiction than exists. He is sort of an awkward figurine, grandly elevated, cher-ished by the establishment. Meanwhile, a whole more accomplished liberatory fiction – more fully human – and often quite aesthetic – in crucial part a more vital development of the novel – has been denied, if not entirely. Where puerile realists show the world all crazy lit up and out, and flaneuring modernists show the world all fastidious miasmic within, liberatory novelists show the world more whole and forward looking, and moving.

Misrepresentation 36 – limits on the real: The more that Wood carries the term "realism" or "real" or "reality" the less water it holds. "…we are likely to think of the desire to be truthful about life – the desire to produce art that accurately sees 'the way things are'– as a universal literary motive and pro-ject, the broad central language of the novel and drama…" Here we see (a repeat of) "the way things are" as "reality" that stories "bring…to mind" – never "possibilities" that stories bring to mind, or even "real possibilities," which is the language not of the status quo. Fiction may reveal reality and possibility, both, in exploring the nature of the human condition achieved and potential – or what is the imagination for?

"Realism, seen broadly as truthfulness to the way things are, cannot be mere verisimilitude…" Well, yes it can. Some stretches of life actually do have a natural story shape, more or less, and may be encountered most pithily in flash dramas that occur in actual moments in time, where present, past, and future all but fuse in concise narrative. One might think of the anecdotal stories of a mo-ment found in Reader's Digest features "Life in These United States" or "Humor in Uniform." Surely some people invent some of these supposed-to-be actual anecdotes to collect the hundreds of dollars that are paid for them – and who can tell the difference between what is fiction and what is actual? That's "mere" verisimilitude as story. Certain poignant autobiographical moments are stories in verisimilitude, as are certain autobiographies, if one allows some cuts for concision. Such stories are essentially "mere" verisimilitude. Some people actually do live storybook lives or at least story quality stretches of life. It seems to me that anecdotes show virtually everyone to live some such moments, at the least. "Realism, seen broadly as truthfulness to the way things are, cannot be verisimilitude"? On the contrary, one can say what the novel is (or may be) far more reliably than what it is not – as Wood himself can be said to point out much earlier in HFW – "The novel is the great virtuoso of exceptionalism: it always wriggles out of the rules thrown around it" – except that verisimilitude as reality in story and life may not be so exceptional after all.

Virtually all content, ideology, verisimilitude, fancy, and direct reference may work and be worked in story to great effect. All does well to both challenge and reaffirm afresh existing actuali-ties and possibilities about the world or about fic-tion. And if any lively fiction aims to teach, and to be liberatory, and to bring people together, and to unmask any and all unjust conditions of life, and to explore their opposite, then fiction (or criticism) with all its great resources is perfectly free to do so just as well as do anything else. Fiction and criti-cism may reveal and catalyze forces of change – by way of experience, by way of understanding and vision. Misrepresentations of life and fiction obviously do not help, and too often function (wittingly or not) to support or propagate deplorable status quo realities. It is important to know how fiction works for the establishment, and often against the people at large, what myths and falsehoods it relies upon to convey its ostensible "lifeness," its wooden or smooth jargon – that is often not so much lifelike or lively or even all that living let alone fully alive in crucial ways. Detailed here, these three dozen misrepresentations and retrograde delimited reali-ties of establishment literature show some of the nature

and scope of the real eviscerations of fiction and life – and also how writers may work well beyond the broken views and repressive grasp. ...

PART FIVE – HUGO AND FLAUBERT

Rather than Victor Hugo's society-rocking fiction and daunting aesthetic achievement, today James Wood and many a writing circle celebrate the (by comparison) wan and dreary writing of Flaubert as seminal and essential – "Novelists should thank Flaubert the way poets thank spring; it all begins again with him." Ignored is the complex more comprehensive and profound let alone liberatory writing of Victor Hugo in Les Misérables, and other works. Flaubert instead is pushed as a central writing workshop and establishment presence – a situation again that comes close to "tragedy manifesting itself as comedy."

Flaubert has long been the (would be apolitical political) tool of the establishment, the obsessive stylist and yet dull shovel used to try to bury the literary and sociopolitical accomplishment and influence of Hugo and others. "It all begins again with Flaubert." It's laughable. Flaubert is a footnote to Victor Hugo (and Montaigne). Hugo writes in his great novel, "Geometry deceives; only the hurricane is accurate," as if he is already countervailing, one might imagine, the contemporary establishment endlessly trumpeting (heedless of the irony) nuance and limnits and the denned in closets of subtlety by those who chew in prose more than they take in of life, the fastidious intimatists and obsessivists of status quo sensibility. Geometry is excellent where not blown away by hurricanes of reality that often far more fully inform narrative and reveal the human condition, the timeless uni-versal and the profound today.

Again, Robb, noting the ethical, normative power, as well as the aesthetic multivalent approach employed by Hugo:

> Les Misérables etches Hugo's view of the world so deeply in the mind that it is im-pos-sible to be the same person after reading it – not just because it takes a notice-able percent-age of one's life to read it. The key to its ef-fect lies in Hugo's use of

a sporadically om-niscient narrator who reintroduces his char-acters at long inter-vals as if through the eyes of an ignorant observer – a narrator who can best be described as God masquerading as a law-abiding bourgeois....

The title itself is a moral test.... Originally, a *misérable* was simply a pauper (*misére* means 'destitution' as well as 'misfortune'). Since the Revolution, and especially since the ad-vent of Napoleon III, a *misérable* had become a 'dreg', a sore on the shining face of the Sec-ond Empire. The new sense would dictate a translation like *Scum of the Earth*. Hugo's sense would dictate *The Wretched*. ...

Every character struck a chord and had such a profound effect on the French view of French society that even on a first reading one has a vague recollection of having read the novel before.

The establishment – anxious to bury Hugo at his most talented and progressive, determined to beat back "a work of serious fiction for the masses...one of the last universally accessible masterpieces of Western literature, and a disturbing sign that class barriers had been breached," devoted to fixing lit-erary taste to be not too liberatory let alone revolu-tionary – committed itself to defending the in-defensible, and strained to clear its ignominious name.

The oxymoronic opinions of critics betray the unease created by Hugo – that the lower orders might also have their litera-ture: "*a cabinet de lecture* novel written by a man of genius", according to Lytton Strachey half a century later, still fighting "bad taste". In other words, Les Misérables was a jolly good book, but Victor Hugo never should have written it.

Too potentially upsetting of the proper order of things. And so the establishment institution-ally and individually does what it can to bury or, fail-ing that, castrate Hugo's work, not least by turning "Javert, the tenacious respecter of authority, 'that savage in the service of civiliza-tion', into the villain [rather than the oppressive social apparatus, which] is to deprive the novel of its dynamite, to point the finger at a single policeman instead of at the system he serves." Again there is no conspiracy; there is a vested culture that highly values the status quo. In literary circles, one hears or reads much about or of Hugo's countrymen and contem-poraries Balzac and Flaubert, who like fraternal twin blankets, one of renowned substance the other of renowned style, function to disappear Hugo, to great extent in prominent US literary realms.

Preferring excess style to excess content, threat-ened by the master writer who combined great content with great style, the establishment presents Gustave Flaubert and Henry James and their kind, and a somewhat different contempo-rary sort of interior obsessive Philip Roth, as "literature" in the preeminent ideal. And the people? Are they "an-tique," "quaint," hope-lessly partisan? Long live Flaubert! and Bovary! that great adulterer, and suicide. Should we wonder that students "joke" that they enter lit studies so excited to read great literature and then within a few years feel instead "suicidal"?

Graham Robb notes in his tremendous bio-graphy:

> The "dangerous" aspect of *Les Misérables* is almost as evident today as it was in 1862. If a single idea can be extracted from the whole, it is that persistent crimi-nals are a product of the criminal justice system, a human and therefore a mon-strous creation; that the bur-den of guilt lies with society and that the rational re-form of institutions should take prece-dence over the punishment of indivi-duals.

Compared to Les Misérables, the prose, the plot, the intellectual and normative scope of Flaubert's most famed novels are often stultify-ing, petty, or worse, yet Madame Bovary "now stands virtually unchallenged not only as a seminal work of Real-ism, but as one of the most influential novels ever written..." to cer-tain people. "A 2007 poll of con-temporary authors, published in a book entitled *The Top Ten*, cited *Madame Bovary* as one of the two greatest novels ever written…" such is the general conclusion at Wikipedia and within establishment literature.

Today, nearly a century and a half on, we might wonder why no novelist has so well created a Les Misérables for our time, if such is the case. Or we might wonder why no novelist has so well imag-ined Jonathan Swift's contemporaneously explicit brief masterwork "A Modest Proposal" at epic length, with its scathing criticisms, marvelous wit, and most especially the (landlord-despised) point-ed "solutions and panaceas" (basic remedies) mixed with great touch – as literary as popular, as explicit as subtle, as clear-cut as nuanced, as cyclonic as limned, as elucidating as "mind-melding," a revolutionary work of epic fiction. Someday may such novels come if they have not already, thumping good reads that limn the hell out of nuance, in non-trivial ways that clarify and churn with power. Explosively subtle and subtly explosive, powerfully analytical and analytically powerful, emotionally charging and charging emotionally, with critics worthy of the contents and contents worthy of critics, epic liberatory works that may be transformed to film, video and stage, works that rally people and help force or engender change. This too may be the style and voice of the novel and criticism, at least outside the dens of the establishment. Such is the force and potential of fiction – fact rich to fuel hunger, metaphor drenched to intensify thirst for what may and must be. This is why it matters most how fiction works – and that it does.

In the Great Deluge, Historian Douglas Brinkley has closely researched and written (and partly lived) a remarkable nonfiction account of the week of the 2005 Hurricane Katrina catastrophe in the US, easily one of the great narratives of today. For-tunately, the prose not only limns aplenty and dan-ces in nuance and subtlety, not least of analysis, but also necessarily spouts, even spouts off, and rocks and booms too. And it would have done well, done better, to do so all the more, in liberatory partisan popular fashion. After all, the phenomenon of Hur-ricane Katrina was not only a great event of nature (worthy of tremendous limning in its own right), the carnage, the slaughter wreaked, and waged, was far more crucially a great crime of the estab-lishment that deserves to be emblazoned on the everlasting page as an orgy of essentially premedi-tated state-corporate killing, mass murder. That it was. And that is centrally how it must always be known. Novelists should be tasked to bring home this reality in far greater force than has yet been achieved.

Future creation of liberatory fiction involves nothing so simple as solely the documenting of his-tory, or solely a reproducing of Classical, Victorian, Romantic, Enlightenment, Modern, Postmodern, or other forms, say, Progressive, Liberatory, or Revo-lutionary. Hugo was no partisan hack but a great artist in both his complexity and simplicity, and his works fomented liberatory, even revolutionary im-pressions and helped create progressive effects, at the least. Though his accomplished aesthetics and ground breaking roles are often slighted, not only noted establishment scholar Victor Brombert "finds in Hugo's novels" (as reported by the New York Times a quarter century ago, in an apparently unat-tributed article):

> an anticipation of a distinctively modern-ist sensibility, at least insofar as such a sensibil-ity presupposes a collapse of the distinction between history and myth, thought and em-otion, external perception and inward mood – the kind of world found in the novels of Joyce, Woolf, Kafka, and Proust. Far from being the late romantic he is conventionally thought to be, Hugo appears in Brombert's account as one of the first modern-ists…[es-pecially] in the fascination with inscriptions, traces, effacements, mirror effects, and dis-solving processes, and in the belief that not only history but reality itself is a "text". Hu-go as "deconstructive" novelist? The sugges-tion is shocking, and in fairness to Mr. Brombert it must be admitted that he only *suggests* this thesis indirectly….[yet] a case may be made for Hugo as a postmodernist.

A case may well be made that Hugo's fiction

was both more clearly pointed (or communicative) *and* more complex than Flaubert's work (or that of modernism and even much Victorianism, etc). Some of the work of Hugo – including his 1829 short novel The Last Day of a Condemned Man is described as "starkly modern" by Peter France, the editor of The New Oxford Companion to Literature in French, a work of fiction that "would have a profound influence on later writers such as Albert Camus, Charles Dickens, and Fyodor Dostoevsky," who called it Hugo's "masterpiece," a work that Hugo pitted contemporaneously against the death penalty, nothing quaint about it, an act of utility discouraged by Wood and apparently depressing to him, a state that suits the status quo. Rather than spring, Flaubert may be much more of a fall of fic-tion.

In Victor Hugo and the Visionary Novel, Victor Brombert notes that in Hugo's early novel, the con-demned man's

> imprisonment in a futureless present, the radicalization of a confined subjectivity, called for a special control of narrative tech-nique. Well before modern writers had de-veloped a rhetoric of existential immediacy, Hugo...created a disrupted yet associative mental discourse that allowed for no respite from the self...[which impressed] Dostoev-sky, as it had impressed Flaubert... The "di-ary" rhythm seems to point forward to the rhetoric of disjunction achieved by Sartre in *La Nausée*.... The structural and rhetorical complexity of this apparently simple ac-count is evident from the very first chapter, which is locked in on itself by the verbless exclamation "Condemned to death!" ...[The novel] blurs all distinctions between object and subject.

> A double metaphor transforms the image of captivity into an inner psychological space, as well as into the imaginary space of writing. The key metaphorical inversion, turning the prison image upside down, ap-pears as early as the third paragraph: "my mind is imprisoned in an idea."

Brombert notes that in an 1852 letter Flaubert "ex-presses his admiration" for The Last Day of a Con-demned Man and "praises the total absence of di-dacticism in Hugo's novel. It's impact, according to Flaubert, is directly related to the absence of auth-orial commentary," but Brombert points out that

> Flaubert was not quite correct when he stated that only the preface – written several years after the novel – was didactic. For the text is reader-conscious, and reader-orient-ed, in morally committed terms. The Con-demned Man explicitly hopes that the diary of his anguish will provide a memorable les-son...for all those who judge and condemn.

As Brombert notes "the pervasive voyeur-ism" in Hugo's famed 1831 novel Notre-Dame de Paris (The Hunchback of Notre Dame), one may wonder if there is so very much in the works of Flaubert that cannot be found in the early works of Hugo (Notre-Dame and Condemned were written when still in his twenties). One wonders further if "mod-ernism" is not something of a neurotic or immature literature, a regression or reversion from present-ing the real, the full human condition. ...

PART SIX

A FURTHER REALITY CHECK

FOR ESTABLISHMENT CRITICISM OF FIC-TION

CRITICISM OF THE PARCHED

William Deresiewicz Reviews How Fiction Works

Is there no current liberatory criticism, no viable alternative to the status quo criticism of fiction and other literature as William Deresiewicz claims in the Nation magazine?: "The very idea of heroic criticism, like that of heroic art, is...no longer credi-ble" given "the abandonment of the political di-mension of radical critique over the past several decades" and "any sense that politics and culture are connected, or that their criticism should be con-nected...."

Actually, some liberatory criticism is being pro-duced in the academy let alone elsewhere, especial-ly online, along with some other liberatory lit as well. Consider-able progress has been made in criti-cism in re-cent decades, especially originating large-ly out-side of commercial critical circles, given the work of Edward Said, for example, among oth-ers.

Dominant criticism is too much impover-ished Deresiewicz notes but far more impover-ished than he touches on. This long into the age of the internet in particular, to not look read-ily beyond the domin-ant journals and maga-zines for other current criti-cal tendencies is to be remiss, at the least, to perpe-tuate the grip of the closeted approach to literature decried in the article, especially since about the only alterna-tive presented is the limited too often biased or retrograde dominant criticism of decades past. Even as Deresiewicz claims James Wood's ex-ample would lead criticism into a desert, his own article already leaves readers there, for not only does Deresiewicz bury contemporary lib-eratory criticism, he buries such criticism of the past, a ten-dency in American criticism more vi-tal, more cru-cial than the bulk of the critical tradition he cites.

He elides accomplished critic Maxwell Geis-mar, the increasingly progressive Geismar who wrote at the same time as the dominant critics Deresiewicz lauds ("the New York crit-ics"), Geismar who was for a time no stranger to the pages of the Nation but has subsequently been written out of history, along with much of the roots, current realities, and possibilities of liberatory lit. Deresiewicz finds him-self with Wood and the New York critics among the dominant lit dunes of their own making.

This far the establishment says, and then this tiny little bit farther, and no more ... until some future additional miniscule adjustment.

It may be that the establishment scarcely flounders more than when it claims to see that it is flounder-ing. A recent example is Zadie Smith's article "Two Paths for the Novel." Comments interspersed for clarity below after sequential select article excerpts:

> From two recent novels, a story emerges about the future for the Anglophone novel. Both are the result of long jour-neys. Nether-land, by Joseph O'Neill, took seven years to write; Remainder, by Tom McCarthy, took seven years to find a mainstream publisher. The two novels are antipodal—indeed one is the strong re-fusal of the other. The violence of the re-jection Remainder represents to a novel like Netherland is, in part, a function of our ailing literary culture. All novels at-tempt to cut neural routes through the brain, to convince us that down this road the true future of the novel lies.

On the contrary, some great novels are ex-pressions of aesthetic, normative, and concep-tual diversity showing that the "future" of the novel may well run down many paths, in vari-ous ways.

> In healthy times, we cut multiple roads, al-lowing for the possibility of a Jean Genet as surely as a Graham Greene.

There are no great, say, combinatory novels? Victor Hugo's Les Misérables has been noted for its wide diversity of qualities and effects: Victo-rian, mod-ern, postmodern, romantic/ideal, epic, classic, real-istic, progressive, and so on. Or see Ngũgĩ wa Thi-ong'o's recent Wizard of the Crow.

> These aren't particularly healthy times. A breed of lyrical Realism has had the free-dom of the highway for some time now, with most other exits blocked.

I suppose Smith means "entrances" rather than "exits"? In any case, "lyrical Realism" is technique or genre, a technical mode basically. It may be reac-tionary or revolutionary, liberal or conservative, etc, depending upon the contents and ideologies explored. The central great weaknesses of contem-porary fiction stem from much vacuity of content, not technique, due largely to establishment con-straints on norms – one may only say so much, go so far, in key directions. Various virtual taboos un-dercut the quality and life of much contemporary fiction, much as they do that of establishment med-ia in general. One can see plenty of crucial realities and possibilities discussed in the most progressive independent media that are basically blocked from establishment fiction.

> For Netherland, our receptive pathways are so solidly established that to read this novel is to feel a powerful, somewhat dispiriting sense of recognition.

Yet as Smith notes later, the familiar is often pleas-ing or comforting, far from dispiriting.

> It seems perfectly done—in a sense that's the problem.

People are not typically dispirited by dances, cars, movies, or novels because they are "perfect" – if they ever could be. The perfect where possible is no problem, in general. On the contrary.

> It's so precisely the image of what we have been taught to value in fiction that it throws that image into a kind of existential crisis, as the photograph gifts a nervous breakdown to the painted portrait.

Apparently, Smith laments that the best establish-ment fiction amounts to little more than pointless reproductions of what already exists; the "lyrical realism" of the Balzac-Flaubert approach to litera-ture is upstaged by reality – no wait, technique, it must be technique, that one, the B-F mode is the problem! mind numbingly worn out. Technique is all. The world – not so much. This view of Smith's is actually far more mind numbingly worn out than the technique, much of which shows scant signs of being dead necessarily, though the stories such approaches are permitted to produce through establishment publishing houses are often far from the most crucial stories of our time. (And there should certainly certainly always be plenty of room for wide diversity of technique. The key question is, What does one do with it? whatever the selected technique(s), To what purpose and upon what princi-ples does one wield it? any or all technique.)

> Netherland [seems set up to be] the post-September 11 novel we hoped for. (Were there calls, in 1915, for the Lusitania novel? In 1985, was the Bhopal novel keenly antic-ipated?) It's as if, by an act of collective pray-er, we have willed it into existence.

Public issues, public reform, sociopolitical crises, revolution – the novel has concerned itself with exploring many crucial issues and events among the public since its inception. Smith knows Dickens, one would think. Public interest and concern are great motive factors for exploring public issues in the novel, as has always been the case, moreso than "collective prayer" – whatever that means. Smith's naïve plaint seems hardly credible.

> But Netherland is only superficially about September 11 or immigrants or cricket as a symbol of good citizenship. It certainly is about anxiety, but its worries are formal and revolve obsessively around the question of authenticity. Netherland sits at an anxiety crossroads where a community in recent cri-sis – the Anglo-American liberal middle class – meets a literary form in long-term cri-sis, the nineteenth-century lyrical Realism of Balzac and Flaubert.

Again, more credulity required here. The "Anglo-American liberal middle class" is only "in recent crisis"? As Franzen asked of fellow novelists post 9-11: "Where have you been?" The Civil Rights struggle, the Cold War, the nuclear arms race and other weapons of mass destruction, climate change and longstanding environmental hazards, inequali-ty, continuous union busting and economic uncert-ainty and oppression, militancy and ongoing series of wars of aggression, the list is virtually endless of longstanding intense sociopolitical conflict confronting every class. Establishment fiction, like the dominant media in general, has not remotely kept pace – status quo realism, contra-realism or not. Moreover, much of the world, the US in particular, entered the age of propaganda about 100 years ago with the stupendous rise of the public relations in-dustry, advertising, corporate dominance, which is a central ongoing causal crisis of our times. "Modernism" has not helped fiction catch up to its age, this age. It seems to have had more the opposite effect, at least in the US. And the same can be said of contemporary Victorian type fiction and "post-modernism." Nevertheless, the technical modes of choice are often by-and-large not where the main problems lie, not where the roots are deepest. Rath-er, critical and central content, focus, emphasis go wanting. Again – not only in fiction but in domin-ant media and institutions generally. Pinning the blame or one's hopes on some technique or another to cure or rescue fiction misses the heart of the problem essentially, mistakes or ignores the sour-ces, and mars much chance for progress, for greater accomplishment in and by way of art.

> Critiques of this form by now amount to a long tradition in and of themselves.

Again, fixing on problems of form misses the prob-lem, which lies elsewhere. This is the establishment blind. Willfully so? Conveniently, at least. It's so easy, so safe to talk about technique, to hopelessly bemoan or tinker with change in technique to little crucial effect. It's almost a way of removing art from the humanities, the human realm, and insert-ing it into severely blinkered conceptual nether-worlds.

> Beginning with what Alain Robbe-Grillet called "the destitution of the old myths of 'depth,'" they blossomed out into a phe-nom-enology skeptical of Realism's metaphysical tendencies, demanding, with Husserl, that we eschew the tran-scendental, the meta-phorical, and go "back to the things them-selves!"; they peaked in that radical decon-structive doubt which questions the capacity of language itself to describe the world with

accuracy. They all of them note the (often unexamined) credos upon which Realism is built: the transcendent importance of form, the incantatory power of language to reveal truth, the essential fullness and continuity of the self.

Ah, theory! Virtually all of which is near ir-relevant to the main problems of the novel these many dec-ades, again, which are not theoretical or conceptu-al per above but normative and broadly intellectual.

> Yet despite these theoretical assaults, the American metafiction that stood in op-posi-tion to Realism has been relegated to a safe corner of literary history, to be studied in postmodernity modules, and dismissed, by our most famous public critics, as a fascinat-ing failure, intellec-tual brinkmanship that lacked heart. Barth, Barthelme, Pynchon, Gaddis, De-Lillo, David Foster Wallace – all mis-guided ideologists, the novelist equiva-lents of the socialists in Francis Fuku-yama's The End of History and the Last Man. In this version of our literary his-tory, the last man standing is the Balzac-Flaubert model, on the evidence of its ex-traordinary persistence. But the critiques persist, too. Is it really the closest model we have to our condition? Or simply the bedtime story that comforts us most?

Once again all blame on the model, the mode or modes, and not a peep about the normative – the moral and political and social, the ideologi-cal and intellectual bankruptcies that persist in fiction often no matter what mode is employed. Both of these trends referred to by Smith are devoid of much vi-tal substance due to reasons often unrelated to their various modes of tech-nique.

> Netherland, unlike much lyrical Realism, has some consciousness of these argu-ments, and so it is an anxious novel, un-usually so. It is absolutely a post-catastrophe novel but the catastrophe isn't terror, it's Realism. ... the founding, consoling myth of lyrical Real-ism – the

self is a bottomless pool. What you can't find in the heavens (anymore), you'll find in the soul.

That "the self" may be viewed as "a bottomless pool" by lyrical realism or any other mode is no necessary problem, but when such limited ex-plora-tion becomes something akin to the end-all be-all of fiction, the malignancy or lack is evident, as Smith sees, but then fixates on tech-nique as culprit, even cause. Bottomless pools of self can be explored in techniques far different from lyrical realism, as can "bottomless pools" of superficial or otherwise limi-ted public explo-ration, which is the central prob-lem. Shifting technique does not necessarily shift the impov-erished norms. Shifting the impover-ished norms may take advantage of many tradi-tional techniques, while also using and creating oth-ers. Smith's status quo suggestions amount to tinkering with the lights out. A far more viable alternative: begin art creation with more libera-tory norms, purposes, principles, guideposts, and / or liberatory "stuff" of all variety. Doing so can raise the shades, throw open the windows, and unlock the doors of the dim and closeted workshop.

Smith describes a passage of Netherlands and concludes: "this is another rule of lyrical Realism: that the random detail confers the authenticity of the Real. As perfect as it all seems, in a strange way it makes you wish for urinals." Smith very politely trashes Nether-lands and dominant contemporary fiction in her article even as she very politely calls Nether-lands "the most masterful recent example" of establishment fiction's "dominant mode." She very politely compares much focus of the novel un-favorably to "urinals." She has good reason to ren-der her critiques with absolute politeness, because her works are accomplished and typical examples of establishment fiction too.

It's a credit to Netherland that it is so anx-ious. Most practitioners of lyrical Realism blithely continue on their merry road, with not a metaphysical care in the world, and few of them write as finely as Joseph O'Neill.

It's not so much any "metaphysical" con-cerns that novels skip past, again, that so gut fic-tion, as the badly slighted, distorted, or outright ignored cru-cial sociopolitical ones.

I have written in this tradition myself, and cautiously hope for its survival, but if it's to survive, lyrical Realists will have to push a little harder on their subject.

The "subject" being the self? If so, on the contrary, by now the self as subject in status quo fiction has been "pushed" too much into a fine paste, refined out of much nourishment – as even this status quo author observes – though greater exploration of the public can fur-ther reveal the self. Emphasis pub-lic. After re-counting and quoting another passage of Neth-erlands, Smith notes: "An interesting thought is trying to reach us here, but the ghost of the lit-erary burns it away, leaving only its remain-der: a nicely constructed sentence, rich in sound and syntax, signifying (almost) nothing." More sending of "masterful" establishment fiction to the urinal, a necessary task. Unfortunately Smith's gaze forward is blank, virtually empty of forward motion, progress. And her fiction?

Netherland doesn't really want to know about misapprehension. It wants to offer us the authentic story of a self. But is this really what having a self feels like? Do selves al-ways seek their good, in the end? Are they never perverse? Do they always want mean-ing? Do they not sometimes want its oppo-site? And is this how memory works? Do our childhoods often return to us in the form of coherent, lyrical reveries? Is this how time feels? Do the things of the world really come to us like this, embroidered in the verbal fancy of times past? Is this really Realism?

In other words, is there any real motion for-ward here in our understanding of anything? Apparently not, and maybe more than stasis there is retrograde motion in this "masterful" example of status quo fiction – at least if we are left longing for urinals.

If Netherland is a novel only partially aware of the ideas that underpin it, Tom

McCar-thy's Remainder is fully conscious of its own. But how to write about it? Immediately an obstacle presents itself. When we write a-bout lyrical Realism our great tool is the quote, so richly patterned. But Remainder is not filled with pretty quotes; it works by ac-cumulation and repetition, closing in on its subject in ever-decreasing revolutions, like a trauma victim circling the blank horror of the traumatic event.

It plays a long, meticulous game, opening with a deadpan paragraph of comic sim-plici-ty:

Smith's description here of Remainder sounds the opposite of promising, apparently against her in-tentions: the novel functions in a sense "like a trauma victim circling the blank horror of the traumatic event" and "plays a long, meticulous game…" That's some game. To what purpose this "circling … game" one might reasonably wonder – or is this just another es-tablishment crossword puzzle of a novel for privileged people to while away the hours?

The theater of the absurd that Remainder lays out is articulated with the same care-ful pedantry of Gregor Samsa himself. In its brutal excision of psychology it is easy to feel that Remainder comes to literature as an assassin, to kill the novel stone dead. I think it means rather to shake the novel out of its present complacency. It clears away a little of the dead wood, of-fering a glimpse of an alternate road down which the novel might, with diffi-culty, travel forward. We could call this constructive deconstruction, a quality that, for me, marks Remainder as one of the great English novels of the past ten years.

Seemingly sick of literary psychology and symbol-ism working miasmic, to scant fresh point, Smith thus turns to consideration and appreciation of Re-mainder, acclaiming its for-mal innovations for cre-ating "newly revealed spaces that" provide "the opportunity for mul-tiple allegories" of wide vari-ety. Not only does this seem a straw-grasping turn from one mode of formalism to another mode of formalism but to formalism once removed, so to speak, as alle-gory. Lyrical realism having failed or maxed out by Smith's literary lights, apparently her own work not least, it's time to lay one's hopes on other forms of realism and allegory. One might anticipate a few years down the road either some ostensibly re-enlightened return to the former formalism or some other formalist grasp, maybe at epic verse? or a novel in sonnets? Formalist hunch-ing games can do little, except secondarily, to ad-dress the novel's most persis-tent lacks. It's not that formalist insights can provide no help for more vital achievement in literature and much else. The problem is that once again formalism is being tasked to provide virtually all the help to cure ill-ness and fix problems (in literature and life) largely beyond its pith and ken.

In this dominant constriction and lack, Smith is representative of the literature establishment, very much in line with what Paul Lauter found decades ago in a review of society and literary criticism. This excerpt below is from the editor of the Norton Anthology of Theory and Criti-cism, Vincent B. Leitch, in his book American Literary Criticism from the 30s to the 80s (Chap-ter Thirteen: "Leftist Criticism from the 1960s to the 1980s"):

When the MLA put together its centen-nial issue of PMLA in May 1984, it com-mis-sioned Paul Lauter to write about the impact of society on the profession of lit-erary criti-cism between 1958 and 1983. Lauter was a radical associated with the Movement in the sixties…. According to Lauter, the MLA be-tween the fifties and the eighties had ex-panded and diversi-fied immensely, yet 'the hierarchy of the profession remains funda-mentally unal-tered, so as yet does the hier-archy of what we value'…. This conclusion was based on two surveys of hundreds of syl-labi collected from around the nation in the eighties. Just as the reigning critical ideo-logy in the late 1950s was 'formal-ism,' so the dominant mode of criticism in the 1980s was 'formalism,' however expanded to include hermeneutics, semiotics, and poststructural-ism, all of which criticism 'accepts the form-alist stance by analyzing texts, including its own discourse, primarily as autonomous ob-jects isolated from their social origins or functions'…. What most dismayed Lauter about such fashionable criticism were its alignment with linguistics and philosophy rather than history and sociology, its tenden-cy to become obscurant self-referential meta-criticism in a debauch of professionalism, its preference for a limited canon of elitist texts, its increasing abnegation of practical exege-sis and humanistic values, and its deepening occupation of the core of the profession…. [Even the rebirth of Marxist criticism in the 1970s deviated from "history and sociology" in that]: What was odd about the Marxist criticism of this [1970s] Renaissance associ-ated with the post-1950s new left and the Movement was its complete disregard of the old left. Mention was never made of V. F. Calverton, James T. Farrell, Granville Hicks, Bernard Smith, Edmund Wilson, or other Leftist Critics prominent in the thirties. The native tradition of radicalism stemming from the nineteenth century had been for-gotten during the heyday of the new left….

In H. Bruce Franklin's view, what was wrong with academic literary profession-als was their thorough immersion in the bour-geois ideology of formalism, which itself was rooted in the counterrevolutionary anti-proletarianism of the thirties. 'In the present era, formalism is the use of aestheticism to blind us to social and moral reality'…

Rather than an instrument or weapon of rul-ing class oppression, literature was potenti-ally liberating [in the view of Louis Kampf], provided it was set within a living context close to daily life and removed from its sac-rosanct place in the great tradition. 'In spite of our academic merchants, literature is not a commodity, but the sign of a creative act which ex-presses personal, social, and histor-ical needs. As such it constantly undermines the status quo.' The task of the radical critic was to destroy received dogmas and proced-ures, letting literature be an instrument of agitation and resistance and a force for free-dom and genuine liberation. 'As members of the educated middle class, we must learn that our words should discredit our own culture. Those of us who are literary intel-lectuals and teachers ought to illustrate in our work that the arts are not alone available to those who are genteel…'

"Two Paths for the Novel"? Make that directions and the basic options become: forward, sideways, or back. Smith seems headed sideways, and in the spare technical light of her workshop can scarcely do more than hope not back. Form is not the base of fiction, except in a sense so broad that it can best be understood as content. In The Secrets of Story-telling: Why We Love a Good Yarn, Scientific American reports:

As many as two thirds of the most respected stories in narrative traditions seem to be var-iations on three narrative patterns, or proto-types, according to Hogan. The two more common prototypes are romantic and heroic scenarios – the former focuses on the trials and travails of love, whereas the latter deals with power struggles. The third prototype, dubbed "sacrificial" by Hogan, focuses on agrarian plenty versus famine as well as on societal redemption. These themes appear over and over again as humans create nar-rative records of their most basic needs: food, reproduction and social status.

Interested in revitalizing fiction? One could do worse than start there, with the basic proto-types: love, power, survival – and more. "Two Paths for the Novel" shows how the establish-ment too often thinks about creating quality lit: as almost sheer ex-ercise in technique, or form.

It seems to me that creative works instead spring fundamentally from an intersection of con-tent, impulse, and principle or purpose. Forms and techniques can be used for progres-sive or retro-grade purposes, so form does not drive key under-lying elements or necessarily engender quality – which makes it safe for the establishment to consi-der in depth within certain parameters, too often ad nauseam and in irrelevant ways. Excessive fo-cus on form abdicates discussion of more vital and pressing normative matters.

Of Form and Content

I don't argue that lyrical realism is not over-repre-sented in lit production. I've not expressed much opinion on the question, because it seems to me beside the point, and diversion-ary from the crucial issues, at least as typically discussed by the estab-lishment. I think forms of fiction should be diverse, as my own fiction happens to be, and so too should content be greatly diverse, across the fields of fic-tion.

Near the end of my comments on Smith's ar-ticle, I point to what Scientific American notes as the ba-sic story founts or "prototypes," which can be de-veloped with any variety of technique or form, as part of pointing out that "what" is written about in story or as story is more fun-damental than "how" story is approached for-mally. New content ac-counts for much of the deserved success of the multicultural expansion of storytellers and stories in fiction in recent decades, which is not primari-ly due to any es-pecially new form brought to the table. One of the great needs has been for diversity of content – diversity of reality and possibility and access – as has been partly supplied in the expan-sion. New forms have arrived too but more valu-able by far has been the content, artfully presented in various ways. Now after these decades the fresh-ness of that expansion may begin to seem more conventional, and in any event does not come cen-trally into play with some writers or stories. So what to do to regenerate or revitalize story, as story must always be regenerated? More expansion of many sorts is still badly needed. Additionally, the Scientific American article provides some pointers: look to

the enduring well of story types. Further, I've long suggested the importance of focusing on various progressive and ever more liberatory stor-ies of wide variety. These are essentially normative issues, not technical or formal con-cerns basically. We are speaking of art, so for-mal concerns are also going to be important, even central in some ways, though not most ba-sic. In my view, Smith mistak-enly (or at least baselessly) points primarily to problems with form rather than with novel content and norms, in the productions of the too oft stag-nant establishment. I agree that more diversity of form would be refreshing and valuable but there are far more fundamental problems sap-ping fiction of its vitality than technical con-cerns – and no key shift in form alone can ad-dress those problems.

For example, there are no overt establishment novels about the supreme crime of the US con-quest of Iraq. In fact, the idea of explicit antiwar novels has been smeared by the literature estab-lishment these years. This represents far more an impover-ishment of literature and life than the fact that there are quite a number of lyrical realism establi-shment novels that explore some aspects or effects of the US invasion and occu-pation. The worth of altering the form of the lat-ter novels pales in com-parison to creating vir-tually any type of the former, as lyrical realism or not. And the "supreme crime" of the US con-quest is one of many central and vital stories that gets filtered out of the fiction publish-ing industry (as I've discussed at length) and out of the dominant media essentially, as many prog-ressive media analysts point out. Smith looks for what "ail[s] literary culture" else-where, and draws conclusions that seem to me to be a central part of the ailment, views that are generally (not necessari-ly in specific) represen-tative of the form obsession of literature estab-lishment thought, far from novel or crucial.

NETHERLAND

AND THE NOTION OF THE POST-9/11 NOVEL

Guardian Books: "'No better mind has gone

to work on where we are post-9/11,' author and judge Lee Abbott told the Washington Post," about Joseph O'Neill and his PEN/Faulkner award win-ning novel Netherland. It "made the longlist for the Booker prize and was the book-ies' favourite to win before it was snubbed for the shortlist...." "It was described by the New York Times as 'the wittiest, angriest, most exact-ing and most desolate work of fiction we've yet had about life in New York and London after the World Trade Centre fell', while James Wood in the New Yorker called it 'one of the most re-markable post-colonial books I have ever read'."

Meanwhile, Shelley Ettinger at Read Red com-ments, O'Neill

> means well, no doubt, and he is it seems try-ing to get at several complexities about iden-tity and immigration and friendship and his-tory with the novel's title, but it strikes me that what he's cooked up is more like Never-land, one more post-colonial fantasy of what life is like for those driven across the world by the crimes of colonialism – as told by the inheritor of the riches stolen from their fore-bearers. There's a liberal smugness to it, or at least that's how it sits with me.

Discussion of the notion of the post-9/11 novel and literature in general leaves out the question of whether or not 9/11 is much of an appropriate touchstone, given the great catas-trophe that was kicked off in the March 2003 ground invasion of Iraq, an extension of the murderous US-UN sanc-tions era kicked off by invasion more than a decade prior.... Our suf-fering defines a literary era but the far more massive suffering we inflict on others does not.

That's retrograde, it seems to me, even though much of the "post-9/11 lit conceit may be of liberal or progressive intention. The un-thinkable has been filtered out prior to the dis-cussion. Along these lines, other significant moments or era shifts – the various US inva-sions, the shift to a finance based economy in recent decades, the rise of the PR industry be-ginning about a century ago, the fall and rise of widespread activist movements – seem like far

more meaningful markers of changing socio-political and cultural eras that would most in-sightfully and most dramatically inform litera-ture.

Of course 9/11 is in its own right a "novel event" – as Noam Chomsky notes:

> It is correct to say that this is a novel event in world history, not because of the scale of the atrocity – regrettably – but be-cause of the target. How the West chooses to react is a matter of supreme impor-tance. If the rich and powerful choose to keep to their tradi-tions of hundreds of years and resort to ex-treme violence, they will contribute to the escalation of a cycle of violence, in a familiar dynamic, with long-term consequences that could be awesome. Of course, that is by no means inevitable. An aroused public within the more free and democratic so-cieties can direct policies towards a much more hu-mane and honorable course.

> The horrendous terrorist attacks on Tues-day [9/11] are something quite new in world af-fairs, not in their scale and character, but in the target. For the US, this is the first time since the War of 1812 that its national terri-tory has been under attack, even threat. It's colonies have been attacked, but not the national territory it-self. During these years the US virtually exterminated the indigenous population, conquered half of Mexico, intervened vio-lently in the surrounding region, con-quered Hawaii and the Philippines (kill-ing hundreds of thousands of Filipinos), and in the past half century particularly, ex-tended its resort to force throughout much of the world. The number of vic-tims is col-ossal. For the first time, the guns have been directed the other way. The same is true, even more dramatically, of Europe. Europe has suffered murder-ous destruction, but from internal wars, meanwhile conquering much of the world with extreme brutality. It has not been under attack by its victims out-side, with rare exceptions (the IRA in Eng-land, for

example). It is therefore natural that NATO should rally to the support of the US; hundreds of years of imperial violence have an enormous impact on the intellectual and moral culture.

As it turned out, the horrific events of 9/11 were quickly overshadowed by far more calamitous events of the conquests of Afghanistan, Iraq, and beyond. The post-9/11 era quickly became the Con-quest of Oila era, the conquest of vast swaths of western Asia. Meanwhile the literature establish-ment remains fixated on the notion of the 9/11 nov-el or the post-9/11 novel – an emphasis, again, that recalls our suffering rather than the orders of mag-nitude greater devastation wreaked by us. To where has the "post-9/11 novel taken us? To the prize winning Netherland, for one.

In the current American Literary History issue, in his essay on the literature of "9/11 and its after-math" – "Open Doors, Closed Minds: American Prose Writing at a Time of Crisis" – Richard Gray points out that:

> many of the texts that try to bear witness to contemporary events vacillate…between large rhetorical gestures acknowledging trauma and retreat into domestic detail. The link between the two is tenuous, reducing a turning point in national and international history to little more than a stage in a senti-mental education.

Responding to Richard Gray's essay in the same issue, Michael Rothberg notes in "A Failure of the Imagination: Diagnosing the Post-9/11 Novel":

> The failure Gray diagnoses is not simply a formal one, but also ultimately a political one. In place of the necessary imaginative reworking Gray calls for, he finds that in novels treating 9/11 by US-based writers, "The crisis is, in every sense of the word, domesticated." Post-9/11 fiction frequently claims to be grappling with public and col-lective history: "Private life shrank to noth-ing," reflects a character in Deborah Eisen-berg's collection Twilight

of the Super-heroes (2006); "all life had become public," echoes another in Don DeLillo's novel Fall-ing Man (2007) (qtd in Gray). Despite such sentiments, however, Gray points out that in most of those works "all life…is personal; cataclysmic public events are measured purely and simply in terms of their impact on the emotional entanglements of their protagonists.

After examining Joseph O'Neill's Netherland, which Michael Rothberg finds valuable but limited, and "without dispensing with the immigrant mod-el Richard Gray proposes," Rothberg suggests:

> What we need from 9/11 novels are cogni-tive maps that imagine how US citizenship looks and feels beyond the boundaries of the nation-state, both for Americans and for others. Such an imagination will necessarily be double and will be forced to balance two counter-vailing demands: to provincialize the claims of "'the first universal nation'" and to mark its asymmetrical power to influ-ence world events. While it is true that the great extraterritorial literature of our new age of war and terror has not yet been writ-ten, the novel remains a necessary form for such a political and aesthetic project.

These are two thoughtful and valuable essays by Gray and Rothberg. However, the severe limita-tions of both Gray's essay and Rothberg's response is that they both fail to look beyond the novels produced by the literature establishment, an estab-lishment deeply embedded in the larger corporate-state establishment that has every incentive not to produce fiction that takes too seriously or looks too keenly at the "political…failure" of contemporary fiction, whether it be labeled post-9/11 fiction, Iraq conquest fiction, global fiction, or otherwise. Any reference in these two essays to significant post- 9/11 fiction from established academic journals or presses – or are such operations so negligent or trivial in this regard that scholars wouldn't think to consult them or wouldn't find much of note?

My own experience and observation is that es-tablishment ideology serves as a real block in both academia and commerce, in regard to progressive or liberatory fiction publishing and much else. I've been in and out of the academic programs, I've ex-perienced first hand the mindsets, and done plenty of research along these lines. Ideology supports the status quo to severe degree – and in particular ways, on particular topics still virtually total – es-pecially unconsciously but consciously as well. I've blanketed academic journals and commercial mag-azines and publishing houses with progressive or revolutionary literary fiction of certain types, my own and others, and have met basically a complete stone wall. This is not the case with some of my work that is less ideologically challenging. Nor is this the case with progressive venues such as Counterpunch, ZNet, Pemmican, and the Texas Observer. My own experience is not at all unique along these lines. "Left" artists or artists who take up too acutely too progressive explorations and portraits often face these blocks throughout US history – today is not particularly special, though some progress has been made, especially in multi-cultural realms.

The situation is somewhat similar in critical realms. Gordon Hutner (who is the Editor of Amer-ican Literary History) in his excellent collection of criticism American Literature, American Culture unfortunately elides a vital and especially libera-tory tendency of criticism in the early 1900s – crucial, central work that goes missing too in Vincent Leitch's Norton Anthology of Theory and Crit-icism, and is near totally written out of history.

Plenty of work along these lines remains to be done. Should be done now, and could be, in-defin-itely. One single explicit investigative an-tiwar nov-el from the academy or anywhere – or even a short story let alone a fiction feature film – about the great crime of the US conquest of Iraq and beyond could be a significant step forward. There exist a ton of journals, including many that are well re-spected, employing plenty of time, effort, and ex-pense to publish in fiction

a lot of redundant work or fluff – not to mention some work that isn't even much competent. I think many people sort of sense the kind of living death of many journals, which may account for why so many people care so little for being published, apart from reasons of career utility or a sort of narrow brand name prestige.

Many of these fiction journals or fiction sections

would be far more valuable if they were far more distinctly and crucially mission driven, rather than calling for virtually any work, "the best," a thou-sand times over.

In the meantime, the notion of the post-9/11 novel shows itself to be all but as severely limited in discussion as are the fictions said to embody it, and is greatly skewed from the start.

———————————

*Though very, very far from ideal, the prospects and reality are currently some degree better on the nonfiction side of things – for a number of reasons, I think, one being simply that the academy produces far more original nonfiction than fiction. Other reasons somewhat related are probably more relevant, having to do with the lightning-in-a-bottle tendencies and oft inherent popular potential of art. Possibly, fiction or the novel in particular can be felt as threatening or inappropriate, for it can be so articulate and so emotional or fully engaging, sometimes seemingly in whole.

Q&A WITH ANTHONY ASC:

LITTELL AND BOLAÑO

Q: Anthony, why is the fiction of Jonathan Littell and Roberto Bolaño currently all the rage in edu-cated circles?

A: Once more to the liberal cesspool. Once more to the conservative craphouse. Clear enough?

Q: Could you expand?

A: As widely reported and discussed, Littell's prize-winning mammoth novel, The Kindly Ones, which publishers are paying hundreds of thou-sands of dollars for the rights to publish (and mar-ket), tells the fictive story of a "former Nazi SS of-ficer, who in addition to taking part in the mass extermination of the Jews, commits incest with his sister, sodomizes himself with a sausage and most likely kills his mother and stepfather." It's a novel about atrocity featuring a sociopathic psychopath, conveniently far removed from the sociopathic atrocities being perpetrated today by the respect-able, by the more or less normal individuals and officials of the sociopathic corporate-state.

Q: And Bolaño?

A: He was instantly canonized. In the US, at least, Bolaño was instantly exalted once translated. Per-vasive through his fiction is a deeply amoral pose. Established "taste" finds this deeply appealing. He strikes the pose purposefully as the centerpiece of his work. It provides a certain suspension, levity, tension – striking an amoral pose in extremely mor-ally fraught situations. Though there are some exceptions to this general Bolaño rule, amorality pervades character and plot and setting. It is the dynamo – more alive than character and plot and setting. Similarly, the weightless is also rendered amoral. For example, early in his long novel 2666 (Time magazine's "Best Book of 2008), Bolaño es-sentially guts the writing of moral and intellectual freight and poses the characters (scholars) as per-ceiving weight and meaning where there is none. The narrative view remains amoral, clinical, for there is precious little apparent consequence of any kind, of anything. Bolaño's writing is not entirely sterile, as one can see the ironies tweaked and played and driven. Bolaño has a lot of experience of the world and he shares it. And there is some value in that. He is an experienced guy building experienced worlds of, well, experience – especially as compared with much of the fluff and pap pub-lished otherwise. He has been around and he takes readers around with him in a very nonthreatening (if unpromising) amoral way. So the establishment loves him. He is no threat to anybody's wealth. He may in passing amorally illuminate a bit of the status quo. He will not cross examine it but skips off like a spaceship approaching the atmosphere of earth

approaching the atmosphere of earth at too shallow an angle. He just skips off, back into space, away from the density and the most compelling gravity. Some people like that; more have been trained to it; many others merely tolerate it, or ideologically laud the style and effect, for various reasons including those heretofore noted. Bolaño sketches scenes with play and pathos and goes relatively easy on the satire. He alludes to matters of great weight but even in Nazi Literature in the Americas draws little more than what he intends to, comic blood. Even when overviewing mass murder in gory detail in 2666, the notes, as they feel, scarcely leave the state of the clinical.

This is a strategy one might plausibly adopt when writing for money. Apparently, Bolaño wrote the bulk of his fiction for money and with some desperation given the illness he died of age 50.

Q: How much of Littell and Bolaño have you read?
A: Do you disagree with my observations?

Q: Actually, I share your views. What can I say?

I've known you always. We have similar views on things. Bolaño seemed quite a character, some of which surely comes through in his fiction. So, like you, I suppose, I read through his stuff to see what he was all about, what all the hype was about, and while he comes up with some interesting passages, turns of phrase, insights, and gets across some ad-venture, the whole time I was reading I could not help but think that this guy sounds like a quintes-sential MFA student, with some talent and with a relative lot of experience. I mean, he reads like a more-or-less mundane workshop – maybe a bit brighter? – overall, in general, I'm saying – bunch of experience, jumpy moments, curio phrasings, and…at the end…ho-hum, not so much. Sort of a drifter, an experimenter, with some interesting and insightful work, yet work that seems sort of frank about struggling to engage even itself, work that works to keep itself awake by constantly toying, playing games. I mean, half the time, the guy sounds bored, and his characters sound bored, and are like, god, I gotta keep going to get something down here, to get some money. The writing shines in patches, as it had better, because overall the work can come off as one big shrug – who cares? Did Bolaño, really? Why? What is at stake? And who cares? You know, the poor guy seemed bored, typically, even with the whole topic of writing. Sort of passionless and pathetic, you know? Like the dude was writing, okay, but in the end mostly writing for grub. And who cares? Sort of pathetic. Sorry, that's how I see it. That's how it feels. He has some interesting achievements but in a sea of the dullard, even the abject. It seems not impossible to see Bolaño's work as too often abject, or just flat boring, and bored. And yet not always unlively, at least in relation to many of the current even more dreadful literary standards.

A: You see now, you are even more harsh and scandalous than I. Your temperamental views are bound to even more greatly offend the establish-ment than my views – which I would call more considered and analytical. (I've read the bulk of Bolaño's translated work.)

Q: I'm "harsh"? You joke, yes? I feel I barely rise to the level of scrappy.

A: I haven't read the Littell book. No appeal. I'll probably scan through it in a bookstore to get a sense of it, see if it's in some way worth looking in to. So you see I cannot and do not comment on his novel now, only the discussion of it. None of the discussion about the book encourages me toward it, neither the pans nor the many praises. Sensation! goes the essential infatuation with these books. Some critiques delve a bit but root themselves in this: sensation! Thin stuff. Relatively thin and dreck stuff these critiques and the bulk of these books. That said, Bolaño has a few moments in his works. How could he not, as a more-or-less heads up guy who devoted something of an inspired effort to literature. A pity, the life within his work, like his own flesh and blood, too brief – though the establishment moves to enshrine and exalt his way forever.

Q: Anything else?

A: Where's the great novel with the title about

the official Respectable Ones – The George Bushes, the Condi Rices, the Donald Rumsfelds, the Colin Powells, the Dick Cheneys, the CNNs, NBCs, NYTs, etc? Of course, the Obama administration is continuing the central elements of their policies. Obama has made some limited liberal change in domestic budgeting but in his Republican-lite handling of the financial implosion he is (as with foreign policy) setting himself up for continued ridicule and extensive outrage. The brilliance of the Republicans for the existence of the overall system is to be even worse than the Democrats. Littell and Bolaño seem to have a somewhat similar or analo-gous relationship. They come across as pre 9/11 works in a post invasion of Oila and economically challenged world. The stars of the literary world.

THE TERMINAL GLIDE PATH

OF THE ESTABLISHED

Pointed incoherence is hallmark of Jonathan Fran-zen's thoughts about the social novel (fiction that is especially sociopolitically engaged). This telling garble is demonstrated in the 1996 essay Franzen wrote on the social novel – both the original and revised version, "Perchance to Dream" in Harpers and "Why Bother?" in How to Be Alone – and recurs most recently in an interview this January 2009 at 5th Estate where Franzen states with trade-mark non sequitur:

> [When] young I actually thought I was the only one with [more-or-less progressive sociopolitical] perceptions. ... I think the difference now is that I recognize that there's a small but non-zero segment of the popu-lation that feels and thinks in all of those literary ways....

Franzen falsely conflates "literary" with enlight-ened sociopolitical views. Franzen has shifted from trying to reveal public reality for a broad audience to writing for a much smaller audience that shares his sense of the "literary," whatever the sociopoliti-cal.

And yet, with no evidence or compelling analysis, he states:

Only written media, and maybe to some extent live theatre, can break down the wall between in and out (i.e., between internal reality and the reality of the world).... All the things that would become impossible politically, emotionally, culturally, psycho-logically... this is, indirectly, what the novel is trying to preserve and fight in favour of.

The claim that "only written media...the novel..." can so effectively cohere the private and the public to "preserve and fight" for various "political... cultural" realities refutes his claim 5 paragraphs earlier:

> It's not necessarily fair to measure our cul-ture's engagement with political reality by the health of the social novel, now that we have shows like The Wire and now that we have CNN.

Directly stated, Franzen's claim is that the social novel is relatively outdated and ineffective; how-ever, somehow, political and cultural life can still be preserved and fought for by literary novels that are not sociopolitically engaged. This claim is so vague, near vacuous, even outright contradictory, as to be absurd. Franzen concedes the vague but not the vacuous, contradictory, and absurd:

> I know I'm expressing this in very vague terms, but I think [literary] epiphanic moments have a social and political valence as well...

This is a null statement since virtually everything has "a social and political valence."

When the established encourage the gutting of highly liberatory social and political features from novels, they speak smooth in apologizing for it by claiming that novelists, literary novelists, can only go so far down the road of public engagement be-fore realizing their prison yard limits, and throw-ing up their puny hands, and even blaming them-selves:

> We may just be little specks. As a percentage of the total world population, we [literary readers and writers] are ever smaller specks, and what we are is ever more mediated by the structures we've created for ourselves to live in.

In other words, literary readers and writers exist in a terminal "ever smaller" condition, and what can one do but go down with the sinking ship?

All who say Aye! follow Franzen and that of which he is symptomatic – the establishment writ large.

Could this explain why some literature majors joke they enter the field feeling full of hope and graduate feeling "suicidal"?

Or this?:

Fight of flight? Franzen twists his tongue around both but in effect has chosen the latter.

Or this?:

The New York Times claims antiwar novels are "belligerent." Does Franzen agree? Irrelevant?

Or this?:

As for Franzen "nowadays":

> I make fun of the ambitions I had when I was 22 and thinking, I will write the book that unmasks the terrible world, I will cause the scales to fall from the public's eyes, and they will see how stupid the local news at 11 is, and they will realize how cliché-riddled the pages of their local newspaper are and how corrupt their elected officials are. And they won't stand for it any more. Exactly what kind of utopia I thought would ensue was never clear.

Good to take from this that it is never a bad idea to clarify one's political vision before embarking on a political novel.

And this?:

In the meantime – so much for powerful literary and popular public works, novels and stories that go out to all the high schools and community col-leges and universities across the land, to soldiers and their families, to hard hit citizens, so much for any flood of revealing Hurricane Katrina novels and Conquest of Iraq novels and other sweeping novels of economic, corporate, and state vicious-ness. So much for these stories thriving in commer-cial magazines and overspilling the literary jour-nals. So much for any track record of it all these past many decades – the flood of vital stories that any healthy culture and society let alone education-al institutions would be immersed in and ex-cited about, powered and instructed by.

We may even suppose that someone lacking the supreme poise, the eloquent composure of respon-sible and respected opinion might won-der if such pointed convolutions of the estab-lished are not emblematic and just flat out typi-cal of the suicidal and homicidal drift and stride of – not the students – the establishment.

No chance "antiwar" novels might be something other than "belligerent"?

ZADIE ANTOINETTE?

Once More to the Orthodox

The literature establishment is constantly grasp-ing for some standout voice or another to cover up its too often eviscerated and eviscerat-ing core. In his recent New Yorker commentary "Zadie Smith Reports from Dream City," Hendrick Hertzberg urges: "Please, I beg you: drop whatever you're doing and read Zadie Smith's brilliant meditation on Barack Obama..." 'Speaking In Tongues,' in the New York Review of Books "....a wonderful essay" of "sparkling words" that is "so absorbing...an exhilarating slalom" that shows "how well [Presi-dent] Obama is positioned...to summon us so thrillingly to a vision of 'the *United* States of America' and a belief, as he said in his Inau-gural, 'that the old hatreds shall someday pass; that the lines of tribe shall soon dissolve'...." Apparently, the master state(s) will remain.

Smith's lecture gives grand voice to the estab-lishment, for it is a voice rich and eloquent, how-ever antique, not least in its ideological or-thodoxy. Per usual, the speech borders on par-ody at its most ideological moments in familiar guise of aestheti-cism denouncing ideology, a would be post-ideological stance.

Ms. Smith acknowledges that she has been well trained. She states her "regret" at losing her Willes-den voice the voice of her youth that "was a big, colorful, working-class sea" for her college voice, her Cambridge voice, acquired in:

> a smaller, posher pond, and almost uni-vocal; the literary world is a puddle. This voice I picked up along the way is no longer an exotic garment I put on like a college gown whenever I choose—now it is my only voice, whether I want it or not. I regret it; I should have kept both voices alive in my mouth. They were both a part of me. But how the culture warns against it!

Despite Smith's being trained into a "puddle," and her stated regret, she finds that all is not lost, and of course it is not. Unfortunately, the intellectual or literary recompense she hails is her adoption or assumption of the standard line of the status quo that not only declaims it prizes no ideology at all but (equally false) that ideol-ogy in literature functions as a lesser thing, a devaluation of literature, a betrayer of literary ideals and life. She believes literature can be ideology free – a belief that only the privileged puddle can afford to float (and even then only in the short term). Dream City indeed. It is the dream of a both servile and ruling status quo ideology:

> ...the final stage, which I [Smith] think of as the mark of a certain kind of genius: the voice relinquishes ownership of itself, de-velops a creative sense of disassocia-tion in which the claims that are particu-lar to it seem no stronger than anyone else's. There it is, my little theory—I'd rather call it a story.

Such a theory, which is part of an ideology, is cer-tainly a story – one that is happily en-sconced in the status quo and especially in this formulation per-petuating of it. The resultant loss is great to both art and life beyond.

Liberatory partisan art, on the other hand, pur-posefully intends that "the claims that are particu-lar to it" are "stronger" – that is, more liberating – than oppressive, ignorant, or deceit-ful claims and other forces. Such progressive or liberatory revolu-tionary art is in many ways no story to which Smith and the establishment can commit, or even refrain from decrying. Any "apparent didactic moral of…story" must be "undercut by the fact of the play itself" – an es-tablishment valuation of art. No matter that Jonathan Swift's great short story "A Modest Proposal" fundamentally disproves such a bind-ing view. Swift's central and even sec-ondary points are apparent and clear, far from "under-cut" or slighted, while quite ironically, aestheti-cally, artfully presented. A number of liber-atory, explicit, and overt points are emphasized and liberatory effects generated all the more by the art. The same goes for great novels such as Les Misérables and Wizard of the Crow, a cou-ple prime examples.

The point cannot be repeated enough: great art can do everything Smith and the establish-ment claim it cannot do along these lines, just as well as it can attend to and achieve their very status quo preferences, beliefs, and ideologies in denial. High-ly accomplished art can certainly be rendered op-pressive, blinkered, and of very confused or regret-table ideology and effect. Or it can be rendered quite clearly and extensively liberatory. It's a choice, not something inevita-bly inherent. Smith shares quite a number of thoughtful observations and perceptions in her essay, so it's too bad and more damaging that she also stands upon establ-ishment bankrupt-cies.

Little to nothing is unorthodox about any-thing Smith says in regard to literature, and yet Smith laments the current state of literature in some of her contemporary articles. At what point might one feel compelled to break with at least some part of the underlying ortho-doxy, i.e., the ideology?

Granted it may not be easy given that a cen-tral tenet of much status quo orthodoxy is that it does not exist. This very prominent author has at least felt compelled to question in print some-thing of what she perceives as dysfunctional or-thodoxy (in "Two Paths for the Novel"). Even though the arti-cle crashed and burned, it was at least a step, if only sideways, like this one "Speaking in Tongues" which in any event cov-ers more ground, possibly more fertile but it seems to me just as orthodox, well trod.

Liberatory critique and art do not destroy quali-ty or exceptionally accomplished art that may be more or less establishment: Shake-speare, for exam-ple, but liberatory work can help put the bard's work in more clear perspective – bring out faults, flaws, and weaknesses of all variety, as well as highlight countervailing strengths. Failure to see that the works of Shakespeare and the works of all other artists contain ideological lines "particular to it" is failure on behalf of critics, not an absence of strong or pointed ideological reality and effect in and around the work, whatever the artists' inten-tions, or however well carried out.

No bread for the people? Let them eat cake! But of course people need nutritional bread, they need it available, they can help make it and in various ways need to, the vital stuff rather than the many mounds of cake and moldy crusts and worse.

They as in we "claiming" for movement for-ward, progress, and critiquing thought and work that holds people back. Plurality of voices? Yes, of course. It's called real democ-racy. Or libertarian socialism. And so on. And that's a kind of ideology, a kind of principle, a kind of ideal. To not eviscerate at the core we need to understand and be open about the reali-ties and possibilities of art, the far more full lib-eratory potential in our time and many another.

THE VITIATION OF AMERICAN LITERATURE

"In a word, the revolutionary critic does not believe that we can have art without craftsmanship; what he does be-lieve is that, granted the craftsmanship, our aim should be to make art serve man as a thing of ac-tion and not man serve art as a thing of escape.

– V. F. Calverton,

James Wood opens his essay "The Tunnel," a re-view of John Wray's novel Lowboy, by claiming:

> Fiction is at once real and imaginary. Not real at one moment and flickeringly illusory the next, like the fading pulse of a dying man, but both at once, as if a ghost had a pulse. Fiction is one giant pseudo-statement, a fact-checker's nightmare. Like one of our own lies, it can be completely "wrong" about the world and yet completely revela-tory – completely "right" – about the psych-ology of the person issuing the error. Thus, one of fiction's most natural areas of inquiry, from Cervantes to Murakami, concerns states of confusion, error, or madness, in which a character's crazy fictions become inter-twined with the novel's calmer fictions, and the reader's purchase on the reliable world becomes intermittently tenuous.

Wood's emphasis here – a kind of tautological claim that the very nature of fiction is "at once real and imaginary…as if a ghost had a pulse" and acts to produce in readers an "intermittently tenuous purchase on the reliable world" – functions to misrepresent or mask his implied observation that fiction as a curious mix of fact and make-believe

allows readers a mostly reliable grip on the world, even when involving a character who also mixes fact and make-believe.

Third sentence in, Wood claims, "Fiction is one giant pseudo-statement, a fact-checker's night-mare." Which is a basic misrepresentation. In fact, fiction is not inherently "one giant pseudo-state-ment, a fact-checker's nightmare." Many key (and even minor) facts in works of fiction can be readily checked, if need be. There are plenty of ways auth-ors can convey the reality or actuality of crucial facts in any novel.

"…one of fiction's most natural areas of in-quiry …[makes] the reader's purchase on the re-liable world becomes intermittently tenuous." This is another way of saying, actually de-emphasizing, that fiction mainly affirms in read-ers a sense of reality. In fact, readers may gain an increasingly stronger understanding of reality, whether "intermittently tenuous" or not, due to one of fiction's "areas of inquiry" far more "natural" generally and that follows far more readily from basic elements of Wood's opening discussion. In other words, from say Gilgamesh to Wizard of the Crow, long works of fiction portray "a character's crazy fic-tions … intertwined with the novel's" other il-luminations of life that help "the reader's pur-chase on the reliable world become" deeper, more firm, more comprehensive, more useful. Emphasis affirmative – not "intermittent"and not "pseudo" and not a fact-checking "night-mare."

So it is that Wood opens this latest review by skewing understanding of fiction and offering a tautological view. Why would one tautologi-cally emphasize that fiction in general may cause a read-er's sense of reality to fall apart off and on, when the far more traditional and far greater functions and uses of fiction are to heighten reality and per-ception? And why would one then two thirds of the way through the review contradict oneself by claiming that Lowboy far from making reality "intermittently tenuous," actually "induce[s]" "epistemological schizophrenia in the reader, whereby" the pro-tagonist's "groundless visions" (unrealities) are "inhabit[ed]" by readers who are left with mere "glimpse[s]" of reality?

Which is it? What is mainly "purchased" by such fiction for readers? Reality or not? Wood con-tradicts himself regarding the work at hand, while misrepresenting fiction in general. Oh, no! one might argue on Wood's behalf – he states that: "You can imagine replying to someone who was curious about what it's like to be schizophrenic, 'Well, start with John Wray's novel.' Lowboy may often be lost to himself, but he is not lost to us." In other words, Wood claims, the book keeps readers firmly grounded in reality, even if just barely – in glimpses – as readers inhabit schizophrenia – and even though "fiction is one giant pseudo-state-ment, a fact-checker's nightmare." Fortunately the facts don't matter, except when they do. Fiction is not so confusing after all, no matter that it can be "completely 'wrong' about the world," for it can be "yet completely revelatory – completely 'right' – about the psychology of the person issuing the error." And what exists in fiction beyond psychol-ogy? Anything? Any fact-checker?

We might examine the implications of this tru-ism a moment longer: "Like one of our own lies, [fiction] can be completely 'wrong' about the world and yet completely revelatory – completely 'right' – about the psychology of the person issuing the error." There is a severe problem here but first the accuracy: of course a lie, whether actual or invent-ed, can reveal the psychology of a person or char-acter, just as it's obvious that pigs on a farm can stand in for vicious tyrants in an allegory, no mat-ter how mistaken it might be outside of story to lit-erally think of pigs as vicious tyrants. The problem is that fiction as "the real and the imaginary" is far more than "psychology." One can be literally com-pletely wrong about the world and think one is completely right, not least in this Age of Propa-ganda that cranks out many lauded fictions and facts quite utterly irrelevant or trivial, mistaken or oppressive – including any number of psychologies however accurate in depiction. There is far more to fiction than psychology. For example, sociology. And a few vital relations between the socio and the psycho for which a great fact-checker of an author comes in handy.

There are some other problems. Take the first sentence of the review. It's a very simple sentence, but a very wrong sentence especially as Wood elaborates it. "Fiction is at once real and imagin-ary." By which is meant "at once real" and make-believe. The problem: fiction is not necessarily real or make-believe "at once." An author or any work of fiction short or long may choose to directly address the reader in all reality at any point, and this may be indicated explicitly or not. In such instances, at the least, there is nothing necessarily make-believe "at once," no such necessary element or phenomenon. The factual, the actual, may stand alone. Or the factual, real element may be inter-twined with the make-believe, and it may be integrated in say some alternating sequence but not necessarily "at once" in some transmuted fashion. The novel or story in such instances may be strictly real or actual (whether mistaken or not is another matter). One might simply wave one's hand and claim, well then such passages are not "fiction" but in doing so one guts many fictions, many quality works of fiction – novels and stories, plays and poems – of essential and sometimes central features (that are real and not simultaneously fantastic).

One cannot even necessarily say that any auth-or's direct address or every passage of every poem, story, or novel is written in a (fictive or make be-lieve) persona distinct from the author anymore than one can say that about a moment by moment exchange of a couple actual workers talking on an actual job.

Moreover, primary etymology of "fiction" includes "to fashion," or "to shape." A fiction can consist entirely of factual matter and actual opinion or belief, in which case it might be literally under-stood as an illusion, a lie, a fake, or an invention. Stories, novels, plays, poems – that is, fiction – are commonly thought of as inventions, which does not imply or necessitate that all key elements of all such fiction are "at once" both real and make-believe. So it is that make-believe (or the fantastic, if one prefers a sound of higher diction) does not always permeate all fictions, nor instantiate itself "at once" with fact – not even in all "fantasy," "sci-ence-fiction," or "speculative" novels, let alone in "realist," "naturalist," and "documentary" novels.

All this said, something greater is at stake in Wood's review than the question of whether or not fiction more adeptly portrays or illumines reality and possibility or make-believe, or how well and in what way fiction illumines both, "at once" or sep-ately. Something more urgent gets buried by this review.

It's a type of review that could have been writ-ten hundreds of years ago about Cervantes' Don Quixote. For that matter, this kind of review could have been written thousands of years ago about the Epic of Gilgamesh, for in not atypical Wood fashion it engages…forget the penetrating and broad public realities…it goes even sub-domestic, into the psycho-clinical, maybe touching on "the so-called absolutes and eternals, with the ultimate emotions and the perennial tragedies," but disdain-ing "solutions…panaceas," which in Wood's view are inevitably:

> the novel's weakness, which is precisely that it is about 'a paranoid schizophrenic,' ex-plicitly flagged as such by the pub-lisher, rather than about someone who is losing his mind, as, say, Knut Hamsun's 'Hunger' and Thomas Bernhard's 'Concrete' are about people losing their minds. Books like Ham-sun's and Bernhard's ex-ult in the unread-able, the indecipherable. 'Lowboy' is excep-tionally tender and acute, but it is at times in danger of falling into the legible stability of case history, in which the reader might check off recog-nizable symptoms, usefully assisted by the subject's mother, who is on hand to provide the necessary background infor-mation, and validated by the acknowl-edged medical sources.

So why not urge Wray to better craft the nar-rative given his fiction's objectives rather than urge him to change his objective for no good reason? And Wood offers no good reason, in fact no tangible reason at all, other than a possi-ble "weakness" that seems as if it would indi-cate a dip in craft more than anything else. There is nothing impossible about creating a quality novel about "a paranoid schizophrenic," no matter if it has been done to death.

Wood adds: "The book is less bold, less play-ful-ly demanding, than Rivka Galchen's recent novel, 'Atmospheric Disturbances,' which ex-plores a simi-lar mental deviancy from what Galchen wickedly calls 'a consensus view of re-ality'." So we turn to Wood's prior review of Galchen's novel and learn:

> Galchen has a knack for taking a thread and fraying it, so that a sentence never quite ends up where you expect. Here Leo is talk-ing about his desperation, as the husband of a woman who has been "replaced." [The husband insanely thinks his wife is an imposter, a simulacrum – "Last December a woman entered my apartment who looked exactly like my wife."] We begin the sen-tence thinking that it might throw some light on his mind, but end it in darkened counsel … Galchen can take the slightest observation of Leo's and warp it, to reveal lunatic undu-lations: "I don't know if Harvey ac-tually had one arm notably longer than the other, but he gave off that impres-sion." His language is strange, pungent, dangerously ripe: "As the simulacrum sleep sighed, her whole thorax centime-tered out against me – then receded." Walking into a pastry shop, Leo takes a quick, fantastical inventory of the people in it, and then:

> "What did you say?" someone said maybe to me.

> "Nothing," I said to almost no one.

At which point we consider that Alex Com-fort may have written the most incisive words yet about such work, or at least about work ap-proximating these lines. He noted in 1948 in The Novel and Our Time that: "We have a tedious mass of books by lunatics who think they are psychologists and by neurotics who think they are lunatics. The literary magazines are full of the praises of schizophrenia."

Wood concludes in the Galchen review that such novels "are short works, in part because first-person lunacy is a stretch. 'Atmospheric Disturb-ances' is too long by forty or fifty pages." At which point we see that Wood's en-thusiasm is more or less terminal for long fic-tion.

Except as marginalized exception, what more can one expect of establishment fiction and criti-cism other than lively blinkered short works and intricate blinkered long works, of various warp, as if written by ideologue hedgehogs?

We do well to turn to a critic like Alex Comfort in The Novel and Our Time who notes of fiction in this age of "barbarism":

> The responsible writer sees everyone naked, and is as naked himself. He is not devoid of political and moral judgments, but he makes them equally. In reading, therefore, ask: Is this writer capable of recognizing a human being? Is he able to reject the art of diverse weights, for which an act identical in every respect is a heroic but regrettable necessity when done by Our Side and a contemptible atrocity when done by Their Side? Is his judgment of human decisions level or weighted: does he know filth from food, whatever the wrapper? If he does, he is capable of being a great artist under bar-barianism, and if not, he is another part of barbarism made manifest.

Is the literary culture effectively tamed, reduced, and marginalized so greatly that such questions – let alone answers – do not arise, let alone prepon-derate, in the dominant, established circles? There exists plenty of evidence by which to draw conclu-sions.

One may not agree entirely here with Comfort, yet he comments with considerable insight:

> Whether we [novelists] are able to influence human conduct will depend very largely up-on the number of people in a given asocial society who react by rational aggression to-wards that society rather than by irrational aggression towards their fellow individuals. The social role of the novel will depend very largely, in coming years, upon the persist-ence of sufficient rationally disobedient individuals to make novel-writing of the kind I have described possible.

> While interpretation rather than an attempt to convince is the chief object of art, the novel is more apt than any other literary form to exert direct pressure upon the growth and forming of ideas, and it will do so whether we intend that or not… Because of the essential humanity which a writer must possess to write major novels, I am confident that it will play a large part in the events which precede the end of asociality, and should it pass out of currency as a form, it will be replaced by the unanimous litera-ture of tyranny or the spontaneous social literature of a free society, depending upon how far its readers are able to share and im-bibe the responsibility of its best practition-ers.

Establishment culture is complicit not least in the ongoing US atrocities against western Asia and beyond and at home. The established culture is so complicit it forefronts the notion of the post-9/11 novel and buries the notions of, to take a few ex-amples, the explosion of incarceration novel, or the lethal state of health care novel, or the conquest of Oila novel – these far more enduring, or far more reaching, or far more calamitous realities and cri-ses than the post-9/11 sensibility, which essentially empha-sizes our suffering at the hands of others and not the far greater suffering we inflict on those among us and on others abroad.

It's a class thing. "The Tunnel," indeed. It's an imperial thing. The USA was founded as an em-pire, Noam Chomsky notes:

> The United States is probably the only coun-try in the world that was founded as a 'nas-cent empire' – it's what George Washington called it. The colonies he said, were a nas-cent empire and they were just beginning their imperial conquest. They had to con-quer the national territory. Thomas Jefferson [who] was the most libertarian of the found-ers effectively called for conquest of the Western hemisphere. The expansion of the colonies to what is now the national terri-tory, is just imperialism. Historians of imperialism warn against what they call the 'salt water fallacy'. Namely you only call it imperialism if you cross saltwater. But that is a fallacy. I mean if the Mississippi River was the size of the Irish sea, the conquest of the national territory would be called imper-ialism. From the point of view of the indig-enous population, it's

the same whether you cross water or not. So yes the expansion it-self was constant war against the indigenous population. The conquest of Florida, which was an undeclared war, the first executive war in American history without congres-sional authorization, the Mexican war con-quered half of Mexico, then the expansion in the Caribbean, into the pacific, and af-ter the Second World War, interventions every-where. It's hard to find a year of peace.

Meanwhile the dominant literature of the empire colludes, plays the imperial game, facili-tates the conquests that ongo. By now at least, and long since for many or most imaginative writers and critics, they cannot say they do not know or could not know, even as their writing belies they do.

Even when they believe otherwise, there ex-ists a certain connection between writers of a certain class and inhumanity, as Chomsky points out:

> If you have gone to the best schools and graduated from Oxford and Cambridge, and so on, you have instilled in you the under-standing that there are certain things it would not do to say; actually, it would not do to think. That is the pri-mary way to pre-vent unpopular ideas from being expressed. The ideas of the overwhelming majority of the population, who don't attend Harvard, Princeton, Ox-ford and Cambridge, enable them to react like human beings, as they often do. There is a lesson there for activists.

A lesson for novelists as well, and all authors, whether deeply invested in the libera-tory or not.

KUNKEL, BOLAÑO, NGŨGĨ,
AND THE STATE OF FICTION

Frequent New York Times contributor and novel-ist Benjamin Kunkel has an article "Dystopia and the End of Politics" in the estab-lishment journal Dissent that is the most recent in a lengthening line of State of Fiction (SoF) commentaries by various authors, picking up with James Wood's book How Fiction Works (and related articles), tracing through a series of challenges to HFW, hopping to Zadie Smith's "Two Paths for the Novel," and then shifting to Kunkel's piece with no basic new turns

in the thinking of the status quo writers amid all declarations and pronouncements lavish, banal, seeking. Some parts of these essays hit the mark in noting the severe limits of various novels and their types, yet the status quo State of Fiction analysts can't or won't turn their heads far enough to note or to compensate for, let alone adequately   ad-dress, ideological binds administered by the caging hands that feed, in academia and commerce.[1]

In Dissent, the longtime cold war journal of Swiftian title, Kunkel writes like a character out of a Roberto Bolaño novel, rendering himself chaotic-ally familiar and essentially inept. Cha-otic because reasonable insight mixes with mis-prision leading to hapless assertions and vacu-ous conclusions.[2] As for content, Kunkel, focus-ing on all too prevalent sterile lit sur-rounds, looks to fly to fertile land, plunging in-stead into sand. Kunkel's article stands as one of the many pinched walls and series of iron bars of the literature establishment, likewise the writings of Bolaño, at least as they function in the US, though Bolaño's work is less familiar and less inept and contains a number of endur-ing qualities. (Kunkel's writing can come across as less sophisti-cated or refined than that of the larger lit establish-ment, possibly willfully so, thus it may appear more evidently flawed to some, more bemusing to others, and so on. That the sentences in his Dissent article hang like de-bris clouds freeze-framed after a building col-lapse merely provides extra asthmatic effect. Kunkel may seem an easy or unnecessary object of criticism, but he remains an establishment outcropping, visible enough for critique.)

Bolaño's work lands hit and miss. 2666 is more miss than hit, as is nearly all his work, but at least something hits in perhaps each of his books. The same cannot much be said of

Kunkel's work in general, in my view, where the persistent miss typically voids most any solid let alone tin-pan hits. (Obviously this refers to Kunkel's work to this point; of course Bolaño had years on Kunkel, al-so very different early experiences and points of origin.) Though there's a lot of chaff in Bolaño's work, it contains some edible kernels while more importantly at least hinting at underlying fertile ground of significant mass, whereas in Kunkel's work, once one finally digs past the fluff and sludge, one typically finds little more than meager crust. Bolaño is convenient, a safe fashionable auth-or for the US literature establishment for an assort-ment of (some) reasons I've gone into elsewhere in regard to other authors, at Fiction Gutted, for ex-ample. Bolaño is so fashionable that it might at first be curious that Kunkel makes no reference in Dissent to such a current bright star in his general attempt to assess and move forward some part of the current state of fiction – curious until one reads Kunkel's more-or-less workmanlike 2007 article on Bolaño in the London Review of Books where little crucial flash or sense of connect may be found either:

> ...to the extent that [Bolaño's] fiction refuses to behave anything like fiction, is this a mark of its triumphant reality? Or (the depressive obverse to the mania of belief) is the world of Bolaño's generation, and perhaps the world generally, too refractory to order and understanding to permit its transformation into literature, leaving inconclusive testimony the only honest form?
>
> To these questions the answer would seem to be a ringing ... simonel. In the first section of The Savage Detectives, García Madero wonders about the Mexican slang term: "If simón is slang for yes and nel means no, then what does simonel mean?"

Ambiguity. More or less. Kunkel then gives over the entire last paragraph of his LRB essay to Bolaño's fiction, the last word being "Simonel." For what it's worth, this is Kunkel in part replacing his nonfiction with fiction, with Bo-laño noted for re-placing fiction with nonfiction (or its appearance). The latter may well turn out to be more valuable and renewable an approach in fiction[3] (if not much as employed by Bolaño) than Kunkel would think to accredit. He leaves Bolaño on a rather detached drifting note, though with regard for this "strange" and "significant" writer.

Near the end of the literary science fiction sur-vey that is his Dissent article, Kunkel states, "In sum, when the contemporary novelist contem-plates the future – including, it seems, the future of the novel – " ... "the result is political novels with-out politics, social novels without society, and romances free of love, amounting, in the end, to 'literature' that isn't" due to the inability of con-temporary authors to depict "character" and "love" and "political problems" – rather barren stories that may even perpetuate the problems, for Kunkel claims this literature is "accidental and symptomat-ic" and one in which "the likelihood of disaster is only abetted." So this is "literature," Kunkel notes valuably with some basis for reason "that isn't."

Unlike Bolaño's nonfuturistic fiction? Or too much like? Where to turn for the future of fiction, or even the present? It takes more than the "luck" that Kunkel hopes toward, for novelists to "reveal – and not only by accident – what" some ostensible "at-mosphere of dread is doing to us" let alone other realities and possibilities.

When one thinks of Bolaño's fiction, one might first light upon as its central elements, perhaps, youth and chaos, or art and chaos, or more basical-ly, live energy and chaos – a sort of loose tracking and swirling impressionism. Due to the statements and implications of Benjamin Kunkel or Zadie Smith or James Wood and other such State of Fic-tion commenters either plaintive or grasping or mistaken, one might be led to think that literature has fallen into rudderless drift (there is wholesale drift, as in distraction, not rudderless), or that it gapes as if near paralysis at chasms or blank walls (virtually endless stupefying canyons indeed but depends on where you look), or that the confusion of the world this time around the pulsating block may just have overtaken the capacity of the novel to portray and transform (an old excuse no serious artist should accept)…just about all lines of ques-tion may be made to seem bleak and mistaken even in the new seeking. This may be what inevitably happens when liberatory lit tendencies in literature are too much buried, not least in a time of increas-ingly obvious and outrageous injustice and oppres-sion. Even so, it remains possible to think to illumi-nating effect along sundry other critical lines also, so circumscribed are the challenges these State of Fiction works set for themselves. For example:

Mary McCarthy: "It could be said that the real plot of War and Peace is the struggle of the char-acters not to be immersed, engulfed, swallowed up by the landscape of fact and 'history' in which they, like all human beings, have been placed: freedom (the subjective) is in the fiction, and necessity is in the fact." Seemingly overwhelming chaos is no new challenge.

Or Victor Hugo in Les Misérables: "Geometry deceives. Only the hurricane is accurate." The precise and contained tremble before controlled explosions.

Or take a mix of approaches consciously prog-ressive and popular: the accomplished fact of Ngũgĩ wa Thiong'o's massive global epic novel from Africa, Wizard of the Crow (2006), with plenty of thoroughly and well depicted "charact-ers," and great "love" and tremendous "political problems" too.[4] This novel rates among the all time greats, possibly standing apart from any other novel written yet this century, or even in a very long time.

Point being: these molehill-made-mountain problems are completely obliterated by existing alternatives. Of course not everyone should write like Ngũgĩ. Everyone needs to figure out things in their own way, find what works for them, as must even Ngũgĩ again for his next work, and one need not have read Ngũgĩ 's Wizard to see how insuffi-cient are the questions asked, the challenges raised in status quo SoF articles, but if one wishes for a contemporary novel that answers all those concerns and more, one is readily available. A novel like Ngũgĩ's great Wizard of the Crow delivers everything the status quo SoF authors claim to seek and fail to find. Moreover, Wizard of the Crow is a vital (normatively) progressive even revolutionary novel. So the next time one of these flailing and plaintive State of Fiction works dribbles, murks, or cheeks from the literature establishment, some power ought to be able to assign an old-fashioned book report to these neo-scholastics to turn their eyes from North America and Europe for at least a moment, lest the working discussion of fiction remain stuck in either the ignorant or the widely known, and the misleading or otherwise bereft. They could do worse than to write their first report on Wizard of the Crow, and then for their second report get an even more global take and an at least equally liberatory view of some existing and poten-tial paths of literature by reading the collection of fiction at Liberation Lit journal. Wizard of the Crow is a novel that shows much greater existing realities and possibilities for fiction than are typic-ally found, by far, including what may be some minimal necessities for vital fiction in this age of increasingly preposterous rot. The Lib Lit collection is not exactly irrelevant in this regard either. The fundamental problems, the pressing problems of status quo fiction are normative. Searching for an-swers by way of technique and form is hopeless, and in some cases manipulative.

Kunkel concludes: due to "the multiplication of new threats…[n]ow it can seem to us again that we and the people we love (or would wish to love) will have to live with an anxiety every bit as per-vasive as the old [cold war] fear, though perhaps less acute. With luck some novelists will be able to reveal – and not only by accident – what this at-mosphere of dread is doing to us."

Woe is "us," is it? We might first do well to look at what and how and why our fear – much of it purposefully fraudulently manufactured and main-tained – has been used to smash Iraq and Iraqis, Afghanistan and Afghanis, Pakistan and Paki-stanis, and far more. When we take on that task, we don't see many such Anti Oil Conquest novels pouring out of the establishment. Quite the oppo-site – they are screeded against and screened off by the paymasters of the status quo SoF writers and the like. This great lack within fiction, which ex-tends into normative realms far beyond overseas conquest, deep into our more intimate public space, has nothing to do with any inherent technical difficulty in depicting such epics and tales, and instead has everything to do with the blinkers, hoods, lines, and limits that so greatly circumscribe, distort, and ultimately render small the conclusions of Kunkel's plaint, and those of other status quo State of Fiction would-be visionaries, searchers, and the like. Technical difficulties will arise and render themselves distinct from pre-vious ones, but this can occur only in the process of attempting to meet the normative challenges first, of which status quo state of fiction writers have thus far proved themselves to have precious little to say, and even less of any worth. Thus fiction is gutted needlessly – and to put it even more plain –

barbarically. Pity the classroom. Pity the magazines. The world.

We need to pick up with Ngũgĩ and others, and we need to pick up from where Maxine Hong Kingston and others leave off in their criticism ("The Novel's Next Step," in Critical Fictions: The Politics of Imaginative Writing; 1991 – Philomena Mariani, Ed.) – Kingston:

I'm going to give you a head start on the book that somebody ought to be working on. The hands of the clock are minutes away from nuclear mid-night. And I am slow, each book taking me longer to write... So let me set down what has to be done, and maybe hurry creation, which is about two steps ahead of destruction…. All the writer has to do is make Wittman [hero of her novel, Tripmaster Monkey] grow up, and Huck Finn and Holden Caulfield will grow up. We need a sequel to ado-lescence – an idea of the humane beings that we may become. And the world will have a sequel…. The dream of the great American novel is past. We need to write the Global novel….

---

¹ They're owned. Just a well known fact about capi-talist culture – somebody owns what goes on – especially when paying direct money for it – someones typically far removed from the authors yet intimately invisibly connected, manifesting the prerogatives of capital: the various ideological bounds. It's an old story everbreaking in clear sight, badly warping and mangling status quo attempts at State of Fiction discussion.

² Some immediately refuted by others online.

³ More complex and more ideologically bound and assaulted public and private conditions may require more intensely fact-infused or ideologically overt and incisive fictions. (These prolems deserve much more extensive exploration and interdisciplinary attention than they receive.)

⁴ Of no small consequence for a larger discussion of these concerns are Ngũgĩ 's extremely vital ideas in relation to fiction and the world, some pithily found, more-or-less in passing, at The Litblog Co-op, for example.

WHAT WOULD NOT DO TO SAY

THE "CLEANSING" OF GEORGE ORWELL

A Real Shove from Above

In many ways, George Orwell's greatest book is Homage to Catalonia, which documents his direct participation in the Spanish Revolution (civil war), a great book of a crucial revolution that is essen-tially elided from James Wood's sociopolitical take on Orwell's life and works in his April 2009 New Yorker article, "A Fine Rage" slugged *"George Orwell's revolutions."* Orwellian: the most liberatory of "revolutions" involving George Orwell is essen-tially nowhere to be found in "A Fine Rage… George Orwell's revolutions."

Wood claims Orwell "idealizes" the working class, then immediately cites Orwell's description of what Wood labels "the best kind of proletarian home." If "best" does not tend toward the "ideal" what does? A month earlier in the New York Review of Books, Julian Barnes notes in "Such, Such was Eric Blair" that Orwell "described the condition of the working class with sympathy and rage, thought them wiser than intellectuals, but didn't sentimentalize them; in their struggle they were as 'blind and stupid' as a plant struggling toward the light." Hardly ideal.

Wood describes Orwell as having "Rousseauian tendencies" (to be a sort of nature lover, Wood means), and additionally calls him a "puritan," and labels him an "upper-class masochist" who wanted not to "level up society" but to "level it down" – and then, a "puritan masochist" whose "real struggle... was personal...the struggle to obliterate privilege, and thus, in some sense, to obliterate himself. This was at bottom a religious mortification." And "perhaps Orwell had, by the late nineteen-forties, soured on socialism, along with capitalism." No longer then a masochist suicide? Please. Wood would do well to save the amateur psychoanalysis hour for himself. "Orwell feared what he most desired: the future." Orwell had "a tendency toward drab omnipotence." Such is Wood's New Yorker style piety, vacuity, and smear.

Wood describes a "judgment against Dickens" by Orwell as being "unwittingly comic." Orwell: "However much Dickens may admire the working classes, he does not wish to resemble them." Wood wonders, "Why would anyone want to...resemble ...the working classes...least of all the working classes themselves?" He adds "...the problem with 'admiring' the working class is that it doesn't, on its own, help anyone to get out of it at all." Which is evidently why Orwell, far beyond admiration, risked his life in fighting on behalf of the working classes during the Spanish Revolution, as described in Homage to Catalonia.

Clearly Orwell saw more virtues and value in "the working classes" than Wood does. In fact, it is the many pressures applied by the working classes against the ruling classes that help to shrink the size of the more oppressed classes and ameliorate conditions within. Gifts are rarely granted from above, not without being forced from below by those who do the work – an active feature of many working classes that is admirable, and worth resembling.

In Spain, Orwell was willing to fight and to risk dying among the working classes who were in revolutionary mode, attempting a liberatory revo-lution that certainly did not spring from the privi-leged ruling classes but rather pushed against them – a "real shove from below," a means to change mocked by Wood: "Ah, that will do the trick." Does principled, justified force from below not sometimes produce real concessions from above? Does not much progress, let alone a revolution, often require it? Does Wood forget how the American colonies once sent his homeland's Kingdom packing? The Spanish revolt of the working classes was largely a liberatory revolution that the wealth of the world left on its own, to be crushed. Other working class revolutions succeed or lay ground-work for progressive movements to come, to gain power under more peaceful conditions. One may see the Americas not least, including contempora-neously, for inspiring examples.

Before and during the Spanish Revolution (civil war), largely working class Spanish socialists and anarchists organized popular workers groups and movements, struggled, fought, and in part success-fully replaced Republican Spain's oppressive liber-al capitalist rule, while holding off the fascism of Franco, for a time at least, greatly transforming peoples lives on a large scale, until the revolution was crushed by force – and mocked or ignored by others.

Establishment Innuendo

There is no little reason to want to embody the gen-uine qualities and enlivening characteristics of the working classes in a variety of ways. Orwell shows why most dramatically in Homage to Catalonia, the revolution blanked from Wood's New Yorker article on "George Orwell's revolutions":

> [In Barcelona 1936] it was the aspect of the crowds that was the queerest thing of all. In outward appearance it was a town in which the wealthy classes had practically ceased to exist. Except for a small number of women and foreigners there were no 'well-dressed' people at all. Prac-

tically everyone wore rough working-class clothes, or blue overalls or some variant of militia uniform. All this was queer and moving. There was much in this that I did not understand, in some ways I did not even like it, but I recognized it im-mediately as a state of affairs worth fighting for. Also, I believed that things were as they appeared, that this was really a workers' State and that the entire bourgeoisie had either fled, been killed or voluntarily come over to the workers' side; I did not realise that great numbers of well-to-do bourgeois were simply lying low and disguising them-selves as proletarians for the time being.

[See an expanded excerpt of Homage to Catalonia appended.] What occurred in Barce-lona, revolu-tionary Spain in 1936 was extraordinary, partially witnessed and participated in by Orwell, and had been long built toward by working class organiz-ing – popular progressive action. Had western "democracies" lifted a fin-ger to assist the anarchists and liberatory social-ists, rather than purposefully failing to support them and even working against them, the world could well be a far better place today. But little official sympathy and far less than needed ap-preciation and understanding of such popular movements exists or is tolerated still today and little, none, or negative appreciation is mainly engendered by the most highly acclaimed promi-nent fiction and prominent literary criti-cism of our time – as we see in the essential blanking of Hom-age to Catalonia and its cru-cial import in Wood's sociopolitical review of Orwell and his works.

Regarding various features of Orwell's work, Wood belittles the thoughtful observations (Wood calls them "attacks") of post-colonial analyst Edward Said on the one hand, and quotes approv-ingly and snidely from Philip Larkin, "a racist who wrote of stringing up strikers," as Terry Eagleton notes. Such tenor and shading readily come across to many casual readers, let alone to close readers. As does plenty of other establishment innuendo: "So the question hangs over Orwell, as it does over many well-heeled revolutionaries: Did he want to level up society or level it down." If such a "ques-tion hangs over...many well-heeled revolutionar-ies" (hanging above one's head by a thread like the deadly Sword of Damocles, one presumes), then similarly loaded questions hang over *all* establish-mentarians, and espe-cially over prominent ones like James Wood, only moreso. At best, the former has much to lose, and the latter has much to save. The innu-endo is of some potentially frightening change posed by revolutionaries, never mind that estab-lishmentarian forces have long been deadly and oppressive for many, and are potentially fatal for the species entire. Such is the status quo or reac-tionary rhetoric, the basic line of Wood's essay. This is the voice of not only the counter-revolution-ary, which one assumes Wood real-izes, it's the voice of the anti-humane, the in-human, which he either fails to grasp or does not want to, joining a long line of Harvard type intellectuals committed in opposition to libertar-ian socialism – an overt acceptance of which, re-cent polls indicate, is on the rise in the US, the basics ever more popular.

Establishment PR

The basic ideology of James Wood to this point is that of a status quo liberal, that is a neo cold war-rior, an ideology that may delude itself to presume it is largely progressive, while es-sentially manifest-ing itself as status quo, with reactionary tendencies.

James Wood is typical of the New Yorker, or maybe somewhat more reactionary. His article on Orwell presents the New Yorker's kind of mental cleansing for and by the liberal and con-servative readers of the magazine, the mindset of ruling class culture and society. It's not only the voice of going along with the ruling estab-lishment to get along, it's the voice of the blink-ered and the blinding. "If you have gone to the best schools," notes Noam Chomsky –

and graduated from Oxford and Cam-bridge, and so on, you have instilled in you the un-derstanding that there are cer-tain things it would not do to say; actu-ally, it would not do to think. That is the primary way to pre-vent unpopular ideas from being expressed. The ideas of the overwhelming majority of the population, who don't attend Harvard, Princeton, Oxford and Cambridge, enable them to react like human beings, as they often do. There is a lesson there for activists.

Activists and artists in general. (One such lesson: read and write through Liberation Lit – liblit.org – and other liberatory venues.) Though sometimes beneficial in truncated ways, the New Yorker's lit-erary and other art efforts are often slight, wrong, corrosive, or beside the point. Much of the literary establishment takes its cue from the New Yorker, or otherwise more-or-less shares its class-based affinities, not infrequently with much admiration and the wish to resemble.

Wood points to the contemporary relevance of Orwell's "coinages" in his novel 1984, such as "'doublethink' and 'Newspeak' and 'Big Brother' [that] now live an unexpectedly acute second life" – only "now"? "unexpectedly"? – "in the supposedly free West" but Wood makes no mention that Orwell wrote 1984 based in substantial part on his experience of working as a propagandist for BBC during World War II, where he was surrounded by and part of propaganda techniques, including those of the sort commonly used by the Nazis. Jutta Paczulla notes in the Canadian Journal of History (Spring-Summer 2007):

> When writing Nineteen Eighty-Four, Or-well drew on the MOI [Britain's Ministry of Information] as a model for the novel's Min-istry of Truth. Not only does the Ministry of Truth building in the novel resemble that of the MOI, but Room 101, where the Eastern Service Committee held its meetings, be-comes the room in which Winston, the cen-tral character in Nineteen Eighty-Four is tor-tured and broken. Moreover, the atmos-phere cre-ated by the mutual censorship conducted by [Orwell's] BBC colleagues is reflected in the novel's atmosphere of para-noia and anxiety.

Introducing the first book of the recent two volume edition of Orwell's work that prompts Wood's arti-cle is George Packer, another of the New Yorker's liberal apologists for imperialism, as detailed by Edward Herman in "George Packer and the Liberal Struggle to Support Im-perialism" Z Magazine 2005. Packer claims there is:

> a strange gap in Orwell's work – for he nev-er wrote a novel or nonfiction book about the most historically important event of his life [World War II, during which] he spent 'two wasted years' as a producer in the East-ern Service of the BBC.

Setting aside the question of whether or not WWII or the Spanish civil war or some other event was "the most historically important event in Orwell's life," the point is apparently inconceivable to both Packer and Wood that Orwell's famed novel 1984 is based substan-tially on his time working for the BBC during World War II. While Orwell directs the satire of 1984 most evidently toward the Soviet Union, also Franco Spain, the satire applies directly to the propaganda institutions and capacities of the liberal "democracies" where Orwell lived and breathed some of the atmosphere and propaganda realities and irrealities that he de-scribes and con-jures up in 1984. Newspeak, doublethink, Big Brother, memory hole – all are longstanding spe-cialties of the BBC, and domi-nant US media, as Orwell came to know and experience ever more intimately during World War II. Thus, the "strange gap" is resoundingly filled and the centrality of Orwell's coinages to the West today is not only not unexpected by unbiased observers, but an under-standing of the Orwellian has long since been re-marked upon and employed in independent media analyses of the dominant corporate media of the US, England, and allied states.

About his state propaganda work at the BBC, Orwell expressed publicly that he kept the "propa-ganda slightly less disgusting than it might other-wise have been"…while writing privately in his diary:

You can go on and on telling lies, and the most palpable lies at that, and even if they are not actually believed, there is no strong revulsion. We are all drowning in filth.... I feel that intellectual honesty and balanced judgement have simply disappeared from the face of the earth....

"Orwell's problem," as Noam Chomsky describes it, permeates the establishment in the US and be-yond: How is it that oppressive ideological systems are able to "instill beliefs that are firmly held and widely accepted although they are completely without foundation and often plainly at variance with the obvious facts about the world around us?" As evidenced in James Wood, George Packer, et al, Orwell's problem has not lessened since Orwell's lifetime, and now the Obama administration is a leading part of the problem. There is no mention in Wood's article about the Orwellian nature of to-day's top rulers. No mention that President Obama and his administration's rhetoric of "change" and "security" purposefully mask the essential preserv-ation of the status quo, let alone continue and escalate the militarism – a state of affairs that recalls "doublethink" and "Newspeak" and "Big Brother" as much as "Fox News...during the last Presidential election" recalls 1984's "Hate Week."

By mentioning only Fox News election coverage, Wood softens his weak nod to the relevant immediate, neatly placing Orwell and Hate Week distinctly in the past. (Meanwhile, for similar ongoing Hate Years in regard to immigration see CNN and Lou Dobbs...) This helps the establishment generally and the Obama administration in particular to "manage expectations" raised by sweeping progressive campaign rhetoric. It gives ruling party Orwellisms a pass. It overlooks the brazen duplicitous propaganda of the current rulers – never mind that they all along as background clinically and soberly revealed that their sweeping progressive flourishes were not to be taken seriously, that is honestly. In this empire of lies, to fuel this empire of lies, the financial institutions – the core funders of both the Democrats and the Republicans that are currently thieving bottom-less dollars from taxpayers by way of the Obama administration – gave more money to candidate Obama than to candidate McCain. For now at least, the Obama crowd are more the establishment's preferred front faces than are the "Hate Week" "Axis of Evil" demonizers. Wood gives an Orwellian pass to the current rulers.

Like a "good liberal" – though many liberals (Hillary Clinton, for example) ludicrously prefer to be thought of as "progressive and perhaps soon as "socialist" – Wood lauds the establishment line about the basic economic status quo, giving the impression that "upwardly mobile working classes" change society enough to justify it. At least Wood gives no indication otherwise. Where has he written for libertarian socialism or for much or any vision of emancipation from class and conquest? That's no minor or irrelevant part of literature, or shouldn't be. He gives a few nods to the oblique or round-about, say, the allegories of Saramago, while part-and-parcel with the establishment he largely ignores or distorts central works and tendencies in literature that are especially libera-tory and compre-hensive and basic – for example: of the Victorian era, Victor Hugo's anti death penalty novel The Last Day of a Condemned Man (1829) and his anti-class-exploitation novel, Les Misérables (1862); of the "modernist" era George Orwell's liberatory partisan nonfiction narrative Homage to Catalonia (1938); of today Ngũgĩ wa Thiong'o's unsurpassed novel Wizard of the Crow (2006). Les Misérables and Wizard of the Crow are as great as any novels ever written, plus of more profound, comprehen-sive, and quality norms than perhaps any. Wood has never mentioned these tremendous works, or others of the sort, while writing out of history the liberatory tendency of which they are part – sent down the Orwellian memory hole – and instead expounds at length along the establishment's bunkered path.

The Sinister Fact

Where are today's liberatory critics? At Counter-punch. ZNet. Liberation Lit and related sites. And scattered in some limited handfuls in virtually in-visible academic journals. The status quo discour-ages them and filters them out. One does not be-come either a New Republic or a New Yorker critic by taking a much liberatory route. Instead one pro-pounds a liberal (and conservative and reactionary) literature of class oppression, repression, distor-tion, or marginalization. In fact, one had better take issue with those who do venture too close, too deep into the more fully liberatory, as Wood does in chastising Orwell for not appreciating the appeal and benefits of "upward mobility," while essential-ly blanking any mention that Orwell went out of his way to put his life on the line for full working class emancipation. Wood, at best, sometimes lauds improvements in the conditions of oppression, while mainly propounding the point of view of the victors, the basic status quo, the so-called "conven-tional wisdom" of which Wood is largely a synthe-sizer and delimiter in literature. Orwell dared more – intellectually, not to mention otherwise – and in doing so achieved far more of vital insight and work than Wood and the New Yorker can allow. With the New Yorker goes the vast majority of the literary establishment, academic and otherwise, minimal ranging aside.

In addition to extraordinary work that is especially accomplished, like Wizard of the Crow, there are other less accomplished but extremely important and powerful popular novels like Harriet Beecher Stowe's Uncle Tom's Cabin that also get regularly slighted and dismissed by the relatively prominent, including Keith Gessen in his introduction to the second book of the recent two volume edition of Orwell's work. No slight intend-ed! Gessen would no doubt protest, though unless he can read the future, he has no way of knowing that Orwell is wrong, let alone "howlingly wrong when [Orwell] says that *Uncle Tom's Cabin* will out-live the complete works of Virginia Woolf."

First, Uncle Tom's Cabin and Woolf's complete works both remain of general interest, both may try one's patience, both are valuable and compelling. Second, due to historical and social reasons, Uncle Tom's Cabin is at least as culturally integral as Woolf's complete works, possibly moreso and plausibly *considerably* mo-reso. Meanwhile, the novel continues to sell well, as do Woolf's works. Third, speaking of the accuracy of "outliving," in his 1945 essay "Good Bad Books," Orwell explained:

> Perhaps the supreme example of the 'good bad' book is Uncle Tom's Cabin. It is an un-intentionally ludicrous book, full of prepos-terous melodramatic incidents; it is also deeply moving and essentially true; it is hard to say which quality outweighs the oth-er. But Uncle Tom's Cabin, after all, is trying to be serious and to deal with the real world. How about the frankly escapist writers, the purveyors of thrills and 'light' humour? How about Sherlock Holmes, Vice Versa, Dracula, Helen's Babies or King Solomon's Mines? All of these are definitely absurd books, books which one is more inclined to laugh at than with, and which were hardly taken seriously even by their authors; yet they have survived, and will probably con-tinue to do so. All one can say is that, while civilisation remains such that one needs dis-traction from time to time, 'light' literature has its appointed place; also that there is such a thing as sheer skill, or native grace, which may have more survival value than erudition or intellectual power. There are music-hall songs which are better poems than three-quarters of the stuff that gets into the anthologies…[which] I would far rather have written…. And by the same token I would back Uncle Tom's Cabin to outlive the complete works of Virginia Woolf or George Moore….

By now, Orwell's "backing" of Uncle Tom's Cabin over George Moore appears ever more solid, and time will have to tell regarding the works of Vir-ginia Woolf. At this point, both Uncle Tom's Cabin and Woolf's works seem they may be equally dura-ble, as much as any other outcome. That's far from a "howlingly wrong" estimation of the books' com-parative durability after these few decades, let alone of their ultimate durability. But Gessen like Wood conveys a smug, presumptuous, corrosive, and misleading "conventional wisdom." Gessen conveys an establishment impression that libera-tory works like Uncle Tom's Cabin do not measure up to certain establishment favorites (let alone sur-pass them socially or culturally), and even are laughingly not worth the time of day – an impres-sion that comes across, intended or not – that great estimations of the lasting nature of such liberatory works are to be laughed at to the point of howling. The indoctrination goes deep. Uncle Tom's Cabin more enduring than Woolf's complete works? Everyone knows that's a howler! Wait a minute. The fact is, Stowe's novel and Woolf's works both con-tinue to be strong sellers. The jury is still out, and the verdict has not remotely begun to be returned conclusively. But Harvard grad Gessen is howling, his mind educated to its foregone conclusion, how-ever empirically challenged, however theoretically lacking. Which is actually what may sensibly draw a laugh in all this. Upton Sinclair's kindred novel to Uncle Tom's Cabin, The Jungle, is doing well also. How finely written is much of, say, the Bible or the several millennia old epic of Gilgamesh? How enduring?

The New Yorker's lead story for the issue of Wood's essay on Orwell asks as title: "Can Iran Change?" More telling to ask, Can the US? Can the New Yorker change? Can status quo criticism? I suppose they can – at the point of revolution, prob-ably best arrived at step by step. This article on Orwell is certainly no step, except backwards. To further help see why such work gets published as it does, we turn again to Orwell in "The Freedom of the Press," an excerpt from his suppressed preface to Animal Farm:

> The sinister fact about literary censorship in England is that it is largely voluntary. Un-popular ideas can be silenced, and inconven-ient facts kept dark, without the need for any official ban.... The British press is ex-tremely centralized, and most of it is owned by wealthy men who have every motive to be dishonest on certain important topics. But the same kind of veiled censorship also op-erates in books and periodicals, as well as in plays, films and radio. At any given moment there is an orthodoxy, a body of ideas which it is assumed that all right-thinking people will accept without question. It is not exactly forbidden to say this, that or the other, but it is 'not done' to say it, just as in mid-Victor-ian times it was 'not done' to mention trou-ser in the presence of a lady. Anyone who challenges the prevailing orthodoxy finds himself silenced with surprising effective-ness. A genuinely unfashionable opinion is almost never given a fair hearing, either in the popular press or in the highbrow period-icals.

This from even Orwell, who was far from always the most progressive or revolutionary (sometimes the flip opposite) writer or thinker one might find or imagine.

Moving Beyond Class Structure

While there are some real individual and social gains from "upward mobility," there are those cen-tral and fundamental features of life in an oppres-sive system that no amount of "upward mobility" can touch, and which Wood scarcely approaches in the New Yorker article, or ever much concerns himself with, unlike Orwell. Class mobility is far from any guarantor of overcoming as a society the unjust and devastating class structure and imperial nature of states. In fact, class mobility greatly func-tions to preserve the fundamentally inegalitarian and anti-democracy hierarchies found throughout "the West" and beyond. In a review of Paul Lauter and Ann Fitzgerald's anthology, Literature, Class and Culture, Lisa A. Cooper notes:

> As Laura Hapke points out, in working-class writings, students' belief systems are called into question as they read works 'that chal-lenge rather than celebrate upward mobili-ty,' and upward mobility and this idea of a shared notion of success is what most mid-dle or upper class students have been taught to give credence to in capitalistic society.

Additionally, class mobility works both ways in the US, the much lauded land of upward mobility (more and more a relative myth). Leaving even the recent economic collapse aside – the ongoing multi-trillion dollar thefts from the populace by the wealthy ruling classes – the US prison system con-tinues to grow like the tortur-ing monster that it is. Even the establishment New Yorker recently gave some decent related insight into this, in its article "Hellhole" by Atul Gawande, on the widespread practice of torture in US prisons that is long term-solitary con-finement (among other official barbari-ties). By 2006, "1 of every 31 adults in the US was on probation or parole or incarcerated in jail or prison" – the highest rate of incarceration and the largest prison population of any country anywhere – not to mention those imprisoned or living and dying under US guns all around the globe. The sun never sets on the US garrisons and guns of the world, as with the British Em-pire of old. Neither does the sun set on its Em-pire of lies and its other deceptions and misrep-resentations, fostered near and far by establish-ment media and other institu-tions of the status quo.

Since class-based society fosters mobility both up and down, does that mean its inhabi-tants whether privileged or virtual vassals, serfs, and real prisoners are doubly free? Or should they be working, thinking, and organiz-ing internationally and domestically toward progressive and revolu-tionary accomplish-ments that achieve and surpass those temporar-ily gained in Spain, and more perm-anently elsewhere – or should one wish to be and "re-semble" the relatively privileged classes and their typical literary criticism (and fiction), such as in the New Yorker that sees fit to send con-tinuous-ly down the memory hole key libera-tory realities and possibilities?

Apparently some particular class or reader-ship might be tempted to "gloat" over any of Orwell's shortcomings, for Wood is compelled to add that "it is too easy to gloat over his con-tradictions." Gloat? Now who – which people, which classes – would want to "gloat" over Or-well's "contradic-tions"? The ones whom Or-well at his best wrote on behalf of and fought alongside? Or...the privileged classes. Orwell

noted in 1946: "Every line of serious work that I have written since 1936 has been writ-ten, di-rectly or indirectly, *against* totalitarianism and *for* democratic socialism, as I understand it." So who are these anti-democratic-socialists so cra-ven as to apparently instinctively "gloat" over the contradictions, perceived and otherwise, of Orwell? The implications are striking.

In The Lion and the Unicorn: Socialism and the English Genius, Orwell wrote that ruling types could:

> keep society in its existing shape only by be-ing unable to grasp that any im-provement was possible. Difficult though this was, they achieved it, largely by fix-ing their eyes on the past and refusing to notice the changes that were going on round them.

Orwell:

> They are not wicked, or not altogether wick-ed; they are merely unteachable. Only when their money and power are gone will the younger among them begin to grasp what century they are living in.

Orwell:

> Even among the inner clique of politicians who brought us to our present pass [World War II] it is doubtful whether there were any conscious traitors. The corruption is more in the nature of self-deception... And being un-conscious, it is limited. One sees this at its most obvious in the English press. Is the English press honest or dishonest? At nor-mal times it is deeply dishonest. All the pap-ers that matter live off their advertisements, and the advertisers exercise an indirect cen-sorship over news. Yet I do not suppose there is one paper in England that can be straight-forwardly bribed with hard cash.

Orwell:

> The underlying fact was that the whole posi-tion of the monied class had long ceased to be justifiable.

Wood's emphasis on "upward mobility" gives the impression that the upper classes are the hope of the working classes, a place to escape to, where they may become the new managers and class sys-tem enforcers – devil take the hindmost. It sure worked like nothing else in Weimar and Nazi Germany. Journalist Alex Constantine observes:

> To quote [historian] Felix Gilbert, 'At the time the Nazis took over, recovery from the recession was beginning' and Germany was economically prospering...
>
> Economic prosperity, however, as catch-words like public works and infrastructure programs reveal, also meant the continued Americanization of Germany's economy under Hitler. Indeed, the dictator himself seems to have welcomed America's efficient methods of production. Hitler was, for in-stance, a proponent of mass-consumption, as shown by his statement from September 1941: 'Frugality is the enemy of progress. Therein we are similar to the Americans, that we are fastidious.' [Historian] Detlev Peukert underlines Hitler's pro-American stance, arguing that, not unlike the U.S., the Third Reich consciously aimed to represent 'the dawning of the new achievement-orientated consumer society based on the nuclear family, upward mobility, mass media, leisure and an interventionist welfare state [...].'

And mass incarceration. Alongside "upward mo-bility." Ah, that will do the trick. Things sure turned out well. That was quite a path, that route of mass confinement and upward mobility. Quite a final solution. Today: the great American lockup and Good Americans moving up to help admini-ster and expand Empire USA, the Good British al-ways ready to lend a helping military hand. "The descent into barbarism" of Germany in a mere de-cade from much admired heights of Western civil-ization – forgotten already? Conditions today are especially volatile and disastrous for many, and not only socially – also environmentally and militarily– in part due to the establishment notion of "eco-nomic growth" that conquests and trashes the earth. Conditions are grave. (Meanwhile there exist far more constructive realities and movements in the arts and culture, in society and politics however marginalized – efforts that struggle for all the en-ergy, growth, support, and progress they can pos-sibly achieve.)

Orwell:

> There they sat, at the center of a vast empire and a worldwide financial network, drawing interest and profits and spending them – on what? The British ruling class obviously could not admit to themselves that their use-fulness was at an end. Had they done that they would have had to abdicate. For it was not possible for them to turn themselves into mere bandits, like the American millionaires, consciously clinging to unjust privileges and beating down opposition by bribery and tear-gas bombs. After all, they belonged to a class with a certain tradition, they had been to public schools where the duty of dying for your country, if necessary, is laid down as the first and greatest of the Command-ments. They had to feel themselves true pa-triots, even while they plundered their coun-trymen. Clearly there was only one escape for them – into stupidity.

Into the mental cleansing of history.

Valuing the Work of Orwell

Near the end of his New Yorker article on Orwell, James Wood tutors the establishment to not "gloat" at Orwell's "contradictions." That would be "too easy." Not too mention pitifully superficial, ignor-ant, and outrageously reactionary, particularly due to Wood's blanking of Orwell's most liberatory un-derstandings and efforts.

"Instead," Wood declaims, "one is gratefully struck by how prescient Orwell was, and by how much he got right" and how "curiously precise: he was...because of his contradictions...":

This combination of conservatism and radi-calism, of political sleepiness and insomnia, this centuries-long brotherhood of game-keeper and poacher, which Orwell called 'the English genius', was also Orwell's gen-ius, finding in English life its own ideologic-al brotherhood. For Good and ill, those Eng-lish contradictions have lasted.

So you see, Dear Readers of the New Yorker, we cannot gloat for we would be gloating at the "con-tradictions" of ourselves, for we are not essentially keepers of the status quo, we too are like Orwell at his best, propagandizing for democratic socialism, as he understands it, in everything we write, and in so very much that we do – just so, history has been obliterated into fantasy, in the pages of the New Yorker by the award winning critic (2009 American Society of Magazine Editors' National Magazine Award for criticism).

In this splendid fiction according to James Wood – cultured good liberals and conservatives, or prog-ressive pretenders, need not worry – need not even know – that Orwell was ever so very revolutionary after all, for Wood has leveled such history to the ground, and below. In this he is professionally as-sisted in the Orwell volumes I and II introductions by George Packer also of the New Yorker and Keith Gessen of n+1 in various ways, including fix-ations and ultimate focus on Orwell's nice-ties of form and style. At least English novelist Julian Banes in the New York Review of Books, though a basically establishment write up, spends some time depicting the manufacture of Orwell's reputation as National Treasure, then closes by quoting Orwell and emphasizing that:

> "The central problem—how to prevent pow-er from being abused—remains unsolved." And until then, it is safe to predict that Or-well will remain a living writer.

Even this slim point of emphasis is beyond Wood, Packer, and Gessen for whom Orwell is far more to be cherished and known for his *writing* and his na-tionally treasured "English gen-ius." To Wood and his chorus, Orwell is "us" after all, in the end – the more-or-less talented and privileged status quo. For which we are grateful. He is our brother through and through. Not that there is nothing to that. After all, Orwell was early in his life an Im-perial policeman, and though he emphasized how he despised it, at the end of his life he was a police informer, pointing out leftists or perceived leftists, including Charlie Chaplin. So there is certainly that establishment strain in Orwell.

Except, brazenly unrevealed in Wood's largely socio-political article is Orwell's most vital, greatest socio-political work. Moreover, Orwell pointedly noted that one group had opted out of "the English genius" that Wood says is "Orwell's genius," part of an "ideological brotherhood": *the intellectuals*. They opted out of the English genius, the brotherhood, according to Orwell, and Wood pointedly omits this crucial fact – again, brazenly, especially in this day of the easy check internet. "Nearly everyone," Orwell writes, "whatever his actual conduct may be, responds emotionally to the idea of human brotherhood," that which Wood describes as the "centuries-long brotherhood of gamekeeper and poacher," thus misrepresenting England as a land of legal workers and illegal workers – with no owners, no landlords to employ the gamekeepers or to prosecute the poachers, no monied rulers.

Contra Wood, Orwell in fact explicitly includes in the "brotherhood" the "millionaires" and the "class-structure" and "all ranks of society ... [where] ... the most atrocious injustices, cruelties, lies, snobberies exist everywhere," which he claims are all part of a "cultural unity," except for that one group, long since, the intellectuals. Orwell observes in his 1940 Dickens essay that the "brotherhood" has long been broken, that:

> In one sense it is a feeling that is fifty years out of date. The common man is still living in the mental world of Dickens, but nearly every modern intellectual has gone over to some or other form of totalitarianism. From the Marxist or Fascist point of view, nearly all that Dickens

stands for can be written off as 'bourgeois morality'. But in moral outlook no one could be more 'bourgeois' than the English working classes. The ordinary people in the Western countries have never en-tered, mentally, into the world of 'realism' and power-politics. They may do so before long, in which case Dickens will be as out of date as the cab-horse.

And in its most liberatory forms actual democratic socialism may have a chance. The intellectuals – those who staff and run the governments, those who fill the privileged schools – opted out of the "brotherhood" one hundred and twenty years ago. And it is the establishment intellectuals, like Wood, who have a real stake, ruling stake, in keeping up "the lofty old schools" on both sides of the Atlantic, "much as always," despite "all the transformations," to "educate the upper classes to govern the country," to "wreck" cities and countries and continents and to have their "lovely" homes and "parties." Orwell's "brotherhood," his ostensible "genius," the "English genius," includes considerably more than Wood indicates (the "millionaires, the landlords – the owners) and considerably less (the "intellectuals"), and meanwhile, the brotherhood's masses (working classes) would be "as out of date as the cab-horse" in revolutionary Spain, or in any functioning democracy or socialism worth of the name. For this genius that Wood mischaracterizes we are grateful? So who is "leveling down" and taking insight and possibility with it?[1]

And so it is that Wood leads readers blindly away from many of Orwell's most valuable, out-raged, and revolutionary insights[2] in the article titled with Orwellian flair, "A Fine Rage" and slugged, "George Orwell's revolutions."

Should journals of literature and other art aspire to the crucially gutted literary work so typically vaunted and displayed in the New Yorker and in periodicals of similar ethos? Are there no counter-vailing literary forces at work? No striking prog-ress? No real revolutions in the brewing? None ad-vancing step by step? Would anyone, could any-one, remotely know by reading the prominent literary voices of the US

US and the West? Is there no "sinister fact," no voluntary suppression in the dominant media, the establishment media, any-more? Nothing Orwellian in the New Yorker?

NOTES:

[1] *Worth quoting in its entirety is this comment by "driedchar" to a particular blog post of George Packer, "Reading Orwell: George Packer" in the New Yorker April 23, 2009. "Driedchar is a big fan of John Updike, as noted in another comment. It doesn't get much more establishment than Updike, a long time New Yorker writer. Yet such is the egregiousness of Wood's misrepresentation of George Orwell that even from various points in the establishment one may feel compelled to point out Wood's "irksome … condescension to Orwell and to the working class" and to "the mugging" that Wood delivers, courtesy of the New Yorker, in his article that George Packer calls "excellent." The comment:*

I agree with most of what Packer has to say, except his reference to James Wood's "A Fine Rage" as an "excellent essay." Wood's piece is filled with questionable statements. For example, when he says, "There is a difference between being revolutionary and being a revolutionary, and journalists are not required to be tacticians," he implies that Orwell didn't really understand the realities of revolt. He fails to mention that Orwell fought (voluntarily) on the front lines against the Fascists in the Spanish Civil War. Wood takes a sentence in Orwell's "The Lion and the Unicorn" ("However horrible this system [Fascism] may seem to us, it works.") out of context and uses it to conclude: "So the example of efficient Fascism is what inspires the hope of efficient socialism." Wood fails to point out that in "The Lion and the Unicorn," not to mention many other essays and reviews, Orwell is at pains to distinguish between Fascism and socialism. For example, in "The Lion and the Unicorn," Orwell says, "Hitler's real self is in Mein Kampf, and in his actions. He has never persecuted the rich, except when they were Jews or when they tried actively to oppose him. He stands for a centralized economy which robs the capitalist of most of his power but leaves the structure of society much as before. The State controls industry, but there are still rich and poor, masters and men.

Therefore, as against genuine Socialism, the moneyed class have always been on his side." Orwell goes on to describe Fascism as "spectacular, conscious treachery." Wood is wrong to connect Orwell's socialism with Hitler's fascism. He is also wrong to allege Orwell's "reputation's later theft at the hands of the right wing." What exactly is Wood referring to here? Is it something disparaging T. S. Eliot and/or Malcolm Muggeridge said about "Animal Farm"? Wood does not substantiate his allegation; he merely says Orwell's reputation was stolen by the Right. As far as I know, no such "theft" ever took place. Wood describes Orwell as a "puritan masochist." Puritan apparently because he is sensitive to squalor; masochist because he repeatedly immersed himself in squalor? A fairer interpretation is that Orwell was onto a great subject – poverty and working class suffering – and that he was very good at describing it. The most irksome aspect of Wood's piece is his condescension to Orwell and to the working class. He says of Orwell, "But it is too easy to gloat over his contradictions.... Gloat? Implicit in that is Wood's enjoyment of the mugging he's administering. Regarding the working class, Wood quotes Orwell on Dickens: "However much Dickens may admire the working classes, he does not wish to resemble them." Woods then asks, "Why on earth should Dickens have wanted to resemble the working classes? Why would anyone want to, least of all the working classes themselves?" Well, I for one identify with the working classes and proudly consider myself part of them. I believe Wood is coming across here as quite a snob. I have only touched on a few of the many troublesome and problematic aspects of James Wood's "A Fine Rage." Far from being "excellent," as Packer describes it, it is thoroughly rotten and regrettable.

[2] An excerpt from George Orwell's Homage to Catalonia:

I had dropped more or less by chance into the only community of any size in Western Europe where political consciousness and disbelief in capitalism were more normal than their opposites. Up here in Aragon one was among tens of thousands of people, mainly though not entirely of working-class origin, all living at the same level and mingling on terms of equality. In theory it was perfect equality, and even in practice it was not far from it. There is a sense in which it would be true to say that one was experiencing a foretaste of Socialism, by which I mean that the prevailing mental atmosphere was that of Socialism. Many of the normal motives of civilized life – snobbishness, money-grubbing, fear of the boss, etc. – had simply ceased to exist. The ordinary class-division of society had disappeared to an extent that is almost unthinkable in the mon-ey-tainted air of England; there was no one there except the peasants and ourselves, and no one owned anyone else as his master. Of course such a state of affairs could not last. It was simply a temp-orary and local phase in an enormous game that is being played over the whole surface of the earth. But it lasted long enough to have its effect upon anyone who experienced it. However much one cursed at the time, one realized afterwards that one had been in contact with something strange and valuable. One had been in a community where hope was more normal than apathy or cynicism, where the word 'comrade' stood for comradeship and not, as in most countries, for humbug. One had breathed the air of equality. I am well aware that it is now the fashion to deny that Socialism has anything to do with equality. In every country in the world a huge tribe of party-hacks and sleek little professors are busy 'proving' that Socialism means no more than a planned state-capitalism with the grab-motive left intact. But fortunately there also exists a vision of Socialism quite different from this. The thing that attracts ordinary men to Socialism and makes them willing to risk their skins for it, the 'mystique' of Socialism, is the idea of equality; to the vast majority of people Socialism means a classless society, or it means nothing at all.... In that community where no one was on the make, where there was a shortage of everything but no boot-licking, one got, perhaps, a crude forecast of what the opening stages of Socialism might be like. And, after all, instead of disillusioning me it deeply attracted me....

This was in late December 1936 [in Barcelona], less than seven months ago as I write, and yet it is a period that has already receded into enormous distance. Later events have obliterated it much more completely than they have obliterated 1935, or 1905, for that matter. I had come to Spain with some notion of writing newspaper articles, but I had joined the militia almost immediately, because at that time and in that atmosphere it seemed the only conceivable thing to do. The Anarchists were still in virtual control of Catalonia and the revolution was still in full swing.

To anyone who had been there since the beginning it probably seemed even in December or January that the revolutionary period was ending; but when one came straight from England the aspect of Barcelona was something startling and overwhelming. It was the first time that I had ever been in a town where the working class was in the saddle. Practically every building of any size had been seized by the work-ers and was draped with red flags or with the red and black flag of the Anarchists; every wall was scrawled with the hammer and sickle and with the initials of the revolutionary parties; almost every church had been gutted and its images burnt. Churches here and there were being systematically demolished by gangs of workman. Every shop and cafe had an inscription saying that it had been collectivised; even the boot-blacks had been collectivized and their boxes painted red and black. Waiters and shop-walkers looked you in the face and treated you as an equal. Servile and even ceremonial forms of speech had temporarily disappeared. Nobody said 'Señor' or 'Don' or even 'Usted'; everyone called everyone else 'Comrade' or 'Thou', and said 'Salud!' instead of 'Buenos dias'. Tipping had been forbidden by law since the time of Primo de Rivera; almost my first experience was receiving a lecture from a hotel manager for trying to tip a lift-boy. There were no private motor-cars, they had all been commandeered, and the trams and taxis and much of the other transport were painted red and black. The revolutionary posters were everywhere, flaming from the walls in clean reds and blues that made the few remaining advertisements look like daubs of mud. Down the Ramblas, the wide central artery of the town where crowds of people streamed constantly to and fro, the loud-speakers were bellowing revolutionary songs all day and far into the night. And it was the aspect of the crowds that was the queerest thing of all. In outward appearance it was a town in which the wealthy classes had practically ceased to exist. Except for a small number of women and foreigners there were no 'well-dressed' people at all. Practically everyone wore rough working-class clothes, or blue overalls or some variant of militia uniform. All this was queer and moving. There was much in this that I did not understand, in some ways I did not even like it, but I recognized it immediately as a state of affairs worth fighting for. Also, I believed that things were as they appeared, that this was really a workers' State and that the en-tire bourgeoisie had either fled, been killed or voluntarily come over to the workers' side; I did not realise that great numbers of well-to-do bourgeois were simply lying low and disguising themselves as proletarians for the time being.

Together with all this there was something of the evil atmosphere of war. The town had a gaunt untidy look, roads and buildings were in poor repair, the streets at night were dimly lit for fear of air-raids, the shops were mostly shabby and half-empty. Meat was scarce and milk practically unobtainable, there was a shortage of coal, sugar and petrol, and a really serious shortage of bread. Even at this period the bread-queues were often hundreds of yards long. Yet so far as one could judge the people were contented and hopeful. There was no unemployment, and the price of living was still extremely low; you saw very few conspicuously destitute people and no beggars except the gypsies. Above all, there was a belief in the revolution and the future, a feeling of having suddenly emerged into an era of equality and freedom. Human beings were trying to behave as human beings and not as cogs in the capitalist machine. In the barbers' shops were Anarchist notices (the barbers were mostly Anarchists) solemnly explaining that barbers were no longer slaves. In the streets were coloured posters appealing to prostitutes to stop being prostitutes. To anyone from the hard-boiled, sneering civilization of the English-speaking races there was something rather pathetic in the literalness with which these idealistic Spaniards took the hackneyed phrase of revolution. At that time revolutionary ballads of the naivest kind, all about the proletarian brotherhood and the wickedness of Mussolini, were being sold on the streets for a few centimes each. I have often seen an illiterate militia-man buy one of these ballads, laboriously spell out the words, and then, when he had got the hang of it, begin singing it to an appropriate tune.

LIBERATORY LITERATURE

It is useful to understand "liberatory" in two basic ways for literature. In the past the term in lit has been used mainly in regard to "women's lib" of the '60s, '70s as far as I'm aware – I don't recall that the lit critics of the '30s and so on use it, though it near-ly gets into the title of one of

VF Calverton's books, and maybe it is used in passing somewhere or an-other. More or less progressive critics of that time used words more like "revolutionary" and "prole-tarian" and "Marxist" or "materialist." One broad basic sense of liberatory is in reference to about any sort of freeing or advancing or progressing phenomena of literature, especially in regard to norm-ative issues (morals and ethics…politics and cul-ture) and less so (secondarily or as derivative) aesthetically. So, for example, the multicultural expansion of recent decades is liberatory in this sense even when it occurs in basically a liberal and conservative or other status quo framework. In this sense, "liberatory" is a synonym for "progressive" (or "enlightened" – as in of the Enlightenment – or moving toward "ideal") however limited or bound that progress may be. Elements of liberalism and conservatism contain some liberatory aspects also (especially in having some roots in the Enlightenment or other relation to it). All this understands liberatory in a very broad sense of the term.

The primary and most crucial sense in which we might understand liberatory is to distinguish prog-ressive or revolutionary literature from status quo work that blocks or slows progress (let alone revo-lution) actively or passively, inadvertently or knowingly. Again, the term refers in this use main-ly to normative respects of literature as revealed in a story's substance, effects, functions, and conse-quences. Revolutionary lit, or to be more clear, lib-eratory revolutionary lit is the strongest sense in which the term might be used – again referring essentially to normative revolution, whether or not the aesthetics are also much revolutionized or ad-vanced.

"Liberatory" may be used to indicate typically progressive or revolutionary instances of literature that the establishment discriminates against (know-ingly or not), ideologically opposes (very often while claiming and believing otherwise). There will always be a need to push for increasingly libera-tory lit and life conditions, so it's no fixed or ulti-mately knowable thing, even in the ideal, though very concrete instances, understandings, and para-meters can be known and realized and fought for and against…and certainly are. Plenty of documentation. The central work of Victor Hugo and others has been ideologically opposed and repres-sed in many ways by the establishment for its lib-eratory features (asinine ideological takedowns of even the canonical Shelley for his progressive/ rev-olutionary features are still a regular phenomenon, or Shelley's most liberatory elements are elided – e.g., see Adam Kirsch for the trademark shock troop establishment flourish and smear, with grat-uitous repugnance). Meanwhile authors like Joyce and Conrad and Dostoevsky have been for the most part the toast of the establishment in ways that help repress far more liberatory novelists, the latter two novelists especially for their political novels, often held up as preeminent political nov-els. This is a great comfort to the establishment for it hides the far more progressive, liberatory, even revolutionary great political novel of, for one cen-tral example of the West, Les Misérables, which is easily a match for any novel ever written, "politi-cal" or otherwise, let alone Hugo's great body of work. More than a match. Reactionary or status quo novels are held up as the model and encourag-ed, supported, acclaimed and one can see what largely follows, normatively, the basically estab-lishmentarian acclaimed works, such as those of Henry James, TS Eliot, Ralph Ellison, Vladimir Nabokov, Saul Bellow, even Philip Roth, these very status quo functional, stylistically or inwardly obsessed scribes for the establishment, and their facilitators. Probably reviews of individual authors are a problem in this regard, rather than periodic liberatory thematic or normative reviews and overviews of lit.

There are particular sociopolitical and historical reasons that make it worth referring to the work of progressive critics of the early part of last century – primarily to recall and emphasize that efflores-cence of more or less liberatory criticism and how buried it has been, forcibly buried, not accidentally. Edward Said is a great recent liberatory critic, and there are a number of others, some of whom I quote at the Socialit subsite, right on up through the decades, as some of the authors write at least in various works and moments. Recent decades have seen another efflorescence of such criticism – much of it with or due to multicultural roots – and it remains striking and problematic that this criticism shows essentially no conscious connection with some of the central groundwork laid decades earli-er. Still written out of history, out of the Norton anthology and everyday lit knowledge, it remains a terrible loss (among others). In any event, taking a look at the century long bibliography and excerpts at the socialit site, it's striking and telling how eth-nically and gender and otherwise diverse much of the better sociopolitical criticism becomes in recent decades. Some visible progress there, to an extent.

A few comments on the more or less progressive or at least sociopolitically engaged critics of the '20s and '30s: James Farrell had more than a bit of the reactionary in him, and Upton Sinclair by and large was somehow maybe not as radical or liberatory ultimately as VF Calverton, Bernard Smith, and Kenneth Burke in their most liberatory moments. For that matter, Calverton published at least one good very early anthology of "Negro" literature in the 1920s. He wrote his first noted and first "lasting" book of criticism/theory too about that time, The Newer Spirit, in his mid twenties. (VF Calverton is a pseudonym for George Goetz – a couple of good fairly recent though obscure biographies of him exist.) That said, Sinclair's Mammonart on whole is rather remarkable. Farrell's book of criticism much less so and is in some ways regressive. The sometimes progressive Granville Hicks wrote a book of criticism (The Great Tradition) similar in spirit to Farrell, was encouraged to, to mitigate the effect and influence of Calverton's Liberation of American Literature, which Hicks was substantially writing against. Calverton was repressed by the general literary establishment, not least by the ostensibly progressive one, Communists/Stalinists and others, for that one of his many books (though not only that book), much like the increasingly progressive critic Maxwell Geismar was heavily repressed by the state-capitalist establishment of the '60s and so on. What a mix and mess it all was, in some ways quite lively, going on basi-

cally outside the academy. In recent decades some of this sort of thing has been going on inside the academy (much of it unfortunately obscure and distant because written by and for relatively niche scholars). In the meantime MFA programs are too much untouched by liberatory criticism – fiction and poetry programs both. It seems only something of an exaggeration to say that plenty of poetry programs would sort of implode if they took seriously Bernard Smith's understanding of TS Eliot, while MFA fiction programs' affinity for Flaubert and the like is largely debilitating.

There are certain imaginative writers and critics who harp comically on formalist concerns, as if they are missing a gene, or possess an absurd extra one, though they are sometimes not completely without sense in their own crevicular way, and they sometimes cull useful works to reference. One "pulls a string" to create art, variously, lifts up and off the top of one's head, but the strings are found in life, high and low, near and far, of myriad revelation and stuff, and not entirely in other strings, or heads. For which we can all be eternally thankful. To describe limited formalist critics as, say, aesthetic incestivists seems largely accurate thought that disparages "aesthetic," which relies on far more than form for its many effects. Much of my art, for example, and not mine alone, has been catalyzed – if not ridden – by sheer white light anger, outrage, or the bitter reality of various injustice – and yet whether then turned comedic, dramatic, satiric, romantic, or fantastic it is sprung from fact and experience, understanding and image and situation, which proceeds to lend shape. Without the stuff of life, there is no art, not beyond the abstract. Literature that refers merely to itself renders the origin of lit impossible and the end of lit its head biting air where its tail would have been – something for and from another planet. The aesthetic abstract can be a catalyst – what can't be? – but not the most vital, the most crucial essence of art, at least not in the novel, possibly not even in its most extreme works.

While authors and activists may be better artists and revolutionaries for thinking well about such technical issues, also for considering what it might mean to come from and for another planet, on normative grounds not least, and while particular aesthetic dynamics may help create powerful art, what basically makes up aesthetics in the novel if not in large part the biting or beautiful stuff of vital normative concerns? Because establishment lit lacks so much of crucial and central import, after a certain point, often soon arrived, aesthetic refineries do not amount to much.

"Some critics consider any mention of content a display of bad taste. Some, more innocent and more modern, have been taught – schooled – to look at paintings in such a way as to make them wholly unaware of content…. But again, we must look upon form as the shape of content…"

– accomplished painter Ben Shahn in The Shape of Content (1957) noting a good rule of thumb for art, from a great essay and book.

Are Henry James, TS Eliot, Saul Bellow, Philip Roth and writers in their veins "inwardly obsessed scribes" as I note? Though my critical emphasis is on how establishmentarian they are, and though I could leave it at that in my various criticisms, I often don't and either refer to such writers as obsessive stylists, or sometimes as obsessive interiorists to help indicate as much what they are not doing, as what they are instead focused on. While the latter may be the most difficult to defend or at least most controversial, I've always gotten the sense that they don't really care all that much about many of the less intimate societal ranges they wander through. It's something like what Robert Alter says in speaking of authors (Pynchon, Barth, Barthelme…Vonnegut) who "finally [do not take] history very seriously," or at least scarcely represent it profoundly or even substantially, Alter concludes, "despite the overwhelming density of actual historical detail in the [novels]." Since James, Bellow, Roth et al seem no more outwardly interested than these authors, or even much less, I make the distinction I do. Their fascination, obsession seems to me to be in the psychological, the inward, moreso than the focus of other types of novelists, the societal gamers, or the hyper quirky, who seem more interested in gaming social landscapes and myriad other elements. I do think that James, Bellow, and Roth have outward curiosity and see themselves as in large part publicly focused. I just don't buy any such intent for much especial actuality. That's controversial, probably, and deserves extensive exploration (someone could probably make a career of it) though not probably by me. Also, often this is how their work is treated, for the fascination of character focus…and it seems to me the particular works ultimately encourage that mainly. So I would extend a version, perhaps greatly modified, of Alter's view to these authors as well.

I get the sense that authors like DeLillo really are much more interested in the outward public societal phenomena that they detail than are these inwardists, as I sometimes refer to them, though still confined in basically status quo veins, and again often or typically passing off appearance of interest for real interest or great substance. (As for TS Eliot, it's a similar argument though maybe revolving more around how his example as a sort of aesthete is used or misused in lit realms.) Lit needs interiorists and virtually all other variety of novelists of course but taken altogether there is basically what Ivan Illich calls a "radical monopoly" for the status quo against much liberatory fiction (not that he was speaking of fiction but of other establishment productions, ideas, and institutions).

A key, highly regarded US novel, establishment novel at least, of the 20th century is Ellison's Invisible Man. It sort of has everything (well, a lot) and it has the obsessions with style and interiority as well as outwardness in linking maybe the most radical era of the century with maybe one of the most repressive, the general socialist upsurge and the "anticommunist" backlash. Without going into extended analysis of the novel, I'll note that in my view Invisible Man is an example of often highly accomplished art that is often highly deplorable, or simply weak, flawed. Others have pointed out some of this in detail. Is the novel liberatory? It has its moments, but on whole no. It's quite an establishment or reactionary novel.

In fiction generally, stylistic obsession, interior obsession, exterior obsession do not determine quality necessarily but can be heavily used in status quo veins to take up plenty of space toward blocking out much liberatory exploration or effects, especially the interior and stylistic, though they can also be used for liberation, as some authors consci-ously attempt outside of status quo ideology and other parameters. (See again a number of the works at Liberation Lit, for example.)

There is no point in gutting "liberatory" of its full range of meaning, and of course no one owns the word. Take A House for Mr. Biswas, an early novel by Nobel prize winning author VS Naipaul. Is it liberatory? Can't say, I've not read Biswas aside from an excerpt years ago, but as James Wood describes the novel it seems it may be somewhat liberatory broadly defined, or at least in moments, as with some other liberal or even con-servative works. That's not the main sense in which I use the world liberatory. Why? Take, for example Naipaul's book Guerrillas. It's an odious novel. Some aesthetics aside. Guerrillas and central parts of Invisible Man are representative of what has been called the "liberal cesspool" though "reactionary mendacity" and "conservative crap" also apply, heavily. Hey, award a Nobel prize, a National Book Award. Praise to the skies (while tossing in an occasional rebuke).

And so the establishment tsunamis on. Thus the need for imaginative writers and critics who write in sheer progressive partisan fashion, to try to help offset the establishment tsunami. It's inaccurate and unfair to claim that such liberatory writing is more political or more ideological than other ways of approaching novels because establishment criticism and fiction is extraordinarily political and ideological too, however privately focused, or unconsciously created and acting, or consciously falsely denying its political and other normative import. Moreover, liberatory writing is often more objective than ostensibly apolitical establishment work, which is frequently warped and debased by the ideology of the paymasters.

Writers would do well to be aware that we live in what has long been the "Age of Propaganda" especially in this country but also of course far be-yond (documented also at the Socialit subsite) – the central and massive institutional and cultural rise of public relations and advertising, by now more than a full century worth. It cannot help but have a profound (perhaps radical) effect on the novel, imaginative literature, for a variety of reasons… also on criticism, which is why liberatory writers may frequently need to repeat points, or especially qualify them near to tedium, or go on at length, or emphatically focus otherwise, because such writers are basically not just repeating conventional wis-dom where everyone nods and goes along with it, having heard and absorbed it before. The propa-ganda with deep and vast institutional roots may be the main monster one writes into and against. Most novels seem to blithely chirp or smudge on oblivious to this new world of the past 100 years or more, a lot like the US Presidential candidates chirping and chipping away at one another while the normative, let alone economic, ground upon which they stand has long been in free fall to the fabled fires of their systems' own making, though they are pleasantly provided protective suits and bubbles within which to live, or exist. They're fro-zen idiotically in time this way. They are the play-ers of official (publishable) appearance, and so they play, and it is so pitifully boring and so limited and so often vacuous, when not sheer fraudulent or ignorant. Are we talking about novels or elections here? Yes – both. That's why some of the stronger novels focus on the private intimate (e.g., Franzen's The Corrections),* because they can be real there (or even ideal) to a much larger extent than one can be in the Orwellian outer world, the public realms … the official, the established, the inculcated and cultured empire of lies – ringed by ostensibly responsible and respectable (if also mouthy and abrasive) gatekeepers who drivel on in a sort of soap opera lunacy.

This is what beheads much would be crucial and accomplished fiction of the public. 500 Palestinians dead? Fine, fine – Israel was feeling a touch nervous. Millions of Iraqis slaughtered? Oh well – the US has been feeling a bit insecure. Tril-lions of dollars worth nothing? So be it – the bank-ers know best. In any case, the bankers and corpse rats own the owned, by fiat, fenced off and disor-ganized in the face of ruling wealth, the Guiding Light of the world. Hail to the Chief, here he comes, Mr. America, and Congress too, bought and paid for, well salaried, ever fresh from bloodbath, put on bright display by their corporate cohorts and a complicit and marauding official culture – lunatic inmates and their financial guards farcing about and running the asylum. Such is the life or class essence of officials and executives and profes-sionals and others in ruling realms: brutal soap opera farce. To get published by the establishment plenty of the most vital public matters have to be written about in truncated or remote absurdist allegory like back in the days of Tsarist Russia, though today the tsunami of propaganda and such, including its style, much of which is trope, can dis-appear much power of allegory – that otherwise oft poor substitute for more direct forms.

The novel that Western fiction may have the most to learn from is Ngũgĩ wa Thiong'o's Wizard of the Crow, of which I've written elsewhere (here and here) – including this:

While not from the US but Africa as Ngũgĩ points out, Wizard of the Crow is far more a global novel than [reviewer] Esposito indicates, and far more a US novel than he hints. Commenting at Amazon.com, Patricia Kramer writes, "The satire is biting, the laughs come often but then the reality of our country's present policies sets in. We would be lucky to have a Wizard of the Crow right now in America."

Such a pointed global epic from the US…would preferably be one that advances well beyond even the mighty Wizard. Such a novel and any clear-eyed criticism will have to wait, and if and when that day arrives, will have to be fought for. That's the reality.

———————————————

*The Corrections is high tech soap opera, more or less well wrought, or at least addictively wrought at a rather verbally refined level, plenty of pastry and sugar that people are famil-iar with (people in fairly ambitious yet somehow dead end lives, as they feel, bred by the millions in this fragmented culture) with just enough nutrition or appearance of nutrition, and not socially devoid either (that is, seemingly). While the work is accomplished, it's far from unflawed, a very status quo novel, and I agree with Mailer that it suffers from a great lack, not hard to realize what sort, I think.

I've always thought that contrary to most opinion the opening page or so is extremely poorly wrought, almost obnoxiously so in its description of nature and so on, yet somewhat sweeping, intriguing nevertheless. It's as if you can tell Franzen was scarcely at all interested in what he was writing right there but that he really felt supercharged to get to what comes next. Sheer supposition though. I don't recall anything normative (or aesthetic) that's much progressive let alone revolutionary about The Corrections. It's a type of head in the sand fiction in regard to much insight about public matters and the larger human condition.

ESTABLISHMENT IDEOLOGY –

SUFFOCATING AND OPPRESSIVE

The Complicit Culture

In literature, as in politics, and plenty of life, there can be a big difference between liberal and left. Lit-erature is not somehow mystically ideology free. Don Quixote, as with many other classics, was written as propaganda. A lot of progressive views are to the left of the basic liberal views of period-icals like The Nation, n+1, The Guardian, London Review of Books, the New Yorker, etc. Substantial left views should be heard in national publications, especially since left views, as I understand them, and as polls reveal, are largely popular views. Instead, many left views are severely drowned out "even" in liberal media, as great media watch or-ganizations like FAIR and Media Lens demon-strate. (Of course in my view conservative and reactionary views are typically as bad as or worse than liberal views.)

Obviously there are some ideological differences between basically liberal publications. There are significant differences between, say, The Nation and the New York Times, and so on. Alexander Cockburn, for example, is a left columnist for the predominantly liberal Nation magazine (though his column space was halved a few years back). The New York Times has no corresponding left columnist, though Paul Krugman occasionally comes close. The Nation is basically a liberal pub-lication with some left tendencies, and its commen-tary on literature reflects its predominantly liberal emphasis, with many left views blocked out and discredited. The New Yorker, though predomin-antly liberal, lies to the right of the Nation. Though liberalism and its variants evince some genuine qualities, they also possess predominant and atro-cious deficiencies, crucial to reveal.

Curiously, even progressive and left publications have poor lit coverage, including the very left Z Magazine, also the progressive Texas Observer. I've disagreed fundamentally with Z's liberalish assessment of the ideological nature of the film Good Will Hunting, for one example. I've also long disagreed with the Texas Observer's choosing to run the essentially liberal fiction it sporadically publishes rather than progressive fiction that would befit the publication. The Texas Observer also recently interviewed, for example, a Palestin-ian American poet who declaims standard liberal status quo ideology about politics in poetry, a pov-erty that can be readily dissected.

Liberatory writers are often decried as ideological by the establishment, a way of spurning and denouncing such fiction for not fitting within the establishment's ideological constraints.

> "Radical critics…have a set of social priorities with which most people at present tend to disagree. This is why they are commonly dismissed as 'ideological', because ideology' is always a way of describing other people's interests rather than our own"
> – Terry Eagleton.

Of course there are important differences between literature and politics, and between the ideology of literature and the ideology of politics. It goes with-out saying, I would think. For example, much ide-ology in imaginative literature has often tended to be more indirect and implicit in articulation and expression than has much nonfiction. Yet there are also crucial similarities, overlaps, intersections. The next time Richard Eder calls antiwar novels cat-egorically "belligerent" in the New York Times, someone from the literature establishment ought to write a letter to the editor about it, which might even get published. Apparently no one of note in the literary world bothered. The NYT certainly did not publish my letter. And some established critic might bother to review the unique, progressive, revelatory Liberation Lit anthology when it comes out in paperback, or even as it currently exists on-line. Established critics could do it pro bono some-where if need be. And if not, why not? Of course, they had better re-examine their ideological under-standings in literature and in general or they will further expose their deficiencies, and poorly ac-count for the literature and life they would discuss.

The idea of left or liberatory or progressive fiction has been buried, long since, as I detail at length in my writings. VF Calverton, editor of the Modern Quarterly for 17 years (for a brief time co-edited by Edmund Wilson and others of note), has penned some of the most central understandings of liberatory fiction in his book The Liberation of American Literature (1932) – along with Bernard Smith in Forces in American Criticism (1939), also Kenneth Burke in The Philosophy of Literary Form (1941), and Upton Sinclair in Mammonart (1924). With the partial exception of Burke's book, these crucial texts have been buried. The attempt to bury Calverton's views was strongly carried out even in his own lifetime (he died at age 40 in 1940 after publishing more than a dozen books). Sinclair had to self publish Mammonart (in book form), and so on.

The rise of New Criticism was in many ways directly opposed, centrally opposed, to the rise of a variety of "progressive" literatures – revolutionary, materialist/marxist, liberatory, propagandistic, par-tisan, documentary, etc. In the establishment in the US, New Criticism (varieties of formalism, narrow aestheticism, then abstract art, and later theory rather than the "old criticism" sociopolitically en-gaged) was given plenty of state/corporate support and funding, and succeeded to the point of burying even a conception of what liberatory or progressive literature basically means, or might, the progres-sive and revolutionary thinking and action that rose out of the ashes of World Wars I, II, and the Great Depression.

Central works of this vital tendency of liberatory criticism certainly do not make it into the Norton Anthology of Theory and Criticism, nor into even Gordon Hutner's excellent historical anthology of criticism. It's basically wiped out of history. Vincent Leitch, the editor of the massive Norton Anthology, is one of the very few people who even seems to know something of what has been lost. Even the rebirth of Marxist criticism in the 1970s deviated from "history and sociology" in that, as Leitch notes: "What was odd about the Marxist criticism of this [1970s] Renaissance associated with the post-1950s new left and the Movement was its complete disregard of the old left. Mention was never made of V. F. Calverton, James T. Farrell, Granville Hicks, Bernard Smith, Edmund Wilson, or other Leftist Critics prominent in the thirties. The native tradition of radicalism stemming from the nineteenth century had been forgotten during the heyday of the new left...."

"Complete disregard," yes, though it seems "forgotten" is partly the wrong word, and it is not "odd" because the propaganda tide against it has long been intense, heavily funded and supported, and the persecution significant to overwhelming.

Leitch continues, "In H. Bruce Franklin's view, what was wrong with academic literary profession-als was their thorough immersion in the bourgeois ideology of formalism, which it-self was rooted in the counterrevolutionary anti-proletarianism of the thirties. 'In the present era, formalism is the use of aestheticism to blind us to social and moral reality' ..."

The greatest counterrevolutionary achievement in US literature is that virtually no one knows the history of progressive, liberatory criticism, or even what it means.[1] It's not even clear that more than a small minority know much what is meant by counterrevolutionary and revolutionary – the normative implications and distinctions.

England is apparently no better. The England based Booker prize awarded its 2008 prize to Aravind Adiga's novel The White Tiger that even others in the establishment can see is lacking. Amitava Kumar via the Boston Review finds "Adiga's villains utterly cartoonish, like the characters in Bollywood melodrama. However, it is his presenta-tion of ordinary people that seems not only trite but also offensive."

Compared to what Kumar has "witnessed," Adiga "knows next to nothing" about the reality he writes about. Adiga's work is "false"…"wrong"… "belies…truth" and is at times, though not always, literarily poor: "utterly cartoonish, like the charact-ers in Bolly-wood melodrama." The establishment struggles to deliver even to the level of some laud-able liberal sensibilities.

In other words, according to Kumar, the 2008 Booker Prize novel is too often a lie, let alone poor-ly wrought. Much of the establishment focuses on how well wrought something is, and typically scants or distorts normative analysis, especially failing to examine or to understand how revelatory the work may or may not be in progressive let alone revolutionary veins, or how much of a lie it may or may not be, not least given the ideological assertions and implications and consequences therein and there from.

Skewed or false norms are more fundamental than craft refinements. Moreover, normative accomplishments and weaknesses are not only inte-grally interrelated with form, they exist and func-tion as a major part of aesthetics. To scant or distort normative elements or to critique as if they do not exist or matter much – to emphasize or merely show that The White Tiger is not a very good novel in literary terms (the typical status quo critical re-view) – is to eviscerate story and discussion of it, or at best to remove discussion to abstract technical grounds uncertainly, superficially, or falsely grounded.

Overt liberatory revolutionary fiction is so an-athema to the lit establishment that it is filtered very much out, de facto censored. This is no game of who is more progressive than whom – it is an institutional and normative analysis of what is tol-erated and encouraged by the establishment, and what is not. It is no game that so much of the lit establishment in the US virtually writes central, great liberatory novelist Victor Hugo out of history, particularly in lieu of Flaubert (a prominent MFA, political, and formalist establishment favorite), though it's pretty close to farce and sheer ignorance and worse. Flaubert is like Hugo's appendix – even establishment scholar Victor Brombert seemed to gain some inkling of this late in his career. Hugo has more to say about literature in his book *William Shakespeare* alone than anything I've seen by or about Flaubert. Moreover, Hugo's great novels, The Last Day of a Condemned Man, Les Misérables in particular, and Ninety-Three (even leaving aside Notre-Dame de Paris, and others), dwarf the best that Flaubert could manage, and over a 45 year span. It's not only a question of the works of Hugo being far more liberatory than those of Flaubert, but more generally intelligent and otherwise ac-complished, even in many ways aesthetically so, and not least. Hugo has been far more influential than the lit establishment typically knows, or al-lows, tolerates, wishes, or is comfortable with – the cap has been held on.

Progressive periodicals scarcely serialize fiction anymore, long since, places where authors like Up-ton Sinclair and even the soon to be reactionary Ralph Ellison were early published. It's all self and small scale collective publishing now. Meanwhile the establishment creaks and stinks on enormously, if not entirely. Ideologically status quo authors are safe for the establishment – their prominence and renown has necessarily nothing to do with literary quality or other vitality, though enforced lack of opportunity can surely crush the potential of liber-atory

authors and others discriminated against – including at one time or another, and to various ex-tents today, black writers, native writers, women writers, slave writers, prison writers, and so on.

In recent years in circles of relative prominence it has been left to Terry Eagleton but especially and moreso to the great John Pilger to take to task the lit establishment for its various complicities in war and aggression, and other atrocities, in Pilger's var-ious Silence of the Writers articles. It remains mon-strously spectacular how little overt antiwar fiction has been published, for example.

Such authors must really be incompetent. They must be immensely stupid or untalented, the explicit and liberatory antiwar writers.

Or just taboo, in a complicit culture.

MALCOLM FINCH
AND THE LIMITS OF LIBERAL FICTION

Or rather, Atticus Gladwell.

It's telling that one of the most valuable pieces of criticism of fiction to come out of the New Yorker in a while was not written by any of its literary critics but by another staff writer, Malcolm Gladwell. It's telling additionally that on the eve of the 50th anniversary of the central US novel To Kill a Mockingbird, a review of the novel and its fit in society was either declined by the entire lit crit staff and all adjunct literary reviewers of the New Yorker or was directed away from all of them. Maybe they were all on vacation, forced or otherwise. One can see why. After all, George Packer, James Wood, and Keith Gessen were recently exposed for their severe distortions of another socially central writer, George Orwell; and Louis Menand recently admitted in a review of Pynchon's latest novel that "I could be missing something, of course. I could be missing everything" in regard to the existence of allusions in the text of a writer famed for allusions. Perhaps New Yorker subscribers don't mind such cavalier attitude to their subscription funds.

Regardless, Gladwell's article, "The Courthouse Ring," goes only a small step forward in New Yorker criticism. Who knew that an early 1960s portrayal of an early 1930s Southern lawyer in a small town would reveal "the limits of Southern liberalism" rather than "instruct us about the world"? Well but Gladwell may mean that the (white) masses hold this belief that goes against reason. But the masses encouraged and "led" by whom? The publishing and lit industry? The corporate-state, its media and schools? Surely not.

Though Gladwell usefully spells out some points of concern, the sociopolitical limits of Harper Lee's novel are much greater than Gladwell states. Not only were "civil-rights activists … arriving in the South as Lee wrote her novel," they had arrived in force for the Scottsboro trial (in Alabama) in the early 1930s, when the novel was set. However, as James A. Miller notes in "Harper Lee's To Kill a Mockingbird: The Final Stage of the Scottsboro Narrative," the novel guts the larger world from Lee's trial of a black man falsely accused of rape by a white woman despite (or maybe because of) its echo of these same central features of the Scottsboro trial. In Lee's novel, with its Scottsboro-type crime against the (black) people in guise of crime of the (black) people, Miller notes:

"There is no Helen Marcy [an organizer / journalist of the Communist Party] and no Hollace Ransdall [a western/northern investigative journalist for the ACLU]; no organizers from the International Labor Defense [ILD] …, no reporters from the national press, no national and international protesters, no U.S. Supreme Court hovering in the background. The case of Tom Robinson is a local matter…"

Tom Robinson, the falsely accused and Finch's client, was convicted and then, fleeing in real fear for his life, killed. And Finch became a US hero:

"the number one hero in American movie history, according to a recent American Film Institute survey." [Miller]

Meanwhile:

"According to a 1991 'Survey of Lifetime Reading Habits' conducted by the Book-of-the-Month Club and the Library of Congress's Center for the Book, Mockingbird was regarded by its 5,000 respondents as one of three most influential books in people's lives, second only to the Bible." [Miller]

So a novel that Eric Sundquist plausibly notes "is the most widely read twentieth-century American work of fiction devoted to the issue of race" guts from its story the key progressive realities, let alone possibilities, of the world in which it was set and published. The lit establishment is more inclined to smear Communism, as in Ralph Ellison's highly acclaimed novel Invisible Man, and to delimit or to cut vital human rights actions and movements from history. In regard to the sociopolitical elements of the factual Scottsboro narrative and the fictional To Kill a Mockingbird narrative, and keeping in mind that the sociopolitical not only impacts but actually makes up a large portion of the personal elements of life, the Scottsboro narrative is far more sweeping and revealing than the by comparison demoralized and demoralizing To Kill a Mockingbird narrative. But the literary establishment has come to embrace Invisible Man as a top or the top US literary novel of the 20th century and has done little to effectively critique To Kill a Mockingbird.

Likewise, hundreds of thousands of copies of F. Scott Fitzgerald's 1925 novel The Great Gatsby are sold each year. Meanwhile, Claude McKay's 1929 novel Banjo, which is at least as accomplished and probably far more vital, remains virtually unknown. The Great Gatsby ranks 2nd on the Modern Library's list of the 100 Best Novels of the 20th Century. Banjo does not appear.

While To Kill a Mockingbird has some great qualities, it badly guts and stunts not only reality but the imagination. "The limits of Southern liberalism" is the caption of Gladwell's article on the famed novel, but the novel had huge New York and national imprint and involvement in its production and creation and further dissemination (the film), as well as having strong current relation (in a variety of ways). The work greatly typifies the limits of liberalism in general: limiting and "underselling" key human rights elements of fiction and life. Thus, Gladwell's article itself is a study in the limits of liberalism but of the national or corporate-state variety and is not the beacon of enlightened norms it implies it is, except to very limited degree – albeit one that was too much for other parts of the liberal-conservative-reactionay establishment and fellow travelers to tolerate.

The article, as a stunted look back and around, mirrors the novel in unfortunate ways, and yet again like the novel, it has some value, in ways that writing would do well to build upon and move beyond. Far beyond.

I suppose that would take some guts. Guts or money. Guts like those of the lionized, the much vaunted Atticus Finch, perhaps, coupled with all too often opposed progressive scope, vision, and movement forward. Guts and money and progressive work to make up for and to surpass that which has been mentally cleansed, censored, or buried, quite professionally. Atticus Gladwell and the limits of liberal fiction. It's long since time to move beyond that world.

Reading, Writing & Politics – A Blogger Takes on the Literary Establishment
Shelley Ettinger

My Correspondence with Mr. AYW
January 7, 2009

Not long ago I had an email exchange with an Ac-claimed Young Writer, a successful novelist, a reg-ular on the readings circuit whose several books have won critical lauds and sold well. He initiated it with a note telling me that he'd chanced across this blog, was enjoying it, and was happily sur-prised by a mention here of one of his books. (That mention is no longer up.) He said he hoped I liked his book and to let him know.

In fact I had just finished reading his book, and had just finished thinking about whether I would blog about it. I'd decided not to, partly because I was sick with the flu and didn't feel I could write as clear and thoughtful a posting as I should. Now, having received an email from the novelist himself, I thought about whether I should answer his ques-tion honestly and tell him what I thought of his book. Probably my mulling about this wasn't all that clearheaded, given the fever and all. Probably I should have just let it go. I didn't. I decided instead to send him a substantive reply including my reservations about his book.

Those reservations centered on this white writer's treatment of Black characters, one in particular. So, while praising his writing, and yes, he's a good writer, which he already knows, I criticized his handling of race. My criticism was rather gentler than it would have been had I gone ahead and blogged about the book (although, having now read several reviews and articles about the book and the author I can conclude that apparently no one else has even raised a peep about this issue, which I find appalling though not surprising) but I did express it. My email was courteous and re-spectful but it did not demur from saying what I thought.

Soon enough my inbox showed another email from the acclaimed young writer. His reply to my reply held to my courteous, friendly tone. He thanked me for my "kind words and thoughtful response" to his book and re-sponded briefly and, to his cred-it, not terribly defensively to my critique. Then he got to the meat of things: an eight-paragraph-long treatise, complete with quotations from several of the bourgeois literary pantheon, on why a political approach to reading, and even more so to writing, is a fallacious and indefensible aesthetic position.

Well my my.

Where did that come from? He, after all, had asked me what I thought of his book. I'd never asked him what he thought of my reading habits.

He had not, in fact, simply chanced upon my blog. He'd found it in the course of a google search of himself, actually a google search of his name plus the phrase "best books of 2008." This I know from the service that tracks visits to my blog. Yes, Mr. Acclaimed Young Writer was hungrily searching for more acclaim. Can't fault him for that, and so what? Writers are a notoriously neurotic lot; if I ever manage to get my novel published I'll no doubt search high and low for any hint of praise. Once he found his way here via the google search, he pored over the site until he found one little mention of his book (again, it's no longer up). My hunch is that, singlemindedly searching for his own name as he was, he had not in fact looked at this blog very carefully at all, let alone been enjoying it, before he emailed me. This blog whose title is "Read Red" with the subtitle "ruminations on the reading life of a communist." Once he'd received my communist reader's criticism of his book, however, he sized me and my blog up and decided to school me on what a sorry, shoddy approach communist reading, let alone class-conscious writing, is.

And thus ended my correspondence with the auth-or of what several critics did indeed find one of the more noteworthy books of 2008. It will take anoth-er post, which I hope to get to soon, to address the substance of his stance against political fiction, un-original, tired and steeped in bourgeois sensibility as it is. His argument hews faithfully to the line espoused by the entire literary establishment; since one purpose of this blog is to oppose and expose that line for what it is, and since I haven't done so explicitly in some time, by golly I'll have to step up to the plate.

There's another topic buried here, which I'll also try to bring to light soon. It has to do with my own relationship to literature in the abstract and, concretely, to actual writers. Such as the actual author whose email started all this, or the one whose book I read and loved and emailed asking if I could in-terview her for this blog but who never replied, or the ones who've ignored my requests that they link to my blog, or the ones who have read my (critical or laudatory) posts about them and their books but not contacted me; and the ones who do link to me and do reply to my queries and are open to the thoughts and ideas of a red reader. Such as, also, the state of my so-called career as a writer and what effect this blog will have on it. It took me years to stop worrying about how blogging as a communist reader would muck up my chances at publication and just make the leap, and I'm not worrying about it any more, not exactly, but I do think about it, by which I mean I think about the whole question of writing and publishing and poli-tics and activism and, well, that's what this whole damned thing is about, isn't it, so this is, as always, to be continued.

I don't think Mr. AYM is still checking in here, red reading being so decisively not his cup of tea, but I'm grateful to him for giving me much to think and blog about.

My Response to Mr. AYW, Part 1
January 21, 2009

When last we left the Acclaimed Young Writer, he had contacted me to ask how I liked his book, then, after I'd politely criticized it, responded with an eight-paragraph lecture on why "reading as a com-munist," as he paraphrased my stance announced in the subtitle of this blog, "shouldn't be part of art appreciation." His treatise expounded on the aes-thetic bankruptcy of looking at art, let alone creat-ing it, based on a political point of view.

Because it was a private email exchange, I'm not naming him, and I won't extensively quote him either. A friend suggested I invite him to make his comments public, to sort of debate me, here. But I'm not doing that. He is an Acclaimed Young Writer. He gives lots of readings and interviews and has all kinds of outlets to speak and write his piece. His opinion on the topic of political art conforms to the conventional wisdom; it's propagated everywhere and anywhere by him and by most other prominent writers and writing teachers. In fact, the "art and politics are antithetical" viewpoint is pretty much the only viewpoint anyone in this country ever gets exposed to. Me, in contrast, I'm an obscure writer who's claimed this teeny tiny corner of the blogosphere as a place to air my dissenting point of view. He gets to spout his bourgeois-masquerading-as-neutral spiel everywhere but here. Here, I speak my proletarian piece.

Mr. AYW's anti-political-literature argument in his email to me opened with a bizarre, reactionary (and misspelled) attack on a short story writer for her "reverse-mysogyny," then rambled about a bit before alighting on the main point, that "using political considerations to determine a reading experi-ence" is wrong, and concluding that a political ap-proach is "not an aesthetic position I have a great deal of sympathy with." To buttress his argument he quoted Bellow, Kundera and Woolf. Shockingly, this trio – the scrivener of the middle-class white male experience, the professional anti-communist, and the brilliant bourgeois whose progressivism didn't extend to relations with the servants – all agree with Mr. AYW.

The position, boiled down, is that true art can have no political viewpoint. That creativity cannot spring from any political purpose or express any political ideology. And that it is equally impossible to appreciate art from any but a non-ideological approach.

Sound familiar? Of course it does. It's the position of the entire arts establishment in this country. Well, almost. A writer you might have heard of sees things differently. [Toni Morrison: "All of that art-for-art's-sake stuff is BS. What are these people talking about? Are you really telling me that Shake-speare and Aeschylus weren't writing about kings? All good art is political! There is none that isn't! … Slavery can never be exhausted as a narrative. Nor can the Holocaust; nor can the potato famine; nor can war. To say slavery is over is to be ridiculous. There is nothing in those catastrophic events of hu-man life that is exhaustible at all."]

Because it's been a while since I wrote here about this whole question of political art, and because the points I want to make will take some time, some thought, and some blog space, I'm going to make those points in a series of posts. Starting today, with points number one, two and three.

Virtually every time I've ever seen the case made that a politically conscious approach to art is illegit-imate, and this certainly applies to the case made by Mr. AYW, it relies on three logical (actually poli-tical!) bases. None is explicitly stated. Each is as-sumed to be understood. Each is mind-bogglingly wrong.

1. The argument that true art can't be political is not really made as an argument backed up by rea-son or evidence. Rather, it's an assertion, backed up by – nothing! It is presented prima facie, as though the assertion needs no proof because it is self-evident to any reasonable person. Actually, the more I review the standard cant the more I'd say that almost always it merely amounts to this. Art can't be political, obviously! Mr. AYW's email, including its citation of quotations, was a prime example of this ap-proach. None of what he wrote me, and none of his "expert" backup, amounted to anything but stating, and re-stating, and re-re-stating, the as-sertion, as though reciting it frequently enough

magically makes it true.

2. This is a variation on #1 but it's worth noting separately. The anti-political-art assertion amounts to a tautology. A tautology, as in my favorite ex-ample from the Bill Clinton presidency, is a logical fallacy in the form of a circular argument: thus-and-so is true because so-and-thus is true. In Clin-ton's case, when he signed the viciously anti-gay Defense of Marriage Act in 1996 and was asked why he opposed same-sex marriage, he said, "I'm against same-sex marriage because marriage is between a man and a woman." Tautology. Similarly, Mr. AYW and his ilk rely on the tautology that true art can't be political because, why?, well, because if it's political it can't be art. How's that for deep thinking!

3. The entire position against a political approach to art claims to be above the fray – posits itself as apolitical, as it has to in order to not appear baldly hypocritical – when in fact the argument itself is deeply, in fact entirely, political. It is not an argu-ment equally against fascist and working-class art although it may claim to be. Who ever defends fascist art and must be answered? No, it is an argu-ment against working-class, or class-conscious, or, heaven forfend, communist art. It is the argument of the class in power, the ruling class, the capital-ists, against the exploited class, the workers. The position that art cannot be political is a position for the status quo, which is an utterly political position. This is so even if the arguer doesn't realize that she/he is arguing for the exploiting class, even if she/he denies it. How can that be? I'll delve deep-er in future posts.

Hey, Mr. AYW, Part 2
January 22, 2009

In the first part of my reply to the Acclaimed Young Writer's lecture to me about the errors of my red reading (and writing) ways, I closed by saying that anyone who stakes out the art-can't-be-political position is herself/himself taking a thoroughly political stance – even if she/he denies it, even if she/he doesn't realize it. How so? Well, for one thing, no literary or critical utter-ance can avoid falling out on one or the other side of the class struggle. The class struggle is the overarching context for all public (and most private) life. As long as we live in a class society, and oh, Mr. AYW, we do, the struggle between the ruling class and the exploited class is always on. It may be less visible at some times than at others, but, like the invisible air we breathe, it surrounds us, we move through it, and though we can deny or ignore it that doesn't change the fact that it's there. As long as it's there, as long as the oppressed, suppressed side tries to ex-press itself, artistically or in any other way, well then anyone who opposes that expression is taking the side of the oppressors, the suppressors, the class in power, the capitalists.

You can claim all you like that you're not for one or the other side, you're only on the side of fine art. When you insist that work that is ex-plicitly parti-san to the working-class side of things cannot be true art – without offering up one iota of reasoned argument or evidence to prove this is true, instead just asserting it over and over and over – you ex-pose your allegiance to the bourgeois side of the class divide.

Mr. AYW didn't only assert that political art is not really art. To drive home the point, he flipped it and insisted that art, true art, is never political. This is either naive or dishonest. It ig-nores a couple key realities: (1) that any art that appears to be neutral automatically becomes an artifact in support of the status quo, and the status quo is capitalist exploita-tion and ine-quality, so "neutral" art is bourgeois art; and (2) that there is a great, great, great deal of "great literature," so deemed by the literary estab-lishment, that is profoundly, manifestly, un-apolo-getically and clearly political. (Calling Mr. Sol-zhenitsyn!) Apparently, the no-politics rule doesn't apply if the politics in question conform to the rul-ing class's ruling ethic.

But it's not just about which side are you on, as the great old song asks. It's also about which side's ideology pervades your conscious mind as well as your unconscious, dare I say, your ar-tistic, creative mind.

One hundred sixty-one years ago in The

Commun-ist Manifesto, Karl Marx and Freder-ick Engels wrote, "The ruling ideas of each age have ever been the ideas of its ruling class." Applied to our time and place, this means that the ideas of the capitalist class are dominant. The ideology of this ruling class permeates all social relations, all human ex-pression, all cul-ture.

This is one of the great hidden secrets of our soci-ety. Yet how could it possibly be otherwise? Those who own and control everything – not only the means of industrial production but also the news media, the entertainment industry, publishing, museums, education – own and control culture as well. Everything, and brother I mean everything; everyone, and sister I mean everyone; is in the grip of bourgeois ideology. We only break out with the most extreme effort of conscious will. It is enorm-ously difficult to take off the bosses' lenses that block and distort our vision and understanding and, yes, cramp our creativity, and to replace them with red-tinted glasses. Most of us, born and bred in this culture as we were, manage it only partially, I think, or with slow, fitful progress. Until we do, our thoughts, feelings, dreams and art remain im-bued with bourgeois ideology. Mired amid the cul-tural muck of the enemy class camp.

This doesn't mean we're bourgeois. The vast major-ity of us are of the other layer, the work-ers and op-pressed. Mr. AYW, I have no idea of your class status or personal wealth. Yours is a bourgeois con-sciousness, however. Your ar-gument against poli-tical art does the work of the bourgeoisie whether that's your intent or not.

I'll continue my rant another day. In store: more examples of highly political literature that is em-braced by the art-can't-be-political crowd, *and* ex-amples of left or people's or communist literature that in my view indisputably rises to the level of art, *and* some actual reasoned argu-ment to show why political art is not a contra-diction in terms.

Socially Engaged Fiction
February 2, 2009

Some novels that are extremely political and ex-tremely fine: here is a mere brief list off the top of my head and in no particular order, con-sisting en-tirely of well known books written in English that I have read.

• *Blonde* by Joyce Carol Oates

• *Cloudsplitter* by Russell Banks

• *Song of Solomon* by Toni Morrison

• *Jude the Obscure* by Thomas Hardy

• *The Brief Wondrous Life of Oscar Wao* by Junot Diaz

• *The Wall* by John Hersey

• *Johnny Got His Gun* by Dalton Trumbo

• *The Grapes of Wrath* by John Steinbeck

The plot, as they say, thickens. It seems that not on-ly are reactionary or anti-struggle books praised by the U.S. literary establishment de-spite its oft-stated view that literature and poli-tics are antitheticcal. Progressive, *though not revolutionary,* fiction that directly and explicitly takes on great social questions can be and often is well received. This is also, or even more, the case when it comes to translated fiction, espe-cially from Africa, Latin America, the Caribbean and Asia, about which I hope to com-ment more soon.

It's so obvious that the anti-political-literature case is not truly believed even by those who argue for it that I won't belabor the point further. The issue, then, becomes why they keep saying it. And what they really mean.

To be continued.

One Last Tussle with Mr. AYW
February 10, 2009

In a series of earlier posts prompted by an email exchange a couple months ago with an acclaimed young writer, I've addressed the hol-low bourgeois heart of the assertion, proclaimed always and ev-erywhere by the literary establishment in this coun-try, that art and politics don't mix, that literature cannot succeed as art if it is political. I've noted that this it is political. I've noted that this assertion is simply that, with never any proof to back it up. I've argued that the class struggle pervades everything, including art, and that there is no such thing as a neutral stance in literature any more than in any other field of endeavor. I've countered the anti-political-art cant with some examples of highly political work – both reactionary and progresssive – that this selfsame literary establish-ment itself recognizes as fine art, which shows that even they don't believe their own dogma.

What's left are two points, more or less. One is to address the question of why they promulgate this lie despite its so extremely obvious falseness. The other is to counter with some reasoning with which we can once and for all dispose of this whole sad spectacle of artists fronting for the capitalist class's interests.

1. Why? When they themselves love and laud ov-ertly political fiction across the bourgeois spec-trum, from Solzhenitsyn to Diaz, why do they claim overtly political fiction can never succeed? Much of it, of course, is unthinking. It's a sort of rote repetition of received wisdom. Its source, how-ever, is no mystery. It is bourgeois ideology, which is the underpinning of all culture under capitalism. I'm not talking conspiracy theories; I'm not saying there are secret meetings where the billionaires hand out envelopes to MFA professors with their marching orders. I'm talking the concrete as well as the subjective workings of class society, in which all norms, culture, beliefs, the whole shebang, arise from and are owned and controlled by the ruling class, either directly or indirectly.

What threatens the rule of the capitalist class? Well, ultimately, revolution of the workers and oppress-sed. But even before it gets to that point, any ex-pression, artistic or otherwise, that can find its way out into the world and find a way to dissent from bourgeois ideology, that takes the side of the work-ing class, that exposes not only the terrible ills of this racist, exploitive society but, much more im-portant, identifies their cause, that is, capitalism, that espouses overthrowing this horrid system of oppression and exploitation – boy oh boy, anything like

that has got to be quashed. That's the why. It's one part of the capitalists' ongoing battle to save their system and thus their riches. It's what moti-vates the ongoing war against truly political art, even as they champion right-wing and can allow the championing of mildly left-wing political art.

2. Which leads to the how. How do they enforce the almost complete banning of truly revolutionary literature? By spreading the big lie that such cannot be art.

So here's the truth: oh yes it can.

I'm not a literary scholar, so I'm at something of a disadvantage in this polemic, but I do know that nowhere throughout the rest of the world is this lit-erature-can't-be-political nonsense taken seriously. Much, possibly even most, fiction, and even more so poetry, written in Asia, Africa, the Caribbean, Latin America, and even to some extent in Europe, has a clear political slant. Much of it espouses revo-lutionary ideas and ideals. Most of it is never trans-lated into English or published in this country. Hmm. I wonder why.

Except if the author is dead and/or the struggle with which her/his work occupies it-self is suffi-ciently distant in time and geography to pose no threat to U.S. imperialism. I'm thinking of Bolaño, whose *The Savage Detectives* I found utterly unalive, quite inferior to some truly fine fiction about the U.S.-backed Pinochet fascist junta in Chile, and who, guess what, is championed as the great dead Latin American "political" novelist.

Then there are writers whose work is truly radical, Marxist writers even, but whom the U.S. critical establishment manages to at once praise and mar-ginalize as if their work is of only local interest in their own part of the world and of no real rele-vance or threat here. I'm thinking of, among others, Ngũgĩ wa Thiong'o, whose mar-velous novel *Wiz-ard of the Crow* I recently read. This book is brilliant on many levels. And it is nothing if not political. My guess is that in this country it is read simple-mindedly as a parody of "African corruption," rather than in its true, complete aspect as a head-on, full-throttled,

multifaceted exposé of British colonialism and
U.S. imperialism and what they have wrought
in the lands they've ravaged. Or at least that this
is how they hope to co-opt it.

Finally, wearily, we come to this. In his email
to me, the Acclaimed Young Writer backed up
the lierature-can't-be-political assertion with
this ex-ample: debate team captains, he said,
can't become novelists because they can't create
complex, subtle, literary writing. Well jeez, I've
been dying to reply, sez who? Is this truly all
you've got? A claim that a debater can't become
a novelist, not a good one, anyway? Wouldn't it
be fun if someone did some research and found
out which novelists did indeed serve on their
high school or college debate teams? I'm betting
there are plenty. But I shouldn't make fun of his
point, because surely he didn't mean to say
something as goofy as that debaters can't be
good writers. What he meant, I believe, was that
writing fiction is different than debating. And of
course he's right. Fiction is different than debate. Although of course it's not true that debaters can't also be novelists, debating and fiction
writing do require different skill sets. They are,
as it were, dif-ferent arts.

Dig one level deeper, pooped as we are, and
we reach his real meaning. A debater should
win lis-teners over to a point of view, a political
belief. A novelist should not.

Why not? He does not and cannot say, for it
would require acknowledging that his supposedly apoli-tical position is in fact a political position.

So there you have it. Not a proof that fine fiction cannot be political, for we've already seen
there are scads of examples of fine fiction that is
indeed poli-tically motivated, politically expressive, and poli-tically oriented. (Okay, I've listed
not quite scads, but I could if anyone requires
more proof, more lists.) Just a precept. It should
not be.

It would not be good for capitalism. Even if
he doesn't, won't, can't acknowledge it, this is
the crux of Mr. AYW's case.

A Gringa Diary

Tamara Pearson

Diary of life in the revolutions and uprisings
of Bolivia and Venezuela

ANOTHER WORLD? (why this blog):

For over 500 years South and Central America have been pillaged, exploited, sold and
abused, its peo-ple killed directly and indirectly
in mines and on farms that send the riches overseas – first by the Spanish and Portuguese, and
now predominantly by US imperialism.

Now, South America is standing up – from
Chavez calling George Bush a devil, to an indigenous presi-dent in Bolivia, to old Cuban
black men singing music like their country loves
it more than money, to the 14 year old who
works at the community radio station which
used to be a police station with bullying and
corrupt police, but was taken over by the local
barrio, to women forming collectives to run
farms, and the old man who sold cheese on a
stall and finally got a uni degree, to the crowds
that surround trucks which give away books on
history and the agreements that are being
formed between Latin countries so they can
IGNORE the U.S. – and offering an alternative.
Un mundo mejor es posible – Another, better
world is possible.

A DIARY (what is this?):

There's lots of information in the media and on the internet about the struggles in South America – some of it right wing bullshit, some of it so-so, alot of it good progressive news and information writ-ten by the people on the ground in those countries. It's easy to get the stats and information (even in English) – see some of my links – but what I'd like to do with this blog is provide more of a feeling of what it's like to live in these countries, to look at the revolutions from a more personal perspective. This blog will be an honest depiction (for exaggeration or romanticisation never helps) of life in a rev-olution. Like a diary, I'll describe life as I live it, from the rubbish in the street, to the doctors and the food missions, to conversations I have and peo-ple I get to know.

GRINGA? (who am I?)

These days Venezuelans emphasise to me that I am not a gringa – I'm not from the US, and some have gone so far to say that I'm a 'sister'.

I'm an internationalist and I believe our struggle has no borders, but I also grew up in a different re-ality – a first world imperialist country – with all the privilege that that brings (material wealth, if not the life wealth of cuba – a country that loves and is full of music, study, learning, healthy and happy people). And so I can never claim to see or watch or participate in this revolution in exactly the same way as local people do.

That perspective has its advantages and disadvan-tages. Things others are used to, I notice more. Our eyes are always more wide open in 'foreign' places. But it is also worth hearing this stuff from the words of Venezuelans who, for example, have lived through the dictatorships, struggled to obtain a living space, or went without education.

APRIL 14, 2009
Free health care IS life or death to some

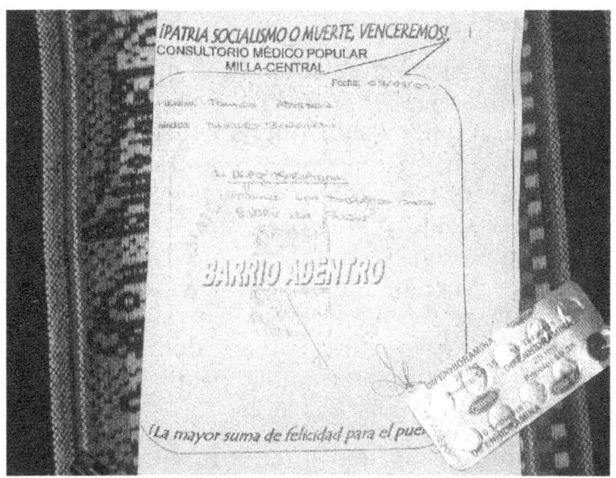

Today (now yesterday) I am in my room working – sitting at the desk or sitting up in bed, typing about Manuel Rosales that worm of a man... And outside I can hear the traditional Chavez songs being played over a loudspeaker – perhaps its in a plaza or perhaps its one of those roaming trucks. It is the anniversary of the counter coup, the 13th of April that beat the coup of 11th of April, an inspiring symbol that for ever defeat of theirs against us we will jump up again – 2 days later or 100 years later, and take it back and make it better. I hope.

Other than that, it has been semana santa (Easter – from last Thursday till Sunday, but many having that whole week off) and its all been a bit – light. Light on news, few meetings, everyone out with their family, and nothing open but churches during the official Easter bit. A good time to get sick – I've felt like a wee hypochondriac these days. Tooth aches and head-aches and sneezing all over the place and then a funny routine of pill taking. Sheesh.

So first I went to the local barrio adentro – a doc-tors surgery in what used to be a house, and per-haps still is upstairs, 2 blocks from my house, with a Cuban woman working mornings and a Venezu-elan man in the afternoons (this set up is becoming quite common I think, as more and more Venezu-elans start to work in the barrio adentros). I walked right in, sat down, and told the doctor about my sneezing (feeling like a fool cos it's just sneezing! But it's all the time and keeping me awake, for 2 weeks now) and he was heaps friendly, we chatted about stuff, and he gave me some medicine and wrote me a script with instructions about how of-ten to take it. The script is in the photo – it says at the top... 'homeland, socialism or death, we will win...popular medical centre, milla-central' and at the bottom 'the greatest amount of happiness for the people'. Love it!

A few days later I went down to the CDI – integral diagnostic centre, which I think is bar-rio adentro 2 – second stage of health care. It has more equip-ment, an emergency centre, x-rays, rehabilitation etc, and a dentist. The system with the dentist is you go down there at either 7am or 1pm, and the first 20 people get a num-ber or get written down on a list (but don't worry, there usually aren't 20 people). I got there at 1, was written down as the 5th person on the list, and after 2 hours got to see the den-tist. We got along instantly, I guess I was in a good mood and also often bond with the Cu-bans because we're both doing the foreigner-living-in-Venezuela thing. She checked my teeth, told me the usual stuff, and said I should get one of my back teeth, a wisdom tooth, I guess, removed. I knew that, I should have got it taken out ages ago but dentists are so expen-sive in Australia and I don't trust them either – all private, they tell you that you need all sorts of things that you don't. I asked her – so what do I do to get the tooth removed? And she said, well just come back when you have some time off work.. Me: "Well how about now?" Her..."Ok."

Ah shoot! I am one hell of a coward. Never had a tooth removed or any kind of operation in my life. Sat there squirming and not wanting to open my mouth. Oh well I eventually let her stick a few needles in then wiggle and pull my tooth out and it was over in 2 minutes. She gave me some anti-biotics and told me to keep my mouth closed for half an hour – and done. No swelling or pain – well not much pain. Can't be-lieve I put that off for so long. But it was of course all free, including the antibiotics. Its mas-sive when you think about it – about some peo-ple who have to go into debt in other countries because of their tooth problems, or in other countries, who just have mouths only half full of teeth, because dentists are not part of their world. In Aus I think you can see a dentist for free if you get treated by a Sydney University student, but I know from experience that the waiting list is 6-12 months. Made my wait of 2 hours not seem like much at all.

THURSDAY, APRIL 2, 2009
Community meeting in the plaza

It was really sweet the way one of the communal council leaders stood in the plaza and using a loud speaker system, called on the people around him – sitting under the trees, standing in shop doors, walking past – to join the community assembly.

The 5 promoters at the communal council assembly

It was a full weekend – the Socialist Front had their annual two day conference with various debates, group discussions and plenaries, and the commun-al council of Belen (the sector just a few blocks from my house) also tried to call a community as-sembly – necessary to elect commissions etc of the communal council, and which requires a minimum of 10% (in this case 100 people out of the community of 1000) to be legitimate.

"Attend the meeting of the community! The assem-bly is where we can solve all our problems! It's not for politics!" the guy said over the loud speakers.

They had set up chairs in the plaza, a white board, the speakers, and had enough copies of the com-munity council laws, as well as a map of the sector that corresponds to Belen, to hand out to everyone. I thought it was great, because everyone could real-ly see what was going on, and the plaza is so beaut-iful, and is the general meeting place of the area, so there was a nice atmosphere. People from shops who didn't join the meeting, stood in their door-ways and watched, while a few other people looked on from their balconies.

While we waited I talked with the loud speaker guy (J...) and he was really emphatic that everyone should participate, and should join one of the com-mittees (sport, culture, education etc) but also that communal councils are not political, that it doesn't matter whether you are 'yellow or white or red' (politically speaking) the most important thing is that you are committed to the community. Of course I agree and disagree – the councils are an initiative of the Chavez government, you can't just forget that, but it's also true that if by politics he meant *electoral* politics – that the PSUV (or whichever political party or organisation) is the place for that.

The meeting was the second assembly called so far. According to the law, if you don't get quorum at the first assembly, you can call another, and if there isn't enough at that you can call another, and that third assembly is legitimate despite the numbers.

Their first assembly only had 6 people. This one ended up having 32 people – not quorum but a big improvement and still impressive I think. The 'pro-moters' (a temporary committee of 5 set up simply to get the council going, once its elected the pro-moters dissolve) encouraged everyone at the meet-ing to be 'multipliers' (a common term these days in Ven politics) so that the third assembly would have quorum.

I was happy with the attendance – that is there was about half half gender wise, and a good range of ages – young, old, middle aged.

I was also impressed with how serious they were about following the communal council laws – diligently getting all attendees to sign in, checking that they were within the sector's area, outlining all the responsibilities of the promoters, how elections work etc.

As it turns out, despite only living two blocks away, I'm technically part of a different communal council, but they still said it was cool if I come to the next assembly (which will be in 2 weeks) to ob-serve, and later I talked to one of the leader's of my actual council and she's keen to get me involved in that.

THURSDAY, MARCH 26, 2009
Setting up women's committees in the councils

Mothers of the Barrio Mission – a mission that recognises the value of women's work in the home, recognising that many often do the work of two parents, and struggle in poverty. The mission is meant to help these women by linking them into other missions – health, culture, food and educa-tion etc and also gives economic help to the applic-able families. The women are also meant to meet, creating solidarity between them and organising the implementation of the program – that is, help-ing themselves.

Thanks to J for suggesting we go to IMMFA (Mer-ida Institute for Women and the Family) to see what the folks there are up to. Apparently they were pretty cool when they were first set up then there was a new 'team' and they started to just fo-cus on domestic violence, and now there's a new team again and some of the original team and they are getting more into the structural side of things, the active side of things.

At the moment the big thing is setting up women's committees in the communal councils. We both said that we wanted to set up one in our communal council – and a woman gave us the information and documentation necessary, which we can then take back to the councils for them to discuss (fin-ally my communal council in Belen is starting to meet – there's a meeting on Saturday, lets see how it goes...).

The women's committees should, according to the woman at IMMFA, organise workshops on self esteem, and have a social focus, create consciousness and ideology, not just be anti-violence. At least 5 women are needed to form the committee, which then elects a spokesperson, who becomes the committee's link to IM-MFA. But the committees are also supported by Banmujer (Women's bank) and Mothers of the Barrio. Committee members must be "committed to the revolution and have human sensibility," – that is, care about the community they're involved in.

This is interesting, because mostly the communal councils have been quite apolitical – dominated by opposition or by Chavista but mostly organising things like local fairs and lighting and stuff, and I guess the fact that the Chavistas control the mini-stries, is a way to inject politics into them.

IMMFA also offered to send people to the councils to help with the setting up of the committees. The procedure is roughly – convoke an assembly (which needs a certain percentage of the community to attend in order for it to be le-git – attendance should be taken), someone from IMMFA can ad-dress it and talk about the law of women and about the purpose of the committees because "the women need to know why the committee is necessary," and I guess from there, elect the committee.

IMMFA is also in the process of making a new women's shelter – good, there are very few of those.

I asked the women we talked to what social-ism was for her (hehe my cheeky method for trying to gauge where a person or institution "is at" politically) and she said "it's equality, quality of life."

Later we talked to the president, and I asked her all sorts of bizarre questions (why is 'family' in the ti-tle of the institution, how do you feel about gay rights etc') trying to put my finger on what was 'not radical enough' about the organisation for me.

On gay rights, she was clear that there should be no discrimination and that gay people shouldn't be excluded but she made some weird comments about some of them being a bit wild and undisci-plined in their sexual behaviour or unfaithful or something like that, which is a silly stereotype and has nothing to do with being gay or straight, and really promiscuity, if there's no deception, is really not that bad a thing. It's just taste. Basically though she said it all came down to culture, which to me is possibly true – just like sexism – but also a bit too wishy washy and dismissive. 'Culture' can so often be an excuse not to challenge things, kind of like saying 'look that's how we are'.

Oh well the law on equality should be passed soon, that will be awesome, lets see what affect that has. It deals with gay rights, right to marriage (wow) and there's also the Law about the Right of Women to a Life Free of Violence which has some pretty full on stuff about vio-lence against women – 18 months to 6 years in prison for 'psychological violence' and a whole gamut of other classifications of violence.

As to the family part of the title, she said that was to "prevent aggressive minds" – the ag-gression that is passed on through generations and so on, rather than women's so called main role in society being the family. Good.

She was also pretty cool on the whole beauty con-test stuff, saying she was against it as it didn't treat women has thinkers.

Lastly, she said that all the 'first' ladies of all the mayors were going to get together to do some cam-paigning and organise municipal-based committees Again, better than nothing, but it's a bit strange, choosing people based on who they are married to, assuming that they are political because their hus-band is.

THURSDAY, MARCH 19, 2009
Coming back

It was a 40 hour Sunday…yee gods, and I'm still jet lagged, after being back three days – waking up at funny hours and falling asleep at the drop of a hat in the middle of the day…

I spent a night in Buenos Aires on the way back. Not long enough to have an opinion right? But still, its so different to Venezuela. For a starters, almost everyone (in the city) is white(ish), and they sound like they are talking French and use funny words like vos and tenes. There was a cool street full of bookshops though. I was there Sunday night and most stuff was closed, but I wanted to get some political books you can't get here, and had the name of an editorial. Although that was closed, the hos-tel guy suggested I got to Corrientes street, which had second hand and discount book shops, one after the other, full with classics, Marxist books, history of Argentinean struggle, anarchism etc. Mega cheap too. Pity I'm not a super human (in terms of carrying it all back to Merida), I would have bought heaps.

Arriving back in Merida was a relief. Not just be-cause I'd spent the last 3 days/nights on planes and buses and not sleeping so good, but the amount of politics just hits you. The taxi driver from the Bus terminal was listening to revolutionary radio, then I went to stock up on vegies and had a che shirt on and the women there asked me about that and kinda wouldn't let me leave, hehe. So much has happened in the last two weeks, in Ven news and local news, po-litical life is so busy and I'm so ex-cited to get back into it, although as usual it's a bit over-whelming as well.

There isn't much else to tell as I've mostly just been sleeping and trying not to sleep, washing clothes, seeing M again (mmmm :) etc...but I did see my friend Z in Caracas, and to steal her story...she told me she'd been in the Mercal, where they had whole chickens for 5Bs ($2.5) and another woman in the queue chucked a tantrum because it turned out you had to buy a chicken AND something else and she said stuff about being oppressed like in Cuba etc.

Really shows how people can see things through the perspective they've already decided to have. Because of course the same woman wouldn't scream about capitalist oppression if she went to a shop where there was a two-for-one sale (ie you *have* to buy two things to get the discount). Sheesh, and as Z said, its not like she *had* to buy the cheap chicken, she could have gone to a private butcher and paid more if she wanted!

FRIDAY, MARCH 6, 2009

Journies

Bellas Artes, Caracas

It was holiday time...for me...and for uni students, so me and M could take some time off and spend a few days travelling around Venezuela. We went to sleepy and hot Coro, where it seems that everyone is Chavista (even wearing election t-shirts *after* elections, badges, hats and things, the bus and taxi drivers tuned into

left radio station etc) and where it is too hot to walk fast. There are plazas every two blocks (as M comment-ed, incredulous) and full of seats with people sit-ting and taking it easy, and I felt it too – the heat literally slows you down.

After a few days there (doing NO work at all, just cooking up amazing pasta sauce (hehe if I say so myself), reading in hammocks, checking out a waterfall, and sleeping...) we went to Caracas to see a few friends. We got lost straight away, Caracas doesn't have the convenient street numbering that Merida does and its so big... urg. Next day we went to Bellas Artes to meet Z, and it really does defy the stereotypes about Caracas. First you do not feel in danger there, unless you have been so affected by all the media that you just feel fear wherever you go... Secondly, its quite beautiful. Murals really in-tricately done with awesome political messages, some even made out of mozaic. The road to the art museum lined with artisan sellers and second hand and record sellers. The circle shaped plaza area in front of the museum full of jugglers, skaters, kids playing soccer, buskers, dudes doing tricks etc. Oh the night before was the 20th anniversary of the Caracazo, there were fireworks that echoed off the tall buildings around us and a movie about it on TV.

Then I was off to the airport to go back to auslandia for a few weeks. Urg a 135B exit tax, shoot that was a surprise. A conversation on the way to Argentina with an opposition woman who works in admin for the government primary education system, and who says that Chavez gives guns and motor bikes to criminals and the stats about poverty decreasing are "rubbish" and things are "worse than ever." Really, how can you be so stupid, really literally, swallowing the right wing propaganda, and with passion.

Here in Australia, after about 1 year 8 months a-way, I didn't get the kind of culture shock I expect-ed but a lot of things I was used to before I came to Venezuela did surprise me. I walk around Sydney now with my eyes wide open, noticing everything ...down to how everyone waits at crossings before crossing and how everyone has prams! I hadn't noticed until now that no one has prams in Vene-zuela. It seems like such a luxury.

The most striking thing has been the consumerism, which I'm always grumbling about as being really strong in Venezuela (and it is) but here its kind of like you can't do anything at all without spending money – socialising must involve going to a cafe and buying food. The way people are all dressed up in the most un-practical and artistic (in the style sense not in the sense of expressing anything) clothing just to walk around in the street, making me feel relatively dirty or something in my casual and comfortable clothing.

Of course you notice the internationalism – there are different colours in Ven but everyone is pretty much Venezuelan in some way, or if not, from Col-ombia or something. In Aus, I guess being a devel-oped country, it attracts people from mostly Asia plus other countries and walking around in UTS (University of Technology Sydney) you really no-tice that and its pretty cool, but we should always remember why... its not like Australia is some how better, its just that England fucked over a bunch of other countries, got rich, sent its criminals here, killed the indigenous, but with its wealth was able to build a country with somewhat better in-frastruc-ture and less poverty than the countries it stole the wealth from, so of course now lots of people want to come here.

Guys don't stare at you. It is much harder (and fur-ther) to find a free doctor. Chemists however, are much more helpful. But despite all the cleanliness and orderliness here in Sydney, despite all the wealth, there's this apathy and a feeling of anger (guy swearing to himself in the medical centre waiting room) that you do not find much in Venezuela.

The final main thing I've noticed that is dif-ferent is marching. I went on the International Women's Day march today, and I felt like we had so much more of an impact, with all the people we passed staring at us in a kind of mix-ture of curiousity, shock, etc that never happens in Venezuela – for two main reasons I think – marches happen so of-ten they aren't a big spec-tacle or surprise, and the content of marches is generally electoral rather than issue based. I imagine if a bunch of women marched down the streets of Merida, demanding to be listened to with the same kind of respect that men are, abortion rights and so on, there'd be a bit of gaping too. Oh and I guess the other thing is that marches in Venezuela are generally kind of cele-bratory – we've sort of won you know. Where as in Australia there's a demand, an an-ger, a breaking with the norm etc.

WEDNESDAY, FEBRUARY 25, 2009
Or maybe I'm just too impatient :)

Like when three bad things happen in a row and you call it a bad day, or two good things happen and you feel that things are looking up, lately I've been feeling that the Venezuelan left is too laid back and lacks a sense of urgency (and a sense of what this process means for ac-tivists in other coun-tries). Of course it's not true, like any country or group it's a broad range of people with various lev-els of com-mitment and seriousness. What leads me to that conclusion though were two main events...

One was an anti-bull fighting protest. Every year in February, as I've mentioned before, is the 'Sun fair/ Feria del sol' with its two main features – the beau-ty queen contest and the bull fighting. People pop up all over the place selling (or wearing) those cow boy hats, and there's a parade and lots of tourists and lots of shops and lots of spending of money, and a concert that was so loud I could hear the shouting at 3am from about 7 blocks away...

The whole bull thing is pretty gross – I don't re-member all the gory details but basically the bulls are given a bunch of drugs which makes them eas-ier, I think, to chase and kill, but also disoriented and angry I think. Then they are killed and it's a slow death and people drink and cheer.

(Seriously, bulls are male cows right, as in cows... those peaceful, boring, all-day-grass eat-ing things, hardly natural fighters?)

So likewise, every year there are protests against it, although it sounds a bit like the women's day pro-tests – once a year, rather than an ongoing cam-paign (for animal rights or against consumerism or against the Spanish-isation of Meridenian culture etc). Leaflets are handed out, articles are written, grafitti is done, murals are made sometimes, and there was the march.

It was advertised to start at 9. Being used to Vene-zuela but not wanting to miss anything, I got there at 9.30. There was no one there, so I texted M, and he got me to go to his place where some people were still making placards. At like, 11:30 they/we left his place and went back to the plaza. There, ORCA – an animal rights group, had put out a bunch of banners along the path – which I thought was cool, people were stopping to read them. There were people dressed up as bulls (horns, black cape, colourful dagger things in their back) and radio Ecos – al-ternative radio – was being played over loud speakers, talking about the bull-fights, how they are harmful to children and so on. I didn't stay for long (had things to do) but M says they marched at about 12.30.

I'm not sure what annoyed me really – per-haps it was the time in general (not accessible for workers) and that people didn't seem wor-ried about being 2 hours late. In the end of course it doesn't matter if you are late but it was the attitude, the laid back-ness off it all.

(which, I feel like repeating, isn't at all general-ised, there are people here who go to the extent of not allowing themselves a social life because they are so busy with activist stuff).

Then, later in the week, there was an anti-feria con-cert. It was organised by the anarchists but sup-ported by ORCA and a few other groups like the CLAN (student far left collec-tive). It took place in the courts in the barrio near the main city bridge thing, and it was a cool idea – its important to take back culture space in this way, and it was fairly vis-ible to the public going past over the bridge, so it was making a public statement as well. The anarch-ists made veggie burgers and sold them to raise a bit of money, but the actual concert was free. There were some anti-feria newsletters and at the start the various groups gave short speeches.

The thing is, most of the audience – hmm I dunno what you'd call them – not Goths, but people dressed in black. Piecings... (And the clowns :). That is they are clowns by day, busking in the pla-za sometimes, and they were hanging out at the concert, doing amazing things with skateboards just for fun as people waited for the bands to set up). But the people in black are supposedly anti-system, anti fash-ion for example, yet they are as dressed up as anyone, just in a different colour – women in revealing clothes and things. (I'm not against revealing clothes in general but if you want people to notice more than your body and you're against the objectification of women..).

At both events there was little effort to get people involved – organised in some kind of or-ganisation, no matter what it be, but to get them to go beyond *attending* marches or concerts.

Finally, I was reading an anarchist newspa-per – 'el libertario' and it got me angry too – be-cause it was ONLY criticising the government. That is, it wasn't a mixture of constructive criti-cism and noting posi-tive things, nor was it a mixture of criticism of the government and capi-talism and the opposition. So for this reason, it sounded more like the opposition to me, to the point where I got suspicious and asked M where it gets its money from. It refers to the 'boliburgesa' (ie the Bolivarian revolution bour-geoisie) and lied, frankly, about a lot of the posi-tive sides of this process – saying that there's so much crime because the government isn't fighting poverty, for example.

It's an ongoing struggle, one a bunch of us talked about last night – how to get a useful bal-ance of healthy, constructive criticism but not romanticise this rather imperfect proc-ess/revolution either.

"WE WONNNNN" they screamed as they hugged each other

(photo: not great quality; it's hard to photo-graph moving red flags at night without strong lights; I just love the look of the woman's face as we heard the results annouced – few could fit in the small room where the TV was, and she had climbed the window bars to see it better)

"And the yes option, with 6 million votes…" and all the people who had raced inside the headquar-ters of the PSUV office, including media, SQUEEZING inside, and outside, and hanging from the window bars, let off a cheer, quickly shushed by everyone…hence we didn't hear the percentage, but we did hear that the opposition got 5 million votes and the whole crowd moved out onto the road to set off fire works and chant and chant and then a sponta-neous singing of the first verse and chorus of the national anthem, fists in the air… and then I found myself on a motorbike…

But going back to the beginning… I had woken up at 5.30 (I WOKE up at 3 to the sound of the Diana, and went back to sleep). The Diana was still being played off the back of a truck at 5.30 and then at 7. I wanted to get photos of people voting as the sun comes up – the booths are meant to open at 5.30 though it depends when the booth workers (who are 'conscripted' in the same way jury workers are in Australia) get there. Unfortunately it seems the sun rises real quick, so I didn't manage to, but I still saw people lining up at 6.30, at various booths, and going into vote.

I went back down to one booth at 3 and there were no queues outside. I think it was that ex-perience (thinking that voter turn out was less, even though I knew it was simply that voting was much quick-er) – and hearing that Caracas – where there are more Chavez supporters, had good voter turn out, which made me think we'd probably won. Later I heard some unofficial re-sults, and at around 8, walked outside, and had to walk all the way to the PSUV building (about 20 blocks) cos there weren't any buses, and un-like in the November elections, it was just cars and bikes with red flags going around the streets honking… and I just knew we'd won.

Even though I haven't been that excited about this election campaign – in my opinion there are so many other things we need to be doing with our time – I still felt like running all the way to the PS-UV. I guess it was the symbol-ism of it. Revolution victory over crazy, selfish opposition. And the fact that we haven't had a victory like that in a while, and we so needed it.

The regional election was a mixed victory, and we lost the referendum in 2007. So boy were people proud and happy, and as I walked down the road people yelled at me 'how did you vote?" and I said 'for yes' (a white lie, easier than stopping to explain that I can't vote) and they cheered, and even taxis had red flags, and security guards up late working were cheering at the cars, like no one was afraid last night to come out again, politically, and say 'Yep I feel strongly about that, and we won!'.

A small crowd, perhaps a hundred or so had al-ready gathered in the plaza and were watch-ing the screen for the results, and chanting and whistling and high-fiving the honking cars that were going past.

I walked down some more, to one of the main booths, the one that had been empty at 3. Wow. I walked through people in red tshirts and people with red flags and people just all beaming and hap-py and chatting then sud-denly I was in a different crowd, no red, no smiles. And I realised that the Chavez support-ers were standing on one side, waiting for the results, and the opposition on the other. Boy did they look dejected.

The red side were trying to get some music going, and put a mobile phone with a revolutionary song on it to the megaphone. Then they gave up on that and just chanted and chanted and the opposition were so quiet. At one point a small group of them chanted, for like, 10 seconds, 'No is No' and I felt like saying sarcastically, boy how deep, you guys really have thought about all the problems in the world. Sheesh.

The red side started to move closer and closer to the booth, and it was a real physical example of how the results (still not announced) had given us confidence, to just take back our space. A lot of the opposition people left.

Then, finally, I did actually run down to the PSUV office. Because I felt like it – it's nice to run on emp-ty roads at night – and because I knew the an-nouncement would be made soon.

From the PSUV office, after the announcement, a friend put me on the back of someone's motorbike, as there were calls to go back to the plaza, where people were playing drums and dancing.

Motorbike guy honked all the way up there, literal-ly, and we got mixed up with all the cars heading to the plaza, blocking up the road for like 10 blocks up. By now (about 10) there were a good thousand or so people in the plaza (that's A LOT, for Merida, at least double the amount celebrating the 10 year anniversary of Chavez government, and it was just people living nearby, others went to their closest plazas to celebrate), red flags galore, the drums, ska music off the back of a truck and people danc-ing, people hugging (including strangers). Bloody awesome night (and not a drop of alcohol to be seen. Who needs alcohol when you have the sort of victory that they say in every other country, is im-possible…)

Two of our mates followed us on a motorbike to watch out for cops, and the four us (women, one older) drove around and stopping at various tempting smooth walls to spray 'We exist to change the world not for the pleasure of men!' and 'Our bodies are not for profit' and 'objectification is the first step to rape' and 'Ferisol = machismo' etc. Ha that was so fun. We did it in response to the annual Sun Fair (Feria del Sol = Ferisol) here in Merida which also involves a beauty queen com-petition.

Hopefully it was noticed in amongst all the other graffiti, one thing I love about Venezuela. The op-position writing 'no means no' all over the place and amendment supporters writing 'si va' which I can't work out how to translate literally, I guess it means 'yep the amendment will pass!'.

Gosh we've received so much opposition propa-ganda about the amendment – under our door. Some of it is so crazy:

– Cuba is the only country in Latin America where indefinite presidential elections exist (pictures of Fidel looking crazy and evil – a picture of him in 1959 and in 2009; stupid people he's not even presi-dent anymore) – In Cuba the youth only have one exit: the sea.

– Do you think that the concentration of power in the hands of only one person is best for a demo-cratic country? (ie a bunch of arguments trying to say that getting rid of term limits = dictatorship. Funny, we have that – no term limits

– in Australia, and unlike Venezuela we DON'T have the ability to recall.)

– Do you think its good for Venezuela that private property is eliminated?

– Would you have voted for Chavez in 1998 if you had known he'd take us to Communism? (I wish!! But not yet.)

– Do you think citizen security has been a priority of the Chavez government?

– Do you think the hate that this government has encouraged is good for Venezuela? (dude they are the negative ones.)

Meanwhile, the PSUV hasn't been so good with putting leaflets under doors, but they have had even more red tents than the elections last Novem-ber, going all out handing out leaflets from those.

The closing motorcade yesterday made me happy. Cars and trucks full of people in red with flags and 'si' stickers and posters plastered all over their cars went past the plaza, and kept going and kept go-ing, and I stood there for an hour taking photos and talking to people, and left to make a phone call and walked home and the cars were still going past, there were that many.

There were old and young and social mission peo-ple and I just love it that they were all SO HAPPY and blowing whistles and raising their fists and just so proud to be red, to be socialist, to be pro-Chavez. Proud of their politics. What it felt like at the time – and I wrote in my diary, 'Pride parade of the previously poor.'

Then Marcos Diaz (governor of the state of Merida) rode past on his bike, and he's a big man so you notice him, but he was just riding along with ev-eryone else, it was cool. I'm not too happy with the guy right now cos he's supporting the Sun festival (and the consumerism, imperialism – Spanish cul-ture – torture of animals (bulls) and sexism that it represents) but it was an awesome moment. The woman who walks around the plaza with a tray of rice pudding in little cups, selling them, just beamed when he rode past. "What a guy!"

He gets around and everyone knows him and his politics are a bit wrong in my opinion but I also think he's genuine and a good guy.

THURSDAY, FEBRUARY 5, 2009
Telling, shooting, celebrating, resisting

Telling Tales

Sometimes Merida feels like such a fairyland, I can never get over the purple night skies. Even in the Museum, with abstract paintings on the walls, in the middle the roof opens up, and there are plants and a fountain. The other night there was even a tiny blue humming bird moving amongst the flow-ers and the participants just like the fairy in Peter Pan…

Anyway it was Telling Tales night, and in one cor-ner of the patio chairs were set up, and people got up and basically did just that – just told quick stor-ies, a few poems, and others sang and played the guitar. Even a kid – she must have been about 9 or something, got up and told this weird story about earthquakes and a kid who didn't want to do his homework, in full confidence. I liked it I guess be-cause it wasn't about performance and compete-tion, it was just a nice night of sharing stories.

Student and police and National Guard violence

I didn't see most of it, in fact I just saw the end, where the National Guard, in 3 tanks, moved slow-ly down the main road next to the law and human-ities faculties of Los Andes University, seemingly shooting at the students (I saw this guy poke out of the top of the tank like a rabbit from its hole, and aim his gun at the students, but it must have been blanks or some-thing, I don't think they wanted to actually kill them, but rather scare them away) and throwing tear gas, and the students, from behind the fence and with their faces covered in t-shirt improvised balaclavas, threw large rocks and bottles back at the National Guard. My friend says he also saw them throw something like dynamite.

The whole thing seemed pointless to me – on both sides. The students were clearly not harming any-thing – that is they were not hurting each other nor property, (earlier, apparently they had been fight-ing directly with the police) so why didn't the Na-tional Guard just leave? And then the students (op-position students) weren't going to achieve any-thing by throwing rocks at tanks. Later they burnt tires, also more symbolic in my opinion, blocking the road and making fire…

Earlier that week Chavez had said that student vio-lence would not be tolerated and students would be arrested, so it seemed like one big media stunt on both sides – to me. 'The Chavez government causes instability!' says the opposition. 'The oppos-ition is violent!' says the Chavez government. And its true, the opposition IS immaturely violent at times, to cause instability, but I'd go for the oppos-ite strategy and not provoke it further with tanks.

I went around taking photos quite close to both students and tanks (everyone always tells me not to do that, that 'they'll take your camera' but they never do – I think the fear of the violent opposition is exaggerated and also, they are all adrenalin charged, unthinking, macho youth who wouldn't do that to a woman…), and got a face full of tear gas quite a few times and later stupidly washed my face in water which just made it sting more.

(For a better chronology of the actual events and background see venezuelanasis.com/news/

4148/)

10th anniversary of the revolution

I have to admit I had kind of forgotten about the anniversary. There wasn't a lot of build up to it, and some workers, who perhaps hadn't watched the news over the weekend, were taken by surprise on Monday morning when they found out they didn't have to work. Most shops, banks, restau-rants etc were closed.

As I walked down to the main plaza and could see the crowd of red and hear the music, I started to feel a bit elated. There were many more people there, than for example the Palestine solidarity pro-tests, and there was this environment of celebration

On the other hand, a lot of activists I know weren't there, I really don't think it was built that well. 10 years of – what ever you want to call it – revolu-tion, opposition to imperialism, dignity for the poor, progressive government – is something to really be excited about, something really special. There should have been balloons, live bands, dancing, many more people.

I guess all the leadership, organizer type people are bogged down in the amendment campaign. Most of the speeches were directed to this – to making sure that there can be another 10 years of Chavez government, of the kinds of things that were achieved in the last 10 years.

After that I invited a friend over for lunch, and she cooked hehe, whilst I sat with her kid at my com-puter – a 4 year old who told me how to find her favourite 'princess game' online and who, when I opened up the paint program (lacking any other games or tiny child friendly stuff on my computer), told ME how to use it.

Hippies shut down

Outside the Bolivar library (literally a Bolivar li-brary – with a bunch of his books and letters and things), the hippies sell their really amazing artes-enia – mostly hand made jewellery, bags, scarves, little animals made out of wire or coke cans. And truth be told, some of them also sell pot.

Recently they disappeared. Apparently they were shut down, most likely by the local police, ordered to do so by the opposition city mayor.

Since then, they have come back, with large signs stuck to their stalls saying that they are buhoneros – informal stall workers, just like anyone else, with children to feed and rent to pay.

Man, the hippies are part of the arty life that is Merida, and pot is not a harmful drug – only if its abused, just like beer can be abused. (Of course, selling pot is illegal in Venezuela, but being a buhonero in general is illegal – that means all those road side hotdog and burger stands that pop up at night, or the people selling fresh orange juice in the morning. All of them are trying to survive and in my opinion add to street life, and should be left alone).

(photo: a plaza in Cucuta)

Well I've just been working, writing, studying, walking around in a bit of a frustrated daze, won-dering what is holding us back and why.

I think on the one hand, with the voting on the amendment coming up, everyone is very orientated – clear about what the priority is (drop everything for the voting), and on the other hand rather disorientated.

We had one election, and then another, and it sounds a bit spoilt perhaps – but I'm a bit sick of elections (and I've only been here for a bit over a year – compared to the other activists here who've done like 11 elections (or 12?) in 10 years...).

One thing I noticed after the regional elections at the end of last year, is people suddenly became more open about their criticisms – they didn't like this candidate, x is corrupt, we need to reorganise, we need to do this and that, – and then the amend-ment election was called and suddenly all those things were put aside again.

Although it would definitely vary according to lo-cation, I think the PSUV branches (as opposed to the leadership) have been the least involved in the amendment campaign. More it has been the missions, the communal councils, and the organised left. By organised left I guess I mean the socialist front, the PPT, the PCV, some of the community radio people, some of the youth. In the socialist front – which is meant to be an open discussion space for the various cadre socialist parties, community activists and individual committed revolutionaries – there has been a lot of debates about its purpose.

People like me are frustrated. The PSUV (here in Merida city) doesn't take a lot of initiative (ie it was the socialist front, not the PSUV who called for Pal-estine solidarity rallies) and so some people were proposing at the meeting the other night that the socialist front set up committees and elect positions (very similar to what the PSUV has – fundraising, logistics, environment committees etc), and others argued strongly against this, suggesting we shouldn't be setting up a 'parallel party' and that the PSUV branches are where we should be doing things.

But most branches aren't meeting! I guess I feel frustrated because we have been handed this mas-sive opportunity that doesn't exist in other coun-tries – where the word 'socialism' is household talk, where – no matter where people are on the political spectrum, at least they are somewhere and politics is relevant and discussed and important, where we have money, resources, government log-istical support – for the ideas of socialism, but where we are caught in this constant cycle of elec-tions, rather than I

guess taking over workplaces, media, or deep-ening general ideological knowl-edge – including awareness of women's rights, the environment – basic grassroots initiative.

(Elections do have the potential to embrace a lot of these things – to get people more organised, to deepen people's experience and ability as protag-onists, and to have debate that deepens conscious-ness – but my experience is that has been limited. The debate around this amendment could be about what real leadership is, about the role of the indivi-dual verses the organised collective and so on, but instead has been simplified really to pro Chavez or not and maintaining the achievements of the revol-ution – a valid thing for sure but not overly empowering in my opinion).

Probably it's my fault – I'm too impatient. Like in most countries, perhaps the revolutionary task right now is more propagandistic and ideological, and it's not the time for taking over workplaces etc.

Oh well. Last Tuesday we had a 'thank god Bush is gone' type party. Ha it was fun. E made a card and everyone wrote 'farewell' messages to Bush that were full of spite, hatred, and hope 'We will win'. Ha.

Then Friday I went with P down to the border as I do every 3 months, and spent a day in Cucuta feel-ing depressed because its centre is basically a giant shopping centre (with a couple of nice plazas I guess – including a giant iguana that was walking around and people in the plaza threw water on it, taking care of it – which I thought was sweet).

But god, some streets of Cucuta its like – shops and then more 'shops' on the side of the street, selling socks, stationary, underwear, singlet tops, over and over again, and you walk through it and think it will stop soon and it just goes on forever.

Fashion in Venezuela and Colombia for women is very much tiny brightly coloured singlet tops, fit-ted t-shirts etc. Its fine, whatever, I don't really care – but if a woman wants to look like she's doing anything but going to a disco, it's a bit hard to find stuff. Hmm. I think it was P who was saying that he'd seen a poster for one of the few women gover-nors or mayors who got elected, and she had bright red lipstick on. We shouldn't have to decorate our-selves like that to be taken seriously!

There's something weird going on with the ex-change rate too. If you change Venezuelan Bolivars in cash in the shops in Cucuta you only get half of what they are officially worth – so its strangely profitable to withdraw Colombian pesos from an ATM if you have a US or Aussie bank account for example, then change them into Ven Bolos. My point on this is not to give everyone a tip about how to make money, but rather the massive econ-omic impact this has.

Venezuelans who manage to obtain a credit card daily cross the border to shop in Cucuta or to buy stuff and then sell it for a profit back here.

While I was in Colombia, funnily enough so was Chavez, meeting up with Uribe and one thing he said was that about $6 billion changed hands be-tween Colombia and Venezuela last year. I have a feeling a good part of that is going from Venezuela to Colombia. Meanwhile Colombians come here to get free medical care (for things like when they are pregnant). Its like you want the capitalist advan-tages, you go to Colombia (*things* here are quite expensive and there isn't a lot of variety), and then for the socialist side of things you come here.

Anyway, I guess it was my every-3-month remind-er about how dead life is under capital-ism – obvi-ously Cucuta is a bit of an exaggera-tion, most cities have a bit of culture, a bit of criticism and debate, something else to life than shops.

SUNDAY, JANUARY 18, 2009

The one place where abortion isn't taboo

Last Saturday I went to a meeting of the "Ideolo-gical formation and attention for women centre," which as far as I can tell is the only decent feminist organisation fighting for women here – the rest are all wishy washy or-ganisations that do what ever Chavez says (or see supporting Chavez in elections as feminist activity), and mostly see feminist stuff as fight-ing against violence and poverty (which it is) but not challenging women's role in society (mother, active in the background only, cook-ing, caring, object of beauty) and generally against abortion. As the woman who was telling me the history of the group said "We organise activities for women's rights, not for women as mothers or as housewives."

This group was formed in 1992 and has al-ways been independent of the government, con-stantly battling to stay alive financially, obtain-ing office space (for meetings, teach ins, and sexual assist-ance – abortions, gynaecology con-sultations as well as an open space where any women with problems could drop in, and con-stantly getting kicked out of that office space, as well as internal political disa-greements that saw the group split awhile ago into a 'Women's house' in Ejido, and the more cam-paigning and education oriented group in Merida.

On top of that people have constantly abused what money they did receive – such as dona-tions from Belgium where the woman in charge misspent the money on other things. In general they have sur-vived by paying for things out of their own pockets

This meeting had 6 women at it, 3 of which have been in the organisation pretty much from the start, and 2 somewhat younger women, plus me. There were 3 main points of discussion:

*things to buy (a sign to put downstairs: the of-fice is conveniently located right on the main plaza, but upstairs and out of sight, a few more chairs etc).

*publicity: organising a campaign against sexist imagery and language in the papers. A lot of pap-ers use virtually pornographic images of women – supposedly next to an article about exercise or something, to sell themselves. Com-bining this with a campaign against the beauty contest that is a cen-tral part of the annual Feria del Sol, coming up next month (see my entries on that last year).

*workshops: We decided on a range of themed workshops which would be aimed at teenagers, including: sexual education, the (new) law against gender based violence, rights of women, sexist lan-guage, religion and women, women and revolution (which was assigned to me to give, eek), women and community organisations and cooperatives…

We also discussed meeting with a range of the women's organisations to coordinate some of this, and 8 March (international women's day).

Frankly, it was one of the best meetings I've been to in a while, with lots of concrete decisions made, little venting, and it was just really nice to be around women who talk about the right to abortion as if its obvious (where as my experience has been, even around supposedly revolutionary people, that it's a pretty taboo topic and generally opposed). Apparently a lot of doctors here will say that they don't do abortions, but if you come back offering a decent amount of money, they

will.

We finished off the meeting with some cheap Champaign to celebrate getting active again.

Then: "Come to the vigil for Palestine in the Plaza," my text message said at 9.30 last night. Ok! The radio collective people had put up a screen in the plaza and were displaying photos and commentary about the struggle in Palestine. It's a neat idea – people walking past can stop and watch, and then the organisers can talk to them. It's just that buses stop at about 9.30 here (depending, sometimes as late as 10.30), so there weren't so many people about. In front of the screen they had arranged can-dles in the shape of the Palestinian flag.

FRIDAY, JANUARY 9, 2009
Big meetings, medium protests, tiring bureaucracy

On Wednesday the campaign for the amendment was officially launched, with people from missions and communal councils around the state coming in to the city (second photo). Ahh we were told it started at 10 and I knew that I could safely arrive around 10:30… By 12 people were still queuing to register and getting stamps to enter, which no one checked :). We were given lunch and water and booklets about the achievements of the revolution, and also most got some t-shirts as well (that said, 'those who care about the country, come with me' – Chavez).

A young guy, kind of head of the communal coun-cils, gave a speech about the stages of the campaign and he said all the communal councils should form 'yes' committees – and he asked 'who's here from a communal council' and a good 100 hands went up, he called on one guy to stand up 'which one are you from?' '…some place…Tovar' (which is a good 2 hours away) and he said he needs to make a promise, a kind of commitment, to the campaign.

Another regional leader who's also in the FFS spoke. He's a real down to earth good guy, it was weird to see him wearing the characteristic red pocket style Chavez shirt.

"We want Chavez to stay in power because we want to the people to continue ruling," he said.

Similar such events were going on in other states, and a talk by Chavez was transmitted to the meet-ing.

Yesterday, we had a protest against the Israeli bombing of Gaza (top photo). It was a different group of people at this event. For a start-ers – a lot less – probably all up 3 or 400 (as people arrived and left and different times – the rally went from 2 till about 5). Mostly cadre type people – the sort of people who'd be revolution-aries even if all the Chavez stuff hadn't hap-pened, or who don't get excited when there is free stuff and who do it all because its important not because its their job.

Anyway there were speeches, an open mike, some singing, a large banner in the street where people could write messages, some flag burning – first in the road next to the plaza, then outside Macdon-alds (of the Israeli flag and the US flag), and people also handed out leaflets and wrote on the backs of taxis and cars 'free Palestine' and so on. Ska-P music and other current bands played in the back-ground. Apart from one guy getting carried away and chanting 'death to the Jews' – which I'm gunna talk about with him next time I see him (and at the next meeting I also intend to briefly raise the issue that some people are confused between Zionism and Juda-ism – they aren't the same) – it was a pret-ty de-cent protest, in the sense that there was a lot for people attending to do. Protests where people give speeches and everyone just stands there and listen annoy me a bit – I think its good to have peo-ple actively participating.

The other night the national TV station had an old Cuban movie about bureaucratism. It was part of tribute to the revolution, with a Cu-ban movie every night for 5 nights or something in a row. It was hil-arious – this guy's aunt needs her pension but can't get it without a la-bour card – as a housewife, she doesn't have one and her husband's was buried with him. So because of bureaucracy she can't get her pen-sion and then they have to go through all this sh&t to get the husband umm…unburied… and then buried again, and its all very crazy.

It really really reminded me of ONIDEX (the pass-port/visa issuing government organisation here). Sheesh, I went to the one here and went up stairs to the 'extranjeria' for foreigners – asked again about what my work would have to do get me a working visa, and the woman was like 'its all on the web-site'. I told her, no, I've visited the website, the in-formation is NOT there (it really isn't) and she in-sisted it was…no its not, I said, I've looked like 50 times…and she just wouldn't help. What does the extranjeria exist for, what do the people in that room do exactly if they don't know that? There's only like 15 foreigners or something (excluding ex-change students) in Merida. Seriously, what do they do in that room?

And they counted UP to 60…55, 56, 57, 58, 59…60! Which makes sense when you think about it, but caught me by surprise so it took me a few seconds to realise it was the new year in Latin America. Like a long lasting orgasm, the city went off in fire works…there was quite a show going off at the Chinese owned supermarket, there were fire works coming off our roof, some big ones from the road on the other side of the baseball court, little ones coming from all the different streets and building tops…then the clouds came down as the night got cold and it was hard to see much at all when they mingled with the dust from the fireworks.

This year as it changed to a new year, I thought about the Palestinians. I made resolutions and things earlier in the day, but I felt like being a bit more serious this year.

I actually felt like staying at home and reading about the events of the year, perhaps writing a poem about it…I wanted to pay a tribute to all the people who struggle and sacrifice silently to make this unjust world a better place, and never receive any kind of recognition…and to say that for me, this year, the fireworks are for them…but the internet was down and my boyfriend was really insistent that I spend the new year with him.

If I had known how that would turn out, I really really wouldn't have gone. His mum is an evangel-ical Christian (he's not) and Venezuelans generally feel a pretty strong moral obligation to spend new years with their family. Anyway I'm ok with peo-ple having their religions, their different beliefs, even when one guy said the only history worth studying was the bible, I was like…ok, don't agree, but ok. But after the fireworks they started doing this kind of praying of a kind I have never seen in my life before, or anything close. It started off with one guy making predictions about the new year, (or what god had supposedly told him would happen next year) and it was this really mixed thing about how the financial crisis was caused by peo-ple not believing in jesus and how Venezuela and Merida have been chosen, and stuff about Israel being in conflict cos Jews don't believe in Jesus and ohh…if it had stopped there it would have been ok. At least, its interesting to learn about different kinds of people…but THEN they started doing this thing where some of them stood up and they all closed their eyes and started saying "Thanks to god" outloud, with this guy talking in a language I swear he'd just made up (but it was god talking through

him) and they started shaking and holding their hands in their air as god entered them, and then walking around each other talking half in Spanish and half in made-up-language, making each other faint and cry, and they were on the floor crying out about things and so on and so on and THIS lasted for 4.5 hours. It was painful and depressing. Later a few of them asked me why I don't believe in god and stuff and I think I was pretty good at being polite in the way I responded, con-sidering. They also said some stuff to M, my boy-friend, that made me feel they thought I was a bad influence on him and they had little respect for me, and on the whole I felt pretty horrible.

Well on the 26th, I also went with M to visit some of his relatives in a rural town 2.5 hours from Mer-ida, and within the border of Zulia state. A differ-ent bunch of people entirely :).

The town is pretty cute and laid back, its one of the main plantain (bananas used for cooking, making chips etc – I'd never heard of them until I came here although I understand they are more common in the US) growing areas. His cousin met us at her house and we ate the traditional Christmas-time hallacas. She used to work in barrio adentro as a nurse, and is now training to be a primary school teacher with mission sucre (although she has to travel in to El Vigia to do it – about half an hour away) and her and her family also run the Mercal next door. Despite all that she didn't seem passionately political and isn't involved in her communal council 'because it doesn't function very well'. Her brother is in the national guard and has a kid by a girlfriend and another kid by his wife, and another girlfriend, and is about 20. He also wasn't that poli-tical, preferring to talk about his new mobile phone and his computer and what kind of phone does M have, and his cost 600Bs and so on.

Then we hopped in a truck (and they picked up some bananas on the way to sell) and went over to the 'abuelo's place' (abuelo literally meaning grandfather but used in this context to mean old guy – some relative, but not M's grandfather). He has a pig farm. Yuck dude. Pigs are really big!! These must have been some other kind of pigs to what I've seen in Australia. Urg. Anyway, good for them I guess. They also had a bunch of fruit trees in their yard.

That night I hung out with, finally, the third group of 'different' people – fellow revolutionaries and members of the FFS. At first the conversation both-ered me a bit – it was mostly gossip, or speculation, about who is in the group for real, and who is just in it for the connections, in order to get jobs with the state (Chavista) government. A story about how one of the guys there had been approached by someone who wanted work and had heard he had connections, this guy – the one asking for work – had worked for the previous governor as well. And the FFS guy responded, well, we can always use help, volunteers, there's a lot to do... hehe. Anyway I guess I understand... we never talk about this kind of stuff at meetings and to vent about it once a year or so is a reasonable necessity.

Then the conversation got more interesting – about the problems of the revolution (which isn't a revo-lution, or is more a (contradictorily) peaceful revo-lution) and the involvement of the Cubans, and what will happen if the amendment isn't voted for and so on. One comment that worries me is that the elected PSUV regional leadership (8 people and 8 substitutes) almost all have other positions now – as mayors, mission leaders and things, so they aren't so available to be doing regional organising. It was really good, sincere, useful criticism and sort of exploded my head a little with all that needs to be done and all there is to worry about etc.

Finally, I had a crappy experience with private chemists...I had brought some medication with me from Australia, and am running out of it. The Bar-rio Adentros provide it for free, but it's slightly dif-ferent, and so I went from chemist to chemist try-ing to see if they had the exact same stuff. They gave me all sorts of things, telling me they were the same, and yet when I looked at the ingredients they were completely different, and some went as far as to tell me the ingredients were the same, they just had a different name in Spanish (gosh I'm not stupid!!). When I expressed my shock at the price, they'd then say they had something else... It's all totally a business! They weren't at all worried about making sure the medicine was what I needed, just in selling me what they could!

God so it's a relief the barrio adentros are here, it would have been crap being sick in Venezuela be-fore they existed – the chemist medicine is really out of range for most people and they try their best to convince you you need more than what you really do.

Because intellectualism is for everyone and creativity is rebellious

Tamara Pearson

Karl Marx lay down on the couch, poured some cheap sherry into a glass jar, and balanced it carefully on his bare chest. A Nigerian oil worker sipped on palm wine as President Yar'Adua spoke of nationalism and country as though blowing through a straw. A young Swiss housewife poured herself a shot of whiskey. A Venezuelan writer and community council representative walked into The Widow, and asked for a beer and pastel. And then they all wondered. Really, really, is it possible to collectively and democratically make a new kind of world?

~

The first essay I wrote at university started off with dialogue. My teacher, an ex communist party member, gave me a distinction for the "thorough research" but told me to refer to the university first year student guide about how to write an essay. Essays do not contain dialogue or narrative. They are clearly structured arguments with a beginning that summarises the ...blah blah. I did not put dialogue into an essay again. To do so, was to lose marks. To lose marks was to possibly fail a course and increase the debt I still owe the Australian government.

~

During high school and university, I worked in supermarkets. I wore a big black jumper in winter. I liked big jumpers, and black and white was the "checkout chick" uniform. One day the manager told me I was sloppy, and if I did not profession-alise myself, I would lose my job.

~

Capitalism is very limited. It tells us that more money is more happiness and that career paths are the only paths to success and a fulfilling life. Schools train us to be workers, not to think, or explore, discover, to love learning. They also teach us to be competitive, not to work together, in preparation for the future career life. We learn quickly to stay inside the square. To dress how we're told, to write resumes like this, poetry like that, to wear make up at job interviews if we are women, to get married, to get a mortgage, to work then go home and watch TV. And to write boring essays.

~

If we can't think outside the squares, how can we think beyond capitalism?

FOR A CREATIVE REVOLUTION FREED FROM FORMAL NON FICTION AND SPEECHES

Where capitalism puts fences around us, guiding where we walk and how, as revolutionaries seeking to create the opposite world, we should not *limit* ourselves to non fiction and speech oriented forums as our main tools for arguing against capitalism and for revolution. We shouldn't worship these methods as the most serious, legitimate, disciplined ones and as the highest expression of what we are striving for.

These tools are important and I would never argue that they should not be used, but rather we need to also see poetry, song, art, novels, dance, and so on as equally legitimate and strive more to use them. Where capitalism is boringly restrained in its ideas of beauty, life, and humanity, communi-cation, and thought, we need to be more creative.

INTELLECTUALISM IS FOR EVERYONE

Intellectualism, that is- thinking and theorising and understanding the world and society, is for every-one. Currently the left 'first world' intellectual world is dominated by, frankly, white, mature aged, university educated men. That is, people who in this unequal world, feel that they have a right to write, a right to be listened to. A right that a lot of blue collar workers, many women, youth, the uneducated, immigrants, and so on, do not feel they have and do not assert, despite their life experience being education enough to have a voice in this future world that we want to construct.

Capitalist education institutions and so on create and perpetuate this disparity. From an early age we are taught that politics is academic, that it is done by the Napoleons and Politicians of the world and that it is not for everyday people. It is an *abstract* theory to write essays about not something *lived* in our our houses and workplaces. They make politics exclusive and most people feel hostile towards and unwelcome to participate in the academic world.

The disparity between those who write and comment on politics is equally present between those who read that writing. Therefore, in order to increase participation in revolutionary thought, and to also reach more people, we need to embrace more creative methods with which people feel more comfortable.

Australian Aboriginals, to generalise a little, told their history and the history of their land with oral stories and cave drawings. Diego Rivera painted murals depicting Mexico's history, its 1910 revolu-tion and its society. He painted his first one in a school in Mexico city armed with a pistol, to defend himself against right wing students. Mafalda, an Argentinian comic series about a 6 year old girl who criticises the world with an acuteness rendered all the more shattering because it is a child saying it, is read by millions still, forty years after its creation. Here I have even seen a version of the Communist Manifesto, written in comic form. Its argument however is still exactly the same.

Rather than being abstract, politics is felt, lived, real, and personal. It's in our psychology, our relationships, our self esteem, our worry, stress, depression, happiness, our daily routine, our expectations. Novels, therefore, are one good medium for making politics real and making the link between the reader's own personal struggles and the larger historic class struggles. A link the dominant capitalist ideology would rather we didn't notice. There have been a lot of good novels written about struggles- Marge Piercy's novel on the early women's movement, Sembene Ousmane's novel about the Senegal train strikes, Frank Hardy's novels about the Australian communist party... These novels bring those battles to life and enable a reader far away by distance or time, to connect to those struggles in a way the BBC news for example, really doesn't (Those poor bombed people in Iraq, but that has nothing to do with me..).

I went to a small art exhibition in the culture centre, on the 3rd floor. The rooms were empty, an attendant slept in a corner. The paintings talked to no one. In the long term, I think we'd like a world where everyone feels comfortable walking into art galleries and talking with people about the messages of the paintings. In the short term, let's take those paintings down from the 3rd floor and put them in the street.

Let's destroy the old conception of intellectualism which sees thinking, ideas, theories, stuck in dry day long lectures in stale white halls away from the places where people are meeting and venting and working and struggling.

REVOLUTION SHOULD BE A DEMOCRATIC, MASS DISCUSSION, NOT CENTRED ON INDIVIDUALS

According to the largely accepted history, Napoleon did this, Bolivar did that, and Captain Cook 'discovered' Australia. The way history is told reflects the history teller's values and perpetuates them, as history is used to justify what is done in the present. History is talked about (in the classroom, in most published books, and in newspapers) in terms of single person actors, who are also generally men and people of power. Even history that ventures to recognise that there were strikes and movements, likes to pick out one or two special leaders, who are also 90% of the time, men. And in Australian history, they are usually not immigrants, Aboriginals, or gay people. Likewise, the writers of history - the famous quoted ones, are mostly the same sort of people, and rarely those who were actually involved in the strikes, the movements, affected by the depression or whatever. Imagine the psychological impact this has on working class people or on women or non white people etc. How are we supposed to value ourselves as actors in society if we are not written about as such? And doesn't all this apply to the way we talk about and do politics as well?

History and politics should be 'written' by the actors as well as the outside observers. Besides, the single-actor point of view really obscures the econ-omic classes. Even capitalism doesn't have single actors- George Bush was more a spokesperson for a whole class rather than an actor on his own, and of course a direct puppet for a range of US business and political interests.

Likewise, when (some people) quote Alan Woods as though he is the only person with any ideas, or when we organise forums and one person talks for two hours and then there are 15 minutes for questions (questions, not comments mind you), or when only a small percentage of us (revolution-aries) are writing articles that influence what we do and how we view the current political situation, aren't we just perpetuating their message that history and politics have a few key actors and that's it. That isn't to say that there are not leaders and there are not people with great ideas. But there are some things we can do better and differently. We can make forums more participatory and less passive. We can encourage the most repressed and exploited people to argue in ways that they are comfortable with, and respect those ways.

Participatory educational forums, discussions, and meetings simply require the implementation of basic progressive teaching techniques. Minimal Teacher Talking Time (even in a classroom situation where the teacher supposedly knows everything and the students nothing- such as second language teaching) means students are actively participating more and learning more.

A student listening for an hour learns a few things. A student somewhat active, by taking notes, learns a little more. A student participating in pair work, group work, standing up and doing interviews and going around a class room asking others what they think, with the teacher quietly organising the discussion, learns the most. Pair and small group discussion before larger group discussion also gives participants a chance to think about what they want to say and bounce it off over people, to organise and develop their ideas, and to get into 'talking mode' (as opposed to the passive listening mode we fall into during long lectures), and they are then more likely to contribute to the all in larger group discussion, no matter how much more 'educated' or experienced the leading talker or facilitator is. They are also more likely to listen to what the lead speaker has to say. We need to start using such methodology in our forums, making them less 'teacher', one-person-knows-all centric, and more participatory.

~

It was a community day in Los Curos, a town climbing the slopes of the Andes of Venezuela. Children made kites in the newly restored park, others danced in the tennis courts, doctors gave out vaccinations, poetry writers handed out their books and discussed them, artists sold their sculptures, and on the side of the tennis court community members painted a mural. There was a really old man, there were two roughly 19 year old, rather gorgeous young men, there were kids about 12 - and they all painted together. Art, dance, story telling and so on have the advantage that they can be the work and expression and argument of a collective of people, not just one person.

~

Or there is that mural in Bellas Artes in Caracas, if you haven't seen it, I wish you could. It tells Ven-ezuela's history in colour and virtually without words. We stopped there for half an hour one day, walking slowing along the wall- starting at the fruit poured into the sea, ending at the man watching Disney, I think it was, on TV. It was history in colour, in its beauty and injustice, with nameless crowds of people being repressed, and rebelling. They (the dominant class) would have history be black and white, numbers, dates, names, and dryness.

They'd have our history of struggle be dusty and forgotten and misunderstood.

PEOPLE COMMUNICATE AND LEARN IN

DIFFERENT WAYS

Related to education, we also need to acknowledge that a lot of people do not learn by reading large volumes of non fiction. This is not just related to the points mentioned about 'the right to read' and so on, but it is also a scientific fact that some people are usually either visual, audio, or movement-based learners and communicators.

Education under socialism, and our methods for arguing for socialism in the struggle for that society, should cater for the different ways people learn and shouldn't elevate reading large volumes as the most serious, some people simply do not learn that way, and there is nothing wrong with that.

Remember making spelling lists in primary school? Writing the words over and over again. Or I think of my comrade BR, who had a brain seizure (sorry I forget the medical term) and she had to learn to read all over again. Or deaf people. Or peo-ple who don't speak the local language. Or people who for whatever reason, have short attention spans. The world we're fighting for is a more inclusive world, lets see that reflected in the ways we argue for that world.

CREATIVE METHODS OF COMMUNICATION
ARE POWERFUL AND REBELLIOUS

That song 'I was only 19' about the Vietnam war and how..."The ANZAC legend

neglected to mention

the mud

the fear

the blood

the tears

the tension..."

... gives me throat lumps even though I wasn't born yet when the Vietnam war happened. It makes me hate imperialism and nationalism and see that soldiers are nothing but unprepared tools in Their war.

~

The new military government in Chile in 1973 understood the powerfulness of song and art. They tortured and killed Victor Jara. They banned many traditional Andean instruments. Jara himself said:

US imperialism understands very well the magic of communication through music and persists in filling our young people with all sorts of commercial tripe. With professional expertise they have taken certain measures: first, the commercialization of the so-called 'protest music'; second, the creation of 'idols' of protest music who obey the same rules and suffer from the same constraints as the other idols of the consumer music industry - they last a little while and then disappear. Meanwhile they are useful in neutralizing the innate spirit of rebellion of young people. The term 'protest song' is no longer valid because it is ambiguous and has been misused. I prefer the term 'revolutionary song'.

~

The innate spirit of rebellion of young people.

Funnelled into university

Essays

Funnelled into suit jobs

Assembly line jobs

House mortgages

Or

Into street art, rock revolution, history rap, rhythmic rebellion, general strikes, and a whole new world.

~

Powerful. Threatening. I'm talking about the Subversive songs of the South African anti-apartheid movement. The poetry of Pakistani women who are not even listened to by other revolutionaries, let alone seen in the street. The bible or the Koran or the Torah, one long creative and poetic novel you might say, which combined with that organised and powerful institution of religion, has been extremely powerful. The Jungle, by Upton Sinclair, that argued for socialism but is remembered for the disgust it caused over meat industry practices, and at least saw reform in that area. Catcher in the Rye was banned from schools for a while in the US, for the influence it was having on children and teenagers. But noone's banning our academic journals. (At least not now). Because that's just theory (apparently).

CREATIVE FORMS BRING US TOGETHER AND NEGATE THE BORDERS AND ALIENATION OF CAPITALISM

My boyfriend is a young Venezuelan with dark black eyes who does not speak English. We argue about Cuba and Denmark and the role of the individual in revolution and if there is a managerial class and if parties and power are inevitably bad. He says yes, I say no.

~

We sat on warm but wet university grass, him and I, and he read out poetry by a local Meridenian, about the earth and global warming, about beauty. And I melted. We were born on opposite sides of the world, we are different colours, different genders, and from different revolutionary backgrounds. But poetry brings us together.

~

Poetry reminds us that we want the same thing, despite all that.

A new blue world.

~

After we won the referendum in February this year, people spontaneously gathered in the main plaza to celebrate. There were red flags everywhere. Some young guys played drums to the rhythm of Caribbean passion. People danced. Strangers danced to strangers' music, danced together.

~

Capitalism makes us strangers. Art helps negate that. Together with solidarity in long struggle.

AND CREATIVE FORMS ARE HUMANISING

There are statistics about the number of homeless people in the United States. There are photos, of tents, and of grey people in grey clothing, expressionless. Then, police and bored youth beat up homeless people and get away with it. They are following a similar psychology to that which sustains racism and maltreatment of others. The one that says Iraqis are evil, are not human, are all the same. That homeless people are evil, are not human, are all the same. 1 billion starving people are starved, thinned black people with long faces, are all the same, are not us, are not our problem.

And then there was a youtube video. A home-less man, an ex prisoner, sang a song and played his guitar.

There was a drawing, of more expressionalistic value than any high priced gallery-ed art: An Iraqi child had drawn fences around his house and his family broken on the lawn.

An African woman wrote a novel about lesbian-ism and love.

And suddenly that kind of dehumanizing ideo-logy that turns Capitalism's victims into a powerless insignificant mass, is broken.

We are intelligent, we are creative, we are hurting and human and varied.

We are worth fighting for.

~

We pick up pen or paintbrush or puppets and we unravel the tangle and we start to understand what is going on and we tell other people about it. Our revolution should be done with reason and humanity. With emotion, passion, and seriousness and commitment. Creativity can express that.

Creativity is the ability to imagine that this world is wrong, despite the propaganda. And it is the abil-ity to imagine that another world is possible.

~

We are responsible for this delicate world

for its midnight migraines, its thrashing fevers, its fallen trees,

its fallen masses of thirdworld,

their voices stolen and put in a box somewhere,

One day that box will explode and a rainbow of confettied sounds will pour out and paint the planet a different colour, a colour we don't know yet.

~

We all know it takes a good argument to convince people that socialism is possible. The historical arguments, the class and materialist arguments. But to really know that socialism is possible and to dedicate our lives to fighting for it, we must be able to imagine it- like any goal, we need to know its real and reachable.

Struggles and systems like those in Cuba, Ven-ezuela, Nepal, etc- show us that. They make it all concrete. Solidarity in the workplace, or multitudes marching, show us that. But so does art, in all its forms. Marge Piercy's 'Woman on the edge of time' enabled me to really imagine a new world. A photo of happy, young, female doctors in Cuba, enabled me to imagine that.

~

Art is full of questions. And questioning, we stop seeing capitalism as natural.

AND BECAUSE IT'S A WAR OF IDEAS AND AGAINST OUR CULTURAL DOMINATION

Zafra Miriam is teaching dance in a few of the steep hillside barrios of Caracas. She told me,

"Up in Los Frailes there's this girl. She's about 12 I think but she looks 15. She dresses hot. Of course she has no idea what she's doing, she's just following industry standards. Anyway, the community up there is quite organised and they were putting something together for Mothers' Day. She does this dance with a couple of girls, one who was 8- don't get me started...It was pure child porn to the worst possible reggaeton... and I talked to the girl. I said, "Dance is a form of communication, you know that. What is it you're trying to say?" No answer. "What is it you want them to say back to you?" No answer. I told her to think about it, told her she has so much more to offer the world than ass wiggling."

Zafra said, "it's about treating them with respect, about supporting street art, not being a slave to the industry produced stuff...any learning situation where people confront a challenge in a supportive group is a form of community building...and we're exploring music that's not reggaeton, it's a kind of cultural revolution."

Fidel Castro said, 'Lies affect knowledge, conditioned reflection affects the capacity to think'.

~

Capitalism's hegemony affects our spirituality- not religion, I mean our heart, our desire to struggle, our humanity, our attitude towards our fellow beings, our curiosity.

~

On the capitalist assembly line of human beings there are a few key machines: Education, Media, and the Need to Survive. This assembly line makes human beings who *want* to work for rich, who *want* to buy their products, who look up to them and aspire to be like them. Who basically want to be exploited over and over again in so many different ways.

Our education of ourselves is one of our biggest weapons against one of their biggest weapons. They have a whole set of machinery set up to convince us to have THEIR values. We have to fight that machine with all the weapons we've got. Bring it on.

~

"Have you read my latest book of poetry?" Endes asks me in the artists' plaza where there is cheap coffee and people painting portraits.

Another time, watching a pre-election car parade I saw Omar. "Ah Tamara, good to see you, how are you? What have you been doing?" Etc. And he left me with a copy of his book of short stories.

Thanks to the government's publishing program the number of *out and proud* local poets has multiplied massively. Then there are all the murals, the free books (children's books, history, theory, classic novels) handed out from the backs of trucks, at fairs, at protests, at youth camps and from tents in the plaza. There are the children in the barrios learning to play the violin. There is dance, theatre, choir, poetry reading in the plaza and in the pub, TV and filming collectives and Community radio. Not to mention the literacy programs and the Boli-varian University.

I think there is a lot of room for improvement in the cultural revolution here (for want of a better phrase), but now I think people here are better armed with their own real history, with tools to communicate, with the ability to express themselves and to be creative. And like that, they will be harder to repress.

It will be harder to convince them that work is not exploitation and that buying is liberating and that the world is free when it is not.

~

Let's rap against imperialism standing on milk crates in pedestrian tunnels. Let's put struggle poetry on stickers and put those stickers on ATMS, in public toilets, on vending machines and parking meters. Let's print more stories, write more novels, paint more murals, put comics in our newspapers and dance at our social events. Our arguments, our messages belong in meetings, in schools, in protests, in the memories of warn out repressed people about to sleep. In late night pub conversations, in park and plaza conversations, as shared conversations between strangers watching a play. Let's take the war of classes, of media, of ideas, into what ever spaces we can, involving more and more people. Take the abstraction out of politics and put it into the street and the living world.

This is a call for the left and for revolutionaries to break with old paradigms of education and argument and to take art, or culture, seriously. To use it to wake people up, to communicate, to argue, to show people how beautiful that other world we are proposing, is.

LIBERATORY CRITICISM

Below, a chronological collage of liberatory critical views (excerpts) on imaginative litera-ture and other art from the past 145 years, largely though not entirely US-based, includ-ing viewpoints ranging from the minimally progressive to the revolu-tionary. While most of the viewpoints below are typical of the author or the work from which they originate, a few are merely incidentally liberatory rather than representative of some larger progres-sive focus of the author or work.

Adrienne Rich, A Human Eye (2009):

Antonio Gramsci wrote of the culture of the future that "new" individual artists can't be manufac-tured: art is a part of society – but that to imagine a new socialist society is to imagine a new kind of art that we can't foresee from where we now stand. "One must speak," Gramsci wrote, "of a struggle for a new culture, that is, for a new moral life that cannot but be intimately connected to a new intui-tion of life, until it becomes a new way of feeling and seeing reality and, therefore, a world intimate-ly ingrained in 'possible artists' and 'possible works of art.'"

In any present society, a distinction needs to be made between the "avante-garde that always re-mains the same" – what a friend of mine has called "the poetry of false problems" – and a poetics searching for transformative meaning on the shore-line of what can now be thought or said. Adonis, writing of Arab poetry, reminds Arab poets that "modernity should be a creative vision, or it will be no more than a fashion. Fashion grows old from the moment it is born, while creativity is eternally modern." …

Most critical writing on poetry in the United States (I can't speak of elsewhere) has reached a pretty low point: degenerated into biographical juicy bits extracted from or read into poems; or "poststruc-turalist" jargon. Any poet whose work is both artistically searching and ideologically dissenting knows how shallow, therefore ultimately dismis-sive, even favorable critical response can be, isolat-ing poems from their historical and social fields of energy – save perhaps as the poetry can be related to a recognized aesthetic movement. (But aesthetic movements, too, belong to historical and social processes, and need critiquing in that light.)

This is a serious loss for poets (who might bene-fit from more informed and penetrating criticism); for readers (who might welcome discussion that could bring their reading of poetry into focus with a world they know all too well, help them become the great readers Whitman declared a great poetry would need); and for the trajectory of all whose desire for social justice is inseparable from their need for beauty.

The imagination of an unrealized, human social order is as passionate and ineluctable as the artist's search for unrealized expression. …

John Pilger, "Hollywood's New Cen-sors", ZNet (2009):

These are extraordinary times. Vicious colo-nial wars and political, economic and environ-mental corruption cry out for a place on the big screen. Yet, try to name one recent film that has dealt with these, honestly and powerfully, let alone satirically. Censorship by omission is virulent. We need an-other Wall Street, another Last Hurrah, another Dr. Strangelove. The parti-sans who tunnel out of their prison in Gaza, bringing in food, clothes, medicines and weap-ons with which to defend themselves, are no less heroic than the celluloid-honoured POWs and partisans of the 1940s. They and the rest of us deserve the respect of the greatest popular medium.

David Walsh, "Novelist John Updike dead at 76: Was he a 'great novelist'?" WSWS (2009):

The need to bend the truth, avoid certain re-alities, above all, not look too probingly at America's so-cial foundations affected his art, deflecting it and blunting it. In the more than 20 novels, there is far too much waste, secondary material, running in place, even showing off. As well, frankly, there is a good deal of mean-spiritedness directed toward those who fall out-side of or reject Updike's limited middle-class American universe.

Shelley Ettinger, "Lush Lies" Read Red (2009):

I'm not a fan of detective novels, mysteries, police procedurals. In my experience they're usually just not very interesting. There's a same-ness. Every time someone urges one on me tell-ing me that no kidding, this one's different, I find it, yep, the same as all the others. They're unimaginative. The writ-ing is blah. All that aside, for me the main impedi-ment to enjoying this genre is that for the most part the heroes are police.

In the real world, police are the furthest thing from heroes there is. Police are racist killers. Po-lice are assassination squads occupying the commun-ities where poor and oppressed people live. Police are the security force in the employ of the ruling class. At base, police are the capi-talist state in its rawest form: armed might fa-cilitating the project of capitalism, which is ex-ploitation.

One of the unforeseen and, well, embarrass-ing, refrains of this blog seems to be how time after time I get snookered, hoodwinked, into reading a book that I shoulda oughta known wasn't for me. It's usually because of some com-bination of re-views, of which I'm generally wary since they're pretty much always imbued with bourgeois con-sciousness yet which still sometimes pique my interest, and friends' rec-ommendations, which I really shouldn'ta oughtn'ta trust any more than the establishment literary critics but I foolishly do.

And so I spent the last two days reading *Lush Life* by Richard Price. Waste of time. A fast read, the guy can write, sure sure. At the end, though, what have you got? You've got a book in which the heroes are cops; in which every white mid-dle-class character ends up alive, with a future, with hope; and every Black and Latino character (other than cops) ends up dead or futureless or hopeless; a book that pretends to be realistic and yet in which not a single cop ever lays a violent hand on a Black or Latino youth; a book in which every Black and Latino youth is a liar and a criminal of one sort or another. A book whose author clearly thinks he un-derstands the op-pressed, how they think, how they talk, how they live – whose narrative armors itself with a sort of faux compassion for people who nev-ertheless are, when you come right down to it, por-trayed as so other, so exotically brutally icky, that the reader is set up from start to finish to identify only with the cops, with the murder victim's family and friends, and never, no how, no way, with the oppressed. What a menda-cious, backward, upside-down view of reality and of who the real criminals in this society are. What a waste of two precious days of reading time.

Sandra Cisneros, The House on Mango Street interview – The Leonard Lopate Show wnyc.org (2009):

Q: You studied at the prestigious Iowa Writers' Workshop. What was it like being there as a Chi-cana woman who grew up in Chicago?
A: Well it wasn't so prestigious to me. It was rather horrible. I like to tell people that I'm a writer *despite* the University of Iowa Writers' Workshop. It taught me what I didn't want to be as a writer and how I didn't want to teach. I think that we often don't hear from the dissi-dent voices of people who were enrolled there, people of color, women, work-ing class people, because there are so few of them there, and when they do survive that experience, perhaps they're not in a place where they can voice their

opinion.

Q: So it sounds like you absolutely hated it, but I mean was there in a sense –

A: Well that's putting it mildly, yes. …

Q: Had anybody ever written a book like *The House on Mango Street* before you wrote it? Was this kind of literature around? Was it readily available? Was there a milieu that was sort of writing about this sort of stuff then?

A: I think that perhaps a literary critic could argue that there were models for a book like this. I wasn't aware of them at the time, but certainly they came to me later and are my favorite books. *Maud Martha*, by Gwendolyn Brooks. It's a series of vignettes written by a poet. And *Lilus Kikus*, written by the Mexican writer Elena Poniatowska. There's a book called *Canek*, by Ermilo Abreu Gómez, a writer from the Yucatan, Mexico. And so there are dif-ferent models for story cycles that I've discovered. They're usually written by women or people of col-or. They're an alternate way of storytelling, and they're novels but not in the linear way that we're used to… I think of her [the main charac-ter in *The House on Mango Street*] as being in the border zone between childhood and adulthood. I used her at first to voice my own censored pe-riod at Iowa to gain a voice in which I could say things I could not say as a young woman in my twenties, and eventu-ally she became a voice for many of my concerns about my young students, not simply my remem-brances. So in the begin-ning she was me, and later as the book travelled from Iowa to Chicago, she became a spokesper-son for things I wanted to say, injustices that I witnessed as a teacher working with young Latinas in the Pilsen community of Chicago.

Q: How did writing the book help you answer some of the questions that you had growing up, some of the concerns that you wanted to ex-press?

A: Well, you have to think of yourself as a young woman in [your] twenties; you are breaking all of the traditions that are part of your culture; you're living away from home; you've gone away to school; you don't want to get married; you don't want to have children; your brothers are still living at home. You're working for minimum wage, sometimes part time, and you're working in a com-munity with other young women that are going to lead the lives you don't want to lead, and you have lots of questions. You're teaching them how to write poetry. Perhaps you're teaching them how to read literature, and perhaps you're teaching read-ing skills. And everyday you go to work and you think, What the hell am I doing? Shouldn't I be teaching this girls how to control their fertility? How can I help these guys that are getting beat up every day when they walk to class because they live in a gang infested neigh-borhood? How can I keep them safe? What am I doing with my own life, and what is my own political direction? Do I really want to write? Is that the most important thing in my life? And how is writing going to change the world? These are questions that I wasn't taught at Iowa. And they were of great concern to me in my twenties. I thought perhaps I might give up writing. Maybe I would take some other skill that I could use with my young women, some-thing that might change their lives, something that would save them, something that would give them a better life, other than to write po-etry. How is a poem going to save them? What's the use of literature? Why do we teach literature to people who have such sad and desperate lives? And why am I a writer? You know, these were all questions I thought about…

Barbara Foley interviewed by Joseph G. Ramsey, Reconstruction 8.1 (2008):

JR: It's been over 20 years now since you first pub-lished Telling the Truth: the theory and practice of documentary fiction, and a decade and a half since Radical Representations came out. How far has the study of proletarian litera-ture and left culture of the mid-20th century more generally come since the 1980s and early 90s? What have been the most remarkable changes in how people relate to radical and pro-letarian literature, since you first entered the field?

BF: A lot has been accomplished as regards the study of proletarian literature over the past cou-ple of decades; I could list some two or three dozen books, as well as scads of articles, which show that this body of literature is now routinely accorded a good deal of respectability. Hey, literary proletari-anism is even seen as integral to modernism (which of course the literary radicals of the time realized – they were all for "making it new.") Radical Repre-sentations (1993) helped to do some of the ground-clearing of the knee-jerk anticommunism that had guided almost all discussions of leftist literature up to the late 1980s; I am glad wrote the book.

BF: To this day, though, anticommunism continues to color a lot of the commentary on literary radical-ism. It has gone into the groundwater of much con-temporary theory, taking the form of a critique of "class reductionism" and "master narratives," the relegation of class to a matter of identity, and the embrace of various "intersectionality" models for examining what Terry Eagleton calls the "holy trin-ity" of gender/race/class. So much work remains to be done.

H. Bruce Franklin, "Inside Stories of the Global American Prison" Texas Studies in Literature and Language (2008):

Despite the assault on the literature of the Ameri-can prison [which Franklin documents in detail], it has been breaking into literature courses and anth-ologies. The 2006 edition of the Heath Anthology of American Literature, which is used in classrooms around the world, actually included a whole sec-tion labeled "Prison Literature." Although this "cluster" consisted of a mere twenty-seven pages out of the more than three thousand in the multi-volume anthology, that was enough to provoke the disapproval of the New York Times Book Review, whose editor Rachel Donadio, complained that it took up more space than that given to "the great poet Elizabeth Bishop." Even more reprehensible, according to Donadio, is the fact that this prison literature section "includes works by Kathy Boudin, a former member of the Weather Under-ground who served more than 20 years for her role in a 1981 robbery

and murder." Implying that the five authors included in this section collectively are not worth as much space as Bishop, Donadio names only Boudin, failing even to give the names of such widely celebrated poets as Etheridge Knight and Jimmy Santiago Baca.[8] Nor does Donadio say even a word about any of their actual work, including Boudin's three beautiful, extreme-ly moving poems. Masquerading as literary criticism based on aesthetic criteria, this editorial com-mentary in the New York Times Book Review thus offers a minor but revealing example of how domi-nant cultural institutions collaborate with the poli-tical apparatus to suppress prison literature....

It is no surprise that modern prisoners [decades ago] helped lead the rediscovery of slave literature, because chattel slavery did not disappear in 1865 – it merely morphed into the modern American pris-on ... merged ... with the more modern [forms of slavery] pioneered by the American prison.... When the time came to globalize this institution, the men chosen for the job were some of its most notorious officials.[9]

The literature of slaves told the inside stories of antebellum slavery and thus helped destroy it. So too, the literature of prisoners tells the inside stor-ies of the American prison and thus threatens its dominion and expansion. The deepest insights into the American global prison, including its culture and political logic, come from this literature it tries to repress.

Footnote [8] – Franklin notes: A torrent of prison literature was pouring out to the American public [over three decades ago] in mass-market paper-backs, newspapers, magazines, and major motion pictures. This era ended with the downfall of the Nixon regime in 1974, the final defeat of the United States by Vietnam in 1975, and the reactionary epoch that soon followed. In 1976 came the Big Bang, the spectacular explosion of the prison-industrial complex. As a necessary corollary to this pris-on cosmos, there began a relentless campaign to silence prisoners and ex-prisoners [by passage of new laws and implementation of other measures.... Moreover, today] gone from the so-called "penitentiary" or "correctional facility" is any pretense of reformation or rehabilitation [exceptions to the rule aside]. In the typical

American prison, degradation, brutalization, and even overt torture are the norm.

Footnote [9] – Franklin details: After the invasion of Iraq, Lane McCotter, who had been forced to resign as the director of the Utah Department of Corrections be-cause of torture carried out under his administration, was put in charge of reconstructing Saddam Hussein's Abu Ghraib. John Armstrong, former director of the Connecticut Department of Corrections, who had been driven out of his position because of sexual and other tortures revealed by the ACLU and Amnesty Interna-tional, became deputy director of operation for the entire Iraqi prison system….

Peter Birnie, "Theatre: Stuff Happens and war ensues, thanks to W., Rummy and Condi" , Vancouver Sun (2008):

The Firehall Arts Centre is about to present Hare's controversial 2004 play Stuff Happens, about the lies told on the road to war with Iraq. I ask him if the political play, which is a rare bird on the princi-pal stages of Canadian theatre, fares better in Lon-don's West End.

"No," he declares firmly. "You have no idea. At the moment in London there is a revival of a play called The Chalk Garden, by Enid Bagnold, which is a play about aristocrats handing crumpets to each other. It is exactly the play that John Osborne [Look Back in Anger] vowed to drive out of the British theatre forever. It's actually the play that created the feeling that we must change our theatre and we must make it contemporary.

"Well, needless to say, this revival of The Chalk Garden has been praised to the skies by the British critics, who are kind of heaving a sigh of relief and saying, 'Thank God, we've got nice people saying nice things on the stage again!'" What's not nice for Hare is the reluctance of people on this side of the pond to produce Stuff Happens.

"It took an artistic director in Los Angeles," Hare says, "Gordon Davidson at the Mark Taper Forum, who did it as the last play of his 35-year tenure as artistic director, and said, 'I can only do this play because I'm leaving after I do

it.' The fact that it sells out wherever it's performed," Hare continues, "doesn't seem to sway minds at all. People would rather have empty theatres where people are passing crumpets to each other than full theatres with plays about contemporary events. I don't know why."

Tara Parker-Post, "Healthful Messages Wrapped in Fiction", NYT (2008):

At the annual scientific conference of the Obesity Society this month in Phoenix, researchers from the Duke medical school presented some remarkable findings on "Lake Rescue" (B*tween Productions, 2005), a Beacon Street book that focuses on the struggles of an overweight girl named Chelsea Briggs.

Chelsea is teased at school and is so self-conscious about her weight that she skips gym class. On a camping trip, she connects with an ath-letic camp counselor who was also overweight as a child. She gains confidence in her skills as a pho-tographer, and when a group of campers get lost on a hike she helps lead them to safety. And in the course of all this, she gains a renewed appreciation for fitness and healthful eating.

The Duke researchers studied 81 girls enrolled in the university's six-month childhood obesity program, called Healthy Lifestyles. Thirty-one girls were given a copy of "Lake Rescue"; 33 others got a 2006 Beacon Street book, "Charlotte in Paris," that carries a positive message of self-esteem but doesn't focus on weight or healthful eating. And 17 girls received the regular program counseling, but no book.

After six months, the girls who got "Lake Rescue" posted a decline in average body mass index scores of 0.71; those who didn't read the book had an average *increase* of 0.05. That seemingly minor difference means the girls who read "Lake Rescue" will achieve a healthy weight in a few years if they maintain their regular growth rate and do not gain any more weight.

"The results of the study are not striking in how big they were but that it worked at all," said Dr. Sarah C. Armstrong, a pediatrician who directs the Healthy Lifestyles program. "It's such a positive, easy intervention. The next step is to follow these girls long term."

The researchers were also struck that the girls who read "Charlotte in Paris" also did better than the girls who didn't receive any book at all. The reasons are not clear, but one theory is that though reading is a sedentary activity, it does take time away from less healthful activities, like snacking in front of the TV…

David Edgar, "Doc and dram", The Guardian (2008):

The war on terror brought politics back on to the world stage, and it's no surprise that politics re-turned to theatrical stages as well. But the predom-inance and resilience of verbatim, wit-ness and testi-mony theatre needs explaining. The big subjects of this decade appear to lend themselves to tradition-al, mimetic representa-tion. So why have so many post-9/11 plays pre-sented their research interviews as reportage rather than dramatising them in scenes? Why is the first question for an audience at a contempo-rary political play not "how have they shown the horrors of terrorism and war?" but "will it be stools or chairs?"

The rise of a theatre of reportage rather than en-actment is all the more surprising in view of what preceded it. … Dozens and dozens of ver-batim and witness plays have appeared, many about the war on terror, some about other con-temporary issues, following on from Jessica Blank and Erik Jensen's The Exonerated (pre-sented from 2000 to 2005 and now televised), a compilation of the stories of six people wrongly incarcerated on American death rows. … Thea-tre of Fact is the other side of the coin of 50s and 60s absurdism. Both forms sought to ex-press phenomena they could no longer explain.

…much journalism-posing-as-theatre is liter-ally and proudly that. In the 2003 play about railway privatisation, The Permanent Way, David Hare and his collaborators did the kind of in-depth, investi-gative, historically analytical job on a contempor-ary political story that con-ventional journalism rarely does any more, oc-cupying space abandoned both by long-form print journalism and by tradi-tional television documentary. In Deep Cut, report-er Brian Cathcart is quoted as saying that "journal-ism

dropped the ball" after the internal inquiry in-to the four deaths, implying that theatre has now picked it up.

Similarly, you could say Hare's 2004 play about the build-up to the invasion of Iraq, Stuff Happens, was performing the role that televi-sion drama-documentary has performed in the past. Drama-documentary was developed by Granada in the 70s to report stories that could not be portrayed by conventional journalism; since then its priorities have shifted from doc to dram…

And far from evading polemic, fact-based thea-tre has tended to make clear where it stands, there-by making an impact beyond the usual audience for political theatre… …Fact-based theatre calls at-tention to, and thus ques-tions, the credibility of the evidence on which we base our view of the world. Unlike naturalis-tic drama, which invites us to sus-pend disbe-lief, verbatim drama wears its sources on its sleeve.

Nick Turse, "Hollywood Movies and the US Military", TomDispatch (2008):

"Liberal Hollywood" is a favorite whipping-boy of right-wingers who suppose the town and its signa-ture industry are ever-at-work under-mining the U.S. military. In reality, the military has been deep-ly involved with the film indus-try since the Silent Era. Today, however, the *ad hoc* arrangements of the past have been replaced by a full-scale one-stop shop, occupying a floor of a Los Angeles office building. There, the Army, Navy, Air Force, Mar-ines, Coast Guard, and the Department of Defense itself have es-tablished entertainment liaison offices to help ensure that Hollywood makes movies the mili-tary way.

What they have to trade, especially when it comes to blockbuster films, is access to high-tech, tax-payer funded, otherwise unavailable gear. What they get in return is usually the right to alter or shape scripts to suit their needs. If you want to see the fruits of this relationship in action, all you need to do is head down to your local multiplex. Chances are that *Iron Man* – the latest military-entertainment masterpiece – is playing on a couple of screens.

Eileen Jones, "'Stop Loss': Patriotic Bluster Dressed up As a Protest Movie", AlterNet / The eXile (2008):

'Ah signed up thinkin' Ah was goin' there fer mah country.' Hayseed accents can't hide the film's glamorization of war. … [Stop Loss is] a protest movie about the war that – follow me closely here – doesn't actually protest the war. Because that would be a bummer, getting us into that whole thing again about Bush and Cheney and the WMDs that weren't there and the no-exit-strategy. Not to mention the 4,000 dead Americans we're sort of peeved about. We support our troops, you know! In this movie Peirce insists on supporting our troops so hard it's impossible to figure out what's ailing us, watching these fine boys with their fine parents all having fine values in this fine country of ours. Nagging questions hang over the whole pro-ject: if our Texas-style patriotism is so great, and our mission to defend America is so great, and we've got hordes of studly young guys leaping at the opportunity to go fight whoever they're told, and they're all great, too, and their families and communities are great, then uh … what's the prob-lem? Why isn't everybody happy?

Well, for one thing, it turns out that if you go fight in a war, you can get SHOT. Yeah! It's true! Even a righteous American, with a big gun, and a Kevlar vest, and a Hummer! That's the movie's first-act revelation. We see our boys in Iraq, doing their jobs chasing insurgents into local people's apartments, and those bastards start SHOOTING at 'em!

Debra Linn, "Book Club Activism" readinggroupguides.com/blog/ (2008):

Edwidge Danticat's family memoir Brother, I'm Dying riled us up. Outraged us, actually. We were incensed by the treatment her uncle received when he arrived in Miami from full-on upheaval in Haiti. Our book club had received the call to action, our chance to start living up to our name, Page Against the Machine, an oppor-tunity for book club activism

Book club activism sounds high-minded and formal, but really, just about any book can spur your club to action. It rises organically from your connection to the book. What Is the What by Dave Eggers leads to activism about Sudan. Water for Elephants to the Humane Society or PETA, per-haps.

Susan Bell, "Talking Bodies: Sociologist Studies Art's Role in Health Movements"; Bowdoin: Academic Spotlight (2008):

Works of art can anchor social movements," says Bell, Bowdoin's A. Myrick Freeman Professor of Social Sciences. "Think of the AIDS quilt, or the Clothesline Project that is used to bring attention to issues of sexual assault and domestic violence against women. Images can be a powerful way to signal, engage, shock. People respond viscerally. It opens up a conversation." In a surprising twist on her discipline, Bell has turned to analyses of works of art to guide her in her research. In recent publications in journals in-cluding Health, Sociology of Health and Illness, and Qualitative Research in Psychology, Bell has made a case for incorporating the analysis of visual narratives into sociological work as documents and barometers of human experience.

Mark Vallen, "1930s: The Making of 'The New Man'" Art for a Change blog (2008):

The American surrealist painter, Peter Blume (1906 -1992), was once highly regarded as an American figurative painter, though today he is unfortunate-ly almost entirely forgotten. Employing the same techniques utilized by Renaissance artists, Blume's paintings made use of a near photographic realism, but his narrative works were permeated with sur-realist vision and social realist spirit. Blume spent 1932 in Rome, Italy, on a Guggenheim grant, the same year the Italian fascist movement celebrated the tenth anniversary of its so-called "March on Rome," the coup d'état that brought dictator

Benito Mussolini and his National Fascist Party to power. After returning to the U.S. Blume brooded over what he had witnessed before starting work in 1934 on *The Eternal City*, a painting that would take him three years to complete and which is now part of *"The New Man"* exhibit.

As he was working on the final touches of his painting in 1936, Blume wrote a proclamation against war and fascism titled *"The Artist Must Choose"*. In his essay he exclaimed; "We, as artists, must take our place in this crisis on the side of growth and civilization against barbarism and reaction, and help to create a better social order." ...

Upon completing *The Eternal City* in 1937, Blume exhibited the painting at the Julien Levy Gallery in Manhattan. Even though the message of Blume's anti-fascist work was unambiguous, especially when combined with his written proclamation, numerous critics voiced thick-headed and imper-ceptive remarks concerning the work. The New York Sun's widely read art critic, Henry McBride, made this vinegary comment about Blume and his painting: "He won, it seems, a Guggenheim fellow-ship, and went to Italy nominally as an art student but actually as a political spy, and returns with a picture that pretends to mock Mussolini. This, of course, is an odd undertaking for an American artist." Edward Alden Jewell, art critic for the New York Times wrote: "The political aspects of this treatise are not altogether clear. We are left in doubt as to whether the propagandist considers this modern dictator a self-sprung megalomaniac or a figurehead manipulated by social forces that have taken control of the situation in Italy. Scarcely more convincing is the religious symbol employed. There is nowhere evident the great transfiguring principle itself of Christian love and Christian sacrifice."

That Edward Alden Jewell referred to Blume as a "propagandist" is revealing, especially since *The Eternal City* was the only explicitly po-litical paint-ing ever created by Blume. The open hostility that American art critics displayed towards Blume's painting was but one indication of the growing disfavor to fall upon figurative and social realist artists in the late 1930s. In a letter to the New York Times in 1943, painters Mark Rothko, Adolph Gottlieb, and Barnett Newman called for an art that would transcend real world issues in favor of pure abstraction. Refuting realism, they declared that meaning in art can only "come out of a consummated experience between picture and onlooker", further stating that "We want to reassert the picture plane. We are for flat forms, because they destroy illusion and reveal truth." Abstract Expressionism soon came to dominate American art, and to the detriment of us all, the realism practiced by Peter Blume was declared hopelessly passé by "serious" critics, collectors, and museums.

Peter Bradshaw, "'Redacted'" Guardian (2008):

Perhaps without quite realising it, De Palma is ap-plying his extensively developed idiom of slash, splatter and gore. After a while, Redacted starts to feel like a sort of politicised exploitation-horror pic-ture. I am still not entirely sure if it is just the dir-ector's default position for representing violence, or if the wayward genius in him senses that, in the era of Abu Ghraib, this is the truest way of repre-senting the essentially grotesque nature of the mili-tary adventure in Iraq. ...

Michael Weldon, "Michael Weldon Interview" by Ryan Lambie; Den of Geek (2008):

DoG: *On your website you say that movies are more politicized now than at any time since WWII or the Cold War. Could you give any examples?*
MW: This is a huge topic. Many movies, producers, and production companies, and some stud-ios, stars and directors have close ties to the Ameri-can DOD (Department Of Defence), arms dealers (American and Israeli), oil companies, and/ or the ruling Republican Party and neocon Bush backers. The Hollywood/D.C. connection has existed for a long time to some extent but it's stronger now than ever. After 9/11 Karl Rove met with studio heads and top producers and directors and convinced most of

them to be part of the war on terror and to be more patriotic and pro FBI, CIA, Armed Forces …

If an American movie features spies, the military, and military hardware and does not explic-itly criticized the government and the Iraq war – it has the full cooperation of the DOD. Some of our tax dollars actually go to providing military planes, boats, weapons, soldiers, advisors… to pro military movies that we pay too much to see – then go buy DVDs of! Many major movies have government agents and agencies right in the credits if you know where to look. Even most people who look back at WWII era movies or early Cold War era movies and realize that they were propaganda, don't real-ize what's happening now. Major pro war movies don't have to use modern hardware though (see *300*)…

This is equally true with American TV. The maj-ority of today's popular drama shows (many pro-duced by Jerry *Top Gun* Bruck-heimer) glorify gov-ernment agencies and agents, while stealing crazed psycho killer plots and autopsy gore from mostly cheap and ob-scure horror movies. Some like the Rupert Mur-doch-backed 24 (Dick Cheney's favor-ite show) exist pretty much to keep us scared, vot-ing Republican, and to justify torture. I could go on about politics on channels owned by Fox, Disney, Viacom…

Karl Wenclas, "More CIA Fun Stuff" Attacking the Demi-Puppets (2008):

1.) Did the CIA [concern itself with] The Paris Review? I'd say yes. After all, it was their money which created the publication!
2.) Their agenda was served by presenting an inter-nationally credible journal ("Paris" Review) which presented a liberal – not radical – example of American literature.

Recall what the trend in American letters and American criticism had been before 1950. Socially active writing was strongly on the march.

(A better journal to look into is Partisan Review, once an organ for the likes of Philip Rahv, which in its later days became the home of neocons! How did this happen? We know that Par-tisan Review was another which received CIA funds.)

Raymond Carver is the perfect example of how the trend in literature, firmly in place by the 70's, put there by the likes of Paris Review, had working class writers like Ray Carver – supposed icon of the working class – writing "minimalist" work which a Susan Minot and other trust-funders could model their own work after! Amazing, really. Working class art– but find in Carver's published work much on the job, or unions, or strikes, or the boss, or anger. Not there. Why was this?

Missing are POLEMICS – the polemics of American writing of the Thirties and Forties.

What did I find with my own writing "career." After I published a couple strong (albeit strongly edited) work in lit journals in the early 90's, I had lit editors and writers telling me that literature was not supposed to be polemical.

Orhan Pamuk: "Orhan Pamuk with Carol Becker" The Brooklyn Rail (2008):

I would say the literary globalization of the world had been completed years ago, when nobody was talking about globalization. With this, I imply that the art of the novel is well and kicking and that ev-eryone from all over the world has access to and is using it. It is now a common heritage of humanity. It has what I would call an intense elasticity in that it can absorb national problems and represent na-tional dramas, so that you can use and impose your particular understanding of this form into your corner of the world, or discuss your national de-bate, whatever it is, such that it will hold the nation together, because it is a text that everyone can ar-gue with. Let me give you an example: I wrote *Snow*, a political novel, thinking everybody would be angry, and, yes, everyone was angry; but every-one was also reading, discussing and talking about it. I think the art of the novel, as a form, is one of the great arts humanity has developed that has continuity, that changes and survives. Over the last twenty years, we have witnessed a return to the 18th century Diderot kind of novel, which is a form that combines essays and novels together. Actually, I consider myself a sort of a representative of that "encyclopedic" novel. In other words, you can put anything into novels; novels are encyclopedias. Mallarmé's words to that effect say that in the end, everything in the world, for the imaginative novel-ist or imaginative literary person, is in fact made to end up in a book. That's how I see the world as well, because I am a novelist, and I care about the informative, encyclopedic quality of the novel.

Hermione Hoby, "Know literature, know the world", Guardian Books Blog (2008):

A team from Manchester University and the Lon-don School of Economics claim that stories and their writers can do just as much as academics and policy researchers, perhaps even more, to explain and communicate the world's problems. Fiction, they boldly venture, can be just as useful as fact. The report is named The Fiction of Development: Literary Representation as a Source of Authorita-tive Knowledge…

The list of novels whose literary power is bound up with their power to push social change is poten-tially huge. Dickens, of course, is an obvious con-tender, as is Harper Lee with To Kill A Mocking-bird, but from more recent years I'd add Rose Tre-main's novel, the Orange Prize-winning, The Road Home.

Surely her protagonist Lev has done more to elucidate the plight of migrant workers than any worthy but dull research findings. Rational beings that we are, we will nonetheless always be more affected by emotion than we are by logic. As the re-port's authors remind us, "having a "good story" is essential if one wants to make a difference in the world".

Unsurprisingly George Eliot, puts it better:

"Appeals founded on generalisations and statistics require a sympathy ready-made, a moral senti-ment already in activity; but a picture of human life such as a great artist can give, surprises even the trivial and the selfish into that attention to what is apart from themselves, which may be called the raw material of moral sentiment."

Ammu Joseph, "Twists in the Tale", The Hindu (2008):

In her essay for The New York Times series, Writers on Writing, Sara Paretsky mentions a letter from a furious reader demanding to know why her books were "infested" with political issues when all she wanted was to be entertained. Her response: "When you're writing about law, justice and soci-ety, you are either challenging or supporting the status quo."

Jeremy Hsu, "The Secrets of Storytelling: Why We Love a Good Yarn", Scientific American (2008):

[Stories] do far more than entertain…

…how do the emotional and cognitive effects of a narrative influence our beliefs and real-world decisions? The answers to these questions seem to be rooted in our history as a social animal. We tell stories about other people and for other people. Stories help us to keep tabs on what is happening in our communities. The safe, imaginary world of a story may be a kind of training ground, where we can practice interacting with others and learn the customs and rules of society.

As many as two thirds of the most respected stories in narrative traditions seem to be variations on three narrative patterns, or prototypes, accord-ing to Hogan. The two more common prototypes are romantic and heroic scenarios—the former foc-uses on the trials and travails of love, whereas the latter deals with power struggles. The third proto-type, dubbed "sacrificial" by Hogan, focuses on agrarian plenty versus famine as well as on societal redemption. These themes appear over and over again as humans create narrative records of their most basic needs: food, reproduction and social status.

The power of stories does not stop with their abili-ty to reveal the workings of our minds. Narrative is also a potent persuasive tool, according to Hogan and other researchers, and it has the ability to shape beliefs and change minds.

Advertisers have long taken advantage of

narra-tive persuasiveness by sprinkling likable characters or funny stories into their commer-cials. A 2007 study by marketing researcher Jennifer Edson Escalas of Vanderbilt University found that a test audience responded more posi-tively to advertisements in narrative form as compared with straight-forward ads that en-couraged viewers to think about the arguments for a product. Similarly, Green co-authored a 2006 study that showed that labeling informa-tion as "fact" increased critical analysis, whereas labeling information as "fiction" had the opposite effect. Studies such as these sug-gest people accept ideas more readily when their minds are in story mode as opposed to when they are in an analytical mindset.

Works of fiction may even have unexpected real-world effects on people's choices. Merlot was one of the most popular red wines among Ameri-cans until the 2005 film *Sideways* de-picted actor Paul Giamatti as an ornery wine lover who snub-bed it as a common, inferior wine. Wine-makers saw a noticeable drop in sales of the red wine that year, particularly after Sideways garnered national attention through several Oscar nominations.

As researchers continue to investigate story-tell-ing's power and pervasiveness, they are also look-ing for ways to harness that power. Some such as Green are studying how stories can have applica-tions in promoting positive health messages. "A lot of problems are behaviorally based," Green says, pointing to research docu-menting the influence of Hollywood films on smoking habits among teens. And Mar and Oat-ley want to further examine how stories can en-hance social skills by acting as simul-ators for the brain, which may turn the idea of the so-cially crippled bookworm on its head.

One thing is clear – although research on sto-ries has only just begun, it has already turned up a wealth of information about the social roots of the human mind…

Jesse Hamlin, "Dedicated to the cause –

documentary celebrates activist Tillie Olsen", San Francisco Chronicle

(2008):

In the film, [Alice] Walker credits Olsen with "changing the landscape of feminist writing and reading," alluding to Olsen's role in getting the Feminist Press to republish forgotten works by women, among them Rebecca Harding Davis' 1861 "Life in the Iron Mills" and Agnes Smed-ley's 1929 "Daughter of Earth."

In the film, Olsen says she started writing about the lives of the working people she grew up with because "it was nearly impossible to find them in any of the books I read." While still in her teens, she began writing the novel "Yon-nondio," which she took up again and pub-lished in the early '70s. In this Depression-era tale of a family struggling to survive, the mother, Anna, dies of a botched abor-tion she performs on herself.

Chalmers Johnson, "Imperialist Propa-ganda: Second Thoughts on Charlie Wilson's War" , TomDispatch (2008):

My own view is that if Charlie Wilson's War is a comedy, it's the kind that goes over well with a roomful of louts in a college fraternity house. Sim-ply put, it is imperialist propaganda and the trage-dy is that four-and-a-half years af-ter we invaded Iraq and destroyed it, such dan-gerously misleading nonsense is still being of-fered to a gullible public. The most accurate re-view so far is James Rocchi's summing-up for Cinematical: 'Charlie Wilson's War isn't just bad history; it feels even more ma-lign, like a con-scious attempt to induce amnesia'."

Stanley Heller, "Brzezinski and Char-lie Wilson's War" Counterpunch (2007):

Imagine, they made a funny movie about how the US helped turn Afghanistan into a kill-ing field. It's the film "Charlie Wilson's War, a lighthearted look of how a skirt-chasing Con-gressman and a no-non-sense CIA thug helped bring mountains of weap-ons and money to the fanatic, women-despising "freedom fighters" who gave us 9/11. It's certainly material for a "laugh riot."

Mark Vallen, "Rise and Fall of the City of Mahagonny", Art for a Change (2007):

Brecht understood theatre not just as a form of en-tertainment, but as a vehicle that could help work-ers understand and analyze their political situation, he felt theatrical performances should appeal to reason and not simply give way to sentimentality. In the 1957 book, *Brecht on Theater*, the playwright described his theory of "alienation effect" theatre as being that "which prevents the audience from losing itself passively and completely in the char-acter created by the actor – and which consequent-ly leads the audience to be a consciously critical observer." The original Brecht production of *Ma-hagonny*, as with his other plays, utilized various contrivances to prevent viewers from being lulled into a theatrical fantasy. Stage settings were delib-erately sparse and flooded with harsh lights, with no attempt to hide stage lighting equipment. Slo-gans and explanatory text were projected upon stage walls, and actors carried placards onstage bearing political messages. With outbursts of songs whose lyrics drove home his political points, Brecht would use music itself to interrupt stage action.

Julia Stein, "Best Novel I Read in 2007: Bleak House" California Writer (2007):

What's great about Dickens' he makes judgments: against lawyers corruption, against the corrupt Court of Chancery, against the brutalization of the poor and the homeless. Well, right now the United States is also a Bleak House dominated by corrup-tion: the corruption of the Iraq War totals billions. What is missing in a lot contemporary fiction is Dickens' moral judgments.

I read Cormac McCarthy's *The Road*, a novel which won a recent Pulitzer Prize for fiction, but the well-written novel has a father and son trying to survive in post-apocalypse America. In many ways I thought *the Road* was metaphori-cally saying this country is now so bad off all a decent person can do is suffer it – I find that a huge cop out. Give me Dickens any day of the week instead.

Laura Flanders, " The Kite Runner: A Stirring Tale of Redemption", Alter-Net (2007):

Some will say it's unfair to hold the movie of a novel to task for repeating the propaganda version of U.S. history, but the myth of the United States as macho rescuer is not only misleading, it's deadly – for people in Afghanistan and around the world. Shed all the tears you like as you're watching, but don't leave the remorse in the cinema. Try as it might, Hollywood can't purge our guilt, or dis-suade us of the need to act.

Kim Sykes, "Thinking About New Orleans", Critical Mass (2007):

Q. Tell me about the writing of fiction you have written since Katrina.

A. There is little room for nonsense, beating around the bush, sort to speak. I get straight to the point. My characters say what they mean and mean what they say.

Q. How is your life going now? How have you been able to manage? Where are you living now, where are you working now, what are you work-ing on?

A. I'm working on the novel called "The Angry Bird," which takes place in northern Louisiana. I wrote in a hurricane scene. I talk a bit more about government. Life goes on. Most of my family are back in their homes. They seem to be settling some. So am I. My well-being is directly related to theirs.

Q. When you sit at your writing, what do you see now? Is that different from before Katrina?

A. Of course. How do I explain it except to say that I see past the bull.

Q. Has your own creative material/style/voice changed radically? Permanently? If so, how?
A. My characters have more of an opinion. More to say of substance. More thoughtfulness.

Peter La Chapelle, "Is Country Music Inherently Conservative?" HNN (2007):

Peter La Chapelle, Assistant Professor in the His-tory Program at Nevada State College and author of Proud to Be an Okie: Cultural Politics, Country Music, and Migration to Southern California, anal-yzes the historical connections between country music and left-wing and right-wing politics:

Perhaps the national amnesia about country's liberal, populist, and leftwing roots will fade as artists as varied in politics and style as Merle Hag-gard, Iris DeMent, Willie Nelson, the Old Crow Medicine Show, Butch Hancock, I See Hawks in L.A., Bobby Braddock, Tom Snider, Nanci Griffith, Steve Earle, and Allison Moorer sing out against the Iraq War, or other more mainstream artists such as Tim McGraw and Tracy Lawrence bemoan its consequences.

Martin Smith, "Norman Mailer and the 'Good War'" Counterpunch (2007):

Each Obituary did at least mention The Naked and the Dead, Mailer's first and most important novel. It is one of the great antiwar classics in literature and a book that speaks to all activists committed to ending the brutality of wars for empire.

Yet The Naked and the Dead is barely known today outside of academic circles – because it chal-lenges the standard assumptions about the Second World War as "the good war," and un-masks the hidden motives of U.S. involvement.

The Naked and the Dead is the story of a sui-cide mission by a reconnaissance patrol that is ordered to assess a Japanese rear position on the island of Anopopei. If the soldiers survive and return, Gen-eral Cummings plans to send out a company for a surprise attack, a daring tactical move that would likely lead to his promotion.

Jeffrey St. Clair, "Mailer and Us: the Writer as Fighter", Counterpunch (2007):

Some of those texts don't stand up all that well: the Picasso biography reads like notations from an art history lecture at the MOMA, Tough Guys Don't Dance a mediocre Ross McDonald novel, The Deer Park, his novel about Holly-wood, should have been better, the Marilyn books are almost as pa-thetic as his long-running obsession with Jack Ken-nedy.

Still for fifty years Mailer stood at the top of the pile: The Naked and the Dead, Barbary Shore (a novel about official paranoia that is perhaps more relevant today than when it was published), An American Dream, Armies of the Night, Miami and the Siege of Chicago, Harlot's Ghost. All better books than anything written by that favorite of the book critics Philip Roth. Only Vidal comes close to Mailer's long-running achievement.

It's hard to name a better novel written in the 1970s than The Executioner's Song. Even Thomas Pynchon's Gravity's Rainbow seems dwarfed by that sprawling portrait of Gary and Nicole Gilmore and the inexorable descent toward the firing squad in that spooky prison outside Provo. It's a big book with an immediate voice: clear and chilling. A-mong other virtues, Mailer captures the strange-ness and beauty of life in Utah better than any book since Wallace Stegner's Mormon Country.

Tony Muhammad, "Trials of a Hip Hop Educator: Bridging the Gap", The Hip Hop Cosign (2007):

As a public school educator that grew up on Hip Hop and who still loves many aspects of its cultur-al elements, I often incorporate it into my day to day lessons. Sometimes my opening activities would involve having my students critically anal-yze some form of controversy related to their fav-orite rappers or an explanation of the meaning of a quote by an influential personality such as KRS-One, Chuck D or Afrika Bambaataa. Our meaning-ful discussions would then be tied in with the les-sons of the day. Art and poetry would be included in much our comprehensive learning activities, which the students have admitted to me help them understand historical events and complex words better. I have found that since I have been teaching this way it has increased both student interest and involvement in a major way.

Anne Feeney, "'The Big Red Song-book'", Monthly Review Zine (2007):

The 2007 publication of The Big Red Song-book is long overdue. Folklorist Archie Green has been in possession of 29 editions of the leg-endary Little Red Songbook of the IWW since Wobbly folklorist John Neuhaus entrusted them to him in 1958. Pub-lished between 1909 and 1956, the IWW songbooks in the Neuhaus col-lection vividly embody the hu-mor, philosophy and history of the working class. Millions of copies of these little songbooks have been sold, giving the IWW its well-deserved repu-tation as a "singing union." For those of you saying "IWWWhat?" – here's a little history…

Paul Piwko and Sarah Bromley, "Dropkick Murphys: Friends to the Working Class", ZNet (2007):

The Murphys started in Boston in the mid-90s as a band of young men from working class and union households. Says vocalist and bassist Ken Casey, a founding member: "We were sing-ing about real life stuff at a time when [the] standard 18 year-old punk rock message [was] 'Fauthority' and 'F- the police'." The Murphys' "real life" lyrics hit home with fans from back-grounds similar to their own. "People from that walk of life started to gravitate towards the band, and in the early days – back in the mid-'90s – places like Detroit, where labor is-sues are real life and death stuff, were our biggest foot-holds."

John Pilger, "Why They're Afraid Of Michael Moore", ZNet (2007):

Moore's "threat" is his unerring view from the ground. He abrogates the contempt in which elite America and the media hold ordinary peo-ple. This is a taboo subject among many journal-ists, especial-ly those claiming to have risen to the nirvana of "impartiality" and others who profess to teach journalism. If Moore simply presented victims in the time-honoured, ambu-lance-chasing way, leav-ing the audience tearful but paralysed, he would have few enemies. He would not be looked down upon as a polemicist and self-promoter and all the other pejorative tags that await those who step be-yond the in-visible boundaries in societies where wealth is said to equal freedom. The few who dig deep into the nature of a liberal ideology that regards itself as superior, yet is responsible for crimes epic in proportion and generally unrecog-nised, risk being eased out of the "mainstream", espe-cially if they are young – a process that a form-er editor once described to me as "a sort of gen-tle defenestration". None has broken through like Moore, and his detractors are perverse to say he is not a "professional journalist" when the role of the professional journalist is so often that of zealously, if surreptitiously, serving the status quo. Without the loyalty of these profes-sionals on the New York Times and other august (mostly liberal) media in-stitutions "of record", the criminal invasion of Iraq might not have happened and a million people would be alive today. Deployed in Hollywood's sanctum – the cinema – Moore's Fahrenheit 9/11 shone a light in their eyes, reached into the mem-ory hole, and told the truth. That is why audiences all over the world stood and cheered.

David Bauder, "[Human Rights First] Group: TV torture [by Americans] in-fluencing real life", AP (2007):

The advocacy group Human Rights First says there hass been a startling increase in the number of [Ameican] torture scenes depicted on prime-time television in the post-2001 world.

Even more chilling, there are indications that real-life American interrogators in Iraq are tak-ing cues from what they see on television, said Jill Savitt, the group's director of public pro-grams…

A former U.S. Army specialist who ques-tioned prisoners in Baghdad's infamous Abu Ghraib pris-on and several other facilities around Iraq... said he saw instances of mock executions like that in [the TV drama] "24." Once, some fellow interroga-tors asked an Iraqi translator to pretend he was be-ing tortured to strike fear in a prisoner, after they had just watched a similar scene on a DVD...

Prior to 2001, the few torture scenes on prime-time TV usually had the shows' villains as the insti-gators, Savitt said. [Now torture on TV is used by the shows' American "heroes".] In both 1996 and 1997, there were no prime-time TV scenes containing torture, according to the Parents Television Council, which keeps a pro-gramming data-base. In 2003, there were 228 such scenes, the PTC said. The count was over 100 in both 2004 and 2005.

They found examples on "Alias," "The Wire," "Law & Order," "The Shield" – even "Star Trek: Voyager."

There's been a surge in general in the level of violence tolerated in prime time.

...Herrington said he's concerned that much of what's on TV is misleading.

Television interrogation frequently works to a ticking clock: someone needs to find out the loca-tion of a bomb from a prisoner within the hour or it will explode. That's so rare in real life that it's es-sentially mythology, he said...

Bill Fletcher, "Environmental Crisis and Despair", ZNet (2007):

When Rosa Luxemburg suggested that the future was one of "socialism or barbarism" there was a tendency by many people – even in the midst of World War I – to view this as hy-perbole. As it turns out, it was rather prescient. This warning through juxtaposition is critical but not enough. Under-standing that we must turn away from barbarism – in whatever form – and toward socialism and the end of capitalist exploitation is a critical awareness but it must be translated into organization and action....

...it is important to dream. By dreaming I mean to suggest that we consider possibilities for the fu-ture that improve the human condi-tion. Being a sci-ence fiction fan and a Star Trek devotee I always re-member a scene from the film Star Trek: First Con-tact. Captain Piccard,

having traveled back (from the 24th century) to the middle of the 21st century, is speaking with a scientist from that era. She asks how much the starship Enterprise cost to build. His response was quite interesting. In effect he said, the eco-nomics of the 24th century are quite different from yours. For us the acquisition of wealth is no longer the driving force of our existence. We seek to better ourselves. It is that notion that must work itself into our everyday realities and serve as the inspiration for action.

John Freeman, "Novel tilt at Turkish society", The New Zealand Herald (2007):

...in Turkey...according to 35-year-old writer Elif Shafak, a new generation of writers is using the novel – a form that came to them from the West – to reimagine their society from within.

"Novelists have played a very, very critical role as the engineers of social and cultural trans-forma-tion in Turkey," says Shafak, when we meet in a New York hotel. "Maybe in that re-gard we are clos-er to the Russian tradition than the Western tradi-tion."

The debate over what these novels say about Turkish society, and how they say it, lurched to the forefront of life in Istanbul in recent years, as the Turkish Government began prosecuting writers for "offending Turkishness".

Nobel laureate Orhan Pamuk and several dozen other writers were tried under this code of Turkish law. Shafak, too, was put on trial be-cause of pas-sages from her new novel, *The Bas-tard of Istanbul*, which referenced the long fallout of what many call the Armenian Genocide, when up to one million Armenians were forci-bly removed from Turkey and killed.

The book has become a best-seller in Turkey, selling more than 60,000 copies, but not without fallout for Shafak. Writing in the *Washington Post*, Shafak explained how critics within Tur-key claimed she "had taken the Armenians' side by having an Armenian character call the Turks 'butchers' in a reference to the Ottoman Empires deportation and massacre of Armenians during World War I."

While Shafak was acquitted, others were not

so lucky. In January, her "dear friend", journalist Hrant Dink, the Armenian editor-in-chief of a Turkish newspaper, was murdered on a street in Istanbul, allegedly by an ultra-nationalist teenager.

"The debate on literature and art is very much politicised," she says, her voice revealing palpable anguish, "sometimes very much polarised. I think my work attracted it because I combined elements people like to see separate."

Badri Raina, "Teach Them Not to Think", ZNet (2007):

After the initial attempts by a section of Christian-bourgeois souls (Dickens, Carlyle, Chadwick, May-hew, Mrs. Gaskell, even the honourable, although not Christian, Benjamin Disraeli who first enunciated the thesis that England was in fact not one na-tion but two – the rich and the poor), to seek re-formative state interventions on behalf of the new urban poor who now swamped the industrial towns, towards the middle of the nineteenth cen-tury the inevitable exhaustion of goodwill fol-lowed.

Where a Dickens had made visits to York-shire schools (captured unforgettably in Nicholas Nick-leby) in the thirties and returned to raise a cry for amelioration, such sentiment expressed from out-side the lived experience of the suffering classes, was to wear thin in a growing fright at the spread of what was to be christened "mass culture."

Dickens of course had repudiated the Chart-ists who had erroneously hoped he would go over to their side (a story rather less often re-cited about him). Some flavour of that history may be savoured in what G.M.Reynolds was to write in the Weekly Newspaper of june 8, 1851:

"This wretched sycophant of Aristocracy – this vulgar flatterer of the precious hereditary peerage – is impudent enough to consider him-self the peo-ple's friend! A precious friend in-deed when he ridi-cules universal suffrage (the elementary principle of Chartism)..."

Suddenly, as industrial England entered the fraught social contentions of the sixties, a whole falange of opinion-makers closed ranks to argue that writers, poets, "creative" individuals of all description had best wash their hands off this fruitless business of meddling with social mat-ters. It was best that they devoted themselves to their precious private visions of abiding truths above and beyond the piss and mire of this thing called history.

The ringing thesis here was to come from Mat-thew Arnold, who, in his perniciously in-fluential Culture and Anarchy (1865) drew the first distinc-tions between "high culture" and the culture of the "populace" – the latter in his view constituting "an-archy." Pleading for an intellectual aristocracy, a return to the classics was advocated. The aesthet-ics of Liberalism was thus inaugurated; and specially endowed individuals were henceforth to seek for eternal verities and universal truths outside the con-crete processes of social and political contention.

England's first Education Act of 1870 was to be the first pusillanimous policy decision to-wards consolidating inequality even though, don't you know, it was all about furnishing a sound educa-tion on the best principles of Eng-lish "humanism."

As the manufacturers and the colonizers bus-ied themselves in profit-making, education came form-ally to be regarded not as a rational aid to under-standing how society came to be thus constituted, but in a forked programme to equip, on the one hand, the labouring classes with the minimal skills that industry needed from time to time (more pro-foundly, as Marx was to point out and Althusser in our time was to nail, in order to keep in place the "reserve army of labour" or in order to ensure the "re-production of the relations of production"), and, on the other, to make available to the leisured classes the delectable riches of speculation.

Not for nothing was Arnold to argue that po-etry would be the religion of the future. That in-junction was devotedly to be pursued by "mod-ernists" like T.S. Eliot for whom, beginning with the twenties of the last century, the world was indubitably a "wasteland". As you would ex-pect, the cure for the unvarying "human condi-tion" was to be found in the Church. All that just when a revolution had happened in the then czarist Russia, and when Gandhi, the Con-gress, and the revolutionaries in India were making big strides to alter the "human condition" in the colony – and, as a fallout, in some two-thirds of the colonized world.

Seiji Yamada, "Transformers, Militarism in Disguise", ZNet (2007):

Transformers – a film about robots from space that can change into cars and trucks – was released just prior to the July 4th. The storyline is that evil robots have come to destroy earth. Good robots team up with the U.S. military to defeat the evil robots.

On the face of it, *Transformers* would appear to be a film directed at the pre-teen male audience, but I'd like to examine some of its underlying as-sumptions. The story starts with American military forces in Qatar under attack from an unknown enemy – which is, as it turns out, an evil robot. Indeed, in real life, Camp As Sayliyah in Qatar serves as the forward headquarters for Central Command – from which the U.S. military conducts its current wars in Afghanistan and Iraq. We see a platoon survive the initial attack to defend Arab villagers from another evil robot. So, the first assumption is that the U.S. has an unquestioned right to project its military in other people's lands – and that it is there for the benefit of those other people ...

In the end, it turn out that both the good and bad robots are aliens from outer space – but pow-erful weapons are manufactured by "our side" aren't labeled WMDs. Perhaps it is useful to view *Transformers* as a parable about the role of militar-ism and the weapons industry in our present-day mythology. The evil robots are akin to WMDs in the hands of rogue (Axis of Evil) nations. The good robots are akin to "our" high-tech weaponry. *Transfomers* serves as a morality play for the next generation to be taught the lies of our times.

Ted Glick, "The U.S. Left Turns a Corner", ZNet (2007):

In the words of Rickke Manazala, "culture is essen-tial to sustaining our work." Culture is not an ad-junct, an add-on, something pigeon-holed and sec-ondary. All throughout the USSF, from the puppets at the opening day march to the Indigenous drum-mers and singers at the fi-nal plenary, this truth was made manifest.

The leadership of the USSF understood that nar-row "correct politics" or efficient organization alone do not do it. As Lillian Cotto Morales said, "we need to know one another as people so we can then talk politics and strategy."

Terry Eagleton, "Only Pinter Remains", The Guardian (2007):

For almost the first time in two centuries, there is no eminent British poet, playwright or novelist pre-pared to question the foundations of the western way of life. One might make an honourable excep-tion of Harold Pinter, who has wisely decided that being a champagne socialist is better than being no socialist at all; but his most explicitly political work is also his most artistically dreary.

The knighting of Salman Rushdie is the estab-lishment's reward for a man who moved from be-ing a remorseless satirist of the west to cheering on its criminal adventures in Iraq and Afghanistan. David Hare caved in to the blandishments of Buck-ingham Palace some years ago, moving from radi-cal to reformist. Christopher Hitchens, who looked set to become the George Orwell de nos jours, is likely to be remembered as our Evelyn Waugh, having thrown in his lot with Washington's neo-cons. Martin Amis has written of the need to pre-vent Muslims travelling and to strip-search people "who look like they're from the Middle East or from Pakistan". Deportation, he considers, may be essential further down the road.

The uniqueness of the situation is worth under-lining [given the lineage of:] Shelley ... Blake ... By-ron ... Arthur Hugh Clough ... Carlyle ... Ruskin ... William Morris, Oscar Wilde, remembered by the English as dandy, wit and socialite; and by the Irish as a socialist republican."

The early decades of the 20th century in Britain were dominated by socialist writers such as HG Wells and George Bernard Shaw. When Virginia Woolf writes in Three Guineas of "the arts

arts of dom-inating other people ... of ruling, of killing, of ac-quiring land and capital", she places herself to the left of almost every other major English novelist.

...The 1930s witnessed the first body of consciously committed left writing in Britain. Taking sides was no longer seen as inimical to art, but as a vital part of its purpose.

In the postwar welfare state, however, the rot set in.

Ann Talbot "The Amis-Eagleton controversy: The British literary elite and the 'war on terror'", WSWS (2007):

In giving Eagleton a kicking, the British literary elite are sending a message to younger and less well-established academics, to aspiring writers and to students that Marxism is not acceptable and that they had better adopt the same degenerate stance as Amis if they expect to be published, get pro-moted or be awarded any grade above a gamma minus.

Mahir Ali, "Knight at the End of the Day", ZNet (2007):

SIR Salman Rushdie – it has a certain ring to it, doesn't it? A faintly ridiculous ring, much like Sir Mick Jagger or Sir Ian Botham, and not a million miles removed from Lord Ahmed or Baroness Uddin. The British honours system is an absurd and undemocratic anachronism that ought to have been abolished decades ago, yet it seems many people in Britain and across the lands once colonized in the name of the crown still covet the silly titles and the right they thereby gain to embellish their names with initials that invoke a non-existent entity: the British empire.

Lord Anybody and Sir Anything cannot expect to be taken too seriously in the 21st century, any more than those whose lopsided lexicon is heavily laden with terms such as apostasy and blasphemy. And after the cash-for-honours scandal that has rocked the Blair administration in recent years, it is somewhat surprising that anyone with an ounce of self-respect would wish to supplement their sur-name with combi-

nations of letters such as KBE, MBE, CBE or OBE. However, it seems relatively few recipients are able to resist the temptation.

Fewer still are able to imbue their rejection of a title with the sort of outrage that the poet Benjamin Zephaniah expressed a few years ago: "OBE me? Up yours! I get angry when I hear that word 'em-pire'; it reminds me of thousands of years of brutal-ity. Stick it, Mr Blair and Mrs Queen, stop going on about empire.'

Last year the venerable folk singer Roy Bailey decided that he could not, in good conscience, hold on to an MBE he had made the mistake of accept-ing earlier in 2006, and decided to return it as a means of expressing "my horror and opposition to our failure to call for an immediate ceasefire in Lebanon and to our complicity with the USA's policy of supporting Israel's actions in Palestine". He went on to mention the death and destruction in Iraq and Afghanistan...

Tony Christini, "Antiwar novels are 'belligerent'?" Letter to the Editor rejected by The New York Times (2007):

Richard Eder writes, "'The Welsh Girl' is a distin-guished, beautifully written example of a small but enduring genre. Call it the counterwar novel. Not antiwar, exactly; it lacks the belligerence." Antiwar like, say, "Homefront"? I wonder what a pro-war novel, or a status quo war novel, could then be called? "Compassionate," I suppose.

There is scarcely an explicit antiwar novel about the US invasion and occupation of Iraq. Why is that? Might it be that the US has a culture a lot like that of Germany of the 1930s and 1940s? Too many "good Germans" and "good Americans"? Too many critics and others who think antiwar novels are "belligerent"?

As Tony Kushner notes (in "Theater"): "I do not believe that a steadfast refusal to be partisan is, fin-ally, a particularly brave or a moral or even inter-esting choice. Les Murray, an Australian poet, wrote a short poem called 'Politics and Art.' In its entirety: 'Brutal policy / like inferior art, knows / whose fault it all is.' This is as invaluable an ad-monishment as it is ultimately untrue."

Tom Wallace, "Rachel's Words' Silenced Again", ZNet (2007):

Once again the play "My Name is Rachel Corrie" has been cancelled, this time in South Florida.

In New York and Toronto the play was cancelled due to pressure from the Jewish community or those that claim to speak for the Jewish Com-munity. The play was successfully staged in NYC at the Minetta Lane theater. It is currently enjoying an extraordinary run at the Seattle Repertory Thea-ter and many more are planned.

Wherever it has been staged, there has been sup-port from the Jewish community as well as criti-cism. The Jewish community is not monolithic and no-one speaks for "it," though many claim to.

Gina Whitfield, "My Name is Rachel Corrie Staged in Seattle", ZNet (2007):

The purpose of art is to inspire us to be more than we are, to question our own assumptions or our entrenched ideas. *My Name is Rachel Corrie* certain-ly achieves this; it is an impassioned call to action. The depiction of her life forces the audience to question their assumptions about a young radical, who was in fact not dogmatic or hateful, but whose spirit was caring and who was desperately trying to find good and genuine beauty amidst a hideous conflict. Her words, which form the core of the play, often brought the audience to tears, describ-ing the appalling conditions of life endured under occupation...

My Name is Rachel Corrie, however, has had to struggle to get a run on stage at all... It's unlikely to be at a theatre any nearer to you anytime soon. *My Name is Rachel Corrie* made its West Coast debut last week at Seattle's Repertory Theatre. The one-woman play is based on Corrie's life and untimely death. The Olympia Washington native was killed four years ago, in March 2003, at the age of 23. She was crushed by an Israeli bulldozer while she tried, along with an International Solidarity Movement team in the Gaza Strip, to protect a Palestinian home from demolition. Rachel Corrie's life, her personal and political passions, and her desire to contribute to peace in the Middle East are compell-ingly acted out by Seattle's Marya Sea Kaminski, who brings her talents to a play that has encount-ered many obstacles in being brought to stage. The play is based on Corrie's journals and email cor-respondence, which were published in the UK Guardian after her death, and was originally con-ceived by actor/director Alan Rickman and Guard-ian editor Katharine Viner. Corrie's writing is both the inspiration and the script; the young woman was a colourful and talented writer, eloquently de-scribing her wish to not be complicit in her count-ry's central role supporting the Israeli occupation. The play is effective both because of Kaminski's delivery, but also because it injects the personal hopes and dreams of a young woman – loves lost, career plans, and family dramas – in addition to Corrie's evolving political views.

The play has sparked controversy wherever it has been produced or, more accurately, wherever people have attempted to produce it. This has left the British creators screaming censorship, and left many in the artistic community questioning just how free speech is in North America, where the play hits political nerves. *My Name is Rachel Corrie* was deemed "too hot" for the Big Apple, for in-stance.

Robert Fisk, "Shakespeare and War", Counterpunch (2007):

My own experience of war has changed my feel-ings towards many of Shakespeare's characters. The good guys in Shakespeare's plays have become ever less attractive, ever more portentous, ever more sinister as the years go by. Henry V seems more than ever a butcher. "Now, herald, are the dead number'd?" he asks.

"This note doth tell me of ten thousand French
That in the field lie slain: of princes, in this number,
And nobles bearing banners, there lie dead
/ One hundred twenty six: added to these

Of knights, esquires, and gallant gentle-
men,
Eight thousand and four hundred…"
Henry is doing "body counts". When the herald
presents another list–this time of the English
dead, Henry reads off the names of Edward,
Duke of York, the Earl of Suffolk, Sir Richard
Kikely, Davy Gam, Esquire:

"None else of name: and, of all other men,
but five and twenty… O God, thy arm was
here…
Was ever known so great and little loss,
On one part and on th'other?"

This is pure Gulf War Part One, when General
Norman Schwarzkopf was gloating at the disparate casualty figures–while claiming, of
course, that he was "not in the business of body
counts" – while General Peter de la Billière was
telling Britons to celebrate victory by ringing
their church bells.

Yasmin Hernandez, "Yasmin Hernan-dez by Donna Hernandez", Colorlines (2007):

What is the role of the artist in changing the po-litical landscape? How does your work do this?

For the artists who choose this path, our role
is to expose injustice. A single painting cannot
save anyone but can serve as a catalyst to evoke
a change in someone to begin the work that can
in-deed save us. With my own work, I seek to
fill voids with innovative methods of presenting
the images we don't usually see, but should. I
paint brown goddesses because young women
of color often have trouble viewing themselves
as sacred. I paint mothers as saints because the
everyday wom-an is worthy of praise. I paint
freedom fighters because today we are taught
that to resist is to be a troublemaker and that to
go against the powers that be when we are in
disagreement is to be un-grateful. I paint the
harsh realities in a world that masks truth behind a bling-bling generation.

John Sinno, "An open letter to the Academy of Motion Picture Arts and Sciences", Cinematical (2007):

I would like to point out that there was no
mention of the Iraq War during the Oscar tele-
cast, though it was on the minds of many in the
theatre and of millions of viewers. It is wonderful to see the Acad-emy support the protection
of the environment. Unfortunately there is more
than just one incon-venient truth in this world.
Having mention of the Iraq War avoided altogether was a painful remind-er for many of us
that our country is living in a state of denial. As
filmmakers, it is the greatest pro-fessional crime
we can commit not to speak out with the truth.
We owe it to the public. I hope what I have said
is taken to heart. It comes from my con-cern for
the cinematic art and its crucial role in the times
we're living in.

P. Sainath, "And all the world's a stage", The Hindu (2007):

*While theatre struggles to survive in the metros
[of India], it thrives in Vidharbha where it draws
audiences of thousands for plays that go on through
much of the night. Atma Hatya is a Marathi play
running to audi-ences of thousands at every show in
eastern Vidharbha. The theme of this jhadi patti play
is farmers suicides.*

It was well past midnight when the farmer
said he was fed up with the way things were
going. He could not take it any more, he told us.
A farmer's life was not worth living. It was
pretty cold by this time. Yet no one budged and
you could feel the tension in the air. The play is
called *atma hatya* (sui-cide) and we were part of
an audience of 6,000 watching transfixed at that
late hour. Theatre may be struggling to survive
in the metros, but here in rural Vidharbha, it
thrives. This is the season of *jhadi patti rang
bhoomi*. Which loosely translates as "theatre of
the jungle belt."

Everybody is part of it. "We have farmers,
tailors painters and vendors in our plays," says
Ghulam Sufi of the Venkatesh natya mandali
that is staging *Atma Hatya*. "That's one reason
why it resonates so much with ordinary people." …

The play's message is positive. Suicide is no
solution. Fight the idea in your homes. An earlier Borkar play that broke records – *I killed my
husband* – fought superstition. Some villages

have used a play's proceeds to give soft loans to farmers. Others to get some work done locally. For the last two decades, *jhadi patti* has taken on social and political themes with a strong accent on justice. (Election year has local politicians scrambling to be seen on stage.) Now the region's farm suicides are under the spotlight.

"This is Maharashtra's most unique theatre form," says Professor Pramod Mungate of the St. Francis de Sales college in Nagpur. Professor Mun-gate, who heads the Marathi department there, is studying *jhadi patti* on a University Grants Com-mission project. "In Nagpur, only big names draw us to a play. In eastern Vidharbha, there will be nine plays held at Kurud village on February 9 simultaneously. They will all have big audiences for mostly part-time actors. *Jhadi patti*'s appeal has not shrunk despite the coming of multiple television channels. It's truly a people's movement, rooted in their lives. No sponsors or commercial patrons. This has audience. This has response. This is theatre."

Andrew Gilbert, "Tim Robbins and S.F. Mime Troupe director uncover 'echoes of our current situation' in Orwell's classic", San Diego Union-Tribune (2007):

For Tim Robbins, the actor, director and play-wright known for his politically charged work, the relevance of a theatrical production based on Or-well's devastating dystopian tale about the mech-anics and methodology of totalitarianism was as apparent as the morning headlines.

"Beyond the obvious idea of torture and moni-toring civilians, I was floored when I re-read the 'War Is Peace' chapter," said Robbins, speaking by phone from the Manhattan home he shares with Susan Sarandon and their three school-age boys. "It's the book within the book, and it talks about what war represents within Oceania and why it's necessary, and you'll see echoes of our current situation. If you want a quick view into what in-spired me to do this play, look at just that chapter."

Matt Cheney, "Q&A: Ngũgĩ wa Thiong'o", Litblog co-op (2007):

Q: How did you settle on the structure and design of *Wizard of the Crow*? It is such a large, rich, all-encompassing book ... how did you decide what to put in, what to leave out, and which characters' stories to tell at particular times?

Ngũgĩ: The writing of *Wizard of the Crow* was more of a possession than conscious plotting. The struc-ture developed with the story. As they dawned on me, many incidents were a surprise to me too, of-ten eliciting laughter. However editing later does allow for reduction of redundancies.

Q: Much has changed in Kenya, in Africa, in the world since you began work on *Wizard of the Crow* – did those changes affect how the book progressed when you wrote it or translated it?

Ngũgĩ: No, no, because the essence of globalization within Africa and between Africa and the West remains the same despite surface changes. That is why I call it a global epic from Africa. ...

Q: Who are writers whose work you would like to see gain a larger audience?

Ngũgĩ i: I would like to see more translations from works written in the original languages of Asia, Africa, Native South American and Native America. I am always curious as to what treasures are hidden in those languages.

Peter A. Welsch, "Paths of Glory" Sampo: The Journal of Abundant Media (2007):

I randomly listened to Metallica's *One* [one day], which was inspired by Dalton Trumbo's anti-war novel *Johnny Got His Gun*. I first read that book when I was in middle school and it inspired me to declare myself a pacifist. [That] has me thinking about the role that militarism plays in our culture and society, especially considering the online row that has resulted from William Arkin's item at the *Washington Post Online*, "The Troops Also Need to Support the American People."

Glenn Whipp, "'G.I. Jesus' soldier wanders in psychic desert after Iraq" San Bernardino Sun (2007):

Joining the burgeoning number of Iraq-related doc-umentaries this week is "G.I. Jesus," a trippy free-wheeling fictional feature that looks at the war from the vantage point of a young Mexican Marine who has been promised citizenship in return for military service.

The film is a sometimes surreal, sometimes fun-ny, sometimes sloppy (befitting its budget) look at a very real issue. Latinos, most of them from Cali-fornia, comprise (in some estimates) more than a third of the United States' deployed force in Iraq, and many of them are "Green Card" troops, immi-grants who join the military in exchange for the promise of citizenship.

"G.I. Jesus" doesn't spend much time won-der-ing why a war fought in the name of the United States is being waged by so many for-eigners. The movie, written and directed by first-timer Carl Colpaert, is more interested in satire and "Man-churian Candidate"-style sur-realism than prosely-tizing.

But by the end, you can't help add the ques-tions the film raises to the laundry list of doubts current-ly circulating about the U.S. presence in Iraq. ...

An hour into things, "G.I. Jesus" takes a dramat-ic left turn, extending a middle finger to material-ism and extolling the virtues of cheap beer and good Mexican food over the killing of innocents. It's a message that cuts across bor-ders and politics – or at least it should.

Tony Christini, "Art, Literature, and the CIA" (compilation) A Practical Policy 2007:

Mark Vallen, "Abstract Art and the Cultural Cold War" Art for a Change (2005): For those who still re-gard art as being above politics consider the fol-lowing. The Central Intelligence Agency fi-nanced, organized, and assured the success of the American abstract expressionist movement, using artists like Jackson Pollock, Sam Francis, Willem de Kooning, Barnett Newman, Robert Motherwell, and Mark Rothko, as weapons in the struggle against the Sov-iet Union. Frances Stonor Saunders has presented this matter of public record in her well document-ed book, The Cultural Cold War – The CIA and the World of Arts and Letters.

Saunders informs us that during the height of the Cold War in the 1950's, the CIA secretly pro-moted abstract expressionism as a means of dis-crediting the socialist realism of the Soviet Un-ion.

James Petras, "The CIA and the Cultural Cold War Revisited" Monthly Review (1999): The CIA's cul-tural campaigns created the prototype for to-day's seem-ingly apolitical intellectuals, aca-demics, and artists who are divorced from popular struggles and whose worth rises with their distance from the working classes and their proximity to prestigious foundations. The CIA role model of the successful professional is the ideological gatekeeper, exclud-ing critical intellectuals who write about class struggle, class exploitation and U.S. imperialism – "ideo-logical" not "objective" categories, or so they are told.

The singular lasting, damaging influence of the CIA's Congress of Cultural Freedom crowd was not their specific defenses of U.S. imperial-ist poli-cies, but their success in imposing on subsequent generations of intellectuals the idea of excluding any sustained discussion of U.S. imperialism from the influential cultural and political media. The is-sue is not that today's in-tellectuals or artists may or may not take a pro-gressive position on this or that issue. The prob-lem is the pervasive belief among writers and artists that anti-imperialist social and political expressions should not appear in their music, paintings, and serious writing if they want their work to be considered of substantial artistic merit. The enduring political victory of the CIA was to convince intellectuals that serious and sus-tained political engagement on the left is in-compat-ible with serious art and scholarship. Today at the opera, theater, and art galleries, as well as in the professional meetings of academ-ics, the Cold War values of the CIA are visible and pervasive: who dares to undress the em-peror?

Richard Cummings, "The Real Agenda" LewRockwell .com (2003): Robie Macauley, a top literary editor at Harcourt, Brace, was, while he functioned in his literary capacity, the head of the CIA Africa desk. I know he was, because he told me so not long before he died. He explicitly said to me that his literary career was his cover. When his obituary appeared in the New York Times, it listed his accomplishments in the literary field, but failed to mention in his real career with the CIA. I rang up the author of the obituary and said, "You left out Robie's career with the CIA." There was a long pause. Then he said, "We can't put everything into an obituary."

Karl Wenclas, "The Empire Strikes Back" and "A Crazy Tale" (2007/2008): Yale poet WWII vet Cord Meyer won an O. Henry Prize in 1946 for best first-published story. He became President of the United World Federalists, "which envisioned a globe under the calm and rational dominion of one government." In 1951 he joined the CIA. "He would rise to become the number two man in the agency's clandestine operations...." "Along the way, he secretly financed labor unions, youth groups, writers' organizations, and literary jour-nals."

This info is from a 2007 bio of the Kennedys, *Brothers* by David Talbot, former editor of Salon. Elsewhere in the book, Talbot mentions that by 1977 there were over 400 U.S. journalists considered "assets" by the CIA. Do any remain? (We know that CNN's Anderson Cooper worked for the CIA after Yale.)

Celia McGee, "Literary Star is Reborn" by Celia McGee NYT (2007): The renewed attention to Har-old Humes is no doubt aided by the growing inter-est in American writing of the 1940s and '50s ... But also intriguing to many is the documentary's revelation of a CIA connection to the history of The Paris Review. In the film, Matthiessen, best known as a novelist, environmental activist and advocate of American Indian rights, admits publicly for the first time that he was a young CIA recruit at the time he helped start the magazine, and used it as his cover.

"Immy cajoled me into talking about it," Matthi-essen said.

Humes, who tussled with Matthiessen and Plimpton about this secret after Matthiessen con-fided in him in the mid-'60s, died in 1992 in St. Rose's Home, the New York City cancer hospice founded by Nathaniel Hawthorne's daughter. Immy Humes found correspondence between the three co-founders about Matthiessen's clandestine affiliation in a suitcase of papers...

H. Bruce Franklin, War Stars (1988): ...explores ov-er two hundred movies, novels, and stories, from obscure pre-World War I fiction that influenced Truman's decision to drop atomic bombs on Japan to such modern classics as Catch-22, Slaughter-house Five, and Dr. Strangelove. He demonstrates how the American imagination continually shapes ingenious new superweapons while engendering their antitheses in art and action.

Frances Stonor Saunders, The Cultural Cold War: The CIA and the World of Arts and Letters (1999): A spectacular history of the ways the CIA's cold war operation included the creation of a safe Western Culture. They channeled money for conferences, founded magazines, mounted art exhibitions, ar-ranged concerts and flew orchestras around the world.

Nick Currie (Momus), "The CIA calls the tune and the tune is called freedom" imomus (2006): On November 29th Arte television aired When the CIA Infiltrated Culture, a documentary based on three years of research into a secret, highly ambitious "Marshall Plan of culture": the CIA's efforts to promote "the freedom of individual choice" in postwar Europe by... subsidizing the arts. Using front organiza-tions like the Farfield Foundation and the Congress for Cultural Freedom, the CIA channeled millions of dollars into the European cultural scene during the 1950s and 60s in an attempt to alter the intel-lectual DNA of the continent. If you wanted the CIA on your side, paradoxes abounded: "no ideol-ogy" had to become your ideology. You had to ban-ish politics from your work for entirely political reasons. You were free to be anything except criti-cal of "freedom", and you could pick any individu-al stance except a pro-collective individual stance. What's more, your anti-government, pro-market position had to be bankrolled by the government and protected from the market.

Since the aesthetic favoured by pro-Soviets in Europe tended to include stuff like political com-mitment, realism, melody, and representation – the communists deplored "decadent formalism" above all – the CIA (somewhat incredibly, to our eyes) threw its weight behind atonal music and Abstract Expressionism. Concerts and exhibitions of the most inaccessible, anti-populist, non-commercial avant garde artists flourished. "The ideology of the CIA was that the West had to be the most modern of the modern," says Gunter Grass, interviewed for the documentary.

Tony Christini, "Fiction Gutted – The Establishment and the Novel" A Practical Policy (2008): When the highly accomplished and leading progressive liter-ary critic, Maxwell Geismar, challenged the very quality and reigning adoration of Henry James' fiction, he was silenced, and rather prominently in one instance, on national TV by two high level functionaries of the CIA, representing the interests of the corporate state rather than the populace. The two men who played a key role: William vanden Heuval and Irving Kristol – the former a "protégé" of the "father" of the CIA and the latter the CIA flack and "father" of neoconservatism who several years earlier had passed on his position as editor of Commentary magazine to Normon Podhoretz (a student of leading establishment lit critic Lionel Trilling, who [as an establishment liberal] was a sort of forerunner of James Wood). When William vanden Heuvel (father of the current editor/ pub-lisher of The Nation Katrina vanden Heuvel) tag-teamed with Irving Kristol (the father of current prominent Fox TV political pundit and New York Times columnist Bill Kristol, also editor of the Washington DC based political magazine, The Weekly Standard) – when these central figures of the political establishment hastened to appear on national TV over four decades ago to attack direct-ly to the face of the silenced progressive literary critic Maxwell Geismar, on the occasion of the publication of Geismar's book of criticism about Henry James ("a primary Cold War literary fig-ure"), Kris-tol and vanden Heuvel, two exemplars of the status quo, serving retrograde state interests, executed a prominent role in destroying Geismar's accomp-lished literary career and ending his run on a na-tional literary television show, Books on Trial ("or something similar," in Geismar's recollection). Geis-mar posits William vanden Heuvel as "a rich, culti-vated, charming, and liberal member of the upper echelons of the CIA [who] had a large hand in em-broiling [the US] in Vietnam," while Irving Kristol "as it later turned out was almost always affiliated with many State Department or CIA literary proj-ects in editing, publishing, and the academic world …a hired hand of the establishment."

Meredith Terretta, "The Flight to Freedom: A Review of Ngugi wa Thiongo's Wizard of the Crow", ZNet (2007):

Most of the reviewers of Ngugi's latest novel, Wiz-ard of the Crow, corral the book into two major themes they find in its 760 pages. The first exposes corrupt dictators in postcolonial Afri-can states who govern through the skillful ma-nipulation of the second – witchcraft and magic as part of a stub-bornly "primordial," "supersti-tious" Africa refus-ing to keep up with the pace of modernity. But reviewers, hemmed in by centuries of the West's misconstrued image of Af-rica as exotic and intro-verted, have missed the point Ngugi makes when he describes his book as a "global epic from Afri-ca." Shift the focus from Africa, and the novel still has plenty to resonate with readers, ranging from the global politics of the Christian right to the ex-tinction of multilingualism. Other universal themes pro-liferate throughout the novel: women's agency in political and social activism (present to a de-gree unprecedented in Ngugi's fiction), quotid-ian hu-mor as an act of political resistance, envi-ronment-alism, and questions of racial and cul-tural identity against the backdrop of globaliza-tion.

In Wizard of the Crow, the Ruler of the fic-tive African nation of Aburiria approaches the Global Bank – the god of multi-national corpo-rate capital-ism – to borrow funds for his efforts to reach God with a sky-scraper in an official, national project called Marching to Heaven. When the Global Bank and Western leaders seem to balk at financing the Ruler's grandiose project, the small-time dictator aspires to sell the nation and its people's labor to global capitalism; he envisions Aburiria as the first corporony – the "corporate colony," leading the way to the world as "one corporate globe divided into the incorporating and the incorporated."

Courtney E. Martin, "After Laughter, Action", Baltimore Sun (2007):

Satire, of course, has a long and proven history as the source of bona fide social change. Aristopha-nes' Lysistrata, Upton Sinclair's The Jungle, George Orwell's Animal Farm – all of these led to new public awareness that then led to protest, even some pragmatic reforms. But does the one-millionth joke about President Bush's preschool perception of global geography really regain the trust of the in-ternational community?

It seems that the difference between a satire such as Animal Farm and The Daily Show is that the latter too often makes us comfortable, satiated, even happy, as opposed to the very motivating and sometimes terrifying disequilibrium caused by Orwell. Rebels distributed copies of Animal Farm, a novella satirizing totalitarianism, to displaced Soviets in Ukraine right after World War II. The occupying American military discovered them and confiscated 1,500 copies that would later be handed over to the Russian authorities whom the Ameri-cans were, at least temporarily, trying to aid. The vicious and powerful humor contained within that small book sure scared the corrupt leaders of that time.

Clearly, the huge audience for sarcastic, sophist-icated slapstick means an increase in public aware-ness of current events. This is an undeniable bene-fit, beyond the salutary giggle, of consuming this kind of news. The National Annenberg Election Survey released in September 2004 reported that The Daily Show 's viewers knew more about elec-tion issues than people who regularly read news-papers or watched news.

But what are we doing with this knowledge, besides rehashing it at the water cooler the next morning?

Paul Mooney "Unfree thinker", Phayul.com (2007):

The demure-looking Woeser seems like anything but a threat to the Chinese state. Yet the govern-ment has banned the Tibetan writer's books, some-times restricts her movements, and last summer shut down her two blogs.

Still, the censors have not fully succeeded in sil-encing the prolific writer, who works away on a computer in her simple apartment in a Beijing sub-urb, surrounded by the many Tibetan religious and cultural images that cover the walls.

Tibet experts heap praise on the 40-year-old writer, who is living in self-exile in the capital, say-ing her writings on Tibet have had an enormous in-fluence.

Robbie Barnett, professor of contemporary Tibetan studies at Columbia University, says Woeser is the first Tibetan to play the role of public intellectual in China in the sense of using modern media. He says thousands of Tibetans have expressed their opposition through demonstrations and leaflets, but Woeser's statements are "signed, enduring and have a very wide impact".

Professor Barnett says Woeser is more of a cul-tural figure than a political one, likening her to public intellectuals such as Harold Pinter and Ar-thur Miller. "She writes as a humanist, as an author struggling to describe the emotions and experi-ences of individuals she's met in a world where many of their most important memories and wishes have been forbidden," he said.

Tseten Wangchuk, a journalist with the Tibetan Service of the Voice of America in Washington, says when he was in China, Tibetan intellectuals privately discussed the Tibet problem. "But she was the first one who really brought this from private conversational circles to the public domain," he said. "In that sense, this was a big break-through for Tibet."

Having never learned to read or write in her

own language, Woeser is forced to express herself in Chinese. Wangchuk says Woeser is representa-tive of a new generation of Tibetans who are using the Chinese language to challenge the central gov-ernment in a highly articulate manner. He estimates there are between 200 and 300 blogs set up by Tibetans around the world. "It's no longer just a state narrative, and that in itself is pretty impor-tant," he said. ...

Woeser says she was also strongly influenced by the works of Edward Said, the author of Oriental-ism, and a long-time advocate of the Palestinian cause. Said's theory of post colonialism particularly gave her a new framework for looking at China's rule over Tibet.

Woeser says she's determined to write "the truth" about Tibet. "As a writer, I felt I needed to write about these things, the real Tibet, and not the false Tibet presented by the government," she said.

In an interview with Radio Free Asia she described how, for years, the party's literary and art workers had "revised Tibet, repainted Tibet, re-sung Tibet, redanced Tibet, refilmed Tibet, re-sculpted Tibet".

"Actual history was changed in this image, col-oured by red ideology," she said. "The memories of generations of Tibetans were changed."

Marina Krakovsky, "Novel Delights" Psychology Today (2006):

Reading fiction, it turns out, is a surprisingly social process. A study at the *Journal of Research in Person-ality* showed that frequent readers of narrative fic-tion scored higher on tests of empathy and social acumen than did readers of expository non-fiction. A follow-up study showed that fiction could actu-ally hone these skills: People assigned to read a *New Yorker* short story did better on a subsequent social-reasoning task than did those who read an essay from the same magazine.

"All stories are about people and their inter-actions – romance, tragedy, conflict," explains Ray-mond Mar, a doctoral candidate in psychology at the University of Toronto and lead author of both studies. "Stories often force us to empathize with characters who are quite different from us, and this ability could help us better understand the many kinds of people we come across in the real world."

Valerie Weaver-Zercher, "From Imagination To Action", Sojourners (2006):

Novelists in the United States who dare to...exam-ine social and political problems rather than con-ceal them – often find their work viewed with sus-picion, says Barbara Kingsolver, author of ac-claimed novels such as *The Poisonwood Bible* and *The Bean Trees*. Kingsolver established the Bell-wether Prize for Fiction, which is awarded bienni-ally to a first novel that emphasizes issues of social justice, as a way to counteract what she calls a "phobic feeling about socially conscious literature from the literary gatekeepers" in the United States.

Seth Sandronsky, "James Brown", ZNet (2006):

Music superstar James Brown's influence was widespread. Count me in as a longtime fan of his. Brown's recent passing marks the end of an era.

What I wish to add to the many accolades and tributes to him is just this. His song "Say It Loud, I'm Black and I'm Proud" during the freedom up-surge of African Americans nearly four decades ago had an impact that, I think, is being side-stepped. This says more about commentators than Brown. Allow me to explain.

The lyrics in his 1968 song that I note aptly de-scribed the conditions of black workers. They were laboring for low wages. Their employers' idea of upward mobility was a cruel hoax in ways big and small.

Craig Crosby, "Civil disobedience a must in class", Kennebec Journal (2006):

"The most I had ever done was very conventional actions toward change, like writing letters," said McGarvey, a senior environmental policy major. "I had not done any kind of social protest. I was a lit-tle dubious about what would happen. It was a lot more than I had hoped for. I was very surprised."

McGarvey's experience is exactly what Unity College associate professor Kathryn Miles had in mind when she first developed the focus for the fall semester's American literature class. From Walt Whitman and Henry David Thoreau through speeches by Martin Luther King Jr. and Edward Abbey's "The Monkey Wrench Gang," the students read the best-known literature of social protest and civil disobedience ever written in this country.

More than just reading, however, the 18 students in Miles' class had to identify an issue, devel-op plans to effect change through an act of protest and then carry it out. Some chose well-traveled roads, such as the war in Iraq, while others were moved by the more obscure, such as a Maine law that prohibits owning exotic reptiles.

The project was designed to let the students put into practice the philosophies they read in the books, Miles said. McGarvey, for example, based much of her protest on Martin Luther King Jr.'s "Letter from Birmingham Jail" in which King writes, "one has a moral responsibility to disobey unjust law."

"Now, more than ever, we can't have higher education in a high tower," Miles said. "I really wanted them to do something to make a difference. I feel like we don't have the luxury of keeping aca-demia abstract. I feel like we have to apply it and do something. I think that, by and large, we as a culture, and this age group, tends to be fairly polit-ically apathetic. Sitting back and complaining is just not an option."

Juan Santos, "On Apocalypto", The Fourth World/ Znet (2006):

Mel Gibson's Apocalypto is not a mere adventure tale, it's not just another excruciatingly brutal por-trayal of apocalyptic violence for its own sake, and the Village Voice is dead wrong when it says that unlike Braveheart and The Passion of the Christ, Apocalypto is "unburdened by nationalist or reli-gious piety," – that it's "pure, amoral sensational-ism."

Despite its extreme brutality Apocalypto isn't just Gibson's latest snuff film with a religious theme. The film is a morality play, and there are only two things one needs to remember to get a hint of the ugly moral intent behind Mel Gibson's depiction of the Maya.

The first is that, despite Gibson's vile portrayal of the Maya as a macabre cult of deranged killers straight out of Apocalypse Now!, there is no evi-dence that the Mayan people ever practiced wide-spread human sacrifice, and they certainly didn't target the innocent hunter-gatherers and horticul-turalists Gibson chooses to portray as the victims of a Mayan death cult.

Gibson knows better. He studied the terrain in depth and had no practical limit to the funds he could expend on research. His portrayal is a con-scious lie, one he uses to justify the premise that the Mayan city states collapsed because they deserved to collapse, and that they deserved to be replaced by a "superior" culture in the genocide known as the Conquest.

Bantu Mwaura, interviewed by Doreen Struahs and David Paul Mavia (2006):

There is a stark difference between the way theatre is approached in Africa and the way it is ap-proached in the West. So in Africa… theatre has never been, never used to be, that thing that you go to put up in some very specific well-established building somewhere and then everybody comes. We did our theatre, we engaged in performance, in everything that we did.

And every time I go and see a play at the French Cultural Centre, it is Heartstrings (Kenyan theatre troupe) doing these British comedies and bedroom farces. And it really annoys you. But you look at the audience and many a time they have full houses, and people are enjoying themselves. But they are enjoying themselves not because that's what they want, but because that's what they have. There is no alternative. If you gave them an alter-native like Wahome Mutahi did, they'd pack those pubs, and I know people who went to see those Wahome plays every time they were performed – twice, thrice, four, five, ten times…

In our national politics, once something is seen as "left" nobody wants to deal with it. Even the most radical people, when they talk about it, they are, like: "Yeah, these lefties, you know." ...And many a times that ideological left that we don't want to deal with is actually where most of our solutions lie... the mainstream has been able to make the left sound as if it is abominable... So if you really want ... to make people not think about it, just call it leftist. Then everybody will want to have armslength.

Christopher Phelps interviewed by Scott McLemee, "Impure Literature" Inside Higher Ed (2005):

Q: Let me ask about teaching the book, then. How does *The Jungle* go over in the classroom?

A: Extremely well. Students love it. The challenge of teaching history, especially the survey, is to get students who think history is boring to imagine the past so that it comes alive for them. *The Jungle* has a compelling story line that captures readers' atten-tion from its very first scene, a wedding celebration shaded in financial anxiety and doubts about whether Old World cultural traditions can survive in America. From then on, students just want to learn what will befall Jurgis and his family. Along the way, of course, Sinclair injects so much social commentary and description that teachers can eas-ily use students' interest in the narrative as a point of departure for raising a whole range of issues about the period historians call the Progressive Era.

Q: Right. All kinds of problems come from taking any work of literature, even the most intentionally documentary, as giving the reader direct access to history.

A: Nowadays *The Jungle* is much more likely to be assigned in history courses than in literature courses, and yet it is a work of fiction. You point to a major problem, which we might call the construc-tion of realism. I devote a good deal of attention to literary form and genre in my introduction, be-cause I think they are crucial and should not be shunted aside. I note the influence upon *The Jungle* of the sentimentalism of Harriet Beecher Stowe, of naturalist and realist writers like William Dean Howells and Frank Norris, and of the popular dime novels of Horatio Alger. Sinclair was writing a novel, not a government report. He fancied him-self an American Zola, the Stowe of wage slavery.

A good teacher ought to be able to take into ac-count this status of the text as a work of creative literature while still drawing out its historical va-lue. We might consider Jurgis, for example, as the personification of a class. He receives far more lumps in life than any single worker would in 1906, but the problems he encounters, such as on-the-job injury or the compulsion to make one's children work, were in fact dilemmas for the working class of the time.

In my introduction, I contrast the novel with what historians now think about immigrant enclaves, the labor process, gender relations, and race. There is no determinant answer to the question of how well *The Jungle* represented such social realities. Many things it depicted extremely well, others abomina-bly, race being in the latter category. If we keep in mind that realism is literary, fabricated, we can see that Sinclair's background afforded him a discern-ing view of many social developments, making him a visionary, even while he was blind in other ways. Those failings are themselves revelatory of phenomena of the period, such as the racism then commonplace among white liberals, socialists, and labor activists. It's important that we read the novel on all these levels.

Q: Sinclair wrote quite a few other novels, most of them less memorable than *The Jungle*. Well, OK, to be frank, what I've heard is that they were, for the most part, awful. Is that an unfair judgment? Was *The Jungle* a case of the right author handling the right subject at the right time?

A: That's precisely it, I think. Sinclair was uniquely inspired at the moment of writing *The Jungle*. I've been reading a lot of his other books, and although some have their moments, they sure can give you a headache. Many of them read like failed attempts to recapture that past moment of glory. He lived to be ninety and cranked out a book for every year of his life, so it's a cautionary tale about allowing pro-lixity to outpace quality. The book of his that I like best after *The Jungle* is his 1962 autobiography, a book that is wry and whimsical in a surprising and attractive, even disarming, way.

Michael Denning, "The Novelists' International", Culture in the Age of Three Worlds (2004):

In the middle of the age of three worlds (1945-1989), the novel looked dead, exhausted. In the capitalist First World, it was reduced to increasingly arid formalisms alongside an industry of formulaic genre fictions. In the Communist Second World, the official conventions of socialist realism were ritualized into a form of didactic popular literature. Into the freeze of this literary cold war erupted Gabriel García Márquez's *Cien años de soledad* [*One Hundred Years of Solitude*] (1967), the first international bestseller from Latin America and perhaps the most influential novel of the last third of the twentieth century. In its wake, a new sense of a world novel emerged, with *Cien años de soledad* as its avatar, the Third World as its home, and a vaguely defined magical realism as its aesthetic rubric.

Like world music, the world novel is a category to be distrusted; if it genuinely points to the transformed geography of the novel, it is also a marketing device that flattens distinct regional and linguistic traditions into a single cosmopolitan world beat, with magical realism serving as the aesthetic of globalization, often as empty and contrived a signifier as the modernism and socialist realism it supplanted. There is, however, a historical truth to the sense that there are links between writers who now constitute the emerging canon of the world novel – writers as unalike as García Márquez, Naguib Mahfouz, Nadime Gordimer, José Saramago, Paule Marshall, and Pramoedya Ananta Toer – for the work of each has roots in the remarkable international literary movement that emerged in the middle decades of the twentieth century under the slogans of "proletarian literature," "neorealism," and "progressive," "engaged," or "committed" writing…. And though the novelists of this movement were deeply influenced by the experimental modernisms of the early decades of the century, they rarely fit into the canonical genealogies of Western modernism and postmodernism. Though the royalties were small, the writers not all proletarians, and the audience often more a promise than a reality, the movement transformed the history of the novel. By imagining an international of novelists, it reshaped the geography of the novel. It enfranchised a generation of writers, often of plebeian backgrounds, and it was the first self-conscious attempt to create a world literature. From Maxim Gorky to Gabriel García Márquez, from Lu Xun to Pramoedya Ananta Toer, from Richard Wright to Ngũgĩ wa Thiong'o, from Patrícia Galvão to Isabel Allende: the novelists' international spans the globe and the century….

The turning point was the world upheaval of 1917-1921. In the wake of the European slaughter, regimes and empires were challenged: there were revolutions in Czarist Russia and Mexico, brief lived socialist republics in Germany, Hungary and Persia, uprisings against colonialism in Ireland, India, and China, and massive strike waves and factory occupations in Japan, Italy, Spain, Chile, Brazil, and the United States. The "imaginative proximity of social revolution" electrified a generation of young writers who came together in a variety of revolutionary and proletarian writers' groups….

Their books were experiments in form, attempts to reshape the novel. Several challenges immediately presented themselves: the attempt to represent working-class life in a genre that had developed as the quintessential narrator of bourgeois or middle-class manners, kin structures, and social circles; the attempt to represent a collective subject in a form built around the interior life of the individual; the attempt to create a public, agitational work in a form which, unlike drama, depended on private, often domestic, consumption; and the attempt to create a vision of revolutionary social change in a form almost inherently committed to the solidity of society and history. The early novels are often awkward and un-novelistic….

The worldwide migration from country to

city was one of the central historical events of the age of three worlds…"the death of the peasantry"…. Out of the clash of peasant and proletarian worlds came the most powerful new form to emerge from the proletarian literary movements: magical or marvelous realism. Though magical realism is often considered as a successor and antagonist to social realism, its roots lay in the left-wing writers' movements….

[Magical realism's] insistence on the specific reality of the colonized world at the moment of liberation in India, Indonesia, and China, a moment that finds its historical precursor not in the French Revolution (as the Bolsheviks did) but in the Haitian Revolution.

If this is true, one can see why the notion of magical realism resonates far beyond the Caribbe-an islands and coasts where it began. The term comes to represent a larger shift in the aesthetic of the novelists' international, from the powerful censoring of desire in the early novels (the works of the epoch of worldwide depression are novels of lack and hunger, and the utopian novel is rare) to an unleashing of desire and utopia, foreshadowing the liberation ideologies of the New Left. This is why it is common to see magical realism as the antithesis of an earlier social realism….

Magical realism finds its most celebrated avatar in Gabriel García Márquez's *Cien años de soledad*. The 1967 novel, part of the celebrated boom in Latin American fiction, came to stand for the moment of Third World hopefulness in the wake of decolonization…[yet] *Cien años de soledad* stands as both a sign of the crisis in the literary desire to represent workers that had animated a generation of plebian writers and as an attempt to bear witness to that desire. [The results are mixed at best, and] …nearly a century after the first calls for an international proletarian literature and socialist realism, that desire seems not only defeated, but nonexistent and unimaginable. [*Note: It might be of no small significance that Denning is writing here several years before the publication of Ngũgĩ wa Thiongo's great world novel,* Wizard of the Crow.] Yet like the strike story in *Cien años de soledad*, the aspirations and aesthetics of the novelists' international remain the forgotten, repressed history behind the contemporary globalization of the novel.

Margo Hammond and Ellen Heltzel, "The Plot Thickens at the New York Times Book Review" poynter.org (2004):

…if you're perplexed or simply bored with what passes for smart fiction these days, the *Times* feels your pain. More attention will be paid to the pot-boilers, we're told… So there's the recipe: Empha-size non-fiction books. Demote literary fiction. Pro-mote (judiciously) commercial novels… Whether or not the *Times'* analysis of the market and its read-ers is correct, it's based on logical reasoning. In the views expressed by its decision-makers, too few works of fiction rise to the level of a 'novel of ideas' – that is, stories that express the concerns and issues of the day as Dickens did.

Andrew O'Hehir, "'The Fountain at the Center of the World' by Robert Newman" salon.com (2004):

The anti-globalization movement may not quite have found its Dante or its Homer in British writer Robert Newman, but it's found something, all right – maybe its Theodore Dreiser. Newman, the auth-or of two previous novels published in the United Kingdom, makes a splashy, messy American debut with 'The Fountain at the Center of the World,' an ambitious and occasionally thrilling book that takes you from a NAFTA-impoverished Mexican village to the sleek corporate hallways of the City of London to the now-legendary street demonstrations at the World Trade Organization's 1999 Seat-tle meeting. Newman is himself a veteran street-level activist, having worked with such groups as Reclaim the Streets, Indymedia, Earth First! and the longshoremen of Liverpool. He writes about the decentralized, ragtag fringes of the contemporary left with affection and a wry eye for detail...

Heather Lee Schroeder, "Political fiction inspires thought, debate on issues" The Capitol Times (2004):

So much of the fiction that crosses my desk has turned inward to focus on issues of interpersonal relationships. Frankly, I find the endless round of 'coming of age' novels and intensely focused stories about individuals rather boring. If the heart of ev-ery story is conflict, then I think the difference be-tween a memorable story and a forgettable story lies in the author's ability to weigh the internal con-flicts of the characters against the greater and exter-nal struggles of the world around them. Not only does political fiction entertain readers, but it also will bring them to a place they have never been or never dared venture. Great political fiction also can spur them on to learn more or think more about greater social issues. Think, for example, of the en-during popularity of Charles Dickens. His writing was of the moment – relevant and sharply focused on both the struggles of individuals and the larger machine in which they toiled – yet it speaks to us today about all sorts of social ills we're still trying to manage.

Ardain Isma, "Novel Injustices: Whither the Contemporary Novel?" justresponse.net (2004):

Far from romanticizing the Haitian masses' deplor-able conditions, [Jacques Stephen] Alexis saw in his 'marvelous realism' the best if not a unique way to beautify the Haitian literature, and with it, the 'marvelous symbiosis,' connect-ing the mind, body and soul of every Haitian in order to bring to light a new and true Haitian nation – one that would be based on justice for all. Alexis saw in the people's daily life an ar-tistic treasure, one not only to pre-serve and cherish, but also to be put at the forefront of the struggle to bring humanity together within the framework of democratic governance and the rule of law.

Ira Chernus, "Presidential Fiction: The Story Behind the Debates", tomdispatch.com (2004):

For most of human history, most people have lived in abject poverty. They survived, in part, on stories. They told stories to interpret their suffering or to distract themselves from their suffering, to parti-cipate vicariously in magnificent events and give meaning to an exis-tence that might otherwise seem meaningless. In most cultures, the truly powerful stories – myths, legends, or sacred narratives – were re-ligious ones. In the United States, where we have no religious myths that we all share, the his-tory of the nation has become our most powerful shared myth. Like all religious stories, the most popular versions of American history are a mixture of fact, fantasy, and wish-fulfillment. Judging from the first debate, it's not clear that Kerry and his campaign strategists understand the power of this potent brew. The Bush campaign understands it all too well.

Fred Kaplan, "Truth Stranger than 'Strangelove'", New York Times (2004):

'Dr. Strangelove,' Stanley Kubrick's 1964 film about nuclear-war plans run amok, is widely heralded as one of the greatest satires in Ameri-can political or movie history. For its 40th anni-versary, Film Forum is screening a new 35 mil-limeter print for one week, starting on Friday, and Columbia TriStar is releasing a two-disc special-edition DVD next month. One essential point should emerge from all the hoopla: 'Strangelove' is far more than a satire. In its own loopy way, the movie is a remarkably fact-based and specific guide to some of the oddest, most secretive chapters of the Cold War... Those in the know watched 'Dr. Strangelove' amused, like everyone else, but also stunned. Daniel Ellsberg, who later leaked the Pentagon Papers, was a RAND analyst and a consultant at the De-fense Department when he and a mid-level offi-cial took off work one afternoon in 1964 to see the film. Mr. Ellsberg recently recalled that as they left the thea-ter, he turned to his colleague and said, 'That was a documentary!'

Larry Beinhart, "Politics & Mysteries" thelibrarian.biz (2004):

In a mystery (and all the sub-genres) crime is per-sonal. Hands on. Painful. It has blood and conse-quences. If some distant and cool and im-personal act of policy impels the criminal act, that allows us, the readers, to make the transla-tion from the insti-tutional to the personal. Poli-tics offers us some-thing real and vital for the story to be about. The story, ideally, takes us past the rhetoric and the posturing, to the reality of the politics. A great symbiosis. That explains why lots and lots of writ-ers would combine politics and mysteries. But they don't. Even when they do, it's rarely about politics as policy. It's mostly politics as a setting… Fiction, specifi-cally mystery fiction, is the tool that I have available to me to talk about unreality of our public mythologies.

Underground Literary Alliance, literaryrevolution.com (2004):

American fiction should be something rele-vant to American people's lives, instead of the lame, over-ly wrought, navel-gazing crap that the congloms make sure gets first-rate display at your local chain bookshop… Our main criticism is that American Lit 'n' Letters has become pro-fessionalized, elitist, art-destructive, corrupt, meaningless, soulless, and just plain crazy sick to look at. This has everything to do with the strangulation since the '90s of indep-endent publishing houses (and, to a big extent, more independent thought) by conglomerates. Basi-cally: it's corporate lit from here on out unless somebody does something about it. We of the ULA are out here doing something about it. We're acti-vists of the aesthetic variety. We want to provoke cultural change against its cur-rent tide towards the focal points of power and capital concentration. We're screaming for sys-temic change now.

Andre Vltchek, "Are We Alone, Arundhati Roy?" zcommunications.org (2004):

Two years ago…[Arundhati Roy and I] dis-cussed politics and we discussed mounting problems in India, but we also talked about the state of litera-ture, a topic about which we both felt passionate. Almost all great modern writers seemed to be in a lethargic sleep or too fright-ened to address impor-tant global issues. Or maybe there were almost no great writers left. Philosophy, politics, social criti-cism and vision had been replaced by frivolous, entertaining plots. The pitiful state of today's world, its dis-parities and scandalous post-colonial arrange-ment, topped the list of issues hardly dis-cussed on the pages of contemporary novels. Fic-tion had become politically and socially detached and therefore historically and morally irrele-vant. Instead of aiming at retaining their status as 'the conscience of society', most of writers opted for much more modest goals, turning themselves to entertainers and showbiz figures.

On Robert Newman's third novel, The Fountain at the Center of the World (2003-2004):

It reads like what you'd get if Tom Wolfe clamb-ered inside the head of Noam Chomsky – it ele-gantly and angrily scorches a lot of earth…the talis-manic 'Catch-22' of the antiglob-alization protest movement, the fictional com-plement to Naomi Klein's influential treatise '"No Logo."

– Dwight Garner, *The New York Times*.

To summarise a plot that swings long and hard be-tween the symbolic and the naturalistic: Chano Sal-gado is a Mexican political dissident; his wife has been shot in the head by armed mi-litia for having had the temerity to attend a po-litical meeting; he is persuaded to blow up a big corporation's pipelines that are sucking the local groundwater dry; his young son Daniel has dis-appeared; on the run, Chano miraculously meets up with his long-lost brother Evan Hatch, who is a PR executive advis-ing the very corporations that are ensuring Chano's continuing oppression.

Evan is dying of a beetle-borne disease called chagas, and has travelled to Mexico in search of a bone-marrow match with his brother. Daniel and Chano and Evan all end up at the WTO protests in Seattle. The book is about power and powerless-ness, about Latin America and North America, and about evil, harm, suffering and pain… It's like boot leg Chomsky … *The Fountain at the Centre of the World* is a serious and intelligent book. It's a novel that confronts everything that is wrong with the world and demands that which is right, and it therefore makes a lot of British fiction seem rather tender-minded in comparison.

— Ian Sanson, *The Guardian*.

War novels need not revel in bloodshed and closely document inhumane horrors to be viscerally effect-ive. Nor must they even be about war in the con-ventional shock-and-awe sense. So you could say the best war novel on the shelves now is Robert Newman's *The Fountain at the Center of the World.*

— Sam McManis, *Tacoma Tribune*.

… [a] spirited attempt to reconcile the larger forces at work in the world through fiction. Could this herald a resuscitation of the English 'literary politi-cal novel', almost dead in the water since the best work of Malcolm Lowry and Graham Greene? [Newman] has … taken a rare risk for our mort-gage-panic, leather-sofa era, to remind us how the personal is political – and vice versa.

— Jean McNeil, *The Independent*.

The Fountain At The Centre Of The World is perhaps the first novel to really explore the human story be-hind the placard waving and polemics of globalisa-tion … it is fiction that tells a truth about a world that is only too real.

— *The Ecologist*.

It is rare to find such a politically engaged novel. There has been plenty of fiction that has had a poli-tical edge or implications, but this book is much more than that. It is openly partisan… uncomfort-able reading for advocates of the current global set-up.

— Nicolai Gentchev, *The Socialist Review*.

A political novel whose lines are drawn too starkly – say, one in which the characters the novelist agrees with are sympathetic and their political opponents unsympathetic – would be tiresome. Newman has for the most part avoided that trap, though it's never in doubt which side he's on. He allows ideology to hit up against its opposition and its own failings. – Karen Olsson *The Texas Observer*

Newman has written a big, generous book, filling canisters with facts and philosophy from the likes of Noam Chomsky, Greg Palast, Susan George, and Bill Hicks, then igniting them with keen observa-tions of everyday life in Mexican villages where international factories suck up all the water … in border jails, and on police-lined streets. Finally, he hurls them at the shock troops of globalization. The troops and everyone else – Radical Cheerleaders and TV correspondents, National Guardsmen and international activists – are blanketed in a cloud of truth-and-laughing gas that stings, burns, and, yes, brings tears.

— Suzanne Charlé, *The American Prospect*.

After absorbing this tale, you'll be left with an obv-ious question. Is globalisation our future, or an at-tack on the human race? Too weighty for you? It shouldn't be. The author's style and the flowing sense of foreign adventure alone make it a good yarn. Learning Spanish to influence a story is real commitment. Incredibly, his descriptions create similar feelings to those left by Gabriel Garcia Marquez. The story is intricately constructed, told from the heart and definitely worth a go, whatever your viewpoint.

— Adam Corres, *Diverse Books*.

Alice Lovelace, "Art Changes" Keynote speech at the conference, The Art of Juvenile Justice: Innovative Practices for Transforming Youth – Coalition for Juvenile Justice Southern Region Training Conference (2003):

In college, I studied criminal justice. I was idealist-ic. Certain that I would be able to have a positive influence in the criminal justice system and create change. One of my professors pulled me aside one day and asked if I had ever been in a prison. I had not so he took me to work with him in a minimum-security facility – but even here there were those doors that shut with a cold clink, the steel bars, and the eyes always on you. The next day, I returned to school and changed my major to Liberal Arts.

I still wanted to make social change. Never-the-less, I accepted as a fact that in 1973 I could not make social change within the system. Therefore, I studied literature and creative writing with the idea that these would be my tools, my weapon to make change. As a result, I have taught poetry and creative writing in a women's jail, spent 18 weeks working with women in a pre-release center, worked in a halfway house, in youth detention cen-ters, and youth-at-risk facilities.

I have carried with me one message and that is that ART CHANGES. This has been the real-ity of my life.

I have seen art change – Art can change the indi-vidual, change someone's mind, or change the way a society thinks about itself and others. Art can change one's understanding of self or another, changes with the times, and is changed according to who rules. I have witnessed art change as it moves from one place to another only to be changed by place. Art changes. Art can expand any environment, only to create its own space. I know that art changes with reality and that art can change reality...

The arts reach students not reached by other pro-grams and methods. Research has shown that young people who are disengaged are at the great-est risk of failure. Researchers have found that the arts provide a reason, and some-times the only rea-son, for these youth to be en-gaged. Arts programs are credited with reduc-ing absenteeism and lessen-ing dropout rates. The arts can be the key that fin-ally unlocks their potential to develop skills and learning they can tap into long after their lessons are over.

Arts programs have traditionally had great success with students who might have other-wise slipped through the cracks. Programs from inner city youth that used an arts-based model have shown an 80% college attendance rate. Arts pro-grams for incarcerated youth have shown that students overcame behavioral prob-lems by 75% and were 50% less likely to commit another crime. These changes are attributed to the fact that in-volvement in the arts has shown that young people grow in self-confidence. They learn techniques of self-control. They clarify and strengthen their self-identity and learn alterna-tive ways of settling dis-putes. They learn to empathize with others. They learn valuable col-laboration skills and are more op-en to accept people who are not like them.

We know that learning in and through the arts can help level the playing field for young people and especially those from disadvantaged circum-stances. The arts provide young people with auth-entic learning experiences that en-gage their minds, hearts, and bodies. The learn-ing experiences are real and meaningful for them.

Why? Because the arts engage multiple skills and abilities. When young people participate in the arts, whether it is visual arts, dance, music, theatre, creative writing, drama, fabric arts, pho-tography or other disciplines, they develop cog-nitive, social, and personal competencies...

Howard Zinn, Artists in Times of War (2003):

I suggest that the role of the artist is to tran-scend conventional wisdom, to transcend the word of the establishment, to transcend the or-thodoxy, to go beyond and escape what is handed down by the government or what is said in the media... It is the job of the artist to think outside the boundaries of permissible thought and dare to say things that no one else will say... It is absolutely patriotic to point a fin-ger at the government to say that it is not do-ing what it should be doing to safeguard the right of citizens to life, liberty, and the pursuit of happi-ness... We must be able to look at our-selves, to look at our country honestly and clearly. And just as we can examine the awful things that people do else-where, we have to be willing to examine the awful things that are done here by our government.

John Pilger (2002-2003):

"Hollywood Hurrah" johnpilger.com: Even in finely crafted films like *The Deer Hunter* and *Platoon* that look as if they might break ranks, there is an im-plicit oath of loyalty to imperial culture. This was true of *Three Kings*, a movie that seemed to take issue with the Gulf war, but instead produced a familiar 'bad apple' tale, exonerating the militarism that is now rampant. So dominant is Hollywood in our lives, and so collusive are its camp-following critics, that the films that ought to have been made are unmentionable. Name the mainstream movies that have shone light on to the vast shadow thrown by the American secret state, and the mayhem for which it is responsible. I can think of only a few…

"Our Writers' Failure (I)" zmag.org: Martin Amis represents a problem: that some of the most ac-claimed and privileged writers in the English lan-guage fail to engage with the most urgent issues of our time. On 1 June, the Guardian published a long essay by Martin Amis, entitled 'The voice of the lonely crowd'. It was about 11 September and the role of writers. What did Amis think about on the momentous day? He thought he was 'like Joseph-ine, the opera-singing mouse in the Kafka story: Sing? "She can't even squeak."' By that he meant, I guess, that he had nothing to say about 'the conflicts we now face or fear', as he put it. Why not? Where was the spirit of Orwell and Greene? Where was a modest acknowledge-ment of history: a pass-ing reflection on the impact of rapacious great power on vulnerable societies, which are the roots of the current 'terrorism'?

"Our Writers' Failure (II)" New Statesman: On 17 June, I wrote about Martin Amis's recent Guardian essay, 'The voice of the lonely crowd,' in which he described the response of acclaimed writers like himself to 11 September as a 'pitiable babble.' In fact, they were and remain mostly silent.

"The Silence of Writers" zmag.org: For the great writ-ers of the 20th century, art could not be separated from politics. Today, there is a disturbing silence on the dark matters that should command our attention. In 1935, the first Congress of American Writers was held at the Carnegie Hall in New York, followed by another two years later. By one ac-count, 3,500 crammed into the auditorium and a thousand more were turned away. They were electric events, with writers discussing how they could confront ominous events in Abyssinia, China and Spain. Telegrams from Thomas Mann, C Day Lewis, Upton Sinclair and Albert Einstein were read out, reflecting the fear that great power was now rampant and that it had become impossible to discuss art and literature without politics.

B. R. Meyers, A Reader's Manifesto: An Attack on the Growing Pretentiousness in American Literary Prose (2002):

[The book begins with an epigraph:] "Those who write preciously are like people who get dolled up to avoid being confused and confounded with the mob, a danger run by no gentleman even in the worst clothes. As a certain sartorial pomp…betrays the plebian, so does a precious style betray the commonplace mind." – Schopenhauer

In late 1999 I wrote a short book called *Gorgons in the Pool*. Quoting lengthy passages from prize-winning novels, I argued that some of the most acclaimed contemporary prose is the product of mediocre writers availing themselves of trendy stylistic gimmicks. The greater point was that we readers should trust our own taste and perception instead of deferring to received opinion. A banal thing to say? I only wish it was. For the past few decades our cultural establishment has propagated a very different message.

MB: Your literary scholarship has focused mostly on poetry. Why have you made that particular choice?

CN: Poetry has had a very long cultural history, as prayer, as chant, as curse, as the song of the subject and the song of the chorus. Nothing poetry has be-come was foreordained. History might have gone differently. But as things have worked out poetry's inscaped language registers a culture's idealiza-tions and its traumas with unique compression and power. There's nothing else quite like it. Save for technology and science, poetry embodies all you need to know on earth.

MB: How did you get interested in the Spanish Civil War as a research topic?

CN: If you're interested in the 1930s, then, to some degree you are interested in Spain. It is the great international story for the Left in that decade and ever since then the surviving veterans have had substantial cultural capital on the Left. It's also a remarkable place to think about the meaning and limits of individual agency within political move-ments and in relation to world politics. Some on the right insist the 40,000 international volunteers who came to help the Spanish Republic were noth-ing more than Stalin's dupes. Some on the Left, including me, argue their motives and actions have relative autonomy.

The Spanish Civil War also presents an astonishing convergence of art and politics, a site where artists contributed worldwide and where all the arts acquire a powerful relationality. But my own interest came conventionally for an English professor – by way of Edwin Rolfe's poetry. He served in the Lincoln Battalion and became its poet laureate. I went to Spain with photocopies of his diaries, retraced his footsteps, and eventually conducted over 3,000 interviews with his friends, family members, and contemporaries.

MB: Have you met many members of the Abraham Lincoln Brigade?

CN: Yes, most of the surviving members, though many of them have died since I began this work in the late 1980s. I've written a couple of obituaries for the first time and will no doubt write others. So there's some sadness that I really met this generation of the 1930s in its twilight years, though mostly I am grateful to have known a group of men and women who carried their political commitments through most of the century. Not everyone ages gracefully, to be sure, and people in their 80s can be extremely demanding, but I've had the great pleasure of spending many many hours with veterans of 1930s politics and 1950s witch hunts who possess remarkable intelligence, energy, insight, and courage. Overall, they are a tremendous inspiration. I count myself very lucky to have started these Spanish Civil War projects in time to talk with so many who were there. Over and over again I met people in their seventies who could run me ragged, who kept going all day long with unfailing energy and whose understanding of current politics and events was sharp and utterly unclouded by sentiment. And it's most often not my peers but these veterans of twentieth century history who unsparingly tell me whether I've got things right in my own work.

MB: *Revolutionary Memory* has more than fifty illustrations drawn from your personal collection. Each of the items practically represents an entire category of neglected radical creative expression: IWW poetry cards, working-class and battlefield manuscripts, pamphlets from John Reed clubs, illustrations from scores of radical magaizines.

What happened to this rich history of political poetry so that it was largely ignored? How do we come to 'forget' such an enormous zone of our political and cultural heritage?

CN: A lot of the active forgetting took place during the McCarthy period. That's when the canon of modern literature was solidified; it was done dur-ing a period of fear when the academy willingly collaborated in the project of McCarthyism. Some English professors were essentially extensions of the House UnAmerican Activities Committee. The modern literary canon was codified on the basis of political anxiety. It's also true that once that hap-pens it happens on multiple levels. It means that work is no longer mentioned in literary histories. It means that work is no longer in print and in book-stores. It means that work is no longer in antholo-gies and not written about in scholarship. Then the next generation just never reads or hears any-thing about alternative literatures.

In the late 40s and early 50s you still get occa-sional mentions of America's long leftist literary traditions accompanied by dismissals but eventu-ally the dismissals no longer take place, and the mentions never take place. A whole his-torical nar-rative is constructed in which certain things no longer have a place.

Like others working to expand the canon, my experience over the last twenty years has been of repeatedly discovering continents on earth that you didn't know were there before. Each time it hap-pens to me I experience the same as-tonishment and incredulity. How could I not have known about this? I have a PhD. I thought I studied this period. How could I not have known about all these things that were part of that historical moment? There are whole discur-sive registers that are just absent from the active historical memory.

MB: Can any of this forgetting be attributed to the relationship between the new left and the old left, or the relationship between the acad-emy and the new social movements?

CN: In the 60s and early 70s the campus left in-clud-ing myself involved in Vietnam protests was large-ly ignorant of the historical and liter-ary-historical traditions to which it was in-debted unbeknownst to itself, and whose heri-tage we should have been celebrating at the same time. I taught anti-Vietnam poetry during that time, but I didn't know that it might have been helpful to teach the anti-imperial-ist poetry about the Spanish American war in those same classes. I didn't know there was any. I knew that poems were being written in 1969 about Viet-nam, but I didn't know that anti-imperialist and anti-racist poems had been written at the turn of the century and that they spoke to Viet-nam quite directly. To recognize those historical continuities, to recognize the role of literaryness in resisting im-perialism, to recognize that it had a history in our own country utterly changes your sense of your relationship to those continuities, to that past, to your discipline, and I think most of us were clueless about it. Of course the old left was struggling to keep alive its own traditions that were already under as-sault, and already being not just forgotten but actively suppressed.

MB: Increasingly you are working with forms widely dismissed as ephemeral.

CN: Preserving ephemera is another matter; some-one has to treasure them and recognize the value of the material form itself. American New Criticism tended to value texts but not the variety of material forms in which they were is-sued. To me nothing is more exciting than learn-ing that a particular poem was distributed at a particular meeting on a given day. Even librari-ans can be slow to learn the value of ephemera. *Revolutionary Memory* reproduces the first page of a condensed version of the poem "On Guard for Spain," marked for a 1937 wartime per-formance in Britain. It's the only known surviv-ing copy so annotated and amended. By law the dealer who offered it to me had to give the Brit-ish Muse-um first refusal. I assumed they would buy it in a second, since the performances of it have been ad-dressed both in published ac-counts at the time and in recent scholarship. But they turned it down, so I eagerly sent my check. Of course I buy these things not to own them but rather to put them into circu-lation, to dis-seminate them again or for the first time.

Arundhati Roy, "Come September", ZNet (2002):

"The theme of much of what I write, fiction as well as nonfiction, is the relationship between power and powerlessness and the endless, cir-cular conflict they're engaged in. John Berger, that most wonder-ful writer, once wrote: 'Never again will a single story be told as though it's the only one.' There can never be a single story. There are only ways of seeing. So when I tell a story, I tell it not as an ideologue who wants to pit one absolutist ideology against another, but as a story-teller who wants to share her way of seeing. Though it might appear otherwise, my writing is not really about nations and histories; it's about power. About the paranoia and ruthlessness of power. About the physics of power. I believe that the accumulation of vast un-fettered power by a State or a country, a corpora-tion or an institution – or even an individual, a spouse, a friend, a sibling – regardless of ideology, results in excesses such as the ones I will recount here."

Tony Kushner, "How Do You Make Social Change?" (2001):

I do not believe that a steadfast refusal to be parti-san is, finally, a particularly brave or a moral or even interesting choice. Les Murray, an Australian poet, wrote a short poem called 'Politics and Art.' In its entirety: 'Brutal policy / like inferior art, knows / whose fault it all is.' This is as invaluable an admonishment as it is ultimately untrue.

Arundhati Roy, Power Politics (2001):

It is the writers, the poets, the artists, the singers, the filmmakers who can make the connections, who can find ways of bringing it into the realm of common understanding. Who can translate cash-flow charts and scintillating boardroom speeches into real stories about real people with real lives. Stories about what it's like to lose your home, your land, your job, your dignity, your past, and your future to an invisible force. To someone or some-thing you can't see. You can't hate. You can't even imagine.

Kathryn Hume, American Dream, American Nightmare: Fiction Since 1960 (2000):

Around 1960, American Fiction cast aside many canonical limits and became a carnival of bustling diversity. Did the excitement of these develop-ments blind critics to a surprisingly bleak outlook in many of these novels? For all the flash and en-ergy of the narrative voices, a disconcerting amount of the fiction expresses bitter disillusion-ment with America and the American Dream. This study considers roughly one hundred novels... Ob-viously disappoint-ment with America is not found in all novels of the period, nor in all the books by these particular novelists. Writers more concerned with language than story, who locate 'art's deepest morality at the heart of linguistic creativity of which fiction is capable,' and those for whom aesthetics, theory, and philosophy are the burning issues may not feel attracted to political rumina-tions... My map of the novelistic landscape since 1960 is not meant to be exhaustive. It explores the surprising expanses of the Slough of Despond rath-er than focusing on the higher plateaus whose in-habitants pursue their own ends and feel no worry for the state of the country.

Winston James, A Fierce Hatred of Injustice (2000):

The ethos of colonial education was to inculcate into the colonized – the conquered – the superiority of the metropole and its culture. As Frantz Fanon demonstrated in *Black Skin, White Masks*, language constitutes once crucial and strategic site of struggle. The acquisition of and facility with the language of the imperial power are signs, as well as prerequisites, of social elevation. France and Portugal were perhaps the most explicit of the colonial powers on this question, providing special privileges in their colonies to natives who mastered the European tongue. This was and is nothing less than a calculated policy of cultural genocide, systematic *deracination* in both senses of the term – uprooting and whitening: "Wherever colinalism is a fact the indigenous culture begins to rot." For the aspiring colonial, the culture of the "mother country," becomes what Mervyn Alleyne terms the "target culture." According to the ethos of colonial education, there was no beauty, no nobility, no history, no culture, in short nothing of any worth – barring the natural resources and markets for the metropolis manufactured goods – in that which existed locally.

The task of the colonial educator, then, in the far-flung hinterland of Empire was to elevate the hapless colonized – "Ham's children," "the Natives," "the Wogs" – from their pathological condition, to lead, coax, cajole and coerce them out of the long night of their heathen darkness into the clear light of day of Western civilization. Colonial education inculcated black inferiority. How else could it persuade black people to relinquish and malign their own culture? Force alone could never work. Commander Bodilly, an Englishman stationed in Jamaica as a resident magistrate, spelled this out as recently as the early 1930s in an interview: British rule in the colonies depends upon a "carefully nurtured sense of inferiority" in the governed.

Colonial domination, direct as well as indirect, is never devoid of local collaboration. This is the key to its longevity: it imbues in the colonized a sense of its indispensability….

Noam Chomsky, email (1999):

About Orwell's 1984, I thought, frankly, it was one of his worst books. Could barely finish it. Some parts (e.g., about Newspeak) were clever. But most of it seemed to me – well, trivial. The problem is not a very interesting one; the modes of thought control and repression in totalitarian societies are fairly transparent. In fact, they often tend to be rather lax. Franco Spain, for example, didn't care much what people thought and said: the screams from the torture chamber in downtown Madrid were enough to keep the lid on. It's not too well known, but the Soviet Union was also pretty lax, particularly in the Brezhnev era. According to US government-Russian Research Center studies, Russians apparently had considerably wider access to a broad range of opinion and to dissident literature than Americans do, not because it is denied them but because propaganda is so much more effective here. Orwell was well aware of these issues. His (suppressed) introduction to Animal Farm, for example, deals explicitly with "literary censorship in England." To write about that topic would have been important, hard, and serious – and would have earned him the obloquy that attends departure from the rules.

Caricature can be very well done. Swift is mar-velous, for example. Animal Farm is pretty good, in my opinion. But 1984 I thought was a serious decline from his best work.

Caricature is an art, and not an easy one. But when well done, a very important one. As for deal-ing with Orwell's problem,* I try to do it in the ways I know how to pursue; 1000s of pages by now. No doubt there are other ways, maybe better ways. But others will have to find what works for them.

*[Orwell's problem: how is it that oppressive ideo-logical systems are able to] "instill beliefs that are firmly held and widely accepted although they are completely without foundation and often plainly at variance with the obvious facts about the world around us?"

Barbara Kingsolver, "In support of a literature for social change" The Bellwether Prize for Fiction bellwetherprize.org (1999):

Fiction has a unique capacity to bring difficult is-sues to a broad readership on a personal level, cre-ating empathy in a reader's heart for the theoretical stranger. Its capacity for invoking moral and social responsibility is enormous. Throughout history, every movement toward a more peaceful and hu-mane world has begun with those who imagined the possibilities. The Bellwether Prize seeks to sup-port the imagination of humane possibilities.

Defining a literature of social change: Socially responsible literature, for the purposes of this award, may describe categorical human transgress-sions in a way that compels readers to examine their own prejudices. It may invoke the necessity for economic and social justice for a particular eth-nic or social group, or it may explicitly examine movements that have brought positive social change. Or, it may advocate the preservation of na-ture by describing and defining accountable rela-tionships between people and their environment. The mere description of an injustice, or of the per-sonal predicament of an exploited person, without any clear position of social analysis invoked by the writer, does not in itself constitute socially respons-ible literature. 'Social responsibility' describes a moral obligation of individuals to engage with their communities in ways that promote a more respectful coexistence...

These authors notwithstanding, issues of social responsibility have in recent decades held a less commanding place in U.S. literature than in the wider world. Social commentary in our art is fre-quently viewed with suspicion. Its advocacy does not fall within the stated goals of any major North American publisher, endowment, or prize for the arts. The Bellwether Prize was conceived to ad-dress this deficiency. We would like to see the place of conscience in our nation's artistic land-scape restored to the same high position it holds elsewhere in the world. By means of this prize we hope to enlist North American writers, publishers, and readers to share in this crucial endeavor.

Ngũgĩ wa Thiong'o, Ngũgĩ wa Thiong'o Speaks (1967-1999), (Eds. Sander and Lindfors) (via Litblog co-op) (2006):

1999: I associate my concept of art with creativity, movement, change, and renewal. I'm thinking of a much more ethical society than what we have now. This "reign of art" would subsume or transcend the coercive nature of the state: a more ethical, more human society that is constantly renewing itself; art embodies this. I remember, historically speaking, a time when there was no state because I grew up in a society where literally there wasn't a state, at least in its centralized form. Art precedes the formation of the state. The state embodies a static concept of conservation, holding back. Of course, when the state is also controlled by a class, it is an instrument for much more holding back of society. Creativity, art embodies the principle of what our hands do anyway: change.

1988: Literature is indeed a powerful weapon. I believe that we in Africa or anywhere else for that matter have to use literature deliberately and con-sciously as a weapon of struggle in two ways: a) first, by trying as much as possible to correctly re-flect the world of struggle in all its stark reality, and b) secondly, by weighting our sympathies on the side of those forces struggling against national and class oppression and exploitation, say, against the entire system of imperialism in the world to-day. I believe that the more conscious a writer is about the social forces at work in his society and in the world, the more effective he or she is likely to be as a writer. We writers must reject the bourgeois image of a writer as a mindless genius.

1984: Art cannot be outside that which affects hu-man beings. Art, literature, is about life, about the quality of human lives, about human relationships.

Therefore whatever affects the quality of human life, whatsoever affects the changing pattern of hu-man relationships is connected with a legitimate area of art. As such, any art which divorces itself from those social forces that impinge on human lives can only be an art which is denying itself its real life-force. So politics, economics – everything which has to do with the struggle of human beings – is a legitimate concern of art.

1977: Fiction cannot be the agent of change. The people are the agent of change. All writers can do is really try to point out where things went wrong. They can do no more than that. But fiction should be firmly on the side of the oppressed. Fiction should firmly embody the aspirations and hopes of the majority – of the peasants and workers.

1967: I am very suspicious about writing about uni-versal values. If there are universal values, they are always contained in the framework of social reali-ties. And one important social reality in Africa is that ninety percent of the people cannot read or speak English. The problem is this: I know whom I write about, but whom do I write for?

John Whalen-Bridge, Political Fiction and the American Self (1998):

The academic study of the political novel begins confidently in 1924 with Morris Edmund

Speare's founding study *The Political Novel...* The American version [of the political novel], claimed Speare, has a more activist-pragmatic aim than the English: 'A comparison [...] of the American with the English political novelist brings out one striking fact: that whereas in England the writers have often enough been interested in presenting the political panor-ama for the sake of panorama, – shall we say, art for art's sake – American novelists have been main-ly concerned with Reform' (334). Some political novels lean toward political activism, some toward art for art's sake. Speare observes that American novelists in particular were distinguished by their zeal for reform. This activist difference could help explain why the prejudice against political fiction is stronger in America than in other countries.

Speare's recognition of the partisan nature of political fiction is presented in disarmingly direct fashion. Contemporary readers who are so quick to find in Speare quaint signs of class privilege over-look the ways in which this reader from 1924 is a-head of today's culture contests, wherein it must be continually reasserted that political struggle is an appropriate end of art. The demand for an absolute separation of politics and aesthetics is today rarely voiced as an imperative, but occasionally we hap-pen upon it whole cloth. In the section of its book-let entitled 'What the Endowment Does Not Sup-port,' the National Endowment of the Humanities makes it clear that it will support no projects that 'Are directed at persuading an audience to a parti-cular political, philosophical, religious, or ideologi-cal point of view, or that advocate a particular program of social change or action' (6). This policy gives us a negative definition of the political novel to complement Speare's positive description. His judgment that the American political novel is en-gaged in the business of Reform has become a much more controversial position since he first wrote it, and the reason is found in critical stan-dards and even government policies that attack works of art that 'advocate a particular program of social change.' Art must affirm the status quo to re-ceive NEH funding.

The political novel exposes itself to economic and critical perils that are somewhat more focused than those faced by other novels; its author will re-ceive fewer government grants, or it may be sin-gled out for reproach in reviews. This condition has not always obtained to the same degree, and there have been moments in this century when challenges to the idea that politics and literature are unmixable discourses were particularly strong. Speare's study is, nonetheless, the last one pub-lished in the United States to speak of the political novel without apology (22-23).

Alan Wald, "On 'The Radical Novel Reconsidered," interviewed by Chris Faatz for Reading the Left no. 4 (1998):

...there is a legitimate tradition of Marxists who see literature as prophetic in its peneration to funda-mental issues in life, and, of course, literature is of-ten the repository of utopian hopes for a future egalitarian society. As I emphasized in answering the first question, Left literature can also record the powerful as well as painful experiences of our predecessors, enabling revolutionaries of the pres-ent to enrich their consciousnesses. I personally believe that there is a tremendous amount of insight into the radical personality to be gleaned by Polonsky's THE WORLD ABOVE and Saxton's THE GREAT MIDLAND – including the matters of romantic and sexual relations. I also have found tremendous inspiration for anti-racist commitment in Maund's THE BIG BOXCAR and Sanford's THE PEOPLE FROM HEAVEN. From Bonosky's BURN-ING VALLEY I saw for the first time the potential for a Catholic commitment to become the site of revolutionary politics. But one thing of which I am definitely skeptical is the whole tradition of Marx-ist parties trying to "lead" a cultural movement, es-pecially by encouraging the creation of a "revolu-tionary" literature. Whatever one's intentions at the outset, this leads too often to judging literature by immedi-ate political line or by interpretations of mainly one feature of the writing (ignoring the ambiguities and contradictions of the reception pro-cess). In my view, James T. Farrell's A

NOTE ON LITERARY CRITICISM remains a useful beginning guide to the problems in this area, even though Farrell, writing in the heat of the 1930s, is a bit overpolemical (and satirical) in his characteriz-ations of various positions.

Graham Robb, Victor Hugo (1997):

[On the reception of his novel *Les Misérables*, Victor Hugo observes,] "The newspapers which support the old world say, 'It's hideous, infa-mous, odious, execrable, abominable, grotesque, repulsive, shape-less, monstrous, horrendous, etc.' Democratic and friendly papers answer, 'No, it's not bad.'"

[Robb adds,] Mme Hugo, who was in Paris giv-ing interviews, tried to persuade Hugo's spineless allies to support the book and invited them to din-ner; but Gautier had flu, Janin had 'an attack of gout', and George Sand excused herself on the grounds that she always over-ate when she was invited out...

...Perrot de Chezelles [a public prosecutor], in an 'Examination of *Les Misérables*', defended the ex-cellence of a State which persecuted con-victs even after their release, and derided the notion that poverty and ignorance had anything to do with crime... The State was trying to clear its name. The Emperor and Empress performed some public acts of charity and brought philan-thropy back into fash-ion. There was a sudden surge of official interest in penal legislation, the industrial exploitation of women, the care of or-phans, and the education of the poor. From his rock in the English Channel, Victor Hugo...[exiled] had set the parliamentary agenda for 1862.

Les Misérables etches Hugo's view of the world so deeply in the mind that it is impossible to be the same person after reading it – not just be-cause it takes a noticeable percentage of one's life to read it. The key to its effect lies in Hugo's use of a sporadi-cally omniscient narrator who reintroduces his characters at long intervals as if through the eyes of an ignorant observer – a narrator who can best be described as God mas-querading as a law-abiding bourgeois...

The title itself is a moral test.... Originally, a *misé-rable* was simply a pauper (*misére* means 'destitu-tion' as well as 'misfortune'). Since the Revolution, and especially since the advent of Napoleon III, a *misérable* had become a 'dreg', a sore on the shining face of the Second Empire. The new sense would dictate a translation like *Scum of the Earth*. Hugo's sense would dictate *The Wretched*.

The oxymoronic opinions of critics betray the un-ease created by Hugo – that the lower orders might also have their literature: "*a cabinet de lec-ture* novel written by a man of genius", accord-ing to Lytton Strachey half a century later, still fighting "bad taste". In other words, Les Misérables was a jolly good book, but Victor Hugo never should have written it.

The "dangerous" aspect of *Les Misérables* is al-most as evident today as it was in 1862. If a sin-gle idea can be extracted from the whole, it is that persistent criminals are a product of the criminal justice sys-tem, a human and therefore a monstrous creation; that the burden of guilt lies with society and that the rational reform of institutions should take prec-edence over the punishment of individuals.

Sharon M. Harris, Redefining the Political Novel: American Women Writers, 1797-1901 (1995):

Feminist theorists in many fields – history, litera-ture, philosophy, political science, sociol-ogy, among others – have challenged assump-tions un-derlying narrow definitions of the po-litical. In the field of political science, Louise A. Tilly and Patri-cia Gurin, editors of *Women, Poli-tics, and Change* (1990), have made significant contributions toward redefining 'politics' to in-clude women as members of the polity. How-ever, they exclude 'power strug-gles in the family' from their definition of politics, 'which is limited to the arena of the state or collect-ive units within it...' (6). While their revised defini-tion offers significant insights into how we can reconsider the idea of politics and the political, their exclusion of the family is disturbing for two reasons. First, while they do include collec-tivism within the broad framework of the political, they denote is as 'protopolitical' (7). Second, their exclu-sion fails to recognize the family *as a collective unit*. I would argue not only that the family is a col-lective unit but also that, in po-litical terms, the fam-ily, in its patriarchal structure and values, is a mi-crocosmic representation of 'the state.' To exclude the family from the political, especially in studies of pre-twentieth-century America, is to deny that arena in which women have most experience and from which their knowledge of the need for change most often has been drawn...

It is notable that the novelists surveyed in the essays contained in *Redefining the Political Novel* were interested in exploring the many avenues by which, overtly or covertly, the political both syn-thesized and dictated the social, especially in terms of women's lives. These works bring to the fore-front debates by women novelists on the nature of political orders (both macrocosmically and in their microcosmic representations of family and social structures), the suppression of classes and races that are not part of the dominant culture in Ameri-can society, and the means by which women's art forms have been controlled and defined under pa-triarchy.

The contributors to this book are acting in ac-cord with Nancy Fraser's demands: they have re-cognized the ways in which women novelists have consciously politicised the genre of the novel, be-yond merely attending to overt politi-cal machin-ery. This book's chapters explore ways in which these novelists have exposed, satirized, addressed, and challenged unspoken political ideologies in art, in the workplace, in all facets of existence under patriarchy.

Frederic Jameson, "'Art Naïf' and the Admixture of Worlds" The Geopoliti-cal Aesthetic (1995):

...we need to invent some new questions to ask of Third-World cinema, and of the Third World gen-erally, as the last surviving social space from which alternatives to corporate capitalist daily life and so-cial relations are to be sought. The fear, to be sure, that the West will have been so successful in de-stroying radical political movements in the Third World as to leave only sterile passions of national-ism and religious fundamentalism (and this is the sense in which, as I've argued elsewhere, these last may also ironically be counted among the current forms of the postmodern). 'Otherness', meanwhile, is a peculiarly booby-trapped and self-defeating concept, and the slogan of 'differ-ence' while politi-cally impeccable in all the obvious senses, is form-alistic and empty of concrete social and historical specification – where it does not, indeed, relax and lend itself to the usual late capitalist celebration of multi-cultural pluralism. (It has, in short, all the ambiguity of an essentially liberal, rather than rad-ical, value.)

My own feeling is that new forms of political art ...are so far to be felt dimly stirring in the general area of the didactic... As an astute observer noted, we are not averse to learning things (facts, recipes, history) out of postmodern books and even out of postmodern novels, in a readerly impurity hitherto taboo and excluded from the practice of the high modernist classics.... Whatever its overt politics and its specific messages, the co-existence of artistic production and political struggle cannot but be stimulating and fertile for the former (and perhaps for the latter as well).

Margaret Randall, "Introduction to Roque Dalton's *Clandestine Poems*" (1995):

I first met Roque in Mexico, in 1964. Poets from some of the Latin American countries and the Uni-ted States were gathered in Chapultepec Park, en-gaged in marathon readings where we reveled in and applauded each other's work.... Roque arrived on the scene fresh from a jail break. He later often laughingly told us he thought he was the only Lat-in American poet who escaped a CIA firing squad because an earthquake had tumbled the walls of the prison they were holding him in, an episode that is reflected in his (tragically) posthumous *Po-brecito poeta que era yo* (*Poor Little Poet, I Was*)...an extraordinary novel about his generation's grappling with the search for inner and outer liberation.

Roque was reality to us then, in our Mexico City of the mid-sixties. Many of us still thought that "politics was outside the realm of art." Roque made us see that wasn't so. He taught us, among many other things, that a simplistic sense of "so-cialist realism", in terms of creative expression, was nothing more nor less than a lack of respect for the work we were doing. That art was life, and that political commitment (not in the narrow sense we had been taught to view it, but in the fullest sense) was simply that: a commitment to life. That art, to be revolutionary in the first place, had to be good.

Jane Smiley, "Say It Ain't So, Huck: Second Thoughts on Mark Twain's 'Masterpiece'", Harpers (1995):

Ernest Hemingway, thinking of himself, as always, once said that all American literature grew out of *Huck Finn*. It undoubtedly would have been better for American literature, and American culture, if our literature had grown out of one of the best-selling novels of all time, another American work of the nineteenth century, *Uncle Tom's Cabin*, which for its portrayal of an array of thoughtful, autono-mous, and passionate black characters leaves *Huck Finn* far behind.... The power of *Uncle Tom's Cabin* is the power of brilliant analysis married to great wisdom of feeling. Stowe never forgets the logical end of any relationship in which one person is the subject and the other is the object. No matter how the two people feel, or what their intentions are, the logic of the relationship is inherently tragic and traps both parties until the false subject/object rela-tionship is ended. Stowe's most oft-repeated and potent representation of this inexorable logic is the forcible separation of family members, especially of mothers from children... The grief and despair [the] women display is no doubt what T.S. Eliot was thinking of when he superciliously labeled Uncle Tom's Cabin 'sensationalist propaganda,' but, in fact, few critics in the nineteenth century ever accused Stowe of making up or even exaggerating such stories. One group of former slaves who were asked to comment on Stowe's depiction of slave life said that she had failed to portray the very worst, and Stowe herself was afraid that if she told some of what she had heard from escaped slaves and other informants during her eighteen years in Cincinnati, the book would be too dark to find any readership at all... One of Stowe's most skillful techniques is her method of weaving a discussion of slavery into the dialogue of her characters... Stowe also understands that the real root of slavery is that it is profitable as well as customary...

When Stowe's voice, a courageously public voice – as demonstrated by the public arguments about slavery that rage throughout *Uncle Tom's Cabin* – fell silent in our culture and was replaced by the secretive voice of Huck Finn, who acknowledges Jim only when they are alone on the raft together out in the middle of the big river, racism fell out of the public world and into the private one where whites think it really is but blacks know it really isn't...

Like little Eva, who eagerly but fearfully listens to the stories of the slaves that her family tries to keep from her, our children want to know what is going on, what has gone on, and what we intend to do about it. If 'great' literature has any purpose, it is to help us face up to our responsibilities instead of enabling us to avoid them once again by lighting out for the territory.

Dorothy Allison, Skin: Talking About Sex, Class & Literature (1994):

The difficulty faced by lesbian and feminist writers of my generation becomes somewhat more under-standable if we think about the fact that almost no lesbian-feminist writer my age was able to make a living as a writer. Most of us wrote late at night af-ter exhausting and demanding jobs, after evenings and weekends of political activism, meetings, and demonstrations. Most of us also devoted enorm-ous amounts of time and energy to creating pres-ses and journals that embodied our political ideals, giving up the time and energy we might have used to actually do our own writing. During my in-volvement with Quest, I wrote one article. The rest of my writing time was given over to grant appli-cations and fundraising letters. I did a little better with Conditions, beginning to actually publish short stories, but the vast majority of work I did there was editing other people's writing and again, writing grants and raising money. Imagine how few paintings or sculptures would be created if the artists all had to collectively organize the creation of canvas and paint, build and staff the galleries, and turn back all the money earned from sales into the maintenance of the system. Add to that the difficulty of creating completely new philosophies a-bout what would be suitable subjects for art, what approaches would be valid for artists to take to their work, who, in fact, would be allowed to say what was valuable and what was not, or more tell-ingly, what could be sold and to whom. Imagine that system and you have the outlines of some of the difficulties faced by lesbian writers of my gen-eration.

As a writer, I think I lost at least a decade in which I might have done more significant work be-cause I had no independent sense of my work's worth. If Literature was a dishonest system by which the work of mediocre men and women could be praised for how it fit into a belief system that devalued women, queers, people of color, and the poor, then how could I try to become part of it? Worse, how could I judge any piece of writing, how could I know what was good or bad, worth-while or a waste of time? To write for that system was to cooperate in your own destruction, certainly in your misrepresentation. I never imagined that what we were creating was also limited, that it, too, reflected an unrealistic or dishonest vision. But that's what we did, at least in part, making an ethical system that insists a lightweight romance has the same worth as a serious piece of fiction, that there is no good or bad, no 'objective' craft or standards or excellence.

Paul Garon, "[Reviewing Walter B. Rideout's] The Radical Novel in the US: 1900-1954" Firsts [magazine] (1994):

[Walter B. Rideout's book, The Radical Novel in the United States, 1900-1954] defined the radical novel as "one which demonstrates, either explicitly or implicitly, that its author objects to the human suffering imposed by some socioeconomic system and advocates that the system be fundamentally changed." The final clause is the most important, for many novelists sympathized with the victims of the system without advocating fundamental chan-ges to the system itself.

Michael Hanne, The Power of the Story: Fiction and Political Change (1994):

Can a novel start a war, free serfs, break up a mar-riage, drive readers to suicide, close factories, bring about a law change, swing an election, or serve as a weapon in a national or international struggle? These are some of the large-scale, direct, social and political effects which have been ascribed to certain exceptional novels and other works of fiction over the last two hundred years or so. How seriously should we take such claims?

In their crudest form, assertions of this kind are obviously naïve, oversimplifying the complex ways in which literary texts can be said to 'work in the world' and oversimplifying, too, the causal proces-ses required to account for a major social or politic-al change. But is it possible to modify or refine such claims in the light of contemporary theory and his-torical research so that the mechanisms by which each text has engaged with the political forces of the time are adequately described? This book ex-plores that general question through the close ex-amination of five works, from several different countries and periods, for which remarkable direct political effects of one kind or another have been claimed…

Storytelling, it must be recognized from the start, is always associated with the exercise, in one sense or another, of power, of control. This is true of even the commonest and apparently most in-nocent form of storytelling in which we engage: that almost continuous internal narrative mono-logue which everyone maintains, sliding from memory, to imaginative reworking of past events, to fantasizing about the future, to daydreaming... It is a curious thing that, in the liberal democracies, the word 'power' is used more frequently than any other by publishers and reviewers to indicate, and invite, approval of a work of narrative fiction... This flooding of popular critical discourse with the term 'power' does not, of course, indicate a wides-pread belief in the capacity of narrative fiction to 'change the world.' The use of 'power'...indicates little more than approval of the novel's capacity to involve and move the individual reader emotional-ly. Indeed the term is so devalued as to imply a denial that narrative fiction can exercise power in a wider social and political sense... Power, as is usu-al in a liberal democracy, is treated as individual and unproblematic, rather than collective, structur-al, and problematic.

Two important corollaries follow from this: a) there is no public acknowledgement that literature plays a role in the maintenance of existing power structures and b) literature is seen as incapable of playing a seriously disruptive role within such a society... If, in a liberal democracy, a piece of imag-inative writing seeks or achieves social or political influence that goes beyond such a limited concep-tion of its proper power, it must either be nonlitera-ture masquerading as literature or a literary work being manipulated and misused for nonliterary, propagandistic purposes... In overtly authoritarian states whose form of government does not rely on liberal bourgeois conceptions of constitutionality, such as Russia under the Tsars or the Soviet Union under Stalin, these assumptions are entirely re-versed. Literature is *required*, by a combination of censorship and patronage, to contribute to the maintenance of power as constituted at the time. The government's insistence on retaining tight control over what is written and published reflects the belief, which is most often shared by the regime's opponents, that fictional writing possesses an extreme potential for disruption.

Barbara Foley, "Art or Propaganda"
Radical Representations: Politics and
Form in U.S. Proletarian Fiction, 1929-

1941 (1993):

The 1930s literary radicals, I have demonstrated, brought various considerations to bear in their def-initions of proletarian literature. There was, how-ever, no party line on the subject. As Jack Conroy remarked retrospectively about the debates over what proletarian literature was, 'We used to talk about it endlessly and never arrived at any definite conclusion'... Even if writers did not feel bound to one or another definition of proletarian literature, [certain] critics argue, they felt obliged to conform to a rigid didacticism involving stock characters, formulaic plots, and a programmatic optimism. Art had to be a weapon and, as such, an instrument of propaganda. But since art and propaganda are an-tagonistically opposed, left-wing didactic literature was condemned to mouthing slogans and preach-ing conversion to the cause.

In future chapters we will have the opportunity to determine whether proletarian novels were in fact as formulaic and predictable as their detractors charge. What I shall argue in this chapter is that there is very limited validity to the charge that rou-tinely accompanies accusations of political strait-jacketing – namely, that Third-Period Marxist crit-ics, as mouthpieces for the party line, sought to im-pose a specifically propagandistic view of literature upon the writers in the party orbit. I shall show that left-wing literary commentators only rarely promoted the notion that literary works should im-part or promote specific tenets of party doctrine; insofar as the critics had a coherent aesthetic theor-y, this theory was almost exclusively cognitive and reflectionist rather than agitational and horta-tory. Indeed, I shall argue that in certain important ways the American approach to questions of representa-tion and ideology was committed – as was the dominant tendency in all Marxist criticism of this peri-od, Soviet and European – to a number of premises about literary form that were bourgeois rather than revolutionary. Literary radicals might applaud pro-letarian novelists whose works encouraged revolu-tionary class partisanship. Gold hailed Conroy as 'a proletarian shock-trooper whose weapon is lit-era-ture'; the novelist Ruth McKenney wrote Isidor Schneider that his *From the Kingdom of Ne-*

cessity was 'a more powerful weapon than any tear gas the other side can manufacture.' In general, how-ever, commentators, critics and novelists alike, held back from theorizing – let alone legislating – any of the representational maneuvers specific to this lit-erary weaponry. Their espoused commitment to the notion that all literature is propaganda for one side or another in the class struggle was countered by a deep antipathy to viewing proletarian litera-ture as propagandistic in any of its distinctive rhetorical strategies. The 1930s radicals never fully re-pudiated the bourgeois counterposition of art to propaganda: to them, proletarian literature con-tained very different values and assumptions, but as literature, it was just like any other kind of writ-ing. Ironically, to the extent that they were pre-scripttive in advocating any given set of aesthetic principles, the Marxist critics urged a largely de-politicized conception of mimetic practice that co-existed only uneasily with many of the values and ideas that they congratulated writers for articulat-ing in their texts (129-131).

Edward Said, *Culture and Imperialism* (1993):

Much of what was so exciting for four decades about Western modernism and its aftermath – in, say, the elaborate interpretative strategies of critical theory or the self-consciousness of literary and musical forms – seems almost quaintly abstract, desperately Eurocentric today. More reliable now are the reports from the front line where struggles are being fought between domestic tyrants and idealist oppositions, hybrid combinations of realism and fantasy, cartographic and archeological descriptions, explorations in mixed forms (essay, video or film, photograph, memoir, story, aphorism) of unhoused exilic experiences...

The major task, then, is to match the new econ-omic and socio-political dislocations and configur-ations of our time with the startling realities of hu-man interdependence on a world scale...

The fact is, we are mixed in with one another in ways that most national systems of education have not dreamed of. To match knowledge in the arts and sciences with these integrative realities is, I be-lieve, the intellectual and cultural challenge of the moment...

Surely it is one of the unhappiest characteristics of the age to have produced more refugees, mi-grants, displaced persons, and exiles than ever be-fore in history, most of them as an accompaniment to and, ironically enough, as afterthoughts of great post-colonial and imperial conflicts...

The émigré consciousness – a mind of winter, in Wallace Steven's phrase – discovers in its marginal-ity that 'a gaze averted from the beaten track, a hatred of brutality, a search for fresh concepts not yet encompassed by the general pattern, is the last hope for thought'...

The modern history of literary study has been bound up with the development of cultural nation-alism, whose aim was first to distinguish the na-tional canon, then to maintain its eminence, author-ity, and aesthetic autonomy... [There has been] an absolute requirement for the Western system of ideology that a vast gulf be established between the [ostensibly] civilized West, with its traditional com-mitment to human dignity, liberty, and self-determination, and the [supposed] barbaric brutality of those who for some reason – perhaps defective genes – fail to appreciate the depth of this historic commitment, so well revealed by America's Asian wars, for example...

A novel is the choice of one mode of writing from among many others, and the activity of writ-ing is one social mode among several, and the cate-gory of literature is something created to serve var-ious worldly aims, including and perhaps even mainly aesthetic ones. Thus the focus in the desta-bilizing and investigative attitudes of those whose work actively opposes states and borders is on how a work of art, for instance, begins *as* a work, begins *from* a political, social, cultural situation, begins *to do* certain things and not others...

Contamination is the wrong word to use here, but some notion of literature and indeed all culture as hybrid...and encumbered, or entangled and ov-erlapping with what used to be regarded as extran-eous elements – this strikes me as *the* essential idea for the revolutionary realities today, in which the contests of the secular world so provocatively in-form the texts we both read and write (317).

I keep coming back – simplistically and ideal-isti-cally – to the notion of opposing and allevi-ating co-ercive domination, transforming the present by try-ing rationally and analytically to lift some of its burdens, situating the works of various literatures with reference to one another and to their historical modes of being. What I am saying is that in the configurations and by virtue of the transfigurations taking place around us, readers and writers are now in fact secular intellectuals with the archival, expres-sive, elaborative, and moral responsibilities of that role (319).
It is no exaggeration to say that liberation as an in-tellectual mission, born in the resistance and op-position to the confinements and ravages of imper-ialism, has now shifted from the settled, estab-lished, and domesticated dynamics of cul-ture to its unhoused, decentered, and exilic en-ergies, energies whose incarnation today is the migrant, and whose consciousness is that of the intellectual and artist in exile, the political figure between domains, be-tween forms, between homes, and between lan-guages. From this per-spective then all things are indeed "counter, original, spare, strange" [Gerard Manley Hop-kins]. From this perspective also, one can see "the complete consort dancing together" con-trapuntally…(332).

George Garrett, My Silk Purse and Yours (1992):

Most of the writers (practically anybody you ever heard of) are involved in a close symbiotic relationship, cozy you might say, with the pub-lishing world. Without the acquiescence and tacit support of the writers (especially the most successful ones), the whole creaky system might collapse. They can fool you, though, the writers. Take PEN, for example, forever using our dues to battle against some form of overt censorship here and there, against racial separation and segregation in South Africa if not, say, Kenya or Ghana, firmly committed against torture eve-rywhere in the world except in certain Eastern

Bloc nations, and mostly keeping their own mouths shut about the inequities and injustices, trivial and profound, perpetuated on the American public by the same folks who give writers their advances against royalties and publish their books. Whatever the price is, it doesn't include a vow of silence or even very much self-sacrifice.

Steven Best and Douglas Kellner, Postmodern Theory (1991):

Though the postmodern emphasis on disintegra-tion and change in the present situation points to new openings and possibilities for social trans-formation and struggle (286)…it lacks positive notions of the social (283)… It ignores the reality of phenomena such as substantive grass roots politics in countries like the United States (284). It pro-motes nihilism and pessimism "as the only possible basis of historical emancipation," while having no conception of what could or should emerge from the detritus of modernity. Finally, it has not formu-lated an adequate political response to the degraded contemporary conditions described.

bell hooks, "Narratives of Struggle," Critical Fictions: The Politics of Imaginative Writing (Philomena Mariani, Ed.) (1991):

Critical fictions emerge when the imagina-tion is free to wander, explore, question, trans-gress. Years ago, I heard Ivan Van Sertima speak about *They Came Before Columbus*, his work documenting the presence of Africans in the 'New World.' Com-menting on black libera-tion struggles globally, he asserted that it is not just our minds that have been colonized, but our imaginations. Thinking about the imagination in a subversive way, not seeing it as a pure, uncor-rupted terrain, we can ask our-selves under what conditions and in what ways can the imagination be decolonized. Globally, literature that enriches resistance struggles speaks about the way the individuals in repressive, dehumanizing situations use imagination to sustain life and maintain critical awareness. In oppressive settings the ability to construct images imaginative-ly of a reality not present to the senses or perceived may be the only means to hope. How many of us in our daily life think about the connection between our capacity to imagine and resistance struggle? Often in radical circles, the imaginative mind is perceived as threatening, as though it will obstruct and disrupt progressive action. Certainly it is use-ful in a culture of domination to project the sense that the imagination is primarily useful as a means to produce fantasy…

…it is difficult for the writer in the United States to find publishers for critical fictions. Again it must be reiterated that a growing interest on the part of publishers and consumers in works by writers of color does not mean that the works that are pub-lished and most talked about are necessarily critical fictions. Although work by black women writers seems to be receiving unprecedented attention at this historical moment in this society, much of that work is in no way subversive. Perhaps it is a bitter commentary to think that writers may strategically include passages or chapters in work so that it ap-pears to be a critical intervention even as the over-all work in no way breaks with prevailing oppress-sive and repressive norms. Such moments may merely reflect contradictions. Interest in works by black women writers should not blind us to the reality that this society does not support or affirm the production of critical fictions by black women…

Maxine Hong Kingston, "The Novel's Next Step," Critical Fictions: The Politics of Imaginative Writing (Philomena Mariani, Ed.) (1991):

I'm going to give you a head start on the book that somebody ought to be working on. The hands of the clock are minutes away from nuclear midnight. And I am slow, each book taking me longer to write… So let me set down what has to be done, and maybe hurry creation, which is about two steps ahead of destruction… All the writer has to do is make Wittman [hero of her novel, *Tripmaster Monkey*] grow up, and Huck Finn and Holden Caulfield will grow up. We need a sequel to adol-escence – an idea of the humane beings that we may become. And the world will have a sequel… The dream of the great American novel is past. We need to write the Global novel... The danger is that the Global novel has to imitate chaos: loaded guns, bombs, leaking boats, broken-down civilizations, a hole in the sky, broken English, people who refuse connections with others... How to stretch the novel to comprehend our times – no guarantees of inher-ent or eventual order – without having it fall apart? How to integrate the surreal, society, our psyches? (200).

Alix Kates Shulman, "The Taint" Critical Fictions: The Politics of Imaginative Writing (Philomena Mariani, Ed.) (1991):

A feminist critic I much admire…proposes that the smallest and least mushy category [of feminist writing], the most neglected and thereby the most interesting one, is Feminist Fiction with capital F's – that is, fiction by political women for whom the contemporary women's movement was one of the major experiences of their lives, an experience leaving its traces in virtually all their thought and work. This, she contends, is probably what most people think of when they hear the term Feminist Fiction, anyway: politically engaged fiction…

Together we review the fiction we know and come up with a short list of Feminist Works, including books by Margaret Atwood, Angela Carter, Marilyn French, Ursula K. Le Guin, Maxine Hong Kingston, Marge Piercy, Joanna Russ, Jane Rule, Alice Walker, Fay Weldon, Monique Wittig…

The list my friend and I compiled seemed sur-prisingly short. Why? Perhaps because revolutions, social or political, may be just too noisy and intense to give rise to an extensive literature, which must be created in hours and years of reflective calm. From experience I know well that activists' ener-gies are directed outward, writers' energies inward. It's probably as easy to record a revolution from the midst of it when everyone is working at fever pitch as it is to write a novel standing in a rush-hour subway train... (83-84).

Toni Cade Bambara, Black Women Writers at Work (Claudia Tate, Ed.) (1990):

I start with the recognition that we are at war, and that war is not simply a hot debate between the capitalist camp and socialist camp over which economic/political/social arrangement will have hegemony in the world. It's not just the battle over turf and who has the right to utilize resources for whomsoever's benefit. The war is also being fought over the truth: what is the truth about human na-ture, about the human potential? My responsibility to myself, my neighbors, my family and the human family is to try to tell the truth. That ain't easy. There are so few truth-speaking traditions in this society in which the myth of 'Western civilization' has claimed the allegiance of so many. We have rarely been encouraged and equipped to appreciate the fact that the truth works, that it releases the Spirit and that it is a joyous thing. We live in a part of the world, for example, that equates criticism with assault, that equates social responsibility with naïve idealism, that defines the unrelenting pursuit of knowledge and wisdom as fanaticism...

I do not think that literature is *the* primary instrument for social transformation, but I do think it has potency. So I work to tell the truth about peo-ple's lives; I work to celebrate struggle, to applaud the tradition of struggle in our community, to bring to center stage all those characters, just ordinary folks on the block...

It would be dishonest, though, to end my com-ments there. First and foremost I write for myself...

Audre Lorde, Black Women Writers at Work (Claudia Tate, Ed.) (1990):

I see protest as a genuine means of encouraging someone to feel the inconsistencies, the horror of the lives we are living. Social protest is saying that we do not have to live this way. If we feel deeply, and we If we feel deeply, and we encourage ourselves and others to feel deeply, we will find the germ of our an-swers to bring about change. Because once we recognize what it is we are feeling, once we rec-ognize we can feel deeply, love deeply, can feel joy, then we will demand that all parts of our lives produce that kind of joy. And when they do not, we will ask, 'Why don't they?' And it is the asking that will lead us inevitably to social change. So the question of social protest and art is inseparable for me. I can't say it is an either-or proposition. Art for art's sake doesn't really exist for me. What I saw was wrong, and I had to speak up. I loved poetry and I loved words. But what was beautiful had to serve the purpose of changing my life, or I would have died. If I cannot air this pain and alter it, I will surely die of it. That's the beginning of social protest.

Pancho Savery, "The Third Plane at the Change of the Century: The Shape of African-American Literature to Come" (1990), Left Politics and the Literary Profession (Davis and Mirabella, Eds.):

What follows is a brief history of the two great cul-tural explosions in African-American history, the Harlem Renaissance and the Black Arts movement, and a discussion of the writers of the Third Plane, writers who have come to prominence since the late 1960s.... Writing fifty years ago in his classic of literary criticism *To Make a Poet Black*, Saunders Redding pointed out that two problems plagued African-American literature. On the one hand was the desire of black people to 'adjust...to the Ameri-can environment.' This created what Redding called a 'literature of necessity,' motivated by ends. On the other hand was the motivation by means. African-American writers were plagued by what DuBois called in *The Souls of Black Folk* 'this double-consciousness.' In Redding's words, 'if they wished to succeed they have been obliged to satisfy two different (and opposed when not entirely opposite) audiences, the black and the white.' Until very recently, Redding's outline has remained true. African-

American writers have been pushed and pulled, and the result has been that consistent qual-ity has been rare. In *To Make a Poet Black* and in subsequent works Redding praises a very small number of writers working before the 1940s. Chief among these are Sterling Brown, James Weldon Johnson, Langston Hughes, Jean Toomer, and Zora Neale Hurston. What unites these writers is an 'acknowledgment of their debt to the folk material'.

D. J. Taylor, "Writers, Politics and Society," *A Vain Conceit: British Fiction in the 1980s* (1989):

Though an air of genteel quietism has hung lazily over the English novel, manifesting itself occasion-ally in the conviction that art is some-how 'above' politics or that no civilized person would ever want to bother himself with the governance of his country, there is a long and fairly honourable tradition of writers interven-ing or interfering in domestic politics. Naturally, this is not something that officialdom has ever welcomed. Characteristically the relationship between writers and politicians has always been uneasy, a fragile dialogue liable to distortion, resentment and cheerful malice. It is said that Macaulay declined to review *Hard Times* on ac-count of is 'sullen socialism', and how much so-cialism is there in *Hard Times*? But then it used to be customary to refer to Cubist paintings as 'Bolshevist', and even today, in the wake of countless revisionist biographies, it is never quite possible to rid Kipling of the tag 'Imperial-ist writer'.

That this sort of resentment persists is a testi-mony to the compartmentalization of modern life. Even today the notion that a novelist might have political ideas floating about in his head and might want to give them a public airing is calculated to make the average newspaper col-umnist seethe with rage. The 1987 General Elec-tion campaign was remarkable for the ardour with which right-wing papers attacked various writers, dramatists and whatnot who had made the indelicate mistake of announcing that they intended to vote Labour. In this atmosphere of suspicion it is hardly surprising that the most

recent engagement between the pen and the Statue Book, Lady Antonia Fraser's little dinner for a group of anti-Thatcherite writers and the establishment of the June 20 group, quickly de-clined into a riot of personal attacks. What did Lady Antonia think she knew about it? What, for that matter, did any pen pusher think that he or she knew about anything? It is a queer para-dox, this. Journalists on all sides cry out for writers to be 'relevant' and as soon as they per-form an act as relevant as expressing a political preference they are somehow seen to be en-gaged in a sort of spir-itual trespassing.

Yet the gathering *au côté de chez Fraser* did at least ventilate the comparatively musty issue of what a writer thinks about the way in which soci-ety is controlled and administered. This re-solves itself into a number of broad questions; not so much: why should a writer bother to have political opinions and presume to prose-cute them…but: is it possible, amid the dense and unpromising chaos that surrounds us, for writers to influence people? If so, how? If not, why not? On the face of it noth-ing could be more straight-forward. X the novelist writes a book read by reader Y who, after mature reflec-tion, allows it to colour his views as to matter Z. This ignores the fact that no art is simply mes-sage, but admits the power of novels to effect change. When Upton Sinclair wrote *The Jungle*, his famous exposé of the turn-of-the-century Chicago meat-packing factories, there was a public outcry and the laws were changed within months. You can just imagine the bureaucratic recrimination, the legal rearguard actions, the closing of ranks on the part of vested interests that would spring neatly into place if, for in-stance, someone were to write a novel set in Suf-folk village about the carcinogenic effects of the local power station. In 1904 the mech-anisms which linked art and society were substan-tially more clear-cut (24-25).

Nadine Gordimer, "The Essential Gesture," The Essential Gesture (1988):

Responsibility is what awaits outside the Eden of creativity… The creative act is not pure. History ev-idences it. Ideology demands it. Society exacts it…. Roland Barthes wrote that…a writer's 'enterprise' – his work – is his 'essential gesture as a social being'.

One thing is clear: ours is a period when few can claim the absolute value of a writer without refer-ence to a context of responsibilities. Exile as a mode of genius no longer exists… What right has society to impose responsibility upon writers and what right has the writer to resist? I want to examine not what is forbidden by censorship – I know that story too well – but what we are bidden. I want to consi-der what is expected of us by the dynamic of col-lective conscience and the will to liberty in various circumstances and places; whether we should respond, and if so, how we do.

'It is from the moment when I shall no longer be more than a writer that I shall cease to write.' One of the great of our period, Camus, could say that. In theory at least, as a writer he accepted the basis of the most extreme and pressing demand of our time. The ivory tower was finally stormed; and it was not with a white flag that the writer came out, but with manifesto unfurled and arms crooked to link with the elbows of the people. And it was not just as their chronicler that the compact was made; the greater value, you will note, was placed on the persona outside of 'writer': to be 'no more than a writer' was to put an end to the justification for the very existence of the persona of 'writer'. Although the aphorism in its characteristically French neat-ness appears to wrap up all possible meanings of its statement, it does not. Camus's decision is a hid-den as well as a revealed one. It is not just that he has weighed within himself his existential value as a writer against that of other functions as a man among men, and found independently in favour of the man; the scale has been set up by a demand outside himself, by his world situation. He has, in fact, accepted its condition that the greater responsibility is to society and not to art.

Long before it was projected into that of a world war, and again after the war, Camus's natal situa-tion was that of a writer in the conflict of Western world decolonisation – the moral question of race and power by which the twentieth century will be characterized along with its

discovery of the satan-ic ultimate in power, the means of human self-annihilation. But the demand made upon him and the moral imperative it set up in himself are those of a writer anywhere where the people he lives among, or any sections of them marked out by race or colour or religion, are discriminated against and represssed…

Whether a writer is black or white, in South Africa the essential gesture by which he enters the broth-erhood of man – which is the only definition of so-ciety that has any permanent validity – is a revolu-tionary gesture.

The transformation of experience remains the writer's basic essential gesture; the lifting out of a limited category something that reveals its full meaning and significance only when the writer's imagination has expanded it. This has never been more evident than in the context of extreme experi-ences of sustained personal horror that are central to the period of twentieth-century writers.

Their essential gesture can be fulfilled only in the integrity Chekhov demanded: 'to describe a situ-ation so truthfully … that the reader can no longer evade it'.

Vincent B. Leitch, American Literary Criticism from the 30s to the 80s, Chapter Thirteen: "Leftist Criticism from the 1960s to the 1980s" (1988):

When the MLA put together its centennial issue of PMLA in May 1984, it commissioned Paul Lauter to write about the impact of society on the profess-sion of literary criticism between 1958 and 1983. Lauter was a radical associated with the Movement in the sixties… According to Lauter, the MLA be-tween the fifties and the eighties had expanded and diversified immensely, yet 'the hierarchy of the professsion remains fundamentally unaltered, so – as yet – does the hierarchy of what we value'… This conclusion was based on two surveys of hundreds of syllabi collected from around the nation in the eighties. Just as the reigning critical ideology in the late 1950s was 'formalism,' so the dominant mode of criticism in the 1980s was 'formalism,' however expanded to include hermeneutics, semi-otics, and poststructuralism, all of which criticism 'accepts the formalist stance by analyzing texts, including its own discourse, primarily as autonom-ous objects isolated from their social origins or functions'… What most dismayed Lauter about such fashionable criticism were its alignment with linguistics and philosophy rather than history and sociology, its tendency to become obscurant self-referential metacriticism in a debauch of profess-sionalism, its preference for a limited canon of elitist texts, its increasing abnegation of practical exegesis and humanistic values, and its deepening occupation of the core of the profession"… [Even the rebirth of Marxist criticism in the 1970s deviated from "history and sociology" in that]: "What was odd about the Marxist criticism of this [1970s] Renaissance associated with the post-1950s new left and the Movement was its complete disregard of the old left. Mention was never made of V. F. Cal-verton, James T. Farrell, Granville Hicks, Bernard Smith, Edmund Wilson, or other Leftist Critics prominent in the thirties. The native tradition of radicalism stemming from the nineteenth century had been forgotten during the heyday of the new left…

In H. Bruce Franklin's view, what was wrong with academic literary professionals was their thorough immersion in the bourgeois ideology of formalism, which itself was rooted in the counterrevolutionary antiproletarianism of the thirties. 'In the present era, formalism is the use of aestheticism to blind us to social and moral reality'…

Rather than an instrument or weapon of ruling-class oppression, literature was potentially liberat-ing [in the view of Louis Kampf], provided it was set within a living context close to daily life and re-moved from its sacrosanct place in the great tradi-tion. 'In spite of our academic merchants, literature is not a commodity, but the sign of a creative act which expresses personal, social, and historical needs. As such it constantly undermines the status quo.' The task of the radical critic was to destroy received dogmas and procedures, letting literature be an instrument of agitation and resistance and a force for freedom and genuine liberation. 'As

mem-bers of the educated middle class, we must learn that our words should discredit our own culture. Those of us who are literary intellectuals and teach-ers ought to illustrate in our work that the arts are not alone available to those who are genteel…'

Gloria Anzaldúa, Borderlands—La Frontera: The New Mestiza: (1987):

In the 1960s, I read my first Chicano novel. It was *City of Night* by John Rechy, a gay Texan, son of a Scottish father and a Mexican mother. For days I walked around in stunned amazement that a Chic-ano could write and could get published. When I read *I Am Joaquín* I was surprised to see a bilingual book by a Chicano in print. When I saw poetry written in Tex-Mex for the first time, a feeling of pure joy flashed through me. I felt like we really existed as a people. In 1971, when I started teach-ing High School English to Chicano students, I tried to supplement the required texts with works by Chicanos, only to be reprimanded and forbidden to do so by the principal. He claimed that I was supposed to teach 'American' and English litera-ture. At the risk of being fired, I swore my students to secrecy and slipped in Chicano short stories, poems, a play. In graduate school, while working toward a Ph.D., I had to 'argue' with one advisor after another, semester after semester, before I was allowed to make Chicano literature an area of focus

Even before I read books by Chicanos or Mexicans, it was the Mexican movies I saw at the drive-in – the Thursday night special of $1.00 a carload – that gave me a sense of belonging… We'd watch Pedro Infante in melodramatic tear-jerkers like *Nosotros los pobres*, the first 'real' Mexican movie (that was not an imitation of European movies). I remember seeing *Cuando los hijos se van* and surmising that all Mexican movies played up the love a mother has for her children and what ungrateful sons and daughters suffer when they are not devoted to their mothers… When watching Mexican movies, I felt a sense of homecoming as well as alienation. People who were to amount to some-

765

thing didn't go to Mexican movies, or *bailes* or tune their radios to *bolero, rancherita*, and *corrido* music...

The whole time I was growing up, there was *norte-ño* music sometimes called North Mexican border music, or Tex-Mex music, or Chicano music, or *can-tina* (bar) music. I grew up listening to *conjuntos*, three- or four-piece bands made up of folk musi-cians playing guitar, *bajo sexto*, drums and button accordion, which Chicanos had borrowed from the German immigrants who had come to Central Tex-as and Mexico to farm and build breweries. In the Rio Grande Valley, Steve Jordan and Little Joe Her-nández were popular, and Flaco Jiménez was the accordian king. The rhythms of Tex-Mex music are those of the polka, also adapted from the Germans, who in turn had borrowed the polka from the Czechs and Bohemians.

I remember the hot, sultry evenings when *corridos* – songs of love and death on the Texas-Mexican borderlands – reverberated out of cheap amplifiers from the local *cantinas* and wafted through my bedroom window.

Corridos first became widely used along the South Texas/ Mexican border during the early con-flict between Chicanos and Anglos. The *corridos* are usually about Mexican heroes who do valiant deeds against the Anglo oppressors. Pancho Villa's song, '*La cucaracha*,' is the most famous one. *Corridos* of John F. Kennedy and his death are still very popular in the Valley. Older Chicanos remember Lydia Mendoza, one of the great border *corrido* singers who was called *La Gloria de Tejas*. Her '*El tango Negro*,' sung during the Great Depression, made her a singer of the people. The everpresent *corridos* narrated one hundred years of border his-tory, bringing news of events as well as entertain-ing. These folk musicians and folk songs are our chief cultural myth-makers, and they made our hard lives seem bearable.

I grew up ambivalent about our music. Country-western and rock-and-roll had more status. In the 50s and 60s, for the slightly edu-cated and *agringado* Chicanos, there existed a sense of shame at being caught listening to our music. Yet I couldn't stop my feet from thump-ing to the music, could not stop humming the words, nor hide from myself the exhilaration I felt when I heard it (59-61)...

In the ethno-poetics and performance of the sha-man, my people, the Indians, did not split the art-istic from the functional, the sacred from the secu-lar, art from everyday life. The relig-ious, social and aesthetic purposes were all in-tertwined... The aes-thetic of virtuosity, art typical of Western European cultures, attempts to manage the energies of its own internal sys-tem such as conflicts, harmonies, resolutions and balances. It bears the presences of qualities and internal meanings. It is dedicated to the validation of itself. Its task is to move humans by means of achieving mastery in content, tech-nique, feeling. Western art is always whole and always 'in power.' It is individual (not commu-nal). It is 'psychological' in that it spins its ener-gies be-tween itself and its witness (67-68)...

My Chicana identity is grounded in the Indian woman's history of resistance. The Aztec female rites of mourning were rites of defiance protest-ing the cultural changes which disrupted the equality and balance between female and male, and protest-ing their demotion to a lesser status, their denigra-tion. Like *la Llorona*, the Indian woman's only means of protest was wailing.

So *mamá, Raza*, how wonderful, *no tener que ren-dir cuentas a nadie*. I feel perfectly free to re-bel and to rail against my culture. I fear no be-trayal on my part because, unlike Chicanas and other women of color who grew up white or who have only recent-ly returned to their native cultural roots, I was tot-ally immersed in mine. It wasn't until I went to high school that I 'saw' whites. Until I worked on my master's degree I had not gotten within an arm's distance of them. I was totally immersed *en lo mexicano*, a rural, peasant, isolated, *mexicanismo*. To separate from my culture (as from my family) I had to feel competent enough on the outside and se-cure enough inside to live life on my own. Yet in leaving home I did not lose touch with my ori-gins because *lo mexicano* is in my system. I am a turtle, where I go I carry 'home' on my back...

Not me sold out my people but they me. So yes, though 'home' permeates every sinew and carti-lage in my body, I too am afraid of going home.

Though I'll defend my race and culture when they are attacked by non-*mexicanos, conosco el malestar de mi cultura*. I abhor some of my culture's ways, how it cripples its women, *como burras*, our strengths used against us, lowly *burras* bearing humility with dignity. The ability to serve, claim the males, is our highest virtue. I abhor how my culture makes *macho* caricatures of its men. No, I do not buy all the myths of the tribe into which I was born. I can understand why the more tinged with Anglo blood, the more adamantly my colored and coloress sisters glorify their colored culture's values – to offset the extreme devaluation of it by the white culture. It's a legitimate reaction. But I will not glorify those aspects of my culture which have injured me and which have injured me in the name of protecting me.

So, don't give me your tenets and your laws. Don't give me your lukewarm gods. What I want is an accounting with all three cultures – white, Mexi-can, Indian. I want the freedom to carve and chisel my own face, to staunch the bleeding with ashes, to fashion my own gods out of my entrails. And if go-ing home is denied me then I will have to stand and claim my space, making a new culture – *una cultura mestiza* – with my own lumber, my own bricks and mortar and my own feminist architect-ture (21-22).

Noam Chomsky, biographies, interviews (~1987):

"If you want to learn about people's personalities and intentions, you would probably do better read-ing novels than reading psychology books. Maybe that's the best way to come to an understanding of human beings and the way they act and feel, but that's not science. Science isn't the only thing in the world, it is what it is...science is not the only way to come to an understanding of things." "If I am inter-ested in learning about people, I'll read novels rather than psychology." "I think the Victorian novel tells us more about people than science ever will...and we will always learn more about human life and human personality from novels than from scientific psychology." "We learn from literature as we learn from life; no one knows how, but it surely happens. In fact, most of what we know about things that matter comes from such sources, surely not from considered rational inquiry (science), which sometimes reaches unparalleled depths of profundity, but has a rather narrow scope." "It is almost certain that literature will forever give far deeper insight into what is sometimes called 'the full human person' than any modes of scientific in-quiry may hope to do." "[Yet] I've been always resistant consciously to allowing literature to influ-ence my beliefs and attitudes with regard to society and history." "There are things I resonate to when I read, but I have a feeling that my feelings and atti-tudes were largely formed prior to reading litera-ture." "Look, there's no question that as a child, when I read about China, this influenced my attitudes – Rickshaw Boy, for example. That had a powerful effect when I read it. It was so long ago I don't remember a thing about it, except the impact. And I don't doubt that, for me, personally, like anybody, lots of my perceptions were heightened and attitudes changed by literature over a broad range – Hebrew Literature, Russian literature, and so on. But ultimately, you have to face the world as it is on the basis of other sources of evidence that you can evaluate." "If I want to understand the nature of China and its revolution, I ought to be cautious about literary renditions." "Literature can heighten your imagination and insight and under-standing, but it surely doesn't provide the evidence that you need to draw conclusions and substantiate conclusions." "I can think of things I read that had a powerful effect on me, but whether they changed my attitudes and understanding in any striking or crucial way, I can't really say." "People certainly differ, as they should, in what kinds of things make their minds work." "I don't really feel that I can draw any tight connections [personally]."

Barbara Harlow, Resistance Literature (1987):

The struggle for national liberation and in-depend-ence, particularly in the twentieth century, on the part of colonized peoples in those areas of the world over which Western Europe and North America have sought socio-economic control and cultural dominion has produced a significant cor-pus of literary writing, both narrative and poetic, as well as a broad spectrum of theoretical analyses of the political, ideological, and cultural parameters of this struggle. This literature, like the resistance and national liberation movements which it reflects and in which it can be said to participate, not only demands recognition of its independent status and existence as literary production, but as such also presents a serious challenge to the codes and can-ons of both the theory and the practice of literature and its criticism as these have been developed in the West... (xvi).

Resistance narratives, at the same time that they, each in its own way, propose historically specific analyses of the ideological and material conditions out of which they are generated, in Nicaragua, South Africa, El Salvador, Palestine, or elsewhere, contribute to a larger narrative, that of the passage from genealogical or hereditary ties of filiation to the collective bonds of affiliation... The connection between knowledge and power, the awareness of the exploitation of knowledge by the interests of power to create a distorted historical record, is cen-tral to resistance narratives. The tradition to which Foucault is referring is a tradition which these narratives seek directly to transform. Within the texts and their analytical representation of the social his-tories of their characters that tradition is critically examined. The texts themselves, however, are im-mediate interventions into the historical record, attempting to produce and impart new historical facts and analyses, what Edward Said has referred to as 'new objects for a new kind of knowledge...' This requires that the historical record and the present agenda be rewritten... (116).

Resistance literature, as this study has attempted to show, has in the past played a vital role in the his-torical struggle of the resistance movements in the context of which it was written (200). That same lit-erature continues to enlist readers and critics in the First as in the Third Worlds in the active recon-struction of inter-rupted histories. Omar Cabezas, former FSLN guerrilla and author of *The Mountain is Something More than a Great Expanse of Green* (published in English as *Fire from the Mountain*), and now head of the Nicaraguan Ministry of the Interior's Political Section, still maintains that:

> To have participated as a guerrilla, to have written this book, son of a bitch: it's dealt a real blow to the enemy. You feel like you could die after something like that. After that book and one more. Or that book and two more. Or that book and five more. Or just that book. What I want to say is it's dealt a blow to imperialism. I saw a photo, once, of a dead guerrilla in a Latin American country, and they showed everything he had in his knapsack: his plate, his spoon, his bedroll, his change of clothing, and *The Moun-tain is Something More than a Great Expanse of Green*. And I think back to when I was a guerrilla; when a guerrilla carries a book in his knapsack, it really means something.

Ngũgĩ wa Thiong'o, "Preface," Decolonising the Mind (1986):

Inevitably, essays of this nature may carry a holier-than-thou attitude or tone. I would like to make it clear that I am writing as much about myself as about anybody else. The present predicaments of Africa are often not a matter of personal choice: they arise from an historical situation. Their solu-tions are not so much a matter of personal decision as that of fundamental social transformation of the structures of our societies starting with a real break with imperialism and its internal ruling allies. Imperialism and its comprador alliances in Africa can never never develop the continent.

Ishmael Reed, "Which State?" (1986), Writin' Is Fightin': Thirty-seven Years of Boxing on Paper (1990):

The current literary establishment, which denies that it exists, is not only a powerful influence upon American intellectual and cultural trends but on political trends as well – both the left wing and right wing of the New York branch having advised political administrations since the 1960s… The problem with the current literary-industrial com-plex of publishers, crit-ics, writers, and slowpoke academia is that it can see cultural repression when it happens in other states but can't recognize it when it's prac-ticed by its own state, the literary state…

In 1976, ten years ago, a group of white and nonwhite ethnic writers decided that, instead of engaging in a time and energy consuming con-fron-tation with the commercial literary institu-tions, we could best serve the literature we championed by establishing new institutions. We began the Before Columbus Foundation, devoted to the promotion of multiethnic litera-tures. The Before Columbus Foundation dis-tributes books and magazines pub-lished by more than two hundred multiethnic presses and, beginning last year, represented these presses at international book fairs…

We are not in opposition to the literary state; we'd like to enter into a dialogue with it. We'd like to cooperate with it. We'd like it to join us in projecting the United States as a planet-nation – a nation that is generated by diversity and cultural exchange between people from dif-ferent backgrounds …

We are not crude writers engaged in ugly rhet-oric against things we disapprove of. We're merely requesting that the literary industrial complex face up to the important changes that have occurred in American literature since the 1960s.

Ngũgĩ wa Thiong'o, "The Language of African Fiction" (1984), Decolonising the Mind (1986):

… the biggest problem facing the growth and the development of the African novel is finding the appropriate 'fiction language', that is with fiction itself taken as a form of language, with which to effectively communicate with one's targeted audi-ence: that is, in my case, the peo-ple I left behind.

There were two interrelated problems of 'fic-tion language', vis-à-vis a writer's chosen audi-ence: his relationship to the form, to the genre itself; and his relationship to his material, that is to the reality be-fore him. How would he handle the form? How would he handle the material before him?

The first question has to do with how the novel as a form has developed…

Language; plot; realism of social and physical detail; features of oral narratives: all these were elements of form and I knew that form by itself, no matter how familiar and interesting, could never hold the attention of my new kind of reader for long. They have more important things to do than indulge in pretty rearrange-ments of familiar features of orature or of the urban and rural land-scape. Content with which the people could identi-fy or which would force them to take sides was necessary. Content is ul-timately the arbiter of form. A proper marriage of content and form would de-cide the reception accorded the novel. So the most important thing was to go for a subject matter, for a content, which had the weight and the complexity and the challenge of their everyday struggles.

And this brought me to the next problem: my relationship to my material, that is to the his-torical reality of a neo-colony.

A writer's handling of reality is affected by his basic philosophic outlook on nature and so-ciety and his method of investigating that na-ture and society…

But what happens when reality is stranger than fiction? … (75-78).

[Some African rulers] are actually begging for a re-colonisation of their own countries with themselves as the neo-colonial governors living in modern for-tresses. they are happier as the neo-slave drivers of their own peoples; happier as the neo-overseers of the U.S.-led economic haemorrhage of their own countries.

How does a writer, a novelist, shock his read-ers by telling them that these are neo-slaves when they themselves, the neo-slaves, are openly announcing the fact on the rooftops? How do you shock your readers by pointing out that these are mass mur-derers, looters, robbers, thieves, when they, the perpetrators of these anti-people crimes, are not ev-en attempting to hide the fact? When in some cases they are actually and proudly celebrating their massacre of children, and the theft and robbery of the nation? How do you satirise their utterances and claims when their own words beat all fictional exaggerations?

As I contemplated the neo-colonial reality of Kenya I was confronted with the question of the fictional form of its depiction. But a writer, any writer, has only one recourse: himself, those images that often flit across the mind, those mental reflections of the world around. The chemistry of imagination transforms the quantity of these different images, reflections, thoughts, pictures, sounds, feelings, sights, tastes, all the sense impres-sions, into a coalescence of a qualitatively different but unified image or sets of images of reality.

In search of the image that would capture the reality of a neo-colony that was Kenya under both Kenyatta and Moi, I once again fell on the oral tradition.

Satire is certainly one of the most effective weapons in oral traditions.

And then one day I got it...(80-81).

Terry Eagleton, "Conclusion: Political Criticism," Literary Theory: An Intro-duction (1983):

What you choose and reject theoretically, then, depends upon what you are practically trying to do. This has always been the case with literary criticism: it is simply that it is often very reluctant to realize the fact. In any academic study we select the objects and methods of pro-cedure which we believe the most important, and our assessment of their importance is governed by frames of interest deeply rooted in our practical forms of social life. Radical critics are no different in this respect: it is just that they have a set of social priorities with which most people at present tend to disagree. This is why they are commonly dismissed as 'ideologi-cal', because 'ideology' is always a way of describing other people's interests rather than one's own.

A. P. Foulkes, Literature and

Propaganda (1983): (from the Introduction and Conclusion):

If we refer to the nineteenth century as the Age of Ideology, then it seems even more appropriate to regard the present century as the Age of Propagan-da... The relationship of literature and art to propa-ganda is not at all straightforward, and would in any case be dismissed as insignificant by many modern critics, whose evaluative criteria would lead them to make a distinction between 'real liter-ature' and 'tendentious' writing. Even so, George Orwell, who stated that 'all art is to some extent propaganda'..., was probably closer to the truth than Hitler, who on one occasion was heard echo-ing the popular view that 'art has nothing to do with propaganda' ... Not the least of ironies con-tained in these seemingly contradictory statements is the fact that Hitler's remarks were addressed to Josef Goebbels who, as head of the Reich Ministry for Popular Enlightenment and Propaganda, had attempted to create a state apparatus for thought control which could have served as a model for the perfect totalitarian state depicted in Orwell's novel *Nineteen-Eighty-Four*... Propaganda does not often come marching towards us waving swastikas and chanting 'Seig Heil'; its power lies in its capacity to conceal itself, to appear natural, to coalesce completely and indivisibly with the values and accept-ed power symbols of a given society. When Hitler claimed that art had nothing to do with propagan-da he was anticipating a perfectly integrated Na-tionalist Socialist Germany whose art would spon-taneously and unthinkingly reproduce the desired images and perceptions. Even in the early revolu-tionary period of the Third Reich, Goebbels, who had objected to the word propaganda being used in the title of his Ministry, insisted that 'news is best given out in such a way that it appears to be without comment but is itself tendentious'... If a simple principle can be derived from the discus-sion so far, it is that the recognition of propaganda can be seen as a function of the ideological distance which separates the observer from the act of com-munication observed.... Hitler's assertion that art has nothing to do with propaganda does not con-tradict Orwell's statement that all art is propagan-da, but is rather contained within it, for the propa-ganda-free art which Hitler envisaged was an art within which the values and beliefs of National Socialism would be dominant, invisible and totally natural. This 'illusion of pure aestheticism' was for Orwell a reminder that 'propaganda in some form or other lurks in every book, that every work of art has a meaning and a purpose – a political, social and religious purpose – that our aesthetic judge-ments are always coloured by our prejudices and beliefs'... Although there is no ready-made method for detecting propaganda, we can become aware of the general categories in which it manifests itself and we can attempt to classify its techniques and forms... This approach does not mean that we must study literature as a set of documents rather than as a set of aesthetic objects. For in effect it denies the validity of such a distinction by assuming that the propagandistic or demystifying moment of literary communication may be inseparable from its aesthetic function...

Susan Rubin Suleiman, Authoritarian Fictions: The Ideological Novel as Literary Genre (1983):

In ordinary critical usage, the term 'roman à thèse' has a strongly negative connotation; it designates works that are too close to propaganda to be artist-ically valid. No self-respecting writer would con-sent to call his novels by that name. A roman à thèse is always the work of an 'other'... There do exist a few critical studies, published quite a while ago, that discuss [certain] novels...as 'political novels' or as examples of 'committed' or engagé literature. Neither of these categories corresponds exactly, however, to the roman à thèse. The political novel as a generic category is at once too broad (Stendhal's *La Chartreuse de Parme* is, as Irving Howe has shown, a superb political novel, but it is not a roman à thèse) and too narrow (Mauriac's 'Catholic novel,' Le Noeud de vipers, is a roman à thèse, but not a political novel). As for 'littérature engagée,' it is too imprecise a term to designate a genre; furthermore, I feel it is too specifically associated with the name of Sartre, who did not invent the term but who made it current – and who, incidentally, went out of his way to distinguish 'engagé' novels from roman à these (although it may once again have been a matter of rejecting the name rather than the thing itself).... As a starting point, I propose the following definition: *a roman à thèse is a novel written in the realistic mode (that is, based on an aesthetic of verisimilitude and representation), which signals itself to the reader as primarily didactic in intent, seeking to demonstrate the validity of a political, philosophical, or religious doctrine....* One could...claim that every novel, indeed every work of fiction..., can be read as expounding a 'thesis,' to the extent that it is always possible to extract from it a general maxim of some kind.... Following this line of reasoning, one would soon have to conclude that the roman à thèse is everywhere and nowhere – in other words, that it is a phenomenon of *reading* (viewed from a certain angle, all works are didactic) rather than of writing. At that point, there would be no reason to try to define a *genre* called roman à thèse, for the concept of genre implies that there exist certain properties that texts have in common, not that (or not only that) there exist certain modes of reading – or as is commonly said nowadays, certain interpretive strategies – that can be applied to any and every text. [However]...I consider undeniable...: there exist nontrivial differences between and among texts, as well as between readers, or between interpretive strategies that readers deploy in order to understand a text. Novels that are roman à thèse have certain identifiable traits which distinguish them from other novels and other genres. One of these traits, and no doubt the most important one is that romans à thèse forumulate, in an insistent, consistent, and unambiguous manner, the thesis (or theses) they seek to illustrate.... Whether its thesis is conservative or radical, defending the status quo or calling for its abolition, the roman à thèse is essentially an authoritarian genre: it appeals to the need for certainty, stability, and unity that is one of the elements of the human psyche; it affirms absolute truths, absolute values (3-10).

Introductory quotations from Susan Rubin Suleiman's Authoritarian Fictions (1983):

Literature, as it has been understood by all the masters, is an interpretation of life. It eliminates in order to prove.

–Maurice Barrès

All literature is propaganda. … Art, for us, is what makes propaganda effective, what is capable of moving men in the direction we wish.

–Paul Nizan

Then comes the modern question: why is there not today (or at least so it seems to me), why is there no longer an art of intellectual persuasion, or imagina-tion? Why are we so slow, so indifferent about mobilizing narrative and the image? Can't we see that it is, after all, works of fiction, no matter how mediocre they may be artistically, that best arouse political passion?

– Roland Barthes

…it is the very notion of a work created for the ex-pression of a social, political, economic, moral, etc. content that constitutes a lie.

–Alain Robbe-Grillet

Toni Cade Bambara, "Foreword," *This Bridge Called My Back: Writings by Radical Women of Color* (Moraga and Anzaldúa, Eds.) (1981):

This Bridge documents particular rites of passage. Coming of age and coming to terms with commun-ity – race, group, class, gender, self – its expecta-tions, supports, and lessons. And coming to grips with its perversions – racism, prejudice, elitism, misogyny, homophobia, and murder. And coming to terms with the incorporation of disease, strug-gling to overthrow the internal colonial/pro-racist loyalties – color/hue/hair caste within the house-hold, power perversities engaged in under the guise of 'personal relationships,' accommodation to and collaboration with self-ambush and amnesia and murder. And coming to grips with those false awakenings too that give us ease as we substitute a militant mouth for a radical politic, delaying our true coming of age as committed, competent, prin-cipled combatants.

There is more than a hint in these pages that too many of us still equate tone with substance, a hot eye with clear vision, and congratulate ourselves for our political maturity. For of course it takes more than pique to unit our wrath ('the capacity of heat to change the shape of things' – Moraga) and to wrest power from those who have it and abuse it, to reclaim our ancient powers lying dormant with neglect ('I wanna ask billie to teach us how to use our voices like she used hers on that old 78 record' – gossett), and create new powers in arena where they never before existed. And of course it takes more than the self-disclosure and the bold glimpse of each others' life documents to make the grand resolve to fearlessly work toward potent meshings. Takes more than a rinsed lens to face unblinkingly the particular twists of the divide and conquer tactics of this moment: the practice of withdrawing small business loans from the Puerto Rican grocer in favor of the South Korean wig shop, of stripping from Black students the Martin Luther King scholarship fund fought for and de-livering those funds up to South Vietnamese or white Cubans or any other group the government has made a commitment to in its greedy grab for empire…

The Bridge can help get us there. Can coax us into the habit or listening to each other and learning each other's ways of seeing and being. Of hearing each other as we heard each other in Pat Lee's *Freshtones*, as we heard each other in Pat Jones and Faye Chiang, et. al.'s *Ordinary Women*, as we heard each other in Fran Beale's *Third World Women's Al-liance* newspaper. As we heard each other over the years in snatched time moments in hallways and conference corridors, caucusing between sets. As we heard each other in those split second interfac-ings of yours and mine and hers student union meetings. As we heard each other in that rainbow attempt under the auspices of IFCO years ago. And way before that when Chinese, Mexican, and Afri-can women in this country saluted each other's attempts to form protective leagues...

Denis Donaghue, NYT (1981):

[Summing vital views of Mary McCarthy with which he disagrees]: Mary McCarthy's new book transcribes the Northcliffe Lectures she gave some months ago at University College, London. Her main argument is that the classic novel in the 19th century grew up and grew strong upon ideas and arguments provoked by public issues, politics, religion – the questions of Free Trade, Empire, women, Reform and so forth. It was assumed that a serious novel would deal with such questions in their bearing upon the themes of power, money, sex and class. The novelist's relation to his readers was sustained by a shared assumption that these matters constituted reality. Miss McCarthy believes that this assumption was undermined by Henry James, and that James's sense of the novel has dominated the general understanding of fiction from that day to this. She argues that in the typical Jamesian fiction ideas, concepts and public issues are mostly replaced by images, hints, guesses, sensations, nuances of sensibility. James's characters, she says, are mostly interested in themselves and in one another, not in anything as external as Free Trade. They visit art galleries, but they never argue about the pictures they have seen.

According to Miss McCarthy, the damage James did in practice was given currency and respectability by T.S. Eliot's theories: It was Eliot who praised James for having "a mind so fine that no idea could violate it." Eliot's influence was such that readers started thinking that ideas are crude things, good enough for journalism but not for a work of art. The serious novelist in our own day, Miss Mc-Carthy argues, is discouraged from dealing with ideas or from making debate and argument an important part of his fiction.

about the political novels of Pynchon and Barth—is the astonishing degree of puerility it exhibits, [including an ending that] like much of the sexual and scatological imag-inings of Pynchon, Barth, and others, finally directs us more to the psychology of the writer than to any political referent, expressing ultimately a child's fantasy of a brutal, threatening father, based on paranoid fear and resentment… One may wonder why so many gifted and serious novelists have chosen to treat politics in such a fundamentally unserious fashion…

One would think that the political novel, perhaps more than other kinds of fiction, requires adult in-telligence… The novel's great strength as a mode of apprehension is in its grasp of character, and the political novel at its best can show concretely and subtly what politics does to character, what character makes of politics…

It may well be that at this point in history we all need the aid of the novelist's imagination simply to help us imagine what seems to be more and more unimaginable – the real world in which we have to live, make decisions individually and collectively, and still struggle to shape a livable political future.

[Alter claims, Norman Mailer in The Deer Park] confronts centrally for the first time the special power of American society to mask, sham, evade, forget reality, to seduce its individual members in-to giving up on engagement in the real world; and the ultimately political nature of his moral imag-ination is reflected in his effort here to show how this American style of cotton-candy insulation from reality allows a society to perpetrate horror and obsceneity at home and abroad with hardly a twinge of conscience.

Robert Alter, "The American Political Novel" (1980) Motives for Fiction (1984):

What is particularly troubling about this book [Robert Coover's novel The Public Burning] – and virtually the same could be said

Lennard J. Davis, "A Social History of Fact and Fiction" Literature and Society (Ed. Edward Said) (1980):

In the late sixteenth and early seventeenth century … the word novel seems to have been used inter-changeably with the word news— and both were applied freely to writings about true or fictional events.... [although by the eighteenth-century] what we have seen is that the novel, at least in sem-antic terms, seems to have moved from a parity with journalism to a separate identity as a fictional work ... [yet] the primacy of centrality of language as representation in eighteenth-century novels [such as *Robinson Crusoe*] shows us how fictional narrative is actually part of powerful discourse associated with journalism...transcribing reality into language ... with the aim of increasing the number of those privy to information, of creating political ideologies, and of embodying social consciousness in the printed word. The nexus between news and novels is a powerful one because it allows us to see that fictional narratives, by participating in a journalistic discourse, are also parts of an information-disseminating system that is by definition social. Raymond Williams has aptly referred to literature as social language and social practice – and I think by showing that novels were part of the journalistic discourse, we can add dimensions to the concept of 'social language.'

For the eighteenth-century novelists the factual side of public things was not entirely outside their realm of interest. With the advent of the category of the purely fictional and its antithetical category of the purely factual—a division our modern world acknowledges and relies upon—has also come a weakening and an isolation to the novelistic dis-course. Fiction is now perceived for the most part as a separate and specialized discourse that has been canonized and valorized as aesthetic, and therefore removed from the world of public events. Even those contemporary novelists who oppose this limitation are working against a general and widely accepted view of fiction. Novels still report on the ideologies of our cultural moment, but they are treated as being part of a discourse that is no longer immanent, no longer energized as is news by its continual impingement on the world of things... This is all the more ironic when we consi-der that before 1725 the literary and the journalistic elements of newspapers were virtually indistin-guishable, serialized novels resting cheek by jowl with fabricated news stories, invented biographies, and the details of continental wars. The price we have paid for pure fiction is that now novels are re-garded as supplementary, and authors who openly profess to be writing fictions are treated as people who are in a major sense not telling the truth.

Mary McCarthy, Ideas and the Novel (1980):

As I was saying, if you are going to voice ideas in a novel, plainly you will need a spokesman. In the traditional novel such semi-official figures are fam-iliar to us and, on the whole, welcome. We quickly learn to recognize which of the character will be a stand-in for the author, that is, which one we can trust as appointed representative with full powers to comment on what is happening and draw the necessary conclusions. There is nothing wrong with this; events in life seldom speak for themselves. Whether it is world events that confront us or local skullduggery – an ecological scandal or somebody running off with a friend's wife – we frequently want somebody to explain them to us, sketch in the background, suggest where our sym-pathies should lie. There is no reason we should be worse off in a novel, as long as the novel is as-sumed to have some reasonably close connection with our immediate life or a life we are acquainted with through reading and report.

The novel in its classic period – the nineteenth century – took on that burden without protest. Pro-test only began to be heard toward the end of the century, when the novel, aggrieved by how much it had been expected to carry on its increasingly slender shoulders, made the first motions toward emancipation. Up until James, the novelist had been a quite willing authority figure, a parent, aunt, in Tolstoy's case a Dutch uncle. The popular novelist (and there was no other kind, the art novel not having been discovered) was looked up to as an authority on all sorts of matters: medicine, religion, capital punishment, the right relation between the sexes. If the role was uncongenial or momentarily wearisome, he had the resort of the short story or the tale to turn to, neither of which carried such heavy responsibilities to the common life (30-31).

Edward Said, Ed., "Preface," Literature and Society (1980):

Anyone who has attended the English Institute over the past decade will agree that an important intellectual shift took place during that period. Not every paper presented then exemplified the shift, but a significant, or at least a noticeable, number did. The simplest way of describing this change is to say that many people became interested in criti-cism, not as a kind of literate, discriminating gloss on a 'primary' text, but as an activity that, in draw-ing on such disciplines as linguistics, psychoanaly-sis, anthropology, and philosophy, made much of itself as a highly specialized, often tendentious theoretical mode of discourse. One result is that the accepted reliance on the work of literature as coming before criticism not only in time but also in value was given up. A critic now seemed to draw many of his or her insights from another critic, and looked to other criticism rather than to poetry, say, for his or her best thought. Certainly this has often been the case with criticism since Coleridge, but rarely before has criticism seemed so self-suffi-cient…and the net effect has been a new sense of freedom and speculation in the production of criti-cism.

But there have been drawbacks, and where we come to the putative mission of a volume like this one, none of whose authors can be considered *arrière* when it comes to using and understanding the most recent developments in the New New Criticism, as it has come to be called. My own estimate is that a paradoxical situation exists today. On the one hand there has never been so much attention to and debate about criticism; on the other hand, rarely has there been such a removal of criticism and critical attention from the ongoing production of society and history. (I would like to be understood here as speaking self-critically, since my own work and my own sympathies have always been engaged with the New New Criticism.) A mode of thought developed in the social, political, and cultural circumstances of Paris or Vienna or Berlin gets adopted in the American academy as a mode of thought, just that, and it has rapidly tended to become an orthodoxy mindlessly followed by a whole band of academic enthusiasts. To read an 'advanced' critic today is often to read writing that is essentially a highly rarified jargon. The historical sense, the rudiments of scholarship and curiosity (which in the past have always characterized even the most abstract of serious theorists), seem no longer to have much to tell a new theorist. Above all, in much of the New New Criticism the issues debated do not involve values or social and cultural questions or urgent philosophical questions; they most often are about 'texts' (so that one is made to feel that there are only texts), they deal in complex abstractions whose main reference is to other complex abstractions, their dense language belies a thin texture of ideas, experience, history.

Having said all this, I must not seem to be say-ing that I agree with many of the attacks on the New New Criticism now appearing in journals here and abroad. Most of those attacks are made from the rather empty standpoint of 'humanistic' scholarship, which seems no less marginal, un-worldly, and rarified than some of the theory being attacked. No: the New New Criticism has provided the current generation of literary and humanistic students with invaluable insights into cultural ac-tivity, and these must not be thrown out wholesale in the interests of a discredited conservative philos-ophy of gentlemanly refinement, or sensibility … (vii-ix).
In sum, this volume of essays from the English In-stitute demonstrates the vitality of the interchange in criticism between literature and society. No at-tempt has been made to have these essays make any monolithic affirmation (or definition) of either a literature or a society, though this is not to say that our critics pretend to value-free neutrality. At very least, then, this volume is a collective act of critical consciousness, as much to be regarded for critical knowledge as for social-historical engage-ment" (xi).

Michael Wilding, Political Fictions (1980):

A radical criticism needs to be responsive to

a radi-calism of form as well as content. Marxist criticism has not traditionally been happy in this area. Marx, Engels, Lenin, Plekhanov, Trotsky, Lukács, all pre-ferred the products of nine-teenth-century realism to any other available fic-tional modes. As a result, works of radical con-tent and radical form have tended to be ne-glected by both conservative and radical critics. The fictions dealt with there demon-strate a search for alternatives to realism – through ver-nacular picaresque, dream vision, imaginary book, found manuscript, collage, utopian pro-ject-tion, dystopian fable, neo-neoclassicism, and through various mixed modes. This is not an at-tempt to offer an alternative 'great tradi-tion' or indeed any tradition at all. The varieties of experi-ment are all different in nature. But what they pre-dominantly share is a constant search for the ap-propriate mode, radical both formally and politic-ally, revolutionary as fic-tion as well as in the trans-mitted consciousness, the better to transmit that consciousness (19-20).

Jack London's *The Iron Heel* details the lengths to which capitalism will go to hold off the achieve-ment of socialism... The ballot is tied to big busi-ness; if by some chance the so-cialists win an elec-tion, despite attempts by big business to prevent that from happening, then the trusts will remove the elected socialists from power...

The Iron Heel [reflects] present realities...a world of USA-based multinational corporations working in accord with and through secret agencies, like the CIA, to topple socialism and set up reactionary regimes in South America, Asia, and Australia...

The conscious and deliberate complementing of popular romance narrative with the docu-mentary tone of the footnotes and the theoreti-cal discuss-ions within the body of the novel, the juxtaposition of narrative flow with frag-mentation, produce the unique tone of *The Iron Heel*. London is writing about revolution, and produces a revolutionary ex-periment in form...

[In the novel] an important, major compo-nent...is the tragic – something continually problematic for socialist art. London recognizes the problem – so includes and then subsumes the tragic into an over-all optimistic, positive framework. But he does this not by reducing the tragic; in no way does he un-dercut it. The indi-vidual tragedy of Everhard and the revolution is clear enough; but the wider time-span places the tragic into a finally positive scheme. In this same context, the positive hero so beloved of so-cialist criticism is presented by London in a novelistically satisfying way. The positive as-pects of [the main character Ernest] Everhard are dominant, and would satisfy any socialist realist; but the problems associated with the positive hero, the tiresomeness that seems a re-current concomitant, are here mitigated and qualified by London's broader dimension – put-ting the positive hero in a tragic situation, plac-ing the positiveness in an his-torical period that is unreceptive and in appropri-ate to such posi-tiveness...

And the final distinction of *The Iron Heel* is this pos-itive note that subsumes the tragic. It is not a naïve positiveness. The details of three centuries of re-pression are spelled out fully enough. But what the novel so persuasively as-serts, is that ultimately the Brotherhood of Man will triumph; that the period of repression is in-evitably doomed. The force of will of the plutoc-racy may be able to extend it – ev-en as long as three centuries. But in the end social-ism will eventually emerge (92-126).

John Colmer, "The Writer as Critic of Society," Coleridge to Catch-22: Im-ages of Society (1978):

A study of the writer as a critic of society that ends with science-fiction fantasies and anti-war novels such as A Clockwork Orange, Fahrenheit 451, Slaughterhouse 5 and Catch-22 had better acquire what academic respectability it can by starting with the ancient Greeks, with Plato in fact. In Plato's Republic, that early blueprint for a benevolent dic-tatorship and first example of Utopian fantasy, no place can be found for the imaginative writer. In justification Plato gives three reasons. The poet, he argues, deals with reality at two removes. He tells lies about the gods and heroes, a complaint that is not difficult to translate into terms that would be applicable to any modern dictatorship. And he ap-peals to emotions, when he should appeal to man's noblest faculty, the reason. 'We shall,' says Plato 'bow down before a being with such miraculous powers of giving pleasure; but we shall tell him that we are not allowed to have any such person in our commonwealth; we shall crown him with fil-lets of wool, anoint his head with myrrh, and con-duct him to another country' (Republic, Book 10). Regretfully, because Plato is certainly not unaware of the sublime powers possessed by the inspired poet, but firmly and magisterially, this stern moral puritan dismisses the poet from his ideal state. Here, then, in Plato's Republic, we have the first memorable statement of the clash between two ideals of order: the inspired order of the artist and the imposed order of the state, an opposition that permeates Romantic and post-Romantic literature. And in exiling the artist from his ideal state, Plato is the first to create for him that very modern role, the Outsider…

The successful critic of society, it may be suggested, is the writer who learns the wisdom of in-direction. He is the writer who learns to combine instruction with delight, without in any way com-promising his integrity of blunting the force of his social criticism. Some literary forms are especially suited to methods of indirect attack: satire, for ex-ample. From the time of the Greeks onwards, satir-ists have invented a variety of ways to maintain apparent detachment and the indirect approach, while pressing home their attack. The three com-monest forms are the beast fable, the imaginary journey, and the Utopian fantasy. The beast fable has been used by the Greek dramatist Aristophanes in the Frogs, by Chaucer in the Nun's Priest's Tale, and by George Orwell in Animal Farm. Swift's Gulliver's Travels provides a model for the imag-inary journey, while the history of literary utopias stretches – to take it no further – from More's six-teenth-century Utopia, to Butler's Erewhon (1872), Morris's News From Nowhere (1891), and Hux-ley's Brave New World (1932). It is essential for the satirist's purpose to shock us into seeing our own familiar world through unfamiliar eyes; some radi-cal change of perspective is therefore absolutely necessary. Each

of the three devices, the beast fable, the imaginary journey, and Utopian fantasy achieves this end.

Maxwell Geismar, Reluctant Radical: A Memoir (1977) [first published 2002]:

One of my later discoveries of my radicalized self was how many of our liberal friends, how many people in general, including particularly the typical American male, have remained per-petual adoles-cents…

The desires and dreams of adolescence die hard, if they ever do. We still yearn for the peace and security of childhood when nothing was certain, when the promise of the future, however vague, still sparkled before us, when we could cherish the illusion of enduring and uncritical happiness and comfort – within the protective womb of family and society.

In my view, however, the great artists are those who have gone beyond the confining web or co-coon of their past, who have been able to look through their world and really understand it. This is perhaps the acid test of maturity: to outlive, to go beyond those entangling bonds of youth and ac-cepted status. Then only do we become ourselves and know who we are; then only do we confirm our judgments by our own inner authority rather then by tribal law or custom.

And yet…and yet how difficult such a moral position is to maintain, so lofty and isolated and comfortless at times, sustained only by the great individuals of history and even then at some cost usually to their humanness. This is one reason that the radicals whom we met later in life clung to each other for support in their common exile. This is why they knew each other and why they joined together – despite their often bitter ideological con-flicts – to support one another in an American society they all opposed.

So it was that at the most rewarding peaks of our new life in the sixties and seventies, I had, on my bad days, recurring fits of self-doubt and re-morse and regret. The truth is, I missed the com-forting and reassuring perks of power and place, not to mention the cash, of my former ca-reer – or the attention I had received as a promising star on the American literary scene. I enjoyed the attention and consideration I received from authors and publishers alike as a featured reviewer in the mass media and in the academic journals. On those low days of mine, when I thought about the money I might have made as a popular writer rather than a radical one, I'd ask myself: Would I have done this, given up all this, if I had known what I was in for? Would I do it all over again, knowing the conse-quences?

I recalled the veiled threats I had received from various members of the literary establishment after the publication of the James book, threats which at the time I had dismissed so lightly. There were warnings, too, by younger friends in academia that they, the accepted pundits, were out to get me, and I should be careful! Well, I had been careful, in my own view. I published a highly praised, carefully wrought volume on Mark Twain positing Twain as the polar opposite of Henry James. And the Twain scholars were even more incensed by my Twain book than the Jamesians were by my James study! What I had done by critical feel, by my deepest per-sonal instinct and judgment in literary affairs, they now attributed to my desire, after the Henry James book, to expand a notorious career! I, who had the worst fears of notoriety all my life, who had craved honorable respectability, who had avoided the ob-vious dodges of creating a name, who had always shunned sensationalism.

It was ironic at least...

I had already reviewed *The Naked and the Dead* in the *Saturday Review* in 1949, and *Barbary Shore* in the same magazine in 1951, and would write about *The Deer Park* (1955) in *American Moderns*. I had praised Mailer's first novel while noting it was consciously literary and derived from such writers as Thomas Wolfe and John Dos Passos... I had panned *Barbary Shore* as being a novel of ideas that were "fashionable by current standards" but that were also mistaken...

As early as this second book Mailer had cut him-self off from the revolutionary currents of the world historical scene around him. Becoming as he did one of the sharpest critics of American capital-ism, knowing it was a corrupt and rotten social system – as he said over and over again – he had no feasible alternative to what he was condemning.

Hence his own work became infested with the corruption he was describing. Even more impor-tant, all that he could place against this decadent society was the solitary image of himself apart from it. Apart, but basically no different from it in his motivation and his literary achievement. In turn that treacherous ego of Mailer's would increase and enlarge itself into monstrous proportions.

That was the mistake I sensed in *Barbary Shore* as far back as 1951. Mailer was far smarter than either Styron or Jones in seeing what was wrong around him, but that intellectual brilliance was supported by no vision or ideological framework.

As a social critic, Mailer was also a failed novel-ist. That special poison, which can paralyze a creat-ive personality, also contaminated his other writ-ing, his values, and his personal-ity. In this sense Mailer's career can be described as one long ego trip designed to keep the failure of the artist away from the artist's own consciousness.

Robert Alter, "History and the New American Novel" (1975) in Motives for Fiction (1984):

If much of this fiction has been obsessed with the war and the terrible revelation of the nature of history embodied in the war, the writers, following the general logic of obsessions, have addressed themselves more to the materials of recurrent fan-tasy than to their ostensibly objective referents. What I am suggesting is that these novelists, even (or perhaps especially) when their surface details are most insistently historical, have been concerned with something very different from history. In-deed, one frequently finds their adversary impulse toward contemporary reality accompanied by a predisposition to dismiss it impatiently, not to bother with imagining it in any complex way. This quality was shrewdly observed a number of years ago by Burton Feldman in a trenchant critique of black humor (*Dissent*, March-April 1968): "For all the violence of its assault on

American culture, black Humor gives no sense that this enemy is worth attacking. It is only there, a middle-class moonscape; and then Black Humor slips off into fantasy and parody…"

"Middle-class moonscape" is an apt description of the America evoked in the fiction of Kurt Vonne-gut, where outraged social criticism, sentimental moralism, and science-fiction fantasy form a piqu-ant if not altogether credible mé-nage a trios. The case of Vonnegut is an instructive one because the comic-strip clarity of his novels lucidly illustrates a conception of history largely shared by Pynchon and Barth, though perhaps partly camouflaged through the complicated elaboration of design in their more ambitious work. Vonnegut's stylistic, structural, and psychological simplicity, coupled with a genuine verve of narrative inventiveness, makes him the most easily accessible of these writ-ers and thus the most widely read. I would attribute at least some of his popularity, however, to the need of many readers over the past decade for a novelist who could write away history while seem-ing to write about it.

Pynchon, Barth, Barthelme, and Vonnegut… fin-ally [do not take] history very seriously, despite the overwhelming density of actual historical detail in the [novels]… If the end of history is at hand, his-torical time being only a welter of statistical events, without causal links, all bent on destruction, there is no objective ground for narrative structure; cal-culated formal design must substitute for anything like development in the novel; and perhaps most critical, there are no criteria for selectivity in the novelist's shuttle between history and invention…

If history is no longer a realm of concatenation, if there are no necessary connections among dis-crete events and no possibility of a hierarchy of materials ranged along some scale of significance, any associative chain of fantasies, any crotchety hobbyistic interest, any technical fascination with the rendering of odd trivia, can be pursued by the novelist as legitimately as the movement of sup-posedly "significant" actions. The end of history [in novels], in other words, is a writer's license for self-indulgence, and Pynchon utilizes that license for page after dreary page of *Gravity's Rainbow* as he describes at incredible length varieties of turds in a sewer, varieties of revolting wine-jelly candies in a British cupboard, varieties of bizarre sexual combi-nations in a very long daisy-chain, and so forth.

The lack of selectivity leads to local flaws; the unwillingness to make differential judgments about historical events results in a larger inadequacy of the novel as a whole….

I have no quarrel at all with fantasy or flaunted artifice in the novel but only with their deployment in ways that are ultimately self-indulgent and mechanically repetitious, that tend to turn the imaginative energies of fiction into a crackling closed circuit.

Tom Wolfe, The New Journalism (1973):

…the most serious, ambitious and, presumably, talented novelists had abandoned the richest ter-rain of the novel: namely, society, the social tab-leau, manners and morals, the whole business of 'the way we live now,' in Trollope's phrase. There is no novelist who will be remembered as the novelist who captured the Sixties in America, or even in New York, in the sense that Thackeray was the chronicler of London in the 1840's and Balzac was the chronicler of Paris and all of France after the fall of the Empire. Balzac prided himself on being 'the secretary of French society.' Most serious American novelists would rather cut their wrists than be known as the 'secretary of American so-ciety,' and not merely because of ideological considerations. With fable, myth and the sacred office to think about – who wants such a menial role?

That was marvelous for journalists – I can tell you that. The Sixties was one of the most extraordi-nary decades in American history in terms of man-ners and morals…

Novelists routinely accepted the unpleasant task of doing reporting, legwork, 'digging,' in order to get it just right. That was part of the process of writing novels. Dickens travels to three towns in Yorkshire using a false name and pretending to be looking for a school for the son of a widowed friend – in order to get inside the notorious Yorkshire boarding schools to gather material for Nicholas Nickleby.

Social realists like Dickens and Balzac seemed so often to delight in realism pure and simple that it was held against them throughout their careers. Neither was regarded as a literary artist in his own lifetime (Balzac was not even invited into the French Academy).

Raymond Williams, "The New Metropolis" in The Country and the City (1973):

It is often said now, in a guilty way, that the British people as a whole benefited from the system of imperialism. If we add up the figures of the movement of wealth we cannot doubt that this is true. The rise in the general standard of living depend-ed, in large part, on the exploitation of millions who were seen only as backward peoples, as natives. Much of the guilt and hatred and prejudice bred through those generations was still there when, ironically, unemployment in the colonies prompted a reverse migration, and following an ancient pattern the displaced from the 'country' areas came, following the wealth and the stories of wealth, to the 'metropolitan' centre, where they were at once pushed in, overcrowded, among the indigenous poor... London was at one of its peaks as an imperialist city when it created its desperate cenrtre of poverty and misery in the East End. For wealth from the Empire, channeled through so few hands, was a critical source of the political and economic power which the same ruling class continued to exercise. The advantages of living in a developed industrial society, even at the lower ends of the scale, were of course more widely diffused. Even then, internally, these workers were directly exploited. But for many of these advantages British workers had to pay: with blood in repeated wars which had little or nothing to do with their immediate interests; and in deeper ways, in confusion, loss of direction, deformation of the spirit. It is the story of the city and the country in its harshest form, and now on an unimaginably complex scale.

It is now widely believed in Britain that this system has ended. But political imperialism was only ever a stage. It was preceded by economic and trading controls, backed where necessary by force. It has been effectively succeeded by economic, monetary and commercial controls which again, at every point that resistance mounts, are at once supported by political, cultural and military intervention. The dominant relationships are still, in this sense, of a city and a country, at the point of maximum exploitation.

What is offered as an idea, to hide this exploitation, is a modern version of the old idea of 'improvement': a scale of human societies which theoretically culminates in universal industrialization. All the 'country' will become 'city': that is the logic of its development: a simple linear scale, along which degrees of 'development' and 'underdevelopment' can be marked. But the reality is quite different...

We are already familiar with the [novels] of Englishmen who experienced the tensions of this process...but we have only to go across to the Indian and African and West Indian writers to get a different and necessary perspective. The tea plantation is seen from the other side in Mulk Raj Anand's *Two Leaves and a Bud* (1937). Chinua Achebe's *Things Fall Apart* (1958) ends with a white man collecting material for a book on 'The Pacification of the Primitive Tribes of the Lower Niger', and this ironic challenge is telling because we have all read such accounts, but now see the process from within a rural community as the white men – missionaries, district officers – arrive with their mercenary soldiers and police. What is impressive about *Things Fall Apart* is that as in some English literature of rural change, as late as Hardy, the internal tensions of the society are made clear, so that we can understand the modes of the penetration which would in any case, in its process of expansion, have come. The first converts to the alien religion are the marginal people of the traditional society. The alien law and religion are bitterly resented and resisted, but the trading-station, in palm-oil, is welcomed, as an addition to the slash-and-burn subsistence farming of yams. The strongest man, Okonkwo, is destroyed in a very complicated process of internal contradictions and external invasion.

We can see the same complications, at a later stage and in different societies in the resistance movements of the country people against English power, in the Kenya of James Ngugi's *Weep Not, Child* and *A Grain of Wheat*, or in the Malaya of Han Suyin's *And The Rain My Drink*. What has been officially presented, to English readers, as savagery followed by terrorism, is seen in its real terms: so many different rural societies – unidealised, containing their own tensions – invaded and transformed by an uncomprehending and often brutal alien system. It is significant that the idealization of the peasant, in the modern English middle-class tradition, was not extended, when it might have mattered, to the peasants, the plantation-workers, the coolies of these occupied societies. Yet in a new and universal sense this was the penetration, transformation and subjugation of 'the country' by the 'city': long-established rural communities uprooted and redirected by the military and economic power of a developing metropolitan imperialism...

...when we look at the power and impetus of the metropolitan drives, often indeed accelerated by their own internal crises, we cannot be in any doubt that a different direction, if it is to be found, will necessarily involve revolutionary change. The depth of the crisis, and the power of those who continue to dominate it, are too great for any easier or more congenial way.

Within this now vast mobility, which is the daily history of our world, literature continues to embody the almost infinitely varied experiences and interpretations... Yet we have got so used to thinking of common experience through the alienating screens of foreignness and race that all too often we take the particularity of these stories as merely exotic. A social process is happening there, in an initially unfamiliar society, and that is its importance. But as we gain perspective, from the long history of the literature of country and city, we see how much, at different times and in different places, it is a connecting process, in what has to be seen ultimately as a common history.

Maxwell Geismar, "Introduction," New Masses: An Anthology of the Rebel Thirties (Ed. Joseph North) (1969):

I welcome this anthology for several reasons, but mainly because it is part of something which I have begun to think of as our 'buried history' in the Cold War period. Recently a group of American historians have been digging into, one might say, 'excavating,' the true facts of this Cold War Culture – the curious period from the mid-forties to the mid-sixties – and the results are very interesting. We have had almost a quarter of a century of con-formity, comfort, complacency and mediocrity in American literature – this epoch of 'instant master-pieces' – and only now can we begin to put the pieces together and find a consistent pattern...

...it was the Cold War that brought about the downfall, in 1949, of one of the most brilliant jour-nalistic enterprises in our literary history. At the war's end, a new epoch of repression was about to start. Another great achievement of the Depression years was the WPA Federal Theater Project; and Halle Flanagan's history of this, in her book *Arena*, ends with the congressional investigation and fore-closure of the Federal Theater by political figures who are, by Divine Grace or special dispensation, still active in Washington today... What was the real truth, the true historical dimension, of the Cold War? As I said in opening this Introduction, a new group of Cold War historians have been giving us a whole new set of impressions, which, alas, most of those who lived through the period, and are so cer-tain of their convictions, will not even bother to read and to think about.

For if they did...the Schlesingers, the Galbraiths, the Kristols, the Max Lerners, the Trillings, the Bells, the Rahvs, the Kazins, the Irving Howes: all these outstanding, upstanding figures of our politi-cal-cultural scene today ... they would have to admit both their own illusions for the last twenty years, and the fact that they have deliberately deluded their readers about the historical facts of our period. Since it was they who fastened the Cold War noose around all our necks, how can we expect them to remove it? – even though, as in the cases of

Mary McCarthy and Dwight MacDonald, and the estimable *New York Review of Books*, they have bowed a little to the changing winds of fash-ion today. Due to student protests at base, and student confrontations on Cold War issues, Prof-essors Bell and Trilling have indeed moved on from Columbia to Harvard University – but after Harvard what?

Mr. Trilling has even 'resigned' from con-temp-orary literature, saying at long last that he does not understand it – but only after he led the attack for twenty years on such figures as the historian Ver-non Parrington, the novelist Dreiser, the short-story writer Sherwood An-derson, and other such figures of our literary history. And only after the Columbia University English Department had tak-en the lead in set-ting up Henry James as 'Receiver' in what amounted to the bankruptcy of our nation-al lit-erature. The Cold War Liberals, historians, crit-ics and so-called sociologists, also clustered around a set of prestigious literary magazines like *Partisan Review, The New Leader, Encounter* of London, *Der Monat* of Berlin, which had in ef-fect set the tone and the values of the 'Free World' culture. When it was revealed, about two years ago, that these lead-ing cultural pub-lications and organizations (the various Con-gresses and Committees for 'Cultural Free-dom'), as well as some student organizations and big unions of the AFL-CIO, were in fact be-ing financed and controlled by Central Intelli-gence Ag-ency – the game was up... (10-12).

John Berger, The Success and Failure of Picasso (1965):

Stupid people often accuse marxists of welcoming the intrusion of politics into art. On the contrary, we protest against the intrusion. But it is pointless to deny such times. They must be understood so that they can be ended: art and men will then be freer. Such a time began in Europe in 1914 and con-tinues still.

Vernon Hall, Jr., A Short History of Literary Criticism (1963):

That Karl Marx could not have envisioned the extremes to which the Soviet totalitarians would put his literary theories is obvious. We know, for instance, that his colleague Frederick Engels wrote the following in a letter to an early 'proletarian' novelist who asked for Engel's help in populariz-ing his novel: 'Look at your hero-ine, with her dialectical materialist eyes and her economic de-terminist nose and her surplus value mouth. You take her in your arms and you kiss her. I know I wouldn't want to' (145).

Robert E. Spiller, Ed. et. al., Literary History of the United States (1963):

When President Lincoln greeted Harriet Beecher Stowe with the words, 'So you're the little woman who made the book that made this great war,' he was speaking as a political realist who had learned by experience to respect the power of the pen. It was not for him to refer slightingly to 'mere litera-ture.' Without *Uncle Tom's Cabin*, in the opinion of Sumner, there would have been no Lincoln in the White House.

But the historian must avoid hyperbole. In spite of the enormous vogue of Mrs. Stowe's novel, it is doubtful if a book had much power to change the course of events. More persuasive than her tender pleadings was the harsh propa-ganda carried on by Abolitionists for over thirty years. And mightiest of all was the trend of lib-eral opinion through the nineteenth century, which was bound to sweep out of existence even the most beneficent and patri-archal of feudal survivals. In the last analysis slav-ery was abolished because men could no longer en-dure the thought of it. Shrewd common people were the first to sense how the tide was turning (563).

Edwin Muir, The Estate of Poetry (1962):

There is a greater poetry than that of the bal-lads; they [ballads] do not contain those univer-sal state-ments of life which we find in Dante and Shake-speare; but they were once a general possession as Shakespeare has never been. And that great poetry can, or once could, be a general possession is a fact which we should not forget: those of us who write poetry, and those of us who criticize it. If we could keep it in mind, I think it would give us a more just and adequate idea of poetry... (22).

[A reporter] also quoted Mr. [T. S.] Eliot as saying that 'criticism of poetry began and ended in enjoy-ment,' which I think is the traditional practice. But the observation that is most illuminating in this report is that 'a genuine poem may arouse a very great number of differing responses, yet there will be always something in common between them,' and that this is what poetry is for. There have been some very strange responses to poems, as Mr. Richards has shown so convincingly in his book, Practical Criticism, responses which seemed plain-ly to contradict one another. Yet, even allowing for this, there will be something in common between people's varied responses to a poem, and the poem exists for that purpose. If we believe this, poetry takes on a wider significance than it is currently allowed, and lets in the ordinary unanalytical reader, and with him human nature. People will read poetry for enjoyment, since that is what it is intended for; and they will not, except in a few exceptional cases, take it up as a strict methodical study. And it may be said that they will get more help, both in enjoyment and understanding, from the traditional critic who tells them what the poem means to him, than from the new one who warns them that it cannot possibly mean what it appears to mean, so that he has no choice left but to explain it. The divorce between the public audience and the poet is widened by this critical method; or perhaps one should rather say that the method legalizes the divorce as a settled and normal state. And that is what we feel to be wrong... (76-77).

I've been trying to measure the gap between the public and the poet, and to find some explanation why it is so great. I began with the time when there was neither poet nor public, when the anonymous song or ballad was transmitted from generation to generation by the peasantry, and poetry was a pos-session so common that poet and audience were lost in it; we have been irreversibly changed. At best we can gain from that or oral poetry that beauty that or oral poetry that beauty which is in it, and the knowledge that po-etry is not a thing reserved for a few, since it was once, and for a long time, treasured and fostered by so many. If, knowing this, we could be brought to modify our contemporary notion of poetry as a rar-ified and special and often difficult thing, it might have a salutary effect on our criticism and our prac-tice of poetry as well...(94).

The first allegiance of any poet is to imaginative truth...but it does not mean that he should turn in-ward into the complex problems of poetry, or be concerned with poetry as a problem. That is some-thing which has commonly happened in the last fifty years. There was some excuse for it after the years of experiment associated with Mr. Eliot and Mr. Pound. To them, about 1910, poetry seemed to have come to a dead end, and intense thought had to be given to it. The experiments of that time and the succeeding years have become a part of literary history. As they were new and strange when they were first attempted, they were found difficult by the reader; and they seem to have left for a time in the minds of poets and critics the belief that poetry should be difficult. The experiment-ers have done their work, and we should be thankful to them. There have been many experimenters in English poetry: Chaucer was one; and Spenser, Milton, Dryden, and Wordsworth were all experimenters. The experiment-ers of forty years ago did some-thing to poetry and something for poetry. One kind of poetry was written before T.S. Eliot, and another kind after him. But the point of an experiment is that it should solve the particular problem set for it. This was done in the twenties... There remains the temptation for poets to turn inward into poetry, to lock themselves in to a hygienic prison where they speak only to one another, and to the critic, their stern warder. In the end a poet must create his aud-ience, and to do that he must turn outward. Even if he is conscious of having no audience, he must imagine one. That may be the way to conjure it out of the public void. Yeats, who had to wait for it long, declared that you must have an audience, and that he could not write without one. Anyone reading his poetry must feel that the audience was an imaginary one long before it became real. To imagine an audience, one must hold up before himself the variety of human life, for from that div-ersity the audience will be drawn. The poet need not think of the public – its vastness and imperson-ality would daunt anyone; he should reflect instead that in no other age than ours – I mean the last hundred years or so – has a poet had to deal with it. He has to see past it, or through it, to the men and women, with their individual lives, who in some strange way and without their choice are part of it, and yet are hidden by it (108-110).

Mary McCarthy, "Characters in Fiction" On the Contrary (1961):

The distinctive mark of the novel [as com-pared to other forms of fiction] is its concern with the actual world, the world of fact, of the verifiable, of fig-ures, even, and statistics. If I point to Jane Austen… Eliot…Tolstoy…Faulkner, it will be admit-ted…dif-ferent as they are … they have one thing in com-mon: a deep love of fact, of the empiric element in experience. I am not inter-ested in making a formal definition of the novel…but in finding its quidditas or whatness, the essence or binder that distinguish-es it from other species of prose fiction: the tale, the fable, the romance. The staple ingredient present in all novels in various mixtures and proportions but always in fairly heavy dosage is fact.

The word novel goes back to the word "new," and in the plural it used to mean news – the news of the day or year Literary historians find the seed or the germ of the novel in Boccaccio's *Decameron*, a col-lection of tales set in a frame of actual life … the Great Plague of 1348…where more than a hundred thousand people died between March and August. The figures and dates come from *The Decameron*, along with a great deal of other factual information about the Black Death… Many of the great novel-ists were newspaper reporters or journalists [and "students" of criminals and prisons] "confirmed prison-visitors"… Defoe…Dickens…Dostoevsky… and Victor Hugo…Tolstoy….

Coming to the twentieth century, you meet the American novelist as newspaperman: Dreiser, Sin-clair Lewis, Hemingway, O'Hara, Faulkner himself … There is another kind of "fact" literature closely related to the novel … the travel book, which tells the news of the ex-otic … The passion for fact in a raw state is a pe-culiarity of the novelist. Most of the great novel-ists contain blocks and lumps of fact… [includ-ing some whole essays…and "durable in-formative matter"]. A novel with descriptions and facts eliminated would only be a scenario and not a novel at all. It could be said that the real plot of *War and Peace* is the struggle for the characters not to be immersed, engulfed, swal-lowed up by the landscape of fact and "history" in which they, like all human beings have been placed: freedom (the subjective) is in the fiction, and necessity is in the fact….

Novels carried the news – of crime, high society, politics, industry, finance, and low life … The epic, I might put in here, is the form of all literary forms closest to the novel; it has the "boiler plate" ["dur-able informative matter"], the lists and catalogues, the circumstantiality, the concern with numbers and dimensions. The epic geography, like that of the novel, can be mapped, in both the physical and social sense…. Whenever the chance arises, Jane Austen sup-plies a figure.

The loss of the hero…the power of the author to speak in his own voice or through the undis-guised voice of an alter ego, the hero, at once a known and an unknown, a bearer of human freedom…upset a balance of nature…and the languishing of the 'characters' followed …

…experiments of the twentieth cen-tury…went in two directions: sensibility and sensation. To speak very broadly, the experi-ments in the recording of sensibility were made in England (Virginia Woolf, Katherine Mans-field, Dorothy Richardson, Eliza-beth Bowen, Forster), and America was the labora-tory of sensation (Hemingway and his imitators, Dos Passos, Farrell). The novel of sensibility was feminine, and the novel of sensation was mascu-line. In Paris, there was a certain meeting and merging: Gertrude Stein (a robust recorder of the data of sensibility) influenced and encour-aged Hemingway; Joyce, who experimented in both directions, influenced nearly everyone... The effect of these two tendencies on the subject matter of the novel was identical. Sensation and sensibility are the poles of each other, and both have the effect of abolishing the social. Sensibil-ity, like violent action, annihilates the sense of character. Beginning with our own...

Sensation and sensibility are at their height in the child; its thin, tender membrane of per-ception is constantly being stabbed by objects, words, and ev-ents that it does not understand. In lieu of under-standing, the child 'notices'... Now two character-istics of the child are that he cannot act (to any pur-pose) and he cannot talk (expressively); hence he is outside, dissociated. And it is just this state, or the dissociated out-sider, that is at the center of modern literature of sensibility and sensation alike ... It is modern but it is not new. The inability to say the appro-priate thing or to feel the appropriate thing, combined with a horrible faculty of noticing, is an almost clinical trait in the character of Julien Sorel and in most of the Stendhalian heroes.

Tolstoy was a master of the tragicomedy of inappropriate feelings, gestures, and sensa-tions... [But] the difference between Tolstoy (Stendhal too) and the fragmented impression-ism of twentieth-century literature, where the real world is broken up into disparate painterly images out of focus and therefore hypnotic and trancelike [is that with Tol-stoy and Stendhal] the point, however, is there, in-escapably so...

Once these discoveries had been made [Woolf, Joyce] in the recording of the perceptual field (i.e. of pure subjectivity), the novel could not ignore them; there was no turning back [from the] frag-mented impressionism [by way of] a curious back door...

That is the entry found by Joyce in *Ulysses*, where by a humorous stratagem character is shown, as it were inside out, from behind the screen of con-sciousness. The interior mono-logue every human being conducts with him-self, *sotto voce*, is used to create a dramatic por-trait... [Such a technique] restricts readers to a narrow field of vision or to several narrow fields in succession...

These books are impersonations, ventrilo-quial acts [including two of her own novels, she notes]; the author, like some prankster on the telephone, is speaking in an assumed voice – high or deep, hol-low or falsetto...[and so] the reader, tuned in, is left in no doubt as to where he is physically, and yet in many of these books he finds himself puzzled by the very vocal con-sciousness he has entered: it is good or bad, im-partial or biased? Can it be trusted ...? [The reader] senses the author, cramped inside the character like a contortionist in a box, and sus-pects (often rightly) some trick.

Or so I feel when I do it myself. It is exhila-rating but not altogether honest... All fictions, of course are impersonations, but it seems to me somehow less dubious to impersonate the out-side of a person ... These impersonations, moreover, are laborious; to come at a character circuitously, by a tour de force, means spending great and sometimes dispro-portionate pains on the method of entry... One is reminded of cer-tain young actors whose trademark is doing character parts, or vice versa, of certain old ac-tresses whose draw can be summed up in the sentence 'You would never guess she was sixty.'

Maxwell Geismar, American Moderns – From Rebellion to Conformity (1958):

The present volume began as a collection of articles and reviews writing in the Nineteen-Forties and Fifties for a more or less popular audience... Some of these articles are in the po-lemical vein which a critic uses with reluctance when his second nature, or his first, is to in-quire, to balance, and to evaluate. The central focus of the volume is on the transition-al dec-ade from the Second World War to the mid-dle of the twentieth century – from McCarthy to Sputnik. The historical setting is that of the un-easy 'peace,' the tensions of the Cold War, the return to 'normalcy,' and the epoch of confor-mity.

Or was it euphoria? In literature the period marked the decline of the classic modern American writers at the peak of their popular reputation. In criticism there was the movement towards higher and higher levels of aesthetic, or scholastic, absol-utism...

There was indeed a state of general inertia in the arts, as the familiar sequel to an age of anxiety: of problems urgent and not resolved, while the sur-face of the globe, and outer space too, vibrated in the throes of change. The American literary scene of the Forties and Fifties must have presented to the rest of the world an odd and ironic spectacle at times; and perhaps the polemical note was indic-ated; and meanwhile I trust that this spectacle may also be instructive... (ix-x).

[An] emotional syndrome of fear, terror, obses-sion-al hatred, and perhaps underground attrac-tion, of which [John] Dos Passos is the clearest example, has colored and conditioned our whole intellectual climate during the last dec-ade.

It accounts for our strange concentration of anxi-ety on the one ritualistic theme of an-ticommunism, by which every other issue has come to be meas-ured. Thus our crucial domes-tic battles have been fought out on the popular level, while our intellec-tual journals have hardly dared to mention them. Our best literary work has come from writers who are outside this intellectual orbit, where panic has slowly subsided into inertia. One notices that Dos Pas-sos himself, settled in the shadow of Monticello, has lost just those attributes of the old republic which made a whole line of country squires – from Jefferson to Franklin Roosevelt – such a potent force in our social revolution.

Dos Passos, indeed, has become a frightened landlord, guarding his ancestral estate. And as I write these lines, another old-fashioned South-ern agrarian, William Faulkner, has just de-clared that in the final crisis he will have to stand by Missis-sippi, and shoot down the Ne-groes in the streets. Well, good-bye to all that (83).

Faulkner had humor, often ironic and bitter, in the series of dramas and tragedies he wrote about the Old South. But the meaning of his humor about the New South, personified in the Snopes clan of *The Hamlet* (1940) is a very differ-ent matter.

Those who are surprised at the recent state-ments on integration which have come from the Nobel Prize Moralist – America's literary spokes-man before the world – might do well to look at Faulkner's novels. Not at the rational and moral statements in them, either, but at their prevailing imagery and true dramatic ac-tion. The critics who have been celebrating this artist as the foremost symbol of the progressive, modern, 'civilized' South have not understood the real psychological forces in his work. Faulk-ner is, or was, a major artist simply because he revealed the darkest recesses of the Southern psyche: the folds and flaps of fear, ignorance, and prejudice.

But he is a writer who is more than half in-fatu-ated with, or strangled by, the psychic de-mons he has conjured up. Never mind the rhetoric on state occasions. He too belongs with the class of South-ern men whom Ellen Glasgow described as having learned to talk and to preach before they learned to think...

The Southern scene does offer great dramatic possibilities for a writer today, and Faulkner is in a unique position to render a true service to his cul-ture, his tradition, and his art. But this writer is not serious any more. The 'humor' of the Snopes chronicle is a hasty gag rather than genuine social satire. It almost seems that the artist's contempt for all phases of modern life, which was clear as early as *The Sound and the Fury*, has prevented him from learning the truth about the modern South.

Why else should two out of three books prod-uced after the Nobel Prize (with its much-publi-cized nobility of artistic aspiration) strike us as not only poor, but trivial or cheap? (While the third book, *The Fable*, is at best mediocre.) This is the real tragedy for Faulkner, for the South, for American letters; and the mass of un-discriminating adulation given to this author re-cently has been no real help ...

So be it; and perhaps it is this dark and reces-sive fear, rooted in the phobic depths of Faulk-ner's own fancy, which has led him to his pre-sent position on the racial question. Is Faulkner himself now living among the phantoms that his own dark and fertile imagination has, in the past, conjured up so magni-ficently? But in the plain light of day, what non-sense it all is!" (101-

106)...

East of Eden is a tricky and meaningless parable – on the conscious level – of man's 'fall' through woman's vice. On the unconscious level – in this case, unconscious to the author – we may feel be-neath the novel's sentimentality, and even below the humanitarian principles which are the remain-ing link with the best period of [John] Steinbeck's work, a certain malice and hostility toward human life itself. The good writers often acknowledge this in their own literary vision, and build upon it. The lesser one write romances which both reveal and deny it, and sometimes it comes to dominate or de-stroy their spirit (166-167)...

Like his closest literary forebear, Dos Passos, [Nor-man] Mailer has no confidence in human nature itself, and perhaps no mature experience with it. The social values in [Mailer's third] novel, too, if they are intelligent, decent, liberal, are based on a biological void.

How tragic it is to be without illusions, even if they exist, in a writer's craft, only to be dispelled. That is probably Norman Mailer's central flaw, his central need; and meanwhile curious undertones of juvenile malice also appear in his work. He may be the latest type of Bad Boy in our national letters, whose problem is to grow up (178-179)...

In a desperate spiritual revulsion against a devour-ing infantile egoism, is the answer really to repudi-ate our whole notion of Western individuality? Is there really no such thing (as Zooey tells Franny) as time or change or growth in our concept of human personality? In the Zen quest for 'No-Knowledge' (as Buddy Glass tells his split-half Zooey), is it true that all legitimate religious study must lead to un-learning 'the illusory differences between boys and girls, animals and stones, day and night, heat and cold?'...a negation of the 'mind'...in favor of the pure and primary world of childhood sensation. That lost world of childhood indeed to which somehow or other, [J.D.] Salinger, like the rest of the *New Yorker* school, always returns! That pre-Edenite community of yearned-for bliss, where knowledge is again the serpent of all evil: but a false and precocious show of knowledge, to be

sure, which elevated without emancipating its in-nocent and often touching little victims... The root of the matter is surely here, and perhaps all these wise children may yet emerge from the nursery of life and art (208-209)...

The suffering, the humility, the moral goodness in [Saul Bellow's] books, the honest and ironic realiz-ation of human weakness: these are the traits that appeal to us. But this note of resignation, of accept-ance, does not appear in Bellow's work after the violence and passions of life, as it commonly does in the work of major artists. It appears in Bellow's fiction *instead of* the emotional storm and stress it should transcend. The central image of the hero in his novels and stories is not indeed that of the rebellious son, but of the suffering, the tormented, and the conforming son.

To use the phraseology of Salinger, this hero is the good boy, the sad sack; or to use the term of depth psychology, he is the castrated son (221).

George Steiner, "Marxism and the Literary Critic" (1958), in Language and Silence, 1967:

There is the intricate, yet ultimately persuasive, distinction which Marxist theory draws between 'realism' and 'naturalism.' It goes back to Hegel's reflections on the Iliad and the Odyssey. Hegel found that in the Homeric epics the depiction of physical objects, however detailed and stylized, did not intrude upon the rhythm and vitality of the poem. Descriptive writing in modern litera-ture, on the other hand, struck him as contingent and lifeless... Compared to Homeric or even to medieval times, modern man inhabits the physi-cal world like a rapacious stranger. These ideas greatly influenced Marx and Engels. It contributed to their own theory of the 'alienation' of the individual under capitalist modes of produc-tion. In the course of their debate with Lassalle and of their study of Balzac, Marx and Engels came to believe that this problem of estrangement was directly germane to the problem of realism in art. The poets of antiquity and the 'classical real-ists' (Cervantes, Shakespeare, Goethe, Balzac) had achieved an organic relationship between objective reality and the life of the imagination. The 'naturalist,' on the other hand, looks on the world as on a warehouse of whose contents he must make a feverish inventory. 'A sense of reality,' says a contemporary Marxist critic, 'is created not by a reproduction of all the features of an object but by a depiction of those features that form the essence...while in naturalistic art – because of a striving to achieve an elusive fullness – the image, also incomplete, places both the *essential* and the *secondary*, the unimportant, on the same plane.' This distinction is far reaching. It bears on the decline of French realism after Balzac and Stendhal, and tells us something of Zola's obses-sive attempt to make of the novel an index of the world. By virtue of it, we may discriminate be-tween the 'realism' of Chekhov and the 'natural-ism' of, say, Maupassant. Through it, also, we may ascertain that Madame Bovary, for all its virtues, is a slighter thing than Anna Karenina. In naturalism there is accumulation; in realism what Henry James called the 'deep-breathing economy' of organic form... (321-322).

At the origins of the Marxist theory of lit-era-ture there are three celebrated and canonic texts. Two of them are citations from Engels' letters [to Kautsky and Harkness]; the third is contained in a short essay by Lenin ["Party Organization and Party Literature"]... Engels is not objecting to a *littérature engagée* as such but rather to the mixture 'of mere empiricism and empty subjectivity' in the bourgeois novel of the period. Obviously dissatisfied with this treatment of the problem, Lukács reverted to it in 1945, in his 'Introduction to the Writings on Aesthetics of Marx and Eng-els.' Here he contends that Engels was distin-guishing between two forms of *littérature à thèse* (it is significant that the English language and its critical vocabulary have developed no precisely equivalent expression). All great literature, in Lukács' reading, has a 'fundamental bias.' A writer can only achieve a mature and responsible portrayal of life if he is committed to progress and opposed to reaction, if he 'loves the good and rejects the bad.' When a critic of Lukacs' sub-

tlety and rigor descends to such banalities – banalities which directly challenge his own works on Goethe, Balzac, and Tolstoy – we know that something is amiss. The attempt to reconcile the image of literature implicit in Lenin's essay with that put forward by Engels is a rather desperate response to the pressures of orthodoxy and to the Stalinist demand for total internal coherence in Marxist doctrine. Even the most delicate exegesis cannot conceal the plain fact that Engels and Len-in were saying different things, that they were pointing toward contrasting ideals (305-307).

Marxist-Leninism and the political régimes en-acted in its name take literature *seriously*, indeed desperately so. At the very height of the Soviet revolution's battle for physical survival, Trotsky found occasion to assert that 'the development of art is the highest test of the vitality and signifi-cance of each epoch.' Stalin himself deemed it essential to add to his voluminous strategic and economic pronouncements a treatise on philology and the problems of language in literature. In a Communist society the poet is regarded as a fig-ure central to the health of the body politic. Such regard is cruelly manifest in the very urgency with which the heretical artist is silenced or hounded to destruction. To shoot a man because one disagrees with his interpretation of Darwin or Hegel is a sinister tribute to the supremacy of ideas in human affairs – but a tribute nevertheless (323).

Irving Howe, Politics and the Novel (1957):

This book is meant primarily as a study of the rela-tions between literature and ideas, though a consi-derable part of it, I should say, consists of literary criticism. My interest was far less in literature as social evidence or testimony than in the literary problem of what happens to the novel when it is subjected to the pressures of politics and political ideology. In discussing nineteenth century writers I have employed more or less conventional methods of criticism, while in treating twentieth century writers I have found myself placing a greater stress upon politics and ideology as such; but this was not the result of any preconceived decision, it was a gradual shift in approach that seemed to be re-quir-ed by the nature of the novels themselves.

Because it exposes the impersonal claims of ide-ology to the pressures of private emotion, the poli-tical novel must always be in a state of internal warfare, always on the verge of becom-ing some-thing other than itself. The political novelist – the degree to which he is aware of this is another prob-lem – establishes a complex system of intellectual movements, in which his own opinion is one of the most active yet not entirely dominating movers. Are we not close here to one of the 'secrets' of the novel in gen-eral? – I mean the vast respect which the great novelist is ready to offer to the whole idea of opposition, the opposition he needs to allow for in his book against his own predispositions and yearnings and fantasies. He knows that his own momentum, his own intentions, can be set loose easily enough; but he senses, as well, that what matters most of all is to allow for those rocks against which his intentions may smash but, if he is lucky, they may merely bruise. Even as the great writer proudly affirms the autonomy of his imag-ination, even as he makes the most se-vere claims for his power of imposing his will upon the un-formed materials his imagination has brought up to him, he yet acknowledges that he must pit him-self against the imperious presence of the neces-sary. And in the political novel it is politics above all, politics as both temptation and impediment, that represents the necessary.

The criteria for evaluation of a political novel must finally be the same as those for any other novel: how much of our life does it illu-minate? how ample a moral vision does it sug-gest?—but these questions occur to us in a special context, in that atmosphere of political struggle which domi-nates modern life. For both the writer and the reader, the political novel provides a particularly severe test: poli-tics rakes our passions as nothing else, and whatever we may consent to overlook in read-ing a novel, we react with an almost demonic rapidity to a detested political opinion. For the writer the great test is, how much truth can he force through the sieve of his opinions? For the reader the great test is, how much of that truth can he accept though it jostle *his* opin-ions?

[A] mistake that many American novelists make: the notion that abstract ideas invariably contam-inate a work of art and should be kept at a safe distance from it. No doubt, when the armored columns of ideology troop in en masse, they do imperil a novel's life and live-liness, but ideas, be they in free isolation or hooped into formal sys-tems, are indispensa-ble to the serious novel. For in modern society ideas raise enormous charges of emotion, they involve us in our most feverish commitments and lead us to our most fearful be-trayals. The political novelist may therefore have to take greater risks than most others, as must any artist who uses large quantities of 'impure' matter; but his potential reward is accordingly all the greater. The novel, to be sure, is incon-ceivable without an effort to present and to penetrate hu-man emotion in its most private, irreducible as-pects; but the direction in which the emotion moves, the weight it exerts, the objects to which it attaches itself, are all condi-tioned, if not indeed controlled, by the pres-sures of abstract thought.

Ben Shahn, The Shape of Content (1957):

Some critics consider any mention of content a dis-play of bad taste. Some, more innocent and more modern, have been taught – schooled – to look at paintings in such a way as to make them wholly unaware of content.... But again, we must look up-on form as the shape of con-tent...

...form is the right and only possible shape of a certain content. Some other kind of form would have conveyed a different meaning and a different attitude. So when we sit in judgment upon a cer-tain kind of form – and it is usually called lack of form – what we do is to sit in judgment upon a cer-tain type of content...

While I concede that almost every situation has its potential artist, that someone will find matter for imagery almost everywhere, I am generally mistrustful of contrived situations, that is situa-tions peculiarly set up to favor the blossoming of art. I feel that they may vitiate the sense of indep-endence which is present to some degree in all art... One wonders how Cé-zanne would have progressed if he had been cordially embraced by the Academy. I am plagued by an exasperating no-tion: What if Goya, for instance, had been granted a Gug-genheim, and then, completing that, had stepped into a respectable and cozy teaching job in some small – but advanced! – New Eng-land col-lege, and had thus been spared the agonies of the Spanish Insurrection? The un-avoidable conclusion is that we would never have had 'Los Caprichos' or 'Los Desastres de la Guerra'...

Thus, it is not unimaginable that art arises from something stronger than stimulation or even inspi-ration – that it may take fire from something closer to provocation, that it may not just turn to life, but that it may a certain times be compelled by life. Art almost always has its ingredient of impudence, its flouting of estab-lished authority, so that it may substitute its own authority, and its own enlight-enment...

I believe that if the university's fostering of art is only kindly, is only altruistic, it may prove to be also meaningless. If, on the other hand, the creat-ive arts, the branches of art scholar-ship, the vari-ous departments or art are to be recognized as an essential part of education, a part without which the individual will be deemed less than educated, then I suppose that art and the arts will feel that degree of inde-pendence essential to them; that they will ac-cept it as their role to create freely – to com-ment, to outrage, perhaps, to be fully visionary and exploratory as is their nature.

Art should be well-subsidized, yes. But the pur-chase of a completed painting or a sculp-ture, the commissioning of a mural – or perhaps the public-ation of a poem or a novel or the production of a play – all these forms of recog-nition are the re-wards of mature work. They are not to be con-fused with the setting up of something not unlike a nursery school in which the artist may be spared any conflict, any need to strive quite intently to-ward command of his medium and his images; in which he may be spared even the need to make desperate choices among his own values and his wants, the need to reject many seeming benefits or wishes. For it is through such conflicts that his val-ues be-comes sharpened; perhaps it is only through conflicts that he comes to know himself at all.

It is only within the context of real life that an artist (or anyone) is forced to make such choices. And it is only against a background of hard reality that choices count, that they affect a life, and carry with them that degree of believe and dedication and, I think I can say, spiritual energy, that is a pri-mary force in art. I do not know whether that de-gree of intensity can ex-ist within the university; it is one of the prob-lems which an artist must consi-der if he is to live there or work there.

Wimsatt and Brooks, Literary Criti-cism: A Short History (1957):

In Czarist Russia of the mid-19th–century, a didactic theory of literature was strongly invited not only by political and social conditions but by the actual pre-eminence of a generation of socially conscious novelists... The greatest Rus-sian literary figure to participate in the 19th-century complex of socio-realistic theory and the writer whose pronounce-ments on art have impinged with most authority on the English literary mind, was undoubtedly Tol-stoy—'the conscience of Russia' in his time, 'the conscience of the world' 'the conscience of human-ity'... He was in his middle age a violent convert to a kind of Christian thinking. A period of furious tractarian activity followed the production of the great novels. And it is a religious theory of litera-ture that near the end of his life issues in his thund-erously deliberate denunciation of all that he him-self and all that European artists for 300 years had created.... The destruction of the idea 'art for art's sake' and the reconstruction of art as a monitor and propagandist for the social process is the gist of Tolstoy's preachment.... In America the idea of a socially activist literature appears during the first decades of the 20th cen-tury with the 'muck-raking' movement (of which Upton Sinclair's *Mammonart*, 1924, may stand as the sufficient symbol) and after that in the overtly Marxist criticism of the later twenties and the thirties—the work of such writers as Michael Gold, editor of the *New Masses*, Joseph Freeman, editor of the anthology *Proletarian Literature in the United States,* 1935, and V.F. Calverton, editor of the *Modern Quarterly*... [Ignored here, among others, W.E.B. DuBois, editor of *Crisis*]

A major monument was Vernon Louis Parring-ton's three-volume *Main Currents in American Thought* (1927-1930)...

Walter B. Rideout, The Radical Novel in the United States – 1900-1954 (1956):

Taken in its entirety, then, a half-century of the rad-ical novel has had its effect on and made a contri-bution to American literature. It has also affected and contributed to American life, not just uniquely, however, but as part of the whole larger course of the novel of social protest, that tradition which has proliferated so variously in the troubled twentieth century and which extends back into the nine-teenth through the early Hamlin Garland and the Utopians, through Mark Twain, in some of his moods, back to, and well before, Harriet Beecher Stowe, whose Uncle Tom's Cabin did as much to change the face of the nation as, perhaps, all the proletarian novels put together. This tradition, which is certainly a great, though not the only one, the radical novel of the present century has helped to continue. Despite their orientation toward Marx-ism, the Socialist, the proletarian, the independent-ly radical novelists have not been able to obscure the fact that in essential ways they represented yet another manifestation of the American middle-class conscience, which has been the major force behind the literature of social criticism from Har-riet Stowe down even to the present day. Viewed as part of a developing process, the radical novel shares in the value of the whole, the value of pro-test against the still limited democracy that is an affirmation of the democracy that can be. For protest is valuable, quite as valuable as that acceptance without which no continuing social organization is possible. Whether wrongheaded or right, protest will always be essential in order to stir our civiliza-tion into self-awareness and thus prevent it from stiffening into an inhuman immobility. In the fre-quently unwise thirties this rather elementary final statement would have been assumed. That it must now be asserted indicates that the fifties have their own particular lack of wisdom...

[In the 1992 introduction, Rideout notes: Rereading The Radical Novel in the United States for the first time in decades...it struck me as a reasonably good book...though I did wonder how I could have had the patience to get through so many awful novels in order to reach the fewer worthwhile ones... In a few reviews, two linked objections emerged... first, that I had too rigidly limited my subject by defin-ing a radical novel as 'one which demonstrates, either explicitly or implicitly, that the author objects to the human suffering imposed by some socioeconomic system and *advocates that the system be fundamentally changed.*' Granted this definition required me to discuss many bad novels and not to discuss certain better ones; but even bad novels can be illustrative, and it seemed, and still seems, to me that such a sociopolitical defi-nition enabled me to treat in some depth a specifically sociopolitical gen-re of fiction aimed at fundamental change rather than at reform which would improve the system but not change it basically. Better a limiting defini-tion, I would argue, than one which might turn out to be imprecise and overinclusive...

My point may be clearer if I move to a second ob-jection, a corollary of the first, that I should have written about the much more extensive fiction of 'social protest.' Suppose I had written or tried to write the kind of book these reviewers had wanted me to instead of the one I did. Quite aside from the probability that the ratio of bad to good social pro-test novels would be about the same as bad to good radical ones, I would have been faced with two problems: how should 'the fiction of social protest' be defined, and how could I, or anyone, hope to cover thoroughly in a single volume a very large and disunified field? For really, in American fiction just of the first half of the twentieth century there were many different kinds of social protest going on...

Joseph L. Blotner, The Political Novel (1955):

In The Charterhouse of Parma the witty and ur-bane Stendhal says, 'Politics in a work of literature are like a pistol-shot in the middle of a concert, something loud and vulgar yet a thing to which it is not possible to refuse one's attention.' His own work contradicts the great French novelist, yet his comment is perfectly accurate for many other nov-elists. Politics in some modern novels of political corruption, such as Charles F. Coe's Ashes, do seem loud and vulgar, and in books like Upton Sinclair's the reader may hear not one pistol shot but a cannonade. But this is not to say that the use of political material must disrupt a work of literature. The trick, of course, is all in knowing how. Harriet Beecher Stowe wrote an artistically weak, politically successful work in Uncle Tom's Cabin, while Fyodor Dostoyevsky produced a politically unsuccessful, artistically enduring classic in The Possessed...

A political novel written from a point of view favoring a particular faction is a political instru-ment in effect even if not in intent. A writer may sternly tell himself at the outset that he will be completely impartial, only to have reviewers note all sorts of bias, real or imagined, of which he may not have been conscious. This happened to Tur-genev when he published Fathers and Sons, and it continues to happen every year. The intensity of the authors' feelings varies from obsessive preoc-cupation to passing interest. The novels in this chapter were included because they contain defi-nite opinions, sometimes appeals, on political sub-jects. Some of them never exhort the reader or seem to lead him by the hand to the author's point of view. But each of them contains material capable of influencing the reader's opinions about some phase of political activity. If a novelist gains a reader's support for a cause, arouses his distaste for a course of action, or simply produces a reeval-uation of previously accepted

beliefs, his work has served as a political instrument just as surely as a pamphlet mailed by a national committee or a handbill stuffed into the mailboxes of a sleeping city.

Ralph Ellison, "The Art of Fiction: An Interview" (1955), Collected essays, 2003; Shadow and Act, 1964:

I recognize no dichotomy between art and pro-test. Dostoevsky's Notes from the Underground is, among other things, a protest against the limi-tations of nineteenth-century rationalism; Don Quixote, Man's Fate, Oedipus Rex, The Trial – all these embody protest, even against the limitation of human life itself. If social protest is antithetical to art, what then shall we make of Goya, Dickens and Twain?

Gilbert Highet, People, Places, Books (1953):

Satire is just as valuable a type of writing as lyric poetry or fiction; but it is far harder to bring off... In order to write satire of any kind, one has to have a number of special talents, and also a special atti-tude to the public... The public usually does not believe that anything is deeply wrong with society, and it often thinks that satirist is a sorehead. It has grown up and found a job and got married and brought up its children in the existing social frame-work. Why should it believe that the whole thing is tunneled through by gangsters, and bought and sold by crooked politicians, and redesigned to give the biggest profits to the ruthless and the corrupt? No, surely not. Therefore the satirist, who believes these things, usually strains his voice shouting, to making the public hear; and then the public is ev-en less inclined to listen... They are very amusing and penetrating, these contemporary satires. The only trouble is this: they don't seem to matter much... This, I regret to say, is the mid-twentieth century. What we need is a satirist bold enough to attack the crooks who run national politics in many countries; the parasites who make vast for-tunes by buying something on Monday and selling it on Tuesday, usually to the government; the idealists who ship five million families off to labor camps in order to make their theories come right; the soreheads whose pride was hurt once and who are determined to start a war to take care of the bruise: the rats in the basement, the baboons play-ing with dynamite. Satire will not kill these ani-mals; but it will make clear the difference between them and human beings, and perhaps inspire a hu-man being to destroy them.

They are very amusing and penetrating, these con-temporary satires. The only trouble is this: they don't seem to matter much. Miss McCarthy spends a lot of care and observation on proving that the Dandelion League colleges are eccentric, confused, and hyper-emotional. Mr. Waugh exposes the burial ceremonies of the Californians with an odd blend of charm and callousness, like sweet-and-sour sauce. But such subjects are not terribly im-portant. This, I regret to say, is the mid-twentieth century.

Nelson Algren, Nonconformity (1953):

We live today in a laboratory of human suffering as vast and terrible as that in which Dickens and Dos-toevsky wrote. The only real difference being that the England of Dickens and the Russia of Dostoev-sky could not afford the soundscreens and the smokescreens with which we so ingeniously con-ceal our true condition from ourselves.

So accustomed have we become to the testimony of the photo-weeklies, backed by witnesses from radio and TV, establishing us permanently as the happiest, healthiest, sanest, wealthiest, most inven-tive, tolerant and fun-loving folk yet to grace the earth of man, that we tend to forget that these are bought-and-paid-for witnesses and all their testi-mony perjured...

'Whin business gits above sellin' ten-pinny nails in a brown-paper cornucopy,' Mr. Dooley decided, 'tis hard to tell it from murder.'

But behind Business's billboards and Business's headlines and Business's pulpits and Business's press and Business's arsenals, behind the car ads and the subtitles and the commercials, the people of Dickens and Dostoevsky yet endure.... The lost and the overburdened...are still torn by the para-dox of their own humanity; yet endure the ancest-ral problems of the heart in conflict with itself. Theirs are still the defeats in which everything is lost, theirs victories that fall close enough to the heart to afford living hope. Whose defeats cost ev-erything of real value. Whose grief grieves on uni-versal bones.

And it is there the young man or woman seek-ng to report the American century seri-ously must seek, if it is the truth he seeks. ...

Mike Gold, "The Dreiser I Knew" (1950)

The Mike Gold Reader (1954):

A titan of the novel ... Theodore Dreiser was respected by the avant-garde for his *Sister Carrie*, which the puritans had suppressed for many years. He had formerly attained an American success as an executive; he had been the highly-paid editor of an enormous slickie, the *Delineator*. He quit this success in mid-career to starve in the Village and write truthful novels. The "genteel tradition" was the main enemy then, the pastel-shaded culture of the industrial pirates who needed a mask of refinement for their crimes. They and their literary office-boys ranted whenever a new book by Dreiser appeared. They accused him of pornography, of clumsy and amateurish craftsmanship, of slander against the pillars of society.

They prevented his books from selling, yet the man grew into a national figure. He persisted. Year after year he turned out his powerful novels, his portraits of oppressed womanhood, his studies of the rapacious American financier, or the shabby tragedies of the lower middle class...

The decadence of capitalist culture becomes painfully clearer every day in America. There is a sterility of heart and mind in the works of the T. S. Eliots and Hemingways that should frighten a cautious conservative. Such lack of love as dominates our literature is surely a sign that society is rotting at the core. Without cement you cannot build a house; without human solidarity you cannot have a social order. It is the Marquis de Sades, it is the Nietzsches who dominate the spirit of America's modern authors. But it is love like Tolstoy's and

Rolland's that was present in Theodore Dreiser, a warm and fruitful love that is bountiful as Mother Nature, that can heal and save, and explore the stars and create a new and better humanity.

Ann Petry, "The Novel as Social Criticism" (1950), African American Literary Criticism, 1773-2000 (Hazel Arnett Ervin, Ed.):

How should Uncle Tom's Cabin, Germinal, and Mary Barton be classified? As proletarian litera-ture? If Gentleman's Agreement is a problem novel what is Daniel Deronda? Jack London may be a proletarian writer but his most famous book The Call of the Wild is an adventure story. George Sand has been called one of the founders of the 'problem' novel but the bulk of her output dealt with those bourgeois emotions: love and passion. I think one of the difficulties here is the refusal to recognize and admit the fact that not all of the concern about the shortcomings of society originated with Marx. Many a socially conscious novelist is merely a man or woman with a conscience. Though part of the cultural heritage of all of us derives from Marx, whether we subscribe to the Marxist theory or not, a larger portion of it stems from the Bible...

Alex Comfort, The Novel and Our Time (1948):

I am assuming without argument that whatever the writer's conception of art, he writes to interpret something to somebody – in other words, he has a subject and an audience, and his problem is to bring them into contact, by making his own experi-ence comprehensible" (10).

Because of the involvement of the novel form with the entire structure of Westernism, beside and in which it has developed, its history is the history of a continuous movement to the present point, the point at which the writer is completely divested of any literary disguises, at which his success or fail-ure depends on his power of comprehension as much as on his power of imaginative creation. The period of early industrialism and the rise of social-ism coincided closely with the period at which conscious insight into history began to be a prime qualification for the novelist, and the novel itself reached its greatest heights in the hands of those writers who were capable of fulfilling those condi-tions before they became inescapable... To see the whole process we need to look at France and Rusia, but in English literature alone there is a well-marked turning point in Dickens and Thackeray. Before them, narration, style, humour, and a sense of magnitudes qualify a novel for major achieve-ment; after them, the criterion is an increasingly responsible understanding of social and historical events...

The responsible writer sees everyone naked, and is as naked himself. He is not devoid of political and moral judgments, but he makes them equally. In reading, therefore, ask: Is this writer capable of recognizing a human being? Is he able to reject the art of diverse weights, for which an act identical in every respect is a heroic but regrettable necessity when done by Our Side and a contemptible atroci-ty when done by Their Side? Is his judgment of hu-man decisions level or weighted: does he know filth from food, whatever the wrapper? If he does, he is capable of being a great artist under barbar-ianism, and if not, he is another part of barbarism made manifest (24-26).

Writers who publically underrate the temptation of money are certainly not proof against concrete of-fers in nine cases out of ten, and the collapse of fiction-writers one after another into acquiescence is even more depressing than it would be if state cen-sorship prevented anyone non-acquiesant from be-ing printed openly.... The mechanics of the [cor-porate publishing] situation make it almost inevi-table that it should be the writer's first book which is the best, the others representing downward degrees of conformity.... (29-30).

When readers accuse novelists of possessing a bloodshot style, they need to be aware of the vast inflation which has taken place both in the curren-cy and the appreciation of violence. The normal nineteenth-century intensificatories have been in-flated out of existence in advertising puffs and in hysterical reportage, and to present normality to a public whose pity is equally choked by custom of fell deeds is a matter of achieving shock-effect (45).

We have a tedious mass of books by lunatics who think they are psychologists and by neurotics who think they are lunatics. The literary magazines are full of the praises of schizophrenia (58).

Whether we [novelists] are able to influence human conduct will depend very largely upon the number of people in a given asocial society who react by rational aggression towards that society rather than by irrational aggression towards their fellow indi-viduals. The social role of the novel will depend very largely, in coming years, upon the persistence of sufficient rationally disobedient individuals to make novel-writing of the kind I have described possible.

While interpretation rather than an attempt to convince is the chief object of art, the novel is more apt than any other literary form to exert direct pressure upon the growth and forming of ideas, and it will do so whether we intend that or not…. Because of the essential humanity which a writer must possess to write major novels, I am confident that it will play a large part in the events which precede the end of asociality, and should it pass out of currency as a form, it will be replaced by the unanimous literature of tyranny or the spontane-ous social literature of a free society, depending upon how far its readers are able to share and im-bibe the responsibility of its best practitioners (80).

Eugene Almazov, "The 'Tendentious' in Literature" Mainstream magazine (1947):

The question, then, is not whether a writer is, or is not, tendentious; but rather what are the tendencies he follows. The antagonists of tendentious art in modern literature are people who remain aloof from the questions occupying the mind of our disturbed world. They are indifferent to the fate of the millions who want bread, work and conditions which will enable them to find delight in the beautiful.

S. Finkelstein, "National Art and Universal Art" Mainstream magazine (1947):

In its lesser, as well as its greater achievements, the national art of the nineteenth and twentieth century had qualities which made it a powerful force opposed to the art-for-art's sake neo-classicism and the individualistic, anti-social, pessimistic and introspective individualism which dominated so much of the art of the times. One of these qualities was a vitality which came from the entrance into this art of the masses of people, through a language which they themselves have helped fashion. This quality may be seen in the sheer abundance of human beings who fill the pages of Dickens, Mark Twain and Gorky….

With the masses of people there entered into this art their philosophy of life, a realistic acceptance of the world reaffirmed in the face of its multitude of hardships. And so if we find irony and protest in the work of these folk-inspired and national artists, we also find the most full-throated laughter…great comic artists in complete contrast to the romantics' emphasis on the "man alone," his pseudo-tragic feeling caused by a self-imposed withdrawal from the real world.

Still another quality of this art was its imaginative use of whatever materials came to hand. While these artists fought for their integrity as honest artists, against censorship, they did not regard a practical use for their art as an intrusion upon their freedom. It was an intrusion only when its conventions were dictated by a ruling-class forcing its own fears of reality upon the artist. When a new medium for art brought these artists closer to a mass audience, and allowed them to speak honestly with it, the medium itself set their ideas flowing. Thus Goya created his epic history and portrayal of the Spanish people in the etching and lithograph; Daumier did the same for the French people, between the 1830 revolution and the Commune, in the form of the lithograph and newspaper cartoon. Dickens grew on the penny serial, Mark Twain on frontier journalism, the Irish poets and prose artists on the Abbey Theatre.

This national art was and is highly experimental. Its experimental qualities were obscured in the later nineteenth century, when critics were enraptured by the one line of romanticist, impressionist, symbolist and expressionist experiments, the deliberate invention of ambiguities, the probing into dream and the subconscious. It remained for the twentieth century to discover the fresh and truly groundbreaking character of the national movement in the arts, and to carry this movement in the idioms of art the constantly changing aspect of the world and people, the search for new materials and media for art, which led to the scientific analysis of the languages of art, the vast enlightening study of ancient, folk, Asiatic, Indian and African cultures, which has made our own age, in the sheer knowledge of its tools, the most educated in history.

A new obscurantism has appeared in critical theory, clinically discussing the styles of such art with an ignorance of the search for greater realism and power in communication behind it. Whitman's free verse is studied without Whitman's democracy; Picasso's cubism without his humanity; Bartok's polytonality without his folk core. Such tendencies have been fostered by some of the artists themselves, such as Stravinsky and Gertrude Stein, who moved increasingly in their art away from human images and broad emotions, and by the small-minded imitators who far outnumber the genuine creative minds.

The most striking quality of national art is that almost alone among modern art movements it seeks to recreate the epic line. The bourgeoisie, who had raised the epic to such heights when they were battling against feudalism, almost destroyed the epic when faced by the struggles of the working class, fostering every theory that would remove art from a devotion to contemporary history and the fullness of society. The epic, except in false neo-classic imitations, is the study of human beings in terms of history, with human knowledge of nature and of social forces replacing the myths that had served such a function in ancient times....

A national art is one that operates simultaneously on different levels: the small forms of immediate popular impact and daily use, the grand line of the social epic, the scholarly research into the past, the laboratory experiment. It is broad in its base, allowing the richest differentiation among the peoples and localities who make up the nation, and profiting from the wealth of idiom developed by the people through their active participation in cultural life.

The movement for a national art is now faced with the practical problem of having the political space in which to grow. In America, cultural as well as political democracy is under increasing attack by reaction. The artist who hires out his talents is forced to give up his integrity and to work hobbled by the most stifling restrictions of form and content. The great public realms of radio, newspaper, motion picture, magazine and book trade, as important to the public domain as education and food, are increasingly forbidden to artists who want to remain artists and to serve the public as honest masters of the means of human communication. The great areas of the American land, the working class and the national minorities who together make up the majority of Americans, are denied the cultural life through which their artists can grow and develop in home soil, speaking to audiences of their own people, rising in stature (as artists can only rise) through constant living contact with an audience. The great masses of people are robbed of the healthy folk and popular culture which can only come through the restoration of creative participation in art to the people. The growing monopoly of every public form of communication, of the means of production and distribution of art, has produced a grotesque mockery of a national cultural life. Yet the potentialities exist in America for a renaissance unequalled in history.

Today the working class is the leading force in the fight for democracy and for a thriving American nation that will serve the welfare of its people. The struggle of a national culture is part of this struggle for a democratic America, and just as the working class must realize the powerful ally it can have in the artist, so the artist striving to grow as an artist must understand that his ally is the working class. Art is the expression among people of their joy in life, their growth, their understanding and mastery of the world. It is the exchange of their experiences and ideas. The very variety of language and forms a national art can take makes for unity among peoples, for the very depth and insight with which art portrays the unique character of a people gives it the power to transcend national boundaries, becoming a force through which people can better understand one another, work together and build a world without exploitation of human beings and wars among states.

Philip S. Foner, The Social Writings of Jack London (1947):

'No American writer,' said Fred Lewis Patee of Jack London, 'has had a career more representative of his time.' To this one should add that no Ameri-can writer was a more articulate and splendid spokesman for his time. For it was Jack London more than any other writer of his day, who broke the ice that was congealing American letters and brought life and literature into a meaningful rela-tion to each other.

The end of the nineteenth century found the na-tion in a state of great social and political unrest. It found expression in the rise of the labor movement, furious battles between labor and capital, and the political conflict between farmers, workers and small businessmen on one hand and the powerful monopolies on the other. Yet throughout this turb-ulent period there was a curious dichotomy be-tween literature and life…

Beginning with Rebecca Harding Davis' 'Life in the Iron Mills' in The Atlantic of April, 1861, proba-bly the earliest treatment of the lives of industrial workers that approached realism, American fiction since the Civil War had occasionally piped a rather feeble note of social criticism…

Upon this scene stepped several young writers who at the turn of the century blazed new trails in American literature. Influenced by the European naturalistic and realistic tradition, and conscious of the growing class conflicts in their own country, they resolved to introduce into the thin, pale, bloodless, sentimental, insipid writing of the day, themes, characters and styles which were reflec-tions of American life itself….

The new trend in American literature made its debut with the publication at the author's expense of Stephen Crane's *Maggie: A Girl of the Streets* in 1893. Six years later, Frank Norris, a devoted disci-ple of Emile Zola, laid the plans for his "Epic of Wheat…

Crane and Norris were the pioneers of realism in modern American literature, but their writings did not reflect the most important issue confronting the American people in their day – the furious battle between capital and labor…

But another American writer was emerging who was interested not only in exposing cruelties and oppressions in the economic system, but in remak-ing it and building a new and better social order. This was Jack London. Like Crane and Norris he was a realist, but unlike them he was also a social-ist, and from his belief in Marxism as a philosophy of history he drew the ability to describe, better than any of his predecessors or his contemporaries and most of those who followed him, the modern social struggle out of which would inevitably come the regeneration of mankind…

London knew of the life of which he wrote; knew how workers lived and talked and how to transfer the details of their lives to the printed page with amazing fidelity. And the workers read this writing, and reread it and passed it along until the pages were shredded…

February of 1908 saw the book published which brought lasting fame to London's name the world over, *The Iron Heel*, a rare and prophetic novel…the most revolutionary novel in American literature… With an amazing insight into the mechanism of the capitalist system, London was able to catch tenden-cies in motion in modern society which went un-noticed by most of his socialist colleagues…

The Iron Heel is the name that London gives to the oligarchy of American capitalists who seized power when there was danger of a socialist victory at the polls…

The book met with instant derision by the maj-ority of the critics. The *Indianapolis News* was one of the few papers to praise it. 'Power is certainly the keynote of this book,' it said.

'Every word tingles with it; it is so strong that it is almost brutal... The lift of the book sweeps the reader to his feet; it con-tains a mighty les-son and a most impressive warn-ing.' Elsewhere the book was denounced as reck-less sensation-alism, dishonest, a dull tract mas-querading as a novel. *The Dial* declared that 'such books as this...have a mischievous influence upon un-balanced minds, and we cannot but deplore their multiplication.' *The Independent* concluded that 'semi-barbarians, to whom this sort of stuff appeals, may possibly tear down our civiliza-tion; they will never lay a single brick of a no-bler civiliz-ation.' *The Outlook* summed up the viewpoint of the press with the observation: '...as a work of fiction it has little to commend it, and as a socialist tract it is distinctly uncon-vincing.

The socialists were divided in their reactions. The more militant leaders like Eugene Debs, Bill Haywood and Mary Marcy praised it unstint-ingly and urged that its lessons be taken to heart by the entire movement. But the middle class leaders of the Party were even more vehement in their de-nunciations than the bourgeois crit-ics... (3-96).

George Orwell, "The Freedom of the Press" (1943) (Excerpt from suppressed preface to Animal Farm):

The sinister fact about literary censorship in Eng-land is that it is largely voluntary. Unpopu-lar ideas can be silenced, and inconvenient facts kept dark, without the need for any official ban... The British press is extremely centralized, and most of it is owned by wealthy men who have every motive to be dishonest on certain important topics. But the same kind of veiled censorship also operates in books and periodi-cals, as well as in plays, films and radio. At any given moment there is an ortho-doxy, a body of ideas which it is assumed that all right-thinking people will accept without question. It is not ex-actly forbidden to say this, that or the other, but it is 'not done' to say it, just as in mid-Victorian times it was 'not done' to mention trouser in the presence of a lady. Anyone who challenges the prevailing orthodoxy finds himself silenced with surprising effectiveness. A genuinely un-fash-ionable opinion is almost never given a fair hear-ing, either in the popular press or in the highbrow periodicals.

Alfred Kazin, On Native Grounds: An Interpretation of Modern American Prose Literature (1942):

Our modern literature was rooted in those dark and still little-understood years of the 1880's and 1890's when all America stood sud-denly, as it were, between one society and an-other, one moral order and another, and the sense of impending change became almost op-pressive in its vividness. It was rooted in the drift to the new world of factories and cities, with their dissolution of old standards and faiths; in the emergence of the met-ropolitan culture that was to dominate the litera-ture of the new period; in the Populists who raised their voices against the domineering new pluto-cra-cy in the East and gave so much of their bit-terness to the literature of protest rising out of the West; in the sense of surprise and shock that led to the crudely expectant Utopian literature of the eighties and nineties, the largest single body of Utopian writing in modern times, and the most transparent in its nostalgia. But above all was it rooted in the need to learn what the reality of life was in the modern era. In a word, our modern literature came out of those great critical years of the late nine-teenth century which saw the emergence of modern America, and was molded in its struggles ... We live in a day when the brilliance of some of our critics seems to me equaled only by their bar-barism. In my study in Chapter XIV of the twin fanati-cisms that have sought to dominate criticism in America since 1930 – the purely sociological and the purely textual-'esthetic' approach – I have traced some of the underlying causes for the aridi-ty, the snobbery, the sheer human insensi-tiveness that have weighted down so much of the most seri-ous criticism of our day...

[On the other hand, literary critic Edmund Wil-son's] capacity for exposition was such that as he presented it the mere summary of a novel seemed to draw light at every point...

Roger Dataller, The Plain Man and the Novel (1940):

The propaganda novel is quite simply a story with a purpose. Not that every novel may not be inter-preted as a story with a purpose; but there are some authors whose educative mission burns so ardently within them that it becomes impossible to consider any kind of writing save that of direct en-treaty. There is little masking of the challenge. The banners flutter, the trumpets blare. The slogan flies to its appointed target. 'And now, men and women of America,' cries Mrs. Beecher Stowe, at the con-clusion of Uncle Tom's Cabin, 'is this [slavery] a thing to be trifled with, apologized for, and passed over in silence? Farmers of Massachusetts, of New Hampshire, of Vermont, of Connecticut, who read this book by the blaze of your winter-evening fire; strong-hearted, generous sailors and shipowners of Maine – is this a thing for you to countenance and encourage?' Such is the voice of the authentic prop-agandist. The pointed moral, and a tale adorned thereby...

It would be erroneous to suppose, however, that every type of propagandist found a field so favour-able for opportunity as Mrs. Harriet Beecher Stowe. All too often in history the re-former has been com-pelled to clothe his meaning in parable and allegor-y. This was Rabelais's method in dealing with the corruption of the mediaeval Church, and that of Swift and Vol-taire with the vileness of eighteenth-century government. The heavy-witted saw only the facile story: the man of critical intelligence the rapier point beneath...

The propaganda story, then, from sheer pres-sure of events, may shape itself to the half-concealed, the oblique approach. Perhaps the most famous exam-ple of this method is to be found in Nicolai Gogol's Dead Souls. Primarily, Dead Souls is as much con-cerned with the problem of chattel slavery as Uncle Tom's Cabin; but Gogol's treatment is as far re-moved from that of Mrs. Harriet Beecher Stowe as the timber profusion of eighteenth-century Mos-cow from the primly ordered architecture of Hart-ford, Connecticut...

How many real Socialists did [Upton Sin-clair's] The Jungle make? It is difficult to say. Very few in-deed, if municipal elections be-tween 1906 and 1936 count for anything. But perhaps the sum total of literary influence can-not be assessed by the mathe-matical habit. That Charles Dickens assisted the reform of the Poor Law, and Charles Reade that of the Victorian prison system, is undeniable; but ex-act meas-urement is beyond the reach of even the most ardent of social investigators. Such novels in-fluence; but downright conversion is another mat-ter. It is doubtful indeed if a novel of propaganda ever really converted anyone. That it may empha-size an atmosphere in which con-version becomes possible is perhaps as far as the Plain Man would care to go (35-46).

Kenneth Burke, "Literature as Equipment for Living," The Philoso-phy of Literary Form 1939):

Here I shall put down, as briefly as possi-ble, a statement in behalf of what might be catalogued, with a fair degree of accuracy, as a sociological criticism of literature. Sociological criticism is cer-tainly not new. I shall try to suggest what partial-ly new elements or em-phasis I think should be added to this old ap-proach. And to make the 'way in' as easy as possible, I shall begin with a discussion of proverbs. Examine random speci-mens in The Oxford Dictionary of English Prov-erbs. You will note, I think, that there is no 'pure' litera-ture here. Everything is 'medicine.' Proverbs are designed for consolation or vengeance, for ad-monition or exhortation, for foretelling (253).

Kenneth Burke, "The Nature of Art Under Capitalism," The Philosophy of Literary Form (1939):

The present article proposes to say some-thing further on the subject of art and propa-ganda. It will attempt to set forth a line of rea-soning as to why the contemporary emphasis must be placed largely upon propaganda, rather than upon 'pure' art... Since pure art makes for acceptance, it tends to become a social menace in so far as it assists us in tolerating the intolerable. And if it leads us to a state of acquiescence at a time when the very basis of moral integration is in question, we get a paradox whereby the soundest adjunct to ethics, the aesthetic, threatens to uphold an unethical condition. For this reason it seems that under conditions of competitive capitalism there must necessarily be a large corrective or propa-ganda element in art. Art cannot safely confine itself to merely *using* the values which arise out of a given social texture and integrating their con-flicts, as the soundest, 'purest' art will do. It must have a definite hortatory function, an educational element of suasion or inducement; it must be par-tially *forensic*. Such a quality we consider to be the essential work of propaganda. Hence we feel that the moral breach arising from vitiation of the work-patterns calls for a propaganda art. And incidentally, our distinction as so stated should make it apparent that much of the so-called 'pure' art of the nineteenth century was of a pronoun-cedly propagandist or corrective coloring. In pro-portion as the conditions of economic warfare grew in intensity throughout the 'century of progress,' and the church proper gradually adapted its doctrines to serve merely the protection of private gain and the upholding of manipulated law, the 'priestly' function was carried on by the 'secular' poets, often avowedly agnostic.

Our thesis is by no means intended to imply that 'pure' art or 'acquiescent' art should be aban-doned. There are two kinds of 'toleration.' Even if a given state of affairs is found, on intellectualist-ic grounds, to be intolerable, the fact remains that as long as it is with us we must more or less con-trive to 'tolerate' it. Even though we might prefer to alter radically the present structure of produc-tion and distribution through the profit motive, the fact remains that we cannot so alter it forth-with. Hence, along with our efforts to alter it, must go the demand for an imaginative equip-ment that helps to make it tolerable while it lasts. Much of the 'pure' or acquiescent art of today

serves this invaluable psychological end. For this reason the great popular comedians or handsome movie stars are rightly the idols of the people. Likewise the literature of senti-mentality, however annoying and self-deceptive it may seem to the hardened 'intel-lectual,' is following in a direction basically so sound that one might wish more of our pre-tentious authors were attempting to do the same thing more pretentiously. On the other hand, much of the harsh literature now being turned out in the name of the 'proletariat' seems inadequate on either count. It is ques-tionable as propaganda, since it shows us so little of the qualities in mankind worth saving. And it is questionable as 'pure' art, since by substituting a cult of disaster for a cult of amenities it 'promotes our acquiescence' to sheer dismalness. Too often, alas, it serves as a mere device whereby the neur-oses of the de-caying bourgeois structure are sim-ply trans-ferred to the symbols of workingmen. Perhaps more of Dickens is needed, even at the risk of excessive tearfulness (271-278).

Bernard Smith, Forces in American Criticism (1939):

Socialist criticism in America may conveni-ently be dated from the founding of the *Comrade* – 'An Illus-trated Socialist Monthly' – in 1901... The Comrade appeared at the beginning of the muckrake era. It was superior to the muckrakers in the clarity of its vision as to the basic cause of social evils and the way to cure them... The aims of socialist critics were propagandistic, and it was inevitable that they should be paramount in a time when Ameri-can critical systems were divided between art for art's sake, art for mo-rality's sake, and various com-promises be-tween those two exhausted theories of esthetic purpose.[28] Consider the essays and lec-tures on

---

[28] 'Propaganda' is not used here as an invidious term. It is used to describe works consciously written to have an im-mediate and direct effect upon their readers' opinions and actions, as distinguished from works that are not con-sciously written for that purpose or which are written to have a re-mote and indirect effect. It is possible that conven-tional crit-ics have learned by now that to call a literary work 'propa-ganda' is to say nothing about its quality as lit-

the contemporary theatre by the anarchist Emma Goldman. Miss Goldman made no bones about her intentions. Her essay on 'The Modern Drama' in *Anarchism and Other Essays* (1911) was frankly a salute to its subject as an instrument for the dissemination of radical thought...

The socialist's affinity with realism was stated forcefully in the leading editorial of the Masses in February 1911 – the second issue of a magazine... which was a successor, on a more mature and 'pol-iticalized' level, to the Comrade. It said: 'It is natur-al that Socialists should favor the novel with a pur-pose, more especially, the novel that points a So-cialist moral. As a reaction against the great bulk of vapid, meaningless, too-clever American fiction, with its artificial plots and characters remote from ac-tual life, such an attitude is a healthy sign...'(289-292).

Its militancy is the most obvious character-istic of American criticism since the war. In the whole of nineteenth century there was only one critic, Poe, who was deliberately and consis-tently disputa-tious. No one else made polemics the basis of a crit-ical method. Whitman was a maverick, but he was exclamatory rather than argumentative. Now how-ever, it is customary for critics to be bellicose, and there are few who have let politeness stand in the way of contro-versy. The reason is not hard to find. Criticism in our time has been largely a war of traditions – a struggle between irreconcilable ideologies... (302).

The academy was growing up. It was begin-ning to share the emotions of serious adults who were try-ing to adjust themselves to an America become rich and imperialistic. In its own special field, literary history, it was begin-ning to achieve mature and realistic interpreta-tions. In 1927 it came of age: V. L. Parrington, professor of English at the University of Wash-ington, published the two completed vol-umes of his *Main Currents in American Thought*. With that work the academy was at last brought face to face with the ideas, sentiments, and his-

torical methods of today... Parrington's *Main Cur-rents* arrived to supply the most needed things: an account of our literary history which squared with recent works on the history of our people and a realistic technique for analyzing the relationship of a writer to his time and place – in addition to a mil-itantly progressive spirit. Professorial and literary circles had consciously been waiting for such a work, and if the one that did come forth was far more radical than some people cared for, it simply could not be rejected. The author was a professor too; his scholarship defied scrutiny; and his ideas were couched in terms that were native American, most of them having come over shortly after the Mayflower. One must emphasize Parrington's radi-calism because it is probably the most significant as-pect of his work. He sharpened, gave point to the economic interpretation of literary move-ments because of his desire to reveal the moti-vating interests and real direction of specific works of literature... (330-331).

There was one critic who apparently pos-sessed all the virtues – fine taste, poetic sensi-tiveness, intel-lectuality, an experimental incli-nation. His literary scholarship was beyond dis-pute, his writing deft and memorable. He was, moreover, a poet of the first rank, which gave his criticism of the art an ex-traordinary auth-ority. He was universally respect-ted: by Pound, by the later expatriates, by the im-presssionists of the *Dial*, by the *Hound and Horn* group. This critic was T. S. Eliot. His volume of essays, *The Sacred Wood*, published in 1920, is still con-sidered to be one of the truly distinguished works of esthetic criticism produced in this cen-tury... The reader will note that he is here de-scribed in the past tense. His works are many now, but *The Sacred Wood* alone is a consider-ation of esthetic problems. In the rest the em-phasis is on the esthetic effects of moral and social beliefs. His development is one of the 'consequences' touched upon in the following chapter... (358-359).

[T.S. Eliot wrote,] 'There are two and only two fin-ally tenable hypotheses about life: the Catholic and the materialistic [i.e., Marxist]. It is quite possible, of course, that the future may bring neither a Chris-tian nor a materialistic

---

erature. By now enough critics have pointed out that some of the world's classics were originally 'propaganda' for something.

civilization. It is quite possi-ble that the future may be nothing but chaos or tor-por. In that event, I am not interested in the future; I am only interested in the two alternatives which seem to me worthier of interest....' Eliot chose not only the Catholic hypothesis, but also its po-litical corollaries. His literary opinions were thus given a firm philosophical base to rest upon, and from that fact he drew the reasonable conclusions ... [that] 'Literary criticism should be completed by criticism from a definite ethical and theological standpoint. In so far as in any age there is common agreement on ethical and theological matters, so far can liter-ary criticism be substantive. In ages like our own, in which there is no such common agreement, it is then more necessary for Christian readers to scruti-nize their reading, especially of works of im-agina-tion, with explicit ethical and theological stand-ards. The 'greatness' of literature cannot be deter-mined solely by literary standards; though we must remember that whether it is lit-erature or not can be determined only by liter-ary standards.' To this has esthetic criticism at last come – to a realiza-tion that non-esthetic cri-teria are the ultimate tests of value. Whether they be called philosophical, moral, or social cri-teria, they are still the ideas that men have about the way human beings live togeth-er and the way they ought to live. The quest of beauty had become the quest of reality. It had become, in essence, literary criticism as socially conscious and as polemical as the criticism of the Marx-ists...

Eliot spoke of alternatives, not of choices... He be-lieves that one of the alternatives has greater value, is nobler, is in a sense more real, than the other. The question is therefore not simply one of person-al taste. It is a question of evidence and reason. But the alternative he fa-vors admits of no evidence and derogates from reason. His philosophy is, in the last analysis, wholly mystical. It is not capable of being tested and verified and improved. The alter-native he rejects is, on the other hand, the one that is fa-vored by those who are determined to be as sci-entific as one can be in a non-physical field. The literary criticism of the neo-classicists is a criti-cism composed of obiter dicta inspired by in-tangible emotions. The literary criticism of the materialists stands or falls by the findings of the social scient-ists, psychologists, and historians. Eliot's alterna-tive involves a revulsion against democracy; the materialists are partisans of de-mocracy. The liter-ary criticism of his school tends to create a litera-ture that will express the sensibilities and experi-ences of a few fortunate men. The criticism of the opposing school tends to create a literature that will express the ideals and sympathies of those who look forward to the conquest of poverty, ig-norance, and in-equality – to the material and intel-lectual eleva-tion of the mass of mankind.

To whom does the future belong? In January 1939 Eliot announced that the Criterion, the lit-erary journal he had edited since 1922, would no longer be published. His Europe had crum-bled; the cul-ture in which he had put his faith was dying. The Criterion had served its pur-pose. Eliot had arrived at a mood of detach-ment. There was nothing he could hopefully fight for now. But those who be-lieve in scien-tific methods, in realism, in social equality and democracy, are hopeful and are fight-ing (384-387).

T. K. Whipple, "Literature as Action" Study Out the Land (1939):

Perhaps we are most accustomed nowadays to considering a book in terms of its author: we ask how it expresses his personality, or how it illustrates the age to which he belonged. But I suggest that the primary question should be, "What is its relation to us, to its living readers?" There is nothing novel in this question: "What does literature do to and for its readers?" is the stock question of all classical criticism. But I wish to go a little further, beyond the effect on the isolated individual reader, and to inquire whether the most important thing about a book is, not its relation to some past age in which it was produced, but rather its relation to the pre-sent age in which it is read. I ask you for a while to think of literature as a living force acting on the present world – that is, as a form of social action

We should expect, should we not, to care

most for those books which best meet our most vital needs – that is, the most vital needs of the present world? But what are they? You can hardly get two people to agree. One of the commonest answers might be, "Need of values" – that is, of something to care about and to live for. And there is much in this answer, but I think we shall arrive at a better solution if, instead of seeking it in the individual's mind, we look outside, at society, where we find the individual's difficulties written large in social conflicts. My own explanation would be that the present is a time of unusual and profound social disharmony, which I would explain thus.

In most respects society has become collective, tightly knit together, every member closely interdependent on every other, most of our undertakings and activities involving vast cooperation. But in certain respects it has remained individualistic, notably in control or power, in certain aspects of our property system, and above all in the distribution of profits. The crux of the situation, then, as I see it, is the struggle between two societies, the old individualistic one which is dying, and the new rising collective one which is growing stronger and stronger. But because of the inertia or cultural lag our minds belong largely to the past; mentally we are incorrigible individualists. Many of us can no longer accept the old values; but neither have we accepted the new. Here, I admit, is a guess in the dark – but if we looked for our satisfaction in successful social functioning, might we not feel the lack of values less acutely? Only – how is one to attain successful social functioning in the existing state of affairs?

You may wonder what these questions have to do with literature. For is not literature a fine art, and does it not therefore lift us out of the turmoil into a serener air? Is it not a form of contemplation, disinterested and detached? In a way, I think it is, sometimes, a kind of disinterested contemplation, though I doubt whether it is detached. And is not the fruit of contemplation sooner or later to issue in action? A detached contemplation of human struggle, wrong, and suffering, with a secret smile of aesthetic pleasure at the spectacle, may befit the gods, but surely it is too godlike an attitude to befit mere human beings.

Literature does act upon us, in a thousand ways. Among other things, it affirms values; writers make us care about things, feel about them, as they do…. One of the functions of literature as of all the arts is too often overlooked: the communication of power, the enhancement of energy. It leaves us more alive, stronger; we feel that virtue has come into us. This heightening of vitality or increase of life accounts in large measure for the joy and delight that art gives us. But the point I wish to stress is that literature not only gives us this augmented power, but, by the values it asserts, directs it. All good writers do this, but most of them act only on part, often a small part, of one; the best or greatest, however, act so upon all of one, on the whole man. They heighten and harmonize and direct our power to think, to feel, to imagine – and to will and to act. They intensify and enlarge our consciousness and awareness. And they do all this to us not as isolated individuals only, but as social beings, for by their own awareness of personal and social relations they enhance ours….

The cults of hedonism, of escape, of isolated individualism, or of no values, of futility, despair, are all denials of the whole man; even the best of them, the cult of detached and disinterested contemplation, is so, if we believe that the man who does not act is incomplete. If there is anything in my guess that our most vital need is to adapt ourselves to the new rising collective side of society and to find our satisfaction in successful social functioning, it would seem to follow that the best literature for us is that which not only most heightens our energy, but which also brings the whole man into play, into action, as a social being. For the following reasons.

The major conflict of our time, I said, is between two groups of forces. The first, which is still in control and rules our world, derives from the economic individualism of the past: it is based upon the principle of the survival of the fittest in the struggle for profits. Because they belong to the past, these forces resist change; they are forces of reaction and repression. In literature, any of the many cults of inaction plays into their hands. But, above all, these forces are allied with the literary cult of violence, force, cruelty, and death, the cult of instinctive action, of unconsciousness, which opposes rational thinking and human feelings and positive social functioning; the cult of incompleteness and self-mutilation.

The other group of forces, which derives from the collective side of our society, the rising, growing, but not yet dominant side, is directed rather toward the future and toward progressive social cooperative activity. It stresses, not the fight of individuals for profits, but rather the importance of social function with suitable reward. Because it is constructive and not repressive, this side needs all the knowledge and thought and awareness it can get, and, because it is not in control, all the disciplined will leading to vigorous social action. It can use and must get the whole man, at his best.

In this great conflict impartiality is impossible and undesirable. Any man who denies the acquisitive values – and who was ever so blind as to go into literature as teacher, critic, or poet with the hope of piling up profits? – anyone who aims at wholeness, or who would like to play a positive role and function in society to the best of his ability, must choose the second side. Therefore the best literature for us is the sort that best conditions us to do so....

Edmund Wilson, "The Historical Interpretation of Literature" (1938), The Triple Thinkers (1948):

I want to talk about the historical interpretation of literature – that is, about the interpretation of litera-ture in its social, economic and political aspects. To begin with, it will be worth while to say something about the kind of criticism which seems to be fur-thest removed from this. There is a comparative criticism which tends to be non-historical. The es-says of T. S. Eliot, which have had such an im-mense influence in our time, are, for example, fundamentally non-historical. Eliot sees, or tries to see, the whole of literature, so far as he is acquainted with it, spread out before him under the aspect of eternity...

Another example of this kind of non-historical crit-icism, in a somewhat different way and on a some-what different plane, is the work of the late George Saintsbury. Saintsbury was a connoisseur of wines; he wrote an enter-taining book on the subject...

There is, however, another tradition of criticism which dates from the beginning of the eighteenth century. In the year 1725, the Neapolitan philoso-pher Vico published La Scienz Nuova, a revolu-tionary work on the philoso-phy of history, in which he asserted for the first time that the social world was certainly the work of man, and attempt-ted what is, so far as I know, the first social inter-pretation of a work of literature...

In the field of literary criticism, this historical point of view came to its first complete flower in the work of the French critic Taine, in the middle of the nineteenth century. The whole school of historian-critics to which Taine belonged – Michelet, Renan, Sainte-Beuve – had been occupied in interpreting books in terms of their historical origins. But Taine was the first of these to attempt to apply such prin-ciples systematically and on a large scale in a work devoted exclusively to literature. In the *Introduction to his History of English Literature*, published in 1863, he made his famous pronouncement that works of literature were to be understood as the upshot of three interfusing factors: *the moment, the race and the milieu...*

To Taine's set of elements was added, dating from the middle of the century, a new element, the econ-omic, which was introduced into the discussion of historical phenomena mainly by Marx and Engels. The non-Marxist critics them-selves were at the time already taking into ac-count the influence of the so-cial classes.... But Marx and Engels derived the so-cial classes from the way that people made or got their liv-ings – from what they called the *methods of production*; and they tended to regard these econ-omic processes as fundamental to civilization.

The insistence that the man of letters should play a political role, the disparagement of works of art in comparison with political action, where thus ori-ginally no part of Marxism. They only became as-sociated with it later. This happened by way of Russia, and it was due to the special tendencies in that country that date from long before the Revolu-ion or the promulgation of Marxism itself. In Rus-sia there have been very good reasons why the political implications of literature should particularly occupy the critics. The art of Pushkin itself, with its marvelous power of implication, had certainly been partly created by the censorship of Nicholas I, and Pushkin set the tradition for most of the great Russian writers that followed him. Every play, every poem, every story, must be a parable of which the moral is implied. If it were stated, the censor would suppress the book as he tried to do with Pushkin's Bronze Horseman, where it was merely a question of the packed implica-tions protruding a little too plainly. Right down through the writings of Chekhov and up almost to the Revolution, the imaginative literature of Russia presents the peculiar paradox of an art that is technically objective and yet charged with social messages. In Russia under the Tsar, it was inevitable that social criticism should lead to political conclusions, because the most urgent need form the point of view of any kind of im-provement was to get rid of the tsarist regime. Even the neo-Christian moralist Tolstoy, who pretended to be nonpolitical, was to exert a subversive influence…. Even after the Revolu-tion had destroyed the tsarist government, this state of things did not change…

In my view, all our intellectual activity, in whatev-er field it takes place, is an attempt to give a mean-ing to our experience – that is, to make life more practicable; for by understand-ing things we make it easier to survive and get around among them…

And this brings us back to the historical point of view. The experience of mankind on the earth is always changing as man develops and has to deal with new combinations of ele-ments; and the writer who is to be anything more than an echo of his predecessors must al-ways find expression for something which has never yet been expressed, must master a new set of phenomena which has never yet been mastered…

James T. Farrell, A Note on Literary Criticism (1936):

Literature must be viewed both as a branch of the fine arts and as an instrument of social in-fluence…. I suggest that the formula 'All art is propaganda' be replaced by another: 'Literature is an instrument of social influence…'. [Litera-ture] can be propagan-da…and it can some-times perform an objective so-cial function that approaches agitation.

Joseph Freeman, Proletarian Literature in the United States (1935):

To characterize an essay or a book as a politi-cal pamphlet is neither to praise nor to condemn it…. In the case of the liberal critic, however, we have a political pamphlet which pretends to be something else. We have an attack on the theory of art as a political weapon which turns out to be itself a pol-itical weapon…

Michael Gold "Gertrude Stein: A Literary Idiot" New Masses (1935):

In essence, what Gertrude Stein's work rep-resents is an example of the most extreme sub-jectivism of the contemporary bourgeois artist, and a reflection of the ideological anarchy into which the whole of bourgeois literature has fallen.

What was it that Gertrude Stein set out to do with literature? When one reads her work it ap-pears to resemble the monotonous gibberings of paranoiacs in the private wards of asylums. It ap-pears to be a deliberate irrationality, a delib-erate infantilism. However, the woman's not in-sane, but possessed of a strong, clear, shrewd mind. She was an excellent medical student, a brilliant psycholog-ist, and in her more "popu-lar" writings one sees evidence of wit and some wisdom.

And yet her works read like the literature of the students of padded cells in Matteawan.

Example: "I see the moon and the moon sees me. God bless the moon and God bless me and this you see remember me. In this way one fifth of the bana-nas were bought."

The above is supposed to be a description of

how Gertrude Stein feels when she sees Matisse, the French modernist painter. It doesn't make sense. But this is precisely what it is supposed to do – not "make sense" in the normal meaning of the term…

A leisure class, which exists on the labor of oth-ers, which has no function to perform in so-ciety except the clipping of investment coupons, develops ills and neuroses. It suffers perpetually from boredom. Their life is stale to them. Taste-less, inane, because it has no meaning. They seek new sen-sations, new adventures con-stantly in order to give themselves feelings.

The same process took place with the artists of the leisure class. Literature also bored them. They tried to suck out of it new sensations, new adven-tures.

They destroyed the common use of language. Normal ways of using words bored them. They wished to use words in a new, sensational fash-ion. They twisted grammar, syntax. They went in for primitive emotions, primitive art. Blood, violent death, dope dreams, soul-writhings, be-came the themes of their works.

In Gertrude Stein, art became a personal plea-sure, a private hobby, a vice. She did not care to communicate because essentially there was nothing to communicate. She had no responsi-bility except to her own inordinate cravings. She became the priestess of a cult with strange liter-ary rites, with mystical secrets…

Marxists…see in the work of Gertrude Stein ex-treme symptoms of the decay of capitalist culture. They view her work as the complete at-tempt to an-nihilate all relations between the artist and the so-ciety in which he lives…

Is there not an "idle art" just as there is an "idle rich"? Both do nothing but cultivate the insanity of their own desires, both cultivate strange indulgen-ces. The literary idiocy of Gertrude Stein only re-flects the madness of the whole system of capitalist values. It is part of the signs of doom that are writ-ten largely eve-rywhere on the walls of bourgeois society…

John Dewey, Art as Experience (1934):

The moral office and human function of art can be intelligently discussed only in context of cul-ture. A particular work of art may have a definite effect upon a particular person or upon a number of persons. The social effect of the novels of Dick-ens or of Sinclair Lewis is far from negligible. But a less conscious and more massed constant ad-justment of experi-ence proceeds from the total environment that is created by the collective art of a time… (344).

The theories that attribute direct moral ef-fect and intent to art fail because they do not take account of the collective civilization that is the context in which works of art are pro-duced and enjoyed. I would not say that they tend to treat works of art as a kind of subli-mated Aesop's fables. But they all tend to ex-tract particular works, regarded as especially edifying, from their milieu and to think of the moral function of art in terms of a strictly per-sonal relation between the selected works and a particular individual. Their whole concep-tion of morals is so individualistic that they miss a sense of the way in which art exercises its humane functions. Matthew Arnold's dic-tum that 'poetry is a criticism of life' is a case in point…(346).

NYT/Diego Rivera, "Row on River Art Still in Deadlock" (1933):

The painter [Diego Rivera], whose subject matter and treatment in other murals for public buildings have provoked numerous disputes on the ground that they set forth ideas too radical for general pop-ular view in what followers of Rivera would call "capitalistic structures", spent a turbulent day giv-ing interviews expressing his indignation and con-sulting with his attor-ney, Philip Wittenberg…. "I refuse to compro-mise", said Rivera. "I will not change my mural even if I lose in the courts. It is a question of the right of the artist to complete his work and have it viewed".

Speaking partly in English and partly through an interpreter, Rivera set forth his views in detail. His fresco, he insisted, was not Communist propagan-da, but the propaganda of the artist for his ideas. The official Commu-nist group, he explained, had criticized both the fresco and himself for his work in collaboration with the Rockefellers...

The painter dwelt on the role of the artist in society in general terms and said he was "like the iceman or delivery boy, and sometimes like the engineer or the expert electrician". He opposed the idea of the artist as apart from the social group and contended that the idea of "art for art's sake" was fostered to "drug" the public by persons profiting by the pres-ent system...

John Sloan, president of the Society of Independent Artists, which first showed Rivera's work here some ten years ago, said he could not overestimate the importance to this country of having Rivera's work here. "In my opinion, Rivera is probably the greatest living mural painter – probably the great-est for several centuries – in the direct line of des-cent from the old masters."

Alon Bement, director of the National Alliance of Art and Industry, who saw the Rivera paintings Tuesday afternoon, said he was disappointed that "so great an artist as Rivera should have been wil-ling to relinquish his fine standing as a mural pain-ter and condescend to become a mere propagan-dist."

V. F. Calverton, The Liberation of American Literature (1932):

Genuine proletarian criticism has seldom sought to deny the importance of literary values because of its desire for social significances. On the contrary, except in the United States, revolutionary critics have often been harder taskmasters from the point of literary quality than aesthetic critics...

The revolutionary critic should demand as much of the art he endorses as the reactionary [critic]. No revolutionary critic, for example, should deny that art in itself, in whatever form, is a trade just as pot-tery-making is, and as a trade it has its technique which has to be mastered if that which is produced is to be worthwhile. Revolutionary art has to be good art first before it can have deep meaning, just as apples in a revolutionary country as well as in a reactionary country have to be good apples before they can be eaten with enjoyment. The fact that the pottery or the apples are the products of a revolu-tionary culture – that is, made or grown by revolu-tionists – does not itself, or by any kind of special magic, make them good. It simply gives them a new form of ideological identification... [Great rev-olutionary] films are great not because they are [only progressive in ideology] but because they are great first in their formal organization, and then greater still because of the social purpose which they serve.

The revolutionary proletarian critic does not aim to underestimate literary craftsmanship. What he contends is simply that literary craftsmanship is not enough. The craftsmanship must be utilized to create objects of revolutionary meaning. Only through this synthesis does the revolutionary critic believe that art can serve its most important pur-pose today. Revolutionary meanings without liter-ary craftsmanship constitute as hopeless a combi-nation from the point of view of the radical critic as literary craftsmanship without revolutionary pur-pose. If proletarian literature fails in so many instances in America, it is not because it is propagandistic – most of the literature of the world has been propagandistic in one way or another, in-cluding even that of William Shakespeare and George Bernard Shaw – but because it is lacking in qualities of craftsmanship.

In a word, the revolutionary critic does not be-lieve that we can have art without craftsmanship; what he does believe is that, granted the craftsman-ship, our aim should be to make art serve man as a thing of action and not man serve art as a thing of escape.

Proletarian writers are not necessarily proletarians ...but they are writers who are imbued with a prol-etarian ideology instead of a bourgeois one. They are writers who have adopted the revolutionary point of view of the proletarian ideology in their work. That often they fail in such expression is in-evitable in a transitional stage of society in which we are living in today. This much should be clear, however, and that is that proletarian writers are not to be confused with literary rebels. Literary reb-els believe in revolt in literature; left-wing, that is proletarian, writers believe in revolt in life. The lit-erary rebels, for example, who became the advo-cates of free verse as opposed to conventional verse must not be associated with proletarian writers, who are opposed to the society in which we live and aim to devote their literature to its trans-forma-tion. Proletarian writers, then, are more interested in social revolt than in literary revolt. As a group they are convinced that present-day industrial so-ciety is based upon exploitation and injustice; that it creates distress and misery for the many and brings happiness only to the few; that its dedica-tion to the ideal of profit instead of use is destruct-ive of everything fine and inspiring in life; and that until its private-property basis is destroyed and replaced by the social control of all property, the human race will never be able to escape the horrors of un-employment, poverty, and war.

More than that, proletarian writers believe that their literature can serve a greater purpose only when it contributes, first, toward the de-struction of present-day society, and, second, toward the crea-tion of a new society which will embody…a social, instead of an individualistic ideal. Unlike Ibsen, they do not ask questions and then refuse to an-swer them. Unlike the iconoclasts, they are not content to tear down the idols and stop there. Their aim is to answer questions as well as ask them, and to provide a new order to replace an old one. Their attitude, therefore, is a positive instead of a nega-tive one (459-462).

Diego Rivera, "The Revolutionary Spirit in Modern Art" Modern Quarterly (1932):

All painters have been propagandists or else they have not been painters. Giotto was a propagandist of the spirit of Christian charity, the weapon of the Franciscan monks of his time against feudal oppression. Breughel was a propagandist of the strug-gle of the Dutch arti-san petty bourgeois against feudal oppression. Every artist who has been worth anything in art has been such a propagandist. The familiar ac-cusation that propaganda ruins art finds its source in bourgeois prejudice. Naturally enough the bourgeoisie does not want art employed for the sake of revolution. It does not want ideals in art because its own ideals cannot any longer serve as artistic inspiration. It does not want feelings because its own feelings cannot any longer serve as artistic inspiration. Art and thought and feeling must be hostile to the bour-geoisie today. Every strong artist has a head and a heart. Every strong artist has been a propa-gandist. I want to be a propagandist and I want to be nothing else. (….) I want to use my art as a weapon.

Diego Rivera, MoMA exhibition (1931):

All art is propaganda. The only difference is the kind of propaganda.

Edmund Wilson, Axel's Castle (1931):

I believe therefore that the time is at hand when these writers, who have largely domi-nated the literary world of the decade 1920-30, though we shall continue to admire them as masters, will no longer serve us as guides. …the private imagina-tion in isolation from the life of society seems to have been exploited and explored as far as for the present is possi-ble. Who can imagine this sort of thing being carried further than Valéry and Proust have done? And who hereafter will be content to inhabit a corner, though fitted out with some choice things of one's own, in the shuttered house of one of these writers – where we find ourselves, also, becoming conscious of a lack of ventilation?

The reaction against nineteenth-century natur-alism which Symbolism originally rep-resented has probably now run its full course, and the oscillation which for at least three cen-turies has been taking place between the poles of objectivity and subjectivity may return to-ward objectivity again: we may live to see Valéry, Eliot and Proust displaced and treated with as much intolerance as those writers – Wells, France and Shaw – whom they have themselves displaced. Yet as surely as Ibsen and Flaubert brought to their Naturalistic plays and novels the sensibility and language of Romanticism, the writers of a new reaction in the direction of the study of man in his relation to his neighbor and to society will profit by the new intelligence and technique of Symbolism. Or – what would be preferable and is perhaps more likely – this oscillation may finally cease. Our conceptions of objective and subjective have unquestionable been based on false dual-isms; our materialisms and ideal-isms alike have been derived from mistaken conceptions of what the researches of science implied – Classicism and Romanticism, Naturalism and Symbolism are, in reality, therefore false alternatives. …our ideas about the 'logic' of language are likely to be very superficial. The relation of words to what they convey – that is, to the processes behind them and the processes to which they give rise in those who listen to or read them – is still a very mysterious one. We tend to assume that being convinced of things is something quite different from having them suggested to us; but the suggestive language of the Symbolist poet is really perform-ing the same sort of function as the reasonable language of the realistic novelist or even the severe technical languages of science (231-234).

Alain Locke, "Art or Propaganda?" (1928) African American Literary Criticism, 1773-2000 (Hazel Arnett Ervin, Ed.):

Propaganda itself is preferable to shallow, truck-ling imitation. Negro things may reasonably be a fad for others; for us they must be a religion. Beauty, however, is its best priest and psalms will be more effective than sermons.

Vernon Louis Parrington, Main Currents in American Thought: An Interpretation of Ameri-can Literature from the Beginnings to 1920 (1927):

I have undertaken to give some account of the gen-esis and development of American letters of certain germinal ideas that have come to be reckoned trad-itionally American – how they came into being here, how they were opposed, and what influence they have exerted in determining the form and scope of our characteristic ideals and institutions. In pursuing such a task, I have chosen to follow the broad path of our political, economic, and social development, rather than the narrower belletristic; and the main divisions of the study have been fixed by forces that are anterior to literary schools and movements, creating the body of ideas from which literary culture eventually springs. The pres-ent volume carries the account from early begin-nings in Puritan new England to the triumph of Jefferson and back-country agrarianism. Volume II concerns itself with the creative influence in Ameri-can of French romantic theories, the rise of capital-ism, and the transition from an agricultural to an industrial order; and Volume III will concern itself with the beginnings of dissatisfaction with the reg-nant middle class, and the several movements of criticism inspired by its reputed shortcomings…

That our colonial literature seems to many readers meagre and uninteresting, that it is commonly squeezed into the skimpiest of chapters in our handbooks of American literature, is due, I think, to an exaggerated regard for esthetic values. Our literary historians have labored under too heavy a handicap of the genteel tradition – to borrow Pro-fessor Santayana's happy phrase – to enter sympa-thetically into a world of masculine intellects and material struggles. They have sought daintier fare than polemics, and in consequence mediocre verse has obscured political speculation, and poetasters have shouldered aside vigorous creative thinkers. The colonial period is meagre and lean only to those whose 'disedged appetites' find no savor in old-fashioned beef and puddings. The seventeenth century in America as well as in England was a *saeculum theologicum*, and the eighteenth century was a *saeculum politicum*. No other path leads so directly and intimately into the heart of those old days as the thorny path of their theological and political controversies; and if one will resolutely pick his way amongst the thorns, he will have his reward in coming close to the men who debated earnestly over the plans and specifications of the Utopia that was to be erected in the free spaces of America, and who however wanting they may have been in the lesser arts, were no mean archi-tects and craftsmen for the business at hand. The foundations of a later America were laid in vigor-ous polemics, and the rough stone was plentifully mortared with idealism. To enter once more into the spirit of those fine old idealisms, and to learn that the promise of the future has lain always in the keeping of liberal minds that were never discour-aged from their dreams, is scarcely a profitless un-dertaking, nor without meaning to those who like Merlin pursue the light of their hopes where it flickers above the treacherous marshlands.

This much is clear [as of 1920]: an industrialized so-ciety is reshaping the psychology fashioned by an agrarian world; the passion for liberty is lessening and the individual, in the presence of creature com-forts, is being dwarfed; the drift of centralization is shaping its inevitable tyrannies to bind us with. Whether the quick concern for human rights, that was the novel bequest of our fathers who had drunk of the waters of French romantic faith, will be carried over into the future, to unhorse the machine that now rides men and to leaven the sodden mass that is industrial America, is a question to which the gods as yet have given no answer. Yet it is not without hope that intelligent America is in revolt. The artist is in revolt, the intellectual is in revolt, the conscience of America is in revolt…

W.E.B. Du Bois, "Criteria of Negro Art" (1926), The Crisis magazine:

…all art is propaganda and ever must be, despite the wailing of the purists. I stand in utter shame-lessness and say that whatever art I have for writ-ing has been used always for propaganda for gain-ing the right of black folk to love and enjoy. I do not care a damn for any art that is not used for propaganda.

Upton Sinclair, Mammonart: An Essay on Economic Interpretation (1924):

The book purposes to investigate the whole process of art creation, and to place the art function in rela-tion to the sanity, health and progress of mankind. It will attempt to set up new canons in the arts, overturning many of the standards now accepted. A large part of the world's art treasures will be tak-en out to the scrap-heap, and a still larger part transferred from the literature shelves to the his-tory shelves of the world's library.

Since childhood the writer has lived most of his life in the world's art. For thirty years he has been studying it consciously, and for twenty-five years he has been shaping in his mind the opinions here recorded; testing and revising them by the art-works which he has produced, and by the stream of other men's work which has flowed through his mind. His decisions are those of a working artist, one who has been willing to experiment and blun-der for himself, but who has also made it his busi-ness to know and judge the world's best achieve-ments.

The conclusion to which he has come is that mankind is today under the spell of utterly false conceptions of what art is and should be; of utterly vicious and perverted standards of beauty and dig-nity. We list six great art lies now prevailing in the world, which this book will discuss:

Lie Number One: the Art for Art's Sake lie; the no-tion that the end of art is in the art work, and that the artist's sole task is perfection of form. It will be demonstrated that this lie is a defensive mechan-ism of artists run to seed, and that its prevalence means degeneracy, not merely in art, but in the so-ciety where such art appears.

Lie Number Two: the lie of Art Snobbery; the no-tion that art is something esoteric, for the few, out-side the grasp of the masses. It will be demonstrat-ed that with few exceptions of a special nature, great art has always been popular art, and great artists have swayed the people.

Lie Number Three: the lie of Art Tradition; the no-tion that new artists must follow old models, and learn from the classics how to work. It will be dem-onstrated that vital artists make their own tech-nique; and that present-day technique is far and away superior to the technique of any art period preceding.

Lie Number Four: the lie of Art Dilettantism; the notion that the purpose of art is entertainment and diversion, an escape from reality. It will be demon-strated that this lie is a product of mental inferiori-ty, and that the true purpose of art is to alter real-ity.

Lie Number Five: the lie of the Art Pervert; the notion that art has nothing to do with moral questions. It will be demonstrated that all art deals with moral questions; since there are no other questions.

Lie Number Six: the lie of Vested Interest; the no-tion that art excludes propaganda and has nothing to do with freedom and justice. Meeting that issue without equivocation, we assert:

> *All art is propaganda. It is universally and ines-capably propaganda; sometimes unconsciously, but often deliber-ately, propaganda.*

As commentary on the above, we add, that when artists or art critics make the assertion that art excludes propaganda, what they are saying is that their kind of propaganda is art, and other kinds of propaganda are not art.

Morris Edmund Speare, The Political Novel: Its Development in England and in America (1924):

The political novel has now become definitely es-tablished as a genre in English letters... It is a lit-erary form which found its sources in that large parent body of English imaginative thought of an earlier century, a parent body which gave rise, in the nineteenth century, to so many diversified types of novel writing. In the twentieth century it has already challenged the attention of several of the most thoughtful English and American writers. A history of what novelists have already done must, perforce, energize the novelists of tomorrow to try their hands, in turn, at a peculiarly fascinat-ing medium of expression, and one which is but in its first stages of development...

What is a political novel? *It is a work of prose fic-tion which leans rather to 'ideas' than to 'emotions'; which deals rather with the machinery of law-making or with a theory about public conduct than with the merits of any given piece of legislation; and where the main purpose of the writer is party propaganda, public reform, or exposition of the lives of the personages who main-tain government, or of the forces which constitute gov-ernment. In this exposition the drawing-room is fre-quently used as a medium for presenting the inside life of politics.* This is my definition of a *genre* in English letters whose history I shall attempt to trace... (viii-ix).

In the political world [an author] had to know his material not as a reporter knows the facts which he has covered in an 'assignment,' nor even as some scholar probes and garners the fruits of his study, but rather as the fisherman knows the sea or the ploughman follows his furrow. To be able to wed politics to art and bring about a consummation where neither the first became tractarian or statisti-cal nor the other too honey-sweet, required not on-ly an imagination of a particularly high order, but a knowledge of material which had been gathered at first hand, with the accuracy which only a partici-pant himself could possess. One had to be able to think in political formulae, to adorn his thoughts in the natural imagery of the political life. Then only could he interpret it intelligently and interestingly to the reader (15).

We deal here with a *genre* of the novel which, if ex-cellently developed, must make its appeal to the reader not primarily as a social force but as an *in-tellectual force*. Dickens and Thackery, in 19th cen-tury literature are, for example, essentially *social writers*. Their men and women, for the most part persons out of everyday life, may even be por-trayed before us as monsters of a caricature...yet... they live in our minds long after we have forgotten the plot in which they appeared; they seem to be creatures of flesh and blood, more true to our ev-eryday life than are one half of our acquaintances. The *social writer* throws an air of common human-ity about his creations; he deals with incidents that are not unusual to the daily lives of all of us; his streets, and homes, and schools, and interiors we have visited and known for many years...

But the writer in the world of politics is not deal-ing with a common humanity... By the very reach and grasp which the genre of the political novel possesses, it is the most embracing in its material of all other novel types... Wars, indus-trial adventure, economic adjustment, commer-cial progress, diplo-macy in foreign lands, social experiences of every kind, education, art, sci-ence, discovery and explor-ation, expansion and internal development – all are grist for his mill, all may be gathered into his drag-net, if the writer pleases to make use of them...

And yet, peculiarly enough, in spite of the full-ness of representation which this material allows its writer, in spite of the reach of the arc of life which he may include in a single work in this *mil-ieu*, the political novelist must, indeed, be the most selective of all novel writers. Dick-ens and Thack-eray, and Henry James, as social writers, deal with men and women as men and women: the variety of common human emo-tions they may report is end-less, and the more usual and familiar they are to us the better it is for those writers. But the political novelist, if he is to be true to his craft, must be dominated, more often than not, by *ideas* rather than by *emo-tions* ... the presentation of powerful forces working across large areas, of customs and forces potent in their influences upon the na-tional life, and not the simple habits and preju-dices and country-church yard epithets of an unsung human-ity. That is what we mean by an *intellectual* inter-pretation of the novel, not a so-cial one...

There is yet another aspect in the contrast be-tween the political novelist and the work of the so-cial writer. The latter, by the very nature of his material, uses scenes, passions, and moods all of which fall within the shadow of an ordi-nary read-er's ordinary life. They may appeal, therefore, in-stantly to his comprehension; they lie at once with-in the range of his interpreta-tion; they call forth his natural sympathies. The extent which this common social appeal of the novelist makes upon the read-er's own experi-ences marks often the measure of his subse-quent popularity. But in the political nov-el the most dramatic and the most productive char-acters are, by their very greatness, the more re-moved from the ordinary world of ordinary men and women...

The political novelist has, therefore, by the in-tel-lectual milieu in which he is at work, many diffi-culties to overcome before he may draw a spark and then fan it into a flame of enthusiasm in the minds and hearts of the reading class, which is ev-erywhere a democratic class. He finds that success in this field requires that he perform adequately a two-fold task: he must not only be able to create his character, and paint his situation accurately, but he must also bring down from the heights on which they live both character and situation; he must translate both for us into our own experience and embody them in such forms that we may under-stand them and be fascinated by them. The act of do-ing so may not require a greater technique than that employed by the social writer; but it is an en-tirely different technique. The former writes of things and in language so that he who runs may read; he does not have to educate his audi-ence as well...

And if he succeeds in endowing his charac-ters and his situations with warmth, color, and vitality, and if his world of statesmen, diplo-mats, and all lesser figures – man, woman, and idealized youth – are spread in an intelligible pageant before us, there is yet a philosophy of politics, so to speak, to represent in a legiti-mately artistic manner....

The attempt, then, to combine impersonated characters with fiction, and to add to the result some significant political or social moral, aside from acting as a check upon the genius of every writer in this field except only the greatest writer... is fraught with peril. It is unfortunate indeed that in this milieu the critic is swift to find what may easily be termed 'propaganda' when it is actually nothing but an impassioned view of some political ideal of the novelist's... It is not difficult to make out a case for the state-ment that in a sense all art is propaganda... How far one may keep one's self out of a book where ideas are brought into full play, how far one may present sharply and appealingly and yet not be accused of 'bringing firearms into an orchestra,' is a difficult question to answer. Some-one has said that one of the main tenden-cies in American literature since 1870 has been its use as an instrument to agitate, and to carry out investiga-tions and reforms of various kinds. Has then all that recent literature – and particularly the novel of the last five decades – been forever damned as works of art? […] Has that destroyed their validity as great artists?

In one form or another what may seem the il-leg-itimate marriage of Beauty with Use will always be a skeleton in the novelist's closet, which he must ei-ther destroy or disown… (21-28).

So vast and varied is the [American] landscape, that we have already taken for granted the fact that 'the great American novel' will never be written because no such work could ever contain a picture of the energy of New England with the charm of the South, and reflect the buoyancy of California and the intrepidity of the middle West. And yet, in the genre of the political novel there seems to be offered the one great vehicle where something of the fusion of north, south, east, and west may take place, and where the writer may produce in fiction what is truly typical of the American people just as Walt Whitman produced it in poetry. Here is a form which offers a great latitude of plot development, permits an untold variety of background, and can present countless numbers of national and local types each novel in situation. And in spite of all this flexibility of content, the political novel must deal with one thing common to all, – the great Experiment of popular democracy in America (335)

Emma Goldman, The Social Significance of Modern Drama (1914):

[George Bernard Shaw wrote,] 'I am not an ordin-ary playwright in general practice. I am a special-ist in immoral and heretical plays. My reputation has been gained by my persistent struggle to force the public to reconsider its moral. In particular, I regard much current morality as to economic and sexual relations as disastrously wrong; and I regard certain doctrines of the Christian religion as under-stood in England today with abhorrence. I write plays with the deliberate object of converting the nation to my opinions in these matters' (96).

This confession of faith should leave no doubt as to the place of George Bernard Shaw in modern dramatic art. Yet, strange to say, he is among the most doubted of his time. That is partly due to the fact that humor generally serves merely to amuse, touching only the lighter side of life. But there is a kind of humor that fills laughter with tears, a hu-mor that eats into the soul like acid, leaving marks often deeper than those made by the tragic form….

'Major Barbara' is one of the most revolutionary plays. In any other but dramatic form the senti-ments uttered therein would have condemned the author to long imprisonment for inciting to sedi-tion and violence.

Shaw the Fabian would be the first to repudiate such utterances as rank Anarchy, 'impractical, brain cracked and criminal.' But Shaw the drama-tist is closer to life – closer to reality, closer to the historic truth that the people wrest only as much liberty as they have the intelligence to want and the courage to take (107).

George Bernard Shaw (1909), Collected Letters (1972):

I, as a Socialist, have had to preach, as much as anyone, the enormous power of the environment. We can change it; we must change it; there is abso-lutely no other sense in life than the task of chang-ing it. What is the use of writing plays, what is the use of writing anything, if there is not a will which finally moulds chaos itself into a race of gods.

Frank Norris, The Responsibilities of the Novelist (1903):

'The novel must not preach,' you hear them say. As though it were possible to write a novel without a purpose, even if it is only the purpose to amuse. One is willing to admit that this savors a little of quibbling, for 'purpose' and purpose to amuse are two different purposes. But every novel, even the most frivolous, must have some reason for the writing of it, and in that sense must have a 'pur-pose'. Every novel must do one of three things – it must tell something, (2) show something, or (3) prove something. Some novels do all three of these; some do only two; all must do at least one…

The third, and what we hold to be the best class, proves something, draws conclusions from a whole congeries of forces, social tenden-cies, race impuls-es, devotes itself not to a study of men but of man. In this class falls the novel with the purpose, such as 'Les Miserables'. And the reason we decide up-on this last as the high-est form of the novel is be-cause that, though setting a great purpose before it as its task, it nevertheless includes, and is forced to include, both the other classes…

[The novel] may be a great force, that works to-gether with the pulpit and the universities for the good of the people, fearlessly proving that power is abused, that the strong grind the faces of the weak, that an evil tree is still growing in the midst of the garden, that undoing follows hard upon unright-eousness, that the course of Empire is not yet fin-shed, and that the races of men have yet to work out their destiny in those great and terrible move-ments that crush and grind and rend asunder the pillars of the houses of the nations" (203-207).

Leo Tolstoy, What is Art? (1898):

This investigation has brought me to the conviction that almost all that our society con-siders to be art, good art, and the whole of art, far from being real and good art and the whole of art, is not even art at all but only a counterfeit of it… In our society the difficulty of recogniz-ing real works of art is further increased by the fact that the external quality of the work in false productions is not only no worse, but often bet-ter, than in real ones; the counterfeit is of-ten more effective than the real, and its subject more interesting…

William Morris, On Art and Social-ism (1883):

You may well think I am not here to criti-cize any special school of art or artists, or to plead for any special style, or to give you any instructions, however general, as to the prac-tice of the arts. Rather I want to take counsel with you as to what hindrances may lie in the way towards making art what it should be, a help and solace to the daily life of all men… Since I am a member of a Socialist propaganda I earnestly beg those of you who agree with

me to help us actively, with your time and your talents if you can, but if not, at least with your money, as you can… Help us now, you whom the fortune of your birth has helped to make wise and refined; and as you help us in our work-a-day business toward the success of the cause, instill into us your superior wis-dom, your superior refinement, and you in your turn may be helped by the courage and hope of those who are not so completely wise and refined. Re-member we have but one weapon against that terrible organization of selfishness which we at-tack, and that weapon is Union.

George Eliot, Leaves from a Note-book:
Authorship (1879):

…man or woman who publishes writings inevitably assumes the office of teacher or in-fluencer of the public mind. Let him protest as he will that he only seeks to amuse, and has no pretension to do more than while away an hour of leisure or weariness – 'the idle singer of an empty day' – he can no more escape in-fluencing the moral taste, and with it the ac-tion of the intelligence, than a setter of fash-ions in furniture and dress can fill the shops with his designs and leave the garniture of persons and housees unaffected by his indus-try.

Victor Hugo, William Shakespeare (1864):

To work for the people, – that is the great and urgent necessity.

The human mind – an important thing to say at this minute – has a greater need of the ideal even than of the real.

It is by the real that we exist; it is by the ideal that we live.

Now, do you wish to realize the difference? Ani-mals exist, man lives.

To live, is to understand. To live, is to smile at the present, to look toward posterity over the wall. To live, is to have in one's self a balance, and to weigh in it the good and evil. To live, is to have justice, truth, reason, devotion, probity, sincerity, common-sense, right, and duty nailed to the heart. To live, is to know what one is worth, what one can do and should do. Life is conscience. Cato would not rise before Ptolemy. Cato lived.

Literature is the secretion of civilization, poetry of the ideal. That is why literature is one of the wants of societies. That is why poetry is a hunger of the soul. That is why poets are the first instruct-tors of the people...(257).

We have just said, "Literature is the secretion of civilization." Do you doubt it? Open the first stati-stics you come across. Here is one which we find under our hand: Bagne de Toulon, 1862. Three thousand and ten prisoners. Of these three thousand and ten convicts, forty know a little more than to read and write, two hundred and eighty-seven know how to read and write, nine hundred and four read badly and write badly, seventeen hun-dred and seventy-nine know neither how to read nor write...(258).

The transformation of the crowd into the people, – profound labour! It is to this labour that the men called socialists have devoted themselves during the last forty years. The author of this book, how-ever insignificant he may be, is one of the oldest in the labour; "Le Dernier Jour d'un Condamné" dates from 1828, and "Claude Gueux" from 1834. He claims his place among these philosophers be-cause it is a place of persecution. A certain hatred of social-ism, very blind, but very general, has been at work most bitterly among the influential classes. (Classes, then, are still in existence?) Let it not be forgotten, socialism, true socialism, has for its end the elevation of the masses to the civic dignity, and therefore its principal care is for moral and intel-lectual cultivation. The first hunger is ignorance; socialism wishes then, above all, to instruct. That does not hinder so-cialism from being calumniated, and socialists from being denounced. To most of the infuri-ated, trembling cowards who have their say at the present moment, these reformers are public enemies. They are guilty of everything that has gone wrong...(259).

The democratic idea, the new bridge of civi-lization, undergoes at this moment the formida-ble trial of overweight. Every other idea would certainly give way under the load that it is made to bear. Demo-cracy proves its solidity by the absurdities that are heaped on, without shaking it. It must resist every-thing that people choose to place on it. At this mo-ment they try to make it carry despotism...(260).

That history has to be re-made is evident. Up to the present time, it has been nearly always written from the miserable point of view of accomplished fact; it is time to write from the point of view of principle, – and that, under penalty of nullity...(347).

CONTRIBUTORS

Adetokunbo Abiola

Nigerian journalist and writer. Published the novel, *Labulabu Mask*, with *Macmillan Nigeria*. Published short stories in magazines, notably *BBC Focus on Africa* magazine, *Flask Review*, and *Sage of Consciousness Review*. Also writes poetry and drama, as well as being an amateur photographer. Currently working on short story collection.

Alaa Kadhim al-Jabiri

Born in 1979 in Baghdad. An Iraqi government em-ployee and a student at Baghdad's University of Mustansiriya, College of Arts, Department of Phi-losophy. A poet, short story writer, and newspaper columnist. He is married and has three children.

Michael Albert

One of the nation's leading authorities on political economy, U.S. economic policies, and the media. A veteran writer/activist, he currently works with *Z Magazine* and the website Znet. Schooled in the new left and anti-Viet Nam war movements and an activist ever since, Albert primarily focuses on matters of movement-building, strategy and vision, creating alternative media, and developing and advocating the economic vision called participatory economics ("Parecon" for short). Albert has authored sixteen books – including *Parecon: Life After Capitalism* (Verso) and *Thought Dreams: Radical Theory for the 21st Century* (Arbeiter Rin) as well as his classics *Looking Forward* (with Robin Hahnel) and *Stop the Killing Train,* both available from South End Press. He recently penned a memoir, *Remembering Tomorrow: From the SDS to Life After Capitalism*. In *Remembering Tomorrow,* Albert charts his own trajectory as the child of a middle class suburban New York family to his political awakening on a Boston campus as revolution and dissent seized the nation. His story is one of swimming against the tide, when it turned against the iconoclasm and tumult of the Sixties, and continuing on with his part in the project for economic justice and social change. Albert has extensive organizing ex-perience, has written hundreds of articles, and has spoken at venues all over the world and throughout the United States. He ideas are both accessible and provocative. His perspective combines attention to race, gender, power, and class, and pursues equity, diversity, solidarity, and self-management. Speaks on movement matters, anti-war, globalization, media, and particularly economic vision for the future. He has a Ph.D. in economics from the University of Massachusetts.

Bruce Allen

Assistant Professor of English at Juntendo University in Japan. He writes about about environmental literature and has focused particularly on the work of Michiko Ishimure. His translation of her novel *Lake of Heaven* will be published by Lexington Books in Fall 2008.

Kim Alphandary

An artist and freelance journalist whose work appears in *NarcoNews, Columbia Report, Insurgent American* and *Z Magazine.* Kim specializes in U.S. foreign policy in Latin America and Central Asia.

Appalachian Author

Liberation Lit would like to learn the identity of the author of "Please Attack Appalachia."

Doreen Baingana

Author of *Tropical Fish: Stories out of Entebbe,* which won a Commonwealth Prize in 2006, among others. She considers Kenya one of her literary homes.

Simiyu Barasa

Kenyan filmmaker and writer. He was Writer/Director of the Feature film *Toto Millionaire* (2007) and has written for numerous Kenyan dramas like *Makutano Junction, Tahidi High* and *Wingu la Moto.* He was on the Editorial Board of *Kwani? 3,* Kenya's literary journal, and his fiction has appeared in *Africa Fresh: Voices from the First Continent.* His opinions have appeared in *New York Times, Nigerian Guardian,* and *South African Southern Times.*

Ross Birrell

Researcher and part-time lecturer at Glasgow School of Art and editor of the Studio 55 e-journal *Art and Research*. His solo exhibitions include *Envoy*, Ellen de Bruijne Projects, Amsterdam (2003) and Bürofreidrich, Berlin (2003) and at the Freismuseum, Leeuwarden (2005). Group exhibition include *TIMECODE*, Dundee Contemporary Arts (January 2009). *Greyscales/CMYK*, Tramway (2002), the 4th Gwangju Bienalle, Korea (2002), *Utopia Station*, Sindelfingen (2003), *Adam*, Smartspace Projects Amsterdam (2005), *Romantic Conceptualism*, Kunsthalle Nürnberg/BAWAG Foundation Vienna, (2007) and *Das Gelände*, Kunsthalle Nürnberg (2008). In 2007 Birrell was awarded an SAC Artist's Film & Video Award to make a collaborative film with David Harding based on the context of the Cuban song *Guantanamera* and the Cuban national poet, Jose Marti shot on location in Cuba and Miami 2008/09. Previous collaborations with David Harding are *Port Bou: 18 Fragments for Walter Benjamin* (2005) and *Cuernavaca: A Journey in Search of Malcolm Lowry* commissioned by Kunsthalle Basel (2006). Birrell's publications include 'The Gift of Terror: Suicide Bombing as *Potlatch*', *Art in the Age of Terror* (London: Paul Holberton Press, 2005), reprinted in *Concerning War: A Critical Reader* (BAK: Utrecht, 2006), *Leituras Da Morte* (Annablume: Sao Paulo, 2007) and *brumaria* 12 (Madrid, 2008). He is represented by Ellen de Bruijne Projects, Amsterdam.

Ernest Callenbach

Writer and editor best known for his visionary novel *Ecotopia*, a political and environmental classic that has sold almost a million copies. Other books include *Living Cheaply With Style*, *Ecotopia Emerging,* and *Ecology: A Pocket Guide*. Coauthor (with Michael Phillips) of *A Citizen Legislature*, and of *Eco-Management: The Elmwood Guide to Ecological Auditing and Sustainable Business*. He founded the critical journal *Film Quarterly* in 1958 at the University of California Press and served as its editor until 1991. Lives in Berkeley, California. His website is ernestcallenbach.com.

Laura Carlsen

Director of the *IRC Americas Program* in Mexico City, where she has been a writer and political analyst for more than two decades.

Cari Carpenter

Professor of English at West Virginia University; author of *Seeing Red: Anger, Sentimentality, and American Indians*; an active member of Appalachian Prison Book Project.

Tony Christini

Novelist, teacher, cofounder of Mainstay Press and Liberation Lit. Blog: apracticalpolicy.org.

Stephen F. Eisenman

(Ph.D. 1984, Princeton; Professor) has dedicated his career to the proposition that the best scholarship requires a critical engagement with the present as well as the past. He thus researches, writes and reads across many disciplines, and is active in contemporary social and political movements. He is the author of seven major books and exhibition catalogues, including *The Temptation of Saint Redon* (1992), *Gauguin's Skirt* (1997), and *The Abu Ghraib Effect* (2007). He is also the editor and principle author of the most widely used textbook in its field, *Nineteenth Century Art: A Critical History*. Professor Eisenman has curated many exhibitions in the United States and Europe. Throughout 2008-2009, Stephen Eisenman has been working with a group of Chicago artists, lawyers, and activists to end torture in a notorious Illinois prison. His article on the subject, "The Resistible Rise and Predictable Fall of the American Supermax," will be published in *Monthly Review* in 2010. In 2009-2010, Eisenman with serve as Chair of the General Faculty Committee, the leading governance organ of the faculty of Northwestern University.

Mike Eldon

Member of *Concerned Citizens for Peace*.

Joe Emersberger

A writer living in Canada with an interest in Haiti. Co-editor of *HaitiAnalysis.com*. Contributor of articles to *ZNet* and *Narco News*.

Shelley Ettinger

Work in Nimrod, Cream City Review, Stone Canoe, Mississippi Review, Mizna, Word Is Bond and other journals. Awarded fellowships to the Saltonstall Foundation Arts Colony in 2008 and the Lambda Literary Foundation LGBT writers' retreat in 2007. Recently completed her first novel and is at work on a second novel and a collection of short fiction. A longtime trade unionist and activist in social-justice movements, Shelley works at New York University where she is a member of the clerical workers' union AFT Local 3882. Read Red (readwritered.blogspot.com) is her blog about literature and the class struggle.

Dayo Forster

A novelist whose first book, *Reading the Ceiling*, was published by *Simon and Schuster* in 2007. She lives in Nairobi where she also works part-time as a financial sector development consultant.

H. Bruce Franklin

One of America's leading cultural historians, H. Bruce Franklin is the author or editor of eighteen books and more than 200 articles on culture and history published in more than a hundred major magazines and newspapers, academic journals, and reference works. He has given over five hundred addresses on college campuses, on radio and TV shows, and at academic conferences, museums, and libraries, and he has participated in making four films. He has taught at Stanford University, Johns Hopkins, Wesleyan, and Yale and currently is the John Cotton Dana Professor of English and American Studies at Rutgers University in Newark. Before becoming an academic, Franklin worked in factories, was a tugboat mate and deckhand, and flew for three years in the United States Air Force as a Strategic Air Command navigator and intelligence officer. Franklin has published continually on the history and literature of the Vietnam War since 1966, when he became widely known for his activist opposition to the war. His pioneering course on the war and his book *M.I.A. Or Mythmaking in America* have had a major national impact, and he is co-editor of the widely-adopted history text *Vietnam and America: A Documented History*. His latest book, *Vietnam and Other American Fantasies, offers a sweeping vision of American culture* into the 21st century. Another area where Franklin's work has achieved international distinction is the study of science fiction and its relation to culture and history. In 1961 he offered one of the first two university courses in science fiction, and his book *Future Perfect* played a key role in establishing the importance and academic legitimacy of the subject. His *Robert A. Heinlein: America as Science Fiction* won the Eaton Award for 1981; in 1983 he won the Pilgrim Award for Lifetime Scholarship of the Science Fiction Research Association; in 1990 he was named the Distinguished Scholar of the International Association for the Fantastic in the Arts; and in 1991 he was Guest Curator for the "Star Trek and the Sixties" exhibit at the National Air and Space Museum of the Smithsonian Institution. Franklin's first book, The Wake of the Gods: Melville's Mythology, has been in print continually since 1963 and is regarded as a classic work of scholarship and criticism. He is a past president of the Melville Society, and continues to publish about Melville. *Prison Literature in America: The Victim as Criminal and Artist* established Franklin as the world's leading authority on American prison literature. His 1998 anthology *Prison Writing in 20th-Century America* is already widely influential. A prominent activist, Franklin were specifically targeted by the FBI COINTELPRO effort. Franklin's political views and actions during that period were public, and continued despite being targeted by the FBI's COINTELPRO, which used disinformation, *agents provocateurs*, and violent acts to discredit leftist organizations. Documents obtained under the Freedom of Information Act show many attempts by the FBI to "neutralize" Franklin. Stanford fired Franklin, even though he had academic tenure, for leading a group of students to occupy the computer center in 1972 and urging students and faculty to strike in protest against the invasion of Laos and Stanford's involvement in the war.

Jerry Fresia

PhD from the University of Massachusetts in political science. Has written extensively on the political-economy of the United States. Left academia to pursue a career in painting, an activity he has studied formally and has practiced his entire adult life. Exhibitor and Executive Director of two outdoor exhibition groups while in San Francisco. Has taught at numerous US colleges and universities. Has taught art privately for 20 years.

Eduardo Galeano

Born in Montevideo, Uruguay, in 1940. He began working as a journalist at the age of 14, publishing drawings and stories in the weekly "El Sol". At 24 he published his first novella "Las dias siguientes". Between 1959 and 1963 he worked for the weekly "Marcha" and later (1964-1966) became director of the daily "Epoca". During the military dictatorship he lived in exile first in Argentina, later in Spanish Catalonia. In 1985 he returned to Montevideo. Galeano is an icon of progressive Latin American literature. His two monumental works "Open Veins of Latin America" (1971) and the trilogy "Memory of Fire" (1982, 1984, 1986) made a tremendous impact on Latin American and world intellectuals, unveiling the brutality of colonialism and post-colonialism, but also capturing readers into its original, magic and highly poetic prose. The latest book of Galeano is called "Bocas del Tiempo" (2004).

Stanley Gazemba

Trained as a journalist. Lives in Kangemi, Nairobi. Writes for *Sunday Nation* and *Msanii* Magazine (Published by RAMOMA). Author of the novel *The Stone Hills of Maragoli*, which won the 2003 Jomo Kenyatta Prize for Literature. Author of 5 childrens' books: *Poko at the Koras, Poko and the Jet, Shaka Zulu, The Herdsboy and the Princess,* and *Tobi and the Streetboy.* Attended the Caine Prize Writers' workshop in Cape Town, South Africa, in 2003. A fellow at the Breadloaf Writers' Conference, Vermont, USA in 2007. Member of *Concerned Kenyan Writers.*

Shalini Gidoomal

Kenya-born journalist and writer who has worked extensively for a variety of UK national news-papers and magazines including the *Independent, News of the World, Today, Architectural Digest, GQ* and *FHM*, and has contributed short stories to various anthologies including *Kwani? 4* and two Caine Prize anthologies. She is a member of *Concerned Kenyan Writers, Concerned Citizens for Peace*, and is editorial co-ordinator for *GenerationKenya 45.*

Theodore A. Harris

Collagist, poet, and mural painter. His visual art, poetry, and manifestos have appeared in publications such as; Real News, Long Shot, The Hammer, Unity & Struggle, New Letters, Ratta Pallax, Paterson Literary Review, Switch Blade, AMEN (published in Madrid), Left Curve, AWOL, Heart, The Gaither Reporter, African American Review, Black Renaissance Noire, Quarterly Black Book Review, XCP: Cross Cultural Poetics, Callaloo, Common Roots Common Ground, WHAT IF?, The Other Side, Cal Literary Arts Magazine, Tangent, Theatre Journal, Souls, X Mag, African Voices, Nommo, Radical Society, boundary 2, South Atlantic Quarterly, Chain, Fiction International, 1913, Temple University Faculty Herald, and in many anthologies. Mr. Harris' work has been exhibited in solo, traveling, and group shows through out the U.S. His work is collected in private and public collections such as the Saint Louis University Museum of Art, Center for Africana Studies University of Pennsylvania, and Lincoln University. Mr. Harris has lectured on his work at Colleges and Universities such as Haverford College, Stanford University, Saint Louis University, University of Pennsylvania, Temple University, Hammonds House Museum and Resource Center for African American Art among others.

Ishimure Michiko

She has often been referred to as the "Rachel Carson of Japan". Her bestselling book *Paradise in the Sea of Sorrow: Our Minamata Disease* (Kugai jodo; waga minamata byo, 1972) alerted many Japanese to the dangers of industrial pollution and shaped the conscience of a generation of politically and environmentally aware writers and activists. Ishimure has gone on to develop the Minamata story into a trilogy. She has also written a wide range of poetry, essays, novels, and noh drama and is the recipient of several international literary prizes as well as Japan's Asahi Prize and the Philippines' Magsaysay Prize. She continues to be involved with the struggle for the rights of Minamata victims, and for the rights of other victims of prejudice and modernization. Her 1997 novel *Lake of Heaven* (in Japanese, *Tenko*) was published in English by Lexington Books in Fall 2008.

Ron Jacobs

The author of the first comprehensive history of the Weather Underground – *The Way the Wind Blew: A History of the Weather Underground*. His articles, essays and reviews have appeared in *Counterpunch, Monthly Review, Monthly Review Zine, Alternative Press Review, Berlin Jungle World, Works in Progress, State of Nature,* and elsewhere.

Dahr Jamail

In late 2003, weary of the overall failure of the US media to accurately report on the realities of the war in Iraq for the Iraqi people and US soldiers, Dahr Jamail went to Iraq to report on the war himself. His dispatches were quickly recognized as an important media resource. He is now writing for the Inter Press Service, The Asia Times and many other outlets. His reports have also been published with The Nation, The Sunday Herald, Islam Online, the Guardian, Foreign Policy in Focus, and the Independent to name just a few. Dahr's dispatches and hard news stories have been translated into French, Polish, German, Dutch, Spanish, Japanese, Portuguese, Chinese, Arabic and Turkish. On radio as well as television, Dahr reports for Democracy Now!, the BBC, and numerous other stations around the globe. Dahr is also special correspondent for Flashpoints. Dahr has spent a total of 8 months in occupied Iraq as one of only a few independent US journalists in the country. In the Mid-East, Dahr has also has reported from Syria, Lebanon and Jordan. Dahr uses the DahrJamailIraq.com website and his popular mailing list to disseminate his dispatches.

Kim Jensen

A writer who has lived and taught in California, France, and the Middle East. She and her husband Palestinian painter Zahi Khamis have been active in human rights movements for many years. Her writings have appeared in a wide variety of newspapers and magazines. In 2001 she won the Raymond Carver Prize for Short Fiction. She currently lives in Maryland, with Zahi and their two children. She is on the editorial board of the *Baltimore Review* and is Assistant Professor of English at the Community College of Baltimore County.

Judy Kibinge

Filmmaker, writer and artist. She lives in Nairobi.

Martin Kimani

Lives and works in Addis Ababa, Ethiopia. He has previously been a Teaching Fellow at the Joint Ser-vices Command and Staff College in Shrivenham, UK and an Associate of the Conflict Security and Development Group of King's College of the University of London where he is a doctoral candidate. He can be reached at martinkimani@gmail.com.

Peter Linebaugh

Teaches history at the University of Toledo. Author of *The London Hanged* and (with Marcus Rediker) *The Many-Headed Hydra: the Hidden History of the Revolutionary Atlantic*. His essay on the history of May Day is included in *Serpents in the Garden*. His latest book is the *Magna Carta Manifesto*. He can be reached at: plineba@yahoo.com.

Stephanie McMillan

Her work has appeared in dozens of publications including *Monday Magazine* (Canada), *Comic Relief, Impact Press, Clamor, Comic News, The Funny Times, Megh Barta* (Bangladesh), *San Francisco Bay Guardian, Casseurs de Pub* (France), *Boston's Weekly Dig, Anchorage Press,* and *The Word* (Canada). A collection of her cartoons, "Attitude Presents Minimum Security" was published in 2005. Her work is also included in "Attitude: The New Subversive Political Cartoonists" (2002), as well as in various textbooks and several books in the Opposing Viewpoints series by Gale Publishing Group. She is a founding member of Cartoonists With Attitude, a group of ground-breaking social commentary and political cartoonists formed in 2006, many of whom appear in N.B.M. Publishing's "Attitude" series of books edited by Ted Rall.

Vivek Mehta
Member of *Concerned Kenyan Writers*.

Mwandawiro Mghanga
Former Kenyan exile, student leader, and current MP for Wundanyi Constituency in Kenya.

Tony Mochama
A poet and journalist who lives and works in Nairobi.

Betty Muragori
Has a degree in Botany and zoology from the University of Nairobi and a Masters degree in Environmental Studies from Clark University in Massachusetts, USA. Together with a friend, Betty started a consultancy, Sienna Associates in March 2003.

Wambui Mwangi
Scholar and writer. She lives in Toronto and Nairobi, teaches at the University of Toronto, and blogs occasionally on Diary of a Mad Kenyan Woman. She is the Director of GenerationKenya.

Shabnam Nadiya
Writer, poet, and translator. Her work has appeared in the anthologies *Galpa: Short Stories by Women from Bangladesh* (Saqi Books, UK), *From the Delta, Different Perspectives: Women Writing in Bangladesh*, *The Escape and Other Stories*, and *1971 and After* (all from University Press Ltd, Bangladesh), and *New Age Short Stories* (New Age/writers.ink). Her prose, poetry and translations have also been published in various print and online periodicals, including *World View, Storyglossia, Her Circle, Bonfire, Texts' Bones, The Beat, Words Without Borders, Cerebration*, and *Kali O Kalam*. Recently, she won the 3rd Prize at the Another Look Short Story Contest 2006 (Torrevieja, Spain). Nadiya lives in Dhaka, Bangladesh, with her husband and daughter.

Mukoma Wa Ngugi
Author of *Hurling Words at Consciousness* (poems, AWP 2006), *Conversing with Africa: Politics of Change* (KPH, 2003) and editor of a forthcoming anthology – *New Kenyan Fiction* (Ishmael Reed Publications, 2008). His political essays and columns have appeared in the *Progressive Magazine, Los Angeles Times, Christian Science Monitor, Radical History Review, zmag.org, Monthly Review, South African Labor Bulletin, The Progressive, South Africa's Mail and Guardian, Chimurenga, Amandla, Against the Current, Kenya's Business Daily Africa*. He has been interviewed by *Democracy Now, Aljeezera, KPFA – Africa Today, BBC Africa Have Your Say* and *the BBC World Service* amongst other places. He is a political columnist for the *BBC Focus on Africa Magazine* as well co-editor of *Pambazuka News* pambazuka.org.

Yvonne A. Owuor
A storyteller who lives in Nairobi. She has contributed numerous short stories to different publications worldwide. Her story about the consequences of regional civil strife, "Weight of Whispers," won the Caine Prize for African Writing in 2003. She has at last finalised work on her first novel, working title *Red Rain*. A contributor to *Kwani?*, and a traveller, she is suddenly rabidly possessive about her country, Kenya.

Stephen Derwent Partington
Teacher in Kenya and poet. He lives and works just outside Machakos. A collection of poems, *SMS & Face to Face*, was published by Phoenix, Kenya.

Shailja Patel
An award-winning Kenyan poet, playwright, theatre artist, and political activist. She is author of *Migritude I: The Mother (Lietocolle)*, and two collections of poetry: *Dreaming In Gujurati*, and *Shilling Love*. Her work has been translated into ten languages. She performs internationally at venues ranging from New York's Lincoln Centre to Durban's Poetry Africa Festival. Recent honours include the inaugural Fanny-Ann Eddy Poetry Award from IRN-Africa, the 2009 Guest Writer Fellowship at the Nordic Africa Institute, and a New Tactics In Human Rights Grant. Shailja is a founding member of Kenyans for Peace, Truth and Justice, which works towards a just and equitable democracy in Kenya.

Tamara Pearson

A Gringa Diary blogger. Australian community worker in Venezuela.

Marge Piercy

Author of seventeen novels including *The New York Times* Bestseller *Gone To Soldiers*; the National Bestsellers *Braided Lives* and *The Longings of Women* and the classic *Woman on the Edge of Time*; seventeen volumes of poetry, and a critically acclaimed memoir *Sleeping with Cats*. Born in center city Detroit, educated at the University of Michigan, the recipient of four honorary doctorates, she has been a key player in many of the major progressive political battles of our time, including the anti-Vietnam war and the women's movement, and most recently an active participant in the resistance to the war in Iraq.

Potash

Authors the blog *A Kenyan Urban Narrative*. His blog has suffered the bane of lesser writers: Demise in the face of critical acclaim. Having lost his street credibility to the embrace of Nairobi's Literati, Potash's blog is no longer the gritty voice of Nairobi's underground. His old friends from his street days have taken to whispering, with mounting anger and loathing, that Potash has gone out and got himself a regular job and a pinstriped suit. The bigger question is: Who reads him any more?

Mahmud Rahman

Born in Dhaka, what was then East Pakistan. Lived on Mymensingh Road, witness to the motorcades of royalty and dictators, to the passing of horse carriages in favor of buses and auto rickshaws, and to the alternating cycles of mass demonstrations and military curfews and gunfire. Schooled – with conflict – by Catholic missionaries from the American Midwest. Active in the movement for the liberation of Bangladesh. Refugee in India during 1971 war. Adult life in the U.S. shaped by the background of racial violence in the Boston of the 70s and the collapse of industry in the Detroit of the 80s. A writer over decades, devoted to fiction since the mid-90s. In May 2004, graduated with an MFA in Creative Writing from Mills College in Oakland, California.

Margaret Randall

Lived in Latin America (Mexico, Cuba, Nicaragua) for close to a quarter century. When she returned to the U.S. in 1984, the government ordered her de-ported because of the content of some of her books. With the support of many good people, she waged an almost five-year battle to remain in the country of her birth, winning it in 1989. Most recent among her more than eighty books are STONES WITNESS (University of Arizona Press, 2007) and the forthcoming TO CHANGE THE WORLD: MY YEARS IN CUBA (due out in fall 2008 from Rutgers University Press). Randall lives in Albuquerque, New Mexico, with her life companion, the artist and teacher Barbara Byers.

Adrienne Rich

Author of more than sixteen volumes of poetry, including *Diving into the Wreck, The Dream of a Common Language, The Fact of a Doorframe: Selected Poems 1950-2001, An Atlas of the Difficult World: Poems 1988-1991, Collected Early Poems: 1950-1970, Dark Fields of the Republic: Poems 1991-1995, Midnight Salvage, Fox,* and *The School Among the Ruins*, as well as *Of Woman Born: Motherhood as Experience and Institution* and *What is Found There: Notebooks on Poetry and Politics*. Rich's newest book of poems is *Tele-phone Ringing in the Labyrinth* (2007). She published a new collection of essays, *A Human Eye: Essays on Art in Society*, in May 2009 with Norton.

Andrew Rihn

Writer and student. His poetry has appeared online at *MR Zine, Poetic Injustice, Dissident Voice,* and *Poets Against the War*. He lives in Canton, OH.

Arundhati Roy

Indian novelist, activist. Trained as an architect. Won the Booker Prize in 1997 for her novel *The God of Small Things*. Since winning the Booker Prize, she has concentrated her writing on nonfiction, publishing collections of essays as part of her work for social causes. In response to India's testing of nuclear weapons in Pokhran, Rajasthan, Roy wrote *The End of Imagination*, a critique of the Indian government's nuclear poli-cies. It was published in her collection *The Cost of Living,* in which she also rallied against In-dia's massive hydroelectric dam projects in the central and western states of Maharashtra, Madhya Pradesh and Gujarat. Roy was awarded the Sydney Peace Prize in May 2004 for her work in social campaigns and advocacy of non-violence. In June 2005 she took part in the World Tribunal on Iraq. In January 2006 she was awarded the Sahitya Akademi award for her collection of essays, 'The Algebra of Infinite Justice', but declined to accept it. "The Briefing" is her first work of fiction since *The God of Small Things.*

P. Sainath

Rural affairs editor of The Hindu and the author of *Everybody Loves a Good Drought.*

Kalundi Serumaga

Part of the immediate post-independence gen-eration (born in the early sixties). Grew up in Uganda, apart from formal education, was trained as an actor for the Abafumi Theatre Comapany in adolescence. Found himself in Kenya after family had to flee Amin persecution of the artistic community. Spent adolescence and very early 20's growing up in Kenya as part of the very politically active Ugan-dan exile community, which cost father (Robert Serumaga 1939-1980: actor, writer, soldier, politician, thea-tre director) his life. Moved to UK. Remained very active in Uganda exile community politics there. Acquired two degrees: Govern-ment/Man-agement (BA) and Independent Film-making (MA). Returned to Uganda in early '90s. Is active in the media and artistic scenes. Worked as Director, Uganda National Cultural Centre/National Theatre for 5 years and later Director for a global, very confused NGO. Left while still sane. Works now as an In-dependent film maker, media and artistic con-sultant, as well as host of a politically focused radio shows in Kampala that several politicians (including President Museveni) have reportedly vowed never to return to, having been inter-viewed there. Recently had on-air contretemps with one Dr. Alfred Mutua. Completed a docu-mentary on the land disputes among Uganda and Kenya's Kalenjin people (was in KIFF). Currently completing a documentary on the cri-sis of the Anglican church in Africa, from an Af-rican perspective. Campaigner for native rights in Uganda, as well as founder of the Serumaga Centre For The Arts.

Cindy Sheehan

Cindy Sheehan is the mother of Spc. Casey Aus-tin Sheehan who was KIA in Iraq on 04/04/04. She is a co-founder and President of Gold Star Families for Peace and the author of two books: *Not One More Mother's Child* and *Dear President Bush.*

Carol Simpson

The pen-name of an artistic team who have been doing cartoons about work and business for 20 years. Estelle Carol does the drawings and Bob Simpson writes the gags. They are union car-toonists. Estelle is a member of the *Graphic Art-ists Guild* and Bob belongs to the *National Writ-ers Union.* They fire off cartoons aimed at Amer-ica's corporate establishment and its wholly owned subsidiary, the U.S. Government. Their work can be found in labor, alternative and business publications across North America and around the world.

keith harmon snow

An independent war correspondent, photogra-pher and human rights investigator recognized for more than a decade's work contesting offi-cial narratives on war crimes, crimes against humanity and genocide before international bodies, keith is the 2009 Regent's Lecturer in Law & Society for the prestigious Regent's Lec-tureship at the University of California, Santa Barbara. A three time Project Censored award winner, his investigations in Central Africa supported the legal proceedings (Spain) that led to the issuance of international arrest warrants against 40 military officials affiliated with the current Rwanda government on charges of war crimes, crimes against humanity, and genocide. From 2004 to 2007 he worked in Ethiopia, South Sudan and the Democratic Republic of Congo, reporting for *National Public Radio* on Congo's presidential elections, and as a field researcher for Genocide Watch and a United Nations consultant on vulnerable populations and genocide. He has worked independently in 42 countries, 17 in Africa, including Afghanistan, China, India, Indonesia, Mongolia and Nicaragua. His work has appeared in numerous print and on-line publications and he contributed to the award-winning *Encyclopedia of Religion and Nature*. A former corporate manager with GE Aerospace Electronics Laboratory, he has written extensively on the pathologies of nuclear power, mining, climate warfare, and other militarization. He has made more than 40 presentations at prestigious colleges and universities in the U.S., Mongolia and India. He often facilitates workshops in consciousness, spiritual awakening and personal development. He is also an organic farmer and the founder of the Wildcat Sanctuary for Peace in Williamsburg, Massachusetts.

Paul Street

Writer, speaker, activist, historian, and satirist based in Iowa City, IA and Chicago, IL. He is the author of *Empire and Inequality: America and the World Since 9/11* (Boulder, CO: *Paradigm*); *Racial Op-pression in the Global Metropolis* (New York: *Rowman & Littlefield*, 2007); and *Segregated Schools: Education-al Apartheid in Post-Civil Rights America* (New York: *Routledge*, 2005). Paul can be reached at: paulstreet99@yahoo.com.

Mark Vallen

Born in Los Angeles California in 1953, Vallen has been creating images for as long as he can remem-ber. By 1971, at the age of 17, he had already pub-lished cartoons in the *Los Angeles Free Press* news-paper. In the same year he published his first street poster, a pre-Watergate artwork titled, Evict Nixon! He studied art at the prestigious Otis Parsons Art Institute of Los Angeles, where he was influenced by the great African American social realist, Char-les White. But despite his schooling, the artist con-siders himself to be largely self taught. He forged a style shaped not so much by how others painted, but what they painted. Vallen has a firm commitment to figurative realism, and he's derived inspir-ation from the rich heritage of artists working as social critics and documentarians. His influences range from Goya and Daumier, to the German Ex-pressionists and Mexican Muralists. His popular web log is Art For A Change where he discusses art theory and news related to the arts.

Joseph Veramu

Leading Fijian novelist and head of the Lautoka Campus of The University of the South Pacific. Author of *Growing Up in Fiji*, a social commentary on Fijian child rearing practices; the story collections, *The Black Messiah*, and *Sunrise to the Coup*; the novels *Moving Through the Streets*, and *Rising Above the Labyrinth*; and *Let's Do it Our Way*, a book about education and development. He has also written a children's story-book, *The Shark*, and he is editor of two collections of myths and legends, *The Two Tur-tles and the Ungrateful Snake and The Snake Prince*.

Andre Vltchek

Philosopher, novelist, filmmaker, investigative journalist, poet, playwright, and photographer, Andre Vltchek is a revolutionary, internationalist and globetrotter. In all his work, he confronts Western imperialism and the Western regime imposed on the world.

He covered dozens of war zones and conflicts from Iraq and Peru to Sri Lanka, Bosnia, Rwanda, Syria, Iraq, Palestine, DR Congo and Timor-Leste.

His latest books are *Exposing Lies of The Empire*, *Fighting Against Western Imperialism* and *On Western Terrorism* with Noam Chomsky.

Point of No Return is his major work of fiction, written in English. *Nalezeny*, is his novel written in Czech. Other works include a book of political non-fiction *Western Terror: From Potosi to Baghdad* and *Indonesia: Archipelago of Fear, Exile* (with Pramoedya Ananta Toer, and Rossie Indira) and *Oceania – Neocolonialism, Nukes & Bones*.

His plays are *'Ghosts of Valparaiso'* and *'Conversations with James'*.

He is a member of Advisory Committee of the BRussells Tribunal.

Investigative work of Andre Vltchek appears in countless publications worldwide.

Andre Vltchek has produced and directed several documentary films for the left-wing South American television network teleSUR. They deal with diverse topics, from Turkey/Syria to Okinawa, Kenya, Egypt and Indonesia, but all of them expose the effects of Western imperialism on the Planet. His feature documentary film 'Rwanda Gambit' has been broadcasted by Press TV, and aims at reversing official narrative on the 1994 genocide, as well as exposing the Rwandan and Ugandan plunder of DR Congo on behalf of Western imperialism. He produced the feature length documentary film about the Indonesian massacres of 1965 in 'Terlena – Breaking of The Nation', as well as in his film about the brutal Somali refugee camp, Dadaab, in Kenya: 'One Flew Over Dadaab'. His Japanese crew filmed his lengthy discussion with Noam Chomsky on the state of the world, which is presently being made into a film.

He frequently speaks at conferences, revolutionary meetings, as well as at the principal universities and academies of science worldwide.

He presently lives in Asia and the Middle East. His website:

http://andrevltchek.weebly.com/

And his Twitter is: @AndreVltchek.

Rasna Warah

A columnist with Kenya's *Daily Nation* newspaper, Rasna Warah has been variously described as a recovering UN employee, a slum journalist and a failed novelist. Her work has appeared in various national and international publications, including *Kwani?*, South Africa's *Mail and Guardian*, *BBC On-line*, *People and the Planet*, *Habitat Debate* and *Sus-tainable Development International*. She has contri-buted to various books and anthologies, including the *State of the World 2007* by the World-watch Institute and was editor and co-author of UN-Habitat's *State of the World's Cities 2006/7*, which examines living conditions in the world's slums. She is also the author of *Triple Heritage: A Journey to Self-discovery* (1998), which looks at the social, economic and political history of Asians in Kenya. She has edited and compiled an anthology that crit-iques the way development is practised in Africa, and is currently looking for potential publishers.

Buff Whitman-Bradley

Peace and social justice activist in northern California. He is the author of two books of poetry, *b. eagle, poet*, and *The Honey Philosophies*. In addition to writing, he produces documentary audios and videos, including the award winning *Outside In*, a film about people who visit prisoners on San Quentin's death row.

Mike Whitney

Lives in Washington State. *Counterpunch* columnist.

Marina Wiedemann

Painter, cartoonist and architect, born in Leningrad (USSR) and since then lived in Czechoslovakia (now Czech Republic) and Germany. Socialist realist by her style, Ms. Wiedeman is widely acclaimed artist. She works on various projects for the United Nations (particularly UNESCO) and exhibits in Germany, Czech Republic, and elsewhere.

Jenny Ruth Yasi

Activist singer-songwriter, behavior scientist, organic grower and small town Founding Mother for an island community off the coast of Maine. Awarded the 2004 OMNI International Peace Writ-ing Fiction Award. Also won the Carbonneau Prize from Stonecoast Writer's workshop, and has been published in *Words and Images 2000*, *Harbor Voices*, and anthologized in *Women Behaving Badly*. Her recent non-fiction mostly concerns canine be-havior, and has been published regionally as well as nationally. Blogs via Whole Dog Camp.

Mickey Z.

Until the laws are changed or the power runs out, Mickey Z. can be found here: mickeyz.net/.